The Economics of Money, Banking and Finance

Visit the *Economics of Money, Banking and Finance*, fourth edition
Companion Website at **www.pearsoned.co.uk/howells** to find valuable
student learning material including:

- Learning objectives for each chapter
- Multiple choice and written answer questions to help test your
  understanding
- Annotated links to relevant sites on the web
- An online glossary to explain key terms

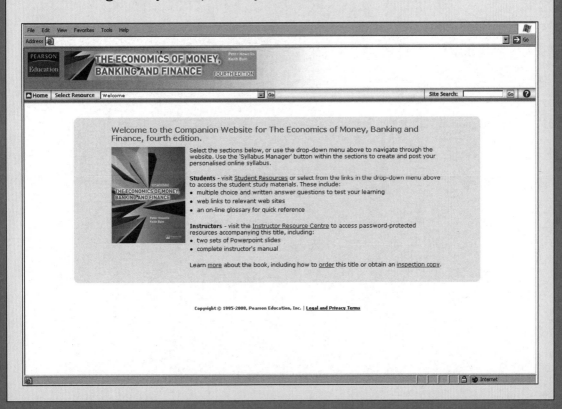

We work with leading authors to develop the
strongest educational materials in economics,
bringing cutting-edge thinking and best learning
practice to a global market.

Under a range of well-known imprints, including
Financial Times Prentice Hall, we craft high
quality print and electronic publications which
help readers to understand and apply their content,
whether studying or at work.

To find out more about the complete range of our
publishing, please visit us on the World Wide Web at:
www.pearsoned.co.uk

FOURTH EDITION

The Economics of Money, Banking and Finance

A European Text

PETER HOWELLS and KEITH BAIN

An imprint of **Pearson Education**
Harlow, England • London • New York • Boston • San Francisco • Toronto • Sydney • Singapore • Hong Kong
Tokyo • Seoul • Taipei • New Delhi • Cape Town • Madrid • Mexico City • Amsterdam • Munich • Paris • Milan

Pearson Education Limited
Edinburgh Gate
Harlow
Essex CM20 2JE
England

and Associated Companies throughout the world

Visit us on the World Wide Web at:
www.pearsoned.co.uk

First published 1998 by Addison Wesley Longman Limited
Second edition published 2002
Third edition published 2005
Fourth edition published 2008

© Pearson Education Limited 1998, 2002, 2005, 2008

ISBN: 978-0-273-71039-4

British Library Cataloguing-in-Publication Data
A catalogue record for this book is available from the British Library

Library of Congress Cataloging-in-Publication Data
Howells, P. G. A., 1947–
 The economics of money, banking and finance : a European text / Peter Howells and Keith Bain. — 4th ed.
   p. cm.
 ISBN 978-0-273-71039-4
1. Finance—Europe. 2. Banks and banking—Europe. 3. International finance. I. Bain, K., 1942– II. Title.
HG925.H695 2008
 332.1094—dc22

                 2008003078

10 9 8 7 6 5 4
12 11 10

Typeset in 9/11.5 GraphicSabon by 73
Printed by Ashford Colour Press Ltd, Gosport, Hampshire

Brief contents

Contents

Part 6   Current Issues

Supporting resources

Visit www.pearsoned.co.uk/howells to find valuable online resources:

Companion Website for students
- Learning objectives for each chapter
- Multiple choice and written answer questions to help test your learning
- Links to relevant sites on the web
- An online glossary to explain key terms

For instructors
- Complete, downloadable Instructor's Manual
- New to this edition, two sets of PowerPoint slides that can be downloaded and used as OHTs. Slides are arranged to suit courses on Economics of Money and Banking and on Economics of Financial Markets

Also: The Companion Website provides the following features:

- Search tool to help locate specific items of content
- Email results and profile tools to send results of quizzes to instructors
- Online help and support to assist with website usage and troubleshooting

For more information please contact your local Pearson Education sales representative or visit www.pearsoned.co.uk/howells

Guided tour

SETTING THE SCENE

Chapter openers list in bullet points **what you will learn in this chapter** to highlight the main topics covered.

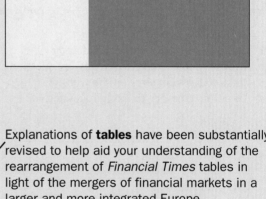

Chapter 15   Money markets

What you will learn in this chapter:

- The major instruments which are created and traded in the money markets
- The characteristics of those instruments and how they are priced
- The main participants in the money markets
- The size, growth and recent development of these markets
- The use of money markets by the authorities for policy purposes

AIDING YOUR UNDERSTANDING

important, accounting for a third of written premiums in 2005. Property insurance (buildings and contents), which generated more than a quarter of the sector's premium income in the same year, came a close second.[5] The payment of premiums creates a pool of funds at the companies' disposal. Eventually most or all of it will be used to meet claims. However, provided sufficient funds are available or can be quickly recovered to make claims payouts as they fall due, the remainder can be placed in earning assets by the companies and thereby provide a further source of income. It follows that investment opportunities arise for general as well as long-term insurance companies. However, to say this does not fully capture the importance of investment for the viability of general insurance business. Although premiums covered claims in 2005, this is not always the case. For example, in 2002 the UK motor and property sectors operated at an overall underwriting loss of £0.2bn.[6] In other words, premiums received by companies failed to cover the cost of claims met by them. The ability of companies to satisfy fully their obligations to clients who had incurred insured losses was due to the returns they were able to earn by investing monies paid by these same clients in premiums. In fact, competitive pressures within the general insurance sector sometimes drive premiums down so low in relation to likely claims levels that companies have been known to plan for underwriting losses to be made good by investment income – a practice known as *cashflow underwriting*.

While the investment function is thus no minor matter for general insurers, it is absolutely central to

long-term insurers, many of whose products are primarily savings vehicles, as we have already noted. This contrast explains the difference in asset growth between the long-term and general insurance sectors apparent in Table 3.4, which indicates that the funds available for the former to invest were some 12 times larger than those available to the latter in 2006. (In fact, a broadly similar picture emerges from balance sheet data in Table 3.5. Long-term insurance companies had net assets worth £1,118bn at the end of 2005, compared with £122bn for general companies.) Together with pension funds and unit trusts, long-term insurance companies were the major institutional investors in 2006.

We noted earlier that the major legislation affecting insurance companies dates from the 1982 Act. This makes it an offence for anyone to conduct insurance business without authorization and resulted from concern following the collapse of a number of (general) insurance companies in the 1970s. The power of authorization lies with the FSA and is granted to each company with respect to particular classes of insurance business. In addition to providing authorization, the FSA subsequently monitors the performance of companies, particularly with respect to solvency margins, and has the power to intervene in a number of ways. It may require a change in investment strategy, prevent the renewal of existing policies or the issuing of new ones. In the event that a company should fail in spite of this scrutiny, policyholders have some degree of protection under the Policyholders' Protection Act 1975. The 1982 Act also imposes

Table 3.4   UK non-deposit-taking financial institutions – net acquisition of selected assets, 2006 (£m)

	PF	LTI	GI	UT	IT
Short-term assets	10,705	9,480	89	10,772	616
British government securities	9,573	5,466	–3,127	5,693	254
UK company securities	–11,707	–2,944	3,836	1,830	–2,332
Overseas securities	8,452	13,534	2,738	9,092	–510
Other	13,820	11,172	–755	4,521	173
TOTAL	30,843	36,708	2,781	31,908	–1,779

Source: ONS (2007) *Financial Statistics*, March, table 5.3c. Crown copyright material is reproduced with the permission of the Controller of HMSO and the Queen's Printer for Scotland under the Click-Use license.

[5]   Source: Association of British Insurers.
[6]   ibid.

Explanations of **tables** have been substantially revised to help aid your understanding of the rearrangement of *Financial Times* tables in light of the mergers of financial markets in a larger and more integrated Europe.

AIDING YOUR UNDERSTANDING
(*Continued*)

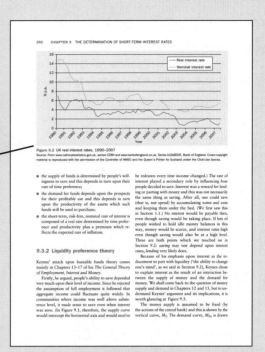

Figures offer visual representation of key concepts in the book.

PRACTICING AND TESTING YOUR UNDERSTANDING

Exercises interspersed in the chapter help you to reflect on what you have just learned and to check your understanding. Answers are provided at the back of the book.

Key concepts and chapter summaries help you review and consolidate your understanding of each chapter.

Questions and problems offer longer review questions to practice and test yourself at the end of a chapter.

Further reading provides full references of sources to refer to for further details on topics covered in the chapter.

APPLYING ECONOMICS TO THE REAL WORLD

Boxes explain how theory works in the real world using examples of real markets and companies in different countries across Europe.

More From The Web introduces you to useful websites and advises you on how to access the best financial information on the web.

An appendix of **case studies** at the back of the book provides illustrations and examples from recent news. Full extracts from the *Financial Times* are analysed in detail and open-ended questions can aid useful discussion.

When we produced the second edition of this book some four years ago we made a number of structural changes from the first edition. In producing the third and now this fourth edition, we have left the structure untouched. There are, however, some significant changes to content and some of these may influence the way in which tutors and students wish to use the book.

Updates

Firstly, as always, we have updated the material where necessary. Since we have always had great faith in the power of illustration and example both to motivate and to explain, we have always used copious extracts from the *Financial Times* (and other sources) with the result that updating is a major task. While finding more recent illustrations involved a lot of work, it was not particularly difficult. This suggests to us that the issues we thought important in the second edition have continued to be so. Markets remain volatile and their movements continue to pose a challenge to orthodox theories of valuation; financial products continue to be mis-sold; the innovative ingenuity of financial firms continues to drive the dialectic relationship with regulators.

Some things do change, however. Europe is more integrated and, from 2007, much larger. Although we still devote four chapters to the financial systems of eight different countries, we can no longer say anything distinctive about the monetary policies of more than half. With the mergers of financial markets currently taking place, we shall soon lose another set of distinctive features. A future edition may well have to recognize a genuinely 'European' (i.e. continental)

financial system. This trend is very noticeable in the *Financial Times* and the current arrangement of its tables. These have been revised substantially since our last edition and updating our comments and guidance on those tables has been a major effort.

When we put together the first edition of this book, the main issue for monetary policy was the independence of central banks. More recently, it has become widely recognized that monetary policy impulses flow directly from the policy rate set by the central bank, rather than by any evolution in the quantity of money itself. This diminishes sharply the importance that used to be given to understanding the demand for money and we have reflected this in the changes made to Chapter 13. The anomalies confronting the efficient market hypothesis have not gone away; if anything they have increased and this has given rise to interesting developments under the heading whereby some economists, dissatisfied with simply *assuming* that agents make the best use of all relevant information, have gone and asked the psychologists what they have discovered *by experimentation* about the way in which people process information. This approach, often labelled **behavioural finance**, has produced some interesting results.

From our point of view, the biggest event, even since the second edition, has been the explosion of relevant material available on the Internet. Central banks and governments, for example, have been at the forefront of publishing statistics, research papers, policy documents etc. as part of the enthusiasm for transparency and openness. Everything published by the Bank of England is freely available on its website. Representative trade bodies have been almost as good. It is now a fairly easy task to get information both about volumes and values of trades and also about trading procedures from associations representing national stock exchanges. Organizations representing insurance companies, unit and investment trusts describe their products in great detail and usually provide useful statistics. Individual firms also have websites which may be aimed primarily at marketing their products but can often provide information of more general value. French banks, in particular, seem to have a highly developed sense of educational responsibility. In the last few years, the most striking development has been the growth of websites devoted to the study of a particular issue, the 'efficient market hypothesis' or 'behavioural finance' are examples. In every book we have ever written we have stressed the importance of students learning how to find out for themselves. This was the main reason behind our original decision to write a book about financial activity which drew repeatedly on the coverage provided by the *Financial Times*. But while the *FT* remains probably the preeminent printed source of financial news and comment, the Internet has rapidly become a major resource. For this reason we began, with the third edition, to feature the most helpful Internet sources. We have continued this through the feature headed '**More From The Web**' scattered widely through the book. While these are obviously meant to be helpful, two notes of caution are necessary. Firstly, we can only refer to the sites we know of and use. There must be many others, possibly hundreds, and possibly better, that we do not know about. Secondly, the Internet technology not only provides very low cost of entry, it also offers very low costs of editing and design. The consequence is that websites are frequently 'updated' and re-designed. We have found that many links that we recommended in the third edition no longer work and we have replaced these. Even so, the directory structure of websites can frequently change and documents are moved from one directory to another. Anyone who has given the Internet address of a document to a student knows the frustration that can be caused by the subsequent error message insisting that it is not at that address. There is not much we can do about this. It is one of the weaknesses of the Internet. What we have done, however, is to explain how we navigated, step by step, to the appropriate source. This means that even if the directory structure changes (invalidating any URL we may have given), readers will know in what part of the website we found the document and may still be able to navigate to it. Unfortunately for us, the *Financial Times* frequently redesigns its website but always remains easy to navigate around.

Using the book

As we said at the outset, the book remains divided into six parts:

- Introduction
- Financial Institutions and Systems
- Theory
- Money and Banking
- Markets
- Current Issues

With the exception of 'Introduction' which is a single chapter, each of the other five parts can form the basis of a one-semester course. Sequence is not important except that students should cover the material in 'Theory' before attempting either 'Money and Banking', 'Markets' or 'Current Issues'. Tutors should bear in mind that there is a Companion Website which provides suggested answers to end-of-chapter questions as well as additional work, yet more reading and exercises.

Additional materials

In addition to the book's Companion Website and the detailed guidance to what is available on other websites, tutors using this edition have access to two sets of 'PowerPoint' slides. With many textbooks, the practice has been to use these slides to provide a visual synopsis of each chapter so that the structure of the book determines the structure of the slide sequence.

We have opted for a different approach, which is to provide two sets of slides that we know, from experience, could be used as the basis for a taught course. Both sets of slides are based upon two courses taught at the University of the West of England, Bristol. These are whole-year courses (approximately 24 weeks) in, respectively, the Economics of Money and Banking (EMB) and the Economics of Financial Markets (EFM). Both courses are based on this book, but they require students to consult a range of other sources both printed and web-based. The EMB course uses material selected from the first four parts of the book. The EFM course uses material taken from the 'Introduction', 'Theory' and 'Markets' parts. Each group of slides, corresponding to a lecture, makes it clear to which chapter it relates, together with any additional material that students need to consult.

PGAH
KB

Acknowledgements

A feature of this book is the guidance it gives to students on reading the financial press. We have reproduced extensive material, both tables and commentary, from the *Financial Times*. We are pleased to acknowledge that this project would not have been possible without the permission and cooperation of its publishers.

In addition, we need to thank all those who have encouraged and helped us to put this new edition together – and have pointed out errors in earlier editions. Most directly involved are Hans-Michael Trautwein and Murray Glickman. Murray has taught from the book for a number of years and has made helpful suggestions throughout. Iris Biefang-

Frisancho Mariscal, at the University of the West of England, Bristol, has pointed out errors (and provided the corrections!). It is her course on the Economics of International Financial Markets that forms the basis of the EFM slides available with this edition. Paula Harris and her colleagues at Pearson Education have given us unfailing support since the first edition and helped us appreciate the developing possibilities of the Internet for this one. To all these, and to the students at the Universities of East London and the West of England at Bristol who showed us what was needed, we are immensely grateful.

PGAH
KB

Publisher's acknowledgements

We are grateful to the following for permission to reproduce copyright material:

Table 1.2 from *Banken Statistik*, February (Deutsche Bundesbank 2007); Table 2.1 adapted from Franklin Allen and Douglas Gale, *Comparing Financial Systems*, Table: 'Classifying Financial Systems', page 4, © 1999 Massachusetts Institute of Technology, by permission of The MIT Press; Table 3.1 adapted from *Bankstats*, www.bankofengland.co.uk (Bank of England); Table in Box 3.1 from *Handbook of Payment Statistics* (APACS 2007); Table 3.2 adapted from *Bankstats*, www.bankofengland.co.uk (Bank of England); Table 3.4 from *Financial Statistics,* March (ONS 2007). Crown copyright material is reproduced with the permission of the Controller of HMSO and the Queen's Printer for Scotland under the Click-Use licence; Table 3.5 from *Financial Statistics*, January (ONS 2004). Crown copyright material is reproduced with the permission of the Controller of HMSO and the Queen's Printer for Scotland under the Click-Use licence; Table 3.6 from *Financial Statistics*, May (ONS 2007). Crown copyright material is reproduced with the permission of the Controller of HMSO and the Queen's Printer for Scotland under the Click-Use licence; Table 4.3 from *Bank Mergers and Banking Structure in the United States 1980–98*, Board of Governors of the Federal Reserve System Staff Study 174, Washington, DC: Federal Reserve System, August (Rhoades, S. A. 2000); Chapter 4 unnumbered table on p. 120 from 'Mortgage finance and housing' in *Financial Services Fact Book 2007*, http://www.iii.org/financial2/about/ (Insurance Information Institute 2007); Table 5.1 from *Banken Statistik*, February (Deutsche Bundesbank 2007); Table in Box 5.2 from *Kapitalmarkt Statistik*, March 2005 and June 2007 (Deutsche Bundesbank 2005 and 2007); Table 5.2 from *Kapitalmarkt Statistik*, June (Deutsche Bundesbank 2007); Table 5.3 from *Monthly Report June 2007*, http://www.bundesbank.de/download/volkswirtschaft/monatsberichte/2007/200706mb_en.pdf (Deutsche Bundesbank 2007); Tables 6.10 and 6.11 from *Rapport Annuel, 2006*, Annexe Statistiques, www.ffsa.fr (Fédération Française des Sociétés d'Assurance 2006); Table 6.13 from *Relazione Annuale, 1995* and *Statistical Bulletin, II 2007* (Banca d'Italia 1995 and 2007); Table 6.14 from *Economic Bulletin*, 37, November 2003 and *Annual Report 2006* (Banca d'Italia 2003 and 2006); Table 16.15 from *Annual Report 2006* (Banca d'Italia 2006); Table 16.16 from *Annual Report 2006* (Banca d'Italia 2006); Table 16.17 from *Annual Report 2006* (Banca d'Italia 2006); Figure 7.1 from *Den svenska finansmarknaden 2007*, August (Sveriges Riksbank 2007); Table 7.2 from *Den svenska finansmarknaden 2006* (Sveriges Riksbank 2006); Table 7.5 from Tables A5 and A6, OECD (1994); Figure 9.2 based on data from CZBH series, www.nationalstatistics.co.uk. Crown copyright material is reproduced with the permission of the Controller of HMSO and the Queen's Printer for Scotland under the Click-Use licence; Figure 9.2 from www.bankofengland.co.uk, Series IUQABEDR (Bank of England); Table 12.1 from *Monthly Bulletin, August*, also available from www.ecb.int (European Central Bank 2007); Table 12.2 from www.federalreserve.gov.uk, reproduced with permission of the Board of Governors of the Federal Reserve System; Figure 13.4 from *Bank of England Quarterly Bulletin*, May, reproduced with permission of the Bank of England (Bank of England 1999); Tables 15.2 and 15.3 from CONDUCT OF MONETARY POLICY IN THE MAJOR INDUSTRIAL COUNTRIES: INSTRUMENTS AND OPERATING PROCEDURES by Batten et al. Copyright 1990 by International Monetary Fund. Reproduced with permission of International Monetary Fund in the format Textbook via Copyright Clearance Center; Tables 15.2 and 15.3 from *Monthly Bulletin*, various issues, Frankfurt am Main, European Central Bank (ECB undated); Table in Box 16.7 and Table in Box 16.9 from *International Banking and Financial Market Developments*, Basel, Bank for International Settlements (BIS 1997); Table 21.1 from The economics of 1992: a study for the European Commission in *European Economy*, Vol. 35 (OPOCE 1988). Reproduced with permission of Pricewaterhouse Coopers; Table 21.2 from Euro area and national MFI interest rates (MIR): July, http://www.ecb.int/stats/money/interest/interest/html/interest_rates_2007-07.en.html (European Central Bank 2007); Tables 21.3 and 21.4 from Eurostat, News Release, 23/2007, 19 February 2007 © European Communities, 1995–2007; Tables 22.2, 23.1 and 23.2 from European Central Bank Statistical Data Warehouse http://sdw.ecb.europa.eu (European Central Bank); Tables 22.3 and 22.4 from WORLD ECONOMIC OUTLOOK: SPILLOVERS AND CYCLES IN THE GLOBAL ECONOMY by IMF. Copyright 2007 by International Monetary Fund. Reproduced with permission of International Monetary Fund in the format Textbook via Copyright Clearance Center.; Table 22.5 from *Convergence Reports*, December 2006 for all countries except Lithuania (May 2006), Bulgaria and Romania (European Central Bank 2006).

We are grateful to the following for permission to reproduce the following texts:

Chapter 2 Box 2.2 Insurers threaten flood cover by Paul Brown, *The Guardian*, 20 April 2004. Copyright Guardian News & Media Ltd 2004; Chapter 2 Box 2.3 Leader: Where ignorance is bliss, *The Guardian*, 18 May 2004. Copyright Guardian News & Media Ltd 2004; Extract in Box 12.2 from *The Monetary Policy of the ECB 2004*, Box 3.7, ECB (2004); Extract in Box 14.1 from www.bankofengland.co.uk/monetarypolicy/remit.htm, Bank of England; Text in Box 21.1 from The Second Banking Directive 89/646/EEC in *Official Journal of the EC*, L386, Vol. 12, 30, December 1989, Annex,© European Communities.

We are grateful to the Financial Times Limited for permission to reprint the following material:

Chapter 2 Box 2.3 Leader: Discrimination in insurance policies, © *Financial Times*, 25 June 2003; Chapter 2 Box 2.5 Private equity must be readier to explain what it does, © *FT.com*, 14 February 2007; Chapter 3 Box 3.2 Merger savings come slowly for Agricole, © *Financial Times*, 11 March 2004; Chapter 3 Box 3.3 Mis-selling: Scandal dates back to Conservative era, © *Financial Times*, 20 September 2003; Chapter 3 Box 3.4 'Mis-selling' warning hangs over pensions saving plan, © *Financial Times*, 16 December 2006; Chapter 3 Box 3.5 Data for Fidelity Investment Services Ltd, © *Financial Times*, 9 June 2007; Chapter 9 Box 9.2 Bank of England keeps rates on hold, © *FT.com*, 6 September 2007; Chapter 9 Box 9.2 US Fed chief holds steady on interest rates, © *Financial Times*, 1 September 2007; Chapter 9 Box 9.2 ECB puzzles markets by leaving rates unchanged, © *Financial Times*, 2 April 2004; Chapter 10 Box 10.1

Market Insight: Fed's weapon of words pops balloon of high expectations, © *Financial Times*, 30 January 2004; Chapter 11 Box 11.1 Good gambling news proves a winner for hotel group, © *Financial Times*, 24 April 2004; Chapter 15 Box 15.1 UK interest rates www.ft.com/marketsdata, © *FT.com*, 5 October 2007; Chapter 15 Box 15.2 ECB lifts interest rates and signals further rise, © *Financial Times*, 8 March 2007; Chapter 16 Box 16.5 Credit rating boost for Croat eurobond debut, © *Financial Times*, 18 January 1997; Chapter 16 Box 16.6 UK GILTS – cash market, © *Financial Times*, 19 September 2007; Chapter 17 Box 17.5 Media, © *Financial Times*, 6 October 2007; Chapter 18 Tables 18.4, 18.5, 18.6, 18.7, Financial Times data, © *Financial Times*, 3 October 2007; Chapter 18 Box 18.5 Dollar index sinks to lowest ebb, © *Financial Times*, 29/30 September 2007; Chapter 19 Tables 19.1, 19.2 and 19.3 Financial Times data, © *Financial Times*, 3 October 2007; Chapter 20 Tables 20.1 and 20.3 Financial Times data, © *Financial Times*, 3 October 2007; Chapter 20 Table 20.2 Financial Times data, © *Financial Times*, 16 March 2004; Chapter 20 Table 20.4 Financial Times data, © *Financial Times*, 27 April 2004; Chapter 20 Box 20.4 Price of being bucked by the trend, © *Financial Times*, 20 March 1991; Chapter 25 Box 25.4 Split cap victims pick up the pieces on offer, © *Financial Times*, 11 November 2006 and Second payment to splits victims, © *Financial Times*, 23 August 2006; Chapter 26 Box 26.1 Gartmore Turnround, © *Financial Times*, 8 October 2007; Chapter 26 Box 26.2 Don't be a mug when buying growth stocks, © *Financial Times*, 29 May 2004; Case study 1 Global settlement: Blodget pays out $4m and gets life ban, © *Financial Times*, 29 April 2003; Case study 2 We Are All Venture Capitalists Now, © *Financial Times*, 11 March 2000; Case study 2 What a difference a year can make to a dream, © *Financial Times*, 10 March 2001; Case study 3 Markets behaving badly, © *Financial Times*, 7 April 2001; Case study 3 FINANCE WEEK: It takes a cracker . . . : Tracker funds look the better bet but even they have problems. The Long View, © *Financial Times*, 11 March 2000; Case study 4 Inflexible King finally forced to bend, © *Financial Times*, 20 September 2007; Case study 5 Pound slips after Bank minutes, © *Financial Times*, 17 October 2007; Case study 6 LEADER: The regulator judged, © *Financial Times*, 22 June 2006; Case study 6 LOMBARD: When a financial failure would be a success, © *Financial Times*, 6 June 2007; Case study 6 The right response to Northern Rock, © *Financial Times*, 1 October 2007; Case study 6 MPs grill FSA chiefs over Northern Rock, © *Financial Times*, 9 October 2007; Case study 6 FSA owns up to Rock failings, © *Financial Times*, 10 October 2007; Case study 6 FSA in the dock, © *Financial Times*, 9 October 2007; Case study 8 Lex: Parmalat, © *Financial Times*, 19 December 2003.

We are grateful to the following for permission to use copyright material:

Case study 6 Return regulation to the Bank of England from *The Financial Times Limited*, 2 October 2007, © Peter Oppenheimer.

In some instances we have been unable to trace the owners of copyright material, and we would appreciate any information that would enable us to do so.

Symbols, abbreviations and other conventions

AI	Accrued interest	i_d	Domestic interest rate
α	The cash ratio of the non-bank private sector $(= C_p/D_p)$	i_f	Foreign interest rate
		$I£$	Irish punt
β	Banks' reserve ratio $(= (C_b + D_b)/D_p)$	K	The return on an asset
β	Beta-coefficient (of an asset)	$\hat{K}$	The expected return on an asset
B	The monetary base	$\overline{K}$	The required rate of return on an asset
BFr	Belgian franc	K_m	The rate of return on a 'whole market portfolio'
C	Coupon payment		
c	Coupon rate	K_{rf}	The risk-free rate of return
C_b	Notes and coin held by the banking system	L	Italian lira
C_c	cost of carry	L_g	Bank loans to the government
C_p	Notes and coin held by the non-bank private sector	L_p	Bank loans to the non-bank private sector
		M	The par or maturity or redemption value of an asset
cy	Current yield		
Δ	Change in	M_D	Demand for money
d	Rate of discount	M_S	Supply of money
d	The Eurobank redeposit ratio	$M1$	M1 monetary aggregate
D_b	Deposits of the banking system at the central bank	$M2$	M2 monetary aggregate
		$M3$	M3 monetary aggregate
D_g	Deposits of the government	$M4$	M4 monetary aggregate
D_p	Deposits of the non-bank private sector	N	Total employment
DKr	Danish krone	n	Total number (e.g. of time periods)
DM	Deutschmark	n_{im}	Length of time from date of issue to maturity
Dr	Greek drachma	n_{lc}	Length of time since last coupon payment
€	euro	n_m	Length of time to maturity
Ecu	European currency unit	n_{sm}	Length of time from settlement of purchase to maturity
E_F	Forward exchange rate expressed in direct quotation		
		n_{tc}	Length of time to next coupon payment
E_R	Real exchange rate expressed in direct quotation	n_{xc}	Length of time from ex dividend date to next coupon payment
E_S	Spot exchange rate expressed in direct quotation	n_{xt}	Length of time between ex dividend date and date of calculation
Es	Portuguese escudo	P	The purchase or market price (the price level in the aggregate)
FFr	French franc		
FM	Finnish markka	Pm^c	The premium price of a call option
Fl	Netherlands guilder	P_s	Spot or cash price
i	Nominal rate of interest	P_x	Strike or exercise price of option

P_x^f	Discounted option strike price	S_R	Real exchange rate expressed in indirect quotation
π	The rate of inflation		
π^e	The expected rate of inflation	S_S	Spot exchange rate expressed in indirect quotation
Pta	Spanish peseta		
Q	The number of coupon payments before redemption	σ	The standard deviation (of an asset's return) risk
r	The real rate of interest	σ^2	The variance (of an asset's return) risk
ry	Redemption yield	Σ	Summation (of a series)
RR	Required bank reserves	t	Time period
smy	Simple yield to maturity	T	Total number of time periods
S_F	Forward exchange rate expressed in indirect quotation	TR	Total bank reserves
		V	Velocity of circulation
S_f	Shareholders' funds	$\dot{W}$	Rate of change of money wages
Sch	Austrian schilling	Y	Aggregate real output, national income
SDR	Special Drawing Right	$¥$	Japanese yen
SFr	Swiss franc	$£$	Pound sterling
SKr	Swedish krona	$\$$	United States dollar

Part 1 Introduction

Chapter 1 # The role of a financial system

What you will learn in this chapter:

- What a financial system consists of

- Who uses it and for what purposes

- The distinctive features of financial institutions

- The distinctive features of financial markets

- Why the performance of the financial system is relevant to the rest of the economy

1.1 Introduction

In this chapter we want to provide preliminary answers to the points listed on the previous page: what is a financial system, who uses it, what does it do, does it matter how it does it? Our answers are preliminary in the sense that these questions concern us throughout the book and each later chapter is looking at some aspect of these questions in more detail. The intention here is to provide an introduction – a definition of key terms and the explanation of some basic principles – for readers who have had no prior contact with financial economics, and an overview of the field, as we see it, for all readers.

We begin by defining a financial system as:

> a set of markets for financial instruments, and the individuals and institutions who trade in those markets, together with the regulators and supervisors of the system.

The users of the system are people, firms and other organizations who wish to make use of the facilities offered by a financial system. The facilities offered may be summarized as:

- intermediation between surplus and deficit units;
- financial services such as insurance and pensions;
- a payments mechanism;
- portfolio adjustment facilities.

Notice that while different parts of the system may specialize in each of these functions, they all have one thing in common: they all have the effect of channelling funds from those who have a surplus (to their current spending plans) to those who have a deficit. Consider each case in turn. Banks, historically speaking, began as institutions whose function was to accept deposits from those who wished to save and to lend them to borrowers on terms which were attractive to the latter. Only later did they begin to offer a means of payment facility, based initially upon written cheques but now largely electronic. Thus, to have access to the current payments mechanism, one needs to hold bank deposits and these can be on-lent. Similarly, insurance companies and pension funds have a primary purpose which is to offer people a means of managing the risk of some major, adverse event. However, the contributions made by policyholders creates a fund which is usually invested in a wide range of securities. This purchase of securities involves a flow of funds (directly or indirectly) to those who issued the securities as a means of raising funds. The income from the securities goes to meet the expenses of the companies' operations, including some payments to policyholders. Portfolio adjustment facilities have to provide wealth-holders with a quick, cheap and reliable way of buying and selling a wide variety of financial assets. When wealth-holders buy financial assets they are **lending** (again directly or indirectly) to those who issued the assets. These facilities are obviously supplied by financial markets, but they are also supplied to smaller investors by 'mutual funds' such as unit trusts. Thus, all kinds of financial activity have the effect in some degree of channelling funds from lenders to borrowers.

It is important to bear in mind that economists are usually interested in the way in which a financial system channels funds between the **end users** of the system, that is, between **ultimate borrowers and lenders**, rather than the **intermediate borrowers and lenders** – the financial intermediaries who also borrow and lend but only, as their name implies, in order to channel funds between end users. In developed economies, incomes are generally so high (by world standards) that there are many people who wish to lend; and the state of technology is such that real investment can only be undertaken by **borrowing** funds to finance its installation and to see firms through the often lengthy period before it earns a return. Given that there is a desire to lend and to borrow, we can get some idea immediately of why modern economies have quite highly developed financial systems.

Faced with a desire to lend or to borrow, the end users of financial systems have a choice between three broad approaches.

Firstly, they can engage in what is usually called **direct lending**. That is to say that they deal directly with each other. But this, as we shall see, is costly, inefficient, extremely risky and not, in practice, very likely.

Secondly, they may decide to use **organized markets**. In these markets, lenders buy the liabilities issued by borrowers. If the liability is newly issued, then the issuer receives funds directly from the lender. To this extent the process has some similarity to direct lending, but dealing in liabilities traded in organized markets has advantages for both parties. Organized markets reduce the search costs that would be associated with direct lending because organized markets are populated by people willing to trade. They also reduce risk since there are usually rules governing the operation of the market which endeavour to exclude the dishonest and the extremely risky. For lenders, there is the big advantage that they can sell their claim on the borrower if, after making the loan, they find they need funds themselves. Indeed, the more typical transaction in organized markets is that where a lender buys, not a newly issued liability, but a liability which was originally bought from the borrower by another lender. In this case the lender is refinancing a loan originally made by someone else, though the borrower is completely unaware of this secondary transaction. The best known markets, of course, are the markets for company shares in Tokyo, London, New York and Hong Kong. But there are organized markets for a vast range of financial instruments, as we shall see in Part 5 of this book.

We have suggested that organized markets may be used by **ultimate lenders** and borrowers. But they are used also by financial intermediaries who themselves provide a third channel for the transmission of funds between borrowers and lenders. When a lender deals through an intermediary, s/he acquires an asset – typically a bank or building society deposit, or claims on an insurance fund – which cannot be traded but can only be returned to the intermediary. Similarly, intermediaries create liabilities, typically in the form of loans, for borrowers. These too are 'non-marketable'. If the borrower wishes to end the loan, it must be repaid to the intermediary. The advantages of dealing through intermediaries are similar to those of dealing in organized markets: lenders and borrowers are brought together more quickly, more efficiently and therefore more cheaply than if they had to search each other out; and the intermediary is able, through superior knowledge and economies of scale, to reduce the risk of the transaction for both parties. One of the ways in which they do the latter is to hold highly diversified portfolios of assets and liabilities and this involves them as traders in organized markets. Indeed, most markets are probably dominated by intermediaries rather than by end users of the financial system. Figure 1.1 summarizes these three possibilities schematically.

We go next, in Section 1.2, to the question of who the end users are and the supplementary question of what are their motives and interests; in Section 1.3 we shall look at the essential characteristics of financial institutions and their role as intermediaries; in Section 1.4 we look at the broad range of financial markets and suggest some ways in which they may be

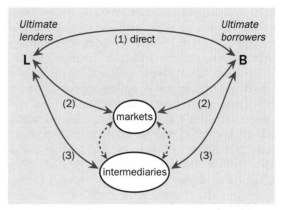

Figure 1.1 The options for lenders and borrowers

ordered and classified as well as introducing some of the basic principles underlying supply and demand in financial markets; in Section 1.5 we look at how all this financial activity relates to the functioning of the 'real' economy.

Remember, as you read these sections, that most issues are dealt with in more detail later in the book. We shall point this out as we go along.

1.2 Lenders and borrowers

In this section we turn our attention to the end users of the financial system – lenders and borrowers – and to their reasons for lending and borrowing. We shall see that these motives differ and in some cases conflict. The role of a financial system is to reconcile these differences, as cheaply and effectively as possible. Remember that lenders and borrowers here are *ultimate* lenders and borrowers. Their motives as lenders and borrowers are different from those of financial intermediaries who are also lending (to ultimate borrowers) and borrowing (from ultimate lenders) and frequently lending and borrowing between themselves. We must not confuse the two.

1.2.1 Saving and lending

As we noted earlier, it is one characteristic of developed economies that incomes are higher than many people require for current consumption. The difference between income and consumption we call **saving**.

In these economies, aggregate saving is positive. These savings can be used to buy 'real' capital assets such as machinery, industrial equipment and premises. Savings used in this way are being used for *investment*.[1]

However, many people will be saving at a level which exceeds their **real investment** spending. Indeed, this is generally true for households whose needs and opportunities for real investment are limited. Many households save without undertaking any real investment. The difference between saving and real investment is their **financial surplus**, and they are often described as **surplus units**. It is this financial surplus that is available for lending and it is this that gives rise to *a net acquisition of financial assets*. Notice that we say 'available for lending'. It does not have to be lent. It is perfectly possible for those with a financial surplus to accumulate what used to be called **hoards**. That is to say, they could use their surplus to build up holdings of money. Borrowing from the vocabulary of computing, we might say that the accumulation of money holdings is the 'default' setting. This is what happens to those with a financial surplus if they make no conscious decision to do otherwise. They receive their income in money form (usually by the transfer of bank deposits). They use some of that (money) income to make consumption purchases. If consumption is less than income they have positive saving. Assume, for simplicity, that their real investment is zero. Their saving is simultaneously a financial surplus and if they make no positive decision about its allocation it will, by default, accumulate in the form of bank deposits. If they do this, they are not lending.[2]

This distinction between saving and lending, revolving around people's desire to hold money as a financial asset, was once a crucial issue in economics. It lay at the centre of contrasting views about the determination of interest rates, as we shall see in Section 9.3.

We can sum up what we have just said in the following identity:

$$(Y - C) - I = NAFA \qquad (1.1)$$

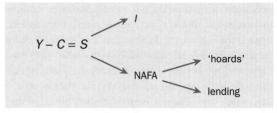

Figure 1.2 Possible uses of saving

where $(Y - C)$, income minus consumption, is saving; I stands for real investment; and $NAFA$ stands for the *net acquisition of financial assets*. Figure 1.2 summarizes the position more schematically, and also emphasizes the point that the net acquisition of financial assets is equal only to *potential* lending. The accumulation of 'hoards' is an acquisition of financial assets (money) but is not, as we know, lending.

What conditions have to be met to induce those with a surplus to lend? As a general principle we shall say that lenders wish to get the maximum **return** for the minimum of **risk**. It is also assumed that lenders have a positive attitude towards **liquidity**. We look at each in turn.

The *return* on a financial asset may take one or more of a number of forms. It may take the form of the payment of interest at discrete intervals. This is the case, for example, with a savings deposit which is, in effect, a loan to a savings institution. Interest is also paid on bonds, though there is also the possibility with a bond of selling at a profit and making a capital gain. With company shares, the attraction of capital gain for some investors is at least as important as the periodic payments, which are variable because they are ultimately related to the firms' earnings. Some assets, when newly issued, are sold at a discount to the price at which they will later be redeemed, their maturity value. This discount functions, therefore, rather like a capital gain – one pays less for the asset than one receives on its disposal. This discount can be expressed as a fraction (usually of the maturity value)

---

[1]   UK readers need to be careful with the use of the term 'investment'. Economists use the term strictly to refer to the purchase of real, physical, assets whose purpose is to contribute to the production process. The printed and broadcast media, following the financial press, use the term investment to refer to the acquisition of financial assets. These are quite distinct activities. It is probably too late to insist on the use of 'investment' being confined to its original sense. When there might be any ambiguity, we shall use the term 'real investment' to refer to the purchase of capital equipment.

[2]   Readers who are puzzled by this (because they are tempted to think that the accumulation of money balances, if it is in the form of bank deposits, still results in lending because banks have more deposits to lend) should think carefully and then read footnote 1 in Chapter 9. Definitions of money and details of the money supply process are dealt with in Chapter 12.

and in this form, known as a *rate* of discount, it can be compared with other rates of return. Discounting is most commonly used in connection with treasury or commercial bills – tradable securities of short duration. We look at the returns on different types of asset, and at the factors determining those returns, in our discussion of individual markets in Part 5 of this book.

Risk in a financial context is usually taken to refer to the probability that outcomes may differ from what was expected. It takes a number of forms. For the moment we may note that lenders are faced with the possibility of **default risk** (the borrower fails to repay when expected); **income risk** (the asset fails to yield the return expected); **capital risk** (the asset's nominal value differs from what was expected) and **inflation risk** (the risk that the price level changes unexpectedly, causing a change in the real value of assets). One of the main disadvantages in direct lending, and hence one of the main advantages in using organized markets or specialist intermediaries, is that many lenders would find it impossible to assess accurately the risk of lending to individual borrowers. And if they could, the level of risk to which they found themselves exposed would deter them from lending, perhaps at all or certainly at anything but a very high rate of return.

Other things being equal, lenders are also assumed to prefer opportunities that offer the greatest *liquidity*. By liquidity we mean the ability to retrieve funds quickly and with capital certainty. Notice that two conditions are involved – speed and value. Any asset can be sold quickly – even a house in a depressed housing market – if the seller is prepared to incur a sufficiently large capital loss. The reasons for this positive attitude towards liquidity are quite complex but they are connected with risk and uncertainty. In making a loan, a lender is calculating that s/he does not need access to the funds for a given period. In an uncertain world, however, these calculations can go wrong resulting in inconvenience, embarrassment or, for a firm, perhaps even bankruptcy. The ability to retrieve funds quickly, and at a value that can be depended upon, is a positive attraction in any lending opportunity.

1.2.2 Borrowing

At the same time that some people have income which is in excess of their current consumption needs, there will be those – firms, households, public authorities – whose incomes are insufficient for their current spending plans. This will usually be because they are planning to spend on large, expensive, 'real' assets of a kind which last for many years. Their need to borrow this year, therefore, may be offset in future by years when saving is the norm. For households, such purchases will typically be major consumer durables, cars or even houses perhaps. For firms, it will be real capital equipment which they hope will add to their cashflow in future and will help them to service and repay the loan. In certain circumstances, however, one can envisage people borrowing in order to purchase financial assets. Notice that this is not likely to be a common situation since it is saying that borrowers can borrow funds at a lower cost than the return that they can get from the financial assets they purchase. This is extremely rare for the personal sector. It is usually much more expensive for individuals to borrow funds than it is for firms or public bodies. A personal loan will cost much more than a firm has to offer on its shares or bonds. But there may have been cases, the Wall Street boom of 1928–29 and the big bull market of the mid-1980s, where people and non-financial institutions have thought, rightly or wrongly, that they could borrow in order to earn a profit from financial assets.

MORE FROM THE WEB
Consumer borrowing

To find the latest figures for net new lending to UK consumers month by month go to the statistical section of Bank of England's website: www.bankofengland.co.uk/statistics.

Click on 'Statistical releases' then 'Bankstats' and then on 'Tables'.

The figures you want are on page 2 of Table A5.6. The table also shows the total amount of consumer credit outstanding.

Similar figures, for the total amount of bank credit outstanding to French consumers at the end of each quarter, can be found in the statistics section of the Banque de France's website: www.banque-france.fr/gb/stat_conjoncture/series/series.htm.

Click on 'Total domestic debt' then on 'Breakdown by agents'.

Those who wish to spend (on consumption and real investment) in excess of their income are said to have a **financial deficit** and they are sometimes referred to as **deficit units**. We saw earlier that surplus units must acquire financial assets as a consequence of their financial surplus; deficit units must either shed financial assets (accumulated in the past) or incur financial liabilities (debts). The latter are *borrowers*. Both groups are engaged in the 'net acquisition of financial assets'. The vital difference is that for the former the net acquisition is positive while for the latter it is negative.

The interests of borrowers are mainly twofold. Firstly, they will wish to minimize *cost*. The cost to the borrower is the yield to the lender and may take any one of the number of forms we described above. Notice though that in addition to wanting to borrow at minimum cost, borrowers may also have definite preferences about other terms on which they borrow. For example, a young firm engaged in rapid expansion may prefer to borrow by issuing shares. In the early stages, earnings may be small, a high proportion will be ploughed back into the business and dividend payments will then be small. But shareholders may be willing to hold shares on these terms because they look forward to capital gains as the firm expands. The alternatives, bond issues for example, mean that the firm commits itself to an outflow of funds right from the start. This cash drain could be critical in the early stages of expansion.

Secondly, and in contrast with lenders, borrowers will wish to maximize the period for which they borrow. This has two benefits. It reduces the risk that the lender will have to be repaid at a time which is inconvenient to the borrower, and also reduces the exposure of the borrower to the risk that the loan might have to be replaced at a time when interest rates have risen.

Table 1.1 summarizes the contrasting interests of lenders and borrowers. A (+) indicates a desire to maximize and a (−) shows a desire to minimize.

Table 1.1 The priorities of lenders and borrowers

Lenders		Borrowers	
Return	(+)	Cost	(−)
Risk	(−)	Length of loan	(+)
Liquidity	(+)		

1.2.3 Lenders, borrowers and the net acquisition of financial assets

Let us summarize. Lenders are a subset of those with a financial surplus. Surplus units are those whose income exceeds consumption and any spending on real capital assets. Their financial surplus ensures that their net acquisition of financial assets is positive. Lending results from the acquisition of financial assets which create loans for borrowers.

Borrowers are a subset of those with a financial deficit. Deficit units have income which is insufficient to meet their planned spending on consumption and real capital assets. Their financial deficit ensures that their net acquisition of financial assets is negative. This 'negative acquisition' may involve disposing of existing financial assets or it may involve acquiring liabilities. Those that take the latter course are borrowing.

We are all familiar with the rule that any asset must be someone's liability. (Even notes and coin, which are sometimes dignified with the special label 'outside money', are technically speaking liabilities of the government.) It follows, therefore, that in the aggregate, financial surpluses and deficits must cancel out. This is simplest to see if we imagine a closed economy. A closed economy is conventionally divided into three sectors: households, firms and the government sector. As a general rule, it is assumed that households run a financial surplus. As we have noted, households spend very little on real investment. By contrast, the business sector is assumed to run a deficit. If the government sector runs a balanced budget, then it follows that the size of the household surplus must match the size of the firms' deficit. If, as frequently happens, the government sector runs a deficit, then the household surplus must match the combined deficits of government and firms. The same principle must hold if we expand the model to incorporate an external sector. *In the aggregate, sector deficits and surpluses must sum to zero.*

In most economies it is possible to find values for all our relevant terms. Figures for income (Y), consumption (C), saving (S) and real investment (I) can be found in the *national income accounts*. The usual practice is then to transfer the difference between S and I to what are called the *financial accounts*. Capital grants (K) and transfers (KT) are then added in order to yield the financial surplus or deficit and the main function of the financial accounts is to show how sector surpluses or deficits are financed. One of the accounts, for example, will show the household sector's total sales and purchases of each class of financial asset or liability. The net balance of these sales and purchases matches, in theory, the size of the surplus. Inspection of any country's financial accounts reveals two striking features. The first is that a sector's net transactions in financial assets and liabilities very rarely match the size of the surplus or deficit exactly. There are usually quite large residual errors in financial accounts. The second is that the total volume of transactions (as opposed to their net balance) is much greater than that required to fund a deficit (or dispose of a surplus). The reason is obvious on reflection. People trade in financial assets not just to fund this year's deficit or to dispose of their current surplus. They are, in addition, continually rearranging their financial wealth in response to what they see as important changes in the risk and return characteristics of assets.

1.2.4 Lending, borrowing and wealth

As in all branches of economics, it is important in financial economics to distinguish between stocks and flows. While flows are very important, and it is flows that we have so far been discussing, there are times when stocks matter.

For example, a person with a current financial surplus is adding to his or her stock of financial wealth. A person with a current financial deficit must either run down his or her stock of assets or add to his or her stock of debt. A (flow) surplus leads to an increase in the stock of net financial wealth; a (flow) deficit leads to a reduction in that stock.

Notice that we talk here, as we did with the flows of lending and borrowing, of 'net' positions. People will hold simultaneous debtor and creditor positions. People with mortgages on their homes will also hold building society deposits. A firm may have very substantial long-term debt as a result of recent expansion while simultaneously holding a large sum in a high-interest bank account.

This looks strange at first sight. After all, financial intermediaries make their profit by, *inter alia*, charging more to borrowers than they pay to lenders. For some people, many individuals for example, this differential or 'spread' is very large. Surely, one would think, debtors with financial assets would be better off if they disposed of the assets and used the funds to reduce their indebtedness. However, this overlooks the advantages that come from having access to 'ready money'. It ignores the advantages of liquidity. When we discussed the desires of lenders, liquidity was specified as one of the characteristics that lenders preferred in a loan. But the advantages of liquidity apply to everyone, not just to lenders. A net debtor who uses a savings deposit to pay off part of the debt sacrifices the benefit and convenience that liquidity confers – the ability to meet unforeseen demands for payment or the ability to make a purchase at an unforeseen bargain price. When it comes to calculating costs and benefits we should say that our debtor would certainly derive some benefit by using the whole of the deposit to pay off part of the loan. (The benefit would be a saving in interest payments equal to the size of the deposit multiplied by the differential between the borrowing and lending rates.) But this benefit would be accompanied by some cost – the loss of liquidity. The question for the rational debtor is whether he or she values the liquidity services flowing from his or her savings deposit at more or less than the saving in interest payments being currently forgone by holding the savings deposit. There are two important points to draw from this discussion. The first is that financial decisions typically depend upon 'spreads' or differentials between interest rates. However, we are used in economics to the idea that people make decisions on the basis of *relative* prices, so there is nothing new here. The second is that the costs and benefits of financial assets and liabilities are not fully captured by their *pecuniary* characteristics. People hold zero-interest sight deposits because the liquidity benefits outweigh the value of interest that could be had from a time deposit.

Clearly, in making decisions to acquire financial assets and liabilities, people are faced with a very complex choice. The choice is not just about whether to be a borrower or a lender but about the amount of both borrowing and lending that they should undertake. It also involves a choice about the best mix of types of asset and liability for their particular circumstances. When they are making these decisions, people are said to be exercising their **portfolio choice**. As we have seen, exercising portfolio choice involves arranging the portfolio, the mixture of assets and liabilities, in such a way that, for a given cost, the benefit derived from each asset or liability is equal at the margin. When this is the case, there is no incentive for further re-arrangements and investors are said to be in **portfolio equilibrium**. The study of the principles underlying portfolio choice is known as the study of **portfolio theory**. We shall look at these principles in Chapter 8.

1.3   Financial institutions

Financial institutions come in lots of different forms and offer a variety of services. Broadly speaking, we may say that financial institutions specialize in one or more of the following functions:

- providing a payments mechanism;
- providing a means of lending and borrowing;
- providing other services, such as foreign exchange, insurance and so on.

Notice, however, that whatever their most obvious function might be, they all have the effect that the institution mediates between those who have a financial surplus and those who have a deficit. Whatever their apparent purpose, they all share the characteristic that they offer many different types of loans to borrowers and create a wide range of assets for lenders. 'Banks' which provide the payments mechanism, for example, do this by accepting deposits which they lend on to borrowers. Other institutions, for example, offer insurance cover or benefits which are paid to the saver conditional upon certain events taking place – the ending of the savings contract or retirement. The firm provides these benefits as a result of investing its clients' contributions in a variety of financial assets. We shall see in Chapter 2 that when we discuss the financial institutions which (together with markets) make up a financial system, we often divide such institutions into two groups. The first is 'banks', or what in most countries we might call 'deposit takers', and 'other' (or non-deposit-taking) financial institutions. The former are discussed in Chapter 12. Discussion of the latter is distributed through the chapters devoted to each country's financial system in Part 2 of the book. This is partly because banks in any financial system fulfil broadly similar roles and operate in broadly similar ways, while individual countries show wider variation – reflecting their individual histories and development – in non-bank institutions. The major reason for this distinction, however, is that deposit-taking institutions have one peculiar feature which distinguishes them from other financial institutions,

and economists regard the distinction as potentially important. This is that their liabilities are used as money. An expansion of bank business, therefore, almost invariably involves an increase in the money supply. We shall see in Section 1.5, and in Chapters 12 and 13, that the creation of money may have particular effects on the economy. This means that banks tend to be subject to special regulation, since a bank failure can have very damaging effects upon the payments mechanism, and also that they are continually affected by the monetary policy that governments choose to pursue. For the rest of *this* section, however, what we say about financial institutions applies equally to banks and non-deposit takers.

1.3.1   Financial institutions as firms

Financial institutions are firms and we can analyse their behaviour in much the same way as economists would analyse the behaviour of any firm. We can imagine them taking various inputs – premises, labour, technology, raw materials – and producing outputs of various kinds. They do this with much the same objectives in mind as any other firm and in the process costs and revenues behave much as they do for other firms. We look at each in turn, noting distinctive features of financial firms where appropriate.

Like most firms, financial institutions hire labour and own or rent specialist premises. In recent years, there have been sharp increases in labour productivity as market pressures have forced firms to cut costs. This has been helped in large measure by technological developments, particularly in computing. Technology has also had its effects upon the 'land' element of inputs. For many years it was accepted, particularly by deposit-taking institutions, that a high street presence was essential to the attraction of customers. This led to large-scale investment in expensive premises located in prime sites. Indeed, the cost of premises for retail financial institutions was a significant barrier to entry. The past 15 years, however, have seen the rapid growth of telephone banking and 'direct line' insurance companies providing services by telephone and computer terminal and using the cost savings on premises to offer competitive prices to customers.

Where inputs are concerned, the most distinctive feature for non-deposit institutions is the funds that savers wish to lend. These are invested with the institution in order to earn insurance or pension benefits, or to accumulate shares in managed funds of securities. The 'cost' of these inputs consists of the cost of administering the account together with the financial benefits themselves which the institution has to pay out. For deposit institutions the essential input is 'reserves'. We shall see in Chapter 12 how, provided a bank or building society has adequate reserves of notes and coin and its own deposits held usually with the central bank, it has great freedom to create loans and deposits at its own discretion. There is an organized market for these reserves (the 'interbank market' which we shall discuss in Chapter 15) and the cost is the rate of interest prevailing in that market, a rate of interest which is strongly influenced by the central bank.

As with other firms, we can distinguish between those costs that are fixed over some range of output and those that are variable. Also, quite conventionally, we can assume that the marginal cost of production is rising in the short run. Attracting more funds will normally mean offering greater inducements in the form of interest, or bonuses or other services, and so the unit cost of such funds will increase with their volume.

On the face of it, the outputs of financial institutions are 'loans' though these loans may take many different forms and may not always be easy to identify as such. In the case of banks and savings institutions the loans that they make to clients are obvious and show in their balance sheets as loans or 'advances' to customers. The loan nature of outputs from non-deposit institutions is not quite so obvious. Many of the funds received by insurance and pension companies are used to hold a diversified portfolio of securities purchased in financial markets. Where these securities are newly issued, the funds flow to the issuing firm and are, in effect, functioning as a loan. Many purchases, however, are purchases of existing securities from existing holders. In this case, financial institutions are in effect refinancing loans originally made by some other person or organization. We shall see in Section 1.4 that the existence of an active market for 'secondhand' securities, that is, for existing loans, is essential if new securities (new loans) are to be acceptable to lenders at a reasonable price.

However, to say that outputs are loans, in some form or other, is to tell less than half the story. Taken as a group, financial institutions offer a wide variety of services ranging from share dealing and share issues to tax and other forms of financial advice to the personal and corporate sectors. Indeed, in Part 2 we shall see that in some financial systems these so-called 'off-balance-sheet activities' have grown rapidly in recent years. Furthermore, in making funds available to borrowers, either directly or indirectly, financial institutions are making important changes to the nature of those funds. This transformation process itself may be said to be creating something and is often said to be the basis for regarding financial institutions as *financial intermediaries*. We turn to this crucially important transformation process in the next section.

Continuing our parallels with other types of firm, financial institutions derive revenue from their outputs. Most obviously, this revenue accrues from the interest that borrowers pay on the loans made by financial institutions. Where institutions are holding portfolios of securities their revenue comes from the dividend and interest payments on those securities. Where institutions offer off-balance-sheet services to customers, they charge fees. Like other firms, financial institutions will maximize profits when the difference between total revenue and total cost is at its greatest, that is, at the point where marginal cost equals marginal revenue.

This is not to say that financial institutions are necessarily profit *maximizers*. It is a characteristic of financial activity that it is subject to economies of scale for reasons we shall see in Section 1.3.2. Thus most financial systems tend to be dominated by large institutions. It is clear from their publicity, as well as their behaviour, that other objectives, such as size, growth and market share, are important to them.

1.3.2 Financial institutions as 'intermediaries'

Right at the beginning of this chapter we saw that, whatever specialist services an institution might provide, a major part of any financial institution's activity was to make loans to ultimate borrowers out of the funds which ultimate lenders made available to them. In doing this, we said that they were involved in a process known as **intermediation** and that intermediation had important characteristics and consequences. What are these?

Rather obviously 'intermediation' means acting as a go-between between two parties. The parties will often be the ultimate lenders and borrowers but sometimes they will be other intermediaries. What are the characteristics of intermediation? The first thing to say is that intermediation involves a good deal more than simply introducing or bringing together two parties. One *could* imagine a firm offering a service whereby it maintained a register of potential lenders and potential borrowers and tried to match them up. This would work rather like a computer dating agency and, rather like such agencies, our firm would charge a commission for successful introduction. But this is not intermediation. If such activity has a name it is best described as broking. The process of intermediation requires that something be created by the transformation of inputs into outputs. At its simplest we might say that what intermediaries do is:

> to create assets for lenders and liabilities for borrowers which are more attractive to each than would be the case if the parties had to deal with each other directly.

Essentially what this means is that intermediaries transform funds which are made available to them normally for short periods into loans which are made available to ultimate borrowers for longer terms. This is sometimes summed up by saying that intermediaries 'borrow short and lend long'. What is being created in this process is liquidity and we can see this most clearly if we contrast the situation of direct lending with lending via an intermediary.

Take the case of someone wishing to borrow £130,000 to buy a house, intending to repay the loan, say, over 25 years. Without the help of an intermediary our borrower has to find someone willing to lend £130,000 for this same period and at a rate of interest which is mutually agreeable. The borrower might just possibly be successful. In that case the lender has an asset (the interest-bearing loan) and the borrower has a liability (the obligation to pay interest and eventually the obligation to repay the principal). In practice, however, even if the would-be borrower employed a broker, it seems unlikely that the search would be successful. Not many people wish to lend £130,000 to a comparative stranger and for a long period of time. Even if a potential lender could be found, the scale of risk involved (in lending to an unknown individual) and the illiquidity of the loan (the funds cannot be recovered at the lender's discretion for 25 years) would mean that the rate of interest demanded would be so high that the borrower would decline the offer.

Suppose now that some sort of savings institution were to emerge, and that it specializes in taking large numbers of small deposits, which it pools and lends as

fewer larger loans and for long periods. It pays interest on the deposits and charges a higher rate of interest on the loans. Ultimate lenders and ultimate borrowers both benefit and indeed benefit by so much that they are prepared to lend and to borrow on such terms that allow the intermediary to make a profit. What are the benefits?

Firstly, provided that the institution keeps some proportion of the funds it receives in liquid form, and provided that depositors do not all wish to withdraw deposits at once, depositors can have instant access to their funds even though the vast majority of funds have been lent for a long period. The corresponding advantage to the borrower is the availability of long-term loans, even though, perhaps, no one wishes to lend for a long period. This is a process known as **maturity transformation**.

Secondly, a benefit for lenders is that the institution can *pool* lots of small deposits which taken in isolation would be unattractive to borrowers. These deposits can then earn a rate of interest from being lent which would not have been possible before. The corresponding benefit to borrowers is that they can borrow large sums even though lenders may not wish to lend large sums.

Thirdly, by operating on a large scale, the savings institution can *reduce risk* for both parties. Partly it does this by employing staff, paid out of the interest-spread between borrowing and lending rates, to assess the risk attaching to the loans it makes. Although each individual case is assessed on its merits, there are many similarities between cases, so the staff become specialists and highly competent by virtue of experience. Institutions also reduce risk by virtue of their ability to *diversify*. They can diversify by lending to a wide variety of people and organizations in such a way that an adverse event is likely to affect only a small proportion of loans. They can also diversify their sources of funds, so that a difficulty in raising funds from one source can be offset from elsewhere. Diversification is one of the characteristics of financial intermediaries that tends to benefit from economies of scale.

Lastly, the institution reduces **search and transaction costs** for both parties. Lenders know where the institution is. They make their deposits and walk away. Borrowers likewise know where the institution is. They telephone, write, or call in. Furthermore, although each transaction is in some sense unique, each can be fitted into a broad category – housing mortgage, personal loan, business overdraft, etc. This means that the terms on which funds are accepted and lent can be standardized. There is a set of rules for each type of deposit or other contribution and a set of rules for each type of loan. Lenders and borrowers accept these terms (or go elsewhere). This avoids the individual negotiation and drawing up of contracts, with attendant lawyers' fees and so on, that would be necessary if lenders and borrowers were to deal directly.

Clearly, this is quite a list of potential advantages. But it serves to emphasize what we said above, namely that *intermediaries create something*, they do not just pass (unmodified) funds between two parties. If we persist with the idea that something is created, the best general term to use is *liquidity*. This does not quite capture all of the advantages but from an economic point of view it captures everything that matters. What intermediaries are doing is making funds available (to lenders and borrowers) cheaply, readily and with a minimum of risk. We look now at why this matters and then, in the rest of this section, we look at some of the principles which underlie the behaviour of intermediaries and which allow them to create liquidity in this way. This is a complicated story and it may be helpful to sketch it first with the help of Figure 1.3.

We shall explore firstly the general consequences of financial intermediation. The first of these is the creation of financial assets and liabilities that would not otherwise exist. The second is the creation of liquidity. We shall indicate that the latter is probably more important from an economic point of view. It is also a complex process. We shall suggest that the creation of liquidity relies in turn on four processes:

maturity transformation, *risk reduction*, the *reduction of search and transaction costs* and *monitoring*. Furthermore, we shall suggest that all four depend to a significant extent upon *economies of scale*.

The first consequence of financial intermediation is that in the presence of financial intermediaries there will be more financial assets and liabilities than there would be without. The growth of financial activity relative to other forms of economic activity therefore implies that financial assets are growing relative to real assets. Box 1.1 provides a simple illustration of this point.

In the direct lending case, our lender lends £130,000 to a borrower. As a result of the transaction, there is a financial asset of £130,000 (the loan seen from the lender's point of view) and a financial liability of £130,000 (the debt seen from the borrower's point of view). Strictly speaking, there has been no *creation* of anything. Prior to the loan the lender had a financial asset of £130,000, presumably in money form, so as far as the lender is concerned there is only a change in the composition of financial assets. Equally, there is no change in the total of borrowers' liabilities. Our borrower has incurred the liability of £130,000 in order presumably to buy a real asset, a house perhaps. This asset has been transferred from a previous owner and the funds have been used to pay off the previous owner's debts.

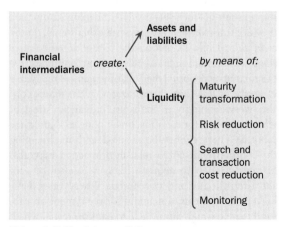

Figure 1.3 The intermediation process

BOX 1.1 The creation of assets and liabilities

(a) Direct lending

Lender			Borrower	
Liability	Asset		Liability	Asset
	130,000			130,000
Total	130,000			130,000

(b) Via an intermediary

Lender(s)		Intermediary		Borrower	
Liability	Asset	Liability	Asset	Liability	Asset
	25,000	130,000	130,000		130,000
	26,000				
	40,000				
	39,000				
Total	130,000 (A)	130,000 (B)	130,000 (C)		130,000 (D)

Total assets (= A + C) = 260,000
Total liabilities (= B + D) = 260,000

Suppose now that funds from several lenders equal to £130,000 are placed with an intermediary which then lends them out: additional assets and liabilities have been created. The (ultimate) lenders still have assets of £130,000 and the (ultimate) borrower has the liability of £130,000. To that extent, things are as they were in the direct lending case (except that we have multiple lenders). But in between the end users, the intermediary has also an asset (the loan) of £130,000 and liabilities (the deposits) of £130,000. Total financial assets and liabilities are now £260,000.

Whether the mere creation of additional financial assets and liabilities matters to the rest of the economy depends upon whether people's spending behaviour is affected by the total quantity of assets and liabilities. Remember that for every extra asset created there is an extra liability. There is no increase in *net* wealth. There is no straightforward answer to this question and we shall return to it again briefly in Section 1.5. What is much more likely to matter is the creation of liquidity which has accompanied this creation of assets and liabilities. Consider the position of the lenders to the intermediary. They have interest-earning assets which they can recover at short notice. Many economists take the view that people spend more (as a proportion of their income) when they know they have liquid assets they could draw on in an emergency. Certainly, our lenders in the second case seem to be in a more enviable financial position than the lender in the first, who could be in serious trouble if expenditure happened to exceed income. Furthermore, our lenders may also benefit from intermediation by having interest-earning assets which they would not have had at all otherwise, if for example there were no market for small loans. In the latter case, there would be less lending and borrowing in total. Perhaps the borrower in our example would have been unable to find funds. His real expenditure would not then have taken place, with possible repercussions on the rest of the economy.

We turn now to the second consequence of intermediation and to the question of how intermediaries are able to create liquidity, to 'borrow short and lend long'. A liquid asset is one that can be turned into money quickly, cheaply and for a known monetary value. Thus the achievement of a financial intermediary must be that lenders can recall their loan either (or both) more quickly or with a greater certainty of its capital value than would otherwise be the case. Notice

that liquidity has three dimensions: 'time' – the speed with which an asset can be exchanged for money; 'risk' – the possibility that the asset may be realizable for value different from that which is expected; and 'cost' – the pecuniary and other sacrifices that have to be made in carrying out the exchange. At the same time, an intermediary has to offer liabilities to borrowers which are more attractive than direct lending and this almost always means offering loans which are larger and for longer periods than would otherwise be the case. On the face of it, borrowers' and lenders' wants conflict (as we saw in Section 1.2.1). How can they be reconciled and a profit drawn from their reconciliation?

In Figure 1.3, we have suggested that the reconciliation involves four processes: maturity transformation, risk reduction, search and transaction costs and monitoring. We look now at each of these in turn. We shall see that the processes overlap somewhat; nonetheless, thinking in terms of four processes is still helpful.

Maturity transformation. Maturity transformation means that intermediaries accept funds of a given maturity, that is, funds which are liable for repayment to lenders at a given date or with a given degree of notice, and 'transform' them into loans of a longer maturity. Any deposit-taking institution will provide a dramatic illustration of this process. This is because they accept deposits of a very short maturity, some indeed repayable 'at sight' or on demand, and yet simultaneously make loans which need not be repaid for several years. In the UK, building societies transform deposits into loans for periods up to 25 years.

The funds accepted by institutions appear as liabilities in their balance sheets while the loans into which they are transformed appear, with other items, on the asset side. Table 1.2 shows the consolidated balance sheet of German banks. Notice that liabilities are dominated by deposits, the bulk of which are repayable at notice of less than three months, while assets consist overwhelmingly of loans and advances, most of which will be for periods much longer than three months. These cannot be recalled without breaking the contract with borrowers. In practice, it may also be very difficult to demand repayment even of very short-term loans and overdrafts. Where these have been made to firms, a demand for repayment or a refusal to renew may simply lead to bankruptcy, in which the bank will have to compete with other creditors for

Table 1.2 German banks' balance sheet (end December 2006)

Assets, €bn		%	Liabilities, €bn		%
Cash in hand and balances			Sight and time deposits	4,040	56.2
at central bank	66	0.9	Savings deposits	595	8.3
Market loans	2,089	29.1	Savings bonds	108	1.5
Bills	2	0.003	Bonds and bills	1,688	23.5
Securities	1,508	21	Other	422	5.9
Advances	3,050	42.4	Capital	337	4.7
Other	475	6.6			
Total	7,190	100.0		7,190	100.0

Source: Deutsche Bundesbank (2007) *Banken Statistik Monthly Report*, February, table IV.2. Reprinted with permission. Percentages may not sum to 100.0 because of rounding.

repayment from any remaining assets. Notice, however, that while the majority of assets are therefore relatively illiquid, some remaining assets are very liquid. Banks can draw on their deposits at the central bank without notice and can sell bills and other securities for cash quite quickly. We shall see in a moment that retaining a small pool of highly liquid assets is part of the key to maturity transformation.

The ability of financial institutions to engage in maturity transformation depends fundamentally upon *size*. The advantages of scale come in two major forms. Firstly, with large numbers of depositors or other types of lender, intermediaries will have a steady inflow and outflow of funds each day. There will be fluctuations. On some days there will be net inflows and on some days net outflows. The larger the numbers the more stable these net flows will be. There will be variations in the flows in response to external shocks. There may be seasonal variations. There will certainly be variations too in response to other firms' behaviour. If competitors raise interest rates, net inflows will decline. But all these variations become more predictable as the number of lenders increases. The significance of this is that it is only *net* outflows against which intermediaries need to hold liquid assets as reserves. The reason that banks can hold so little cash in relation to all their other assets is that even at their maximum, net outflows on any particular day are extremely small in relation to the total stock of assets and, crucially, banks *know this with virtual certainty*.

Secondly, large size implies a large number of borrowers or a large quantity of funds which can be spread across a wide variety of assets. The larger the volume of assets, be they loans, securities or anything else, the greater the scope for arranging them in such a way that a small fraction is always on the point of maturing. This guarantees a steady stream of liquid assets. At best, assets can be arranged so that they mature so as to coincide with anticipated days of major net outflows. In the limiting case, a perfect match would mean that firms need hold no liquid assets.

Risk reduction. Financial intermediaries are able to reduce risk through a number of devices. The two principal ones are diversification and specialist management. The scale of operations is also relevant here. As a general rule, the opportunities for risk reduction increase with size.

It seems intuitively obvious that holding just one asset is more likely to produce unexpected outcomes than holding a collection or 'portfolio' of assets. This is the basis on which small savers are recommended to contribute to a managed fund, or to buy unit trusts. The managers of the funds can collect contributions from a large number of small savers and then distribute a comparatively large sum among many more assets than an individual saver could possibly afford to do, bearing in mind transaction costs. Precisely the same process is at work in a deposit-taking institution. The intermediary accepts a large number of small deposits, creates a large pool and then distributes that pool among a number of borrowers who, the intermediary can ensure, are borrowing to fund different, that is, diverse, types of activity. (The pool also enables the intermediary to adjust the size of loan to the needs of borrowers which will usually be much larger than the size of the average deposit.) Clearly, the larger the size of the institution the larger its pool of funds. Since the cost of setting up a loan, or buying securities, is more or less constant regardless of size, large loans and large security purchases have lower unit transaction costs than small ones. A large institution has the advantage therefore that it can diversify widely and cheaply even though it deals in large investments.

Precisely how and why diversification leads to a reduction in risk is a complex, technical question. For the moment, we can probably agree that the reason that common sense encourages us to diversify has something to do with the fact that assets do not all behave in the same way at the same time and that, therefore, if we hold enough different assets there will be occasions when the behaviour of some tends to offset the behaviour of others. The key certainly does lie in the fact that there is less than perfect correlation between movements in asset returns. What is harder to understand is that by combining assets in a portfolio, one can actually reduce the risk of the portfolio below the average of the individual risk of the assets contained within it. Box 1.2 gives an extreme illustration of how 'diversifying' from just one to two assets reduces portfolio risk below the average for the two individual assets.

In addition to being able to reduce investors' risk by diversification, intermediaries also offer the risk reducing benefit of specialist expertise. It is extremely difficult and costly for individuals to research the status of would-be borrowers and their schemes. There are newspapers and magazines which claim to offer useful information about companies and their plans and sometimes they go so far as to offer 'tips' to would-be investors, but the quality of this information is much less than that which can be obtained by intermediaries recruiting and training 'analysts' who specialize in assessing the risk and likely performance of particular groups of potential borrowers. And here again, scale is important. As more information and experience is acquired it becomes easier to spot the essential characteristics of borrowers and their projects which make them into low, medium or high risks with high, medium or low potential returns.

Search and transaction costs. At one extreme, one can imagine the costs, pecuniary and otherwise, of direct lending where an individual lender has to search for, contact and arrange for an individually negotiated,

---

BOX 1.2 The gains from diversification

Imagine an investor faced with the opportunity to invest in either or both of two shares, A and B, the returns on which behave independently. Suppose that both are expected to yield a return of 20 per cent in 'good' times and 10 per cent in 'bad' times. Assume, furthermore, that there is a 50 per cent probability of each share striking good and bad conditions. Then it follows that investing wholly in A or wholly in B produces the expected return:

$$\hat{K} = 0.5(20\%) + 0.5(10\%) = 15\%$$

Notice that although the expected return averaged over a period of time will be 15 per cent per year, in any one year there will a 50 per cent chance of getting a high return and a 50 per cent chance of getting a low return. There is absolutely no chance whatsoever of getting the expected return! Risk, in the sense in which we have been using it, is infinite. Remember that this conclusion applies whether we hold A or B.

Now consider the possible outcomes if one half of the investor's funds are allocated to each of A and B. Since good and bad conditions can arise *independently* for each of A and B, it follows that four outcomes are possible, each with an equal probability of 25 per cent. The outcomes and the associated returns are:

Outcome	A	B	Return
1	Good	Good	20%
2	Good	Bad	15%
3	Bad	Good	15%
4	Bad	Bad	10%

Over the years the expected return will be:

$$\hat{K} = 0.25(20\%) + 0.25(15\%) + 0.25(15\%)$$
$$+ 0.25(10\%) = 15\%$$

The expected return is still 15 per cent, but in any one year receiving the expected return is now the most likely outcome!

legally binding contract to be drawn up. More realistically, one can also imagine the costs faced by small savers trying to diversify their wealth across a range of securities. On each of these a minimum commission has to be paid and, being fixed, this therefore rises as a proportion of the value of the transaction as the transaction gets smaller. Looking at it another way, savers with small funds have to earn a bigger gross return to offset their higher transaction costs. A saver with less than £50,000 to invest and looking for diversification across a minimum of, say, 15 securities is likely to find the charges made by unit trusts and managed funds (typically 5 per cent of the initial investment and 1 per cent annual management charge) attractive. The lower costs available through an intermediary result, of course, from the ability to pool funds and to trade in large blocks of securities where the dealing commission is very small as a proportion of the value.

The same process is at work with deposit-taking institutions. One standard contract covers each class of deposit and each type of loan. The intermediaries' search costs are incorporated in the cost of prime site premises and in their advertising. The consequence of such spending is that lenders and borrowers know what services are available and where. Although prime sites and advertising are very expensive, once again the scale of operations almost certainly means that these search costs, absorbed by intermediaries, are less than the search costs that would be incurred by lenders and borrowers if they had to deal with each other directly.

We said at the beginning of this section that financial intermediaries clearly offered some benefit to borrowers and lenders since the latter were prepared to deal via the intermediary on terms which allowed the intermediary to make a profit (from a mixture of fees and the 'spread' between rates charged to borrowers and paid to lenders). Having seen what it is that intermediaries do (and how they do it) we are now in a position to see formally how benefits arise and why they are worth paying for.

We denote a lender by L and a borrower by B and we suppose that they have agreed to lend/borrow at a rate of interest, i, *in the absence of an intermediary*. Without an intermediary, however, both will be involved in search and transaction costs and these will eat into the return that the lender gets and will add to the costs for the borrower. If we denote the costs to the lender and borrower respectively as C_L and C_B and imagine that they are expressed as a percentage of

the agreed loan then the *net* return to the lender, i_L, will be:

$$i - C_L = i_L \qquad (1.2)$$

and the *gross* cost to the borrower, i_B will be:

$$i - C_B = i_B \qquad (1.3)$$

Consequently, the difference between the actual cost to the borrower and the actual return to the lender, that is, having regard to their respective costs, is $(i_B - i_L)$ and is the sum of their combined search and transaction costs:

$$C_B + C_L \qquad (1.4)$$

Our argument in the last few paragraphs of course has been that financial intermediaries can reduce search and transaction costs. Let us then suppose that by dealing via an intermediary the costs for our borrower and lender would have been C_B' and C_L' respectively, where:

$$C_B' < C_B \quad \text{and} \quad C_L' < C_L \qquad (1.5)$$

However, in order to supply the services that enable these cost reductions to take place, the intermediary makes a charge, Ψ. This is assumed again to be expressed as a percentage of the loan. Indeed, it could take the form of charging a higher explicit interest rate to the borrower and paying a lower explicit rate to the lender. Clearly, in these circumstances there is an opportunity for profitable intermediation to be beneficial to both borrowers and lenders provided that:

$$(\Psi + C_B' + C_L') < C_B + C_L \qquad (1.6)$$

Notice that the possibilities for profitable intermediation in (1.6) hinge solely upon intermediaries being able to reduce costs for lenders and borrowers cheaply. That is to say that the reduction in costs must be greater than the charge made by the intermediary:

$$(C_B + C_L) - (C_B' + C_L') > \Psi \qquad (1.7)$$

We can see from our discussion above that this is a condition that should be widely met. We have tried throughout this section to argue that the costs faced by lenders and borrowers dealing directly are very considerable and that the savings available via intermediaries are substantial.

This illustration shows nothing of the other advantages of intermediation, those that arise from maturity transformation and risk reduction, for example. To incorporate these, we have to return to the agreed rate

---

BOX 1.3 Financial intermediaries and transaction costs

Looking at Equations 1.2–1.7, we can illustrate financial intermediaries' ability to reduce costs to borrowers and lenders while at the same time making a charge for their services which yields them a profit.

Suppose that B agrees to borrow £10,000 from L for one year at 20 per cent interest (so, $i = 0.2$). Imagine now that L reckons that drawing up a contract and checking on B's creditworthiness is going to cost him £500. Similarly, B calculates that he has spent £100 on advertising for a lender.

As a result, L calculates his *net* return as £2,000 − £500 = £1,500 ($i_L = 0.15$),
while B calculates his *gross* cost as £2,000 + £100 = £2,100 ($i_B = 0.21$)

The difference between the actual return and the actual cost is then £2,100 − £1,500 = £600, which is also the sum of their combined transaction and search costs (£500 + £100).

Suppose now that both parties are confronted by the possibility of using an intermediary which reckons its search costs at £30 and its transaction costs at £70 for a loan of this kind. On these costs it charges a 30 per cent mark-up for overheads and profit. Ignoring interest, the total cost of using an intermediary compared with direct lending, will be:

(£30 + £70 + £30) against (£500 + £100)

The difference is £470, a considerable saving. Notice that this saving comes about as the result of the difference between the costs of the private transaction (£600) and the costs of the intermediated transaction (£100) *minus* the charge made for the intermediation (£30). As we say in the text, provided the difference between the two levels of cost exceeds the intermediary's charge, then B and L will gain from using the intermediary.

Clearly, then, it is not difficult to see why borrowers and lenders may be willing to pay an intermediary for something which they could do them for themselves. An intermediary may just have lower total costs. But now consider whether there might be further advantages in the form of a lower rate of interest. The 20 per cent was agreed between the borrower and lender, having regard to the level of risk, the maturity preferences of the two parties, alternative possibilities, etc. An intermediary, with all its resources for risk assessment, screening, etc., may well think that 12 per cent is a reasonable rate to charge, while the lender, being able to lend to the bank at zero risk, with the option to retrieve the funds at a moment's notice, may well feel that 7 per cent is an acceptable return.

---

of interest, i. This, it will be recalled, was agreed between borrowers and lenders in the absence of an intermediary which was later introduced in order to reduce transaction and search costs, *ceteris paribus*. In practice, of course, we would expect the presence of intermediaries not just to reduce these costs but also to make lending and borrowing much more attractive in many respects. We could accommodate this in our illustration by allowing the agreed rate of interest, i, in (1.2) and (1.3) to tumble at the same time as costs were being reduced, in (1.5). This would not alter our illustration of profitable intermediation. It would simply mean that the agreed rate of interest assumed for the illustration would be much lower once intermediaries were introduced. The benefits from the cost-reducing aspects of intermediation would still depend upon the condition in (1.7), whatever the level of interest rates.

Monitoring. It is generally recognized that financial decisions between two parties are often characterized by asymmetric information. In particular, borrowers are likely to be much better informed about the uses to which they propose to put the funds than lenders can be. This asymmetry is another of the many disincentives to direct lending: the ultimate borrower knows how he is going to use the funds and can form a reasonable judgement of the likelihood of success and the likely rate of return on the project. The borrower may choose to share that information honestly and openly with the ultimate lender or may prefer to conceal it. But there is very little that the ultimate lender can do to check the accuracy of the information.

This asymmetry can often be alleviated by financial markets. As we shall see in Chapters 16 and 17, access to bond and equity markets usually requires that borrowers make specified information publicly available on a regular basis and there are severe penalties for firms that fail to do so or who produce information that seeks to mislead. Given that this information is available from all borrowers to all market participants, 'the market' can use its experience to develop its own 'rating' system, classifying certain types of firms and certain types of projects as more risky than others and pricing the loans accordingly.

However, market solutions to the asymmetry are not always available. Firstly, access to securities markets is expensive. The very requirements that make the information available impose costs on firms, and small firms in particular will not feel it worthwhile to meet the administrative costs of a stock exchange listing. Furthermore, the issue costs associated with raising new funds by selling new shares, for example, are considerable and contain a large fixed cost element. Again, small to medium-size firms will not find new security issues cost-efficient for the size of loan they require. Secondly, for persons and unincorporated businesses, markets are simply not appropriate.

The alternative solution is for intermediaries to take on the monitoring task. This involves the development of skills in discriminating between more and less risky projects and firms. One way in which this is done, of course, is to demand information as a condition of the loan; another is to develop a long-term association with successful clients so as to gain access to 'inside' information; yet another is to monitor carefully the *ex post* outcome of projects in which they have invested depositors' funds. These activities have a high fixed set-up cost but are subject to economies of scale, with the result that while individuals are excluded from doing their own monitoring, the cost to each depositor when the service is provided by the bank is quite small.

Notwithstanding the various monitoring mechanisms available to banks, some degree of asymmetry is likely to remain. Banks can and do find themselves exposed to bad-risk loans. The imperfect nature of the monitoring process gives rise to the conventional bank-type loan where the borrower is required to provide collateral for the loan and where the terms of the loan sometimes give the bank the power to make the borrower bankrupt.

1.4 Financial markets

In economics a market is any organizational device which brings together buyers and sellers. It does not need to be a physical location – though many towns and cities have 'market squares' and many of those host periodic markets. Some financial markets exist in specific locations but most use electronic trading methods which allow dealers to be dispersed. For example, markets for foreign exchange by necessity 'bring together' buyers and sellers located in countries all over the world. The latest communication technology now permits financial institutions in the United States to deal in shares in Tokyo as readily as they can in New York. Until 1986, share dealing in the UK was concentrated on the trading floor of the London Stock Exchange. With the introduction of new technology, however, dealers quickly dispersed to their companies' offices.

1.4.1 Types of product

What is it that is traded in financial markets? The answer clearly is some sort of financial asset or liability. But briefer terms like 'financial instruments' or 'financial claims' are sometimes used.

Financial instruments come in a bewildering range of types. Table 1.3 lists just a small sample of instruments traded in financial markets. This is a very small sample from the range of financial instruments for which markets exist. Nonetheless, it is sufficient for us to discuss and illustrate different systems of market classification and thus to draw attention to similarities and differences between the markets for certain types of instrument.

First of all, one can distinguish between those markets for instruments that can be traded directly between holders and potential holders and those that cannot. Table 1.3 provides examples of the former. However, we still talk of markets for pensions or life assurance and even, for that matter, of markets for bank deposits. Such instruments cannot be traded directly between third parties. Holders of unwanted pension or life assurance benefits can dispose of them only by 'selling them back' to the issuers in exchange for money. The

Table 1.3 A sample of financial instruments

Securitized mortgages	Bond futures
Certificates of deposit	Currency futures
Treasury bills	Bond options
Central government bonds	Currency options
Local government bonds	Equity options
Eurocurrencies	Interest rate futures
Equities	Currency swaps

same is the case with bank or savings deposits. Nonetheless, for all these products there is a demand and there is a supply, and the terms on which the demand is satisfied will reflect supply and demand conditions.

Alternatively, one can distinguish markets for instruments that pay a fixed rate of interest from those for instruments where the rate of interest (or the rate of return) is variable. Government bonds probably provide the largest class of fixed interest assets. Most local government bonds and treasury bills are also fixed rate instruments. In France, Italy, Spain and Germany many housing mortgages carry a fixed rate of interest. In the UK, by contrast, most carry a variable rate. As a general rule, bank deposits pay variable interest (though occasionally time deposits pay a fixed rate), while equities, or company shares, pay dividends which are highly variable.

Another popular basis for distinguishing between markets is the *residual maturity* of the instruments traded in them. Some instruments – treasury and commercial bills, interbank loans, certificates of deposit – have a very short maturity when initially issued, generally less than three months, and thus have on average a much shorter residual maturity. Markets for these instruments are often called 'money markets' – markets for short-term money. This contrasts with 'capital markets' – markets for long-term capital. These include the market for company shares – instruments with a theoretically infinite life. They also include the market for government and corporate bonds which are commonly issued with initial maturities of 10–25 years, and the market for mortgages.

Finally, a distinction is often made between 'primary' and 'secondary' markets. This does not lead to a distinction based on the trading of different instruments but rather upon subsets of a given instrument. A primary market is a market for a newly issued instrument. (In a primary market an instrument can only be traded once.) The primary market for company shares, for example, consists of firms issuing new shares, the underwriters of the issue and those members of the general public willing to buy new issues. Notice that it is only in the primary market that firms actually raise (borrow) new funds. The corresponding secondary market is the market for existing instruments, in this example, for company shares that were first issued sometime in the past. No new funds are being raised. This does not, however, make secondary markets unimportant. Firstly, the existence of an active secondary market makes new issues more liquid than they would otherwise be. The fact that they can be easily sold on makes them more attractive to buyers and thus new issues can be sold at a higher price (and capital raised at lower cost) than would otherwise be the case. Secondly, new issues have to offer a combination of risk and return comparable with that available on issues being traded in the secondary market. The secondary market, in other words, is determining the cost of new capital. Thirdly, since the trading in secondary markets amounts to trading in claims on existing *real* assets, the secondary market provides a mechanism whereby the ownership and control of organizations can change hands. Many would argue that this is essential if 'good' management is to replace 'bad'.

As financial innovation proceeds, so new instruments emerge, and with them new markets. As a general rule, new instruments tend to fill the gaps between existing ones, often offering a combination of attractions currently available only in different instruments. This process is said to be taking us towards a 'complete' set of markets, a situation which economists tend to regard as desirable since it means that the facilities exist to satisfy the needs of every borrower and lender. As this happens, so it becomes more difficult to draw demarcations between markets, a problem of which regulators are only too well aware.

The behaviour of financial markets, like the behaviour of other markets, can be analysed using the apparatus of conventional economics. In Part 5 of the book we look at a variety of markets in detail.

1.5   The financial system and the real economy

We have just seen that the function of a financial system is broadly to facilitate lending and borrowing. This enables people to arrange their expenditure over time in a way which is to some degree independent of their income. Lenders can store wealth for later consumption; borrowers can buy in advance of their income. As well as displacing expenditure through time, this is also displacing the use of resources between people. Lenders temporarily surrender a claim to goods and services while borrowers get the use of those goods and services. When we talk about 'the real economy', therefore, we mean that part of the economy which produces the real goods and services to which claims are being made as opposed to the financial part of the economy whose job is to enable the claims to be transferred on attractive terms. Clearly, the efficiency with which the real economy functions is of paramount importance since it ultimately determines the real standard of living. Countries which feel that their real economy is failing to perform as it should (and in rich economies this is usually judged by comparing the rate of growth of output with that of other rich economies) sometimes look to the financial system as one of the possible causes: is it too large, too small, inefficient, 'short-termist'? In this section, we consider two broad headings under which one can generalize about the relationship between financial activity and the real economy. These are: the composition of aggregate demand, and the allocation of resources. We shall also look at one particular situation which illustrates what can happen when the financial system is prevented from allocating resources in order to benefit the real economy. This is the case of 'financial repression'.

We look firstly at the possibility that the financial system can affect the *composition of aggregate demand*, by altering the balance between consumption and saving, and investment. This possibility arises because one major function of a financial system is to make it easier for agents to borrow and to lend. If we try now to formalize this a little we can say that one consequence of a well-functioning financial system is that, at any given rate of interest, lenders will be more willing to lend and borrowers will be more willing to borrow than they would otherwise be. This applies whether we think about the advantages and convenience of using financial intermediaries like banks and building societies or about financial markets. Efficient markets with low transaction costs make it easy for holders of securities to buy and sell. Securities become more attractive to lenders than they would be if they had to buy and hold the security until it matured. Consequently firms, and others, can borrow more cheaply by issuing securities at lower rates of interest than would otherwise need to be the case. Figure 1.4a illustrates the effect using a familiar diagram. On the vertical axis, we have the rate of interest, i, and on the horizontal axis, the flow of funds lent and borrowed. The figure shows the supply of funds under conditions of a developed financial system, S, and the demand for them, again in a system which offers a range of choice of favourable conditions to borrowers. The flow of funds is shown by F^* at a rate of interest i^*. If lenders were not able to lend with security and for short periods, and if borrowers could only find one or two lenders after intensive and costly searching, the supply of funds would be much less, shown by S', and the demand for them also much less, shown by D'. In these circumstances the flow of lending and borrowing would be much less at F', and much more costly at i'.

Figure 1.4b shows the effect upon real investment expenditure. Firms are assumed to undertake all those

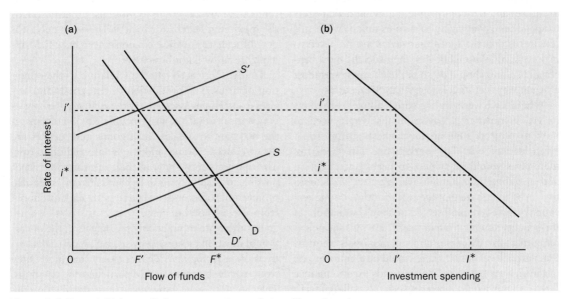

Figure 1.4 Financial intermediation encourages saving and investment

investment projects which yield an expected rate of return at least equal to the cost of funds (here, the rate of interest in Figure 1.4a). Marginal projects are assumed to have diminishing expected yields. Thus, for a given state of expectations regarding the rates of return on investment projects we say the flow of real investment spending is expected to be negatively related to the cost of funds and we can draw an explicit relationship, I in Figure 1.4b. Combining the two diagrams, we can see that in the more favourable lending–borrowing conditions the cost of funds will be i^* and the flow of investment will be I^*. Without the advantages of a developed financial system, the cost of funds would have been i' and investment spending would be I' only.

In conclusion, then, we may say that the existence of a developed financial system offering a full range of instruments to match the needs of borrowers and lenders is likely to encourage higher levels of saving and lending, relative to consumption, and that this will facilitate higher levels of investment. Assuming that the investment projects are well chosen, we should see the economy enjoy a higher rate of growth than would otherwise be the case.

Secondly, we can think about the possibility that the financial system may have some effect upon the real economy through the *efficiency with which it allocates resources*. This arises because the function of a financial system is to reallocate resources through time (allowing spending now against income earned in future) and between people (allowing deficit units to spend funds belonging to surplus units). What this requires is that the funds that savers are prepared to make available should flow to their socially most beneficial use, and should do so in the cheapest and most efficient way. Let us consider what this requires.

Whether we were dealing with lending via markets or via intermediaries, savers' funds would need to flow to projects offering the highest returns for a given level of risk. The markets and intermediaries themselves would be subject to perfect competition and operating at minimum average cost. We should then need to be sure that the rate of return on the real capital employed represented society's valuation of the benefits flowing from its use. There must be no externalities, for example, and no monopoly returns. For a given level of risk, there would be a uniform rate of return on projects and on the funds used to finance them and this would represent society's willingness to trade consumption now for consumption in the future.

Most importantly, a project offering above average returns would be producing above average benefits. It would also have access to unlimited funds. With no monopoly conditions, such projects could be undertaken in larger numbers (adding more to aggregate benefits) until the returns on the project and on the funds equalled those available on other projects.

Introducing firms into the picture leads us to some other notable conclusions. Since, in theory, a firm is nothing but an administrative device for organizing real capital projects, the returns available to the owners of firms are simply the returns available from its capital projects. So long as the returns on the projects are greater than the returns required by the owners, more funds can be raised and the firm will expand (raising the general level of welfare all the time, remember) until the returns on capital just equal the cost of funds required by the owners. The owners, of course, are the shareholders. Their shares have a market value and if shareholders are happy that the firm's projects yield just the rate of return that they require, there will be no excess buying or selling and the share price will be in equilibrium. This is the price at which the firm has to issue new shares if it wishes to expand. The price reflects, again, the cost of funds. If the price were higher, funds would be cheaper; if the price were lower, funds would be dearer.

We have come a long way in a short distance, but what all this amounts to is a summary of the conditions that would have to prevail for us to be sure that funds were always going to those uses that produced the maximum benefit for society. Unfortunately, it is not difficult to imagine circumstances in which this happy result will not be achieved.

Firstly, there are conditions relating to the operation of firms. The production of real goods and services is sometimes associated with negative externalities which means that the price people pay overestimates the real gain to society. Such goods and services are overproduced. Some industries are monopolistic. Their projects earn above average returns and it is not possible for such returns to be eliminated by additional production. Such goods and services are underproduced from a social point of view.

But there are in practice some defects in the operation of most financial systems as well. Financial activity is often *segmented*. That is to say that funds flow from particular sources to particular destinations. They are not free to flow to the most socially productive use. The reasons for this are sometimes informal or historical – households with surplus funds think first of accumulating interest-bearing deposits because securities have been seen as assets for the rich. Sometimes there are legal reasons – institutions that take small savings are obliged to channel a large proportion into government debt because it is seen as 'safe'. Sometimes the reasons are institutional – the minimum denominations of treasury and commercial bills are far too large for private savers, or minimum commissions are too large. The desire to break down such segmentation, and the argument behind it that this would make the system more efficient, has been a major driving force in policies of financial deregulation in recent years.

Another reason why an optimum allocation of funds may not occur lies in either the poverty or *asymmetry of information*. Acquiring information about the best returns available takes time and thus has a cost attached to it. Many people will think such costs not worth incurring. For many years, most European governments have been able to borrow from households more cheaply than from any other source and this may be as much the result of households' reluctance to search for better returns as it is the result of a desire for high security. This gives, in effect, a subsidy to public sector borrowing and investment. Asymmetric information may also play a part in people's choice of financial assets in such a way that they buy assets that are unsuitable. In recent years, many households have claimed that they bought certain types of savings policy which claimed to guarantee repayment of their mortgage without realizing that the value of their savings was linked to the performance of the stock market. In the worst case, the asymmetry of information may scare people away from saving at all for their long-term security. Or it may lead to mis-pricing of financial products and services. For example, if insurance companies cannot distinguish high-risk from low-risk clients, they will have to charge premiums at a 'worst case' level. This means that insurance is too costly for low-risk clients who then try to live without insurance.

Yet another reason for resource misallocation rests with the markets part of the system where **speculation** may sometimes be at work. This can arise because part of the return for holding some assets comes as a result of an appreciation of the asset's value – a capital gain. Clearly, such gains are expected as a natural result of holding company shares over a long period (since we expect the nominal value of dividends to rise) and may be as important to investors as the periodic dividend payments. Notice that provided the price goes up investors make a gain; it does not matter *why* the price goes up. We may know that the market price should only reflect the productivity of the underlying assets but investors would be foolish, acting against their own self-interest, if they failed to buy (or to hold) shares whose prices they were sure would rise for other reasons. Profitable investment is not only, therefore, a question of buying shares of firms that are about to enjoy large profits; it is also about buying the shares of firms that other people *think* are going to enjoy good times. You may even get rich by buying shares in firms that other people think are about to do well. Indeed, maybe the firm's profitability has nothing to do with it at all – you only need to be able to spot those shares that other people are about to buy (for whatever reason). This behaviour gives rise to what are sometimes known as 'fads' or speculative bubbles. Asset prices begin to rise, perhaps for good economic reasons to begin with. But once people think that the rise is going to continue there will be some who buy just because they believe the price is going to rise, not because they believe there is any fundamental reason why it should. This is known as acting on the 'bigger fool' hypothesis. ('I know that I am buying these shares whose price is artificially high but next week I shall sell them at a profit to someone who is even more foolish.') And if enough buyers join in, the price *will* rise. At least, for a while. But we have to remember that while gambling on asset price movements may seem like harmless fun, or at least something that can only harm the gambler, a change in an asset's price is a change in the cost at which funds can be raised. A rise in the price of shares, for example, makes raising capital cheaper; it encourages expansion; it makes it easier for the firm to take over ownership of its rivals. This is fine if there are sound underlying reasons – the firm may be more productive and better managed than its competitors – but it is a serious failing of the market if it happens for no reason other than a 'fad'.

We return to 'fads' in Section 11.5 while the general question of financial **market efficiency** is one to which we return in Chapter 26.

Another issue which has come to the fore in recent years in discussions of how well financial systems function and the extent to which they improve or hinder the performance of the real economy is the issue of **financial repression**. Unlike the composition of aggregate demand and resource allocation, financial repression is not itself a cause of good or bad economic performance, rather it describes a case where the composition of aggregate demand and resource allocation together both turn out for the worse. Financial repression refers to the prevalence of undue interference by governments in financial systems. Consequently, a repressed financial system is a state-dominated financial system. The role of financial repression (and its antidote, 'financial liberalization') has mainly been discussed in connection with less developed countries where the question is whether liberalization would encourage investment, improve resource allocation and increase the rate of economic growth. However, since the key cause of repression is an autocratic and overbearing state, the concept is also relevant to countries like Russia, China and India, which are making the transition towards market economies and also to the new 'succession' states in the EU, some of which have an economic history of highly centralized state control, particularly over their financial systems.

Bearing in mind that financial repression is merely a context in which the two functions we have already discussed are likely to be done badly, we must be content with a fairly brief outline of why high levels of state interference are likely to produce results which mean that the financial system inhibits economic growth.

Let us be clear first of all that when we refer to government interference we are not talking about the kind of interference that is involved in normal regulation of the financial system. There are many features of financial repression, but just two are quite widespread and these give a good illustration of why repression almost invariably produces adverse results. The first is lending and deposit rates capped at an artificially low level; the second is regulations requiring banks to hold unnecessarily high reserves or holdings of government bonds.

Given our discussion at the beginning of this section, the idea of low interest rates as an encouragement to investment may seem like a good idea. It increases the number of real capital projects that pass the test of earning a return in excess of the cost of capital. There are, however, two related problems. One concerns the quantity of investment while the other concerns its quality. As regards the quantity, capping the rate of interest below the market-clearing rate, limits the amount of investment that can be undertaken to the supply of loans at that interest rate. Far from getting more capital investment, we get more schemes that pass the test but *fewer* that can actually be funded.

This creates the second problem which is that there is excess demand for the limited funds that are available. Consequently, lenders have to devise some system of rationing. There are various possibilities. These range from favouring established or large clients to funding enterprises which are favoured by the state or by some powerful local official. At worst, the funds go to those prepared to offer the largest bribes or other favours. The essential point is that none of these rationing methods is going to favour the most profitable projects – the ones which theory tells us should provide the greatest social benefit. The only way to improve the quality of investment is to allow interest rates to *rise*, thereby screening out the low-return, low-utility projects.

Along with the capping of interest rates at artificially low levels state interference in the financial system often involves the requirement that banks and other intermediaries hold high levels of government debt or reserves with the central bank – higher than they would naturally choose. As with the capping of interest rates, there is a superficial justification for this in that government bonds are generally among the least risky assets in an economy and one can therefore argue that holding more bonds increases the stability of the firm. Holding additional reserves gives a bank additional protection against liquidity risk. But these are not the reasons for imposing these ratios and in any event one would normally argue that financial firms are the best judges of their own exposure to risk. The reason for insisting on minimum holdings of government debt is that it helps the government finance its deficit. This is linked to the capping of interest rates since it enables the bonds to be offered at a rate of interest which is below what the market would require if it were free to choose. It is a form of forced lending to the government. Artificially high reserve requirements also help the government finances. This follows because the reserves (which include deposits with the central bank) generally do not pay interest. The commercial banking system is therefore being obliged to make interest-free loans to the central bank which it can then use to lend at interest. This increases the profits of the central bank and, since the central bank is usually a nationalized firm whose profits accrue to the ministry of finance, income to the government.

1.6 Summary

The primary function of a financial system is to reconcile the diverging interests of end users, lenders and borrowers. The system itself consists of a group of institutions and markets, both of which help people to lend and to borrow. Financial institutions are often described as 'intermediaries' because of their particular ability to create the liquidity that lenders and borrowers want. This ability relies upon the transformation of maturity and risk and the reduction of costs. These processes are facilitated by the size of intermediaries.

The effects of a financial system are to make lending and borrowing cheaper and to increase liquidity. This in turn encourages investment and may also increase the overall level of spending in the economy. The efficiency with which the financial system channels funds from lenders to borrowers is also important for resource allocation.

Key concepts in this chapter

Borrowing	Maturity transformation
Capital risk	Monitoring
Default risk	Organized markets
Deficit units	Portfolio choice
Direct lending	Portfolio equilibrium
End users	Portfolio theory
Financial deficit	Real investment
Financial repression	Return
Financial surplus	Risk
Hoards	Risk reduction
Income risk	Saving
Inflation risk	Search costs
Intermediate borrowers and lenders	Speculation
Intermediation	Surplus units
Lending	Transaction costs
Liquidity	Ultimate borrowers and lenders
Market efficiency	Ultimate lenders

Questions and problems

1 Distinguish between surplus and deficit units.

2 Discuss the advantage to deficit and surplus units of using financial intermediaries and organized markets.

3 Suppose you wished to save for your retirement, in an economy with no financial system. What assets would you accumulate and why? What advantages would you have if you were able to contribute to a conventional pension fund?

4 With which financial institutions do you deal? Identify those with which you deal as a deficit unit and those with which you deal as a surplus unit. Which of them are deposit-taking institutions? Which of them are not?

5 Distinguish between broking and intermediation.

6 Why do people hold financial assets and liabilities simultaneously?

7 How are financial intermediaries able to engage in maturity transformation?

Further reading

A D Bain, *The Financial System* (Oxford: Blackwell, 2e, 1992) Ch. 1

D Blake, *Financial Market Analysis* (London: McGraw-Hill, 2e, 2000) Ch. 1

M Buckle and J Thompson, *The UK Financial System* (Manchester: Manchester University Press, 4e, 2004) Chs 1, 2

J H Haslag and J Koo, 'Financial Repression, Financial Development and Economic Growth' Federal Reserve Ban of Dallas, available at http://www.dallasfed.org/research/papers/1999/wp9902.pdf

M Levinson, *Guide to Financial Markets* (New York: Bloomberg, 3e, 2003)

J Madura, *Financial Markets and Institutions* (New York: South-Western, 6e, 2002) Ch. 1

F Mishkin, *The Economics of Money, Banking and Financial Markets* (New York: Pearson-Addison Wesley, 8e, 2007) Ch. 2

Radcliffe Report, *Committee On the Working of the Monetary System* (London: HMSO, 1959)

J Toporowski, *The End of Finance* (London: Routledge, 2000) Chs 1, 2

S Valdez, *An Introduction to Global Financial Markets* (Basingstoke: Palgrave, 5e, 2006) Ch. 1

Websites

www.bankofengland.co.uk
www.banque-france.fr
www.ecb.int

Part 2 Financial Institutions and Systems

Chapter 2 | # An introduction to financial systems

What you will learn in this chapter:

- How financial systems differ

- The different roles played by deposit and non-deposit intermediaries

- The different risks faced by DTIs and non-DTIs

- How DTIs and non-DTIs deal with these risks

- How the different roles and different risks affect the structure of their balance sheets

2.1 Introduction

At the beginning of this book, we defined a financial system as consisting of a set of financial markets and institutions and the people who use them – the ultimate lenders and borrowers. Under global pressures, the free movement of capital is an obvious example, national financial systems are coming to look more and more alike. However, it is not yet quite true that all financial *systems* are the same. The differences lie mainly in the institutions and in approaches to the regulation of financial activity.

By contrast, financial markets and the instruments traded in those markets are remarkably similar from one country to another. The instruments – bills, bonds, equities and so on – fulfil a common purpose wherever they are traded and inevitably, therefore, they are priced according to the same principles in all countries. Indeed, most of the instruments are internationally traded with the result, for example, that US equities are close substitutes for German equities in the portfolio of a French investor. The few differences that exist between *markets* in different countries amount to differences in size and differences in institutional arrangements for the trading of instruments. These differences are neither large nor very important, but we have picked out the main details in each of the market chapters in Part 5 of this book.

In this part of the book we concentrate upon the institutions which make up the financial systems of Germany, France, UK, Scandinavia, USA and Italy. To begin with, though, we look at different ways of classifying financial systems, an issue that has become complicated in recent years, and then we provide a summary of different types of financial institutions, their functions and the principles which underlie their activities.

2.2 Classification of financial systems

In the existing literature, financial systems are widely interpreted as lying somewhere along a continuum with '**market-based**' systems at one end and '**bank-based**' systems at the other. However, the position on this continuum tends to be associated with other, important, characteristics so an effective classification system requires additional dimensions. For example, if financial markets play a large part in corporate financing and those markets are particularly active, then takeovers, often hostile, will likely be commonplace in disciplining firms (and managements) which underachieve. It has even been argued that market-based systems tend to encourage a degree of '**short-termism**' in the decisions of managers who are conscious of the need continuously to maximize shareholder returns. There are implications, in other words, for corporate governance. Conversely, if markets play a small role, firms will be more dependent upon banks for finance. Banks will therefore have to take a close interest in firm behaviour, suggesting an alternative form of corporate discipline, and they may have to be structured differently from banks which operate in a 'market-based' system. So, if we wish to classify financial systems in this way, we need to think not just about the role of markets but also about the nature of the banking system and the style of corporate governance. Table 2.1 is adapted from Allen and Gale (2000) and shows the relative standing of the major financial nations with respect to the dimensions we have just discussed.

We turn our attention now to each of these three dimensions, but before we do so it is worth noting that each is defined by its role in the process of corporate financing. This reflects a particular model of financial activity which sees its fundamental role as

Table 2.1 Classifying financial systems

	USA	UK	Japan	France	Germany
Markets	Very important	Very important	Important	Fairly unimportant	Unimportant
Banks	Competitive	Concentrated	Concentrated	Concentrated	Concentrated
External corporate discipline	Takeovers	Takeovers	Banks	Banks/takeovers	'Hausbanken'

Source: Adapted from Franklin Allen and Douglas Gale, *Comparing Financial Systems*, Table: 'Classifying Financial Systems', page 4, © 1999 Massachusetts Institute of Technology, by permission of The MIT Press.

channelling surplus funds from households to firms wishing to invest. We have already seen that financial systems do a good deal more than this and, at the end of this section, we shall see that even if one focuses solely on the 'channelling of funds' function it is by no means obvious that the household → firm route is the only, or even main, one that financial systems are concerned with today. Nonetheless, where classifying systems is concerned, the criteria are dominated by the corporate financing process.

The original idea that financial systems could be placed along a 'bank-based/market-based' continuum was based upon the quantitative importance of sources of funds. In practice, what this means is that banks provide a markedly larger share of corporate funds in bank-based systems than do markets. But we need to be careful not to exaggerate the role of banks and markets in each system. In the bank-based systems (France, Germany and Japan) banks provide typically something approaching 20 per cent of net corporate financing, while markets provide only 3–4 per cent. In the so-called market-based systems (UK and USA) it is true that banks provide very little financing (virtually no long-term financing) but at the same time the issue of new equity and bonds accounts for only 10–15 per cent, while banks provide virtually nothing. In neither system does external finance, bank and market-based combined, contribute more than 20 per cent of the total. The fact is that the bulk of corporate finance comes from internally generated funds, in all systems.

When it comes to the nature of banking systems, different countries have very different histories. In the USA the banking system is characterized by a large number of independent, competitive banks. This stems partly from a deep-seated, historical, dislike of the centralization of economic power (particularly if this meant its concentration in a few northeastern states). Regulations therefore restricted banks to operating within their home state and prevented the development of a nationwide system of branch banking. In 1933 the Glass–Steagall Act prevented banks from helping firms to make new issues of securities (a legacy ultimately of the 1929 Wall Street crash). Although these restrictions were progressively lifted (in the 1980s) their effect has been to limit banking activity to short-term lending to firms and to consumer credit and home loans.

By contrast, banking in the other main countries is highly centralized. In the UK it is dominated by the

big five: Barclays, Lloyds TSB, RBS-NatWest, HSBC and HBOS. In Germany it is dominated by the big three. In Japan and France the situation is similar. Even so, there are differences. In Germany and France there is a large mutual/cooperative banking sector which had its origins in providing (cheap) credit for particular trades and activities. In France, the dominant commercial banks have often been owned by the state, although since 1982 they have been privatized. In Germany, the major banks are 'universal' banks – providing a full range of financial services to firms and households. In the UK and in France, the tradition was one of specialization (hence the terms 'retail banks' contrasting with 'wholesale' or 'investment' banks) but these too are moving in the German direction.

When it comes to distinguishing between 'market-based' and 'bank-based' financial systems, it may well be that the main distinction lies in the implications for corporate governance rather than in crude measures of the proportions of funds raised. In all five of the countries we have so far mentioned (and in most others) the boards of directors of large corporations are legally responsible to shareholders for their conduct of the firm. However, it is only in the UK and USA that boards of directors accept that the maximizing of shareholder value is the main day-to-day objective. At the other extreme, Japanese companies have traditionally tried to maintain stable conditions of employment for their employees and this has been accepted by shareholders, at least until recently. There is now pressure for change, being exercised, ironically, through the financial markets. Between these two extremes, the situation in Germany is much more complex in practice than the legal supremacy of shareholders would suggest. In Germany a system of 'co-determination' means that workers are represented on the supervisory boards of companies and therefore have some stake in managements' decisions. In France, the situation is similar though there workers' representatives have only rights of consultation. In all three bank-based systems, complex patterns of shareholdings exist between firms and holding companies, and cross-holdings are commonplace. Furthermore, in Germany and Japan it is commonplace for a firm to have a long-term relationship with one major bank (the 'Hausbank' in Germany) which provides long-term loans to the firm as well as corporate advice. The bank may also be a major shareholder in the firm. In Germany, the majority shareholding in many large firms still remains in the hands of the founding family and its descendants. For all these reasons, takeovers, especially hostile takeovers, while legally possible in bank-based systems, are extremely rare. External pressure on managements comes, therefore, primarily from banks. The magnitude of this difference, between bank and shareholder pressure, and the strength of feeling against the US/UK system, was highlighted by Franz Müntefering, chairman of Germany's ruling Social Democrats in April 2005, when he described investment companies as 'locusts' for buying and selling companies on the basis of their ability solely to maximize short-term profits.

The relative importance of banks and markets has other implications, which will occasionally emerge in the following chapters. If firms are less reliant on equity capital and if such capital as there is is held largely by banks and founding families, then it follows that equities must form a relatively small part of the savings of the vast majority of households. Typically, households will hold a higher proportion of their wealth in fixed-interest securities or in deposits. Furthermore, there may be implications for the funding of pensions. If equity markets are smaller, then pension funds may also be driven to hold a higher proportion of fixed-interest securities, the income from which may not deliver adequate incomes to people in retirement. Indeed, it may be that the state has to accept a larger role in pension provision in bank-based systems. If the population structure is ageing (generally the case in Europe) this then raises questions about the acceptable level of taxation and the effects on incentives.

Finally, before we leave the question of how we should characterize financial systems, recall once more that the characteristics we have focused on all relate to the way in which a financial system meets the requirements of corporate finance. This, we said, is based upon a model in which households save in order to lend to firms which invest. This is a model with a long history and no doubt was an appropriate description of the role of a financial system for many years. However, it is a feature of all developed financial systems in recent years that more and more activity, particularly lending activity, has been devoted to meeting the needs of the personal or household sector. In the UK, as we shall see later, households borrow more from banks than do industrial and commercial companies and non-bank financial firms combined. Even if there remains net lending from households to

firms, it may be small because firms rely so heavily upon retained funds. This intersectoral lending may then easily be dwarfed by lending between deficit and surplus units within the same sector. Households lending to households may be much more important.

2.3 Banks and other deposit-taking institutions

Banks and other deposit-taking institutions are financial intermediaries whose assets consist overwhelmingly of loans to a wide variety of borrowers and whose liabilities consist overwhelmingly of deposits. We shall refer to such institutions henceforth as DTIs for short. The deposits of many such institutions are included in national definitions of the money supply and this inevitably means that many DTIs are involved in the payments mechanism. The European Central Bank has a convenient label for this subset of DTIs. It calls them MFIs or 'monetary financial institutions'. For reasons we come to later, DTIs offer an increasing range of financial services in addition to lending, deposit-holding and payments.

As a subset of financial intermediaries, banks share the fundamentals of them all. This means that they help channel funds from lenders to borrowers and they do this by a combination of maturity transformation, risk reduction and a lowering of transaction costs as we described above in Section 1.2.3. In the next few paragraphs we concentrate on what it is that makes banks different from other financial intermediaries.

The distinction between banks and NDTIs lies with the very particular nature of banks' assets and liabilities. As we know, the former are predominantly loans while the latter are overwhelmingly deposits. For borrowers, financing a deficit by a bank loan involves a very special type of obligation. Firstly, the loan is for a fixed nominal amount. Even in the case of an overdraft, where the borrower can vary the amount borrowed, the amount to be repaid is fixed in nominal terms. Ignoring the question of default, there is no question of the bank being repaid some amount that is different from the amount that it lent. The situation is the same with deposits. A depositor has a claim on the bank which is fixed in nominal terms and can expect to be able to withdraw exactly the amount that she paid in. This is quite different, for example, from the situation where a borrower obtains funds by selling his own obligations in an organized market. Because they can be traded, the value of those obligations can fluctuate. If the value falls, for example, the borrower can buy back the obligations for less than he originally borrowed and the lender will get back less than she lent. This form of lending is obviously riskier for the lender than entering into a fixed nominal value contract.

The nature of the compensation is also distinctive. This too comes as a fixed nominal sum – a rate of interest. In some cases the rate of interest on the loan, and on the deposit, may be absolutely fixed for the period of the loan. More commonly, the rate of interest varies with market rates. Nonetheless, even in the latter case the borrower and the depositor know what they have to pay and what they are entitled to. Contrast this with, say, the dividends that are paid on company shares. The lender (the shareholder) receives a dividend which varies with the success of the borrower's business. The lender has a stake in the business which requires her to share some of the risk.

The kinds of contracts in which banks specialize are known as **debt contracts** while contracts which involve the lender sharing in some of the risk of the project financed by the loan are known as **equity contracts**. Broadly speaking, it is this distinction that separates Islamic finance from western finance. Islamic finance prohibits debt-type contracts.

Why do we need these distinctive, debt-type, contracts? The answer lies with **asymmetric information** (AI).[1] This refers to any situation where one party to a contract has more or better information, relevant to the deal, than the other party. As a general rule, in a financial context, it is assumed that borrowers have superior information about the risk and likely return on the funds they have borrowed than the borrowers have. Hence a bank is usually at an informational disadvantage compared with its borrowers; on the other hand, the bank has an informational advantage over depositors.

Debt-type contracts are one way of dealing with the presence of asymmetric information which might otherwise discourage lending/borrowing. To understand why, put them to one side for a moment and consider other ways of dealing with the problem. In financial markets, AI is reduced by imposing 'rules of disclosure'. A firm cannot issue shares for trading on

the London Stock Exchange unless it has a record of satisfactory trading for a number of years and is prepared to publish detailed, and independently audited, accounts every six months. The exchange will also have strict rules about 'insider trading' whereby anyone close enough to the firm to have information which is not widely available, must not use it. This gives potential lenders (buyers of the shares) a reasonable amount of information about the firm and its activities as well as reassurance that they are not going to be disadvantaged by other market participants with superior information. The situation is further improved by large numbers of analysts, market-makers and financial advisers who have a financial incentive to discover relevant information and publicize it.

However, these arrangements are costly and while they may work for large firms with an established trading record, they are no help to a firm which is just starting up and has no trading record. Even a medium-sized firm with a good trading history may hesitate at the costs of complying with the requirements of a major stock exchange (which is why many exchanges have 'subsidiary' or 'junior' exchanges with less strict rules for 'newcomers'). Clearly these arrangements are completely unsuitable for households and individuals be they borrowers or lenders.

Debt contracts, offered by banks, are an alternative way of reducing the impact of asymmetric information. From a depositor's point of view the only relevant information required concerns the probity of the bank. The depositor cannot know this perfectly, but three things about a bank should reassure him. Firstly, the bank has a reputation to safeguard. Without the widespread confidence of its depositors no bank will prosper. Secondly, most jurisdictions impose strict licensing requirements for banks and in return for this 'interference' they offer a degree of deposit insurance to bank clients. Thirdly, depositors know that they have a very low-risk asset since the value of their deposit is fixed in nominal terms and there is a guarantee that the compensation depends upon a known rate of interest. Neither the principle, nor the compensation is dependent on the performance of the bank.

Similarly, a debt contract provides a bank with a high degree of security when lending to small borrowers or borrowers who, for various reasons, do not wish to disclose details of their affairs to the market.

---

[1] For more examples of asymmetric information and its consequences, see Sections 2.4.2 and 2.4.3 below.

This still leaves the bank exposed to considerable risk which, in effect, they have accepted in order to protect depositors, but this can be managed by a range of devices. Traditionally, one of these has been building up a relationship with the borrower over a long period (**relationship banking**). In this relationship, the borrowing client expects to get a range of high quality financial services (including loans and advice) on very competitive terms; for the bank, dealing with the same client repeatedly means that the bank acquires information about the client and his business. And again, as with depositors, the bank knows that ultimately the borrower must repay a fixed amount and pay interest which is independent of the borrower's business.

Hence we can see that banks are differentiated from other intermediaries by the nature of their core assets and liabilities. But the debt-type contracts that we have just examined have a number of important consequences that add to the differentiation. This applies particularly to deposits, since these are widely used as means of payment. Apart from notes and coin, no other asset (at the moment) is used in this way. What makes an asset suitable for use as money is quite a long story which we discuss further in Section 12.2. But among the characteristics that have led people to use bank deposits is the fact of their possessing a fixed nominal value. Obviously, the person who accepts a transfer of a bank deposit as a means of payment expects its nominal value to be known, this is not the issue. It would be possible for the payer to write out an order to his **unit trust** manager saying that (for example) £100 of units should be transferred to the payee. Provided the law recognizes this contract and the unit trust company agrees to offer this facility, the payee would be sure of £100. The importance of the fixed nominal value rests with the payer. The widely accepted argument is that people would not be willing to *make* payments from an account whose value was not known with certainty. If you have £1,000 in the bank, that £1,000 is guaranteed provided that you make no changes to it (by adding or withdrawing). This is not true for a mutual fund. The value of your fund may be £1,000 at the beginning of the day and (say) £900 or £1,100 at the end. This is a bit like saying that you would never know exactly how much you have in the bank. It is widely believed that depositors would be reluctant to write cheques drawing an uncertain amount.

The use of deposits as means of payment itself has a profound implication for banks and their behaviour.

This is because deposits become a sort of 'residual' or 'discretionary' financial asset. If people wish to spend, they transfer deposits out of the bank. If they have unforeseen expenditures, they will expect to transfer deposits without notice. If they have a surplus of income in one particular period, this will result *automatically* in an increase in their bank deposit. After the accumulation of several surpluses, a depositor may decide to withdraw most of it in order to buy a more interesting financial asset and the deposit shrinks dramatically. What all this means is that there is a degree of instability about bank deposits that does not apply to the liabilities of other financial intermediaries. A pension fund, for example, receives a steady build-up of liabilities as a result of a strict contractual agreement. Equally, it only suffers withdrawals when individuals reach retirement – something that is pretty predictable.

The implication for banks is that they face a relatively high degree of 'liquidity risk'. This is the possibility that they face unforeseen withdrawals of deposits. This requires them to hold a sufficient quantity of 'reserves' which generally earn low interest. Furthermore, since deposits function as a means of payment, the failure of a bank to permit clients to use their deposits on demand, or even the rumour that a bank might have difficulties, would produce a 'run' on other banks. Since the whole structure of banking relies on banks having only a small fraction of assets in the form of reserves, these other banks are bound to fail and the country's payments mechanism will collapse. The terrible consequences of a contagious bank panic has led most central banks to adopt a role as 'lender of last resort' in order to guarantee sufficient liquidity to banks – subject to certain conditions.

The making of loans and the holding of deposits constitute the core, defining, activities of a bank. However, there is plenty of room for differentiation between types of bank and much of this differentiation rests on the other products and services offered by banks or DTIs. Major banks in France, Germany and Japan offer a comprehensive range of financial services to a comprehensive range of clients – households and firms. These include **retail** or **commercial banking**. This is the traditional banking business of holding deposits, bundling them together as loans, operating the payments mechanism etc. **Corporate banking** provides similar services, albeit restricted to large firms. Corporate banks also offer a range of advice and consultancy services of particular relevance to the finance and operation of large firms.

Investment banking is similar to corporate banking, in that clients are firms rather than households, but here the emphasis is upon the flotation and underwriting of new securities issues. Investment banks also act as intermediaries between publicly quoted firms and their stockholders. In addition, investment banks may also be involved in making markets for company securities (see Chapter 17) and here their activities shade into those of **asset management**. Asset management has least contact with the traditional banking business of deposit-taking and loan-making. It involves primarily the administration of pension funds, institutional assets and mutual funds, sometimes combined with market-making. In Germany, Japan and France, it is commonplace for a single banking company to be involved in all these activities, though for organizational purposes they may be allocated to separate 'divisions' of the firm. This reflects a tradition of **'universal' banking**, one firm offering all types of banking service, in these countries.

Banks in the UK have made much progress along a similar road (see Figure 3.1). Banks in the USA are more numerous, geographically restricted and are still to some degree restricted in the services they can offer. However, as with banks in the UK, the trend is towards universal banking. The degree of progress can be represented by the degree of autonomy between the corporate divisions. Banks that wish to act as market-makers in securities in the USA can do so, but only by setting up separately capitalized subsidiaries, and elaborate 'firewalls' are required between different branches of a bank's activities. Alongside the major banks, most countries have a range of smaller DTIs whose sources and uses of funds are restricted by law or, increasingly, only by custom and choice. These include the UK building societies and the US savings and loan societies (S&Ls or 'thrifts'). In France and Germany there are large mutual and cooperative banking sectors with institutions that are limited to particular geographical areas or to providing services for particular groups or professions. The French Crédit Agricole is a classic example of a bank which began in this way.

Unfortunately for students of money and banking, the full range of 'banking' services we have just described represents quite different types of activity. Corporate banking is clearly related to retail banking, distinguished by the differing needs of firms and households, but investment banking and asset management have little to do with deposit-taking or the payments mechanism. When talking about 'banks', therefore, it is often important to distinguish between banks whose clients are mainly persons, households and small firms ('retail' banks) and those which offer specialized services to large firms. The question is, what level of differentiation serves best? In the next few chapters we have chosen generally to distinguish between retail banks (offering services mainly to households and small firms) and 'the rest' which offer a range of specialist services largely to firms. We refer to these as **'wholesale'** banks, but it should be remembered that this term embraces activities ranging from deposit-taking and lending to firms through to asset management. When it matters, we make the distinction again.

We turn now to the traditional business of banking, in which all banks (except the asset managers) are active to some degree. This is usually described as bundling together a large number of small, short-term deposits in order to create a smaller number of larger loans, of longer maturity. This description needs to be viewed carefully. It is perfectly true that if we look at the balance sheet of any bank we shall see that deposits which can be withdrawn at short notice dominate the liability side, while loans (or 'advances') with a longer maturity dominate the asset side. It is also true that there are many more deposits than loans. There certainly is a mismatch of maturity and size and so banks are engaged in both maturity and size transformation. However, the description must not be read as implying causality. It is not the case that banks *receive* large numbers of small short-term deposits which they then *convert* into loans of a different scale and maturity. Deposits do not cause loans. A moment's reflection makes this perfectly clear. When banks respond to a demand from clients it is a demand for loans to which they respond. Customers simply do not go into a bank 'demanding' deposits. An individual customer can add to his or her deposit by paying in cash, but that cash must have been received from someone else who drew cash *from* his or her deposit. Equally, a customer may find his or her deposit increased because he or she has been paid by his or her employer, but that payment is a transfer of a deposit from another bank account. Cash comes into the hands of the public by being obtained from a bank. It is just not true that there is a vast pool of unwanted cash outside banks as a whole waiting to be paid in, in order to increase deposits.

By contrast, clients certainly do ask for loans, and banks, being commercial organizations, do what they can to accommodate all creditworthy demands. Consider now what happens when a successful applicant makes use of the loan. He or she can do so only by making payment to someone else. The likelihood is that the single loan will be used to finance a series of smaller payments. Throughout the system a number of payees receive an addition to their deposits. Hence the appearance of the balance sheet: many small short-term deposits matching fewer, larger long-term loans. But deposits do not cause the loans, rather loans create deposits.

A major difference between retail and wholesale banks, as we implied above, is that making loans and holding deposits form a larger part of retail bank business than they do for wholesale banks. Further differences of detail arising from loan/deposit activity are fourfold. Firstly, deposits are particularly small and numerous for retail banks. Secondly, retail clients have insisted upon access to banking services via extensive branch networks; these are expensive and banks are trying to change this behaviour. Thirdly, a high proportion of retail deposits are sight deposits, used for payment, and therefore retail banks are central to the payments system. Fourthly, retail bank deposits are mainly in the domestic currency while the majority of deposits for wholesale banks are often held in foreign currency.

Given the presence of sight deposits among their liabilities, it follows that banks are engaged in a high degree of maturity transformation. Even if we include all time deposits in the denominator, the average maturity of assets is much longer than liabilities. This is particularly true for retail banks, but it is true only in lesser degree also for wholesale banks. The risks faced by banks are of three broad types. The first, '**asset risk**', is a potential problem for all financial intermediaries; the same is true of the second, '**liquidity risk**', though the deposit nature of bank liabilities means that banks are particularly exposed; the third, '**payment risk**', is almost unique to banks. We look at each in turn and at the action(s) which banks may take to protect themselves. We conclude with some remarks about the regulation of banking activity.

Asset risk. As the term suggests, asset risk refers to the statistical probability that the market value of assets may at some point differ from the value recorded in a bank's balance sheet. Problems arise, naturally

enough, when the market value falls below book value. Sudden changes in value can be caused by a wide variety of events. For example, borrowers may default – either on payment of interest or even on the repayment of the loan. (Because loans make up a large and distinctive part of bank assets, the possibility of loan default is often separated from other types of asset risk and given its own name 'credit risk'.) Interest rates may rise, causing a fall in the present value of all assets. Occasionally, banks may be forced to sell assets in order to meet demands for withdrawal by their depositors. If this happens on a significant scale across the system, then the sudden excess supply of certain types of asset will force down the price and banks go 'bankrupt'.

Protection against asset risk comes broadly in three forms. Firstly, banks are naturally protected to some

MORE FROM THE WEB
What banks do

Banks today are among the largest financial institutions in Europe, with branches and subsidiaries throughout the world. Furthermore, they offer a range of services which goes well beyond the traditional banking functions of making loans and holding deposits. Most have websites where the structure and history of the bank can be seen, together with a list of its products and services. Try the three examples below.

www.Commerzbank.com

Commerzbank is one of the big three German universal banks.

www.creditagricole.fr

This is one of France's largest banks.

In both cases you should be able to find a chart showing the structure of the bank and the range of products and services. You should also be able to click on 'History' to see how they have come to their dominant position after starting out as lenders and deposit-holders.

Commerzbank and Crédit Agricole are both 'universal' banks offering a full range of banking services. Goldman Sachs, by contrast, is an international investment bank. To see the range of services offered by an investment bank, go to www.goldmansachs.com and click on 'Client Services'. How much reference do you see to deposit-taking and lending? On what you see of Goldman Sachs, what are the main activities of an investment bank?

degree against default by the diversification of their loans across a wide range of borrowers. This is one reason why stability tends to increase with size. The more clients there are, the easier it is to diversify lending across a wide range of different types of borrower with different types of project. Except in a major economic upheaval, it is unlikely that all borrowers of different kinds will simultaneously be unable to service a debt. More typically, a small number of borrowers may be in difficulty at any time, but these poorly performing loans will be insignificant among the majority which are performing normally. (We look at the relationship between risk and diversification in Section 8.3.) But banks can, and do, go further. Secondly, they can screen loan applicants – by asking for information about the purposes of the loan and by checking the credit record of the potential borrower. If the loan is a large one, it may even pay the bank to monitor the performance of the project which it is financing. This is unlikely to happen frequently in the case of retail banks lending to households, but wholesale banks will typically include some clause about their monitoring rights in contracts for large loans made to large firms. Thirdly, they can protect themselves against interest and forced sale risk by holding short-term assets. This has two advantages. If the pool of short-term assets is carefully arranged, a bank can ensure that it has a continuous stream of assets maturing in the normal way and at normal prices. In the event of a sudden need for funds, it can simply not reinvest. Even if this does not meet the crisis, more assets will be maturing in the very near future and the crisis might be averted until this happens. There is also a technical advantage in holding short-term assets when interest rates are volatile. Short-term assets are less price-sensitive to interest rate changes than are long-term assets. The reasons for this are explained later when we look at the riskiness of fixed interest bonds (in Section 16.4). For the moment, we can simply imagine an asset with only six months to maturity. This period can, at most, include only one interest payment, followed by maturity at a specified price. Whatever happens to interest rates on other assets, it can have little effect on the value of our asset, since interest is a very small part of the payments which the asset will shortly deliver.

Liquidity risk. As we saw earlier, liquidity risk is an especial problem for banks because it arises from the distinctive nature of their deposit liabilities. Liquidity risk refers to the possibility that a bank may not have the funds with which to meet the demand for payment when it falls due. Notice that this is not necessarily a question of solvency. Assets may well match liabilities but payment on demand requires *liquid* assets to be available in sufficient quantity. This is a question rather of the *composition* of assets and liabilities and relates obviously to the process of **maturity transformation** in which all financial intermediaries are to some degree engaged. It is particularly acute for banks, since their liabilities will normally include sight deposits, which must be convertible into notes and coin on demand. Furthermore, it must be possible for clients to instruct their banks to make immediate payments to clients of other banks.

Notice that while we are all exposed to liquidity risk, the degree of exposure and above all the *potential consequences* for banks puts them in a unique position as a result of the 'convertibility' promise that attaches to sight deposits. Households can suffer a liquidity crisis when, for example, a utility bill arrives earlier than expected or is for an amount that is unexpectedly large and it has inadequate funds immediately available with which to pay the bill. But the 'crisis' is usually manageable. As a general rule, the household has 14 days in which to raise the necessary funds, which it can do by withdrawing funds from a savings account or selling some assets or borrowing. If this is not long enough, payment can usually be delayed for a further period before the utility company terminates the electricity or gas supply. The situation is similar for firms: payment can usually be delayed for long enough to allow funds to be raised. Even with non-DTIs, a request for repayment by investors does not usually have to be acted on immediately. A period of notice is usually required. But for banks it is completely different. A request to convert sight deposits to cash *must* be met on demand. Any failure to do so, or even a rumour that the bank might have difficulty in so doing, will be enough to close the bank, *however solvent it may be*. This is because the rumour will result in everyone trying to withdraw cash at once and no bank can meet that demand. As we shall see now, the process of banking depends fundamentally on the *inability* to meet any demand for cash beyond a small fraction of outstanding sight deposits.

One obvious solution would be to hold liquid assets exactly equal to these demand liabilities (a 100 per cent 'reserve ratio'). In practice, this would mean holding a matching quantity of notes and coin, or notes and coin combined with deposits at the central bank which banks can exchange for notes and coin instantly. The problem with this solution is that such liquid assets (even including deposits at the central bank) yield little interest since notes and coin make up the bulk of such assets. These are low-earning assets and as such act as a tax on banking activity. As a general rule, taxes on the production of any good or service are better avoided since they increase the cost and reduce the quantity of what is produced. Furthermore, in the case of banks there is a question of distortion. If a high reserve requirement is placed upon a bank then it is immediately placed at a competitive disadvantage against other financial intermediaries. Experience has shown that this encourages a cat-and-mouse type game between banks and the authorities where banks try to reconstruct themselves or set up subsidiaries in such a way that they fall just outside the definition of a bank for the purposes of the regulation.

Fortunately, what experience has also shown is that the probability of all sight deposits being withdrawn at a moment's notice in an established banking system is infinitesimal. On any particular day, some deposits will be withdrawn (as cash or transferred to another bank as payment) but by the same token, deposits from other banks will flow in. All that is required is sufficient funds to meet the *net* payments plus a margin for unexpected events. Once again, size helps. The larger the client base, i.e. the greater the *number* of flows, (a) the smaller are the net flows relative to the total stock of deposits and (b) the more predictable the flows. The latter is an example of the **Law of Large Numbers**, which we explore in more detail in Section 2.4.1, and it means that net flows can be calculated with greater accuracy. These mean that banks can, in practice, operate with very small reserve ratios. These can be specified by a central monetary authority ('mandatory' ratios) or they may be left to banks' discretion, normally with a requirement that the central bank be notified of any planned change ('prudential' ratios). In the early years of banking, when banks were small and confidence in the convertibility of deposits into cash was less well established than it is today, it was found necessary for the system to have a 'lender of last resort' – a role assumed by the central bank. This meant that if the system were faced with an unexpected demand for convertibility, banks which had insufficient reserves but were otherwise solvent and well managed, would be guaranteed adequate liquidity by being able to borrow from the central bank. Such a role is rarely required today. Central banks are occasionally required to give leadership in a financial crisis but this is more frequently connected with financial markets than the liquidity of the banking system. Where banks are concerned, the central bank's role has undergone a subtle change. Instead of helping banks in occasional crises, central banks now typically provide liquidity on a day-to-day basis in order to smooth out fluctuations in bank reserves which arise from payments between public and private sectors, and to ensure that banks always have funds available to meet the demand for loans which grows with the level of economic activity. This gives rise to the joke that central banks are now lenders of *first* resort but, more seriously, it enables banks to operate with even lower reserve ratios (and a lower 'tax') but it gives the central bank immense power over the banking system from another direction – the setting of short-term interest rates.

Holding sufficient notes and coin and other assets, such as deposits at the central bank which are virtually cash assets, is an obvious way of dealing with the liquidity risk that arises from the possibility that holders of sight deposits may demand instant withdrawal. It does not, though, avoid the penalty that these assets do not earn interest. Hence there is always commercial pressure to restrict these to a minimum level (with the help of the central bank these days) and hold assets which may be slightly less liquid but do nonetheless earn some positive return. This is why, compared with other intermediaries, banks tend to hold a large quantity of short-term money market assets such as bills and short-dated government bonds. As we saw earlier in this section, these can be quickly sold, with little risk to their value in the event of a liquidity shortage and yet they still yield a positive return. In most countries, recent years have seen the rapid growth of the 'interbank' market as one of the wider group of money markets. The interbank market allows banks with surplus funds to deposit those funds with other banks, at interest, for very short periods – often overnight. This is another source of liquidity which banks short of reserves can tap. It reduces their need to hold surplus reserves against unforeseen events. In doing this, the interbank market spreads the existing stock of liquidity across the system as a whole more closely according to need. Banks with a surplus of reserves can lend to banks who are short and would otherwise be constrained in their lending/deposit-taking.

This in turn helps the system as a whole to create a quantity of loans and deposits closer to the limits set by the availability of aggregate reserves.

Payment risk. Payment risk arises specifically from banks' role in the payments mechanism. When the client of bank A makes payment to a client of bank B, this initiates an instruction from bank B to bank A to remit funds to bank B (assuming bank A's client has funds available). This transfer takes place between the two banks' deposit accounts with the central bank, described above. Clearly, this takes time. Traditionally, the instructions have taken the written form of a cheque. After the payee pays this into his account (at bank B) the cheque has to find its way (through a clearing mechanism) to the payer's bank, A. It has then to be verified and instructions given to the central bank to credit bank B. If bank B makes funds available to its client as soon as the cheque is paid in, it runs the risk that funds may not be available in the drawer's account. It has then paid out funds which it will not receive. As we all know, the banks' solution to this particular risk is to delay payment on a cheque until the cheque has been 'cleared' and funds received, a process which can take several days. The same risk (and the same solution) applies with automated debits and credits – standing orders, direct debits, electronic salary payments etc. – though here the delay is usually rather shorter.

It is easy to understand that cheque clearing takes time – pieces of paper are being sent through the post after all – and that banks could be at risk of premature payment. It is less obvious that they run the same risk with electronic transfers or with systems that are deliberately designed to allow same-day clearing. In the UK, interbank payments are handled by five companies. The first is the Cheque and Credit Clearing Company which deals with (roughly) cheques and other paper-based instructions. The Bankers' Automated Clearing System (BACS) handles a large number of electronic payments, especially where these are automated, regular, payments. MasterCard and Visa handle payments by debit and credit cards. Finally, the Clearing House Automated Payments Company (CHAPS for short) handles same-day-large-value payments. The system is used mainly by financial institutions. (The Bank of England recently estimated that 60 per cent of CHAPS transactions involved foreign exchange.) The nearest that the personal sector comes to using it is in the process of house purchase when

funds may go through the CHAPS system within minutes, in exchange for the door key. Until recently, the CHAPS system itself gave rise to a high degree of payments risk even though settlement took place within the same day. This arose because the UK banking system worked on the basis of 'deferred net settlement' for *all* transactions. This meant that all interbank transfers were accumulated until the end of the trading day, when transfers would be 'netted out'. Payments from bank A to bank B, for example, would be offset against payment instructions from B to A and only the balance would actually be paid. Provided that the banks imposed a payment delay of the kind we described above, no risk was involved. But the CHAPS system gave the payee the right to draw funds the moment that the payment instruction was accepted by the payer's bank. This could be early in the morning, in which case the payee's bank would obviously be exposed to the risk of default by the payer's bank

MORE FROM THE WEB
The payments system and payment risk

The payments system in the UK is operated by several companies. Fortunately, they all make returns to the Association for Payment Clearing System, APACS, which has a very good wesbite at www.apacs.org.uk

At the APACS website you can find information about the different types of payment instruments handled by the three companies as well as statistical information about the value and volume of payments made by each of these instruments. If you click on 'Payment Facts' and then on 'Cheques' you will see a detailed explanation of the procedures involved in paying by cheque and why it takes cheques several days to pass through the clearing process. The length of time it takes shows why a bank would be exposed to payment risk if it paid out as soon as the cheque was presented.

An excellent discussion of the general principles involved in designing a payments and settlement system is provided by the Bank of England. At the Bank's homepage, www.bankofengland.co.uk, click on the link to the Centre for Central Banking Studies and then on 'Handbooks'. The one you want is No. 8 by David Sheppard. A review of recent developments in UK payments systems can be found in the Bank of England's *Payment Systems Oversight Report*, at: http://www.bankofengland.co.uk/publications/psor/psor2006.pdf.

until funds were received at the end of the day. This may sound like a rather theoretical risk, but the sums involved are huge. The paper and electronic systems together cleared payments totalling approximately £4,663bn during 2006. In the same year, CHAPS handled over £109,000bn.

The average size of a CHAPS transaction in 2006 was c. £2.7m but many were over £100m. Some of these payments exceeded the total value of the capital invested in the bank involved in the transaction. In other words, the failure of one of these large transactions could have wiped out the entire net worth of a bank, leaving its shareholders with nothing and very likely having to organize a panic sale of assets which then leaves it unable to meet its other liabilities (we come back to the role of shareholders' funds in a moment). The bank is quite literally 'bankrupt'. Remember too that if a bank fails there is always the risk of contagion as depositors try to recover what is not just part of their wealth but crucially also their means of payment. No wonder the Bank of England was alarmed at the risks some banks were taking through the CHAPS system.

The only solution to this is for the appropriate funds to accompany each individual payment instruction. If a customer of bank A pays £1m to a customer of bank B at 09.30 in the morning, bank A must remit £1m at the time of the instruction, regardless of what the balance of its transactions with bank B might be at the end of the day. Such a system is known as 'real-time gross settlement' (RTGS) and has been adopted for CHAPS payments since 1997. This brings CHAPS into line with the European Monetary Union payments system (known as TARGET). In November 2007, the UK will see the introduction of a new 'Faster Payments Service' which will settle BACS payments on an almost real-time basis. Consequently, this will leave only paper-based payments operating outside the RTGS principle and these payments are in steady decline.

Regulation. As we have just seen, banks provide a readily accessible home for clients' savings. We also noted, however, that some bank deposits (probably most sight deposits) perform an additional function as a means of payment. This is particularly true for retail banks. Hence we can see that if a bank should fail, its clients would not only lose part of their wealth: they also lose their means of buying goods and services. A loss of wealth is naturally enough distressing for anyone, but losing that part of wealth which functions as

money can have dire consequences. For example, a loss of (non-money) financial wealth need involve no instant secondary effects. Victims may look for someone to sue, and they may increase their savings rate in future to restore the lost wealth, but this is not likely to cause disruption to the rest of the economic or financial systems. A loss of the means of payment, however, requires urgent action since bills still have to be paid and some of those bills (eating, travel to work etc.) will fall due immediately. The danger with any bank failure, therefore, is that those affected will immediately withdraw deposits which they may hold with other deposit-taking institutions (triggering liquidity risk for all DTIs). Furthermore it is immediately followed by the distress selling of financial assets as people try to raise money in near-panic circumstances. This pushes down asset prices (triggering asset risk for *all* financial institutions). For this reason, a bank failure may easily be 'contagious'. Other institutions which are perfectly solvent and liquid in normal circumstances may also fail through liquidity and/or asset risk. This reminds us why a 'lender of last resort' was so important in the early stages of banking development. It also explains why banks tend to be subject to a high degree of regulation and supervision, of a quantity and a kind which is unusual for NDTIs.

We have already met one obvious form of regulation – the mandatory reserve requirement. By specifying that banks should hold a minimum ratio of notes and coin plus bankers' balances at the central bank to their outstanding deposit liabilities, monetary authorities (usually the central bank itself) could try to eliminate liquidity risk. However, we have also seen that this can be considered as the equivalent of imposing a tax on banks and encourages business to divert to alternative institutions. The trend is to allow banks to set their own reserve requirements and to rely upon the central bank as a source of liquidity in the event of a shortage. Furthermore, liquidity risk is only one form of risk faced by banks and so reserve ratios are only a partial antidote to bank risk.

In the last 25 years or so, regulation has become much more sophisticated, concentrating upon the full range of bank risk and seeking to impose some degree of consistency across systems so that banks can compete internationally on a reasonably level playing field. The organization mainly responsible for the design (but not the enforcement) of the regulations is the Bank for International Settlements, based in Basel. The 'Basel Committee's' approach has been to switch attention from bank liabilities to bank *assets* and from liquid reserves to a bank's *capital*. Furthermore, in both cases, they focus not just upon total quantities but also upon composition. The critical test, however, remains a bank's ability to meet a specified ratio – of risk-adjusted total assets to bank capital. The basic principle behind such a ratio is that the risks of carrying on a banking business should be borne by the shareholders rather than the bank's clients, and that the bank's capital should be sufficient to absorb any losses that could not be met out of current profits.

In order to understand the role of a bank's capital in limiting clients' exposure to risk, we need to understand the structure of a firm's balance sheet and the relation between assets and liabilities. A glance at Box 2.1, which shows a simplified version of the balance sheet of a typical bank, may help. Throughout this book we shall often refer to the 'balance sheet identity' meaning that assets must always be matched by a combination of liabilities and 'equity' or capital. (In short $A \equiv L + E$ where E stands for 'equity'.) A balance sheet must always balance and this is clearly true for XYZ. But for readers unfamiliar with the structure of financial statements this must seem a strange idea. After all, many of the items shown as assets and liabilities on the XYZ's balance sheet are securities which are traded in volatile markets. Their value must fluctuate from day to day. Equally with non-traded assets, customer loans, for example, the value can fluctuate. After all, the value of a loan which goes into default is probably zero. How can it be therefore that, whatever it does, a firm is guaranteed to find that its assets match its liabilities plus equity? The

answer lies in the behaviour of the E part of our identity. Another way of approaching this is to think of E as expressing the 'net worth' of the company or the difference between its assets and liabilities. For a thriving firm, E will be positive, so yet another way of thinking about equity is to think of it as the *excess* of assets over liabilities. On the other hand, where E is negative, a firm has negative net worth, its assets are insufficient to match its liabilities and it is technically insolvent (and in the UK it is required to cease trading).

In order to understand the importance of banks' equity in preserving a bank's solvency, consider what happens if there is a negative shock to bank assets. The balance sheet must constinue to balance, but in practice a firm's liabilities are given. (Indeed the term 'liability' has a legal meaning signifying that it is an obligation to someone that *must* be honoured.) In the case of banks, this is very clear since many of its liabilities take the form of deposits whose very nature, as we stressed above, requires them to have a fixed nominal value. In these circumstances, a negative shock to assets must result in a reduction in a firm's equity and thus in effect in the value of the firm to its shareholders. This happens because the equity consists of:

- the value of the funds originally committed to the firm (when it was first incorporated);
- plus any funds committed later by subsequent share issues;
- plus the accumulated earnings retained from each year's profit;
- plus this year's retained earnings.

BOX 2.1 XYZ bank, consolidated balance sheet (€m)

Assets		Liabilities	
Cash and balances at the central bank	5,000	Sight deposits	109,000
Money-market loans	210,000	Time deposits	110,500
Loans and advances	222,000	Savings deposits	86,500
Securities	105,000	Repos	35,000
Insurance company investments	64,500	CDs, bonds and securities	83,400
Accrued income and other assets	155,500	Reserves of insurance companies	54,750
		Loans from other MFIs	22,100
		Accrued expenses etc.	184,750
		Other liabilities	25,000
		Shareholders' funds, equity	51,000
Total	762,000	*Total*	762,000

Although the first two items alone strictly make up 'shareholders' funds' – the funds that shareholders have committed to the firm – the whole of this equity (the firm's net worth) belongs to shareholders and is one component in the value of the shares they own.

Imagine now the case where a borrower with a large loan defaults. If there is absolutely no chance of the bank recovering any part of the loan, the loan's value as an asset falls to zero. In the simplest case, a bank will 'write off' the value of this loan in the year of default. In effect, it is deducted from any profit the firm may have earned. The retained earnings for the year in question are reduced and the equity will be less than it would otherwise have been. In an extreme case, the default could be so large that it exceeds the whole of the value of the equity. Then the firm has negative net worth and will not have sufficient assets to meet its liabilities. In these circumstances it is insolvent and, since we are talking about a bank, will not be able to repay all customers' deposits. We noted the consequences of such a failure in connection with payment risk above. Given that payment and asset risks are all risks that banks must face – however good their asset management – it is clearly important that banks have sufficiently large equity or capital that they can meet all reasonably conceivable shocks without experiencing negative net worth and threatening the wealth of depositors who have dealt with the bank in all good faith and are in no way responsible for the problem. This is why the Basel Committee decided many years ago to specify minimum levels of capital that a bank must have in relation to the risks that it faced. If something goes seriously wrong with the bank, there should be sufficient equity to ensure that the shock is borne entirely by shareholders and not by (innocent) clients of the bank.

Under the Basel Committee's 1988 proposals ('Basel I', adopted by most industrial countries in 1993) assets are divided into five groups or classes, each with its own risk-weighting, lower weights being given to less risky assets. Thus, cash has a weight of 0, loans to the discount market are weighted at 0.1, local authority bonds 0.2, mortgage loans 0.5, while commercial loans have the full weight of 1. The method of assessment, broadly speaking, is to multiply the market value of each asset by its risk factor and then to aggregate the risk-adjusted value. This is then compared with the bank's capital base.

Capital, in turn, has a two-tier classification. Tier I or core capital consists essentially of shareholders' equity, disclosed reserves and the current year's retained profits, which are readily available to cushion losses – these must be verified by the bank's auditors. Tier II or supplementary capital comprises funds available but not fully owned or controlled by the institution such as 'general' provisions that the bank had set aside against unidentified future losses and medium- or long-term subordinated debt issued by the bank.

When it comes to the ratios, tier II elements are not permitted to make up more than 50 per cent of an institution's own funds. More fundamentally, the Basel Committee recommended a lower limit of 8 per cent for the ratio of total capital to risk-adjusted assets, though national bank supervisors had some discretion in applying this to different types of bank. Monitoring and enforcement of these requirements lies with national bodies. In the UK until 1998 this was the Bank of England but is now the Financial Services Authority. Subject to enforcing the Basel Committee's capital requirements, national regulators may impose further restrictions. The UK FSA, for example, recognizes a 'tier III' level of capital.

Notice that these requirements, just like a simple reserve ratio, are built upon the weighing and comparing of items in a balance sheet. Indeed, it is difficult to see how else regulators could proceed. To show that rules are being observed or breached there has to be documentary evidence and the obvious documentary evidence must be a firm's accounts. Basing regulation upon the composition of balance sheets has, however, had an interesting though perhaps predictable consequence. It has encouraged banks that wish to expand, but find the capital requirements constraining, to develop 'off-balance-sheet activities'. These are activities which generate revenue (and ultimately profit) without requiring a corresponding entry in the balance sheet. An early example is provided by the so-called 'bill leak' in the UK during the 1970s. For most of the 1970s UK banks were restricted (by the 'supplementary special deposit scheme') to allowing their eligible liabilities (roughly deposits) to grow only at a maximum specified rate. This restricted banks' ability to lend and both loan and deposit growth could be checked from banks' accounts. Corporate clients took to issuing commercial bills (see Section 15.2) in order to borrow directly in the money markets. Firms and banks then quickly realized that both could benefit if banks were to 'accept' or guarantee the bills at the time of issue. The guarantee made the bills more secure from the markets' point of view

---

MORE FROM THE WEB
More on the 'Basel Accord' and bank risk

At the time of writing, the Basel capital requirements described on this page are still under review – a process which has been going on for some years.

The work of the Basel Committee, and the progress of the revisions, is described on the website of the Bank for International Settlements: www.bis.org/bcbs.

The firm of BarrettWells also hosts a website which deals with 'risk' in a broad financial context and at a much more sophisticated level than we can do here. The best starting point for exploring the site is: www.barrettwells.co.uk/sitelist.html.

---

and so firms were charged a lower rate of interest; at the same time banks charged a fee for the guarantee, thus replacing some of the profit they were forgoing by having their normal lending business restricted. A more widespread practice today is the practice of 'securitization'. A bank which finds the capital requirements constraining typically establishes a subsidiary which then 'buys' loans from the parent bank. In order to do this, it sells bonds (i.e. securities) to the market. The bank passes the loan interest to the subsidiary which then passes it on, less a premium for expenses and profit, to the bondholders. So far as the originating bank is concerned, the loans have disappeared 'off-balance-sheet'. The capital:asset ratio is increased and expansion can resume. Finding ways of measuring and controlling the risk of these so-called 'contingent liabilities' was one of the stimuli to a major revision of the Basel I requirements. A new set of regulations, 'Basel II' try to capture a wider range of risks. These began to be implemented in 2007 and are described in more detail in Chapter 25.

2.4 Non-deposit-taking institutions – insurance companies and pension funds

In the preceding section, we looked in some detail at deposit-taking institutions and in particular at banks. As we saw there, deposits are a unique kind of liability: individuals who hold deposits can require the financial institutions whose liabilities they are to pay them their value in money on demand ('at sight') or at short notice – in other words, more or less at the holders' discretion. In contrast, a non-deposit-taking institution (NDTI) is under no obligation to provide clients with anything like ready access to the funds they have placed with it. What is more, clients are often bound by contract to make payments *to* the NDTI. For example, an endowment policy commits the policyholder to making regular payments (premiums) to an insurance company over many years.

NDTIs are often collectively referred to as the 'institutional investors'. This is because of their role in taking in savings from households and firms and pooling them before investing in securities of many different kinds. As we shall see, investing institutions have the advantage of being able to buy and sell in large quantities and thus to enjoy low unit transaction costs. They also offer the benefits of professional analysts who should have an information advantage (over private investors) when it comes to asset selection. The term 'institutional investor' covers pension funds, insurance companies and mutual funds. By size, the first two are by far the largest and we look at the main principles under which they operate in the rest of this section. Mutual funds are the subject of Section 2.5.

Differences in the size and role of the institutional investors provide the main differences between financial systems around the world, but especially in Europe. For example, the assets of institutional investors in the G7 countries amount to approximately the same value as the combined G7 GDP. But there are very big differences between countries. In the UK and USA, their assets are nearer twice the size of corresponding GDP while in continental Europe the figure is nearer 50 per cent. It follows from this that the markets for institutional investment (the range of products offered, for example) are much nearer to maturity in the Anglo-Saxon countries than in continental Europe. From this, it is a reasonable guess that much of the evolution in continental financial systems is likely to come via the investing institutions, rather than through markets. Historically, the reasons for this continental/Anglo-Saxon split lie with supply-side factors such as deregulation and enhanced competition and demand-side factors such as higher wealth and demographic factors which led, some years ago, to a concern that individuals should take a much larger responsibility for their own pensions by accumulating an equity-based investment fund. Much of continental Europe is still dominated by **'pay-as-you-go'** social security systems, raising the same demographic issues. How to pay for pensions, and the implications that this has for financial institutions and other firms, is a recurrent theme through these next few chapters.

Insurance companies

The endowment and other policies that *life insurers* (often referred to as **life offices**) issue are, as we have just noted, long-term contracts. The maturity date of a policy of this kind is almost invariably at least 10 years from its inception date and often much longer. Policyholders pay regular premiums in return for the prospect of a payout, on death or at maturity, that will, they hope, represent a worthwhile return on these premiums. In most cases, policyholders take out life insurance primarily as a means of building up savings.

General insurers (otherwise known as *non-life offices*) offer cover against day-to-day risks, of which the most important categories are home, marine, vehicle and liability to third parties.[2] In contrast to life insurance, non-life policies are generally issued and renewed on an annual basis.

Reinsurance represents a third major area of insurance activity. Reinsurance enables one insurer to 'lay off' risks it considers excessive on business it has 'written'.[3] It does so by itself buying insurance from another office.

Pension funds

Occupational pensions are paid to retired people who have been members of pension schemes run by their employers during their working lives. Many schemes require both employees and the employer to make regular contributions into a fund – the *pension fund* – which is invested in stock market securities and other assets. If the fund is to remain continuously solvent, contributions received, supplemented by the returns earned on them, need to be sufficient to meet liabilities to pay pensions out of the fund, as these fall due. The administration of the scheme and/or the investment of the fund may be entrusted to a life insurance company.

2.4.1 Some principles of insurance

The Law of Large Numbers: from dice throws to insurance

The outcome of a particular event may be very difficult to predict. However, in many situations, the *average* outcome of a large number of similar events is, in contrast, highly predictable. The Law of Large Numbers (LLN) is based on this fact. It is true to say that insurance would not be possible if the LLN did not 'work'. For that reason, we need to examine it in some detail.

Even though the connection between dice throws and insurance may not seem immediately obvious, thinking about patterns of scores that emerge when one or more dice are thrown repeatedly turns out to be a useful way of gaining an insight into how the LLN operates in insurance. First we consider a single die. Then we look at average scores from simultaneous throws of a *pair* of dice.

In the terminology of statistical theory, the score on one throw of a single die represents one member of an infinite 'population' of possible 'observations'. What is the population? It consists of the scores on all the throws of the die in question that there have been in the past and all those that there might potentially be in the future. Suppose the die is *unbiased*, that is, any one score is equally as likely as any other. Each observation, in other words, the score on any one throw, must be a whole number between 1 and 6, and the probability of it being any one of these numbers is 1/6. It follows that:

- the population mean, μ, the mean of scores of the whole (infinite) population of possible throws of that die, equals:

$$1/6(1) + 1/6(2) + \ldots + 1/6(6) = 3.5 \qquad (2.1)$$

and that

- the standard deviation[4] of the whole population of possible scores, σ, is equal to

$$\sqrt{\left[\frac{1}{6}(1-3.5)^2 + \frac{1}{6}(2-3.5)^2 + \ldots + \frac{1}{6}(6-3.5)^2\right]} \approx 1.71$$

$$(2.2)$$

---

2   Third-party liability insurance involves the insurer in covering the insured against the risk of having to pay compensation for some act or omission as a result of which a third party suffers damage or loss. For example, a failure by an employer to provide safe working conditions could lead to claims for damages from workers who have suffered illness or injury as a result. Employer liability insurance exists to protect the employer against the risk of such claims. In the next section of this chapter, we refer to the dramatic case of the massive accumulation of insurance claims that resulted from employer liability for the contraction by employees of asbestosis and related diseases.
3   That is, on policies it has issued to its own clients.
4   If you need to revise the meaning and calculation of a standard deviation, go to Section 8.2.

Now we can say that any one throw of the die represents one *sample*, of size 1, from this population. As only one die is thrown, the average score for the sample *is* the score shown on the die.[5] We can call the average score on any sample, whatever its size, the *sample average*. Obviously, the value of the sample average will vary between one sample and the next. It follows that the sample average is itself a *variable* which has its own **mean**[6] and **standard deviation**. In this one-die case, sample averages, being identical to the scores on different throws, will be distributed around their population mean in an identical way to these scores. Thus we can say that the sample average of single throws of a die will have $\mu = 3.5$ and $\sigma = 1.71$.

Table 2.2 depicts the distribution of sample averages for single throws of an unbiased die. Note that the distribution is *uniform*, that is, it is flat and does not peak around any particular value.

Suppose, now, a pair of dice are thrown at the same time. The score on each die will again be a number between 1 and 6. Consequently, one throw of a pair of dice could produce any of 36 different outcomes, from a [1,1], (i.e., a 1 on the first and a 1 on the second die) to [1,2], (a 1 on the first and a 2 on the second), and so on through to [6,6]. All 36 possible outcomes are shown in Table 2.3.

Throwing a pair of dice together produces samples of size 2. The total and average score in each sample will now be different, and we have to divide the total

Table 2.2

Probability =	1/6	1/6	1/6	1/6	1/6	1/6
Value	1	2	3	4	5	6

Table 2.3

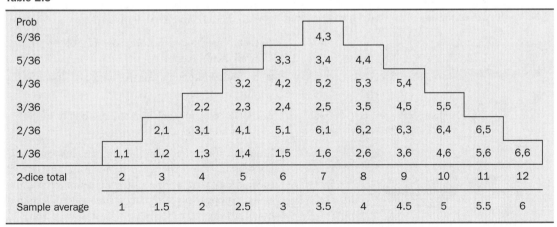

Prob											
6/36						4,3					
5/36					3,3	3,4	4,4				
4/36				3,2	4,2	5,2	5,3	5,4			
3/36			2,2	2,3	2,4	2,5	3,5	4,5	5,5		
2/36		2,1	3,1	4,1	5,1	6,1	6,2	6,3	6,4	6,5	
1/36	1,1	1,2	1,3	1,4	1,5	1,6	2,6	3,6	4,6	5,6	6,6
2-dice total	2	3	4	5	6	7	8	9	10	11	12
Sample average	1	1.5	2	2.5	3	3.5	4	4.5	5	5.5	6

---

[5] In general terms, average = total ÷ number of observations. When only one die is thrown the number of observations is 1, the average equals the total, so the average score is simply the score itself. It may therefore seem strange that we differentiate between the average and the total in this case. However, there is a good reason for doing so, and this should become clear shortly when we consider the case of two dice thrown simultaneously.

[6] It may seem odd to talk in terms of the 'mean' of an 'average', but a moment's thought will show that doing so makes sense. Suppose we take repeated samples of some type or other (e.g., samples of 10 students' weights) and then record the average weight in these samples. The average of each individual sample (of 10) will be a member of the whole population of averages of samples (of 10), and this population must have a mean.

by 2 to obtain its average. By throwing the pair of dice again and again, we would obtain repeated samples and thus a series of sample averages. Just as in the one-die case, the value of the sample average can vary between 1 and 6, but this time with gradations of 0.5. These are shown in the bottom row of Table 2.3. The probability of the sample average taking any particular value can be read off along the vertical axis.

What happens to the mean and the standard deviation of the sample average when we increase the number of dice thrown from one to two? Outcomes remain distributed symmetrically around the value 3.5, leaving the mean unaffected, i.e., μ remains equal to 3.5. But note the effect on the *way* sample averages are distributed around this mean. Comparing Table 2.3 with Table 2.2, we can see that this ceases to be uniform once the sample size is increased to 2. Rather, when a pair of dice are thrown at the same time, a sample average that is close to the mean is more likely than one that is much higher or lower than it.[7] In other words, when the sample size increases, the dispersion of sample averages around their mean is reduced. This is illustrated by the fact that, when the number of dice thrown rises from 1 to 2, the standard deviation of sample averages, σ, can be shown to fall from 1.71 to 1.21. Now think about the questions in Exercise 2.1.

These questions illustrate the operation of the LLN. As the size of the sample we take increases, the

variability of sample averages around the mean of the population of samples diminishes. Indeed, as the sample size grows towards infinity, the standard deviation of the sample averages diminishes towards zero. *Thus, the more we increase the size of the sample, the less chance there is that the averages of samples we take will differ significantly from the mean and therefore from one another.*

Applying the Law of Large Numbers to insurance

We are now in a position to move on from talking about dice to discussing the application of the LLN to insurance. Consider an imaginary insurance company that offers households cover against burglary. Suppose policies are renewed annually. Each household covered in each year represents a single observation (with two possible outcomes: *loss* or *no loss*). The population consists of all the possible observations of all the possible households in all the possible years in which these households might exist – an infinite population.

Suppose that every household faces a 1 in 100 chance that it will be burgled in any one year and that, if a burglary occurs, it will suffer a loss of £2,500.[8] We can write: E(loss) = 0.99(0) + 0.01(2500) = £25, where E(loss) denotes the (statistically) expected loss per household. Note straightaway that:

- each household will *either* lose £2,500 *or* nothing at all in any year;
- no household will incur the 'expected' loss of £25; and
- the outcome for each household is highly variable – either no loss or 'big' loss.

From the point of view of the company insuring these households, the 'experience' of insuring any one of them in any year will be either 'no claim' or '£2,500 claim'. Suppose the company insures 100,000 households in any year. Its overall claims experience in each year can be thought of as a sample comprising 100,000 such individual claims experiences. Each year will represent a different sample.

Exercise 2.1

We could increase the number of dice thrown together to 3, 5, 10 or more and work out the sample average each time we throw any specific number of dice.

(a) What will happen to μ and σ, the mean and standard deviation of the sample average, as we increase the number of dice thrown?

(b) What will happen to σ as the number of dice thrown increases towards infinity?

(Answers appear in the text.)

---

[7] For example, Table 2.3 tells us that, when a pair of dice are thrown, the probability of an average score lying between 2.5 and 3.5 is $^{15}/_{36}$ or, in other words, more than 41 per cent. In contrast, the chance of an average score of 2 or less or, on the other hand, 5 or more is, in either case, $^{6}/_{36}$ or less than 17 per cent.
[8] Assume, for simplicity, that no household is burgled more than once in any year.

Now the number of households that suffer burglary in any one year's sample will vary. However, the mean number of households burgled in any one year will be 1,000. It follows that the mean household loss through burglary, taking one year with the next, will be £2.5m/100,000 = £25. Thanks to the LLN, our insurer can expect the number of households suffering a burglary in any year to be close to the mean of 1,000.[9] It follows that the insurer can be fairly confident that:

■ its average loss per household insured (its sample average) in any year will be close to £2.5m/100,000 = £25,

and therefore that,

■ if it charges each householder a premium of £25, it will be able to meet total claims for loss out of the premium income it will receive.

You should now be able to answer the question in Exercise 2.2.

Exercise 2.2

Insurance does not prevent losses from happening. How then is it possible that insurers are able to cover individual policyholders financially against the risk of loss?

(The first paragraph of the next section of this chapter contains an answer to this question.)

2.4.2 Insurers' residual risks and other limits to the insurance principle

Insurance reduces neither the frequency with which events that result in loss occur nor the amounts lost when they do. Rather, as far as policyholders are concerned, it eliminates the risks associated with the *possibility* of loss. For, by taking out insurance cover, an individual converts the *chance* of a large loss into the *certainty* of a very small one: if the event insured against occurs, the insured loses no more than the premium paid; if it does not, he or she loses no less than this amount. Thanks to the LLN, an insurance company can in this way eliminate risk faced by its clients

without at the same time being obliged to take on an equivalent amount of risk itself. This is because the LLN will make the total value of claims for loss that the company will be called upon to meet each year a reasonably predictable sum. As a result, insurance reduces the overall amount of risk faced by society as a whole. Nevertheless, we need to recognize that the LLN does not entirely eliminate the risks the insurance company faces. It merely reduces them to manageable proportions. This is because, however well the LLN operates, three sources of *residual* risk remain to confront the insurer. We give them the names:

■ random fluctuation;

■ **mis-estimation**;

■ **parameter change**.

We look next at each in turn and then at a list of other conditions which must apply in order for the LLN to operate effectively.

(1) Random fluctuation

In the example we used to illustrate the LLN, the mean of average annual burglary losses per household, taking one year with the next, was £25. However, the average loss itself will differ from year to year, because each year represents a different sample and, as we know, sample averages vary randomly around their mean. As a result, the insurer will sometimes come up against 'bad years' in which the average household loss through burglary turns out to be above and, on occasions, considerably above, the mean of £25. If, as suggested in the preceding section, premiums are set equal to this mean, the insurer will face a financial shortfall in such years, as the cost of settling claims will exceed premium income, possibly by a large margin.

For the purposes of illustration, let us assume that the average annual burglary loss per household is normally distributed around its mean of £25, as shown in Figure 2.1. Then in some years ('bad' years), the outcome will be at the lower tail of the distribution. Although the probability of a 'bad' year (represented by the shaded area in Figure 2.1) may be small, the point to remember is that the risk of 'bad' years cannot be entirely eliminated. It is part and parcel of the way the LLN operates. That said, an insurance company can protect itself in a number of ways.

---

[9] We consider some qualifications to this statement in the next section.

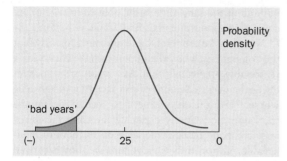

Figure 2.1

which it provides cover, the more likely it is that high levels of claims in some classes of business in any given year will be offset by low claims levels in others. Once again, the effect will be to reduce the variability of its annual financial outturn.

A final option open to insurers wishing to mitigate the risks inherent in random fluctuations in their claims experience is to obtain reinsurance. By 'laying off' some risk in this way, the company will earn lower surpluses in good years but limit the net cost to itself of settling claims even in bad ones.

(2) Mis-estimation

So far, it has been convenient to simplify our discussion of insurer's risk by assuming that our insurer *knows* the size of the true population mean loss through burglary of the households it insures. However, if we think about it, we will quickly realize that this assumption cannot be realistic. For the population of burglary experiences is infinite and the value of the mean loss resulting from such experiences cannot therefore be known for certain by insurers or anyone else.

Nevertheless, insurers will wish to relate the premiums they charge to their clients' likely average experience of loss. In practice, therefore, they will have no alternative but to make *estimates* of the value of the mean losses incurred by policyholders. They will do so by using their own past experience of providing cover for clients or obtain data on claims experiences elsewhere in the wider insurance industry.

To illustrate the problems inherent in having to rely on an estimate of the mean loss, suppose that the insurance company in our example computes the average burglary losses per household in each year of the last 10 and then uses the average of these averages as its estimate of the mean loss. Now, this estimate is the average of a sample 10, and we know that, even if samples are not biased in any way, their averages will vary randomly from the true population mean. As a result, the company faces the risk that any estimate it makes will be a *mis*-estimate of the mean loss.

Mis-estimation could take the form either of an under- or an overestimation. Either way, inaccuracy in the company's estimate will increase its risk of insolvency. Consider underestimation first. If the company bases the premiums it charges on an underestimate of the mean loss, premiums will be set at an unduly low

Firstly, so long as the average losses per household in different years are distributed randomly around their mean, years in which shortfalls are recorded will tend to be matched by years in which the cost of settling claims turns out to be lower than premium income and the insurer's accounts consequently show a surplus. The company can, of course, add surpluses to its financial reserves, drawing on them to preserve its solvency in years in which shortfalls occur. It has to be recognized, however, that the insurer still faces the risk of a total volume of claims so high in some years that previously accumulated surpluses will prove insufficient to cover current shortfalls in premium income. Even though this risk may seem a remote one, it represents a threat to the company's solvency and therefore to its ability to offer policyholders what they are ultimately looking for from an insurer – peace of mind. One prudent course of action the company can take is to add what is known as **loading** to the premiums it charges, that is, to set premiums above the mean level of average annual claims per household. The purpose would be to enable it to enlarge the size of its financial reserve, giving itself a better chance of withstanding highly adverse claims experiences.[10]

Secondly, the insurer could try to expand the scale of its operations. If it can increase the amount of business it does (that is, increase the volume and value of the policies it writes), it should be able to extend the effect of the LLN and thereby reduce further the variability of its average claims experience around the mean annual loss and with it the possibility of an unmanageably high claims level in any particular year.

Thirdly, it could try to diversify its business portfolio further. The more diverse the range of risks for

---

10　State regulation of insurance companies aims to guard against this risk. The regulatory system in the UK is discussed in Chapter 25.

level and, as a result, there are likely to be an unduly high number of years in which premium income is insufficient to cover total claims. The danger is all the more likely because the company's low rates of premium are likely to attract business towards it and away from competitors. Note that because this business increases the risk of financial shortfalls it is in fact unprofitable at the rates of premium the company charges.

If, on the other hand, the company overestimates the mean loss, this could well lead it to set its premiums at an unduly high level. As a result, it will be in danger of losing business to competitors, business that would have been on average profitable even at lower rates of premium. As a result, the volume of business it will write will be smaller than otherwise and it will derive less benefit from the LLN. This means that the variability of its annual financial results will be higher than otherwise. It should be clear that the security of its position is thereby reduced. The problem of mis-estimation is illustrated in Figure 2.2. Suppose that curve *A* depicts the *true* distribution of annual average losses through burglary. If the insurer had some way of knowing where this true distribution lay, it could base its premiums on the true mean average loss figure (£a). Unfortunately, it can only try to estimate the position of curve *A* by using sample data based on its own or other companies' claims experience. Because sample averages vary around the true mean, it may wrongly come to believe that the distribution of annual average losses is represented by curve *B*. In that case, it will base its premiums on a figure of £b, an underestimate of the mean average loss. On the other hand the data it has available may lead the company to believe, just as wrongly, that curve *C* depicts the distribution of annual average losses. It might then base

premiums on an overestimate of the mean average loss, believing it to be as high as £c.

What can an insurance company do to protect itself against the risk of mis-estimation of the mean loss? Obviously, reinsurance will allow a company to limit the adverse consequence to itself of mis-estimating the mean policyholder loss. Secondly, adding a loading to premiums in recognition of this risk in order to build up a company's financial reserve will be useful in that it will help carry it through years of financial shortfall produced either by the unduly low premium levels that would result from an underestimation of the mean loss, or the unduly high one that would result from an overestimation. Eventually any mis-estimation will become apparent from experience, and the company can then adjust premium levels appropriately – provided it can survive that long. Building up its reserve will increase its chances of doing so.

Both under- and overestimation of the mean loss will, as we have noted, result in financial problems for an insurer. Hence, in the case of mis-estimation, errors in one direction will not offset errors in the other. It follows that diversification of a company's range of business will do nothing to mitigate the risk of mis-estimation. The other side of this particular coin is that this risk is a reason for insurers to take diversification gradually. For, as we have also just noted, the risk of mis-estimation diminishes over time, as an insurance company accumulates experience of an emerging pattern of claims within a particular class of business. A core of established business will therefore tend to add to the stability of the financial results a company achieves. This core can in turn offer it a financial cushion enabling it to withstand the potential adverse financial consequences of taking on new classes of business, with the inherent risk of mis-estimation that entails. However, a major proviso here is that the scale of the new business taken on at any one time must not be too large.

(3) Parameter change

Actuaries seek to provide a rational basis for an insurer's pricing structure by estimating risks of losses across the various classes of business as reliably as possible from the data to hand as a basis for determining premiums. Mis-estimation is one example of actuarial error. As the preceding discussion has shown, it results from random variation in sample averages, and the possibility of such sampling error cannot be eliminated even if the characteristics (or *parameters*)

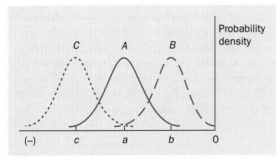

Figure 2.2

of the population from which samples are drawn are stable over time. The scope for actuarial error is, however, very much broadened by the fact that stability in these parameters cannot by any means be counted on. On the contrary, they are dependent on social, environmental, technological and other factors and will change as the latter do. It follows that the past is not necessarily a good guide to the future however well we have learned to analyse the former.

To illustrate this point, consider Figure 2.3. Suppose that initially actuaries have accurately estimated the position of the distribution of annual average burglary losses (curve 1). Relying on their advice, the insurance company, basing its premiums on an estimated mean average loss of £25, encounters no difficulty in meeting claims out of premium income. As time passes, however, social conditions change, causing the incidence of burglary to rise and as a result changing the parameters of the annual average loss distribution so that its position is now represented by curve 2. The mean average annual loss is now £35. However, because they have no choice but to rely on past data, actuaries take some time to identify this parameter shift. In the meantime, if the insurance company continues to base its premiums on the now unduly low estimate of annual average losses of £25, it could find its solvency under threat.

The scale of asbestos-related losses suffered by Lloyds 'names' in recent decades is perhaps the most spectacular illustration of the potentially devastating consequences of parameter change for insurers to have emerged in the last 30 years. In the 1950s and 1960s, before the health hazards associated with asbestos were properly understood, Lloyds names underwrote large numbers of health and safety insurance policies in the USA. Asbestos was then very widely used as a fireproofing material. Awareness of the causes of asbestosis and related conditions, however, developed in the 1970s, and asbestos-related insurance claims submitted to Lloyds reached 6,000 per annum by the early 1980s and 24,000 per annum ten years later. By the early 1990s, names had settled asbestos-related claims totalling £8bn. In all, some 34,000 individual underwriters lost money as a result of these claims. Many were forced to sell their houses and businesses to meet their debts. Recriminations over the crisis continued. In November 2000, after a high-profile hearing lasting several months, a judge in the High Court in London finally dismissed a massive claim for compensation against Lloyds mounted by more than 230 names who had lost money as a result of asbestos-related claims.[11]

Clearly, building an adequate level of reserves can go some way towards helping an insurance company limit the threat to its solvency that parameter change poses, as indeed can reinsurance. Diversification, too, may help, so long as cases of beneficial and adverse parameter change tend to cancel one another out and insurers as a whole tend to err in the same direction at the same time. In that case, if one company fails to anticipate beneficial parameter changes and as a result charges unnecessarily high premiums on a particular class of business, others will tend to have done the same. As a result, an underwriting surplus will be generated for the sector as a whole which will be available to cover losses as a result of failures to anticipate negative parameter changes affecting other classes of business.

Other limits to the insurance principle

Insurance works on the principle that it is possible for an intermediary – the insurer – to organize a financially solvent risk-pooling arrangement which removes the exposure to some risk that a group of individuals would otherwise face. In the discussion so far we have shown how this principle relies on the Law of Large Numbers. At the same time we have made it clear that, however well the LLN operates, insurers remain exposed to certain residual risks.

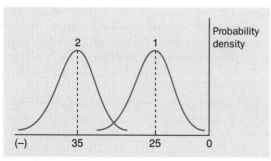

Figure 2.3

---

11   See 'Lloyds names "fleeced in £4bn fraud"', *The Guardian*, 7 March 2000, and 'How the names lost their shirts', *The Guardian*, 4 November 2000.

In fact, for the LLN to operate effectively, a number of other conditions must also be satisfied. The most important of these can easily be stated. They are that the exposures an insurer is called upon to cover must be:

- large in number;
- part of a known phenomenon;
- statistically independent of one another;
- homogeneous in character;
- unaffected by the fact of insurance;
- borne by individuals who can afford to insure themselves.

Quite commonly, one or more of these conditions will not be met. As a result, the applicability of the insurance principle will very often be severely limited – as this section explains.

(1) Small numbers of exposures

Some perils are specific to relatively few individual cases, with the result that there may only be a small number of exposures to them extant at any one point in time. For example, injury to a virtuoso concert pianist's hands would mean a massive loss of earning capacity for the performer concerned. But how many truly virtuoso pianists are there?

An insurance company which offered cover to a small number of clients facing an uncommon risk would be likely to find that its year-to-year claims experience in relation to this risk was highly variable. Consequently, the risk to the company that claims levels could turn out to be considerably higher than premium income would be significant in every single year that it wrote such business. As we know from our earlier discussion, an insurer operating in such conditions would be highly exposed to the risk of insolvency. For this reason, insurers will tend to be reluctant to cover classes of risk characterized by small total numbers of exposures and, in these circumstances, the risks in question could prove to be more or less *uninsurable*.[12]

Now, to take just one example, there is a multitude of highly specific risks in the field of the performing arts and entertainment alone, not only risks to pianists' hands but risks to tenors' voices, to ballet dancers' legs and to various parts of other celebrities' bodies which we leave to the reader to imagine. One way in which insurers seek to meet the demand for cover despite the threats to them posed by small numbers of exposures is to respond to this multiplicity of risks by organizing multiple underwriting syndicates, each of which underwrites one specific risk. Within each syndicate, any one insurer takes on only a small proportion of the overall risk, and each insurer may participate in a number of different syndicates. There is then a good chance that the risks concerned will become more readily insurable because:

(a) each individual insurance company will be able to limit the loss to itself that would arise from a high level of claims in respect of any one risk in any year;

(b) provided there was not a strong positive correlation between the different risks covered, the total of claims any insurer would be likely to be called upon to meet in any year as a result of involvement in various syndicates should also lie within acceptable bounds.

The formation of such syndicates enables insurers to create underwriting *portfolios*. The discussion in Section 8.3 shows how holding a portfolio of stock market securities can reduce an investor's risk. It

---

[12] A risk can be said to be uninsurable when no insurer is prepared to offer cover against it or, on a less strict definition, when cover is only available at prohibitively high rates. For example, suppose £500 was the lowest annual premium quoted for insurance of an item worth £1,000. Unless there was a very high probability that it would be lost or damaged in any year, the owner of the item would be likely to regard insurance as too expensive to contemplate and the item would for all intents and purposes be uninsurable.

should be clear that underwriting portfolios offers insurers similar benefits in terms of risk reduction.

(2) Unknown phenomena

We have seen that insurers try to set premiums by reference to estimates of average expected claims levels on policies of different types. These estimates are based on past claims history and other indicators such as officially published statistics on crime, mortality and morbidity rates. What, however, if the risk clients wish to be insured against is a hitherto unknown one? In a fast changing world, novel risk situations arise continuously. Obvious topical examples relate to the spread of new information technologies. For example, in the latter part of the 1990s there was widespread international concern that the arrival of the new millennium would be marked by computer failure on a monumental scale. But nothing comparable to this danger had ever arisen before and therefore there was nothing in insurers' combined past underwriting experience that they could have used to guide them in setting premiums for covering millennium-bug-related risks. Similarly, the risk of cyber-vandalism (such as the spreading of computer viruses) is becoming an increasingly serious one for organizations worldwide and one against which it would be natural for many to wish to insure themselves. However, until society gains much more familiarity with this phenomenon, premium setting will be little more than guesswork.

When the risk is a new one, insurers could quite easily underestimate claims levels by a substantial margin and, as a result, set premiums at much too low a level to cover them. Furthermore, the problem could be compounded by small numbers of exposures: if a risk is novel, the numbers of individuals confronted by it may not be large. The risks to an insurer inherent in offering cover against novel kinds of loss exposure could threaten to make some of them uninsurable. Here again, though, the formation of underwriting syndicates may offer individual insurers sufficient protection of their own positions to persuade them that writing some business of this kind is viable.

(3) Positively correlated risks

Returning yet again to the burglary example used earlier to illustrate the LLN, suppose now that the incidence of burglary in a particular neighbourhood varies from year to year. In particular, suppose that there is either a crime wave and many houses in the same vicinity are broken into over the same period, or

the whole area is relatively crime free for that length of time. In these circumstances, it is clear that the chances of burglary facing any two houses in the neighbourhood will not be statistically independent. If one house has been burgled recently, the chances will be relatively high that neighbouring properties will shortly suffer the same fate. On the other hand, if there have been no attempts to break into any one house in the locality recently, nearby properties will be relatively safe for the time being.

We are here describing a situation in which individual risks are positively correlated with one another. In Box 8.2 we show how diversifying our holdings of risky assets usually reduces risk. This is because the returns on two assets are usually less than perfectly correlated. Technically speaking, the correlation coefficient of returns between assets x and y, $\rho_{x,y}$, is less than $+1$. But note that the risk reduction effect is at its maximum when $\rho_{x,y} = -1$ and diminishes as the value of $\rho_{x,y}$ approaches $+1$. The same is true of any set of random variables, including sample averages. The point to emphasize is that the presence of positive correlation between individual exposures to a given risk diminishes the variance-reducing effects of the LLN and, as a result, makes insurers' claims experiences more variable. In some years this will work to the insurer's advantage since it will result in a low level of claims. However, if it is true that losses tend to occur together, there will be other years in which claims may well far exceed premium income. To protect themselves against positive correlation between risks, insurers may raise premiums, possibly to prohibitive levels, or even refuse cover entirely.

Another way in which insurers try to limit their exposure to highly correlated risks is by inserting *exclusion clauses* into policies which offer cover against loss from a range of causes. An important current example in the UK is subsidence of the land on which buildings stand, which is now widely the subject of exclusion clauses in property insurance policies. Subsidence became an increasing problem when extremely low rainfall in some years in the early and mid-1990s significantly depleted amounts of water contained in the ground under buildings in many localities, leading to shrinkage and shifting of the subsoil and movement in foundations (with consequent structural damage to buildings). Insurers have responded to this experience by redrafting the terms of policies in ways which significantly restrict their liability to pay compensation when subsidence occurs.

The likelihood that adequate insurance will not be available to protect people against catastrophe risk[13] suggests that, as a device for protecting members of society against the consequences of adverse events, insurance has some major limitations. For risks are no less serious for being highly correlated. On the contrary, highly correlated risks are arguably often the *most* serious kind, since they can inflict massive losses on whole communities at the same time – witness the effects of major natural disasters like hurricanes. Yet those who suffer in such circumstances will often be denied the benefit of insurance precisely because of the catastrophic nature of the risk to which they are exposed.

Exercise 2.4

Read the article in Box 2.2. Insurers give the name 'catastrophe risk' to some situations in which there is a high positive correlation between claims experiences on different exposures.

Can you explain, in terms of catastrophe risk, why insurers are responding to the increasing risk of flood in the way the article describes?

Why might damage caused by such events as war, riot, civil commotion also be subject to exclusion clauses in household policies?

BOX 2.2 Insurers threaten flood cover

By Paul Brown, environment correspondent

British insurers are threatening they will withdraw flooding cover from about 220,000 homes if the government cuts the spending on flood defences as part of Treasury economies.

Britain is unique in Europe in offering universal flood insurance but companies, having paid out £5bn in the last five years – twice as much as in the previous five – believe it may be no longer be viable to do so.

Following the disastrous floods of 2000, the worst event in 300 years, spending on defences was stepped up by the government to cope with decades of neglect. Many of those affected were new houses built on flood plains without adequate defences which would be rendered unsaleable by withdrawal of insurance. Without insurance, most banks and building societies will not agree a mortgage, so only cash buyers would be able to purchase.

After the 2000 floods the insurance industry agreed with the government that it would continue to insure all properties for at least two years until the long-term intentions of the government on repairing and creating new flood defences became apparent. The government solved the problem by stepping up expenditure but is threatening to cut it again, now that there have been no serious floods for 18 months.

Jane Milne, head of household and property insurance for the Association of British Insurers (ABI) said 'The average home in Britain spends £295 on household insurance including flooding. The average cost of a flooding claim is between £15,000 and £30,000. You do not need many flooding claims to eat up a lot of insurance premiums.'

The insurance companies believe that properties should by protected to the extent that flooding could be expected to return not more often than one in 75 years, in order to make insuring them a viable risk.

In a submission to Gordon Brown, the chancellor, the ABI says that despite the increased expenditure one in 10 of the 1.8m properties threatened by flooding will be in greater danger than the one in 75 year risk that companies have set. The association has told Mr Brown that it is prepared to continue covering those properties after that date if the Treasury continues its level of spending on defences, which will be £564 million in 2006.

The expenditure is enough to protect an extra 80,000 properties a year, so it will still take at least three years to improve the barriers of the most vulnerable properties, without any money being spent on repairing existing deteriorating defences.

Ms Milne said 'It is not a threat to withdraw cover so much as a sound business decision that we cannot afford to take these risks. In the light of climate change we have to keep the risk of flooding under constant review.'

The submission to the Treasury comes just before the government's Office of Science and Technology foresight programme this week releases its scenarios for the next 100 years on how Britain will cope with climate change and flooding.

Source: *The Guardian*, 20 April 2004. © Guardian News & Media Ltd 2004. Reprinted with permission.

---

[13] A concept explored in Exercise 2.4.

Recently, a term has been coined to describe a situation in which economic or social conditions deny particular social groups benefits that the financial system offers: *financial exclusion*. The kind of exclusion that may arise when risks are catastrophic in nature creates a case for the *socialization* of some such risks, that is, for the government to take responsibility for providing compensation to victims out of public funds when losses reach high enough levels.[14] Such outlays could be viewed as being financed by a kind of enforced premium charged to the community at large. However, note the key difference that, if compensation for loss is paid out of the public purse, the cost falls on individual members of society in proportion to their liability to pay tax, *not* according to their degree of exposure to risk of loss. This is at odds with normal insurance principles, according to which those who are most exposed to risk are required to pay most (in premiums). However, catastrophe risk is the problem it is precisely because normal insurance principles do not apply. Furthermore, it is by no means obviously fair that those members of society who are less fortunate than most (i.e., those most exposed to risk of loss) should be expected to pay the most.

There is an international dimension to catastrophe risk. Evidence is mounting that the world faces greater exposure to natural disasters, such as floods, as a result of global warming. There is evidence, too, that the homes of the poorest within a given country's population are often concentrated in the areas that are most exposed to such risks. Normal insurance arrangements cannot be made to protect such people for reasons which should be clear. If they are not to be left to cope as best they can when disasters occur, socialization of risk, whether through governmental or charitable aid agencies, has a role to play.

(4) Non-homogeneous client groups

In our earlier illustration of the LLN, we implicitly assumed that the risk of burglary was identical for all policyholders. In other words, we treated the insurer's client group as if it were *homogeneous*. This was useful in that it helped to simplify the analysis in a way that enabled us to focus on essentials. But it overlooked the major problems that arise when homogeneity is not the case. As we now make clear, the nature of the problem produced by non-homogenous client groups depends critically on whether the insurer is or is not able to identify the material differences between clients that do exist.

We begin by looking at *identifiable non-homogeneous client groups*. It is unfortunately true that young drivers are particularly accident-prone. Any insurance company that did not differentiate premiums according to driver's age would soon find itself undercut in the market for mature drivers' business by other companies which offered this group lower premiums to reflect their lower risk. Insurers will therefore use their claims experience to divide a given class of clients into as many subgroups as possible. They will always be alert to new ways of doing so. For example, insurers increasingly exploit the opportunities inherent in the fact that addresses in the UK are differentiated by postcode,[15] something which in effect subdivides the population into tiny, readily identifiable, geographical subgroups.

The ability of insurers to differentiate between subgroups within a class of policyholders can be something of a mixed blessing. On the one hand, it enables insurers to match premiums more closely to an individual's liability to incur loss. On the other hand, it can seriously limit the social usefulness of insurance in some circumstances. Consider the position of the chronically sick and disabled, who are particularly exposed to health-related risks, or of inner city communities, who face particularly high crime-related risks. Both subgroups are readily identifiable by insurance companies, which, when requested to provide cover to members of them, will quote higher-than-normal premiums (which may make them prohibitively expensive) or even refuse cover altogether.

Financial exclusion of this kind was one of the factors which gave rise to the system of *National Insurance* that has existed in Britain over many decades.

---

[14] Or, as suggested in the article in Box 2.2, for the government to bear the cost of reducing the risk of loss to levels acceptable to the private sector.

[15] Where the first half, and first digit of the second half, of the postcode of a group of UK addresses are the same, the addresses concerned are said to be in the same *postal sector*. There are some 9,200 of these in the country as a whole. Insurers have sought to differentiate clients by postal sector for many years. However, advances in IT are making it increasingly possible for insurers to analyse their claims experiences in a far more detailed way by using the whole postcode. There are more than 1.5 million different postcodes, each containing about 15 addresses.

It offers some protection against the adverse financial consequences of unemployment, sickness and old age but is not strictly speaking insurance since contributions are uniform or income-dependent and not related to risk.

In the future, genetic testing looks set to become an unprecedentedly powerful prognostic tool, making it possible to examine an individual's DNA structure to determine his or her degree of predisposition to a wide range of diseases, conceivably even at birth or in the womb. The scope for differentiating between high- and low-risk clients that genetic testing potentially offers insurers could have some profound and surprising consequences. A moratorium on the use of genetic tests results was in operation until 2006. However, as genetic testing becomes more sophisticated in the future, the temptation on insurers to make it compulsory will grow. Some individuals could then in effect be born uninsurable across a wide range of health risks. That could in turn lead to a demand for some kind of social insurance provision, which would be the only viable option for such individuals.

In fact, genetic testing might eventually allow insurers to differentiate so finely between subgroups among their prospective clients that business in some classes of private health insurance could become impossible. For, with the results of such tests routinely available to insurers and applicants, the former would, as just noted, be reluctant to offer cover to those of the latter who would most strongly desire it, i.e., those whom tests showed to be at high risk. On the other hand, the clients whom insurers would most like to have – those shown to face low health risks – would have little reason to seek insurance! In such circumstances, insurers would only be able to obtain business they did not want and they might well find that their technologically advanced techniques had caused the business they did want more or less to dry up.

This futuristic scenario would constitute a case of what insurers call **adverse selection**.[16] To explore this important concept more fully, we refer once again to our burglary example and show that, when differences exist within insurers' client groups that insurers are *unable* to identify, the problem of adverse selection is particularly serious. Note that we are dealing here with *non-identifiable non-homogeneous client groups*.

In our earlier example, the reader will recall, burglary on average affected 1 house per 100 each year and each burglary resulted in a loss amounting to £2,500, so that E(loss) = 0.99(0) + 0.01(2,500) = £25. Our insurer had 100,000 clients. Suppose now that half of these households were in a high-risk category (with a 3 in 200 chance of suffering a burglary in any year), while the other half were at low risk (only 1 chance in 200 of loss). Notice that the expected loss of a household will now depend on whether it is in the high- or the low-risk group. For the high-risk group, expected loss equals 0.015(2,500) = £37.50, whereas for low-risk households E(loss) = 0.005(2,500) = £12.50.

If we assume for simplicity that the burglary risks faced by different households are uncorrelated, what premium will the insurer need to charge to cover expected claims, assuming all households pay the same premium? Clearly, the premium required will need to be equal to the average expected loss of high- and low-risk groups combined, i.e., $\frac{1}{2}$(37.50) + $\frac{1}{2}$(12.50) = £25. Now the example has been designed to produce a figure that is the same as if all households faced the same degree of risk. However, when clients fall into high- and low-risk groups, charging all policyholders a standard premium that reflects the average degree of risk may be fraught with difficulties for the insurer. For example, suppose that differences in lifestyle determine whether a household is in the low- or the high-risk group. Some families, for example, rarely leave their homes unoccupied and some are very careful about locking up when they go out or go to bed. Others are rarely at home and some are extremely careless about their domestic security arrangements. In all these respects, individual behaviour will influence the level of burglary risk a household will face. However, the situation may well represent one of asymmetric information because householders will be aware of their own lifestyles and therefore be in little doubt themselves as to whether they are in the high- or the low-risk category. But it might be very difficult for insurers to obtain reliable information on the habits of different households.

---

[16]   As the two contrasting articles in Box 2.3 illustrate, developments in genetics are leading to calls for discrimination on grounds of genetic make-up to be banned, which have in turn prompted concern that such a ban would expose insurers to adverse selection of a closely related kind.

BOX 2.3 Discrimination and adverse selection in insurance

(a) Discrimination in insurance policies

Consider these two statements. As men are more dangerous drivers than women, they should pay more for motor insurance. Someone who is found to be genetically predisposed to a certain illness should not pay a higher premium for life insurance. Seemingly inconsistent, they reflect the status quo in Britain. The policies are also right but have recently been questioned.

In Brussels, Anna Diamantopoulou, the European Union's employment and social affairs commissioner, has produced draft legislation banning sex discrimination in insurance. And the Department of Health yesterday published a white paper on genetics, which mused about genetic testing and insurance. While the white paper judiciously recognised the inherent, difficult trade-off between outlawing discrimination and ensuring a viable insurance industry, the draft legislation from Brussels did not.

The underlying principles are the same. Sexual discrimination is ethically repugnant and has been outlawed in many areas. The government also accepted that 'a core ethical principle . . . is that no one should be unfairly discriminated against on the basis of his or her genetic characteristics'.

But in applying the principle of non-discrimination to insurance markets, public policy must have regard to the importance of asymmetric information. If customers choose insurance on the basis of private information, the market will be distorted and, in the extreme, can cease to exist. To avoid this problem of adverse selection – that only the worst risks want to buy insurance at the price offered – insurance companies segment the market into broad risk groups.

For gender, this is simple. A person's gender is rarely in doubt and the broad risks are well known. Women are safer drivers so pay less for motor insurance, but live longer so receive lower retirement annuities. Society would lose if insurance companies were forced to be blind to gender.

With genetic testing, things are much more difficult. First, genetic tests have the potential to identify the risk of a specific individual's developing a particular disease – which could make him or her uninsurable. People could be excluded from getting a mortgage or protecting their family against their death. Second, forced disclosure of test results could inhibit some people from taking the tests, to the detriment of public health. Third, the relevance of genetic tests remains difficult to interpret for insurance purposes.

The current voluntary insurance industry moratorium on using genetic test results for life assurance policies up to £500,000 is therefore sensible. Some time after 2006, it may be the case that the combination of risk pooling and widespread genetic testing becomes incompatible. That point has already been reached as regards gender. Sex-neutral insurance policies would create great adverse selection, would not deal properly with discrimination and must not be introduced.

Source: *Financial Times*, 25 June 2003. Reprinted with permission.

(b) Where ignorance is bliss

A genome is not a horoscope. Destiny is not DNA. With the exception of a few, very rare diseases, causes of death are not genetically determined and neither are courses of life. Everything else the genome tells us is a matter of probabilities. But our knowledge of these probabilities is improving all the time, thanks to the knowledge and technologies brought about by the human genome project. Tests are becoming widely available which will make it possible to distinguish much more finely which probabilities apply to individuals. This is information which could be worth a great deal not just to the people directly concerned, but also to their insurers, their employers, those who pay their pension funds, and even the general public.

So why has the Human Genetics Commission proposed a law that would in principle ban discrimination on the grounds of genetic makeup and why is this such a good thing? One answer lies in a paradox. Insurance benefits from knowledge, but it depends also on ignorance. If we had complete knowledge of outcomes, life insurance would be impossible. Those whose genetic constitution promised long life would not buy it, and no one would sell to those who really needed it. Something like that is already happening in America, where health insurance is increasingly a privilege of those who do not need it. So there is a clear benefit to society in ensuring that insurance is available to everyone, especially in a society like ours, where the ability to own a house is dependent on getting an insurance policy along with your mortgage.

Another reason is that the knowledge gained from genetic testing will be multiplied the more people are tested, precisely because it is a knowledge of probabilities and statistical effect. So nothing must be done that might make people fear the consequences of being tested. But the most important reason is a moral one. What the commission proposes is a statement of a human right, one to which everyone should be entitled by virtue of being human. That is why it should be incorporated into legislation.

Source: *The Guardian*, 18 May 2004. © Guardian News & Media Ltd 2004. Reprinted with permission.

Without a reliable way of differentiating between policyholders, our insurance company may be tempted to charge a uniform £25 premium. High-risk householders would be likely to regard this rate as a bargain and flock to insure themselves: after all, they know that their expected loss if uninsured is as high as £37.50. However, a household in the low-risk group may take a very different view. Knowing that its expected uninsured loss is only £12.50, it may consider a premium of £25 as exorbitantly high and, even if it is risk averse, it could well decide not to take insurance. As a result, charging a standard premium could leave the insurance company dangerously exposed to adverse selection – plenty of high-risk customers and relatively few low-risk ones. With this imbalance in its clientele, it will be likely to experience average claim levels higher – possibly a lot higher – than £25, and its solvency will be threatened.

There are a number of ways in which insurers may be able to protect themselves against adverse selection. For example, companies will engage actively in risk screening, that is, using past experience to identify as accurately as possible characteristics (e.g., age, occupation) which will add to or diminish the likelihood that a policyholder covered against a given risk will incur losses and make claims. Individual applicants will then be charged a premium appropriate to the category to which the insurer believes they belong. However, past claims experience must be accumulated *before* risk screening can become possible. Until then, the insurer would be unable to identify good and bad risk characteristics and could remain exposed to adverse selection.

The same kind of difficulty arises when insurers offer reduced premiums in the form of no-claims discounts to policyholders who have rarely, if ever, made claims in the past and who are, on that basis, regarded as being of low future risk. No-claims discounts would be most effective if the insurer could carry on doing business with the same clients year after year. However, all existing policyholders eventually 'pass on' and the company will need a flow of new applicants to take their places. If accepted, some new clients will, of course, turn out to be good risks. However, with no past record to go on at the point of initial application, the company may have no way of telling which applicants are in this category and therefore no reliable method of attracting them with offers of reduced premium rates.

By sharing information, insurers can in practice reduce the need to accumulate past experience of their own and as a result make more extensive use of risk-screening and no-claims discounts. For example, British insurers have access to CUE (the Claims and Underwriting Exchange), a computer database of general insurance claims and individuals' claims profiles.

Some other devices for discouraging or reducing the cost of adverse selection do not rely so critically on the accumulation of past data. For example, policies of many kinds contain restrictive clauses which exempt the insurer from liability when the policyholders' behaviour may have been a significant factor leading to loss. Thus, some home protection policies will not compensate householders for burglary losses in the absence of evidence of forced entry (which would indicate that the householder concerned had not taken the reasonable precaution of locking all doors and windows). Similarly, standard holiday insurance policies do not cover 'hazardous pursuits' such as skiing and mountaineering.

As well as responding negatively to the threat of adverse selection in these kinds of ways, insurers can also respond positively by trying to promote behaviour that will reduce the incidence of loss. For example, property insurance policies frequently offer discounts on the standard premium to policyholders who have fitted specified security devices.[17]

Insurers sometimes also impose 'excesses', that is, they insist that the policyholder meets the first £x of any claim him- or herself. The existence of an excess is in itself a negative response to the problem of adverse selection, for it is a device for making high-risk clients bear more risk themselves. However, excesses become a more positive kind of response if they are voluntary and accompanied by the offer of reduced premium rates to policyholders willing to accept them. For they then turn into a technique by which an insurance company can hope to make its policies more attractive to a low-risk clientele and to promote loss-reducing behaviour among policyholders. Once again, voluntary

---

[17]   It would be enormously expensive for an insurance company to check that all policyholders who claimed to have fitted the devices in question were telling the truth – part of the problem of asymmetric information. However, it would not really need to do so. It could instead simply make checks only when policyholders made claims and then refuse to pay out when these revealed that false information had been provided.

excesses will 'work' for an insurance company even if it does know which clients are low risk and which high risk.

(5) The effects of insurance on the behaviour of the insured

Suppose an insurance company gathers information about the experience of burglary among uninsured people and discovers that, as in our earlier example, the risk of burglary in any one year is 1 chance in 100, with an average loss of £2,500 if burglary does occur. Suppose it then begins to provide cover against burglary, charging a premium equal to expected loss of uninsured households, i.e., £25 per annum.

Now a company which, like this one, based premiums on the record of loss among uninsured people may find that these are insufficient to meet claims as a result of the phenomenon of **moral hazard**. This problem arises because once individuals are insured they may take less care to avoid loss, simply because they know that, should a loss be incurred, the insurance company will ultimately bear the cost. Even worse, they may do things which increase the size of their exposure. For example, they may acquire more valuable possessions, comforted by the knowledge that they will receive compensation in the event of loss.

It follows that, in practice, insurers will need to set premiums at above the average uninsured loss level or find ways of reducing the problem of moral hazard, or both. Fortunately, techniques available to help insurers cope with adverse selection, e.g. risk screening, no-claims discounts, restrictive clauses, discounts for loss-reducing behaviour, excesses and so on, will also tend to be useful in helping them deal with moral hazard. The reader should make sure he or she understands why.

Finally, we must consider the question: *is insurance affordable*? An obvious but important fact about insurance is that it is useful only to the extent that potential users can pay for it. This is often not the case, a point touched on earlier in our discussion of natural disasters. We have noted also that some social groups in this country, for example the irregularly employed and the chronically sick, are in particular need of the protection afforded by some types of insurance but will in many instances find it difficult to obtain cover. The problem for such people is often compounded by the fact that, even if cover is available, their situation means that they are on low incomes and therefore cannot afford its cost – double financial exclusion.

A case in point is the healthcare system of the USA, which is based predominantly on private insurance and from which tens of millions of citizens are excluded by their low incomes or employment situation. Indeed, the existence of the National Health Service in the UK can be understood in part as a response to this limit of the insurance principle, namely that insurance works only if those who face the risks can afford to pay for cover.

2.4.3 Pension systems: what are they and why have them?

We now turn our attention to pension funds, the other major class of NDTI identified earlier. These institutions operate as part of a **pension system**, and in order to begin to understand the principles governing their operation, we need first to say something about what a pension system is and why (if indeed at all) it might benefit society to have such a system.

What is a pension system?

A pension system may be briefly defined as a framework of arrangements, based on statute or private contract or both, under which individuals gain specified entitlements to a regular income in retirement (a pension) in return for the payment of specified sums (contributions) made by themselves or their employers during their working lives.

Notice that the system could, at one extreme, be an entirely voluntary one, in which individuals freely entered into contracts committing themselves to making payments to intermediaries and the latter, in turn, committed themselves to financing the payment of pensions on specified terms when the individuals eventually retired.

At the other extreme, a pension system might be compulsory and government-operated: workers and perhaps employers too might be legally obliged to make payments to the state (such as National Insurance Contributions in the UK) and the state might commit itself to paying pensions directly to retired individuals according to rules laid down in statute.

Systems representing all kinds of intermediate positions between these two extremes are possible. For example, the law might *require* employees and employers to enter into pension contracts with financial intermediaries whose terms were specified by statute. Workers and firms might be allowed to contract with any intermediary approved by the government, i.e., they might be given a choice *between* intermediaries. However, they would be obliged by law to enter into a contract of the prescribed kind with one such organization or another. Such a system would thus be based on compulsion even though no money passed through the government's hands at any stage. Alternatively, the system might be such that employers voluntarily entered into contracts with financial intermediaries (or made internal financial arrangements) with a view to providing pensions for their employees on retirement, but obliged their workers to accept such arrangements, including making contributions from salary, as part of the contract of employment.

Why pensions?

Now that we have defined what we mean by a pension system it should be apparent that it is not something that will necessarily exist in all countries at all times. For, in the absence of a pension system, individuals could still provide for their old age by accumulating savings during their working lives and then financing their needs during retirement by spending the income (dividends, interest etc.) generated by their capital, by gradually drawing on it ('dissaving') or both. Given that this is possible, is there any reason why a pension system should be needed at all? We can perhaps usefully subdivide this question into two:

1 Does a pension system of a purely voluntary kind offer any advantages to individuals who wish to provide for their old age?

2 Is there any case for state intervention in relation to the financial provision made for the elderly?

Considering the first of these sub-questions, we should immediately note that trying to plan for one's retirement in the self-sufficient kind of way just described poses a serious financial problem. For, if I wish to fund my old age by spending the returns my capital generates and by gradually drawing it down, I must plan to have the right amount of savings at the point of retirement to allow me to do so. But to plan that, I must accurately forecast my lifespan. Now, to stay alive on this Earth as long as possible is a more or less universal human desire, but what if I live longer than I had forecast when I formulated my life savings plan? Put bluntly, my funds may come to an end before I do! We are referring here to the problem of *longevity risk*, namely the risk that I may live longer than

expected(!) and may therefore have run down my capital so far while still alive that it does not afford me a satisfactory standard of living throughout my lifetime.

An obvious advantage of a pension system, even one based purely on voluntary contracts, is that it may help to overcome this problem. Suppose that, instead of accumulating capital on my own account, I enter into a contract with an intermediary under the terms of which I make payments before retirement and in return am guaranteed a regular income throughout my lifetime, *however long that turns out to be*. Such a contract would effectively eliminate my longevity risk.

How could such a contract be financially viable from the point of view of the intermediary? The answer is that, if it can persuade a large group of individuals to enter into contracts of this kind, it can hope to exploit the LLN to ensure that the longevity risk thereby removed from the shoulders of individuals concerned is not simply transferred onto itself. For, given reliable enough data on life expectancy and suitable actuarial skills, it can set the payments it requires an individual to make at the right level to ensure that they will be sufficient to finance the pension payouts made to a person who lives an average lifespan. Now, of course, some individuals to whom the intermediary is contracted will live longer than others. But, with a large enough client base, it can expect that the long stream of payments it will have to make to individuals who live to a ripe old age will be offset by the much smaller total payouts made to those who are not so fortunate. One arguably distasteful but nevertheless essential feature of pension schemes financed by contributions is that those who die young subsidize those who live on!

Even if I could forecast my lifespan accurately, trying to finance my retirement in a self-sufficient way by accumulating my own savings would also expose me to *investment risk*. For in deciding how hard I would need to save during my working life in order to ensure the standard of living I desired in old age, I would need to forecast the rate of return my savings would earn as they accumulated before I retired as well as the rate of return my capital would earn afterwards. If, as things turned out, I had overestimated either my pre- or my post-retirement returns, I would discover – too late to do anything about it – that I had not saved hard enough!

I may be able to reduce or even eliminate this investment risk by entering into a pension contract with an intermediary of the kind already described. Once again, any reduction in risk that arises will be due to the scale of the intermediary's operations, which will enable it to hold a more diversified asset portfolio than any individual will be able to achieve and to cover the costs of more expert fund management than an individual is likely to be able to afford.[18]

Longevity and investment risk suggest reasons why individuals might choose to participate in a pension system of a purely voluntary kind. They do not in themselves, however, justify the involvement of the state in financial provision for the elderly. We now turn to consideration of a range of other factors which, in the view of many observers, do suggest grounds for government intervention of one form or another in this area.

Adverse selection

One way in which I could act individually to avoid longevity risk is by buying what is known as a **retirement annuity**. This would involve me in using some or all of my savings to make a lump sum payment to an *annuity provider* at the point of retirement. In return the latter would agree to pay me a regular pension (the annuity) for the rest of my life. Exercise 2.5, to which the reader should now turn, is intended to highlight a major drawback of a voluntary arrangement of this kind.

Exercise 2.5

(a) If someone purchases a lifetime annuity on retirement, does longevity risk disappear or is it transferred? Explain your answer.

(b) Who would be more likely to purchase such an annuity: Mr X, whose life expectancy is short because of a medical condition he has developed, or Ms Y, whose family tends to live to a ripe old age? Why?

(Answers: Part (a), see end of book; part (b), this page.)

Because of his medical condition, Mr X could expect to receive only a short stream of pension payments if he purchased the annuity. To put the same point a little more technically, the annuity would represent poor value for him because his longevity risk is low. The standard of living he could expect to enjoy over his expected short life would be likely to be higher if he invested his money on his own account for the time being, rather than paying it over to the annuity provider, and subsequently spent it as he wished. Exactly the opposite is true for Ms Y, however. Her longevity risk is high and the annuity for her would be likely to be an extremely good buy.

It should be clear from our comparison of the positions of Mr X and Ms Y that an annuity-providing intermediary in a voluntary system would face a major adverse selection problem. It would welcome clients like Mr X since the lump sum payments it would receive from them would be likely to be large in relation to liabilities it would incur in return. But the intermediary will find it difficult to attract the likes of Mr X. On the other hand, clients like Ms Y would be distinctly unattractive to the annuity provider, since they would bring formidable liabilities with them relative to the lump sums they would pay. However, conscious of the high levels of longevity risk they faced, they would be the first people at the intermediary's door demanding to be allowed to buy a pension.[19]

It follows that a purely voluntary pension system might never get off the ground, since, as a result of adverse selection, intermediaries might not find it financially viable to offer pension annuities. As a result there would be market failure: the financial system would be incapable of fulfilling the function of helping individuals overcome the longevity risk that they would face if left entirely to their own devices in the matter of providing for old age. The possibility of market failure of this kind suggests a first argument for state involvement in pension provision. Only if the state *obliged* people to purchase pension annuities might it be financially viable for intermediaries to provide them. If that is true, an element of state compulsion might be viewed as desirable as the only practical means of ensuring that protection against longevity risk was made available.

---

[18]   In some circumstances a pension scheme will be capable of transferring risk away from the individual at the point of retirement. See the discussion of defined benefit versus defined contribution pension schemes in Section 2.4.4 below.

[19]   Notice the contrast with life insurance. Life insurers welcome long-lived individuals and are chary about providing cover to people with known medical conditions that may shorten their lives. For pension providers, everything is reversed!

Financial 'myopia'/improvidence

The future is uncertain, and each of us only gets old once (if at all). Providing for old age is therefore not something we can learn to do from personal experience, particularly since we will not have a chance to learn from our mistakes. It follows that individuals left to their own devices may fail to save sufficiently before they retire. They may not be far-sighted enough to see a need to do so. Or they may just be plain improvident: they may decide to enjoy the present and to let the future take care of itself. Whether myopic or improvident, by the time the individuals concerned have discovered the error of their ways (which may not be until old age has arrived) it may be too late.

If it is accepted that a civilized society cannot simply allow individuals who have been 'feckless' in their younger days to live in destitution in their old age, then some state-initiated system to provide pensions for them is required. In fairness the benefits of such a system would probably have to be extended to everybody else. The costs of the system could conceivably be met out of taxation, which would immediately introduce an element of compulsion. Furthermore, it is likely that some people will save less for themselves if they believe the state will provide for their financial needs in retirement. If it is thought desirable that society should be protected against this form of moral hazard, compulsion of a more direct kind will be necessary: future beneficiaries will have to be required to make contributions towards the cost of the pensions they will in due course receive. At the same time, even if the principle is accepted that citizens should be made to pay in a direct way for the pensions they will receive, it is not necessary for the state to have any involvement in the actual financing of pensions. Individuals could pay their contributions to private sector intermediaries during their working lives and the latter could in turn pay the former their pensions after retirement. The state's role would then be restricted to using its power to require citizens to enter into these financial arrangements and to providing a regulatory framework for them.

Poverty alleviation/redistribution

Even though they may be neither 'myopic' nor improvident, people in some social groups may not save enough for their old age because they simply have not

been able to afford to do so. For example, they may have experienced a lifetime of poorly paid or casual jobs or else their careers may have been interrupted significantly by sickness, family responsibilities or unemployment. If *all* sections of society are to enjoy an adequate retirement income, deliberate provision will need to be made for people in this (possibly) large category. Such arrangements are also likely to result in a redistribution of income and wealth towards the poor, something that will be regarded as desirable if it is felt that market economies tend to produce unfair and random economic inequalities.

To the extent that the purpose of a pension system is poverty alleviation or redistribution, it would obviously be inappropriate for its beneficiaries to be expected to meet the costs of the pensions they are intended to have. Since that is so, designing a pension system with objectives of these kinds but based on financial contracts between individuals and private sector intermediaries is likely to prove problematic. This points to one of the dilemmas surrounding the so-called 'stakeholder' pensions recently introduced by the UK government.[20] These are intended to enhance the living standards in retirement of poorer sections of the community who have not hitherto enjoyed the benefit of occupational pensions. Yet the stakeholder pension is an essentially private arrangement by which a portion of a worker's salary is deducted at source and paid into a pension fund that will ultimately have the responsibility of paying a pension reflecting the size and quantity of the contributions he or she has made. So the stakeholder pension does not shift the burden of providing for old age from the poor or relatively poor intended beneficiaries – unless employers also contribute to workers' pension funds.

Social solidarity

A further related justification for having a pension system derives from the motive of social solidarity. As members of the same society, we will have a concern for one another's wellbeing and will also recognize the latter stages of life as a period when individuals are particularly vulnerable. We may therefore feel it right to offer one another collectively some kind of assurance that, regardless of financial circumstances or choices made earlier in life, old age, should we reach it, will be a time of financial security. In that case, our feelings of

---

[20]   Stakeholder pensions are discussed further in Section 3.5 below.

social solidarity are likely to lead us to wish to ensure that a pension system exists capable of guaranteeing everyone an acceptable standard of living in retirement.

Note that a pension system motivated by social solidarity could take many forms. It might be state-operated and financed out of taxation. Equally, however, it could be based on a legal framework which ensures a level of contribution to private sector pension schemes that enables the intermediaries responsible for their operation to offer a standard of pension provision high enough to meet society's expectations.

Clearly, pension systems can differ widely in their design and characteristics. In the next section, we examine some key differences and consider their implications for pension funds in particular.

2.4.4 Characteristics of pension systems

Pension systems can be distinguished according to the principles on which they:

- are financed, that is, how benefits are paid for;
- determine the entitlement to benefit of different individuals.

These differences and their implications form the focus of the discussion for the remainder of this chapter.

Financing pensions: 'pay-as-you-go' and 'funded' schemes

The UK state pension scheme is financed on a **PAYG** ('pay-as-you-go') basis: national insurance contributions received from *today's* generation of workers go to pay the pensions of *today's* retired generation. In a significant way, this arrangement reflects underlying economic reality. Suppose I want to ensure that I have bread to eat after I retire. During my working life I could, for example, build an oven in which the bread I will eat after retirement will be baked. This would be a *real* equivalent of saving for my retirement. However, even though I can provide myself with real capital for my old age in this way, I can only eat as a pensioner if the next generation of workers does the work needed *at that future time* to bake the bread I will eat and

grow the wheat from which it will be made. In other words, since the current labour of others is always needed to support the generation of pensioners that is alive at any point in time, it is true to say that the latter are in a real sense maintained economically on a pay-as-you-go basis by the current working population, *however their living costs are paid for*.

Notwithstanding these considerations, PAYG is an unsuitable basis for financing the occupational pension schemes[21] operated by individual firms in the private sector for two main reasons:

1 if the workforce of a private firm diminishes over time (e.g., because the business is declining), its pensioners could outnumber its current workforce so greatly that current contributions into the firm's pension fund do not cover its current liabilities to pay pensions;

2 the firm may cease trading, leaving pensioners (and employees hoping for a pension in the future too) unprovided for.

State-financed schemes, whether operated to provide pensions for public sector employees or the general population, do not face these particular problems and, in any case, the state could in principle always levy taxes (or 'print' money) to make good any funding shortfall. However, state provision is under threat in the UK and many other relatively rich countries because of the twin demographic implications of (i) rising life expectancy, which implies an expanding pension population, and (ii) stagnant or declining numbers of people of working age to provide for their own and everybody else's needs.

These two developments together mean a rising **dependency ratio**, defined as the ratio of economically dependent people to those who support them.[22] This, it is widely feared, could mean steep increases in taxation for the working population that could impact badly on the living standards of workers and their families, especially if economic growth is weak, and produce disincentive effects that could have adverse effects on economic growth.

Set against this it should be recognized, however, that in increasingly wealthy communities there is scope for increasing the level of taxation without actually

---

[21] Recall that occupational pensions and the role of pension funds in providing them are briefly outlined at the beginning of Section 2.4 above.

[22] The elderly are a major economically dependent group but not the only one. The very young (those below working age) are also economically dependent, as are those who are unable to work through severe illness or disability.

reducing living standards. In other words, even if some of the benefit of economic growth is taken away from today's producers in extra taxation, they may still be left with sufficient gains to enjoy a gradually rising standard of living. Secondly, it should be noted that the spending capability pensions offer to the retired community may help to stimulate aggregate demand and, in particular, demand for labour-intensive services (personal care, for example). This could be genuinely beneficial in an era when technological advances are causing labour to be shed in many sectors of the economy.

For the reasons outlined above, UK law requires private occupational pension schemes to be fully funded. The underlying principle of a **funded scheme** is that each generation of workers finances itself. But the current generation of workers belonging to any scheme is still in the process of making contributions and will only draw pensions in some future period. How can we tell whether it is truly succeeding in financing its own future pension provision? The answer is that we have to compare the current asset and liability positions of the pension fund in question, something which is complicated by the long time spans involved.

The contributions already made by workers who have yet to retire will give them rights to future pension payments as determined by the rules of the scheme. These, together with the obligations to pay pensions to former workers already in retirement, represent the currently accrued liabilities of the fund. Note that they are liabilities to make payments at a succession of dates stretching into the (fairly) remote future. Note also that if the scheme's estimate of its own future liabilities is to be reliable, it needs to forecast accurately the average longevity of its current and future retired scheme members.

On the other hand, the present assets of the fund equate to the sum of all contributions received to date *plus* all returns gained as a result of investing these *minus* all monies so far paid out in pensions. These are available to meet future pension payouts and, in the meantime, to invest with a view to acquiring additional assets in the future that will also be available to finance the payment of pensions.

For a scheme to be fully funded, the total of its present assets must be sufficient, given projected rates of return on future investment of these monies, to ensure that all liabilities that have so far accrued to pay pensions in the future can be met as they fall due. The scheme's actuaries will be concerned particularly with

the validity of assumptions made about longevity rates and projected rates of return on the future investment of funds held by the scheme. If they are satisfied with the reasonableness of these assumptions then the fund can be said to be *actuarily sound*. Clearly *actuarial soundness* is a key requirement for a fully funded scheme.

Factors such as those identified in Exercise 2.6 could present a risk that an occupational scheme might at some point in time become underfunded. That would cast doubt over its ability to pay the full rate of pension due to its retired members, present or future. So long as there is a chance that a scheme could become underfunded, its members thus face what is in effect an investment risk. The reader should recall that the reduction of investment risk was one of the justifications put forward earlier for the existence of a pension system.

If a scheme appears underfunded, the pressure will be on the employing firm, in the first instance, to step up its contribution rate so as to remedy the situation. If the degree of underfunding is so great that the additional need for contributions from the employer would be excessive, the current generation of workers might also be required to make higher contributions. Either way, the current generation of pensioners is completely protected against this investment risk. Currently working members are also fairly well protected, since they will not have the primary responsibility for making good any funding shortfall.

Exercise 2.6

Suppose the pension scheme of a given firm is fully funded at the present time. How, if at all, will the following changes affect the financial state of the fund?

(a) An increase in the rate of benefit paid to retired members.

(b) A decrease in the contribution rate paid by workers or by the employer.

(c) An increase in the life expectancy of retired members.

(d) A decrease in the profitability of the fund's investments.

(e) An increase in labour turnover within the firm.

(f) A round of redundancies before retirement within the firm.

(g) An increase in the rate of inflation.

The real threat to the financial security of both actual and prospective pensioners arises from the possibility that, at the point in time at which a state of underfunding has developed, the firm has ceased to trade. Now, in order that accrued liabilities can be met, a firm's pension fund is designed to carry on even if the firm itself closes down. However, suppose that after the firm's closure a significant fall in the projected rate of return on the fund's investments occurs. In such circumstances there would be no source of finance from which to top up the fund's assets and its trustees would find themselves with no option but to reduce the level of pensions members receive.

Determining benefits

Having considered funding aspects, we now go on to examine the benefits side of pension provision. Essentially, schemes divide into two major classes in terms of the way in which benefits to be paid to members are determined: these are 'defined benefit' and 'defined contribution' (sometimes called 'money purchase') schemes.

Defined benefit schemes set down precise rules governing how much each individual will receive in pension payments. For example, the size of an individual's UK state pension depends on how complete his or her contribution record is.

Many occupational schemes are defined benefit schemes in which the individual's pension right is determined on a *final salary* basis. The pensioner receives:

- an annual pension equal to a specified fraction of his/her final salary (e.g., 1/80) for every year s/he has worked

and generally also

- a lump sum on retirement equal to a fraction (e.g., 3/80) of final salary for every year worked.

If I am a member of a defined benefit scheme, I can at any time make a reasonably reliable forecast of my pension income by working out how many years of service I will have achieved by the time I retire and estimating what my final salary will be. The characteristics of a defined benefit scheme, coupled with safeguards against underfunding already discussed, offer members of such schemes a high degree of security. The employer bears the brunt of any investment risk. It is true that, if benefits are defined in nominal (money) terms, the value of the pension can be undermined by inflation. However, in many schemes pensions are index-linked, so that the inflation risk too is borne by the employer.

Exercise 2.7

Carl has worked for 23 years in a firm whose pension scheme is designed on an 'eightieths' basis. His salary in the year preceding his retirement was £26,400. What will his annual pension be and what lump sum will he receive on retirement?

These risk transfers obviously represent a disadvantage of defined benefit schemes as far as employers are concerned. However, they also possess a number of other limitations which should not be overlooked.

Without doubt, defined benefit schemes offer real security in old age to individuals who expect to clock up a long period of service with an employer and to be earning a reasonable final salary by the time they retire. However, many people will not be in continuous, reasonably well-paid employment. For example, some will suffer illness or unemployment, and many will have to interrupt their careers to care for children or elderly relatives. For people in these categories, the defining of benefits will not in itself be sufficient to ensure a reasonable level of pension entitlement.

Furthermore, although making pension entitlement dependent on length of service and final salary is intended to achieve fairness between members of a scheme, inequities such as that illustrated in Exercise 2.8 can arise.

Exercise 2.8

Stuart and Barbara have both recently retired on the same pension from the company for which they have worked. This is because both received the same final salary and both had the same length of service with the company.

However, Stuart spent most of his working life on a lower salary grade and was promoted to the same salary level as Barbara only 18 months before retirement. Barbara, on the other hand, had worked at this higher grade for most of her career.

Is it fair that both should receive the same pension?

(Answer: this question raises a matter of personal judgement but, in thinking about it, the reader should bear in mind that over her career Barbara will have made much larger contributions to the company's pension fund than Stuart will have done.)

Another issue of equity that arises out of the nature of defined benefit schemes is that people who change jobs frequently may lose out:

■ There may be a minimum period of service before the individual's right to a pension becomes 'vested'. If he or she leaves the job before the end of that period he or she will have accrued no pension entitlement.

■ Even if the right is vested, it will be frozen until the individual retires. If pension entitlement is fixed in money terms it is not protected against inflation. Even if it is index-linked, the individual remains at a disadvantage as it is likely that the Retail Price Index will rise more slowly than the salary he or she would have earned by staying in the company and to which the pension would have been tied.

■ The individual loses the opportunity to enhance the value of his or her early contributions by achieving promotion at a late stage (consider Stuart's case in Exercise 2.8).

The economy looks set to be characterized by high job insecurity for the foreseeable future. Many people could therefore be disadvantaged by these features of defined benefit schemes.

The features of defined benefit schemes which give rise to these equity considerations may also have implications for economic efficiency. Because they create a financial incentive for workers to stay with the same employer, they will tend to discourage labour mobility. As a result, staff turnover may be reduced and this may in some ways benefit firms and through them the wider economy. By the same token, however, defined benefit schemes will reduce labour market flexibility. This will tend to make it more difficult for growing firms, perhaps the most dynamic enterprises in the economy, to attract labour that they can use effectively. Economic growth could suffer as a result.

In view of the risk burden defined benefit schemes place on employers as well as the equity and the efficiency issues they raise, some commentators have suggested that it might be useful if they were widely replaced by *defined contribution* (otherwise known as **money purchase**) schemes. An example of the latter kind of scheme is the UK 'personal pension'. Here the individual pays in contributions over his or her working life which are invested to produce a fund that is

---

Exercise 2.9

1 Under a defined contribution scheme:
   (a) who bears (i) investment risk, (ii) inflation risk – the employer or the employee?
   (b) would the obstacles to labour market flexibility referred to above disappear?
   (c) would adequate pensions be ensured for those in low-paid or irregular employment?

2 Should the government encourage a shift from defined benefit to defined contribution schemes?

---

used when the person retires to buy an annuity payable for the rest of his or her life. The size of the eventual pension received therefore depends on:

■ the value of contributions paid in – the individual may have some discretion over this;

■ the returns earned on these contributions;

■ the market rate for annuities at the time of retirement.

Note that, under a money purchase arrangement, the worker will not know the size of his or her pension until the day he or she retires. Other aspects of defined contribution schemes are explored in Exercise 2.9 above.

2.5 Non-deposit-taking institutions – mutual funds

Mutual funds are, strictly speaking, *any* funds in which investors' savings are pooled, on an equal basis, for investment purposes. In this sense, the insurance companies and pension funds that we have just been discussing could be regarded as mutual funds. However, the pooling of funds for investment purposes comes about as a side-effect of their main objective, which is to provide a particular kind of financial product. Thus the term 'mutual fund' is more commonly restricted to organizations for whom the pooling of investment funds is their primary business. The phrase is thus used to describe a fund of savings collected in order to exploit the economies of scale that exist in the transactions costs associated with trading in securities – equities, bonds or money market instruments.[23] In a

---

23 The term 'mutual' is also used to describe a particular form of ownership of a financial organization, one where ownership rests with the savers and borrowers. Among many examples are building societies in the UK (Chapter 3) and some banks in Germany (Chapter 5). This is quite different from the meaning of mutual here.

mutual fund, small savings are placed with a fund manager who uses them to buy, hold and sell securities with a view to achieving the objectives of the fund, which may be 'growth', 'income' or 'balanced' (a mixture of the two). Alternatively, the fund may concentrate upon particular sectors of the securities market ('technology', 'special situations', 'smaller companies') or upon particular geographical regions ('Pacific', 'SE Asia', 'North America'). If the objective of the fund is primarily to generate income, it may invest exclusively in bonds or in money market instruments (a 'money market mutual fund'). Traditionally, there are two types of mutual fund: 'open ended' or more popularly 'unit trusts', and 'closed-ended' or '**investment trusts**'.

In order to meet the costs of trading in the securities, the fund will make a small annual charge to investors and there may also be a charge for entering and leaving the fund. The benefits to investors, however, are that these charges are much smaller than they themselves would face if they tried to buy a similar portfolio of securities as individuals. This is because of considerable economies of scale in transaction costs – it costs no more to process a very large deal than it does to handle a small one – and this is reflected in brokers' fees and commissions. Thus an individual buying, say, £10,000 worth of shares in a company might find that s/he was paying, say, 3 per cent in fees, whereas a fund manager buying, say, £10m worth might pay only 0.5 per cent. This in turn means that an individual would find it very expensive to build up a diversified portfolio, whereas, as a member of a mutual fund s/he can have a small share in say, 100 companies. Finally, there may be an advantage to unsophisticated investors with little knowledge and little time to increase it, in putting their funds with a professional manager and his or her team of analysts (though evidence discussed in Section 26.4 does not strongly support this).

As we said above, the term 'mutual fund' has come to mean a fund which pools savings in order to buy, hold and sell securities. A glance at the financial press in any developed country will reveal hundreds of funds available to savers, all offering the advantages of relatively cheap diversification. (Section 8.3 discusses these advantages.) Similar as all these funds are in their objectives, the structures which are used in order to achieve those objectives vary in detail between countries. Traditionally, there have been two fundamentally distinct types of mutual fund and most

countries offer both. Mutual funds can be either 'open-ended' or 'closed-ended', or, as they are more popularly known, 'unit trusts' and 'investment trusts'. We look at these now. Then, at the end of the section, we look at two new types of collective investment vehicle, which have attracted much publicity in the last year or two – the 'hedge fund' and 'private equity'.

An **open-ended fund** is one in which the size of the invested fund varies in response to two things. Firstly, the size of the fund varies with fluctuations in the value of the assets held by the fund. This is true to a greater or lesser extent of all mutual funds. What is special about open-ended funds, however, is that the flow of savers' contributions to the fund will also cause a change in fund size. An inflow of savings causes the fund to expand while an outflow causes it to shrink. In the UK, such funds are known as 'unit trusts' or 'open-ended investment companies' (OEIC). There are differences in structure and in pricing practice (see Section 3.6) but neither of these concern us here. To understand how an open-ended fund works we need to understand the concept of a 'unit', since the inflow (or outflow) of funds causes a change in the number of units in existence but not their price.

Imagine an open-ended fund which is being created from new. The management advertises its intention to open a fund with specific objectives, let us say capital growth from shares in mainly US companies. They invite savers to invest as much as they wish (though this will usually be subject to some minimum amount, say £500) by a specified date. Let us assume that subscriptions amount to £100m. This is immediately invested in US shares with a small amount, say 5 per cent, retained as bank deposits. The fund is then divided into units with an arbitrarily chosen price. In the UK, an opening price of 50p is quite common. Fixing the price obviously fixes the number of units. In our example, the price of 50p means that 200m units are created. These units are then allocated to savers in a quantity which matches the amount that they originally subscribed to the fund. The result is that the company has a portfolio of shares and 'cash' equal in value to the funds subscribed by savers and savers have a claim on this portfolio, represented by a number of units of 50p, which just matches what they subscribed. Now suppose that no additional funds are subscribed and no savers cash in their units. The value of the fund will vary *directly and only* with the value of the underlying shares. If the price rises such that the whole portfolio becomes worth £150m, then it follows that the value of each unit will have increased to £150m ÷ 200, or 75p.

Imagine now that new savers wish to join the fund and others wish to leave. On any particular day, units will have a price, calculated as we have just seen. New savers can buy units at this price while existing savers who wish to withdraw from the fund can sell units at the same price. Let us assume that, on balance, an additional £7.5m flows into the fund. The managers will create an extra 10m units credited to the new savers and invest the new savings in more US shares. The effect of the inflow has been to expand the size of the fund (by 10m units = £7.5m). The reverse would have happened in the case of withdrawals. Meanwhile, the value of the units will vary if, and only if, the value of the fund's investments changes. In an open-ended fund, therefore, inflows and outflows from savers affect its size, not its value. Its value depends solely upon the value of the underlying assets.

By contrast, a **closed-end fund** is one whose size is unaffected by its popularity with savers. 'Inflows' and 'outflows' have no effect at all on the *size* of the fund and this is because strictly there can be no inflows or outflows to the fund itself. A closed-end fund is one where the fund is established by the savings originally subscribed and then the doors are closed. As with an open-ended fund, subscribers' contributions are used to buy assets which reflect the objectives of the fund ('income', 'growth' etc.) and subscribers are once again given shares in the fund at a price which determines the number of shares in issue. What distinguishes the two types of fund is what happens next. Suppose that additional savers wish to join the fund, attracted perhaps by its objectives and the assets that it owns. Since the fund is closed, their savings cannot be added to the fund. If they wish to acquire a share in the fund, they have to buy existing shares, already held by other savers. With a closed-end fund, additional savings cannot increase its size, they can only increase its value. Equally, people 'leaving' the fund cannot diminish the size of the fund – *they cannot withdraw their savings from the fund itself*. This structural difference gives rise to two further distinguishing features.

The first relates to the pricing of units or shares in the fund. We have seen that the value of units in an open-ended fund changes only when there is a change in the value of fund assets. By contrast, since joining and leaving a closed-end fund means buying or selling its shares, attempts to join and leave will affect the price of the existing shares. This means, therefore, that the value of shares in a closed-end fund can change for *two* reasons. First of all, the value of the shares will bear *some* relation to the value of the underlying assets. If the assets in which it is invested rise dramatically in price, for example, then the fund is more valuable and, other things being equal, the shares in the fund will also be more valuable. But for closed-end funds, other things may not be equal. The value of the shares in the fund will only rise if people see them as more valuable and wish to buy them at the price which reflects the value of the underlying assets. As a rule, we may expect this to be the case but it *need* not happen, or it may not happen with precision. In fact, it is quite common for the value of shares in a closed-end fund to stand at a discount to the value of the assets in which the fund is invested. (We look at why this might be the case in Box 2.4 overleaf.) So, the second fundamental difference between an open-end and closed-end fund is that while the price of shares (units) in an open-end fund is determined exclusively by the value of the assets in the fund, the price of shares in a closed-end fund is determined by demand for the shares. The value of the underlying assets is relevant only in so far as it affects this demand. During the equity market recovery of 2003–04, the price of shares in most investment trusts lagged behind the general rise in the level of share prices and the discounts to net asset values widened.

The second difference between the two types of fund means that closed-end funds are, as a rule, cheaper to operate. This follows from the fact that savers' decisions to buy or sell the shares have very little impact on the fund's managers. Their job is to invest the funds originally subscribed when the fund was first established. If the fund becomes popular (and the share price rises) that is of no direct consequence to the managers. In an open-ended fund, however, this popularity would mean an inflow of funds which would have to be invested. Likewise, with sales. If savers 'leave' a closed-end fund they merely sell their shares (whose price may fall). The fund itself is unaffected. In the case of an open-ended fund, however, the managers will have to sell underlying assets in order to repay savers who wish to quit. An open-ended fund entails much more buying and selling and therefore higher operating costs. As a result, while a closed-end fund might charge investors around 0.5 per cent (of the value of the fund) per annum, charges for a unit trust or OEIC might be around 1.5 per cent.

BOX 2.4 Why do investment trusts trade at a discount?

Because the price of shares in investment trusts is determined by the demand for them, their price can deviate from the value of the underlying assets. One might expect such deviations to be short term and equally distributed between discounts and premiums. However, discounts are much more common and can go on for years (though varying in size). At first sight, this bias is curious and difficult to explain. Consider what it means. If an investment company owns shares whose current market value is £500m and the market value of its own shares is £450m, the discount is 10 per cent. A large investor, interested in the underlying shares then has a choice. He can either buy the shares in the open market for £500m or he can buy all the shares in the investment company for £450m, close the firm and keep the underlying shares, saving himself £50m. This looks like an anomaly which ought not to exist in a competitive, well-informed, market. The fact that the discounts persist suggests that shares held by an investment company are less attractive to would-be purchasers than the same shares bought in the open market.

There are several factors which explain the paradox. The first is that if a single buyer tried to buy up the shares of the investment company, it is very likely that the share price would rise and the discount would be eliminated, certainly once it became clear that a takeover was planned. The second is that the rate of return on shares owned by an investment company are bound to be less than they would be if held directly since the investment company has operating costs which have to be met from the return on the portfolio before the company's shareholders can benefit. This is acceptable to 'small' investors because the charges are less than the costs they would have to face if they tried to create the same portfolio on a small scale. The same would apply to anyone who bought up all the company's shares – its operating costs would still have to be met. However, any potential buyer of the investment company is likely to be another financial institution, or at least another company. Such a buyer would not be interested in paying for the management of the fund. The buyer would wish to sack the management and employees and hold the underlying portfolio directly. This eliminates the future management charges, but winding up the company would involve costs which would include paying compensation to the management and employees of the fund.

It should be clear from this description that a closed-end fund has many of the characteristics of a publicly quoted company. One cannot put funds into the company itself, but, if one wishes to benefit from the skills of the managers, one can buy shares in the company. And this is effectively what closed-end funds are – listed companies whose job happens to be investing in other companies' shares (or other securities) rather than the production of goods and services. This is why the details of shares in closed-end funds are usually listed along with the details of shares in all other publicly quoted firms in the financial press. In the UK, such funds are called 'investment trusts' and their details are quoted on the 'London Share Service' pages of the *Financial Times*, along with all other quoted companies. (The word 'trust' is thus misleading but has survived from the nineteenth century when these funds were first established as genuine trusts.) Like other companies, they can issue various types of shares to shareholders and they can borrow. The latter is useful when markets are rising, since the interest on the loans will usually be less than the return from the additional assets which can be bought with the loan.

We noted earlier that one of many differences between DTIs and NDTIs is that the latter tend to experience flows of funds which are 'contractual'. People make regular payments into pension funds and insurance policies and these buy them an agreement that the pension fund or insurance company will make payments to them in the event of some specified contingency, accident, illness, retirement, death etc. Both of these conditions make the flows of funds experienced by NDTIs relatively stable and predictable, especially when contrasted with funds entering and leaving DTIs. These tend to be 'discretionary'. People hold additional deposits after they have made all their other expenditure decisions. When they reach a certain threshold, they may be withdrawn and converted to something else. The position for mutual funds is somewhere in between. Most funds operate regular savings schemes, where the saver contributes a fixed monthly amount. This has the advantage to the fund that its inflows have some degree of predictability. On the other hand, they also accept 'lump-sum' investments and these may be quite volatile. In countries (like the UK) where there are tax advantages relating to investment in each tax year, mutual fund inflows may tend to bunch towards the end of the tax year as people make last-minute decisions not to pass the tax-saving opportunity. More generally, mutual fund inflows and outflows are likely to be strongly affected by the performance of markets in which they invest. Stock market slumps, for example, will reduce net investment in mutual funds and could, in the worst case, cause net withdrawals.

In the last few years, the general public has become very concerned about two further types of collective investment vehicle. The first of these is the so-called **hedge fund** and the concept first came to attention in 1998 when 'Long Term Capital Management', a US-based mutual fund in which many financial institutions and wealthy individuals had invested, nearly collapsed. It sent shivers through world financial markets, such was its size, and caused the Federal Reserve to cut interest rates, leading to the allegation that the Fed was developing a new role – of lender of last resort to financial markets – to complement its traditional role of lender of last resort to the banking system. LTCM was widely referred to as a 'hedge fund'. The term hedge fund has since been applied to many other mutual investment projects, not all of which strictly merit the term.

The basic principles of a hedge fund were established by Alfred Winslow Jones, an Australian by birth but later a US citizen with a colourful and varied career, in 1949. A conventional mutual fund buys assets which it expects to give a good rate of return in some combination of income and capital gain. If the managers think that the assets are likely to produce a poor or negative return, their defence is limited to selling the assets and holding money instead. A hedge fund does the same but, crucially, it does four other things. Firstly, it simultaneously engages in 'short-selling', that is it sells shares it does not own but has only borrowed, in the expectation that it will be able to buy them later, when their price has fallen. Secondly, it borrows funds in order to buy assets in excess of the subscriptions that it has received from fund members. In other words, it employs 'gearing' or 'leverage'. Thirdly, there should be no explicit charge to members of the fund because the managers are paid a percentage of realized profits. Thus their remuneration has a strong incentive element. Finally, hedge funds are usually unregulated and are therefore free to deal in derivative instruments (see Chapter 20) giving them another source of gearing.

The basic idea behind a hedge fund, therefore, is to eliminate market risk (the fund's long holdings benefit when the market rises and the short sales show a profit if the market falls) and to make a profit by buying and selling the right stocks. We shall see, when we have studied Chapter 8, that the theory behind this is quite different from the theory that drives most conventional mutual funds. The conventional argument, used to justify the latter, is that one does not have enough information consistently to buy (sell) individual assets just before their price rises (falls) so that 'stockpicking' is highly risky and is unlikely to give a return which is better than holding a diversified portfolio. However, the added advantage of investing in a mutual fund is that it gives a high degree of diversification which eliminates the specific risk associated with individual assets, since good returns will offset poor returns. With sufficient diversification, the level of risk can be driven down to approximate 'market risk', the risk that the whole market may rise or fall. This level of risk is regarded as unavoidable. But a hedge fund is constructed in such a way that market risk is eliminated while the managers concentrate upon spotting 'undervalued' shares (which they buy) and 'overvalued' shares which they borrow and sell short. The icing on the cake is then to magnify the profits by gearing.

Another feature which distinguishes hedge funds from traditional mutual funds is that they aim to earn an *absolute* return. This follows from their design and their use of short-selling in order to make a profit even in falling markets. Hedge funds will advertise a target return which they try to earn, come what may. The managers of conventional mutual funds (unit and investment trusts) would never commit to earning a particular rate of return. They aim to beat an 'index' which shows the average performance of similar funds. In effect, this amounts to competing with each other. The objective in this case therefore is to earn a *relative* return – a return which is better than their competitors', even if at times this may be negative.

The main concerns about the activities of hedge funds stem from the regulatory environment in which they work. Unlike traditional mutual funds (and rather like private equity funds to which we come in a moment), hedge funds are comparatively 'private' organizations. In principle, a hedge fund could be legally structured along the lines of the closed- or open-ended funds we have already discussed and they would be subject to the same regulations. But typically hedge funds are limited partnerships and membership is restricted to financial institutions or high net worth individuals. The significance of this is that investors are assumed to be well-informed and therefore able to look after themselves. In most jurisdictions, therefore, this type of collective activity is very lightly regulated. Furthermore, the fund maybe domiciled overseas in order to avoid taxes on the fund itself. From this it follows that the fund is required to make relatively little information available to the public.

As an indication of the size, but more strikingly the rate of growth, of hedge funds consider the estimates that in 2002 some $61bn in funds were managed from London and $600bn in New York. By the end of 2006, the corresponding figures were $400bn and $1.225trn respectively.

As we have seen, to begin with, hedge funds sought to attract only very large subscriptions so they were accessible only to institutions and the extremely wealthy prepared to enter into a limited partnerhsip. However, with stock markets generally falling during 2000 and 2001, retail fund management groups found it impossible to sell units in conventional funds. The idea that it might be possible to make a profit whichever way the market was moving thus became very attractive as a marketing device. These groups then began to offer 'hedge funds' scaled down for people to invest as little as £5,000 and structures along conventional mutual fund lines and subject to higher levels of regulation. At the same time, it became apparent that the term 'hedge fund' was being misused in a number of these cases and regulators became worried that unsophisticated investors were being drawn into funds which they did not fully understand. The biggest worry is that some of these so-called retail hedge funds lack the short-selling element. This leaves them as highly geared conventional investment funds. They borrow money in order to buy and hold shares which they think will rise. Gearing increases the possible returns but it also increases the risk. It remains to be seen whether retail investors fully understand this risk and how they will react when it turns out that some of these funds are not fully hedged.

In the popular imagination, hedge funds are often linked with **private equity**. Although, as we shall see in a moment, there are distinct differences between the two, they are often linked for four reasons. Firstly, they are lightly regulated and related to that they have low levels of disclosure. Secondly, the investors are limited to professional institutions and high net worth individuals – giving rise to the perception that they are investment vehicles for the privileged few. Thirdly, their managers are compensated on the basis of the fund's profit, rather than via a fixed fee. Finally, some hedge funds have holdings in private equity.

The term 'private equity' refers to any type of equity investment in an asset in which that equity is not freely tradeable on a public stock market. More precisely here, private equity refers to the manner in which the funds for the investment vehicle have been raised, namely on the private markets, as opposed to the public markets. This follows from the fact that access is resricted to financial institutions and high net worth individuals and, again following the hedge fund example, the ownerhsip structure is generally one of a limited partnership. Within the partnerhip, however, the designated 'general partner' is what would be termed the 'fund manager' in other structures and is responsible for making the investment decisions and draws the performance-related fee. The remaining partners make an initial subscription to the fund and commit themselves to making further contributions as the manager finds suitable investment opportunities.

Private equity can be divided into further subcategories depending on the objectives of the fund. 'Leveraged buyout' refers to a fund whose object is buy an existing company, often financing the purchase with a high level of debt, changing the management, improving the profitability and then selling the firm back to he public markets. 'Venture capital' and 'angel capital' focus on start-up or very young companies. 'Growth capital' and 'mezzanine' funds tend to deal in established (but small to medium-sized) firms that they think show potential for rapid growth. Note that private equity tend to be deeply involved in the running of the firms in which they are invested, typically controlling the day-to-day management. This is a major difference from hedge funds, which generally content themselves with simply owning the shares of publicly quoted companies. It also gives rise to a further difference which is that private equity funds are invested in very illiquid assets – often owning a whole firm. This makes it very difficult for partners to withdraw their investment until the fund is finally wound up. This usually happens when the underlying firm is sold on the stock exchange or to another private equity company. There is a market for partnerships, but it is understandably very small.

Finally, there is a substantial difference in size between the two industries. The total (world) value of

> **BOX 2.5 Private equity must be readier to explain what it does**
>
> The elastic has finally snapped. The tension between private equity groups' continuing desire for a low profile and their increasingly high-profile activities has become too great. The past two weeks have provided fresh evidence of buy-out groups' ambition and the opposition it can arouse. An effective response requires private equity to abandon its reclusive habits.
>
> Buy-outs are getting bigger. Just a week ago Blackstone won a bitter takeover battle to acquire Equity Office Properties for $39bn – the largest leveraged buy-out on record. They are also venturing into the heart of national life. A trio of private equity firms is circling J. Sainsbury, one of Britain's biggest food retailers. Animosity towards private equity is growing, too. In the UK, a trade union-led campaign has combined with posturing ahead of the contest for the deputy leadership of the Labour party to turn up the heat on the large buy-out firms. In particular, the GMB union is urging MPs to support the scrapping of corporate tax relief for interest payments on loans.
>
> The politics is dispiriting. With weeks of campaigning among Labour MPs still to come, we can expect more demagoguery. It is at least reassuring that the Treasury says it will not be bounced on the question of tax relief. Of course, the relief matters particularly in leveraged buy-outs, but private equity firms are not the only ones to benefit. There is certainly scope for a tax policy debate about the relative treatment of debt and equity: an atmosphere of visceral hostility towards private equity is not conducive to informed choices.
>
> There are signs, though, that private equity is listening. Damon Buffini, managing partner of Permira, Europe's largest private equity firm, has proposed a meeting with the GMB union. This is a welcome first step toward engagement with critics, not all of whom are agitators targeting favourable borrowing terms as well as their lucrative fees.
>
> The next step is for all these high-earning firms to recognise what comes with entering the mainstream. This requires them to change in two ways. First, where a firm buys a national icon or a large employer, it must accept that it cannot behave as if its actions in restructuring the business have no wider impact on the community.
>
> More generally, the industry needs to get better at justifying what it does. It should be prepared to tackle criticism that the improved performances firms can achieve from the companies they buy come not primarily from brilliant management, but at the cost of riskier positions for creditors, employees and pension funds.
>
> Buy-out firms have learned the hard way that a reputation for asset-stripping is easier to gain than to lose. To prevent its new-found wealth and respectability being jeopardised, it is time for private equity to address its public.
>
> Source: *Financial Times*, 14 February 2007. Reprinted with permission.

private equity funds in 2005 was put at $135bn though this is growing rapidly and will have been increased sharply by the record-breaking deals that took place in 2006.

Because of its lack of disclosure, the private equity industry has been subject to much the same criticism and suspicion as the hedge funds. (It was the activities of both that provoked the outburst from Franz Müntefering in Section 2.2 above.) The *Financial Times* report in Box 2.5 illustrates some of these issues.

2.6 Summary

The defining characteristics of financial systems lie more in the nature of the institutions that make up those systems than they do in the markets. We shall see some of the differences in the next few chapters.

In this chapter we have divided financial institutions into deposit-taking and non-deposit-taking institutions, noted their main features and explained some of the principles on which they work. Deposit-taking institutions, for example, are institutions whose liabilities act as a country's principal means of payment and form the largest part of its money supply. For both reasons, such institutions tend to be highly regulated and to have access to a 'lender of last resort' which can provide liquidity if the deposit takers are threatened with illiquidity. Illiquidity risk is one of the main risks faced by such institutions and comes about fundamentally because deposit liabilities have a shorter maturity than the loans which are DTIs' main assets, but is exacerbated by deposits' use as means of payment and the fact that decisions to hold deposits, as opposed to other forms of financial wealth, are discretionary rather than contractual. These two circumstances give deposit inflows and outflows a degree of volatility which is not experienced by NDTIs.

By contrast, the main NDTIs, insurance companies, pension funds and (to a lesser extent) mutual fund organizations, have inflows and outflows which are contractual and/or can be estimated with some degree of reliability. The fact that inflows and outflows can be estimated depends to a large extent upon the 'law of large numbers' and this enables all financial institutions to engage in some degree of maturity transformation – holding liabilities which are of shorter maturity than assets.

Key concepts in this chapter

Adverse selection	Market-based
Asset management	Maturity transformation
Asset risk	Mean
Asymmetric information	Mis-estimation
Bank-based	Money purchase
Catastrophe risk	Moral hazard
Closed-end mutual fund	Open-ended mutual fund
Corporate banking	Parameter change
Debt contracts	Pay-as-you-go (PAYG) pension scheme
Defined benefit	Payment risk
Dependency ratio	Pension system
Equity contracts	Private equity
Funded pension scheme	Reinsurance
General insurers	Relationship banking
Hedge fund	Retail (commercial) banking
Investment banking	Retirement annuity
Investment trust	Short-termism
Law of Large Numbers	Standard deviation
Life offices	Unit trust
Liquidity risk	Universal banking
Loading	Wholesale banking

Questions and problems

1 Distinguish between 'asset risk', 'payment risk' and 'liquidity risk' as faced by banks.

2 Explain why 'liquidity risk' is a particular problem for banks (when compared with non-deposit-taking institutions). How can banks protect themselves against liquidity risk?

3 How does the presence of 'asymmetric information' help to explain the type of contracts offered by banks?

4 'Provided an insurance company bases the premiums it charges on the claims resulting from a large sample of homogeneous and statistically independent past exposures, its premium income will always be sufficient to meet claims.' Do you agree? Why or why not?

5 Why should it matter to an insurance company whether or not the exposures it is called upon to cover are:

(a) large in number?

(b) part of a known phenomenon?

(c) statistically independent of one another?

(d) homogeneous in character?

(e) unaffected by the fact of insurance?

6 Explain how limits to the applicability of the insurance principle can lead to financial exclusion.

7 How much truth is there in the accusation sometimes levelled against insurance companies that they are in business to provide cover for people who do not need it?

8 Do insurers face a dilemma between trying to differentiate as finely as possible between subgroups within a given class of business and seeking to reduce risk by making use of the LLN?

9 Is it reasonable to argue that provision for old age should be left as a matter for individual choice? If your answer is 'no', what do you consider to be the strongest argument against doing so and why?

10 Distinguish between (i) PAYG and funded pension schemes and (ii) defined benefit and defined contribution schemes. In both cases, identify the main advantages and disadvantages of each member of the pair.

11 Distinguish between 'closed-end' and 'open-ended' mutual funds. Why are management charges in the former generally lower than in the latter?

12 Why do the shares in investment trusts often trade at a discount to the value of the underlying assets in the fund?

13 How do hedge funds differ from private equity funds? Why are they often linked in popular commentary?

Further reading

F Allen and D Gale, *Comparing Financial Systems* (Cambridge MA: MIT Press, 2000)

P Brown, 'Insurers threaten flood cover', *The Guardian*, 20 April 2004

M Buckle and J Thompson, *The UK Financial System* (Manchester: Manchester University Press, 4e, 2004)

B Casu, C Giradone and P Molyneux, *Introduction to Banking* (London: Pearson Education) part I.

E P Davis, *Pension Funds, Retirement-income Security and Capital Markets: An international perspective* (Oxford University Press, 2e, 1998)

E P Davis and B Steil, *Institutional Investors* (Cambridge MA: MIT Press, 2001)

A R Dombret and H J Kern, *European Retail Banks: an Endangered Species?* (Chichester: Wiley, 2003)

F Fabozzi, F Modigliani, M Ferri and F Jones, *Foundations of Financial Markets and Institutions* (New York: Prentice-Hall, 2003)

Financial Times, 'Leader: Discrimination in insurance policies', 25 June 2003

S I Greenbaum and A V Thakor, *Contemporary Financial Intermediation* (Fort Worth: Dryden, 2e, 2004)

The Guardian, 'How the names lost their shirts', 4 November 2000

The Guardian, 'Leader: Where ignorance is bliss', 18 May 2004

The Guardian, 'Lloyds names "fleeced in £4bn fraud"', 7 March 2000

S Heffernan, *Modern Banking* (Chichester: Wiley, 2004)

A D Morrison and W J Wilhelm, *Investment Banking: Institutions, Politics and Law* (Oxford: Oxford University Press, 2007)

B Reszat, *European Financial Systems in the Global Economy* (Chichester: Wiley, 2005)

M Sullivan, *Understanding Pensions* (London: Routledge, 2004)

J Toporowski, *The End of Finance* (London: Routledge, 2000) Chs 5, 6

E Vaughan and T Vaughan, *Essentials of Insurance: A Risk Management Perspective* (New York: Wiley, 1995)

▶

Websites

www.apacs.org.uk
www.bankofengland.co.uk
www.barrettwells.co.uk
www.bis.org
www.Commerzbank.com
www.creditagricole.fr

www.dwp.gov.uk/
http://en.wikipedia.org/wiki/Hedge_fund
http://en.wikipedia.org/wiki/Private_equity
www.goldmansachs.com
www.pensionprotectionfund.org.uk/
http://www.preqin.com/

Chapter 3 The UK financial system

What you will learn in this chapter:

■ The functions of the major institutions comprising the
  UK financial system

■ The comparative size of those institutions judged by stocks
  of assets and by flows of funds

■ Their importance in financing real economic activity

■ Their importance as traders in financial markets

3.1 Introduction

In this chapter, we look at the main characteristics of the UK financial system. As we said in the last chapter, the distinctive characteristics of a financial system lie largely in the institutions which comprise the system and the way(s) in which they are regulated. Accordingly, the chapter proceeds by examining in turn each of the groups of intermediaries briefly described in Chapter 2. Under each heading we indicate the scale of activity and the sources and uses of funds. We also outline the main features of the relevant regulatory regime.

There are various ways in which data can be used to compare the size and behaviour of financial inter- mediaries. Firstly, one can look at the use which is made each year of funds received from savers. For this, we require data on the **net acquisition of assets**. These are assets *purchased* during a period of time, *less* assets sold. This does not of course measure the flow of new lending to ultimate borrowers, since many of the assets purchased will be assets already in existence; these are assets created by earlier lending, the institutions taking over the loan from a previous holder. Neither does it measure the total scale of trading in assets by any par- ticular institution. In the course of a year an insurance company, for example, will buy and sell many assets of any given type. Its total sales and purchases of a given asset constitute the **turnover** in that asset while the net acquisition, as we said, is the difference between sales and purchases. Finally, we could compare **stocks** of assets currently held. This would involve looking at *balance sheet* data and that data would show the sum of net acquisitions cumulated over previous years. Comparisons made in this way would obviously be strongly affected by decisions made in the past.

For banks and building societies Tables 3.1 and 3.2 (respectively) give data on both stocks of assets and also changes in those assets in the most recent year for which data is available. Thus one can judge the size of banks and building societies either in terms of their accumulated wealth or in terms of the flows of funds

which they are directing into new assets. One can also see the direction of those funds.

Our comparison of other (non-deposit-taking) financial intermediaries is based around Table 3.4 which shows data for net acquisitions and thus enables us to compare the scale of funds available for disposal by each institution and the way in which those funds were used in the most recent period for which data is available, and around Table 3.5 which shows stocks of assets. Using all four tables, comparisons can obviously be made between each type of intermediary. For non- deposit-taking institutions we then include a further table (3.6) which shows the part played by each type of institution in the turnover of selected securities.

3.2 Banks in the UK

The UK banking sector has traditionally been highly segmented. Until the last 20 years or so, it was possible to read about the activities of 'retail banks', 'accepting houses', 'discount houses' and so on. And these divi- sions were maintained in the official statistics. Until the mid-1990s, for example, the *Bank of England Quarterly Bulletin* used to publish a list of institutions to whom the Bank of England had granted a banking licence. The list ran to more than 450 institutions and these were allocated to one of seven sections, reflecting their function. The distinctions were maintained in the published statistics so that it was possible to compare the balance sheets of 'retail banks' with, for example, those of 'British merchant banks'. This no longer makes much sense. As we explained in Section 2.3, what we think of as 'a bank' is often just one division (usually the retail division) of a much larger banking *group*. The group as a whole will offer a full range of banking func- tions and even a variety of financial services, like asset management, which we would not usually think of as part of banking at all. Barclays plc is a name which most people in the UK would immediately recognize as a major retail bank, but as Figure 3.1 shows, Barclays is a large conglomerate which operates a retail banking

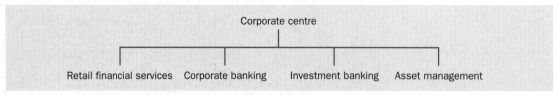

Figure 3.1 The Barclays Group

division alongside corporate and investment banking and asset management functions.

In these circumstances, we can still distinguish between different types of banking *function* or *activity* (retail banking *is* different from investment banking) but we should not think about these activities being the sole activity of a particular *firm*. There are some investment banks in the UK which specialize only in that activity but most banks, and certainly all retail banks, are parts of a much larger group which offers everything. The Financial Services Authority now publishes the list of banking licence holders on its website (www.FSA.gov.uk). In the current list, banks are classified by their 'nationality' – the location of their headquarters.

Table 3.1 shows the assets and liabilities of UK banks in March 2007, distinguishing between sterling and foreign currency items. Bearing in mind our discussion in Section 2.3 about liquidity risk, the first thing to notice is the very small ratio of instantly available 'liquid reserves' to the rest of the balance sheet. For example, if we add 'Notes and coin' and 'Balances at the Bank of England' we have a figure of £25,496m. But this figure does not strictly correspond to 'reserves' since the figure for 'Balances at the Bank of England' includes 'cash ratio' deposits. These are deposits which banks must maintain at the Bank of England, up to 0.15 per cent of their assets, in order to generate income for the Bank. 'Operational deposits' are only a subset of the figure in Table 3.1, amounting in March 2007 to about £14,553m. If we add these to notes and coin to calculate a 'reserve ratio' (reserves/deposits) it amounts to about 1 per cent if we use only

Table 3.1 Assets and liabilities of UK banks, March 2007 (£m)

Sterling assets		Sterling liabilities	
Notes and coin	8,672	Sight deposits	990,221
Balances at the Bank of England	16,824	Time deposits	1,254,524
Market loans	940,963	CDs and other paper	185,121
Advances	1,519,272	Liabilities under sale and repurchase agreements	343,616
Bills	12,300	Sterling capital	297,530
Claims under sale and repurchase agreements	328,218	Other	47,329
Investments	200,727		
Other	96,587		
Total	3,123,563	Total	3,118,341
Foreign currency assets (including euro)		**Foreign currency liabilities (including euro)**	
Market loans and advances	1,608,057	Sight and time deposits	2,047,107
Claims under sale and repurchase agreements	1,198,194	Liabilities under sale and repurchase agreements	945,538
Bills	32,156	CDs and other paper	435,686
Investments	683,760	FC capital	59,496
Other	286,448	Other	326,010
Total	3,808,615	Total	3,813,837
TOTAL ASSETS	6,932,178	TOTAL LIABILITIES	6,932,178

Note: Totals/subtotals do not balance/sum owing to rounding.
Source: Adapted from www.bankofengland.co.uk, *Bankstats* (table B1.2), Bank of England. Reprinted with permission.

sterling deposits and to about half that, 0.5 per cent, if we include foreign currency deposits. In the UK this ratio is a 'prudential ratio', that is, it is chosen by banks themselves in the light of what experience tells them is a safe minimum. There is a requirement, however, that any bank that intends to change this ratio should give prior notice to the Bank of England so that the Bank is always in a position to form a view about the likely availability of liquid assets relative to banks' requirements. Table 3.1 aggregates all banks and the ratio we have just calculated is a broad average. If we could break the table down to show different types of banking functions we would find that this ratio would be higher for retail banking divisions, probably around 2 per cent, and lower for non-retail banking. Such a very low reserve ratio makes the availability of 'second tier' liquidity very important. In the UK this is provided by 'market loans', 'repurchase agreements' and 'bills'. Market loans are loans to the interbank and other money markets, many of them for very short periods or even overnight. The latter can be liquidated on demand or 'at call'. Repurchase agreements (when listed under 'assets') are loans that have been made, again usually to other banks or other financial institutions, by 'buying' assets (usually government bonds) from the borrowing firm on the strict condition that the borrower will repurchase them within 14 days at a higher price. Bills are short-term money market securities with an original maturity usually of three months. By holding a range of 'repos' and bills, banks can ensure that they have a continually maturing stock of interest-earning assets which provide them with a constant flow of funds. In a real emergency, a fraction of these assets can be easily liquidated at a moment's notice. (Details of these money market instruments are given in Chapter 15.)

The bulk of banks' earning assets are held in the form of loans or 'advances' to the 'non-bank, non-building society private sector' ('M4PS' for short!). 'Investments' refers primarily to securities and most of these are short-dated government bonds.

Table 3.1 suggests that sterling business and foreign currency business account for about 45 per cent and 55 per cent of the total, respectively. But this is true only for the banking system as a whole. In retail banking, foreign currency deposits make up less than 25 per cent of the total, while wholesale banking foreign currency business accounts for about 70 per cent. What the table also conceals between different types of bank is the importance of 'sight' or 'demand' deposits

against 'time' deposits (including CDs). Retail banks are central to the payments mechanism. For this reason virtually everyone needs a bank sight deposit account and sight deposits make up about 50 per cent of retail bank deposits. But for wholesale banks, deposits are much more likely to be time deposits. Consequently the degree of 'maturity transformation' undertaken by wholesale banks is less than it is for retail banks and this partly explains why wholesale banks can operate with smaller reserve ratios than retail banks.

Until 1998, supervision of the UK banking system rested with the Bank of England, under the terms of the Banking Act 1987, which required the Bank of England to exercise the following powers:

- licensing of all deposit-taking institutions (except building societies);

- ensuring that institutions have adequate capital, liquidity and controls;

- ensuring that they make adequate provision for bad debts;

- checking that directors of banking institutions are 'fit and proper persons'.

In 1997, however, the Bank of England was given 'instrument independence' for the conduct of monetary policy. The thinking behind this, a desire to free the Bank of political constraints on its actions, is discussed in Sections 14.5 and Section 14.6. But political pressure is only one source of potential interference with a central bank's conduct of monetary policy. A central bank might, for example, be reluctant to raise interest rates if it happens to know that some commercial banks are facing a high level of bad debts which is likely to rise further if interest rates go up. So long as it is responsible for supervising the banking system and maintaining stability, a central bank is likely to delay raising interest rates if it knows that one consequence might be bank failures.

To avoid this conflict of interest, therefore, the supervisory powers listed above were transferred from the Bank of England by the Bank of England Act in June 1998 to a newly established Financial Services Authority (FSA) which is now responsible for the supervision of virtually all financial intermediaries.

Banking, like most forms of financial intermediation, is increasingly an international activity. Banks with headquarters in one country, for example, may operate subsidiaries in many others. This poses a problem for supervisors partly because differences between national rules may lead to distortions in the pattern of banking activity whereby banks concentrate certain types of business in those countries where regulation is lightest and partly because there is a danger that foreign subsidiaries 'fall between the cracks' when it comes to supervision: the home authority cannot exercise supervision in the host country, while the host country supervisor may not feel a responsibility for foreign banks. Thus much effort in recent years has gone into the international coordination of banking supervision. For example, the capital tests imposed by the FSA are enshrined in the EC Capital Adequacy Directive, 1996. These in turn are based upon recommendations of the so-called 'Basel Committee' in 1988 and involve calculating a 'risk-adjusted' measure of bank assets. The details are discussed in Chapter 25, but essentially the calculation involves attaching 'weights' (=1 for commercial loans, 0.5 for mortgage loans, 0 for cash, for example) to each category of assets. The value of assets when adjusted for risk is clearly less than the unadjusted value, but unlike the unadjusted value it will change if assets of the same value, but different risk weights, are substituted for each other. Having calculated a risk-adjusted value for assets, the next step involves calculating the bank's total capital (subject to certain definitions and rules about proportions) and comparing this with risk-adjusted assets. The recommendation, widely accepted in industrial countries in 1993, was that the ratio of capital to risk-adjusted assets should not be less than 8 per cent.

Devising a regulatory system where nothing falls between the cracks requires not only an international set of rules, but some agreement about supervisory responsibilities where firms' activities cross international boundaries, as they usually do. The EC Second Banking Coordination Directive, 1993, places the responsibility for supervision of overseas branches on the home supervisor but lays down rules to ensure cooperation between home and host authorities. Thus branches of banks with headquarters in other EU states are permitted to operate in the UK on the strength of the licence issued in the home country, while the FSA is responsible for the supervision of branches of UK banks operating in other EU countries on the strength of the licence issued in the UK by the FSA.

Banks in the UK are subject to pressures for change which affect banks throughout the western economies although the results have not always been the same as in other countries. The most noticeable trends in recent years have been the increasing automation of banking services (surely a worldwide phenomenon), the concentration of the industry through merger and acquisition (certainly a European and North American trend), the closure of branches (a rather more peculiarly British development involving mainly retail banks) and the increasing use of securitization. Such trends are not independent of one another but we can only discuss each in turn, pointing out the connections. When it comes to mergers, we shall also point to an interesting pattern which these have taken, which is perhaps rather different from what one might expect.

Like most industries, banking has been dramatically affected by technological developments in the last quarter-century. Many of these are linked to improvements in communication and thence to the revolution in information technology. Two of these, which have had far-reaching consequences, have changed dramatically the provision of the core banking activities of deposit-taking and payments.

The first is the development of automated teller machines ('ATMs') or 'cash dispensers' as they are often called. The latter is an interesting misnomer. It is true that when the first machines were introduced in 1967 they did little more than give the customer access to cash in a fixed amount. In 1977 there were about 1,300 machines, which by then offered customers a choice of withdrawal amounts together with a statement of current balance. By 2006 there were 60,468 machines. About 20,000 are sited on bank premises but the growth in these locations has now come to a standstill. The remainder are sited in 'remote' locations such as supermarkets, railway stations, filling stations etc. and growth is much more rapid in these sites, new machines being opened at the rate of about 2,000 a year. Although still primarily used for access to cash (there were 2.7bn withdrawals averaging £65 in 2006) these machines now offer a wide range of services from the ordering of statements and cheque books to changing one's PIN. The size of withdrawals can now be user-specified across a wide range, and developments in communication technology now make it possible to use a card in virtually any machine, including machines located overseas for the withdrawal of foreign currency. Although not yet in use in the UK, machines exist which can scan a cheque and credit specified amounts across a number of accounts. In some branches, machines with touch-sensitive screens provide on-screen links to a variety of product descriptions, take customers through a series of questions and answers before recommending a product or providing a quotation and can create a video-conferencing link with staff at a central location to deal with more complex enquiries.[1]

At least as important to banks, though of lower profile than ATM development, is the progressive automation of the payments mechanism. Box 3.1 shows clearly the trend away from cheque and other paper-based methods of payment and toward electronic-based methods.

Though strictly dependent upon cost structures, merger and consolidation is a feature of most maturing industries and it has been a characteristic of banking since the earliest days. This partly reflects the economies of scale that are present in most financial activity, but it is also partly a product of the benefits of diversification and, until the early twentieth century, it also reflected the increasing integration of the national economy in the UK. When trade was local and then regional, a regional banking system was perfectly adequate. But when markets became national and trade and payments went from one end of the country to the other, a national network of banks had obvious attractions. Hence the history of the current big five (Barclays, HSBC, RBS-NatWest, Lloyds TSB and HBoS) is a continuous history of absorption of the smaller by the larger.

However, the economic need for a national banking system in the UK was met some years ago. With the top four banking groups holding 60 per cent of UK sight deposits, the question confronting further mergers is whether the process has gone too far when it comes to competition and consumer choice. In 2000, the merger between the Royal Bank of Scotland and NatWest was accepted by the competition authorities, but of the two further mergers proposed in 2001 (Halifax with Bank of Scotland and Lloyds TSB with Abbey National) only the former was allowed. Interestingly, the Abbey's merger with the Spanish bank Banco Santander was allowed in 2004 and at the time of writing there appears to be no regulatory objection to the merger of Barclays with the Dutch bank ABN-AMRO. This is because merger with a foreign bank does not reduce competition and consumer choice.

On the face of it, therefore, the integration of the national economy can hardly be called on to justify the continuing trend to consolidation and we maybe have to look to economies of scale and diversification as the driving forces. But before doing so, it is worth considering whether the demands that originally flowed from national integration might be replaced by those that flow from international integration. As we shall see in Chapter 21, the European Union has been striving for years to create a European single financial market by reducing national barriers of all kinds. Furthermore, a large part of the EU now uses a single currency. If patterns of trade once made it important to develop a banking system comprising a few large firms with national coverage, one might well ask whether the further integration of a European-wide economy might have the same effect. And if so, does this suggest that future bank mergers (within the EU) might be across national boundaries? There is a limited parallel in the case of the USA where, until 1984, banks were forbidden to operate across state boundaries. Since the lifting of the restriction about half of all bank mergers have involved crossing state boundaries.

But so far the European experience has been very different. The three mergers we referred to above all involved UK banks. In 1999 merger negotiations between Deutsche and Dresdner banks reached an advanced stage before being broken off, while discussions between two French banks, Banque National de Paris and Paribas, succeeded. In Europe there does

---

BOX 3.1 Recent trends in UK payment methods (no. of payments, £ trillions)

	2002	2006	Annual % change
CHAPS	30,845	109,637	37.3
Cheque	2,393	1,234	−15.3
Automated	2,382	3,429	9.5
Credit card	81	98	4.9
Debit card			
(inc. charge card)	130	223	14.4
Cash at ATMs	149	198	7.4

Source: APACS (2007) *Handbook of Payment Statistics*, various tables. Reprinted with permission.

---

[1]   The figures in this paragraph are taken from APACS (2007) *Handbook of Payment Statistics*.

BOX 3.2 Slow benefits of mergers

BANKING

Merger savings come slowly for Agricole

By Martin Arnold in Paris

Crédit Agricole, France's biggest bank by assets, was yesterday forced to admit that its integration with Crédit Lyonnais was proving tougher than expected as it warned it would achieve less than half its €574m ($707m) planned synergies from the merger this year.

The warning came as the bank reported an 8.5 per cent decline in full-year consolidated net profits to €1.14bn, below analysts' expectations, because of €1bn of exceptional charges and goodwill write-downs to cover the cost of integration.

The mutual bank, which bought Lyonnais for €19.5bn last year, blamed the slower realisation of synergies on delays to closing the deal caused by legal challenges from rival banks, which dragged it out until June.

Agricole said it would only achieve €275m of the €574m synergies it had planned for this year.

It also said synergies would reach €620m in 2005, instead of €738m, before hitting €760m in 2006.

Investors seemed to have already taken the more gradual timing of synergies into account, as Agricole shares closed up 7.3 per cent at a new 52-week high of €21.51.

To account for the costs of integrating Lyonnais, which Agricole said had involved some 25,000 staff worldwide, the bank recorded a €513m restructuring charge against income and €532m of synergy-related costs against shareholders' equity.

It recorded a €203m exceptional goodwill write-down for its stake in Rue Impériale, the investment company merging with the private equity group Eurazeo.

Excluding the effect of exceptional costs and goodwill amortisation, Agricole said net profits rose by 28.5 percent to €2.4bn, giving it an annualised return on equity of

10.6 percent. René Carron, chairman, said 2003 was an 'outstanding year' for the group. 'Net banking income came back to a positive trend and the cost of risk returned close to more normal levels,' he said.

Gross operating income in the fourth quarter rose 49 per cent to €1.14bn, boosted by consumer finance operations, the Lyonnais retail banking network and its asset management, insurance and private banking.

■ Agricole is to be fined $13m by the US Federal Reserve and the banking department of New York for breaking banking regulations in New York, according to the Fed, *reports AFX News in New York*.

The move follows accusations that the bank failed to respect an agreement dating back to 2000 with the regulatory authorities for shortfalls in its accounting system and for failing to provide certain documents.

Source: *Financial Times*, 11 March 2004. Reprinted with permission.

---

seem to be a preference for intra-national mergers: in 1995, of 32 bank mergers within the EU, just eight involved cross-border consolidation; in 1997 when the total more than doubled to 67, only seven involved mergers across national boundaries.

It is not entirely clear why this should be the case. Clearly, cross-border mergers in the EU raise issues of culture and language which are largely absent in the USA. The outcry raised against the manner of Marks and Spencer's withdrawal from French retailing in 2001 shows just how different management and worker attitudes to employment protection are across Europe and one can imagine that while there may be advantages of economies of scale and diversification to be had from national mergers, banks may prefer

this route until forced to look across borders. These preferences will be further strengthened if bank clienteles differ between countries. (The German and British attitudes to credit would hardly encourage Anglo-German bank mergers.) Shareholders, too, have to be persuaded of the merits of a merger and if they perceive sharp cultural and institutional differences, even if the perception overstates the reality, this will discourage firms.

It may be that what we are witnessing is something of a 'pecking-order' approach wherein the easiest mergers are carried out first and these are domestic mergers. However, when the degree of domestic concentration begins to raise competition questions (when two or three banks have 30 per cent shares of the market, for example) banks will then be forced to look across national borders to find new partners. There is a little evidence for this in that such cross-border mergers that have occurred have been concentrated in Scandinavia and the Benelux group of countries. Individual country markets here were small and had the highest degrees of concentration by the mid-1990s. Further mergers were not possible without crossing national boundaries. It is interesting too that both groups of countries have a degree of cultural, if not linguistic, homogeneity that is absent across the EU as a whole. The Abbey–Santander and Barclays–ABN-AMRO, referred to earlier, almost certainly grew out of the regulator's refusal to allow further concentration within the domestic banking industry. One thing is for certain and that is that the prospect of economies of scale (especially with the automation of banking services) and the risk-reduction of diversification (greater surely across national boundaries than within them) will continue to push the banking system towards ever greater concentration.

When Barclays plc announced that it was going to close 171 branches on a single day in April 2000, this caused an outcry among customers and consumer pressure groups. However, Barclays was far from alone in its policy of branch closure and may not even have been in the forefront. The NatWest bank reduced branch numbers from over 3,000 in 1988 to about 1,700 in 2000; HSBC reduced the numbers from 2,000 to 1,600 over the same period. The total number of UK branches fell from over 20,000 in 1989 to 17,000 in 1994 and to below 15,000 by 2000.

The reasons for such closures are twofold though both are closely connected with the increasing automation of basic banking services that we referred to above. Firstly, it is now possible for clients to carry out many of their banking operations by telephone and by internet. In April 2000, for example, Barclays was quoted as having 1.2m telephone banking customers and 800,000 'online' accounts. The latter had grown at a staggering rate from just 20,000 a year earlier. In 2007, Lloyds TSB had over 2m online customers, a figure which had grown from zero in 1999. There is therefore some truth in banks' assertion that the decline of branch banking is demand-led, by customer preference.

However, it is interesting to note what is happening in branches that have remained open and in particular in those into which banks have put most investment. This suggests that there may be other advantages – to

banks and their shareholders – and that banks may not be simply following customer preferences. (The fact that some banks offer 'internet tuition' at selected sites itself suggests that they have some interest in 'encouraging' consumer preferences.) The branches into which banks have put most development effort are in major centres of population. No doubt this reflects the familiar banking economies of scale again. But it also means that these branches are open to a large potential market for a whole range of financial products and services. A careful examination of any of these branches confirms that traditional banking functions (deposits and cash withdrawals) occupy a minority of space in large banking halls which were originally designed for a very labour-intensive operation. The reduction in cashiers and counter space has been facilitated by the development of ATMs which will also be found inside the banking hall, offering the full range of services we referred to above. The remaining space, typically half the floor area, will be devoted to the marketing of a range of products and services, some of which (foreign exchange, personal loans, trustee and executorship) are traditional activities, while some (insurance, mortgages, pensions, mutual funds) most decidedly are not but represent the movement towards universal banking that we discussed at the outset.

'People, paper(work) and premises' are expensive. This is especially true for banks where traditionally there has been little scope for employing unskilled labour and where premises have had to be located in prime business sites. Technology has lifted some of this burden. It enables the closure of peripheral sites and the concentration of activity in fewer larger premises. By automating many traditional banking functions it raises productivity (partly by shifting the work of keying instructions onto customers themselves). Fewer, and less skilled, staff are required for these functions while others can be redeployed to the more profitable task of selling (non-bank) financial services and products. The downside of all this is the restricted access to banking services for those who live away from major centres and do not have access to internet facilities through choice or, more usually, for reasons of income and education. This, together with banks' understandable desire to target their products and services at their most affluent customers, has led to public concern that sections of the community (typically the poor and the elderly) are in danger of suffering 'financial exclusion' (see Case study 7, page 612).

Not only is it more convenient in many cases to make payment by direct debit or other electronic means, we have seen that it also is cheaper for everyone. This is sometimes reflected in discounts to people who pay bills by these methods. Those without a bank account are denied these benefits. A more immediately pressing issue has been the plan by UK government to pay social security benefits directly to bank accounts (rather than in cash over a Post Office counter). Notice that the cost savings from replacing the physical handling of paper and coin by automatic/electronic payment have once again proved irresistible (this time to government). This clearly raises the question of how the 'non-banked' public is to receive these payments, as well as a question about the future profitability of smaller Post Offices for which this work was a valuable source of income. In April 2001 the major retail banking groups announced that they would establish a 'basic' bank account, with limited facilities and no direct costs, for anyone who wanted one and that they would arrange for these facilities to be available via Post Offices. In addition, they agreed to pay £180m spread over five years to help set up a 'Universal Bank' to be run by the Post Office. The centrepiece would again be an account with very limited facilities (no borrowing, for example). The numbers of the potentially excluded are not trivial. When these agreements were announced it was estimated that between two and four million people might benefit.

The closure of bank branches has been a trend largely confined to retail banks, which traditionally relied upon branches as the 'gateway' through which customers accessed banking services. It is of little relevance to wholesale banks. A final trend which has affected all banks to some degree has been the increasing development of **off-balance-sheet activities** and, within this broad category, of 'securitization' in particular. 'Off-balance-sheet activity' refers quite simply to any income-generating activity which does not create a corresponding balance sheet entry. It is worth noting immediately that it is only the very distinctive nature of banking business that makes off-balance-sheet activity remotely interesting. Consider, for example, the case of a firm manufacturing washing machines. Its balance sheet shows its assets and liabilities at a particular moment. Its liabilities will be largely determined by its capital structure (bonds, equity and so on) while its assets will consist largely of its premises and other productive equipment. The

number of washing machines that it manufactures in any particular week is quite remote from the balance sheet. Conceivably the output decision could have some effect upon short-term assets ('amounts due') and upon the size of its bank overdraft, but even this supposes quite a large variation in output. The firm might even be able to add or remove new models from its range without having much noticeable effect upon the balance sheet. Traditional banking activity is quite different. Taking a single additional deposit or making a single additional loan changes the balance sheet immediately. The 'inputs' and 'outputs' of banking business are themselves balance sheet items. Hence, the idea that banks might engage in off-balance-sheet activity is a curiosity, something which is untrue for any other type of firm.

Given this definition, it is clear that many of the activities which banks are promoting through their changing use of branches falls into this category. If a bank sells an insurance policy, it earns a commission which appears ultimately in its profit and loss account. There is no change to its balance sheet (though the insurance company has an additional liability). Similarly, if customers buy into a unit trust, the fund management company pays a fee to the bank and takes the additional liability and asset on to its own balance sheet. The guaranteeing (or 'accepting') of commercial bills which used to be the staple activity of British merchant banks is another example. The bank earns a fee in return for the guarantee. The bill, however, remains the liability of its issuer. It only becomes a liability for the bank if some other event happens first (the bankruptcy, or at least the inability to pay, of the firm when the bill falls due for payment). Because something else has to happen first, guaranteeing is sometimes said to create a 'contingent liability', a liability contingent on something else happening. 'Securitization' refers to the creation of a tradable asset out of a non-tradable one. If a bank lends to a firm by buying its bonds, for example, those bonds can subsequently be traded (sold, for example, if the bank needs liquidity). If it lends by granting a conventional loan, that loan remains on its books until repaid by the borrower. It cannot be disposed of to a third party. In recent years, however, banks have found it convenient to set up separate companies ('special purpose vehicles') for the specific purpose of 'buying' the loans from the bank, using bonds which it issues to the general public. On the bank's balance sheet, 'loans' are replaced with 'money', the deposits with which the public bought bonds from the special purpose vehicle.

Clearly, in most cases the rationale for off-balance-sheet activity is that it is more profitable than traditional banking activity. However, as we shall see in Section 24.3, where we discuss securitization in more detail, it can also be driven by regulation. We noticed earlier that banks are required to maintain an 8 per cent ratio of capital to risk-adjusted assets. Commercial loans have a risk weighting of '1' while money ('cash') has a weighting of '0'. Without changing the *size* of the balance sheet, securitization can have a dramatic effect upon the quantity of risk-adjusted assets.

3.3   Building societies in the UK

As we shall see in a moment, the history, function and regulation of building societies distinguishes them quite clearly from banks. They are, however, deposit-taking institutions and since 1989, when M4 replaced M3 as the official measure of broad money in the UK, their deposits have been unambiguously 'money'. Together with UK banks they form what the ECB refers to as the UK's 'Monetary Financial Institutions' (MFIs).

'Unambiguously' is worth stressing. For most of the 1980s, the treatment of building society deposits was something of a problem. Undoubtedly depositors themselves saw the deposits as money. They could go into a building society branch and draw cash on demand. For larger purchases they could obtain, also on demand, a cheque signed by the manager payable to whomsoever they nominated. In the first case, though, it was the cash that was money while in the second case careful examination of the cheque would show that it was drawn on the building society's bank. It was the building society's *bank* deposit that was functioning as money, not a deposit with the society itself. As we shall see in the next section, competition between banks and building societies drove their products closer and closer together during the 1980s. Eventually, the Building Societies Act 1986 removed some of the formal distinctions. Most importantly, it allowed building societies to issue cheque guarantee cards (so their own deposits became instantly acceptable as means of payment), and it provided for societies to 'incorporate' themselves as banks. At the time, building society deposits were included in a measure of 'liquidity', 'PSL2', but not in M3. After the 1986

Act this differential treatment of building society deposits became very difficult to sustain. A change was finally forced by the decision of the Abbey National Building Society, at the time the second largest society, to convert to banking status in 1989. This would have meant an overnight increase in M3 of about 11 per cent. This large break in the series persuaded the Bank of England to discontinue publication of the M3 measure and to treat M4, first published in 1987, as a replacement for PSL2, as the official measure of broad money. (A brief history of UK monetary aggregates is provided in Chapter 12.) Thus, *from a monetary point of view*, the societies have become indistinguishable from banks.

Building societies began in the eighteenth century as friendly or **mutual societies**, often with a local focus, into which members made periodic payments in order to finance the building of houses. Unlike banks, therefore, a society has no shareholders; its members are the 'owners' and they lend to the society by, technically speaking, buying shares, though these shares are, in effect, deposits. In the early days, it was quite common for building societies to be dissolved once their specific house-building programme was completed. Some, however, became 'permanent' societies, adopting a continuous programme of housing construction and finance and it is these that have survived to today.

The history of the societies is important because it explains why, although in many respects it seems natural to treat them as a form of bank, they have been able to behave rather differently from banks and have been subject to different regulatory regimes. Because they were mutual societies, their regulation was for many years the responsibility of the Registrar of Friendly Societies. Because they were not companies their trade association, the Building Societies Association, was able for many years to operate a system of 'recommended' deposit and mortgage (interest) rates without contravening restrictive practices legislation. These were usually below market-clearing rates and thus provided comparatively cheap funds for house purchase but also created queues for mortgages and led to non-price rationing. The interest rate cartel broke up in 1983 following the entry of retail banks into the mortgage market.

Table 3.2 shows the distribution of UK building society assets and liabilities at the beginning of 2004. Comparing Tables 3.1 and 3.2, it is immediately obvious that the building society movement is only a

Table 3.2 UK building societies, assets and liabilities, March 2007 (£m)

Assets		Liabilities	
Notes and coin	395	Retail shares and deposits	198,848
Bank and building society deposits, inc. CDs	20,556	Wholesale deposits and CDs	47,423
Public sector securities	973	Bonds	30,577
Other liquid assets	30,222	Reserves	32,036
Commercial assets	255,129	Other	1,748
Other	3,357		
Total assets	310,632	Total liabilities	310,632

Source: Adapted from www.bankofengland.co.uk, *Bankstats* (table B1.3), Bank of England. Reprinted with permission.

fraction of the size of the banking system. Just like bank deposits, building society deposits are used as means of payment so that building societies must be ready to meet demand for convertibility to cash and for transfer. It will be recalled that banks do this by holding cash and very small balances at the Bank of England. By contrast, building societies rely much more on deposits, but these deposits are held with the banking system rather than with the Bank of England and are generally interest-bearing. In spite of the freedoms conferred under the Building Societies Act 1986, the bulk of assets remain mortgages secured on residential property (about £186bn out of commercial assets of £255bn). Much of the rest is secured on land or other property and only £763m is unsecured lending to members.

Deregulation has had slightly more impact on societies' sources of funds. Liabilities remain overwhelmingly members' (shares and) deposits but some £78bn consist of wholesale funds, if we assume that building society bonds are largely held by other financial institutions.

During the 1980s, building societies found themselves under increasing competitive pressure. There was competition within the industry following the ending of the interest rate cartel in 1983. But there was growing competition too from retail banks. Societies responded with a number of innovations. They introduced new types of deposits which paid premium rates of interest for regular contributions and for minimum balances. They introduced cheque book facilities and automated cash dispensers. Nonetheless, it was felt, firstly by the societies, but eventually by government, that the existing rules, dating from the eighteenth century, put societies at a disadvantage when compared

with banks, and created an artificial segmentation of the loan/deposit market which inhibited competition. For example, the existing rules restricted societies to lending only on houses or similar property. They could not make unsecured loans and thus could not permit overdrafts. This in turn meant that they could not issue cheque guarantee cards (since they would have been breaking the law if they had honoured the cheque of any customer who went overdrawn) and so their cheque book facilities were of limited use. The first change came in 1983 when the Finance Act enabled societies to pay interest gross on CDs and time deposits over £50,000. This, at last, meant societies could attract 'wholesale' deposits from firms, since firms were responsible for paying tax at whatever rate applied to their particular circumstance. Eurobond issues were permitted from 1985.

But the biggest changes came with the Building Societies Act 1986. This broadened the assets in which societies were allowed to invest to include commercial assets and, crucially, allowed them to make unsecured loans, though both were limited to small fractions of total assets. Since unsecured lending, even in small amounts, meant that they could now provide cheque guarantee cards, building societies were able to offer means of payment facilities on an equal footing with banks. In Chapter 24, we shall see that this broadening of the competitive front between banks and building societies had important implications for a variety of financial developments.

The 1986 Act also gave the societies powers to seek 'incorporation', subject to their giving adequate notice of this intention and subject to a vote by their members. Incorporation meant that they would become limited liability joint stock companies with shareholders

Table 3.3 Conversions of building societies to plc ('bank') status

Abbey National BS	incorporated as bank	July 1989
Cheltenham and Gloucester BS	joined Lloyds Bank Group	July 1995
National and Provincial BS	joined Abbey National Bank plc	August 1996
Alliance and Leicester BS	incorporated as bank	April 1997
Halifax BS	incorporated as bank	June 1997
Woolwich BS	incorporated as bank	July 1997
Bristol and West BS	joined Bank of Ireland Group	July 1997
Northern Rock BS	incorporated as a bank	October 1997
Birmingham Midshires BS	joined Halifax Bank plc	April 1999
Bradford & Bingley BS	incorporated as a bank	July 2000

rather than members. It would also mean that an incorporating society would become a bank, subject to banking rather than building society regulations. As we saw above, the Abbey National Building Society was the first to take this step in 1989. Against expectations, there was no immediate rush to follow, but, as Table 3.3 shows, conversions were commonplace from the mid-1990s, giving rise to a new category of UK bank – 'the mortgage bank' – so-called because of the continued importance of mortgage business. The reason usually given for wanting to do so was that incorporation as a public company would enable the 'society' to raise large quantities of capital which would enable them to offer a wider range of services, at more competitive prices. These arguments were not always persuasive to building society members, some of whom protested vigorously by forming pressure groups. However, after the Abbey National flotation, other societies found that promising shares on generous terms to existing members would guarantee that formal votes would always go in favour of incorporation. The rush to incorporate coincided (in 1996–97) with research from a variety of consumer bodies suggesting that retail customers were generally better served by mutual societies than by plcs, receiving marginally higher interest payments on deposits and being charged less on loans. It remains to be seen whether this evidence will slow the rate of transition or perhaps lead to a more vivid demarcation between mutual deposit takers and banks as the former try to exploit this goodwill. The impact of conversion on customer service and other benefits is discussed in various documents available from the Building Societies Association (www.bsa.org.uk/mediacentre/press/).

The 1986 Act placed the regulation of societies in the hands of a newly created Building Societies Commission. Among other things, the Commission was required to ensure that the conduct of a society's business met the intentions of the 1986 Act. In particular, the Commission was required to check that societies observed the restrictions on their sources and uses of funds (liberalized further by a 1997 Act) and that societies were led by fit and proper persons. In principle, the Commission's powers were considerable, allowing it in the extreme case to withdraw a society's authorization to accept deposits. In 2000, the Commission's powers passed to the Financial Services Authority. Details can be found at www.fsa.gov.uk.

3.4   Insurance companies

People take out insurance because they prefer to incur a small, certain loss (the amount of the premium paid to the insurer) in order to be protected against the risk of a much larger, and possibly catastrophic, loss resulting from adverse 'events' such as fire, theft, accident or ill-health. This principle unites all types of insurance contract. The importance of insurance in Britain today can be gauged from the fact that the value of premiums paid to insurance companies in the UK was equal to more than 12 per cent of GDP in 2002.[2] However, there are major distinctions in the kinds of policy offered by insurance companies and in the types of risk covered. The distinction is so sharp that, although some of the larger firms deal in both, many specialize in one or the other. The distinction

---

[2]   Source: Association of British Insurers.

that is usually drawn is between **long-term** or **life insurance**, and **general insurance**. As an indication of the relative significance of the two sectors, we may note that the premium income generated by UK long-term business in 2005 was £100bn while that for general business, at £32.2bn, was less than a third of this amount.[3]

On 1 January 1999, the *Financial Services Authority* (FSA) assumed responsibility for regulating companies whose activities come within the purview of the 1982 Act. The FSA, a quango, which describes itself as 'an independent, non-governmental body',[4] became the single statutory regulator for all financial business with the passing of the Financial Services and Markets Act 2000.

The 1982 Act defines general insurance and divides it into 17 classes, and long-term insurance, divided into seven classes. The former includes accident and damage to property, vehicles, goods in transit, personal liability and so on. Classes of long-term insurance include life and annuity, permanent health, marriage and birth. An additional class of long-term business is pension fund management, which, as we make clear in the next section, is now a more important part of the activities of the long-term insurance sector than specific insurance business itself.

As we said earlier, long-term insurance contracts enable people to insure against such events as death or permanent illness or disablement. For obvious reasons, life (that is, death-) related contracts dominate. These may be of various forms. A person can insure against death within a specified period, the policy paying nothing if the insured survives. This is known as **term insurance**. Alternatively, a *whole of life* policy insures against death at any time. An **endowment** policy pays a capital sum to the insured at a specified time in the future, or on death if earlier. This sum may be a guaranteed absolute amount, in which case the insured has a policy 'without profits', or there may be a guaranteed minimum plus an entitlement to share in the company's annual profits. On this 'with profits' type of policy, the share in the profits accumulates as a series of annual bonuses which are paid, with the guaranteed minimum, on termination of the contract. Increasingly, the proceeds from endowment policies are linked to the value of units in a unit trust which may or may not be run by the insurance company

itself. Only an authorized insurance company is allowed to provide an **annuity**, the payment to an individual of a regular income from a specified date until death in return for a lump sum paid by the individual to the company, usually at the point when he or she retires. As with other financial products, new types of insurance product are continually evolving, so this should not be treated as an exhaustive list.

It should be clear by now that the motivation behind many long-term 'insurance' contracts is essentially a desire to save for the future, either for one's own benefit or for the benefit of dependants. This means, of course, that while the products are distinct by virtue of their insurance element, life insurance contracts are in competition with a whole range of other products as a home for long-term saving.

The nature of these policies determines the risks to which long-term funds are exposed. Actuarial predictions of a country's mortality record are now very reliable and it is unlikely that a sudden change would find insurance companies struggling to meet their obligations on life policies. More probable is that changes in the products offered by competitors might cause an increase in terminations or 'early surrender' of policies. The most serious risk faced by long-term insurance companies, however, is that changes in economic and financial conditions cause the yield on the asset portfolio to fall below expectations. This would be serious for the companies, since investment income amounts to about one-third of total (investment *plus* premium) income, and for investors, who would share in reduced profits. In recent years, yields have been lower than those insurers have grown accustomed to. One reason is that inflation has been lower than it was in the 1970s, 1980s or even the 1990s. A second is that the climb in stock market indices has been reversed. A third reason is that the rate of return on government securities has been low. This is a problem for some savers who had taken out with-profits or unit-linked life policies of a given projected value as a means of repaying their mortgage at some point in the future. It also means that the value of the annuities individuals are now generally being offered when their pension plans mature is much lower than they had hoped for or expected.

Among the classes of business carried out by the general insurance sector, motor insurance is the most

---

3 Source: Association of British Insurers.
4 See the FSA's Information Guide, downloadable from www.fsa.gov.uk.

important, accounting for a third of written premiums in 2005. Property insurance (buildings and contents), which generated more than a quarter of the sector's premium income in the same year, came a close second.[5]

The payment of premiums creates a pool of funds at the companies' disposal. Eventually most or all of it will be used to meet claims. However, provided sufficient funds are available or can be quickly recovered to make claims payouts as they fall due, the remainder can be placed in earning assets by the companies and thereby provide a further source of income. It follows that investment opportunities arise for general as well as long-term insurance companies. However, to say this does not fully capture the importance of investment for the viability of general insurance business. Although premiums covered claims in 2005, this is not always the case. For example, in 2002 the UK motor and property sectors operated at an overall underwriting loss of £0.2bn.[6] In other words, premiums received by companies failed to cover the cost of claims met by them. The ability of companies to satisfy fully their obligations to clients who had incurred insured losses was due to the returns they were able to earn by investing monies paid by these same clients in premiums. In fact, competitive pressures within the general insurance sector sometimes drive premiums down so low in relation to likely claims levels that companies have been known to plan for underwriting losses to be made good by investment income – a practice known as *cashflow underwriting*.

While the investment function is thus no minor matter for general insurers, it is absolutely central to long-term insurers, many of whose products are primarily savings vehicles, as we have already noted. This contrast explains the difference in asset growth between the long-term and general insurance sectors apparent in Table 3.4, which indicates that the funds available for the former to invest were some 12 times larger than those available to the latter in 2006. (In fact, a broadly similar picture emerges from balance sheet data in Table 3.5. Long-term insurance companies had net assets worth £1,118bn at the end of 2005, compared with £122bn for general companies.) Together with pension funds and unit trusts, long-term insurance companies were the major institutional investors in 2006.

We noted earlier that the major legislation affecting insurance companies dates from the 1982 Act. This makes it an offence for anyone to conduct insurance business without authorization and resulted from concern following the collapse of a number of (general) insurance companies in the 1970s. The power of authorization lies with the FSA and is granted to each company with respect to particular classes of insurance business. In addition to providing authorization, the FSA subsequently monitors the performance of companies, particularly with respect to solvency margins, and has the power to intervene in a number of ways. It may require a change in investment strategy, prevent the renewal of existing policies or the issuing of new ones. In the event that a company should fail in spite of this scrutiny, policyholders have some degree of protection under the Policyholders' Protection Act 1975. The 1982 Act also imposes

Table 3.4 UK non-deposit-taking financial institutions – net acquisition of selected assets, 2006 (£m)

	PF	LTI	GI	UT	IT
Short-term assets	10,705	9,480	89	10,772	616
British government securities	9,573	5,466	−3,127	5,693	254
UK company securities	−11,707	−2,944	3,836	1,830	−2,332
Overseas securities	8,452	13,534	2,738	9,092	−510
Other	13,820	11,172	−755	4,521	173
TOTAL	30,843	36,708	2,781	31,908	−1,779

Source: ONS (2007) *Financial Statistics*, March, table 5.3c. Crown copyright material is reproduced with the permission of the Controller of HMSO and the Queen's Printer for Scotland under the Click-Use licence.

---

[5] Source: Association of British Insurers.
[6] ibid.

regulations on advertising and promotion of insurance products and provides for a 'cooling-off' period. The fact that so many insurance products involve a savings element brings them also within the scope of the Financial Services and Markets Act 2000.

3.5 Pension funds

In Section 2.4.3, we discussed pension systems in general terms and outlined the major different forms such systems could take. There, we emphasized the possibility that a system could comprise compulsory or voluntary elements or a mixture of both, the former being based on statute and the latter on private contracts. The UK pension system, at least as it has existed since the post-Second World War period, has contained elements of both types. In this section we examine the way this system has developed and consider the impact the major developments that have occurred have had on the role of pension funds.

The central compulsory element in the UK pension system is the 'first tier' or basic state pension scheme introduced in 1948. This places a statutory obligation to pay National Insurance Contributions (NICs) on employees whose pay exceeds what is termed the 'lower earnings limit'[7] as well as on their employers. Financed in this way by the current working generation's NICs (but also out of general taxation), the state pension is a PAYG, defined benefit[8] scheme, with entitlement to pension dependent on the individual's contribution record. Since inception, the state scheme has been coupled with a succession of means-tested arrangements providing additional types of financial support to the elderly. In the sense that such support is paid for out of taxation, it can be thought of as in many ways the economic equivalent of a compulsory, PAYG pension arrangement.

From 1948 until the 1970s, the UK pensions framework could probably best be described as comprising two co-existing but unrelated systems. For, separate to, and in parallel with, state provision, a system of company occupational pension schemes operated and, in fact, expanded rapidly.[9] Such schemes were **fully funded** and, in the vast majority of cases, they were

defined-benefit arrangements. They were also voluntary, at least on the part of employers, and existed to enable the latter to offer more attractive total remuneration packages to current and prospective employees.

The Social Security Pensions Act 1975 created an economic linkage between these two systems. This statute established the State Earnings-Related Pension Scheme (SERPS). It thereby extended the compulsory element in UK pension provision, since membership of SERPS was made obligatory for employees in designated earnings categories and membership carried an obligation on employees and their employers to pay higher NICs. However, the Act allowed approved company occupational schemes to be 'contracted out' and employees in contracted-out schemes and their employing firms paid NICs at a correspondingly lower rate. Thus the Act introduced a new financial incentive encouraging the creation and continuation of company occupational schemes.

The next major milestone in the development of the current UK pension was the Social Security Act 1986. This piece of legislation significantly altered the nature of the financial incentives created under the 1975 Act. That Act had permitted only defined benefit schemes offering what it defined as a 'guaranteed minimum pension' to be contracted out of SERPS. The 1986 Act allowed defined contribution schemes also to be contracted out and to attract a corresponding NIC rebate. In so doing, it accelerated the trend, already observable in the more difficult labour market conditions that had existed since the mid-1970s, for companies, especially newly established ones, to offer defined contribution rather than defined benefit schemes.

Even more significantly, the 1986 Act allowed employees to opt out of company schemes altogether. This paved the way for the emergence of the *personal pension*, a defined contribution, contractual arrangement made between an individual, employed or self-employed, and an authorized intermediary (generally an insurance company or a bank). Here the former's contributions are invested by the latter to build up a personal fund on the individual's behalf that becomes available for the purchase of a pension annuity when he or she retires. The NIC rebate that personal pensions attracted was set at a higher level than that available to occupational pension schemes. As we shall see, the

---

[7] With the exception of married women, who could opt out until 1978.
[8] 'PAYG', 'defined benefit' and the other pensions terms used in this section are explained above in Section 2.4.3.
[9] The proportion of employees covered by company schemes rose from 28 per cent in 1953 to 53 per cent in 1967 (Dilnot *et al.*, 1994).

expansion of personal pension provision has been perhaps the most notable – some might say, notorious – development in the UK pension field to have occurred since the late 1980s.

Some employers had traditionally made provision for employees to 'top up' the pensions they would receive under their company's occupational scheme with AVCs, *additional voluntary contributions*. An AVC is a money purchase arrangement by which employees can supplement the pension benefits accruing to them under occupational schemes. Since the 1988/89 tax year all occupational schemes have been required to provide facilities for employees to make AVCs. Usually this necessitates a contractual arrangement between the employer and an outside pension provider, an authorized intermediary who receives and invests the additional contributions employees make. The preceding year, 1987, saw a further new development, the introduction of FSAVCs (*free-standing* AVCs). Like company-organized AVCs, these are money purchase arrangements. However, under an FSAVC, the employee enters into a direct contractual arrangement with a pension-providing intermediary: the employer is not involved at all.

A further chapter in the development of Britain's current pension system was marked by the Welfare Reform and Pensions Act 1999, which created the framework for the *stakeholder pension*, a new defined contribution device introduced in the 2001/02 tax year. This Act placed an obligation on employers to provide access to a stakeholder pension scheme for employees who did not qualify for membership of an occupational scheme – for example, because membership of their company's scheme was restricted to certain grades of staff or because no company scheme existed. The Act sets limits to the charges a stakeholder pension scheme can levy on members' funds and facilitates transfer into and out of such schemes. Its underlying aim was to increase the take-up of funded pension provision outside the ambit of the state scheme among groups in society that had been relatively excluded from such provision in the past.

A further point to note is that occupational schemes as well as personal and stakeholder pensions, AVCs and FSAVCs carry tax advantages for the contributing employee. While membership of occupational schemes was compulsory, before 1988, such advantages were probably of little economic significance. However, since that date, employees have had the right to opt out of any pension provision offered by employers, and tax benefits have therefore represented an inducement

for employees to join or stay in company schemes or else to pay into personal pensions. Even more clearly, they are an incentive for employees to take the more active step of making voluntary contributions towards their future pensions, whether AVCs or FSAVCs.

The outline of the evolution of policy we have provided above suggests that the state has exerted an influence in three main ways: firstly, it has increased the legislative pressure on employers to provide funded pension facilities of one kind or another; secondly, it has extended the scope for individuals to enter into independent contractual arrangements with pension providing intermediaries; thirdly, it has widened financial incentives likely to encourage the growth of funded provision.

Obviously, government policy in the area of pensions has been motivated by a desire to enhance the financial security of the elderly, currently and in the future. However, policymakers' concern in the last quarter of the twentieth century to reconcile this goal with the objective of restraining the growth of public expenditure is also evident in the character of successive pieces of legislation. It is clear too that the prevailing ideological climate, with its emphasis on individual choice and its preference for private over state provision, has had a fundamental impact on policy choice.

Stakeholder pensions represent an attempt to reflect all these concerns simultaneously. Moreover, conflicting policy goals and influences came to the fore in the mis-selling scandal that erupted over personal pensions in the mid-1990s and subsequently merged with a number of other incidents which called into question the merits of long-term savings products, as we shall see below.

In the fiscal year 2002/03, 51 per cent of the income of the average British pensioner household came from state pension and other state benefits. Income from occupational pensions accounted for a further 27 per cent. These figures illustrate the continuing importance extending into the twenty-first century of the twin elements of the post-Second World War pensions framework: on the one hand the compulsory, PAYG, basic state pension plus supplementary means-tested state provision and, on the other, the network of funded, employer-organized, occupational schemes.

As we have shown, the UK pensions system has, since the post-war period, evolved in directions that have considerably enhanced the role of pension funds of all kinds. In 1997 the government committed itself to reinforcing this trend when it set a long-term target of 60 per cent as the proportion of overall pension saving to be achieved through private schemes. The sale of 840,000 stakeholder plans in the first 12 months of the existence of stakeholder pensions (the year to April 2002) seemed to be evidence of early success in moving towards this goal.[10] However, both on the stakeholder front and in relation to occupational pensions more generally, the more recent picture has been distinctly less satisfactory as far as the government's self-imposed '60 per cent' pensions target is concerned.

Considering stakeholder pensions first, take-up appears to have stalled since 2002, the Association of British Insurers reporting that total sales of personal pensions, including stakeholder pensions, had dipped below pre-stakeholder days by late 2003. Furthermore, even though nearly two-thirds of even the smallest firms were, by 2003, making some kind of pension provision for their employees, four out of five stakeholder schemes were found to be 'empty shells' – schemes which existed on paper but had no contributing members at all. There are concerns, too, that the level of contributions being paid into stakeholder schemes will prove too low in many cases to assure participants of decent pensions in the future. In this context it is worth noting that only 13 per cent of employers make contributions of their own to the stakeholder schemes they have set up.

In Section 2.4.3 we noted that investment risk in a defined contribution (DC) scheme falls squarely on the employee, whereas in a defined benefit (DB) scheme it is borne by the employer, at least in the first instance. With the end of the long stock market boom and the sharp decline in stock market indices following the advent of the new millennium, investment risk has materialized in no uncertain terms for employers operating DB schemes. Faced with the prospect of having to raise their own contribution levels substantially in order to maintain the actuarial soundness of schemes, many have opted for more radical measures in addition.[11] The most common action taken has been to close schemes to new employees, a development that has been so rapid and far-reaching that by May 2007 the CBI was estimating that only 16 per cent of company schemes were of the DB kind. As regards membership, 34 per cent of employees were covered by a DB

occupational scheme in 1997 but this had fallen to 19 per cent by 2005. Because the alternative for excluded workers is at best membership of DC schemes, which characteristically set lower contribution levels,[12] and because the proportion of excluded workers will continue to grow over time, this is clearly a worrying development for the government with its 60 per cent target.

The opening years of the new century were also marked by some major new initiatives in state pension provision: the introduction of the State Second Pension (S2P) in 2002; the arrival of the Pension Credit in 2003; and the appearance of the Self-Invested Personal Pension (or 'SIPP') in 2006.

S2P, aimed at low and moderate income earners, has replaced SERPS as a contributions-based, government run, supplement to the basic state pension.[13] Although S2P could be regarded as in some senses a competitor to the stakeholder pension, the two are in practice often complementary, many workers choosing to remain 'contracted in' to S2P even while contributing to their stakeholder pensions. In contrast, the Pension Credit is tax-financed and in no way contribution-dependent. Replacing the Minimum Income Guarantee (MIG), it is a means-tested benefit designed to ensure that the level of income of all members of the elderly population is brought up to a defined minimum. A novel feature of the Pension Credit is its *savings credit* component. This rewards moderate levels of prior saving by offering additional benefit to eligible individuals.

Whether it is conviction or the pressure of circumstances that is the driving force behind these measures, their thrust arguably runs counter to the government's stated goal of increasing reliance on private pension provision, though to say this is by no means to question the desirability of the measures in themselves. S2P may prove in the longer run to be more of a substitute for, than a complement to, private provision. The means-tested Pension Credit may act as a disincentive to private saving despite the existence of the savings credit component.

As the name implies, the Self-Invested Personal Pension is not so much a new product as a modification of the rules governing existing personal pensions. Two changes in particular led to SIPPs attracting a lot

---

[10] Pauline Skypala, 'Stakeholder pensions a success say ministers', *Financial Times,* 13 September 2003.

[11] In a few highly publicized cases companies have chosen to disband their DB schemes altogether rather than meet the costs of making good the decline in the value of pension fund assets. We return to this issue below.

[12] A recent survey of small companies still operating DB schemes open to new members suggests that total employee and employer contributions in such schemes average 21 per cent of salary. The equivalent figure for DC schemes is only 8.6 per cent.

[13] Unlike SERPS, S2P extends opportunities to accrue benefits to individuals prevented from making contributions by caring responsibilities, illness or disability.

of attention. The first was a relaxing of the requirement that the retirement fund had to be used to purchase an annuity immediately on retirement. This requirement became increasingly resented as the returns on annuity contracts declined from the early-1990s with the decline in long-term interest rates. Under the rules of a SIPP the purchase of an annuity can be deferred until the age of 75. In the meantime, a fraction of the fund can be withdrawn in the form of income. The new rules also widened the range of assets that could be acquired by the fund. This included property and antiques and works of art, in addition to the financial assets that were traditionally included in a personal pension fund.

We now look more closely at the functioning of pension funds within the UK pension system whose evolution we have traced.

Turning first to occupational pension schemes, we may note that the trustees of any scheme must make two basic organizational choices. Firstly, they must decide who is going to administer the scheme, that is keep the records, collect the contributions, pay the pensions and so on. Either they will opt to keep these tasks under their own direct control, in which case the scheme will be *self-administered*, or they will pass them over to an external body, almost always a long-term insurance company. In that case the scheme is said to be *insurance-administered*. Secondly, the trustees have to decide who is going to manage the assets of the fund and in particular to determine its investment policy. Here again the choice is between managing the fund themselves, that is, operating a *self-invested* scheme, or allowing an insurance company to act as fund manager. An *insured* scheme is one where both administration and fund management is delegated to an insurance company.

Self-administered, self-invested schemes are predominantly large, often with many thousands of members and large enough to enable the economies of scale that would justify internal management to be achieved. In contrast, insured schemes are overwhelmingly small schemes with less than 1,000 members. Hence the role of insurance companies in the management of occupational schemes is a relatively minor one. With the advent of personal pensions, insurance companies have been able to expand their activities in the pensions field, particularly since only authorized insurance companies

are allowed to provide the annuities which personal pension funds will eventually be used to purchase.[14] It is noteworthy that, in 2005, 76 per cent of the total premium income of the UK long-term insurance market was derived from pensions business (occupational and personal).[15]

As we noted in Section 2.4.3 projected rates of return on a pension fund's assets need to be sufficient to ensure that the scheme is at all times fully funded. In the case of defined benefit schemes, the responsibility to make good any shortfall rests in the first instance with the employer. Trustees of such schemes and, in particular, employer representatives among them, will therefore be concerned to ensure that the fund achieves healthy long-term returns. A decline in projected rates of return does not bring with it the same kind of threat of underfunding as a defined contribution scheme. However, it does pose a threat to the value of the pension that currently contributing members will receive. The achievement of healthy long-term returns is therefore just as important an objective for defined contribution schemes. In contrast, the flow of monies into and out of pension funds is, in the short run, regular and highly predictable. It follows that liquidity is not a significant factor in pension fund management.

These twin considerations go a long way towards explaining the composition of the asset portfolios of the pension fund (PF) and long-term insurance (LTI) sectors at the end of 2005 that are set out in Table 3.5. (Recall, as we noted earlier, that nearly three-quarters of the business of the LTIs is in the pensions field.)

In both the PF and the LTI sector, short-term assets amounted to c. 3 per cent and 5 per cent respectively of the total at the end of 2005. This is hardly surprising, for such assets offer liquidity but generally low rates of return to their holders. On the other hand, more than half of the assets of both sectors consisted of company securities. Again this is easily explained given that, in recent decades, high dividend growth and significant capital appreciation have combined to produce high levels of average yields on company stocks around the world. Holdings of overseas securities accounted for more than 17 per cent of LTI assets and 24 per cent of the assets of the PF sector. Once again, the pursuit of higher returns is part of the

---

[14] This is because annuities are regarded as long-term insurance business. In contrast, the management of pension funds is regarded as investment business under current regulations, which banks and building societies as well as insurers are allowed to carry on.
[15] Source: Association of British Insurers.

Table 3.5 UK non-deposit-taking financial institutions – holdings of selected assets, end 2005 (£m)

	PF	LTI	GI	UT	IT
Short-term assets	27,067	57,530	11,771	13,944	0
British government securities	94,329	163,746	19,862	25,216	769
UK company securities	247,264	442,338	20,721	185,784	25,710
Overseas securities					
company	203,562	165,452	12,645	121,500	24,002
government	19,037	16,065	7,341	6,386	168
Unit trust units	103,347	159,343	1,158	0	140
Land, property etc.	31,613	61,037	1,470	0	117
Other	188,736	52,878	46,965	12,122	2,358
TOTAL	914,955	1,118,389	121,933	364,952	53,264

Source: ONS (2004) *Financial Statistics*, January, tables 5.1b, 5.1a, 5.2a, 5.2d, 5.2c. Crown copyright material is reproduced with the permission of the Controller of HMSO and the Queen's Printer for Scotland under the Click-Use licence.

explanation here. However, fund managers have also invested abroad to achieve greater stability in returns through diversification. For while stock market indices in different financial centres tend to move broadly in line with one another, the correlation is less than perfect.[16]

By the opening years of this century, it was widely recognized that long-term contractual saving in the UK, largely the province of life assurance and pension funds, was in serious trouble. At the core of the problem was the failure of many people to make the necessary arrangements to provide themselves with an adequate income in old age. The rule of thumb adopted by the pensions industry is that people should aim for a net pension of approximately two-thirds their net pre-retirement income, though one should note that given the way the UK tax system affects retired people, this would be achieved with a gross pension equal to about one-half of gross earnings. The extent of the long-term savings problem, together with some recommendations for tackling it, were the subject of the Sandler Report in 2002.

Looking at the causes of the problem, we can identify four factors, each of which played a specific role, but we should always remember the background that we explored in Section 2.4.3, where we commented on the tendency of many people to focus on the present at the expense of the future – 'financial myopia'

as we called it – with the result that they would probably undersave.

The first problem originated with the government's decision in 1988 to encourage people to opt out of the State Earnings-Related Pension Scheme (SERPS), and out of employers' schemes if they so wished, and to make payments into a personal pension scheme. This was to be achieved largely by opening up pension provision to a wide range of financial intermediaries. The arguments in favour of increasing private provision were twofold. The first derived from demographic changes. With falling birth rates and increasing longevity, the dependency ratio would rise in the twenty-first century to a point where, it was argued, PAYG schemes would pose an unacceptably high burden on taxpayers. The second was an argument about economic efficiency. The way in which most employers' occupational schemes functioned discouraged worker mobility because it was difficult to transfer pension rights from one firm to another.

The end result of the government's action was an outbreak of high-pressure selling of private pension schemes which persuaded many workers to quit their occupational pensions. For many people this turned out to be a mistake, principally because in an occupational scheme the employer would make a contribution on behalf of each employee. By 1996 it was estimated that some 500,000 people had been sold personal

---

[16] See Section 8.3 for an explanation of why diversification of asset portfolios can reduce risk even where returns are positively correlated, so long as the correlation is not perfect.

pensions which put them in a worse position than if they had remained in their occupational scheme. The then regulatory body, the Securities and Investments Board (SIB), ordered that the victims must be found and compensated. But in February 2001 the Financial Services Authority, the new regulatory body, estimated that only 200,000 had actually received compensation (amounting to £2.2bn). Progress continues but is very slow and it is quite likely that the difficulties in getting compensation have done more to reduce investors' confidence in the financial services industry generally than the original mis-selling.

The trouble that began with PAYG schemes in the 1980s spread to funded schemes at the end of the 1990s. We have seen that the difference between a defined benefit (DB) scheme and a defined contribution (DC) scheme is that in the former the employer is committed to paying the specified benefits whatever that may cost. During the 1990s, with rising stock markets, pension funds often built up a 'surplus' of funds over and above what was likely to be needed to pay the defined benefits in the foreseeable future. In these circumstances some firms gave themselves a 'pensions holiday' by suspending payments into the fund. With the sharp fall in share prices in 2001 and 2002, however, the picture changed dramatically and some firms found that they faced pension funds deficits. This was made worse by a new accounting procedure (FRS17) that required the deficit/surplus to appear on a firm's balance sheet. The result, as we noted above, was that firms began to close their DB schemes to new employees, offering them only DC arrangements. This was bad enough for new employees but what attracted public attention was the decision by a few firms (Rentokil in December 2005 was a recent example) to impose the switch on workers already contributing to a DB scheme. This was widely seen by the general public as a breach of faith (even though it was not actually illegal). Once again, the term 'pension' had got itself attached to some very negative publicity.

The end of the long stock market boom in 2000 lay behind yet another problem: it coincided with what now looks like an era of low inflation with correspondingly low interest rates. The combined result has been that investment funds which had grown at average rates of c. 15 per cent from the mid-1980s suddenly ceased to grow or grew only very slowly. Consequently, many savers who had taken out long-term savings schemes with a view to achieving a target level of wealth by a specified date found that they would be disappointed.

Of course, one might argue that savers who felt disappointed were suffering from 'money illusion'. Their nominal wealth had grown more slowly but their real wealth had benefited from the slow rise in prices.

The problem which could not be cured by removing money illusion arose in those cases where people were saving in order to repay their mortgage loan on a specified date. These 'interest-only' mortgages were designed to be repaid from the proceeds of an endowment life assurance policy. Contributions (fixed for the life of the policy) were set by the insurance company at the beginning of the contract and were set in line with the past experience of nominal investment returns so as to achieve a target value when it terminated on a set date. The way in which many of these endowment policies were structured ('with profits') required the insurer to add a fraction of its investment returns to the value of the policy each year. This was then supplemented by an additional or 'terminal' bonus paid on maturity. This meant that a 25-year endowment policy, maturing in 2002, for example, would have the benefits of many years of good annual bonuses. Nonetheless, terminal bonuses played such a large part in the final payout that a policy maturing in 2002 would have paid only about two-thirds the amount of a similar policy maturing before the crash, in 1999.

The consequence was that even savers with endowment policies nearing maturity in the early twenty-first century suddenly discovered that their fund would not be sufficient to settle their mortgage debt when the obligation fell due. For those savers without the benefit of many years of high returns, the situation was even more bleak. The problems became public when the FSA required life companies to begin sending out warning letters after 2001. Many savers claimed that they had no idea that their endowment policies exposed them to stock market risk. If true, this amounts to another case of mis-selling. But true or false, coming on top of the earlier issues, the 'with-profit endowment' problem further undermined the reputation of the long-term savings industry.

Finally, at least at the time of writing, there was the case of the Equitable Life Assurance Society. Equitable Life was a very old and highly regarded mutual life assurance company. Its products were regarded as some of the best in the business, producing returns which put the company always near the head of the league tables. Over the years it had built up a clientele which was skewed towards the professional classes and many in public life, including members of parliament and the judiciary, owned pension or other long-term savings products with Equitable Life. In his report, which finally appeared in 2004, Lord Penrose dated the origin of Equitable's problems to policies adopted by its management in the 1980s to pay out the maximum bonuses consistent with what were thought at the time to be the minimum safe level of reserves. What first alerted the public to a problem with the society, however, was the outcome of a decision in the 1970s to offer a guaranteed minimum income from annuity policies. This guarantee was given when, as we have seen, nominal returns were good (comfortably above

the guaranteed level) and neither the company nor its clients gave much thought to the possibility that the guarantee would ever be called on. But during the 1990s, with signs that inflation and interest rates were falling around the world, the society had to face the risk that at some time in future the company would not be able to meet the guarantees. Its solution (decided in 1995 but not made public until 1998) was to cut the bonuses that it paid to those savers who had a guaranteed annuity policy so that, although the guaranteed *rate* would be paid, it would be paid on a smaller sum than would be available to those without the guarantee. As a result all clients would get the same returns and Equitable would be safe.

Unfortunately, after a series of legal actions, the House of Lords ruled this practice illegal in 2000. This forced the company to close to new investors, to switch its investment portfolio largely into safe but low-yielding bonds and to impose penalties on investors who decided to terminate their policies early rather than accept the future poor returns. Even these measures were not sufficient to ensure the survival of the society and, in March 2004 when Penrose reported, the outlook was very uncertain.

Given the professional nature of Equitable's client base, it is not surprising that a number of action groups were formed with a view to trying to get compensation for investors. This ensured that the plight of Equitable Life remained in the headlines in the following years. Then, when Lord Penrose's report drew attention to the very poor record of supervision by a succession of regulatory bodies (they had known, he said, about the guarantee problem since 1993 but had done nothing to check on how the society was going to deal with it), savers once again got the message that long-term saving, even with one of the most venerable financial firms in the UK, was a highly risky business.

In the light of all these problems, the UK government introduced the Pensions Act 2004. The Act was particularly concerned with the level of underfunding of occupational pensions revealed after the stock market crash in 2000. Recall that two problems resulted from this. The first was the progressive shift by employers away from defined benefits schemes; the second was the loss of pension entitlements by workers who were unlucky enough to have contributed, often for many years, to a scheme which was underfunded at the time that their firm went bankrupt. The 2004 Act established a pension regulator to review the operation of individual schemes, to root out fraud and

---

BOX 3.4 'Mis-selling' warning hangs over pensions saving plan

By Robert Budden

The blueprint for pensions saving for millions of future employees was unveiled by the government this week.

It is expected to see up to 10m people putting £4bn–£5bn a year into new personal accounts in a move that will help narrow the UK's pension saving gap. The new personal accounts, which go live in 2012, will not be compulsory. But employees who are not already enrolled into a better pension scheme run by their employer will automatically be enrolled into the new vehicles, although they will retain the right to opt out.

But the scheme has already attracted criticism from many, including product providers and MPs who argue that, when combined with the government's complicated system of means-tested benefits, many lower-paid workers risk being little better off from making contributions to the new personal accounts. Frank Field, a former Labour welfare reform minister, warned that the scheme posed 'the biggest risk of the mis-selling of pensions for a quarter of a century'.

Under the proposals announced this week, money paid into a personal account will automatically be channelled into a default fund, likely to be a low-cost fund tracking the stock market. This will also include a 'lifestyling' function, so that this money will be shifted into less volatile investments such as cash or bond funds as the employee approaches retirement.

There will be further fund choices, including most likely funds run by well-known industry figures, although the charges on these funds will almost definitely be higher. Ethical and social funds are also likely to be made available to investors. The government still believes that its centrally-administered model will allow fund charges on its default option to be just 0.3 per cent annually, which would make these funds significantly cheaper than other mainstream pension options. Under the proposals, transfers in and out of the scheme will not be allowed at least up until 2020, when this restriction will be reviewed. Employers will be required to put in a minimum 3 per cent contribution on earnings between £5,000 and £33,000 a year with employees contributing 4 per cent and tax reliefs effectively adding a further 1 per cent benefit.

Source: *Financial Times*, 16 December 2006. Reprinted with permission.

---

maladministration of funds (warning on the degree of underfunding) and simplifying pension fund rules. One problem that preoccupied the regulator through 2007 was how to ensure that workers could be protected in the event of a takeover while the pension scheme was underfunded. The particular difficulty here was how to value the extent of the deficit.

The Pension Protection Fund was established to provide compensation to workers who lose their pension rights when closure of their employing firm results in the winding-up of the firm's occupational scheme. The PPF is financed by a levy on pension funds in general. This obviously carries with it the drawback that pension funds that are struggling to get out of deficit are having to face an additional cost, but the alternative, funding from general taxation, has been rejected. While the PPF may make a contribution to repairing damaged public confidence in the private pensions industry (an issue to which we return later in this section), the levy which supports it could well prove damaging to the financial health of pension funds in general.

Finally, the 2006 White Paper set out plans for a major overhaul of the UK pensions system. Since we are talking about long-term savings some of the changes (regarding contributions, for example) are planned to take place in the next few years. By contrast, some changes to benefits and entitlements will not occur for thirty years or more. The details can be read on the website of the Department for Work and Pensions. But in brief they entail requiring all firms to offer an occupational scheme which meets minimum criteria laid down by the Department for Work and Pensions; requiring all employees to be automatically enrolled in their employer's scheme unless they specifically opt out; making the state pension more generous and restoring the link to changes in earnings and raising the normal retirement age for men and women to 68. Box 3.4 highlights the key proposals; it also mentions a number of reservations which underline the scale of the problem that the new proposals have to overcome.

3.6 Unit trusts

As we said in Chapter 2, unit trusts are examples of 'open-ended' trusts, in the sense that net investment into the trust means that the managers can create more 'units', buy additional assets and thus enlarge the size of the underlying fund.

The first unit trusts appeared in the UK during the 1930s. By the outbreak of war in 1939 there were about 90 trusts managed by 15 companies. The number of trusts (and management companies) grew slowly until the 1960s when it expanded very rapidly, falling back again in the 1970s and taking off again in the 1980s. These growth rates broadly coincided with trends in UK stock prices. In the mid-1980s the value of funds was about £20bn. By 2006 this figure had increased eighteenfold to about £365bn.

The attractions to investors are several. Firstly, a 'small' saver is able to reduce risk by investing quite cheaply in a much wider portfolio of assets than would be the case by buying securities directly. The unit trust company, in other words, is exploiting the market imperfection which is the economy of scale available in securities trading. Secondly, holdings can be liquidated very quickly. In Chapter 17 we note that securities trading in the UK is divided into fortnightly account periods and accounts are settled only after the end of each period. By contrast, the holder of units in a trust can sell the units back to the managers and receive payment, normally within 10 days. Notice that units can only be traded between the investor and the trust manager. There is no secondary market.

Each trust is always the responsibility of two companies. Firstly, there is the company responsible for day-to-day management of the trust (the **trust manager**). This may be a specialist unit trust management company or it may be part of some larger financial grouping. We saw in Section 3.2, for example, that retail banks have their own unit trust management companies. The management company makes the detailed investment decisions, issues certificates of ownership, pays income to investors and so forth.

In addition, each trust has a **trustee**. These are mainly specialist subsidiaries of major banks. The job of the trustee is to see that the fund is managed within the terms of its trustee deed. This deed specifies the objective of the trust and lays down broad conditions governing the management of the funds. The trustee company is acting to some degree as guardian of the investors' interest.

There are, of course, expenses involved in the running of unit trusts: the management company and the trustees are entitled to reward for their services. For the management company, income derives from two sources. Firstly, there is the 'spread', the difference between the *bid* (the trust's buying) and *offer* (the trust's selling) prices. Unit trusts are permitted to operate a spread as wide as 15 per cent of the fund's net asset value. On a central value of £1, for example, the bid price could be as low as 93p while the offer price could be 107p. However, competition between management companies keeps the spread closer to 6–7 per cent (97–103p). In addition, the management company is entitled to charge an annual management fee of 0.5–1 per cent of net asset value. This is normally deducted from the fund's investment income before deciding upon the distribution to be made to unit holders. The trust company receives an annual fee, normally calculated as a very small proportion of the trust's net asset value.

Box 3.5 overleaf shows data for the group of unit trusts managed by Fidelity Investment Services Ltd. The data was taken from the *Financial Times* of 9 June 2007. Reading from the top, it shows the name of the management company and its address and telephone number. It also shows, in the expression '(1200)F', the time of day at which the units are revalued and indicates that the managers will normally deal at 'forward prices' (F), that is to say at the prices which prevail at the *next* valuation after the receipt of buy/sell instructions. The first column gives the abbreviated name of each trust, which tells investors something about the objective of the trust or the geographical area in which it invests. The first column of figures shows the management company's initial charge. The next two columns show the latest bid–offer prices. Notice that there is a price spread only where there is a positive initial charge. The next column shows the change in value of the units since the previous day's valuation. The final column shows the gross yield (the dividend (or coupon) divided by price). As their names suggest, a number of the Fidelity funds listed invest in money market instruments and/or large time deposits. This explains why they have a zero initial charge and why, in the final column, the yields are so similar, being roughly the short-term rate of interest prevailing at the time. The broader-based 'Wealthbuilder' and 'Fidelity Portfolio' invest in a wide range of assets. They have an initial charge of 3.5 per cent and the current yields are very low, suggesting that the investments made by the fund are intended primarily to generate a return through capital gains.

In recent years, many unit trusts have converted to 'OEICs'. OEIC stands for 'open-ended investment company'. This is a variation on the unit trust type of fund management in the sense that it preserves the fundamental feature of unit trusts, namely that they are open-ended. The main difference is that an OEIC is structured as a company, rather than a trust, and

---

BOX 3.5   **FT**

Fidelity Investment Services Ltd (1200)F   **(UK)**

130 Tonbridge Road, Tonbridge TN11 9DZ   Private clients 0800 414161
                                                                Broker dealings 0800 414181

Authorised Inv Funds

Moneybuilder Global	0	183.1xd	183.1	−1.90	0.07
Wealthbuilder	$3^1/_2$	68.39	70.78	−0.74	0.59
Cash Fund	0	100.0xd	100.0	....	5.37
Cash Accum units	0	172.16	172.16	+0.02	5.37
Gross Accum Cash	0	115.95	115.95	+0.01	5.38
Moneybuilder Cash	0	100.0	100.0	....	5.38
Fidelity Portfolio	$3^1/_2$	227.9xd	235.8	−2.50	1.02

Source: *Financial Times*, 9 June 2007. Reprinted with permission.

'units' are replaced by 'shares'. It is doubtful that savers are aware of these differences and many unit trusts have converted to OEICs since 1997 with no impact at all on their savers. The noticeable difference is that the pricing of OEICs allows only one price to be quoted: the buying and selling prices are the same and this simplification for savers is usually given as the main reason for conversion from unit trust to OEIC. Given the single price, it follows that managers cannot draw income from the bid–offer spread and have to take it from the income of the fund. OEICs themselves are not a novelty; they have been the standard form of open-ended mutual fund in continental Europe for many years.

Table 3.5 on page 93 shows just how strongly, in relation to their total investible funds, unit trusts are concentrated in equities. This explains what we said at the beginning of this section, namely that the growth in unit trusts (both asset values and numbers of clients) varies with stock market performance. Thus the creation of new units virtually ceased after the crash of 1987, but began again within a year. Growth in the 1990s averaged about 18 per cent per annum, though this included a year of negative growth in 1994. Much the same happened following the 2000 crash. Sales were static for four years and recovered only when share prices recovered from 2004. This suggests a rather naïve approach on the part of retail investors – tending to buy when prices are high and avoiding the market when prices are low. Total assets at the end of 1995 were £112bn, so Table 3.5 shows that their assets nearly trebled in value in the eleven years to 2006.

One of the reasons for the rapid growth of unit trusts as a form of saving during the 1990s was the encouragement offered to 'small' savers by UK governments. This began with Conservative governments offering savers relief from both income and capital gains tax on equities and unit trusts held in a *Personal Equity Plan*. One such plan could be taken out in each tax year and the amount that could be invested in it was £5,000. The Labour government which took office in 1997 replaced 'PEPs' with 'ISAs' or *Individual Savings Accounts*. These managed to combine increased flexibility with additional complexity, but the principle remained the same: up to a fixed annual amount (£7,000), savers could protect their investments from both income and capital gains tax.

The intermediary role of unit trusts is, strictly speaking, limited to their purchase of newly issued equities (or bonds). This is always the case where tradable assets are concerned. Whether the assets are being bought by an individual or an organization, the only act that transfers funds from a lender to a borrower is the purchase from the borrower of his or her *newly issued* liabilities. All other transactions simply involve the reassignment of previous loans. Unit trusts are important actors in the primary markets but their purchases of newly issued UK company shares (for example) are dwarfed by both their *total* net acquisitions of UK equities (newly issued plus existing) and their total *turnover* (total sales and purchases) of equities. As Table 3.4 (page 88) shows, unit trusts made net purchases of UK equities amounting to about £1.8bn in 2006 against a background (Table 3.6) of their total buying and selling of UK equities amounting to about £200.7bn. By comparing Tables 3.4–3.6 we can see that total trading in securities by unit trusts amounted to nearly £527bn of which some £31.9bn represented net acquisitions while their total asset holdings were £365bn.

We noted in the last chapter that **open-ended funds** are generally more expensive to run than **closed-ended funds**. This is inevitable, since savers' desire for more investment in unit trusts means that managers have to buy additional securities while a desire for units means that funds are withdrawn from the fund and the managers have to respond by selling assets. This is why, in the mid-1990s, unit trust management companies started looking for ways of reducing costs in a sufficiently dramatic way that 'low cost' could be made part of their marketing. It coincided also with a more analytical approach to the assessment of mutual fund performance in the popular financial media. What this analysis showed, again and again, was that most managed funds failed to beat the returns that would have been available to savers if they themselves had simply constructed a miniature portfolio replicating one or other broadly based share index. Holding a replica of the FTSE-100 index (i.e. a portfolio of the largest firms), or the FTSE-350 or the 'All-share', would have given better returns than holding units in many professionally managed funds. This discovery is entirely consistent with the efficient market hypothesis (EMH)

which broadly says that share prices incorporate all relevant information so rapidly that no one has an information advantage which enables them to sniff out bargains. Attempts to do so simply add to costs. Indeed, examining the performance of mutual funds is one common way of testing the EMH and these tests have shown repeatedly that there is rarely any advantage to professional management (see Section 26.4).

When eventually the financial press caught up with this and suggested that investors might do better to 'hold the index', some management companies responded by creating funds which did precisely this. Thus emerged the so-called '**tracker funds**' whose purpose was simply to earn the return that would be earned by a portfolio constructed to replicate a specific index. Such a fund, in theory at least, could not do worse than the index on which it was based and, since performance against the index was a popular measuring rod in the financial media, the managers would be spared the humiliation of failing to beat the index.

Furthermore, there was the advantage that 'tracker' funds would be relatively cheap to run. They could not remove the fundamental disadvantage of open-ended funds, that inflows and outflows required asset purchases and sales, but they did remove any need for expensive research and analysis about which assets to buy and sell. The index dictated what shares should be in the fund and in what proportions: the manager had simply to buy and sell across the whole fund in order to keep its constituents in line with the index. A computer could do it, and in many cases did.

Tracker funds turned out to be one of the most popular innovations of the mutual fund industry

Table 3.6 UK non-deposit-taking financial institutions – turnover of selected securities, 2006 (£m)

	PF	LTI	GI	UT	IT
Listed UK ordinary shares	171,150	172,325	4,035	200,692	21,039
Other listed UK company securities	58,302	91,922	13,589	39,781	700
Overseas ordinary shares	219,285	137,719	1,284	224,549	31,897
Other overseas company securities and government securities	120,043	99,525	23,330	61,499	2,131
Total	568,780	501,491	42,238	526,521	55,767

Source: ONS (2007) *Financial Statistics*, May, table 5.3a. Crown copyright material is reproduced with the permission of the Controller of HMSO and the Queen's Printer for Scotland under the Click-Use licence.

during the 1990s by giving retail investors who wanted a diversified exposure to equity returns a rate of return which matched that of the stock market as a whole at lower cost (and no less success) than had been previously possible, at least from unit trusts. Just how safe it was, of course, depended upon the degree of diversification. Tracking the FTSE-100 index meant holding a portfolio of shares in the one hundred largest UK companies. Conventional wisdom has always suggested that most of the risk-reducing benefits of diversification can be obtained by holding about 20 different assets, *provided that they are genuinely diversified* (see Section 8.3). A potential problem with tracking an index was illustrated in 2000. This was the year of the 'dotcom' boom when the market value of many technology companies gave them a capitalization that put them (temporarily) among the UK's largest one hundred firms. Thus they were included in the FTSE-100 index which became rather heavily skewed towards technology companies and was consequently rather undiversified. Since then, a similar problem has arisen with banks and then oil companies dominating the FTSE-100. Consequently many funds have chosen to track a broader-based index, such as the FTSE-350 or even the All-share.

3.7   Investment trusts

Investment trusts differ from all the other institutions we have discussed in this chapter in a number of significant ways. The chief of these is that while all previous intermediaries are 'open-ended', investment trusts are 'closed'. By open-ended we mean that any number of savers can lend any volume of funds to the intermediary at any time. Any increase in the demand for the liabilities of open-ended intermediaries means that more funds are potentially available to ultimate users.

In the case of investment trusts, however, what savers buy is shares in a trust which is, in effect, a firm whose business it is to own stocks and shares. At any moment, the number of shares in the trust is fixed. Thus new savers can buy shares only from existing shareholders and so when we speak of a flow of funds into investment trusts we must recognize that extra funds do not go into the trust at all. There is no increase in lending by the trust to ultimate lenders. All that happens is that the market price of the shares rises.

The fact that an increase in the demand for an investment trust's shares does not mean that more funds are made available to ultimate borrowers raises the question of whether investment trusts should be considered as intermediaries at all. Intermediation, the transfer of funds between ultimate lenders and ultimate borrowers, requires that two conditions are met. The first is that funds flow from savers into the trust; savers' decisions must make a change to the funds available to the trust. The second is that the trust passes these additional funds to a borrower; in practice, the trust must use the funds to buy liabilities newly issued by borrowers (this is the same condition that we met with unit trusts in the last section). These two conditions *could* in principle be met. It could be the case that the investment trust company makes a new issue of its own equities (or bonds) and uses the additional funds to buy equities (or bonds) *newly issued* by another firm. The point is, however, that this coincidence is far from the norm. Investment trust companies will sometimes make new issues to expand their capital base and they will sometimes buy securities newly issued by borrowers. But most of the time the first link fails in the sense that a decision to switch savings 'into' an investment trust means simply buying its existing shares (no new funds are made available to the trust) while the second link fails because most of the time the IT company itself buys existing securities (no new funds are passed on to borrowers).

Investment trusts' claim to intermediary status rests primarily upon the fact that (like unit trusts) they are active in the primary market. When firms raise new capital, investment trusts are among the institutions who will subscribe. However, while Tables 3.4 and 3.5 show that equity holdings are very important to investment trusts, they also show that the investment trust sector is very small when compared with the other financial institutions.

While 'channelling funds' is the obvious sense in which any institution can claim intermediary status, we should never lose sight of the fact that activity in the secondary market makes a subsidiary but important contribution to the lending/borrowing process. An active secondary market for *existing* securities gives such securities a liquidity which makes them more attractive to investors and thus lowers the dividends that issuers have to pay in order to induce lenders to buy them. The more liquid the market, *ceteris paribus*, the lower the cost of capital to firms.

As we have already said, investment trusts are not trusts at all in the strict sense of the word. They are simply firms whose business happens to be the trading of securities. This is reflected in both the way that investment trust companies are regulated and the way in which their share prices are quoted. Like other publicly quoted firms they are subject to the full range of Companies Acts and to the regulations that the London Stock Exchange imposes upon firms wanting a stock exchange listing. Finally, the Inland Revenue 'approves' investment trusts for purposes of tax treatment (principally their exemption from capital gains tax on their sales of securities).

The history of investment trusts predates that of unit trusts by quite a long way. The first to be established was the Foreign and Colonial Government Trust in 1868. As the name implies, the purpose of this particular trust was to enable UK investors to get access to the returns from overseas government bonds which generally paid higher rates than were available on UK government bonds. In fact, the higher returns available from overseas investment, especially in the period before 1914, was a major driving force behind the early growth of investment trusts and it remains true even today that investment trusts tend to be more outward looking than unit trusts. In spite of this early start, it is clear from our tables that the investment trust sector has grown much more slowly than the unit trust movement, in spite of their cost advantage. The reasons for this are not entirely clear. One reason may be the fact that investment trust share prices need not be a precise reflection of the value of the underlying assets. As we saw in Chapter 2, the value of one's holding in an investment trust company depends immediately upon the demand for its shares and this is only indirectly linked to the value of the underlying assets. In fact, Box 2.4 shows that investment trust shares are often priced at a discount and this may create an unfortunate impression amongst retail investors, though in fact it means that the underlying assets can be purchased more cheaply through an investment trust than if they were bought directly. And what really matters to the investor's return is whether the discount changes. For a constant rate of discount, investment trust shares will move directly with the value of the underlying assets.

The fact that investing in investment trusts involves buying company shares may also have played a part in limiting their retail appeal. The advantage of buying unit trusts is that one deals with the managers directly, by picking up the phone or filling in a coupon in a newspaper. Until recently buying investment trust shares meant dealing through a stockbroker which many savers would have found off-putting. In the last few years, investment trusts have worked hard at marketing their shares to small savers, with television and newspaper campaigns, and now offer their shares directly to the public.

Since investment trusts are simply limited public companies whose job is to hold and trade firm and government securities, it is hardly surprising that their share prices are listed in the same way as those of any other quoted company. In the *Financial Times*, for example, they appear with all other shares, on the 'London Share Service' pages in a category headed 'investment companies'. A minor difference from other share prices is that the 'yield' and 'P/E' columns (see Section 17.5) are replaced, for investment trust shares, by 'NAV', standing for 'net asset value', and 'dis or pm'. NAV shows what the share price should be if it were to match the value of the underlying assets and 'dis/pm' calculates the difference between the actual share price and NAV as a percentage of NAV. From what we have said above, it will be appreciated that most investment trust shares show a negative figure (for discount) in this column.

3.8 Summary

A financial system consists of a set of markets, institutions and their ultimate users. As a result of competition, improving communications technology and a general movement towards deregulation of economic and financial activity, systems are becoming increasingly homogeneous. However, some differences still remain and these are reflected rather more in institutions than in markets.

A common practice is to divide institutions into those that take deposits (often included in official measures of 'money') and those that do not. In the UK, we need further to divide deposit-taking institutions into banks and building societies. In their main activities, there are considerable similarities between retail banks and building societies, though the former have greater freedom in both sources and uses of funds. Partly for this reason, some larger building societies are considering converting to banks and becoming subject to banking rather than building society regulation.

Bank (and building society) assets consist overwhelmingly of non-marketable loans supplemented by a small proportion of short-dated, highly liquid government securities. The bulk of company securities, and of longer-dated government bonds, are held by non-deposit-taking (or 'other') financial institutions. This is because (with the exception of general insurance companies) their liabilities are held largely as long-term savings products by the public who want protection from inflation and a share in the real growth of the economy. For this they are prepared to accept some degree of risk that their savings will fluctuate in value over time.

Key concepts in this chapter

Annuity	Off-balance-sheet activities
Closed-ended fund	Open-ended fund
Endowment	Stocks held
Fully funded	Term insurance
General insurance	Tracker fund
Life insurance	Trust manager
Long-term insurance	Trustee
Mutual society	Turnover
Net acquisitions	Yield

Questions and problems

1 Explain how deposit-taking institutions differ from other financial institutions in their sources and uses of funds.

2 Distinguish between a 'mutual' and a 'joint stock' (plc) enterprise. List some of the advantages of conversion from mutual to plc status.

3 What are the major differences between UK general and long-term insurance companies and why do they exist?

4 Identify the major legislative changes that have had an impact on pension provision in the UK since 1948. Comment on their objectives and major effects.

5 Explain carefully the composition of the asset portfolios of the UK pension fund and long-term insurance sectors by reference to the objectives and problems of pension fund management.

6 Distinguish between a 'funded' and a 'pay-as-you-go' pension scheme. How would you expect the market for ordinary company shares to be affected by a general switch from PAYG to funded schemes?

7 Distinguish between the 'net acquisition of assets', 'turnover in assets' and 'holdings of assets at end of period'. What might you expect about their likely size relative to each other?

8 Why do you think that people tend to buy equity-based investments after prices have started to rise and sell after prices have started to fall? Is this a rational investment strategy?

Further reading

APACS, *Handbook of Payment Statistics*, 2007

Bank of England, 'Risk measurement and capital requirements for banks', *Quarterly Bulletin*, 35, 1995, 177–81

Bank of England, 'The Bank of England Act', *Quarterly Bulletin*, 38, 1998, 93–9

Bank of England, 'Financial market developments', *Quarterly Bulletin* (every issue)

M Buckle and J Thomson, *The UK Financial System* (Manchester: Manchester University Press, 3e, 1998) Ch. 17

B Casu, C Giradone and P Molyneux, *Introduction to Banking* (London: Pearson Education) part I

E P Davis and B Steil, *Institutional Investors* (Cambridge MA: MIT Press, 2001)

Department for Work and Pensions, 'The Pensioners' Income Series', www.dwp.gov.uk

A Dilnot, R Disney, P Johnson and E Whitehouse, *Pension Policy in the UK: An Economic Analysis* (London: The Institute for Fiscal Studies, 1994)

C A E Goodhart, *Money, Information and Uncertainty* (London: Macmillan, 3e, 1999) Ch. 5

P G A Howells, 'UK building societies: The end of mutuality?', *British Economy Survey*, Spring 2000

P G A Howells, 'The FTSE-100: What does it really tell us?', *British Economy Survey*, Autumn 2000

P G A Howells and K Bain, *Financial Markets and Institutions* (London: Pearson Education, 5e, 2007)

London Stock Exchange, *Stock Exchange Quarterly*

London Stock Exchange, *Stock Exchange Quality of Markets Fact Sheet* (quarterly)

Office for National Statistics, *Financial Statistics* (monthly)

Office for National Statistics, *Financial Statistics*, April 2007, table 5.3c (t3.4), tables 5.1a–5.3d

Pensions Regulator, *The Purple Book*, www.pensionprotectionfund.co.uk

M Sullivan, *Understanding Pensions* (London: Routledge, 2004)

Websites

www.abi.org.uk (Association of British Insurers)

www.bankofengland.co.uk, *Bankstats*

www.dwp.gov.uk (Department for Work and Pensions)

www.fsa.gov.uk (Financial Services Authority)

www.londonstockexchange.co.uk

www.pensionadvisoryservice.org.uk

www.pensionprotectionfund.co.uk

www.thepensionservice.gov.uk

Chapter 4 The US financial system

What you will learn in this chapter:

■ The organization of the US banking system

■ The relationship between US bank legislation and the
development of the banking system

■ The reasons for the recent large changes in the structure of the
US banking sector

■ The reasons for the savings and loans crisis of the late 1980s

■ The nature of the US central bank system

■ The nature of non-depository financial institutions in the USA

Introduction

The US financial system is often grouped with that of the UK as a market-based system, indicating that the finance of firms comes largely from the issue of securities, and thus via markets. In fact, in some periods, the net contribution of bond and equity issues to corporate finance has not been particularly high and has certainly been lower than that in the UK. Nonetheless, it remains true that Wall Street (the location of the New York Stock Exchange) is central to the US financial system both psychologically and in terms of its influence on economic policy.

The psychological importance of Wall Street stemmed in part from the role of securities markets in the financing of firms during the period of the USA's most rapid growth; but in part also from the image that the USA had of itself as a young, confident, risk-taking nation in which almost anyone could become rich overnight. The stock market became the focus of one element of the American dream. The sharp price rises on Wall Street in the 1920s and the crash in 1929 are widely accepted as indicators of the economic boom and the subsequent worldwide depression of the 1930s. Commodities markets first developed in the USA, as did trading in futures, financial futures and options. US markets in these instruments remain the world's largest. The 'get rich' aspect of financial markets has remained important, as shown, for instance, by the junk bonds scam of the 1980s (discussed in Box 4.4).

Although the role of securities markets in providing finance to industry has declined, the importance of the stock exchange in the lives of average Americans has increased since the 1970s with the growth of mutual funds and the development of pension funds. This was caused partly by the limitations imposed by law on the US banking system and partly by the increased volatility of inflation and interest rates in the world economy in the 1970s. Banking laws and the attitudes that gave rise to them have thus played an important role in the development of the system as a whole and, like all national financial systems, that of the USA is highly individual. Comparisons can, of course, be drawn and there are ways in which the US system has more in common with that of the UK than with that of, say, Germany. One example of this is the strength of securities houses which concentrate on business lending and investment activity. However, there are

many ways in which the US system is dramatically different from that of the UK.

The importance of the US financial system to economic policy is not recent. For example, it is widely held that the contractionary policies of the US Federal Reserve System in 1928 contributed significantly to the onset of the Great Depression. These contractionary policies were introduced specifically to curb stock market speculation. We have had a recent example of concern regarding the potential of problems in financial markets to spill over to the real economy with the difficulties experienced by banks in the **subprime** section of the housing market. Banks, having lent heavily to borrowers regarded as high-risk, unsurprisingly found that, as interest rates rose, they faced larger than usual defaults on loans. This had a significant impact on the US stock market and fears of consequent falling demand and increasing unemployment influenced the behaviour of the US central bank. This case is dealt with in Section 4.5.

The size of the US economy and the continued dominance of the dollar in international transactions has meant that the US financial system has become central not only to the US economy but also to the global economy. Financial markets in all countries pay great attention to the ups and downs of the Dow Jones Industrial Average index and to the NASDAQ index. In addition, large banks and other financial firms outside the US may have significant exposure to financial risks within the US. Again, the 2007 subprime lending fears provide a good example of this.

Deposit-taking institutions in the USA

The US banking system has a number of characteristics that distinguish it from those of other countries. Firstly, there are a very large number of banking organizations. Although the number of banks has fallen sharply in recent years, particularly through mergers and acquisitions, there remained at the end of August 2007 a total of 7,355 commercial banks, down from 7,769 at the end of 2003. This shows a decline in the rate of reduction of the number of commercial banks from the height of merger activity in the middle 1990s. At the end of 1990 there had been 12,343 commercial banks.

Secondly, until recently, legislation limited the growth of US banks and their ability to expand from their home states to other states within the country. The restriction on expansion within the USA was one of a number of reasons for large banks from the financial centre, New York, choosing, from the 1960s on, to establish branches offshore, and playing a major part in the development of the Eurocurrency markets.

Thirdly, there is a dual system of licensing, with banks being chartered by both the federal government and individual states. Fourthly, for a significant part of the twentieth century, other restrictions on the operation of banks were in force, limiting interest payments on deposits and providing for a strict separation of investment banks from commercial banks.

Finally, a central bank was not established until 1913 – although there had been two much earlier attempts to do so. The central bank that was then established was not a single institution but a system of 12 **Federal Reserve Banks** overseen by a Board in Washington DC.

Most of these characteristics can be explained by two major fears within the USA – the fear of centralized authority and the fear of domination by moneyed interests. These fears reflect the origins of the US nation state – settlement from Europe had been by separate, relatively small groups often fleeing from religious or political domination. The first significant united action by settlers was the struggle against the distant authority of Britain. The two fears combined to produce a determination to prevent the financial system being controlled either by large institutions in the financial centre of New York or by political forces concentrated in Washington. This led to severe geographical restrictions on the development of US banking – banks were not permitted to have branch offices. The result of this was the continued existence of a very large number of banks, most of them small. It was only in the 1970s, and particularly the 1980s and 1990s, that this structure began to change.

The limitations on the development of banks, together with a general distrust in the population of financial institutions, left the system vulnerable to **bank runs** on individual banks. These frequently developed into **multi-bank panics**. Fourteen such panics have been identified in the years between 1800 and 1933, 11 of which led to widespread restriction of convertibility of deposits into currency. This strongly influenced the nature of bank legislation and this, in turn, had a marked impact on the way in which the system developed. Laws passed during the 1930s sought to restrict what was seen as damaging competition

among banks, to prevent firms from engaging in a mixture of banking and non-banking business, and to provide a system of insurance of bank deposits. Ironically, the system that had been developed to limit the number of bank failures and to provide greater security for depositors was held by many to be largely responsible for a new wave of failures in the 1980s and early 1990s.

4.2.1 The classification of US depository institutions

Classification of the US banking system is complicated by a number of the system's features. Firstly, there is the classification of depository institutions into commercial banks, thrifts (saving institutions) and credit unions. Commercial banks are deposit-accepting institutions (depository institutions) which engage in a variety of financial activities. Under the *Banking Act, 1933* (widely known as the **Glass–Steagall Act**), commercial banks were effectively restricted to banking activities. The act prohibited them from originating, trading or holding securities other than those of the federal government, state and local governments. Other securities business was restricted to investment banks, which were non-depository institutions. However, the *Glass–Steagall Act* was repealed in 1999, allowing commercial banks to take on the activities of investment banks.

Thrifts are subdivided into **savings and loan associations** (S&Ls) and **savings banks**. Thrifts have longer-term assets and liabilities than commercial banks. Their assets principally consist of long-term bonds or house mortgages. Until the early 1980s, mortgage advances were required to be fixed-interest loans. Their liabilities are almost exclusively savings and time deposits.

S&Ls are primarily involved in real estate and housing finance. They can be traced back to the early 1830s when they began to be set up as credit cooperatives to provide housing finance and to act as a safe repository for small savers. They became the second largest type of financial institution in the USA, behind only commercial banks, but have declined both in number and asset size following the savings and loans crisis of the 1980s (discussed in Box 4.1). Most S&Ls were organized as mutual associations (owned by their members rather than by stockholders). Indeed, in the majority of states they were required by law to

---

BOX 4.1 The savings and loans crisis of the 1980s and 1990s

The *Banking Act, 1933*, had introduced federal deposit insurance through the FDIC. This was extended to S&Ls by the setting up of the Federal Savings and Loan Insurance Corporation (FSLIC) in 1934. The schemes required the payment by members of flat-rate premiums unrelated to the degree of risk of assets. The Act also prohibited interest payments to owners of FDIC-insured demand deposits and authorized the Federal Reserve System (the Fed) and the FDIC to set limits for rates paid on insured savings deposits of various maturities. This was implemented by the Fed under Regulation Q. Although these interest rate ceilings were not extended to thrifts until 1966, their imposition on banks allowed thrifts also to raise funds at low cost without fear of competition for deposits from the banks. S&Ls flourished during the 1950s and 1960s as housing became a national priority. Mortgage lending tripled in the 1950s and in the 1960s the assets of S&Ls again doubled.

However, commercial banks began to find their way around the limitations through the use of Certificates of Deposit, placing increased pressure on S&Ls. The Fed responded by using powers granted to them in 1966 to allow S&Ls to offer interest rates on deposits half-a-point higher than the limit on banks. But in the 1970s inflation rates became more volatile and the Fed met increased inflationary pressure by tight monetary policy which forced market interest rates well above Regulation Q ceilings. Money market mutual funds developed in the mid-1970s to offer savers higher rates of return, putting both banks and thrifts under severe competitive pressure for deposits.

In 1980, interest rate ceilings were removed, allowing banks and thrifts to compete for deposits, but the problem continued until 1982 when they were allowed to offer an unregulated deposit account directly competitive with the money market mutual funds. But the higher interest rates sharply increased costs and, since S&Ls were still largely invested in much lower yielding fixed rate mortgages, most thrifts lost money. Net worth declined to what would have been crisis levels in the absence of federal deposit insurance.

No action was taken since it was assumed that the problem would disappear when interest rates again fell. Indeed, S&Ls were encouraged to expand and their capital requirements were lowered from 5 to 3 per cent of assets. Informally, the standards were lowered even further by the introduction of less stringent accounting principles and a cut in the number of examiners of thrifts.

Variable rate mortgages were allowed in 1981 but there was considerable consumer resistance to them. Congress expanded the lending activities permitted to thrifts to allow them to diversify their portfolios but this only made things worse as S&Ls sought to return to profit by engaging in very risky activities, including the purchase of junk bonds (see Box 4.4), secure in the knowledge that they were covered by the FSLIC. The number of loan defaults began to rise and S&Ls to fail.

Problems during the period were intensified by poor management of S&Ls and by fraud which was uncovered in many of the loans when institutions were taken over by FSLIC. The resources of FSLIC came under great pressure as it sought to dispose of the assets and liabilities of failed S&Ls. The FSLIC became insolvent and in 1989 its duties were transferred to the new Savings Association Insurance Fund (SAIF) at the FDIC. In 2005, the US Congress passed legislation merging the SAIF with the Bank Insurance Fund (BIF) of the FDIC to create one insurance fund, the Deposit Insurance Fund (DIF).

---

be mutual associations. Their very rapid growth in the nineteenth and early twentieth centuries can be seen as a reflection of the fear of 'moneyed interests' mentioned above. The collapse of house prices in the Great Depression of the early 1930s led to the failure of nearly 2,000 S&Ls (out of a total of just under 13,000) and to two important pieces of legislation – the establishment of the Federal Home Loan Bank system (1932), which provided a central credit facility to lend to troubled institutions, and the introduction of deposit insurance with the establishment of the Federal Savings and Loan Insurance Corporation

(FSLIC) in 1934. This was similar to the Federal Deposit Insurance Corporation (FDIC), established under the *Glass–Steagall Act*, to provide deposit insurance for commercial banks. Problems began to arise, however, in the late 1960s and 1970s.

Savings banks were first set up in the early nineteenth century as mutual philanthropic institutions aimed to encourage the poor to save. They grew rapidly throughout the century, although they remained heavily concentrated in the northeast and middle Atlantic regions of the country. They, too, engaged in mortgage lending while also holding large

Table 4.1 Changes in number of FDIC-insured banks 1984–2007

	Number				Assets ($bn)
	end 1984	end 1994	end 2004	June 2007	June 2007
Commercial banks	14,381	10,452	7,631	7,350	10,411
Savings institutions	3,414	2,152	1,345	1,265	1,850
Credit unions	15,193	11,991	9,209	8,504	766
Total	32,988	24,595	18,185	17,119	13,027

Sources: Federal Deposit Insurance Corporation (FDIC) *Statistics on Banking*, tables 101 and RC; Credit Union National Association (CUNA), annual reports.

quantities of government and corporate bonds. Savings banks have always been safer than other depository institutions. During the Depression only eight of the 598 savings banks failed and they also performed much better than S&Ls during the 1980s crisis. This was partly because they responded more flexibly to the changing economic and financial circumstances than did S&Ls and, from the late 1960s on, began diversifying their assets away from mortgages towards securities. Recently, a number of surviving S&Ls have converted to savings banks to escape the S&L name. Regulatory changes since the Second World War have, however, eroded the boundaries between savings banks and other financial intermediaries. All savings banks are now federally insured and many of the larger banks have shed their mutual status, although a higher proportion of savings banks have remained mutuals than has been the case with S&Ls. Fewer than 40 per cent of thrifts have remained mutual.

Credit unions deal primarily in small, fixed-term, personal loans. Their funds come entirely from persons (and individual deposits are very small). Credit unions too were established as mutuals. Under the *Federal Credit Union Act* their membership was limited to groups having a common bond of occupation or association. They were thus essentially local in nature. Although, unlike commercial banks and other thrifts, they were not legally prohibited from operating across state lines, the common bond requirement restricted the interstate activities of credit unions to a few large institutions serving the armed forces or large multinational corporations. However, in 1982, the regulator of federally chartered credit unions, the National Credit Union Administration (NCUA), ruled that in some cases a single credit union could

serve more than one unrelated group, each of which shared a common bond. Much freer interpretations of the term 'common bond' have followed, resulting in credit union mergers. In 1991, the NCUA also allowed credit unions to share branches, giving them an inexpensive way of expanding geographically. Despite these changes, the credit union sector remains small in relation to other deposit-taking institutions.

Table 4.1 provides a comparison of the numbers of different types of federally insured depository institutions at the end of 1984, 1994 and 2004 and the end of June 2007 and also gives the total assets of the different types of depository institutions at the end of June 2007.

As Table 4.1 shows, at the end of June 2007, credit union assets totalled $766bn compared with $10,411bn for commercial banks and $1,850bn for savings institutions (thrifts). That is, credit union assets were only 7.4 per cent of commercial bank assets. Not only are credit unions much smaller in total than commercial banks and savings institutions but also the average size of credit unions in terms of assets is small in comparison with both banks and savings

MORE FROM THE WEB

If you want to be really up-to-date with the number of US banks, try the FDIC website: www.fdic.gov. On the home page, click on 'Bankers' under quick links by user in the top left-hand corner of the screen. Then, under the heading 'Top Picks', click on 'Institution Directory'. Here you will find up-to-date statistics on FDIC-supervised institutions as well as historical data.

Table 4.2 Distribution of consumer savings[1] ($bn)

	31 December 2006		31 December 2002		
	Outstanding	Mkt share %	Outstanding	Mkt share %	% Change 2002 to 2006
Commercial banks	4,117.2	60.9	3061.1	54.6	34.5
Savings institutions	811.7	12.0	744.9	13.3	9.0
Money mkt mutual funds	1,005.1	14.9	1,106.5	19.7	−9.2
Credit unions	621.1	9.2	500.1	8.9	24.2
US savings securities	202.4	3.0	194.9	3.5	3.8
Total	6,757.5		5,607.5		20.5

[1] From Credit Union Call Reports and Fed Reserve H6 release.

Sources: Credit Union National Association (CUNA), Annual Reports, 2003 p. 9 and 2006 p. 9: http://advice.cuna.org/download/curepd06.pdf; Statistical Abstract of the United States; US Census 2000, table 809; Federal and State-Chartered Credit Unions – Summary.

institutions. The average size of the three types of depository institutions at the end of June 2007 was:

- commercial banks $1.416bn
- savings institutions $1.462bn
- credit unions $90.075m

That is, the asset base of the average credit union is well under one-tenth the size of that of the average commercial bank.

Table 4.2 shows the distribution of consumer savings in the USA at the end of 2002 and 2006. Here we can see that the main change over the four-year period was the steady increase in market share of the commercial banks at the expense of the **money market mutual funds** and, to a lesser extent, the savings institutions. The fall in market share of the money market mutual funds largely reflects the relatively poor performance of the stock market in the early years of the century. Indeed, the market share of consumer savings of these funds had fallen as low as 13.7 per cent by the end of 2005 before recovering a little in 2006. There is no indication in these figures of a significant advance for credit unions.

Secondly, there is the dual nature of the chartering system with financial institutions being granted licences (charters) to operate either by individual states (**state-chartered banks, state-chartered savings institutions**) or by an agency of the federal government (**nationally chartered banks, nationally chartered savings institutions**). This had its origin in the strong desire for local independence so important in the development of the US governmental system. Still today, state financial authorities continue to encourage new banks to take out state charters and existing financial institutions to convert to a state charter. They claim greater knowledge of local conditions, closer geographical proximity to their primary regulator and hence better communication with regulators. They might also claim lower fees and more favourable local banking regulations. This makes evident a possible danger of a dual regulation system – the possibility that one of the chartering agencies will have weaker regulations or will enforce them less well, allowing banks to join the weaker agency, lowering the overall effectiveness of control. In the US system it has been argued that federal banking authorities are less strict in the supervision of financial institutions than are many state bank regulators.

In the past, states used their power to charter banks to restrict the ability of banks to open branches

MORE FROM THE WEB

For an example of an attempt to persuade financial institutions to take out a state charter, see the website of California's DFI, the Department of Financial Institutions:

http://www.dfi.ca.gov/cacharter/advantages.asp

For the argument in favour of the dual charter system see the website of the Wyoming Department of Audit:

http://audit.state.wy.us/banking/banking/Benefits_of_charter_choice.pdf

even within their own states and virtually to prevent cross-border activities of banks by not allowing those chartered in other states to open within their borders. **National banks** were prevented from opening branches until the *McFadden–Pepper Act* of 1927 when they became subject to the banking restrictions that applied to state-chartered banks in the state in which they were operating.

At the end of June 2007, there were 1,677 nationally chartered (22.8 per cent of the total) and 5,673 state chartered commercial banks. A much higher proportion (59.8 per cent) of saving institutions have national charters – at the end of June 2007, there were 756 nationally chartered and 509 state-chartered savings institutions. Although it has often been predicted that the proportion of state charters would steadily fall, the movement has been in the opposite direction in recent years with the number of national charters of commercial banks falling from 25.9 per cent since the end of 2003. However, a much higher proportion of larger banks are nationally chartered.

A third distinction arises because of the deposit insurance provisions of banking law mentioned above. Although the first insurance fund to protect depositors was set up by New York State as early as 1829, the present, nationwide system of deposit insurance was established by the *Glass–Steagall Act* (*Banking Act, 1933*). This, in reaction to three banking panics between 1930 and 1933, set up the Federal Deposit Insurance Corporation (FDIC) to implement the federal insurance of bank deposits. Participation in the scheme was mandatory for all Federal Reserve member banks. Other banks could participate if approved by the FDIC. A very high percentage of banks currently participate in the scheme although there remain a few uninsured banks.

To be approved by the FDIC, banks must follow specified liquidity and reserve requirements. The FDIC then classifies member banks according to their risk-based capital ratio. If this ratio falls below 6 per cent, the bank is said to be significantly undercapitalized, the FDIC can change the management of the bank and force it to take other corrective action. If the ratio falls below 2 per cent, the bank is declared insolvent. The insurance scheme covers all bank deposits with member banks up to a current limit of $100,000. It does not cover investment products sold by member banks. Since 1989, the FDIC has also insured thrifts (see Box 4.1).

Deposits with credit unions are insured by the National Credit Union Share Insurance Fund (NCUSIF) which is managed by the National Credit Union Administration, another agency of the Federal Government. Again, there are some small credit unions that are not part of this deposit insurance scheme.

A fourth distinction is that between independent banks and banking organizations or **bank holding companies** (BHCs) – companies that have controlling interests (i.e. directly controlling more than 5 per cent of voting shares) in one or more US banks. The ability to form a bank holding company has existed for more than a century but it became a popular form of organization only after the Second World War. Forming a bank holding company provided a way around some of the restrictions imposed on banks by legislation. This was particularly true of restrictions on the formation of bank branches both within and between states since a bank holding company could form separate banking subsidiaries in other parts of its home state or in other states. Up until 1956, bank holding companies could also have controlling interests in companies engaged in activities other than banking. This led to fears that bank assets would be used to finance the losses of non-banking subsidiaries, increasing the risk attached to banks. Thus, the *Bank Holding Company Act, 1956*, prevented multi-bank holding companies from engaging in non-banking activities that were not, in the judgement of the Federal Reserve, closely related to banking. Multi-bank holding companies were also limited to owning banking subsidiaries in their home states, unless other states expressly permitted their entry. Since no state permitted such entry prior to 1975, the 1956 Act ruled out the possibility of multi-bank holding companies engaging in interstate banking. In 1970 the law was extended to cover the activities of one-bank holding companies. We discuss recent changes to the *Bank Holding Company Act* in Section 4.2.2.

Fifthly, there is the relationship between banks and the **Federal Reserve System** (widely known as the Fed). Under the *Federal Reserve Act, 1913*, all nationally chartered banks were required to become members of the Federal Reserve but membership was optional for state-chartered banks. Membership gave access to Federal Reserve services but imposed obligations such as reserve requirements designed to guarantee the liquidity of banks. The *Depository Institutions and Monetary Control Act, 1980*, extended the Fed's benefits and obligations to all depository institutions but state banks may still be classified as member or non-member banks of the Federal Reserve System.

As at the end of June 2007, only 15.6 per cent of state-chartered commercial banks were Fed members (883 out of 5,673).

Membership or not of the Fed also determines which of the three institutions responsible for the supervision of commercial banks supervises state-chartered commercial banks. All nationally chartered banks (1,677 at the end of June 2007) are supervised by the Office of the Comptroller of the Currency (OCC), an independent bureau of the Department of the Treasury established in 1863 specifically to supervise banks chartered by the Federal government. State-chartered banks that are members of the Federal Reserve (883 at the end of June 2007) are supervised by the Fed itself. The state-chartered banks that are not members of the Federal Reserve are supervised by the FDIC.

A final distinction is made in official banking statistics between large and small commercial banks. Large banks are currently defined as those that have consolidated assets of $300 million or more. At 30 June 2007 there were 1,686 such banks, ranging from the Bank of America with consolidated assets of $1,252,402m to the Heritage Bank of Nevada with consolidated assets of $300m.

4.2.2 Changes in the structure of depository institutions

As Table 4.1 shows, between the end of 1984 and the end of June 2007, the total number of FDIC-insured depository institutions (commercial banks and thrifts) fell by over 50 per cent to 8,615. The number of credit unions also declined by 44 per cent in this period.

The numbers of savings institutions (down 63 per cent) declined more rapidly than those of commercial banks (down 49 per cent) between 1984 and 2007.

This partly reflected the number of failed savings and loan associations in the 1980s and 1990s (discussed in Box 4.1). In addition, there was a considerable shift away from independent banks to bank holding companies which now hold over 97 per cent of the total assets of the banking system.

Amel (1996) identifies five reasons for the considerable structural changes within depository institutions:

■ mergers and acquisitions;

■ legislative changes affecting interstate expansion;

■ legislative changes affecting expansion by branching;

■ changes in credit union membership regulations;

■ failures of depository institutions.

Merger activity among healthy banks rose to record levels during the 1980s as banks sought to reduce costs, partly as a result of increased competition from non-depository institutions. This was spurred by technological change which broadened access to the commercial paper market and reduced the role of commercial banks in lending to large corporations. Technological change also probably reduced costs for large firms relative to small firms. From an average of about 200 in the years between 1970 and 1980, the number of bank acquisitions jumped to a total of nearly 8,000 between 1980 and 1998. Whereas acquisitions in the 1970s were principally of small banks, banks merged or taken over in the 1980s included larger institutions. The mergers that took place between 1980 and 1998 involved $2,400bn in acquired assets – equal to 55 per cent of all banking assets in existence in 1980. Some of the mergers that took place, particularly between 1995 and 1998, were among the largest in US banking history. Table 4.3 shows a breakdown

Table 4.3 Bank mergers and failures in USA, 1980–98

Period	Number of mergers	Assets acquired ($bn)	Large mergers [1]	Number of failures
1980–84	1,838	204.989	15	172
1985–89	2,515	415.914	56	858
1990–94	1,993	574.111	76	412
1995–98	1,639	1,249.507	101	15
Total	7,985	2,444.522	248	1,457

[1] Mergers involving more than $1bn of assets are classified as large.

Source: S.A. Rhoades (2000). Reprinted with permission.

of the number and size of mergers in sub-periods between 1980 and 1998 and compares the number of acquisitions with the number of bank failures in the same period. It can be seen from the table that the number of mergers reached a peak during the mid- to late 1980s, a period when industry profit rates and share prices were very low. Rhoades (2000, p. 31) suggests that this is a little surprising because mergers are thought to be more likely during periods of high share prices and profits. However, as Table 4.3 shows, the mid- to late 1980s was also a period of many bank failures and there may have been good buying opportunities for banks that were performing relatively well. In terms of assets acquired, the peak period was in the second half of the 1990s.

Bank mergers and acquisitions have continued in recent years although at a slower rate than in the 1980s and 1990s. In 2006, there were 255 announced mergers and acquisitions among banks and 46 among thrifts.

The large decrease in the number of US banks led to a considerable increase in the nationwide concentration of bank deposits in the largest banks. This has continued. By the end of 2006, the ten largest banks held 51.7 per cent of banking industry assets and the largest 100 banks 78.5 per cent of total assets. The 50 largest bank holding companies held 76 per cent of all bank holding company assets.

It is noteworthy that despite the reduction in the number of banks and the explosion in the number of ATMs during the same period, there were continuing increases in the number of banking offices and in the number of cheques cleared. At the end of 1990, the 12,329 commercial banks had a total of 62,346 offices. By the end of 2006, the 7,479 commercial banks had 81,329 offices. This growth in the number of banking offices suggests that the restrictions on the development of branch networks had in the past limited the number of banking offices. It further suggests that local markets continue to be relevant geographic markets and that ATMs and other forms of retail electronic banking are not yet substitutes for banking offices although that may still happen in the future.

A major element in the increased number of acquisitions was the changed attitude of the US government and of federal agencies towards mergers in the finance industry. Under US law, any bank wishing to acquire another bank must obtain approval from the appropriate federal bank regulator and from the Department of Justice, which is the primary authority for administering US competition laws. From 1980 onwards, the administration of President Reagan spoke out strongly in favour of bank mergers in general and found few that it believed should be challenged.

These changed attitudes were also reflected in legislation and in the interpretation of legislation. Many individual states liberalized their banking laws to allow greater geographic expansion within their borders and interstate banking began to get under way as an increasing number of states passed laws allowing entry by banks from some or all other states. The first step towards allowing out-of-state bank holding companies to own banks was taken by Maine in 1975, although this only applied to banks from other states which granted similar rights to Maine bank holding companies. By 1983, however, all of the New England states had enacted similar reciprocal laws and by the end of 1994 every state but Hawaii had introduced laws allowing some degree of interstate banking. On 29 September 1995, bank holding companies were given the right to purchase banks throughout the USA for the first time since the passage of the *Bank Holding Company Act, 1956*. The *Riegle–Neal Interstate Banking* and *Branching Efficiency Act, 1994*, which permitted the expansion also from 30 September 1997, allowed banks to branch across state lines. This overrode all remaining restrictions on bank holding company expansion, including the state laws in Hawaii.

Legal interpretations by federal agencies led to the reduction of restrictions on state-chartered banks. In many states, the laws restricting intra-state branching had not applied to thrift institutions. The Office of the Comptroller of the Currency (OCC) argued that national banks were in competition with state-chartered thrifts and thus ruled that national banks could branch to the same extent as thrifts. This would have put state-chartered banking organizations at a disadvantage relative to national banks, and states responded by relaxing their restrictions on intra-state branching by state-chartered banks.

The OCC also took advantage of a long-standing rule which allowed national banks to move their head offices up to 30 miles and retain the previous head offices as branches. In 1985, the OCC ruled that a national bank that had an office within 30 miles of a state line could make that its head office and then branch into the adjacent state. The ruling had little effect until 1994 when it began to be used by bank holding companies for branching across state lines against state laws. A few bank holding companies merged banks in more than two states by repeatedly moving their head offices near a state border, then across the border, then across the new 'home state' to within 30 miles of another state border and so on. This practice encouraged some states to allow interstate branching by state banks before the 1997 date set by the *Riegle–Neal Act* so that state-chartered banks were not at a disadvantage to national banks that branched interstate. Both the OCC rulings mentioned here survived a number of court challenges.

Federal agency interpretation was also important in breaking down the separation of securities and banking business. The *Banking Act of 1933* (Glass–Steagall) had allowed banks to carry out securities business through separate subsidiaries provided they were not engaged principally in such non-banking activities. From the early 1980s on, the Fed and the OCC began to interpret this provision more liberally, allowing banks to expand in a small way into new markets – first commercial paper, then mortgage-backed bonds, corporate debt and equities. In 1982, the OCC authorized several national banks to conduct discount brokerage businesses through subsidiaries and in 1983 the Fed permitted the then second largest US bank holding company to acquire the largest US discount brokerage company. In 1986, the Fed ruled that a bank holding company subsidiary, until then doing only a discount brokerage business, could provide customers with investment advice. The OCC then authorized brokerage subsidiaries of national banks to provide investment advice. After 1986, some bank holding companies were able to extend their underwriting activities considerably.

The final factor in the consolidation of US depository institutions was the large number of failures in depository institutions in the 1980s and early 1990s. Between 1984 and 1994, 1,276 banks, 1,129 thrifts (predominantly S&Ls) and 987 credit unions failed. The crisis had an impact on interstate expansion by thrift institutions as the federal regulators sought to sell the failing firms at least cost to the thrift deposit insurance fund. In 1986, the Federal Home Loan Bank Board proposed that buyers of failing thrift institutions be allowed to branch into any three states of their choice. In 1990, a federal appeals court upheld the right of the organization set up specially to dispose of failing thrifts[1] to allow purchasing banks to convert failed thrifts into branches, even if this violated state branching laws. In May 1992, the Office of Thrift Supervision, the successor agency to the Federal Home Loan Bank Board, acted to allow nationwide branching by all thrift institutions.

In November 1999, the *Gramm–Leach–Bliley Financial Services Modernization Act* (GLBA) was passed. This repealed the *Glass–Steagall Act* of 1933 and greatly amended the *Bank Holding Company Act* of 1956. It allowed bank holding companies to become a new entity called a **financial holding company**, which may make minority or controlling investments in any company, including non-bank financial companies such as securities and insurance firms. Some restrictions still remain as banks may not 'routinely manage or operate' their portfolio companies. This made it possible for bank holding companies to have a much freer hand in merchant banking and generated a number of cross-industry mergers. By the end of 2006, 643 (599 domestic, 44 foreign) bank holding companies had qualified as financial holding companies.

The US banking system has changed rapidly in a short time.

4.3 The Federal Reserve System

The Federal Reserve System (the Fed) was created by the *Federal Reserve Act, 1913*. Unlike most central banks in Europe, the Fed had not evolved into a central bank from an ordinary bank of discount, deposit and note issue. The Fed was a compromise between two central banking traditions – that of the corporate central bank, chartered by the state but owned wholly or in great part by private investors, and that of having the government's fiscal authority (the US Treasury) act also as the central bank. The first was tried with the First Bank of the United States (1791–1811) and the Second Bank of the United States (1816–36) but both were strongly opposed on the grounds that a large and privileged corporation with a monopoly of the federal government's banking business was incompatible with America's democratic ideals. Neither charter was renewed. In 1840–41 and from 1846 to 1914, the federal government acted as its own banker, establishing a number of sub-treasuries in

---

[1] The Resolution Trust Corporation (RTC).

major cities. Treasury officials gradually realized that funds might be added to or withdrawn from the private sector on a discretionary basis to prevent financial panics and as an element of macroeconomic policy. However, this led to a widespread fear of political control of money and finance, particularly that the Treasury would have a long-run bias towards 'easy money' and inflation and that it would favour some financial, geographic and economic interests over others. A financial panic in 1907 led to the setting up of a commission of enquiry and its report led to the *Federal Reserve Act, 1913*.

This gave both bankers and the Treasury a voice in central bank policy formulation but aimed to prevent control of policy by either New York bankers or Washington politicians. The system consists of 12 regional Federal Reserve Banks, each having authority in a specific geographical area, and a coordinating Federal Reserve Board in Washington DC. The capital stock of each of the regional Reserve Banks was subscribed by the member banks in its district. Member banks received a fixed dividend on their capital contribution with any profits in excess of these dividends going to the Treasury. They also received the right to participate in electing six of the nine directors of their Federal Reserve Bank. The other three directors of each Bank were appointed by the Federal Reserve Board in Washington. The regional Reserve Banks were given a monopoly (originally only partial) of the nation's note issue, became fiscal agents of the government, banks of rediscount and reserve for member banks, and lenders of last resort in their districts.

MORE FROM THE WEB

The websites of the 12 regional Federal Reserve Banks provide a great deal of information and interest. Go to www.federalreserveonline.org and you will find links to an explanation of the Federal Reserve System and links to all 12 regional reserve banks. If you would like to play some games, try Boston (http://www.bos.frb.org) – click on 'Consumer Information' and then 'Personal Financial Education'. Several other regional Reserve Bank sites have educational resources as does the Fed itself (http://www.federalreserve.gov) – click on 'Consumer Information' along the top of the home page. The Fed also has a website dedicated to education, http://www.federalreserveeducation.org/Fed101/.

Each Bank set its own discount rate and engaged in its own open market operations. It was hoped that this decentralized structure would ensure a sufficient supply of credit in each region.

Member banks held legally prescribed reserves as deposits in their Reserve Banks and in return were entitled to rediscount their eligible commercial paper at the Banks when in need of temporary liquidity. They were also able to use the Fed clearing facilities including electronic funds transfers and the currency and information services of the Banks. The original Federal Reserve Board comprised five members appointed to staggered 10-year terms by the US President, and the Secretary of the Treasury and the Comptroller of the Currency as *ex-officio* members. The Fed was intended to be independent of:

(a) private financial business interests;

(b) duly constituted government authorities (executive and legislature); and

(c) partisan political interests.

The job of the Federal Reserve Board was to oversee and supervise the operations of the Reserve Banks, coordinate their activities, handle the system's relations with the federal government, bring about a uniform banking and monetary policy in the USA, and participate in the regulation and supervision of the banking system. It was given little authority to initiate policies. Its late appearance meant that the Fed had to share regulatory and supervisory duties with already established federal agencies and state banking authorities. Under the present division of responsibilities, the Fed oversees bank holding companies, foreign banks and state-chartered banks which belong to the Federal Reserve System. The FDIC monitors other state banks at the federal level and runs the fund guaranteeing depositors in the event of failure.

The Office of the Comptroller of the Currency (OCC) oversees nationally chartered banks while the Office of Thrift Supervision oversees S&L institutions. (See Box 4.2 for a summary of the supervisory authorities.)

The Fed's responsibility for all bank holding companies has meant that, as bank holding companies have become more popular, it has come to be the primary federal overseer of banks, now holding about 90 per cent of the nation's deposits.

It is widely held that the Fed performed badly in the Depression. Friedman and Schwartz (1963), for

---

BOX 4.2 US banks supervisory authorities

Board of Governors of the Federal Reserve System (FRB)

The US central bank. It supervises those state-chartered banks that are members of the Federal Reserve System as well as bank holding companies and non-bank subsidiaries owned or controlled by bank holding companies. Non-bank subsidiaries of holding companies include institutions such as mortgage banking companies, finance companies, securities brokers and dealers, investment or merchant banks, and trust companies. The FRB also has overall responsibility for all foreign banks operating in the USA but directly regulates only the agencies and branches of those foreign banks with state licences. Finally, the FRB also licenses and supervises some special purpose institutions, known as Edge or Agreement corporations, which are generally authorized to finance international transactions.

Federal Deposit Insurance Corporation (FDIC)

An independent agency that supervises those state-chartered banks which are not members of the Federal Reserve System as well as insuring the deposits of banks and thrifts through the Deposit Insurance Fund (DIF), the result of the recent merging of the Bank Insurance Fund (BIF) and the Savings Association Insurance Fund (SAIF). The FDIC also regulates the small number of branches of foreign banks that are permitted to accept deposits.

Office of the Comptroller of the Currency (OCC)

An independent bureau of the Department of the Treasury, the OCC was established in 1863 to supervise all banks chartered by the Federal government. These banks all have the word 'national' in their names or carry the abbreviations 'NA' or 'NS&T'). The OCC also regulates the agencies and branches of foreign banks that have a federal licence (these cannot be identified as having a federal licence from their names).

Office of Thrift Supervision (OTS)

The primary regulator of all Savings and Loan Associations (S&Ls), whether federally chartered or state chartered. The OTS was established as a bureau of the Department of the Treasury on 9 August 1989.

National Credit Union Administration (NCUA)

Supervises all credit unions and insures credit union deposits.

Federal Financial Institutions Examinations Council (FFIEC)

Established on 10 March 1979, the FFIEC is a formal interagency body empowered to prescribe uniform principles, standards and report forms for the federal examination of financial institutions by the FRB, the FDIC, the NCUA, the OCC and the OTS and to make recommendations to promote uniformity in the supervision of financial institutions.

---

example, blame it for not suspending convertibility until it was too late. Part of the blame was placed on the decentralized structure of the system since during the Depression serious disagreements had arisen over monetary policy both among the Federal Reserve Banks and between the Banks and the Board. The Federal Reserve Bank of New York and, somewhat later, the Board, favoured policies to stimulate the economy, but several other regional banks had sufficient power to resist such policies.

In the *Glass–Steagall Act* of 1933 but particularly in the *Banking Act* of 1935, Congress moved to centralize authority in the renamed Board of Governors of the Federal Reserve System, led by a Chairman with enhanced powers. All seven members of the new Board were directly appointed by the President with the advice and consent of the Senate. The Federal Open Market Committee (FOMC) was set up and the Board was given the authority to adjust reserve requirements of its member banks. The FOMC comprised the seven members of the Board of Governors, the president of the Federal Reserve Board of New York and four other Reserve Bank presidents, serving on a rotating basis. This gave the Board members a permanent majority on the Committee and ensured a unified monetary policy.

The form of the Federal Reserve System established by the 1935 Act remains in place today. As the Bank of England did until its reform in 1997, the US central bank carries out all possible functions of a central bank, being:

- the bank to the banking system;
- the bank to the US government;
- the body responsible for monetary policy;
- the operator of the payments system;
- a major part of the system of supervision and regulation of depository institutions.

BOX 4.3 The functions of the 12 district Federal Reserve Banks

Although monetary policy has, since 1935, been centralized and rests with the Board of Governors of the Federal Reserve System, the 12 district Federal Reserve Banks continue to play a number of important roles.

- They provide 5 of the 12 members of the Federal Open Market Committee (FOMC) and have the specific task of helping the Committee stay in touch with the economic conditions in all parts of the country.

- They supervise banks and bank and financial holding companies, helping to maintain the stability of the financial system.

- They provide financial services to depository institutions.

- They market and redeem government securities and savings bonds and conduct nationwide auctions of Treasury securities as well as maintaining the Treasury's funds account.

- They provide payments services – the safe and efficient transfer of funds and securities throughout the financial system.

- They distribute coins and currency.

- They are heavily involved in research and have an educational role.

- The Federal Reserve Bank of New York carries out open market operations and intervenes in foreign exchange markets on behalf of the Board of Governors.

It also has a responsibility for the protection of consumers' rights in dealing with banks and for promoting community development and reinvestment.

In the 1935 reforms, the regional Reserve Banks lost their power to determine interest rates but they continue to have many functions. The modern role of the 12 regional Reserve Banks is set out in Box 4.3.

The Chairman of the Board of the Federal Reserve is now widely regarded as one of the most powerful economic policymakers in the world. Nonetheless, a potent distrust of the Fed remains in American society. This is strongly reflected in Greider (1987) who sees the Fed as a non-elected body with an anti-inflationary bias that restrains economic growth in order to preserve the value of financial assets, most of which are owned by wealthy people.

4.4 Non-depository institutions in the USA

Non-depository institutions in the USA consist of securities firms, insurance companies, mutual funds, pension funds and finance companies.

4.4.1 Securities firms

Securities firms consist of securities brokers and dealers, investment banks and advisers, and stock exchanges. There are over 5,000 firms in this sector of the financial industry. At the end of 2006, the assets of securities firms stood at $2,741.7bn, an increase of 28.9 per cent

over the year. Mergers and acquisitions are important here as well as among banks and savings institutions. In 2006, there were 179 mergers and acquisitions among securities firms. Of these, 50 (28 per cent) involved the purchase of securities firms by banks. This was slightly below the average for the period 2001–06, which saw a total of 322 purchases of securities firms by banks out of a total of 1,015 mergers and acquisitions in the industry (31.7 per cent). This steady movement by banks into the securities industry followed the easing of restrictions on the non-banking activities of commercial banks, notably in the *Gramm–Leach–Bliley Act, 1999*.

The securities industry is overseen by the Securities and Exchange Commission (SEC) which regulates the issue of securities, and the various securities exchanges. The SEC was established by the US Congress in 1934 to protect investors and to maintain the integrity of financial markets. The *Securities Act* of 1933 required publicly owned companies to disclose financial information to provide transparency and to give investors access to important information. The *Sarbanes–Oxley Act* of 2002 was enacted to increase the accountability of the boards of publicly held companies to their shareholders. In addition, the Federal Reserve Board has some regulatory influence on the industry through determining the credit limits or margin requirements in securities markets.

There is also self-regulation of the industry. From 1936 onwards, this was carried out by the National Association of Securities Dealers (NASD) which later changed its name to NASD, Inc. NASD was created under amendments to the *Securities Exchange Act* of 1934. All brokerage firms which were not members of

---

BOX 4.4 The growth of junk bonds

Junk bonds are corporate debt instruments that the credit-rating agencies regard as 'below investment grade' because they judge that the issuing companies might not be able to meet interest or principal payments. In the late 1970s the market consisted largely of debt securities of companies that had been successful in the past but had run into difficulties ('fallen angels'). However, from 1984 onwards, Michael Milken, of the securities firm Drexel Burnham Lambert, transformed the market by selling high-yield bonds as a means of raising finance for corporate raiders and shell companies without earnings or assets to undertake leveraged buyouts. The bonds yielded an average of 350–450 basis points more than Treasury bonds of similar maturities, but with a very wide range. For instance, bonds issued by a steel company, LTV, which sought legal protection from its creditors in 1986, yielded around 35 per cent. Milken found a ready home for the bonds among insurance companies and thrift institutions which were seeking to diversify away from fixed-interest lending and were willing to take risks to maintain returns, pension plans, the mutual funds and even the public directly. In 1980 there had been 46 issues of junk bonds for a total of $1.38bn. By 1986 this had grown to 210 issues for a total of $29.83bn.

Drexel charged very high commissions to the issuing firms (up to three or four per cent of the principal) and paid very high bonuses to their traders. In 1987 Milken received $550m for his services. However, in 1989 Drexel was heavily fined for mail and securities fraud and the following year Milken was heavily fined and later jailed for securities violations which included cheating some customers and helping others to break securities law. The value of most junk bonds declined sharply in late 1989 and S&Ls were required under the *Financial Institutions Reform, Recovery and Enforcement Act* of 1989 to sell their junk bond holdings. Drexel Burnham Lambert went bankrupt in February 1990.

---

another approved self-regulating organization were required by law to be members of NASD. In practice, that meant that almost all brokerage firms were required to be members of NASD. However, on 26 July 2007, the SEC approved the formation of a new self-regulating organization for the industry to be known as the Financial Industry Regulatory Authority (FINRA). This will involve the merging of the NASD with the enforcement arm of the New York Stock Exchange, NYSE Regulation, Inc.

In recent years the large US securities firms have spread throughout the world. At the same time, although foreign banks have not made major inroads into US retail banking, foreign-owned institutions, notably the very large Japanese banks, have entered strongly into wholesale banking and the securities industry in the USA.

Securities firms come to the attention of the public principally when there is a major collapse or court case. For example, in the 1980s, the US securities industry was perhaps best known in relation to the issue of junk bonds. This is dealt with in Box 4.4. In the late 1990s, there was the case of Long Term Capital Management in which the near collapse of a **hedge fund** led to problems in many financial markets in different parts of the world. This and several other problems involving securities firms are dealt with in Chapter 20. The false description of client firms by Merrill Lynch, which came to light in the spring of 2002 is dealt with in Case study 1 (see page 590).

4.4.2 Insurance companies

Unsurprisingly, the USA has the largest insurance market in the world. A survey of world insurance premiums carried out by Swiss Re, a major reinsurance and financial services group, estimated that total insurance premiums for 2006 were $3,723bn (life insurance $2,209bn; non-life $1,514bn). The estimate for US insurance premiums was $1,170bn, nearly a third of the total. In the USA it is more common to divide insurance into three groups: property/casualty (covering motor vehicle, home and commercial insurance), life/health (life insurance and annuity products) and health (private health insurance plans).

All types of insurance are regulated by the states. Each state has its own set of statutes and rules. State insurance departments are responsible for insurer

---

MORE FROM THE WEB

The website of the SEC (http://www.sec.gov) gives an outline of its history and responsibilities and has an educational section. Click on 'Divisions and Offices' on the home page, then on 'Investment Management' and then 'Investor Info'. For information on the new self-regulatory organization, FINRA, see http://www.finra.org/index.htm.

solvency and market conduct. There have been several proposals for the introduction of federal regulation to provide a more uniform system, perhaps with companies being given a choice between being state-regulated or federally regulated along the lines of the banking system, but these ideas continue to be resisted. The National Association of Insurance Commissioners (NAIC), a non-profit organization established in 1871, provides a basis for coordination among the states. The NAIC is, however, not itself a regulator. It proposes model laws and regulations but the states decide whether and to what extent to implement the models.

In the 1970s and 1980s, life insurance companies ran into the same disintermediation difficulties as the S&Ls. At the beginning of the 1970s the assets of life insurance companies were long-term fixed interest (usually acquired years before when interest rates were low). Liabilities were very largely whole life policies. As market interest rates rose in the 1970s and as money market mutual funds developed offering much higher returns than were available on life policies, the competitiveness of the life insurance industry was much reduced.

Life insurance policies in fact consist of two elements – the insurance element and one of saving and accumulation. Policyholders found that they could unbundle their policies by taking out short-term life policies and undertaking the accumulation element in other ways. Between 1970 and 1984, premiums on life policies fell from 3.12 per cent to 1.99 per cent of disposable income while whole of life policies declined from 82 per cent to 22 per cent of new policies written. Lapses and surrenders of both old and new policies doubled to 12 per cent of all policies in force in 1984. Attempts by US companies to follow the UK practice of acquiring claims to real streams of goods and services (such as the earnings of industrial and commercial enterprises or holdings of real estate and property) were restricted by state regulations covering the types of assets life offices could hold. Nonetheless, they diversified as much as possible, often into riskier products with higher rates of return including junk bonds and doubtful commercial real estate loans. The sharp downturn in the junk bond market in 1989 caused problems for a number of, mainly small, life insurance companies. Forty-three companies failed in 1989, another 30 in 1990 and more in 1991, including some rather larger companies. The NAIC promoted nationwide standards for capital adequacy and for state guarantee funds.

Insurance companies also responded to the pressure on their profits in the 1970s and 1980s by seeking to market more flexible types of policies and to enter new product markets. Some companies began to offer certificates of deposit or cash management accounts in direct competition with commercial banks while others merged with brokerage firms and began to offer a wide range of securities-related services. Insurance companies also began to offer mutual funds to investors.

The *Gramm–Leach–Bliley Act, 1999*, which removed the long-lived restriction on mergers between commercial banks and securities and insurance firms, paved the way for cross-industry mergers, particularly involving bank holding and insurance companies. However, there have been fewer mergers between banks and insurance companies than had been expected. Banks have naturally wished to add insurance products to the range of products they offer but have more often achieved this by buying existing agencies and brokers or establishing their own agencies rather than by buying insurance companies. Some of the largest insurance brokerages now belong to banks. Equally, insurance companies have been more likely to set up thrift or banking divisions rather than to seek to acquire existing banks. Nonetheless, there has been a continued steady movement towards the concentration of the industry.

4.4.3 Mutual and closed-end funds

Mutual funds are open-end funds run by investment companies which invest pools of money into a number of investment options. Open-end funds have a much higher share of the total market than closed-end funds. Mutual funds have been in existence since the 1920s and are regulated by the Securities and Exchange Commission (SEC) under the *Investment Company Act, 1940*. The Act sets fiduciary standards as well as reporting and disclosure requirements.

Funds usually specialize in particular types of investment, including growth stocks, income-producing stocks, small-firm stocks, short- or long-term bonds, tax-exempt bonds, precious metals or international stocks. A simple classification of mutual funds by the type of asset in which they invest gives us:

- equity funds;
- bond funds;
- money market funds;
- hybrid funds.

We saw in Box 4.1 that the development of money market mutual funds (MMMFs) from 1975 onwards had a profound effect on banks, thrifts and insurance companies. They specialize in high-grade, short-term securities that offer market returns on cash equivalents, and permit cheque-writing privileges. Thus they were able to offer rates of return that reflected the higher rates of short-term interest produced in the late 1970s by world economic events and the Fed's response to them. Between the beginning of 1979 and the end of 1982, the assets of money market mutual funds jumped from $12bn to $230bn. By 1985, they held nearly 50 per cent of the assets of the mutual funds industry.

Mutual funds as a whole continued to grow rapidly after 1982. Between 1985 and 2006, the net assets of the industry grew from $495.4bn to $10,413.6bn. The percentage of households investing in the funds increased from 5.77 per cent in 1980 to a peak of 49.6 per cent in 2002 before falling back slightly. At the end of 2006, 48 per cent of all US households held an investment in mutual funds. Much of this is indirect, being held through managed investments such as the popular retirement accounts (IRAs), which had benefited from changes in taxation rules in the 1990s. According to the triennial survey of consumer finances conducted by the Federal Reserve, at the end of 2004, 15 per cent of US families held a direct investment in mutual funds (not including money market mutual funds), down from 17.7 per cent in 2001, another reflection of the worsening equity market performance in 2001 and the following years.

The equity market boom of the 1990s led to a particularly rapid growth of equity-based mutual funds. In 1990, equity funds accounted for only 22.5 per cent of industry assets. By 2000, this had reached 56.9 per cent. The 2001 stock market fall caused this percentage to fall to 41.7 by the end of 2002 but this subsequently increased steadily so that by the end of 2006 again nearly 57 per cent of all mutual fund assets were in equity funds. The next largest group was money market funds with just under 23 per cent of industry assets.

consumers for the purchase of motor vehicles or large household items such as furniture or domestic appliances, for home improvements or for the refinancing of small debts. Business finance companies lend to wholesalers and manufacturers, engage in factoring (purchasing accounts receivable at a discount) and engage in motor vehicle, aircraft and equipment leasing. Finance companies also offer credit cards and in recent years have moved strongly into the real estate market, which is considered separately in Box 4.5. Some finance companies are subsidiaries of bank holding companies or insurance companies or themselves have subsidiaries which offer banking or commercial services. Some are affiliated with motor vehicle or appliance manufacturers.

As financial intermediaries, finance companies compete with banks, savings institutions and credit unions. The sector is twice as large as the credit union sector, about the same size as thrifts and one-fifth as large as commercial banks. Because they are non-depository organizations, funds are raised not from the deposits of savers but through bank loans, the issue of commercial paper or bonds or the securitization of their loans, although some states allow finance companies to seek customer deposits under particular circumstances.

Finance companies are for the most part regulated by the states and regulations vary between states. There are generally, however, limits placed on the size and the maturity of loans finance companies can make and on the interest rates they can charge.

Pension funds have developed in much the same way as in the UK. The performance of their portfolios is very susceptible to market conditions. Criticisms of the operation of pension funds led to the *Employee Retirement Income Security Act, 1974* (revised in 1989) which introduced rules regarding the length of membership of the fund needed before a pension would be paid and about transfers from one fund to another. It also stipulated that contributions should be invested in a prudent manner. Pension funds are also subject to state regulation.

4.4.4 Other non-depository institutions

Other non-depository institutions include finance companies, mortgage bankers and brokers and pension funds. Finance companies specialize in the provision of short- and medium-term credit to firms and households. Consumer finance companies lend to

| 4.5 | The home mortgage market and subprime lending |

We have seen that commercial banks, thrifts, credit unions and finance companies are all involved in mortgage lending. So too are life insurance companies and government-sponsored enterprises like Fannie Mae which operates in the secondary mortgage market, aiming to ensure that mortgage bankers and other lenders have enough funds to lend to home buyers at low rates. In recent years the home mortgage market has expanded rapidly, with loans outstanding doubling from $501.1bn to $1,019.2bn between the end of 2002 and 2006. In 2006, loans in the residential mortgage section of the market accounted for more than 40 per cent of the growth in lending by banks. The division of the mortgage market among the various lenders at the end of 2006 was:

	Loans outstanding $bn
Commercial banks	637.0
Savings Institutions	137.6
Credit unions	90.2
Finance companies	107.8
ABS[1] issuers	46.6

[1] Asset-backed securities issuers.

Source: Insurance Information Institute (2007) *Financial Services Fact Book 2007*, http://www.iii.org. Reprinted with permission.

The market expansion had been assisted by the low interest rates of the period and contributed to a house price boom which continued from 2001 to 2005. The expansion in home mortgages was also partly due to the big increase in subprime and non-traditional mortgages offered. The subprime category of residential mortgages:

> typically includes loans made to borrowers who had one or more of the following characteristics at the time the loans were originated: weakened credit histories that include payment delinquencies, charge-offs, judgements, or bankruptcies; reduced payment capacity as measured by credit scores or debt-to-income ratios; or incomplete credit histories.[2]

Subprime mortgages are riskier than average and so carry higher than average interest rates. Consequently, in periods with low interest rates, rising house prices, and hence few defaults, they offer lenders high profits.

With house prices high, even defaults present few problems to lenders. It was not surprising then that subprime lending expanded greatly, reaching around 20 per cent of all new mortgages by 2005.

Mortgages in the USA had traditionally been simple fixed interest rate mortgages. However, this began to change as lenders designed products to attract new borrowers into the market. It has been suggested that regulators encouraged this trend. In a speech in March 2007 to the US Senate Committee on Banking, Housing and Urban Affairs, the Committee Chairman, Chris Dodd said:

> Despite those warning signals, in February of 2004 the leadership of the Federal Reserve Board seemed to encourage the development and use of adjustable rate mortgages that, today, are defaulting and going into foreclosure at record rates. The then-Chairman of the Fed said, in a speech to the National Credit Union Administration: 'American consumers might benefit if lenders provided greater mortgage product alternatives to the traditional fixed-rate mortgage.'[3]

Non-traditional or 'exotic' mortgages include fixed rate mortgages that quickly convert to variable rates; adjustable rate mortgages (ARMs) in which the interest rate is adjusted periodically according to a preselected index; interest-only mortgages (mainly ARMs) in which the borrower pays only the interest on the capital for a set term and then, usually after five to seven years, has to refinance the balance in a lump sum or start paying the principal; and 'pick a payment' loans, for which borrowers choose their monthly payment (full payment, interest only, or a minimum payment which may be lower than the payment required to reduce the balance of the loan). Almost all of these not only carry higher interest rates but also involve (possibly sharply) increasing interest rate payments as interest rates rise in the economy. In addition, in 2006 there was a significant increase in the number of 'piggyback mortgages' (80/20 mortgages), that is, two loans taken out in tandem and worth up to 100 per cent of the value of the property. This meant that a growing number of borrowers had no equity in their houses and had little incentive to go on paying when their interest payments rose sharply. This was especially the case when house prices began

---

[2]   US Federal Reserve, 'Profits and balance sheet developments at U.S. commercial banks in 2006', *Federal Reserve Bulletin*, July 2007, A37–A71.

[3]   US Senate, 'Opening statement of chairman Chris Dodd – Hearing on "Mortgage market turmoil: causes and consequences"', 22 March 2007, http://banking.senate.gov/index.cfm?Fuseaction=Articles.Detail&Article_id=125&Month=3&Year=2007.

to fall causing the size of the loan to be repaid to be greater then the market value of the house.

One of Senator Dodd's criticisms of the authorities was that four months after Alan Greenspan's encouragement to lenders to provide alternative types of mortgage loans, the Fed Open Market Committee started pushing interest rates up and, over the following 24 months, made 17¼-point increases, taking the Fed Funds rate from 1 per cent to 5¼ per cent.

The way in which many of the mortgage loans were financed also contributed to the problems that later developed. All types of lenders had engaged in the expansion of subprime mortgages but commercial banks were not greatly involved. In a survey conducted in 2006, only about 5 per cent of US commercial banks reported that subprime mortgages made up more than 20 per cent of the residential mortgage loans on their books. Much of the subprime lending had been carried out by non-depository finance companies often financed by bundling the mortgages into mortgage-backed securities (MBSs) sold on to investment banks, hedge funds and other investors. This passed the risks associated with the subprime mortgages on to other institutions. As long as financial markets remained confident and willing to buy these securities, the lenders could go on expanding. In fact, life in financial markets is much more complex than this as Box 4.5 suggests. However, by the last quarter of 2006, the market was slowing down. Construction of new houses was in decline, the increase in house prices was slowing

---

BOX 4.5 Mortgage-backed securities and hedge funds

Mortgage-backed securities (MBSs) are created when mortgage lenders bundle up a group of mortgages to create a security which is then sold on. Unfortunately, credit rating agencies are only likely to give an MBS backed by subprime mortgages a low rating (less than investment or 'junk' grade). This would mean that it would not be held in many portfolios and could only be sold at a large discount, making the funds raised by the mortgage lender to finance its lending expensive.

Enter an investment bank. It is prepared to pay rather more to the mortgage lender because it is able to slice a large quantity of MBSs into a number of tranches in order to create a mixture of assets of different degrees of risk. These are known as Collateralized Debt Obligations (CDOs). Perhaps 80 per cent of the CDOs will be sufficiently low risk to be granted an investment grade rating by a credit rating agency and these can be sold on easily. Ten per cent may be middle risk (mezzanine) and 10 per cent high risk (equity). As long as things go well (low interest rates, rising house prices), the equity assets produce high returns, but they lose value first and very rapidly if the housing market turns down. The investment bank will not wish to keep the medium- and high-risk CDOs and so has to devise a way to get rid of them.

One method is to set up a hedge fund to trade in the medium- and high-risk CDOs. The bank puts money into the hedge fund and uses this to buy the equity CDOs from itself. The equity CDOs are not traded on a market and so have no market value, but when the housing market is doing well, as between 2001 and 2005, and there is little chance of the underlying subprime mortgages defaulting in large numbers, the equity CDOs are less risky and so a higher value can be attributed to them in the hedge fund's books. Indeed, because the CDOs have most of the risk associated with the mortgages concentrated in them they can be marked up faster than house prices are rising and the hedge fund seems to be doing spectacularly well. Investors from outside invest in the hedge fund. The hedge fund can then seek to raise the profit rates further by using the equity CDOs as collateral to borrow from another bank. The hedge fund is said to be 'leveraging risk' by doing this. It uses the loan to buy more equity CDOs from the investment bank which, in turn, buys more MBSs from the mortgage lenders who initiate more subprime mortgages. This increases demand in the housing market and helps house prices to keep rising.

As the value of the CDOs are marked up even higher with rising house prices, it is able to borrow again and so the process continues. But one can see the problem if, as at the beginning of 2007, house prices begin to fall and the proportion of subprime mortgage defaulting begins to rise. The outside bank that has lent to the hedge fund asks for its money back but the hedge fund has used it all to buy equity CDOs to which the hedge fund may still attribute a high value on its books but will have next to no value if the outside bank tries to sell them on the open market.

This is, in essence, what happened to the two Bear Stearns hedge funds, Bear Stearns High-Grade Structured Credit Fund and Bear Stearns High-Grade Structured Credit Enhanced Fund, which were two of the high-profile failures in the subprime mortgage collapse.

MORE FROM THE WEB

For more details on CDOs and what investment banks might do with them see 'Subprime mortgage collapse: why Bear Stearns is just the start', *Money Week*, 15 October 2007, http://www.moneyweek.com. For a list of failed, failing or, at least, ill subprime mortgage lenders, see the Implod-o-meter on http://ml-implode.com.

down and concern started to be expressed about delinquency rates of subprime mortgages. A loan is defined as 'delinquent' when payment is 30 to 60 days behind and no payments are currently being made. Loans that are more than 60 days overdue are labelled 'seriously delinquent'. The position deteriorated in the first quarter of 2007 and the number of defaults in the subprime market increased rapidly. This continued throughout the year.

As the defaults increased, investors became nervous and began to switch towards more secure investments. The demand for subprime mortgage-backed assets dried up and the finance companies found that they could no longer raise the finance to back their mortgages or could only do so at large discounts. Finance companies began to fail in large numbers. Others closed departments, put off staff or were taken over by other banks. Banks demanded higher interest rates for lending in the interbank market and the 'credit crunch' developed. Hedge funds that had invested heavily in subprime mortgage-backed assets failed or needed to be rescued. In the middle of 2007, international markets became nervous and the US crisis became of global concern, playing a major part in the problems of Northern Rock (Case study 4, see page 603). At the other end of the chain, many poor and vulnerable people, who had been encouraged far beyond their means, lost out.

4.6 Summary

The US financial system is highly individual, having developed to reflect two major concerns present since the early days of the country – the fear of moneyed interests and the fear of being controlled either by large institutions in the financial centre of New York or by political forces concentrated in Washington.

This led to a complicated dual system of regulation and to state and federal laws limiting the ability of banks to open branches and to engage in interstate banking. This ensured that there would be a large number of small banks and that, in turn, contributed to the tendency of the system to suffer from bank runs and multi-bank panics.

Legislation that aimed to restrict the activities of banks and to insure their deposits followed, producing a large reduction in the number of bank failures from the 1940s to the 1970s. However, with changes in the international economic environment in the 1970s, problems arose and the 1980s saw a new burst of bank failures especially among savings and loan associations. This, together with the effects of technological change and a number of legislative changes at both federal and state levels, has produced a major consolidation of the US banking system which is continuing. In recent years, banks have become free to open branches and to engage in interstate banking. In addition, the barrier erected between commercial and investment banking in the 1930s has been eroded.

The US central bank (the Federal Reserve System) is also quite different from other central banks and the form it has taken also owes much to long-lived attitudes and to historical developments. There have also been a number of important developments among non-depository financial institutions, not least with the establishment of money market mutual funds in the 1970s and the very rapid growth of equity mutual funds in the 1990s.

A housing market boom between 2001 and 2005 was partially fuelled by a big increase in the number of subprime mortgages, many of which were non-traditional in kind. When interest rates rose sharply between 2004 and 2006 and particularly when house prices began to fall in 2007 there was a large increase in subprime mortgage defaults. Uncertainties following on from this led to a credit crunch and the failure of many mortgage lenders and some hedge funds. The US subprime mortgage crisis had a global impact and led to bank problems and hedge fund failures in other countries.

Key concepts in this chapter

Bank holding companies
Bank runs
Federal Reserve Banks
Federal Reserve System
Financial holding company
Glass–Steagall Act
Hedge fund
Money market mutual funds
Multi-bank panics
Mutual funds

National banks
Nationally chartered banks
Nationally chartered savings institutions
Savings and loan associations
Savings banks
State-chartered banks
State-chartered savings institutions
Subprime
Thrifts

Questions and problems

1 Why are US financial markets so important to the rest of the world?

2 Consider the relationship between US bank legislation and the structure of the banking industry in the USA.

3 Discuss the advantages and disadvantages of a banking system with large numbers of small, independent banks.

4 Why was investment banking separated from commercial banking in the USA? Do the arguments which were used for doing this in the 1930s still apply today?

5 Are there advantages in having a regionally based central bank? Compare the structure of the Federal Reserve System with that of the German *Bundesbank*.

6 What did S&Ls and insurance companies have in common in the 1970s? Why did that cause them problems?

7 How did the subprime mortgage crisis of 2006–07 compare with the savings and loans crisis of the 1980s? Did it have anything in common with the junk bond problem?

Further reading

D F Amel, 'Trends in the structure of federally insured depository institutions, 1984–94', *Federal Reserve Bulletin,* 82, 1996, 1–15

M Friedman and A Schwartz, *A Monetary History of the United States, 1867–1960* (Princeton: Princeton University Press, 1963)

W Greider, Secrets of the temple: How the Federal Reserve runs the country (New York: Simon and Schuster, 1987)

F S Mishkin, *The Economics of Money, Banking and Financial Markets* (London: Addison Wesley, 8e, 2007)

P Newman, M Milgate and J Eatwell (eds), *The New Palgrave Dictionary of Money and Finance* (London: Macmillan, 1992)

S A Rhoades, 'Bank mergers and banking structure in the United States 1980–98', *Board of Governors of the Federal Reserve System Staff Study 174* (Washington DC, August 2000)

Websites

www.allcountries.org/uscensus/
http://audit.state.wy.us/banking
www.bos.frb.org/
www.cuna.org/data
www.fdic.gov
http://ml-implode.com
www.moneyweek.com
www.occ.treas.gov/
www.sec.gov

Chapter 5

The German financial system

What you will learn in this chapter:

- The monetary and financial upheavals in Germany's past

- The role of these upheavals in creating a financial 'stability culture'

- The characteristics of 'universal banking'

- The dominant role played by banks in the German financial system

- The comparatively small use made of 'plc' status by German firms

- The small role played by securities and equities in particular in German savings

5.1 Introduction

Between 1960 and 2000, the German economy emerged as the strongest in Europe and its financial system acquired an outstanding reputation for stability. For example, in Chapter 21 we note that other countries tried, from time to time, to link their currencies to the Deutschmark in order to acquire some of the reputation that it enjoyed as a currency with a low risk of depreciation.

The strength of the Deutschmark was often said to be the result of certain institutional features of the German financial system, in particular the independence of its central bank, the *Bundesbank*. This is not the whole story, as we shall see in the next section. A more fundamental explanation takes us back into Germany's economic and financial history. More than any other European country in the twentieth century, Germany has suffered the effects of violent currency fluctuations.

The first and most spectacular of these had its origins in the financing of Germany's 1914–18 war efforts, when the *Reichsbank*, the central bank, had provided finance to the government by accepting large quantities of treasury bills. This is as close as it is possible to get to financing a budget deficit by 'printing money' in a modern financial system. The government issues its own treasury bills and the central bank credits the government account with corresponding deposits. As government deposits were spent, the broad money supply increased by a corresponding amount and, naturally enough, notes and coin increased in step as some of the deposits were converted to cash. An indication of the rate of expansion is given by the fact that notes and coin in circulation increased by 50–60 per cent per year, 1917–21. After 1920, punitive reparations payments imposed by the Allies made matters worse. The payments had to be made in US dollars and the only means of paying for these dollars, given the state of the German economy, was to buy them with Marks created by selling treasury bills to the *Reichsbank*. While war finance was the cause of the emergency, the *Reichsbank* occasionally protested at the unorthodox methods of finance, but once the cause of the deficits was seen to be 'unfair' reparations

imposed by the Allies, the *Reichsbank* gave up and agreed that 'it would continue to take into its reserves all the treasury bills the government wished to issue' (Marsh, 1992, p. 99). Predictably, the Mark fell rapidly in value against other currencies and, in an attempt to end the process, in 1922 the Allies forced the passage of a law making the *Reichsbank* independent of government. It made not the slightest difference and the episode is thus an interesting illustration of the limited power of independence. Independent central banks succeed in the pursuit of low inflation because the community wants them to succeed. Where there is a view that inflation has some merit (as a means of undermining unfair reparations), central bank independence can achieve very little. Consumer prices rose at an exponential rate. At the worst, in 1923, prices rose nearly two billion fold. When stabilization finally occurred in November 1923[1] the exchange rate was M4.2 trillion per US dollar.[2] At inflation rates of this magnitude, conventional payment systems, based on money, collapse and exchange takes the form of barter, with all the inefficiencies and disruption that follow. Savings in the form of financial wealth, especially where the assets are of fixed nominal value, are also destroyed.

The hyperinflation of 1922–23 is now more than 80 years away. But there was a more recent reminder of its effects, particularly upon savings, in the conversion of the Mark in another post-war setting, in 1948. The Reichsmark, as it had by then become, was virtually worthless and, under Allied supervision, the *Bank deutscher Länder*, forerunner of the *Bundesbank*, embarked on a process of converting Reichsmarks into Deutschmarks. Current payments, including wages and salaries, were converted at a one-for-one basis in June 1948. But savings were converted in October 1948 at the rate of DM6.50 to RM100. Once again, financial wealth was drastically reduced.

It is this experience that has made *all* German institutions and administrations strongly inflation averse (and also perhaps more risk averse) than those of other countries. These aversions predate the *Bundesbank*'s success. They explain *why* the *Bundesbank* was established with such a high degree of independence and they explain why the *Bundesbank* has had a comparatively simple task in maintaining low rates of

---

[1] By linking the note issue to the value of agricultural and industrial land, a commodity in (relatively) fixed supply. See Marsh (1992) Ch. 4 for details.
[2] 1 trillion = 1,000 billion.

inflation: it has enjoyed widespread support throughout German society. The aversions and the low inflation record also explain some other characteristics of the German financial system which we shall touch on in this chapter, particularly the low levels of equity holdings in household portfolios and the correspondingly low levels of equity finance in German firms.

In the rest of this chapter we shall look at German banks and other deposit-taking institutions (in Section 5.1); at non-deposit-taking institutions (in Section 5.3) and at the use of bond and equity markets by institutions and households (in Section 5.4).

5.2 Banks and other deposit-taking institutions

The central bank in Germany is the *Bundesbank*. It was formally established in 1957 (following the *Bank deutscher Länder* founded in 1948) with a constitution that made the stability of the currency its principal objective. Its constitution also stresses its independence from government, though the *Bundesbank* is technically owned by the central government, which has the power to appoint the president and other members of the directorate. The *Bundesbank* is organized along federal lines. Each state (*Land*) has a central bank (effectively regional offices of the *Bundesbank*) and each of these has one representative on the governing body of the *Bundesbank*. So far as the mechanical aspects of central banking are concerned, commercial banks hold operational balances with the *Land* central bank, which maintains balances with the *Bundesbank* in Frankfurt. Intra-regional payments are thus reflected in banks' balances at the *Land* central bank while net transfers between banks in different regions will be reflected in changed *Land* central bank balances at the *Bundesbank*. The *Bundesbank* is not responsible for supervision of the banking system, this is the job of the Federal Banking Supervisory Office, although the data required for monitoring bank behaviour is collected and published monthly by the *Bundesbank* as part of a whole series of banking statistics (see Deutsche Bundesbank *Banken Statistik* (monthly)).

With the launch of stage three of economic and monetary union on 1 January 1999 responsibility for deciding and implementing the single monetary policy in the euro area was transferred to the

Eurosystem – the ECB and the 11 (13 from 2007) central banks of the member states. Within this system, member central banks are required to implement the monetary policy decided upon by the ECB but otherwise retain most of the functions that one would expect to see in a national central bank. For example, the *Bundesbank* continues to function as the issuer and monitoring authority for euro banknotes; with its regional counterparts (the *Land* central banks) it continues to act as the bankers' bank as described in the last paragraph; it is banker to the Federal Government; it is the guardian of Germany's foreign exchange reserves, though it needs the approval of the ECB for foreign exchange operations above a certain level; and it is responsible for monitoring national and international payments mechanisms and stability of German financial markets. What it does not do is decide upon the euro-wide 'refinancing rate', the rate at which the ECB, via the national central banks, is prepared to make funds available to the banking system. So far as the German banking system is concerned, its liquidity remains guaranteed by the *Land* central banks and then the *Bundesbank*, but the (repo) rate at which liquidity is forthcoming is set by the ECB.

Partly because of Germany's record in maintaining price stability between 1948 and 1999, the *Bundesbank* has had considerable influence on the evolution of the ECB and the Eurosystem. This extends to an apparent preoccupation with monetary growth rates, long after most other countries abandoned them. The ECB publishes what it calls a 'reference' growth rate for broad money and uses departures from this target as one indicator of what should happen to interest rates. But it should be clear that it is the short-term interest rate that is the operating instrument (just as it was under the *Bundesbank*) rather than the monetary base. It has inherited much of the *Bundesbank*'s pragmatism as well: the rate of monetary growth has rarely been below its reference rate but this has never stopped the ECB from cutting interest rates when other indicators required it. Clearly, monetary trends were only one input into the decision-making process.

Under the *Bundesbank*, inflation targets were set in the light of what seemed reasonable at the time. There was never any attempt to use monetary policy to combat what the *Bundesbank* called 'unavoidable inflation'. Above all the approach 'underline[d] the *Bundesbank*'s conviction that control of the money supply for the sake of combating inflation and ensuring steady economic growth can only be success-ful if the policies and behaviour of public authorities, enterprises and trade unions are guided by the same objectives'. Furthermore, banks were (and are under the ECB) subject to mandatory reserve ratios but the system uses lagged reserve accounting – reserves today must match deposits of an earlier date – and so there was no attempt to control reserves directly. Like other central banks, it provided reserves on demand to ensure the stability of the financial system. Also, like other central banks, the *Bundesbank* varied short-term interest rates to influence the *demand* for loans and only through that the demand for reserves and monetary growth.[3]

Unlike the UK, USA and Japan, Germany has a tra-dition of **universal banking**. This means that any recog-nized bank is able to provide a full range of banking services and many other services that elsewhere would be called financial rather than banking services. Thus they can offer the usual range of retail banking services but also engage in wholesale and investment banking. They can even buy and sell securities on behalf of cus-tomers. In the UK and USA it often appears that a single bank offers this range of services, but strictly speaking it does this only by creating separately capi-talized subsidiaries with names similar to the parent. Switzerland also has a tradition of universal banking while Spain, France and the Netherlands lie somewhere between the universal and the segmented traditions.

That said, it does not follow that banks are *obliged* to offer a full range of services with equal emphasis. Box 5.1 lists the categories of banking institutions rec-ognized by the Federal Banking Supervisory Office. Banking statistics are published by the *Bundesbank* using these categories, and a summary of recent figures appears in Table 5.1 overleaf.

Using the concept of universal banking it is possi-ble to divide the list of institutions into two groups: universal banks and specialist credit institutions. Uni-versal banks in turn comprise the commercial banks, the saving banks and the credit cooperatives, while the remaining banks comprise the specialist category. When we go into more detail in a moment we shall see that the reason for distinguishing between commercial banks, savings banks and credit cooperatives is not because their functions differ – their names may

---

BOX 5.1 The classification of German banks

Universal banks
Commercial banks
 The 'big five' banks
 Regional and other commercial banks
 Branches of foreign banks
Land banks
Savings banks
Regional institutions of credit cooperatives
Credit cooperatives

Specialized credit institutions
Mortgage banks
Building and loan associations
Banks with special functions

---

suggest this but since they all offer 'universal' services this cannot be the case – but because their ownership structure is very different. Commercial banks are private sector institutions, savings banks are public sector institutions while credit cooperatives are 'mutuals'. We look first at the universal group and then at the specialized institutions.

Commercial banks are privately owned banks, ranging in size from the 'big five' (Dresdner, Commerz-bank, Deutsche Bank, HypoVereinsbank and Deutsche Postbank), through regional banks, to branches of foreign banks. The big five (the *Großbanken*) all date from the beginnings of the unified German state in the 1870s. As universal banks, they offer retail, wholesale and investment banking though, by comparison with other universal banks, their business is concentrated especially in investment banking, the financing of firms and foreign trade. Only in recent years have they made a major effort to compete for retail deposits. The *Großbanken* account for approximately 18 per cent of all banking business (by assts) in Germany. Next come the universal banks known as *Kreditbanken*.

Smaller, but still significant among commercial banks, are some regionally based banking groups such as the Berliner Handels and Frankfurter Bank (the *Regionalbanken*). Their description as **'regional' banks** is a reference to their geographical origin and the fact that their branches tend still to be concentrated in

---

[3] This passage is based on evidence given by representatives of the *Bundesbank* to the UK Treasury and Civil Service Select Committee in November 1980. The evidence is particularly revealing of just how limited the *Bundesbank* felt its power to be and how heavily it relied on pushing in the direction that public opinion in general wished it to go.

Table 5.1 Selected assets and liabilities of German banks, end 2006 (€bn)

	No.	Assets					Liabilities					Total assets/ liabilities
		Cash and balances at central banks	Bills	Other securities	Advances	Other	Sight deposits	Time deposits	Saving deposits	Other	Capital	
Big banks	5	13.3	1.0	209.5	915.6	159.2	320.6	581.9	62.8	273.3	60	1,298.6
Regional and other commercial banks	158	9.1	0.2	95.4	479.6	36.1	203.2	232.8	34.7	110.9	38.8	620.4
Branches of foreign banks	93	1.2	0.1	8.7	115.4	4.1	33.3	88.9	0.0	4.1	3.2	129.5
Land banks	12	4.2	0.3	294.2	1,051.3	90.3	134.5	707.8	15.3	519.8	62.9	1,440.3
Savings banks	457	21.5	0.5	252.8	712.8	39.4	227.2	280.1	302.2	165.4	52.1	1,027.0
Regional institutions of credit coops	2	1.0	0.0	82.9	135.8	22.8	40.8	138.9	0.0	51.7	11.1	242.5
Credit coops	1,257	13.4	0.3	132.7	398.8	61.8	144.8	160.3	178.7	89.0	35.2	608.0
Mortgage banks	22	1.5	0.0	249.2	599.7	28.4	2.6	331.0	0.8	520.8	23.6	878.8
Building and loan associations	26	0.0	0.0	28.6	147.3	18.0	2.1	155.2	0.4	28.8	7.4	193.9
Banks with special functions	16	0.7	0.0	153.2	414.6	182.0	10.6	240.1	0.0	456.9	42.9	750.5

[1] Mainly bearer bonds.

Source: Deutsche Bundesbank (2007) *Banken Statistik Monthly Report*, February, table IV. Reprinted with permission.

those regions. However, they have branches throughout Germany (and abroad) and they are publicly quoted, limited companies in the same way as the big five. With effect from January 1999, this category contains data for what were previously reported separately as '**private banks**'.

Much smaller in aggregate are the branches of foreign banks (*Zweigstellen auslädischer Banken*). The German financial system has always been fairly open to foreign participation and currently some 90 foreign banks have branches in Germany, mostly operating in Frankfurt.

The *Landesbanken* began life as regional girobanks, banks whose main function was to operate a payments system. While continuing with this function, often in association with other banks as we shall see, they now offer a full range of banking services including international banking. As Table 5.1 shows, they are large institutions, measured by total assets.

Much smaller, but also more numerous, are the savings banks, or *Sparkassen*. As separate firms they number around 500, with approximately 20,000 branches between them. Many date from the nineteenth century when they were founded by local and regional government authority. Their function was to provide finance for local and regional infrastructure and to make loans to disadvantaged groups in the community. This was done by attracting small, retail, deposits from households and firms. In return for their public-spirited lending policy, the solvency of savings banks is guaranteed by the owning public authority which imposes some restrictions on the riskier areas of banking business. Consequently, they are subject to lower capital adequacy requirements (see Section 2.3).

The emphasis upon attracting 'small' deposits from the widest range of clients meant that the savings banks were in the strongest position (within the early German banking system) to develop a cheque payment system. This they did after 1900 by associating themselves with a regional girobank which conducted the clearing operations. The latter developed into the *Landesbanken* (see above) while the savings banks have maintained their emphasis upon retail deposit-taking.

Cooperative banks (*Kreditgenossenschaften*) constitute the third category of universal banks and are, as their name implies, mutual organizations owned by their members. Their origin was often linked to particular trades and professions, deposits being taken from members of the profession and loans being made to

enterprises in that field, the objective being to further the interests of the profession. Such banks are quite common in continental Europe. The biggest and best known – with obvious origins – is France's Crédit Agricole. In Germany there are nearly 1,800 with some 16,000 branches. There are many similarities between the savings and cooperative bank sectors. The individual coops have, for example, remained committed largely to retail deposit business on the liability side while making loans to a regional cooperative bank on the asset side. As with the *Landesbanken*, it is these regional cooperatives (called *Genossenschaftliche Zentralbanken*) that are the genuinely universal banks.

We turn next to the **specialist credit institutions**. These, obviously, are classified by function; we shall find various patterns of ownership within each category.

Germany has both *mortgage* banks (*Hypothekenbanken*) and *building and loan associations* (*Bausparkassen*). Both accept deposits but also finance their lending by the sale of bonds known as *Pfandbriefen*. Legally, the *Hypothekenbanken* are usually private companies while the *Bausparkassen* are owned by public authorities or are mutuals. The function of both is to provide finance for construction though the mortgage banks have also taken up considerable holdings of general government debt. Rather like the UK building society sector, the *Bausparkassen* have benefited from the increasing aspiration of people to own their own homes and from tax incentives which encourage borrowing for home purchase.

The instalment credit banks are mostly subsidiaries of the biggest commercial banks. Their lending consists largely of overdrafts to customers who also hold deposits with the bank and have their main income credited to an account held at the bank.

The remaining specialized credit institutions are institutions established by the state for some specific purpose, often linked to post-war reconstruction problems. They include the Equalization of Burdens Bank (*Lastenausgleichsbank*) whose main function was to settle claims for damages and to help with restitution claims by refugees. The Reconstruction Loan Corporation (*Kreditanstalt für Wiederaufbau*) was founded in 1948 to administer public funds for reconstruction purposes and now handles much of Germany's aid to developing countries. There are also specialist institutions dealing with the requirements of forestry and agriculture. There is also a Post Office Savings Bank (*Deutsche Postbank*) which holds personal sector deposits and operates a payments mechanism.

5.3   Non-deposit institutions

When we compare the German financial system with that of the UK or the USA, the first striking feature is the *presence* of 'universal' banks which we discussed in the previous section. The second is the *absence* of pension funds. In both the USA and the UK, pension funds constitute a major division of the 'institutional' investors and the importance of their behaviour, in securities markets in particular, is considerable. In Germany, however, the major provider of pensions is the state which operates a **pay-as-you-go** (as opposed to a **funded**) system in which pensions are paid out of current taxation; no investment fund is created. Where companies operate a pension scheme, they retain contributions within the firm as working capital so that pension payments are a charge on the firms' profits. For savers who wish to make further provision for old age, there are tax incentives to do so by subscribing to life insurance policies and, as we shall see, insurance companies have grown rapidly in recent years. In common with other European countries, Germany now has a rising proportion of retired to working population which is beginning to cause problems for the state scheme. It seems likely, therefore, that the future will see increasing private sector provision of pensions but that in itself does not necessarily mean the growth of a 'pension fund sector'. It may simply mean the further expansion of insurance companies.

The two major non-bank groups of financial institutions in Germany, therefore, are the insurance companies, which function as we described for insurance companies in Section 2.4, and the investment funds, which function broadly as open-end mutual funds. They occupy a similar position to unit trust companies in the UK, though the instruments held by savers are known as 'certificates' rather than 'units'.

Box 5.2 gives some impression of the comparative size of these institutions as well as the distribution of their asset holdings. It also shows the effect on their balance sheets of the fall in equity prices in 2001–02.

BOX 5.2 Financial assets of German non-bank institutional investors

End-of-year figures (€bn)

Item	2003	2005	Item	2003	2006
Insurance enterprises			**Investment funds**		
With banks[1]	27.8	20.1	With banks[1]	42.4	34.3
In shares	361.7	406.6	In shares	227.7	310.3
In debt securities	432.9	499.8	In debt securities	401.9	420.0
Participating interests	134.9	131.7	In other forms[3]	16.7	42.0
In other forms[2]	106.6	102.0			
			Total	688.7	806.6
Total	1,063.9	1,160.2			
			Percentages		
Percentages			With banks[1]	6.2	4.3
With banks[1]	2.6	1.7	In shares	33.1	38.5
In shares	34.0	35.1	In debt securities	58.4	52.1
In debt securities	40.7	43.1	In other forms	2.3	5.1
Participating interests	12.7	11.4			
In other forms[2]	10.0	8.7	Total	100.0	100.0
Total	100.0	100.0			

[1] Primarily time deposits, including registered debt securities and claims on banks arising from borrowers' notes.
[2] Mortgages, claims arising from borrowers' notes and book-entry securities as well as participating interest in non-banks.
[3] Primarily loans against borrowers' notes.

Source: Deutsche Bundesbank, *Kapitalmarkt Statistik*, March 2005 and June 2007, tables VI.1 and VII.1. Reprinted with permission.

The difference in size is immediately apparent (the combined assets of UK insurance companies converted at the current exchange rate would amount to approximately €1,824bn). Looking at the distribution of asset holdings, it is apparent that investment funds hold higher proportions of securities. That said, the proportions are more similar now than they have been in the past and this represents a shift by insurance enterprises away from assets held with banks (primarily time deposits) towards securities of all kinds, a shift that would certainly be necessary if pensions are to become more fully funded in future. However, in both cases the equity holdings remain considerably smaller than they are for corresponding institutions (long-term insurance companies and unit trusts) in the UK.

5.4 The use of bond and equity markets in Germany

Universal banks and the lack of a pension funds sector are just two of the distinctive features of the German financial system. Others, which we shall discuss in this section, are:

- the limited use of equity finance by firms;
- the small size of equity markets relative to GDP;
- the small number of publicly quoted firms;
- the portfolio preference among households for deposits and bonds over equity;
- the dominant role of bank intermediation in channelling funds from surplus to deficit units.

Table 5.2 shows both the stock and new issues of equities and bonds in 2006. The importance of bond finance is immediately apparent, mainly because banks and other financial institutions rely very heavily upon bond finance. Equity finance is more important to non-financial firms but it is important to get this into perspective.

If companies do not issue large numbers of shares, then households cannot hold them as a large part of their financial wealth. Table 5.3 overleaf shows German households' acquisition and holdings of financial assets in 2006. As regards company shares, the table shows households actually *reducing* their direct shareholdings and also their holdings in mutual funds which would have given them indirect exposure to share ownership. Other striking features are the large holdings of monetary assets (34 per cent of all financial

Table 5.2 German capital markets

Amounts outstanding, by issuer, end 2006 (€bn)	
Shares	
Banks	127.8
Insurance companies	129.0
Other financial	22.0
Industrial and commercial Corporations	1,000.9
Total	1,279.7
Bonds	
Banks	1,809.9
All corporations	99.5
Public sector	1,134.7
Total	3,044.1
New issues during 2006 (€bn)	
Shares Total	0.7
Bonds	
Banks	58.3
All corporations	15.6
Public Sector	55.5
Total	129.4

Source: Deutsche Bundesbank (2007) *Kapitalmarkt Statistik*, June, tables II.2, II.4a, IV.2, IV.3. Reprinted with permission.

assets) and savings schemes with insurance companies (25 per cent) and the low investment in pensions (5 per cent). The latter reflects the continued prevalence of PAYG schemes in Germany. In terms of trends (not shown), there is some evidence of a declining commitment to monetary assets (the proportion stood at 41 per cent ten years ago) and of an increasing investment indirectly in shares via mutual funds (from 7 to 11 per cent of financial assets over ten years).

As we said in the opening to this chapter, part of the reason for household's aversion to equity investment lay with Germany's exceptionally turbulent financial history. This turbulence has led to a strong anti-inflation consensus since 1948 and with low inflation one of the main arguments for equities as a form of saving disappears. Taxation has also worked against household equity investment for much of the period, subjecting shareholders to double taxation (taxation of the company's profits and then taxation of the dividends paid to shareholders) and high rates of capital gains tax.

Table 5.3 German households and non-profit institutions, financial account, 2006 (€bn)

	Net acquisition	Holdings
Assets		
Currency and sight deposits	19.65	611.20
Time deposits	31.86	271.30
Savings deposits	−16.02	580.00
Savings certificates	7.04	72.40
Money market paper	0.98	2.00
Bonds	36.00	480.00
Shares	−5.00	372.30
Other equity	2.95	211.80
Mutual funds	−8.37	524.70
Claims on insurance cos.	55.44	1,107.80
Claims from company pension commitments	7.90	248.40
External	6.76	
Other		46.70
Liabilities		
Loans		1,556.10
Other	4.89	9.70
Total/balance	**134.30**	**2,962.7**

Source: Deutsche Bundesbank (2007) *Monthly Report*, June, adapted from tables VII.1 and VII.2. http://www.bundesbank. de/download/volkswirtschaft/monatsberichte/2007/ 200706mb_en.pdf. Reprinted with permission.

MORE FROM THE WEB

Data on the balance sheets of German financial institutions can be found in *Bankenstatistik*, a monthly statistical supplement published by the Bundesbank, while data on securities issues can be found in *Kapitalmarkt Statistik*. Both can be found on the DB's website: www.deutschebundesbank.de

From the home page click on 'Statistics', then 'Publications', then 'Statistical Supplements'. *Financial Accounts for Germany, 1996–2006* is listed on the website under 'Special Statistical Publications'.

Another very useful website offering statistics and commentary on the German banking scene is that of the German Banking Organization. The address is: www.germanbanks.org. See also the information about the German banking system at Hans Engelbrecht's home page: www.Hans.engelbrecht. com/banksys.htm.

Some useful information is also available from the Frankfurt Stock Exchange. Its address is: www.deutsche-boerse.com (the most useful link is probably 'Private Investors').

In recent years, governments have tried to tip the balance further towards equity financing and shareholding. Tax reforms in 1977 abolished the double taxation of dividend income and introduced a capital gains tax exemption for gains on shares held for more than six months. More recently, in 1994, the Companies Act was amended to simplify the formation of an **AG** and also removed employees' rights of co-determination, for AGs with fewer than 500 employees. When Deutsche Telekom was privatized in November 1996 the flotation was designed, like UK privatizations in the 1980s, with features to appeal to personal shareholders. It remains to be seen whether this, and other planned privatizations, do much to fire an enthusiasm for equity investment. But it may be worth noting that the Federal Government disposed of holdings in several major undertakings during the 1960s and did so on

terms designed to attract broad groups of shareholders. The initial sales of these *Volksaktien* were initially successful but within a few years most had found their way to institutional investors – a story rather similar to that of the UK in the 1990s.

The main reason for the increased interest in equities, however, especially on the demand side, lies in the recognition by government and, more reluctantly, the general public, that alternatives have to be found to the dominant position of PAYG pension arrangements.

In 2001, the German government introduced a major reform of the German pension system called the 'Riester reform' (after the German Minister of Labour, Walter Riester). This had as its main objectives:

■ The stabilization of contribution rates which threatened to reach unsustainable levels as a result of demographic changes. More specifically, the aim was to keep contribution rates below a maximum of 22 per cent of earnings while keeping the level of pension as a fraction of income (the 'replacement rate' above 67 per cent). The corresponding figures at the end of 2001 were 19 per cent and 70 per cent. Without reform, the contribution rate was projected to rise to 40 per cent by 2035.

■ Secure the long-term stability of the replacement rate. The proposals aimed for a slow reduction over

20 years to a minimum rate of 67 per cent compared with the 70 per cent of 2002. But new methods of calculation in the proposals mean that the actual replacement rate will come down to 64 per cent.

- Increase the take-up of private, funded, supplementary pensions by offering various types of tax subsidy. The decision remains at the discretion of individual savers.

The crucial question obviously is whether the package will succeed in stabilizing the replacement rate at reasonable cost. This depends crucially on whether people can be induced to participate (voluntarily) in a supplementary private pension scheme.

The subsidies are quite large – up to 40–50 per cent of their contribution for some groups. But the initial take-up was slow. By early 2003 it had reached 35 per cent of all eligible workers. Many polls, however, suggested that a majority of workers would have favoured a compulsory scheme and so it remains to be seen whether the take-up will continue to increase.

More serious for the success of the scheme is the suggestion that demographic trends will not allow a replacement rate of 67 per cent with a maximum contribution of 22 per cent of earnings. Research at the University of Mannheim (Börsch-Supan and Wilke, 2003) suggests that if this cap on contributions is maintained then replacement rate will fall quickly below 67 per cent and eventually stabilize at around 62 per cent. Those worst affected will be older current workers (born before 1970) who will not have time to build up sufficient savings to maintain income above this 62 per cent level.

The result of growing doubts about the adequacy of these reforms has led to a further proposal, the 'Rürup proposals', published in August 2003, at the centre of which is a proposal to raise the retirement age from 65 to 67 years, beginning in 2011 and proceeding in monthly increments until 2035. Initial reactions were very hostile and it remains to be seen whether these proposals make it into law without major modification.

5.5 Summary

The German financial system is one which, historically speaking, has been dominated by banks. Consequently, financial flows have been channelled through credit institutions rather than through markets. The result is that firms' balance sheets show high levels of bank finance, followed by bond finance, with equity finance in a minority role. This has further consequences: Germany has relatively few public limited companies, and security markets, although large by comparison with some countries, are small relative to the German economy as a whole. Inevitably, therefore, households' asset portfolios are dominated by bank instruments, with equities, held directly or indirectly, playing a very small part.

The reasons for this are partly historical, resulting from Germany's turbulent financial history which has created strong inflation aversion, making fixed interest and fixed nominal value assets relatively attractive. Pension funds, major participants in securities markets elsewhere, are largely absent in Germany because existing pension arrangements make them unnecessary. Additionally, there is a corporate culture which has favoured private ownership and the private conduct of business generally. Until recently, public limited liability status was also discouraged by tax and other regulatory measures. These have diminished in recent years and it may be that the immediate future will see an increase in market mediation, particularly if there is a change towards 'funded' pension arrangements.

Key concepts in this chapter

AG	*Großbanken*	Regional banks
Commercial banks	Pay-as-you-go pension	Specialist credit institutions
Cooperative banks	scheme	Universal banking
Funded pension scheme	Private banks	

Questions and problems

1 Why has the *Bundesbank* placed such strong emphasis upon maintaining low rates of inflation? Comment on the significance of

   (a) 'independence' of the *Bundesbank*; and

   (b) popular support in helping to achieve that objective.

2 Explain what is meant by 'universal banking'.

3 Distinguish between 'commercial banks', 'savings banks' and 'cooperative banks'.

4 Why does Germany have a very small pension fund sector?

5 How would you explain the comparatively small role historically played by equities in the financing of German firms and in German household asset portfolios?

Further reading

A Börsch-Supan and C B Wilke, 'The German pension system: How it was, how it will be', *MEA Working Paper*, 34 (Mannheim: University of Mannheim, 2003)

Deutsche Bundesbank, *Bankenstatistik* [February 2004 tables 3, 12, 13 (t5.1)] (Frankfurt am Main: Deutsche Bundesbank)

Deutsche Bundesbank, *Kapitalmarkt Statistik*, various issues [May 2004 tables II.2, II.4a, IV.2, IV.3 (t5.2), (box 5.2)] (Frankfurt am Main: Deutsche Bundesbank)

Deutsche Bundesbank, *Monthly Reports* (Frankfurt am Main: Deutsche Bundesbank)

Deutsche Bundesbank, *Financial Accounts, 1996–2006* (Frankfurt am Main: Deutsche Bundesbank) [tables II.1 and II.2]

E D M Gardener, P Molyneux and B Moore, *Banking in the New Europe* (Basingstoke: Palgrave–Macmillan, 2003)

German Financial Markets Yearbook, 2002 (London: Euromoney plc, 2003)

D Marsh, *The Bundesbank* (London: Heinemann, 1992)

N Walter and R Von Rosen (eds), *German Financial Markets* (Cambridge: Woodhead Publishers Ltd, 1995) Chs 3–6

Websites

www.bundesbank.de
www.deutsche-boerse.com
www.deutschebundesbank.de
www.germanbanks.org
www.hans.engelbrecht.com/banksys.htm
www.mea.uni-mannheim.de

Chapter 6 The French and Italian
financial systems

What you will learn in this chapter:

■ The main features of the French and Italian banking systems

■ The size and significance of non-depository institutions

■ The comparatively small use made of equity finance by French
and Italian firms in the past

■ The role of social and political influences upon the past
development of the systems

6.1   Introduction

For many years there has been a tradition of describing France as an '**overdraft economy**'. This term originated in the work of J R Hicks in 1974 and describes an economy in which the flow of funds between surplus and deficit units takes place largely through intermediaries, that is, banks, rather than through markets. In simpler language, we might say that such economies rely on 'indirect' rather than 'direct' finance. It is essentially the same distinction that we first met in Chapter 2 where we distinguished between 'bank-based' and 'market-based' financial systems.

Until the 1970s it certainly was reasonable to describe France as a bank-based or overdraft economy, whether one focused on stocks or flows. However, since the 1970s there have been numerous changes (which we note below) which have moved the French financial system more towards the use of markets. In this respect, there are similarities between the French and the German systems (as we saw in the previous chapter). As in Germany, the French financial system is dominated by banks, and securities markets are (relative to the UK, USA and Japan) underdeveloped. Correspondingly, firm and household balance sheets are still dominated by bank instruments, but the picture is changing quickly.

Another characteristic of the French financial system is that historically it has always been highly centralized and regulated. Furthermore, the changes that have taken place in recent years have been much more closely connected to decisions by the French state to change the regulatory framework than is generally the case in other countries where they have been spontaneous responses on the part of the private sector to changed financial conditions.

Between 1945 and 1984 French banking regulation favoured the specialization of banking institutions. This contrasts with the German tradition of 'universal' banking which we looked at in the previous chapter. However, by the early 1980s three things were apparent. Firstly, the increasing trend towards a single European market was opening the French financial system to competition. Secondly, banks in other European countries, subject to lighter regulation, were better placed to exploit economies of scope. Thirdly, plans to encourage the development of French securities markets might cause a rapid switch of bank clients to deal directly in markets if the

banking system remained compartmentalized and required agents to deal with several banks at once. In fact, changes in regulations in 1985 and 1986, which allowed firms to issue money market instruments and thus to borrow directly from markets, reduced French banks' intermediary role quite sharply. The 'financial intermediation ratio' which expresses bank lending to non-bank borrowers as a proportion of their total borrowing fell from 71 per cent in 1978 to 41 per cent in 2001. Since then, the decline has virtually stopped (at 40 per cent in 2004). This is slightly lower than the ratio for the USA (48 per cent) and the UK (46 per cent) and much lower than Germany at 68 per cent, all in 2004. However, it may be of some interest that the figures for the UK and USA have been on a rising rather than falling trend since 2000 as a result, largely, of increasing borrowing by households (virtually of whose borrowing comes from banks and similar institutions).

The realization that the structure and regulation of French banking had to change led to the Banking Act of 1984, which was based upon the principles of universality (all credit institutions free to offer a full range of financial services) and thus also upon harmonization (all credit institutions subject to the same rules). Henceforth all credit institutions would come under the same regulators and supervisors. (The three most notable institutions not covered by the 1984 Act were the central bank – the *Banque de France* – the *Caisse des Dépôts et Consignations* and the financial arm of the Post Office.) That said, the Act recognized that credit institutions would continue to fall into several distinct groups. These categories are still widely used and are listed in Box 6.1, together with the number of such institutions in May 2007. (If we add the financial arm of the Post Office to the institutions listed in Box 6.1 then we have France's monetary financial institutions or MFIs.) Until 1990 the total number of institutions remained steady at about 2,000. Since then the number has declined fairly steadily to about 1,000 at the beginning of 2003, largely through merger but also by the outright closure of smaller, often family-owned, institutions. Unlike in the UK, however, the reduction in the number of *firms* in France has not resulted in a significant reduction in the number of *branches*.

In 1996, the Financial Activity Modernization Act made an important change to the 1984 Act by extending the remit of the *Commission Bancaire* to investment firms (we return to this in a moment). More

---

BOX 6.1 French credit institutions

	No. at end May 2007
Banks – members of the Association Française des Banques	229
e.g. *BNP-Paribas, Société Générale*	
Mutual or cooperative banks	89
e.g. *Groupe Crédit Agricole, Crédit Mutuel*	
Savings and provident institutions	29
Caisse d'épargne et de prévoyance des Alpes,	
Caisse d'épargne et de prévoyance d'Alsace	
Municipal credit banks	19
Caisse de crédit municipal d'Avignon,	
Caisse de crédit municipal de Bordeaux, etc. . . .	
Financial companies	384
e.g. *Abbey national France, Lille (Nord),*	
Crédit immobilier de France-Manche,	
Société financière de grands magasins, Paris	
Specialist financial companies	7
e.g. *Crédit Foncier de Paris (land bank)*	
Euronext-Paris	
Société de développement régional (various)	

Source: Comité des Etablissements de Crédit et des Entreprises d'Investissement (2007) *Liste des Etablissments de Crédit au Mai 2007.* Available at: http://www.banque-france.fr/fr/supervi/telechar/popetscred/lisetcre.pdf.

---

recently an Act of 1999 introduced a Deposit Guarantee Fund. These three pieces of legislation provide the framework for the operation of French banks and other credit institutions.

In the rest of this chapter we shall look firstly, in Section 6.2, at the structure and operation of the banking sector. We then turn, in Section 6.3, to specialist and non-deposit institutions. Then in Section 6.4 we look at financial markets and their importance.

In Sections 6.5 and 6.6 we move on to look at the Italian financial system, which definitely remains bank-based. It contrasts, however, with the French system in that one part of the securities market has become highly developed – the market for public sector debt. Corporate finance has come almost entirely from retained earnings and borrowing from banks. The one thing that all the financial systems we have looked at have in common is that they have been subject to great change in recent years. As usual, the final section, 6.7, summarizes.

MORE FROM THE WEB
The website of the *Banque de France*

The website of the *Banque de France* (the French central bank) can be accessed at: www.banque-france.fr.
Among many resources, it offers:

Banking and Financial Information
An area explaining the structure and regulation of the French monetary and financial systems.

Monthly Digest of the Banque de France
A monthly update of monetary and financial developments in France. Its 'Editorial' and 'Economic and Monetary Highlight' provide information and commentary on recent developments. The 'Statistics' section contains the latest of a wide range of monetary and financial statistics.

Statistics
Long runs of monetary and financial statistics.

6.2   The French banking system

As with other banking systems, it is reasonable to begin our review by starting with the most central organizations and then working down to local institutions. The *Banque de France* is France's central bank. Founded in 1800, the *Banque* was nationalized in 1945. It was made 'autonomous' from government by legislation in 1993 but it remains a limited company whose capital is 100 per cent owned by the state. It is headed by a governor and two deputies, appointed by the government for a term of six years, renewable once. The 1993 Act protects them from being dismissed except by reason of criminal acts. The main decision-making bodies within the *Banque* are the *Conseil de la Politique Monétaire* and the *Conseil Général*, the former having responsibility for monetary policy and the latter looking after day-to-day administrative matters. The government also makes appointments to these bodies for fixed terms but with similar protection. As the central bank, the *Banque de France* manages the government accounts, the foreign exchange reserves and holds the operational deposits of commercial banks. Since the introduction of the single currency in 1999, the *Banque de France* has occupied the role of a national central bank within the European System of Central Banks (ESCB) headed by the European Central Bank (ECB). The ECB sets a single interest rate (strictly three rates) which applies across all members of the monetary union. The role of the NCBs is then:

- to collect information (including national monetary and financial stastistics) according to a standard framework laid down by the ECB;

- to report to the ECB on economic and monetary conditions within the national state;

- (for the *Banque de France*) to supply reserves and foreign currency to French banks at interest and exchange rates laid down by the ECB.

In addition to these functions, the *Banque de France* also plays a significant role in the supervision of the French banking system.

Figure 6.1 shows the structure of the regulatory bodies created by the 1984 Act. Recall that we are dealing here with 'credit institutions'. Unlike the UK, which has opted for a single supervisory agency (the FSA), at least until recently France has preferred separate and specialized supervisors for banks, the insurance industry and financial markets. After 1984 the insurance industry was supervised by the *Commission de Contrôle des Assurances* (CCA) while the stock market was the responsibility of the *Commission des Opérations de Bourse* (COB). Until 2003, supervision of other markets was the responsibility of the *Conseil des Marchés Financiers* (CMF) while another range of provident institutions was supervised by the *Commission de contrôle des*

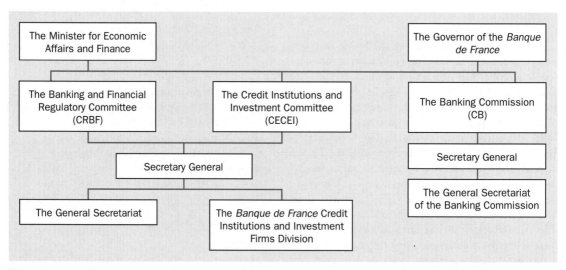

Figure 6.1

mutuelles et des institutions de prévoyance (CCMIP).
One potential problem of specialist supervisors arises
from the need for coordination. The danger of incomplete supervision arising from this type of
arrangement was recognized in 2003 when the COB
and CMF were merged (and joined also with the
Conseil de discipline de la gestion financière or
CDGF) to form a single market regulator (the
Autorité des Marchés Financiers or AMF). At the
same time, the CCA and CCMIP merged to give a single authority for (non-credit) financial institutions,
the *Commission de contrôle des assurances, des
mutuelles et des institutions de prévoyances* (CCAMIP).
Even so, in a system of universal banking, credit institutions will act as agents for clients in access to financial markets and may even engage in proprietary
trading on their own behalf and, in these circumstances,
banking and market supervisors must be willing to
share information and to cooperate. Where credit institutions are concerned, the key committees in the
regulatory structure are shown in the second line of
Figure 6.1 and amongst these it is the *Commission
Bancaire* (CB) which provides the link from banking
supervision to the supervision of markets carried
out by the AMF and other financial institutions by
the CCAMIP.

The regulation of financial activity in France rests
ultimately with the Minister for Economic Affairs and
Finance. Where the activity refers to credit institutions, the Minister appoints the Governor of the
Banque de France, subject to the approval of the
French Council of Ministers. The Minister appoints
the members of all three committees in the second line
of Figure 6.1 and chairs the *Comité de la Réglementation Bancaire et Financière* (CRBF). Furthermore, he
is represented on the other two, the *Comité des Etablissements de Crédit et des Entreprises d'Investissement* (CECEI) and the *Commission Bancaire* (CB)
which are chaired by the Governor. Essentially the
CBRF lays down the regulations governing the behaviour of credit institutions (checking for consistency
with the AMF where credit institutions are engaged in
investment activity). The CECEI issues authorizations
and licences to operate as a credit institution in France
and the CB:

■ supervises the financial position of credit institutions;

■ ensures that they adhere to the rules laid down by
the CRBF; and

■ imposes sanctions for breaches of these regulations.

MORE FROM THE WEB
The *Commission Bancaire*

The CB is the main body responsible for the day-to-
day supervision of credit institutions in France. Since
most credit institutions also carry out securities
dealing and have contacts with financial markets and
insurance, the CB works closely with other regulatory
bodies such as the CCA and AMF. Details of the CB's
responsibilities, powers and activities are contained
in Fact Sheet no. 120 'The Commission Bancaire'
available from www.banque-france.fr. Click on
'Welcome' and then enter 'Fact Sheet no. 120' in the
search box. An explanation of the CB's role and its
relation to the CECEI and CRBF can be found at
www.banque-france.fr/gb/banque/main.htm. Click
on 'The Banque de France and the ESCB' and then on
'Regulating and supervising the banking system and
investment firms'.

The major banks in France are members of the
Association Française des Banques. (For purposes of
statistical reporting their aggregated data often appears
under the heading 'AFB banks'.) This group includes
famous names like *Société Générale*. It also includes
BNP-Paribas, formed in 1999 by a merger between
Banque National de Paris and *Paribas*. The French
banking system as a whole is represented by the
Fédération Bancaire Française (founded in 2000).
Since 1945 all the major French banks have experienced
periods of state ownership. A wave of nationalization
was justified in 1982, by a socialist government, on
the grounds that small and medium-sized firms were
at a persistent disadvantage and that the banks were
reluctant to finance sections of industry which the
government saw as being of strategic importance. The
results were disappointing and since 1986 the movement towards private ownership has been justified
by the need for banks to be able to raise more capital
and have more freedom to compete in the emerging
single market. Even so, the state has retained large
stakes – directly or indirectly – in the privatized banks.
Freedom of behaviour does not necessarily follow
ownership, however. The *Banque de France* and the
Ministry of Finance have always exercised considerable influence over the French banking system by the
use of 'moral suasion'. Since the 1984 Act, AFB members have functioned more or less as universal banks,
offering retail, investment and wholesale banking

services and a money transmission mechanism. The AFB has about 250 members, a figure which was fairly stable up until 2000. Since then, the number has declined, largely as a result of merger. In recent years they have been under great pressure from the mutual and cooperative banks and the **savings banks** (see below) for deposits.

Mutual and cooperative banks have broadly similar origins, structures and functions. They are owned by their 'members', usually their depositors. Their origins lie in the nineteenth century when their purpose was to provide a source of credit for people with limited income. Because they did not need to earn a profit for shareholders, their lending rates would be comparatively low. The rates paid to members were also comparatively low but were nonetheless attractive to members, who were mainly small depositors and not welcome at the larger private banks. So far as structure is concerned, we can take the *Crédit Mutuel* as typical of the group of mutual banks. At the base of the pyramid, there are local offices grouped into several cooperative companies. Each of the local offices is a member of a regional federation (22 in all). The function of the regional offices is to provide clearing facilities between local offices, to pool and on-lend their surpluses and to make loans to local offices where necessary (creating in effect an interbank market for mutuals). There are two national organizations: the *Caisse Centrale de Crédit Mutuel* and the *Cofédération Nationale de Crédit Mutuel*. The former acts as a bank to the regional organizations while the latter is a more 'political' body, speaking on behalf of the movement and representing their common interests.

The other cooperative and mutual banks are organized upon similar pyramid lines – local branches, regional offices and a national organization. Their objectives are also similar, taking deposits from and lending to members who tend to be households or local public bodies or cooperative and mutual organizations. As the names of the organizations suggest, their members tend to be drawn from a particular field of activity – fishing, agriculture and so on. The *Crédit Agricole* has been particularly succesful in competing for deposits with the large AFB banks and absorbed *Crédit Lyonnais* in 2003.

The *Caisses d'Epargne*, **savings banks**, are also cooperative institutions providing a full range of services for retail depositors, with the distinctive features, however, that loans must not be for commercial

and trade purposes and interest on deposits is tax-free up to a maximum threshold. Like the other financial networks, the savings banks have a regional layer of organization (the SOREFIs) and two national bodies. The *Centre National des Caisses d'Epargne et de Prévoyance* represents the interests of the movement and provides regulatory oversight while the *Caisse des Dépôts et Consignations* (CDC) manages the funds collected by the savings bank network.

The CDC is another institution whose activities fall outside the 1984 Banking Law provisions. It occupies a central role in the French financial system and participates extensively in the long-term securities markets. Although it takes deposits (indirectly via the *Caisses d'Epargne*) its activities are so extensive that we discuss it in more detail in the next section.

Municipal credit banks, collectively known as the *Crédit Municipal*, are established by local authorities. They accept deposits from the general public, again with an emphasis upon personal savings, and make loans to public sector employees and organizations. They also provide a home for the local authority's spare funds. Since each is created by its own local authority, each *Crédit Municipal* is independent of the others, but there is a national organization, the *Central Union des Crédit Municipaux*, which represents their common interests.

Finally, before leaving this list of deposit-taking, 'banking' institutions, we should note that the French postal service also offers money transmission services, clearing cheques drawn on generally small, retail deposits. It is not allowed to make loans. It also collects savings for the National Savings Fund, one of many funds managed by the CDC.

We noted in the introduction to this chapter that the French financial system has traditionally been highly centralized and highly regulated. Both of these characteristics, as applied to the banking system, require further comment. With the development of a single market there is an inevitable tendency towards homogenization of systems, products and procedures. It is thus a common theme in the recent development of most European financial systems that rapid change has been necessary to meet the threat of competition posed by more lightly regulated institutions with a background in the UK (or even in the USA). France, Italy and Germany have all had to give more freedom to their banking systems in recent years. In France, for example, lending rates were controlled by the *Banque de France* until 1967. The

MORE FROM THE WEB
Credit Institutions licensed by the CECEI

A full list of individual institutions approved by the CECEI can be found on the website of the *Banque de France*. These are listed by the categories shown in Box 6.1, but subdivided into several levels of subcategory.

A glance at the list, especially the sections dealing with mutual/cooperative banks and municipal credit banks helps to illustrate the 'pyramiding' structure of these institutions as discussed above. The list can be found at: www.banque-france.fr.

Much other useful information from CECEI about the French banking system can be found at the *Banque de France* website by clicking on 'Supervision et réglementation' and then on 'Rapport Annuel du CECEI'.

legislation which liberalized lending rates also lifted restrictions on the opening of bank branches with the result that many large banks opened new branches, one form of non-price competition, to the point where some areas of France became 'over banked'. Since 1986, banks have been closing branches in an attempt to cut costs and restore profits.

The deregulation of deposit rates has, however, been more gradual. The 1967 act actually prohibited interest payments on sight deposits, a state of affairs which was defended by banks for many years on the grounds that it enabled them to provide 'free' services on current accounts. The continuing controls on deposit rates was a major reason for the outbreak of *non-price* competition in the 1970s. Such restrictions create fertile ground for financial innovation to sidestep the controls. (See, for example, the development of US money market mutual funds in Chapter 4.) By 1996 deposit rates and bank commissions, and fees generally, were deregulated. This was partly a response to circumventory innovations but also to the development of a single market, in which banks from most other countries paid market-determined rates on all deposits, and also to a desire to see greater clarity in the pricing of banking services, with explicit prices for each service and less cross-subsidization.

The advent of the euro has brought the development of a single European market in financial services

one step nearer and it was always doubtful whether, in these circumstances, French banks could continue to resist payment of interest on current accounts, when the practice was virtually universal elsewhere. The restriction was lifted in 2001.

One consequence of lifting this restriction is that it has intensified further the competition already encouraged by recent deregulation and which has seen the number of French banks and other financial institutions almost halving since 1990. This is just one example of the general trends that we discussed in Section 2.3 being played out in a particular system. Another is the advance of technology which has affected payment and money transmission practices much as it has in the UK. In 2000, the Dutch financial services group ING began offering internet banking facilities to French clients, offering attractive deposit rates (on *all* positive balances) and generally low charges. This was a timely demonstration of just how competitive the removal of national barriers combined with new technology would make the European financial marketplace in future. Most major French banks have now followed suit.

The aggregate balance sheet of French MFIs (excluding the *Banque de France*) is shown in Table 6.1 overleaf. The bulk of liabilities shown in Table 6.1 are the liquid assets of French residents.

In recent years, French banks have been subject to many of the same pressures and trends that we have already seen working on UK banks (Chapter 3). There has been a shedding of staff and a consequent increase in productivity. The effect can be seen in the last few years where income growth has been almost static but costs as a fraction of income have fallen from 74 per cent to 64 per cent in the 10 years since 1994. There has been the same trend towards diversification of activities and a greater concentration on services and financial products as banks have modeled themselves upon the 'universal' banking firm. An increasing involvement with financial markets – the securitization of loans and off balance sheet activity – has also been a feature of the French as of other systems. The consequence has been a steady rise in non-interest income as a fraction of total income from 20 per cent in 1995 to 30 per cent in 2000 and almost 35 per cent in 2004.

Automation of payment activity is also apparent. Table 6.2 shows much the same decline in the use of cheques that we see in other banking systems, though the process has been rather slower in France.

Table 6.1 Balance sheet of French MFIs, end March 2007 (€bn)

ASSETS			LIABILITIES		
National territory			National territory		
Current account with the Banque			MFIs	1,118.2	
de France			General government	22.2	
Loans	2,849.2		Other sectors	1,233.7	
MFIs		1114.0	Sight deposits		404.2
General government		158.0	Time deposits ≤ 2 years		79.0
Private sector		1,577.3	Time deposits > 2 years		287.7
Securities (exc shares)	491.4		Deposits redeemable at		
MFIs ≤ 2 years		169.7	notice ≤ 3 months		424.8
MFIs > 2 years		69.5	Repurchase agreements		38.0
General government		159.4	Other euro area countries –		
Private sector		92.7	deposits	366.5	
Money market fund units	85.2		MFIs		289.7
Shares and other equity	297.2		Other sectors		76.8
Assets of other euro			Rest of the world –		
area countries	927.2		deposits	1,031.3	
Rest of the world	1,050.1		Not broken down by area	2,826.9	
Not broken down by area	898.3		Debt securities issued ≤ 2 years		339.7
TOTAL	6,598.5		> 2 years		559.3
			Money market fund units		466.5
			Other liabilities		1,089.3
			Capital and reserves		372.1
			TOTAL	6,598.5	

Source: Banque de France, http://www.banque-france.fr/gb/stat_conjoncture/stat_mone/page4c.htm.

Table 6.2 Number of transactions by means of payment (total for the year, in millions)

	2001	2002	2003	2004	2005	% change 2005/2001
Cheque	4,338.6	4,349.5	4,261.5	4,133.8	3,916.3	−9.7
Credit transfers	2,175.5	2,564.2	2,587.5	2,599.2	2,408.4	10.7
Direct debit	2,063.5	2,183.8	2,353	2,542.7	2,512.8	21.7
E-money	2.8	18.4	18.1	16.0	17.0	507.1
Plastic card[1]	3,670.7	4,095.6	4,351.5	4,650.0	5,243.8	42.9
Total	12,251.1	13,211.5	13,571.6	13,941.7	14,098.3	15.1

[1] Excludes e-money.

Source: BIS, *Statistics on Payment and Settlement Systems* (the 'Red Book') at www.bis.org/statistics/payment_stats.htm, table 7.

The result is apparent in Table 6.3, where a comparison with different payment systems can be made across a wide range of countries. Interestingly, however, although the trend is downward, the French have remained more attached to the use of the cheque than other Europeans as the table shows.

As a measure of its economic importance we can note that the banking sector's contribution to French GDP has varied between 2.6 and 3.1 per cent since 2000. Furthermore, the four largest French banks (by **market capitalization**) constituted 12.3 per cent of the total value of firms quoted on Euronext Paris.

Table 6.3 Number of transactions by means of payment – international comparisons, 2005

	No. of transactions per person per year					Percentage of total transactions				
	Cheques	Credit transfers	Direct debits	E-money	Cards[1]	Cheques	Credit transfers	Direct debits	E-money	Cards[1]
Belgium	1.5	78.1	20.9	9.7	70.5	0.8	43.2	11.6	5.4	39.0
France	62.5	38.4	40.1	0.3	83.6	27.8	17.1	17.8	0.1	37.2
Germany	1.3	81.4	80.8	0.5	28.8	0.7	42.2	41.9	0.2	14.9
Italy	8.0	18.0	8.0	0.4	20.6	14.6	32.8	14.5	0.6	37.5
Netherlands	–	75.0	62.7	9.0	86.2	–	32.2	26.9	3.9	37.0
Sweden	–	56.6	17.7	–	117.6	0.1	29.5	9.2	–	61.2
UK	32.1	49.8	45.2	–	104.4	13.9	21.5	19.5	–	45.1

[1] Excludes e-money.

Source: BIS, *Statistics on Payment and Settlement Systems* (the 'Red Book') at www.bis.org/statistics/payment_stats.htm, tables 8a and 7c.

Table 6.4 Comparison of stock market capitalization of major banks, end 2006 (€bn)

	Paris	New York	London	Frankfurt	Milan[1]
Total capitalization of the market	1,702	11,689	2,876	1,242	778
	BNP-Paribas 76.9 (4.5%)	Citigroup Inc. 207.4 (1.8%)	HSBC Holdings 159.9 (5.5%)	Deutsche Bank 52.8 (4.3%)	UniCredito 69.3 (8.9%)
	Société Générale 59.3 (3.5%)	Bank of America Corp. 181.7 (1.6%)	Royal Bank of Scotland grp 93.6 (3.3%)	Commerzbank 19 (1.5%)	Intesa Sanpaolo 40.3 (5.2%)
Capitalization of the major banks	Crédit Agricole 47.7 (2.8%)	J P Morgan Chase 127 (1%)	Barclays 70.8 (2.5%)	Deutsche Postbank 10.5 (0.9%)	Capitalia 18.6 (2.4%)
	Natixis 25.9 (1.5%)	Wells Fargo & Co. 91 (0.8%)	HBOS 63.5 (2.2%)	Landesbank Berlin 8 (0.6%)	Mediobanca 14.6 (1.9%)

[1] More recent figures for Italian banks (alone) are given later in the chapter.

Source: CECEI (2006) *Rapport Annuel*, p. 118.

Table 6.4 lists the banks concerned and allows comparison with the situation in other major financial centres.

There has also been the same trend towards concentration that we have seen in the UK and other banking systems. Although Box 6.1 shows that there were approximately 350 banks in 2006, France's banking system is now dominated by the 'top-5' which account for about 80 per cent of retail deposits and 52 per cent of total bank assets (up from 47 per cent in 2001 – see Table 6.5). This concentration has come about largely through mergers, and a noticeable trend in recent years has been the growth of cross-border merger. For example, the takeover of CCF by HSBC in 2000 was regarded as a notable exception to the rule that mergers were usually between domestic banks. Since then, *Caisse d'Epargne* has merged with the French subsidiary of the Italian group San Paolo IMI (in 2003).

Table 6.5 Banking sector top-5 concentration ratios, selected EU members

	2001	2005
Germany	20.2	21.6
Italy	29.0	26.7[1]
Luxembourg	28.0	30.7
UK	28.6	36.3
Spain	43.9	42.0
Austria	44.9	45.0
Ireland	42.5	46.0
Poland	54.7	48.6
France	47.0	51.9
Sweden	54.6	57.3
Greece	67.0	65.6
Denmark	67.6	66.3
Netherlands	82.5	84.8
Belgium	78.3	85.2
EU average	59.1	59.6

[1] Mergers among Italian banks since 2005 have greatly increased the top-5 concentration ratio in Italy. It may now (October 2007) be greater than France (see later in this chapter).

Source: CECEI (2006) *Rapport Annuel*, p. 147.

6.3   Specialist and non-deposit institutions

Before looking at the role of other financial institutions (and in the next sector at markets) it is helpful to get some impression of the scale of lending and borrowing in France in recent times and at who the main borrowers and lenders have been.

Table 6.6 shows how the financial deficit of non-financial firms in France was financed in 2006.

Table 6.6 Borrowing by non-financial firms, 2006 (€bn)

Debt	
Commercial paper (CP)	21.1
Bonds	−10.6
Borrowing from credit institutions	53.6
Share issues	97.6
Total	161.4

Source: Banque de France, http://www.banque-france.fr/fr/ publications/telechar/bulletin/etu161_1.pdf.

What Table 6.6 shows is that non-financial firms raised external finance in some form of debt instrument amounting to €63.9bn. Of this, €53.6bn took the form of borrowing from banks or other credit institutions. What the table does not show is that both of these figures represent very large increases on previous years. Debt finance in total increased fivefold between 2004 and 2006 (borrowing from banks increased by rather less). Share issues amounted to €97.6bn, up from €77.7bn in 2004. Overall, the €161.4bn of funds raised was nearly double what had been raised in 2004. This near-doubling of the need for external finance represents a sharp rise in firms' levels of real investment but it was combined with a reduction in self-financing from retained profits (down from 75 per cent of total financing in 2004 to 60 per cent in 2006).

French households, like most of those in the rest of Europe, the UK and USA, have increased their level of indebtedness in recent years. The growth rate has been about 11 per cent p.a. At the end of 2006, household debt stood at 68.4 per cent of household disposable income, or, to put it in terms of net savings, the debt amounted to about 4.5 years-worth of saving at 2006 rates. Within the 11 per cent overall growth, borrowing for house purchase increased by 15 per cent while consumer and other forms of unsecured credit increased by only 5 per cent. Most of this borrowing came from banks and other credit institutions.

Table 6.7 shows the gross acquisition of financial assets by French households. It shows the demand for

Table 6.7 French households, gross acquisition of financial assets, 2006

	€bn	As % of total
Notes and coin	4.5	3.2
Sight deposits	10.2	7.2
Savings deposits	24.3	17.2
Time deposits	7.0	5.0
Regular savings schemes	−23.9	−17.0
Life assurance	88.8	63.0
Bonds	−0.6	−0.4
Money market mutual funds	1.2	0.8
Other mutual funds	3.5	2.5
Quoted company shares	−5.0	−3.5
Total	140.9	100

Source: Banque de France, http://www.banque-france.fr/fr/ publications/telechar/bulletin/etu161_1.pdf.

short-term assets being satisfied largely by increased holdings of bank deposits while long-term assets take the form of contributions to life assurance schemes. The other entries are largely inconsequential with the exception of payments into regular savings schemes (largely deposit-based) from which withdrawals totalled over €23bn, in part because of fiscal changes in January 2006 which made them less attractive. This pattern of *acquisition* is somewhat different from the *stocks* of financial assets accumulated by French households. The lastest figures for these (end-2004) show that the financial wealth of French households was divided relatively evenly between deposits (33.3 per cent), life insurance (30.9 per cent) and securities (27.7 per cent), where the latter include shares but also bonds and indirect ownership via mutual funds. Over the past ten years, French households have shifted a part of their financial savings from deposits to life insurance, whose share grew by

10 percentage points while that of deposits declined by 8 points. These proportions of holdings are not out of line for the richer countries in continental Europe, but the acquisitions in 2006 show a much larger concentration on life assurance at the expense of securities. If continued for long enough, this pattern of acquisition will eventually have its effect upon the distribution of holdings of financial assets, but we must be careful not to read the figures for one year as indicating a trend.

Table 6.8 summarizes the issue and acquisition of selected financial instruments by firms and households.

As the tables above imply, the bulk of French non-bank financial institutions consists of mutual funds and insurance companies.

As in the UK, French mutual funds, *organisms de placement collectif en valeurs mobilières* (OPCVM) come in open- and closed-end form. The latter are

Table 6.8 Issue and acquisition of selected financial instruments in 2006, €bn

Company shares – net issue	180.8		Bonds – net issues	173.5	
By: non-financial firms		97.6	By: non-financial firms		−10.6
insurance companies		5.4	public authorities		24.2
banks and financial institutions		12.8	banks and financial institutions		25.3
non-resident firms		65.9	non-resident firms		132.4
Company shares – net acquisitions	180.8		other		2.2
By: households		9.8	Bonds – net acquisitions	173.5	
non-financial firms		66.8	By: insurance companies		55.6
public authorities		−14.2	mutual funds		51.3
insurance companies		10.2	financial firms		17.6
mutual funds		23.0	rest of world		34.8
banks and financial institutions		51.6	other		14.2
non-residents		42.8	Commercial paper – net issue	141.2	
Mutual fund units/shares			By: non-financial firms		21.1
Acquisition of in monetary MFs	38.7		public authorities		−19.9
By: households		1.2	banks and financial institutions		112.7
non-financial firms		10.8	non-resident firms		27.2
insurance companies		5.9	Commercial paper – net acquisitions	141.2	
other mutual funds		12.2	By: non-financial firms		10.4
Acquisition of in non-monetary MFs	120.4		insurance companies		0.9
By: households		3.5	mutual funds – money market		8.1
non-financial firms		−8.1	mutual funds – non money market		24.6
insurance companies		39.6	banks and financial institutions		15.8
other mutual funds		42.2	other		23.6
financial firms		21.3	non-resident firms		57.8
non-residents		18.6			

Source: Banque de France, http://www.banque-france.fr/fr/publications/telechar/bulletin/etu161_1.pdf.

known as **fonds commun de placement** (FCPs) while the former are *sociétés d'investissement à capital variable* (**SICAVs**). There are thousands of funds from which investors can choose, many of them general, but many also with specific investment objectives contained in their title. One obvious distinction is between funds which invest broadly and those which focus upon money market instruments. In fact, as the tables suggest, this particular distinction is regarded by the French authorities as more important than the open/closed distinction.

The authorization of mutual fund management companies lies with the *Autorité des Marchés Financiers*. The AMF, we have seen, was formed in 2003 by the merger of the *Commission des opérations de bourse* (COB), the *Conseil des marchés financiers* (CMF) and the *Conseil de discipline de la gestion financière* (CDGF). It was hoped that the result of the merger would be a regulatory body with a higher profile (better known to investors) and with greater effectiveness (a lower probability of a problem 'falling through the cracks'). Its visibility is important since one of its roles is to provide protection to investors in mutual funds. In this role, it oversees the accuracy of information given to investors and checks that management companies follow the rules for collective investments as required by their licence. A list of authorized management companies is available at www.amf-france.org. In July 2007 there were 517 such companies.

While there are many similarities between the mutual fund industry in France and other countries, it is noticeable (as we have seen) that the French system makes less of the distinction between SICAVs and FCPs than the US and UK systems make of the distinction between investment and unit trusts. For example, the distinction on which the AMF concentrates in its 'glossary of savings' (see 'More from the web: The AMF') is that investors in SICAVs are shareholders while investors in FCPs are not. There is no focus on the closed-/open-end nature of each. Equally, when it comes to balance sheet data the *Banque de France* divides mutual funds between 'general purpose', 'bond', 'equity' etc. funds but puts SICAVs and FCPs together under each heading. Table 6.9 summarizes their holdings of assets. Two points are immediately clear. Firstly, the sector is dominated by 'general' funds and that they are the main holders of equities. However, the equity funds, although smaller overall, are very heavily invested in equities as a proportion of their portfolios (about 92 per cent of the total).

The other major form of institutional saving in France occurs via insurance companies. These, and other financial firms offering protection and prudential services, have been regulated since 2003 by the *Commission de contrôle des assurances, des mutuelles et des institutions de prévoyances* (CCAMIP), formed from the merger of the *Commission de contrôle des mutuelles et des institutions de prévoyance* (CCMIP) and the *Commission de Contrôle des Assurances* (CCA).

As in many other countries, the French insurance industry is divided between firms (sometimes subsidiaries of universal banks) which specialize in either 'life' (or long-term) assurance or 'general' insurance. One way of comparing their relative sizes is to look at the total assets of each group. At the end of 2006, the value of life company assets was €1161bn and that of general insurers was €140bn. The composition of those assets is shown in Table 6.10. Compared with the UK, it is noticeable that both types of insurer are less heavily committed to the equity market. The higher liquidity of general insurers, however, conforms to the general pattern – with predictable and long-term liabilities, life insurers have little need for liquidity.

Another way of comparing size is to look at the premium income earned by each group. In Table 6.11 we show the evolution of premium income for both over a period of years. This allows us to make some observation about the rate of growth in recent years.

The relative size of the two sectors is again confirmed. More interestingly, the general sector appears to have grown rather more slowly (c. 4 per cent p.a.)

MORE FROM THE WEB
The AMF

The AMF, the *Autorité des Marchés Financiers*, is the regulatory authority for French financial markets. Its website can be accessed at: www.amf-france.org.

The website explains the history, the responsibilities and the powers of the AMF. But more useful, probably, is a glossary of terms relating to the mutual funds industry which can be accessed by clicking on 'OPCVM et produits d'épargnes' on the home page.

The website is not very useful for statistical material. This is better found at www.banque-france.fr by clicking on 'Statistics' and 'Time Series'.

Table 6.9 French mutual funds, assets, end December 2006 (€bn)

	Loans	Money market paper	Securities (excl. equity)	Equities and related	Fixed assets	Other assets	Total assets
General purpose	38,213	96,658	631,003	563,201	30	17,248	1,346,353
Bond and fixed interest	−2,957	4,197	173,022	11,801	0	5,635	191,698
Equity funds	1,817	4,118	6,955	308,816	0	10,693	332,399
Diversified funds	8,839	20,499	102,651	188,207	30	3,951	324,177
Guaranteed funds	6,469	4,106	12,758	50,560	0	−2,632	71,261

Source: Banque de France, time series data, 'Assets breakdown of French non-monetary mutual funds', http://www.banque-france.fr/gb/stat_conjoncture/series/statmon/html/statmon.htm.

Table 6.10 French insurance companies – distribution of assets, end 2006 (%)

	General	Life
Cash and deposits		
Loans	5.7	3.3
Other		
Equities and variable income mutual funds	30.8	28.3
Bonds and fixed income mutual funds	56.7	65.5
Fixed assets	6.8	2.9
Total	100	100

Source: Fédération Française des Sociétés d'Assurance (2006) *Rapport Annuel*, Annexe Statistiques p. 73. The report is also available at www.ffsa.fr. Reprinted with permission.

> **MORE FROM THE WEB**
> **French insurance companies on the web**
>
> The website of the insurance regulatory organization is at www.cca.gouv.fr. This gives details on the history, powers and procedures of the CCAMIP. Beyond that, it has little of general interest about the insurance industry in France. This is better provided by the insurance companies' trade association, the *Fédération Française des Sociétés d'Assurance*. From its home page you can access a useful glossary of insurance terms called 'Glossaire' (useful when it comes to reading other material on the site) and a section called 'Ressources' which offers a copy of the annual report (*Rapport Annuel FFSA*), statistics (*Statistiques*) and other items. The annual report is particularly helpful. It contains most of the useful statistics (www.ffsa.fr).

Table 6.11 French insurance companies – premium income, 2002–06 (€bn)

	General	Life
2002	51.4	93.1
2003	54.0	101.7
2004	56.3	116.4
2005	58.7	133.2
2006	60.7	155.2

Source: Fédération Française des Sociétés d'Assurance (2006) *Rapport Annuel*, Annexe Statistiques p. 71. The report is also available at www.ffsa.fr. Reprinted with permission.

than the life sector (c. 12 per cent p.a.). There are probably two factors at work here. The first is demographic.

Firstly, remember that many of these premiums in the life sector are buying long-term savings products while in general insurance, premiums are mainly buying protection for houses and property.

In Germany and in France there has been a long tradition of state pension provision and in state schemes it is common for those currently retired to draw pensions paid for directly from the taxes and other contributions of those in work. Such schemes are known as 'pay-as-you-go' schemes and consist of straightforward transfers. No fund is accumulated and financial markets and institutions, consequently, are by-passed. The basic state pension in the UK functions in a similar way, but in the UK, because the state pension is paid at a very low level, many people belong additionally to an employers' pension scheme and recently some have paid into private pension schemes of their own choosing. In both these cases contributions during working life accumulate in a fund which can be invested in long-term financial assets. Because of the 'pay-as-you-go' tradition pension funds as such are virtually non-existent in France and Germany and so the job of providing long-term savings to generate income in retirement falls to the life assurance industry.

The feasibility of a pay-as-you-go scheme depends critically upon the age structure of the population. If, say, seven or eight workers are paying taxes to support one retired person, the individual tax burden is acceptable; it may not be acceptable if the population as a whole 'ages' and each pensioner has to be supported by only three or four workers. Ageing populations are a characteristic particularly of Germany, but also at the moment of France and Italy and in all these countries the state is pressuring workers to make greater efforts to provide for their own pensions. The growth of the life assurers is therefore to some extent an offshoot of public policy.

The second reason has to do with the behaviour of financial markets. The benefits of long-term saving through an intermediary that invests largely in stock and bond markets is that the saver benefits from the rising value of assets in those markets. However, while the long-term trend for such values is upward, there can be sharp fluctuations in the short term. There was a sharp fall in equity prices in 2000–01 (the end of the 'dotcom' boom) which did not begin its reverse until 2003. Thereafter, investors saw the value of stocks, and stock-related savings, rise quite steadily until August 2007. 'Following the market' is probably not the best investment strategy but it is easy to understand how unprofessional investors, which is what most households are, decide to buy savings products whose prices are already rising.

6.4   Financial markets in France

The high degree of regulation to which the French financial system was subject until recently affected financial markets as well as institutions. This regulation helped to maintain sharp segmentation between institutions and limited the development of securities markets. (Before 1985, there were no money market

securities and the French 'money market' was, in effect, simply an interbank market.) Several consequences naturally followed. Firstly, financial assets available to the general public were highly liquid, consisting either of 'money' or of savings deposits. From this, in turn, it followed that banks and other financial intermediaries played a more important role (compared to markets) in the French financial system and that they had to perform a higher degree of maturity transformation than intermediaries in systems where securitization was commonplace.

As in the UK, securities trading goes back many centuries. An Order of the Royal Council of State authorized a Paris stock exchange in 1724. However, the Revolution saw many upheavals (including a brief ban in 1795) and it is easier to date its recent history from 1801. For most of the nineteenth century, its fortunes went hand-in-hand with the liberalization of company law that facilitated the incorporation of joint stock companies (1867 and 1900). As we noted earlier, the French government took several steps to modernize the financial system during the 1980s and on the securities front this involved the setting up of the *Marché à Terme International de France SA* (MATIF) and the *Marché des Options Negotiables de Paris SA* (MONEP). The former was a futures exchange offering contracts on government bonds and later on commodities while the latter was an equity options exchange. A 1988 Act reformed the (main) stock exchange, bringing provincial exchanges under its control and naming it the *Société des Bourses Françaises SA* (SBF). The same Act opened up membership of the market to a wide variety of institutions including international banks (in a manner similar to the UK's 'Big Bang'). On 1 June 1999, the four French market operators, MONEP, MATIF, SBF and the recently formed *Société du Nouveau Marché*, for newly incorporated firms, merged to form a new company, *ParisBourse^{SBF} SA*. At this point, trading in virtually all French securities came under one market administrator.

More recently, in 2000, the exchanges of Brussels, Amsterdam and Paris merged to form *Euronext*, a holding company (based in the Netherlands) of which *Euronext Paris* is a subsidiary. At the beginning of 2002, the Euronext group expanded further with the acquisition of the London International Financial Futures Exchange (LIFFE) and the Portuguese Stock Exchange in Lisbon. Finally, in April 2007, the Euronext group merged with the New York Stock Exchange to form *NYSE Euronext*.

MORE FROM THE WEB
History of the Paris Bourse

A more detailed history of securities trading in Paris, including the latest developments involving Euronext, can be found at: www.euronext.com. Click on 'About us', then 'Business' and then 'History'. The history of individual exchanges can be accessed from here.

At the time of writing, the Euronext home page lists 'Other Euronext exchanges' on the left-hand side. Clicking on 'Paris' takes you to the Euronext Paris website. Clicking on 'Indices and statistics' gives access to a large amount of information about the Paris market. A useful place to start is with 'Annual statistics'. This is the source for most of the statistics used in this section.

The section on education/information contains a wide range of documentation explaining the operation of the market at a practical level. 'Euronext: organisation and procedures' is a good place to start.

Table 6.12 gives a number of statistics relating to cash trades in bonds and equities during (or at the end of) 2006. Trading in fixed income securities ('bonds') is confined almost entirely to the main market and

Table 6.12 Securities trading on NYSE Euronext, 2006

	Main market
No. of listed shares – domestic[1]	730
Capitalization[1]	€1,841bn
Turnover[2]	€1,577.6bn
Of which Equities	€1,534.8bn
Government bonds	€0.79bn
Other bonds	€3.32bn
New capital raised on[2]	
Newly listed shares	€9.76bn
Existing shares	€27.77bn
Newly listed bonds	€56.38bn
Existing bonds	€63.35bn

[1] End-December.   [2] Total for year.

Source: www.euronext.com, *Euronext Paris Factbook 2006* at http://www.euronext.com/fic/000/020/200/202003.xls.

accounted in 2006 for less than 1 per cent of the total value of trading. Trading in corporate bonds accounted for about 83 per cent of total bond turnover. Over €37bn of new capital was raised either by new issues of existing shares or the listing of entirely new shares. However, the amount raised from bonds was much greater at €119bn.

As in the UK (see Table 6.9), direct shareholding plays a relatively small part in the portfolios of French households. Investment in equities is indirect via the mutual funds and insurance companies that we saw in the last section and trading in equities accordingly is dominated by these institutions. In the terms that we use in Section 16.6, the Euronext Paris markets (like most continental bourses) work on the basis of electronic matching of orders. For the most frequently traded securities the matching is 'continuous' in the sense that the placing of a buy or sell order will be carried out immediately provided that there is a matching order already on the book. For less liquid securities orders are accumulated and dealt with in two batches (at 10.30 and 4.30). As we explain in Section 16.6, this auction or order-driven type of trading does away with the market-maker, the firm that holds stocks of equities on its own account, and quotes continuous prices at which it is prepared to deal. The participants on the Euronext Paris markets are broadly of two kinds. The first are 'trading members'. These include duly authorized credit institutions, brokerage houses and investment companies that have become market members in order to execute buy and sell orders on the market. Depending on the type of authorization granted, they may trade on behalf of clients and/or on their own account. Clearing members, as their name suggests, are responsible for seeing buyers receive the securities and sellers receive payment within the time specified by market regulations.

Despite all these changes, however, the balance sheets of French firms still show a heavier reliance upon bank-intermediated finance than their counterparts in the UK and USA. Consequently, the savings of French households are still concentrated in bank liabilities, though money market assets, held indirectly via mutual funds, have taken an increased share in recent years. We shall see that equity and bond (direct plus indirect) holdings play a larger role than they do in Germany but they are unlikely to reach UK and USA proportions until funded pension schemes become the norm.

6.5 The development of the Italian financial system

In the terms of the discussion on financial systems in Section 2.2, the Italian financial system is clearly bank-based rather than market-based. Firms have raised funds principally through the banking system. Founding families continue to play an important part in the ownership of many firms, limiting the role played by the equity market. Takeovers and mergers remain relatively uncommon among non-financial firms. Although Italy accounts for approximately 18 per cent of the euro area's GDP, Italian companies were, in the three years to the end of 2006, responsible for only 4 per cent of the value of mergers and acquisitions in the area.

The bond market remains predominantly a market in government bonds and has in the past contributed little to corporate finance. The relationship between banks and firms has typically been close and important. Thus, the Italian system has similarities with the other systems in continental Europe, although it also has a number of individual features.

As with the USA, the basis for the development of the system for the following 60 years was laid in the 1930s. Italy had only become a united country in 1870 and, by the standards of northern Europe, much of it was economically underdeveloped. Its social and economic history had left it with a shortage of private capital willing and able to engage in banking. Prior to the 1930s there had been a succession of bank failures and financial crises and the position deteriorated during the economic crisis of the 1930s. The Italian response was strikingly different from that of the USA in that public intervention frequently followed and, as a result, most of Italy's banks became state-owned, either directly or under the control of charitable, non-profit-making foundations that were themselves government supervised.

However, the *Banking Act, 1936*, derived from the same determination to ensure the stability and security of the system which had been the driving force behind the 1933 *Glass–Steagall Act* in the USA – and it followed much the same approach. The law created a rigid demarcation between financial institutions in providing corporate finance. Commercial banks (standard credit institutions) were only allowed to conduct short-term (up to 18 months) deposit and lending business while medium- and longer-term financing was to be provided by investment banks (special credit institutions). This distinction existed nowhere else in Europe. Commercial banks were given slightly more freedom than this suggests since they could grant medium-term loans not exceeding 8 per cent of their deposits as long as loans to any one institution did not rise above 15 per cent of capital, but any such loans had to be individually authorized by the central bank, the *Banca d'Italia*. Banks were also prohibited from acquiring participating interests in industrial companies and the development of branch networks was discouraged by the *Banca d' Italia* which demanded evidence that there were valid economic reasons for any such expansion.

The banking system that developed was one with a very large number of small local banks that faced very little competition. As a consequence, banks became very bureaucratic and did not provide a high level of service. Savings products provided by the banking system were few and unsophisticated. In the larger public sector banks, as in most parts of the Italian state, appointments of top officials became highly politicized and the banks had little chance of raising share capital.

The structure of Italian capitalism also contributed to the way in which the financial system developed. The family remained central to the operation of capitalism much longer than in comparable countries. The average size of firms remained small. Even today, over 50 per cent of Italian manufacturing firms employ fewer than 100 workers. This is true of under 20 per cent of manufacturing firms in the UK. Many of the larger firms continued to have large family shareholdings. This is still true of firms such as Fiat, Pirelli, Olivetti, Benetton and Gucci. Many other large Italian firms were owned either directly or indirectly by the state. Under these circumstances there was very little call for an equity market and, although it has been strengthened over the past 20 years, its contribution to the growth of the Italian economy has been small.

Following the formation of the EU in 1957, the Italian economy grew very rapidly. However, when growth rates in all western economies turned down in the 1970s, much of the burden in Italy fell upon the Italian state, especially since much of the country's heavy industry was state-owned. Continuing regional problems and public attitudes made it difficult for the government to finance increased expenditure through high taxation and Italy embarked upon a series of large budget deficits. Savings ratios in Italy were high and, given the unsophisticated nature of savings vehicles provided by the banking system and the existence of exchange controls that made it difficult for capital to leave the country, the government was able to finance its deficits through the domestic sale of securities, although at an increasing cost in terms of interest rates and payments. The bond market became entirely dominated by government debt.

Firms seeking capital either provided it themselves through retained earnings or entered into special relationships with investment banks. One such bank, *Mediobanca*, a government-controlled bank in Milan, became central in financing operations and oversaw the development of close relationships among a number of the country's largest private firms. This was in part a response to the lack of development of bond and equity markets but contributed to the continued slow development of those markets.

It was not until the late 1980s that things began seriously to change. The pressures for deregulation that we have noted in other countries gradually came to be felt in Italy. Pressure for reform came also from the Italian employers' association, *Confindustria*, which argued that inefficiencies in Italian banking threatened the long-term viability of Italian manufacturing. The Italian Bankers' Association drew attention to unsystematic *ad hoc* lending criteria and undisciplined loan-monitoring procedures. The *Banca d'Italia* acted in a number of ways to try to bring Italian banking practices into line with the rest of Europe. The requirement that commercial banks needed special authorization from the *Banca d'Italia* to grant medium- or long-term loans was removed. Administrative controls and regulations on the investment of banks' funds in government securities began to be revoked from 1984 on. As soon as the law allowed, the central bank fostered competition by encouraging the merger of smaller credit institutions and, after May 1990, it discontinued the policy of limiting and controlling branch networks. A large increase in the number of bank branches followed.

The gradual reduction in restrictions on capital outflow under the terms of the Single European Act, culminating in the removal of the final foreign exchange control by the end of June 1990, had profound effects. Italian financial institutions now had to compete for the funds of Italian savers with foreign savings products; foreign banks increased their presence within Italy. This occurred first in investment banking, with Italian government bond trading becoming dominated by foreign houses including J P Morgan,

Morgan Stanley and Salomon Brothers. Later, Deutsche Bank and other EU banks began to make inroads into the retail market but these remained minor and later met resistance. Italian banks sought to diversify by granting medium- and long-term loans through special subsidiaries and by engaging in near-banking business such as leasing and factoring. Agreements between commercial and investment banks and insurance companies provided for the marketing of the financial products of other institutions.

It was clear that the 1936 *Banking Act* had to be replaced. A bill to reform the Act was tabled in parliament in 1989 but the new Banking Act was not passed until 1 September 1993, coming into force on 1 September 1994. This law, however, incorporated a number of legislative and administrative changes that had been made from 1990 on. Perhaps the most significant of these was the *Legge Amato* (Law no. 218) of 30 July 1990 which authorized the transformation of public banks into limited companies, establishing the full legal parity of public and private financial intermediaries, on the principle that all banks are business firms. In May 1993, banks were allowed participating interests in industrial companies up to the limit of 15 per cent of their own funds. The *Banking Act, 1993*, removed the distinction between short-term and medium- and long-term lending. It also introduced a separation between the banks themselves (now all private law limited companies) and the public foundations owning shares in those banks. The foundations were allowed to sell or exchange shares, leading to increased concentration. The law thus led to the existence of bank holding companies with subsidiaries providing medium-term lending, insurance and other financial services. It was hoped that this would result in four or five large financial institutions able to compete internationally.

This became more urgent with the translation into Italian law of the EU's *Second Banking Directive* towards the end of 1995. This was followed by a rush of notifications of intent to offer banking services in Italy from banks based in other EU countries.

The *Consolidated Law on Financial Intermediation, 1998*, allowed financial intermediaries to offer a wider range of asset management products. Competition intensified as more banks entered the same markets and the presence of foreign intermediaries increased. The increased competition led to a reduction in the spread between bank lending and deposit rates. This fell from 6 to 4 percentage points between the beginning of the 1990s and the end of 2002 but has again increased since 2005, with bank deposit rates adjusting more slowly than lending rates to changes in monetary conditions. At the end of May 2007, the average interest rate paid on current accounts of households and firms was 1.4 per cent whereas the average rate on bank loans with a maturity of not more than one year to households and firms was just over 6 per cent.[1] This increase in spread happens frequently during periods of rising interest rates.

6.6 The current position of the Italian financial system

6.6.1 The banking industry

The Italian banking system has undergone a major restructuring since the passing of the *Legge Amato* in 1990. Although there are still many banks, mergers and acquisitions have reduced their number from 1,176 in 1989 to 800 at the end of March 2007. As Table 6.13 shows, the reduction in numbers has been among the small cooperative and mutual banks whereas limited company banks have increased in number through the processes of mergers and acquisitions and privatization.

Between the end of 1990 and 2002, there were 566 mergers and acquisitions among banks. The target banks in the mergers and acquisitions accounted for nearly 50 per cent of total bank assets. The process of consolidation slackened in 2001 but regained momentum in 2002 when there were 29 mergers and acquisitions, involving institutions holding 5 per cent of the total assets of the system. Merger activity slowed down again between 2003 and 2005 but picked up sharply in 2006. In that year, the share of system assets attributable to Italian groups that have merged with or been acquired by other Italian groups was estimated at 23.5 per cent compared with 7.2 per cent between 2002 and 2005.[2]

The restructuring process was given a strong impetus in December 1993 when IRI, the large government-owned holding company, sold its 64 per cent stake of ordinary stock in *Credito Italiano*. Other early part or full privatizations included *Banca Commerciale Italiana*, IMI, a Rome-based banking and financial services group, and the investment bank, *Mediobanca*. The withdrawal of the public sector from control of the finance industry was slow in comparison with the programmes of privatization in other countries but sped up in the late 1990s, and the years 1997 and 1998 saw the privatization of a number of the larger banks: *Cassa di Risparmio delle Provincie Lombarde, Banca Nazionale del Lavoro, Banco di Napoli, Banca di Roma*

Table 6.13 The Italian banking system – numbers of banks and branches in Italy

	At end 1995		At end March 2007	
	Number of banks	Number of branches in Italy	Number of banks	Number of branches in Italy
				(end March 2007)
Limited company banks[1]	203	16,744	246	24,704
Cooperative banks (*banche popolari*)	96	4,239	39	3,852
Mutual banks (*banche di credito cooperativo*)	619	2,379	437	3,780
Branches of foreign banks	52	78	78	135
Total	970	23,440	800	32,471

[1] Includes central credit and refinancing institutions.

Source: Banca d'Italia *Relazione Annuale*, 1995, table F3, page 292; Banca d'Italia, *Statistical Bulletin, II 2007*, table B.1 5.1. Reprinted with permission.

---

[1]   Banca d'Italia Eurosistema, *Economic Bulletin*, 45, July 2007, p. 24 and fig. 24.
[2]   Banca d'Italia Eurosistema, *Annual Report 2007*, abridged version, p. 144.

and *Istituto Bancario San Paolo di Torino*. The result was that between 1993 and 2002, the share of bank assets possessed by banks controlled by the state or by charitable foundations fell very sharply – from 70 per cent to 10 per cent – and the process of privatization continued thereafter.

The ownership of banks has become more concentrated than is suggested by the simple reduction in numbers of banks through the development and growth of banking groups (equivalent to the bank holding companies in the USA). By the end of 2006, 87 banking groups encompassed 227 of the 793 banks. Although there were still a large number of independent banks, most of these were small mutual banks and more than 80 per cent of all bank branches belonged to the groups.

Mergers have continued among the banking groups and two particularly large mergers in 2006 and 2007 created two banking institutions, large even by European standards. Intesa Sanpaolo, the result of a merger between Banca Intesa and Sanpaolo IMI completed at the beginning of 2007, had, at the beginning of 2007, assets of €580bn (20.2 per cent of the assets of the domestic market). It has 5,800 branches in Italy and has a presence in 10 other countries through 14 subsidiaries. It has large market shares in central and eastern Europe. An even bigger institution, UniCredit-Capitalia, was created through the

---

BOX 6.2 The five largest Italian banking groups

A brief list of the recent mergers that have taken place to form the leading banking groups gives an idea of the speed of the restructuring of the Italian banking system. As at 31 July 2007, the five largest banking groups in Italy in terms of market capitalization[1] were:

1 **UniCredit-Capitalia (market capitalization €81.39bn)**
   Merger completed in September 2007 between UniCredit and the smaller Capitalia. *UniCredit* was formed in 1998 from the merger in 1998 of Credito Italiano (privatized in late 1993) and a number of smaller banks. After 1998, UniCredit expanded principally by acquiring controlling interests in banks outside Italy, especially in eastern Europe. *Capitalia* had been formed in 2002 from the merger of Gruppo Bancaroma (whose principal members were Banca di Roma and Banco di Sicilia) and Bipop-Carire, the product of a 1999 merger between Bipop (Banca Popolare di Brescia) and Cassa di Risparmio di Reggio Emilia.

2 **Intesa Sanpaolo (market capitalization €69.2bn)**
   Merger completed in January 2007 between Banca Intesa and Sanpaolo IMI. *Banca Intesa* had been produced by the addition in 1999 of Banca Commerciale Italiana to the group formed in 1998 through the merger of CARIPLO (Cassa di Risparmio delle Province Lombarde), Banco Ambrosiano Veneto and Mediocredito Lombardo. *San Paolo IMI* was the result of a merger in 1998 between l'Istituto Bancario San Paolo di Torino and IMI (Istituto Mobiliare Italiano). Sanpaolo IMI had later acquired several other banks including Banco di Napoli; Cassa di Risparmio di Padova e Rovigo; Carisbo (Cassa di Risparmio in Bologna); Friulcassa;

Cassa di Risparmi di Forlì e della Romagna; Cassa di Risparmio di Venezia; and Banca dell'Adriatico).

3 **Mediobanca (market capitalization €12.38bn)**
   The only bank in the top five not the result of recent mergers. Mediobanca was established as an investment bank after the Second World War by Banca Commerciale Italiana, Credito Italiano and Banco di Roma, all then in the public sector. It has since been fully privatized and has expanded in recent years by developing partnerships in various areas of banking and in acquiring shares in foreign banks. In 2006, it became the full owner of the Monaco Bank, Compagnie Monégasque de Banque.

4 **UBI Banca (market capitalization €11.5bn)**
   Formed in April 2007 from the fusion of a number of small mutual banks: Banca Popolare di Bergamo; Banco di Brescia; Banca Popolare Commercio e Industria; Banca Regionale Europea; Banca Popolare di Ancona; Banca Carime (the result of a merger among a number of southern Italian banks): Banca di Valle Camonica; Banco di San Giorgio; BLPI (Banca Lombarda Private Investment).

5 **Banco Popolare (market capitalization €11.34bn)**
   Formed in July 2007 through the merging of a number of small mutual banks: Banca Popolare di Verona; Banca Popolare di Lodi; Banca Popolare di Novara; Credito Bergamasco; Banco S.Geminiano e S.Prospero; Banco S.Marco; Banca Popolare di Trentino; Banca Caripe; Banca Popolare di Crema; Banca Popolare di Cremona; Banca Popolare di Mantova; Cassa di Risparmio di Lucca Pisa Livorno.

---

[1] Market capitalization figures from *Il Sole 24 Ore*, 31 July 2007.

merger of UniCredit and Capitalia from the beginning of October 2007. In terms of market value, it became the biggest bank in the euro area. This increased the market share in terms of assets of these two largest groups to 37.5 per cent of system assets and that of the five largest groups to 53.5 per cent. This is higher than the market share of the five largest banks in Germany but below that in France.

In 2007, there were also significant mergers between cooperative banks creating two large cooperative banking groups. The UBI group, the result of a merger between Banche Popolari Unite and Banca Lombarda e Piemontese, had in 2007 total assets of €117bn and 1,970 branches. The later merger between Banco Popolare di Verona e Novara and Banca Popolare Italiana produced Banco Popolare, a new cooperative bank holding company listed on the stock exchange with assets of €120bn. and 2,200 branches.

Following the removal of restrictions on the development of branch networks, the total number of bank branches has been increasing steadily, rising from 23,440 at the end of 1995 to 32,471 at the end of March 2007. This was more than double the number of bank branches (12,174) in existence in 1980. Thus, the tendency for banks to reduce the size of branch networks evident in the UK has not developed in Italy. The great growth in the number of branches in Italy reflects the previous underdevelopment of the Italian system and the limitations imposed until 1990 on the formation of new branches by the *Banca d'Italia*.

One of the more controversial areas in the development of Italian banking in recent years has related to the attempts of foreign banks to acquire controlling interests in Italian banks.[3] Many foreign banks had built up shareholdings in Italian banks but had found difficulty when they had attempted to increase their holdings to significant levels. Any acquisition of more than 5 per cent of an Italian bank have to be approved by the governor of the central bank. Further approvals are needed to take shareholdings beyond 10 per cent, 15 per cent, 20 per cent, 33 per cent and 50 per cent. The then governor, Antonio Fazio, was believed to have used his power to block the attempts by foreign banks to expand within Italy and also to have opposed several all-Italian banking mergers. Both actions would have been in conflict with the aims of the European Commission to produce a more competitive financial system across Europe.

In February 2005, the EU's financial services commissioner, Charlie McCreevy, wrote to the Bank of Italy expressing his concern about reports that foreign banks were being blocked from expanding in Italy. There was particular concern over the attempt by the Dutch bank ABN-AMRO to increase its shareholding in Banca Antonia Popolare Veneta (Banca Antonveneta) beyond the 12.7 per cent it already held. At the same time, the Bank of Italy approved a takeover bid for Banca Antonveneta being made by the smaller Italian bank, Banca Popolare di Lodi (now part of Banco Popolare). In a second case, the central bank supported a bid for the Banca Nazionale del Lavoro (BNL) by a small Italian insurance company, UNIPOL, in opposition to the Spanish bank, BBVA. Following newspaper publication of intercepted telephone calls between the Governor, his wife, politicians and businessmen, there were accusations of illegal practices and the Bank of Italy announced an investigation into the Governor's actions. He was alleged to have passed on inside information and of having improperly approved share buying and takeover operations, and a criminal investigation was started. Court documents revealed that the chief executive of Banca Popolare Italiana, had also sent numerous gifts to Mr Fazio and his family, including jewellery from Cartier. Under great pressure from both the Italian government and the European Central Bank, Fazio (whom the Italian government had no power to dismiss) eventually resigned in December 2005 although he continued to claim that he had done nothing illegal. Mr Fiorani and other Banco Popolare executives were arrested on insider trading and other charges although Fiorani was released after four months in prison without being charged.

A new governor, Mario Draghi, was appointed to the *Banca d'Italia* in January 2006. Following Fazio's resignation, the *Banca d'Italia* halted the takeover of BNL by UNIPOL and the Banca Popolare di Lodi's takeover attempt of Banca Antonveneta also failed. ABN-AMRO acquired Banca Antonveneta in 2006. BBVA re-launched its bid for BNL but was outbid by the French bank BNP-Paribas. However, despite the fact that there had ultimately been foreign takeovers of Italian banks in these two cases, there were still suggestions that the efforts of foreign banks to make significant inroads into Italy had failed.

---

[3] A list of sources for the information given here on the *Banca d'Italia* can be found at the end of the chapter.

Until recently, Italy's banks were the least profitable in Europe with a very low **return on equity (ROE)** compared with European competitors. The low profitability of Italian banks over a long period had been explained by their heavy dependence on traditional loan income with only small amounts of revenue coming from commission or other fee-based income and by their high staff costs. An additional reason for the lower rate of return in Italy had been the higher rate of direct taxation. However, the tax burden was eased by the application of dual income tax from 2000 onwards and reductions in the rate of the regional tax on productive activities that took effect from 2001.

During the early and middle years of the 1990s, the capital bases and the profitability of banks declined. Each year from 1994 to 1997 the 10 largest banks recorded an overall net loss, owing in part to loan losses generated in the past recession. Corporate finances had deteriorated sharply in 1992 and 1993, there had been a crisis in the construction and public works sector and property values had fallen. The long stagnation of the southern Italian economy had continued. In addition, in the middle years of the decade there were high restructuring costs involving voluntary redundancy payments needed to bring about staff reductions. Yet again, the ambitious strategy of mergers, acquisitions and expansion of branch numbers initially led to low earnings retention and declining profit margins because of the poor state of many of the banks acquired. The low profitability and weak capitalization, in turn, had an adverse effect on credit ratings.

However, the performance of the larger banking groups in particular improved considerably in the late 1990s and, overall, the profitability of the Italian banking system moved closer to the European average. In 1995, the average rate of return on equity for all Italian banks was only 4.13 per cent. This had risen to 7.4 per cent by 1998, in comparison with 14.0 per cent in Spain, 10.2 per cent in Germany and 8.3 per cent in France. In 2000, the return on equity rose to an average of 12.9 per cent. For 2006, the return on equity for the system as a whole was 13.8 per cent while for the five largest banking groups, the figure was 15.6 per cent.

This very considerable increase in profitability stemmed from the supply of a wider range of services and improvements in operating efficiency. During the second half of the 1990s, the proportion of gross

> **MORE FROM THE WEB**
>
> The Bank of Italy website, www.bancaditalia.it, provides almost everything you are likely to want in relation to Italian banking – articles, speeches, statistics and comments on the world, euro area and Italian economies. There is an English-language version. The quarterly *Economic Bulletin* is particularly useful. Go to the Bank of Italy's home page, click on 'Publications' and then on 'Economic Publications'.

income generated by services and trading in securities and foreign currencies rose from 26 to 43 per cent. In 2006, non-interest income made up 47.4 per cent of the gross income of the banking system. This was partially the result of the programme of mergers and acquisitions, which enabled the larger banks rapidly to expand their asset management and business services.

Following large staff reductions, staff costs began to fall relative to bank earnings. In 1996 the banks' per capita labour costs had been 31 per cent higher than the average in Germany, France and Spain but the gap narrowed to 17 per cent in 1998. A new national labour contract for the banking industry came into effect in November 1999, restraining wage increases and automatic seniority increments. Action plans were agreed to make work organization more flexible, improve training and upgrade employees' skill levels. In the mid-1990s staff costs were equal to 45 per cent of gross income, significantly higher than for banks in other large countries. By 2000, the figure had fallen to 36 per cent.

The performance of the Italian banking industry is influenced by the strong north–south difference. The weak economy of the south led to crisis in the credit system in the early 1990s, with bad debts up to three times higher than in the north. Two of the largest banks in the area, the *Banco di Napoli* and *Sicilcassa*, ran into serious trouble. The *Banco di Napoli* had to be rescued from a liquidity crisis with huge loans from the Deposits and Loans Fund and from leading banks. In addition, parliament authorized the Treasury to subscribe additional increases in the bank's capital. *Sicilcassa* was taken into special administration. Other smaller banks in the south also found themselves in trouble. Many interventions by the supervisory authorities aimed at avoiding interruption to the supply of financial services in the areas concerned and at transferring sound credit positions to other banks. This often led to banks located in the south being taken over by banking groups whose parent companies are based in the centre and the north. Ownership of the industry is now heavily concentrated in the north.

Banking and other financial services remain much less developed in the south. The growth in the number of bank branches has reduced the number of inhabitants per bank branch for Italy as a whole to just over 1,800. This improvement has occurred in all regions but there remains a marked north–south difference. At the end of 2006, in the north and centre there was a bank branch for every 1,500 inhabitants as against 2,730 in the south and islands. The lower level of competition together with the higher proportion of bad debts means that interest rates on short-term loans are higher in the south than in the north and centre although the differential has fallen in recent years. At the end of 2006 it was approximately 1.3 per cent. The difference is rather less for long-term loans. The gap between deposit and lending rates in 2006 was around 4.7 per cent in the south compared with a gap of approximately 3.5 per cent in the centre and north.

6.6.2 The banking authorities

The *Banca d'Italia* was, until the beginning of 1999, as the Bank of England was until 1997, the bank of issue and the government's principal banker. It also played a role in the supervision of the Italian banking system. It retains the last two of these three roles, having become a member of the European System of Central Banks (ESCB) and having passed over its monetary responsibility to the ECB.

The *Banca d'Italia* was founded in 1893 as a private company but became part of the public sector in 1936. It derives its primary role as responsible for monetary stability from article 47 of the 1947 Italian constitution. This is a vaguely worded article which does not mention the *Banca d'Italia* by name but talks of encouraging savings and controlling credit.

Until 1992, the *Banca d'Italia* was far from being independent of government. The *Comitato Interministeriale per il Credito e il Risparmio* (CICR) was responsible for monetary policy issues and bank supervision policy. It was made up of the Treasury, Finance and other economic ministers, with the governor of the *Banca d'Italia* only being present at meetings in an advisory capacity. The Minister of Finance, together with the Minister for Trade, was responsible for all foreign exchange policy decisions and appointed or dismissed presidents of public banks in consultation with the political parties. The problem of financing the government's large budget deficits led to regular conflicts between it and the *Banca d'Italia*. Until 1981 the *Banca d'Italia* was required to take into its own portfolio any government securities not taken up by the market. Although this requirement was annulled, the government continued to make constant use of a cash advance facility which obligated the *Banca d'Italia* to provide up to 14 per cent of projected budgetary expenditure. In January 1983 the *Banca d'Italia* made use of a 1948 legislative decree under which, when the Treasury persistently exceeded the limits of the cash advance facility, it could suspend its payments to the Treasury and force parliament to resolve the conflict between the central bank and the Executive. Parliament responded by approving legislation requiring the *Banca d'Italia* to grant the Treasury extraordinary additional finance.

As required for membership of economic and monetary union, steps were taken in the first half of the 1990s to increase the power of the central bank relative to that of the elected government. In February 1992, the authority to determine the discount rate was transferred from the Minister of Finance to the central bank and in June 1994 the *Banca d'Italia* assumed responsibility for determining minimum reserve policy. For a time, however, government continued to attempt to influence the bank through the method of appointment of its top officials. The *Banca d'Italia*'s executive directorate is composed of the governor (who has no fixed term) and three other members, all of whom are chosen by the governing council on which sits the bank's 13 regional office chairmen. Appointments must, however, be confirmed by the Italian President in consultation with the government. A conflict over bank appointments occurred in 1994 when the government used its power to veto the appointment of Tommaso Padoa Schioppa to the executive directorate of the bank but could not then enforce the selection of its own preferred candidate. Instead, the *Banca d'Italia* was able to appoint a substitute for Padoa Schioppa from within its ranks. No conflict of this kind has since arisen. Padoa Schioppa later became the Italian member of the Executive Board of the ECB and, from

May 2006, Minister for the Economy in the Italian government.

As supervisory authority, the *Banca d'Italia* evaluates proposed consolidation projects and monitors their implementation. It assesses the adequacy of risk measurement and management systems and calls on parent companies to take prompt action to rationalize branch networks and integrate information systems and procedures. The bank has the power to investigate in cases where increased concentration may reduce competition. It can issue warnings to banks, can order compensating measures such as the closure or sale of branches or a temporary ban on the opening of new branches and, where anti-competitive behaviour is found, can levy fines on the banks involved. The bank initially played a major role in encouraging and supervising the restructuring of the Italian banking sector but has also, notably through the efforts of Antonio Fazio (Governor from 1994 to December, 2005), sought to control the nature of that restructuring.

6.6.3 The securities industry

The potential for securities markets in Italy has been high for a long time because Italian savings have been consistently high by international standards. A comparison of household net savings rates (savings as a percentage of household disposable income) for 2005 across 24 OECD members placed Italy at the top with a ratio of 11.6 per cent, ahead of France (11.5) and Germany (10.7). The ratio of other euro area countries in the table were: Belgium (10.4), Austria (9.1), Netherlands (7.1), Spain (4.6), Portugal (4.0), Finland (0.0), UK (0.0) and Greece (−7.7).

The propensity of Italian households to save as calculated by the Bank of Italy has fallen from 21 per cent of disposable income in 1983 to between 12 and 13 per cent in the first five years of this century. In 2006, it fell to 11.0 but, as we have seen above, this is still high by the standards of most other countries. Italian households also stand out by international comparison for the low level of their debt. Although the liabilities of households have risen considerably in recent years, largely for the purchase of housing, the ratio of financial liabilities to assets in 2006, at 17.6 per cent, remained well below the figures in other major

industrial countries (32.6 per cent on average for the euro area countries, 31 per cent in the USA and 36 per cent in the UK). However, Italian savings products have until recently been unsophisticated and only a small proportion of Italian savings has in the past been professionally managed.

The large budget deficits of the 1970s and 1980s led to securities markets being dominated by the market for public debt. From 1980 to 1991, that debt grew almost sixfold; relative to national income it rose from 59 per cent to 102 per cent. By 1996, general government gross debt was 123.4 per cent of GDP. This limited the development of the equity market and accentuated the corporate sector's preference for bank or internal sources of financing. The Italian government debt market is now the third largest in the world in nominal terms, behind those of USA and Japan. Until recently, most of the relatively small number of private bonds have been issued by publicly owned companies such as public banks or the Italian state railways. Bonds directly issued by the corporate sector have represented only a tiny proportion of the total amount outstanding. At the end of 1995, 88.2 per cent of the total stock of outstanding bonds and government securities consisted of public sector bonds or bills. Banks had been responsible for the issue of 10.5 per cent of the stock and firms for only 1.5 per cent.

After 1996, as part of the Italian government's drive to meet the convergence criteria for membership of economic and monetary union, the public sector deficit began to fall. The general government net borrowing requirement fell to 1.8 per cent in 2000 before rising again, reaching 4.2 per cent in 2005 and 4.4 per cent in 2006.[4] By 2003, government debt had fallen back to 106.2 per cent of GDP. This reduction in the need for the public sector to sell new debt provided some scope for the re-emergence of a corporate bond market. However, recent increases in the net borrowing requirement have prevented the government debt/GDP ratio from falling further. It stood at 106.8 per cent at the end of 2006.

In common with the rest of the euro area, the Italian bond market grew considerably after the launch of the single currency. Between 1998 and 2006 the ratio to GDP of the stock of resident companies' bond issues on the domestic and international markets rose from

---

[4] However, the 2006 figure included extraordinary special costs and the performance was considered an improvement on the previous year.

Table 6.14 Outstanding bonds of Italian companies

	Stocks (at face value; millions of €)		As a % of GDP		
	2005	**2006**	**1998**	**2002**	**2006**
Banks	484,370	544,742	25	32	37
Other financial companies	162,831	185,299	0	7	13
Non-financial companies	46,167	50,626	3	7	3
Total	693,368	780,667	28	47	53
of which: international market	312,345	392,665	4	20	27

Source: Banca d'Italia (2003) *Economic Bulletin,* 37, November, table 1, p. 88.; Banca d'Italia (2006) *Annual Report,* table 13.2, p. 119. Reprinted with permission.

28 to 53 per cent in Italy but much of this growth has been, as Table 6.14 shows, attributable to banks, which use the proceeds of bond issues to fund their loans. Between 1998 and 2002 the stock of securities issued by non-financial firms rose from 3 to 7 per cent of GDP in Italy and from 5 to 8 per cent in the euro area as a whole. Issues continued to grow in 2003 and 2004 but then, against the euro area trend fell back, following the collapse of the two large industrial groups Cirio and Parmalat. By the end of 2006, the stock of bonds issued by non-financial firms had fallen back to the 1998 figure of 3 per cent of GDP compared with 7 per cent for the euro area. In 2006 bonds amounted to under 2 per cent of non-financial firms' total financial liabilities, similar to the proportion in Germany but far smaller than in France, the UK and the USA. By international standards the corporate bond market in Italy remains underdeveloped.

The securities issued by the Treasury are of standard types ranging from treasury bills to floating rate issues. Their names and available maturities are provided in Box 6.3.

Denominations (€1,000) are small enough to allow private investors to participate in the fortnightly auctions through financial intermediaries. The result is that over three-quarters of the public debt consists of securities placed in the domestic market with the greater part held by households, firms and institutional investors. Investment in government securities has spread to all the different components of society: around 40 per cent of pensioners hold government securities, as do more than 35 per cent of white-collar households and nearly 25 per cent of blue-collar households.

The market was reformed in 1988, with a group of institutions becoming market-makers quoting bid–offer prices on various bonds as in the UK and USA. Previously, treasury bonds had been sold by banks forming a consortium and subscribing to a whole issue even if at prices below the equilibrium level. There had been government arm-twisting of financial intermediaries to ensure the sale of bonds. In 1988 also an efficient screen-based secondary market for government securities, the MTS, was established. This has now been privatized and around 200 Italian and foreign intermediaries engage in the trading of Italian government

---

BOX 6.3 Italian government securities

The five types of security issued by the Italian government are:

1 Treasury Bills (BOTs: Buoni Ordinari del Tesoro) – maturities of 3, 6 and 12 months.

2 Zero Coupon Bonds (CTZs: Certificati del Tesoro Zero coupon) – 24 months.

3 Treasury Bonds (BTPs: Buoni del Tesoro Poliennali) – maturities of 3, 5, 10, 15 and 30 years.

4 Treasury Bonds indexed to Eurozone Inflation (BTP€i: BTPs indicizzato all'inflazione) – maturities of 5, 10 and 30 years.

5 Treasury Certificates (CCTs: Certificati di Credito del Tesoro) – 7 years.

For other details see the pretty chart in 'Italian Government Bonds in a Nutshell' on http://www.dt.tesoro.it/ENGLISH-VE/Public-Deb/Treasury-S/Italian-Government-Bonds-in-a-Nutshe.pdf.

bonds and those of other EU governments. In addition, there are retail markets for government and corporate bonds.

The market was reformed in part because of the perceived need to attract foreign investors following the removal of exchange controls which increased the possibility of Italian savings flowing abroad. There has indeed been a considerable growth in non-resident holdings of government securities in recent years. In 1996, non-residents owned only 15 per cent of Italian public sector securities. By the end of 2005 this had risen to 56 per cent. The share held directly by households and non-financial firms had fallen to 11 per cent. However, 2006 saw households and firms again engage in substantial net purchases of public securities while foreign investors cut back sharply their net purchases. The move of households back to government securities indicated a reduce willingness to take risks. This was reflected also in the increase in the proportion of fixed-rate and inflation-indexed securities sold since these are less vulnerable to movements in nominal interest rates. The fall in foreign purchases in 2006 was probably partially the result of increased concern about the quality of Italian debt given Italy's continuing failure to achieve the EU's public finance targets. This led to the downgrading of Italian debt by two of the three big international credit-rating agencies in October 2006. The downgrading itself, however, appeared to have little impact on the market.

Change has been slower to come in equities markets. By the end of 2006, there were still only 284 companies listed on the Italian Stock Exchange in Milan – many fewer than in the other major euro area countries. The relatively underdeveloped state of the Italian stock market is also shown by its capitalization. Price rises contributed to a sharp rise in capitalization in 2006, from €677 billion (49 per cent of GDP) to €779 billion (52.8 per cent of GDP). This was only slightly behind the German Stock Exchange which had a market capitalization of 54 per cent of GDP but well below the four countries with Euronext exchanges – Belgium, France, the Netherlands and Portugal – where the ratio was 101 per cent and far behind the UK (150 per cent) and the USA (145 per cent).

The equity market had grown in the 1980s and 1990s, but progress had been slowed by the way in which the stock exchange operated. A 1913 law had given a monopoly over transactions to brokers. They were meant to be pure brokers, acting only as agents.

However, the market did not work well in the late 1980s. No one was compelled to use the stock exchange and only 20 per cent of transactions went through the exchange; the average availability of a company's share capital on the market was very small. The official market was thus thin and speculative and was a market for insiders. There were no rules of conduct or investor protection. Specifically, there was no law on insider trading and no rules requiring public takeover offers. This all led to many complaints that share deals were frequently rigged by big groups, that small investors were crucified and that the market was characterized by secret pacts and the atmosphere of a private club. A new bill was presented to parliament in 1989 requiring transactions in equities to go through authorized intermediaries on the official market. The distinction between brokers and market-makers disappeared. New firms became market-makers, brokers and fund managers, with Chinese walls being required. The Italian Stock Exchange was privatized in 1997, becoming *Borsa Italiana SpA*. Despite these changes, there were only small increases in the number of companies listed on the exchange in Milan in the 1990s and the early part of this century and the gap with respect to the other euro area countries in terms of the number of listed companies continued to widen. Most of the increase in activity that took place in the Italian equities market in these years was associated with the newly privatized companies, particularly those in the banking sector. Studies seeking to identify the reasons for the limited growth of the Italian Stock Exchange highlight the limited supply of shares: businessmen's fear of losing control and reluctance to disclose the information laid down for listed companies discourage them from going public.

As in other countries, a new market, the *Nuovo Mercato* (NM) was established in 1999 for the listing of high technology stocks. More recently, the principal stock market has been segmented with the intention of making exchange listing easier for small and medium-sized companies. Thus, in December 2003 the Expandi market was established for small firms. Medium-sized firms (with market capitalization below €800 million) in both traditional and technology-based industries are catered for in the Star segment of the market. The tech-Star index is an index of prices of equities of technology-based companies in the Star segment. On 1 October 2007, *Borsa Italia* merged with the London Stock Exchange.

All of these changes are perhaps giving new life to the Milan exchange. New listings have been increasing recently. In 2006, 21 new companies made initial public offerings compared with 15 in 2005. Of these 21, 9 were in the Star segment and 7 in the Expandi market. This, together with the big increase in the number of companies quoted in the Star segment in 2005 (see Table 6.15), suggests a new confidence in raising funds through the exchange on the part of small and medium-sized companies. On the other hand, it might rather be a reflection of the four consecutive years of increasing prices of quoted shares following the large price falls of 2001 and 2002.

6.6.4 Institutional investors

Institutional investors include investment funds, insurance companies, pension funds and asset management companies. Asset management companies were created by the 1998 Consolidated Law on Financial Intermediation. They provide individual portfolio management services for a number of banking groups and manage a large part of the portfolios of Italy's main insurance companies.

The late 1980s and 1990s saw a marked growth in the professional management of savings. According to the *Banca d'Italia*'s survey of household income and wealth, between 1995 and 1998 the proportion of households entrusting their financial savings to

investment funds or portfolio management services rose from 5 to 11 per cent. Between the end of 1996 and the end of 2000 assets under management in Italy in individual and collective investment portfolios nearly tripled. As Table 6.16 shows, by the end of 2006 the total amount under management had risen to over €1,400 billion. However, institutional investors remain relatively unimportant by international standards, principally because of the small presence of pension funds.

As elsewhere, investment funds are divided into open-end and closed-end funds although the Italian market is dominated by open-end funds, over 80 per cent of which are **harmonized open-end** funds. These are the product of a 1985 European directive that sought to harmonize the laws, regulations and administrative provisions relating to undertakings of collective investments in transferable securities (**UCITS**). The directive sets out a number of requirements relating to competition among UCITS across Europe and to the protection of investors. Open-end funds that meet these requirements are then granted a European passport. This allows them to be freely marketed across borders in European Economic Area countries without further authorization. They only need to be registered in the country of destination (host country). Once this is done they are subject to the laws, regulations and administrative provisions in force concerning marketing, advertising and taxation. The directive aimed to simplify cross-border marketing and to help

Table 6.15 Performance of the Italian Stock Exchange, 2001–06

	2001	2002	2003	2004	2005	2006
Annual change in prices[1]	−25.1	−23.7	14.9	17.5	20.0	19.0
Listed Italian companies						
(number at end of year)	288	288	271	269	275	284
of which: in the STAR segment	*37*	*41*	*40*	*46*	*70*	*75*
Total market capitalization[2] (€m)	592,319	457,992	487,446	568,901	676,606	778,501
as a percentage of GDP	*48.6*	*36.3*	*37.5*	*43.1*	*47.7*	*52.8*
Market value of newly listed						
companies (€m)[3]	10,554	5,142	1,412	5,999	6,405	12,919
Turnover: spot market (€m)	620,004	572,940	580,703	641,376	893,853	1,078,390

[1] Percentage change in the MIB index during the year.   [2] Italian companies, at end of period.
[3] Sum of the market value of each of the companies at the IPO price.
Source: Banca d'Italia (2006) *Annual Report*, table 13.3, p. 123. Reprinted with permission.

Table 6.16 Italian institutional investors: assets under management

	End-of-period stocks (€m)		Percentage composition	
	2005	2006[1]	2005	2006[1]
Investment funds[2]	416,628	391,021	30.2	27.6
Insurance companies[3]	417,957	439,535	30.3	31.1
Pension funds[4]	34,655	37,062	2.5	2.6
Individually managed portfolios	512,713	547,580	37.1	38.7
Total	1,381,953	1,415,198	100.0	100.0

[1] Provisional.   [2] Italian investment funds and SICAVs.   [3] Technical reserves.   [4] Total balance sheet assets.

Source: Banca d'Italia (2006) *Annual Report*, table 13.1, p. 117. Reprinted with permission.

to bring about a European capital market. However, member states may also allow the marketing of non-harmonized (non-UCITS) investment funds. These include hedge funds and closed-end funds such as real estate funds and special funds for institutional investors as well as special funds for retirement provision. Harmonized open-end funds are in turn divided into equity, balanced, bond, money market and flexible funds. Table 6.17 shows the market structure of Italian investment funds.

As Tables 6.16 and 6.17 show, 2006 saw a fall in investment fund assets as a result of net redemptions. This was primarily due to the increased preference of households noted above for direct investment in low-risk assets such as government securities and bank bonds. The falls were all among harmonized open-end funds. The gainers were new types of investment funds such as hedge funds and closed-end real estate funds. There was also an increase in the assets held in foreign funds (both harmonized and non-harmonized) controlled by Italian intermediaries (not shown in Tables 6.16 and 6.17). Despite this, the net assets of the harmonized funds controlled by Italian intermediaries fell as a percentage of overall investment fund assets in the euro area by more than 2 points to 10.8 per cent.

Table 6.17 Italian investment funds: market structure[1]

	Number of funds[2]		Net assets		% of total assets	
	2005	2006	2005	2006	2005	2006
Harmonized open-end funds	871	842	352,103	311,582	84.5	79.7
equity	376	346	74,845	68,770	18.0	17.6
balanced	71	64	33,214	30,790	8.0	7.9
bond	306	302	157,359	121,255	37.8	31.0
money market	42	40	72,840	67,009	17.4	17.1
flexible	76	90	13,845	23,758	3.3	6.1
Non-harmonized open-end funds	354	417	50,164	60,047	12.0	15.3
of which: hedge funds	162	206	16,957	23,592	4.1	6.0
Total open-end funds	1,225	1,259	402,267	371,629	96.5	95.0
Closed-end funds	129	191	14,361	19,392	3.5	5.0
Total	1,354	1,450	416,628	391,021	100	100

[1] Includes SICAVs.   [2] Funds in operation at the end of the year indicated.

Source: Banca d'Italia (2006) *Annual Report*, table 13.4, p. 124. Reprinted with permission.

The Italian life insurance industry has grown rapidly in recent years. Between 1990 and 2005, life insurance premiums grew by an average of over 20 per cent from under €5,000m in 1990 to €75,577m in 2005. This far outstripped the rate of growth in non-life insurance. However, in 2006 life insurance premium income fell by 3.7 per cent. By the end of 2004, insurance reserves had risen from around 6 per cent in the 1990s to 9.8 per cent.

Nonetheless, the industry remains underdeveloped by international standards. To see this, we need only consider the figures for life insurance reserves as a percentage of GDP at the end of 2003 in a number of European countries. These were:[5]

UK	87.1%
France	50.2%
Netherlands	45.6%
Belgium	34.7%
Germany	28.6%
Italy	20.8%
Spain	14.7%

There has been a strong tendency towards the concentration of the industry, with several mergers involving foreign insurance companies. Banks play an important role in the market. As elsewhere, ownership links have developed between banks and insurance companies, especially in the field of life insurance, and the cross-selling of products. Business combinations involving banks and insurance companies have frequently been cross-border and have given rise to some of the largest European conglomerates. In Italy, five of the ten largest life insurance companies have links with banks. Some smaller banks are controlled by insurance companies.

Pension funds have been particularly slow to develop largely because of the generous state pension provision.

However, in the early 1990s, the Italian government accepted that it needed to reform pension provision and to reduce state pension provision if they were to meet the requirements of membership of the single European currency. More recently, the concern has been with meeting the requirements of the EU's growth and stability pact. Thus, in 1992 the Italian social security system was radically reformed. This reform introduced supplementary retirement instruments and rules in an attempt to encourage Italian workers to make private pension provision. Despite this, Italy lags far behind not only the USA and the UK, where pension funds have developed most strongly, but also behind euro area economies such as France, Germany and Spain. At the end of 2006, pension fund assets were equal to less than 3 per cent of Italian GDP, against the euro area average of 15 per cent and that for the USA and the UK of approximately 65 per cent. In the 2006 annual report, the Banca d'Italia reported that sample surveys showed that Italian workers are only partially aware of the extent of the cuts made to public pensions and thus of the need to make private pension provision. To try to overcome the problem, new rules on supplementary retirement schemes were approved in 2005 and took effect from the beginning of 2007. These greatly increased the flexibility of the funds held in supplementary retirement schemes. This, together with employer contributions and favourable tax treatment, was expected to increase the flow of funds into pensions.

Individual portfolio management accounts have gradually spread from higher income investors to a wider customer base. As a result, assets held in individually managed portfolios grew very rapidly until 1999 but then slowed. Nonetheless, as

---

[5] Figures from *Overview of the Italian Insurance Market*, presentation by the Associazione Nazionale fra le Imprese Assicuratrici (ANIA) to the International Monetary Fund, Rome, 26 October 2005, on http://www.ania.it/home/.

Table 6.18 Individually managed portfolios: net flows and assets under management

Year	Net flows (€m)	End-of-period stocks (€m)	% of total funds under management
1999	53,609	370,292	33.6
2000	33,087	392,112	34.6
2001	27,343	410,406	36.5
2002	5,715	401,755	36.4
2003	5,364	418,128	35.4
2004	14,296	448,661	35.8
2005	35,410	512,713	37.1
2006	26,719	547,580	38.7

Table 6.18 shows, they have continued to grow both in absolute terms and as a percentage of total assets under management.

The low figures for net fund raising in 2002 and 2003 were the result of the weak performance of stock markets in those years. The decline in 2006 relative to 2005 was ascribed to the return of households to direct investment in government securities and private sector bonds. This was brought about partly by low average yields of the portfolio management services.

The composition of portfolio management accounts has changed as government securities have made way for a growing proportion of shares and corporate bonds. In 2006, portfolio managers made large net sales of Italian government securities and investment fund units and net purchases of Italian equities and foreign securities. At the end of 2006, foreign securities made up 54.7 per cent of the assets held.

In Europe venture capital business has grown rapidly in recent years but, compared with the USA, it has focused less on investments in innovative sectors and new companies. Investment and fund-raising by private equity and venture capital companies has increased but is still far smaller than in other leading industrial countries. About two-thirds of investment related to transactions involving changes in the ownership of large companies while, as in earlier years, funding for business start-ups or companies in high-technology sectors played only a minor role. On average over the decade from 1996 to 2005, venture capital and private equity investment in new companies was equal to 0.27 per cent of GDP in the USA,

0.1 per cent in European countries as a group and only 0.05 per cent in Italy. Closed-end investment funds are important for this type of investment but, as we have seen, this sector is not well developed in Italy. A decree issued by the minister of the Treasury in 1999 made it easier for investors to enter and exit such funds. This led to increased activity in this field for a time but has had no long-term effect. In addition, the underdevelopment of pension funds makes it more difficult to find investors with a long investment horizon. It is also more difficult in Italy for venture capital funds to exit once they judge that they can no longer contribute to the growth of the enterprises than it is in countries with more developed equity markets.

6.7 Summary

Until the 1970s, France could certainly be regarded as having an overdraft economy – one with a bank-based financial system. The system has also been highly centralized and regulated. Many changes have taken place in recent years although these have largely occurred as a result of deliberate decisions made by the French state rather than being a private sector response to changed financial conditions.

The changes introduced by the state were made in response to the movement towards a single European market which was opening the French financial system to competition. The result was the Banking Act, 1984, which had implications for almost all financial institutions. In 1993, as part of the preparation for a move to European Monetary Union (discussed in Chapter 22), the *Banque de France*, France's central bank, was made autonomous from government. As with Germany, however, securities markets, and particularly the market for equities, have been less important in providing corporate finance and assets for households than US and UK markets have been for their savers and borrowers. In both cases this is partly the result of the small pension fund sector, itself a product of generous state pensions financed on PAYG principles.

The Italian financial system is different again. In the past its banking system was highly segmented, its equity market small and the financial system dominated by the large market in government securities. However, the Italian system is now becoming more like those of the other leading countries. The banking system, under severe pressure to become more efficient, changed rapidly in the 1990s through mergers, takeovers and privatization. The government securities market, while still very large, has become relatively less important. The lengthening of average life expectancy, the reform of public pension systems, and more widespread familiarity with financial instruments have strengthened the preference for managed assets and stimulated the demand for complex and sophisticated financial services. The share of equity capital in households' portfolios is increasing, as is the share of savings entrusted to specialized managers.

Greater use is being made of technologically advanced channels for the distribution of financial instruments. It remains that the equity market, the corporate bond market and pension funds are all underdeveloped by the standards of other euro area countries and particularly in relation to the USA and the UK.

This study of financial structures shows us that although the current structures still show the importance of historical, political and social influences, there is a strong tendency with the development of a single European financial market for them to become more alike.

Key concepts in this chapter

Fonds commun de placement
Harmonized investment funds
Market capitalization
Mutual and cooperative banks
Overdraft economy

Return on equity (ROE)
Savings banks
SICAVs
UCITS

Questions and problems

1 Explain what is meant by an 'overdraft' economy.

2 Distinguish between the functions of the *Comité des Etablissements de Crédit,* the *Comité de Réglementation Bancaire* and the *Commission Bancaire.*

3 Give three examples of steps taken to stimulate the development of securities markets in France in recent years.

4 Why have French governments taken these steps?

5 Why was the Italian banking system segmented and uncompetitive until the 1990s?

6 What was done during the 1990s to increase the relative profitability of Italian banks?

7 Why has the market for government securities been the dominant financial market in Italy until recent years?

8 In what ways and for what reasons is the Italian financial system becoming more similar to the financial systems of other developed countries? In what ways does it remain different?

Further reading

Associazione Nazionale fra le Imprese Assicuratrici (ANIA), *Overview of the Italian Insurance Market,* presentation to the International Monetary Fund, Rome, 26 October 2005, at http://www.ania.it/home/
Banca d'Italia, *Annual Report 2006* (Rome: Banca d'Italia, 2007) (annual reports and other publications are available in English and Italian at www.bancaditalia.it/)
Banca d'Italia, 'The growth of the market for Italian corporate bonds', *Economic Bulletin,* 37, November 2003 (Rome: Banca d'Italia)
Banque de France, *Monthly Digest* (Paris: Banque de France)

Denis Marionnet, 'French households' financial investment. Comparisons with Europe (1995–2004)' *Banque de France Bulletin*, Summer 2006 (http://www.banquedefrance.fr/gb/publications/telnomot/bulletin/qsa4.pdf)

Euronext, *Euronext: Organization and Procedures* (Paris: Euronext, 2002)

A Fazio, 'Fact-finding with regard to the relationship between firms, financial markets and savings', *Economic Bulletin*, 38, March 2004 (Rome: Banca d'Italia)

Fédération Bancaire Française, *Overview of French Banking* (2006) (www.fbf.fr)

Fédération Française des Sociétés d'Assurance, *Rapport annuel* (Paris: FFSA, annually)

J R Hicks, *The Crisis in Keynesian Economics* (Oxford: Blackwell, 1974)

INSEE, *Bulletin Mensuel de Statistique* (Paris: INSEE, various)

D K R Klein, *The Banking Systems of the EU Member States* (Cambridge: Gresham Books, 1995)

Sources for information on *Banca d'Italia* found in this chapter:

T Barber, A Michaels and F Kapner, 'A cloud over the Bank of Italy', *Financial Times*, 2 August 2005

I Bickerton, L Crawford, A Jones and A Michaels, 'Companies International: Italy fends off assault by foreign invaders', *Financial Times*, 8 June 2007

T Buck, 'Italy asked to clarify foreign banking participation', *Financial Times*, 14 February 2005

D Dombey, T Barber and R Atkins, 'Europe: Brussels to take action over Bank of Italy', *Financial Times*, 25 November 2005

Financial Times, Leader, 'Fazio bows out', 20 December 2005

A Michaels, 'Rome moves on Fazio amid insider trading probe', *Financial Times*, 16 December 2005

A Michaels, 'Companies Europe: Italian banking strives to shake off shackles of the past', *Financial Times*, 9 August 2007

L Pagni, 'La seconda vita di Fiorani "In tv darò consigli ai truffati"', *La Repubblica*, 14 July 2007

La Repubblica, 'Antonveneta, arrestato Fiorani nel mandato "soldi ai politici"', *La Repubblica*, 13 December 2005

Websites

www.afb.fr
www.amf-france.org
www.ania.it/home/
www.bancaditalia.it
www.banque-france.fr
www.borsaitaliana.it/
www.Bourse-de-Paris.fr
www.cca.gouv.fr
www.dt.tesoro.it
www.efama.org/
www.euronext.com
www.fbf.fr
www.ffsa.fr
www.oee.fr

Chapter 7

Financial systems in Northern Europe

By Hans-Michael Trautwein

What you will learn in this chapter

- The main features of the banking systems in Nordic countries

- The main features of Nordic non-deposit-taking institutions

- The origins of Nordic banking crises in the 1980s and 1990s

- Current trends towards concentration and integration

- The differences and similarities in approach to monetary policy among Northern European countries

7.1 Introduction

The Nordic countries – Denmark, Norway, Sweden and Finland[1] – are small economies in comparison with the countries whose financial systems have been described in previous chapters. Yet the institutions of money, banking and finance in these Northern European countries are of general interest because of their history and because of the current interaction between structural changes in the financial systems and the diversity of monetary policy frameworks in the region. Moreover, the four countries enjoy a relatively high degree of cultural homogeneity, and if their financial institutions continue to merge and cooperate at their current pace, the region will – with less than 25 million inhabitants, but a total GDP that exceeds that of Spain (with a population of more than 40 million) – soon have an integrated financial market that ranks among the ten largest in the world.

The Bank of Sweden, *Sveriges Riksbank*, is the oldest existing central bank in the world. Its history as a public institution dates back to 1668, when it succeeded the world's oldest note-issuing bank, *Stockholm Banco* (also known as *Palmstruchska Banken*). Under the auspices of the parliament, the *Riksbank* (or, as it was called then, *Riksens Ständers Bank*) was actually in operation long before private banks started to do business in the mid-nineteenth century, when the state began to promote private banking in order to develop Sweden's industries and commerce.

The Danish central bank, *Danmarks Nationalbank*, is somewhat younger, but its history is remarkable for its shifts between public and private ownership. The institution was founded as a private bank in 1736 and, due to insolvency, was transformed into a state bank in 1773. Some interesting changes took place in the second decade of the nineteenth century – a period that also saw the foundation of the Bank of Finland, *Suomen Pankki* (in 1811), and the Bank of Norway, *Norges Bank* (in 1816). As Denmark's finances were ruined by the Napoleonic wars, the old state bank was declared bankrupt in 1813 and first replaced by a new state bank, the *Rigsbank*. Since it had no gold or silver reserves, the *Rigsbank* supported its issue of banknotes by a rent charge on all real estate in Denmark.[2] In 1818, the state bank was transformed into the privately owned *Nationalbank*, as the large property holders received shares in the bank in exchange for the rent charge. This privatization of the central monetary institution was reversed in 1936, when the *Nationalbank* was proclaimed to be a 'self-owning' public institution and the government and parliament were given greater insight into its affairs.

As in Sweden, systems of commercial banks or other private banks emerged in Denmark, Norway and Finland only some time after the central banks had been established. The evolution of banking in Scandinavia thus followed a '**top-down approach**' – in contrast to continental Europe and Britain, where commercial banking had developed long before its cyclical instability prompted governments to bring the monetary system under the control of central banks.

Even though its commercial banks were latecomers, Sweden has come to be an extreme case of a bank dominated economy (see Section 2.2). By the mid-1980s, the two biggest commercial banks held '**strategic shares**' in most of the major non-financial companies, of which a large number was ranked among the top multinationals in the world (think, for example, of Volvo, SAAB, Ericsson and SKF). Swedish governments, mostly dominated by the Social Democratic Party, supported this concentration of capital and power as it helped them to centralize economic decisions and to carry out their export-oriented growth strategy. In the other three Scandinavian economies, small and medium-sized companies remained economically and politically predominant, with the exception of one or two big conglomerates. In all four countries, the financial systems were dominated by relatively large domestic banks that were protected from the competition of foreign banks, but at the same time subject to extensive regulation and exchange controls.

This changed in the mid-1980s when a wave of deregulatory measures eliminated credit and interest restrictions, at the same time as Northern Europe was

---

[1] In the following, the terms 'Nordic countries', 'Scandinavia' and 'Northern Europe' are used interchangeably to describe these four countries. Iceland, the fifth member of the Nordic council, is not included in this chapter because of the relatively small size and importance of its financial system.

[2] This trick seems to have set the example for the well-known *Rentenmark* that the German *Reichsbank* introduced to eliminate hyperinflation in 1923; see also Chapter 5 and C A E Goodhart, *The Evolution of Central Banks* (Cambridge, MA: MIT Press, 1988), p. 129.

opened for cross-border capital flows. New markets were set up for a broad range of financial assets. The opening of the markets created a credit boom, a rise in inflation rates, and speculative bubbles in property and equity markets that were supported by huge capital inflows. However, most of the export markets of the Scandinavian industries went into a recession around 1990, while the German *Bundesbank* began to fight the inflationary impulses of the exceptional reunification boom in Germany (see Chapters 5 and 22). As a result, real interest rates in Scandinavia quickly rose to unprecedented levels. The speculative bubbles burst and produced a wave of bankruptcies, which led to a deep recession and severe banking crises in Sweden, Norway and Finland (and milder problems in Denmark) in the early 1990s. These crises were overcome within a few years, but the landscape had changed very much by the turn of the century. The financial sector in Scandinavia has been transformed by a series of domestic and cross-border mergers and acquisitions, in which some big domestic banks and insurance companies evolved into large financial groupings.

Moreover, the four countries are currently characterized by a great diversity of exchange-rate and monetary policy regimes, as illustrated by Table 7.1. Finland, Sweden and Denmark are members of the European Union (EU), while Norway is not. Finland is a founding member of the European Monetary Union (EMU), whereas Denmark and Sweden have opted out – at least for the time being. Denmark has pegged the exchange rate of her currency to the euro (€), whereas Sweden and Norway leave their exchange rates floating.

This diversity, which largely developed after the crisis of the European Monetary System in 1992, may to some extent be explained by policy responses to the deregulatory transformation of the financial systems and, in particular, to the deep recession and the banking crises. As such it may be a transitory phenomenon, even though it has now lasted for more than 15 years. It is an issue open for discussion in how far the respective choices of the exchange rate regime have affected the structures of the financial systems in Scandinavia.

In the rest of this chapter, we shall take a look at the banking systems in the Nordic countries (in Section 7.2), at other financial intermediaries (in Section 7.3), at the domestic and cross-border integration of the financial systems (in Section 7.4), and finally at the diversity of monetary policy strategies in these countries (in Section 7.5). The discussion is largely centred on the Swedish system, both because Sweden is the biggest economy in the region and because the evolution and present state of its financial system is particularly well documented. With Sweden as the benchmark case, the description of the other three systems will mostly be confined to their relevant peculiarities. The last two sections will concentrate on the convergence of financial institutions and the divergence of the monetary policies in the region.

7.2 Banking systems in the Nordic countries

This section contains a short introduction to the structures of the Scandinavian banking systems. The presentation is arranged country by country, setting the focus on the main players in the national arenas. Each subsection provides a brief account of the tasks, organizational features and main instruments of the central bank, followed by a description of the market structure in the banking sector in the respective country.

Table 7.1 Scandinavian diversity of frameworks for monetary policy

	Status quo in autumn 2007	EU membership	
		Yes	No
Exchange rate regime	Currency union (EMU)	Finland	
	Fixed €-exchange rate	Denmark	
	Floating exchange rates	Sweden	
	Floating exchange rates		Norway

7.2.1 Sweden

Sveriges Riksbank, the Bank of Sweden, is the oldest existing central bank in the world. Yet it was only in 1999 that a new law gave the *Riksbank* full independence in its operations to keep the value of money stable (see Section 7.5). In addition to its responsibility for monetary policy, the *Riksbank* also has the tasks of promoting a secure and efficient system of payments and safeguarding the stability of the financial system as a whole, while the responsibility for the soundness of individual financial institutions rests with the Financial Supervisory Authority (*Finansinspektionen*).

The *Riksbank* is managed by an executive board of six full-time members, who are appointed by the general council for six-year terms according to a rolling schedule. The executive board makes all monetary policy decisions, and its members are forbidden to seek or take instructions from the government or any other institution. For transparency, the minutes of the meetings of the executive board are published very shortly afterwards. Apart from selecting the members of the executive board, the general council has a controlling function; its eleven members are recruited from the ranks of the members of parliament.

In its conduct of monetary policy, the *Riksbank* aims at controlling the market level of short-term interest rates. The main instrument used for this purpose is the 'repo rate', the interest rate on the weekly repurchase agreements by which the banks borrow from and deposit money in the central bank. By raising the repo rate, the *Riksbank* signals its intent to curb inflationary expectations. By lowering the repo rate, it signals its willingness to support an expansion of lending and investment.

Sweden has, like Germany, a tradition of universal banking. Most Swedish banks offer a comprehensive range of services in retail, wholesale and investment banking. The most remarkable feature of the Swedish banking system is the dominant position of four big banks, which account for nearly 80 per cent of the balance sheet totals of all 126 banks in the country (see Figure 7.1). Two of the Big Four, SEB and *Handelsbanken*, are old commercial banks with a long tradition of ownership and close management

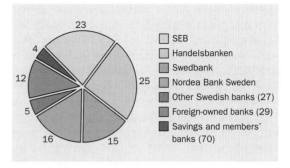

Figure 7.1 Banks' balance sheet totals in Sweden, end 2006 (shares in per cent of total of all 126 banks: SKr 5,150 bn)
Source: Sveriges Riksbank (2007) *Den svenska finansmarknaden 2007*, August, pp. 54–6. Reprinted with permission.

ties with industrial companies. The other two, *Nordea* and *Swedbank*, are newcomers with old roots in other segments of the banking business.

The SEB (*Skandinaviska Enskilda Banken*) is the base of the Wallenberg dynasty, a family that has presided over Scandinavia's biggest industrial empire for most of the twentieth century and continues to exert its influence on a large sphere of companies by way of foundations, strategic shareholding and directorates – not to speak of the bread-and-butter business of bank lending.[3] A list of the major companies under the influence of the Wallenbergs reads like the *Who's Who* of Swedish multinationals: ABB (formerly ASEA), Alfa Laval, Astra, Atlas Copco, Electrolux, Ericsson, SAS, Scania, SKF, Swedish Match, and many others. *Handelsbanken*, the other old commercial bank, shows a bigger balance sheet total than SEB in Figure 7.1, but its sphere of influence in the non-financial sector is not quite as large. *Nordea Bank Sweden*, formerly *Nordbanken*, emerged as a half-privatized company from the state-owned postal bank in the mid-1980s, when Swedish credit markets were deregulated. In the general race for market shares that followed the opening of the markets, *Nordbanken* increased its corporate lending aggressively. Between 1990 and 1992 it suffered such great credit losses that the government had to acquire all privately owned shares and restore the capital base. In the mid-1990s

---

[3] Until recently, Swedish law permitted the issue of shares with very large differences in voting rights. The Wallenbergs have thus been able to secure control positions with relatively small shares of capital. In the mid-1980s, it was estimated that their voting rights exceeded their shares of capital by a ratio of 100:1. Some differences in voting rights are still tolerated, even though they are not in accordance with European Union legislation.

Nordbanken was partly privatized again; since then it has expanded rapidly in the Scandinavian and Baltic banking markets and changed into *Nordea*, a large trans-Nordic financial services group and one of the first Nordic companies to be registered under the legal form of 'Societas Europeae' (see Section 7.4). *Swedbank* was founded as *FöreningsSparbanken* in 1997, when *Föreningsbanken*, the central institution of the agricultural credit unions, merged with *Sparbanken*, the largest of the savings banks. *Sparbanken* was itself a product of mergers of a number of savings banks, some of which had also been in great trouble during the banking crisis of the early 1990s.

Traditionally, SEB and *Handelsbanken* have dominated the market segments of wholesale and investment banking, whereas *Nordea* and *Swedbank* have held stronger positions in retail banking. The restructuring of Scandinavian banking has greatly diminished these differences (see Section 7.4).

7.2.2 Denmark

Danmarks Nationalbank, the Bank of Denmark, has enjoyed independence from the government since 1936, but it is not autonomous in its conduct of monetary policy. Denmark has pursued a fixed exchange-rate policy vis-à-vis the Deutschmark since 1982 and the euro since 1999. Until 1998, its policy measures were designed to shadow the movements of the German currency, and since the start of the European Monetary Union they have to match the policy of the European Central Bank (see Section 7.5). Like other central banks, the *Nationalbank* is also a banker to the banks and to the government. The responsibility for the stability of the financial sector is divided between the *Nationalbank*, as the guardian of the system, and a separate supervisory authority (*Finanstilsynet*) that monitors the soundness of individual financial institutions.

The *Nationalbank* is managed by a board of three governors, who are appointed by the board of directors for unlimited tenure. The board of directors has 25 members, out of whom eight are elected by the parliament, two are appointed by the Minister of Economic Affairs and the other 15 members are elected by the board of directors with a view to involving the business community. A seven-member committee of directors provides a link between the board of governors and the board of directors, without a strict definition of its tasks. The power to decide about the formulation and measures of monetary policy – which, however, have to conform to the exchange-rate target – rests entirely with the board of governors. In its conduct of monetary policy, the *Nationalbank* mainly relies on repurchase agreements, as in the Swedish case, but it still uses the discount rate for signalling its assessment of the market conditions.

The Danish market for banking services is nearly as much concentrated as its Swedish counterpart, even though it is characterized by a relatively large number of small banks. In 2005, the five largest banks accounted for 82 per cent of the balance sheet totals of all 152 banks in the country. The market shares of the biggest two, *Danske Bank* and *Nordea Denmark*, were 36 and 23 per cent respectively. Traditionally, mortgage institutions have been strong in the Danish financial sector. In recent years, the biggest banks and mortgage institutions have been penetrating each others' markets. These trends will be discussed in later sections.

7.2.3 Norway

In most international rankings, *Norges Bank*, the Bank of Norway, has for a long time been considered to be among the least independent banks (Bank for International Settlements, 1997, p. 128). The political authorities, i.e. the government and the parliament, still have a greater influence on the formulation of the guidelines for monetary policy than elsewhere. But since 2001, *Norges Bank* has been more independent in pursuing the prescribed target of maintaining inflation in the range of 2.5 per cent (see Section 7.5). In Norway, too, the tasks of supervising the financial system are divided between the central bank and a separate authority (*Kredittilsynet*). In addition to the usual activities of central banks, Norges Bank manages the 'Government Pension Fund – Global', which was formed from the earlier Petroleum Fund in 2006, and in which a large portion of Norway's revenues from oil and gas production is saved and invested in foreign equities and bonds.

Norges Bank is managed by an executive board whose seven members are all appointed by the King; employees have two members who supplement the executive board when it deals with administrative matters. A supervisory council of fifteen members, all elected by the parliament, is responsible for ensuring that the rules and guidelines for the Bank's activities are observed. In its conduct of monetary policy, *Norges Bank* – like most central banks in Europe – has come to rely on repurchase agreements as the main instrument for the liquidity supply. However, as the Norwegian banks tend to have a structural surplus position vis-à-vis the central bank, the sight deposit rate is considered to be the key rate. Furthermore, *Norges Bank* intervenes frequently in the market, because the government's working account is in the Bank. The liquidity position of banks is thus subject to rapid changes, which make it necessary to supply or withdraw liquidity at irregular and short intervals.

The Norwegian banking sector is characterized by a relatively strong position of savings banks. While the clear division between this segment and the commercial banks has largely vanished in the other Scandinavian countries, it is still perceptible in Norway. Out of the about 150 banks supervised by *Kredittilsynet* in the year 2006, 124 were savings and union banks, mostly small institutes of local character (*Kredittilsynet, The Financial Market in Norway 2006*). The segment is dominated by the SpareBank 1 group, with a market share of 12.4 per cent in the whole banking market. After the acquisition of the Union Bank of Norway in 2003, *Den norske Bank* (DnB NOR) is now by far the biggest commercial bank in the country, with a market share of 40 per cent. The second biggest bank is *Nordea Norway*, the former K-Bank (*Christiania Bank og Kreditkasse*), with a market share of 13.2 per cent. DnB and K-Bank suffered heavy losses in the banking crisis of the early 1990s and had to be rescued by government funding. They recovered quickly, but the majority of their shares remained in the hands of the government funds – at least until 2000, when K-Bank was sold off to *Nordea* (see Section 7.4). The big banks in Norway are comparatively small by Scandinavian standards.

7.2.4 Finland

Finland is one of the eleven founding members of the European Monetary Union. *Suomen Pankki*, the Bank of Finland, is thus a member of the Eurosystem, the core group of the European System of Central Banks. It participates in the implementation of the Eurosystem's single monetary policy which is conducted by the European Central Bank at Frankfurt (see Chapter 23). Banks and other financial institutions in Finland are supervised by 'Financial Supervision' (*Rahoitustarkastus*),

which is located at the Bank of Finland, but operates as a legally independent authority.

Among the Nordic countries, Finland has the largest number of banks and, at the same time, the highest degree of **concentration in the banking sector**. At the end of 2006, a total of 338 banks were operating in the country (Federation of Finnish Financial Services, 2007, pp. 1–4). Most of them were small savings banks and local union banks. The three biggest banks accounted for more than 90 per cent of the balance sheet total of all Finnish banks. The smallest among the Big Three was *Sampo* with a market share of three per cent. The OP Bank Group, a consortium of 243 union banks, had a market share of 27 per cent. Roughly two-thirds of the Finnish banking market are made up by *Nordea Finland*, formerly known as *Merita*. Like various other big banks in Scandinavia, *Merita* was an indirect product of the banking crisis of the early 1990s. It was created by a merger of the two largest commercial banks in the mid-1990s, after extensive rescue operations of the government and the central bank.

7.3 Other financial intermediaries in the Nordic countries

In Section 7.2 we have looked at the Scandinavian systems of central banks and deposit banks, whose core business is to provide payment services and to make loans and hold deposits. In this section, we will take a brief look at other market segments of financial services in the Nordic countries. The firms that operate in those segments are mortgage institutions, other special credit institutions (including state lending institutions), investment companies, mutual funds, insurance corporations and pension funds. Most of these institutions do not, in their activities, differ very much from their British or German counterparts, which have been described in greater detail in Chapters 3 and 5. Furthermore, nearly all private non-bank intermediaries in Scandinavia are closely connected with, or direct subsidiaries of domestic banks. This integrative 'all-finance' or 'bancassurance' approach of Scandinavian banks will be assessed in the next section. In this section, the discussion is confined to two issues: the role of non-bank intermediaries in lending to the non-financial sector and in financial asset holdings of households, and the role of pension funds. It is convenient to

Table 7.2 Balance sheet totals and assets of financial institutions in Sweden, end 2005

SKr billion	Balance sheet total	Lending to the public	Other lending	Interest-bearing securities	Equities	Other assets
Banks	4,583	1,701	1341	724	362	454
Mortgage institutions	1,643	1,528	81	9	3	21
Other credit institutions	637	384	59	182	9	3
Insurance companies	2,253	32	51	1,032	1,051	89
National Pension Fund	821	–	–	253	409	159
Fund management companies	1,316	–	–	310	733	273
Securities companies	38	5	8	–	12	13
Total	11,290	3,652	1,540	2,509	2,580	1,011

Source: Sveriges Riksbank (2006) *Den svenska finansmarknaden 2006*, p. 95. Reprinted with permission.

organize that discussion issue by issue, rather than country by country.

7.3.1 Structures of lending and asset holding

Table 7.2 gives a quantitative impression of the structure of financial intermediation in Sweden. In terms of the balance sheet total, the biggest institutional segment is clearly the banking sector, followed by mortgage institutions and insurance companies. In a system of universal banking the banks' aggregate portfolio is naturally more diversified than the portfolios of the other, more specialized groups of institutions. That implies that the banks, despite their dominant position, are not necessarily the biggest lenders in credit markets or investors in bond and equity markets. Mortgage institutions account for a greater volume of direct lending to the non-financial sector, while insurance companies and pension funds hold more bonds and shares than the banks.

The prominent role of mortgage institutions reflects the high degree of owner-occupied housing in Sweden. Real property constitutes the greatest item among households' net assets in the whole of Scandinavia. Yet the systems of finance for housing differ a lot between the countries. In Denmark, special institutions have traditionally played a far greater role in this market than banks (see Table 7.3). Mortgage institutions lend roughly the same amount in Denmark and in Sweden, but the Danish population is only 60 per cent of its Swedish counterpart. In contrast, the segment of mortgage banking is much smaller in Norway and smallest in Finland where housing is largely financed by way of bank loans, and where insurance companies play a relatively greater role. In Finland, the banks have now even penetrated the insurance business to the extent that, due to separability problems in the data, the country's statistics about the structure of the financial industries are discontinued (which is why the last available figures in Table 7.3 date back to 2002).

Table 7.3 Banks, mortgage institutions and insurance corporations[1] (% of balance sheet totals)

	Sweden (2005)	Denmark (2006)	Norway (2007)	Finland (2002)
Banks	41	39	63	60
Mortgage institutions	15	26	11	1
Insurance companies	20	13	19	28

[1] Excluding public pension funds.

Sources: Sveriges Riksbank (2006, p. 95), Finanstilsynet (2007), Norges Bank (2007, p. 55), Suomen Pankkiyhdistys (2003, p. 5).

These structural differences between the Nordic countries are largely due to two factors. Mortgage banking has enjoyed greater privileges and subsidies in Denmark than in Norway and Finland. In addition, the bond markets of the two northernmost Scandinavian countries were, for a long time, far too small to provide the means for refinancing mortgage loans. In Denmark, on the other hand, mortgage institutions often intermediate between bond markets and firms in the sense that many companies prefer to borrow from them rather than finance their investments through direct bond issues.

The differences in housing finance are of some importance for the transmission of monetary policy: the longer the periods of fixed interest in loan contracts, the lower is the immediate impact of changes in the central bank's lending rate on consumer spending and on overall economic activity. The financial structure in Denmark is dominated by long-term borrowing at fixed rates via mortgage institutions, whereas lending and borrowing at floating (or short-term adjustable) interest rates is highly common in Norway and Finland; in Sweden, the share of fixed-interest contracts is about 50 per cent, but the average duration of fixed interest periods has varied frequently and conversely with the market level of interest rates in recent years. These differences in financial structures lead to the prediction that monetary policy in Denmark works less directly and with longer lags than equivalent measures in Sweden, Norway and Finland.

The liabilities of the financial sector are to a large extent financial assets of the household sector. If we look at the portfolio structures in Table 7.4, we can see

further significant differences between the national systems of financial intermediation. In international surveys, Sweden is frequently ranked as the country with the world's highest ratios of households' shareholding and of shareholders among the population. Table 7.4 shows that direct and indirect shareholding (fund shares) accounted for half of households' financial wealth in Sweden before the 'dotcom'-bubble burst in 2000. This seems to contradict our earlier observation that the Swedish economy is dominated by a few big banks. Yet it should be noted that the wide distribution of shares has been supported by various political measures in reaction to debates about the concentration of capital and power in the country, and that considerable differences between the voting rates of shares (of the same denomination) still exist. A large fraction of the investment funds, through which Swedish households indirectly hold shares, are subsidiaries of domestic banks. This gives the banks another channel of influence on the decision making of the fund managers.

It should be noted that the high proportion of equity in the financial wealth of Swedish households in 1999 followed to some extent from a price effect, since the values of shares were extraordinarily high then. The price effect also accounts for the lower ratios of shareholding in 2003. We have chosen to compare the years 1999 and 2003 because they were peak and trough years in the international financial markets. In addition to other differences between the Nordic countries, they help to indicate the degree of cyclical variability in the portfolio structures of financial asset-holdings of households. The sensitivity to cyclical swings seems to be greater in Sweden and Finland than in the other two

Table 7.4 Financial assets of households (%)

	Sweden		Denmark		Norway		Finland	
	1999	2003	1999	2003	1999	2003	1999	2003
Bank deposits	16	19	29	29	32	35	36	35
Insurance claims	24	31	44	43	34	34	15	23
Fund shares	24	19	6	9	7	5	3	4
Bonds	5	3	13	8	n.a.	2	1	1
Equities	26	19	6	7	14	11	43	33
Other	6	9	2	4	13	13	2	4

Sources: Sveriges Riksbank (2002), Statistiska Centralbyrån (2004), Danmarks Nationalbank (2004), Kredittilsynet (2000), Norges Bank (2003), Statistics Finland (2004).

countries. Finland even tops Sweden in terms of direct shareholding, but the relatively high share of bank deposits suggests a higher degree of risk aversion and a price effect in the valuation of Finnish shares, following the extraordinary boom in the Finnish equity markets in the late 1990s. In Denmark and Norway, by far the largest part of financial assets is held in the form of bank deposits and insurance claims.

The differences in shareholding could lead to differences in the transmission of monetary policy between the Nordic countries, since share values are quite sensitive to changes in the market level of interest rates and value gains and losses frequently have a wealth effect on borrowing and consumer spending. We will take a further look at these issues in Section 7.5.

7.3.2 Pension funds

All the pension systems in Northern Europe rest on three pillars: a general public pension, supplementary occupational pension schemes, and individual private pension saving. The first pillar has often been regarded as the main element of 'the Scandinavian model', a pension system that follows the principle that all citizens have the right to the same pension. This public pension is independent of previous contributions and it is paid from general tax revenues. However, what was meant to be an equal pension for all has become a minimum pension over the last three decades. The second pillar has therefore enormously gained in importance in all four countries, where mandatory schemes have developed along with voluntary schemes at trade union and firm levels. The supplementary pensions in the mandatory schemes depend on previous contributions from payroll taxes and on the salary incomes of the last working years before retirement. These schemes are (at least partially) prefunded in the sense that the contributions of the wage earners are paid into National Pension Funds which invest the money in the financial markets – with the exception of Finland, where the pension funds are managed by private insurance companies.[4]

The National Pension Funds are large investors in the financial markets. The Swedish AP-fonden and its Danish counterpart ATP account for about 7 per cent of the balance sheet totals of financial institutions in their countries, respectively (see also Table 7.2). No separate figures were available for Norway and Finland, but it should be noted that the main objective of the Norwegian Government Pension Fund, formerly the Petroleum Fund (Section 7.2.3), is 'to meet the financial challenge of paying for an ageing population'. The balance sheet total of the Petroleum Fund corresponds to two thirds of the total of all banks in Norway (as of March 2007), and it is growing fast.

In addition to the occupational pension schemes, a number of other pension funds exist in all four countries. So far, they play only a minor role in the capital markets and for pensioners' incomes.

7.4 ## The evolution and integration of financial systems in Scandinavia

In the following we shall take a look at past problems and present trends in financial institutions and markets in the Nordic countries. The first subsection provides a brief account of the development of financial markets and the ensuing banking crises in the 1980s and 1990s. The second subsection describes the ongoing process of concentration in the Nordic financial sector.

7.4.1 Market expansion and banking crises

Before the 1980s one could hardly speak of financial markets in Scandinavia, at least not in terms of transaction volumes in the money, bond or equity markets. The financial systems in all four countries were clearly centred on bank lending, strictly segmented[5] and regulated by interest and credit ceilings, portfolio restrictions and exchange controls. Apart from small interbank markets, there were no money markets. Bond markets were largely confined to primary markets for issues of the governments and the mortgage institutions, and investors were almost exclusively domestic insurance companies and pension funds,

---

[4]   Since the year 2000, Swedish wage earners also have the option to place a part of their contributions to the supplementary pension scheme in mutual funds that are administered by independent companies.
[5]   Separate systems of regulation applied to commercial banks, savings banks, union banks, mortgage-credit institutions, insurance companies and mutual funds.

which were legally obliged to hold certain shares of government bonds in their portfolios. The equity markets were quiet places, too, as the open trading of shares was rather marginal; most of the shares were continuously held for purposes of strategic control or as long-term investments in fund portfolios.

As in many other countries, this changed with financial market deregulation and integration in the 1980s. Many Scandinavian companies had begun to circumvent the exchange controls or to use 'grey' credit markets, when prices, interest rates and exchange rates became increasingly volatile in the 1970s. As the governments and central banks noticed that quantitative regulation no longer ensured control of activities in the financial sector, they abolished controls over banks' lending volumes and interest rates at the same time as they created open money markets and bond markets as arenas for their use of interest rate policy. And they dismantled other portfolio restrictions and exchange controls, so that equity markets became increasingly attractive.

Deregulation did not come everywhere at the same time. In Denmark, the process had already started around 1975, since the country had joined the European Economic Community (EEC, now the European Union) and had to adjust to EEC rules and regulations. In Sweden and Norway, the biggest changes came with the creation of fully fledged money and bond markets in the early 1980s, whereas in Finland, functioning secondary markets for bonds and equities appeared only at the beginning of the 1990s (Oxelheim, 1996, ch. 15).

The years around 1985 nevertheless mark a period of extraordinary credit expansion in all four countries, which clearly had its root in the deregulation of the financial sectors. Unfettered competition in the loan markets led to a sharp increase in bank lending to investments in commercial and residential property as well as equity. As a consequence, a debt–asset price cycle developed that interacted with accelerating inflation. Competition kept nominal interest rates at a low level, and real interest rates were even lower due to inflation. Borrowed funds helped to fuel the rise in asset prices which, in turn, helped to increase the borrowing capacity of firms and households. And the banks pushed on in their race for

market shares and profits. Between 1982 and 1989, house prices in Sweden rose by 50 per cent, commercial property prices by almost 200 per cent, and equity prices by almost 400 per cent (OECD, 1994, Annex III). Similar developments took place in Norway and Finland. In Denmark, the asset price inflation was considerably lower, since the market expansion was both stretched over a longer time and more restricted by the relatively high interest rates that *Danmarks Nationalbank* had to set in order to meet its exchange rate targets within the European Monetary System.

The debt–asset price cycles of Sweden, Norway and Finland proved to be unsustainable when real interest rates surged to unprecedented levels around 1990. A worldwide recession, the breakdown of (trade with) the Soviet Union and the weakened confidence in the (then) fixed exchange rates led the central banks of the three countries to pursue strongly disinflationary policies. The speculative bubbles in the property and equity markets burst and produced heavy credit losses, which brought many of the largest banks of Scandinavia to the verge of collapse – and with them the whole of the financial systems.

Sweden, Norway and Finland thus experienced severe banking crises that quickly proved to be too strong for ordinary 'lending of last resort' by the central banks.[6] The central governments had to intervene, but the type and costs of their rescue operations differed considerably between the three countries (see Table 7.5 overleaf). In Norway and Finland, the rescue operations were largely carried out with resources from the central banks and government funds, whereas in Sweden the central government alone has been involved. The Swedish solution of the problem was quite spectacular and much debated. Between autumn 1992 and the end of 1993, the central government provided unlimited state guarantees for all commitments of banking institutions towards creditors and depositors. Prior to this, the government had injected large funds into the three banks whose equity capital was wiped out by the credit losses. *Nordbanken*, which had been a state-majority owned bank, and *Gota Bank* were completely taken over by the state and stripped of their bigger problem assets which were transferred into two newly created, state-owned '**bad banks**',

---

[6] In Norway, the wave of credit losses had actually started as early as 1988, but there was little recognition that a banking crisis had occurred before similar problems made themselves more strongly felt in Sweden and Finland in 1991; see Reve (1996).

Table 7.5 Assets of major banks and costs of rescue operations in the banking sector (%, as a share of GDP 1992)

	Assets of five largest banks	Assets rescued	Costs of rescue operations
Sweden	121.0	31.0	5.2
Central government			*5.2*
Finland	102.0	16.0	7.4
Central government			*1.7*
Government funds			*3.0*
Central bank			*2.7*
Norway	69.0	46.0	3.0
Central government			*2.8*
Government funds			*0.1*
Central bank			*0.1*

Source: Tables A5 and A6, OECD (1994). Reprinted with permission.

Securum and *Retriva*.[7] Even all the other big banks seized the chance to recycle their bad assets through such tax-and-cost-saving special institutions.

The immediate costs of these rescue operations were considerable, about 5 per cent of 1992 year's GDP in Sweden (see Table 7.5). Since they had to be borne by the taxpayer and since the banks' shareholders were treated rather generously, there was some debate about 'moral hazard' problems. Moreover, it was argued that the bail-out through state guarantees and bad banks tends to undermine incentives to cost-efficiency in the banking business and that it has placed the more prudent banks at a competitive disadvantage. More than fifteen years after the outbreak, the total costs of the Swedish banking crisis are still an issue of controversy. Technically, the handling of the problem assets was quite successful. When *Securum*, the biggest bad bank, was liquidated in 1997, a large share of the problem assets and institutions had been sold off at reasonable prices, so that it was estimated that nearly half of the state's immediate costs of the rescue operations had been retrieved. Yet the bad banks themselves were accused of liquidating too many companies and jobs on their way. And the reshaped 'good'

banks were very restrictive in their lending in the first years after the crisis. It is nevertheless fairly safe to conclude that the total costs of the banking crisis would have been much higher for the Swedish economy, if the state had not bailed out the banks.

7.4.2 Concentration in the Nordic financial sector

We have seen in Section 7.2 that the banking sectors are highly concentrated in all Scandinavian countries. A joint report by the Nordic Central Banks (Danmarks Nationalbank *et al.*, 2006, pp. 10 and 50) shows that, by the end of 2005, the five largest banks accounted for 84.2 per cent of the total balance sheets of Swedish credit institutions; the corresponding figures were 83.1 per cent for Finland, 66.3 per cent for Denmark, and 48.7 per cent for Norway.[8] The degrees of concentration have been relatively high for a long time. They are, as such, a rather common phenomenon in small countries, reflecting the existence of economies of scale and scope in the banking business which imply that banks need to be of a certain size in order to work

---

[7] 'Bad banks' are special institutions whose task is to save 'good banks' by buying some of the latters' problem assets (mostly non-performing loans), presumably at low prices. The 'good banks' are then allowed to write off the losses and save taxes and further costs. The 'bad banks' reschedule the loans, restructure the borrowers' business or sell off the collateral, usually within the framework of special regulations and a predefined period. In the 1990s, the Swedish strategy of 'bad banking' achieved model character for the restructuring of crisis-stricken banking sectors in other countries; see Hawkins and Turner (1999).

[8] It should be noted that these figures relate to the total of all credit institutions, which is why they are lower than the figures provided in Sections 7.2.2 and 7.2.3 where 'mortgage banks' and 'other credit institutions' had been excluded.

efficiently. But the concentration process has been intensified in recent years; and it has taken the Nordic financial sectors several steps closer towards the domestic integration of different segments and towards their **cross-border integration**. This process is, to a large extent, a by-product of the banking crises, because they created an atmosphere in which the consolidation of the banking sector was given strong priority – especially in view of the ongoing integration process on the level of the European Union.

Close to collapse as the Swedish banks were in 1992, they quickly recovered in the following years, with some appetite for expansion in and beyond the Nordic region. In 1993, *Nordbanken* went ahead to buy *Gota Bank*, the other problem bank. What first looked like a club of losers became the core of *Nordea*, now the biggest financial services group in Scandinavia whose total assets (€375 billion in October 2007) amount to nearly as much as the combined GDPs of Denmark and Finland. *Nordbanken* merged with the Finnish Merita Bank in 1997, and their joint holding began to acquire other large banks as well as mortgage institutions and insurance companies in all the Nordic countries. The conglomerate changed its name to *Nordea* in 2001; its history (outlined under www.nordea.com) is the perfect example of cross-border and cross-segment integration of financial activities in the region.

Other banks have expanded in similar ways, though on a smaller scale. Nearly all of the large new holdings have set up subsidiaries in the Baltic countries and some, like Nordea and the Swedish SEB, have even started to acquire larger banks on the Continent. Some banks, like *Swedbank*, have chosen to forge strategic alliances with banks in other countries that have a similar background in savings and union banking.

This wave of mergers, acquisitions and alliances is not a specific characteristic of the Nordic financial sector. As financial institutions prepared for intensified competition in the European financial markets, these things have happened everywhere. Yet it is remarkable that the concentration has almost exclusively been an intra-Nordic affair. Financial institutions from countries outside Scandinavia have so far had little success in penetrating the markets in the Nordic countries (Engwall *et al.*, 2001; Danmarks Nationalbank *et al.*, 2006, p. 42).

Two other characteristic features of the ongoing concentration process are the strategies of all-finance and electronic banking. The term 'all-finance' describes cross-segment integration, that is: a tendency of financial groups, like *Nordea*, to offer the full range of banking and financial services under one brand, including insurance and pension fund management. In addition, Scandinavian banks do currently have a lead in the technologies of electronic banking. What is normally regarded as a disadvantage of the Nordic countries, namely their low population density, has turned out to be an advantage in the diffusion of new techniques. The costs of setting up brick-and-mortar branches of financial institutions are particularly high in sparsely populated countries. This gives the financial services groups extra incentives to exploit the economies of scope from all-finance and the economies of scale from electronic banking. Technical progress and the concentration process interact, since profits from electronic banking tend to grow with network size, and mergers and acquisitions enlarge the networks.

The emergence of transnational financial groups increases the need for cooperation between the supervisory authorities of the countries involved. The supervisory authorities of the Nordic countries have therefore extended their practical cooperation in the control of banks, insurance and investment companies. The central banks regularly publish reports on financial stability in which they increasingly set their focus on the cross-border activities of the financial institutions in their domains.

<table>
<tr><td>**7.5**</td><td>Monetary policy strategies in the Nordic countries</td></tr>
</table>

It has been pointed out in Sections 7.1 and 7.2 that the Scandinavian central banks pursue different targets in varying frameworks of monetary policy. Sweden has an independent central bank that follows an **inflation target** (2 per cent, ± 1 per cent) under flexible exchange rates. Denmark too has an independent central bank, but it has pegged its currency to the euro at an exchange rate of 7.46 DKr/€ in the narrow target zone of ERM II (± 2.25 per cent). Norway has a less independent central bank which, however, can exert more discretion in preserving monetary stability as it has gone over from a **'soft' exchange rate target** to inflation targeting. Finland no longer has a monetary policy of its own, as it is a member of the European Monetary Union; the Bank of Finland supports the European Central Bank in its pursuit of an inflation target, but that target (2 per cent or less) is defined as an average of the whole eurozone, not of Finland alone.

In this last section, we shall discuss the following questions: Why this diversity? And can the national monetary policy strategies diverge when the main players in the private sector converge to large transnational financial groups? The first question is about the recent past, the second is about the near future.

7.5.1 The origins of the diversity

Until autumn 1992 all four Scandinavian countries adhered to similar types of fixed exchange rate arrangements. As an EEC member, Denmark joined the Exchange Rate Mechanism of the European Monetary System (EMS) in 1979, whereas the other three countries pegged their currencies to trade-weighted currency baskets. Yet exchange rate stability was difficult to achieve, as the oil crisis of 1973/74 had set off price–wage spirals that led to relatively high inflation in the Scandinavian countries, reinforced by the effects of income tax progression. Due to the fast increase in unit costs, the Scandinavian industries began to lose ground in their export markets. Devaluations were often used as a way out of this problem, but they tended to come late, to weaken the confidence of investors and to add to the inflation problem by raising import prices. During the 1970s and early 1980s, all four countries were thus caught in vicious circles of inflation and devaluation which eroded both the competitive advantages of the region's export industries and the systems of **credit and exchange controls**.

Due to its constraints in the EMS, Denmark was the first country to break these circles by going over to a rigorous austerity policy, but the change to low inflation and durable exchange rate stability came at the hefty cost of high and persistent unemployment. This was a price that the other countries, in particular Sweden, were not prepared to pay. Instead, Sweden tried to fight its way out of the dilemma by way of a shock devaluation, combined with fiscal consolidation, wage restraints and financial market deregulation. The 16 per cent devaluation of the Swedish crown in October 1982 was meant to stimulate exports and thereby growth and employment, but the Swedish government made it clear that this had to be the last action of its kind, if the inflation trend was to be broken. The crown was firmly pegged to a new target exchange rate vis-à-vis the currrency basket. The **deregulation and liberalization** of the financial sector was meant to subject the wage and price setters in the country to the

discipline of interest rate and loan constraints. Norway and Finland followed suit – though somewhat grudgingly, because the Swedish shock devaluation had put their own export industries at a disadvantage.

The hopes of reining in inflation by way of financial market deregulation were unfounded, as we saw in Section 7.4. The inflationary impulses of wage and tax policies were replaced by the **debt–asset price cycles** in the real property and equity markets. Increasing deficits in the current accounts had to be financed with capital inflows that further contributed to inflation. When the first signs of a recession weakened the confidence of investors and threatened exchange rate stability in 1990/91, Norway, Sweden and Finland pegged their currencies to the ECU (European Currency Unit) in order to win credibility for their disinflationary policies. Like other central countries in Europe, they hoped to be able to achieve price-level stability by way of preserving strict exchange rate stability.

However, these measures backfired on the economies and eventually on the monetary policy strategies. Keeping the exchange rates fixed in terms of the ECU, or rather the Deutschmark as the anchor currency of the EMS, required a policy of high interest rates, since the German *Bundesbank* began to raise its key rate in order to fight the inflationary impulses in the wake of German reunification. The restrictive monetary policies in Sweden, Norway and Finland aggravated the problems with credit losses that had begun to develop in the banking systems.

In the summer of 1992 all hell was let loose, when a referendum in Denmark resulted in a 'No' to the Maastricht treaty and its plans for a European Monetary Union. As the trend towards irreversibly fixed exchange rates in Europe seemed no longer certain, it became attractive to speculate against the currencies of European countries that suffered either from high inflation or from high unemployment. The Danish crown was relatively well protected, since its peg to the ECU was multilaterally defended, mainly by support from the German *Bundesbank*. The northern Scandinavian currencies were unilaterally pegged to the ECU and they were traded in small foreign exchange markets with few big players. This made them much easier targets for speculative attacks.

The Swedish government and the *Riksbank* were determined to defend the symbol of their newly won credibility, the fixed ECU exchange rate, at all costs. In September 1992, the *Riksbank* raised its lending rates to the banks to 500 per cent in order to stop the vicious circle of self-fulfilling expectations which threatened to develop from the massive increase of loans at Swedish banks that were converted into foreign currencies in speculative anticipation of a devaluation of the crown. These draconian measures, rather uncommon in highly developed economies in times of peace, only brought the banking system closer to collapse and invited further speculative attacks. After very costly, but eventually futile interventions in the foreign exchange markets the *Riksbank* abandoned the unilateral ECU parity in November 1992. Finland had gone over to floating exchange rates in September, and Norway followed in November.

To sum up, there is some irony in the fact that the northern Scandinavian countries tried to use the deregulation of the financial sectors as a vehicle for regaining interest rate control and winning credibility for their policies of disinflationary exchange rate targetting. The inflationary dynamics of the deregulation process contributed to the deep economic and banking crises which, in turn, made the exchange rate arrangements unsustainable.

Yet the four Nordic countries have all reacted differently to the **currency crises** of the early 1990s. Denmark survived the speculative attacks and stuck to its ECU peg (now a euro peg), but it did not join the European Monetary Union (EMU) because there is strong political opposition to the project of a single European monetary policy in the country. Once bitten, twice shy, public opinion in Sweden is also dominated by eurosceptical positions, and it is widely argued that it is easier to fight inflation by directly targeting it in the country than leaving monetary policy decisions to some central bank in Frankfurt. In the referendum of September 2003, a clear majority of Swedish voters rejected the government's plans to join the EMU. By contrast, Finland took the bull by the horns and joined the EMS in 1997 in order to become an EMU member right from the start. Norway has preferred to stay outside the European Union altogether, but it adopted a 'soft policy' of stable exchange rates shortly after the turmoil of 1992. The underlying motivation was to keep the Norwegian economy, and in particular its sectors outside the oil and gas industry, under competitive pressure. The difference compared with the earlier unilateral ECU parity was that the authorities did not define a new parity with fluctuation margins, but declared their

intent to react to shocks in the foreign exchange markets by gearing monetary policy to returning the euro exchange rate gradually to its initial range. However, even this soft exchange rate targeting had to be given up in favour of inflation targeting, when the end of the 'dotcom bubble' made the Norwegian krone vulnerable to speculative attacks.

7.5.2 The problems of diversity

So far, all the different choices of monetary policy regimes in Scandinavia can be considered as being successful in terms of both preserving price-level stability and regaining financial sector stability. Yet it is not certain that the diversity of strategies can be sustained in the long run. General macroeconomic developments were unusually favourable in the second half of the 1990s, and the downswing at the turn of the century was softened by globally low interest rates. Even by 2007, the new strategies have not yet been put to the test of sudden increases in real interest rates.

Apart from macroeconomic concerns, problems may also arise from the ongoing concentration in the financial sectors of the Nordic region. In the past decades, the Scandinavian central banks have supported the creation of domestic money and bond markets in order to make use of the banks' competition for liquidity. Now they face fewer and bigger players in those markets. Moreover, the transnational financial groups have more opportunities for cross-border arbitrage and for the circumvention of specific restrictions in the countries. This may contribute to rendering monetary policy less effective or, in the case of Sweden and Norway, less independent in their pursuit of national inflation targets. Take, for example, the risks for financial stability that arise from the high share of shareholding in Sweden. If there is a sudden fall in share prices, as in the years 2000–01, the negative wealth effect on investment and consumer spending tends to be stronger than in other countries. This could induce the *Riksbank* to lower its interest rates in order to meet its inflation target.[9] If the rates come to be lower than elsewhere in Europe, banks could use the Swedish money market for borrowing funds to invest them in other countries, while investors would stay away from the Swedish markets because they can earn more elsewhere. The market levels of interest

---

[9] It should be noted that Sweden had exceptionally low inflation rates in the 1990s, often at or even below the lower boundary of the target zone (1–3 per cent). Due to measurement problems in the inflation rate, this would be considered as deflation which, in turn, tends to have a negative effect on real economic activity.

rates in Sweden would adjust to or even rise above the levels in the eurozone, due to a risk premium.[10]

It may therefore be concluded that the diversity of monetary policy targets and frameworks in Northern Europe will be a transitory episode, born out of crisis of its financial systems and doomed to give way to further integration of the financial sectors even at the monetary policy level – perhaps within the European Monetary Union or some satellite arrangement such as the EMS II. However, the present arrangements have proved more durable than initially expected by most observers.

7.6   Summary

The financial systems in Northern Europe are dominated by a few large domestic banks that have recently evolved into even larger Nordic financial groupings by way of cross-border mergers and acquisitions. Until the 1980s, the domestic banks were protected from the competition of foreign banks, but at the same time subject to extensive credit and exchange controls. The financial sectors were segmented by separate systems of regulation for different financial intermediaries. As quantitative regulations of credit and capital flows became increasingly ineffective in the 1980s, the monetary authorities in Scandinavia created money markets and other arenas for interest rate policies, by which they attempted to meet their exchange rate targets. The financial markets were deregulated and opened for capital flows across the borders.

The opening of the markets created a credit boom, a rise in inflation rates, and speculative bubbles in property and equity markets that were supported by huge capital inflows. Due to a combination of internal over-heating and external shocks, real interest rates in Scandinavia rose to unprecedented levels around 1990. The speculative bubbles burst and produced a wave of bankruptcies, which led to a deep recession and severe **banking crises** in Sweden, Norway and Finland (and milder problems in Denmark) in the early 1990s.

As a consequence, the monetary authorities in Scandinavia began to diverge in their approaches to central bank independence and the setting of targets for monetary policy. While Denmark continued to peg her exchange rate to the ECU (now to the euro), Sweden has left her exchange rate floating and follows an inflation target since 1992. The central banks in both countries have gained operational independence vis-à-vis the respective governments. Norway has kept its central bank under the close control of parliament while going over to a softer exchange rate target and, more recently, to an inflation target. Finland has joined the European Monetary Union, thereby giving up her (formal) independence in all matters of monetary policy.

Thus there is some irony in the fact that the northern Scandinavian countries tried to use the deregulation of the financial sectors as a vehicle for regaining control over bank lending and winning credibility for their policies of disinflationary exchange rate targeting. The inflationary dynamics of the deregulation process contributed to the deep economic and banking crises which, in turn, made the original policies of fixed exchange rates unsustainable and created a diversity of monetary policy frameworks. Yet, as the main players in the Nordic financial systems have begun to converge to large transnational financial groups, the question arises, whether the national monetary policy strategies in the Nordic countries can diverge in the longer run – or whether they, too, will converge in the European Monetary Union (or some satellite arrangement).

Key concepts in this chapter

All-finance *alias* bancassurance	Debt–asset price cycle
Bad banks	Deregulation and liberalization
Banking crises	Inflation target
Concentration in the banking sector	Strategic shareholding of banks
Credit and exchange controls	Strict and soft exchange rate targets
Cross-border integration	'Top-down approach' to the evolution
Currency crises	of commercial banking

---

[10]   However, in the downswing between 2000 and 2003 there was no big difference between the wealth effects in Sweden and in the core economies of the euro area. The *Riksbank* has kept short-term interest rates relatively high and the difference between long-term interest rates in Sweden and in the euro area rarely exceeded half a percentage point.

Questions and problems

1 Describe briefly and explain the differing approaches to monetary policy among the Scandinavian countries.

2 Compare and contrast the structure of the banking systems of Norway, Sweden, Denmark and Finland, paying particular attention to the role of the central bank.

3 How would you explain the banking crises suffered by Norway, Sweden and Finland in the 1980s and 1990s? How did these crises lead to changes in the structure of the financial systems as well as to changes in the targets of monetary policy?

4 Discuss the pros and cons of using bad banks and public subsidies for rescuing (half-)private banks from insolvency.

5 Explain why the market shares of big banks, or the degrees of concentration, tend to be higher in small economies (compared with larger economies).

Further reading

Bank of Finland, *Bulletin, Special Issue: Financial Stability 2006* (Helsinki: www.bof.fi, 2006)

Bank for International Settlements, *Monetary Policy in the Nordic Countries: Experiences since 1992* (Basle: www.bis.org, 1997)

Danmarks Nationalbank, *Monetary Review*, various issues (Central Bank of Denmark, Copenhagen: www.nationalbanken.dk)

Danmarks Nationalbank, *Financial Statistics – Special Report*, 26 April 2004 (Copenhagen: www.nationalbanken.dk, 2004)

Danmarks Nationalbank, Suomen Pankki, Sedlabanki Islands, Norges Bank, Sveriges Riksbank, *Nordic Banking Structures – Report*, 28 August 2006 (Reykjavik *et al.*: http://www.sedlabanki.is/lisalib/getfile.aspx?itemid=4146, 2006)

Lars Engwall, Rolf Marquardt, Torben Pedersen and Adrian Tschoegl, 'Foreign bank penetration of newly opened markets in the Nordic countries', *Journal of International Financial Markets and Money*, 11, 2001, 53–63

Federation of Finnish Financial Services, *Finnish Banking in 2006* (www.fkl.fi, 2007)

Finanstilsynet, *Key Figures 2006 for Financial Instiutions under Supervision* (Danish Financial Supervisory Authority, Copenhagen: www.finanstilsynet.dk, 2007)

Hawkins, John and Philip Turner, 'Bank restructuring in practice: an overview', in *Bank Restructuring in Practice*, ed. by the Bank of International Settlements (Basle: Bank for International Settlements, 1999) 6–104

Kredittilsynet, *The Financial Market in Norway 2006* (Oslo, 2006)

Norges Bank, *Economic Bulletin*, various issues (Oslo: www.norges-bank.no)

Norges Bank, *Financial Stability 1/07 – June*. Reports from the Central Bank of Norway (Oslo: www.norges-bank.no, 2007)

OECD, *Economic Surveys 1993–1994: Sweden* (Paris: OECD, 1994)

Oxelheim, Lars, *Financial Markets in Transition – Globalization, Investment and Economic Growth* (London: Routledge, 1994) Ch. 15

Reve, Torger, 'Learning to Compete in a Deregulated Credit Market: The Failure and Recovery of Norwegian Banking', in *Banking Cultures of the World*, ed. by Leo Schuster (Frankfurt: Fritz Knapp, 1996) 489–500

Statistics Finland, *Financial Accounts* (Helsinki, 2004)

Statistiska Centralbyrån, *Statistics Sweden, Financial Accounts* (Örebro: www.scb.se, 2004)

Suomen Pankki, *Bank of Finland Bulletin*, various issues (Helsinki: www.bof.fi)

Suomen Pankkiyhdistys, *Finnish Financial Markets*, 19th edn (Helsinki: Finnish Bankers' Association, 2003)

Sveriges Riksbank, *The Swedish Financial Market*, various years (Bank of Sweden, Stockholm: www.riksbank.com)

Sveriges Riksbank, *Economic Review*, various issues (Stockholm: www.riksbank.com)

Part 3 Theory

Chapter 8   Portfolio theory

What you will learn in this chapter:

■ How to describe financial assets by reference to their risk and return

■ Why lenders are risk averse

■ Why diversification helps to reduce risk

■ How to calculate portfolio risk and return

■ Why lenders prefer some portfolios to others

■ How financial markets price risk

■ How to price the risk attaching to an individual asset

■ How to calculate the return required on an individual asset

8.1   Introduction

In this chapter we explain how lenders decide on the allocation of their surplus funds, or to put it another way, how they decide what assets to hold. The answer is that they will hold those assets that give them the rate of return they require, in view of the risk which attaches to the asset. So our question has now become 'how do lenders decide on the rate of return that they require on an asset?' Stated briefly, our explanation is that this required rate of return on an asset consists of the **risk-free rate of interest** (set in the economy at large) plus a risk premium (reflecting characteristics of the individual asset). In this chapter we focus largely upon the risk premium. The setting of the risk-free rate of interest is explained in Chapter 9.

Notice that if we can answer this question we can also answer the question, for tradable assets, of what determines their *market price* since the equilibrium price must be that at which lenders think they are getting the right rate of return. Formal demonstrations of this appear in Section 8.5 where we bring together the risk premium and the risk-free rate in models of asset pricing, but it is not difficult to understand intuitively. If we take a simple asset which pays a fixed amount in perpetuity, then the rate of return is clearly the payment (D) divided by the price (P). Suppose all else remains the same (including the fixed payment) while asset holders decide that the return is no longer good enough, perhaps because more attractive assets appear. All they can do is sell. This drives down the price, increasing the payment as a fraction of the price (D/P increases), until a new, higher rate of return emerges which makes the asset attractive again. Thus, in explaining how investors decide upon the required rate of return, we are, in effect, explaining the demand side of a supply/demand framework of asset pricing.

8.2   Risk and return

In choosing what assets they wish to hold people are assumed to be *risk-averse income maximizers* and thus to be seeking the maximum return for a given level of risk or, to put it another way, the minimum risk for a given level of return. The return on an asset is usually expressed as its average or **mean return** (μ) over a period of time. This will consist of any income

(interest or dividend) that the asset earns plus any capital gain (or loss). Thus the return on an asset in period 1, K_1, is given by:

$$K_1 = \frac{D_1 + (P_1 - P_0)}{P_0} \tag{8.1}$$

where P_0 is the price of the asset at the end of the previous period. The (arithmetic) mean return over T periods is:

$$\mu = \frac{\sum_{t=1}^{t=T} K_t}{T} \tag{8.2}$$

Risk is usually defined as *the probability that the actual return may differ from the expected return*. Notice that this view of risk embraces both the possibility that the actual return may exceed what we expect and the possibility that it may be less than we expect. *Actual risk* in this context is therefore symmetrical. However, people's *attitudes* to risk may be asymmetrical. They may be more concerned with the possibility of loss than with the possibility of gain. It is this asymmetric attitude that we are referring to in the phrase **'risk aversion'**. 'Risk' may only mean an equal chance of winning and losing but people do not like it. Why should this be the case?

The generally accepted answer lies in the idea of the *diminishing marginal utility of wealth*. By this we mean that a given addition to wealth is valued less highly than the loss of an equivalent amount. Figure 8.1 illustrates the proposition. An individual is assumed

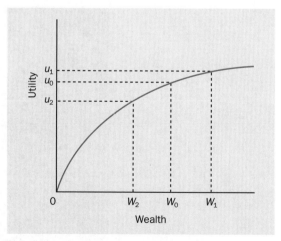

Figure 8.1 The diminishing marginal utility of wealth

to have a given amount of wealth, shown on the horizontal axis by W_0. This yields a certain amount of utility, u_0, shown on the vertical axis. An increase in wealth from W_0 to W_1 increases utility from u_0 to u_1. A decrease in wealth of *an equal amount* is shown by the movement from W_0 to W_2.

Notice now that the reduction in utility is shown by the movement from u_0 to u_2 but that the distance $u_0 - u_2$ is greater than the distance $u_1 - u_0$. That is:

$$\frac{u_0 - u_2}{W_0 - W_2} > \frac{u_1 - u_0}{W_1 - W_0} \qquad (8.3)$$

If it is true that people are risk averse, they will be less willing to hold a risky asset than they will be to hold an asset with little or no risk. Indeed, as we said in Section 1.2.1, they will hold the more risky asset only if they receive a higher reward. But judging between assets on the basis of their risk requires that we be able to measure risk itself. As we shall see in Section 8.4, this can become quite complicated. But we can start with a simple idea. If we define risk as the probability that an individual outcome may differ from what was expected then it seems reasonable to suggest that we measure risk by examining the degree of variation in the return over a period. On our definition, an asset which has shown a wide dispersion of actual returns around the mean is riskier than one where returns have been tightly clustered around the mean value. In technical terms, the dispersion of values around a mean is expressed by the **variance**, σ^2. An alternative is the **standard deviation**, σ, the square root of the variance. The variance is found by:

$$\sigma^2 = \frac{\sum (K_t - \mu)^2}{T} \qquad (8.4)$$

Thus, we can now say that:

> the key characteristics of any asset can be described by the mean value and the variance of its returns.

Notice that the former tells us what an investor can expect to earn from holding the asset over a period of time and the latter tells us the degree of risk associated with those returns.

Unfortunately, the mean and variance of an asset can only be known *ex post*, while investors' decisions must be forward looking. This means that they have to make decisions on the basis of what they *expect* to happen. This raises the very tricky question of just how people form expectations of future economic and financial events. The obvious starting point is that

---

BOX 8.1 Mean and variance

		Share A			
State	P_i	$K_i\%$	P_iK_i	$(K_i - \hat{K})$	$P_i(K_i - \hat{K})^2$
Boom	0.3	18.0	5.4	4.0	4.8
Normal	0.5	14.0	7.0	0.0	0.0
Slump	0.2	8.0	1.6	6.0	7.2
		$\hat{K}_A = 14.0$			$\sigma^2_A = 12.0$

---

expectations are based in some way on what has happened in the past. However, 'in some way' leaves open a lot of possibilities. It seems reasonable perhaps to suggest that people are guided by what they have observed to happen in particular circumstances in the past, together with some assessment of the likely probability of those circumstances occurring again. On this basis, the expected return on an asset, which we write as $\hat{K}$, can be calculated as follows:

$$\hat{K} = \sum P_i K_i \qquad (8.5)$$

where P_i is the probability of a particular state of affairs and K_i is the return expected in those circumstances. The corresponding calculation for the variance is then:

$$\sigma^2 = \sum P_i (K_i - \hat{K}_i)^2 \qquad (8.6)$$

In Box 8.1, share A is expected to produce annual returns ranging from 8 to 18 per cent depending on the state of the economy. The probability of the economy being in a state of 'boom', 'normality' or 'slump' in the next time period varies between 30 per cent, 50 per cent and 20 per cent respectively. The expected return on the share is 14 per cent and its variance is 12.0. Notice that its standard deviation, σ, is 3.46 per cent ($=\sqrt{12.0}$).

8.3 Diversification

It seems intuitively obvious that the degree of risk to which investors are exposed can be reduced by **diversification**. Indeed, this is one of the many benefits that intermediaries offer to lenders (see Section 1.3.2). We can show that this piece of common sense has a firm basis in fact. Furthermore, we can also show that combining assets into a portfolio can usually reduce risk 'more cheaply', that is to say with a smaller sacrifice in return, than would be the case if we simply switched from one (single) risky asset to another less risky (single) one.

The most dramatic effect in risk reduction comes in the early stages of diversification, as we go from one to five to ten assets, say. In fact, after diversification to holding around 20 assets the degree of risk reduction that comes from further expansions of a portfolio is very small.

For simplicity, therefore, we shall illustrate the risk-reducing effect of diversification by expanding from a one-asset to a two-asset portfolio. Assume that we are faced with choosing between the share A in Box 8.1 and another share B which is expected to give a return varying between 12, 8 and 8 per cent (see Exercise 8.1) per annum in the 'boom', 'normal' and 'slump' states. At this point, you should calculate the expected return and variance of share B in Exercise 8.1, before going on.

Obviously we could put all our funds into A or into B, or we could split our investment between the two. Consider firstly the effect upon returns. The general expression for portfolio return is:

$$\hat{K}_p = \sum w_i K_i \qquad (8.7)$$

where w_i is the 'weight' or proportion of the portfolio allocated to each security and K_i is the return on each asset. (We have dropped the subscript t indicating a given time period in order to make the expressions easier to read.) We can apply the general expression in Equation 8.7 to our specific case. If, for example, we put one half of our funds into each of A and B (whose

return in Exercise 8.1 is 9.2 per cent) then we have an expected return of:

$$\hat{K}_p = 0.5(14.0) + 0.5(9.2) = 11.6\%$$

Portfolio return is therefore quite simply the weighted average of its components.

When we consider the effect of diversification upon risk, however, the picture is more complex, but also more interesting. It is not a simple weighted average, though the proportions allocated to each asset do play a part. Using the standard deviation as the measure of risk the general expression for a two-asset portfolio is:

$$\sigma_p = \sqrt{X_A^2 \sigma_A^2 + X_B^2 \cdot \sigma_B^2 + 2X_A(X_B) \cdot \text{cov } K_A, K_B} \qquad (8.8)$$

where X_A, X_B are the relative proportions of assets A and B in the portfolio. The first part of the expression:

$$X_A^2 \sigma_A^2 + X_B^2 \cdot \sigma_B^2 \qquad (8.9)$$

clearly is just a weighted average of the variances of each of the two assets (albeit weighted by the squares of the proportions held). The interesting part of Equation 8.8 is the second part:

$$2X_A(X_B) \cdot \text{cov } K_A, K_B \qquad (8.10)$$

which features the **covariance** of returns between the two assets. The covariance can be written as:

$$\text{cov } K_A, K_B = \sigma_A \cdot \sigma_B \cdot \rho_{AB} \qquad (8.11)$$

Notice that the covariance includes the standard deviation of each asset but it also includes a term, ρ_{AB}, which is the **correlation coefficient of returns** between A and B. While the variance of each asset, σ^2, measures the size of variability or dispersion of returns around the mean value, the correlation coefficient measures the degree to which the returns on any two assets, be they highly variable or not, actually *move together*.

This is clearly important if we are interested in risk and if we define risk in terms of variability. After all, we could imagine two assets each with a large variance which would therefore be very risky if held in isolation. But suppose that whenever the return on one went up, the return on the other went down. We could then combine them in such a way that returns were constant because the variations would cancel out and the portfolio variance and standard deviation would be zero. We come back to this later in this section.

Exercise 8.1 Mean and variance

Share B

State	P_i	$K_i\%$	$P_i K_i$	$(K_i - \hat{K}_i)$	$P_i(K_i - \hat{K})^2$
Boom	0.3	12.0			
Normal	0.5	8.0			
Slump	0.2	8.0			
		$\hat{K}_B =$			$\sigma_B^2 =$

(Answers appear in the text.)

Let us see what happens in the present case. We have most of the information necessary for a solution to Equation 8.8. We shall assume that we split our investment equally between A and B and so X_A and X_B each have the value 0.5. The variances, σ_A^2 and σ_B^2, we have calculated above. What we do not yet have is a value for the covariance term, Equation 8.11. The covariance can be found as follows:

$$\text{cov } K_A, K_B = \sum P_i (K_A - \hat{K}_A)(K_B - \hat{K}_B) \quad (8.12)$$

where K_A and K_B are the returns on A and B in each state of the economy as shown in each of the tables above. (K_A and K_B are in effect short for $K_i(A)$ and $K_i(B)$.) In our case, therefore:

$$
\begin{aligned}
\text{cov } K_A, K_B &= 0.3(18 - 14)(12 - 9.2) \\
&\quad + 0.5(14 - 14)(8 - 9.2) \\
&\quad + 0.2(8 - 14)(8 - 9.2) \\
&= 3.36 + 0.0 + 1.44 \\
&= 4.8
\end{aligned}
$$

Putting everything together (including the variance of share B) we can now solve Equation 8.8 and find the standard deviation of our two-asset portfolio as follows:

$$
\begin{aligned}
\sigma_P &= \sqrt{0.5^2(12) + 0.5^2(3.36) + 2(0.5)(0.5)\,4.8} \\
&= \sqrt{3.0 + 0.84 + 2.4} \\
&= \sqrt{6.24} \\
&= 2.50
\end{aligned}
$$

Let us now summarize our three investment possibilities: putting all our funds into A or all into B or dividing them equally between A and B in a portfolio, C.

	A	B	C
$\hat{K}$	14.00	9.20	11.60
σ	3.46	1.83	2.50

Investing entirely in A, we can expect a return of 14 per cent per annum if we are prepared to accept a standard deviation of returns of 3.46. If this seems too risky, one alternative is to invest entirely in B. This gives us a very large reduction in risk but we have to accept also a reduction in the expected return to 9.2 per cent. Looking at C, we can see that splitting our investment equally between A and B means, predictably, that we have to accept half of the reduction in returns but we can still get *more than half of the risk reduction effect* that we would have had from putting everything into B. A way of expressing this more formally is to say that in going from A to B we reduce risk at the rate of 0.34 for every unit reduction in return (1.63/4.8). In going from A to a split portfolio, C, however, we 'buy' the reduction at a rate of 0.40 for every one point reduction in return (0.96/2.4).

The reason for this reduction in risk per unit rate of return lies in the correlation coefficient of returns between the two assets. If we compare the way in which returns on share A and share B vary in different states of the economy, we can see firstly that they move together in the sense that they both go up when the economy moves from normal to boom but only the return on A goes down when we move from normal to slump. B is what might be called a good 'defensive' security. We can also see that the overall variability of B is less than that of A, which is what we discovered in calculating their variances. These differences mean that the returns are less than perfectly correlated – that is, the correlation coefficient is less than $+1$. We can calculate the correlation coefficient from the covariance by rearranging Equation 8.11.

$$\rho_{AB} = \frac{\text{cov }(K_A, K_B)}{\sigma_A.\sigma_B} \quad (8.13)$$

In this case, the correlation coefficient of returns is:

$$\rho_{AB} = 4.8/(3.46 \times 1.83) = 0.76$$

Perfect correlation is indicated by a correlation coefficient of $+1$ while complete negative (offsetting) correlation is signified by a coefficient of -1. To see why the correlation coefficient is so important in reducing the risk of a portfolio below that of its component parts, consider the effect of these extreme values in the expression for a portfolio, Equation 8.8. Remember that we divided this complex expression into two parts: the first (Equation 8.9) was based on the variances of the portfolio's components, the second (Equation 8.10) featured the covariance of returns between the components. If the correlation coefficient is negative then it follows that the covariance term (Equation 8.10) will be negative. The effect of the standard deviations of the individual securities contained in the covariance will then work to *reduce* the effect of the variances in the first part (Equation 8.8) of the portfolio risk formula and the negative effect will be at its greatest when the coefficient takes the extreme value of -1. On the other hand, for any value greater than zero, the effect of the correlation

Exercise 8.2

1 Calculate the covariance for our hypothetical portfolio, C, by substituting +1 for the correlation coefficient ρ_{AB} in Equation 8.11, leaving all other values unchanged. Then recalculate the standard deviation of the two-asset portfolio. Compare the risk attaching to this portfolio with the risk that you would incur by putting 50 per cent of your wealth into asset A and 50 per cent into asset B.

2 Recalculate the covariance and portfolio standard deviation again, setting $\rho_{AB} = -1$

3 Leaving $\rho_{AB} = -1$, combine A and B in order to produce zero portfolio risk.

(Answers appear in Box 8.2.)

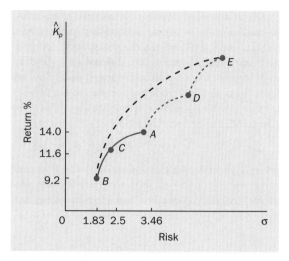

Figure 8.2 Efficient portfolios

coefficient will be that the effect of the standard deviations in the covariance will be *added* to the effect of the variances in the first part of the portfolio risk formula. The covariance's contribution to risk will be greatest when the coefficient takes the value of +1. In these circumstances, there is no benefit from diversification and it follows then that the portfolio's risk must be equal to the weighted average of the standard deviation of its components. This is illustrated in Exercise 8.2.

The conclusion we have come to then, and it is fundamental to understanding the behaviour of individual investors and financial intermediaries, is that:

> provided the returns on assets are less than perfectly correlated, the greater the degree of portfolio diversification, the lower will be the level of risk associated with a given return.

This can be seen in Figure 8.2. Points A and B show the risk and return associated with our two assets A

BOX 8.2 Three answers

When $\rho_{AB} = +1$, and other values remain as they were, the standard deviation of our two-asset portfolio, C, = 2.64. This is because when returns are perfectly correlated, we know from Equation 8.11 that the covariance term in Equation 8.8 simplifies to $\sigma_A \cdot \sigma_B$. Thus Equation 8.8 can be written:

$$\sigma_p = \sqrt{X_A^2 \cdot \sigma_A^2 + X_B^2 \cdot \sigma_B^2 + 2X_A(X_B)\sigma_A.\sigma_B}$$

This in turn simplifies to:

$$\sigma_p = X_A\sigma_A + X_B\sigma_B$$

which is simply a weighted average of the standard deviations of the returns on the individual assets.

When $\rho_{AB} = -1$, and other values remain as they were, the standard deviation of our two-asset portfolio, C, = 0.821. The reasoning parallels that above, except that the simplification of the covariance term to $\sigma_A \cdot \sigma_B$

is accompanied by a minus sign. Thus Equation 8.8 can be written:

$$\sigma_p = \sqrt{X_A^2 \cdot \sigma_A^2 + X_B^2 \cdot \sigma_B^2 - 2X_A(X_B)\sigma_A \cdot \sigma_B}$$

This in turn simplifies to a positive portfolio standard deviation of:

$$\sigma_p = X_A\sigma_A - X_B\sigma_B \quad \text{or} \quad \sigma_p = X_B\sigma_B - X_A\sigma_A$$

We commented earlier in this chapter that if two assets were perfectly negatively correlated then it was possible to construct a zero-risk portfolio. This requires merely that we choose appropriate proportions of each asset, that is, appropriate values for the X's. These values can be found as follows:

$$X_A = \sigma_B/(\sigma_A + \sigma_B), \quad X_B = \sigma_A/(\sigma_A + \sigma_B)$$

To make a zero-risk portfolio from our two assets, A and B, requires $X_A \approx 0.35$ and $X_B \approx 0.65$.

and B from earlier in this section. Point C represents the risk and return that we calculated for a portfolio composed of equal quantities of A and B. Notice, on the vertical axis, that the return associated with C comes exactly halfway between the returns on A and B, while the risk, on the horizontal axis, is less than halfway between the risk of A and the risk of B. C represents a portfolio of equal weights, but we could have any weight for asset A ranging from 0 to 100 per cent and the corresponding weight for B would be the residual. If we were to plot the risk/return combinations for all these different portfolio compositions, then the results would lie on the smooth curve between A and B. Notice that the curve is convex. This is entirely due to the risk reduction effect of diversification.

The curve joining A and B results from combining just those two assets. But in the real world there are many assets and we could combine, for example, A with D or D with E and so on. And we do not have to stop at just two assets. We could combine all risky assets together in almost infinite combinations. This would give us even lower risk for any given rate of return, and this is shown by the dashed envelope curve in Figure 8.2.

8.4 'Market' and 'specific' risk

Figure 8.3 illustrates this conclusion in another way. As more securities are added to the portfolio, so the portfolio's standard deviation diminishes. Notice though that most of the risk reduction effect is achieved by the time the portfolio consists of 20 securities. Beyond that point, portfolio risk appears to settle at an irreducible threshold. Why should this be?

The downward-sloping portion of the curve is explained by our discussion in the last section and hinges on the correlation coefficient of returns. For most assets, the correlation coefficient of returns with other assets is less than $+1$. Think carefully what this means. Something happens that causes the return on asset A, say, to rise. The returns on some other assets also rise but not to the same degree and returns on some assets are unaffected. It might even be that the returns on one or two assets move in the opposite direction. What this indicates is that each asset is affected to some extent by events which are unique to that asset. Combining assets in a portfolio means that the

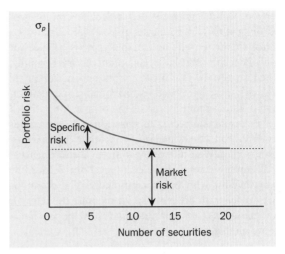

Figure 8.3 Benefits of diversification

effect of a specific event on asset A will be partially offset by the effect of some other event on asset B. As the number of assets increases, the scope for this offsetting also increases. Risk arising out of events unique to particular securities is called **specific, unique** or **unsystematic risk**. Examples of events giving rise to specific risk can be found in good and bad news about individual borrowers – news about individual firms or about the industry in which they operate.

The near-horizontal part of the curve is explained by the fact that in addition to unique events, assets are also exposed to common sources of risk. Most company shares will be adversely affected by a downturn in the economy. Risk arising out of economy-wide events is called **market** or **systematic risk**. Not all will be affected to the same degree: some securities will be very sensitive to market events, some less so. But diversifying from one to many assets, or even changing the composition of the portfolio entirely, cannot eliminate market risk. A rational, risk-averse, investor will do everything possible to diversify away specific risk, but market risk always remains.

Since it measures the dispersion of returns around the mean value from a security held in isolation, standard deviation (or variance) is an attempt to measure **total risk**. That is to say:

Total risk = market risk + specific risk
= standard deviation

However, we have just seen that diversification can reduce total risk by eliminating specific risk. Since anyone can diversify, the only risk which an investor is obliged to face is market risk. Three conclusions must follow. Firstly, no rational risk-averse investor will incur specific risk, since it is unnecessary. Secondly, the only reward that investors can expect to be paid for risk must be related to unavoidable, i.e. market, risk. (Because market risk is the only risk for which investors can expect compensation it is sometimes referred to as 'relevant' risk – all other risk is irrelevant.) Thirdly, standard deviation (by measuring total risk) must overstate the relevant level of risk faced by any investor who behaves rationally. The questions we are left with are 'how do we measure the relevant or market risk of an asset?' and 'how do we put a price on that risk?'

8.5 The capital asset pricing model

One popular way of answering both questions lies in the **capital asset pricing model**, or CAPM. This states that:

> The rate of return on an asset will be equal to the risk-free rate of interest plus a risk premium which depends upon the market price of risk and the quantity of market risk contained within the asset.

Notice two things. Firstly, although it is called the capital asset *pricing* model, our statement of it refers only to rates of return. We come back to this at the end of the section. Secondly, the statement involves three elements. We take each in turn.

The first element is the risk-free rate of interest. The relevance of the risk-free rate is that it puts a floor or threshold under the return on all risky assets. Risky assets must pay a return which *exceeds* the risk-free rate. Furthermore, for a given level of risk, one would expect the additional return to be a constant premium over and above the risk-free rate, whatever may happen to the latter. In other words, if the risk-free rate rises, then we would expect all other rates to be pushed up and the return on all risky assets to rise along with the return on risk-free ones. The risk-free rate should therefore be seen as a 'floating' threshold or baseline from which all other rates are derived by the addition of a premium. In practice, the risk-free rate is often approximated by the return on short-dated treasury bills. We denote it by K_{rf}.

The second and third elements relate to the risk premium to be added to the risk-free rate. The second

element is the 'market *price* of risk'. This can be thought of as the 'going rate' for some sort of 'standard' level of risk. What benchmark do we use? The answer takes us back to the distinction between market and specific risk again. We know that we can eliminate the latter by diversification. The greatest degree of diversification that we could achieve would be to hold a portfolio which contained *all* the risky assets available. The same could be achieved by holding a miniature portfolio which replicated the **whole market portfolio** of risky assets. In practice, what this would mean is holding a miniature portfolio composed of all the risky assets available to us in the proportions that they exist in the whole market. One might imagine that this involves holding a miniature reproduction of the whole stock market, though, strictly speaking, *all* risky assets should mean *all* risky assets – embracing all financial assets and real assets too. The importance of the whole market portfolio, however it is defined, is that it represents the extreme case of diversification and therefore is subject solely to market risk. Any return earned by such a portfolio, over and above K_{rf}, must therefore be the premium uniquely associated with pure market risk.

In practice, the 'whole market portfolio' is often taken to mean the 'whole share market portfolio'. In these circumstances, the return on the whole market can be fairly easily established by looking at the annual yield generated by shares in an 'all-share index', together with movements in the index itself. This we shall call K_m. The difference between this result and the risk-free rate $(K_m - K_{rf})$ is then the market risk premium, or the market price of risk. We can, if we wish, express this price per unit of risk by dividing the premium by the standard deviation of returns on the whole market portfolio. The market risk premium is our benchmark by which we shall judge the premium to be paid on individual assets.

Given this benchmark price, we now need to know how much of this price should apply to any individual asset. This is described in the third element: the *quantity* of market risk in the asset. This is found quite simply by comparing the behaviour of an individual asset with the whole market portfolio. What is compared is the variance of returns. And the logic is that if the whole market portfolio carries a risk premium of, say, 10 per cent, then an asset which shows twice the variability should have a 20 per cent premium, while an asset with only half the variance should have a risk premium of 5 per cent. Figure 8.4

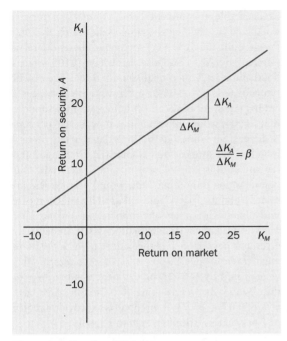

Figure 8.4 The β-coefficient

shows how we might make the comparison between a single asset and the whole market.

Figure 8.4 is essentially a scatter diagram, where each point represents simultaneously the return on the asset (marked on the vertical axis) and the return on the whole market (marked on the horizontal axis). A 'line of best fit' is then drawn through the scatter of points. This can be done either by eye, or more precisely by using a regression technique like ordinary least squares. Clearly, the line when fitted could be 'steep' or 'flat', or it could be at 45°. If the slope is 45° the variation of returns on the individual asset exactly matches the variation of return on the whole market portfolio and the asset has the same exposure to market risk as the whole market portfolio. In these circumstances, the individual asset should earn the same premium as the whole market portfolio. If the slope is 'flat', less than 45°, the asset shows less exposure to market risk and the premium should be smaller; if the slope is steep, greater than 45°, the risk premium on the asset should be greater than that on the whole market portfolio.

But we can be much more precise. Once we have drawn the line, we can measure its slope. In Figure 8.4, the slope is equal to $\Delta K_A / \Delta K_M$. If we fitted the line by regression techniques, the slope of the line would

commonly be represented by β. For this reason, this measure of an asset's exposure to market risk is often referred to as its **β-coefficient**. We can now see that if the line is drawn at 45°, $\beta = 1$. If the line is steeper, then the β-coefficient is greater than 1; if the line is flatter, then the β-coefficient is less than 1.

Putting all of this together, we can now see that the CAPM tells us how to find the required return on a risky asset, A, for example. Letting $\overline{K}_A$ stand for the required return, then:

$$\overline{K}_A = K_{rf} + \beta_A(K_m - K_{rf}) \qquad (8.14)$$

Equation 8.14 is the equation for what is known as the **security market line** or *SML*. (Occasionally, the equation is said to represent the CAPM itself.) Using values for K_A, K_{rf} and K_m taken from Exercise 8.3, we have drawn the *SML* in Figure 8.5. The *SML* shows the additional return (above K_{rf}) required on *an*

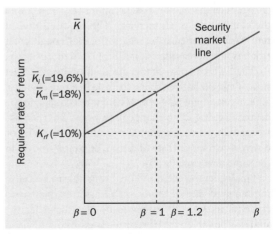

Figure 8.5 The security market line

individual asset whose risk characteristics can be compared with those of a whole market portfolio. It is these characteristics, expressed by β, which are drawn on the horizontal axis. Expressed in terms of *pricing*, rather than *rates of return*, the message of the CAPM is that assets which are 'fairly priced' will yield a rate of return such that they plot on the *SML*.

Notice firstly that an asset with no relevant risk, $\beta = 0$, has a required rate of return equal to the risk-free rate while an asset with $\beta = 1$ has the same required return as the whole market portfolio. If we know the risk-free rate, the market risk premium and the asset's β-coefficient we can read off the required rate of return. For example, in Exercise 8.3 our hypothetical asset had a β-value of 1.2 while the risk-free rate was 10 per cent and the whole market rate was 18 per cent. In this case $\overline{K}_i = 10\% + 1.2(18\% - 10\%) = 19.6\%$.

To understand what might cause the required return to change, we need to be careful, as always, to distinguish between movements *along* and movements *of* the *SML*. Consider firstly movements along the curve. Since the curve plots the required rate as a function of β, movements along the curve will occur whenever anything happens to affect a share's β-coefficient. This means that its exposure to market risk has changed. An increase in exposure will move us up the *SML*, increasing the required rate of return; reductions in risk will move us down the *SML*.

The *SML* itself can change in two senses: its slope may change or it may be subject to a parallel shift. Its slope is given by $(K_m - K_{rf})/\beta$ and expresses the degree of risk aversion in the market. A change in slope will occur if, as we suggested in Exercise 8.3, there is a change in risk aversion. If, for example, there is an increase, then the market risk premium $(K_m - K_{rf})$ and the slope of the *SML* increase. The required rate of return on assets also increases since although their risk has not increased, risk itself is priced more highly.

The *SML* can also change its position by a parallel shift. This will happen when the risk-free rate changes, all else remaining as it was. There is no change in the degree of risk and no change in its price. But the risk-free rate to which the premium is added may go up or down. The required rate of return, of course, moves in the same direction.

Finally, let us return to how being able to establish the required rate of return on an asset enables us to establish its *price*. In order to do this, consider the simplest possible rate of return – a cashflow of fixed amount, paid in perpetuity. An example might be an irredeemable government bond. A *rate* of return is calculated by dividing the actual amount received by the amount that we paid to receive the entitlement (see Equation 8.1). Suppose that we pay £100 for this bond and it pays an annual amount of £6. The rate of return is $6/100 = 0.06$ or 6 per cent. Since there is a ready market for government bonds, we may suppose that £100 is a 'fair' price and this is because 6 per cent is the current going rate on long-dated assets of very low risk. But suppose that circumstances changed and returns on this kind of asset rose to 7 per cent. Our bond, paying only 6 per cent, would become less attractive and its price would fall until it could compete fairly again with other comparable assets paying 7 per cent. Its need to compete with other assets immediately gives us a new price. It is that price at which the bond must trade to give buyers a 7 per cent return. This we can find by solving for x, where x is the price of the bond. By rearranging $0.07 = 6/x$ we have $x = 6/0.07 = 85.71$. If this bond is to provide a return of 7 per cent its price must fall to £85.71.

We can now rephrase our earlier version of the CAPM to make it clear that it really does have pricing implications:

> **The market will price an asset such that** its rate of return will be equal to the risk-free rate of interest plus a risk premium which depends upon the market price of risk and the quantity of market risk contained within the asset.

8.6 Summary

Other things being given, the price paid for an asset determines its rate of return. If we can explain the return required on an asset, therefore, we can explain why the market prices an asset as it does. Our explanation of asset returns is that the required rate of return is equal to the risk-free rate of return plus a fraction or multiple of the premium required for 'average' or 'standard' risk.

The benchmark risk premium is the difference in return between a whole market portfolio of risky assets and the risk-free rate $(K_m - K_{rf})$. This represents the price required by the market for holding a fully diversified portfolio. That is to say it is the price required for holding the minimum level of risk for a given return, since all risk that can be avoided has been eliminated by diversification. It is the only risk that rational, risk-averse, investors will be prepared to hold.

An individual asset attracts a proportion of this whole market risk premium, determined by its β-coefficient. We use the β-coefficient, rather than the standard deviation of returns, as a more relevant measure of an asset's riskiness in this situation because, again, rational investors will hold an asset only as part of a fully diversified portfolio. The β-coefficient is relevant because it measures the risk brought by an asset to a portfolio, taking account of its covariance of returns with the whole market as well as its standard deviation.

Key concepts in this chapter

β-coefficient
Capital asset pricing model
Correlation coefficient of returns
Covariance
Diversification
Market or systematic risk
Mean
Return
Risk

Risk aversion
Risk-free rate of interest
Security market line
Specific, unique or unsystematic risk
Standard deviation
Total risk
Variance
Whole market portfolio

Questions and problems

1 What is meant by risk in a financial context? Why are people assumed to be risk averse?

2 Why does the diversification of asset holdings generally lead to a reduction in risk?

3 Are there any limits to the benefits of diversification? If so, why?

4 Distinguish between market risk and specific risk.

5 Why does the return on assets reflect only their exposure to market risk?

6 If the riskiness of an asset can be described by its variance, why do we need the β-coefficient?

7 Explain how you would expect each of the following events to affect the security market line and the required rate of return on a given share (imagine that each event occurs independently of the others):

    (a) an increase in official short-term interest rates;

    (b) a reduction in the degree of risk aversion in the market;

    (c) an increase in the uncertainty of the share's future prospects.

Further reading

D Blake, *Financial Market Analysis* (London: McGraw-Hill, 2e, 2000) Ch. 13
Z Bodie, A Kane and A J Marcus, *Essentials of Investments* (New York: McGraw-Hill, 2001) Ch. 2
E J Elton, M J Gruber, S J Brown and W N Goetzmann, *Modern Portfolio Theory and Investment Analysis* (Chichester: Wiley, 6e, 2006) Ch. 13
P G A Howells and K Bain, *Financial Markets and Institutions* (London: Pearson Education, 5e, 2007) Ch. 1
K Pilbeam, *Finance and Financial Markets* (London: Palgrave, 2e, 2005) Ch. 7

Chapter 9 | The determination of
short-term interest rates

What you will learn in this chapter:

- The distinction between real and nominal interest rates

- The meaning of liquidity, risk and inflation premiums

- The loanable funds and liquidity preference theories of interest
  and the assumptions behind them

- The Fisher effect and its role in linking nominal and real rates
  of interest

- The origin and limitations of central bank influence over
  interest rates

9.1 Introduction

No one interested in economics or finance would doubt the importance of interest rates. Consider just a few possible reasons:

- the rate of interest is a payment from borrowers to lenders;
- asset values move inversely with changes in interest rates;
- interest rates are part of the cost of firms' investments;
- interest rates affect the exchange rate;
- interest rates affect bank lending and monetary growth.

The first two in this list are particularly important in financial theory. For example, in the last chapter we established that lenders would require a reward which compensated them for the degree of risk that they felt they were running by lending, and this was a reward which was paid *as a premium* on the 'risk-free' rate of interest. Later, in Chapter 11, we shall see that the prices of financial assets change in response, naturally enough, to changes in demand and supply. But we have already seen that the price that people are prepared to pay is determined by the rate of return that they require from an asset, and this is determined partly by the risk-free rate of interest.

In this chapter, therefore, we want to begin to explain how interest rates are determined. We start with the determination of the *short-term, risk-free, nominal rate of interest*. In the next chapter we go on to look at how a whole range of other interest rates, differentiated by term and by risk, are derived from the short-term, risk-free rate. One way of visualizing this two-stage process is to think that we are first going to examine the base or foundation level of interest rates, before going on to look at the superstructure built upon that base.

9.2 Interest rates defined and classified

The rate of interest is a payment from borrowers to lenders which compensates the latter for parting with funds for a period of time and at some risk. Put into real terms, it is often said that lenders are being encouraged to forgo consumption now, in conditions of comparative certainty, in return for consumption later, in an uncertain future. This is a little misleading. In 'rewarding' savers for parting with funds, a rate of interest is, strictly speaking, rewarding savers for giving up the *ability to consume* if they should change their mind about saving. After all, there is a perfectly rational case to be made for people to save (forgo *actual consumption*) at zero, or even negative, real interest rates since they will wish to provide for old age or other future periods of zero income.

Notice that the effect of interest rates is to influence behaviour which stretches over a period of time – lending *for a period*, forgoing the ability to consume *for a period*, investing in capital goods which yield a return *over a period*. The relevant concept of interest rate is thus, strictly speaking, the *expected* rate. However, we can only observe actual interest rates. Unless we state otherwise, we shall assume that expected and actual rates turn out to be the same.

Nominal interest rates are the rates of interest that are actually paid, in money form. They are the interest rates that we use in everyday discussion and which we see quoted in advertisements, in the media and in official announcements. It is useful to think of nominal rates as consisting of four elements. Letting i stand for the nominal rate of interest, then:

$$i = r - \pi + l + \sigma \qquad (9.1)$$

where r is the *real* short-term rate of interest, π is an **inflation premium**, l is a *liquidity* premium and σ is a premium for risk.

The **real rate of interest** is the return that lenders require even if there is no risk and prices are constant. This is the 'pure' return for giving up the ability to spend, for even the shortest period of time. It is generally accepted that lenders prefer to lend for the shortest possible period. If this is the case, then long-term (real) interest rates will be higher than short-term ones and the difference might be described as a liquidity premium. If it is true that lenders require increasing inducements to part with liquidity for increasingly long periods then the inducements must be real (unless we assume that lenders suffer from 'money illusion'). Thus lenders will require compensation for any rise in prices that they expect to occur over the duration of the loan. Lastly, σ is a further premium required to compensate for whatever level of risk is perceived to attach to the loan. As we saw in the last chapter, the size of this premium in any specific case will depend upon the riskiness of the loan in question in relation to 'average risk' in the market and the price required to compensate lenders for average risk. Of the four components making up the nominal rate, σ is not related to time.

Through Sections 9.3 to 9.5, we shall concentrate upon the determination of the risk-free, short-term nominal rate of interest. That is, we shall concentrate upon i, where i is composed of the two elements r and π. We shall use l and σ in the next chapter to explain the structure of interest rates built upon the short-term, risk-free rate.

9.3 'Market' theories of interest rate determination

Many economics textbooks present two apparently conflicting accounts of the determination of interest rates. (Some do it perhaps even without realizing it. The **loanable funds theory** (*LFT*) is the basis of interest rates in the microeconomic section while **liquidity preference theory** (*LPT*) is called on in the macroeconomic chapters.) *LFT* is associated with the 'classical' economists of the nineteenth and early twentieth centuries while *LPT* is a product of John Maynard Keynes' *The General Theory of Employment, Interest and Money* (1936). The merits of the two approaches were the subject of a long and often bitter dispute between Keynes and his pupil (later colleague) D H Robertson.

9.3.1 Loanable funds theory

Briefly, *LFT* explained the level of interest rates as the outcome of decisions to invest and decisions to save. Decisions to invest resulted from the desire to enjoy the future output from capital assets while decisions to save resulted from a desire to accumulate wealth for the future through the rate of interest offered by investors. The essential point, from an economic point of view, was that the rate of interest was freely determined by the interaction of these two sets of decisions. At the going rate of interest, any decision to save (not spend) must be matched by a decision to spend on capital goods. If, for some reason, savers decided to save more, then the excess supply of saving would push interest rates down, and investment up,

until a new equilibrium was reached at which saving and investment were equal. There could be no 'leakage' from the circular flow of income. In *LFT*, it is often said, the rate of interest is determined by the 'real' forces of *productivity* (of capital equipment, determining what borrowers could pay) and **thrift** (on the part of savers, determining their willingness to lend).

As we shall see in Section 9.3.2, this explanation of interest rates was attacked by Keynes in *The General Theory of Employment, Interest and Money*. Before attacking it, he labelled the theory a product of 'classical' economists, though he also pointed out that it had never been very clearly stated. (It might be noted in passing that Keynes was never very clear as to whom exactly he included under the heading of 'classical' economists.) The label undoubtedly comes from the fact that the theory makes a number of assumptions that are common in the approach of Ricardo and Mill and, indeed, in the work of more recent economists who claim to have revived the classical tradition. The assumptions of **loanable funds** theory are:

- the economy is operating at full employment;
- prices are constant;
- there is a fixed supply of money;
- there is perfect information.

From a borrowing and lending point of view, the significance of these assumptions is as follows. With output fixed at full employment there are no fluctuations in income or employment and therefore no fluctuations in the supply of saving resulting from this source. There is no fluctuation either in the demand for money as a result of varying levels of transactions in the economy. With the money supply fixed, there is no alternative source of funds but savings out of current income. No new money is being created which might meet part of the demand for funds. If there is perfect information, there is no uncertainty. There will be no fluctuation in the demand for funds resulting, for example, from shifts in the demand for money as a safe haven for savings. There will be no fluctuation in 'hoards'. All savings will be made available in loanable form in order to benefit from the rate of interest. With no fluctuation in demand for hoards, the only source of demand for loanable funds comes from a desire to invest. Loanable funds theory is an explanation of how interest rates would be determined in an economy in long-run full equilibrium.

The effect of these assumptions is to ensure that the only supply of funds is saving, while the only demand comes from investment and the only influence on either is the rate of interest. We shall now look at *LFT* in more detail, remembering that *LFT* originally assumed constant prices. In these circumstances, the real and nominal rates of interest are identical. An explanation of the real rate is also an explanation of the nominal rate.

The real rate of interest

It is assumed that agents prefer consumption now to consumption in the future, that is to say that they have *positive time preference*. The real rate of interest is the rate of interest that lenders would need to compensate them for postponing consumption until some point in the future, given constant prices. The size of the inducement necessary to bring about the postponement is thus said to measure their **rate of time preference**. Individuals will differ in their rates of time preference, in the way that individual 'tastes' vary towards all activities, but as a general rule we might expect the rate of time preference to fall with increases in income. People with large incomes will find it easier, and more attractive, to postpone consumption now – in order to enjoy a more prosperous old age, for example – than people with incomes scarcely large enough to purchase day-to-day essentials. In the aggregate, therefore, we would expect high-income communities to have a lower rate of time preference and this is just another way of saying that, other things being equal, we would expect saving to increase (as a proportion of income) with increases in income.

As described in the last paragraph, therefore, the real rate of interest can thus be seen as an inducement to *savers*. On the other hand borrowers, or users of those funds, are normally assumed to want them for investment in assets which yield a future stream either of income or of services or of output.

Consider for a moment the purchase of real assets such as plant or machinery. Borrowers will purchase such assets if they have a positive *net present value*. That is to say that the assets will be attractive if they yield some net benefit in excess of their purchase price, running costs and the cost of borrowed funds. Formally:

$$NPV = -P + \sum_{t=1}^{n} \frac{CF_t}{(1 + \overline{K})^t} \qquad (9.2)$$

where *CF* is the cashflow (net of any running costs) in each period *t*, and $\overline{K}$ is the required rate of return. The required rate of return on a project must obviously cover the cost of funds and this will mean matching the risk-free short-term rate of interest plus the various risk premiums that lenders require. Any project that achieves this while leaving $NPV \geq 0$ will justify borrowing the funds to undertake it. Clearly, from Equation 9.2, the ability of a project to fulfil this condition for any value of $\overline{K}$ will depend upon its cashflows, that is to say, upon its **productivity**. The greater the productivity of the asset, the higher the value at which $\overline{K}$ can be set without breaching the condition of a positive *NPV*. Thus, an investor's ability to pay any given price for funds will depend upon the productivity of the real assets. We shall see later, but especially in Chapter 11, that the return on financial assets should also, in theory, reflect the return on the underlying real assets. If we accept this for the time being, then we can see that the demand for funds, that is to say the price that borrowers will be prepared to pay, will depend upon the productivity of real assets.

According to this point of view, therefore, the equilibrium real rate of interest will be that rate at which the supply of funds from savers just matches the quantity demanded by investors. Figure 9.1 illustrates this situation. The supply curve of funds, *S*, is drawn upward-sloping because of its savings component reflecting the fact that the higher the rate of interest

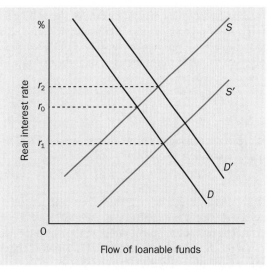

Figure 9.1 Loanable funds theory of the real rate of interest

the greater the number of people who will find that it exceeds their rate of time preference. The demand curve, D, is drawn downward-sloping, indicating that the lower the rate of interest the more projects can be found whose productivity generates a positive NPV. The equilibrium real interest rate is that at which the supply of funds is just equal to the demand, r_0.

Imagine now that the community's rate of time preference diminishes and the supply of lending increases at all rates of interest. This is shown by a downward shift of the supply curve to S'. There is now an excess supply of lending – the number of profitable projects at any rate being unchanged. In the circumstances, the interest rate falls to r_1, more projects become profitable and the flow of lending and borrowing would be again in equilibrium.

Imagine now that, instead, there had been an increase in productivity. At r_0 there would be an excess of profitable projects. The demand curve shifts to D'. Competition for funds would push up the rate of interest. More potential lenders would find that the rate of interest exceeded their rate of time preference, more funds would be forthcoming and a new equilibrium would emerge at r_2.

The rate of inflation

We have just seen that the traditional explanation for a rate of interest payable to lenders by borrowers is that lenders are forgoing consumption for which they require compensation. Depending on their rate of time preference they may, for example, be willing to forgo £100's-worth of current consumption provided that they are in a position to consume £105's-worth in one year's time. If this is the case, then the real rate of interest, r, is 5 per cent:

$$r = \frac{£105}{£100} - 1 = 0.05 = 5\% \qquad (9.3)$$

If prices are constant, a 5 per cent return on £100 requires a cashflow in one year's time of £105.

$$CF_{t+1} = £100 \times (1 + r) \qquad (9.4)$$

With constant prices, a 5 per cent real return is achieved with a nominal rate of interest, i, of 5 per cent. The real and nominal rates are the same and we can write the required augmentation in terms of either the real or nominal rate of interest, that is:

$$(1 + i) = (1 + r) \qquad (9.5)$$

Given the experience of inflationary episodes throughout Europe in the twentieth century, the assumption of constant prices strikes us today as hopelessly unrealistic and might lead us to view loanable funds theory with scepticism. But it is not difficult to graft on to LFT an account of the determination of *nominal* interest rates under conditions of inflation. This explanation simply amounts to saying that nominal rates will differ from real rates by an amount necessary to compensate savers for rising prices and to ensure that borrowers do not benefit from them.

For example, suppose that prices are expected to rise by 8 per cent over the same period. (Notice again that it is the *expected* (or **ex ante**) rate of inflation that strictly matters.) Unless our lender suffers from money illusion, s/he will now require the future cashflow to be adjusted for the rise in the price level. The required cashflow in one year's time, CF_{t+1}, will be:

$$CF_{t+1} = £100 \times (1 + r) \times (1 + \pi^e) \qquad (9.6)$$

where π^e is the expected rate of inflation. The required augmentation is now $(1 + r) \times (1 + \pi^e)$ and this must be reflected in the nominal interest rate. Thus when prices are rising:

$$(1 + i) = (1 + r) \times (1 + \pi^e) \qquad (9.7)$$

and the formula for the nominal rate becomes:

$$i = (1 + r) \times (1 + \pi^e) - 1 \qquad (9.8)$$

Exercise 9.1 Real and nominal interest rates

Given the nominal rate of interest, i, and the expected rate of inflation, π^e, we can find the real rate, r, by rearranging Equation 9.8. Thus:

$$r = [(1 + i)/(1 + \pi^e) - 1]$$

But for low rates of interest and inflation we could rearrange the simpler expression, Equation 9.13:

$$r = i - \pi^e$$

1 Use each of these expressions to find the real rate of interest when nominal interest rates are 8% (= 0.08) and the expected rate of inflation is 4% (= 0.04).

2 Repeat the exercise setting the nominal rate to 20% and inflation to 15%.

3 Observe the difference between the two methods in each case.

Notice that the expression $(1 + r) \times (1 + \pi^e)$ can be expanded as follows:

$$(1 + r) \times (1 + \pi^e) = 1 + r + \pi^e + (r)(\pi^e) \quad (9.9)$$

For modest rates of interest and inflation, the cross-product $(r)(\pi^e)$ is very small and can be ignored. In these circumstances, our outlay has to increase by:

$$1 + r + \pi^e \quad (9.10)$$

In our example, the cashflow required in one year's time can now be found:

$$\begin{aligned} CF_{t+1} &= £100 \times (1 + r + \pi^e) \\ &= £100 \times (1 + 0.05 + 0.08) \\ &= £113 \end{aligned} \quad (9.11)$$

and the nominal rate of interest can be found (from Equation 9.3) by:

$$i = \frac{£113}{£100} - 1 = 0.13 = 13\% \quad (9.12)$$

At 'normal' rates of inflation and real interest rates, therefore, we can say that the required nominal rate of interest is approximately equal to the real rate plus the expected inflation rate:

$$i \approx r + \pi^e \quad (9.13)$$

Equation 9.13 is the equation for the short-term, risk-free, nominal rate of interest. If we replace π^e with π then Equation 9.14 is directly comparable with the first part of Equation 9.1.

$$i \approx r + \pi \quad (9.14)$$

The Fisher effect

By rearranging Equation 9.13, we can see that the real rate of interest is the difference between the nominal rate and the expected (*ex ante*) rate of inflation.

$$r \approx i - \pi^e \quad (9.15)$$

Furthermore, unless they suffer from money illusion, it is the real rate of interest which will matter to the decisions of lenders and borrowers. Unfortunately, we cannot observe the real rate directly since we cannot observe lenders' and borrowers' *expectations*. The only way around this problem, unless we engage in large-scale surveys of what agents expect, is to assume that what they expect generally turns out to be the case. If we do this, then it means that we can subtract the *actual* or realized rate of inflation (which, of course, we can observe after the event) from the nominal rate of interest which we can also observe. This

gives us an **ex post** measure of real interest rates by re-arranging Equation 9.14:

$$r \approx i - \pi \quad (9.16)$$

Equation 9.13 (sometimes written as Equation 9.14) is often known as the **Fisher equation**, after Irving Fisher whose book *Theories of Interest* (1930) provided the first systematic discussion of the relation between real and nominal rates. In fact, Fisher is often credited with the argument that the real rate of interest tends to be stable over long periods. This, after all, is plausible given the explanation of the real rate as the result of time preference and capital productivity. There is no reason to suppose that either of these would be subject to violent short-term fluctuations. The argument then went on to explain variations in the nominal rate as the result of changes in the expected rate of inflation. In actual fact, although Fisher does advance this suggestion as worthy of consideration, he himself recognized that the nominal rate of interest did not follow the rate of inflation very closely and much of the book is taken up with explanations of why such an obviously plausible theoretical idea was not strongly confirmed in practice. In spite of this, the proposition that the nominal rate of interest is made up of a stable real rate and a premium which closely follows the rate of inflation has become known as the **Fisher effect**.

Figure 9.2 overleaf shows the recent behaviour of the UK (*ex post*) real interest rate calculated by subtracting realized inflation from the interest rate on three-month certificates of deposit. Clearly, there have been significant fluctuations.

These fluctuations in the real rate do not necessarily disprove entirely the Fisher hypothesis that the nominal rate consists of a stable desired real rate plus a premium for expected inflation. It could be true that people's expectations of inflation are responsible for the nominal rate but that these expectations are frequently wrong. It is worth recalling, however, that in the world of loanable funds theory, from which the Fisher hypothesis developed, perfect information was assumed.

Because of its origin in the work of 'classical' economists in the nineteenth century, **loanable funds theory** is often regarded as the 'traditional view' of interest rate determination. We can sum it up as follows:

- the short-term, risk-free real rate of interest is the sum paid by borrowers to lenders for the shortest possible period, in a world of constant prices and zero risk;

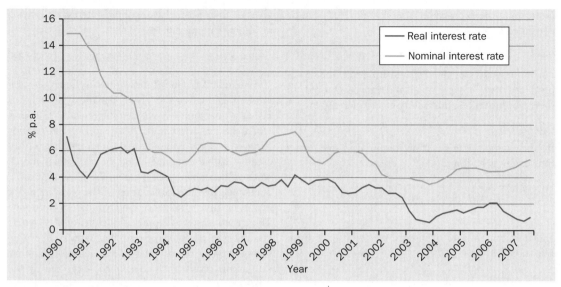

Figure 9.2 UK real interest rates, 1990–2007

Source: From www.nationalstatistics.gov.uk, series CZBH and www.bankofengland.co.uk, Series IUQABEDR, Bank of England. Crown copyright material is reproduced with the permission of the Controller of HMSO and the Queen's Printer for Scotland under the Click-Use licence.

- the supply of funds is determined by people's willingness to save and this depends in turn upon their rate of time preference;

- the demand for funds depends upon the prospects for their profitable use and this depends in turn upon the productivity of the assets which such funds will be used to purchase;

- the short-term, risk-free, nominal rate of interest is composed of a real rate determined by time preference and productivity plus a premium which reflects the expected rate of inflation.

9.3.2 Liquidity preference theory

Keynes' attack upon loanable funds theory comes mainly in Chapters 13–17 of his *The General Theory of Employment, Interest and Money*.

Firstly, he argued, people's ability to save depended very much upon their level of income. Since he rejected the assumption of full employment it followed that *aggregate* income could fluctuate quite widely. In communities where income was well above subsistence level, it made sense to save even when interest was zero. (In Figure 9.1, therefore, the supply curve would intercept the horizontal axis and would need to

be redrawn every time income changed.) The rate of interest played a secondary role by influencing *how* people decided to save. Interest was a reward for lending or parting with money and this was not necessarily the same thing as saving. After all, one could save (that is, not spend) by accumulating notes and coin and keeping them under the bed. (We first saw this in Section 1.1.) No interest would be payable then, even though saving would be taking place. If lots of people wished to hold idle money balances in this way, money would be scarce, and interest rates high even though saving would also be at a high level. These are both points which we touched on in Section 9.2: *saving* may not depend upon interest rates, *lending* very likely does.

Because of his emphasis upon interest as the inducement to part with liquidity ('the ability to change one's mind', as we said in Section 9.2), Keynes chose to explain interest as the result of an interaction between the supply of money and the demand for money. We shall come back to the question of money supply and demand in Chapters 12 and 13, but to understand Keynes' argument and its implications, it is worth glancing at Figure 9.3.

The money supply is assumed to be fixed (by the actions of the central bank) and this is shown by the vertical curve, M_S. The demand curve, M_D, is drawn

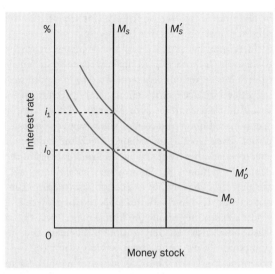

Figure 9.3 Money market equilibrium – the effect of demand shifts

downward-sloping. One might explain the negative slope by reference to 'opportunity cost'. If we assume that money (= cash + bank sight deposits) does not pay interest then at lower interest rates money's attractions as a perfectly liquid asset are greater than they would be when interest rates on alternative assets are high. Keynes' explanation, however, drew upon interesting psychological factors. When interest rates are low, people would expect the next movement to be upward. When interest rates rise, asset prices fall

(Box 9.1 contains an illustration) and holders of assets suffer a capital loss. Thus, at low interest rates money avoids the risk of capital loss. The *position* of the curve depends upon people's need for money in exchange and this in turn depends upon the price level and the level of economic activity. Thus any change in nominal aggregate income causes the curve to shift.

One of the most important of Keynes' insights was to introduce expectations and uncertainty and thus to create a role for money as a safe haven in a treacherous world. We have seen that the downward slope of the curve arises from the increasing strength of *expectation*, when interest rates are low, that a capital loss may be just around the corner. But expectations of interest rate changes are not tied to absolute levels of actual rates. What may look like a low rate (set to rise) in one situation may look 'normal' in another. Thus at any actual rate, circumstances may change so as to cause expectations to change. The current rate, acceptable today, may look too low tomorrow. There will be a rush for money. At today's rate, the demand for money tomorrow may be much greater. Thus, introducing expectations in this way introduces the possibility that the demand curve may shift around. As a rule, anything that increases uncertainty tends to increase the attraction of money. The demand curve shifts upward (to M'_D) and the rush to liquidity pushes up interest rates, from i_0 to i_1. If the money supply were to expand, to M'_S for example, the comparative shortage would be eliminated and the rate of interest would remain at i_0.

BOX 9.1 Interest rates and asset prices

A fundamental principle of economics and finance is that the value of an asset lies in the stream of income or services or other benefits that it produces. In the case of financial assets, the benefit is usually an income stream or 'cashflow'. In order to arrive at a valuation the payments in this income stream have to be discounted – that is to say that the value of the more distant payments has to be adjusted downward to take account of the fact that we have to wait for them.

This is what we saw in Equation 9.2. It shows a cashflow as a series of payments identified as CF_t, where t indicates the time of their receipt. The value of the series is found by discounting each payment by $(1 + \overline{K})^t$, where $\overline{K}$ is the rate of return that we require and t again denotes the period in which the payment is received. One can see immediately that a payment (CF) which lies a long way ahead (that is, has a high t value) will be heavily discounted. This is because the corresponding denominator will have a high t value and will be raised to 'the power of t'.

But, more importantly, notice what happens if we change the value of $\overline{K}$. This also appears in the denominator. If we make it larger, the value of each CF is made smaller. Thus, when we sum the series of discounted CFs their value will be lower, the larger is the magnitude of $\overline{K}$. All we need to remember now is that since $\overline{K}$ is the rate of return that we require, it must reflect the level of returns that are available elsewhere. That is, *it must reflect the going rate of interest*. If interest rates go up, $\overline{K}$ increases and the value of our asset goes down. If interest rates go down, $\overline{K}$ goes down and the value of our asset goes up.

There are numerical examples of changes in interest rates causing changes in asset prices in Sections 10.2 and 11.3.

The significance of all this for Keynes' wider project was first of all that the rate of interest was no longer free to accommodate the flow of saving to the flow of investment. There could, for example, be leakages from the circular flow of income and spending leading to a fall in output and employment. Secondly, the possibility that the demand for money might be unstable meant that nominal interest rates (and therefore real interest rates) might fluctuate in response to psychological factors, causing instability in the real economy.

We can sum up the liquidity preference approach as follows:

- Agents' actions determine *nominal* interest rates. Real rates will depend upon the behaviour of prices and the extent to which price changes are correctly anticipated.

- The nominal rate is determined by the demand for money relative to its supply.

- The demand for money depends upon the price level and upon the level of economic activity but it also depends upon the desire to hold money as a safe asset in an uncertain world.

- The degree of uncertainty that agents feel is highly variable, leading to fluctuations in the demand for money and hence in the nominal rate of interest.

- The supply of money is independent of the demand for it and is assumed to be fixed by the actions of the monetary authorities.

9.3.3 The determination of interest rates: an eclectic approach

Considered alone, neither the *LPT* nor *LFT* is entirely satisfactory. Loanable funds theory is appropriate for a perfectly static setting with output fixed at its full employment level, prices constant, a fixed money supply and perfect information. As we said, in those circumstances there would be no fluctuations in the demand for hoards, savers would lend all that they saved and the only demand for funds would be for investment. We could then say that the real rate of interest paid between borrowers and lenders would

be determined by time preference (for savers) and the productivity of capital (for borrowers).

In economies as we know them, however, this is too simple. Interest is paid not just as an inducement to save but as an inducement to *lend money*, and saving does not necessarily entail lending. Our savers would not earn interest, for example, if they simply accumulated notes and coin or some types of bank deposits. They have to be willing to *lend* the funds that become available from saving; and fluctuations in the demand for money (or 'hoards' in classical language) are perfectly reasonable in economies where output not only grows but fluctuates in its rate of growth and where uncertainty about the future makes occasional 'rushes to cash' entirely rational. Furthermore, in economies as we know them, saving is not the only potential source of funds. Banks are in business to lend and the normal result is a money supply where deposits are expanding as a result of this lending.

We need to take account of both complications and our suggestion is that we do this by thinking of 'new money' as an additional source of funds and of 'hoarding' as an additional demand. We begin with the former.

The supply of funds available to borrowers consists of both the funds that savers are prepared to lend *plus* any increase in the community's total stock of money. We shall see in Chapter 12 that the money supply expands when banks lend, since their lending creates deposits. Furthermore, this additional lending need not entail rising interest rates if employment is below the full employment level. Provided the central bank is prepared to provide banks with the necessary reserves at the going rate of interest, lending (and deposits) may expand for so long as banks can find willing (and creditworthy) borrowers. Whether we focus upon the bank loans or upon the bank deposits that they create, bank lending is an additional source of funds.

Our second complication, recall, is that savers may not wish to lend all that they save. In certain circumstances, they may wish to accumulate funds themselves, usually in the form of bank deposits. Adding to holdings of money is sometimes called additional 'hoarding' or adding to 'idle balances'.[1] Both the potential supply of new money and the possibility that

---

[1] Take care not to think that the decision to accumulate bank deposits makes it possible for banks to lend more and thus to replace the lending that savers have decided not to do. The decision to accumulate deposits does not increase their quantity. If savers had decided to lend (by buying bonds, for example) the deposits would still have been in the banks and they would still have been matched by bank loans. But they would have been owned by borrowers and lending would have been equal to the bank loans *plus* bond issue.

more money may be demanded for hoards are additional influences on the supply and demand for funds which we must add to the traditional account which focuses only upon the actions of savers and investors.

Looking at the supply side, we can now say that the quantity of funds available to borrowers is:

saving − Δhoards + Δnew money

and the equilibrium condition will be that in which:

saving − Δhoards + Δnew money = investment

In practice, this condition is often rearranged to show sources of funds on one side and uses of funds on the other, thus:

saving + Δnew money = investment + Δhoards

Figure 9.4 is a modification of Figure 9.1 and shows the effect of incorporating these complications. The supply curve, *S*, is now labelled to make it clear that the potential supply of funds consists of both saving from income and also any addition to the money stock. It is drawn upward-sloping still because of the savings component which is assumed still to respond to interest rates. The demand curve, *D*, is drawn downward-sloping reflecting still the demand for funds for investment in real capital assets. More of these assets, as we said before, will have a positive *NPV* the lower is the rate of interest, but the curve

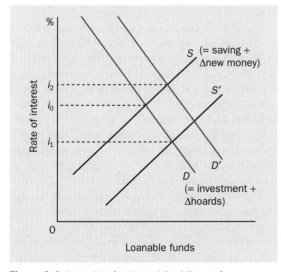

Figure 9.4 Loanable funds and liquidity preference theories combined

also contains a demand for 'idle balances' which causes it to lie further to the right (and may cause it to be unstable).

In Figure 9.4 an increase in income, a decrease in time preference or an increase in the supply of new money each increases the availability of funds and causes the equilibrium rate of interest to fall, from i_0 to, say, i_1. Reversing the disturbance causes the curve to shift upward. On the demand side, an increase in productivity of capital assets or an increase in the demand for money causes the curve to shift outward and, starting from i_0, the equilibrium rate of interest will rise, say to i_2.

Notice that this account allows for a certain amount of flexibility in the relationship between real and nominal rates, at least in the short run. Imagine, for example, a monetary expansion which increases the supply of funds relative to the demand. In Figure 9.4 the supply curve shifts down and the nominal rate falls. More investment is undertaken and, without the classical assumption of full employment, output and employment will expand. With spare capacity, output may rise, again in the short run, with little, if any, effect on inflation. The new nominal rate now lies below the old nominal rate and, if inflation remains unaffected, the new *real* rate lies below the old real rate.

Under the classical assumptions of loanable funds theory this outcome would be impossible. Starting from full employment and constant prices, an expansion in the supply of new money would initiate an increase in spending and prices would rise, producing an increase in the rate of inflation from zero to, say, 5 per cent. Figure 9.5 overleaf shows what would happen from a classical perspective.

We begin with an equilibrium real rate of interest of 4 per cent which, given constant prices, is also the current nominal rate. A monetary expansion, however, causes inflation of 5 per cent and this is recognized accurately and equally by both borrowers and lenders. With inflation at 5 per cent, lenders demand 9 per cent for the current level of lending and the supply curve shifts upward. On the other hand, borrowers know that at 9 per cent they are paying a real rate of only 4 per cent. The demand curve also shifts upward. Notice two things. Firstly, that they both shift by the exact amount necessary to maintain the same levels of borrowing and lending. ('Real' behaviour is unchanged.) Secondly, that the nominal rate is equal to the real rate plus an accurately anticipated inflation premium. In these circumstances, the Fisher hypothesis would be vindicated.

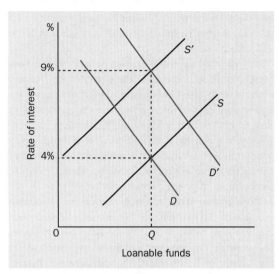

Figure 9.5 The effect of inflation in 'classical' theory

S = saving + Δnew money; D = investment + Δhoards.

9.4   The role of central banks – 'administered' interest rates

The account that we have so far given of how short-term interest rates are determined stresses the role of private decision makers or what might be called 'market forces'. We have mentioned the monetary authorities, in the guise of the central bank, only once in saying that commercial banks can add to funds by creating money and that this need not involve a rise in interest rates if the central bank supplies the necessary reserves at a constant price.

However, to any student who keeps even a casual eye on current affairs this must seem odd. Scarcely a month goes by in any economy without the news-media reporting either that the monetary authorities have raised (or lowered) the level of official short-term rates or that financial markets are speculating that the authorities are about to do so. Box 9.2 shows a selection of typical recent headlines from newspapers doing just that.

If it is the case that short-term nominal interest rates are set by administrative decision then all the earlier discussion of this chapter is redundant. (If, on the other hand, interest rates are indeed set by market

forces, then the currently fashionable argument that central banks should have more independence in their ability to set interest rates becomes pointless.) In this section, therefore, we devote our attention to the influence that central banks, acting on behalf of or independently from their governments, can exert over interest rates. We begin by looking at sources of influence and then go on to consider the constraints and limitations to this influence. But before we do, let us clearly distinguish the terms '**short *term***' and '**short *run***'. Throughout this chapter, our emphasis has been upon short-*term* interest rates. These, we know, are interest rates which apply to loans for short periods or short *terms*. In the rest of this section we shall suggest that these short-*term* rates may be influenced by central bank behaviour for short periods of time, that is to say, in the short *run*. If this influence cannot be exerted over a long period of time, however, then we have to say that **short-*term*** rates are market-determined in the **long *run***. This lesson will be useful in future. We often need to distinguish between the behaviour of short-*term* (or medium-*term* or long-*term*) instruments over a short period of time (the short *run*) and a medium or long period (the medium *run* and long *run* respectively).

The ability of all central banks to exercise any influence over interest rates lies in their role as **lenders of last resort**. This in turn relies upon their role as monopoly suppliers of liquidity in the event of a general shortage of funds. In most European countries, central banks developed this role in the second half of the nineteenth century or the early years of the twentieth. The need for a lender of last resort originated with the need to reassure depositors of the certain convertibility of their deposits into cash. In the early days of deposit banking when banks were numerous, small and local there was always the danger that a perfectly well-run and solvent bank could fail as a result of unexpected cash withdrawals or transfers to another bank. Indeed, in the earliest stages mere rumours of a cash shortage could be sufficient to bring about withdrawals and a failure which was quite unnecessary. Clearly the failure of one bank involves major hardship for its depositors but in the background loomed the nightmare that one failure might lead to more as depositors in sound banks panicked. Without a lender of last resort, the only solution would be for banks to hold very high levels of reserves (= cash + banks' deposits at the central bank). Since these reserves pay

BOX 9.2 Central banks and interest rates

Bank of England keeps rates on hold

By Scheherazade Daneshkhu, Economics Correspondent, and Delphine Strauss

The Bank of England kept its main interest rate unchanged at 5.75 per cent on Thursday but took the unusual step of issuing a statement, prompting speculation that interest rates may finally have peaked.

Financial Times, 6 September 2007

US Fed chief holds steady on interest rates

By Krishna Guha and Jackson Hole and Andrew Ward in Washington

Ben Bernanke said the Federal Reserve would act as needed to ease the impact of financial markets turmoil on the economy but offered no clear signal that it was poised to cut interest rates.

Financial Times, 1 September 2007

ECB puzzles markets by leaving rates unchanged

By Tony Major in Frankfurt

Jean Claude Trichet, the recently-appointed European Central Bank president, confused markets yesterday by playing down the chances of an interest rate cut in the coming months. Just a week earlier he had hinted at a monetary easing.

The mixed signals from the ECB, which held its base interest rate steady at 2 per cent for the tenth month running, cast renewed doubt on the clarity of the bank's policy pronouncements.

Financial Times, 2 April 2004

Reprinted with permission.

a low rate of interest (lower than the rate that banks could earn on alternative assets), they act as a tax on banking activity and make bank intermediation more expensive and less efficient than it would otherwise be.

It is doubtful that many depositors these days give so much as a thought to the possibility that they will not be able to draw on their deposits whenever they feel like it. However, so long as full convertibility between deposits and cash is guaranteed, a lender of last

---

MORE FROM THE WEB
The setting of interest rates

All the major central banks publish detailed information about their latest interest rate decisions and the reasons for them. (This is part of the trend towards 'transparency' in policy-making which we discuss in Section 14.7). For example, the Bank of England and the European Central Bank both highlight the current official rate(s) on their home pages.

From the Bank of England's home page there is a link to the minutes of the latest meeting of the Monetary Policy Committee which is responsible for the decision. From the ECB's home page you can go to 'Press Releases' where you will find a press release stating the latest decision with a link to the 'Press Conference' which is held shortly after the announcement. Both the MPC's minutes and the ECB's minutes shed useful light on how the respective banks came to their latest decisions.

The ECB's website is at www.ECB.int.

The Bank of England is at www.bankofengland. co.uk.

---

resort is essential.[2] This requirement is reinforced where, as is sometimes the case, reserves pay no interest at all since banks then have an incentive to minimize holdings of such reserves. In some systems banks are required to observe a minimum *mandatory* reserve ratio, in which case they will be seeking to minimize holdings of additional, or what are sometimes called 'free', or 'excess', reserves. In cases where the minimum reserve ratio is a matter of choice (a *prudential* reserve ratio) there is no distinction between required and excess reserves.

The consequence of operating with minimum reserves is that banks can find themselves short of reserves at a particular moment for reasons that have little to do with prudence or foolishness. In the UK, for example, the central government banks with the Bank of England, not with the commercial banks. A net payment of funds by the private sector to the central government, therefore, transfers deposits from commercial banks to the government's account at the Bank of England. This withdrawal (of liabilities) is matched on the asset side of the balance sheet by an equal transfer from commercial banks' reserves to the government's account at the Bank of England. Since reserves are only a very small proportion of deposits, this one-for-one reduction in deposits and reserves lowers the ratio dramatically.[3] Such private–public sector transfers are not easily predicted on a daily basis.

An individual bank in difficulty can, of course, remedy the position by borrowing in the interbank market. But in the event of a system-wide shortage of funds, the central bank becomes the monopoly supplier. The precise manner in which central banks operate to relieve shortages (or to mop up surpluses for that matter) varies between systems and reflects the differing histories and institutional arrangements in each system. Central bank relations with the commercial banking system is a theme in each of our earlier chapters on specific countries. However, it is worth noting that whatever the arrangements may be in detail, they fall into two broad categories. Either the central bank may *lend* funds for reserve purposes (often known as helping through the 'discount window') usually at a pre-announced rate of interest or it may *buy* short-dated non-reserve assets from banks at prices which may or may not be pre-announced.

The essential point here, however, is that the central bank is the monopoly supplier of funds and it can behave just like any other monopolist. It can either decide on the quantity of reserves to make available, and allow banks to bid between themselves for the available supply, or it can set the price and supply whatever quantity of reserves is required. In the former case, the quantity is fixed directly and the price follows; in the latter the price is fixed and the quantity demanded follows. Whichever it decides to do, its actions will determine short-term interest rates. This in turn sets a base to the level of interest rates since commercial banks will not engage in lending at rates which do not at least exceed the rate that they would have to pay for lender of last resort facilities. Deposit

---

[2]   Not all would agree today. In the past few years there has been a revival of interest in 'free' banking in which market forces would force banks to behave in a way that would guarantee their stability. See the references to Dowd (1996), Benkston and Kaufman (1996) and Dow (1996) at the end of this chapter. Goodhart (1991) presents a fairly conventional case for the last resort role of central banks.

[3]   For example, in a banking system running with a ratio of reserves to deposits of 1:10, a 5 per cent loss of deposits is matched by a 50 per cent loss of reserves and the reserve ratio is almost halved from 1:10 to 1:19. We look at banks, reserve ratios and the money supply in more detail in Section 12.4.

rates are then set at a discount to lending rates and arbitrage is assumed to keep bank and other short-term interest rates in line. Since banks are generally in the position of wanting to expand their loans and deposits, and because they are continually rolling over previous borrowings, the central bank always has the power to set the price by one means or another. And it is movements in this price, whether it is known in different monetary systems as 'base rate', 'refinancing rate', 'repo rate', 'minimum lending rate', which are the subject of intense interest when commentators report that 'the Bank has raised (or lowered) interest rates'.

On the face of it, we have here an account of interest rate determination which provides a much bigger contrast with our two 'market' theories than they do with each other. *If* the central bank is in a position to set short-term interest rates as a matter of administrative decision, then there is no need for elaborate theories about the level of interest rates.

As usual in economics, however, things are not quite so straightforward. Notice, firstly, that even if we accept the 'administrative' account unreservedly, we are only taking a view about the setting of *nominal* interest rates – the *real* rate will depend upon what happens to expectations about future inflation rates – and we only have an account of the setting of the shortest of short-term rates. (Most central banks would claim to set rates only in the overnight to seven-day range.) Nonetheless, we are still a long way from both loanable funds and liquidity preference. Can we establish firmly that either 'market' or 'administrative' accounts are superior? And if we cannot, then can we reconcile or combine them in some way? Since we observe central banks setting interest rates, telling us that they do so and telling us how they do it, it seems we have either to reject more market-based accounts or look for reconciliation. This may not be so difficult as it seems, because if we consider the central bank's position in more detail we shall see that there are a number of constraints within which it must work and some of these are constraints posed by market forces.

Firstly, saying that central banks set interest rates (even very short-term nominal rates) does not mean that they are free to set these rates at whatever level they choose. Obviously, interest rates have to be set in order to achieve a number of objectives. We are familiar these days with the idea that objectives may pose conflicting demands on instruments. Since 2001, for example, the USA, the Eurozone, and other countries including the UK have all had to face the dilemma of raising interest rates to protect weak currencies with the risk of ending a fragile recovery from recession.

Secondly, even where a single or overriding objective can be identified – these days it is usually a low rate of inflation – there may still be conflicting pressures on the interest rate instrument arising out of disagreement about which intermediate target to focus upon. For example, if inflation is the ultimate target, should the level of interest rates be chosen with a view to minimizing the rate of monetary growth, or to maintaining a high exchange rate?

Thirdly, when all these questions have been resolved, the setting of interest rates will often depend upon what is happening to interest rates elsewhere. For many European countries, the level of short-term interest rates is closely connected with rates available on sterling or dollar assets. For 'open' economies like that of the UK, changes in EMU or US rates inevitably trigger questions about the next movement in sterling rates. This happens because capital is internationally very mobile. Thus, quite slight differences in the profits to be gained from holding dollar rather than sterling assets, for example, cause savers to sell sterling assets and buy dollar ones. Since assets are normally bought and sold in the currency of their denomination, this means that sellers of sterling assets (who now hold sterling) must now sell sterling itself in order to buy dollars. If this continues for only a short time, the price of sterling (in other currencies) begins to fall. If, as is usual, governments have some desired exchange rate for the domestic currency, then domestic interest rates will have to rise.

Fourthly, and more directly relevant in the present context, it is virtually impossible for central banks to set interest rates that do not have the endorsement of financial markets. As we shall see in several later chapters, it is now possible for very large sums of money to be moved between financial centres at a moment's notice and at very low cost. It is very difficult, therefore, for the authorities to impose a level of short-term rates which is regarded as inappropriate by financial markets. Indeed, it is not difficult to find cases where central bank preferences and market preferences appear to have conflicted and where this happens it is usually market sentiment that ultimately triumphs. The experiences of Italy and the UK in being forced from the Exchange Rate Mechanism in September 1992 yield dramatic examples. One can say either that these incidents were demonstrations of the power of market sentiment when the countries concerned tried to maintain exchange rates (as opposed to interest rates) which markets thought unsustainable, or one can make the cases even more relevant by saying that the choice of exchange rate and interest rate were two sides of the same problem. *Given* their desire to maintain their ERM agreed exchange rates, the Bank of England and the Bank of Italy pushed up interest rates to emergency levels. But markets took the view that these interest rates were still not high enough given the exchange rate objective. Faced with the choice of yet higher interest rates or leaving the ERM, the central banks chose the latter course.

Fifthly, if central bank decisions about interest rates can be clearly seen to be influenced by market forces in some rather dramatic situations, we need to look carefully at their decisions in more everyday contexts. After all, outward appearances will be the same (a central bank will make an official announcement, the media will treat it as 'news') whether the central bank is issuing an independent instruction which it expects everyone else to follow, or is confirming a situation which market practitioners have come to regard already as inevitable. Careful study of the financial press, for example, often reveals rises in short money rates, and may even show developing market sentiment that interest rates must rise, in the few days immediately prior to an official announcement. Here, the central bank merely confirms what markets have already decided. And as central banks have concentrated in recent years on making their conduct of monetary policy more 'transparent' it has become even more difficult to tell whether markets are anticipating what the central bank is deciding or whether the central bank is confirming what the markets have already decided.

What all of this suggests is twofold. Firstly, central banks are certainly constrained in their ability to set interest rates and some of the most significant constraints are those imposed by markets' beliefs about what interest rates *ought* to be. Secondly, while central bank behaviour is clearly visible, it will always be reported as news, while market activity is more complex and obscure and receives less media attention. We therefore need to be cautious about interpreting the correlation between central bank interest rate statements and changes in interest rates as cause and effect.

9.5   A synthesis

The safest conclusion is that the setting of short-term nominal interest rates depends upon *both* market forces (which may be driven by some mixture of loanable funds and liquidity preference considerations of the kind we discussed in Section 9.3.3) *and* upon decisions by the monetary authorities. We might be able to make this vague conclusion a little more precise if we think of a 'short-run/long-run' distinction. We might want to say, for example, that for short periods the central bank has considerable power over the determination of short-term nominal rates (and if the economy is operating in a recession this may also yield an influence over real rates). For example, looking at Figure 9.6 (which is based on our earlier Figure 9.4) we might envisage a situation where the flow of funds and the demand for them is initially consistent with an interest rate of i_0 and we might also assume that this is also the authorities' target rate. Imagine now that market sentiment anticipates a rise in interest rates (perhaps because of weakness in the exchange rate). There is an increase in liquidity preference and in Figure 9.6 the demand for funds shifts out to D',

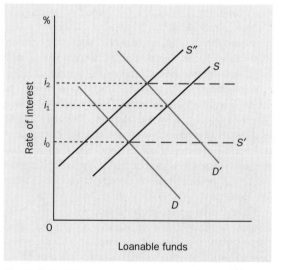

Figure 9.6 Interest rate determination – when the central bank has preferences

threatening to push interest rates up to i_1. If the central bank wishes to maintain interest rates at i_0, it can make it clear to banks that reserves will continue to be made available at the existing level of interest rates so that they can respond to the demand for funds without fear of a reserve shortage. Unlimited funds become available at the going rate and the supply curve effectively becomes horizontal, as shown by the broken line, S'.

In the longer term, however, which may only be as long as it takes for foreign exchange markets to realize what is happening, this policy may prove unsustainable. If continuous expansion of money and credit at the going level of interest rates is unacceptable in foreign exchange markets (perhaps because of its inflationary potential) then the pressure on the exchange rate will grow. The authorities are then faced with the familiar dilemma of conflict in objectives. Notice that the interest rate/exchange rate combination is unstable. Holding rates *given* at i_0 (and expanding money and credit) threatens a continually *declining* exchange rate. If preserving the exchange rate triumphs, the authorities may not just have to 'put' interest rates up to i_1 but may be forced to raise them further, say to i_2, by indicating that henceforth new reserves will be forthcoming only at a new, higher level of interest rates.

9.6 Summary

No one doubts that the behaviour of interest rates is important for both the real economy and for financial markets. The traditional account of interest rate determination focuses upon the 'real' factors of productivity and time preference. These forces set the *real* rate of interest and the nominal rate will simply be the real rate plus an inflation premium. This account treats the act of saving as equivalent to making available 'loanable funds'. Clearly, this need not be the case, as Keynes pointed out. People may save without lending. Furthermore, the ability to save rests also upon a level of income (which was variable) and not just an interest incentive. Keynes' liquidity preference theory focused upon the desire to hold money in relation to the supply that was available. We suggested that these accounts could be combined if one recognized that both the demand for liquid wealth and banks' creation of new money by lending affected the supply of loanable funds.

Both of these accounts, however, focus upon market forces. Neither is immediately reconcilable with what we frequently observe which is that 'the authorities' announce and appear to decide upon interest rate changes. On the other hand, we know that central banks are often constrained by market sentiment in what they can do about interest rates. Therefore a sensible way of looking at interest rate determination is to recognize the fundamental role played by market forces but then also to recognize the influence of central banks in the short run, provided their decisions do not stray too far from market sentiment.

This interplay between the authorities and market participants determines the short-term, nominal, risk-free, rate of interest. For a given rate of inflation, this fixes also the short-term, *real*, risk-free rate.

Key concepts in this chapter

Ex ante	Loanable funds theory
Ex post	Nominal interest rate
Fisher effect	Productivity
Hoards	Rate of time preference
Inflation premium	Real interest rate
Lender of last resort	Short term *vs* long run
Liquidity preference theory	Short term *vs* short run
Loanable funds	Thrift

Questions and problems

1 Distinguish between nominal and real interest rates.

2 Using loanable funds theory, explain the likely effect on the supply of funds and the equilibrium interest rate of:

   (a) an increased desire to save for old age;

   (b) a reduction in taxes on income from savings.

3 Explain the Fisher hypothesis. What is the logic behind the idea that there should be a positive relationship between the rate of inflation and nominal interest rates?

4 What is meant by the terms *ex ante* and *ex post* as applied to real interest rates?

5 Use the loanable funds diagram to explain how you would expect an increase in inflationary expectations to affect:

   (a) the supply and demand schedules;

   (b) the nominal rate of interest;

   (c) the *ex ante* real rate of interest.

6 Estimate the *ex post* real (short-term) interest rate over the past year. How does it compare with the nominal short-term rate?

7 Using liquidity preference theory, explain how you would expect the demand for money and the equilibrium rate of interest to be affected by:

   (a) a growing anxiety that security prices might be about to fall;

   (b) a growing belief that the central bank is about to tighten monetary policy?

8 Explain what central banks can do to prevent a rise in interest rates. What limits the central bank's ability to do this?

9 Using the financial press and/or official publications give a brief outline of the current policy on interest rates.

Further reading

A D Bain, *The Financial System* (Oxford: Blackwell, 2e, 1992) Ch. 5

Bank of England Fact Sheet, *Monetary Policy in the UK* (March 1999). Available at www.bankofengland.co.uk/factmpol.pdf

G J Benkston and G G Kaufman, 'The appropriate role of bank regulation', *Economic Journal*, 106 (436), 1996, 688–97

D Blake, *Financial Market Analysis* (London: McGraw-Hill, 2e, 2000) Ch. 2

S C Dow, 'Why the banking system should be regulated', *Economic Journal*, 106 (436), 1996, 698–707

K Dowd, 'The case for financial *laissez-faire*', *Economic Journal*, 106 (436), 1996, 679–87

C Giles, 'Interest rate rise: Shock for the City's soothsayers', *Financial Times*, 12 January 2007.

C A E Goodhart, 'Are central banks necessary?', in F Capie and G E Wood (eds), *Unregulated Banking: Chaos or Order?* (London: Macmillan, 1991)

P G A Howells, 'The determination of interest rates', *British Economy Survey*, 24 (2), 1995, Section 4

P G A Howells and K Bain, *Financial Markets and Institutions* (London: Pearson, 5e, 2007) Ch. 7

J M Keynes, *The General Theory of Employment, Interest and Money* (London: Macmillan, 1936) Chs 13, 14

T Major, 'ECB puzzles markets by leaving rates unchanged', *Financial Times*, 2 April 2004

Websites

www.bankofengland.co.uk
www.ecb.int
www.nationalstatistics.gov.uk

Chapter 10 The structure
of interest rates

What you will learn in this chapter:

■ The meaning of risk and term premiums

■ Why the 'term' or period to maturity of an asset affects its rate
   of return

■ Why a term premium may still be required even if the asset is
   highly liquid

■ Some of the forms that risk can take for borrowers and lenders

■ Why risk affects the rate of return on an asset

■ Why expected changes in interest rates can affect the current
   structure of rates

■ How persistent borrowing by governments may (and may not)
   affect the structure of rates

10.1   Introduction

In the last chapter we saw that any nominal interest rate, i, could be seen as the sum of four components:

$$i = r + \pi + l + \sigma \qquad (10.1)$$

where r is the real short-term rate of interest, π is an *inflation* premium, l is a *liquidity* premium and σ is a premium for *risk*. We then concentrated upon the determination of the first two components in order to develop a theory of short-term nominal interest rates. But we know from everyday observation that any developed financial system is characterized by instruments offering a vast range of different interest rates (a range which expands again when we think about *rates of return*). This *range*, or *structure*, is the result of instruments offering facilities for borrowing and lending over different periods (or *terms*) and with differing degrees of *risk*.

We turn our attention in Section 10.2 to the way in which the term (l) of a loan may affect the rate of interest and in Section 10.3 we shall look at how it may also be affected by risk (σ). Together they give rise to a range of interest rate *differentials* or **spreads**. In Section 10.4 we shall look at two other factors which are often said to influence the structure of interest rates.

Remember, before we begin, that the rate of interest on any asset depends ultimately upon the supply and demand for that asset. The rate of interest on long-term loans therefore depends upon the willingness of lenders to lend long term compared with the desire of borrowers to borrow for long periods. Similarly, a premium on risky assets reflects the comparative unwillingness of holders to hold such assets. It is rather easy, when explaining differentials as the result of certain types of premiums, to start to think of these premiums as mark-ups which somehow have to be added 'naturally' or 'automatically'. There is nothing natural or inevitable about them. They are created by people's preferences. The market for loans considered as a whole contains a whole range of products which investors see as differentiated by risk and return. The market, in other words, is weakly segmented. The premiums paid on loans of different types reflect agents' willingness to hold assets or incur liabilities with different characteristics.

10.2   The effect of term

As we can see from Equation 10.1, we expect both term and risk to be associated with positive premiums. Indeed, we can turn the equation into a diagram, Figure 10.1.

In this diagram, we can see any nominal rate of interest as being made up of 'layers' corresponding to each of four components. r is the real, short-term, risk-free rate. i is the nominal rate, incorporating only an inflation premium. i' is the nominal rate on a risky loan with n years to maturity. Notice that we have drawn the figure with term to maturity on the horizontal axis and that the liquidity premium is shown to increase with the term. The same positive relationship would very likely appear between the risk premium and the degree of risk if we put risk on the horizontal axis.

Figure 10.1 suggests that for a given short-term rate of interest, long-term loans will cost more than short-term loans. The idea that a liquidity premium *positively* related to the term of a loan is 'normal' has a long pedigree and it can be explained in two ways.

The first, and simplest, explanation is the one we touched upon in Section 1.1. There we suggested that lenders generally prefer to lend for the shortest period while borrowers prefer to borrow for the longest

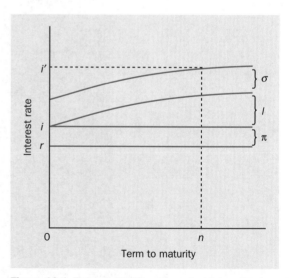

Figure 10.1 The composition of nominal interest rates

possible period. We say 'generally' since preferences will vary between individual investors. Pension funds, for example, are more inclined to hold long-term assets because of their need to earn a guaranteed long-term income. However, if we assume, as seems reasonable, that *on balance* lenders prefer to lend short-term, then borrowers will have to pay lenders a premium for the use of longer-term funds in order to induce them away from their preferred position.

Lenders' preference for short-term loans, in this argument, arises out of uncertainty. Although lenders may *plan* to have funds available for lending for a long period, there is always the danger that they may need to have use of the funds earlier than they planned. Having funds tied up for a long period in those circumstances would then be costly, in either preventing the lender from carrying out urgent spending, or forcing him or her to borrow and pay interest, or leaving him or her unable to pay bills, which might in turn spell bankruptcy or at least major embarrassment. Short-term lending thus has a flexibility – the choice to use the funds once again for spending at short notice or to re-lend if convenient.

Borrowers' preference for long-term loans arises precisely because they wish to avoid the costs associated with having to renegotiate or replace loans when they mature. It helps if we bear in mind that in any economy there are agents who are debtors on a more or less permanent basis (firms, for example). They are not, as individuals might be, borrowing to cover a temporary shortage of funds. They know that when a loan falls due for repayment they will have to replace it and the uncertainty they face is that the conditions (the rate of interest, for example) on which the loan can be replaced are worse than they were when the original first loan was taken out at the start of the investment project. Borrowers are therefore said to be prepared to pay more for long-term loans in order to avoid this **reinvestment** or **rollover risk**.

The **liquidity premium** is thus a premium required to tempt lenders from their short-term preference and it is a cost that borrowers are willing to pay in order to have guaranteed long-term use of funds. Notice that in Figure 10.1 the liquidity premium is shown increasing with the term of the loan *but at a diminishing rate*. Clearly, this suggests that lenders are prepared to discriminate sharply between lending for, say, one year and five years but are much less concerned about the difference between, say, a 20-year and a 25-year loan. One might rationalize this in a rather casual way by saying that the difference in length between a four- and five-year loan is 25 per cent while an additional 25 per cent on the term of a 20-year loan is an additional five years. More strictly, the reason for the diminishing rate of increase in the premium lies in the practice of discounting. The present value of any future income flow depends upon the rate at which we discount it and upon the length of time we have to wait for it. If i is an appropriate rate of discount then the discount term (by which we divide the income) is $(1 + i)^t$, where t is the number of periods for which we have to wait. The effect of raising this denominator to the power t is to reduce the present value of future income payments quite quickly. Payments in 20 years' time are therefore very heavily discounted and lenders will thus be comparatively indifferent between lending for 20 or for 25 years.

It is not difficult to understand that lenders and borrowers may have different preferences regarding the length of loans and that this might explain the existence of positive liquidity premiums. However, the idea that interest rates (and yields and rates of return when we come to them) vary positively with the term to maturity is much more general than its application to loans would suggest. For this we need a second, probably more general, explanation for such premiums. Implicit in our discussion so far is the idea that once a loan is made for x years, it cannot be liquidated until x years have passed (except perhaps at some considerable penalty). This is of course generally true for what we might call **non-marketable loans**, loans of the kind typically made by banks or building societies or even by individuals between themselves. As we said in the introduction to this chapter, the fact that some loans are made for short periods and some for long makes them very highly differentiated products. However, much lending, particularly where large amounts are concerned, is not of this kind. It involves the borrower issuing some form of instrument which is bought by lenders in a primary market. Such instruments, once issued, are tradable in a secondary market. Company shares, corporate and government bonds and bills are obvious examples. In such cases, it makes little sense to say that buyers of newly issued 20-year corporate bonds require a liquidity premium to induce them to lend for 20 years, since they could sell the bonds at any time in a highly efficient market in order to retrieve the funds which they had initially lent. Buying a long-dated bond does not therefore mean that one is making a longer-term loan than if one had bought a short-dated bond and yet it is widely accepted in bond markets that, *other things being equal*,[1] longer-dated bonds will often carry a higher yield than shorter-dated ones.

The explanation lies in the behaviour of asset prices when market interest rates change. A firm (or government) which issues 20-year bonds in order to fund a deficit must obviously do so at a *price* and this must be acceptable to the market. Furthermore, the bonds must yield to their buyers a known series of payments which are desirable, at the price which has to be paid. These payments are often indicated by the 'coupon rate' which appears in the title of the bond. (A '10% Exchequer' bond, for example, carries a fixed payment of £10 to its holder every year.) If market interest rates change, the only way in which this fixed series of income payments to bondholders can adjust with them is if the market price of the bonds changes (falling when interest rates rise, for example). In Chapter 16, we shall give a formal proof that the sensitivity of asset prices to changes in interest rates is directly related to a concept known as 'duration', which itself depends upon the remaining life of the asset. Unfortunately, the mathematics are rather intimidating and, again, it is helpful to know more about the characteristics of bonds before attempting the proof. But we can *illustrate* the effect of term fairly easily. Imagine that we are dealing with a range of fixed-interest bonds which mature at a fixed point in the future. Then the formula for their value is:

$$P = \sum_{t=1}^{n} \frac{C_t}{(1 + i)^t} + \frac{M}{(1 + i)^{n_m}} \qquad (10.2)$$

This expression tells us that the bond's value consists of two elements. These are the sum of the coupon payments ($\sum C_t$) and the final payment of the maturity value (M). Notice that each element of cashflow has to be discounted. t is an index standing for the year (counting from now) in which the payment is made; n_m is the number of years to maturity. In every case we discount by $(1 + i)$ where i is the current market rate of interest for bonds of this duration and risk.

Imagine now that we are looking at two bonds which differ only in their term to maturity – one

matures in two years, the other in five. This means that their redemption values, M, are equal and that their coupon payments C_t are also identical. Suppose that M is £100 and that we are dealing with 10 per cent bonds, so that C_t in each case is £10. The coupon payments are annual. Finally, let us assume that relevant market interest rates are 12 per cent.

The value of the two-year bond consists of the present value of two payments of £10, where the first is received in one years' time and the second in two years' time, plus the value of £100, also receivable in two years' time. From Equation 10.2 we know that each of these payments has to be discounted by the current rate of interest, that is by the term $(1 + 0.12)$. Using discount tables, we can see that the present value of £10 received in one year's time is £8.93. We can also see that £10 two years hence is worth £7.97 now, and that the present value of £100 in two years is £79.72. The total value of these payments, and the present value of this bond, is thus £8.93 + £7.97 + £79.72, or £96.62.

For the five-year bond we have a series of five payments, the first payable in one year and the last in five years. The value of this income stream, again discounted by the factor 1.12, is:

£8.93 + £7.97 + £7.12 + £6.36 + £5.67 = £36.05

The present value of £100 received in five years is £56.74, making the present value of the bond £92.79.

Now suppose that interest rates fall to 8 per cent. We should by now be familiar with the *direction* of the effect, which will be to increase the value of both bonds, but the question is by exactly how much in each case? The answer can be found by working through Exercise 10.1. This should be done before reading on.

When interest rates are 8 per cent, the present value of a 10 per cent bond maturing in two years is £103.56 (£9.26 + £8.57 + £85.73). The value of a five-year bond of identical characteristics in the same circumstances is £107.98 (£9.26 + £8.57 + £7.94 + £7.35 + £6.80 + £68.06). We can now compare the prices for these two bonds at the two different rates of interest. Table 10.1 summarizes the results.

For a four-point change in interest rates, we can see that the price of a two-year bond changes by

---

[1]   The 'other things' which are crucial are (a) expectations that future interest rates remain as they are now and (b) bonds are homogeneous with respect to default risk.

Exercise 10.1 The effect of term on bond values

(a) Following the example in the text, find the present value of a 10 per cent bond, maturing for £100 in two years' time when the rate of interest is 8 per cent.

(b) Find the value of a five-year bond, with the same characteristics, when the rate of interest is 8 per cent.

(c) Compare their present values at this rate of interest.

(d) Now compare the present values calculated with interest rates at 8 per cent with the values calculated (in the text) when interest rates were 12 per cent. Which bond shows the largest price rise when interest rates fall?

Table 10.1 Term and value

Interest rate (i)	Term (n)	
	$n = 2$	$n = 5$
$i = 0.12$	96.62	92.79
$i = 0.08$	103.56	107.98

£6.94 (£103.56 −£96.62), equivalent to 7.2 per cent, while the price of a five-year bond changes by £15.19 (£107.98 −£92.79), equivalent to 16.4 per cent.

Thus, the fact that assets can be sold in secondary markets means that lenders can retrieve their funds (a long-term loan is not illiquid provided it is marketable) but what we have just demonstrated suggests that the risk that prices might be above or below what sellers require is greater for long-dated than short-dated loans. Hence, given certain other assumptions, we might expect a term-related premium to be paid, even on loans which are marketable, if they are loans made at a fixed rate of interest. The relationship between the yield on assets and their term to maturity, a subject known as the **term structure of interest rates**, is a major issue in financial economics, with a number of important applications. To discuss it in depth, we need to know more about the characteristics of assets, particularly bonds, and asset markets, so we defer further discussion until Chapter 16. We accept, for now,

that positive **term premiums** are likely because of the preferences of lenders (for lending short in the case of non-marketable loans and for minimizing capital risk with marketable ones) and the preferences of borrowers (for borrowing long).

10.3 The effect of risk

We said in Section 9.2 that interest rates influence behaviour which involves commitments over a period of time. Loans are made for a period (even if they can be sold on in a secondary market, the original *intention* was a commitment for a period). Debts are entered into for a period of time. It will often be more difficult for a borrower than for a lender to get out of a loan contract since the funds may well have been invested in a long-term project with a long payback period. All of this means that lenders and borrowers are entering into contracts which involve some degree of *risk*.

As we already know from Section 8.2, 'risk' in financial terms refers to the possibility that outcomes may differ from what was expected and it is usually assumed that the degree of risk can be measured and expressed as a probability statement, calculated on the basis of past outcomes. The risk thought to attach to an individual loan or asset is thus obviously one element in the size of the risk premium. Remember (from Section 8.4), though, that there is a second element. This is the 'price of risk'. By this we mean the price of 'average' or 'standard' risk and in Section 8.4 we saw that this is often taken to be represented by the difference in the rate of return on a portfolio of assets representative of the whole population of risky assets and the return on risk-free assets. We called this the 'market price of risk' and we noted that it would rise or fall with changes in the community's degree of risk aversion. The **risk premium**, σ, paid on a particular loan or asset will depend therefore upon the riskiness or the perceived riskiness of the loan itself relative to the representative portfolio multiplied by the market price of average or standard risk. A change in the risk premium, therefore, can be the result of changes in the characteristic of the asset (a change in its own riskiness) or the result of changes in the level of risk aversion in the community at large.

Risk can take many forms. For example, one can distinguish **default risk** (the borrower cannot repay the principal) from **capital risk** (the loan has a lower nominal value when it terminates – a possibility if one has to sell bonds in the open market rather than wait to maturity, for example) and from **income risk** (the possibility that the flow of interest, dividends or other payments are less than were expected).[2]

These forms of risk can have various sources. For example, it is common in the finance literature to distinguish between *business risk*, which means the risk which arises from the nature of the activity to which the borrower intends to apply the borrowed funds, and *financial risk*, the additional risk which arises from the overall pattern of financing that the borrower chooses.

We know also (from Section 8.4) that some risk attaching to individual assets (specific risk) can be diversified away by combining assets in a portfolio. When all the gains from diversification have been exploited, however, the fact remains that some loans will be riskier than others (by virtue of their differing exposure to market risk). It seems reasonable to suppose that savers willing to lend, let us say, £1 million at 10 per cent to a risk-free borrower would require a larger reward if they were to lend the same amount for a risky purpose. Thus lenders require a 'risk premium', a payment over and above the risk-free rate to induce them to lend a given amount. In a diagram, the supply curve of risky funds lies above the risk-free supply curve by the amount of this premium. The premium itself, of course, varies with the degree of risk and the market's attitude to risk.

Thus large corporations may be able to borrow by issuing corporate bonds which offer a rate which is only slighter greater than the rate paid by government on its bonds. On the other hand, we should expect that ordinary company shares will generally pay a better return (dividend payments plus capital growth) than corporate or government bonds. This is because dividends are variable and because the claims of ordinary shareholders, both to profits and to residual assets in the event of bankruptcy, rank well behind the claims of other creditors and of subscribers of fixed-interest capital.

10.4 Expectations and government borrowing

So far, we have said that different types of asset/liability will carry different rates of interest because they are essentially different products. They are differentiated by term and by risk. In this section, however, we shall see that even if we take a subset of instruments which look homogeneous, we may still see a range of interest rates payable on them. Our subset could be government bonds, or treasury bills, or, possibly, interbank deposits. In each of these categories, within any national market, the default risk is uniform (and very close to zero in most countries). European governments are not generally expected to default on their bond or bill obligations and, even if they were, there is no basis to suppose that default is more likely on long- rather than short-dated bonds or vice versa. Similarly, the market for interbank deposits is dominated by a few major banks of equal creditworthiness. Furthermore, within each category the instruments are homogeneous in the sense that they can be instantly traded, regardless of maturity. A three-month treasury bill does not require a longer commitment of funds than a one-month treasury bill.

Exercise 10.2 Interest rates – term and risk

1 Check the financial press to find the current yield on government bonds. Sketch roughly in a graph any relationship that you can see between the return and the term to maturity. (Hint: use redemption yield.)

2 Check the financial press for the return on corporate bonds. How does the return on corporate bonds compare with the return on government bonds? What explanation can you offer for any differential?

3 Let us suppose that we observe a premium in the rate of return on corporate bonds over the rate on government bonds and that over a period of time we see this premium increasing. What conclusions might we be tempted to draw?

---

[2] Notice that lenders making fixed-interest but marketable loans (for example, bonds) are in effect avoiding income risk but only at the expense of accepting capital risk (the risk that they may have to sell before maturity at a price which is different from that which would be expected at maturity). This is the case that we discussed in the last section and one might say, therefore, that what we there called a 'term' premium could be seen as a 'risk' premium to compensate for the interest-sensitivity of bond prices.

And yet it is usually the case that if we plot the interest rate (usually called the 'yield' in this context) against the term to maturity, we observe a pattern to which a smooth curve can usually be fairly closely fitted. This plot is known as a **time–yield curve**.[3]

The most commonly advanced explanation for a systematic relationship between yields and term, among assets which are homogeneous except with respect to term to maturity, is *expectations of future interest rates*. The argument is that if people expect short-term interest rates to be higher (lower) than they are now, *current* long-term rates will be above (below) current short rates; that is, expectations about *future* changes affect the *current* structure. Why the present should be influenced by events which have not yet occurred seems rather mysterious. But a moment's thought makes it at least intuitively obvious. Lenders willing to lend for a period longer than the minimum available clearly have a choice. They can either lend for the shortest possible period and then re-lend at the end of that period and re-lend again and so on, or they can agree to lend now for just one period corresponding to their investment horizon. Assume that the yield curve is stable. This must mean that lenders and borrowers are broadly happy with the current pattern of interest rates and therefore we have an equilibrium position. (If they were not, then there would be a general shift towards lending long, or vice versa, and the yield curve would be changing its shape.) If we have equilibrium, then it follows that lenders are currently indifferent about whether they lend for a series of short periods or one longer period. If we ask ourselves, 'in what circumstances would investors be indifferent between a series of short loans and one long loan?', the answer ought to strike us quickly that they will be indifferent when the returns they expect from both strategies are equal. In other words, the reward for the long strategy must be equal to what lenders think they will get from a series of short loans. The reward for the long strategy must equal the average of the series of short loans. This is where expected future rates enter the picture. Since we can only know the *current* short loan rate, we have to make an educated guess at likely *future* short rates. What we guess must be responsible for any observed difference between

current short and long rates. That is, expected future short rates are implicit in any difference between current long and short rates.

Suppose for simplicity that a short loan is for one year and a long loan is for two years. Suppose, furthermore, that the current short rate (i_S) is 6 per cent while the current long rate (i_L) is 8 per cent. If this differential is stable then lenders are happy with the prospect of what they will earn by lending for one year and then renewing at the expected one-year rate compared with what they would get by lending now for two years. Formally, it must be the case that they expect:

$$(1 + i_S)(1 + \hat{i}_s) = (1 + i_L)^2$$

where $\hat{i}_S$ is the expected *future* short-term (one-year) rate.

Rearranging gives us:

$$(1 + \hat{i}_S)(1 + i_L)^2/(1 + i_S)$$

Substituting actual values gives:

$$(1 + \hat{i}_S) = (1.08)^2/(1.06)$$

$$= 1.1664/1.06 \approx 1.10$$

If $(1 + \hat{i}_S) = 1.10$, then $\hat{i}_S = 1.10 - 1$
$$= 0.10 \text{ or } 10\%$$

In this example, therefore, we can see that if current short rates are 6 per cent and long rates are 8 per cent then this suggests that people expect short rates to rise to 10 per cent before the second period begins.

In this example, therefore, the yield curve slopes upward and long-dated bonds have a higher yield not because they involve a greater sacrifice of liquidity than short-dated bonds but because their current yield persuades those willing to lend for a longer period that they will do just as well from long-dated bonds as they will from holding a succession of short-dated ones, bearing in mind what is expected to happen to interest rates on short-dated bonds in future. Conversely, if the market expected short rates to fall in future, the yield curve would be downward-sloping. The argument then would be that investors would still be willing to hold (lower-yielding) long-dated bonds

---

[3] We shall look at time–yield curves, their construction and interpretation, in more detail in Chapter 16. We shall see, for example, that 'yield' (for bonds in particular) can be measured in a number of different ways. For the moment, readers who wish to scan the bond yield columns of a financial newspaper to form a mental picture or to do a freehand drawing of a current time–yield curve, should use the figures in the column showing 'redemption yield', or its equivalent.

MORE FROM THE WEB

The Bank of England has a subsection of its statistics website devoted to yield curves – what they show as well as data. The address is: http://www.bankofengland.co.uk/statistics/yieldcurve/.
     The UK Debt Management Office publishes a *Quarterly Review* which contains charts showing selected current yield curves. The address is: www.dmo.gov.uk.

because this would give them the same return as a succession of short-dated bonds, bearing in mind that short rates in future would be lower than they are now, and indeed lower than current long rates.

The relationship between yields on assets differentiated only by their term to maturity is known as the *term structure of interest rates* and we shall return to it in Chapter 16 when we study government bonds in more detail. The term structure (the shape of the yield curve) is an issue of great interest to economists precisely because it may be dominated by markets' perceptions of future interest rates. For example, if it does, and if those perceptions were generally correct, then we could use the yield curve and our calculations above to derive **future implied** short-term rates, that is, to calculate what future short-term rates were expected to be. The yield curve would be a useful forecasting tool. Furthermore, if we were to combine the yield curve with the Fisher hypothesis (see Section 9.3.1) then we could derive future implied interest rates and implied *inflation* rates.

To say that expectations of *future* short-term rates determine the relationship between *current* long and short rates is one thing, however; knowing what affects expectations is something else. And yet profitable investment in financial markets would be much easier if we did know how expectations were going to change. For example, we saw in Section 10.2 that bond prices would change inversely with changes in interest rates (and that long-dated bond prices would change by more than short-dated ones). Obviously, therefore, investors will wish to sell bonds if they expect interest rates to rise and to buy them if they expect a fall. Notice then that the expectation itself is sufficient to cause the changes in prices and yields that were expected! For an individual investor, the trick is to be first to anticipate any change in expectation.

One obvious source of influence on expectations will be all those events that markets think may herald a change in inflation. Faster credit growth, rapid falls in unemployment, a rise in imports relative to exports may all suggest that prices will rise more rapidly in future. If one assumes that higher inflation means higher interest rates, without necessarily believing in the full rigours of the Fisher hypothesis, then all these events suggest higher (rather than lower) future interest rates, and the yield curve will steepen.

Frequently anticipating changes in future rates of interest (and anticipating changes in expectations of changes) involves an appraisal of the authorities' monetary policy objectives and thus how policy instruments may be changed in response to events. This is easily understood in the light of our discussion about central banks' influence on short-term interest rates in Section 9.4. If the government is known to desire low inflation above all else, then all of the events that we mentioned in the last paragraph become connected with higher interest rates through a second channel: the authorities' response. For a real example, we may recall that in the early 1980s many governments pursued explicit money supply growth targets. Thus an overshoot, for example, in the figures immediately led to expectations that the authorities would raise short-term rates in order to reduce monetary growth in future. The consequence would be that the yield curve would steepen, showing an expectation of a regime of higher short-term rates in future. A rise in long-term rates means, of course, a fall in the price of longer-dated bonds and one can trace the markets' changing perceptions of what really mattered to the authorities by tracing the changes in events to which bond prices are sensitive. In the early 1980s, as we just observed, the bond market was very sensitive to money growth figures. In the UK, this became less important in the mid-1980s, when money growth targets fell out of fashion and the market (and the yield curve) became very sensitive instead to quite small movements in the exchange rate, as the authorities were believed to have a policy of shadowing the Deutschmark.

Box 10.1 provides an amusing example of the markets' attempts to anticipate the US Federal Reserve's next step on interest rates. In the end, they seem to have come to the conclusion that a minute change of wording in a public statement by the Fed increased the likelihood of a future rise in interest rates. The chart shows the yield curve steepening as we would expect. The discussion also suggests that a degree in

BOX 10.1 Guessing the next step

FT

MARKET INSIGHT

Fed's weapon of words pops balloon of high expectations

By Deborah Hargreaves and Jennifer Hughes

Financial markets have become accustomed to the US Federal Reserve saying it will keep monetary policy accommodative for a 'considerable period'. Although the US central bank on Wednesday kept interest rates unchanged, it altered its phrasing about the outlook and the after-shock rippled rapidly through asset prices.

'There is now a little more certainty that the Fed might do something this year and that went like an electric shock through the market,' said Andrew Milligan at Standard Life.

Wall Street saw a sharp sell-off after the Fed's statement, two-year Treasury yields rose sharply and the dollar gained about two cents against the euro in the immediate aftermath.

Many strategists believe financial markets initially overreacted to the

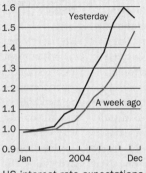

Derived from Fed Fund futures contracts (%)

US interest rate expectations

Source: Thomson Datastream.

Fed's shift in phrasing as it caught investors by surprise.

Market participants had widely expected the Fed to keep the phrase 'considerable period' and had positioned for some dollar weakness. The dollar's rapid rise sparked a

wave of covering of these short-dollar positions.

After further reflection yesterday, many believe the central bank is creating more room to manoeuvre but not necessarily signalling an imminent change of stance.

Deutsche Bank said the Fed's use of the phrase 'considerable period' was contributing to a market perception that it would do nothing this year. Peter Hooper, chief US economist, said the Fed's open market committee may have felt that was too constraining.

The Fed's new statement says: 'The committee believes that it can be patient in removing its policy accommodation'.

Divyang Shah at IDEAGlobal said this was the key to the Fed's stance. It replaced the phrase: 'Policy accommodation can be maintained for a considerable period.'

Source: *Financial Times*, 30 January 2004. Reprinted with permission.

linguistics might be a useful qualification for money market participants.

One issue which has always had a significant effect upon the shape of the yield curve is the level of government borrowing. Financial markets in all countries pay close attention to the monthly government borrowing figures in relation to the anticipated outturn. As we have seen above, this may be for two seemingly conflicting reasons.

Firstly, higher than expected public sector borrowing may cause fears of a willingness on the part of the authorities to tolerate higher inflation than the market would like. In such cases, the markets are assuming that the increase in debt is likely to be financed by

borrowing from the banking sector with a consequent increase in bank deposits and the money supply. Although the form of the link between the rate of growth of the money supply and the rate of inflation remains controversial both theoretically and empirically, there can be no doubt that there is a strong acceptance within financial markets of the proposition that money-financed government debt will cause inflation. As long as that remained true, an increase in government debt would generate inflationary expectations and creditors would demand higher interest rates in future to preserve the real rate of return on their funds. Given the time lags involved in monetary policy, however, we would not be talking here about an immediate increase in the inflation rate, but an increase more than a year hence. The yield curve would steepen from that point on.

On the other hand, if the authorities in question have a reputation established over a number of years of being tough on inflation, the markets may react to higher than expected public sector borrowing in a quite different way – assuming that the government would finance this increase in debt by borrowing from the non-bank public with the possibility that interest rates would need to rise immediately to bring this about. Even if it were possible for the government to borrow more from the non-bank public without interest rates having to rise, inflation-conscious authorities would very likely act to cause interest rates at the short end of the market to rise, precisely because it would be aware of the market fears of inflation mentioned in the previous paragraph. In such a case, an announcement of higher than expected borrowing would produce an expectation of an increase in short interest rates not accompanied by fears of longer-term inflation. The shape of the yield curve would clearly be different in this case from the previous one even though the markets would in both cases expect interest rates to rise at some point.

We have suggested that the assessment by the markets of the likely response of the authorities to higher government borrowing depends on the authorities' past anti-inflationary reputation. Much also depends on institutional arrangements. A strong belief has developed in recent years that central banks which are constitutionally independent of government are likely to operate tougher monetary policies than those which are, in varying degrees, dominated by government. In the former regimes, higher than expected government borrowing would very likely produce an expectation of an immediate increase in short-term interest rates. In contrast, in regimes where the government could put pressure on the central bank such an announcement might produce fears of future inflation. These fears would be all the greater if there were an election in prospect because the markets would assume that the government would be unwilling to raise either taxes or interest rates for fear of losing votes.

In 1997 there was an interesting development in the German yield curve which could be traced to these market attitudes. It was generally expected that, despite strong statements to the contrary, the European Central Bank, which would operate monetary policy after establishment of European Monetary Union, would be less able to adopt a tough anti-inflationary stance than the *Bundesbank* had previously done. For this reason, the markets expected an increase in German inflation after 1999 and German interest rates have increased sharply on financial instruments maturing after that date. This emphasizes the point that it is what is believed in financial markets which is crucial here. Whether any economic analysis underlying these beliefs is sound is of little relevance.

10.5 Summary

Any developed economy offers a wide range of financial instruments to lenders and borrowers. These offer a correspondingly wide range of rates of interest or other forms of return. The minimum return that will be available will be the risk-free, short-term nominal rate of interest. This will be available, obviously, on very short-term loans of zero risk. In practice, the rate on one-month treasury bills might be representative. Everything else will offer a rate of return in excess of this. On top of the short-term, risk-free rate there sits a structure of interest rates. This structure is determined by the willingness of lenders to hold assets which are not risk-free and short-term, relative to their supply. We generalize that two characteristics in particular affect demand. These are 'term' and 'risk' and they affect demand negatively. That is to say that as term and risk increase, lenders, on balance, become less willing to hold such assets and require 'premiums' to induce them to do so. As we have said many times, lenders are assumed to be risk averse and to be attracted by liquidity.

But there many other influences on supply and demand for funds and if these operate in respect of particular classes of funds then they will contribute to the structure of interest differentials. One set of influences is the expectation that people hold about future movements in interest rates. Their investment decisions now will try to take account of future possible returns and those decisions will affect the current structure. Another influence, which has been topical in recent years, has been the public sector's demand for funds. If this demand were uniform across funds of all types, of course it would be irrelevant to the *structure* of rates. But, as we have seen, governments tend to borrow funds at longer maturities and this can, certainly in principle, affect relative returns.

Key concepts in this chapter

Capital risk	Non-marketable loans
Default risk	Reinvestment or rollover risk
Future implied rates	Risk premium
Income risk	Term premium
Interest spreads	Term structure of interest rates
Liquidity premium	Time–yield curve

Questions and problems

1 Why might lenders demand a premium for lending long term?

2 Does your answer to (1) explain why long-dated bonds often have higher yields than short-dated ones? If not, what alternative explanation can you offer?

3 Look at the financial press and find the current interest spread between 5-year and 10-year government bonds. Is there a positive term premium?

4 What conclusion might you draw about possible future interest rates if a positive term premium were to increase?

5 What name do we give to the pattern of yields available on bonds of different maturities?

6 Using the financial press, compare the redemption yield on one or more *corporate* bonds with that on *government* bonds with a similar term to maturity. How would you explain any differential?

7 What conclusions might you draw about future developments in the economy if corporate yields were to rise relative to yields on government bonds?

Further reading

A D Bain, *The Financial System* (Oxford: Blackwell, 2e, 1992) Chs 5, 6

D Blake, *Financial Market Analysis* (London: McGraw-Hill, 2e, 2000) Ch. 2

R Glenn Hubbard, *Money, the Financial System and the Economy* (Reading MA: Addison Wesley, 2e, 1997)

C A E Goodhart, *Money, Information and Uncertainty* (London: Macmillan, 2e, 1989) Ch. XI

D Hargreaves and J Hughes, 'Fed's weapon of words pops balloon of high expectations', *Financial Times*, 30 January 2004

P G A Howells and K Bain, *Financial Markets and Institutions* (London: Pearson, 5e, 2007) Ch. 7

M Livingston, *Money and Capital Markets* (Oxford: Blackwell, 3e, 1996)

F Mishkin, *The Economics of Money, Banking and Financial Markets* (London: Pearson-Addison Wesley, 7e, 2004) Ch. 6

R Reeves, 'Do financial markets react to Bank of England communication?' *Bank of England Quarterly Bulletin*, winter 2005, 431–9

Chapter 11 The valuation of assets

What you will learn in this chapter:

■ How the risk-free rate of interest combines with a risk premium to determine the required rate of return on an asset

■ Why it is that, in equilibrium, a tradable asset will be priced so as to yield the required rate of return

■ How to use the required rate of return to analyse asset price movements within a supply and demand framework

■ The connection between the required rate of return and the 'fundamentals' of an asset's value

■ Some of the implications of a market's failure to price assets according to their required rate of return

11.1 Introduction

In this chapter we want to bring together what we have learned so far from Chapters 8, 9 and 10. In Chapter 1 (Sections 1.4 and 1.5.3) we explained that other things being equal the price of assets moves inversely with their rate of return. Thus it follows that if we know the required rate of return, then (again all else being given) we know the price at which assets will be willingly held. In Chapter 8, therefore, we concentrated on the determination of the required rate of return. This, we said, would be equal to the risk-free rate of return and a risk premium calculated from the price of 'average' or whole market risk and the asset's individual risk characteristics relative to those of the market as a whole. An asset that is 'fairly priced' will yield a return which places it on the security market line. The equation for asset A is:

$$\overline{K}_A = K_{rf} + \beta_A(K_m - K_{rf}) \tag{11.1}$$

and we can interpret Equation 11.1, less formally, as saying that:

the required rate of return = the risk-free rate
+ (the quantity of risk $\times$ the price of risk)

In Chapter 9 we went on to explore the determination of the risk-free, short-term rate of interest. We said that this is the outcome of market forces, represented by the demand for and supply of loanable funds (where this included the money-creating activities of banks) modified, in some situations by the administrative decisions of central banks. In symbols,

$$K_{rf} = i = r + \pi$$

The 'fair' price of an asset will be as illustrated in Figure 11.1. We want now to see formally how it is that the required rate of return determines asset prices and how changes in the required rate cause asset prices to change. We can analyse the behaviour of asset prices using the conventional supply and demand apparatus. The theme of the rest of this chapter, therefore, is how we can incorporate changes in the required rate of return into a supply and demand framework. After some preliminary clarification (in Section 11.2) we shall do this (in Section 11.3) by looking at the markets for two 'stylized' assets: company shares and fixed-interest bonds. We say 'stylized' because we shall only describe these assets and their markets in the barest essentials – only as much as we need to

$$\overline{K}_A =$$

K_{rf}: The short term, risk-free rate of interest. The result of the interaction between the supply of, and demand for, loanable funds, including banks' creation of money, and the intervention of central banks. In the terms of Chapter 9:
$$K_{rf} = r + \pi$$

$+$

β_A: The share's β-coefficient, expressing its riskiness in relation to the riskiness of the whole market portfolio. From Section 8.5 we know that $\beta_A = \dfrac{\text{cov } K_A, K_m}{\sigma_m^2}$

$\times$

$K_m - K_{rf}$: The premium required to induce investors to hold the level of risk associated with the whole market portfolio. This is the only fully diversified portfolio that rational investors will hold (see Section 8.5)

Figure 11.1 The origin of the required rate of return

understand the theory. The detail of these markets, and others, is discussed in Part 5 of this book.

Throughout Part 3 of this book we have been trying to provide an intelligible account of the orthodox theory of portfolio choice and asset valuation. In Section 11.4, therefore, we take a little space to raise some critical questions about the orthodox theory and to suggest that there are other, more controversial, ways of interpreting the processes that we have described so far.

Before we begin, though, we need to be absolutely clear what it is that we are trying to explain. Some preliminary clarification is therefore provided in the next section.

11.2 Supply and demand in asset markets

When we apply a supply and demand framework to the valuation of assets, there are two pairs of distinctions that it is useful to make. The first is the distinction between assets that are tradable between third parties and those which can only be 'bought' and 'sold' between the original supplier and the original buyer. The second distinction is between stocks of assets and flows. We have met both of them before, in Sections 1.4.1 and Sections 1.2.4 respectively. Most of us are likely to be more familiar with supply and demand as applied to flows – of newly created goods and services per period of time, for example. But we shall see that stock demand is at least as important in financial markets.

Tradable assets

Let us assume to begin with that we are dealing with **tradable assets**. These are securities like bonds, bills or company shares which, after issue, can be bought and resold many times. At any particular time, there exists a very large number of these assets. This is a *stock*. There may also be new issues taking place, in which case there is also a *flow* causing the stock to expand. In practice, the stock is likely to be very large relative to the flow and, frequently indeed, the flow will be zero. In equilibrium, this stock must be willingly held. This does not mean that there will be no trading. It simply means that another set of *flows*, the flows of orders to sell, match the flows of orders to buy at the prevailing market price. Clearly, in equilibrium, the price at which the stock is willingly held must be the same as the price at which trading is taking place. A fall (for example) in the price at which trades are taking place can only occur if the numbers wishing to sell at the earlier price increase relative to buyers and this means that more holders of the stock think it currently overvalued than think it currently undervalued. In trading, the price falls to a new equilibrium (sell orders match buy orders) only when once again the balance of those thinking it overvalued is matched by those who think it undervalued. Explaining the price of financial assets, therefore, amounts to explaining what it is that makes holders of the stock of assets willing to hold the stock at a given price. Furthermore, since changes in the stock (as a result of new issues, or cancellations for that matter) are small relative to the size of the stock and discontinuous, discussions of changes in price come down in practice to discussing changes in *demand* for the stock. The question becomes one of 'what makes investors change their view of the value of these assets?' The appropriate diagrams are stock diagrams. The supply curve is vertical (and subject to small rightward movements as new issues take place). The demand curve is downward-sloping and it is shifts in the demand curve that occupy most of our attention when we discuss asset price changes.

This does not make flows irrelevant. Firstly, as we just said, flows of new issues cause the stock to expand. Continuous government borrowing on a sufficiently large scale could cause the stock of bonds to expand so rapidly that the price might fall, for example. Furthermore, we are sometimes interested in the details of the trading process itself. This happens when we come to discuss the role of 'market-makers' in different trading systems. As we noted above, market-makers are dealing in flows of orders to buy and sell and in making a margin or profit out of those orders. When we look specifically at the role of market-makers we shall encounter more familiar supply and demand diagrams with flows on the horizontal axis and upward-sloping supply curves. Trading systems are among the institutional details which we postpone until Part 5 of this book.

Non-tradable assets

Although, of course, we can still bring our conventional supply and demand apparatus to the analysis of markets for **non-tradable assets**, the situation is rather different from the one we have just described. With tradable assets, there is a stock to be traded which exists even if the issuer of the assets decided to issue no more. With banks, savings institutions, insurance companies, pension funds and so on assets can be disposed of only by returning them to the originator and, in complete contrast with securities markets, the originator of the asset cannot stand aside from the demand. If there is an increase in the demand for IBM shares, for example (because people think they are undervalued), this requires no immediate response from IBM. If there is an increase in the demand for insurance contracts from Allianz, by contrast, the firm can supply more. If demand continues at a high level, Allianz may revise the terms on which it issues the contracts, making them less favourable to investors but more profitable to itself, but it cannot stand aloof in the way that a company can from the market for its shares. This gives us a number of problems about the way in which we use our supply and demand apparatus.

Firstly, in most of these cases of non-tradable assets there is no explicit price. There is an explicit yield, or rate of return, which *implies* a price but we normally draw supply and demand diagrams with respect to price. If we draw them with respect to yield, then the slopes must be reversed. As the yield on an asset rises, more investors will be willing to buy it, *ceteris paribus*.

By contrast, the higher the yield demanded by investors, the less willing issuers will be to issue contracts. Secondly, there is the question of whether we are dealing with a stock or a flow. The correct answer to this is that we should deal with whichever seems to provide the most useful insights in a given situation. The apparatus is only a means to an end. In practice, the answer probably depends upon the time period in which we conduct the analysis. Of course, institutions are opening new deposit accounts, new insurance, new pensions contracts and so on all the time. But accounts and contracts are being closed on a continuous basis too. The net flows may be very small or even zero in the short run. In this case we are dealing with a stock. The supply curve is vertical (and the demand curve slopes upward with yield on the vertical axis, remember). On the other hand, if the focus of attention is a longer period, we may prefer to discuss supply as a flow (with the supply curve sloping downward).

11.3 Asset valuation

Real assets are goods that provide a flow of output or services over a period of time. The output or service has a monetary value and so we can talk about assets as goods which yield a future stream of income. *Financial* assets are claims upon the real assets and upon their future income stream. The basic principle in the orthodox valuation of assets is that:

> the (present) value of an asset is equal to the sum of its future income stream (net of running costs), suitably discounted.

Notice that this gives rise, in theory, to an identity between the value of the underlying *real* assets (the sum of their discounted future income stream) and the value of the financial assets whose own income stream is simply the income generated by the real assets passed on to the current owners of those real assets. (We shall see in Chapter 17 that this identity may need to be modified in practice to take account of taxation.) Thus the value of a firm, for example, is equal to the future discounted income stream from the assets which make up the firm and this *should* (assuming no tax) be equal to the market value of the shares in issue.

The practical difficulties of asset valuation revolve around estimating the future income stream (which is

at best uncertain), estimating the running costs, and choosing an appropriate rate of discount. These are very real difficulties. In practice, they are to some extent side-stepped by concentrating upon *relative* valuation. That means that most of the time practitioners in financial markets are looking to see whether an individual asset is over- or undervalued when compared with other assets for which it is a very close substitute. In these circumstances, it does not matter whether we view all assets as over- or undervalued because of an error that we make in estimating future income streams (for example), provided that the error is reproduced across all assets. We shall do the same and thus we focus here upon the third step, the discounting process. The next two sections are devoted to showing that the required rate of return provides the appropriate rate of discount.

11.3.1 Valuing company shares

Ordinary company shares provide their owners with a perpetual claim upon the earnings or profits of a firm. What is actually paid to shareholders is known as a **dividend** and is variable. This variability results firstly from the fact that earnings themselves are variable; secondly, from the fact that other people and agencies (bondholders and the tax authorities, for example) have a prior claim on those earnings and the size of this claim may vary; thirdly, the firm may decrease (increase) its 'payout ratio' if it wishes to increase (decrease) the size of its retained earnings, to finance real investment. This variability, combined with the fact that shareholders' claims on residual assets rank low in the event of bankruptcy, explains why company shares are generally regarded as having comparatively high total risk.

However, since the dividend payment is a claim on earnings and earnings are expected to increase over time (as a result of real productivity gains and inflation), dividends in a well-managed firm usually show an upward trend over a period of years. Clearly, if dividend payments are not to become infinitely large relative to a share's price (or alternatively if there is some 'normal', long-run relationship between dividend payments and prices) it follows that a share's price will also follow an upward trend over a period of years. This capital appreciation may be a significant part of the total return on shares and thus a significant part of their attraction to investors.

The total return on company shares is thus made up of two elements: the **dividend yield** and the **rate of capital appreciation**. The dividend yield is simply the current dividend (D) divided by the market price (P) while the rate of capital appreciation is the capital gain made from holding the share while its price rises. Strictly speaking, it is the difference in price at the end of the period compared with the price at the beginning expressed as a percentage of the price at the beginning. If we denote this difference by g, then:

$$g = (P_1 - P_0)/P_0 \qquad (11.2)$$

and the total return can then be written as:

$$\overline{K} = D/P + g \qquad (11.3)$$

A very simple rearrangement of Equation 11.3 gives us an expression for price:

$$P = D/(\overline{K} - g) \qquad (11.4)$$

In equilibrium, therefore, given their dividend payments and growth prospects, the price of company shares depends upon the required rate of return. In Chapter 17 we shall see that Equation 11.4 is known as the Gordon constant growth model of share valuation. This is because we have implicitly assumed that g, the rate of capital appreciation, is constant. The treatment of the rate of capital appreciation is problematic and thus the Gordon model is just one of several we look at later, distinguished by the way in which they handle the growth issue. What they all share in common, however, is the presence of $\overline{K}$, the required rate of return in the denominator. Provided that this is the case then, with other things (i.e., dividend payments and growth) given, the price must *always* be determined by the required rate of return.

This is easily illustrated by substituting some plausible values in Equation 11.4. If, for example, a company, XYZ plc, were paying a dividend of 25p per share while the rate of capital appreciation were 15 per cent and the overall return required by shareholders were 22 per cent, then the share would be priced at:

$$25p/(0.22 - 0.15) = 357p$$

If now the required rate of return were to increase to 28 per cent, then the new price would be:

$$25p/(0.28 - 0.15) = 192p$$

A further example is provided in Exercise 11.1.

Exercise 11.1 Prices and rates of return

Assume that a share pays a single, annual dividend (D) and that the annual rate of capital appreciation is denoted by g, then we know that the annual rate of return, K, can be found from the expression:

$$K = D/P + g$$

Suppose that the rate of capital appreciation is 10 per cent p.a. and the dividend payment is 30p.

1 Find the current rate of return if the share's price is £3.75.

2 Find the current rate of return if the share's price were £5.00.

3 If the market thought a rate of return of 20 per cent appropriate, what would happen to the share's price?

(Answers appear in Figure 11.2 below.)

Figure 11.2 shows how we can interpret these changes in rates of return and prices in a supply and demand framework. Notice firstly that the supply of shares in XYZ is a *stock*. If XYZ were in process of issuing new shares, the stock would be expanding but with no new issues the existing stock remains available for trading. This is shown by the vertical supply curve, S, in Figure 11.2. (The values in Figure 11.2 are the answers to the questions in Exercise 11.1.)

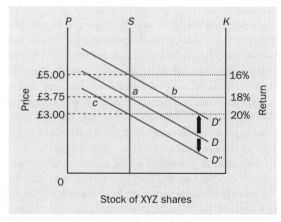

Figure 11.2 The demand for assets and their rate of return

The demand curve for XYZ shares is shown by *D*. It slopes downward on the basis that the lower the price of XYZ shares, *ceteris paribus*, the higher their rate of return and thus the greater the demand for them. The initial equilibrium is shown by the intersection of the two curves and the equilibrium price is £3.75. (Notice that at this price the rate of return is 18 per cent.) At this price (rate of return) sell orders match buy orders.

Let us imagine now, as in Exercise 11.1, that the required rate of return increases to 20 per cent. Shares in XYZ are less attractive at any given price than they previously were. At the original price of £3.75 sell orders exceed buy orders. This is shown by the downward shift in the demand curve from *D* to *D″*. At the original equilibrium price of £3.75 the shortfall in demand is shown by the distance *ac*. The new equilibrium price, the price at which the existing stock is willingly held, in the sense that sell orders match buy orders, is £3.00.

Finally, suppose that there is an increase in demand for the shares. The demand curve shifts to *D′*. At £3.75 there is excess demand, shown by *ab*, and buy orders exceed sell orders. The price rises. Let us suppose that it rises to a new equilibrium of £5.00. At £5.00, Equation 11.3 tells us that the rate of return has fallen to 16 per cent.

In equilibrium, therefore, price settles at a level which equates the **actual rate of return** with the **required rate of return**. Notice that this equilibrium condition also implies that the firm's cost of capital is equal to the required rate of return. The cost of capital is the rate of return which a firm has to pay in order to raise additional funds. If the going rate of return on its existing shares is 16 per cent, then the cost of capital from a new share issue (ignoring transaction costs) is 16 per cent. In other words, the firm has to earn a 16 per cent return on its real capital which it then divides – paying some as dividends and retaining the rest to ensure a rate of growth adequate to make a total return to shareholders of 16 per cent. In equilibrium, the going rate of return and cost of capital will equal the required rate of return. This is important, since we can now see that changes in the required rate of return lead not only to changes in price but also to changes in the cost of capital and thus, presumably, in the allocation of new funds which will always seek the best return

for a given level of risk. In Section 11.4, we shall see that if assets are indeed priced (and the cost of capital is determined) by the required rate of return as we have suggested here, then an argument can be made that resource allocation is optimal. If asset prices and the cost of capital are not determined in the way described in this section, there are adverse implications for resource allocation. This possibility is explored in Section 11.5.

11.3.2 Valuing fixed interest bonds

Unlike company shares, fixed interest bonds provide their holders with a fixed income stream. In the UK, the income payments are known as **coupons**. Coupon payments can be expressed as a **coupon rate** by dividing by the par value of the bond. The coupon rate is often incorporated into the title of the bond alongside other information. For example, *Treasury 10% 2015* is a bond which pays £10 per annum to its holder and will mature (or be redeemed) in the year 2015. Notice that its **residual maturity** is the length of time from now to the redemption date. Its **original maturity** may have been very long (if it was issued many years ago) or it may have been quite short. We simply cannot tell. It is fortunate, therefore, that we are more interested in residual than original maturity. The income stream of such bonds amounts to a series of (known) coupon payments plus a terminal payment, which is also known and which is the redemption value of the bond. In these circumstances, the value of the bond is found by using the following expression (which we first met in Section 10.2):

$$P = \sum_{t=1}^{n} \frac{C}{(1+i)^t} + \frac{M}{(1+i)^{n_m}} \qquad (11.5)$$

However, some fixed interest bonds have no redemption or maturity date. These are sometimes called **perpetuals** or **consols**. The value of bonds with no redemption date can be found by setting $n_m = \infty$ in Equation 11.5.[1] With $n_m = \infty$, Equation 11.5 simplifies to:

$$P = C/i \qquad (11.6)$$

Irredeemable bonds are rather like company shares with zero growth and we can see this if we compare

---

[1] See the appendix to this chapter for some further bond pricing arithmetic.

Equation 11.6 with Equation 11.3. If we eliminate g and we substitute C ('coupon') for D ('dividend') then Equation 11.6 is the same as Equation 11.3, except that Equation 11.6 has i rather than K in the denominator. But a few moments' reflection reveals that K and i are equivalents: they are both rates of return and, in equilibrium, when the asset is fairly priced, both i and K will equal the required rate of return for their respective assets. For example, by rearranging Equation 11.6 we can see that:

$$i = C/P \qquad (11.7)$$

and that i is thus the running yield calculated as the perpetual coupon payment divided by the price paid for the bond.[2] The question remains, however, 'why, in equilibrium, is i (or K) also the required rate of return?' This can be best answered by posing some other questions. 'Why should they not be the rates that investors *require*?' 'If the assets can be easily bought and sold, why should investors accept a price which means that they do not get the return that they require?' Surely, we must expect that if $K \neq \overline{K}$ the price will readily adjust until the two are brought into equality. In *equilibrium* the price will be that which delivers the required rate of return. Looking at Equation 11.6, we can now see clearly why the price of bonds (and other assets) varies with changes in market interest rates. It is because the asset must be priced in such a way that it provides the required rate of return and one obvious reason why the required rate may change is that rates available on other assets in the market change.

As with company shares, therefore, the required rate of return is the appropriate rate at which to discount future income payments and thus, *ceteris paribus*, determines the **equilibrium price** of bonds. In the case of company shares, we used the capital asset pricing model to find the required rate of return. The CAPM says that the required rate is equal to the risk-free rate of interest plus a risk premium derived from comparing the riskiness of the asset with the riskiness of the whole market portfolio. We can also use the CAPM to find the required return on bonds. The theory behind the CAPM requires that we derive a β-coefficient for any risky asset by comparing the variance of returns on the asset with the variance of returns on the 'whole market' portfolio. Interestingly, the extent to which bond prices fluctuate in response to changes in market conditions depends to a large extent upon their residual maturity. The price of bonds with a long residual maturity is more sensitive to changes in interest rates than is the price of short-dated bonds. We shall explore this more fully in Chapter 16, where we show that the concept of *duration* measures the interest sensitivity of a bond's price with respect to changes in interest rates. We have already met the idea in Section 10.2, where we worked an exercise to show that the longer the maturity of an asset the more variable its price in response to a change in interest rates. For the moment, however, one can grasp the basic idea that price sensitivity varies positively with the term to maturity by remembering that bonds pay a series of *fixed* coupons. Thus when market interest rates are falling there is an advantage in receiving fixed payments, and the more fixed payments the greater the advantage. When interest rates are rising, fixed payments are less attractive and the more fixed payments there are, the greater the disadvantage. Thus, when interest rates change, the impact on price is greater for long-dated bonds. The effect of duration can be seen again in Exercise 11.2, which is an exercise in the pricing of two bonds with identical characteristics except that one has a residual maturity of four years while the other is irredeemable.

An irredeemable bond is simply a bond of infinitely long residual maturity. In Exercise 11.2 we see that a

---

Exercise 11.2 Bond pricing

Assuming that the required rate of return is 8 per cent p.a., find the equilibrium price of:

1   a 6 per cent bond maturing in four years' time;

2   a perpetual 6 per cent bond.

Calculate the new equilibrium prices if the required rate of return rises to 9 per cent p.a.
Note: (1) requires the use of discount tables.

(Answers appear in the text below.)

---

2   The demonstration is more complicated for a **redeemable bond**, since 'yield' for redeemable bonds has several meanings. We shall see in Chapter 16 that i in Equation 11.5 is known as the *redemption yield* (and that it is not easily calculated). We shall also see, crucially, that the redemption yield is the discount rate that makes the cashflows over the life of the bond equal to its price.

one-point rise in required rates of return causes a fall in the equilibrium price of the irredeemable bond from:

£75 (= £6/0.08)   to   £66.66 (= £6/0.09)

while the price of the 'short-dated' bond falls from:

£93.37 (= £5.56 + £5.14 + £4.76 + £4.41 + £73.50)

to:

£90.27 (= £5.50 + £5.05 + £4.63 + £4.25 + £70.84)

The change in price of the irredeemable bond is £8.34 while the price change for the short-dated bond is only £3.10. The risk attaching to a bond, therefore, is contained in the interest-elasticity of its price and this in turn results largely from its duration.

We shall come back to the issue of duration and its relevance to bond prices in Chapter 16. For the moment, we only need to appreciate that, in equilibrium, bond prices, just like the prices of any assets, must adjust so as to provide their holders with the required rate of return and that this required rate of return will be equal to the risk-free rate (of appropriate maturity) plus a risk premium. For an individual bond, therefore, anything that changes the level of risk-free rates, or the general level of risk aversion in the market or the riskiness of the bond itself, will cause a change in the rate of return required and thus in the equilibrium price.

Figure 11.3 shows how we can interpret these changes in a bond's rate of return and its price in a supply and demand framework, just as we did with a company share. The supply of a bond available for trading is a *stock* and is shown by the vertical supply curve, S. The demand curve, D, is drawn downward-sloping to indicate that, *ceteris paribus*, the lower the price the greater the quantity of a bond investors will wish to hold because, as we know, the lower the price the higher the rate of return. In Figure 11.3, the initial equilibrium price is £70. Suppose now that market interest rates rise. Among the interest rates to rise will be the risk-free rate and this in turn raises the rate of return required on this bond. Investors are no longer willing to hold the stock of bonds while the rate of return is that rate generated by a price of £70. Sell orders exceed buy orders and the price falls. In Figure 11.3, the demand curve shifts downward to D″ and the new equilibrium price – the price which yields an appropriate rate of return – is shown as £60. If, by contrast, market interest rates fell, the required rate on all bonds would fall. At £70 the bond in Figure 11.3 would yield a rate of return which exceeded that available elsewhere. This would encourage an excess of buy orders over sell orders which we would show by an upward shift in the demand curve to D′. The new equilibrium price is shown as £80. Exercise 11.3 requires the calculation of rates of return associated with each of these levels of demand.

The rate of return on a 7% irredeemable bond trading at £70 is 10 per cent. At £80 the rate of return falls to 8.75 per cent while at £60 the rate of return is 11.67 per cent.

Again, as with company shares, changes in the required rate of return are determining not only prices but also the cost of new funds. A firm whose 7 per cent bonds currently trade at £70 must issue new bonds

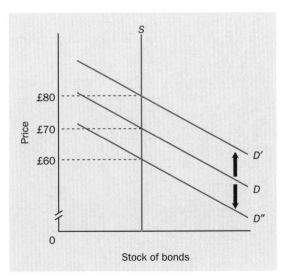

Figure 11.3 Bond prices and shifts in demand

Exercise 11.3 Bond prices and yields

Assume that Figure 11.3 depicts the market for a 7 per cent irredeemable bond.

1 What was the required rate of return at the original equilibrium price of £70?

2 To what level did the required rate rise to cause the equilibrium price to fall to £60?

3 To what level did the required rate fall to cause the equilibrium price to rise to £80?

(Answers appear in the text below.)

which (ignoring issue costs) bring in £70 for a commitment from the firm of £7 paid per year (or alternatively bring in £100 for a commitment of £10). If the bond's price falls to £60, new £100 bonds will not be bought unless the firm is willing to pay at least £11.67 for every £100 raised by the sale of those bonds.

11.4 The 'fundamentals' of asset valuation

The account that we have so far given of the determination of rates of return and of asset prices is a very orthodox or conventional one. In orthodox theory price adjusts in order that the asset provides the rate of return required by investors. When this condition is met, an asset is said to be *fairly valued* and its price equals its 'fair' or 'fundamental' value. This rate of return is derived from the risk-free rate of interest and a risk premium, and the latter in turn is equal to the quantity of undiversifiable risk attaching to the asset multiplied by the price of undiversifiable risk as set by the market for risky assets as a whole. Any change in these components changes the required rate of return and, *ceteris paribus*, the price of the asset. The reason that the price must adjust is that we assume that in the short run the income stream is unchanged. Thus, if we take shares as an example, we are assuming that dividend payments are fixed (by the performance of the company) and that the growth rate of dividends is also fixed (by the growth in productivity of the firm's assets).

Notice two features of this account. Firstly, *price is the dependent variable*. It is the price that adjusts in

order to satisfy investors' requirements for a return. Secondly, the rate of return (and therefore the price) is the outcome of a *rational* process. That is to say that every element in the story can be explained by economic agents trying consistently to maximize the benefit from some *real* economic activity. Figure 11.4 brings together the whole picture as we have developed it in the last four chapters. It uses share prices as an example. We look at the schema first and then try to show how each of the elements can be presented as the outcome of a rational process.

Reading from left to right, the figure reminds us that the required rate of return is equal to the risk-free rate (K_{rf}) plus the quantity of risk (β) times the market risk premium ($K_m - K_{rf}$). This is the CAPM (from Section 8.5). The (nominal) risk-free rate of interest (i) is made up of a real rate of interest (r) (Section 9.3), an inflation premium (π) (Section 9.3) and a term premium (l) (Section 10.2). This is the outcome of the interaction of the supply of and demand for loanable funds in conditions of zero risk, occasionally modified by central bank policy decisions. It is primarily the result of lenders trying to maximize their return from surrendering a current claim to consumption and borrowers trying to maximize the return from the projects in which they invest borrowed funds.

The risk premium on a whole market portfolio ($K_m - K_{rf}$) is the return required over and above the risk-free rate by investors endeavouring to maximize return while minimizing risk. The market risk premium is what they demand for a portfolio from which all diversifiable risk has been eliminated (Section 8.4).

In equilibrium, the required rate must be matched by the actual rate of return and for company shares

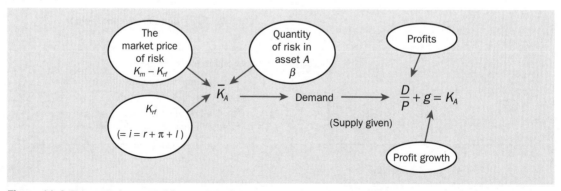

Figure 11.4 The capital asset pricing model

this means the sum of the dividend yield (D/P) and the earnings growth rate (g). The dividend available to shareholders depends upon the profit made by the firm and this depends upon the productivity of the underlying assets which constitute the real capital of the firm and the price which consumers are prepared to pay for the output from that capital equipment. In a perfect world, the price that the community is prepared to pay represents the addition to total welfare provided by the marginal unit of output. Provided that price is just equal to this marginal benefit, then total welfare is being maximized by the output from these assets and shareholders are earning a just reward for their contribution to satisfying these needs. The growth in dividends depends upon the rate of growth of productivity of the underlying assets, a rate which depends upon the firm's management's ability to follow a sound policy of reinvestment and to manage the assets. In the short run, all of these are given, except price.

Price is thus the dependent variable which adjusts in order to meet the requirements of a 'rational' process. Because the rationality lies in the behaviour of agents engaged in *real* economic activity, we tend to describe these determinants of a share's price as its **fundamentals**. If P is determined by $\overline{K}$ (given D and g) we say that price is determined by the underlying fundamentals.

11.5 An alternative interpretation

Before leaving this section of the book, however, it is worth pausing to reflect on the overall picture that we have drawn and to consider how well it, or its implications, reflects the reality which we think we see.

The first point to make perhaps is that where tradable financial assets are concerned, the dominant discourse concerns *prices* and not rates of return. It is true that newspapers report and commentators discuss deposit accounts and insurance and pension policies in terms of rate of return. But where an asset is tradable almost all comment relates to its recent, latest and next-most-likely price movement. Rates of return are just not part of the conversation.

The *Financial Times* interest in the Hilton Group as reported in Box 11.1 shows this quite well. First of all it tells us that the share *price* has almost doubled in the last year. It then goes on to consider how the

BOX 11.1 Good gambling news proves a winner for hotel group
By Peter John

Hilton Group, which owns the rights to the Hilton brand outside the US and operates about 400 hotels in more than 75 countries, is on a three-star rating. The shares have almost doubled in the past 12 months, with the most recent rise prompted by revived broker suggestions that Hilton should hive off its 2,300 Ladbroke betting shops, which represents 80 per cent of profits. It pushed the prospective p/e – based on 2004 earnings per share forecasts of 15.7p – to 16 times, a slight discount to the sector. Hilton insiders do not believe that split will happen but the shares have been driven by positive news in the gambling industry – the removal of betting tax and the liberalisation of fixed-odd betting machines. And just as those aspects start to be discounted in the price, the cyclical recovery of the hotel industry is getting into gear. The latest survey by Deloitte showed London was booming and the consultancy expects the effects to ripple out across the UK and Europe. The slight p/e discount may reflect the continuing caution of US visitors and their return could provide that extra star.

Source: *Financial Times*, 24 April 2004. Reprinted with permission.

current price compares with the price of other hotel/leisure groups. The comparison is done by looking at the 'prospective p/e' meaning the price one has to pay per unit of profit, given current profit expectations. The current price of Hilton Group shares (260p) is about 16 times the amount of profit that the shareholder is buying, slightly less than one would have to pay for the same amount of profit in rival groups. The report finishes by suggesting that this discount could disappear if the number of US visitors to Europe returns to normal. Notice also that while the report is preoccupied with *price* rather than rate of return it focuses upon the *relative* price rather than the *absolute* price. The issue for the *Financial Times* is only whether Hilton's price is 'high' or 'low' compared with the price of shares in similar leisure groups. This is another common characteristic of share price evaluation as it is carried out in practice. But if we were really convinced that there is a specific rate of return which is correct for Hilton Group, bearing in mind the fundamentals, then this rate of return would produce a unique *absolute* price: a price which is fair for the firm given its characteristics, *regardless of what prices may be attached to similar firms.*

This may not be significant. It may be that everyone discussing asset prices automatically carries the corresponding rate of return in his or her head and talks only of 'price' because it is more convenient than 'rate of return'. On the other hand, it may be that the financial community talks in price terms because price is genuinely more interesting, and not simply the reciprocal of a rate of return. This is not a silly idea; one can see why it could happen. For example, if we go back to our share valuation formula, Equation 11.3, we can see that a price change is part of the rate of return. In the long run, dividends increase (*g* is positive). If dividend yields are not to rise to infinity (that is *D/P* is stationary) then *P* must also rise. And we all know that investors are in practice very interested in the capital appreciation of shares which may well be a larger part of the total rate of return than the dividend yield.

But we know that prices change because of changes in demand, whatever may be the ultimate cause of the demand shift. A shift in demand causes a change in price just as effectively if it is the outcome of a (false) rumour about a change in interest rates as it does when it is the outcome of an actual change. And once we separate the desire to buy or sell from actual events and link it to *expectations* of events we open the door to the possibility that demand may shift in response to a very wide range of forces, ranging from those that might be more or less rational in origin to those that have no logical connection with asset values.

Let us think about some possibilities, beginning with events which are strictly rational (in the sense we are using here) and then moving towards the more fantastic (but not impossible). An *actual* change in the risk-free rate of interest causes a change in asset prices because it changes the demand for the asset by changing the **present value** of its future income stream by changing the rate at which we discount that future income stream. Holding the asset when the interest rate changes thus leads to a capital gain (a positive contribution to the overall rate of return) or a capital loss (a negative one). It makes sense, therefore, for investors to try to anticipate changes in interest rates. In these circumstances, demand will shift, and prices will change when agents *expect* a change in interest rates. An *expected* event causes an *actual* event. For an individual investor, however, making a capital gain

or avoiding a capital loss does not require a belief or expectation that interest rates will change in the very near future. It requires only a belief (or expectation) that other investors believe or expect that interest rates are going to change and that they are going to buy or sell on the strength of that expectation. Indeed, it is not necessary even to believe that other investors believe that interest rates are going to change but only that other investors are going to buy (or sell) *for whatever reason.* This gives rise to two features of investor behaviour, one of which is certainly observable, while we cannot be sure about the second. The first is the sensitivity of demand (and price) to actual events which might help to predict interest rate changes. This often involves forming an implicit government policy reaction function. For example, if investors know that the government is particularly concerned about the rate of growth of credit and the build-up of inflationary pressures, the announcement of a big rise in bank lending causes asset prices to fall because investors make the connection between an undesirable credit surge and the likelihood of a rise in official interest rates to try to stop it. In small open economies, changes in the balance of trade often cause asset price changes through the same (interest rate anticipation) mechanism.

The other feature of investor behaviour which follows from wanting to participate in capital gains and avoid capital losses is the apparent 'herd' behaviour which leads a rising asset price (for example) to go on rising even after any fundamental reason for an increase has ended. A situation where this happens is known as a **bubble**. Sometimes, as with the Big Bull Market in the USA in 1928–29, the buying behaviour affects the whole market. The 1987 crash might be an example of herd selling. The technology stock boom and slump in 2000/01 certainly showed aspects of herd behaviour. It is not possible to be absolutely sure whether investor behaviour corresponds to that of a bubble merely by observation. It is always possible to argue that the market's aversion to risk is diminishing or that investors genuinely think that future growth in productivity is going to be much higher than in the past (a lower $\overline{K}$, higher *g*, remember). Or, alternatively, that they genuinely think that the fundamentals are getting very rapidly worse. It is, though, hard to believe that fundamentals, or even people's perception of the fundamentals of asset values, could change so much and so rapidly during the great booms and crashes of asset prices. It is very tempting to think that investors are looking after their own short-term self-interest by sticking with the herd.[3] As John Maynard Keynes once famously remarked, 'it is not sensible to pay 25 for an investment of which you believe the prospective yield to justify a value of 30, if you also believe that the market will value it at 20 three months hence' (Keynes, 1936, p. 155). Indeed, if you were a fund manager who insisted on dealing in assets on the basis of their fundamentals when everyone else was buying in a bubble and making large profits, your clients could accuse you of negligence.

If it *is* true that investors in tradable assets are sometimes buying and selling on the basis of what they expect the price to do in the very near future, rather than on the rate of return offered by the asset, then Figure 11.4 gives a misleading picture. Causalities are reversed. Investors are aiming at a target price for the asset and the rate of the return becomes the dependent variable. In the world we have just described, buying and selling drives the price, as it always does, to an equilibrium where sell orders match buy orders, but the rate of return, instead of determining this price, is itself determined by it.

Which of the two pictures we have just described is the more accurate is an important issue. The rational determination of prices by the required rate of return is essential if resources are to be allocated efficiently as we described in Section 1.5.3. We said there that the return to investors was just enough to compensate them for surrendering their ability to purchase real resources plus whatever degree of risk was involved in so doing. The rate of return that they required was the cost of capital. The fact that consumers were ultimately prepared to pay a price for the goods produced by the real capital assets financed by investors indicated that their welfare gain from the goods produced just matched the sacrifice of the providers of finance. No *net* benefits could result to society by changing either the volume of investment or its composition.

This happy situation is not the outcome if people buy assets just because the price is rising (or sell just because the price is falling). In these circumstances the return to investors could settle anywhere, and where it settles the cost of capital also settles. For example, take the case where a company's share price rises on

the rumour of some new product development and, even when the rumour subsides, the price goes on rising because investors are impressed by its recent capital appreciation. Perhaps its price before the rumour was £2 and the dividend payment was 8p per share. The dividend yield was 4 per cent and this was the cost (in terms of dividend per pound raised) of raising new capital by issuing new shares. Suppose that after a few weeks' buying the price settles at £3. If the firm now decides to raise new capital by issuing new shares then the cost (in dividend per pound raised) is now 8/300 or 2.66 per cent. In the circumstances, the firm may be encouraged to expand, though there is no indication that the benefits to society from the output that it produces have increased. Furthermore, the firm's enhanced share price makes it easier for it to make a bid for other firms (by issuing some of its own shares to shareholders of the target firm). There are resource allocation arguments in favour of takeovers. For example, a poorly performing firm, if correctly valued, will have a low share price and will be a target for more efficient firms which will bring their more efficient management to the poorly performing firm. But where a firm is valued as the result of a bubble, its price is no longer an indication of superior performance. We cannot then expect that benefits will follow if it takes over a firm which is priced more cheaply – but correctly.

11.6 Summary

The present value of an asset is equal to the sum of the future stream of income payments that it provides, each payment suitably discounted. The rate of discount is also the rate of return on an asset and so the appropriate rate of discount is the *required* rate of return. In equilibrium, the asset's price will equal its present value and its actual rate of return will equal the required rate of return.

The required rate of return is given by the risk-free rate plus the quantity of undiversifiable risk multiplied by the market price of risk. An asset whose price is determined according to these principles is said to

---

[3] Another point to remember is that once we recognize the importance of 'perceptions' we should also recognize that people's perceptions are influenced by emotions. Good news in the present may make us more optimistic about future events which have no rational connections with the good news.

be priced according to its fundamentals since the determinants of its price all reflect the rational decisions of agents engaged in real economic activity. If assets are priced according to these principles, a case can be made that capital is being allocated in an optimal way.

However, there are occasions when asset prices behave in a way that suggests that other forces are at work. It is hard, sometimes, to believe that the fundamentals of an asset's value change so fast or so much that they can account for dramatic changes in asset prices. In these circumstances it is tempting to think that price takes on a momentum of its own. Instead of the required rate of return determining the price, the price is driven by some herd-like behaviour on the part of investors with the result that the rate of return becomes the dependent variable and may settle anywhere, with no rational foundation. In these circumstances, we cannot be sure that capital is being allocated efficiently.

Key concepts in this chapter

Actual rate of return
Bubbles
Capital appreciation
Consols
Coupon
Coupon rate
Dividend
Dividend yield
Equilibrium price
Fundamentals

Irredeemable bonds
Non-tradable assets
Original maturity
Perpetuals
Present value
Redeemable bonds
Residual maturity
Required rate of return
Tradable assets

Questions and problems

1 Imagine that the central bank raises short-term interest rates. Discuss and explain the effect on:

(a) the rate of return required by investors in bonds;

(b) the price of ordinary company shares.

2 Suppose that investors expect inflation to increase in future. Explain the likely effect on bond prices. (You may wish to refer to Figure 10.1.)

3 How would a fall in interest rates affect the required rate of return on securities? Using a supply and demand diagram, show the effect of this fall upon the equilibrium price of a security.

4 You are advising a friend who holds company shares whose return plots below the security market line (see Chapter 8). Would you advise your friend to hold or to sell? Explain your answer.

5 Imagine a security whose price has been unchanged for several days. What does this stable price imply about the buying and selling of that security?

6 Suppose that you decide to take a round-the-world cruise and that you will pay for this by (a) selling bonds and (b) withdrawing your savings deposits from a bank. What effect does (a) have on the total quantity of bonds in existence? What effect does (b) have on the quantity of savings deposits? Explain any difference.

7 Explain the basic principle underlying the valuation of any asset.

8 How would you expect the price of (a) a short-dated bond and (b) a long-dated bond to be affected by a given increase in market interest rates? How would you account for any difference?

9   What do we mean when we say that an asset is priced acording to its 'fundamentals'? In what sense might it be argued that securities priced according to fundamentals are priced according to rational principles?

10 From the financial press, collect some recent reports of security market behaviour. Do those reports suggest to you that price changes are driven by changes in desired rates of return or by expectations of future price changes?

11 Suppose that you hold shares in a company whose future profitability you think is likely to decline, but you see that these shares are still being recommended for purchase in the financial press. What would you do?

Further reading

D Blake, *Financial Market Analysis* (London: McGraw-Hill, 2e, 2000) Ch. 13

E J Elton, M J Gruber, S J Brown and W N Goetzmann, *Modern Portfolio Theory and Investment Analysis* (Chichester: Wiley, 6e, 2006) Chs 18, 20

P G A Howells and K Bain, *Financial Markets and Institutions* (London: Pearson, 5e, 2007) Ch. 6

P John, 'Good gambling news proves a winner for hotel group', *Financial Times*, 24 April 2004

J M Keynes, *General Theory of Employment, Interest and Money* (London: Macmillan, 1936)

F Mishkin, *The Economics of Money, Banking and Financial Markets* (New York: Pearson, 7e, 2004), Ch. 7

K Pilbeam, *Finance and Financial Markets* (London: Palgrave, 2005)

Appendix to Chapter 11

When n_m is small, Equation 11.5 is fairly easily solved. However, when n_m is large, calculating the present value of a stream of coupon payments can be tedious. Thus, it is worth remembering that the present value of a stream of income payments can alternatively be written as:

$$\frac{C}{i}\left(1 - \frac{1}{(1 + i)^{n_m}}\right)$$

Substituting this into Equation 11.5, we can then find the price more easily as:

$$P = \frac{C}{i}\left(1 - \frac{1}{(1 + i)^{n_m}}\right) + \frac{M}{(1 + i)^{n_m}} \quad \text{(A11.1)}$$

Note also that if $n_m = \infty$, the value of

$$\frac{1}{(1 + i)^{n_m}} = 0$$

and

$$\frac{M}{(1 + i)^{n_m}} = 0$$

Hence the value of a perpetual bond is:

$$\frac{C}{i}(1 - 0) + 0 = \frac{C}{i} \quad \text{(A11.2)}$$

Part 4

Money and Banking

Chapter 12 | # Banks and the supply of money

What you will learn in this chapter:

- The essential characteristics of money

- Why monetary assets are difficult to identify

- Which assets are officially classified as money

- How changes in the money supply are reflected in banks' balance sheets

- How to analyse changes in the money supply through the monetary base and flow of funds models of money supply determination

- The range of techniques available to the authorities for the purposes of money supply control

12.1 Introduction

In the next two chapters we turn our attention to banks and the supply of and demand for money. There are four reasons for this.

Firstly, banks themselves form one particular subset of financial intermediaries. In most developed countries they also make up a *large* subset of financial intermediaries and so they are worth studying for this reason alone.

Secondly, the liabilities of banks are the principal components of any country's money supply and so the behaviour of banks is intimately connected with changes in the supply of money. We pointed out in Section 1.5.1 that one general effect of any increase in financial intermediation is the creation of liquidity, but if the increased activity involves primarily banks, then the increase in liquidity takes the specific form of 'money'.

Thirdly, many economists take the view that changes in the money supply have important effects upon the economy, especially if the changes are large or sudden. *Exactly* what these effects may be, and whether they have an impact in the short run or in the long run and whether the effects are temporary or permanent, are matters of controversy. But the fact remains that whatever version of this view one accepts, bank behaviour may have effects upon the economy which are rather different from those of other intermediaries.

Fourthly, even if one doubts the importance of money in the economy, anyone interested in finance has to recognize that governments and central banks certainly behave as if it matters. Thus they tend to adopt policies which set at least broad limits to the desirable rate of monetary growth and then take such action as they can to keep monetary growth within those limits. This leads them invariably to make changes to short-term interest rates (as we saw in Section 9.4) – raising them to reduce monetary growth, for example.

For all these reasons, therefore, the behaviour of banks is an important issue. In this chapter, we concentrate upon questions which are related to the theme of money *supply*. This leads us to consider what money is, how the components of the money supply change over time, how money is created and finally what the authorities can do to control its creation.

In Chapter 13, we shall focus upon questions which are related to the theme of money *demand*. This leads us to consider how people decide how much of their wealth to hold in monetary form and how their behaviour is affected by a mismatch between the quantity of money available and the quantity they wish to hold. It is here that the controversy about the effects of changes in money supply have their origin. People may respond in ways that have little lasting effect upon the economy, or their attempts to adjust to monetary shocks may be very important. This behaviour is summed up in what is known as the 'transmission mechanism'. In Chapter 14 we shall look at what governments have thought about the importance of money at various times and how these views have been reflected in policy.

12.2 The definition of money

12.2.1 Some general principles

One traditional way of defining money is to look at what it does, or what we require it to do, and then to see what in practice we use for that purpose. We shall do that in a moment but first let us begin by clarifying some important terms which sometimes cause confusion in discussions of what money is.

We begin with **real wealth**. Wealth (alternatively called *capital*) is a *stock* of assets, including human capital, which can be used to produce a *flow* of goods and services over a period of time. Thus we are all familiar with the idea that we use some of our human capital (in the form of labour) each year in order to produce a flow of new goods (books, computer programs, mobile phones and so on) or services (such as lectures or taxi rides) each year. In any year, we shall consume, that is, use up, a large proportion of the income we produce. The rest is saved. We shall also use up a proportion of wealth in the production of that income. Clearly, wealth consumed or used up in the production of income must be replaced each year or the production process must eventually grind to a halt.[1]

---

[1]   **(Real) income** was famously defined by Hicks (1946) as all that output that could be consumed while leaving us as well off at the end of the period as the beginning. This is restating what we have said, with different priorities. Looking at total output, Hicks insists on deducting sufficient saving to *ensure* that wealth is unchanged. What is left is income which can be consumed or some further saving may be carried out, adding to future wealth.

Saving is an addition to wealth. If saving is sufficient to replace the wealth consumed then we say that *net investment* is zero. If saving exceeds the consumption of wealth then we have positive net investment. Our real wealth increases and opens up the possibility that more of it may be devoted to production in future. The real economy expands. All of these concepts, wealth, capital, income and saving, are expressed so far in *real terms*. That is to say we are talking about *volumes* of goods, services and skills. These volumes determine what we can *really* consume, save, invest and so on. It is these volumes that *really* matter to our welfare. Whatever price or value we place upon these volumes makes no difference to their quantity and no difference to our real welfare.

In everyday language, however, we think and talk about income, saving, wealth and so on in **money terms**. We shall see just why that is in the next paragraph. But it is important to be absolutely clear that 'money' is merely some token in which we choose to reckon these magnitudes and use to carry out exchanges. Classical economists used to describe money as a 'veil' – meaning something which partially hid what was really going on, but which had no effect upon it. In Section 13.3 we shall see that it might be going too far to say that the quantity of money available has no effect at all on real behaviour but it is crucial at this stage to realize that 'money' is something that exists quite independently of the real goods and services, income, wealth and so on which it is being used to measure or exchange. It is because 'money' is so intimately connected with the measurement and exchange of goods and services that there is sometimes a danger of confusion.

Firstly, when it comes to measuring the *total* volume of production, income, saving, wealth and so on we require some common standard in which to express them. In other words, we need a **unit of account**, and that is provided by 'money'. Thus we may talk of this year's national income as £1200bn and we may forecast that over the next year it will grow to £1250bn.

Furthermore, while it may be true that the production of real goods and services determines our real income and the amount that we can save and add to real wealth, we do not individually consume what we produce. Typically, we sell our labour to employers who organize production and pay us wages and salaries in the form of 'money' which they in turn receive from buyers of the goods and services or by borrowing. What this tells us is that modern economies are 'exchange' rather than 'barter' economies. This brings us to another function of money, which is its use as a **medium of exchange**. The movement from barter to the use of money brings with it a large saving of resources. These gains, which come under the general heading of seigniorage,[2] include a large reduction in the information costs involved in comparing relative prices of goods and services throughout the economy.[3]

The movement from barter to exchange, using money, brings also a greater flexibility from being able to separate income and consumption decisions in time. In a barter economy, a decision to save would mean setting aside something that one had produced in the hope that it might be useful at some time in the future or, alternatively, exchanging it now for some other good again in the hope that it might turn out to be what one needed. With money, one can decide to save now, in the knowledge that those savings will definitely be needed at some time in the future but without knowing exactly when, or in exactly what form or for what purpose. When the time comes, the savings, in money form, can be converted into whatever is required. Because saving (adding to wealth) is being carried out by holding 'money', money is said here to be functioning as a **store of wealth**.

Finally, in a monetary exchange economy, it is often advantageous to carry out exchanges and payments at different times. Clearly, it is not much benefit to households to arrange a daily delivery of milk or newspapers to their home if they are required to go to the dairy or newsagent every day to pay for the milk or newspapers. One of the many benefits of a monetary economy is the availability of credit. But credit will only be possible if there is some form in which debts and credits can be recorded to everyone's satisfaction and if there is some acceptable form in which the debts can be finally extinguished. We know, of

---

[2] *Seigniorage* may be defined as the gains which accrue to the issuer of a currency because the issuer (a government, for example) obtains real resources in return for non-interest-bearing, non-repayable debt.
[3] Information costs involved in a non-monetary system can be reduced by the development of more sophisticated forms of barter. Nonetheless, costs within a barter system remain very high.

course, that debts are recorded in money form (money's role as a unit of account again) and it is accepted that they will eventually be settled using 'money'. This is money acting as a **standard of deferred payment**.

These – the unit of account, medium of exchange, store of wealth and standard of deferred payment – are the roles that money is traditionally said to perform. The major ones, by which we mean that they may be a means whereby money may have some effect upon the rest of the economy and about which there is certainly some controversy, are the medium of exchange and store of wealth functions. The next question is: 'does identifying these functions enable us to identify "money"?'

So far as the unit of account, medium of exchange and standard of deferred payment roles are concerned, it seems very clear that 'money' must be something which is universally acceptable. What it is that makes one asset in particular universally acceptable is an interesting question which has fascinated economists over the years. One can lay down certain physical essentials – it must be cheap to produce, highly divisible and convenient to carry – but an asset could have all these qualities and still not function as money. One can appeal to official regulations. Most countries define certain assets as **legal tender**, meaning that people *must* accept them in exchange. In the UK, for example, notes and coin are defined as legal tender, at least for transactions of specified type. But most transactions (by value) are carried out in most economies by a much wider range of assets. The dominant medium of exchange in most economies is bank deposits. One might argue that these are made acceptable by the understanding that they are fully convertible on demand into legal tender and that legal tender itself is ultimately guaranteed by the state. It seems hard to imagine, however, that if the idea of legal tender were to be abandoned, bank deposits would cease to function as the main medium of exchange.

Money's ability to function as a store of value does not rely so heavily upon its general acceptability but requires another characteristic which may also be important in making it acceptable. This is stability in its value. To be persuaded to use money as a store of value, people must be persuaded that its future purchasing power will be little different from what it is now. At the very least, people will wish to be assured

that there is not a general tendency for its purchasing power to diminish. This requirement may not be absolute. Since money yields numerous benefits, it will not lose its attractiveness, even as a store of value, until the rate of depreciation reaches such a pace that it outweighs the benefits. Such rates have, of course, been reached at various time and places. The Weimar Republic and Hungary in the 1920s, some Latin American states in the 1970s and perhaps Russia in 1994–95 yield examples of what happens when confidence in the currency finally collapses because of doubts about its future purchasing power. Those that can do so move their savings out of the country (adopting dollars or euros as alternative stores of value) and exchange takes place using alternative commodities.[4] It is to avoid situations like this, and the disruption to trade that follows, that governments and central banks place such emphasis upon minimizing inflationary pressures. In conditions of hyper-inflation, no amount of legislation about 'legal tender' will make the official currency acceptable.

The important lesson that we must draw from this 'acceptability' criterion is that it does not provide a timeless definition of 'money'. What is widely acceptable now was not generally acceptable even 100 years ago. Indeed, there was a time when people were reluctant to accept government issues of notes and coins of low intrinsic value, preferring to be paid in precious metals. Defining token money as 'legal tender' was initially introduced by monarchs and governments which wished to enjoy the seigniorage benefits of issuing token money of low intrinsic value but found that their subjects were reluctant to move away from gold and silver coins.

More importantly for us, however, is that the acceptability criterion means that 'money' continues to change. This in turn poses problems for authorities wishing to control the amount of money in circulation – especially if they try to do it by 'direct' or non-price methods of control. In most economies, the general public, banks and other financial institutions have become very adept at developing money substitutes. In the next section we shall see that there have been major changes in official definitions of money in recent years and that these have been necessary because of changes in private sector behaviour.

---

4   Quite often cigarettes, since they meet the criteria of divisibility and low carrying costs.

12.2.2 Official definitions

In this section we look at the assets which various monetary authorities choose to recognize as components of their money stock. What is apparent for each country is that money can be defined 'narrowly' or 'broadly'. The normal practice is to attach numbers to these official magnitudes using the lowest numbers to refer to the narrowest magnitudes. In Tables 12.1 and 12.2 we describe the national definitions of money currently in use in the eurozone and the USA. We also give the recent magnitudes of the various components of the monetary definitions so that the approximate proportions can be seen. In an ideal world, the

Table 12.1 Money definitions in the eurozone, end June 2007

Name	Components	Size (€bn)
Reserves	Currency with monetary financial institutions (MFIs) + MFIs' holdings of deposits with the central bank	191.3
M1	Currency in circulation outside MFIs + non-MFIs' holdings of sight deposits	3,784.7
M2	M1 + non-MFIs' holdings of time deposits	6,954.8
M3	M2 + non-MFIs' holdings of repurchase agreements, money market instruments and bonds with <2 years to maturity	8,183.3

Source: European Central Bank (2007) *Monthly Bulletin*, August, tables 1.4 and 2.3. This information may be obtained free of charge through the ECB website www.ecb.int. Reprinted with permission.

Table 12.2 Money definitions in the USA, end June 2007

Name	Components	Size (US$bn)
Monetary base	Currency in circulation and with banks + commercial banks' deposits with Federal Reserve banks	819
M1	Currency in circulation + travellers cheques of non-bank issuers + demand deposits at commercial banks (excluding those amounts held by depository institutions, the US government, and foreign banks and official institutions) + other checkable deposits	1,369
M2	M1 + savings deposits (including money market deposit accounts) + small-denomination time deposits + balances in retail money market mutual funds	7,248
M3	M2 + balances in institutional money market mutual funds + large-denomination time deposits (>$100,000) + repurchase agreement (RP) liabilities of depository institutions, in denominations of $100,000 or more, on US government and federal agency securities + Eurodollars held by US addressees at foreign branches of US banks worldwide and at all banking offices in the United Kingdom and Canada	see note below

Note: In March 2006 the Federal Reserve announced that it would cease publication of an M3 measure because 'M3 does not appear to convey any additional information about economic activity that is not already embodied in M2 and has not played a role in the monetary policy process for many years.'

Source: www.federalreserve.gov (2007) Statistical releases (September) H3 and H6. Reprinted with permission.

definitions would be consistent across countries, and we shall see in a moment that there are indeed some similarities. But there are some significant differences of detail and these illustrate very clearly what we saw in the last section, namely that which assets function as money depends upon their acceptability in that role. This in turn depends upon the particular history and monetary institutions of each country. The fact that the old broad money definition in Germany excluded the equivalent of building society deposits, while in the UK they are included, is a reflection of the different way in which people treat these deposits.

The narrowest definition of money is that which makes up the **monetary base** or **high powered money**. This consists of notes and coin (or 'currency' or 'cash' as it is sometimes called). Most monetary aggregates include assets held only outside banks (that is, by the 'non-bank private sector' or simply 'non-banks' as we describe them in the tables). But the monetary base is unique in including cash held both by non-banks and in the vaults of the commercial banking system. It also includes commercial bank deposits at the central bank. The name 'high powered money' is derived from the base: multiplier model of money supply determination (see Section 12.4). In this model, the monetary base forms a stock of highly liquid potential 'reserves', on the basis of which commercial banks can create **broad money** as a multiple of the monetary base.[5] Since the multiple is often very large, this model predicts a large change in broad money from a small change in the base – changes in the base thus appear very powerful.

The next monetary aggregate in most systems is **narrow money**, sometimes called M1. This consists of notes and coin, but this time only the notes and coin held by non-banks[6] together with non-banks' holdings of bank **sight deposits**. These are deposits which can be used (to make payment or to exchange for cash) on demand. They are sometimes referred to as **demand** or **checking deposits**. Until recently, it used to be a characteristic of sight deposits that they did not pay interest. The benefits to depositors lay in the fact that banks did not charge for the money transmission services to which these accounts gave access. In some monetary systems, however, a distinction can now be made between sight deposits that do pay interest and those that do not. In such systems, this generates a subset of narrow money known as *non-interest-bearing narrow money*.

In many monetary systems there is also an M2 aggregate. As a rule, this is a broader or more inclusive measure of money than M1, though not so broad as M3. Exactly what is included in aggregates broader than M1 is, as we noted above, very much a reflection of the particular characteristics of a country's monetary system. In the USA the difference between M1 and M2 includes some savings deposits but also Eurodollar deposits held with overseas branches of US banks and even some outstanding repurchase agreements. This reflects the fact first of all that such assets are significant in quantity in the USA and also a belief by the Federal Reserve that in the USA people treat them with a degree of 'moneyness' that means they should be included. The same need not apply in other countries. There is one exception to the definition of M2 as lying on a direct line from M1 to M3. In the UK, M2 is used to refer to an aggregate which tries to measure 'retail deposits'. These are deposits held by households, mainly for transactions purposes. Unlike M1, therefore, they include building society deposits. Since M3 did not contain building society deposits this was a leap beyond M3. But UK M2 also excluded large sight deposits held by firms with banks and in that sense was narrower than M1.

The next definition, used in all systems, is that which captures the components of *broad money*. This incorporates **time deposits**, deposits for which, strictly speaking, notice of withdrawal is required. Needless to say, time deposits pay interest. Unlike sight deposits, within any system time deposits come with many different terms attached. They vary with respect to the period to maturity, from one week to one year, for example. They vary in the interest rates they pay – typically higher rates for longer maturities – and they vary in their penalties for early withdrawal. Since the late 1960s, some time deposits have provided their owners with a **certificate of deposit**, stating the

---

[5]   In *International Financial Statistics*, what we have called the monetary base is titled 'reserves'.

[6]   The repeated use of the phrase 'non-bank private sector' or 'non-banks' as an alternative to 'the general public' serves to emphasize an important point, namely, that with the exception of the monetary base, money exists only when it is held outside banks. There is no quantity of monetary assets somewhere in store, waiting to come into circulation. Whatever else money is, it is what people are willing to hold. We return to this when we discuss the demand for money in Chapter 13.

amount and the terms of the deposit. This 'CD' in turn has been tradable in organized markets, giving the underlying deposit something of the liquidity characteristics of a sight deposit.

So far, we have measured the quantity of money by simply aggregating all its components at their nominal value. While this may be an obvious (and straightforward) approach it suffers from both a theoretical and a practical weakness. At the theoretical level, simple aggregation implies that we are dealing with homogeneous assets. We seem to be saying, for example, that *from a monetary point of view*, £1bn of CDs is the same as £1bn of notes and coin. The mere fact that CDs pay interest while notes and coin do not, however, indicates some degree of differentiation since otherwise no one would hold notes and coin. At the practical level, economists are usually interested in the closeness of the relationship between a monetary aggregate and income. This is likely to increase with the extent to which the aggregate is dominated by assets used for transactions. However, as we have seen, it is difficult to know exactly where to draw the line between whole classes of assets for this purpose. Notes and coin and sight deposits are all perfectly liquid and are obvious transactions media but we know that time deposits can be switched to sight deposits quickly and cheaply and that other, apparently less liquid, assets have sufficient liquidity that they could still be relevant to transactions, albeit to a lesser degree. The **Divisia** approach involves weighting each of the component assets according to the extent to which they provide transactions services. If this could be done accurately, then the resulting index should measure the quantity of money available in the economy for transactions purposes and should be more closely linked to expenditure and income.

The weights given to each asset are often said to represent the 'user cost' of the asset. To measure the user cost, we must first choose a benchmark asset which provides *no* transactions services. For example, the Bank of England publishes a Divisia index going back to 1977 based upon the components of M4 and using the rate on three-month local authority deposits (the 3mLA rate) as the benchmark. We then subtract the rate of interest on the component asset from the rate on the benchmark asset (the 3mLA rate). Notes and coin are given a weight of one representing the difference between the 3mLA rate and zero. Each other asset, a_i, is then given a lesser weight, w_i, equal to the difference between the benchmark rate and its

own rate, i_i, as a fraction of the benchmark notes and coin differential. In symbols:

$$w_i = (3\,\text{mLA rate} - i_i)/(3\,\text{mLA rate} - 0)$$

The index, D, is then the sum of the nominal value of each asset adjusted for its appropriate weight:

$$D = \sum a_i \cdot w_i$$

If it is the transactions services of money in which we are primarily interested, then Divisia clearly possesses several attractions.

Before we leave this discussion of the definition of money, we look briefly at the UK aggregates and their recent history. This will provide further illustration of the points that we made above, namely, that what is acceptable as money varies with time and between countries with different institutional arrangements. But it also shows something further. In recent years, governments have often thought it important to control the growth of money, in order to confine it within a 'target' range. (We look at the techniques of control in Section 12.5 and at the theory behind it in Section 13.4.) Inevitably, such a policy requires the choice of one or more aggregates for control and the choice should be made ideally in the light of theory. For example, if it is thought that the growth rate of money matters because of its role as a medium of exchange, it makes sense to target a monetary aggregate like M1, where the components are mainly used for transactions purposes. Table 12.3 shows how the status of various aggregates has changed over the years in the UK.

One might ask why there have been so many changes, with new aggregates being developed while old ones are discontinued and while others change from being 'targeted' to merely 'monitored'. We can offer three reasons. Firstly, there are 'institutional' changes, or changes over time in the way in which people treat financial assets. M1 in the UK, for example, does not include building society deposits, and so it might once have been a suitable 'transactions' aggregate when building society deposits were used overwhelmingly as a savings medium. But when building societies started to provide money transmission services during the 1980s, M1 seemed no longer appropriate and a new, M2, aggregate was developed (see above). In 1989 the Abbey National building society announced that it was going to convert to a bank. As a result, its deposits would become part of M3 (causing a jump of about 11 per cent in the size of M3). Hence it was decided to abandon M3 as the official measure

Table 12.3 UK monetary aggregates

Name	Components	First published[1]	Discontinued[1]	Targeted
Notes and coin	Notes and coin outside the Bank of England	May 2006		
Reserve balances	Banks' holdings of reserve balances with the Bank of England	May 2006		
M0 (wide monetary base)	Notes and coin outside the Bank of England + banks' operational deposits	June 1981	April 2006	1984–2006[2]
NIBM1 (non-interest-bearing M1)	Notes and coin in circulation + NBPS[3] holdings of non-interest-bearing sight bank deposits	June 1975	May 1991	
M1	NIBM1 + NBPS holdings of interest-bearing sight bank deposits	Dec. 1970	July 1989	1982–84
M2	NIBM1 + NBPS holdings of interest-bearing retail deposits with banks and building societies + NBPS holdings of National Savings ordinary accounts	Sept. 1982[4]		
M3 (£M3 until May 1987)	M1 + NBPS holdings of bank time deposits + NBPS holdings of CDs with banks	March 1977[5]	July 1989	1976–86
M3c (M3 until May 1987)	M3 + NBPS holdings of foreign currency bank deposits	Dec. 1970[5]	July 1989	
M3H	A UK version of euro-M3 (see Table 12.1)	August 1992		
PSL1	M3 − NBPS bank time deposits with original maturity > 2 years + NBPS holdings of bank bills, treasury bills, local authority deposits and certificates of tax deposit	Sept. 1979	May 1987	
PSL2	PSL1 + NBPS building society deposits (excluding term shares) + short-term National Savings instruments	Sept. 1979	May 1987	1982–84
M4	M3 + NBPS building society shares, deposits and CDs − building society holdings of bank deposits, CDs and notes and coin	May 1987		
M4c	M4 + NBNBSPS[6] bank and building society foreign currency deposits	May 1987	May 1991	
M5	M4 + NBNBSPS holdings of bank bills, treasury bills, local authority deposits and certificates of tax deposit	May 1987	May 1991	

Table 12.3 *Continued*

Name	Components	First published[1]	Discontinued[1]	Targeted
	+ short-term National Savings instruments − building society holdings of bank deposits, CDs and notes and coin			
'Liquid assets outside M4'	M5 + NBNBSPS holdings of bank and building society foreign currency deposits + further liquid assets of NBNBSPS and overseas sectors (see text)	May 1991		
DCE (Domestic credit expansion)	*Change* in bank lending to the non-bank private and public sectors	Dec. 1972	March 1986	1967–69
'Divisia'		August 1993		1976–79

[1] First published in this form. The data may have been available (by extraction from other series) at earlier dates. Consequently, when first published the series may extend backwards to include earlier values. Likewise, when a series is discontinued, this does not mean that it cannot still be constructed by extraction from other series. This emphasizes our point that publication of data in a particular form reflects an *official or policy interest* in the data in that form.   [2] 'Monitored'.   [3] NBPS = non-bank private sector.   [4] Not to be confused with an earlier M2 aggregate (Dec. 1970–Dec. 1971) which was roughly midway between M1 and M3.   [5] £M3 and M3 included public sector £ bank deposits until March 1984.   [6] 'Non-bank, non-bank building society private sector', sometimes known as 'M4 private sector' (M4PS).

of broad money and switch instead to M4 which would be unaffected by this (and subsequent) conversions. More recently, in 2006, the Bank of England introduced a series of reforms to UK money markets which led to a large increase in the quantity of reserves held by banks. This would have produced a large jump in the magnitude of M0, which included those reserves and so the M0 series was discontinued. Secondly, in some regimes aggregates seem to be subject to 'Goodhart's Law' which states that any past relationship between a monetary aggregate and some other variable will break down the moment that the aggregate becomes the subject of attempted control by the authorities. Thirdly, of course, there are occasional shifts in the theory behind monetary policy. If, instead of focusing upon a transactions medium, we begin to think that it is the general level of 'liquidity' in the economy that influences people's spending plans then policy should shift towards targeting a broader aggregate. Ultimately what Table 12.3 shows is just how difficult it is (or at least has been for the UK) to define 'money' in an unambiguous and lasting way.

12.3 Banks' balance sheets

In the last section we noted that bank deposits feature in all measures of 'money'. Indeed, in all of the M1–M3 measures, for example, bank deposits are the dominant component. Thus it follows that changes in the stock of money entail changes in bank deposits and vice versa. Since bank deposits dominate the liability side of banks' balance sheets, and since balance sheets must also balance, it follows that changes in the money supply require changes in banks' assets as well. In order to explain how changes in the money stock occur, therefore, we need to be familiar with the structure of banks' balance sheets.[7] Table 12.4 shows the balance sheet of a commercial bank, simplified to the essentials we require, and employing some symbols with which we need to be familiar.

How can we relate this balance sheet to our discussion in the last section? Firstly, we saw earlier that the monetary base comprised notes and coin in circulation and with banks as well as banks' deposits at the

[7] For the UK, we shall assume that building societies are included within the general category of 'banks'. This is not quite accurate since building societies hold their own reserves with banks rather than with the Bank of England. It makes little difference to our analysis, however. A detailed explanation of the relationship between balance sheets of building societies, banks and the Bank of England is contained in Howells (1993).

Table 12.4 A commercial bank's balance sheet

Assets		Liabilities	
Notes and coin	C_b	Capital and shareholders' funds	S_f
Deposits at the central bank	D_b	Customer deposits	D_p
Loans to the money markets	L_m		
Investments	I_b		
Loans to the public sector	BL_g		
Loans to the general public	BL_p		

central bank. Clearly, the last two components are assets to banks and they are shown in the top left corner of Table 12.4 as C_b and D_b respectively. The first component, notes and coin in circulation with non-banks, we can denote C_p (standing for 'cash with the public'). Thus we can now write:

$$\text{monetary base} = C_b + D_b + C_p \qquad (12.1)$$

Recall that we said that banks' holdings of the monetary base, $C_b + D_b$, functioned as highly liquid reserve assets. We could thus write:

$$\text{monetary base} = R + C_p \qquad (12.2)$$

where R now stands for bank 'reserves'.[8] Notice that the rest of the asset side is made up of loans to non-banks in some form or another. L_m represents loans made for very short periods (often overnight or 'at call') to the money markets or other financial institutions; I_b represents investments in the form of securities, typically short-dated government bonds or treasury bills. BL_g and BL_p represent loans to the government (or 'public sector') and to the non-bank private sector, respectively. We saw in Section 10.2 that longer-term loans generally pay a higher rate of interest than shorter ones. Thus, looking at the structure of assets we can draw two conclusions. Firstly, yields are likely to increase as we read down the list (C_b of course pay no interest, nor in some systems do D_b); secondly, banks will wish to maximize their holdings

of investments and loans and minimize their holdings of reserves.

Turning to bank liabilities, D_p – deposits of the non-bank public – form the major component of most definitions of money. As we saw in the last section, D_p will consist of sight deposits, time deposits and CDs. On the same principle that we just restated, sight deposits will pay little or no interest, while time deposits and CDs will pay interest which increases with the term for which the deposits are made.

Like any other firm, a bank makes profits equal to the difference between revenues and costs. Revenues will consist of interest from the assets listed above together with fees and commissions charged for the additional services that they offer to customers. Costs will consist of interest paid to depositors, wages and salaries, premises and capital. Focusing on the balance sheet, profits will flow from the difference between the interest received from assets and the interest paid on liabilities. In these circumstances, an obvious question to ask is why do banks hold non- (or low-) interest-bearing reserves ($C_b + D_b$), when other assets would produce a better return?

The answer comes in two parts. Firstly, as we saw in Section 1.3.2, banks engage in 'maturity transformation'. This means that their liabilities are of shorter maturity than their assets and can thus be withdrawn more readily than banks can realize most of their assets.[9] Secondly, banks are central to the payments mechanism which means that withdrawals (and receipts) of deposits are continuous. On some occasions, withdrawals and receipts will cancel and *net* withdrawals will be zero. However, as a general rule they will not and some days will see net receipts and others will see net withdrawals. Box 12.1 summarizes the ways in which net withdrawals may take place.

The public's confidence requires that deposits be convertible into cash on demand and thus banks have to maintain sufficient cash (C_b) or central bank balances (D_b) which they can exchange for cash. Because of their role in ensuring convertibility, the level of **bank reserves** is usually expressed as a ratio to their deposits. This is known as the **reserve ratio**. In some monetary systems, this ratio is set down by regulation (a **mandatory ratio**) and in others it is left to banks'

---

8   UK readers should be careful not to confuse the 'reserves' here with 'banks reserve balances' in Table 12.3. Reserves as defined here include those balances (= D_b) but *also* banks' holdings of some of the 'notes and coin' (= C_b) in Table 12.3.

9   Indeed, this 'playing the yield curve' is precisely why they earn more on assets than they pay on liabilities.

BOX 12.1 **Sources of net withdrawals from banks**

We need to distinguish between withdrawals from individual banks and withdrawals from the banking system as a whole.

Withdrawals from individual banks
- Customers of bank A make net payments to customers of other banks.
- Customers of bank A make net drawings of notes and coin from bank A.
- Customers of bank A make net payments to the public sector.

Withdrawals from the system as a whole
- Bank customers make net drawings of notes and coin from banks.
- Bank customers make net payments to the public sector.

Table 12.5 Loans increase in a multi-bank system (I)

Bank A			
Assets		**Liabilities**	
Notes and coin	C_b	Capital and shareholders' funds	S_r
Deposits at the central bank	D_b (−)	Customer deposits	D_p
Loans to the public sector	BL_g		
Loans to the general public	BL_p (+)		

Bank B			
Assets		**Liabilities**	
Notes and coin	C_b	Capital and shareholders' funds	S_f
Deposits at the central bank	D_b (+)	Customer deposits	D_p (+)
Loans to the public sector	BL_g		
Loans to the general public	BL_p		

own judgement (a **prudential ratio**) though there is usually an obligation on banks to inform the central bank of any intended change. In some systems, the ratio differs for different types of deposit, naturally being highest for sight deposits and decreasing against deposits with increasing terms to maturity.

So far we have considered a static position. We have a given quantity of money, the largest part of which comprises bank deposits, while the rest is made up of the notes and coin from the monetary base which are not held as banks' reserves. Letting M_s stand for some unspecified definition of money, therefore, we have:

$$M_s = D_p + C_p \qquad (12.3)$$

We want now to turn our attention to *changes* in the money supply and how banks' balance sheets are involved in such changes. The essential point to remember in working through the following illustrations is that balance sheets always balance and therefore any change that we make on one side must be matched by an equal change (with the same sign) on the opposite side or by an equal change (with opposite sign) on the same side.

In Table 12.5, we illustrate the process of loan (and deposit) creation using two banks, though to economize on space we have reduced the list of both banks' assets from what we saw in Table 12.4. In particular,

we want to demonstrate three general principles. The first concerns the relationship between loans and deposits. In Table 12.5, bank A agrees to make additional credit facilities available to a customer. But stop to consider that there is a difference between a bank *agreeing* to a customer's demand for extra credit facilities and the extra loan *coming into existence*. The latter can only happen when the borrower writes a cheque on which the bank has to make payment. The loan comes into existence when the bank makes the payment. The importance of this distinction is that it shows that a loan cannot come into existence until someone is paid. That means that for *every loan created, someone must receive an addition to his or her deposit*. Loans and deposits must increase together. The loan comes into existence when the cheque is cleared and at the same time as the payee's account is credited. In bank A then, BL_p is shown with a (+) and we must look for some corresponding and simultaneous increase in D_p. In a multi-bank system, it is quite likely that a customer will make payment to someone who banks elsewhere. In our example, the borrower from bank A makes payments to a client of bank B. Thus in bank B we show D_p with a (+). Notice that we are now violating our fundamental rule that balance sheets must balance. Assets appear to exceed liabilities for bank A, while the position is reversed for bank B. Clearly this cannot be correct. To complete the picture, we have to focus upon 'reserves'. We said earlier in this section that banks need to hold a safe minimum level of reserves in order to meet customer withdrawals. Sometimes they will be withdrawals of cash; sometimes, as here, they will be transfers of deposits to other banks; sometimes, if the government banks with the central bank, they will be transfers to the government's accounts at the central bank. In our illustration, the payment by the customer of bank A to the customer of bank B is matched by a transfer of bank A's deposits at the central bank to bank B's account at the central bank. Thus for bank A, D_b acquires a (−) while D_b for bank B acquires a (+). Notice that this adjustment restores the balance.

The second principle is that of portfolio equilibrium (which we first met in Chapter 8). Consider what has happened to the *composition* of these balance sheets since the creation of the loan. Loans and deposits have increased, relative to all other assets and liabilities. Bank A has a balance sheet unchanged in size but it now has replaced low (or zero) earning assets with higher earning customer loans. Notice also that its reserve ratio has therefore fallen and further adjustments will very likely be necessary. Bank B has a *larger* balance sheet now. It also has a *higher* reserve ratio than it previously had. This is because its reserves have increased by the same absolute amount as its deposits; that is, they have increased in the ratio 1:1 while the initial ratio was less than 1:1. If we assume that the initial balance sheet position was one of equilibrium – that is to say that the bank was happy with the distribution of its assets and liabilities having regard to their relative risks and returns – it is unlikely that this new position is also one of equilibrium. We should expect to see that there will be some further readjustment.

The third principle involves the reserve ratio. In our illustration, loans and deposits have increased equally, *all other assets and liabilities unchanged*. One aspect of the balance sheet composition that must have changed, therefore, is the ratio of reserves to deposits. $D_b + C_b$ are now smaller relative to D_p (and of course to L_p) in bank A than they were before. If we follow Equation 12.2 above and call banks' holdings of cash

MORE FROM THE WEB
The Bank of England's balance sheet

Details of the Bank of England's assets and liabilities (divided between the Issue Department and the Banking Department) are published monthly on the Bank's website. They appear in Table B1.1 of *Bankstats*. (Look under 'Statistical releases'.)

Components of commercial banks' balance sheets at the end of March 2007 appear in Table 3.1. They can be updated from *Bankstats*, Table B1.2.

The Bank of England's website is at www.bankofengland.co.uk.

and central bank deposits 'reserves', we can write the reserve ratio as R/D_p. It is this that has diminished (because D_b has diminished while D_p is unchanged). Whatever a bank may think about the composition of the rest of its balance sheet, this is one relationship about which it can hardly be indifferent. Clearly, if there is a mandatory ratio, the bank is under an

Table 12.6 Loans increase in a multi-bank system (II)

Bank A			
Assets		**Liabilities**	
Notes and coin	C_b	Capital and shareholders' funds	S_f
Deposits at the central bank	D_b (−)[+]	Customer deposits	D_p [+]
Loans to the public sector	BL_g		
Loans to the general public	BL_p (+)		

Bank B			
Assets		**Liabilities**	
Notes and coin	C_b	Capital and shareholders' funds	S_f
Deposits at the central bank	D_b (−)[+]	Customer deposits	D_p (+)
Loans to the public sector	BL_g		
Loans to the general public	BL_p [+]		

obligation to see that this ratio is maintained. Even if the ratio is prudential, a bank has a target ratio based on its own experience of what is a safe level of reserves, given the deposits and withdrawals that its customers make. If this new loan threatens to take the ratio below its desired level, the bank has to think about how to obtain additional reserves. For bank B's reserve ratio to be restored to its original value, by contrast, bank B would have to *increase* its deposits by some multiple of the extra reserves it received.

In the example above, notice that the extra lending was carried out entirely by one bank while the extra deposits appear entirely in a different bank. In practice, in a multi-bank system, we should expect all banks to be making similar decisions. If economic conditions lead customers to ask for more credit, this is not likely to affect one bank any more than another. Thus what we have shown in Table 12.5 is a very incomplete story. In Table 12.6 we show a more realistic picture. Beginning with the position as we left it in Table 12.5, bank B now also makes additional loans to its customers (these later adjustments are shown in square brackets). Thus in bank B, $BL_p[+]$. These will be paid to customers of bank A ($D_p[+]$), with corresponding transfers of central bank deposits from bank B ($D_b[-]$) to bank A ($D_b[+]$). Notice carefully the final position. Both banks have made loans and both banks have clients holding more deposits. In the course of the process, there have been transfers of central bank deposits ('reserves') between the two banks which cancel. Once again our fundamental principles hold. Balance sheets balance; an increase in lending means an increase in money; a change in lending (and deposits), *ceteris paribus*, means a change in the reserve ratio and in the ratio of capital and shareholders' funds to assets and liabilities. Exercise 12.1

Exercise 12.1 Loans create deposits

Imagine a system with just three commercial banks, A, B and C, whose balance sheets are shown below.

Bank A		Bank B		Bank C	
A	L	A	L	A	L
$C_b = 10$	$D_p = 1000$	$C_b = 10$	$D_p = 1000$	$C_b = 10$	$D_p = 1000$
$D_b = 40$		$D_b = 40$		$D_b = 40$	
$BL_p = 950$		$BL_p = 950$		$BL_p = 950$	

where D_p are customers' deposits, C_b is cash (notes and coin) held by banks, D_b are banks' deposits at the central bank and BL_p are loans to the non-bank public. Bank reserves, R, consist of $C_b + D_b$ and a bank's reserve ratio is thus R/D_p. Assume that non-banks hold 500 in notes and coin (C_p).

1 What is the size of the money stock, $C_p + D_p$?

2 Calculate the reserve ratio, R/D_p, for each bank and for the system as a whole.

Suppose now that bank A increases its loans (BL_p) by 10 and that its customers use this lending to pay 5 to clients of bank B and 5 to clients of bank C.

3 Show the new balance sheet position for each bank.

4 By how much has the money supply increased?

5 Calculate the new reserve ratio for each individual bank and the aggregate reserve ratio.

Suppose now that bank B also increases its lending by 10 and that its customers use this lending to pay 5 to clients of banks A and C, and that bank C increases its lending by 10 and that its customers use this lending to pay 5 to clients of banks A and B.

6 What is the size of the money stock now?

7 What is the reserve ratio for each bank?

8 What is the aggregate reserve ratio?

9 What quantity of bank deposits are customers of each bank now holding?

Suppose that customers of each bank now decide to increase their holdings of notes and coin (C_p) by 5.

10 What effect does this have on the total money supply?

11 What effect does this have on the composition of the money supply?

12 What effect does this have on the aggregate reserve ratio?

provides an opportunity to work through a three-bank example of the relationships we have just described.

Before leaving this examination of bank balance sheets and their importance in money supply changes, we need to go one further step and integrate the central bank's balance sheet. This is shown in Table 12.7. Central bank assets, like those of commercial banks, are loans in some form or other. CBL_g indicates central bank loans to government while B_g stands for central bank holding of government bonds. Other assets include building and equipment, F. Liabilities, again like those of commercial banks, are overwhelmingly customers' deposits but customers are the commercial banking system, D_b, and government, D_g. Notes and coin in circulation are also liabilities of the central bank. (We have ignored capital and shareholders' funds.) None of the changes that we have examined so far has had any impact on the aggregate figures in the central bank's balance sheet. In our multi-bank example there were transfers of banks' deposits, D_b, between two banks. This means that the central bank moves such deposits from one bank to another in its own accounts, but this has no effect upon the total. There are, however, some transactions which will affect the aggregates in the central bank's balance sheets.

The most common are those transactions involving the public's exchange of bank deposits for cash and vice versa; and those that involve flows between the public and private sectors. Let us take the case where the public increases its holdings of notes and coin (C_p) surrendering deposits (D_p) as it does seasonally, at Christmas, for example. In commercial banks' balance sheets we have $D_p(-)$ matched initially by $C_b(-)$. It is unlikely that banks will wish to be short of cash

for very long, however, and they will quickly draw more notes and coin from the central bank. This second step sees C_b restored, while the reduction in bank assets is transferred to $D_b(-)$. These transactions have their counterpart in the central bank's balance sheet where banks' exchange of central bank deposits for cash is shown by $D_b(-)$ at the central bank. But so far as the central bank's balance sheet is concerned, this is offset by $C_p(+)$ and the balance sheet still balances, and is unchanged in size.

Suppose now that the general public makes net payments to the government. (The government is running a budget surplus.) At commercial banks, we have the sequence $D_p(-)$ and $D_b(-)$. At the central bank we have $D_b(-)$ matched by $D_g(+)$, as government deposits increase. The money supply has decreased (by the reduction in D_p) and banks have become less liquid: R/D_p has fallen. At the central bank, there may be further adjustments if the $D_g(+)$ is reduced in order to pay off some of the borrowing from the central bank, CBL_g.

Suppose by way of contrast that the government runs a budget deficit. It may borrow from the central bank. In this case, as the government spends the loan: $CBL_g(+)$, $D_p(+)$ (as the general public receives the payments from government). These new customer deposits are matched in commercial bank balance sheets by $D_b(+)$ and this same $D_b(+)$ appears in the central bank's balance sheet as the counterpart to the initial $CBL_g(+)$. Bear in mind also that $D_b(+) = D_p(+)$ and thus banks' reserve ratio, R/D_p, increases and banks are more liquid.

The flows of funds that we have just seen may be described as 'spontaneous'. They have arisen from the imbalance between government expenditure and tax revenue. But it is always open to governments and central banks to buy or sell government debt, regardless of their financing needs. Such sales/purchases will cause induced flows. By buying government bonds from the non-bank public, the central bank initiates the sequence $B_g(+)$, $D_p(+)$ as the public receives payment, and this is matched in commercial bank balance sheets and at the central bank by $D_b(+)$. The money supply is increased and banks are more liquid. Conversely, a sale of government debt to the non-bank public results in the sequence $B_g(-)$, $D_p(-)$ and $D_b(-)$. The money supply is reduced and the banks are less liquid.

In the next section we shall see that there are further flows which cause changes in loans, deposits and the money supply. We list them all in Box 12.3 on page 258.

Table 12.7 The central bank's balance sheet

Assets		Liabilities	
Loans to commercial banks	CBL_b	Deposits of commercial banks	D_b
Loans to government	CBL_g	Deposits of government	D_g
Securities (government bonds)	B_g	Capital and reserves	CR
Fixed and other assets	F		

12.4 Models of money supply determination

We have seen that most measures of money are dominated by bank deposits. In the last section we saw that changes in the quantity of money must involve changes in banks' balance sheets. Furthermore, since balance sheets must always balance, a change initiated at one point must be matched or compensated for by a change at some other point. Our accounting conventions tell us, for example, that *if* banks make new loans, there will be new deposits while *if* people exchange their deposits for government debt, customer deposits diminish along with banks' deposits at the central bank. But simply observing these interactions can tell us nothing about causality. We know what is involved when the money supply changes but we do not know what, *as a rule*, initiates those changes. When it comes to explaining why changes in the money supply occur, we need something further.

One myth which we are not going to perpetuate is that the *cause* of changes in the quantity of money occurs if and only if the central bank changes the size of the monetary base. This is an account of money supply determination which has proved historically popular and has been kept alive by the popularity of the IS/LM model of a simple macroeconomy. In that model, the LM curve is derived on the assumption of a fixed quantity of money which is exactly what is provided by the 'monetary base' or 'deposit-multiplier' account of money supply determination.

The account begins by putting together as a ratio of the stock of broad money (M) and the monetary base (B) and observing that M/B has a value much greater than unity. It is then shown that this ratio is identical to the ratio that we get if we re-write it in terms of the components of M and B. Thus:

$$\frac{M}{B} \equiv \frac{C_p + D_p}{C_p + C_b + D_b} \tag{12.4}$$

where the terms on the right-hand side have the same meaning as they had in the tables of the previous section of this chapter. C_p is cash (notes and coin) held by the non-bank public; C_b is cash held by banks; D_b are deposits held by commercial banks at the central bank while D_p are the non-bank public's holdings of bank deposits – the bulk of the broad money supply. But we know, from Equation 12.2, that $C_b + D_b$, a subset of the monetary base, constitute banks' reserves. Hence we can re-write Equation 12.4 as:

$$\frac{M}{B} \equiv \frac{C_p + D_p}{C_p + R} \tag{12.5}$$

If we now divide each item on the right hand side by D_p we make the discovery that the ratio M/B is identical to the relationship between two further ratios.

$$\frac{M}{B} \equiv \frac{C_p/D_p + D_p/D_p}{C_p/D_p + R/D_p} \tag{12.6}$$

Exercise 12.2 The base-multiplier process

Imagine the same system that we saw in Exercise 12.1, with the same banks and the same balance sheets.

Bank A		Bank B		Bank C	
A	L	A	L	A	L
$C_b = 10$	$D_p = 1,000$	$C_b = 10$	$D_p = 1,000$	$C_b = 10$	$D_p = 1,000$
$D_b = 40$		$D_b = 40$		$D_b = 40$	
$BL_p = 950$		$BL_p = 950$		$BL_p = 950$	

In this exercise, non-banks hold a total of 300 in notes and coin (C_p).

1 Calculate the size of the banks' reserve ratio.

2 Calculate the size of the public's cash ratio.

3 Using Equation 12.6, calculate the size of the multiplier.

4 Recalculate the size of the multiplier if the banks' reserve ratio rises to 0.07.

5 Calculate the value of the multiplier if the public's cash ratio now falls to 0.08.

C_p/D_p is the public's cash ratio while R/D_p is the banks' reserve ratio. If we denote these by α and β respectively, then Equation 12.6 can be written more conveniently as

$$\frac{M}{B} \equiv \frac{\alpha + 1}{\alpha + \beta} \qquad (12.7)$$

and we can then show, by multiplying both sides by B, that the expression on the right-hand side must be a multiplier which accounts for the fact that the quantity of broad money is much larger than the base:

$$\frac{M}{B} \equiv B \cdot \frac{\alpha + 1}{\alpha + \beta} \qquad (12.8)$$

As it stands, Equation 12.8 is simply an identity. However, just a few assumptions give it considerable behavioural content. Recall that the components of the monetary base are all liabilities of (are issued by) the central bank. Then if we assume:

- the central bank is willing and able to control its liabilities,
- the public's cash ratio is stable,
- the banks' reserve ratios are stable,

it follows that the central bank's control of the base will 'produce' a predictable quantity of money. Note also the implication: if the central bank does nothing to change the base, the money stock is *fixed*. Unfortunately, these assumptions are very easy to make with the result that the **base-multiplier account** of money supply determination is still deeply embedded in macroeconomics, ten years after Goodhart described it as being so far removed from reality that its appearance in textbooks 'amount[s] to misinstruction' (Goodhart, 1984, p. 188).

What exactly is so misleading about the approach? Firstly, as we saw at some length in Section 9.4, the monetary policy instrument that has been adopted by all central banks for many years now is a short-term rate of interest, not the quantity of base money. We described the role of the central bank as being that of a monopoly supplier of reserves in a system-wide shortage of liquidity faced with the standard choice open to any monopolist: it can set the price or the quantity. The base-multiplier account requires it to set the quantity but in the real world we know it sets the price. A further fundamental consequence follows from this. If the central bank sets the rate of interest it must then supply the reserves that banks require and

this will depend upon the demand for new loans and deposits *at the going rate of interest*. 'In the United Kingdom, money is endogenous – the Bank supplies base money on demand at its prevailing interest rate, and broad money is created by the banking system' (King, 1994, p. 264). Far from the money supply being a magnitude exogenously determined by the central bank, it is determined, in effect, by the state of the economy.

This then brings us face to face with two further aspects of reality with which the base-multiplier approach cannot deal. We have seen that it presupposes that if the central bank does nothing, the *stock* of money will not change. But because the central bank sets the interest rate, supplies reserves as required and the quantity of money depends upon how much the economic system requires, the money supply is in a state of continuous expansion. If the central bank does nothing, the money supply *expands* at whatever rate agents require. From this it follows that central banks have no policy interest whatsoever in the *stock* of money. Their concern with the quantity of money and credit (if they are concerned at all) is with its *rate of growth*. The ECB is one central bank that says explicitly that it takes account of the behaviour of the money supply, but as Box 12.2 makes clear, the ECB's 'reference rate' for money is a *growth* rate.

This is not to say that it is impossible to imagine a monetary system and policy regime in which the

---

BOX 12.2 The role of money in ECB policy decisions

The prominent role for money in the ECB's strategy is signalled by the announcement of a reference value for the growth of the broad money aggregate, M3. The choice of M3 is based on the evidence . . . that this aggregate possesses all the desired properties: in particular it has a stable money demand relationship and leading indicator properties for future price developments in the euro area. The reference value for the growth of M3 has been derived so as to be consistent with the achievement of price stability . . . the reference value was set at 4½% by the Governing Council in December 1998.

Source: ECB, *The Monetary Policy of the ECB 2004*, Box 3.7. This information may be obtained free of charge through the ECB website www.ecb.int.

focus might be on stocks and where the magnitude of those stocks was determined by the deliberate action of the central bank to control the base. In these circumstances, the base-multiplier approach might yield useful insights. But this is not the world we live in, and a glance at Box 12.4 reveals a list of compelling reasons against modifying the current system in that direction.

When we are dealing with monetary regimes where the central bank sets interest rates and supplies reserves on demand, where the resulting flow of new deposits depends upon agents' demand for loans and where policy is concerned with the resulting rate of growth of money, we are likely to get better insights from the '**flow of funds model**' which focuses explicitly upon the flow of 'new' money and seeks to explain this by looking at the demand for loans. In this model the demand for new lending is assumed as a rule to be positive because the demand for loans, at any given rate of interest, is determined by the level of economic activity and the level of prices. Since both of these tend to increase over time, there is a tendency for firms and households to increase their borrowing from banks over time. The demand for loans is *endogenous* – it is determined by other variables within the economic system. Control of the money supply in this model requires that the authorities control the demand for loans.

Section 12.5 below shows that there are potentially many ways in which this could be done, including '**direct**' **controls** upon bank lending. Such controls were commonplace in the UK until 1971 (and can still be found in the monetary systems of some less developed countries) but all have disadvantages as the details show. The general problem is that direct controls were usually imposed with the intention of restricting the supply of bank lending below the level that would have cleared the market at the prevailing level of interest rates. This creates an excess demand and requires some form of non-price rationing of the available bank credit. Non-price rationing generally results in some combination of inefficiency, inequity and evasion. It is for this reason that we have a widespread consensus that the central bank should set the price of reserves in order to influence the price that banks charge for credit.

Our definitions and symbols are the same as those we have used throughout this chapter. The first step is to remember (from Section 12.3) that banks' deposit liabilities are matched by loans of some form. Then it

follows that *changes* in one must be matched by changes in the other. Thus:

$$\Delta D_p \equiv \Delta C_p + \Delta BL_p + \Delta BL_g \qquad (12.9)$$

but since the money stock consists also of notes and coin, we may write changes in the money stock as:

$$\Delta M_s \equiv \Delta C_p + \Delta BL_p + \Delta BL_g \qquad (12.10)$$

Consider now the origin of ΔBL_g. The starting point is the total of government or public sector borrowing, the *PSNCR* ('public sector net cash requirement'). This can be financed by selling government debt to the non-bank private sector, ΔG_p. It can also be financed by selling foreign exchange for the domestic currency which provides an 'external' source of finance, Δext, or, as a last resort, it can be financed residually, by borrowing from the banking system, ΔBL_g. Since the take-up of newly issued notes and coin, ΔC_p, also provides finance to the government, though in most countries incidentally rather than deliberately, we can write the government financing identity as:

$$PSNCR \equiv \Delta G_p + \Delta C_p + \Delta ext + \Delta BL_g \quad (12.11)$$

(Notice that the *PSNCR* appears without the Δ sign. It is already a *flow*, whose *stock* counterpart is (roughly speaking) the national debt.)

We can now combine Equations 12.10 and 12.11 to show that changes in M_s depend upon the size of the *PSNCR* and its *non-bank* methods of finance, since they together determine ΔBL_g.

$$\Delta M_s \equiv \Delta C_p + \Delta BL_p + PSNCR - \Delta G_p - \Delta C_p - \Delta ext$$

$$(12.12)$$

The two references to ΔC_p obviously cancel and the outflow of foreign currency in exchange for sterling reduces the money supply. Thus making these adjustments to Equation 12.12, we have what is commonly described as the key flow-of-funds identity. In Equation 12.13 we have also reordered the terms to match the most common presentation.

$$\Delta M_s \equiv PSNCR - \Delta G_p - \Delta ext + \Delta BL_p \quad (12.13)$$

Unlike the base-multiplier model, the flow of funds approach focuses attention upon the demand for credit, by both the public and the private sectors. Given the many different ways in which both the public and private sectors can borrow, it follows that there are quite a number of loan-related flows which could have some impact upon the money supply. We saw

---

BOX 12.3 Flows that change the stock of money

- Central bank loans to government (ΔCBL_g)
- Central bank sales or purchases of government debt (ΔB_g) from:
  - the government
  - banks
  - non-bank private sector
- Changes in central bank holdings of foreign currency as a result of transactions with government or foreign exchange market intervention
- Bank loans to the non-bank private sector (ΔBL_p)
- Bank loans to the public sector (ΔBL_g)
- Bank purchases/sales of government debt (ΔB_g) from the non-bank private sector
- Bank purchases of government debt (ΔB_g) directly from government to finance a government deficit

---

some earlier in Section 12.3. Box 12.3 provides a complete list.

We saw earlier that the base-multiplier approach to the money supply process *implied* certain ways in which the authorities should act in order to control the money supply. So too does the flow of funds model, though naturally it directs our attention to the importance of controlling the demand for bank loans. This brings us quite quickly to a major role for interest rates in influencing the growth of money. This is clearly seen if we take each of the variables in turn.

The PSNCR is the balance of government revenue from tax (and charges) and expenditure. It is thus the outcome of fiscal policy instrument settings and the level of economic activity. As such, and in economies where a large part of government spending is cyclically determined and non-discretionary, it is not an obvious candidate for use as an instrument for monetary control. Governments, and their electors, have preferences about public services and about taxation which have their own implications for the PSNCR.

Look now at the second component of Equation 12.13, which tells us that, *ceteris paribus*, the larger the quantity of government debt sales, G_p, to the NBPS, the lower the rate of monetary expansion. Furthermore, *ceteris paribus*, one would expect that larger debt sales would require higher interest rates. An active policy of using debt sales for monetary control purposes requires governments to accept whatever level of interest rates may be necessary to sell the debt. Ideally, this would require government debt to be sold entirely by auction. This is a position towards which the UK has moved slowly over the past 15 years, but most governments have preferred to maintain some control over medium- and long-term interest rates by selling debt only when they think that markets will accept it at current yields and prices.

In Equation 12.13 monetary growth will decrease with increases in the sale of domestic currency by residents in exchange for foreign currency. The limitations to the use of foreign exchange transactions as a monetary policy instrument are obvious. Net purchases by the authorities of domestic currency, aimed at reducing monetary growth, will force the exchange rate up, under a floating exchange rate regime, causing a fall in import prices. This, and the rise in export prices, will weaken the balance of payments which slower monetary growth is often meant to strengthen. Under a fixed exchange rate regime, the device is simply not available.

Clearly, the use of PSNCR, debt sales and foreign exchange transactions for monetary control are subject to formidable constraints. This means that monetary control within this model is forced to focus upon the regulation of lending to the non-bank private sector. This emphasis is further strengthened by the private sector's domination of bank lending flows in most monetary systems. It is not uncommon now for public sector borrowing to be 'fully funded', that is to say, financed without recourse to the banking system. In fact, in 2006 in the UK, additional bank lending to the government (ΔBL_g) was very slightly negative. The government managed to sell more debt than it needed to fund the PSNCR. Given the small role played by the PSNCR and the even smaller role played by the residual financing of it, one might wonder why we arrange the terms so that the flow of funds explanation of monetary growth begins with the PSNCR (as in Equation 12.13). The answer is largely historical. This framework for looking at changes in the money supply developed in the late 1960s when government borrowing was much larger (it reached 10 per cent of GDP in 1976) and its financing was a major problem. If the framework were developed today, no doubt it would be arranged so as to give priority to the private sector's demand for credit. The next section reviews briefly a number of possible ways in which the authorities can influence monetary growth.

12.5 Controlling the money supply

In Section 12.3, we established that changes in the money supply are bound to involve changes in the stock of bank deposits and that the balance sheet identity means that changes in bank deposits must be matched or compensated for by changes elsewhere in the balance sheet. Remember also the principle of portfolio equilibrium. A change in any component of the balance sheet is likely to have further repercussions as banks adjust their portfolios in the light of prevailing risks and returns. In theory, therefore, an intervention at any point in the balance sheet could have some effect upon the money supply. However, the first and fundamental choice that the authorities face is whether to act by 'direct' or quantity controls, or by price. All these possibilities add up to a formidable choice. We summarize them below.

(1) Price effects on bank deposits

A rise in official interest rates (see Section 9.3.3) causes all short-term rates to rise in sympathy. However, if deposit rates can be held down, the return on non-money assets rises *relative* to money and agents will be less willing to hold money. Since money can only exist if it is held by non-banks, this increase in the cost of holding money reduces the money supply (or its rate of growth if we think in terms of flows). The most famous example of this technique was 'Regulation Q' in the USA which limited interest that could be paid on deposits. In the UK, and in other countries, the interest paid on *sight* deposits was limited until the past few years by the commercial decision of banks. So long as deposit rates are restricted or at least 'sticky', the authorities can exert some control over the money stock by varying interest rates.

(2) Quantity effects on bank deposits

Regulations on the rate of growth of deposits were a feature of the 'supplementary special deposit scheme' or 'corset' during the 1970s. It was effective in the short term but banks and their clients eventually devised techniques such as the 'bill-leak' which allowed borrowers to borrow (but from non-banks) and enabled banks to charge commissions (to replace their interest charges). The result of this 'disintermediation' was that borrowing and spending carried on pretty much as though the regulations were not there,

although the money supply (and bank lending) statistics gave the impression of control. This episode illustrates the weakness of all direct controls, namely that they encourage innovative behaviour which undermines the regulations.

(3) Price effects on bankers' deposits at the central bank

This could mean varying the interest rate paid on banks' deposits at the central bank. A rise in rates (r_r) would encourage banks to hold more reserves, β would increase and the multiplier and money supply would fall. Not used.

Alternatively, it could refer to changes in the rediscount or lender of last resort rate (r_d). An increase raises the cost to banks of being short of reserves and having to borrow from the central bank. This would encourage banks to be more cautious, increasing β and reducing the multiplier and the money supply. Changes in r_d are a major technique of monetary control but more likely through the mechanism described in (7) below.

(4) Quantity effects on bankers' deposits

Changing the quantity of reserves available to banks is often presented as the major method of monetary control. As we saw at the end of Section 12.3, the authorities can buy (sell) government bonds which increases (decreases) D_p as well as D_b. The change in the latter causes a change in the ratio of reserves to deposits (R/D_p) and restoring this ratio to its original value requires multiple changes in D_p. The authorities' use of 'open market operations', as described here, is often presented in textbooks as *the* obvious technique of monetary control. It has many disadvantages, however, which mean that it is very rarely used in practice. These disadvantages are set out in Box 12.4.

(5) Price effects on banks' holdings of government securities

Imagine that the authorities increase the rate of interest offered on government bonds and that banks increase their holdings. For commercial banks, I_b rises while D_b falls. At the central bank of course $D_b(-)$, while $D_g(+)$. *Provided that the government does not spend the funds it receives from banks* (shown by $D_g(+)$), there is no immediate change in the money supply but since

BOX 12.4 Monetary base control (MBC) rejected

> Virtually every monetary economist believes that the CB [central bank] can control the monetary base . . . Almost all those who have worked in a CB believe that this view is totally mistaken.
>
> Goodhart, 1994, p. 1424.

The base-multiplier model of money supply determination is presented in almost every macroeconomics textbook as the only explanation of money supply determination. Furthermore, it is *implied* in all those texts which, lacking a formal model, still present the money supply as a curve drawn vertically in interest–money space. And yet, as Goodhart says, no central bank uses open market operations with a view to changing the size of the base in order to achieve a multiple change in deposits. Even in 1981, at the 'high tide of monetarism' when monetary targets were universally adopted, the Bank of England considered explicitly moving to a system of MBC and just as explicitly rejected it. Why the model continues to dominate in textbooks when the real world consistently rejects it is an issue we do not have time to discuss, but we can offer a number of reasons for the rejection.

■ Firstly, MBC is a quantity control. In a pure system of MBC, supply would be fixed (some positive interest elasticity notwithstanding) and fluctuations in demand would have to be absorbed entirely by price. If the authorities were trying to target the base over very short periods, the fluctuations in short-term interest rates could be extreme. The authorities are always reluctant to create situations in which interest rates may be very volatile. Targeting the base, averaged over a longer period, would ease this problem by allowing some day-to-day flexibility in quantities, but so long as quantities are targeted rather than price, price must fluctuate.

■ Secondly, while the base consists of liabilities of the central bank and one might expect the central bank to be fully in control of its own liabilities, this is not always the case. Firstly, the central bank has to know in advance what will happen to its liabilities in the course of ordinary transactions. CBL_b will fluctuate as a result of the central bank's lender of last resort role and CBL_g and B_g will fluctuate if the central bank has to provide residual finance to governments when debt sales to the non-bank public fail to match the PSNCR. Most central banks make daily predictions about these flows and inform banks and money markets of their plans. It is quite common for the financial press to report the predictions and outcomes. The errors are very large.

■ Thirdly, even if the central bank knew what effect its ordinary transactions were going to have on the base this does not mean that it could take the appropriate measures. Knowledge that the base was going to expand more rapidly than desired does not mean that the bank can suddenly organize a bond issue in order to offset it. Again, this problem becomes more acute the shorter the targeting period. But even if the aim were to achieve an average rate of growth on a quarterly basis, frequent sales of government debt could be very disruptive to financial markets. To ensure the sale of the correct *quantity* governments would have to adopt a pure auction form of sale and thus would have to accept the market clearing price. Once again we are back to volatile interest rates, this time at the longer end of the spectrum.

■ Fourthly, in some systems there would need to be major structural changes. For example, it is doubtful whether MBC is compatible with an overdraft system of borrowing where banks agree maximum credit limits with their clients who then use whatever fraction of the limit they need. In the aggregate, this is often of the order of 50–60 per cent. A tightening of monetary policy would inevitably mean that firms would want to use more of their overdrafts; and banks (unable to get reserves) would then face the choice of either allowing the loans and breaching the reserve ratio requirement or defaulting on their promises to borrowers. MBC would also require governments to bank with the commercial banking system rather than the central bank so that payments between the public and private sectors would not cause continuous and large fluctuations in D_b.

■ Fifthly, there is an asymmetry in the operation of MBC caused by the fact that most bank assets are non-marketable. This means that an open market purchase of debt will increase D_p, D_b and β as predicted and banks, being more liquid, can try to increase their lending. But a sale, causing a reduction in D_p, D_g and β, requires banks to reduce loans. But loans are not, as a rule, marketable. They can only be reduced by insisting on repayment (or refusing to renew). This is likely to prove very disruptive to trade, resulting in bankruptcies.

■ Sixthly, if reserves pay no interest then reserve requirements act as a tax on bank intermediation since they increase its cost. This occurs because the remaining, earning, assets have to earn a higher return to compensate for the zero return on reserves. This increases the spread between deposit and

---

BOX 12.4 *continued*

lending rates, which many would regard as the appropriate way of calculating the cost of intermediation. As with any tax, the supply curve is shifted to the left. Less intermediation is 'bought' and 'sold' at a higher price.

■ Finally, MBC raises doubts over the central bank's lender of last resort role. As we have seen, bank

deposits are convertible into cash on demand (albeit with interest penalties in some cases). However, the flows that we have discussed in this section could mean that perfectly well-run and solvent banks might find themselves short of reserves. Would the central bank still offer the convertibility guarantee if such a shortage arose, as it well might, in a period of tight MBC?

---

banks' reserve ratio (R/D_p) has fallen, banks will need to reduce their lending and deposits as a secondary effect. The technique is not used in practice, though a rise in interest rates on government bonds is likely to be a side effect of any rise in official interest rates intended to reduce the money supply (or rate of growth).

(6) Quantity effects on banks' holdings of government securities

An alternative to price inducements to increase or decrease holdings of government debt is regulation. *Requiring* banks to hold more or less government debt has broadly similar effects upon the money supply and on bank liquidity to those resulting from price. However, if the return on government securities is below the rate required to justify the holdings in the absence of regulation, then the regulation acts as a tax on banking and a subsidy on government debt. One could then take the standard view that the effect of the tax will be a lower level of bank intermediation than would otherwise be the case, and a smaller money stock. There have been occasional examples of balance sheet regulations which influence bank holdings of government debt – the UK regulations embodied in *Competition and Credit Control* (1971–81) provide an example – but they are generally rejected now along with most direct controls.

Since 1993, banks in the Group of 10 have had to observe rules on capital adequacy laid down by the 'Basel Committee'. This requires banks to observe a specified ratio of capital to 'risk-adjusted assets'. Government debt has a low risk weighting and banks may sometimes decide to hold more government debt in order to lower the value of their risk-adjusted assets, but these regulations are aimed at improving and maintaining the solvency of banks and not at monetary control. The regulation of banking and other financial activity is discussed further in Chapter 25.

(7) Price effects on bank advances to the non-bank private sector

Through its lender of last resort role a central bank can raise (lower) the level of short-term interest rates. Other things being equal, this moves the non-bank private sector up (down) its demand curve for bank credit. Assuming some negative interest elasticity, bank advances fall (rise). At first glance, the process could scarcely be simpler. However, there are some problems.

Firstly, we are here discussing stocks but in the real world the authorities are concerned with *flows*. In a world where nominal magnitudes are generally increasing it is the rate of increase that the authorities seek to influence. Experience suggests that the demand for new bank lending is not very interest elastic while the flow of such lending is subject to a wide variety of other influences. With a low interest elasticity, the behaviour of the curve itself becomes critical. In a recession, for example, it seems plausible that 'distress borrowing' will, for a period at least, push the curve to the right. If the recession is itself related to the present conduct of monetary policy then we have a malevolent cycle in which a rise in interest rates pushes us up an (inelastic) curve, which simultaneously moves outward.

Secondly, while this mechanism appears not to involve the demand for money, a rise in rates will make bank deposits *more* attractive. We saw in (1) above that if deposit rates were sticky (or could be held down) then any rise in interest rates would make holding money less attractive. This would reinforce the negative effect of a rise in interest rates on lending. However, in many European countries now, even sight deposits bear market-related interest rates. This means that a rise in official rates pushes up money's own rate as well and this secondary mechanism is lost.

Nonetheless, changes in short-term interest rates are currently the favoured mechanism of monetary control.

(8) Quantity effects on bank advances to the non-bank private sector

If price effects on bank advances have been the cornerstone of recent monetary control, quantity effects were their predecessors. Quantity controls usually consisted of target rates of growth of bank credit being laid down by the central bank, with penalties if they were exceeded. The obvious advantage of quantity over price controls is that they avoided fluctuations in interest rates. In particular, a tight monetary policy could be operated without high interest rates. However, any direct control must involve non-price rationing and, with it, the risk of inefficiency and inequity. Furthermore, the control is likely to be evaded as the passage of time pushes the cost of complying towards the cost involved in circumvention. In the present climate, which favours free markets, the disadvantages of direct control are felt to outweigh any advantage.

(9) The size of the PSNCR

Other things being equal, the larger the PSNCR the greater will be the amount that the government has to borrow from banks and, *ceteris paribus*, the greater the flow of new loans and deposits. This is demonstrated in Equation 12.13. Adjusting the PSNCR for monetary control purposes is impractical, however, for reasons which we saw in Section 12.4. Most EU governments are more concerned with reducing their PSNCR in order to meet the Maastricht criteria. These conditions have monetary implications, but rather more for interest rates than for money supply.

(10) Price effects on government debt sales to the NBPS

We have seen that selling government debt to non-banks reduces the money supply. The sequence is $D_p(-)$ matched by $D_b(-)$ for commercial banks. At the central bank, $D_p(-)$ is offset initially by $D_g(+)$. This may be followed by $D_g(-)$ matched by $L_g(-)$. Banks' reserve ratio is also reduced and banks may need to make multiple reductions in loans and deposits (as described in Box 12.4). This is the process that is often described as 'open market operations'.

Selling government debt to the general public at interest rates higher than those currently prevailing is often a feature of a tight money policy, but it is intended more to limit the quantity of new money created by bank lending to government than to achieve a particular quantity change in reserves. The relevant framework is Equation 12.13 rather than Equation 12.8.

Anything that makes government debt, of any sort, more attractive to the non-bank public will have these effects. New savings products, with attractive terms and conditions, have often been developed in phases of tight monetary policy.

(11) Quantity effects on government debt sales to the NBPS

Monetary authorities do not normally impose requirements that the general public should lend to the government. Forced loans have had a bad press since numerous monarchs throughout Europe were variously deposed and/or executed for adopting such a policy.

(12) Price effects on the external impact on deposit growth

The objective here is to cause transactions involving foreign exchange which will make the domestic money supply grow more slowly. In the flow of funds identity Equation 12.13 is represented by Δext. Remember that Δext is shown as contributing positively to a change in the money supply. If we take Germany as an example, then this will happen when overseas citizens buy goods or assets in Germany. Either the overseas buyers make payments to sellers in euros (in which case euros previously held outside Germany and thus excluded from the official measures of money are now included) or overseas buyers buy euros from the *Bundesbank*, which takes foreign currency in exchange. The effect is the same as if the central bank had bought government debt from non-banks, paying them with domestic currency.

In order to reduce monetary growth, the mechanism needs to be reversed. In other words a capital *outflow* needs to be induced. And herein lies the major difficulty with the manipulation of external flows for monetary control purposes. The main objective of a tight money policy is likely to be a reduction in the rate of inflation, usually to a rate which is similar to those of major trading partners. In other words, the purpose of tight money is to ensure that the country's balance of payments either improves or does not deteriorate.

And yet tight money, engineered via external flows, requires that the balance of payments gets worse.

(13) Quantity effects on the external component of deposit growth

Quantitative measures mean exchange controls. Restricting outflows makes the money supply higher than it would otherwise have been while restricting inflows has the opposite effect. Germany has used control on inflows to reduce the rate of monetary growth and one might view the relaxation of exchange controls in the UK in 1979 (in the hope of encouraging outflows) as a sort of negative inflow control. The advantage of exchange controls is that appropriate flows can, in theory, be created without disturbing the balance of payments. However, the first phase of the planned movement to a monetary union (initiated in July 1990) included the removal of all exchange controls between European countries. Now this has been completed it is difficult to see, even if progress towards unification slows to a halt, that this policy will be reversed.

12.6 | Summary

There are numerous theoretical and practical difficulties involved in defining money. The former stem from a circular argument: we cannot say what assets function as money unless we know what it is that money does, but we cannot be sure what role is being played by money itself unless we know which assets we should be studying. The latter stem from the fact that whatever functions as money is defined by custom, and customs change.

In spite of these difficulties the monetary authorities in any country have to take a stand and define money in some practical way. The uncertainty is reflected in the fact that money in most countries is defined both 'narrowly' and 'broadly'. At the moment, all commonly used measures of money are dominated by bank deposits. It follows therefore that anything that causes a change in the size and composition of bank balance sheets is likely to cause a change in the quantity of money and conversely that any change in the quantity of money must be reflected in changes in banks' balance sheets.

There are two ways of modelling the money creation process. One, the base-multiplier approach, focuses upon stocks and makes discretionary decisions by the authorities central to changes in the quantity of money. The other, the flow of funds approach, focuses upon flows and sees expansion as the norm. In this model, the authorities occupy a subordinate role in which they do what they can to influence the demand for new loans and thus the rate at which the money supply expands.

The base-multiplier model points to control of the monetary base, or bank reserves, as the obvious means of controlling the money supply; the flow of funds model points to action to control bank lending. At present, 'market' methods of influence are preferred and that essentially means using interest rates.

Key concepts in this chapter

Bank reserves
Base-multiplier model
Broad money
Certificate of deposit
Demand or checking deposits
Direct controls
Disintermediation
Divisia
Flow of funds model
High powered money
Legal tender
Mandatory ratio
Medium of exchange
Monetary base

Money income
Narrow money
Price effects
Prudential ratio
Quantity effects
Real income
Real wealth
Reserve ratio
Sight deposits
Standard of deferred payment
Store of wealth
Time deposits
Unit of account

Questions and problems

1 Distinguish between 'broad' and 'narrow' measures of money.

2 Why do countries usually have several official measures of money?

3 For your own economy, find recent figures for GDP (at current prices) and for a measure of narrow money and a measure of broad money. Calculate narrow money velocity and broad money velocity.

4 Why is the money supply endogenous?

5 Explain what is meant by the phrase 'loans create deposits'.

6 Using a flow of funds framework, explain the effect upon the creation of new deposits of:

   (a) an increase in the *PSNCR*, *ceteris paribus*;
   (b) a reduction in the central bank's official dealing rate, *ceteris paribus*.

7 Summarize the arguments against quantity controls on bank deposits and bank lending.

Further reading

K Bain and P G A Howells, *Monetary Economics: Policy and its Theoretical Basis* (Basingstoke: Palgrave, 2003)

Bank of England, *The Framework for the Bank of England's Operations in the Sterling Money Markets (the 'Red Book')*, February 2007 (available at www.bankofengland.co.uk)

Deutsche Bundesbank, *Monthly Report*

European Central Bank, *The Monetary Policy of the ECB 2004* (Frankfurt: ECB, 2004)

European Central Bank, *Monthly Bulletin*

C A E Goodhart, 'What should central banks do? What should be their macroeconomic objectives and operations?', *Economic Journal*, November 1994, 1424–36

C A E Goodhart, *Monetary Theory and Practice* (London: Macmillan, 1984)

S Heffernan, *Modern Banking* (Chichester: Wiley, 2004)

J R Hicks, *Capital and Value* (Oxford: Clarendon Press, 2e, 1946)

P G A Howells, 'Banks, building societies and the money supply', *British Economy Survey*, 23 (1), 1993, 13–18

T M Humphrey, 'The theory of the multiple expansion of deposits: What it is and whence it came', *FRBR Economic Review*, Autumn 1987, 3–11

M King, 'The transmission mechanism of monetary policy', *Bank of England Quarterly Bulletin*, August 1994, 261–7

A Mullineux, *Financial Innovation, Banking and Monetary Aggregates* (Aldershot: Edward Elgar, 1996)

Websites

www.bankofengland.co.uk
www.federalreserve.gov

Chapter 13 The demand for money

What you will learn in this chapter:

- The arguments traditionally given for the importance of the demand for money

- The dependence of these arguments on the use of the monetary base as the instrument of monetary policy

- The current view of the transmission mechanism of monetary policy

- The position of the demand for money within the current view

13.1   Introduction

Having considered the money supply process in Chapter 12, we look in this chapter and in Chapter 14 at the importance and practice of monetary policy. We are concerned principally here with the economic significance of changes in monetary policy instruments – in particular with the impact of monetary policy changes on aggregate demand (GDP at market prices). Changes in the level of aggregate demand may in turn affect the price level and/or the level of real income and it is these that are of interest to voters and policy makers. This series of linkages between monetary policy changes, prices and real income (and hence employment) is frequently referred to as the **transmission mechanism of monetary policy**. We look at both the standard economics textbook approach

to these linkages which works through the relationship between the supply of and the **demand for money** (explained in Box 13.1) before going on to consider a more realistic approach which begins with changes in short-term interest rates, the policy instrument actually used by central banks.

In this chapter we consider only the impact of interest rate changes on aggregate demand. In Chapter 14, we develop our treatment of monetary policy and its impact on the rate of inflation and the real economy. We also deal there with the relationship between the central bank and the government and the possible use of rules to govern monetary policy.

13.2   The standard approach to the transmission mechanism

Until recently, almost all explanations of the monetary policy process began with an assumed change in the **supply of money**, with the question of how that change was brought about being treated as a subsidiary issue. In Chapter 12, we saw that central banks do not in practice attempt to control the quantity of money directly. Box 12.4 explains why **monetary base** control has been rejected. It is clear, then, that the money supply is not an instrument of policy. Nonetheless, a strong school of theoretical monetary economics has always argued that the monetary authorities could, and should be attempting to, control the money supply through monetary base control. Sufficient numbers of economists have in the past apparently believed strongly enough in the stability of the link between the monetary base and the money supply that the money supply has commonly been treated as a policy instrument. Thus, most textbook analyses of the transmission mechanism begin with an assumption of a given change in the money supply, *as if* the authorities could automatically bring this about. The explanation of monetary policy within *IS/LM* analysis, the standard form of analysis in macroeconomic textbooks, operates in this way.

IS/LM starts with an assumption of an equilibrium between the supply of money and the demand for money. A change in the supply of money thus produces disequilibrium in the money market. Let us assume for this discussion an increase in the supply of money. Then, the supply of money temporarily exceeds the demand for money. In other words, people

---

BOX 13.1   The meaning of the demand for money

The demand for money is simply the quantity of money that economic agents *wish to hold* at a given time under the existing economic conditions. We have seen that people, in the aggregate, hold a stock of wealth. The income derived from wealth may be consumed or saved. Savings from income add to the stock of wealth. The decision as to how to hold wealth (that is, which types of asset to hold) will influence the amount of income derived from wealth and hence the ability to consume in the future. The decision will involve some trade-off between the expected rate of return on different types of assets, the risk associated with holding those assets and the fluctuations in return on them. This risk may relate to a possible loss in the nominal value of an asset or to a loss in real value through inflation. It follows that we may compare different assets (for example, financial versus real assets; equities versus bonds) and ask how much of each people are likely to hold in their portfolios under different circumstances. Money is one component of wealth and hence in asking about the demand for money we are asking why people choose to hold some of their wealth in the form of money, which pays a zero or low rate of interest, rather than in the form of other assets which bear a higher rate of return. We might also ask the circumstances under which the proportion of wealth held in the form of money will change.

are holding more money than they wish to (they are holding excess money balances). They seek to remove these excess balances. However, if the money stock is fixed exogenously, the actions of individuals cannot reduce the aggregate supply of money. It follows that we are interested in how the attempts of individuals to reduce their holdings of money might change economic variables in such a way as to make them willing to hold money balances just equal to the increased money supply. The transmission, in other words, is said to be through changes in the money supply which produce changes in the economy that in turn cause the demand for money to change. The economy goes on changing until the system is again in equilibrium. In other words, we are asking a rather back-handed question: *what has to change in the economy in order to cause the demand for money to increase by the amount of the increase in the supply of money?* This approach assumes that nothing else changes at the same time. It is an example of comparative static equilibrium. Crucially it assumes that consumer **confidence** and **expectations** are unchanging. This view of the transmission mechanism is illustrated in Figure 13.1. It is not then a surprise, given this approach, that the demand for money function has dominated monetary economics for so long both in theoretical studies that sought to provide a basis for the relationships between the demand for money, interest rates and real income, and in the vast number of empirical studies that have sought to identify the function and examine its properties.

The demand for money was not dealt with directly in the early literature which concentrated instead, through the quantity theory of money (see Section 14.1), on the velocity of money and had no place for the rate of interest. It was assumed that people only held money to allow them to carry out the economic transactions they wished to undertake.

Keynes changed all this in two important ways. Firstly, he paid particular attention to the notion of **liquidity preference** – the degree of liquidity economic agents seek in their asset portfolios under the existing economic conditions. Money is regarded as the most liquid of assets and in a simplified model (such as that of Keynes) in which there are only two assets, money and bonds, a desire for a more liquid portfolio is equivalent to an increased demand for money. The term, the demand for money, quickly replaced the more general idea of liquidity preference.

Secondly, Keynes stressed the relationship between the interest rate and the demand for money, particularly through the speculative demand for money (the idea that people might choose to hold money not because they needed it to allow the purchase of goods and services but rather because of uncertainty about future interest rates and hence the prices of other financial assets). Thus, fears of falls in the prices of financial assets other than money might persuade people to hold more money than they need for transactions motives. This potentially weakened the relationship between the money balances people wished to hold and the value of the transactions they wished to undertake.

Later studies have then concentrated on two issues, the importance of which can easily be seen in Figure 13.1. The first of these has been the interest

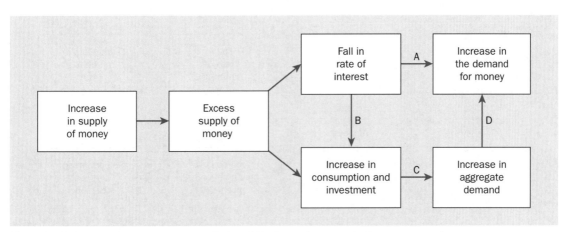

Figure 13.1 Return to money market equilibrium following an increase in the money supply

elasticity of the demand for money. Two opposing views were common in the literature:

(a) If the demand for money were highly interest elastic, the movement back to equilibrium following a change in the supply of money would be brought about largely by link A in Figure 13.2 and this would occur with only a small change in interest rates. Links B, C and D would all be relatively unimportant. The money supply change would bring about only a small change in aggregate demand. Monetary policy would be quite weak. This was the view identified for a long time in textbooks as the Keynesian view of monetary policy.

(b) On the other hand, if the demand for money were interest inelastic, link A would be of little importance. The significant relationships would be those indicated in Figure 13.3: a change in the money supply would need to have a powerful impact on aggregate demand to take us back to equilibrium. Monetary policy would be powerful. This was identified in most textbooks for many years as the monetarist view of monetary policy.

The second important issue was seen to be the stability and hence the predictability of the relationships involved, especially of link A. However weak or strong the linkages were, monetary policy would not be of much value, even if the authorities could determine the size of the money supply, if they did not have a clear idea of what would happen. In Keynes's liquidity preference theory there is a high probability that link A is unstable and unpredictable.

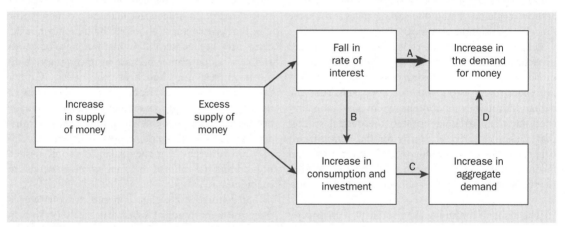

Figure 13.2 Simplified Keynesian view of monetary policy

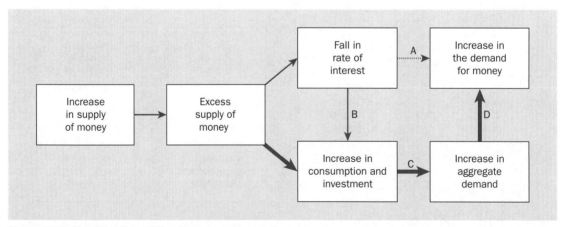

Figure 13.3 Simplified monetarist view of monetary policy

Expressed in this way, everything seems straight-forward. Economic theory could be used to suggest the factors that we need to look at in constructing a money demand function that might help us to predict the aggregate demand for money. Empirical testing could then be expected to resolve the debates about the nature of the demand for money function. And, indeed, this is what many monetary economists have spent much of the last sixty years trying to do.

The testing of money demand functions has usually taken the form of regression analysis in which the aggregate demand for money is expressed as a function of a number of independent variables. Theories of the demand for money tend to suggest a set of independent variables to include in the function something like the following:

- the interest rate on representative non-money assets, possibly including the **rate of inflation**;

- the interest rate on money;

- the transfer costs of switching between money and non-money assets;

- the level of income;

- the variance of income;

- the expected change in the rate of interest;

- an index of prices.

There were several practical problems here. Firstly, there was little point in including the interest rate on more than one non-money financial asset since interest rates on financial assets tend to move together. Furthermore, nominal interest rates may be strongly correlated with the rate of inflation. Thus, including *both* an interest rate on a financial asset *and* the rate of inflation would have disturbed the relationship between either one of them and the demand for money. However, omitting variables that contribute to the explanation of the demand for money causes the equation to be mis-specified. Then, testing the equation might suggest an instability in the demand for money that would be removed if the equation were properly specified. Thirdly, transfer costs are difficult to measure since they vary from one individual to another and from one company to another depending on the circumstances. In any case, they are likely to change only slowly and so have usually been left out of aggregate demand for money equations.

Fourthly, there were no objective *ex-post* measures of the expected variables included in the list above.

The best that could be done was to estimate expected future values of variables on the basis of forecasts using currently available information (making a judgement in doing so as to the best available forecasting model). These estimates could then be entered into the demand for money equation on the assumption of rational expectations – that agents make use of the best available forecasting models. A more usual approach was to replace the expectational variable with an available proxy or to represent it econometrically in some other way (for example, by a dummy variable or a trend term).

Fifthly, wealth and income presented problems. Ideally, a broad, all-inclusive definition of wealth was required, but the broader the definition of wealth, the more difficult it is to obtain a satisfactory measure for it. In any case, since income can be viewed as a return on the holding of wealth (human and non-human), the inclusion of both a broad definition of wealth and income presents problems. Many alternatives were tried including narrower definitions of wealth, the use of permanent income and measures of consumption expenditure. All presented difficulties.

Sixthly, we have no direct measure for the demand for money. All we can do is use the supply of money. If we were to make no other adjustments to the equation, this would be tantamount to assuming that the money market was always in equilibrium. Even if we accept this, we are left with the question of which measure of the supply of money we should use. This is complicated by the variety of definitions of money in use in different countries. Theories are of very little help here although concentration on the transactions demand for money leads in the direction of narrow definitions of money. In practice, econometricians have been happy to accept the definition of money that yields the most accurate predictions and not worry too much about the theoretical justification for it. Problems have arisen, however, from changing definitions of monetary aggregates and financial innovations that change both the roles of financial institutions (and thus the extent to which their liabilities may act as money) and attitudes towards the various types of financial assets.

Finally, there was a problem with the time period covered by the studies. Supporters of the notion of a stable demand for money only claim stability in the long run. However, if the demand for money is unstable in the short run, we need to be able to explain why, and do it in such a way that this instability is compatible with long-run stability. Further, long-run studies (which typically use annual observations or temporally averaged data) face problems because the definitions of many of the variables change over time. In addition, some elements that are omitted from the equation because they are assumed to be constant, such as transfer costs and payment systems, clearly do change over time. In any case, the distinction between long-run and short-run studies is arbitrary. There is no theoretical definition of the long run in macroeconomics other than that it is the period necessary for the economy to return to equilibrium – a definition that is useless for empirical work.

The net result of these problems is that the standard regression equation used in demand for money testing is quite a long way removed from the theoretical arguments we have considered above. A standard aggregate money demand equation, linearized by taking logs, is:

$$\ln m_t = \ln \beta_0 + \beta_1 \ln Y_t + \beta_2 \ln r_t + v_t \quad (13.1)$$

where m is the real value of the money supply (the money supply divided by a price index); Y a measure of aggregate real income; r the interest rate on a representative financial asset; and v a random variable. A common addition is the lagged dependent variable (the real value of the supply of money): $\beta_3 \ln m_{t-1}$. This simply accepts that there are bound to be time lags in adjustment and thus it is a reflection of the idea that a movement to a new equilibrium following a change in one of the independent variables will not be instantaneous. In the early days of testing it was assumed that these time lags would be quite short and thus that the role of the lagged dependent variable would not be very great. The other principal hopes of the testers of functions such as this were that:

1 the signs would be as indicated by the theory, most obviously a negative relationship between r_t and m_t;

2 that the constants would indeed turn out to be constant;

3 that the independent variables (Y_t and r_t) would between them predict a high proportion of the demand for money; and

4 that v would indeed prove to be random, indicating that it did not incorporate a missing variable with a systematic relationship with the demand for money.

13.3 Testing the demand for money – the outcome

Studies in both the USA and the UK up until the early 1970s appeared to produce satisfactory results. The demand for money was found to be **interest elastic** but elasticities were relatively low. The majority of studies produced income elasticities close to unity. The demand for money appeared to be correctly specified in real terms. Time lags between interest rate and income changes and the demand for money seemed from long-run studies to be relatively short, although this was called into doubt in short-run studies. Crucially, demand for money functions appeared to be reasonably stable.

However, in the early 1970s the demand for money function began to show signs of instability in both the UK and the USA. In the USA between 1973 and 1975, real money balances steadily declined, falling by about 7 per cent whereas demand for money equations estimated with data for the 1950s and 1960s had predicted a mild decline in 1974 followed by a recovery in 1975. Thus, existing demand for money equations were seriously *over-predicting* the demand for money, whereas in the UK equations based on the 1950s and 1960s *underestimated* the demand for money.

Equations also broke down in several other OECD countries. The problem showed up in ways other than the failure of equations to predict accurately. For example, extending the data used for estimating equations to include the 1970s produced changes in the coefficient on the lagged dependent variable which suggested unreasonably long adjustment processes.

MORE FROM THE WEB

The web is not of great help on the demand for money but if you enter 'demand for money' in Google, you will find a variety of types of material ranging from very basic outlines and diagrams (for example, on http://economics.about.com, http://www.bized.ac.uk or on http://www.revision-notes.co.uk/revision/) to difficult articles from journals. If you enter addresses directly, you will occasionally be told that you do not have the right to view the material, but if you work through Google (or another search engine) up will pop the pages you want – another wonder of the web.

Things began to go wrong again in both the USA and the UK in the early 1980s when income velocity began to fall sharply and demand for money functions estimated on pre-1982 data seriously underestimated the demand for narrow money in the mid-1980s.

Several explanations of these problems have been proposed, most of which have sought to preserve belief in the view that the demand for money is stable in the long run. Firstly, and least disruptively, it has been argued that the demand for money remained stable even in the 1970s and 1980s but that the equations derived from the pre-1970s studies failed to identify the stability because of faulty specification of the equation or the dynamics in the model. The fault thus lay with the econometrics and the problem could be overcome by altering lag structures or the functional form of the equation, especially by including important variables that had been omitted from the equation, such as a term representing relative prices of consumer durables, non-durables and services in addition to the general index of prices.

Secondly, it was argued that there had been changes affecting the arguments of the function, resulting in unpredictable shifts in the demand for money function and/or in the slope of the function. To retain belief in the long-run stability of the function, it was then necessary to argue that such changes were limited to a particular, dramatic period of time and that once the system had adjusted, long-run relationships would re-emerge. The problems in the early 1970s were attributed to a variety of causes including the change from an international fixed exchange rate system to floating exchange rates and, in the UK, changes in the approach to the control of the money supply. The difficulties in the 1980s were overwhelmingly attributed to financial innovation and institutional change.

MORE FROM THE WEB

If you would like some feel for the quantity and nature of academic research on the demand for money, try http://ideas.repec.org or http://www.ideas.uqam.ca/. Enter 'demand for money' in the search facility on the home page and up will come a long list of papers – in September 2007, the request produced 1,099 responses! When you look at the titles of the individual papers, be prepared to be frightened.

Institutional change is not new. Particular changes may affect the demand for money in different ways and thus to some extent their impacts may cancel out over time. Further, there is little to worry about if the changes occur steadily over time since their effects will be predictable. Problems only arise if changes are sudden and frequent or are induced by levels of, or changes in, other variables within the demand for money function. Financial innovations, for instance, may occur in waves, causing discrete short-term jumps in demand for money functions. Again, a period of prolonged high interest rates may encourage the development of financial innovations, allowing money balances held for transactions purposes to be reduced. Thus, there is the possibility of a ratchet effect – when interest rates are high, it pays to spend time and effort on the development of **financial innovations** such as the introduction of different types of bank accounts or the introduction of automated teller machines. Having been introduced, these innovations are not reversed when interest rates fall again because the costs involved are mainly set-up costs (e.g. computing hardware and software). Thus such financial innovation is likely to have both (a) caused the constant to fall and (b) caused the interest elasticity of the demand for narrow money to increase (as shifts between demand deposits and high-interest-bearing deposits have become much easier).

Attempts to reflect the effects of financial innovation in empirical work have been of several kinds. For example, it was argued that the problems of the 1970s could be overcome by including long-term interest rates in the function and redefining money, overcoming the problems arising from the growth of interest-bearing demand deposits by excluding them from the definition of money. A more usual approach was to incorporate additional variables into the money demand equation. For instance, instead of narrowing the definition of money it was possible to seek to cope with the increased payment of interest rates on demand deposits by adding money's own rate of interest to the equation. Among other variables included have been the change in the number of bank branches per head of population, the ratio of currency to total money stock and of non-bank to bank financial assets and past peak levels of interest rates. Such attempts to adjust equations to reflect institutional change have often not produced satisfactory results. However, this may reflect the difficulty of capturing in equations the many ways in which institutional change may influence agents' actions rather than indicating that financial innovation has not been the principal cause of the apparent instability. A particular problem is that, to the extent that they are induced rather than autonomous, the factors causing financial innovations may be taken into account elsewhere in the equation. Econometricians have largely sought to use cointegration techniques to identify long-run stability amidst the short-run fluctuations.

Thirdly, blame was placed upon the assumption of equilibrium and new approaches to disequilibrium were developed. Associated with these was the development of the **buffer stock** approach to the demand for money – a formalization of the old idea that the existence of money allows the separation in time of sales and purchases (the store of value function of money). A distinction is drawn between 'demanding' money as a means of payment and being willing to 'accept' it temporarily because of the costs associated with adjusting stocks of less liquid assets. This work has built upon precautionary demand for money models which see individuals as being willing to allow their money holdings to fluctuate between a floor and a ceiling.

In short, economists responded to the apparent instability in the demand for money in the 1970s and 1980s with a great deal of imagination. Many journal articles claimed support for reasons why the demand for money function was truly stable. Nonetheless, some economists saw the problems with the function as evidence for the proposition that such a function either could not sensibly be defined at all or was bound to be unstable. One view of this kind derives from the endogenous money hypothesis. This holds that in order to carry out spending plans, agents obtain bank loans. The act of spending these loans creates money in the form of additional bank deposits. As long as banks freely meet the demand for loans, the supply of money can be seen to be adjusting to the demand for them. Spending plans drive the whole process. Since investment plans, in particular, are influenced by waves of optimism and pessimism there is no reason to believe that the demand for money will be stably related to real income. In its extreme form, the endogenous money hypothesis holds that there is no demand for money function independent of the supply of money. People are willing to hold whatever money is created through the banking system.

In summary, there appeared to be some evidence of stability in the long-run demand for money relationship

---

MORE FROM THE WEB

You would like something more on the testing of the demand for money? Well, the web certainly demonstrates that it is international. Enter 'testing the demand for money' in Google and you will get a rich panoply of articles dealing with the demand for money in, among other countries, Korea, Denmark, Turkey, Israel, the UK, Switzerland, Fiji, Pakistan, South Africa, China and India. However, for many of the papers only an abstract is freely available on the web.

---

but short-run adjustment lags were variable, making it difficult to estimate a stable short-run demand for money function for targeted variables. Even if the long-run function were stable, central banks would not know the lags between changes in the money stock, prices and real income.

13.4 A more realistic approach to the transmission mechanism of monetary policy

We have considered the problems in reaching a conclusion about the nature of the demand for money. However, the major difficulty facing this approach to the transmission mechanism is that central banks cannot and do not attempt directly to control the rate of growth of the money supply. Monetary policy is practised through the influence that the central bank can bring to bear on short-term interest rates in the economy. Thus, a realistic approach to the transmission mechanism should begin with short-term interest rates. This approach is summarized in Box 13.2 (Goodhart, 2002).

In Section 15.4 we explain how exactly central banks seek to influence short-term interest rates in the economy. For example, the Bank of England and the ECB set the price of very short-dated gilt repos, but a notable feature of recent developments in central bank operating procedures is the tendency towards convergence. There is little difference wherever we look (Borio, 1997). A mixture of convention and arbitrage then communicate any change in this 'official' rate to other short-term money market rates, more or less instantly. The impact upon longer-term rates is

BOX 13.2 **The interest rate control (endogenous money) approach to the transmission mechanism in six steps (Goodhart, 2002)**

1 The central bank determines the short-term interest rate.

2 The private sector determines the volume of borrowing it wishes to undertake from the banking sector at the current set of interest rates.

3 Banks adjust their own relative interest rates, marketable assets, and interbank and wholesale borrowing to meet the credit demands upon them.

4 These bank actions determine the money stock and its various sub-components (e.g. demand, time and wholesale deposits). This determines the volume of bank reserves needed, taking into account any required reserve ratios.

5 This determines how much the banks need to borrow from, or pay back to, the central bank in order to meet their demand for reserves.

6 In order to sustain the level of interest rates set under Step 1, the central bank uses open market operations to satisfy the banks' demand for reserves established under Step 5.

rather less direct and less certain, though there is a tendency for all rates to move in the same direction.

The next step is to consider the effects on the economy of these changes in interest rates brought about by central banks. To do this, we make use of a Bank of England diagram of the transmission mechanism (Figure 13.4).

You should note the absence of the demand for and supply of money from this diagram. Let us next consider the relationships in a little more detail.

13.4.1 The impact of interest rate changes on consumption and investment

It is widely accepted that consumption expenditure is influenced by changes in the real rate of interest (the nominal rate of interest less the expected rate of inflation). Changes in nominal interest rates brought about by central bank changes in its short-term interest (repo) rate will, given the expected rate of inflation at the time, result in changes in the real rate of interest in the economy. Thus, we need to look at the ways in which real interest rate changes induced by central bank policy affect private sector spending.

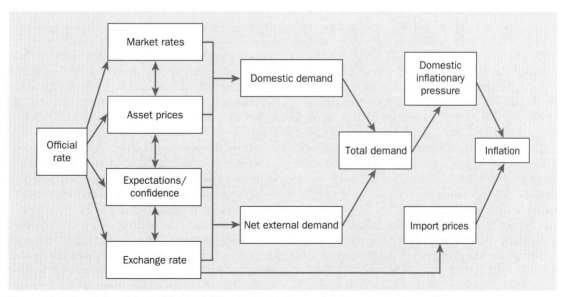

Figure 13.4 The Bank of England's view of the transmission mechanism of monetary policy

Source: Bank of England (1999) *Quarterly Bulletin*, May. Reproduced with permission.

The principal components of domestic private sector demand are consumption and investment expenditure. Consumption expenditure derives from current income but consumption decisions depend also on expected future income, the level of wealth and on the ability to borrow against existing wealth. Thus, monetary policy is likely to influence household consumption through several channels. For example, an increase in interest rates:

- makes saving from current income more attractive;

- increases repayments on existing floating-rate debt and thus lowers disposable income;

- increases the *cost of borrowing* and thus increases the cost of goods and services obtained on credit;

- lowers the price of financial assets and hence influences estimates of private sector wealth;

- lowers house prices or, at least, slows the rate at which they are increasing and this, too, influences estimates of household wealth and lowers the value of the collateral against which households seek to borrow.

If households believe that the interest rate changes will lower aggregate demand, they might also become concerned about the impact on output and employment. Increased worries about future employment will cause households to lower their estimates of expected future income from employment and become more cautious about current expenditure. Any fear of an impending recession might, in addition, cause banks to tighten the conditions they apply to loan applications, making it more difficult for people to obtain credit even if they remain willing to borrow.

Of these various influences, changes in repayments on floating-rate mortgages are particularly important in the UK since loans secured on houses make up about 80 per cent of personal debt, and most mortgages carry floating interest rates. *All of these influences operate in the same direction – we expect an increase in interest rates to reduce consumption expenditure.* Yet, not everyone will reduce consumption expenditure as interest rates rise. The discussion so far has implied that interest rate rises reduce the disposable income of all households, but this will not be true for those consisting of people living off income from savings deposits. Nor is it true for people whose expected future income depends on an annuity to be purchased in the near future. In both of these cases, higher interest rates imply a higher income. Thus,

interest rate changes have redistributional effects. When interest rates increase, net borrowers are made worse off and net savers better off. However, the groups made better off (net savers) are highly likely to be outweighed by those made worse off (net borrowers) and so we continue to expect increases in interest rates to reduce household consumption expenditure.

The same applies to investment expenditure. An increase in interest rates:

- raises external borrowing costs for firms that raise funds through bank loans or from bills or bonds markets;

- increases the rate at which they discount back expected future returns from investment, making investment projects less attractive;

- increases the return from the savings of firms, retained from past profits, raising the opportunity cost of financing investment internally;

- increases the difficulty and cost of raising investment funds through the issue of new capital on the stock market;

- increases the costs of holding inventories of goods, which are often financed by bank loans;

- lowers asset prices, reducing the net worth of firms and making it more difficult for them to borrow.

The way in which firms respond to monetary policy changes also depends on the way in which those changes affect estimates of future aggregate demand since these are a major influence on their forecast future sales and hence on estimated future profits. Thus, if a change in the official interest rate – or, indeed, a failure to change it – reinforces a view that aggregate demand is likely to fall in the future firms may respond by 'restructuring' and cutting back employment by greater amounts than might be expected simply on the basis of the direct effects listed above.

As with households, not all firms will be affected in the same way or to the same extent. Much depends on the nature of the business, the size of the firm and its sources of finance. An increase in interest rates improves the cashflow of firms with funds deposited with banks or placed in the money markets, although this does not imply that they will make use of their improved position to increase investment. It is more likely, indeed, to encourage firms to hold greater quantities of financial assets or to pay higher dividends to shareholders. The cashflow of firms whose short-term assets and liabilities are more or less matched will be little affected by changes in short-term interest rates but are still likely to be influenced by changes in longer-term rates. Further, despite the above list, the impact of changes in the official interest rate on the cost of capital for particular firms is difficult to predict, especially for large and multinational firms with access to international capital markets. Nonetheless, it remains true that for firms taken together increases in interest rates are highly likely to lead to reduced investment expenditure.

Open economy influences also need to be taken into account. Other things being equal, an increase in domestic interest rates should increase the attractiveness of the currency in foreign exchange markets, raising the value of the currency. This damages the international competitiveness of domestic firms since it raises the prices of their goods when expressed in foreign currencies and, in the short run at least, they have little scope for reducing costs of production and lowering domestic currency prices. Thus, they must reduce their profit margins, accept a loss of market share in export markets or both. Problems arise in domestic markets also. Import-competing goods face increased competition from foreign products because their prices are now lower in domestic currency terms. Difficulties are likely to follow also for domestic firms that are not in direct competition with foreign firms because of changes in the composition of household spending that results from changes in the relative prices of domestic and foreign goods. For example, households may respond to a reduction in the domestic currency price of foreign holidays by cutting back on expenditure on books or CDs in order to take a foreign holiday. Of course, it is only those changes in exchange rate that are brought about by monetary policy changes or expected changes in monetary policy that we are concerned with here. Exchange rates may be affected by many other factors.

Again, different sectors will be affected in different ways by monetary policy induced exchange rate changes. The manufacturing sector is the most exposed to foreign competition and thus is likely to suffer most from increases in the value of the domestic currency. Agriculture, financial and business services, and those parts of the service sector heavily reliant on the arrival of foreign tourists are also likely to be strongly affected.

Expectations and confidence about the future clearly play a major role in all of this. It follows that the size of the likely fall in aggregate demand depends crucially on whether:

(a) the present increase in interest rates had been expected; and

(b) the present increase leads to expectations of further increases in future or quick reversals of policy;

(c) expectations regarding future inflation rates.

Inflationary expectations are particularly important since much of the influence of interest rate changes on the expenditure of households and firms relates to changes in real interest rates (the rate of interest adjusted to take into account the expected rate of inflation). Monetary policy operates directly on nominal interest rates. Much of the above discussion takes inflationary expectations as given, in which case a change in nominal interest rates is equivalent to a change in real interest rates. However, monetary policy may well have an influence on inflationary expectations. Indeed, it is commonly the intention of the monetary authorities that it should do so. Hence, if an increase in interest rates lowers market expectations of the future rate of inflation, the real rate of interest will increase by more than the nominal rate. Those areas of expenditure particularly influenced by real rates of interest (e.g. investment expenditure by firms and housing expenditure and expenditure on consumer durables) will be affected more than would have been the case had inflationary expectations remained unchanged.

We can conclude from this section that:

- monetary policy influences aggregate demand in a variety of ways;

- the relationship between interest rate changes and changes in aggregate demand might be quite powerful;

- the relationship between interest rates and aggregate demand is inverse – increases in interest rates reduce aggregate expenditure; reductions in interest rates cause aggregate expenditure to increase;

- nonetheless, the relationship between interest rates and aggregate demand is complex;

- interest rate changes affect the distribution of income as well as the level of aggregate demand.

This last point is of great importance to the monetary authorities. Knowing the direction in which aggregate demand is likely to change when interest rates change is of very limited use. We need to know how powerful a policy instrument monetary policy is, whether the size of the impact of a given change is predictable and how long it will take for the full impact of a change in interest rates to be felt in the economy. Clearly, the size of the impact of a monetary policy change and the length of the time lags involved in the process may well vary from one economy to another. Nonetheless, we can make some general points about time lags.

Time lags in monetary policy

There are several different **time lags** involved in monetary policy. We can distinguish the following:

- the length of time it takes for the authorities to observe changes in the economy and to decide on a change in the official short-term rate of interest (policy decision lag);

- the length of time it takes for the change in the official rate to feed through to other interest rates in the economy (institutional lag);

- the length of time required for interest rate changes to affect the disposable income of households (income lag);

- the length of time required for changes in short-term and long-term interest rates to affect the expenditure of households and firms (expenditure lag);

- the length of time needed for changes in expenditure to be reflected in changes in the rate of inflation, output and employment (real response lag).

Evidence from industrial economies generally suggests that once the monetary authorities have changed the **official rate** it takes about twelve months for the full impact of the change to be felt on demand and production. It takes a further twelve months for the full effect on the rate of inflation to be felt. This in itself presents serious problems for the monetary authorities since it means that they must be constantly looking forward trying to assess the likely state of inflationary pressures two years ahead on the assumption of unchanged policies and then trying to estimate the impact of a policy change. Given that the interest rate is only one influence among many on expenditure, this is clearly very difficult. However, things are even worse because the time lags of twelve months and two years mentioned here are only approximate and are only averages. The

> **MORE FROM THE WEB**
>
> This discussion of the transmission of monetary policy changes is based on the discussion in the Monetary Policy Committee's 1999 paper on the transmission mechanism. It can be downloaded in pdf form on: http://www.bankofengland.co.uk/publications/other/monetary/montrans.pdf.
>
> A slightly older Bank of England paper compares the monetary transmission mechanism in the UK, France and Germany and is available at: http://www.bankofengland.co.uk/publications/quarterlybulletin/qb970202.pdf.

time lags associated with any particular act of monetary policy may be much shorter or much longer – they are highly variable and will depend, among other things, on the state of business and consumer confidence, how this confidence is influenced by monetary policy changes, events in the world economy and expectations about future inflation.

13.4.2 The demand for and supply of money in the transmission mechanism

We pointed out at the beginning of this section that neither the demand for or supply of money appears in the Bank of England transmission diagram. What role, if any, do they then play in monetary policy.

Consider, firstly, the supply of money. It is clear that in this approach to the transmission mechanism, the money supply is endogenous, that is, it is determined within the system. Changes in measures of the money supply will be the outcome of changes in a number of the variables in Figure 13.4, most obviously the official interest rate. However, other variables such as expectations/confidence, asset prices and the exchange rate can change without changes in the official rate. There is thus no suggestion that the central bank can hope to influence the rate of inflation through influencing the money supply, either directly or indirectly. The basic idea of a relationship between the supply of money and **total demand** in the economy still holds and a rapidly expanding money supply continues to have an association with high rates of inflation. From a monetary policy point of view, because of the long time lag between changes in official interest rates and their impact on the rate of inflation, measures of the money supply and/or of the monetary base may be one of several indicators central banks are likely to consult in deciding upon changes in interest rates.

The demand for money is more difficult. Plainly, there is a demand for money in the same way as there is a demand for each of the other assets in which economic agents choose to hold their wealth. Again, there is a relationship between the demand for money and the value of economic transactions people wish to undertake. There may be some value in estimating a demand for money function and testing it for such things as interest rate elasticity and stability. However, it is clear that interest rates in the economy are not determined by the interaction of the demand for and supply of money and, since we cannot measure the demand for money independently of the supply of money, there is no obvious role for it in the practice of monetary policy.

13.5 Summary

This chapter is concerned with the first part of the transmission mechanism of monetary policy – that is the link between changes in the monetary policy instrument and changes in the level of total demand in the economy. Chapter 14 extends the analysis to consider the relationship between the monetary policy instrument and the rate of inflation. The economics literature adopts two contrasting approaches to the transmission mechanism.

The standard textbook approach assumes that the monetary policy instrument is the money supply itself and analyses the impact of changes in the money supply on total demand. This is assumed to disturb an existing equilibrium between the supply of and demand for money. Attempts by economic agents to restore equilibrium are held to bring about changes in the economy that influence total demand. The demand for money function then has a central role in this analysis. *If* the authorities could determine the size of the money supply, they could only make use of this to control total demand and ultimately inflation if the demand for money were a stable function of a small number of variables. Thus, a great deal of effort has gone into trying to show that this is the case.

However, as we have seen in Chapter 12, the authorities cannot control the money supply either directly or indirectly through changes in the monetary base. Nor do they attempt to do so. It thus seems much more realistic to examine the impacts on the economy of changes in the official rate of interest, the instrument that central banks do use. This has the added advantage that we can much more easily take into account the impact of policy changes on the expectations of economic agents. We have seen that in this form of analysis, measures of the money supply might still have a use as one among several indicators of likely future changes in the rate of inflation but that there is no clear role for the demand for money function whether it can be shown to be stably related to a small number of variables.

Key concepts in this chapter

Buffer stock	Official rate of interest
Confidence	Rate of inflation
Demand for money	Rates of interest
Expectations	Supply of money
Financial innovation	Time lags in monetary policy
Interest elasticity	Total demand
Liquidity preference	Transmission mechanism
Monetary base	

Questions and problems

1 Explain why the question of the stability of the demand for money was for long regarded as an important issue.

2 What is meant by the phrase 'a stable demand for money function'?

3 Why is it not possible to add up the demand for money of individual households to obtain an aggregate demand for money for the economy?

4 List the difficulties associated with the empirical testing of demand for money functions.

5 Discuss how useful all of the work done on the demand for money has, in fact, been. Should our response to the difficulties be: (i) 'Let us give up testing the demand for money now, the exercise is pointless'; or (ii) 'We need more research into this important topic'?

6 Why does the Bank of England's Monetary Policy Committee need to be forward looking in making decisions about changes in the Bank's repo rate?

7 How certain and predictable are the various links in the Bank of England's monetary transmission diagram?

Further reading

K Bain and P Howells, *Monetary Economics. Policy and its Theoretical Basis* (Basingstoke: Palgrave, 2003) Chs 5, 6

C E V Borio, 'Monetary policy operating procedures in industrial countries' (Basle: Bank for International Settlements, 1997), Working Paper no. 40

E Britton and J Whitley, 'Comparing the monetary transmission mechanism in France, Germany and the United Kingdom: some issues and results', *Bank of England Quarterly Bulletin*, May 1997, 152–62. http://www.bankofengland.co.uk/publications/quarterlybulletin/qb970202.pdf

C A E Goodhart, 'The conduct of monetary policy', *Economic Journal*, 99/396, June 1989, 293–346

C A E Goodhart, 'The endogeneity of money', in P Arestis, M Desai and S Dow (eds) *Money, Macroeconomics and Keynes*. Vol. 1 (London: Routledge, 2002)

M K Lewis and P D Mizen, *Monetary Economics* (Oxford: Oxford University Press, 2000) Ch. 11

Monetary Policy Committee, Bank of England, *The Transmission Mechanism of Monetary Policy*, May 1999. http://www.bankofengland.co.uk/publications/other/monetary/montrans.pdf

Websites

www.bankofengland.co.uk
www.bis.org
www.bized.ac.uk
http://economics.about
http://ideas.repec.org
www.ideas.uqam.ca
www.imf.org
www.oecd.org
www.revision-notes.co.uk

Chapter 14

Monetary policy

What you will learn in this chapter:

■ That how the effects of monetary policy are divided between
  output and prices is a controversial issue

■ The importance of the role of 'expectations' and
  'price-stickiness' in this debate

■ The basis for the argument that elected governments have an
  incentive to conduct monetary policy with an inflationary bias

■ How this bias might be reduced if the policymaker is
  constrained by 'rules'

■ How this bias might be reduced if monetary policy is placed
  in the hands of an independent central bank

14.1 Introduction

We are now familiar with the idea that the main instrument of monetary policy in most regimes is an 'official' rate of interest set by the central bank in its dealings with the commercial banking system. In Chapter 13 we saw how changes in this instrument produce changes in the rate of inflation – the primary concern of monetary policymakers these days. Box 14.1 shows the way in which the policy objective is framed for the Bank of England. The Bank is expected to support the government's wider policy regarding employment and growth but only *after* it has secured price stability (defined as an annual rate of change in the CPI of 2 per cent). And 'remits' of this kind are now quite commonplace among central banks.

The fact that the monetary policymaker is required to focus primarily on price stability is not accidental. It indicates a widespread belief that the effects of monetary policy fall largely on the price level and its rate of change. In other words, monetary policy has little influence over *real* variables like output and employment and so it is best used to achieve what it is good at, which is price stability, or at least a low rate of inflation.

This position is sometimes claimed to be equivalent to the 'classical' view of money, enshrined in the 'quantity theory of money'. If we write all variables as growth rates then the quantity theory says:

$$m + v = p + y \qquad (14.1)$$

where m is money, p is the price level, y is real output and v is the velocity of circulation (best understood as a

term which is necessary to make both sides of Equation 14.1 balance and is related to the way in which people use money for payments). The crucial point for the classical economists was that v and y changed only very slowly (at their 'natural rates') and their behaviour was completely independent of what was happening to m. Clearly, if v and y were determined elsewhere, then changes in m, the growth of money, must be reflected in p, the rate of inflation. Except that modern monetary policy substitutes a rate of interest for the quantity of money, there are some similarities.

But only *some*. While it is true that monetary policymakers are *primarily* concerned with inflation they are not exclusively so. Every policymaker knows that a rise in interest rates will slow the growth of aggregate demand. After all, as we saw in Chapter 13, that is precisely the mechanism through which the interest rate change is ultimately going to affect inflation. But a slowing of aggregate demand is almost certainly bound to slow the growth (or even reduce the level) of output and this will have some effect upon employment. The controversial issue is not whether real effects occur but whether they are limited to the 'short run' and, if so, how short can we make the short run. And there's the related issue of whether, if the economy is subject to frequent disturbances, policymaking is always operating in the 'short run': the effects never have time to work themselves out fully.

Like most knowledge, the current wisdom that price stability should be the main focus of monetary policy is the result of an evolutionary process. Our understanding of where we are now can therefore be helped by a brief look at this evolution. In the next section (14.2) we shall look at what we have labelled 'the simple Phillips curve'. In Section 14.3 we look at a major criticism of the simple Phillips curve, based on the importance of 'expectations'. In Section 14.4 we turn our attention to the final development of the Phillips curve framework, associated with the 'policy irrelevance theorem'. In Section 14.5 we show how the current conduct of monetary policy can be represented, distinguishing between short-run effects (including those on output and employment) and long-run effects, affecting principally the rate of inflation. After examining the split between short- and long-run effects, the remainder of the chapter looks at the argument that the conduct of monetary policy can be subject to inflationary bias and how this might be limited by the use of policy 'rules' (14.6) and by handing monetary policy to an independent central bank (14.7).

BOX 14.1 The Bank of England's priorities

REMIT FOR THE MONETARY POLICY COMMITTEE

The Bank of England Act came into effect on 1 June 1998. The Act states that in relation to monetary policy, the objectives of the Bank of England shall be:

(a) to maintain price stability; and

(b) *subject to that*, to support the economic policy of Her Majesty's Government, including its objectives for growth and employment.

Source: www.bankofengland.co.uk/monetarypolicy/remit.htm, Bank of England (our emphasis).

14.2 The simple Phillips curve

For 25 years after the Second World War, most governments conducted macroeconomic policy upon the basis that their instrument settings would have an effect upon aggregate demand and that changes in aggregate demand would have 'real' effects, that is, upon output and employment, provided that there was spare capacity in the economy. Furthermore, as a general rule, it was felt that fiscal policy – changes in government spending and taxation – probably had more powerful and predictable demand effects than monetary policy. In the UK at least this view of the **transmission mechanism** was summed up by the Radcliffe Committee which rejected the importance of the money stock but laid greater emphasis upon the vaguely defined concept of 'general liquidity'. As for central bank adjustments to short-term interest rates, their effect was largely symbolic. They might have some effect also upon the availability of liquidity but this could be better achieved by direct controls (Radcliffe Committee, 1959).

More relevant for our purpose, however, is the belief, prevalent at the time, that changes in aggregate demand could have real effects provided that the economy was operating at less than full employment. Little thought was given to what precisely was meant by 'full employment' or to the question of how unemployed resources could persist in an economy where limited resources faced insatiable wants and where markets were free to respond to relative price signals. In the early part of the period, say from 1945 to 1960, the connection between demand and employment was probably based upon a few stylized facts: unemployment was high in the 1930s when demand was low; it was non-existent during the war years when demand for everything outstripped supply; and it did seem to be the case through the 1950s that small increases in unemployment could be reversed by expansionary demand management.

After 1958, the idea that governments could effectively 'choose' the level of employment and output, up to some critical full employment level, enjoyed what appeared to be overwhelming *empirical* support from the work of A W Phillips (1958). The 'Phillips curve' plotted the relationship between the recorded level of unemployment (U) and the rate of change of money wages (C) (as a proxy for inflation since data was not available for the earlier years) from 1861 to 1957. Figure 14.1 shows a curve fitted to this data.

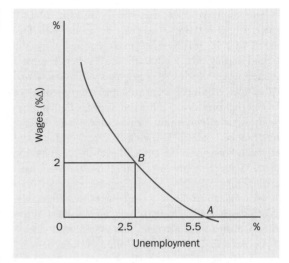

Figure 14.1 The simple Phillips curve

The implication seemed clear. The historical evidence suggested firstly that the economy could be run at various levels of unemployment and, consequently, output. Secondly, it suggested that varying the level of unemployment could be done without any positive inflation until the level of unemployment fell to 5.5 per cent. The third implication, and this is crucial in the light of later developments in this field, was that governments could choose to run the economy at even lower levels of unemployment if they so wished, but in exchange they would have to accept some positive rate of inflation. On the evidence, they could, for example, choose point B in Figure 14.1, achieving an unemployment level of 2.5 per cent provided that they were prepared to accept the inflation rate of 2 per cent. Thus was born the idea of a *stable* trade-off between unemployment and inflation. We firstly illustrate this trade-off and then see that it raises some awkward questions.

Let us assume first of all that we can take the rate of change of money wages as a proxy for the rate of inflation. The Phillips curve then suggests that the rate of inflation is a function of the level of unemployment, which we might write:

$$\pi = b_1 \cdot 1/U \qquad (14.2)$$

As unemployment falls the rate of inflation increases. The sensitivity of the relationship is determined by the coefficient b_1, the curve in Figure 14.1 becoming steeper, for example, with larger values of b_1.

Suppose now a situation where the value of U is such that $\pi = 0$ (5.5 per cent, at point A in Figure 14.1). In this setting, markets, including the labour market, are in equilibrium. Workers receive a money wage which they recognize as having a *real* value which induces them to supply the amount of labour that produces 5.5 per cent recorded unemployment. Equally, employers are prepared to pay the current money wage, knowing its real value, and knowing that given the current level of productivity, demand for their products and so on, they can earn normal profits.

Now imagine that the government introduces a demand shock, with a view to reducing the level of unemployment to 2.5 per cent, and is willing to accept 2 per cent inflation as the trade-off. As U falls, demand pressure increases. Firms produce more in response to the increased demand and hire more workers, paying them a higher money wage to induce extra work. Suppose that they are offered an increase in money wages of 2 per cent. More labour is forthcoming (U falls) because employment has become more attractive since **real wages** appear to have increased by 2 per cent. In Figure 14.1 we move up the Phillips curve from point A to point B, and all appears to be well.

However, it is commonplace in economics to assume that people are rational, utility maximizers and that they are well informed. The first two assumptions carry with them the corollary that agents respond to changes in *real* magnitudes. In our example, unemployment falls (output expands) because workers expect to be better off in *real* terms by the increase in money wages. But if the rate of inflation (at point B) is now 2 per cent, then the contracts which have just been signed no longer deliver a real increase in wages of 2 per cent. In fact, once the inflation rate has fully adjusted to the new pressure of demand, there will be no change in real values at all. The negotiated 2 per cent will only be enough to keep pace with inflation. And if we hold to our assumption that rational agents are only influenced by real changes, we must now expect that workers will revise their plans to supply labour when they find that there is no real wage increase. If the planned *real* wage increase is to materialize under these new inflationary conditions, then the wage contract has to increase **nominal wages** by an amount sufficient to deliver the intended *real* change *plus* an amount sufficient to compensate for inflation. In this case, if $\pi = 2$ per cent, a real increase of 2 per cent requires a money or nominal increase of 4 per cent.

The point of this illustration is that it shows that the assumption of rational, well-informed agents leads us to expect that people take the rate of inflation into account in setting prices, since what they are concerned with is *real* values. If they do not behave in this way, then we have to conclude that they are not rational (something that economists are always reluctant to do!) or that they are not well informed enough to realize what is happening and that they mistake changes in nominal or money values for changes in real ones. This may be more plausible, and it is known as **money illusion**.

We can now see why, if agents take inflation into account, the stable trade-off between inflation and unemployment shown in the 'simple' Phillips curve in Figure 14.1 is threatened. At point B prices are now rising by 2 per cent per annum. The 2 per cent increase in money wages no longer gives an equivalent increase in real wages. Indeed, the real wage is unchanged. If we maintain our assumptions about rational, well-informed agents, we must expect that their behaviour will revert to that which prevailed at the old real costs and rewards. Unemployment (and output) return to their original level. All that has changed is that prices are now rising by 2 per cent per annum. Knowing this, rational agents will take 2 per cent inflation into account in setting future contracts and there is a likelihood that 2 per cent thus becomes established as the new rate of inflation. If this happens then in Figure 14.2 we are at point C.

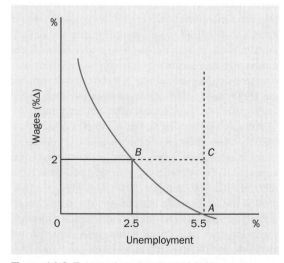

Figure 14.2 Expectations-augmented Phillips curve

The 'expectations-augmented' Phillips curve

In Figure 14.2, we move from point B to point C because agents come to realize what is happening to the rate of inflation. The time it takes for them to realize this and to take it into account in their behaviour obviously depends upon how they 'learn' about the rate of inflation. If they learn slowly, then point B might be an available option to governments for a significant period of time, the transition to C happening only slowly. On the other hand, if the learning takes place quickly, point B will be short-lived. We shall see in the next section that it might even be possible for agents to *anticipate* what is going to happen to inflation. In this case, point B never materializes and we go directly from A to C. If we rule out the latter case for the moment and accept that learning takes time, then what we saw at the end of the last section leads us to the conclusion that the Phillips curve may be downward sloping in the short run but that in the long run it is vertical. The length of the short run depends upon how quickly people learn what is happening to the price level and upon how quickly contracts can be revised.

What we have described as 'learning' is usually described in the monetary policy literature as **expectations formation**. The idea that expectations should play an important role in economic and financial decision making is no surprise to us. In Section 8.2, for example, we noted that decisions to buy assets must be based on the return people *expect* and yet the only firm information that they have concerns past returns. In Section 9.3.1, we drew a distinction between the nominal and real rate of interest, a distinction which depended upon the *expected* rate of inflation. In Section 9.3.2 we saw that Keynes thought the demand for money (and thus the current rate of interest) depended upon how agents thought interest rates were going to change. In Section 10.4 we were interested in agents' expectations of the behaviour of *future* short-term interest rates and listed factors – expected inflation, the rate of credit expansion, the level of government borrowing – that might influence these expectations. In Section 11.5 we saw that asset prices might be affected by what agents thought would happen to asset prices in future. Notice, however, that although we have frequently stressed the importance of expectations and we have sometimes listed factors which seem relevant to a particular set of expectations, we have

said nothing about the manner in which that information is used in order to *form* expectations.

There are essentially three approaches which economists take to 'expectations'. The first is to treat expectations as exogenous. This means that expectations are formed by influences largely outside the economic system. This would be legitimate if we felt that the state of expectation depended upon such 'psychological' factors that no amount of studying human behaviour could ever lead us to general conclusions about a connection between 'economic' events and expectations. This is a position that Keynes sometimes took, in talking about the 'animal spirits' of entrepreneurs, for example. At other times, however, he often wrote as though uncertainty about the future caused agents to rely very heavily upon past experience or 'convention' as he often called it.

The idea that past experience should play a large part in forming people's expectations seems eminently reasonable and forms the basis of a second approach to expectations formation known as **adaptive** or **backward-looking expectations**. In this case, people expect events to continue as they did in the past, where the recent past is more important than the distant past. We might, for example, expect inflation next year to be equal to some weighted average of the past five years, where the weight given to this year's rate is quite large, with the weights given to earlier years declining quite sharply.

Yet another idea suggests that agents form their expectations taking past experience into account but doing so in a way that enables them to construct a 'model' of the economy. This model then gives them some guidance about the likely *future* effect of *current* events. In a sense, therefore, such expectations are **forward looking** but are more frequently called **rational expectations** because this is the way in which we would expect rational economic agents to form expectations. Rational agents should make the best use of all available information and not just the past behaviour of the variable in which they are interested. The theory of rational expectations has had a major impact in economics and finance in recent years. We shall meet it again in Chapter 18, when we look at foreign exchange markets. It is also a major theme of Chapter 26 where we discuss the 'efficiency' of financial markets.

For the moment, we need to understand that the possibility of a Phillips-curve-type unemployment–inflation trade-off depends upon the speed with which people learn about what is happening to inflation; and the speed of this learning depends upon how expectations are formed. It is easy to see why the trade-off should depend upon speed of learning. Assume that learning takes some time so that the transition from B to C is slow. This is because agents failed to take the *future* rate of inflation into account accurately and quickly. If, in our example, workers had *known* that inflation was going to be 2 per cent, they would have asked for 4 per cent. If employers had refused, then workers would not have accepted more employment. We would have gone directly from A to C. The simple Phillips curve disregarded expectations and thus created the impression of a *stable* trade-off between unemployment and inflation. In the next section we shall examine an argument that correct expectations are formed so quickly that there is *never* a trade-off. In this section we look briefly at an intermediate position which shows more precisely what is necessary for monetary shocks to have at least a short-run effect on employment and output.

The simple Phillips curve of Section 14.2 takes no account of expectations. This is clear in Equation 14.2 where the rate of inflation depends solely upon demand pressure, captured by the term $1/U$. This is easily modified to incorporate a role for expectations.

$$\pi_t = b_1 \cdot 1/U_t + b_2 \cdot \pi_t^e \qquad (14.3)$$

(We add the time subscripts, t, since time is about to become critical.) Current period inflation now depends upon the *current* level of demand pressure (as before) but also upon current expectations of inflation. The term b_2 captures the extent to which inflation expectations, howsoever they are formed, are incorporated into current price-setting behaviour and thus into the rate of inflation. If $b_2 = 0$, then we have the simple Phillips curve case where expectations play no part. $b_2 = 0$ therefore indicates total money illusion, while $b_2 = 1$ indicates complete absence of money illusion. We shall assume that $b_2 = 1$, unless otherwise stated. Notice that this does *not* mean that the inflation rate is correctly and instantly anticipated. It only means that whatever expectations people have, these are fully incorporated. As we shall see in a moment, the expectations themselves could be persistently wrong.

The question then is how are inflation expectations formed? The early attacks upon the simple Phillips curve used the assumption that *current expectations* of inflation are based upon *past actual* rates (Friedman, 1968). Current expectations are a weighted average of past actual rates, with the weight on each past rate declining as it becomes more remote. In the terms of our discussion above, these criticisms were based upon an adaptive or backward-looking approach to expectations. The significance of backward-looking expectations formation can be illustrated if we simply assume that expectations are based solely on the most recent past period. If this is the case, then:

$$\pi_t^e = \pi_{t-1} \qquad (14.4)$$

Substituting into Equation 14.3 we then have the rate of inflation given by:

$$\pi_t = b_1 \cdot 1/U_t + b_2\pi_{t-1} \qquad (14.5)$$

Current inflation is thus the outcome of current demand pressure plus last period's inflation rate. There are two very important implications of Equation 14.5.

The first implication is that monetary policy can only influence the inflation rate if it succeeds in changing demand pressure and thus the level of output and employment. To see this, assume that unemployment takes a value such that $b_1 \cdot 1/U_t = 0$. Current inflation will equal last period's inflation. Current inflation can *change* only if demand pressure, and U, change. In the short run, at least, the Phillips curve must have a negative slope and monetary policy has at least a short-run effect upon the real economy.

The second implication is that if demand pressure is such that $b_1 \cdot 1/U_t > 0$, then maintaining that level of pressure must result in *accelerating* inflation. This is just a formal presentation of the criticism of the simple Phillips curve that we saw at the end of the last section. If the government persists with an attempt to maintain unemployment at a level that creates inflationary pressure, the short-run Phillips curve will shift *continuously* upward. Exercise 14.1 provides a numerical illustration.

If there are levels of U such that $b_1 \cdot 1/U_t > 0$ and inflation *accelerates*, there must be some value of U at which $b_1 \cdot 1/U_t = 0$. At this level of U, there is no demand pressure, and inflation is constant. (Inflation in each period is equal to that of the previous one.) This level of unemployment is known variously as the *non-accelerating inflation rate of unemployment* (happily shortened to **NAIRU**) or the **natural rate of unemployment**, 'natural' because this is the level of unemployment that the economy will settle at if governments do not attempt to raise aggregate demand to inflationary levels. In a sense, therefore, this 'natural rate' might be regarded as 'full employment', though it

Exercise 14.1 Adaptive expectations and the rate of inflation

Suppose that the current rate of inflation is determined as specified in Equation 14.4. Calculate the rate of inflation:

1   this year

2   next year

3   in two years' time

if $b_1 = 0.1$, $b_2 = 1.0$, $U_t = 5$ per cent $(= 0.05)$, last year's inflation rate was 2 per cent. Assume that unemployment is unchanged throughout the three-year period.

need not, of course, correspond to a situation where the recorded level of unemployment equals zero. When demand pressure begins to cause inflation there will still be positive unemployment made up of people moving between jobs or lacking the necessary skills or being in the wrong place. And if the official unemployment count depends upon the number of people claiming welfare benefits, as it does in the UK, then changes in the rules governing eligibility for those benefits will cause changes in the recorded number of unemployed associated with zero inflation. The 'natural rate' will certainly be positive and is unlikely to be a constant number.

14.4 The policy irrelevance theorem

If expectations are backward-looking or adaptive, monetary policy will still affect output and employment in the short run, but in the long run, when eventually expectations catch up with reality, it can only affect the rate of inflation. However, while it may be perfectly sensible to suggest that people form their expectations on the basis of the recent past, it may be too simple to suggest that this is the only source of information they use.

Let us suppose that knowledge of the past enables agents to build up an accurate picture about how the economy works. Suppose, moreover, that their 'model' is one in which changes in the rate of monetary expansion cause changes in the rate of inflation after a period of time.[1] If they know this, then their expectations of future inflation will be based upon the government's current monetary policy. Expected inflation is no longer equal to past inflation, but is a function of what people believe current policy will produce. If this is the case, and assuming that agents are working with a quantity theory model, the second (expectations) term in Equation 14.5 needs to be modified to one that features the current rate of monetary growth, $\dot{M}$, relative to the natural rate of growth of output, Y^*.

$$\pi_t = b_1 \cdot 1/U_t + b_2 \cdot (\dot{M}_t - \dot{Y}_t^*) \qquad (14.6)$$

Notice that in making this modification we have made expectations *forward-looking*. What people expect inflation to be is based upon what they think the effects of current policy *will be*.

In the terms that we used above, agents are now forming *rational expectations*, 'rational' because agents, acting in their own self-interest, are making the best use of all available information in making any judgement. Failure to do this will result in them making mistakes (see Chapter 26),[2] and if they make mistakes that they could avoid, then either they are not acting rationally or they are not concerned to maximize their own welfare. Neither of these possibilities is allowed in orthodox economics.

The suggestion that agents form their expectations 'rationally' is credited initially to Muth (1961) though the best known application of it in an economic policy context was by Lucas (1973). Since then, the 'rational expectations hypothesis' (REH) has played a large part in the development of macroeconomics and has come to be associated with what is known as the 'New Classical Macroeconomics', so-called because it combines the rational expectations proposition with the assumption of market-clearing in order to produce

---

[1]   This amounts to saying that they have a 'quantity theory' view of the world. Velocity is stable, so that there is a reliable connection between money and spending. Meanwhile, output can grow only at its 'natural rate'.

[2]   In Chapter 26 we revert to the practice of using ^ over a variable to indicate an expected value. That is common practice in many finance texts; unfortunately, the same convention does not apply to economics texts where it is more usual to denote an expected value with the superscript [e]. We have used both because we think it will help students who may be reading our exposition of a particular issue simultaneously with treatments in other books. We hope that trying to be consistent with other texts is more helpful than being consistent through all of our chapters. Readers who do find our practice confusing should keep one finger in the glossary where we make the meaning of each [e] and ^ variable clear.

much the same predictions about the macroeconomy that 'classical' (pre-Keynesian) economists produced (see Section 14.1).

At this juncture we need only appreciate the crucial point that in saying that people do not make avoidable errors in forecasting inflation, the REH is saying that agents, on balance, make correct forecasts. We can see why, if we consider the ways in which the forecast can differ from the actual outturn. In Equation 14.7 π_t^e is the expectation of next period's inflation formed in period t. π_{t+1} is the rate of inflation that actually materializes in the next period, $t + 1$, while μ is an error term. Thus:

$$\pi_{t+1} = \pi_t^e + \mu_{t+1} \tag{14.7}$$

It is central to the REH that in a series of repeated forecasts the error term, μ, should have a mean of zero and be uncorrelated with previous values of itself and uncorrelated with the actual inflation rate. These conditions ensure that there is no information contained in μ that could be used to improve future forecasts. For example, if the mean value of μ were not 0, we would have forecasts that consistently over (or under-) forecast the outturn. Future forecasts could be improved by making an appropriate allowance. Equally, correlations between the error term and earlier errors, or actual outturns, would suggest a pattern in the forecast errors which we could uncover and use to improve future forecasts.

Returning to the Phillips curve, we can see that the implications of the REH approach are quite startling. We noted in the last section that it was the speed with which agents realized what was happening to inflation that determined how long it took the economy to move through the sequence $A–B–C$ (in Figure 14.2) and thus determined for how long monetary shocks could have any effect upon output and employment. If it is correct, the REH approach is saying that, when agents notice a monetary shock is taking place, their expectations of inflation will adjust *immediately*. We go straight from A to C and monetary policy is impotent as regards 'real' variables. Exercise 14.2 illustrates the different responses we should expect between agents who form expectations adaptively (as in the last section) and those who form them according to the REH.

> **Exercise 14.2 Adaptive and rational explanations**
>
> Imagine that the rate of inflation was 2 per cent last year while the rate of growth of output has been running at about 3 per cent for the past few years. Suppose also that the government announces a target rate of monetary expansion for the next year of 7 per cent with the aim of expanding demand and lowering the level of unemployment.
>
> 1 What would be your best forecast of the rate of inflation over the next year if you formed your expectations adaptively?
>
> 2 What would your forecast be if you formed them in a forward-looking manner?
>
> 3 In the circumstances described, how would you react to the offer of a 4 per cent increase in money wages if you formed your expectations adaptively?
>
> 4 How would you react if your expectations were forward-looking?

Notice, though, that this does not mean that monetary policy *never* has any real effects. We used the phrase 'when agents notice a monetary shock is taking place . . .'. Clearly they cannot incorporate a monetary expansion into their model in order to make the correct inflation prediction if they do not know it is happening or for some reason cannot recognize it for what it is. Monetary 'surprises', therefore, can have short-term real effects, but we need always to remember that agents can learn also about surprises. A government is unlikely to introduce a surprise without reason (to win an election, perhaps). Once that reason becomes understood, a surprise is no longer possible and policy will be impotent once again.

The suggestion that monetary policy is completely irrelevant to real variables unless it is carried out in such a way as to 'surprise' well-informed agents was bound to be controversial. Moreover, it also appeared to be a testable hypothesis and many tests were in fact carried out. The majority of the tests suggested that monetary policy had real effects whether it was anticipated or not.[3]

---

[3]   A problem with all tests of hypotheses about expectations-determined events is that rejections are hard to interpret. They may indicate a rejection of the genuine hypothesis ('expectations *do not* play the expected role') or they may indicate that expectations are actually crucial, but are usually wrong. The problem is that any such test is a simultaneous test of joint hypotheses.

Although monetary policy impotence is a large claim, it may be less striking than one of the *implications* of the hypothesis. This is that the persistent and major deviations of real variables – output, employment, capital formation and so on – from trend, which we have seen in recent years, is due to people being 'surprised' by movements in the general level of prices. To appreciate this implication we return to Equation 14.3. Since variations in the level of unemployment occur with divergences in actual output (Y_t) from equilibrium output, (Y_t^*), we can rewrite Equation 14.3 as:

$$\pi_t = b_1 \cdot (Y_t - Y_t^*) + b_2 \cdot \pi_t^e \qquad (14.8)$$

Continuing with the assumption of no money illusion, ($b_2 = 1$), then:

$$b_1 \cdot (Y_t - Y_t^*) = \pi_t - \pi_t^e \text{ and}$$

$$(Y_t - Y_t^*) = 1/b_1(\pi_t - \pi_t^e) \qquad (14.9)$$

The difference between actual and equilibrium output is a function of the difference between expected and actual inflation, the forecasting error. But under rational expectations we know that the forecasting error should be purely stochastic with mean zero and no auto-correlation. However, the UK, like the USA and most European economies, has experienced major booms and recessions over the years. During the 1950s, the pattern was referred to as 'stop–go' and was certainly thought of at the time as being associated with demand management policies. More recently, in 1980–83 and again in 1990–93 the UK experienced two periods of major recession when output was below potential. In 1987–89 output was above potential. On this evidence therefore, if we persist with an REH-type analysis, we have to say that agents make frequent and large forecasting errors. They seem not to be well informed about movements in the price level. Furthermore, since the deviations persist (and often have the appearance of cyclical behaviour) the forecast errors show incontrovertible signs of auto-correlation.

Given both the quantity and quality of information that is available about current changes and likely future movements in the price level, it is difficult to believe that agents make frequent, large and persistent (that is, auto-correlated) errors in the way the theory suggests. Price level data and leading indicator data is available monthly. It is among the more reliable information that is regularly published. It is also reported in a high-profile way. Furthermore, anyone lacking the necessary information to make a judgement can obtain it quickly and very cheaply. At the same time, we know (from Section 9.4 and Chapter 13) that central banks certainly act as though changes in interest rates have effects upon real variables and we know that (with one exception) fluctuations in the UK economy since the 1950s have been associated with macroeconomic policy responses to pressure on the exchange rate.[4] Policy does seem to have real effects and yet it is hard to believe that people are not well informed.

14.5 The Phillips curve and monetary policy today

We know that central banks conduct monetary policy, fully aware that changes in interest rates have 'real' effects, at least in the short run. And yet the rational expectations hypothesis tells us that this can only happen (with rational agents) if the policymaker succeeds in springing 'surprises', i.e. causing them to make expectational errors. But we have just seen that it seems unlikely that mistaken assessments about the general price level can be responsible for monetary policy's continuing impact on real variables. So what is the explanation? There are several posible answers and most go (again) beyond the scope of this book. But one issue worthy of careful attention is the nature of markets, *in practice*. Much economic theory works on the assumption that market prices are perfectly (that is, continuously) flexible. It is assumed that they work *as if* prices are being continuously adjusted by a mythical auctioneer who gathers all bids so that no trades take place at disequilibrium prices. Consequently, markets always clear. The appeal of this assumption lies, like the REH itself, with the idea that economic agents are fundamentally rational, self-interested individuals and that trading at disequilibrium prices, prices that generate quantities that agents do not want, is inconsistent with such rationality.

---

4 The exception is the 1973–76 'oil shock', though even here part of the recession may be attributed to policy responses to the oil price rise.

But this overlooks a reality which is that such flexibility is conspicuous by its rarity. Later in this book, we shall see that it is a characteristic of only a subset even of financial markets. In dealer or 'quote-driven' markets, for example, dealers quote a two-way price *for a period of time* until sufficient information has accumulated, through inventory changes, to suggest that a change is essential. Many markets for goods and services exist where adjustments take the form of quantities in the first instance. Labour markets are both quantity and price inflexible over long periods. The reasons for these inflexibilities are many and are increasingly well understood. They have to do primarily with costs, information and uncertainty. It takes time to adjust prices, and price adjustments involve real resources. At the least, there is no reason to assume that traders will adjust prices until the cost of sticking with a misaligned price exceeds the cost of changing it. In the presence of uncertainty (about the permanence of an apparent demand shift, for example) and incomplete information (about the quality of goods and services from rival traders, for example) a rational, self-interested response may be to continue as before until the picture clarifies.

> . . . in the real world many markets do *not* clear perfectly and instantaneously, even though market agents behave rationally and efficiently with regards to the formation of expectations under conditions of imperfect and costly acquisition of information. In short, an assumption of rational, efficient market agents does not also validate an assumption of perfectly clearing markets.
>
> Goodhart, 1989, p. 23.

Consider now the implications of having *some* **fix-price** firms in an economy. We begin at the end of a week's trading, in full equilibrium, where everyone knew the pattern of relative prices as well as the general price level: expectations were fulfilled. Expectations are then formed about next week's trading. Now let us introduce a monetary policy 'shock' in the form of a reduction in interest rates. There is an increase in spending. Recognizing this monetary shock, **flex-price** firms raise their prices immediately. The increase in spending is partially absorbed by the price rises and, additionally, the pattern of demand is switched toward the fix-price producers. So long

as there are some fix-price producers, however, the adjustment in the general price level must be incomplete and some increase in expenditure must remain. Output and employment in fix-price firms, and in the economy as a whole, increase. The monetary expansion has real effects.[5] This amounts to saying that although agents may *know* what is likely to happen to inflation in the near future, they cannot, for reasons to do with the way in which prices and wages are set, do anything more than recover the *past* effect of price rises in their negotiations. This means that the inflation rate used in contracts always lags behind what is currently happening to inflation. Of course, if inflation is constant for two periods or more, then lagged-inflation and current inflation will be the same. But if inflation is rising then current inflation will be higher than lagged inflation, and vice versa when inflation is falling. The point is that the two can differ as with expectational errors and the results are the same.

Whether they explain it by 'price-stickiness' or 'surprises', central banks (and governments) are well aware that monetary policy has 'real' effects, certainly in the short run. In other words, they are aware of a trade-off: a deflationary policy is going to have *some* negative effect on output and employment, while output and employment will respond positively to an expansionary monetary policy. We shall now see how we can represent the conduct of monetary policy as it is understood today, using essentially the Phillips curve framework of the last two sections but with some modifications.

The main modification is that we draw the diagram featuring inflation (as before and on the vertical axis) combined with output (rather than unemployment) on the horizontal. This should pose no problem since we would expect (and there is evidence) that output and employment will be connected in some way and that the connection will be inverse. This means that a downward-sloping Phillips curve (in its unemployment version) becomes upward-sloping in its output version. Figure 14.3 shows long- and short-run Phillips curves.

How do we interpret Figure 14.3? The vertical Phillips curve embodies the view, developed above, that when agents are fully informed and fully adjusted to what is happening to the rate of inflation, the level of output (and unemployment) will settle at its natural

---

5   This passage draws heavily upon Laidler (1988).

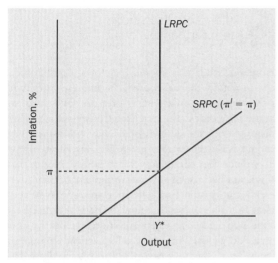

Figure 14.3 Long- and short-run Phillips curves

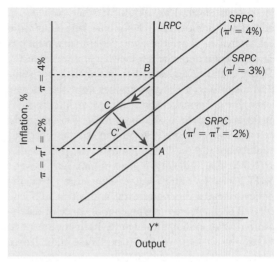

Figure 14.4 Responding to an inflation shock

rate, Y^*. However, in the short run, agents may be surprised by inflation (it differs from what they expect) or, alternatively, they may know what is happening to inflation but it takes time to adjust prices. Until this adjustment takes place, unemployment and output may diverge from the equilibrium. This is entirely consistent with what we saw in Equation 14.9 above. This says that deviations in output from its natural level depend upon the extent to which agents' expectations differ from the actual rate. This can be rearranged, as Equation 14.10, to show the behaviour of output itself.

$$Y_t = Y_t^* + 1/b_1(\pi_t - \pi_t^e) \qquad (14.10)$$

Equation 14.11 expresses the same situation but uses the idea of price stickiness rather than expectational errors. π^l denotes lagged inflation.

$$Y_t = Y_t^* + 1/b_1(\pi_t - \pi_t^l) \qquad (14.11)$$

The actual level of output will be equal to the natural rate plus an amount which depends upon the extent to which current inflation exceeds lagged inflation. Notice, other things being equal (including lagged inflation), that actual output is a positive function of the actual rate of inflation. This is what is shown by the SRPC in Figure 14.3, provided that we recognize that the SRPC is drawn for a given rate of lagged inflation. In fact, we can work out what that the lagged, or established, rate is.

Notice that the SRPC cuts the LRPC at output Y^*, and inflation of π. Hence, at π, $Y = Y^*$. From Equation 14.11 we can see that this requires the condition that $1/b_1(\pi - \pi^l) = 0$; in other words that the lagged rate of inflation, π^l, is equal to the actual rate, π.

To illustrate the operation of monetary policy, we turn to Figure 14.4 where we assume that the current rate of inflation matches the lagged rate (as before) but also that both coincide with the policymaker's target rate, say 2 per cent. We are in full equilibrium (inflation is at target and output at its natural rate) at A. There is then an inflationary shock and inflation settles at 4 per cent p.a., shown at point B. The policymaker then raises the rate of interest and this depresses the level of aggregate demand (through the channels discussed in Chapter 13). Eventually, this reduces the rate of inflation to, say, 3 per cent and we are at C. Notice that lagged inflation is still at 4 per cent so we have moved *down* the existing 4 per cent SRPC. Eventually, lagged inflation catches up (at 3 per cent) and the SRPC shifts appropriately. The policymaker now has a choice. It can keep the interest rate where it is which will maintain the gap between current output and its natural rate. But this involves losses (in output and employment) which most policymakers would be unwilling to sustain provided that they were making progress in returning the economy to the desired position. Most policymakers would ease up on interest rates, making a reduction towards the original level. This allows for some recovery in output and employment. Hence once lagged inflation has shifted to 3 per cent, the deflationary policy is eased and output recovers somewhat and we are at C'. Notice that at C' inflation is less than 3 per cent. Eventually lagged inflation catches up with this new level. The policymaker can ease back on interest rates again allowing for a bit more recovery in aggregate demand so, eventually, 'steers' the economy back to equilibrium at A.

Notice that C denotes a point of tangency between $SRPC$ ($\pi^l = 4\%$) and a curve. This is, in effect, the policymaker's indifference curve and is part of a ring centred on A. There is a whole set of concentric rings centred on A so that, although we have not drawn it, C' is also a point of tangency. These indifference curves tell us how the policymaker views the trade-off between inflation and lost output. If these are equally balanced, then the rings will be perfect circles. If, however and for example, the policymaker is much more concerned about inflation than about lost output, the circles will be ellipsoid ('stretched') in the horizontal plane. Look at Figure 14.4 again. The policymaker had the option to raise interest rates so dramatically that the economy was pushed all the way down $SRPC$ ($\pi^l = 4\%$) and straight back to the target inflation rate of 2 per cent. But until lagged inflation caught up, output (and employment) would be a very long way below their natural rates. This is the choice that a very inflation-averse policymaker would opt for and one can see that would be a point of tangency (the policymaker would be on his/her indifference curve) if the rings were stretched sufficiently in the horizontal plane.

Formally speaking, these attitudes to the inflation/output trade-off are incorporated in what is called the central bank's 'reaction function'. A typical example of such a function is given in Equation 14.12, which says that the policymaker's loss is made up of the extent to which inflation exceeds its target and the extent to which output is below its natural rate.

$$L = \alpha(\pi - \pi^T)^2 + (1 - \alpha)(Y^* - Y)^2 \qquad (14.12)$$

Notice that if the policymaker gives equal weight to deviations in inflation and output, then $\alpha = 0.5$. Notice too that the loss terms are quadratic. This means that the losses increase dramatically as the deviations increase in size.

14.6 Rules and discretion in monetary policy

However, while it is obviously helpful to policymakers to know that a rise/fall in interest rates will reduce/increase inflationary pressure and also to know *why* that is the case (the transmission mechanism), it does not tell policymakers by *how much* they should raise the rate in given circumstances (or by how much they should lower it in others). Notice that this is not because of any uncertainty about their preferences or loss function. The policymaker may be very clear that s/he wishes to follow the path in Figure 14.4 from B to C to C' to A. The question is rather 'by how much do we need to raise the interest rate to take us from B to C (and not beyond)? It is easy to draw diagrams but in practice there are lots of uncertainties: about how big the inflationary shock will be (where exactly is the $SRPC$?), how responsive to a change in interest rates inflation will be this time (what's the slope of the $SRPC$?), and what other events might be just around the corner which will either reinforce any policy move or offset it. Bear in mind (from Chapter 13) that we think that the full effect of an interest rate change (the movement from B to C) can take up to two years to develop and we see that monetary policymaking is fraught with uncertainties.

The Bank of England is guided in this decision by econometric evidence of the past responsiveness of key variables to changes in interest rates. The Monetary Policy Committee then uses these relationships as a starting point and makes a decision based in part on its *judgement* about how events are likely to unfold (Budd, 1998; Bean, 2001). The point is that the MPC has considerable *discretion* in making its interest rate decision. Much the same applies in the USA where the Federal Open Markets Committee makes the judgement and in the ECB where the decision rests with the Governing Council (ECB, 2004, p. 10). The very fact that the decision is made by committee is an indication that judgement and discretion are involved.

How much easier it would be if only the decision could be made by reference to some simple rule. Furthermore, some economists have argued that a rule could be made to *constrain* the decision makers and prevent them using their discretion and that this might be advantageous. We return to this 'constraint' argument in a moment.

Before we do that, however, we need to be clear on what is meant by a 'rule' and we'll think of it for the moment as a 'rule of thumb' – a guide to making the policy decision. For our purposes, a **monetary policy rule** is a formula which tells us how to set the policy instrument (or instruments) in a given set of circumstances. On this definition, a monetary policy rule might tell us how to set either the growth rate of money or (more realistically) the level of short-term interest rates. One of the earliest examples of such a rule was Friedman's (1968) suggestion that policy should be designed to deliver a rate of growth of the money supply which should approximate the long-run growth of real output. This takes us back to the quantity theory again at the beginning of this chapter. If velocity was rising (falling) then the growth rate might have to be modified so that the money growth rate exceeded (was less than) the growth of output, but the idea was to produce a growth in the quantity of money which would be just sufficient to buy the growing level of output. If this could be achieved, there would be no inflationary or deflationary pressure. A more recent version of a rule with the money stock as the policy instrument was formulated by McCallum (1989). This provides a formula for setting the growth rate of narrow money (M0) in the light of changes in velocity (the demand for money) and the deviation of nominal income from its target level.

As we all know, however, the chosen instrument of monetary policy is the rate of interest rather than the money stock. For this reason, the best-known rule in recent years is that devised by John Taylor (1993) to guide central banks in setting interest rates. Essentially, the rule requires decision makers to focus upon the current rate of inflation in relation to the target, and the output gap. If we take the target rate of inflation to be 2 per cent p.a. (again) then formally, the rule can be written as:

$$i = \pi + 2.0 + 0.5(\pi - 2.0) - 0.5(Y^* - Y)$$
$$(14.13)$$

where i is the nominal rate of interest (set by the central bank), π is the rate of inflation and $(Y^* - Y)$ is a measure of the output gap – the extent to which output falls short of its potential. It should be read in three parts. Firstly, it sets the real rate of interest at 2 per cent $(\pi + 2)$ provided (next) that inflation is on target at 2 per cent and (thirdly) that output is at its potential. Going back to Figure 14.4, we could say

that the rate of interest generated by this rule, in these conditions, is the rate required to keep us at A. (Note that according to the rule, the nominal rate in these circumstances will be about 4 per cent). However, the interpretation of the rule becomes more interesting when we are away from equilibrium (in regard to output or inflation or both). Notice that the middle term of the rule says that for every 1 per cent that inflation exceeds the 2 per cent target, the real rate should be raised by 0.5 per cent. Leaving aside the value of 0.5, it seems perfectly reasonable to argue that the bigger the inflation problem, the bigger the interest rate response will have to be.

However, the third term says that the extent to which we need to raise interest rates in these circumstances depends on what is happening to output (and aggregate demand). Specifically, it says that for every 1 per cent by which output is running below its full capacity level, the real rate can be 0.5 per cent lower. The underlying logic of the rule obviously relates quite closely to the analysis of Section 14.5. Firstly, it embodies a target rate of inflation. Assuming that we are at the target rate and output is at its natural rate, then there is some real rate of interest that will hold the position steady (the 'stabilizing' rate of interest). Secondly, if there is an inflationary shock (the *SRPC* shifts upwards) we need to raise the nominal rate, firstly to protect the real rate but then by a bit more to increase it in order to push the economy down the *SRPC* to reduce the rate of inflation). Finally, to the extent that we are 'down' the *SRPC* below the natural level of output there will be deflationary pressures; when they start to take effect on inflation, we can ease off on the nominal (and real) rate of interest.

Exercise 14.3 Using the Taylor rule

Given the version of the Taylor rule in Equation 14.9:

1 calculate the rate of interest that the central bank should set if the rate of inflation is currently 5 per cent, the inflation target is 2 per cent and output is estimated to be two percentage points below capacity;

2 if this succeeds in bringing inflation down to 4 per cent next year, what rate should the central bank set, assuming other conditions are unchanged?

Central banks do not generally admit to setting interest rates in this way, but the increasing openness of monetary policymaking in recent years means that we can see considerable similarities in the way in which policy is operated and the way that it would be operated under a Taylor rule. Firstly, most central banks have accepted that targeting the inflation rate directly is preferable to targeting some intermediate variable (money stock, exchange rate) which might itself deliver the desired rate of inflation. In the UK, the target rate adopted in 1992 was 2.5 per cent per annum as measured by the retail prices index. This was amended in January 2004 to 2 per cent, measured by the annual change in a new 'consumer price index'. The ECB's target is a rate of inflation less than 2 per cent as measured by the 'harmonized index of consumer prices' – effectively the same measure as now used in the UK. The Federal Reserve does not publish an explicit target but appears to be content with inflation rates of less than 2 per cent. Furthermore, we can see from the many central bank publications and press releases explaining their decisions, that the current rate of inflation and its forecast trend, in relation to the target rate, form the starting point of any decision about interest rates. Furthermore, the future path of aggregate demand and its components are carefully assessed in relation to the economy's capacity. In the circumstances, it is hardly surprising that many studies show that monetary policy is often conducted *as if* the policymaker were following a Taylor rule.

We turn now to another aspect of monetary rules: their use in 'constraining' or tying the hands of the policymaker. This particular argument for rules has its origin in the view that monetary policy can often be subject to an 'inflationary bias'. This arises when the policymaker has a target for the level of output which exceeds the equilibrium level i.e. where $Y^T > Y^*$. In the loss function, the output loss is now measured as the difference between actual output and this target level. In other words, Equation 14.12 becomes:

$$L = \alpha(\pi - \pi^T)^2 + (1 - \alpha)(Y^T - Y)^2 \qquad (14.14)$$

This situation is shown in Figure 14.5 where the policymaker's preferred position is shown at *A*. Crucially, the figure shows that if the economy is at

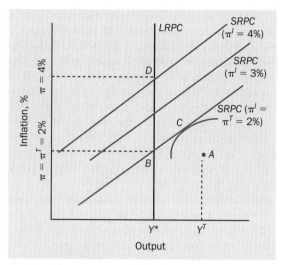

Figure 14.5 Inflation bias

point *B*, where inflation is at its target rate of 2 per cent and output is at equilibrium ($Y = Y^*$), the policymaker can do better (be on a higher indifference curve) by moving the economy to *C* where output will be nearer to target but inflation will be above target. However, we know from our previous analysis that point *C* cannot be sustained. Once the higher rate of inflation becomes embedded in wage and price setting the *SRPC* will move upwards. This will continue until actual output is equal to equilibrium output on the *LRPC* at (say) 4 per cent, at *D*. The policymaker may then embark on a policy of deflation, as we saw in the previous section. This will bring the *SRPC* down until, eventually, we return to *B*. But once *B* has been achieved, the incentive to 'cheat' (i.e. to inflate in order to get to *C*) reappears. Over time, the average rate of inflation *must* exceed the target rate.

Although the argument was expressed rather differently, the desire to avoid inflation bias was part of the argument behind Friedman's (and McCallum's) money growth rules referred to earlier. If we could find, not the equilibrium level of output as such, but its 'natural' rate of growth, then we could find the rate of growth of money stock that would allow demand to grow by just this same amount (having allowed for velocity changes), this would prevent policymakers from aiming at points like *A* in Figure 14.5.[6]

---

[6]   Another part of the rules as constraint argument was that the economy was that monetary policy operated with long (and variable) lags while the economy's future behaviour was difficult to forecast. This meant that 'discretionary' adjustments in monetary policy would create more instability than following a simple rule regardless of economic fluctuations.

In the next section we shall see that the possibility that policymakers might be subject to inflation bias is linked to another set of recommendations (which have been adopted rather more enthusiastically than monetary rules).

14.7 Governments, inflationary incentives and independent central banks

We are familiar by now with the fact that monetary policy is conducted by central banks. This is because policy in practice involves setting interest rates and this has to be done by some agency which is powerful enough to impose its will on the markets in which these interest rates are set. This falls inevitably to the central bank because of its monopoly powers in supplying liquidity to the banking system (see Section 9.4). Hence central banks are inevitably involved in the conduct of monetary policy. However, it is one thing to say that central banks implement interest changes and another to say that they decide what those interest rates should be. In the past many central banks acted as agents for their governments (specifically the Ministry of Finance or the Treasury) and implemented the rate of interest dictated by the government. In these circumstances it is the government that is the policymaker and the central bank is merely its agent. In recent years, however, a strong consensus has emerged that monetary policy is more effective if carried out by a central bank which is independent of government. 'Independence' could mean that it is free to decide on the rate of interest necessary to deliver the inflation target ('**operational independence**') or that it is free to set *both* the target and the instrument ('**full independence**'). The Bank of England is an example of the former case; the ECB and the Federal Reserve are cases of the latter. This movement towards removing government from the decision-making process obviously shares some common features with the arguments in favour of the 'rules' approach to monetary policy that we looked at above. Both, rules and independence, reduce the scope for political judgement in the setting of interest rates. In this section we look at where this desire to restrict the role of government has come from.

In Figure 14.5, we saw that key to the problem was the desire by the policymaker to achieve a level of output which exceeded the long-run equilibrium (point A, to the right of the $LRPC$). The question is 'why' should a policymaker have this preference (the loss function like Equation 14.14 rather than 14.12).

One obvious answer is to see governments as sets of individual politicians who are seeking only to retain power. They thus choose those policies which they believe will ensure their re-election (they seek to maximize votes). So, for example, among the promises made to voters are low inflation and high output (more usually expressed in political debate as low unemployment). The problem is that no one really knows what the precise level of equilibrium (unemployment) is, and it may, of course, vary over time. In a democratic political system, this results, particularly at election time, in promises about inflation/unemployment that are overoptimistic. Political parties engage in a bidding war to persuade voters that each is more likely to achieve A (rather than B) than their opponents. The party in power does what it can to expand the economy in the run up to an election, triggering the sequence that we described in Figure 14.5. Only after the election does it become apparent to everyone that inflation is rising and that the economy is headed for D.

To reduce this inflation, the government might then have to cut demand sharply, inducing a recession as we move down the $SRPC$. This would make the government very unpopular between elections but could put it in a position to expand the economy again in time to win the next election. Such a process is referred to as the political business (or electoral) cycle – an unnecessary cycle with real costs for the economy which is generated by the need for governments to face elections. This would not lead to ever-increasing inflation but would involve real costs for the economy as inflation would fall following each election only at the expense of high, albeit short-term, unemployment. The economy would face a regular and unnecessary stop–go cycle which would create uncertainty and interfere with its longer-term growth prospects.

If the key to this problem is the temptation to aim for A, then the key to the solution is to remove the temptation. One way of doing this is to put policy in the hands of the 'conservative' central banker. 'Conservative' here means that s/he has a greater inflation aversion than a government subject to periodic elections might have. In terms of our loss functions, s/he would be more likely to embrace Equation 14.12 than 14.14 and might even have $\alpha > 0.5$ indicating a greater concern at missing the inflation target than causing a loss of output. Notice, that the policy only 'works' if the central bank has, or can be made to have, this particular outlook. Mere independence alone is not sufficient – the central bank might just share the same preferences as the general public. The importance of creating and maintaining this conservative outlook explains a number of features surrounding independent central banks. We have already met one of these at the very start of this chapter. This is the practice of creating an independent central bank with a 'remit' that *obliges* it to place more weight on inflation than on output. This is often done, as in the case of the Bank of England by ranking policy objectives and ensuring that all other objectives are subsidiary ('subject to') achieving low inflation. It also explains some of the features of contracts of employment for senior central bank staff. A long contract with no prospect of re-employment reduces the incentive to please governments or any other outside interest. In the extreme case, a governor's contract could specify termination in the event of failure to deliver low inflation. We look at some other characteristics of independent central banks when we look at the Bank of England below. The important point is to see them as trying to impose a more 'conservative' set of preferences than those likely to be adopted by government or the general public.

So far, we have linked independence to a set of preferences which aim at Y^* rather than at Y^T. But there is another reason that is sometimes advanced for the claim that independence improves policy outcomes. Again, this can be seen by looking back at our earlier diagrams. If we look at the discussion surrounding Figure 14.4 we observe a central bank embarking on a policy of deflation in order to bring the rate of inflation back down to target following an inflationary shock. We noted that the path back to target followed a triangular route. To reduce the rate of inflation the central bank raises the interest rate which pushes *down* the SRPC. Notice that output is below (and unemployment very likely above) its natural level. There are losses here. And these losses continue for as long as the economy is the left of the LRPC. So far we have said nothing about how long we may be in this position, beyond saying that it depends how long it takes for the SRPC to shift downward to its original position where expected (or lagged) inflation is equal to the target rate. How long this takes depends upon how long it takes for agents to adjust

either their expectations of inflation to what the central bank is trying to achieve (if we take the SRPC to be based upon expectational errors) or their price-setting behaviour (if we are thinking about price rigidities). Either way, it could be argued that these adjustments are likely to take place more quickly if agents 'believe' what the central bank says it is trying to do and expect it to succeed.

In other words the SRPC may shift more quickly (and losses could be smaller) if the central bank has **credibility**. Indeed, in the extreme case, it might be argued that the policymaker could bring about a reduction of inflation without creating a recession if market agents believed that the monetary authorities were genuinely committed to low inflation, that is, if the statements by monetary authorities that they intended to bring about low inflation were held by market agents to be perfectly credible. The difficulty is that market agents, aware of the expansionary incentives faced by elected governments, will not believe government statements. The past behaviour of the monetary authorities will have given the government an inflationary **reputation**. The same could be true, as we have seen, if the policymaker were a central bank which shared the same incentives. But if independence is combined with a different set of incentives which make it clearly in the central bank's interest to aim for low inflation then credibility and reputation could be improved with a consequent reduction in output and employment losses in a period of tight monetary policy.

So far, we may have what looks like quite a strong theoretical case for placing the conduct of monetary policy in the hands of an independent central bank. But there is one problem that is often overlooked. The argument that monetary policy when conducted by government has an inflationary bias is based upon the notion that governments have objectives which are too optimistic when it comes to trying to achieve low inflation and high levels of output. Moreover, agents are assumed to know this, so the policymaker lacks credibility with the result that deflationary policy can be costly in the way that we've just discussed. But it is not clear why elected governments should *persistently* have these inconsistent objectives. Moreover, if private sector agents *know* that governments have unrealistic ambitions why do they continue to elect them? Why is there not a (political) market for a party which promises low inflation and sticks to it?[7]

---

7   One might argue that the first Thatcher and Reagan administrations in the UK and USA respectively came close to this.

But theoretical argument is only part of the case for independence. In the early 1980s there were many studies which claimed to find an *empirical* association between 'good' monetary policy and independent central banks. These looked at the *degree* of central bank independence and attempted to find correlations between this and the rates of inflation in the respective countries. These studies (see, for example, Alesina and Summers, 1993) have, by and large, claimed to find such correlations within developed economies as well as failing to find correlations between the independence of central banks and low rates of economic growth (which might be thought to be a price of tight monetary policy). The implication is that countries with politically independent central banks can maintain lower rates of inflation with no loss in terms of economic growth.

There are, however, several difficulties with these studies too. Firstly, the 'independence' of central banks is not easily measured. Many characteristics may contribute to the degree of independence of a particular central bank from its government (Box 23.2 considers such characteristics). These characteristics must be weighted in order to produce some composite index of independence. Such a process may inevitably be subjective and different researchers might rank central banks differently in terms of independence. Although it was accepted that the *Bundesbank* ranked highly on any index of independence, there was sufficient doubt about other central banks to raise doubts about the apparent correlations between independence and inflation rates.

Secondly, the existence of this correlation provides no guarantee of a causal relationship from central bank independence to low inflation rates. It is at least equally plausible that some third factor has been responsible for both the independence of the central bank and the low rate of inflation or, indeed, that any apparent correlation is entirely accidental. For example, it has been argued that low rates of inflation in Germany have been due principally to a strong anti-inflationary attitude among German people as a result of particularly unpleasant (and politically and socially damaging) episodes of inflation. This has meant that there has, until very recently, been little or no

disagreement among the major political parties over the need to keep inflation rates low. Under such circumstances it was easy for the government to hand power over monetary policy to an independent central bank and there have been relatively few disagreements between the *Bundesbank* and the government over monetary policy.[8] Thus, it may well have been the case that German governments would have followed much the same monetary policy as that chosen by the *Bundesbank*.

Nonetheless, there was during the 1990s a widespread acceptance among economists and politicians of the desirability of politically independent central banks. Although the movement towards making central banks independent embraced non-European economies such as New Zealand and Australia, the key to the changes could be found in the requirement in the Maastricht Treaty on European Union that the European Central Bank (after economic and monetary union) had to be independent of all governments and of the European Commission and that all monetary union member country central banks had also to be independent.[9] This was largely responsible for the increased independence granted to the central banks of France, Spain and Italy. This requirement of economic and monetary union was thought to be needed

---

[8] Notable exceptions to this included disagreement over the rate at which Ostmarks were converted to Deutschmarks at the time of German reunification, and over a government plan to revalue its holdings of gold in early June 1997 in order to meet more easily the conditions for membership of EMU. The government emerged victorious in the first disagreement; the *Bundesbank* won out in the second.
[9] This issue is dealt with in Section 23.3.

to persuade the German people and authorities to participate in EMU since the *Bundesbank* had come to be accepted within Germany as a symbol of the determination to maintain low rates of inflation and to preserve the value of the Deutschmark. This meant that the only way Germany might be persuaded to cede power from the *Bundesbank* to the European Central Bank was if the ECB were made in the image of the *Bundesbank*.

Another major reason for the practical movement towards central bank independence in many countries was the acceptance, in a world of highly mobile capital, of the dominance of financial markets. It has become widely accepted that a country's long-term interest rates might fall if only governments could convince the financial markets of the genuineness of their expressed determination to keep inflation low. One way of trying to achieve this has been to hand control of monetary policy over to the central bank on the grounds that financial markets will have more trust in the anti-inflationary credentials of the central bank than in those of the elected government.

If this in fact occurs, we have a classic example of self-fulfilling beliefs. We have suggested that the theoretical arguments in favour of taking the control of monetary policy out of the hands of elected governments are not strong and that the empirical evidence is also rather weak. It remains that, so long as these views are accepted in financial markets, it will be in the interests of governments to accept them also. Strength is added to this proposition by the view that governments are not, in practice, giving up very much since the increased mobility of international capital has made it increasingly difficult to operate national monetary policies markedly different from those being followed in other countries.

MORE FROM THE WEB
Transparency and other aspects of monetary policy

The Bank of England's home page has a link to 'monetary policy'. This in turn gives access to the minutes and voting decisions of the MPC, a list of MPC members with brief biographies, a list of MPC scheduled meeting dates, the Chancellor's 'remit' to the Bank and much else designed to explain and clarify the conduct of UK monetary policy.

Before leaving this summary of recent trends in monetary policy, it is useful to apply the above discussion to the issue of the independence of the Bank of England. The first major action of the newly elected Labour government in the UK was to announce, on 6 May 1997, that the Bank of England was to be granted operational independence from the UK Treasury and that interest rates would in future be set by the Bank rather than by the government following consultation with the Bank, as had previously been the case. On the surface, this appeared a somewhat unlikely act since it had been accepted that governments more to the political left would be less willing to give up power over monetary policy to a non-elected body.

We have seen above, however, that so long as the markets believe that the independence of the central bank provides a stronger guarantee of a low-inflation policy, governments may see the granting of independence to the central bank as a route to lower long-term interest rates. Such an argument might be more appealing to left-leaning governments which might be suspected by financial markets of continuing to harbour expansionary aims. The move might also be seen as necessary to give the UK government the possibility of joining economic and monetary union should it wish to do so. It remained that the Chancellor's action in making the Bank of England operationally independent angered a number of traditional Labour Party supporters. In the light of this and of the characteristics in Box 23.2, it is worth considering exactly what additional powers were granted to the Bank of England and what was removed from its control.

Let us consider, firstly, the interest rate decision itself. Under the new regime, interest rates in the UK are determined by the Monetary Policy Committee of the Bank of England. This committee has nine members – five from the Bank of England and four nominated by the Chancellor. This meets the independence requirement that Bank members are in the majority. This is less strong than it seems, however, since the government retains control over the appointment of the future governor and deputy governors of the Bank of England. In addition, government-nominated members of the Monetary Policy Committee will have relatively short terms of office (five years) and be subject to re-appointment. The 5-year term contrasts with the 14-year term of office of members of the Board of the US Federal

Reserve. It is generally argued that short terms of office coupled with the possibility of re-appointment allows the possibility of some degree of government influence over existing central bank board members since they may seek to please the government in order to ensure their own re-appointment.

More important, however, is the meaning of the term 'operational independence'. The Chancellor has retained the power to set the inflation target for the economy, leaving to the Bank what might be seen as the relatively technical job of setting interest rates in order to achieve that target. Thus, the Chancellor has preserved the ability of the government to choose a mainly expansionary policy. In practice, the Chancellor could not have raised the inflation target immediately after the 1997 election, allowing an easing of monetary policy, even if he wanted to do so. Such an action would have caused the market to lose immediately its belief that the granting of greater powers to the Bank gave a guarantee of continued low inflation. In this case, any hoped-for gains in terms of a lower risk premium in UK interest rates would not have materialized. Thus, the Chancellor simply carried forward the inflation target set by the previous government. Nonetheless, the Chancellor gave himself some degree of control over the monetary policy stance to be pursued by the Bank.

Two other issues are of some importance. Until independence, the Bank of England, unlike the *Bundesbank* and the Federal Reserve, had three major functions. It was the country's monetary authority (under the control of the Treasury); it was the banker to the British government and as such had the responsibility of financing the UK national debt; and it acted as the supervisory authority over the country's banking system.[10]

In the past, a conflict had often been seen to exist between the first two of these roles. Thus, the need to sell a large amount of government debt may have led the Bank to prefer relatively stable interest rates (to remove uncertainty about future bond prices) at a time when monetary policy appeared to require sharp changes in interest rates. It has been argued that a potential conflict also exists between the roles of monetary authority and banking system supervisor. The point here is that the banking supervisory authority will wish to maintain trust in the banking system by preventing, as far as is possible, the collapse of banking institutions. If there are a number of banks known to be in weak financial positions, the supervisor might be reluctant to tighten monetary policy for fear that this will force the weaker banks to default. The result might be that a central bank with both supervisory and monetary roles would operate, on average, a looser monetary policy than it would if it did not have supervisory responsibility.

The independence that was announced in 1997 was ratified by the Bank of England Act 1998. This same Act transferred the management of the national debt to a newly formed Debt Management Office – an agency of the UK Treasury – and the supervisory responsibilities of the Bank to the Financial Services Authority which was in the process of becoming a single supervisory agency for the whole of the UK financial system. The actions of the British government could be seen to have set the Bank free to determine UK interest rates and to remove all possibilities of conflict of interest, allowing a concentration on monetary policy alone. On the other hand, as we have seen, other aspects of the government's granting of independence to the Bank of England leaves it still subject to government influence to a greater extent than was the case for example with the *Bundesbank*.

14.8 Summary

The conduct of monetary policy in most countries has changed markedly in the course of the past 30 years or so. Until the mid-1970s, monetary policy, along with fiscal policy, was frequently used as one element in a programme of demand management which aimed to smooth out fluctuations in real variables like output and employment. The belief that governments had a choice between high levels of output and employment on the one hand and low inflation on the other was symbolized by the original Phillips curve.

From the mid-1970s onwards, however, the idea that real variables could be influenced for any long period lost conviction. Eventually, as part of the rational expectations revolution, it came to be argued

---

[10] A function performed in Germany by the *Aufsichtsamt*, the Federal Banking Supervisory Office, for precisely this reason.

that no real effects were possible at all. However, while monetary theory took this very pessimistic turn, governments continued to operate monetary policy as though sometimes they could boost or restrain demand with beneficial results. This led to the accusation that democratic governments were bound to operate monetary policy with an inflationary bias and that this ultimately eroded a government's credibility whenever it did wish to reduce inflation. The way to avoid this, it was argued, was to 'precommit' monetary policy to low inflation and the popular way of doing this in recent years has been to hand the operation of monetary policy to an independent central bank.

Key concepts in this chapter

Adaptive expectations
Backward-looking expectations
Central bank independence
Credibility
Expectations-augmented
   Phillips curve
Expectations formation
Fix-price markets
Flex-price markets
Forward-looking expectations
Full independence

Monetary policy rules
Money illusion
NAIRU
Natural rate of unemployment
Operational independence
Policy irrelevance theorem
Rational expectations
Real/Nominal wages
Reputation
Simple Phillips curve
Transmission mechanism

Questions and problems

1 Explain what is meant by the transmission mechanism.

2 Using the simple Phillips curve, show how governments might use an expansionary monetary policy in order to lower the rate of inflation. Why is there a 'trade-off'?

3 Distinguish between real and nominal wages. If you expect the rate of inflation to be 5 per cent over the next year, what change in nominal wages would you require in order (a) to maintain real wages unchanged; (b) to increase real wages by 3 per cent?

4 If the rate of inflation has been running at 3 per cent per annum for the past few years, what increase in nominal wages would you require in order to enjoy a 2 per cent increase in real

wages? Explain the assumptions which you have to make in order to answer this question.

5 Why does the way in which expectations are formed influence the impact of monetary policy?

6 Explain what is meant by a monetary 'surprise' and why this may affect the economy in a way that differs from monetary events that are anticipated. Make clear any assumptions that you need to make.

7 Why is it argued that governments might seek to create inflationary surprises?

8 Explain the ideas behind the notion of the political business cycle. Do they seem to reflect the realities of political behaviour?

9 Why might the 'credibility' of the policymaker affect policy outcomes?

Further reading

A Alesina and L Summers, 'Central bank independence and macroeconomic performance: Some comparative evidence', *Journal of Money, Credit and Banking*, 25 (2), 1993, 151–62

K Bain and P Howells, *Monetary Economics: Policy and its Theoretical Basis* (Basingstoke: Palgrave, 2003)

Bank of England, 'Monetary policy in the UK', *Fact Sheet*, March 1999. Available at www.bankofengland.co.uk/factmpol.pdf

Bank of England, 'The transmission mechanism of monetary policy', *Quarterly Bulletin*, May 1999, 161–7

C R Bean, 'The formulation of monetary policy at the Bank of England', *Bank of England Quarterly Bulletin*, Winter 2001, 431–4

A Blinder, *Central Banking in Theory and Practice* (London: MIT Press, 1998)

K Boakes, *Reading and Understanding the Financial Times* (London: Financial Times Prentice Hall, 2008), Topic 2

C E V Borio, 'Monetary policy operating procedures in industrial countries' (Basle: Bank for International Settlements, 1997), Working Paper no. 40

A Budd, 'The role and operations of the Bank of England Monetary Policy Committee', *Economic Journal*, 108 (451), 1998

European Central Bank, *The Monetary Policy of the ECB, 2004* (Frankfurt: ECB, 2004)

M Friedman, 'The role of monetary policy', *American Economic Review*, 58, 1968, 1–17

C A E Goodhart, *Money, Information and Uncertainty* (London: Macmillan, 2e, 1989) Chs 1, 13

M King, 'The inflation target five years on', *Bank of England Quarterly Bulletin*, November 1997

D Laidler, 'Some macroeconomic implications of price stickiness', *Manchester School*, 56, 1988

R Lucas, 'Some international evidence on output inflation trade-offs', *American Economic Review*, 63, 1973, 326–34

B T McCallum, 'The case for rules in the conduct, of monetary policy: A concrete example', *Weltwirtschaftliches Archiv*, 125, 1989

J Muth, 'Rational expectations and the theory of price movements', *Econometrica*, 29, 1961, 313–35

A W Phillips, 'The relation between unemployment and the rate of change of money wages in the United Kingdom, 1861–1957', *Economica*, 25, 1958, 283–301

Radcliffe Committee, *Committee on the Working of the Monetary System: Report*, Cmnd. 827 (London: HMSO, 1959)

J B Taylor, 'Discretion versus policy rules in practice', *Carnegie–Rochester Series on Public Policy*, 39, 1993

D K Whynes, 'The political business cycle' in D Greenaway (ed.), *Current Issues in Macroeconomics* (London: Macmillan, 1989)

Websites

www.bankofengland.co.uk
www.zei.de

Part 5 Markets

Chapter 15 Money markets

What you will learn in this chapter:

- The major instruments which are created and traded in the money markets

- The characteristics of those instruments and how they are priced

- The main participants in the money markets

- The size, growth and recent development of these markets

- The use of money markets by the authorities for policy purposes

15.1 Introduction

Financial markets can be classified in many different ways. One very simple and very common classification distinguishes between **money markets** and **capital markets**. The distinction is based upon the length of the loan when it is first made (that is, on the 'initial maturity'). In money markets, funds are borrowed and lent for a maximum of one year. However, many loans are for less than one year when they are initially made (many are 'overnight'). This, combined with the fact that many existing one-year loans were made some time ago, means that the average maturity of outstanding debt in money markets is much shorter. Within this two-part classification there are further possibilities. We can distinguish (money) markets for several different instruments; or we can distinguish by the way in which they are traded; or we can distinguish by the identity of the borrower. Table 15.1 provides a list of money markets distinguished largely by instrument. The table begins with those markets where the borrowing/lending is carried out through the issue of securities which can be bought and sold in a secondary market. These are the discount market itself, and the markets for commercial paper (CP) and certificates of deposit (CDs). We then subdivide the discount market by borrower, noting that it trades bills issued by three distinct classes of borrower. By contrast, the interbank market is a 'market' for deposits that cannot be traded. Money market deposits have much the same characteristics. Repurchase agreements involve a sale of securities with an agreement to buy them back in the near future for a price that determines the cost of the funds obtained. One consequence that follows from this variety of short-term instruments is that they are priced (or 'quoted') in two different ways. Some are quoted on a **yield basis**, while others are quoted on a **discount basis**. We note this distinction in the table (by y and d respectively) and explain it in the next section. Finally, we need to bear in mind that most of these markets exist for instruments issued in the domestic currency, and also, increasingly, for instruments denominated in a currency other than that of the country in which they are traded. Such instruments are identified by the prefix 'Euro-', though this is strictly a misnomer since the currency can be *any* currency (US or Hong Kong dollars, or Yen, for example). Hence, most financial centres trading CDs and commercial paper will also trade Euro-CDs (ECDs) and ECP.

Although Table 15.1 shows an apparently wide variety of instruments available to short-term lenders and borrowers, the fact that they are all short-term instruments makes them very close substitutes for one another. This in turn means that price movements (for money market securities) and movements in rates of return (for all money market instruments) are very highly correlated. It also means that differentials between the returns on different instruments are usually very small. This is reinforced by the fact that money markets are usually dominated by large traders – banks, savings institutions, government and corporate treasury departments – to whom small differences in yield can still mean large differences in profit or loss. One consequence of this is the need for a convenient form for expressing fractions of yields or interest rates. This is done by quoting **basis points** (or bp) where one basis point equals 1/100 of 1 per cent. Basis points have become an internationally recognized standard. Of course, it follows equally that some method is needed for quoting small changes in price. Alas, these methods are not universal. In the UK and USA the smallest unit of price change is 1/32 while in continental Europe the unit is 0.01.[1] For some reason, both units have come to be known as *ticks* in everyday use. But saying in London that UK treasury bills are 'up three ticks' suggests a larger price change than a similar remark about *Schatzwechsel* in Frankfurt.

Table 15.1 Money markets

The discount market	
Treasury bills	d
Local authority/utility bills	d
Commercial bills	d
The market for commercial paper	d
The certificate of deposit market	y
The interbank market	y
Money market deposits	y
Repurchase agreements	y

d quoted on a *discount* basis; y quoted on a *yield* basis

---

[1] We have used decimals rather than fractions in all illustrations and exercises.

Distinguishing financial markets into markets for 'short-' and 'long-term' loans is common practice, and useful since instruments within each category are close substitutes for each other. But, while some institutions have a particular need to lend or borrow short term while others specialize in long-term lending or borrowing, most lenders and borrowers use both groups of markets at some time. For example, remember what we said in Section 10.4.1 about the effect of interest rate expectations on lenders' decisions. Imagine a lender who normally prefers to lend for a short period (in the money markets). If he thinks that short-term rates are likely to fall in the very near future, he might prefer on this occasion to lock into current rates for a longer period (via the capital markets). Equally, firms who think that interest rates will be lower in future might decide to borrow short on a temporary basis in spite of their normal preference for long-term borrowing.

As a source of short-term finance, the money markets are, naturally, important to a wide range of institutions. They are important also for another reason which takes us back to Chapter 9, on the *level* of interest rates and Chapter 12 on bank lending and the money supply. This is that central banks exercise their influence over short-term interest rates, via the money markets (either the discount market or interbank market in practice). Money markets are the focus for this official activity for a combination of reasons. Firstly, as we all know, banks offer a guarantee to their clients that their deposits can be converted on demand into cash and therefore banks need to hold the necessary liquid reserves. Secondly, because these reserves (generally) pay no interest, banks hold the minimum quantity; their demand for reserves is highly interest-inelastic. Thirdly, since banks must make settlement on a day-to-day basis, shortages of reserves must be relieved by immediate (that is, *very* short-term) funds. Finally, in a system-wide shortage of funds the central bank becomes the sole supplier. We shall see how this works, in a little more detail, in Section 15.4.

In the next section, we explain the characteristics of each of the instruments being traded in the money markets. In Section 15.3 we look at the use and characteristics of the markets themselves in each of several European centres; in Section 15.5 we note the rapid growth of Eurocurrency markets and the causes and consequences of this growth. Section 15.6 summarizes.

15.2 Money market instruments: characteristics and yields

15.2.1 The discount market

This is a market in which short-term securities are issued and traded. Bills are usually issued with initial maturities of from one to three months, six months, and, less usually, 12 months. For this reason, it would be inconvenient and expensive to set up the arrangements for paying interest in the normal way, for securities which would attract at most one interest payment, and so the practice is to issue the bills at a discount to their *par* or maturity value. Thus a three-month bill with a par value of £250,000 might be issued for £240,000, a discount of £10,000. Clearly it is essential that the amount by which the bill is discounted should be convertible into a *rate* in order to allow comparison with the return on other financial instruments. The simplest way to do this is to calculate the return as a *rate of discount, d*. The formula for the **rate of discount** is:

$$d = \frac{M - P}{M \cdot n_{sm}} \qquad (15.1)$$

where P is the price, M is the par or redemption or maturity value and n_{sm} is the period to redemption (that is, from settlement of purchase to maturity) *expressed as a fraction of a year*. In the UK, a year is reckoned as 365 days while in the US markets and in continental Europe it is taken to be 360 days. In our example, therefore, the discount of £10,000 is equivalent to a *rate* of discount of:

$$d = (250,000 - 240,000)/(250,000 \times 0.25) = 16\%$$

Notice that as the bill approaches maturity, the value of n_{sm}, and thus the value of the denominator, falls. If nothing else changed, therefore, the return on the bill would increase as it approached maturity. To prevent this from happening, it is the bill's price that rises as it approaches maturity.

By rearranging Equation 15.1, it is quite easy to find the price at which a bill must be sold in order to yield a given rate of discount. Suppose, for example, that we wish to lend for two months at a rate of 10 per cent. Then:

$$P = M - d(M \cdot n_{sm}) \qquad (15.2)$$

and thus:

$$P = 250,000 - 0.1(250,000 \times 0.166) = 245,835$$

Equation 15.1 enables us to compare the return on all securities where the return is calculated on a discount basis. But these are not directly equivalent to returns calculated on the more familiar yield (or 'add-on' in the USA) basis. This is because on a discount basis the gain (£10,000) is being expressed as a proportion of the maturity value of the security – the sum received *on redemption*, whereas a conventional rate of interest is calculated by expressing the gain as a fraction of the *outlay*. In our first example, we can see that if we substitute £240,000 (the outlay) in the denominator, the discount of £10,000 converts to a rate of interest of 16.6 per cent. If we let i stand for the interest rate (or 'add-on' rate or **equivalent yield**), then this can be found as follows:

$$i = \frac{M - P}{P \cdot n_{sm}} \qquad (15.3)$$

and it is a simple task to compare Equations 15.1 and 15.3 in order to see that the maturity value in the denominator of Equation 15.1 is replaced by the smaller (discounted) market price in Equation 15.3. *Given* either the yield or the rate of discount we can convert between the two as follows:

$$d = \frac{i}{1 + i \cdot n_{sm}} \qquad (15.4)$$

$$i = \frac{d}{1 - d \cdot n_{sm}} \qquad (15.5)$$

It is important to remember that a rate of discount offers a better return than a yield of the same numerical value.

Bills are often distinguished by their origin. They are issued by central government, local authorities and financial and non-financial institutions. We say more about these distinctions in the next section.

Exercise 15.1

A one-month bill for £100,000 is issued at a discount of £1,000.

Find:

1 the *rate* of discount

2 the equivalent yield

3 the price at which it will trade with two weeks remaining to maturity, market interest rates unchanged.

15.2.2 The commercial paper market

Commercial paper (CP) is the other market in which funds are priced on a discount basis. In effect, a firm issues a promise to pay the holder of the paper at some specified future time. In most countries, access to the market is regulated, usually by specifying that firms must have a stock exchange listing and meet some minimum capital requirement. As a rule, the promise to repay is unsecured by any specific assets and this has led many firms issuing commercial paper to seek a credit rating from one of the major bond rating agencies. The difference between the yield on the highest rated paper and unrated ('junk') paper varies between 100 bp (that is, 1 per cent) and 150 bp. Most paper is issued with an initial maturity between 7 and 45 days. Because of the short duration, there is little by way of a secondary market for commercial paper. The issue is usually handled by a specialist commercial paper dealer, often a subsidiary of a bank, and the dealer will usually offer to repurchase CP from investors.

Yields are calculated in exactly the same way as the (discount) yield on a bill (see Equation 15.1). In Europe, the CP market is a product of the past 25 years or so (only 1991 in Germany), though it began in 1970 in the USA, where it is now very large, accounting for over 80 per cent of the world total of commercial paper in issue. Among the European countries, France has the largest domestic CP market. In the UK the market has remained comparatively underdeveloped, partly because bank lending, as an alternative source of finance, has been comparatively free of restrictions for many years and also because firms prefer the traditional discount market which is very highly developed in the UK and has the attraction that the Bank of England stands as a ready buyer of many bills. (See Section 15.4.)

15.2.3 The certificate of deposit market

A certificate of deposit is a statement to the effect that a lender has deposited a specified quantity of funds for a specified period with a specified bank at a specified rate of interest. It is, in other words, a receipt for a time deposit. As with other money market instruments, denominations are comparatively large (a minimum of £50,000 in the UK, $100,000 in the USA). The significance of having such a receipt lies in the fact that in most countries there exists an active secondary market in which they can be traded, making them into *negotiable* CDs (NCDs). Thus we have a situation with the traditional advantages of a time deposit (the borrower gets a large loan for a fixed period, the lender receives a premium rate of interest as compensation for the loss of liquidity), but one with the added advantage that the lender can, if needs be, have instant access to funds by selling the CD. Because of this liquidity, the borrower pays and the lender accepts a slightly lower rate of interest than would be the case on a corresponding time deposit with no certificate. Just like bills or commercial paper, a CD has a maturity value (equal to the sum deposited plus the interest payment initially agreed upon). However, unlike bills and CP, CDs are priced on a *yield basis*. The interest paid on the CD is often linked to the rate paid on money market deposits (see *interbank deposits* below). Thus, if a three-month interbank deposit paid interest of 10.25 per cent, the equivalent CD might be priced on the basis of LIBID (London Interbank Bid Rate) less 0.25 per cent, that is, 10 per cent. In the circumstances, the 10 per cent payable on maturity is equivalent to the *coupon rate* (c) on a conventional bond and the maturity value in three months' time will consist of the initial deposit (D) *plus* interest payment. In this case, therefore:

$$M = D \times (1 + c \cdot n_{im}) \tag{15.6}$$

where n_{im} is the number of days from *issue* to *maturity* as a fraction of a year. The market price of the CD is then given by discounting the maturity value by the current yield adjusted for the period to maturity. Thus:

$$P = \frac{M}{1 + i \cdot n_{sm}} \tag{15.7}$$

If, as we have assumed here, the coupon rate reflects the yield currently available on comparable three-month instruments at the time of issue, then,

$$M = 100,000 \times (1 + [0.1 \times 0.25]) = 102,500$$

and $P = 100,000$, the issue price.

However, if market rates of return on comparable instruments change, this will be reflected in a change in the price of CDs. Imagine, as an example, that after one month the yield, i, on two-month negotiable instruments falls to 8.5 per cent. Then, using Equation 15.7, we can see that the price of our CD will be:

$$102,500/(1 + [0.085 \times 0.166]) = 101,156$$

(Check that the market price at two months to maturity would have been £100,826 if the yield had remained at 10 per cent.) Given the pricing equation (Equation 15.7), it follows that if we know the price at which a CD of given coupon and given maturity is trading, we can find its current yield. This is done by expressing the gain, the difference between purchase price and maturity, as a percentage of the purchase price and adjusting that percentage to an annualized rate:

$$i = \left(\frac{M}{P} - 1\right) \cdot \frac{1}{n_{sm}} \tag{15.8}$$

Readers should satisfy themselves that Equation 15.8 is equivalent to Equation 15.3.

The first negotiable CD market began in New York in 1961, the sterling CD market opening in London in 1968. Since then markets for negotiable CDs have grown rapidly in all European centres with the exception of Germany. The problem for German banks until recently has been the comparatively high reserve requirement on time deposits. As we noted in connection with quantitative controls on bank balance sheets (Section 12.5), a non-interest-bearing reserve requirement acts as a tax on banking activity. If, for example, a bank issues a €500,000 CD on which the reserve requirement is 5 per cent, then it can on-lend only 95 per cent of the deposit, that is, €475,000. Suppose now that interest rates (and thus the coupon rate on the CD) are 10 per cent. The reserve requirement has the effect of raising the cost of the deposit to the bank by 52 basis points (0.1/0.95 = 0.1052). This puts domestic CDs at a disadvantage with Euro-CDs and with other domestic instruments where reserves are lower. Indeed, the exceptionally rapid growth of the Eurodollar-CD market is partly explained by tough reserve requirements on domestic dollar CDs in the USA. The *Bundesbank* lowered reserve requirements in February 1993 and this did encourage an expansion of the DM-CD market.

Exercise 15.2

1 Find the value of a 5 per cent negotiable six-month CD for £200,000.

2 What would its price be if interest rates were 6 per cent when 146 days remained to maturity?

3 What would its current yield be if its market price were £195,000 with 146 days remaining?

15.2.4 The interbank market

Unlike the other money markets, the interbank market is a market for (non-negotiable) deposits. The deposits can be disposed of only by withdrawing them from the borrower. The initial maturity of the deposits can range from overnight to one year, though the shorter maturities are the more popular. The deposits are the assets of banks with surplus funds and the liabilities of banks who bid for them in order to fund their lending commitments. Thus, the deposits provide an attractive means whereby individual banks can adjust their cash position, being neither too liquid (forgoing profitable lending) or short of liquidity (with the possibility in the extreme case of being unable to honour customers' cheques). The use of the market by banks making continuous adjustments to their liquidity positions largely accounts for the high level of activity at the short end of the maturity spectrum.

The interest rate paid on interbank deposits represents the marginal cost of one important source of funds for banks. A decision to lend may require the lending bank either to withdraw deposits which it earlier made in the market or to attract funds from other banks. Clearly, the loan must offer a return which covers the (opportunity or explicit) cost of funds and thus will be priced on the basis of interbank rate, *plus* a mark-up reflecting the risk thought to attach to the loan. In the UK, the interbank rate is known as LIBOR, London Interbank Offer Rate, and is widely used as a benchmark rate for setting loan and deposit rates by the addition or subtraction of appropriate margins. Equivalent rates can be found in all financial centres (PIBOR in Paris, FIBOR in Frankfurt, for example). As a rule, interbank rates are quite closely related to the official rate of interest set by the central bank since both, the interbank market and the central bank, are potential sources of funds to a bank that needs liquidity. Indeed, the intention of central banks in setting an official rate is to influence interbank rates which are the rates from which banks tend to calculate their lending and deposit rates. We shall see later, in Section 15.4, that the Bank of England introduced a number of innovations in 2006 to ensure a close relationship between the official rate and LIBOR. The Northern Rock case (see Case study 4, page 604) showed that in a crisis interbank and official rates could still diverge quite sharply.

Exercise 15.3

Moneylenders plc arranges a purchase of securities for £5,900,000 with an agreement to resell them in 70 days for £6,000,000.

1 What is the repo rate earned by Moneylenders plc?

2 For what price would they have to be resold in order to provide a return of 10 per cent?

15.2.5 Money market deposits

Money market deposits are large, fixed-term, bank deposits made by non-banks. These are usually large corporations but may be municipalities or other public bodies. In the UK, it is also the custom for local authorities to *borrow* by accepting large fixed-term deposits. These are usually for seven days, though sometimes longer. All such deposits pay interest at rates linked to interbank rate.

15.2.6 Repurchase agreements

A repurchase agreement is an agreement to buy securities from a seller on the understanding that they will be repurchased at some specified price and time in the future. In this deal, the seller is the equivalent of the borrower and the buyer is the lender. The repurchase price is higher than the initial sale price, and the difference in price constitutes the return to the seller. Deals are quoted on a yield basis, using Equation 15.3 (or 15.8). Thus if the *Bundesbank* agrees to a repurchase deal with a German bank, involving treasury bills, it may buy them for €1m, agreeing to resell in three months for €1.008m. If so, the yield can be found as follows:

$$i = (1.008 - 1.0)/(1.0 \times 0.25) = 3.2\%$$

In this example, the sale price of €1m is likely to be slightly less than the market value of the bills at the time of purchase. This margin offers some protection to the lender in case the borrower goes bankrupt or defaults for some other reason. The size of the risk, and thus this margin, depends in large part upon the status of the borrower, but it also depends upon the precise nature of the contract. Some repo deals are genuine sales. In these circumstances, the lender owns the securities and can sell them in the case of default. In some repo contracts, however, what is created is more strictly a collateralized loan with securities acting as collateral while remaining in the legal ownership of the borrower. In the case of default, the lender has only a general claim on the lender and so the margin is likely to be greater.

15.2.7 Reading the *Financial Times*

Commentary on interest rates and money market developments are carried on the *Financial Times* 'Money and Investing' pages. The tables of data, which used also to be published in the *FT* are now increasingly available only from its website.

Box 15.1 reproduces the table that is most relevant to the present discussion. The 'UK Interest Rates' table shows interest rates available on each of the instruments described above, for different periods to maturity as appropriate. Looking firstly at the table as a whole, it amply confirms what we said earlier about the market dealing in instruments with a high degree of substitutability and with very small differences in yields. The difference between 27/32 and 3/4 explains why we need 'basis points'! Looking next

down the 'one month' column we can see that a bank could lend in the interbank market at an (equivalent annual) rate of 6 per cent and could borrow at $6^3/_{32}$ per cent. Other assets of the same maturity yield returns which are very close indeed. If we look further down the one-month column we see that sterling CDs offer only very slightly more. Reading across the table, we see that interest rates rise slightly with increases in the term to maturity up to about six months. At one year, rates are very slightly lower (but not as low as overnight and 7-days). In other words, the 'time–yield curve' slopes upward to begin with. As we shall see in Section 16.5, a popular explanation for the term structure of interest rates is that longer-term rates reflect expectations of future short-term rates. The facts here certainly fit that theory since the Bank of England, at the time, was signalling that it was expecting to have to raise interest rates in the near future.

The 'money markets' section of the *Financial Times* 'markets data' web pages carry a wide range of additional tables. One of these gives short-term market interest rates for maturities up to one year in a variety of international markets. Here one can find

---

BOX 15.1 Reporting the money markets **FT**

UK INTEREST RATES

Oct 4	Overnight	7 days notice	One month	Three months	Six months	One year
Interbank Sterling	$5^{27}/_{32} - 5^3/_4$	$5^{27}/_{32} - 5^3/_4$	$6^3/_{32} - 6$	$6^7/_{32} - 6^5/_{32}$	$6^7/_{32} - 6^5/_{32}$	$6^1/_8 - 6$
BBA Sterling	$5^{13}/_{16}$	$5^7/_8$	$6^5/_{32}$	$6^1/_4$	$6^1/_4$	$6^5/_{32}$
Sterling CDs			$6^7/_{32} - 6^3/_{32}$	$6^{11}/_{32} - 6^7/_{32}$	$6^5/_{16} - 6^7/_{32}$	$6^7/_{32} - 6^3/_{32}$
Treasury Bills			– – –	– – –		
Bank Bills			– – –	– – –		
*Local authority deps	$6.00 - 5.90$		– – –	– – –	– – –	– – –
Discount market deps	– – –	– – –				

Av. tender rate of discount Sep 28, 5.7767pc. ECGD fixed rate Sterling Export Finance. make up day Sep 28, 2007. Reference rate for period Sep 1, 2007 to Sep 30, 2007, Scheme V 6.667%. Finance House Base Rate 5.75pc for Aug 2007
UK clearing bank base lending rate $5^3/_4$ per cent from Jul 5, 2007

Source: Reuters, RBS, * Tradition (UK) Ltd

	Up to 1 month	1–3 month	3–6 months	6–9 months	9–12 months
Certs of Tax dep. (£100,000)	$1^3/_4$	$4^1/_4$	$4^1/_4$	4	4

Certs of Tax dep. under £100,000 is $1^3/_4$pc. Deposits withdrawn for cash $^3/_4$pc.

Source: www.FT.com/marketsdata, 5 October 2007. Reprinted with permission.

US dollar repo rates, Swiss franc, yen and euro inter-bank rates and sterling LIBOR (London Interbank Offer Rate – essentially the BBA rate in Box 15.1). There is also a table showing the official, central bank, rate for major financial centres.

15.3 Characteristics and use of the money markets

The bills that are traded in the discount market usually come from one of three sources.[2] The major, and historically the most important, source is the central government treasury. Such bills are known as *treasury bills* in the UK and USA (usually shortened to T-bills in the latter); *bons de trésor* in France and *Schatzwechsel* in Germany. Although treasury bills circulate quite widely after issue, at least between financial institutions, they are usually sold initially to designated institutions. These are banks and discount houses in the UK; anyone with a central bank account in France; any institution registered also for the purchase of government bonds in Germany and to 'primary dealers' in the USA. Their initial issue usually involves a sale by auction (weekly in the UK, France and USA but with no set timetable in Germany). Auctions can take one of two forms: the **bid-price** auction where successful bidders pay the price that they bid, and **striking-price** auctions where bids are ranked by descending value and all successful bidders pay the (uniform) price of the lowest bid necessary to clear the market. As a general rule, the 'bid-price' auction is the more common. (In the UK, the striking-price method is sometimes used for the auction of bonds, when the process is known as a *tender*. In the UK, therefore, 'auction' tends to mean 'bid-price auction'.) Among money market instruments, treasury bills tend to offer the lowest yield, since they are default-free and also because most central banks are prepared to discount treasury bills on demand for cash which is important to deposit-taking financial institutions who in turn guarantee to supply cash on demand to their depositors. We shall see in Section 15.4 that treasury bills and 'eligible' commercial bills (see below) feature largely in central bank operations to set short-term interest rates.

In much of continental Europe, but not in the UK, there are also large markets for local authority (*municipalité*, *département*, *Länder*) bills and bills issued by public corporations such as SNCF, *Deutsche Bundesbahn* and *Deutsche Bundespost*.

The third major source of bills is large corporations. A *commercial bill* is a promise by one firm to pay another a fixed amount at some specified time in the near future. As with treasury bills, the initial maturities range usually from one to six months. The promise is given in respect of some good or service which has been purchased and the par or maturity value of the bill includes a sum over and above the value of the goods, which is the interest payable to the seller for having to wait for payment. The seller 'draws' a bill on the buyer of the goods who 'accepts' the obligation to pay at a specified time and place. The point about a market for these bills, however, is that once issued they can be traded. The supplier, in our example, need not wait until the bill matures in order to receive payment. The bill can be sold whenever funds are required. Assume for simplicity that short-term interest rates are unchanged since the bill was first drawn up. The price obtained will stand at a discount to the maturity value and the size of the discount will depend upon factors with which we are now familiar. It will depend upon the period to maturity (since this determines the *rate* of discount). It will also depend upon the market's assessment of risk, which in this case means the risk that the issuer of the bill will default. If short-term interest rates *do* change then the discount will get bigger (as rates rise) or smaller (as rates fall).

The fact that the discount rate on commercial bills depends upon the risk of default means that discount rates on commercial bills are generally higher than rates on government or public authority bills. It also gives rise to an important distinction between classes of bills. Some bills may be drawn on banks which have agreed to accept them on behalf of the buyer of the goods. Since the status of such banks is generally well known, their acceptance of bills usually leads to such bills (*bank* bills) carrying a lower rate of discount than they would if they had been accepted by the buyer of the goods. Furthermore, acceptance by certain specified banks, of the highest standing, renders the bill *eligible* for discount with the central bank.

---

[2] For a detailed discussion of the mechanics of bill issue, acceptance and discounting see Valdez (1993) Ch. 5.

This in turn means that the central bank guarantees to discount these bills for cash in the event of a system-wide shortage of liquidity. This immediately gives these bills a special status since they have almost the characteristics of deposits with the central bank while at the same time they provide a positive rate of return. All deposit-taking institutions hold some eligible (commercial) bills and treasury bills as second-line reserves.

In the UK, the commercial bill market received a considerable boost starting in 1974 as a result of what became known as the 'bill-leak'. At several intervals during the 1970s the Bank of England tried to limit bank lending (and monetary growth) by penalizing banks which allowed their interest-bearing deposits to grow beyond set limits (see Section 12.5). As a result, frustrated firms took to raising short-term funds by issuing bills to which banks gave their acceptance. Thus firms, for the most part, got the funds they required while banks were able to replace lost interest income with fee income from supporting the bill issues. For UK banks this was one of the earliest introductions to 'off-balance-sheet' activity, an issue to which we return in connection with regulation of financial institutions in Chapter 25.

In the next section we shall see that central banks conduct **'open market' operations**, of various sorts, in many of the instruments traded in the money markets in order to influence short-term interest rates. It is only with treasury bills, however, that central banks are involved in the 'primary' or new issue market. With all other instruments central banks are operating in the secondary market – the market for instruments already issued by the private sector. Since it is a characteristic of all money market instruments that their minimum denominations are very large (€0.1m for *bons de trésor*, £0.1m for UK commercial paper, $10,000 for US T-bills, for example), it is easy to understand that money markets are markets for 'wholesale funds'. The borrowing and lending involves government and large financial and non-financial corporations. Access to money markets for the personal sector has to be indirect, through some intermediary that is prepared to pool small investors' funds, purchase money market instruments and then pass on money market interest rates (*less* a deduction for expenses) to investors. In the United States, where access to interest-bearing deposits was further restricted by 'Regulation Q' until 1980, the demands of small investors gave rise to the **'money market mutual fund'**. Between 1973 and 1980 US MMMFs' assets grew from nothing to over $200bn.

The impact on banks was considerable, as the personal sector withdrew deposits in order to get the market interest rates offered by MMMFs, and led to the ending of Regulation Q in 1980. From 1982, banks were allowed to offer deposit accounts to 'retail' customers which offered both money market rates and limited checking or payment facilities.

Similar developments occurred in the UK in the late 1970s, though here it was the minimum size of money market instruments rather than regulation that excluded the personal sector from the market. These minimum thresholds led some merchant banks to offer 'high interest cheque accounts' to selected customers. Once again, the principle was to pool retail deposits and use them to buy large denomination CDs, bills or money market deposits. As with US MMMFs, UK banks found that they needed to impose restrictions on such accounts in order to pay the highest possible rates while keeping the operating costs of such accounts to a minimum. In 1980, for example, a typical account required a minimum deposit of £2,500 (equivalent to £7,000 in 2004 – quite high for the personal sector) and set a minimum value for each cheque transaction of £100 (in order to limit the number of transactions for which the account would be suitable).

15.4 Official intervention in the money markets

In Section 12.5 we examined a number of techniques that the monetary authorities in any country could use in order to influence the rate of growth of bank lending and money supply. The list was long, but we could divide the techniques into 'direct' or quantity controls and 'indirect' or 'market-based' controls. We noted in that section that most countries had at some time experimented with some forms of direct control but that in recent years the trend had been towards market-based methods. Indeed, there is now little difference in monetary policy *operating techniques* between the major economies. Essentially, 'market-based' simply means setting the level of short-term interest rates and allowing the market to determine both the quantity and the distribution of money and credit. Clearly, setting the level of short-term interest rates must involve some form of official intervention in the money markets. The main theme of this section is the form that this intervention takes.

In all cases, the central bank uses open market operations in order to exploit its position as the monopoly supplier of bank reserves.

In practice, 'operating on bank reserves' is consistent with the central bank behaving in a number of different ways which can be characterized along a spectrum. At one end of this spectrum, the central bank can set the rate of interest which it wishes to see form the basis for all other short-term rates. In order to maintain this rate, the central bank will have to supply whatever quantity of reserves banks require. In effect, in this situation, the supply of reserves is perfectly elastic at the target interest rate. In Figure 15.1, demand for reserves increases from D_1 to D_2. In order to maintain the target interest rate at i^*, reserves are supplied in whatever quantity is necessary along S_1. Alternatively, the CB can set a quantity target for reserves, engaging in open market operations so as to provide only the target quantity. In this case it must accept whatever level of short-term rate is necessary

to clear the market. In Figure 15.1 the target quantity of reserves is shown by R^*. In these circumstances, the increase in demand takes us along S_2 to an interest rate i'.[3]

Economic theory suggests that the choice between these extremes should depend upon the nature of the origin of the shock to the demand curve. If, for example, the increase in demand for reserves results from an aggregate demand shock which threatens to push demand beyond its trend growth rate, then accommodating the demand for reserves at the going rate of interest enables banks to respond to demands for money and credit which may lead to higher inflation. If, by contrast, the shock stems from an increase in demand for money resulting from financial innovations which cause agents to wish to hold more money in their wealth portfolios, then holding to a rigid reserve quantity target will cause interest rates to rise with a generally deflationary effect upon the real economy. The emerging consensus among central banks during the 1980s was that shocks to the demand for reserves were increasingly the outcome of changes in portfolio preferences. Thus, the tendency was increasingly towards interest rate targeting and reserve accommodation. Behind this, however, was an increasing awareness of the *practical* difficulties involved in operating quantitative controls over the monetary base. These were outlined earlier, in Box 12.4.

In practice, therefore, central banks choose to set the price rather than the quantity of reserves and thus make the setting of short-term interest rates their chosen policy instrument. This they do by making reserves available, at the target price.[4] Changes in officially determined rates are then transmitted by arbitrage (or sometimes simply by conventionally determined mark-ups) to a broad spectrum of short-term rates. Changes in short-term rates then affect the price of bank loans and thus the quantity demanded, as well as affecting the return on a wide variety of assets. If the change in these returns is a change *relative* to the

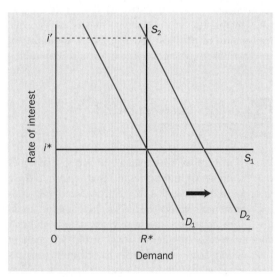

Figure 15.1 Interest versus reserve targeting

---

[3]   This discussion, and Figure 15.1, both involve an element of simplification. Both describe a static situation whereas, in practice, the demand curve is continually shifting to the right. A *quantity* target is not therefore a target set at an absolute level (R^*) in the figure, but a target *rate of growth*. In Figure 15.1, this would appear as limiting the rate at which the supply curve, S_2, was allowed to move to the right. With a quantity target the rightward shift of the supply curve would often be less than the rightward shift of demand, and interest rates would rise. An interest target would require that the supply curve were allowed to shift rightward at the *same rate* as the demand curve.

[4]   We need to be careful to distinguish (minor) day-to-day changes in the demand for reserves which result, for example, from payments between the treasury and the private sector. These are always routinely accommodated since it would be impossibly disruptive to have day-to-day interest rates fluctuating, perhaps quite dramatically, around a stationary mean. The shocks we have discussed here are shocks which are sufficiently major, and sustained, as to require a discretionary policy response.

rate of return on money, then there is an impact also on the quantity of money demanded.[5] Equally, changes in short-term rates in one country change the rate of return on short-term assets in that country relative to others and cause changes in exchange rates via capital flows.

Essentially, central banks can influence interest rates by exploiting their position as lenders of last resort or monopoly suppliers of liquidity in a general shortage. Since the tendency is for most economies to expand over time (and for nominal values to increase where inflation is positive) there is almost always a positive demand for net new bank lending (and net new deposits) at current interest rate settings. This generates the parallel tendency for banks to require recurrent increases in reserves (which as we saw in Section 12.3 are liabilities of the central bank). This is further reinforced by the fact that central banks have always met some of this demand by lending reserves on a short-term basis. The fact that this assistance is continuously maturing means that banks have a continuing need for new assistance which central banks can supply at rates of their own choosing (though subject of course to the (mainly international) constraints which we touched on in Section 9.4). The facilities through which the central bank can provide assistance are virtually the same in all countries. Firstly the central bank can engage in one or other form of *open market operations*. This simply means entering the money markets itself as a buyer (or seller). Alternatively, it can lend directly to banks ('*through the discount window*' as it is sometimes called). The past 15 years or so have seen a considerable convergence in money market intervention techniques (for reasons we explain below). The most obvious is a decline in the amount of discount window lending and greater emphasis upon open market operations, particularly, in recent years, repurchase agreements. Lending via the discount window still takes place in the USA (at 'discount rate') but direct lending is now a marginal source of funds in all developed systems.

'Open market operations' simply means the authorities' buying and selling of securities in markets open to all participants. For example, let us suppose that a central bank wishes to raise interest rates, using open market operations. In such a case, it may offer to buy treasury or eligible commercial bills at a lower price than it did on the last occasion of assistance. This increase in the official discount rate is usually sufficient to signal to all market participants that all short-term rates should change by a similar amount. Alternatively, it may enter the repo market as a buyer, but again offering to buy at a price that represents an increase in the cost of funds to borrowers. If it wishes rates to remain as they are, which is, of course, the more common case, it simply offers to deal at current prices and yields. Box 15.2 overleaf contains a report of the ECB signalling a rise in interest rates.

The fundamental source of its power, as we said in Sections 6.4 and 12.5, is that the central bank is the monopoly supplier of liquidity in the event of a system-wide shortage. Furthermore, the facilities for exploiting this power are very similar in money markets throughout the world. By comparison, the differences between operating techniques are fairly trivial. Table 15.2 on page 315 shows the instruments through which selected central banks conduct their open market operations and the similarities are obvious.

Table 15.3 on page 315 shows the interest rates that the same selected central banks try to influence via these operations. Careful inspection of the final column shows that it is essentially the same range of short-term rates as central banks seek to influence.

We noted above that there has been a convergence of operating procedures in recent years towards open market operations. Both the reasons for this, and the institutional changes necessary to bring it about, vary from country to country. In the USA and the UK the changes were small. In Italy and France the necessary changes were considerable but for Germany rather less. The general principle underlying the shift has been the move towards less direct regulation of markets. When market participants are free to operate with few constraints, direct controls are fairly easily circumvented. Where this is not possible, the controls impose a cost on the service which drives clients elsewhere, a freedom again which comes with deregulation. Recent developments in France provide a useful illustration, though a very similar picture could be drawn based on the UK in the late 1960s.

---

[5] This is a condition which it has always been difficult to achieve when targeting broad money aggregates which contain a high proportion of interest-bearing deposits whose returns move with other short-term rates. Where financial innovation has led to the payment of interest on sight deposits this condition is hard to achieve even for narrow money aggregates.

BOX 15.2 ECB lifts interest rates and signals further rise

By Gerrit Wiesmann in Frankfurt and Chris Giles in London

Eurozone interest rates look set to rise to 4 per cent by June after the European Central Bank raised the cost of borrowing to 3.75 per cent on Thursday and signalled a further increase to come despite recent turbulence on the world's financial markets.

ECB president Jean-Claude Trichet said the new rate was 'moderate' . . . [which] does not mean 'appropriate', heightening economists' expectations that the bank's main rate is likely to hit 4 per cent by the middle of the year. Meanwhile in the UK, the Bank of England left its main interest rate on hold at 5.25 per cent as expected, but investors and economists still expect one more interest rate rise in coming months.

Mr Trichet signalled the Frankfurt-based institution was relaxed about the recent drop in asset prices, although it would 'monitor very carefully' the – not unwelcome – 'reassessment of risk' by investors. He conceded drops seen last week had been 'very rapid', but had not been 'abrupt' enough to worry the central bank. An 'orderly' re-pricing of risk was not a problem given the good fundamentals of the economy.

The ECB also published a new staff economic forecast that showed inflation in the eurozone would this year likely remain below the 2 per cent mark it deems critical for price stability – the first such positive signal since 2000. The central bank's economists for this year project annual inflation in a range with a mid-point of 1.8 per cent, 0.2 points lower than forecast in December. But they also raised the 2008 outlook 0.1 points to 2 per cent.

The ECB's rate rises – Thursday's was the seventh since December 2005 – have recently sparked heckles from some of the eurozone's 13 states who point out that inflation forecasts show that prices are currently stable. But Mr Trichet was keen to stress that the ECB had its eyes on 'the medium-term horizon', which continued to show 'upside risks' to the development of prices. Big wage increases, in particular, posed a 'significant' risk. The ECB's economists raised their forecast for economic growth this year by 0.3 points to 2.5 per cent, and by 0.1 points to 2.4 per cent for next year – a sign the central bank sees that demand in Europe is likely to remain stronger than the ECB's estimate of the potential growth rate of the eurozone. The implication is that the ECB sees inflationary pressure will remain considerable even if the headline rates come down as energy prices moderate this year . . .

The article above reports the ECB's decision to raise interest rates in March 2007. Three points are of interest. The first is the way in the report searches evidence of the *next* change in interest rates. Notice the way in which the reporters pick out the key words and put them in quotes. This is because it is too late for investors to react to the current change. But there might be time to avoid a capital loss (or make a gain) if they can make the correct guess about the next movement and sell (or buy) as appropriate. Recall (from Chapter 11) that asset prices vary inversely with interest rates.

Secondly, notice that the Governor recognizes that asset prices have already been falling and that his decision might push them down further. But he is not concerned about the falling prices which he says is the result of the market 're-pricing' risk. This is code for saying that investors have decided that they generally want higher returns in order to compensate them for the riskiness in financial assets and so the market-risk premium is widening. (See Figure 11.4.)

Finally notice that some members of the eurozone are starting to complain that interest rates are too high, given that inflation is within its target range. But the Governor stresses that he is looking to the future (the 'medium-term') where the evidence is that inflation is likely to rise. Remember our discussion of the transmission mechanism of monetary policy in Chapter 13, where we stressed that a change in interest rates takes about 18 months to have its full effect.

Source: *Financial Times*, 8 March 2007. Reprinted with permission.

Before 1985, the French financial system was highly segmented, with each segment regulated by a different authority and largely by administrative decree. This was because with borrowers and lenders confined to their own specified segment, there was no mechanism (arbitrage or competition, for example) whereby the effect of central bank money market operations could be transmitted generally through the rest of the system and also because, before 1985, there were anyway no money market securities through which the *Banque de France* could conduct open market operations. This, in turn, meant that monetary policy had to be implemented separately in each segment and this required the development of quantitative rules and guidelines for the quantity and distribution of credit for each segment.

Table 15.2 Instruments used in central bank operations

	ECB	UK	USA
Outright purchase	GS, CP[1]	GS	GS
Outright sale	GS, CP	GS	GS
Repurchase	GS, CP	GS, CP	GS
Matched sale and purchase	–	–	GS

[1] GS = government securities (including treasury bills); CP = commercial paper (including commercial bills).
Source: CONDUCT OF MONETARY POLICY IN THE MAJOR INDUSTRIAL COUNTRIES: INSTRUMENTS AND OPERATING PROCEDURES by Batten et al. Copyright 1990 by International Monetary Fund. Reproduced with permission of International Monetary Fund in the format Textbook via Copyright Clearance Center; and table 15.2 from *Monthly Bulletin*, various issues, Frankfurt am Main, European Central Bank (ECB, undated). Information can be obtained free of charge through the ECB website www.ecb.int.

> **MORE FROM THE WEB**
> ***Bundesbank* money market operations**
>
> An interesting explanation of how a national central bank in ESCB uses its domestic money markets to implement the decisions of the ECB is contained in the annual reports of the *Bundesbank*.
>
> These, and the Monthly Reports, are available on the Bundesbank's website: www.bundesbank.de. From the home page, click on 'Economics' and then on 'Annual Report'. The activities are described in a chapter headed 'Operations of the Deutsche Bundesbank'.

There were several reasons for change. Firstly, as we noted earlier, where these controls are effective they impose a cost. As financial markets elsewhere were liberalized, it became both easier and cheaper for French corporations to raise funds outside France. This would clearly become a bigger problem as national barriers to monetary and financial activity were removed in the cause of further European integration. Furthermore, and this was a perfect repetition of the UK experience in the 1960s, direct regulation encourages firms to set up at the margin of the regulations. The target of any regulation has to be defined with precision. Once defined, it is an invitation to those who wish to circumvent it to develop an activity which falls just outside. The result then is that the regulations (and their bureaucracy) either have continually to expand or become ineffective. Finally, when the EMS was established in 1979 and the French authorities committed themselves to stabilizing the franc within it, they required a mechanism capable of reacting quickly enough and with sufficiently broad effects to fluctuations in the external value of the franc. The only mechanism that would operate in a sufficiently widespread and non-discriminatory way was the level of short-term interest, provided, of course, that interest rates in one segment were free to influence interest rates in another. Substantial structural changes to French financial markets were undertaken in 1985 and the move towards a monetary policy based on money market intervention began.

The move from discount window lending to open market operations represents a further step along the

Table 15.3 Official and key money market interest rates

	Rate	Description
ECB	Refinancing rate	Rate charged by ECB on repos and outright purchases of eligible assets (mainly government securities)
United Kingdom	Bank of England dealing rates	The rates at which the Bank of England conducts bond and bill repos
United States	Discount rate	Rate charged by the Federal Reserve on short-term lending to depository institutions
	Federal funds rate	Rate charged in the interbank market for lending between depository institutions

Source: CONDUCT OF MONETARY POLICY IN THE MAJOR INDUSTRIAL COUNTRIES: INSTRUMENTS AND OPERATING PROCEDURES by Batten et al. Copyright 1990 by International Monetary Fund. Reproduced with permission of International Monetary Fund in the format Textbook via Copyright Clearance Center; and table 15.3 from *Monthly Bulletin*, various issues, Frankfurt am Main, European Central Bank (ECB, undated). Information can be obtained free of charge through the ECB website www.ecb.int.

same road towards market liberalization. Lending via the discount window requires the authorities to advertise or 'post' a rate of interest at which it will provide assistance. The authorities are therefore clearly setting short-term rates. There is, firstly, a technical question about whether they are in a position to make the correct judgement about the rate necessary in a particular situation. They may, for example, judge that economic conditions require a rise in interest rates of 50 bp, but raising their lending rate by 0.5 per cent will not *necessarily* cause market rates to rise by the same amount if they have underestimated the degree of liquidity in the market. But in some countries there has been a 'political' problem too. Announcing an official discount rate makes the authorities visibly responsible for the setting of interest rates. In systems like the UK, France and Italy where the central bank was accountable to elected governments, there was sometimes a reluctance to change rates (particularly to raise them) when economic circumstances require. Open market operations give the authorities freedom to exploit the markets' own perception of the shortage/surplus of funds and, less convincingly, to claim that interest rate changes are the result of market forces.

With the movement to independent central banks, it has become unnecessary to disguise who sets interest rates. Indeed, most central banks have embraced the idea of 'transparency', meaning 'openness' in policy making to such a degree that they publish a schedule of dates on which they meet to make the decision and on these dates the central bank's decision is usually a matter of great media speculation.

Since April 2006, when it made a number of changes to the way in which it operates in money markets, the Bank of England's procedures have become even more typical of central banks around the world. Firstly, banks themselves decide on what they think is an appropriate target level of reserve balances and notify the Bank. A change in this target requires six months' notice. A major innovation in April 2006 was for the Bank to pay interest on these reserve balances up to the target (where previously they had been non-interest bearing). The rate of interest is whatever is the official rate prevailing at the time.[6] Once a week, the Bank makes a forecast of banks' likely liquidity position given transactions between the public and private

sectors and other factors affecting banks' reserve position. Since the system tends to expansion, the forecasts tend to show a shortage of liquidity. Given the forecast shortage, the Bank engages in open market operations (making outright purchases of assets and/or entering into repo agreements up to the amount of the forecast shortage) at prices equivalent to the current official interest rate. The repo deals are for one week's maturity. Where it makes outright purchases these are usually treasury bills and 'eligible' (see Section 15.3) bank and local authority bills. However, it is more common for the Bank to engage in repurchase ('repo') deals using government bonds as the underlying collateral. The purpose of these deals is to enable banks to meet their target level of reserves, averaged over a so-called 'maintenance period' which is the period between meetings of the MPC. In order to deal with the Bank as 'counterparties', institutions have to meet certain criteria and enter into an agreement giving them certain obligations to be willing always to provide any short-term finance that the government may require. In practice, the Bank deals with most licensed UK banks and building societies.

MORE FROM THE WEB
UK money markets

The day-to-day issue and redemption of treasury bills in the UK is in the hands of the recently created Debt Management Office. The DMO's website has a feature which explains how it manages the government's short-term financing requirements and how it deals in the UK money markets. The site also provides statistical information on treasury bill tender prices and yields. On the DMO's home page, click on 'Money Markets'. The website is: www.dmo.gov.uk.

Details of the Bank of England's reform of money market operations can be found on the Bank's website and clicking on 'Markets' and then 'Money Markets'. The definitive document describing the operation of the scheme in great detail is the so-called 'Red Book' which can be read at http://www.bankofengland.co.uk/markets/money/publications/redbookfeb07.pdf.

---

[6]   Since balances at the Bank of England now pay interest, banks are understandably willing to hold them in larger quantities than hitherto. There was thus a substantial jump in UK bank reserves in April 2006, though the ratio to deposits is still only about 1 per cent.

The weekly open market operations are carried out on a Thursday, which is also the day of the week on which any interest rate change would be announced by the MPC. In the event of a change, the terms of the Bank's repo deals change accordingly so as to impose the new rate.

Another novelty that accompanied the remuneration of reserves was the introduction of loan and deposit 'standing facilities'. This means that banks with excess reserves could deposit the excess with the Bank (as an alternative to using the interbank market) and banks with a shortage could borrow from the Bank (again as an alternative to the interbank market). The deposit rate was fixed at (MPC rate − 1) per cent while the lending rate was fixed at (MPC rate + 1) per cent. This 'corridor' arrangement is very similar to the system operated by the ECB. The thinking behind the reforms was to limit the fluctuation (or volatility) in interbank rates between meetings of the MPC. By creating the standing facilities and saying that it was always ready to take banks' deposits or to make loans at 1 per cent either side of the official rate, the Bank was effectively constraining interbank rates within this corridor by relying on arbitrage: for example, the moment that interbank lending rates moved more than 1 per cent above MPC rate, borrowing banks would immediately switch to the Bank of England where borrowing was cheaper. The first real test of the new arrangements came in September 2007 with the so-called Northern Rock case (see Case study 4, page 614).

In announcing its willingness to engage in repos (or make outright purchases) each week the Bank is normally expressing its willingness to do so at the going rate. However, if the MPC decides that interest rates should change, the new rate operates with effect from the dealing period scheduled for the day of announcement. Since the Bank's official dealing rate is setting the price of a key source of marginal funds for banks, its immediate effect falls upon interbank rates which change immediately. Since, as we have seen, many other rates are set by formula to LIBOR, these change automatically. Others, linked to LIBOR at a bank's discretion, will change only when the bank thinks making the change justifies the administrative cost. Those money market rates that are set by the trading of money market instruments (bills, commercial paper etc.) change rapidly as possible arbitrage opportunities emerge.

15.5 The Eurocurrency markets

In the introduction to this chapter we noted that most of the instruments we were going to analyse as part of money market transactions existed in both a domestic currency form and a 'Euro-' currency form. A Eurocurrency instrument is, in fact, any instrument denominated in a currency which differs from that of the country in which it is traded. Thus it follows that 'Euro-' instruments can be found all over the world and have no obvious connection whatever with Europe. The 'Euro-' prefix is just a reminder that the practice of trading instruments denominated in foreign currencies began with the US dollar being traded in Europe. Since dollar deposits first began to be held in European banks in the late 1960s, the Eurocurrency markets have grown very rapidly, the stock of Eurocurrency assets being estimated by 1995 at over $6,000bn. In the 1980s alone they expanded over threefold. The Euro*currency* markets predate the markets for Euro*bonds* (which we discuss in the next chapter). We look firstly at the factors behind the growth of Eurocurrency instruments[7] and then at some of the possible consequences.

Under the Bretton Woods system of fixed exchange rates established after the Second World War, the US dollar functioned as an intervention currency, an international means of payment and store of value. The worldwide demand for dollars was met by a combination of US balance of payments deficits and dollar borrowings from US banks, the resulting deposits being held until the early 1960s, mainly with US banks. In the mid-1960s, however, the US authorities began to impose controls on currency outflows which limited access to these (US-stored) deposits for overseas owners. This combined with two further, long-running, disadvantages. The first was 'Regulation Q' which limited interest payments on deposits. The second, mainly relevant to Eastern bloc countries, was the risk that dollar deposits might be impounded for

---

[7] Readers may care to note the similarities between the forces driving the growth of Euro*currency* activity and those behind the growth of the Euro*bond* markets. The latter are listed in Box 16.7. The role played by regulation is particularly striking in the two cases.

political reasons. The result was that non-US owners of dollar deposits began to place them with European banks and, later, with European subsidiaries of US banks.

Since reserve, deposit insurance, capital and other regulatory requirements are usually imposed with respect to banks' holdings of deposits in the domestic currency and act as a tax on deposit business, a further contributory factor to the long-term growth of Eurocurrency business was the ability of Eurobanks to offer their services at more competitive rates than domestic institutions. 'Eurobanks' is actually something of a misnomer. Most are departments or subsidiaries of major banks with a clear national identity. Most countries are involved, although the largest shares lie with banks whose headquarters are in Japan or the USA.

When we come to look at the consequences of Eurocurrency development, it should be said immediately that there is nothing fundamentally different between a bank that specializes in Eurocurrency business and a bank that concentrates on domestic deposits and lending, from an economic point of view. Both help channel funds between surplus and deficit units and, in so far as they create assets and liabilities which are more attractive to end users than would be the case if the latter dealt directly with each other, they help to mobilize funds which might otherwise have lain idle. However, there are two possible consequences of Eurobanking activity which have attracted considerable attention.

The first is the effect upon world money supply and liquidity. If, as we said above, Eurobanks are able to mobilize funds which would otherwise lie idle (through the usual processes of maturity and risk transformation) then private sector liquidity is increased. Furthermore, if we introduce into the banking system a further layer of institutions whose liabilities are money, as is plainly the case with any Eurocurrency, then we introduce the possibility of further multiple deposit creation against a limited

---

BOX 15.3 Money market flows

The following flows will cause changes in money market liquidity. The headings used are the terms employed in *Financial Times* money markets reports for the UK. The explanations, however, are written in general terms, applicable to any money market. In each case, the event is described in such a way that it produces a *reduction* in liquidity to which the central bank will have to respond by supplying additional funds in whatever quantity and at whatever price it thinks appropriate.

■ *Exchequer transactions*
  – Net payments to the exchequer
    If the government banks with the central bank (as it does in the UK), then net payments to government by the private sector will lead to a transfer of funds from banks' balances at the central bank into government accounts.

  – Net official sales of gilts
    The net purchase of government bonds by the private sector is just one way in which net payments may be made to government with the money market consequences described above.

  – Net receipts of sterling on the Exchange Equalization Account
    If the central bank intervenes to support the domestic currency, it sells foreign currency in exchange and thus drains the market of the domestic currency.

■ *Change in the note issue*
  When the public makes net withdrawals of banknotes, retail banks replenish their holdings of notes from the central bank which debits their balances accordingly.

■ *Bills maturing in official hands/sales of treasury bills*
  When bills (or other instruments) held by the central bank mature, payments flow to the central bank from those who issued the bills. The purchase of treasury bills (or other government debt) by money market institutions also causes a flow of funds from the market to the central bank.

■ *Unwinding of previous assistance*
  Previous assistance given by the central bank to the market, a repo deal for example, will be for a fixed period. At the end of that period market institutions will have to repay the loan or repurchase the bills and this requires a flow of funds from the market to the central bank.

■ *Bankers' balances below target*
  If the previous day's clearing has left banks' balances at the central bank below their desired level, banks will withdraw funds lent in the money market.

quantity of reserves. Most Eurobanks hold reserves with major US banks or with major banks operating in the domestic monetary system. Imagine, for example, that a US resident moves dollars from a domestic bank to a Eurodollar bank. In the domestic bank, there is a rearrangement of ownership of deposits (from a non-bank to the Eurobank). In the Eurobank, there is an increase in customer deposits matched, of course, by an increase in reserves. However, the bank's liquidity has increased (on the assumption that its reserve/deposit ratio is less than one). If its response is then to increase its advances and if those advances are redeposited, then a further expansion of the Eurobank's balance sheet is possible. Numerically at least, the significance clearly depends upon two ratios: r, the reserve ratio and d, the redeposit ratio. The multiplier will take the value:

$$\frac{1}{1 - d(1 - r)} \tag{15.9}$$

Estimates of the size of the Eurodollar multiplier range widely, from the very high figure of 18.4 down to 1.15. Part of the explanation for the wide range of estimates lies in the difficulty of identifying reserves held against Eurodollars in Eurobanks which are branches of domestic US banks. The reserves held by the parent bank do not distinguish between the types of deposit against which they are held.

A second consequence, or group of consequences, arises from the increasing difficulty of operating an independent domestic monetary policy. Clearly, any attempt to control domestic monetary expansion can be partially thwarted at least by frustrated UK borrowers taking out Eurodollar (for example) loans and exchanging the proceeds for spot sterling. Such would be a predictable response whether the monetary restrictions came in the form of higher interest rates or some form of MBC. Furthermore, high UK interest rates, which would be part of a restrictive monetary policy, may attract an inflow of Eurocurrencies which could then be exchanged for sterling at a guaranteed price (under fixed exchange rates), increasing both the money supply and UK banks' cash reserves. In principle such an inflow can be sterilized by sales of securities but there is the obvious danger that security sales themselves widen the gap between domestic and Eurocurrency interest rates, leading to an increased inflow. With floating exchange rates it is the exchange rate itself that has to adjust.

15.6 Summary

Money markets enable lenders and borrowers to trade short-term funds. Some markets consist of negotiable securities which can be bought and sold between third parties while others are deposits which can be extinguished only by withdrawal. Since it would make no sense to arrange for interest payments on very short securities, these are usually issued at a discount to their par or maturity values. This means that comparisons between the yields on different money market instruments are not directly comparable. Rates of discount have to be converted to equivalent yields.

The markets are used overwhelmingly by large corporations and by government. The minimum denominations of instruments are very large and trading and trades take place at very 'fine' margins, measured in basis points. However, the personal sector can get access to money market rates of return via a number of indirect routes which require the creation of mutual funds by an intermediary.

From an economic policy point of view, the most important feature of the money markets is that central banks play a dominant role which they can exploit when they wish to change the level of short-term interest rates.

Key concepts in this chapter

Basis points	Money markets
Bid price	Open market operations
Capital markets	Rate of discount
Discount basis	Striking price
Equivalent yield	Yield basis
Money market mutual fund	

Questions and problems

1 Distinguish between 'money' and 'capital' markets. In what circumstances might (a) lenders and (b) borrowers abandon their usual preferences?

2 Why are the interest rate spreads between money market instruments generally very small?

3 Why does the yield on a discount security exceed the discount rate?

4 Which of the following offers the highest return?

   (a) A three-month bill with a discount rate of 8 per cent.

   (b) A three-month NCD with an interest rate of 8.25 per cent.

   (c) A six-month bill with a discount rate of 8 per cent.

   (d) A six-month NCD with an interest rate of 8.25 per cent.

5 The yield on 30-day commercial paper is 7 per cent. What is its discount rate?

6 Who are the main participants in money markets?

7 Explain briefly how the monetary authorities might intervene in the money markets in order to influence the growth of money and credit.

8 Discuss the proposition that the monetary authorities can control either short-term interest rates or the quantity of bank reserves, but not both.

9 How does economic theory suggest that the authorities should choose between an interest rate target and a reserves quantity target?

Further reading

A D Bain, *The Financial System* (Oxford: Blackwell, 2e, 1992) Ch. 12

Bank of England, 'Financial Market Developments', *Quarterly Bulletin* (every issue)

Bank of England, *The Red Book*. Available at http://www.bankofengland.co.uk/markets/money/publications/redbookfeb07.pdf

D Blake, *Financial Market Analysis* (London: McGraw-Hill, 2e, 2000) Ch. 4

C E V Borio, 'Monetary policy operating procedures in industrial countries', *BIS Working Paper* No. 40 (Basle: BIS, 1997)

M Buckle and J Thompson, *The UK Financial System* (Manchester: Manchester University Press, 4e, 2004) Chs 10, 12

European Central Bank, *The Monetary Policy of the ECB, 2004* (Frankfurt: ECB, 2004) Ch. 4

European Central Bank, *Monthly Bulletin*, various issues; *Euromoney*, various issues

Financial Times, 'Bonds and interest', 18 May 2004

Financial Times, 'Bundesbank cuts repo rate to 3%', 23 August 1996

S Gray and N Talbot, *Monetary Operations* (London: Bank of England, 2006). CCBS Handbook No. 24. (Available at www.bankofengland.co.uk/education/ccbs/handbooks/pdf/ccbshb24.pdf)

M Livingston, *Money and Financial Markets* (Oxford: Blackwell, 3e, 1996) Ch. 16

M K Lewis and K T Davis, *Domestic and International Banking* (Hemel Hempstead: Philip Allan, 1987)

K Pilbeam, *Finance and Financial Markets* (London: Palgrave, 2e, 2005) Ch. 5

A Santomero and D Babbel, *Financial Markets Instruments and Institutions* (New York: McGraw-Hill, 2e, 2001) Ch. 11

R Steiner, *Mastering Financial Calculations* (London: F T Pitman, 1998)

R Vaitilingam, *The Financial Times Guide to Using the Financial Pages* (London: Pearson Education, 4e, 2001)

S Valdez, *An Introduction to Western Financial Markets* (London: Macmillan, 1993) Chs 5, 6

Websites

www.bankofengland.co.uk
www.bundesbank.de
www.dmo.gov.uk

Chapter 16   Bond markets

What you will learn in this chapter:

■ The main characteristics of bonds

■ How they are priced and how yields are calculated

■ Why yields vary between bonds of different maturities

■ How these yield differences may be used to obtain information about future interest rates

■ The main participants in the bond markets

■ The size, growth and recent development of these markets

16.1 Introduction

By contrast with bills, and the other money market instruments that we met in the last chapter, the issue of bonds provides a long-term source of funds. Even the shortest-dated bonds have an initial maturity of more than one year, though most, as we shall see, have much longer lives when they are initially issued. Traditionally, bonds offer a fixed rate of interest and bondholders usually have a claim on the issuer which comes before that of other creditors (such as shareholders, for example) in the case of the issuer's bankruptcy. Bonds issued by governments and large corporations who are unlikely to default are therefore regarded as relatively safe investments.

However, most bonds also have a fixed nominal value. This has meant that their real value has often been sharply eroded by inflation. Indeed, we shall see later that bond markets are very sensitive to any event which appears to foreshadow higher inflation, prices fluctuating sharply and inversely with changes in inflation expectations. This means that bondholders are exposed to capital risk if they do not intend to hold the bonds to redemption. The high and variable rates of interest and inflation of the 1970s and 1980s led many bond markets to experiment with innovations such as index-linked and variable rate bonds.

The biggest innovation of all in recent years, however, has been the massive growth in the **Eurobond** market. As we saw with the money markets, instruments can be issued in the currency of the country in which they are traded ('domestic' instruments) or, increasingly, they can be issued in the currency of another country. Yen-denominated bonds issued in London, for example, or HK$-denominated bonds issued in Frankfurt are all known as Eurobonds.

In this chapter we begin by looking in more detail at the types and characteristics of bonds available. In Section 16.3 we then look at the different meanings that can be attached to the term 'yield' as it applies to bonds and at the mathematics of bond yield calculation. This naturally requires us to consider the pricing of bonds, to which we had an introduction in Sections 11.3 and 11.4. Section 16.4 looks at the types of risk to which bondholders are exposed and at the work of the risk-rating agencies. Section 16.5 examines the term structure of interest rates while Section 16.6 looks at the users of bond markets, borrowers and lenders, and at some of the institutional features of bond markets and trading. One of the major developments of recent years has been the rapid growth of international bond markets. Although international bonds share many of the characteristics of domestic bonds, and are priced and traded in similar ways, we have chosen to deal with this particular development, in order to emphasize its dramatic expansion, in a separate section, 16.7. Section 16.8 summarizes.

16.2 Bonds: types and characteristics

As we said at the outset, bonds are traditionally fixed interest, long-term securities. 'Long term' means at least a year, though many are issued with an initial maturity of 20 years or more. For purposes of reporting prices and yields, bonds are often classified by time to maturity but what matters, of course, is the length of time to maturity *from now*, that is, what matters is **residual maturity**.

The classification commonly used is:

<5 years' residual maturity: 'shorts'

5–15 years' residual maturity: 'mediums'

>15 years' residual maturity: 'longs'

In the UK there are six issues of 'undated' government bonds dating from the 1914–18 war.

All bonds are issued with a **par value**. This is the price at which they will be redeemed at maturity. This is not necessarily the price at which they are issued – they may be issued at a discount or premium to their par value. In the UK, the par value is £100, in the USA $1,000, in Germany €100. Conventional bonds pay a fixed amount to their holders at set intervals throughout their life. This amount is set in absolute terms and is known as a **coupon**, for reasons we shall see in a moment. It is a simple task to convert the coupon to a **coupon rate**, by dividing by the par value. Thus a UK bond that paid a £5 coupon per year, or a German bond that paid €5 per year, would both have coupon rates of 5 per cent, and would be referred to as '5 per cent bonds'. Notice that if an investor does happen to buy the bond when its price is equal to its par value and holds it to redemption, then the yield to the investor is also 5 per cent. The investor invests £100 and receives £5 per year until his or her outlay is returned. The characteristics we have so far listed are usually all included in the name or title of a bond. Thus, for example, we may see:

Electricité de France 8¾% 2022

or

Treasury 9% 2008

The title of the former bond indicates that it will pay £8.75 per annum until the year 2022, when it will be redeemed at its par value, while the latter will pay £9 per annum until 2008, when it too will be redeemed. Box 16.6, later in this chapter, features a table from the *Financial Times* listing UK government bonds identified by coupon and redemption date.

As a general rule, the ownership of domestic bonds is 'registered', that is to say that the issuer of the bonds maintains a register of current owners and pays them the coupon when it falls due. (In the UK, USA and Italy, most coupons are paid in two equal, six-monthly instalments, though a minority are paid annually or quarterly. In France, Germany and the Netherlands annual payments are the norm.) However, some domestic bonds and most Eurobonds are **bearer bonds**. That is to say that there is no register: possession of the bond itself is proof of ownership. Owners of bearer bonds claim their interest payments by detaching the appropriate coupon supplied attached to the bond and sending it to the issuer at the appropriate time. The universal use of the term 'coupon' for the interest payment dates from the time when all bonds were bearer bonds. Occasionally, one comes across **zero coupon bonds**. These are bonds which pay no interest but must then be issued at a discount to their redemption value in order to provide a return to investors in the form of capital appreciation. Thus, zero coupon bonds are simply long-dated versions of the bills we analysed in Chapter 15. In recent years, markets have developed for what are known as *strips*. Each strip is the single component cashflow of a bond (usually a government bond) traded separately. Hence, for example, a 5 per cent bond maturing in four years' time could be traded as nine separate strips (eight coupon payments, each with a different maturity plus the maturity value of the bond payable at the end of its life). Each of these would be traded as a zero coupon ('deep discount') bond, maturing on the appropriate date. The advantage of zero coupon/deep discount bonds is twofold. Firstly, their return comes effectively in the form of a capital gain and for some investors there are tax advantages in receiving a capital gain rather than a series of income payments.

Secondly, because no coupons are paid, the 'duration' of a strip is always equal to its residual maturity. Strips will thus be particularly attractive for investors who wish to take a position in bonds based upon an expectation that interest rates are likely to fall. (Duration and its relevance to bond price behaviour is discussed in Section 16.4.2 below.) Bonds with the traditional characteristics that we have just described are sometimes known as **straight**, or **plain vanilla** or **bullet bonds**, to distinguish them from the more recently developed variants which we come to shortly.

Bonds are issued by governments and by large financial and non-financial firms. Where public corporations, such as SNCF or *Deutsche Bundesbahn*, issue bonds these generally share the characteristics of, and are classified with, government bonds. As a rule, (private) corporate bonds show a greater degree of variation in their characteristics than do bonds issued by the public sector. We return to this in a moment.

As with money market instruments, the terminology used in different countries is not always helpful, terms for 'bills' and 'bonds' tending sometimes to merge at the margins.

The terminology of bonds issued by private sector institutions can also pose a problem. The most general term, covering all types of bonds issued by private firms, is **corporate bonds**. Within this category, however, are a number of subdivisions. These arise mainly from differences in the claim on a firm's assets which the bond gives to bondholders, rather than in the financial characteristics of the bond (though the claim on assets naturally affects the risk and therefore the yield attaching to the bond). Table 16.1 overleaf summarizes the terms used to describe government bonds in major European centres.

Debentures are a subset of bonds which are secured on the assets of a firm. They may be secured by a *fixed charge* on specific assets or a *floating charge* on the firm's assets in general. Fixed-charge debenture holders rank above floating-charge debenture holders but it is the floating-charge debenture holders (in the UK) who have the power to ask for a firm to be declared insolvent.

Corporate bonds with no charge over a company's assets are known as *unsecured loan stocks* while those bonds guaranteed by a third party, most usually the parent company or group to which the issuer belongs, are known as *guaranteed loan stocks*. When it comes to risk, guaranteed loan stocks would normally be ranked better (that is, lower risk) than unsecured loan

Table 16.1 Government bond terminology

France	*Obligations Assimilable de Trésor* (OATS)[1]
Germany	*Bundesschatzanweisungen* (2–4 years initial maturity)[2]
	Bundesobligationen (5 years initial maturity)
	Bundesanleihen (10–30 years initial maturity)
Italy	*Buoni del Tesoro Poliennali* (2–10 years initial maturity, fixed rate)
	Certificati Credito del Tesoro (2–10 years initial maturity, variable rate)
	Certificati del Tesoro con Opzione (6 years initial maturity with 3-year redemption option)
UK	Government bonds or 'gilt edge' ('gilts')
US	Treasury notes (1–7 years initial maturity)
	Treasury bonds (>7 years initial maturity)

[1] Note that the French government also issues 2- and 5-year bonds which it calls '*Bons de Trésor à Interêt Annuel*' or '*BTANs*'. '*Bons de Trésor*' is also the term used for 'bills' – see Chapter 15.
[2] All known colloquially as '*Bund*s'.

stocks, but behind floating-charge debentures which in turn rank behind fixed-charge debentures. Again, all of these bonds can offer the traditional characteristics of vanilla or bullet bonds, or they may involve one or more of the additional characteristics listed below.

Some corporate bonds are **convertibles**. In addition to the normal characteristics of a bond, they carry the option to convert at some point in the future either to other types of bond issued by the firm, or more usually to its equity. Other corporate bonds with options attached to them are *callable* or *puttable bonds*, meaning that their redemption date can be decided later at the discretion of the issuer (callable) or the holder (puttable). Some corporate bonds (and some government bonds too) are *double-dated*. That is, their redemption can take place (at the issuer's discretion) at any time between two dates, which are usually included in its title.

As a result of the high and variable inflation rates of the 1970s and 1980s some corporate and government bonds are **index-linked**. This means that their par value is uprated periodically in line with a price index and that the coupon payment is also increased

by the amount of the recent change in the index. The same conditions gave rise to bonds that pay a coupon which is adjusted in line with some other, usually short-term, interest rate. For some reason, such bonds issued by the public sector are known as *variable rate bonds* while their corporate counterparts are known as **floating rate notes**.

Preference shares have characteristics which place them between bonds and equities. We discuss them in Chapter 17, when we examine company shares.

Eurobonds are bonds issued in a currency which is not the currency of the country of issue. The Eurobond market has been the most innovative of all bond markets and we look at it later in Section 16.7. Eurobonds should not be confused with **foreign bonds** – bonds denominated in domestic currency but issued in that country by non-residents. In London, for example, foreign firms may issue **bulldog bonds**, denominated in sterling, while UK firms may issue *yankee bonds*, denominated in dollars, in the USA.

16.3 Bond prices and yields

We already know enough about financial assets to appreciate that the yield on a bond is going to be determined to a large extent by the price that we pay for it and the periodic 'coupon' payment that we receive from the issuer of the bond. While this is true, there are some other considerations which we have to take into account. For each of the additional factors that we take into account, we have a rather different meaning of the term 'yield'. Worse than this, not only do we have different definitions of yield, but 'price' itself has two meanings when we discuss bonds. We look at price first.

In Section 11.3.2 we saw that the valuation formula for a fixed interest stream is:

$$P = \sum_{t=1}^{n} \frac{C_t}{(1+i)^t} + \frac{M}{(1+i)^n} \quad (16.1)$$

or alternatively:

$$P = \frac{C}{i}\left[1 - \frac{1}{(1+i)^n}\right] + \frac{M}{(1+i)^n} \quad (16.2)$$

We also know that if we set $n = \infty$, then Equation 16.2 reduces to:

$$P = \frac{C}{i} \quad (16.3)$$

However, all three formulae suffer from two important simplifications. Firstly, they assume that coupons are paid annually, while in practice most are divided into two equal instalments which are paid at six-monthly intervals. (A few pay coupons in four, three-monthly, instalments.) The second is that the coupon is paid on a set date while deals can be struck on any day of the year and therefore some way has to be found of taking account of the interest that has accrued to the seller but will be received by the buyer after the deal has taken place. Taking coupon intervals first, if coupons are paid six-monthly, then Equation 16.2 should be modified to:

$$P = \frac{C}{i}\left[1 - \frac{1}{\left(1 + \frac{i}{2}\right)^{2n}}\right] + \frac{M}{\left(1 + \frac{i}{2}\right)^{2n}} \quad (16.4)$$

We turn now to the question of accrued interest. Imagine a bond with semi-annual coupon payments. One might buy it, for example, just after a coupon payment, and thus wait nearly six months for the next; or one might buy it with only two months to go to the next coupon payment. If we were to pay the same price for the bond in both cases, then clearly the yield would be lower in the former case (where we get the coupon after six months' waiting) and higher in the latter (where we get the same income after only a short wait). Everyone would wish to hold the latter bond and there would be no market for the former. In practice, of course, the market prices the long-wait bond below the short-wait one, with two consequences. Firstly, the yields are made equivalent by the different prices offsetting the different waiting periods; secondly, the market price of bonds varies cyclically with the length of wait to the next coupon payment. If everything else is unchanged over the year, a bond's price will follow the pattern shown in Figure 16.1.

The increase in the price between each coupon payment date, C_1 and C_2 for example, represents **accrued interest**. Accrued interest is that fraction of the coupon payment which has been 'earned' since the last payment date.

$$AI = \frac{C}{2}\left(\frac{n_{lc}}{182}\right) \quad (16.5)$$

In Equation 16.5, AI stands for accrued interest and n_{lc} is the number of days since the last coupon payment. The market price, incorporating accrued

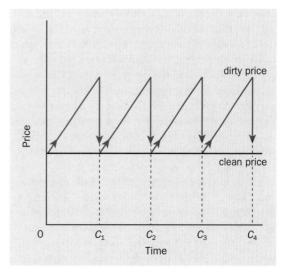

Figure 16.1 Clean and dirty bond prices

interest, is also commonly known as the **dirty price**, meaning that the price, which one usually explains by reference to other, more interesting, variables, is, additionally, contaminated by the position of the bond between its coupon payment dates.

The dirty price can be contrasted with the bond's **clean price**, where the effect of accrued interest is ignored. In most countries, the price actually quoted for bonds – in the financial press and on trading exchanges – is the clean price. However, when the bond is traded it is understood that a buyer will pay to a seller the clean price, plus an amount of accrued interest which is the seller's share of the coupon payment which will later be paid to the new owner.

The formulae that we have used so far ignore accrued interest and therefore, by implication, they are the formulae one would use if pricing the bond immediately after a coupon payment. They are the formulae that one would use for the clean price. Combining Equations 16.4 and 16.5 gives us a formula for finding the dirty price of a bond paying coupons twice a year and including any accrued interest. This is:

$$P = \frac{C}{i}\left[1 - \frac{1}{\left(1 + \frac{i}{2}\right)^{2n}}\right] + \frac{M}{\left(1 + \frac{i}{2}\right)^{2n}} + \frac{C}{2}\left(\frac{n_{lc}}{182}\right)$$

$$(16.6)$$

One might well wonder why this complication is necessary. There are essentially two reasons, one analytical and the other distinctly practical. The first, we have touched on. Bond prices fluctuate for a number of reasons. We shall see in a moment that the main cause is changes in market interest rates, but inflationary expectations and risk also play a part. Changes in these variables cause large changes in bond prices and they are irregular and hard to predict. Thus, these are the interesting variables for bond analysts and they act upon the clean price. The fact that the **market price** also varies continuously as a linear function of the period to the next coupon payment is a mere mathematical necessity. It is of very little interest and thus, as we said above, it 'contaminates' the interesting picture. The practical reason for the distinction lies with taxation. In many tax systems, income is taxed differently from capital gains. A rise in market price resulting solely from the accrual of interest is in effect the result of the coupon or income payment and should be taxed as income. By contrast, an increase in the bond's clean price for other reasons is a change in its capital value and should be taxed as capital gain.

Before we leave the issue of price, there is one further complication. We said a moment ago that the market or dirty price included accrued interest which represented the seller's share of the coupon payment which would be paid in full to the buyer, even though the buyer may not have held the bond for very long. A moment's thought should suggest that it is not administratively practical, in the case of registered (as opposed to bearer) bonds, to make coupon payments to the buyers of bonds who buy the bonds only a few days before the coupon payment date. It takes time for the registrar's office to record a change of ownership and to organize payment to hundreds of thousands of bondholders. There is thus a 'cut-off' date for sales, after which the next coupon payment will go to the previous, rather than the new, owner. After the cut-off date the bond is said to trade **ex dividend**, meaning without the benefit of the coupon payment. This means, of course, that the new owner will have to hold the bond for *more than* six months before receiving a coupon. During this period, instead of the dirty price being made up of the clean price *plus* accrued interest, the market price will actually lie *below* the clean price.

Figure 16.2 shows the situation. If nothing else changes, the clean price is constant throughout the year. The market price, however, fluctuates as we saw in Figure 16.1. The clean and dirty prices are equal on the coupon date, C. After the coupon payment date,

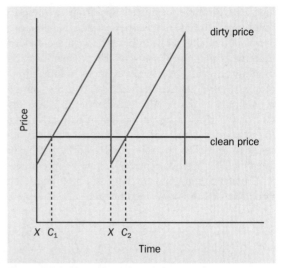

Figure 16.2 The effect of ex-dividend dates

the dirty price accumulates accrued interest. During this period the buyer will get the whole of the next coupon payment and is therefore compensating the seller by passing a share of it to him or her. The accrual of interest (and the increase in the dirty price) continues to the ex-dividend date, X, after which the next coupon payment goes to the seller. In these circumstances, the compensation must flow from seller to buyer. This happens when the dirty price drops overnight and buyers can buy at a price below the clean price until the next coupon payment date. The formula for accrued interest now becomes:

$$AI = \frac{C}{2}\left(\frac{n_{xt} - n_{xc}}{182}\right) \tag{16.7}$$

where C is the coupon payment, n_{xt} is the time in days since the last ex-dividend date and n_{xc} is the time in days from the last ex-dividend date to the next coupon payment.

Notice that the numerator of Equation 16.7 may be either positive or negative, depending on the date on which the calculation is done. In the illustration in Box 16.1, the numerator is positive and so there is a fractional *addition* of interest (0.56 of £4) to the clean price. The seller is being compensated for not receiving the coupon even though he had held the bond for 56 per cent of the coupon period. But it is quite possible for this fraction to be negative. If we were thinking to buy the same bond on 11 November, for example, we should find that the fraction is $-0.1[(11-30)/182]$.

BOX 16.1 Bond prices and accrued interest

Imagine a plain 8 per cent £100 bond which pays its coupon in equal half-yearly instalments on 1 June and 1 December each year. Suppose further, only for simplicity, that it has a long residual maturity and that long-term interest rates are 8 per cent. Its clean price will be £100 and this will also be the dirty or market price on 1 June and 1 December, when there is no accrued interest to take into account. Now let us assume additionally that the bond goes 'ex dividend' 30 days before the coupon payment date. If it is now 10 September, we can calculate the accrued interest using Equation 16.2.

Firstly, the relevant coupon payment will be:

$$C/2 = £8/2 = £4$$

The number of days between the ex-dividend date and the coupon payment date is 30 days (by assumption) and so:

$$n_{xc} = 30$$

The number of days between now and the last ex-dividend date is 132 (= 2 May–10 September) and so:

$$n_{xt} = 132$$

Substituting these values into Equation 16.2 gives:

$$AI = 4\{(132 - 30)/182\} = 4(0.56) = 2.24 \text{ or } £2.24\text{p}$$

On 10 September, therefore, the market or dirty price of this bond will be £102.24p.

Exercise
Find the market price of this bond on 11 November, assuming nothing else has changed. (The answer is in the text.)

In this case, the clean price would be *reduced* by £0.40p ($-0.1 \times £4$). This is because the coupon payment of £4 will go to the seller and the buyer needs compensation for holding the bond but not receiving the next coupon.

It is obviously important for traders to know whether the quoted price is the clean or dirty price, but we shall see now that the distinction is important also because some measures of yield are calculated using the clean price while some use the dirty price.

We begin our examination of bond yields by looking at the more straightforward measures, and moving later to more sophisticated ones. The examination is not exhaustive, however. We confine our attention to 'plain' or 'vanilla' bonds and even then we have omitted some of the least-used yield concepts. Readers who have occasion to calculate 'yields to call' or 'yields to put' or yields on index-linked bonds, are referred to the more comprehensive treatments in Blake (2000).

16.3.1 Running yield

Imagine the simple case where one buys a bond, holding it for a period and then sells it for the price that

one paid. In this case, the return on the bond consists of the periodic coupon payments and the *rate* of return relates this income stream to the price that was paid for it. This is shown in Equation 16.8, where C is the coupon payment, P is the *clean* price and cy stands for what is known as the **running** or **interest** or **current yield**.

$$cy = \frac{C}{p} \qquad (16.8)$$

It might seem strange to use the clean price in this calculation, since we usually think of the yield as the return that we receive in relation to actual outlay which in this case would be represented by the dirty or market price. The explanation for this practice can be derived from Figure 16.2. Figure 16.2 shows that the market price of a bond must vary systematically as a (linear) function of the number of days to the next coupon payment date. Since C is constant, it therefore follows (from Equation 16.8) that the systematic fluctuation in P would produce a systematic and opposite fluctuation in current yield. Indeed, we could, if we wished, draw a figure for the behaviour of running yield over time. It would be the reverse of Figure 16.2 with running yield declining systematically from one

---

BOX 16.2 Why bond prices change – *in the short run*

The stock of bonds is given and prices fluctuate because of shifts in demand (in Figure 11.3 the supply curve is fixed). The demand curve for bonds shifts when bondholders revise their view of the value of holding bonds. If the revision applies to bonds in general, then the bond market as a whole rises or falls (and, remember, yields fall or rise). If the revision applies to one particular bond, or more likely a group of bonds with a particular maturity, then there is a change within the structure of bond prices and yields. Since, for most bonds, the income stream (the coupon payments) is given, changes in investors' valuation must come from changes in i – the rate of discount or the required rate of return. This means that bond prices change because there is a change in the level of risk-free interest rates or in the risk premiums which bondholders attach to those risk-free rates. Thus we would expect the bond market, *as a whole*, to fall when central banks announce a rise in official dealing rates and to rise when interest rates are reduced. The price of bonds issued by particular firms, or sometimes by particular governments, may fall, for example, if bondholders think they see an increase in the risk of default. If a risk-rating agency changes a bond's risk classification, there will certainly be a change in price.

If bond prices only changed with *actual* changes in interest rates or with actual changes in risk, explaining those price changes would be easy. But we often see the bond market rising or falling when nothing else appears to change at all. We must always remember that with tradable securities it is only possible for investors to make a capital gain (or avoid a capital loss) if they can *anticipate* what is going to happen to prices. This leads bond investors to be searching continually for indicators of what is *going to happen next* to interest rates or to risk premiums. And prices will change, because investors will buy and sell, if there is only a change in what people think is going to happen next, even if they are wrong! And once we start to think about what causes changes in people's expectations of interest rates, we create a virtually endless list of possible events. Consider, for example, how bond prices might respond to the following:

(a) an unexpected announcement of an increase in official interest rates;
(b) an unexpected increase in the rate of inflation;
(c) an announcement of rapid credit growth in an economy enjoying a boom;
(d) an announcement of increased retail sales in an economy in the depths of recession;
(e) a government statement that it intended to halve the rate of inflation by the time of the next election;
(f) the publication of better than expected export figures.

Suggestions
(a) prices fall; (b) assuming that the government's policy is to minimize inflation, prices fall in anticipation of a rise in interest rates; (c) as for (b); (d) since the economy is in recession, there is no simple connection with inflation or interest rates and prices may not be affected; (e) depends on whether investors believe their government, but prices probably fall; (f) probably leads to stronger currency and may allow government to reduce interest rates – prices probably rise.

Notice how frequently the mechanism connecting events to price changes involves inflation and interest rates, that investors often need to make a judgement about government policy and reaction, and that this often involves looking at the wider state of the economy.

---

ex-dividend date, jumping back to its initial level on the next ex-dividend date.

16.3.2 Simple yield to maturity

Useful though the concept of running yield may be, it has the severe limitation that it takes no account of any capital gains or losses that investors will experience if they buy the bond when its market price differs from its par value, with the intention of holding it to redemption. Suppose, for example, that instead of long-term interest rates being 8 per cent, in our earlier illustration, they are 10 per cent. Then it follows that our long-dated 8 per cent bond will not have a clean price of £100 on its coupon date, since there will be no buyers for an existing asset that pays 8 per cent when newly issued assets pay 10 per cent. In fact, to make it attractive, its price must stand at a discount to par. If it is a very long-dated bond, its

---

BOX 16.3 Why bond prices change – *in the long run*

Over time, the stock of bonds increases (in Figure 11.3, the supply curve shifts to the right). This happens, firstly, because on balance firms expand and new firms are created, and, secondly, because governments frequently run budget deficits which are financed largely by the issue of new bonds. For a given demand schedule, the rightward drift of a supply curve would lead us to expect a decline in prices (and a rise in yields). But we know that this does not happen. Bond yields certainly rise over periods of time, but they also fall over other periods. There is no continuous upward trend, even though there is a continuous increase in the stock of bonds.

Our supply and demand framework tells us immediately that if the supply curve shifts continuously to the right without a continuous fall in prices (rise in yields), then it must be that something is pushing the demand curve to the right, and it is not difficult to see what that something is. We saw in Section 1.2 that the buyers of financial assets are agents who are running a financial surplus and that this surplus must result in a net acquisition of financial assets. Furthermore, this net acquisition of financial assets is a flow of spending which constitutes an addition to their stock of wealth. Over time, therefore, there is a more or less steady demand for extra financial assets to add to the stock of wealth. In our diagram, the demand curve for bonds moves to the right over time because new lending occurs every year. The extent to which the demand curve shifts per period of time depends upon the size of the financial surplus in that period and the major influence on that is the level of income out of which people can save. When the economy is expanding rapidly, the additional saving, the additional financial surplus and the additional demand for *new* bonds will be large.

We can now see that the long-run trend in bond prices (and yields) will depend upon the relative rates of shift of the supply and demand curves. This in turn depends upon the demand for new borrowing (acting on the supply curve) relative to the demand for new bonds to add to wealth (acting on the demand curve). There is no *inevitable* trend. If, for example, governments run large deficits for a number of years, the demand for the new bonds at the current rate of interest may not expand sufficiently quickly. If that is the case, then prices will tend to decline (and yields will rise). This is a development which is often predicted by politicians who wish to reduce the level of government spending and the size of the deficit. But it could easily happen that annual deficits are not large enough to match the rising demand. If that happens, persistent budget deficits will be accompanied by falling yields and rising prices.

---

clean price is likely to be about £80 (since the £8 coupon paid on an outlay of £80 is equivalent to 10 per cent). Someone buying this bond and holding it to redemption will enjoy a running yield of 10 per cent but will also benefit from a capital gain of £20 when the bond matures. We thus need some means of converting this capital gain into an equivalent annual return which can be added to the current yield. One way of achieving this is to calculate the **simple yield to maturity** or *smy*. The method is shown in Equation 16.9.

$$smy = \frac{C}{P} + \frac{100 - P}{n_m \times P} \qquad (16.9)$$

C and P are the coupon and the *clean* price, as above, while n_m is the number of years to maturity. We can see, therefore, that the simple yield to maturity begins by taking the running yield, calculated as in Equation 16.8, C/P. It then adds to this the capital gain (that is, the difference between the redemption value and the clean price), expressed as a percentage

of the outlay spread over the number of years of the investment.

16.3.3 Redemption yield

The simple yield to maturity is certainly a more useful expression of yield for investors who intend to hold a bond until redemption. But both the current yield and the simple yield to maturity suffer from the shortcoming that they ignore the fact that the coupon payments made over the life of a bond can be reinvested at the going rate of interest and thus understate the overall return that is available to bondholders. **Redemption yield** or *ry* takes account of the coupon payments and the fact that they can be reinvested, as well as any capital gain or loss that might occur between purchase and redemption. Unfortunately, its calculation ceases to be a straightforward matter. The redemption yield is the return that equates the discounted values of the bond's cashflows back to its *dirty* price. In other words, ry is the internal rate of return. Finding the redemption yield involves solving for ry in the rather forbidding expression, Equation 16.10.

$$P_d = \left(\frac{1}{(1 + \frac{1}{2}ry)n_{tc}/182} \right)$$

$$\times \left(\sum_{t=0}^{Q-1} \frac{C/2}{(1 + \frac{1}{2}ry)^t} + \frac{M}{(1 + \frac{1}{2}ry)^{Q-1}} \right)$$

$$(16.10)$$

In Equation 16.10, n_{tc} is the number of days between the current date and the next coupon payment; ry is the yield to maturity; Q is the number of coupon payments before redemption and P_d is the dirty price, that is, the clean price plus accrued interest. Equation 16.10 might usefully be compared with Equation 11.5, the earlier expression that we saw for the valuation of a bond with a fixed period to maturity. In Equation 16.10, the expression between large brackets to the right of the '×', corresponds to Equation 11.5, except that it has been modified to take account of the semi-annual payment of coupons. In Equation 11.5 we used i to discount the future cash payments on our (annual coupon) bond back to its current price; in Equation 16.10 we use ry. Thus i and ry in the two expressions are equivalent. However, we used a second simplification in Equation 11.5. We ignored the relationship between the date of valuation, 'today', and the coupon payment date. By implication, in Equation 11.5 we were assuming that we were valuing the bond on its coupon payment date. In Equation 16.10, the expression to the right of '×' uses ry to discount the future cashflows back to the next coupon payment date but, recognizing that the next coupon payment date may not be today but could be any fraction of a half-year away, we discount that value back to the present, wherever that may be in relation to the next coupon payment date, by using the expression to the left of '×'.

The value of ry cannot easily be found. It has to be done by iteration, using repeated values for ry until the value for the right-hand side of Equation 16.10 converges on the bond's dirty price. For a computer (or calculator with appropriate programmable functions)

it is the work of a moment. Without such technology it can be done by using two approximations. From Equation 11.6 it might be recalled that (by setting $n_m = \infty$) the valuation of a perpetual bond simplified to:

$$P = C/i \qquad (16.11)$$

The same would follow in equation 16.10 if we set $Q = \infty$.[1] Naturally enough, if we set n_m (or Q) very large, but less than infinity, then Equation 16.11 would be approximately true.[2] Recalling that i and ry are equivalent, then it becomes a fairly simple matter, for very long-dated bonds at least, to choose a value for ry in Equation 16.11 which generates a price reasonably close to the current dirty price. By then choosing a second value for ry, so as to generate a second price which 'brackets' the actual price, we can interpolate the precise redemption yield which makes the prospective cashflows equal to the dirty price. Box 16.4 provides an illustration.

For 'short'-dated bonds (less than 15 years), this approximation does not produce satisfactory results, but experience suggests that the following works reasonably well:

$$Approximate\ ry = \frac{C + \dfrac{M - P}{n_m}}{\dfrac{M + P}{2}}$$

where n_m is the number of years of residual maturity. After the initial estimate, the method follows that for long-dated bonds.

Box 16.6, later in this chapter, contains a *Financial Times* listing of UK government bonds and shows the redemption yield in the second column of figures.

16.3.4 Holding period yield

In many circumstances redemption yield will be a more relevant measure of yield than either current yield or the simple yield to maturity. However, it makes two assumptions which will make it inappropriate in certain circumstances. Firstly, and obviously, it assumes that investors hold the bond to redemption.

---

[1]   In Equations 11.5 and 16.11, i is the internal rate of return and the redemption yield on a perpetual bond since i is the rate of interest that discounts the cashflows of a perpetual bond back to its present value. If Equation 16.11 is rearranged to find i, that is, $i = C/P$, it can be seen that the rearrangement is equivalent to the equation for current yield, Equation 16.8. Thus, for a perpetual bond, current yield and redemption yield are identical.
[2]   In practice, the approximation is satisfactory for bonds with residual maturity in excess of 15 years.

BOX 16.4 Interpolating redemption yield

Suppose that we wish to find the redemption yield for an 8 per cent bond with just over 20 years to redemption. The bond is currently trading at £95 and there are 40 days to the next coupon payment.

Using Equation 16.11, we can make a first, rough, estimate:

$$ry = 8/95 = 8.42\%$$

Substituting 0.0842 in Equation 16.10 and solving for the price gives us £99.03. Since the bond is actually trading at £95, then our estimate of the redemption yield is clearly too low.

For a second trial, suppose that we take an estimate of 9.0%. Substituting this into Equation 16.10 gives a price of £93.98. This price lies below the actual market price, but the two prices taken together give us a basis for a more accurate estimate of redemption yield.

Firstly, we can see that the correct redemption yield lies nearer to 9.0% than it does to 8.42%. In fact, if we round our estimated prices to £99 and £94 for simplicity, we can see that the real price of £95 lies 4/5 of the way along the £99–£94 range. This might suggest that the redemption yield that we require lies 4/5 of the way along the interest rate spectrum of 8.42%–9.0%. Four-fifths of this difference is 0.46. If we add this to 8.42% and solve Equation 16.10 once more using a redemption yield of 8.8%, we shall find that the estimated price does indeed match the actual price of £95.

This last step is an example of linear interpolation. If we let the subscripts 1, 2 and a stand for the first estimate, the second estimate and the actual values respectively, then we can summarize this last step formally:

$$ry_a = ry_1 + [(ry_2 - ry_1) \times P_1 - P_a/P_1 - P_2]$$

Less obviously, while it takes into account the effect of compound interest on the coupons when they are reinvested (unlike the simple yield to maturity), it assumes that the coupons can be reinvested at the constant redemption yield. The first assumption is obviously inappropriate to investors who intend to sell before redemption. For them, it is not the par value that matters but the price of the bond at the time they wish to sell. The second assumption will often be inappropriate for many bondholders, especially in a period of

Exercise 16.1 The interpolation of redemption yields on short-dated bonds

Find an approximate yield to maturity for a 5% bond with just over three years to maturity, when there are 50 days left to the next coupon payment and there are six coupons remaining. The bond is currently trading at £92. From this approximation, find the exact yield to maturity.

Hints
1   From the expression above:

    (approximately) $ry_1 = [5 + (100-92/3)]/(100 + 92)/2 = 7.986 = 8.0\%$

2   Substitute 8.0%, and the characteristics of the bond, into Equation 16.10 and calculate a trial price, P_1.

3   Use another trial value (ry_2) which is bound to produce a second trial price (P_2) for this bond such that the actual price (P_a) lies between P_1 and P_2.

4   Use the interpolation formula from the illustration in Box 16.4 to find the exact redemption yield.

5   Substitute the interpolated value for ry into Equation 16.10 and check that it does give the correct market price.

Answer
Taking ry_1 as 8.0% gives a P_1 of £94.76; taking ry_2 as 10.0% gives a P_2 of £90.39. Using the interpolation formula tells us that the redemption yield for an actual price of £92 is 9.263%.

fluctuating interest rates. Ignoring accrued interest (that is, assuming that the bond is bought on a coupon payment date), the **holding period yield** (*hy*) is the rate that satisfies the expression:

$$P_d(1 + \tfrac{1}{2}rh)^{2n_m} = (C/2)(1 + \tfrac{1}{2}i_1)2^{n_m-1} +$$
$$(C/2)(1 + \tfrac{1}{2}i_1)2^{n_m-2} + \ldots$$
$$+ (C/2) + P_1 \qquad (16.12)$$

where i_1, i_2 and so on are the rates of interest at which the first coupon, second coupon and so on can be reinvested, while P_1 is the price for which the bond is eventually sold. Solving for *hy* is done as follows:

$$hy = \left(\left[\frac{(C/2)(1 + \tfrac{1}{2}i_1)^{2n_m-1} + \ldots + (C/2) + P_1}{P_d}\right] - 1\right) \times 2$$
$$(16.13)$$

16.4 Risk and fixed interest bonds

In many respects, bonds appear to be very low-risk investments. Compared with shares, for example, the income stream is fixed. Bonds issued by most governments are default-free. Furthermore, in the case of corporate bonds, bondholders have a comparatively strong claim on any remaining assets in the event of the firm's bankruptcy.

This does not make them risk-free, however. In this section, we shall consider three types of risk to which bonds are subject:

1 default risk;
2 reinvestment risk;
3 capital risk.

16.4.1 Default risk

Bonds, particularly government bonds, may be relatively secure instruments but this does not mean that their issuers *never* default. Corporations do go bankrupt and even governments can have problems. The Bank of Credit and Commerce International failed in 1991; Baring's bank failed in 1995; Eurotunnel unilaterally suspended interest payments on part of its debt in October 1995; the Northern Rock bank got into serious difficulties in 2007. In August 1982 the

MORE FROM THE WEB
Assessing corporate risk

The need for lenders and investors to know as much as possible about the firm to which they might be lending, or in which they may be going to invest has given rise to a number of credit rating agencies. These are commercial organizations which have built up considerable experience over the years in recognizing those characteristics of any organization which increase or diminish its risk. As we explain in the text, this enables them to give a numerical or alphabetical score to firms which they assess.

One of the major credit rating agencies is Standard & Poor's, whose website can be accessed at: www.standardandpoors.com.

Their home page publishes the latest ratings awarded to selected bond issues. More interestingly, clicking on 'Products A–Z' and then on the letter 'C' gives access to 'Credit Risk Assessment Templates'. These give some idea of the factors taken into account in deciding on a rating.

The Fitch website can be accessed at http://www.fitchratings.com/.

Mexican government announced that repayment of principal would be deferred and in 1991 there were doubts about the Italian government's ability to meet all its debt obligations exactly as specified. All such events mean that bond investors have to take default (or *credit*) risk seriously.

As always, investors face considerable costs in acquiring the information necessary for the assessment of the risk they face. This creates the opportunity for **credit rating agencies** to exploit economies of scale and specialist expertise in order to provide assessments of risk. This service is purchased by issuers of bonds who find that a reputable credit rating enables them to borrow on better terms than would be the case if investors had no guidance. The best known agencies are Moody's and Standard & Poor's and Fitch.

Box 16.5 reports a Croatian Eurobond issue receiving a credit rating in January 1997. Notice firstly that the report confirms that getting a rating is expected to be beneficial. But notice also that the rating given to Croatian Eurobonds was 'BBB–'. The picture on the right shows the ratings used by the three agencies and this shows that 'BBB–' (or its

BOX 16.5 Bond credit ratings

Credit rating boost for Croat eurobond debut

By Kevin Done, East Europe Correspondent

Croatia's hopes of a successful debut in the international bond market grew yesterday after it received investment grade ratings from two leading international rating agencies.

The former Yugoslav republic, which is preparing to launch its first foreign currency eurobond next month, was awarded a BBB-rating, the lowest investment grade, by both Standard & Poor's of the US and IBCA, the European agency.

Moody's, the other leading US agency, is expected to release its first assessment early next week.

Croatia is rated at the same level as Hungary and Slovakia. It is also rated the same as Poland and Latvia by S&P and, outside east Europe, it is on a par with Greece and Tunisia.

Mr Bozo Prka, Croatian finance minister, said yesterday that the country would seek to raise $250m in its debut foreign currency eurobond. It would have a maturity of five years, which was 'unimaginable until very recently,' he said.

The issue will be arranged by a syndicate of 15 international banks led by Merrill Lynch of the US and Union Bank of Switzerland. The price will be determined following a 20-day roadshow to institutional investors in Asia, the US and Europe beginning in the Far East this weekend.

Croatia, like other countries in eastern Europe, is hoping to take advantage of the increasingly keen appetite among investors for emerging market risk. Earlier this week both Latvia and Moldova received their first international ratings, with Latvia assessed BBB investment grade by S&P and Moldova Ba2 (BB) speculative grade by Moody's.

Credit ratings reflect the perceived risk of default by a borrower on its debt. A strong rating, implying reduced risk to investors, usually means lower funding costs for the borrower.

IBCA said that the BBB-rating for Croatia reflected both the impressive way the economy had been stabilised, with the lowest rate of inflation of the transition economies and substantial export earning capacity and potential. External debt was still modest compared with both gross domestic product and foreign exchange receipts.

The agency said it believed the risks of Croatia becoming embroiled in another war were now small with frontiers mutually recognised by Croatia, Bosnia and Yugoslavia. The rapid Croatian military build-up meant there was now a balance of power in the region.

Tensions in Bosnia could 'taint Croatia by association', however, and harm both tourist earnings, the 'potential jewel' in foreign currency earnings and foreign direct investment.

It also warned that progress in structural reform had been 'patchy' with particularly slow progress in privatisation. IBCA forecasts growth of 5.5 per cent in GDP this year following an estimated 6.5 per cent in 1996, with inflation remaining around 3.5 per cent a year.

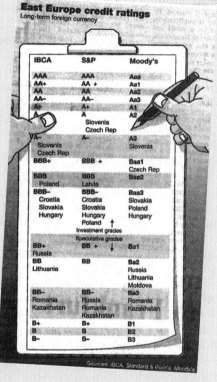

East Europe credit ratings
Long-term foreign currency

IBCA	S&P	Moody's
AAA	AAA	Aaa
AA+	AA +	Aa1
AA	AA	Aa2
AA–	AA–	Aa3
A+	A+	A1
A	A	A2
	Slovenia	
	Czech Rep	
A–	A–	A3
Slovenia		Slovenia
Czech Rep		
BBB+	BBB +	Baa1
		Czech Rep
BBB	BBB	Baa2
Poland	Latvia	
BBB–	BBB–	Baa3
Croatia	Croatia	Slovakia
Slovakia	Slovakia	Poland
Hungary	Hungary	Hungary
	Poland	

Investment grades ↑
Speculative grades ↓

IBCA	S&P	Moody's
BB+	BB +	Ba1
Russia		
BB	BB	Ba2
Lithuania		Russia
		Lithuania
		Moldova
BB–	BB–	Ba3
Romania	Russia	Romania
Kazakhstan	Romania	Kazakhstan
	Kazakhstan	
B+	B+	B1
B	B	B2
B–	B–	B3

Sources: IBCA, Standard & Poor's, Moody's

equivalent) is a long way below the best. In fact, bonds rated from AAA to BBB (inclusive) are sometimes referred to as 'investment grade' bonds since it is only these bonds that professional investment managers are normally prepared to hold. Croatian bonds barely qualify, therefore. On the other hand, it is only when we get down to grade D that we are dealing with bonds which are either in default, or are likely to be in default. It follows from this that the difference in yield required by the market as we move from one grade to another looks comparatively small, usually less than 30 basis points. (But we must always remember, as we saw in Chapter 15, that these small differentials are being paid on very large sums and so quite fine differences have the ability to move large sums of money.) Bonds rated below BBB are known as 'speculative' or even **junk' bonds**. (Note that 'junk', in this context, does not mean 'worthless'.)

The rating agencies are, naturally enough, mainly concerned with the ability of the bond issuer to meet his or her obligations. But in addition to this concern with 'ability to pay', the agencies also take into account the nature and terms of the obligation in the bond and, just in case things go wrong, the protection and claim that bondholders have. The case of Eurotunnel illustrates what is at issue here. Like many large corporations, Eurotunnel has issued more than one type of bond. The differences between these bonds often involve differences in the rights of the bondholders. The suspension of interest in 1995 applied only to the 'subordinate' debt. Holders of this subordinate debt had relatively little power and a low priority claim in the event of the firm's liquidation. Consequently, this debt was rated more speculatively by S&P and carried a higher yield than 'primary debt'.

16.4.2 Reinvestment and capital risk

Since, for conventional bonds, coupon payments are fixed for the life of the bond and since the par or maturity value is also fixed, it follows that purchasing a bond and holding it to redemption provides a known, fixed, rate of return. The redemption yield is fixed. However, we have already seen that the holding period return remains uncertain. This uncertainty arises (a) because we cannot be sure of the yield we can get on the coupon payments when we reinvest them and (b) our circumstances *may* change such that we have to sell the bonds before maturity, and we cannot then be

certain of the price we shall get. Both of these uncertainties derive from a common source: a change in interest rates.

Naturally enough, bond yields must reflect these risks, by incorporating a premium which reflects both the degree of risk and the strength of the market's aversion. We have already met the idea that some bond prices are more sensitive to interest rate changes in Section 11.3.2. It is now time to look carefully at why this is the case and also to explore ways of measuring the degree of interest rate sensitivity. For the latter, we shall examine the concept of **duration**. Two other, less common, measures are *convexity* and *dispersion*. Details of these can be found in Blake (2000, Ch. 5).

Imagine a bond which makes annual coupon payments. Then:

$$\text{Duration} = \frac{\dfrac{1C}{(1+ry)^1} + \dfrac{2C}{(1+ry)^2} + \dots + \dfrac{n_m(C+M)}{(1+ry)^{n_m}}}{P_d}$$

(16.14)

If we now recall (from the appendix to Chapter 11) that we can dispense with the summation by using the alternative expression for the present value of an annuity:

$$P = \frac{C\left(1 - \dfrac{1}{(1+ry)^{n_m}}\right)}{ry} = C/ry(1-[1+ry]^{-n_m})$$

(16.15)

then:

$$\text{Duration} = \frac{\left[\dfrac{C(1+ry)}{ry}\right]\left[\dfrac{1-(1+ry)^{-n_m}}{ry}\right] + \left[\dfrac{n_m(m-C/ry)}{(1+ry)^{n_m}}\right]}{P_d}$$

(16.16)

For purposes of illustration, imagine a bond with a £5 coupon paid annually, redeemable in three years' time, and a par value of £100. If the redemption yield is 8 per cent, then (from Equations 11.5 or Appendix 11.1) its current price must be £92.268.

Substituting these values into Equation 16.16 gives:

$$[(67.5) \times (2.577) + (89.306)]/92.268 = 2.853$$

Notice what happens to duration if the coupon had been £6, redemption yield and period to maturity remaining constant. Firstly, we would of course expect the price of the bond to be higher. Using Equation 11.5 again, $P = £94.36$. Solving Equation 16.16 again using the new coupon and new price but leaving the redemption yield and maturity as before gives:

$$[(81.0) \times (2.577) + (59.537)]/94.846 = 2.829$$

We find that the higher coupon gives us a lower value for duration.

Consider now what happens if we change the redemption yield. Suppose that we leave everything as it is ($C = 6$; $n_m = 3$), but increase the redemption yield to 12 per cent. Firstly, the market price falls to £85.589. More interestingly, duration is reduced to 2.819.

From these illustrations, we can draw three conclusions about duration, maturity, coupon and redemption yield, at least as they apply to *coupon-bearing, redeemable* bonds:

> *Duration and maturity.* For a given coupon, duration increases with maturity. Thus, other things being equal, long-dated bonds are more sensitive to interest rate changes, and therefore riskier, than short-dated bonds.
>
> *Duration and coupon.* For a given maturity, duration diminishes as the coupon increases.
>
> *Duration and redemption yield.* For a given maturity, duration diminishes as redemption yield increases.

From this it follows that the riskiest bonds, that is, those whose prices are most sensitive with respect to interest rate changes, are those with long maturities and low coupons. Furthermore, the riskiness of all bonds is greater when interest rates are low.

These propositions apply to coupon-bearing bonds with a fixed period to maturity. Note that zero coupon (pure discount) bonds and perpetual bonds are special cases which behave rather differently. Firstly, for a zero coupon bond we set $C = 0$ in Equation 16.16. The duration is thus equal to maturity (n_m) and zero coupon bonds have the greatest duration and price volatility for bonds with that maturity. Secondly, for an irredeemable bond, in Equation 16.16 we set $n_m = \infty$. For perpetual bonds then *duration* $= (1/ry) + 1$.

Duration is defined as the weighted average maturity of a bond. The logic behind the idea of 'weighted average maturity' is that for bonds which pay regular coupons, the total cashflow from that bond is spread over a period (from now to the date of maturity).

Depending upon the characteristics of the bond, this cashflow could be heavily weighted towards the immediate future or towards the more distant future. Since changes in the discount rate always have a larger effect upon distant payments than upon short ones, a bond where the weight of payments is soon should be less interest-sensitive than a bond where the weight of payments lies further away. Duration, therefore, is trying to capture the average time that it takes to receive the cashflow. The weights are the relative discounted cashflow in each period and the weighted average is simply the sum of those weights.

This is easier to see if we go back to Equation 16.14 and consider an example which compares duration for two bonds, each paying a 5 per cent annual coupon, trading at par, with $ry = 5$ per cent, but bond A maturing in two years and bond B maturing in three years' time. For bond A:

$$D = (4.776 + 190.476)/100 = 1.953$$

While for bond B:

$$D = (4.776 + 9.070 + 272.114)/100 = 2.859$$

Notice that for both bonds duration is less than the period to maturity. This must be the case since some cashflow in both cases comes from interim coupon payments. In the case of bond A, one may say that the interim coupon payments contribute 0.0478 of the duration value of 1.953, while the final coupon *plus* maturity payment contributes 1.9057. As proportions, these represent 2.44 per cent and 97.56 per cent respectively. For bond B, duration is 2.859, to which interim coupon payments contribute 0.138, while the redemption payment contributes 2.721. As proportions, these represent 4.83 per cent and 95.17 per cent respectively. With the longer dated bond a larger weight attaches to the interim coupon payments.

We can now show formally that duration is a measure of interest rate risk. Assuming still that coupon payments are annual, then the present value of a bond is given (see Equation 11.5) by:

$$P_d = \sum_{t=1}^{n} \frac{C}{(1 + ry)^t} + \frac{M}{(1 + ry)^{n_m}} \tag{16.17}$$

Differentiating with respect to $(1 + ry)$

$$\frac{\Delta P_d}{\Delta (1 + ry)} = -C \sum_{t=1}^{n} \frac{t}{(1 + ry)^{t+1}}$$
$$- M \frac{n_m}{(1 + ry)^{n_m+1}} \tag{16.18}$$

If we now multiply both sides by $(1 + ry)/P_d$ we have:

$$\frac{\Delta P_d/P_d}{\Delta(1 + ry)/(1 + ry)} = \frac{C}{P_d}\sum_{t=1}^{n_m}\frac{t}{(1 + ry)^t}$$
$$- \frac{M}{P_d}\frac{n_m}{(1 + ry)n_m} = -D$$

(16.19)

The leftmost expression in Equation 16.19 is the elasticity of the bond price with respect to $(1 + ry)$. The larger the value of duration, the larger the (negative) elasticity.

16.5 The term structure of interest rates

The **term structure of interest rates** refers to the pattern of interest rates available on assets differentiated *solely* by their term to maturity, and a plot of these rates against the period to maturity is known as a **time–yield curve**. An example is provided in Figure 16.3.

The central issue of term structure discussions is the effect that the period to maturity has upon yields, when all other possible explanations for yield variation have been removed. In order to study the term structure, therefore, we need a large population of assets which are homogeneous, particularly with respect to default risk, but exist in a wide range of maturities.

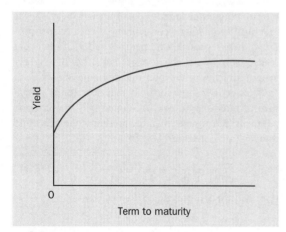

Figure 16.3 A time–yield curve

Not many asset groups can meet these requirements. The most obvious candidates in most countries are government bonds. They are all issued by the same (and therefore constant risk) issuer, and they exist in a wide variety of maturities. Some term structure investigations use treasury bills for the same reason, though the range of maturities is limited to <1 year, of course. Occasionally interbank deposits are used, though the maturities are even more restricted. Because the 'term structure' so often means the term structure of yields on government bonds, and also because one theory (the 'term premium' theory) of the term structure draws upon technicalities which we have just been discussing, this is the obvious place in which to examine it more closely.

Before we begin, however, we need to be clear that one can plot a yield curve for every meaning of the term 'yield' which we identified in the last section. Fortunately, in practice, discussions of the yield curve are almost always discussions of the curve which plots redemption yields against period to maturity. Unless we state otherwise, 'yield' means 'redemption yield' throughout this section.

We examine three theories which try to explain the relationship between term to maturity and yield: the **expectations**, the **term premium** and the **preferred habitat/market segmentation** theories. They are presented in this order which roughly corresponds to their importance in the specialist literature. It is useful to note at the outset that the theories are not mutually exclusive. The yield curve *could* be determined by expected future interest rates, with a term premium reflecting the general level of risk aversion and 'local' premiums or discounts reflecting the abundance or shortage of bonds in a particular part of the maturity spectrum.

16.5.1 Expectations theory

The idea that the term structure could be explained by reference to market expectations of future interest rates dates at least from Irving Fisher (1930) and was discussed extensively by Hicks (1946).[3]

The term structure of interest rates presents investors with a variety of interest rates on assets differentiated solely by their term to maturity. At the very

---

[3]   More recent extensions and modifications of the theory appear in Malkiel (1966) and Roll (1970).

least an investor looking to invest for L-years has a choice between holding a 'long' bond to maturity in L-years at a 'long-term' rate of interest, i_L,[4] which is currently known, and holding a succession of short-dated bonds, only the first of whose rates of interest, i_1, is currently known, reinvesting the proceeds at the end of each period in another short-dated bond whose rate of interest, $\hat{i}_2$, is not known now, but can only be anticipated.

Let us assume that an investor wishes to invest for two years ($L = 2$) and that the investor is risk neutral. Furthermore, let us suppose that s/he knows the current one-year rate of interest (i_1), the current two-year rate of interest (i_L) and holds a confident expectation about the one-year rate ($\hat{i}_2$) that will prevail in one year's time. Then it follows that s/he will be indifferent between these two investment strategies when:

$$(1 + i_1)(1 + \hat{i}_2) = (1 + i_L)^2 \qquad (16.20)$$

Furthermore, knowing i_1 and i_L, we can solve for the expected, or *implied*, future spot rate, $\hat{i}_2$, as follows:

$$\hat{i}_2 = \frac{(1 + i_L)^2}{(1 + i_1)} - 1 \qquad (16.21)$$

In recent years, some authorities have taken to referring to the implied future spot rate as a *forward* rate.

Turning now to the relationship $i_L - i_1$, the relationship between long and short rates, it follows from Equation 16.21 that if $i_L > i_1$, then $\hat{i}_2$ is also greater than i_1, that is to say that the investor expects future one-year rates to be above current one-year rates. Rearranging Equation 16.21 tells us indeed that with $i_L > i_1$, then $\hat{i}_2$ must also be greater even than i_L.

$$i_2 = \frac{(1 + i_L)^2}{(1 + i_1)} - 1 \qquad (16.22)$$

The common sense of this, of course, is that an investor willing to buy a one-year bond now at a rate of interest below the going two-year rate must expect at the end of the first year to be able to replace the first one-year bond with a second which pays a (one-year) rate of interest which is higher than the current two-year rate by the amount necessary to produce an average return over the two years just equal to $(1 + i_L)$. As Shiller (1990) helpfully points out this is analogous

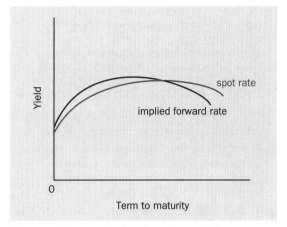

Figure 16.4 The spot rate–implied forward rate relationship

with the marginal cost/average cost relationship. When the yield curve is rising, forward rates must be higher than spot rates of the same maturity and vice versa when the yield curve slopes downward. This is shown in Figure 16.4.

Turning from the individual investor to the market for one- and two-year bonds as a whole, equilibrium, indicated by stable bond prices, will exist when all investors are indifferent between holding two one-year bonds and one two-year bond, that is to say when the market as a whole takes i_L to be an average of the known one-year rate, i_1, and the *expected* future one-year rate $\hat{i}_2$. Were this not to be the case, suppose for example that i_L were greater than the average of the two short rates, then arbitrage between long and short bonds would push up the price of long bonds until i_L was reduced to the average of the short rates. Notice that the argument depends upon complete substitutability between long and short bonds. We return to this in the next section.

The principles which underlie the choice between one- and two-year bonds can, of course, be generalized to cover bonds of all maturities. In our example, we took i_L to be the rate on two-year bonds. Thus reordering Equation 16.20 we have:

$$(1 + i_L)^2 = (1 + i_1)(1 + \hat{i}_2) \qquad (16.23)$$

---

4   Remember that yields throughout the following discussion of term structure are assumed to be nominal redemption yields (yields to maturity). The long-term rate should therefore strictly be written ry_L. However, when we talk about nominal long-term redemption yields, we are talking, most of the time, about what is for many purposes the long-term nominal interest rate, i_L. Through the remainder of this section we have used the symbol i_L for reasons of brevity, and clarity in the mathematical expressions.

BOX 16.6 Bond yields and maturity

The table reproduced below is taken from the London *Financial Times* for Wednesday, 19 September 2007 and shows the behaviour of a sample of UK government bond prices and yields on 18 September. (The *FT* currently publishes a full list only on a Saturday.) The table appears on the 'Market Data' page. The table illustrates a number of points which we have already discussed in this chapter. Notice:

- The title of each bond includes the coupon rate and the year of redemption.
- The bonds are listed in increasing order of their residual maturity.
- The first column of figures shows the current price.
- The next four columns show the change in redemption yield over a selection of periods. Remember that a change in yield indicates an inverse change in price.
- The two columns show the highest and lowest price of the bond in the preceding 52 weeks.
- The final column shows the value of the bonds in issue.

UK GILTS – cash market   www.ft.com/gilts

Sep 18	Price £	Red Yield	Day	Week	Month	Year	High	Low	Amnt £m
				...... Change in Yield			... 52 week ...		
Tr 5pc '08	99.82	5.39	+0.13	+0.16	−0.13	+0.39	100.18	99.42	14,928
Tr 4pc '09	98.34	5.19	+0.14	+0.14	−0.08	+0.23	98.53	97.05	16,974
Tr 4.75pc '10	99.18	5.07	+0.13	+0.13	−0.12	+0.17	100.04	97.05	12,774
Cn 9pc Ln '11	113.22	5.13	+0.13	+0.14	−0.08	+0.27	118.29	111.14	5,664
Tr 5pc '12	99.90	5.03	+0.12	+0.12	−0.08	+0.22	101.75	96.93	14,009
Tr 8pc '13	115.20	5.04	+0.10	+0.07	−0.09	+0.29	120.38	111.64	6,489
Tr 5pc '14	99.89	5.02	+0.10	+0.06	−0.08	+0.31	103.14	95.99	13,699
Tr 4.75pc '15	98.54	4.97	+0.10	+0.05	−0.08	+0.29	101.89	94.37	13,647
Tr 4pc '16	93.22	4.95	+0.10	+0.04	−0.06	+0.30	96.39	89.02	13,500
Tr 4.75pc '20	98.76	4.88	+0.09	+0.06	−0.02	+0.30	103.64	93.94	10,743
Tr 8pc '21	130.64	4.90	+0.09	+0.06	−0.02	+0.32	138.75	124.86	17,573
Tr 5pc '25	102.69	4.77	+0.08	+0.05	–	+0.33	109.55	97.34	16,188
Tr 6pc '28	117.17	4.71	+0.08	+0.06	+0.03	+0.35	126.35	111.19	12,340
Tr 4.25pc '32	94.92	4.60	+0.07	+0.07	+0.05	+0.34	103.01	89.59	17,326
Tr 4.25pc '36	95.53	4.53	+0.07	+0.07	+0.06	+0.34	104.38	90.20	15,668
Tr 4.75pc '38	103.84	4.52	+0.07	+0.07	+0.07	+0.35	114.06	98.49	14,958
Tr 4.25pc '55	97.93	4.35	+0.07	+0.10	+0.13	+0.38	110.87	93.37	11,602
War Ln 3.5pc	77.24	4.53	+0.06	+0.06	+0.05	+0.28	86.41	71.23	1,939

xd Ex dividend. Closing mid-prices are shown in pounds per £100 nominal of stock. Red yield: Gross redemption yield. This table shows the gilt benchmarks and the non-rump undated stocks. A longer list appears on Mondays and the full list on Saturdays, and can be found daily on ft.com/bonds&rates.   Source: REUTERS Ltd.

Source: *Financial Times*, 19 September 2007. Reprinted with permission.

We said at the beginning of this section that the 'term structure' is often studied by looking at yields on government bonds, and that the yields in question are usually redemption yields. Examine carefully the second column of figures in the table. At the very shortest end of the maturity spectrum, the redemption yield is 5.39 per cent. Moving up the maturity spectrum, yields are 5.03 per cent for bonds with five years to maturity. They continue to fall through the maturity spectrum, reaching 4.35 per cent for bonds maturing in 2055. Clearly, on 18 September 2007, the yield curve for UK government bonds was downward-sloping throughout its length. This is unusual and would probably be interpreted as meaning that there was a strong expectation in the gilts market that short-term interest rates needed to be high at the moment but that they would fall in future years to more 'normal' levels.

and thus:

$$i_L = \sqrt{(1 + i_1)(1 + \hat{i}_2)} - 1 \qquad (16.24)$$

Equation 16.24 is very closely approximated by the linear expression:

$$i_L = \frac{i_L + \hat{i}_2}{L} \quad \text{or} \quad \left(\frac{1}{L}\right)(i_1 + \hat{i}_2) \qquad (16.25)$$

where L defines the period to maturity of the bond on which i_L is paid. Thus with i_L paid on a two-year bond, the value of i_L (from Equation 16.25), is:

$$\left(\frac{1}{2}\right)(i_1 + \hat{i}_2) \qquad (16.26)$$

that is to say, a simple average of the two one-year rates. More generally, however, we may say that:

$$i_L = \frac{i_1 \cdot K + \hat{i}_2 \cdot (L - K)}{L} \qquad (16.27)$$

where K is the period of time on which i_1 is paid and $(L - K)$ is the remaining period to maturity on which $\hat{i}_2$ is expected to be paid. According to the expectations theory, therefore, any 'long-term' rate of interest, i_L, is said to be a *weighted* average of expected future short-term rates, where K and $L - K$ (in Equation 16.27) are the weights.

Plotting the (actual) yields on offer at any particular time (in effect plotting the value of i_L from $L = 1$ to $L = \infty$, since undated bonds or 'consols' are available) produces what is called the 'time–yield curve'. Figure 16.5 shows just three possible shapes for this curve, corresponding (1) to the situation where future short rates are expected to rise ($i_L > i_1$ in our example); (2) to the situation where future short rates are expected to remain unchanged ($i_L = i_1$); (3) to the situation where future short rates are expected to fall ($i_L < i_1$).

The diagram needs careful interpretation, particularly with regard to the horizontal axis. It is important to remember that the time–yield curve shows the rate of interest available *now* on assets of varying periods to maturity. *It must not be read as telling us those interest rates that will prevail at a particular time from now.* If the expectations hypothesis holds, then the

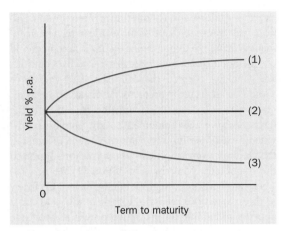

Figure 16.5 Three time–yield curves

yield curve implies forward rates but it does not show them. What it shows are today's rates.[5]

Since, according to the expectations theory, the shape of the curve depends entirely upon the market's expectation of the future level of interest rates, the curve obviously could take any shape. It could approximate any of the three cases in Figure 16.5, but it could also be humped, if investors thought interest rates would first rise and then fall; or it could have a trough, indicating the expectation of a fall followed by a rise. Several humps, troughs or even mixtures of both are possible. The ability of the expectations theory to explain any particular shape is limited only by our ability to supply sufficiently ingenious rationalizations for investors' interest rate expectations. It follows equally that no conceivable shape to the curve could lead us to a firm conclusion about the validity of the expectations theory. However, it is worth noting that the theory draws some informal support from the observed tendency for the time–yield curve to slope downwards when interest rates are historically high, and to slope upwards when rates are near the bottom of their range. This would be consistent with the idea that investors perceive a band of 'normal' interest rates to which they expect future rates to return whenever current rates are at or outside the limits of the band.

One of the most interesting developments in the recent study of the term structure is the possibility of

---

5   Theoretically, the rates reported in a time–yield curve are those which prevail *simultaneously*. In empirical work, therefore, the rates should be those that existed at a single moment. It is not, strictly speaking, appropriate to construct a time–yield curve from data recorded even at different times of the same day. Theoretical purity is not always possible in empirical work, of course, and this requirement explains the tendency for researchers to use rates recorded at the end of a day's trading.

extracting information about future interest and inflation rates from the shape of the yield curve. The argument is that *if* the expectations theory is accepted, and we then add the assumption that those expectations are generally correct, then the shape of the curve should be an accurate predictor of future nominal interest rates. (Indeed, this would be true even if the term structure also contained a term premium, provided such a premium were stable.) Taken in general, the findings from empirical tests have not supported the hypothesis. Mankiw and Miron (1986, p. 216) offer one fairly representative judgement. 'Contrary to the expectations theory, the slope of the yield curve appears to exhibit no predictive power at any time since 1915.'[6] However, in spite of the failure to find widespread evidence in its support, the expectations hypothesis has continued to attract attention. This is undoubtedly due to its attraction, when combined with the 'Fisher hypothesis', as a predictor of inflation in a period when inflation has emerged as a major policy issue and when conventional indicators of the policy stance have failed. We saw in the last chapter that monetary policy in several countries in the 1980s was initially based upon the pursuit of monetary growth 'rules' or 'targets', on the argument that a stable velocity of circulation together with a 'natural rate' of productivity growth would produce a close connection between monetary growth and inflation. Given these rules or targets, policy could then be easily judged for 'slackness' or 'tightness' depending on whether the targets were achieved or under- or overshot. We are not concerned here with the pretty dismal record of failing to hit the targets. More relevant is the fact that in both the USA and the UK a dramatic collapse in velocity destroyed the money–inflation link. The targets, even had they been achieved, no longer indicated anything of significance.

Combining the expectations theory of the term structure with the Fisher hypothesis seemed to offer an ingenious alternative way of interpreting the state of policy. The Fisher hypothesis is that nominal interest rates are composed of a (fairly stable) real rate plus an inflation premium. Thus *if* (after Fisher) expected nominal interest rates *are* composed of a stable *ex ante* real rate plus an inflation premium, and *if* the shape of the yield curve *is* determined wholly by rational expectations of future short rates, then in telling us about future nominal interest rates the yield curve would be telling us about the market's expectation of future inflation and therefore about (the market's interpretation of) the current tightness or laxity of monetary policy. Unfortunately, tests of its predictive ability, both of future short-term interest rates and of the rate of inflation, have not generally suggested that it is particularly effective.

It is not altogether essential, however, for the term structure to be an accurate predictor of future inflation or interest rates for it to have some role in the formulation and evaluation of policy. Provided, for example, that one thought the shape of the curve was generally correct in pointing to the *direction* of change in future rates, then it could still function as a guide, especially if there were little else. This seems to have been the case in the USA and in Germany (and to a lesser extent in the UK) during the period of falling interest rates in 1992–93. The authorities made a succession of small cuts in official discount rates while watching the yield curve for any sign of steepening. Provided all rates came down broadly in step, the policy was 'justified'. But when a cut in short rates caused the curve to steepen this was taken as evidence that the probability of a higher inflation in future had increased and the cuts stopped.

[6] Their explanation is interesting. The failure of the market to anticipate future interest rates accurately coincides with the setting up of the Federal Reserve Board and its subsequent interventions in the money market to set interest rates according to its policy preferences. (This activity was examined in the last chapter.) If this is true, it amounts to saying that, left to itself (for example, before 1915) the market is quite efficient in the judgement it makes about future interest rates, but it simply cannot outguess the next move of central banks committed to using interest rates at their own discretion.

16.5.2 The term premium theory

If the expectations theory is attractive because it is consistent with one frequently observed feature of the curve's behaviour, the term premium theory is attractive for the same reason. But the feature this time is the curve's historical tendency to slope upward except when interest rates are at very high levels, indicating that, as a general rule, higher yields are available on bonds with longer maturities. Clearly, this is a problem for the expectations theory. If the curve does, as a rule, slope upward when current interest rates are in their 'normal' range, the expectations account would lead us to believe that investors expect future interest rates, as a rule, to be higher than today's. It does not seem very likely that investors expect interest rates to rise persistently over time.

The question for the term premium theory therefore is what characteristic might longer-dated bonds possess which makes them *systematically* unattractive, so that investors must be paid some premium to induce them to hold longer bonds? One obvious, but wrong, suggestion might be that investors require a 'liquidity premium' to induce them to 'lock up' their funds for a long period. Hicks, following Keynes in the *General Theory*, advanced the idea that investors required a premium to induce them to hold longer-dated bonds. Hicks, however, was careful to refer to a 'risk premium'. The problem lies in what one understands by 'liquidity'. Strictly, as we have had occasion to point out elsewhere in this book, liquidity refers to the ease with which an asset can be converted into money, *with capital certainty*. Most assets can be converted into money quickly, and even cheaply, if the rate of exchange sufficiently favours the buyer. A long-dated bond is no less liquid than a short-dated one, in the limited sense of investors being able to sell the bond for cash. There is, in most developed countries and certainly in the UK, a highly developed secondary market for government securities (as we shall see in the next section). The possibility that holders of long-dated bonds require a 'liquidity premium' has nothing to do with any difficulty in disposing of long bonds. We must not confuse a bond's term to maturity with the period for which investors must hold it. Terms like 'risk premium' or 'term premium' are less likely to cause this confusion than 'liquidity premium'.

What else might it be about a long-dated bond that requires the payment of a term premium? The answer lies in Equations 16.17 and 16.19. The first shows that the market price fluctuates with interest rates while the second shows that the interest elasticity increases with duration. A future change in interest rates thus causes a capital gain or loss for bondholders who may wish to sell before maturity. Uncertainty about future interest rates has introduced risk. In itself, however, the recognition of risk does not add anything to our understanding of the term structure that is not already supplied by the expectations theory. The expectations theory recognizes that people do not know what future interest rates will be. The yield curve takes the shape dictated by the weight of expectation in the market as to what future rates will most probably be. Only if the expectations theory included an additional supposition (which it does not) that investors generally made upwardly biased estimates of future interest rates would we have any reason to expect a generally upward-sloping curve. If we take the more reasonable view that there is no reason why market participants should consistently under- or overestimate the future level of rates, there must be an actuarially even chance of under- or overestimation and thus, on average, expectations should turn out to be correct. Thus, the specific recognition of risk notwithstanding, there is still no reason to expect a general tendency for the curve to slope upward.

Suppose, however, that investors had an asymmetrical attitude to the actuarial symmetry of winning and losing.[7] Suppose that they attach more *significance* to the possibility of loss than to the possibility of gain. One obvious and frequently suggested justification for this possibility is that wealth is subject to diminishing marginal utility – a given increase yields less satisfaction than the loss of satisfaction which follows from a decrease of equal magnitude. In these circumstances, investors are said to

---

[7]   In fact, an equal chance of interest rates rising or falling by the same amount does not produce a strict actuarial symmetry. The result is biased in favour of *capital gain*. This arises because in the pricing formula we divide by the gross interest rate $(1 + i)$. Suppose that the bond in Equation 11.5 has an annual coupon of £6 ($C = 6$) and pays £100 ($M = 100$) in four years ($n_m = 4$). If interest rates are 10 per cent ($i = 0.1$) then the market value is currently £87.08. If interest rates fall to 9 per cent, the formula prices the bond at £90.11, a capital *gain* of £3.03. A one point *rise* in interest rates, by contrast, causes the price to fall to £84.19, a capital *loss* of only £2.89.

be *capital risk averse* and the market is dominated by **capital risk aversion**. While risk itself may not take us far in explaining the upward-sloping tendency, capital risk aversion most certainly does. Imagine investors faced with the choice between a default-free, demand deposit and a (default-free and so on) security giving the same return but having (obviously) a longer term to maturity than the demand deposit. Suppose also that investors hold confident expectations that interest rates will remain as they are and that they rate the possibility that interest rates may (unexpectedly) rise *equally with the possibility that rates may fall*. Actuarially, investors expect the same return from both investments but clearly, if risk aversion is present, they will choose the deposit unless some interest premium or other form of inducement is offered to persuade them to hold the (risky) security.

In the presence of capital risk aversion we can see why a premium might be demanded for a term security when compared with a zero-term deposit. Furthermore, knowing that the interest-elasticity of bond prices varies with duration, we can now see why longer-term securities are seen as more risky than mediums, and mediums as more risky than shorts and thus why the term premium should increase with the term to maturity.

According to the term premium theory, any long-term rate of interest, i_L thus contains a risk premium, θ_L, which is dependent upon the degree of capital risk aversion in the bond market and the residual maturity of the bond on which it is paid. In Equation 16.28, for example, the risk premium, θ_L, on a bond with (L) periods to maturity is proportional to (L) with the proportion, p, indicating the market's degree of capital risk aversion.

$$\theta_L = p(L) \tag{16.28}$$

As with the expectations theory, mere observation of yield curves does not allow us to endorse or reject the risk premium theory. Any of the curves in Figure 16.5, and indeed any other curve we may care to imagine, *may* contain evidence of a term-related risk premium. Indeed, as we said at the opening of this section, the term premium theory is not inconsistent with a role for expectations. In Figure 16.5 curve (1) is clearly consistent with a positive term premium. *If* we knew that investors expected the current rate, i_1, to continue unchanged ($i_1 = \hat{i}_2$) then curve (1) would be determined *solely* by the term premium and its slope would

be given by p in Equation 16.28. In Equation 16.29, $i_1 = \hat{i}_2$, but $i^* = \theta^* + \hat{i}_2$

$$i^* = (1 + i_1)(1 + \hat{i}_2) + \theta_L - 1 \tag{16.29}$$

However, it is also possible that the market expects future rates to rise ($i_1 < \hat{i}_2$) but by only a small amount, the rest of the positive slope being made up by p. But a term premium is also consistent with curve (2) – investors expect future rates to fall slightly but this is exactly offset by capital risk aversion; it is even consistent with (3) – the market expects future rates to fall sharply but this is partially offset by risk aversion. And if risk aversion can modify any of the curves in Figure 16.5, it follows that it could modify any shape of curve dependent upon any set of expectations about the future level of interest rates.

Figure 16.6 shows a yield curve (1) determined solely by expectations (where investors think interest rates are already high but expect them to rise still further before falling in the long term), and a yield curve (2) where the same interest rate expectations apply, but the shape of the curve is modified by capital risk aversion.

As an explanation of the alleged upward bias in the term structure, the risk premium theory relies upon *capital* risk aversion in the bond market. Capital risk is not the only form of risk to which investors may be averse, however. For some investors, most likely institutions, fluctuations in *income* may be more important. Institutions such as life assurance companies, for example, have long-term liabilities in the form of the returns to investors guaranteed by virtue of the policy when it is issued or sold. These returns have to be earned from assets purchased with contributions

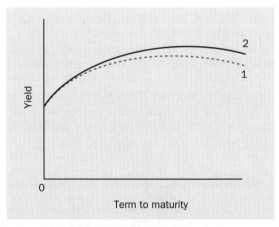

Figure 16.6 Adding a positive term premium

which the company receives long after the contract was written. Clearly, at the time of purchase asset prices (yields) could be high (low). One way to limit the risk is to buy long-dated bonds when yields are high and hold them to redemption. **Income risk aversion** thus pulls in the opposite direction from capital risk aversion. In these circumstances, there is a systematic bias towards long-dated bonds. *Ceteris paribus* one would expect long-dated bonds to have a higher price (lower yield) than short-dated bonds, and the yield curve would tend to slope downwards.

There is no *theoretical* reason for capital risk aversion to dominate and thus for the term premium to be positive. Its sign, as well as its size, is an empirical matter.

16.5.3 Preferred habitat theory

Notice that risk aversion and the term premium theory require us to drop the implicit assumption of the pure expectations theory that the bonds are homogeneous except with respect to their term to maturity. Differences in period to maturity create different risk characteristics to which investors may be sensitive. Preferred habitat, and its more extreme version, market segmentation, theory takes heterogeneity so seriously as to argue that investors have distinct preferences for parts of the maturity spectrum.

For example, pension funds as well as life assurance companies are significant holders of long-dated bonds, while banks and building societies hold mainly shorts. This preference, ultimately related to the pattern of their liabilities, encourages a concentration of skill and expertise in the observation and analysis of 'segments' of the market in order to take advantage of arbitrage opportunities. Moving outside these segments may involve significant costs. The observation that balance sheet and operational pressures may cause investors to focus upon a particular part of the maturity spectrum led Culbertson (1957) to suggest a 'Market Segmentation' theory of the term structure and Modigliani and Sutch later (1966) to their 'Preferred Habitat Theory'.

On both views, the shape of the yield curve will be influenced by the demand for and supply of bonds within each particular segment. Suppose, for example, that government took the decision to fund successive PSNCRs by issuing debt in the 7–10-year maturity range, everything else remaining unchanged. Eventually, we should expect to see the price of 7–10-year bonds fall relative to the price of longer and shorter debt, and yields would rise. *Ceteris paribus*, the yield curve would display a 'hump' in this maturity range. However, if we were to assume complete substitutability throughout the full maturity spectrum, as the expectations theory implicitly does, such a hump would never materialize. As prices began to fall (yields rise), investors from adjacent parts of the spectrum would switch out of (slightly) longer and shorter bonds to take advantage of the emerging higher yields. This in itself would limit the rise in 7–10-year yields but it would also lower the price (and raise the yields) of bonds in the adjacent parts of the spectrum. With complete substitutability, ripples of adjustment would spread along the whole curve, with the result that the whole curve would shift upward while retaining its original shape.

If, however, investors occupied a preferred habitat they would be reluctant to move from their chosen part of the spectrum. Resistance would not be total. We would expect some premium over yields in adjacent spectrums at which a movement would be triggered. (Indeed, our earlier argument that a premium may have to be paid to induce capital (income) risk averters to hold long- (short-)dated bonds could be seen as special cases of preferred habitats.) The size of this premium will depend upon the strength of preference. In these circumstances, the continued issue of bonds in one part of the spectrum will cause a 'hump' to emerge while concentrated redemptions would cause a 'trough'. The significance of the preferred habitat theory is that it presents the maturity spectrum as the sum of many segments each inhabited by investors whose preferences are derived from many influences (not just their attitudes to capital and income risk) and thus admits the possibility of a yield curve with any number of inflexions.

With complete segmentation, resistance to movement from the preferred habitat would be total and the 'humps' and 'troughs' correspondingly larger.

Once again, such behaviour can be combined with other influences. A market dominated by capital risk averters might expect short rates to fall progressively over the next 15 years, but the yield curve could show a trough in the 12–14-year range if, in a segmented market, such bonds were in particularly short supply.

16.6 | Characteristics of the bond markets

Fixed-interest securities are issued in all countries by a wide range of institutions wishing to raise funds for longer than one year. The list includes central governments, local or regional administrations, other public bodies and corporations[8] and private firms. Table 16.2 shows the value of bonds issued in selected markets, distinguishing by broad category of issuer. It shows, in particular, the size of the US bond market, relative to its European counterparts.[9]

Table 16.2 tells us nothing about how these stocks have come about. Governments, as a rule, run budget deficits, which guarantees a continuous flow of new issues from the public sector. Such a persistent flow of new issues, we noted earlier, causes the stock (supply) to expand continuously. But there is also a net flow of new issues from firms, as existing firms expand and new firms are created. One factor which has been particularly relevant to the new issue of corporate bonds in recent years has been the behaviour of interest rates. During the 1970s high and volatile interest rates seem to have discouraged firms from entering into long-term fixed-interest commitments and temporarily the new

issue of corporate bonds slowed to a trickle in most European markets. (These were the same conditions that forced several governments to experiment with index-linked and variable rate bonds in order to fund their deficits.)

16.6.1 Primary markets

In most financial centres, the methods for making *new* issues of corporate bonds are the same as for the issue of new ordinary company shares. In the UK, for example, corporate bonds may be the subject of a 'public offer for sale' either at a fixed price or by auction. Alternatively, they may be issued by a 'placing'. In this case the institution responsible for issuing the bonds places them directly with investors with whom it already has contacts. The institution responsible for handling the issue will be a merchant bank or a securities dealer.

The methods for making new issues of government bonds, however, are often different. This is because the sale and redemption of government bonds is an important instrument of monetary policy and the government needs to be certain that its wishes can be made quickly effective in the market for government bonds. In 1998 the responsibility for managing

Table 16.2 Bond issues and turnover

Exchange	No. of bonds outstanding, end August 2007			New issues[1]	Turnover[2]
	Public sector	Private sector – domestic	Private sector – international	All	All
Deutsche Börse	1,377	13,844	7,831	19,642	18,468
Euronext[3]	341	n/a	2,988	n/a	9,120
Italian exchanges	111	228	204	n/a	10,814
London Stock Exchange	123	7,897	6,390	28,196	201,019
Oslo Børs	134	475	45	1,702	5,799
Spanish exchanges	424	4,268	43	n/a	475,633
Warsaw	209	2,592	293	5,696	33

[1] Funds raised in August 2007, in €m.   [2] Turnover in August 2007, €m.   [3] Amsterdam, Brussels and Paris.
Source: Compiled from data in the Federation of European Stock Exchanges Database. *Last Month Report,* http://www.fese.be/en/?inc=page&id=10.

---

[8] Except in the UK where public sector bond issues are centralized in the government's public sector borrowing requirement (PSNCR).
[9] The yen bond market is also very large, much closer to the US than to European equivalents.

government debt in the UK was transferred from the Bank of England to the newly formed 'Debt Management Office', an agency of the UK Treasury. In the UK, the DMO is responsible for the terms on which new bonds are issued and for the timing of such issues. The traditional method, still used, is the sale by tender in which the DMO offers a specified quantity of stock for sale on a particular day at a minimum price and invites bids. If the offer is undersubscribed, all bids are accepted; if it is oversubscribed, the highest bids are accepted but at a common price – usually the minimum bid price necessary to clear the sale.[10] If the offer is undersubscribed, the DMO retains the unsold stock and releases it onto the market subsequently, when conditions permit. Stock issued in such a way is known as *tap stock*.

The second method of issue involves the auction of stock, in which no minimum price is set. The stock is sold to the highest bidders at the price they bid.[11] This is a method which was first used in 1987 and represents a distinct stage in the evolution of debt management policy. From the point of view of the money supply and credit aggregates, sales by auction have the advantage that the issuer can set the volume, knowing that it will be fully subscribed, since the price will adjust to ensure that this is so. Thus, the desire to sell a given volume of stock consistent with targets for the money supply can generally be met. With a sale by tender the price is set, with the result that the volume of sales becomes uncertain. The two methods simply illustrate the age-old principle that one can control the price or the quantity, but not both.

The third method of issue is for the DMO to 'buy' the stock itself and to release it to the market as conditions permit: the 'tap' method of issue.

In Germany, government bonds are generally 'plain' or bullet bonds, and there have inevitably been large issues following the reunification of Germany in 1990. Long-term government bonds ('Bunds' – see Table 16.1) are issued in three ways. A tranche of any new issue is offered initially at a fixed price to a 'Federal Loans Syndicate' of designated financial institutions. The remainder are then subsequently sold at auction to anyone who cares to bid, while the *Bundesbank* retains a small proportion for future monetary policy operations. Medium-term bonds ('Bobls') are sold to a network of financial institutions

as market conditions permit, rather in the way of the Bank of England tap method. The short-term *Bundesschatzanweisungen* are sold by auction. Auctions of German bonds are bid-price auctions, conducted at regular intervals.

In France, the standard method of issue is by competitive bid-price auction to designated 'primary dealers' ('*Spécialistes en Valeurs du Trésor*') according to a regular timetable.

As the figures in Tables 16.2 and 16.3 (page 351) show, the Italian bond market is dominated by government bonds, reflecting Italy's long history of public sector deficits. Even more than other systems, therefore, the Italian bond market has to be able to cope with large and frequent government bond issues in an orderly way. Dealers in bonds are divided into three groups ('dealers', 'primary dealers' and 'specialists in government bonds') according to the scale of their commitment to make markets in government bonds and to take up new issues. New issues are offered to the latter two groups who are invited to bid in a marginal ('strike-price') auction. In return these dealers have preferential access to the Bank of Italy and are members of the 'MTS', a computerized market for the wholesale trading of government bonds. This market accounts for about 95 per cent of trading in government bonds compared with the Milan Stock Exchange where retail trading accounts for the remainder of trading in government bonds.

16.6.2 Secondary markets

When it comes to trading *existing* bonds, markets can be classified in a number of ways depending upon the way in which the trading is carried out. Figure 16.7 provides a schematic typology, with a selection of bond and equity markets allocated to the type of market which they most closely resemble. Unfortunately for us, the picture is confused by the use of multiple terms with the same meaning.

As the figure shows, the most basic distinction is between **matching** and **dealer markets**. For reasons we shall see in a moment, matching markets are sometimes described as 'order-driven' or 'auctioneer' markets while dealer markets are sometimes called 'quote-driven' markets. In matching/order-driven/auctioneer

---

[10]   This is an example of the striking-price auction we first met in Section 15.3.
[11]   An example of the bid-price auction of Section 15.3.

Dealer ('quote-driven')
  NASDAQ

Matching ('order-driver' or 'auction')
  Hong Kong
  Zurich
  Paris
  Madrid
  Frankfurt
  Milan
  Toronto
Mixed
  London Stock Exchange
  Tokyo
  Amsterdam
  New York

Figure 16.7 Security market trading systems

markets there is a further distinction between *continuous* and *call* (or 'batch') markets. (Dealer/quote-driven markets are always continuous.)

In matching markets, trades take place when dealers can match orders to buy and orders to sell. Hence they are responding to 'orders' and in trying to find a price that will match the maximum number of buy and sell orders they are acting very much like traditional 'auctioneers'. The matching process may be continuous or it may take place at specified times. As Figure 16.7 shows, the majority of bond (and equity) markets are matching markets and the majority of these work on both a continuous and a call basis. There is a call auction at the beginning of the day in which all orders accumulated since the last close of trading are executed, followed by continuous trading throughout the day. Buyers and sellers can normally specify with their order whether they wish it to be exercised immediately or at the next call. Notice that the system does not depend upon auctioneers holding their own inventories. There is no need since they only 'buy' from a seller when they simultaneously 'sell' to a buyer.

By contrast, in a dealer market, the dealer 'makes' a market by holding his own inventories of stocks and announces (continuously) a price at which he is prepared to buy and sell (rather like a dealer in second-hand cars or antiques). The picture here is one in which those who wish to buy or sell know in advance what price is available and they are responding to that price. This is why a dealer market is described as a *quote-driven* market.

What consequences follow from these different structures? As a rule, call (or batch) markets are cheaper to operate than continuous markets. The obvious drawback, however, is that prices are established only at discrete intervals and price changes can be sharper when the trades are called than they would be in continuous markets. On the other hand, although pricing is continuous and large volume deals can be done at low unit costs, continuous markets and dealer markets especially are expensive to operate. As we said above, major financial markets tend to be of the continuous kind. In the light of our previous point it is worth noting that a continuing criticism of the London Stock Exchange since its major reforms in 1986 has been its inability to provide a cheap service for small to medium-sized trades, and that this contrasts sharply with a steep decline in the unit cost of large trades.

The costs of buying and selling securities are twofold. Firstly, dealers may charge a commission. This is usually calculated as some percentage of the value of the transaction of the deal, subject to some minimum and maximum figure. (It is these minimum and maximum thresholds that lead to low unit costs for large deals and discriminate against small investors.) In addition, investors will normally face a 'bid' price, at which the dealer will buy, which is below the price at which the dealer will sell or 'offer' securities. One measure of the quality of a market, as we shall see in a moment, is the narrowness of the bid–offer spread around the equilibrium price.

There are other consequences too – in the speed with which prices change and the causes of price changes. To understand these differences we need firstly to distinguish between *information traders* and *noise* or *liquidity traders*. Information traders are investors who buy and sell securities in order to profit from what they think is their superior information about the securities (or their superior interpretation of information). Noise or liquidity traders are those who trade for any other reason. As a rough approximation we might regard information traders as the 'professionals'. They are the investors who make the best use of available information about the security's fundamental value. Information traders use information to price bonds according to the principles set out earlier in this chapter and they value equities according to the dividend discount models in the next chapter. If we jump to Chapter 26, it is information traders who make financial markets informationally efficient. By contrast, noise traders buy and sell in response to their own view about where the security's price is going next, *whatever the basis of that hunch may be*. We should not dismiss them as 'amateurs' or suggest that they are necessarily foolish. 'Noise trader' is a category that would include the technical analysts or 'chartists' described in Section 17.3.

The reason we make the distinction here is that information traders have a crucial role in dealer markets. Recall that in a dealer market, the dealer stands ready to buy and sell at a quoted price. Information traders give dealers a strong incentive to set the correct price (correct in the sense of reflecting all relevant information). If dealers did not do this, information traders would have an advantage which they would be able to exploit at the dealers' expense, given the commitments that dealers have to make and stand by. Suppose, for example, that a trader believes, in the light of carefully studied information, that a security trading for $4.90 is worth $5. Let us assume that he buys it from a dealer, its price subsequently rises to $5, and he sells it back to the dealer. His 10 cent profit is made at the dealer's expense. It is because dealers must hold inventories of stocks and deal on demand that they must continuously make the best prices. Thus prices will change quickly and *they will change in response to information rather than trades*. In dealer markets, prices may change even when no dealing takes place.

By contrast, prices in auctioneer markets change *only* in response to trading. Information is relevant to market prices only in so far as it causes people to wish to buy and sell, and only then when it causes a liquidity imbalance, an excess of buy orders over sell orders or vice versa.

In most financial centres, secondary trading in corporate bonds is carried out by the same dealers in securities that make markets in ordinary company shares. (We say more about these in Section 17.5.) As a general rule, however, the stock of corporate bonds and the trading in them is very much smaller than that of equities. (Bond markets are large overall because of the accumulation of government bonds.) One consequence is that the bid–offer spread is often much larger than it is on the equities traded by the same firms and certainly much larger than the spreads on government bonds being traded in the same market.

As with new issues, and for the same reason, secondary trading in government bonds is usually subject to arrangements which are rather different from those applying to corporate bonds. Markets in government stock are frequently made by the same firms that deal in equities and bonds but they will be subject to separate and additional regulation by the central bank. In the UK, for example, although any securities dealer can in theory make a market in government stock, since the 'Big Bang' reforms of 1986, the market for government stock has been dominated by the 'gilt-edge market makers' (or GEMMs). They hold government stocks and deal on their own behalf but also act as clients for brokers.[12] The reason for this domination is that, being 'recognized' by the Bank of England, they enjoy certain advantages. These are: (1) borrowing facilities at the Bank of England; (2) access to inter-dealer brokers;[13] (3) a direct dealing relationship with the Bank of England; (4) a facility for making 'late' bids at auctions.

In return for all this, there are considerable obligations. Firstly, while a GEMM may very likely be part of a securities dealer making markets in all types of stock, it must be separately established with its own capital. (In December 1996 the Bank of England announced plans to lift this requirement.) Secondly, GEMMs may not deal in equity shares and while they may deal in other fixed-interest securities these must not be convertible into equities. Thirdly, they agree to make 'continuous and effective two-way prices' at which they are committed to deal up to a specified bargain size. Fourthly, the size of transactions and the risk exposure that a GEMM can accept are subject to regular review and discussion with the Bank of England. (The December 1996 announcement envisaged an easing of the capital adequacy requirements in future.)

Since GEMMs are members of the London Stock Exchange, all of these obligations and regulations are additional to the conditions laid down for membership. Indeed, when we say that in the UK 'most

---

[12] An illustration of the 'dual-capacity' role which became common in London after 1986. See Section 17.5.2.

[13] Inter-dealer brokers (IDBs) are intermediaries who buy and sell stock from and to GEMMs in conditions of anonymity. This enables a GEMM which has purchased (for example) a long line of one particular stock to sell parts of it on to other GEMMs without their knowing that it has this large holding and deliberately lowering their bid prices. In so far as the IDB system makes it easier for GEMMs to trade large blocks of stock without dramatic effects on prices, IDBs contribute the market's 'depth' – a term which is explained in Section 17.5.2.

securities are traded on the London Stock Exchange' it is only the fact that GEMMs are members and subject to its rules that gives this statement any sense today. Before 1986, when all securities dealing took place in one physical location, it was literally true. Brokers would make their way to one jobber for the ordinary shares of British Petroleum and then to another jobber for 'Treasury 9% 2008', as their clients required. But like (virtually) all securities dealing in London since 1986, the gilt-edge 'market' is screen-based and the dealers, rigidly demarcated from other dealers in other securities as we have just seen, are located in offices dispersed through the City of London.

As we explain in Section 17.5, one of the objectives of the Big Bang reforms was to increase the size and capital resources of market-making firms in the London Stock Exchange in order to make its services more competitive with those of other financial centres. One way of assessing the changes in the quality of a market is to look at transactions costs. Before 1986, commissions on average size deals, of £0.5–1m, ranged between £100 and £250. Since the Big Bang, such commissions have disappeared and, furthermore, bid–offer spreads have also narrowed from about 0.125 per cent to 0.0625 per cent for short-dated stocks and from 0.25 per cent to 0.125 per cent for long-dated stocks.[14]

16.6.3 Reading the *Financial Times*

One of the most comprehensive bond market information services readily available to the general public is provided by the *Financial Times*, in its UK and European editions and on its website.

In the UK edition, most of the relevant information is provided on the page headed 'Market Data'. The page includes the table showing prices and yields for UK government bonds which we included in Box 16.6 (on page 338). Another table shows the prices, yields and changes in both, for 'Government Benchmark Bonds' in a wide range of countries. Data for a short- and long-term bond is usually given and this provides an indication of the short- and long-term risk-free rates of interest in these countries. There is also a table headed 'Global Investment Grade' which shows similar information for a range of corporate bonds. A

further table shows the risk ratings and the yields available on a variety of 'High Yield and Emerging Market Bonds'.

16.7 International bonds

In addition to issuing bonds in domestic currency in the domestic bond market, large borrowers may make use of international bond markets. Until recently, it was common practice to distinguish between two types of international bonds. The first are known as Eurobonds. These (like all 'Euro-' instruments) are bonds issued in a currency which is different from that of the market in which they are issued. A Eurodollar bond, for example, must be issued in a non-US market. The second type are known as foreign bonds. These are bonds denominated in the currency of the market in which they are issued, but they are issued by non-residents. Box 16.7 summarizes these classifications.

The first Eurobond was issued in 1963 but growth of the market was subdued until the 1980s. Thereafter, the Eurobond market expanded very rapidly, followed by the market for foreign bonds. It was the spectacular growth of the Eurobond market between 1980 and 1995, together with some special characteristics of the bonds, that made the Eurobond phenomenon a case worthy of special study. In recent years, however, there has been considerable convergence in the characteristics of these bonds and of the markets in which they are traded and it now makes mores

---

BOX 16.7 A taxonomy of bonds

	Bond issues	
	By residents	By non-residents
In domestic currency	A	B
In foreign currency	C	D

A = domestic bonds; B = traditional foreign bonds;
A + C + D = Eurobonds; B + C + D = International bonds

Source: BIS (2002) *International Banking and Financial Market Developments*, p. 21; the full publication is available for free on the BIS website, www.bis.org. Reprinted with permission.

---

[14] That is, from 4 to 2 'ticks' and from 8 to 4 'ticks' respectively.

sense to analyse the success of the international bond market as a whole. We begin with a look at the special case of Eurobonds. We then look at arguments for treating all international bonds together and finally provide some figures and analysis of the international bond markets.

There are many reasons behind the growth of Euromarkets. Like other financial instruments, the attractiveness of Eurobonds to issuers and to holders depends in the short run upon yield relativities. The longer-run trend, however, is the result of several longer-term factors. The oldest of these goes back to the late 1950s and 1960s and lies in the reluctance of east European countries to hold dollar-denominated assets in the USA for fear that they might be frozen if relations deteriorated sharply enough in the depths of the Cold War. A further reason was the succession of large US current account deficits during the 1970s which led to an accumulation of dollar holdings in Europe. However, most of the explanation lies in various fiscal and other regulations in domestic markets which encouraged borrowers and lenders to find ways of trading which were subject to lighter control. This does not mean that there are no restrictions on Eurobond dealing. The International Securities Markets Association (ISMA) has drawn up rules and procedures but we shall see that the heavier regulation of domestic markets provides several incentives to issue Eurobonds. We have highlighted the regulatory stimuli responsible for its growth in Box 16.8.

The main influences on the currency of denomination are the demands of international trade together with a desire for denomination in 'strong' currencies. Therefore, the predominant role of dollar Eurobonds followed by denominations in Japanese yen and Deutschmarks is hardly surprising.

Just as the development of the whole Eurobond market can be seen as an innovative response to regulations governing other long-term financial instruments, there were notable innovations within the market. The dominant type of Eurobond remains the 'straight' fixed rate ('straight' or 'bullet') bond (whose price will be determined in the way that we saw earlier in this chapter). As a proportion of total issues, 'straights' have usually accounted for between 60 and 80 per cent. However, the 1980s saw the development of the **floating rate note** (FRN) and a family of equity-related bonds. At various times in the 1980s FRN accounted for nearly 40 per cent of total Eurobond issues while equity-related Eurobonds reached a peak of 30 per cent of issues in 1989. Years of high equity-related issue have tended to be years of low FRN issue and vice versa, leaving the dominant position of straights untouched. FRNs are bonds whose coupons are set by adding a mark-up to some variable benchmark interest rate, often LIBOR or the interbank rate in

---

BOX 16.8 Regulation stimulates Eurobond markets

There are numerous regulations applying to domestic markets which have encouraged lenders and borrowers to find alternative locations for trading. Among those relevant to the Eurobond market are as follows:

- 'Regulation Q' in the USA limited the interest that could be paid on time deposits. This encouraged US residents to keep dollars outside the USA and thus led to the growth of Eurodollar deposits. With time, holders of deposits looked for other dollar assets into which they could diversify without returning the dollars to US regulation.

- Under legislation introduced in 1963, US corporations were restricted in the amount of capital they could raise domestically in order to fund their overseas operations.

- In most countries, interest on bonds is paid net of tax to domestic holders and withholding tax is deducted on interest paid to overseas bondholders. Eurobonds pay tax gross.

- In most countries, issuers of domestic bonds are required to maintain a register of owners. The cost of maintaining the register is a disadvantage to the issuer and being identified as the owner of bonds is a disadvantage to some bondholders.

- Domestic bond markets usually impose stringent accounting and other disclosure conditions on bond issuers in order that their bonds may be listed (and therefore traded) on recognized securities exchanges. Again this imposes costs but it also slows down the issuing process, exposing the firm to the risk of changes in financial conditions between the decision to issue and raising the funds.

some other centre. Coupons are paid at six-monthly intervals and are re-set each time in the light of changes in the benchmark rate. Equity-related bonds are bonds which give their holders some future access to the issuer's equity stock. **Convertible Eurobonds**, like convertible domestic bonds, give the holder the right to convert into the equity stock of the issuer at some specified time in the future and on terms which are set out at the time of issue of the bond. Alternatively, bonds may have **equity warrants** attached. Warrants give the bondholder the option to convert to equity on specified terms but, unlike convertibles, the warrants are securities in their own right and can be detached and sold separately.

The main issuers of Eurobonds are sovereign governments, banks (including building societies in the UK) and large corporations. In 1993, for example, 25 per cent of all FFr Eurobond issues were made by *Crédit Local de France*, SNCF, *Crédit National* and the European Investment Bank, while two major issuers of DM Eurobonds were the UK and Italian governments, wishing to rebuild their DM reserves. The main holders are banks and large managed funds (life assurance, pension funds and unit and investment trusts in the UK).

The method of issue in the primary market has evolved markedly over time. At the moment, the usual method is for an issuer of bonds (the borrower) to approach a **lead manager** for the issuer, usually an investment bank. The lead manager recruits additional banks to form a **syndicate**, within which some banks will be identified as underwriters and sellers. The function of the underwriters is to guarantee to buy the stock at a set minimum price if it cannot be sold above this price by the sellers. The lead manager then buys the whole issue on terms previously agreed with the borrower and then distributes the bonds throughout the syndicate for onward sale to the public. In this arrangement, known as the **bought deal**, the risk (of failing to sell to the public at the anticipated price) lies with the lead manager and the underwriters. Since 1990 it has been common practice to superimpose upon this arrangement an agreement between members of the syndicate not to discount bonds when selling to the public until the issue has been completely disposed of. This is known as the *fixed price re-offer technique*.

The secondary market for Eurobonds centres on **reporting dealers**. These are usually a subdivision of a merchant bank or of a general securities dealer. Each reporting dealer makes a market in a subset of Eurobonds. The dealers are members of the ISMA (see above) and must submit every day a list of the bonds in which they are prepared to deal and the prices and quantities. The ISMA circulates this information publicly. Prices, however, are 'indicative' and not 'firm' as they would be for market-makers in most domestic bonds. Reporting dealers can also deal among themselves using the facilities offered by inter-dealer brokers (see Section 16.6 above).

Although most European authorities insist that domestic issuers of Eurobonds use lead underwriters in their home country (so it can be said for example that SNCF issues Eurobonds 'out of Paris'), London has become and remains the centre for the bulk of new issues. It also accommodates most secondary market trading. In recent years, and partly because of London's success in attracting such a large share of this rapidly growing activity, the question of what makes a financial centre attractive has begun to receive considerable attention (Grilli, 1989; Cobham, 1992).

In the case of London and the Euromarkets in general, the following factors appear to be of particular relevance. Firstly, dating from its long-established tradition as a financial centre, London has been able to offer a supply of well-trained labour and a supply of suitable premises concentrated within a relatively compact area. There is also a regulatory regime which is seen as being sympathetic to financial activity in its willingness to consult and in its determination to minimize turnover taxes and barriers to competition. Personal and corporate rates of taxation are now low by international standards. These regulatory benefits are reinforced by a stable political system which is unlikely to produce sudden, radical change. Furthermore, the absence of exchange controls since 1979 has made London an attractive location for a wide range of international activity in recent years. More generally, English language and law are both widely used in international financial business. Fortuitous, but important, is London's position in a time zone which allows trading to run consecutively with the trading in the other two main international financial centres, Tokyo and New York.

Table 16.3 shows the rapid growth in the international bond market over the five-year period from 1998 to 2003. Looking at amounts outstanding, the compound annual growth rates for France, Germany and the UK are roughly 23, 30 and 27 per cent. Judged by the flow of new issues (net of redemptions) the growth rates are 29, 19 and 33 per cent.

Table 16.3 International bond issues – by nationality of issuer (US$bn)

	Amounts outstanding		New issues (net)	
	end-2005	June 2007	2005	2007(Q2)
Denmark	67.4	120.4	18.5	19.1
France	966.7	1,382.2	159.5	79.6
Germany	2,169.3	2,783.2	200.4	63.7
Italy	730.4	1,035.8	77.0	55.6
Netherlands	730.5	1,039.1	104.2	35.1
Norway	79.7	122.3	8.6	1.4
Spain	702.1	1,287.7	199.9	92.2
Sweden	176.5	249.7	25.5	23.3
United Kingdom	1,531.7	2,329.4	284.2	131.1
United States	3,554.0	5,095.0	290.5	365.8

Source: BIS, http://www.bis.org/statistics/secstats.htm (table 12A).

Within these totals, the Bank for International settlements estimates that Eurobonds accounted for about 65 per cent of the stock of international bonds outstanding in 1998 and that this fraction had fallen to about 45 per cent by 2003. This is a sharp drop and to bring about this scale of change in a stock suggests that the shift in the composition of the annual *flow* of new issues must have been very substantial indeed. This decline in the (relative) popularity of Eurobonds is just one of the reasons that the BIS gives for paying less attention to the Euro-/foreign-bond distinction.

Other reasons include the fact that many of the regulatory loopholes to which Eurobonds once gave access have diminished as the regulation of domestic markets has eased and bond market structures and regulations have converged. Box 16.9 overleaf summarizes the features of Eurobonds which, compared with foreign and domestic bonds, used to give them a special status. In recent years, however, many bond markets have eliminated withholding tax for foreign and domestic bonds and some have introduced the option of bearer status for domestic bonds. Furthermore, the break-up of the Soviet bloc and the decline in Cold War suspicions which had originally discouraged east European investors from holding dollar assets in the USA has removed another special attraction of Eurobonds. Taken together, these developments have made Eurobonds less 'special' and have made all classes of bonds closer substitutes, one for another. This is reflected in Eurobonds' declining share in the total of international bonds, referred to above.

What, in particular, has caused this dramatic expansion in international bond issues? International bonds are issued by firms, national governments, financial institutions and international organisations of many kinds. The easiest issues to explain are those made by firms which wish to borrow in a foreign currency in order to pay bills in that currency. We might therefore say that one motive behind the growth of the market is 'trade'. But in addition to firms wishing to finance current or capital spending there are investment institutions which are trying to get the best rate of return for themselves or on behalf of clients and to achieve the benefits from diversification across a wider range of assets than are available in the domestic market. These portfolio decisions will be particularly sensitive to interest rate differentials. Where investment institutions are concerned, there may also be a demand for foreign bonds arising from a desire to protect clients funds from domestic political instability, high tax rates or the threat of future restrictions on the use of their capital.

But we know that interest rates fluctuate, and since the break-up of the Bretton Woods agreement in 1972 the same has been true for exchange rates. This suggests that there will be a speculative element in the issue of and demand for international bonds from borrowers and lenders who think that they will be able to profit from such movements. Conversely, some of the trade will reflect a hedging motive – a desire to avoid *losses* from exchange and/or interest rate fluctuations. Almost certainly, if we are looking for an

BOX 16.9 Traditional distinguishing features of world bond markets

	Euro	Foreign	Domestic
Withholding tax	No	Yes	Yes
Form	Bearer	Bearer/Registered	Registered
Issue method	International syndic.	Domestic syndic.	Direct, auction or syndic.
Listing	London or Luxembourg	Local stock exch.	Local stock exch.
Trading	Over the counter (OTC)	OTC/local stock exch.	OTC/local stock exch.
Settlement	Euroclear/Cedel	Local	Local

Source: BIS (2002) *International Banking and Financial Market Developments*, p. 23; the full publication is available for free on the BIS website, www.bis.org.

explanation for the rapid growth of international bond markets we should focus on the portfolio and speculative/hedging uses of these bonds. It is unlikely to be co-incidence that these markets took off at a time when interest and exchange rates were particularly volatile.

16.8 Summary

'Bonds' are securities which enable borrowers to raise funds for long periods but leave lenders with the convenience of being able to sell their loan if they need to retrieve their funds. As a general rule, bonds pay a fixed rate of interest and have a fixed period to maturity. These are the 'plain' bonds on which we concentrated in this chapter. The price of bonds depends upon the coupon which they pay, upon the current level of market interest rates and the residual period of the bond's life. The prices of bonds with a long residual maturity are generally more interest-sensitive than the prices of short-dated bonds. As with all assets, the yield on bonds varies inversely with their price. There are several measures of bond yields.

If we plot the yield on bonds against the residual period to maturity, we often observe a pattern. This distribution of yields is known as the term structure of interest rates and the plot is known as a time–yield curve. There are several theories of what determines this pattern of yields. The expectations theory is particularly interesting since it says that current long-term rates are the average of expected future rates. It is an interesting theory since, if it is true, *and* if expectations are generally correct, then we can derive implied future short-term interest rates and the derivations will generally be correct.

Once issued, bonds are traded in a secondary market, in which there exist a variety of trading arrangements. As a general rule, trading in bonds is carried out by firms which also deal in company shares and other securities, though dealers in government bonds are often subject to regulations which are additional to those of the stock market in which they work. The market for government bonds is generally much larger than the corporate bond market. Most European markets have recently embarked on a series of reforms similar to those that occurred in London in 1986. One significant difference, however, is that European centres have opted for 'continuous auctioneer' ('order-driven') rather than 'continuous dealer' ('quote- driven') markets.

Key concepts in this chapter

Accrued interest	Clean price	Credit rating agencies
Bearer bonds	Convertible bonds	Dealer markets
Bought deal	Convertible Eurobonds	Debentures
Bulldog bonds	Corporate bonds	Default risk
Capital risk	Coupon	Dirty price
Capital risk aversion	Coupon rate	Duration

Equity warrants
Eurobonds
Ex dividend
Expectations theory
   of the term
   structure
Floating rate notes
Foreign bonds
Holding period yield
Income risk aversion
Index-linked bonds

Junk bonds
Lead manager
Market price
Market segmentation
Matching markets
Par value
Preferred habitat
Redemption yield
Reinvestment risk
Reporting dealer
Residual maturity

Running, interest or current
   yield
Simple yield to maturity
Straight (or plain vanilla or
   bullet) bonds
Syndicate
Term premium
Term structure of interest
   rates
Time–yield curve
Zero coupon bonds

Questions and problems

1 Distinguish between clean and dirty bond prices and explain how each is calculated.

2 A bond with four years to maturity and a coupon of 7 per cent has a current market price of £102.50. What is: (a) the current yield; (b) the simple yield to maturity; (c) the redemption yield?

3 A 12 per cent bond will be redeemed at par on 1 March 2013. If the yield to maturity on 2 March 2008 is 8 per cent, what is the price of the bond?

4 Other things being equal, the prices of long-dated bonds are more sensitive to changes in interest rates than are the prices of short-dated bonds. Why is this the case?

5 Outline the possible effects upon bond prices of each of the following events and explain your reasoning. (Assume that each occurs in isolation from the others.)

   (a) The current account shows an unexpectedly large deficit.
   (b) In the midst of a recession, the central bank announces a small cut in interest rates.
   (c) Three months before an election, with the economy growing strongly, the government announces a cut in income tax.
   (d) An increase in the central government borrowing requirement which was widely expected.
   (e) The price of oil falls unexpectedly.

   (f) The *Bundesbank* announces an increase in money supply which exceeds the target range.

6 If the current (redemption) yield on bonds with one year to maturity is 6 per cent, while the yield on bonds maturing in three years is 8 per cent, what does this imply about one-year yields in three years' time?

7 What assumptions have you had to make in Question 6 in order to obtain a forecast of the future spot rate?

8 In what circumstances might the shape of the yield curve tell you something about (a) the future level of interest rates and (b) the future rate of inflation?

9 Why might the yield curve incorporate a *positive* term premium?

10 Who are the main participants in bond markets?

11 Why is it possible for governments to run repeated budget deficits without causing bond yields to rise continuously?

12 Box 16.6 discusses a downward-sloping yield curve and the market's expectations of future short-term rates. In Section 14.6 we saw that the 'Taylor Rule' enabled us to calculate the nominal rate of interest that would be required for a given inflation target and output gap. Do you see any possible connection between the Taylor Rule's prediction and the downward-sloping yield curve? (Remember: the UK inflation target is 2 per cent p.a.)

Further reading

General

Bank of England, 'Financial Market Developments', *Quarterly Bulletin* (every issue)

BIS, *International Banking and Financial Market Developments* (Basle: BIS, 1997)

BIS, *Quarterly Review* (Basle: BIS, February 2002 and March 2004)

D Blake, *Financial Market Analysis* (London: McGraw-Hill, 2000) Ch. 5

K Boakes, *Reading and Understanding the Financial Times* (London: Financial Times Prentice Hall, 2008), Topic 4

Z Bodie, A Kane and A Marcus, *Essentials of Investments* (New York: McGraw-Hill, 4e, 2001) Ch. 10

D Cobham (ed.), *Markets and Dealers: The Economics of the London Financial Markets* (London: Longman, 1992)

J Culbertson, 'The term structure of interest rates', *Quarterly Journal of Economics*, 71 (4), 1957

Debt Management Office, *Quarterly Review*

K Done, 'Credit rating boost for Croat eurobond debut', *Financial Times*, 18 January 1997

Euromoney (monthly) and *Euromoney Country Surveys* (annual) (London: Euromoney Publications)

Federation of European Stock Exchanges, *Stock Exchange Fact Sheet* (Brussels) (monthly)

I Fisher, *The Theory of Interest* (New York: Macmillan, 1930)

V Grilli, 'Europe 1992: Issues and prospects for the financial markets', *Economic Policy*, 4, 1989, 388–421

J R Hicks, *Capital and Value* (Oxford: Clarendon Press, 2e, 1946)

London Stock Exchange, *Stock Exchange Quarterly*

London Stock Exchange, *Stock Exchange Quality of Markets Fact Sheet* (quarterly)

B. Malkiel, *The Term Structure of Interest Rates* (Princeton: Princeton University Press, 1966)

N G Mankiw and J A Miron, 'The changing behaviour of the term structure of interest rates', *Quarterly Journal of Economics*, 101, 1986

F Modigliani and R Sutch, 'Innovations in interest rate policy', *American Economic Review*, 1966

OECD, *Financial Market Trends* (triannual) (OECD: Paris)

OECD, *Financial Statistics*, part 1, § 1 and 2 (monthly) (OECD: Paris)

M Pagano and A Roell, 'Trading systems in European stock exchanges: Current performance and policy options', *Economic Policy*, 10, 1990, 65–115

M Pagano and A Roell, 'Auction and dealership markets: What is the difference?', *European Economic Review*, 1992

K Pilbeam, *Finance and Financial Markets* (London: Palgrave 2e 2005) Ch. 6.

R Roll, *The Behaviour of Interest Rates* (New York: Basic Books, 1970)

R Shiller 'The term structure of interest rates', in B Friedman and F Hahn (eds.), *Handbook of Monetary Economics* (North-Holland, 1990)

R Vaitilingam, *The Financial Times Guide to Using the Financial Pages* (London: Pearson Education, 4e, 2001)

Websites

www.bis.org

http://www.dmo.gov.uk/index.aspx?page=About/About_Gilts

www.fese.be

www.fitchratings.com

www.isma.org

www.oecd.org

www.standardandpoors.com

Chapter 17   Equity markets

What you will learn in this chapter:

■ The types and characteristics of ordinary company shares

■ A variety of approaches to evaluating the market price
  of shares

■ Why share prices behave as they do

■ The characteristics of equity trading arrangements, their main
  participants and recent developments

■ How to read, interpret and analyse equity market reports

17.1 Introduction

For many people, the phrase 'financial markets' means equity markets. This is curious because we shall see that in many financial centres the amount of trading in equities, measured by value, falls a long way short of trading in bonds and a long way short of trading in foreign exchange. And yet general news broadcasts on radio and television invariably quote the latest movement in some index of equity prices, when they would not consider for a moment broadcasting information on bond yields or money market interest rates, both of which have considerable relevance to everyone.

There are several reasons for the disproportionate amount of popular attention focused on equities. Firstly, it is equity markets that have provided the most spectacular fluctuations in the history of financial markets. There are many examples of spectacular crashes (preceded by major booms of course) including: the South Sea Bubble of 1720; the Mississippi Bubble of 1719–20; the Wall Street crash of September 1929 and the crash of October 1987.[1] Secondly, it may simply be that there is more 'news' behind company shares. Most bond markets are dominated by government bonds and their prices are driven, as we have seen, by whole market events such as changes in interest rate expectations. The price of individual corporate bonds can be affected by company-specific events, but the impact will always be limited because of the fixed coupon payment and the preferential claim that a bondholder has on a firm's assets. It is ordinary company shares that hold out the prospect of truly large gains and losses. Company share prices are continually affected by company-specific events and these can be quite colourful, ranging from the company chairman who describes his own products as rubbish, or drowns at sea with the workers' pension funds, to the discovery by a research team of a treatment for AIDS. Since ordinary shareholders have a residual claim on profits and profits can range from the negative to the infinite, the potential for losses and gains is correspondingly large. Thirdly, since shareholders are the legal owners of firms, the buying and selling of shares involves the transfer of ownership.

Sometimes that transfer itself is news, especially if one firm is making an unwelcome bid to take over another, since mergers and takeovers may involve 'rationalizations' and redundancies. These in turn can affect employees of the two firms and perhaps even a regional economy if a large plant is closed.

A fourth possible reason is that many European governments have followed the policy begun 30 years ago in the UK of privatizing hitherto state-owned firms. To take just a few famous examples, since 1993, the German government has privatized Lufthansa and Deutsche Telekom, France has privatized Banque National de Paris and Elf Aquitaine. In Italy, Credito Italiano and Banca Commerciale Italiana are now in private hands. The two main reasons behind these privatizations are, firstly, that state-owned firms providing goods and services which are already provided by the private sector are less efficient, and, secondly, that firms in private ownership are probably more likely to take advantage of cross-border merger and amalgamation opportunities that will arise as the European market becomes more integrated. However, there may be another reason. We shall see below (Section 17.5) that all continental stock markets were very concerned in the 1990s about losing business to London since the reforms that took place there in 1986. One certain effect of these privatizations was to increase sharply the size of domestic markets in securities. For example, the French privatization programme, re-launched in 1993, was planned to raise FFr280bn which was the equivalent of 10 per cent of the value of equities quoted on the Paris Bourse in 1993. Furthermore, like the UK Thatcher governments in the 1980s, the French government linked privatization to attempts to popularize individual direct shareholding. 1992 saw the introduction of the '*Plan d'Epargne en Actions*' which, like personal equity plans in the UK, enabled 'small' investors to invest in shares without becoming liable to capital gains and income tax; in 1993 'Balladur bonds' were introduced to enable savers to buy a fixed interest rate instrument which would be convertible later (in 1997) into the shares of privatized firms. These incentives were also linked to the development of the domestic stock market through the argument that small investors would always prefer to trade in their 'home' exchange. The

---

[1] A useful survey and discussion of these events is contained in Garber (1990). A much more detailed but highly readable account of the 1929 crash is in Galbraith (1961) while the *Bank of England Quarterly Bulletin*, February 1988, contains an article which describes and offers some explanation of the events of 1987.

scope for encouraging individual direct investment is considerable: direct investment in equities is limited to about 5 per cent of households in France and Germany, compared with 20 per cent in the UK (and 40 per cent in the USA). It follows from this that in continental Europe the ownership of company shares is even more concentrated in the hands of financial institutions than it is in the UK. In particular, it is banks that are major shareholders, which is a further contrast with the UK where banks hold only short-dated fixed interest securities and shares are held largely by pension funds, long-term insurance companies and mutual funds.

In this chapter, the next section outlines the characteristics of ordinary company shares. Section 17.3 explains a number of approaches to valuing shares, concentrating upon dividend discount models but touching briefly on other methods, including technical analysis. In the course of these discussions it will become apparent that the events that can cause people to change their view of the appropriate value of company shares are many and varied, compared with those that affect bonds, for example. For this reason, we include a section (17.4) which shows how a selection of typical events can be connected with changes in share prices – individually and in the aggregate, in the short and the long run – using the formal models that we have examined in Section 17.3. Section 17.5 discusses the characteristics of equity markets in Europe and elsewhere, including data on capitalization and turnover. It continues the discussion about trading structures that we began in Chapter 16 and includes a section on interpreting and analysing the equity market data in the *Financial Times*. Section 17.6 summarizes.

17.2 Company shares: types, characteristics and returns

A joint stock firm, often referred to rather loosely as a 'corporation', is one that can raise capital by the issue of bonds and shares to the general public. At the time of its incorporation, such a firm must specify the quantity (and type) of shares that it proposes to issue. In the UK, these specifications are contained in a firm's **memorandum** and **articles of association**.

These documents will specify, for example, the total of **authorized shares**. Authorized shares may be *issued*, that is, they have been sold to shareholders, or they may be authorized but as yet *unissued*. The two main classes of shares are **equity** (or **ordinary**) **shares** and **preferred shares**. In the USA, equities are more frequently referred to as **common stock**. The holders of ordinary shares are legally the owners of the firm. This means that they have voting privileges which allow them to appoint and dismiss members of the board of directors; in most countries company legislation also specifies those decisions about which directors have to consult shareholders and obtain their permission. Because they are the owners of the firm, ordinary shareholders receive a share in the profits of a firm after all prior claims have been met. The prior claims include payments to creditors, including interest to bondholders, and all taxes. With the shareholders' permission, the directors will also retain a proportion of profits (the **retention ratio**)[2] in order to finance new investment projects. The shareholder's share of profit is paid in the form of a **dividend** per share. We can now readily see why equities are generally thought to be riskier assets than bonds. With straight bonds, at least, the income (coupon) stream is fixed. With ordinary shares the dividend per share may vary for one or more of several reasons: the trading success of the firm may rise or fall; interest rate or tax changes may take a larger or smaller slice of profits; changes in the retention ratio will cause dividends to rise or fall, even when post-interest, post-tax profit is unchanged. When issued, ordinary shares have a *par* value, though this is of little interest unless the firm becomes insolvent. The issue price is usually well above the par value and, once issued, it is the market price in which investors are interested.

In addition to receiving a dividend, ordinary shareholders would normally expect to benefit over time from an increase in the capital value of their shares. Each share represents a claim on the *nominal* profits of the firm. These, and thus dividends, will rise over time and if the share price were to remain constant the yield would rise continuously towards infinity. Since the return on shares must bear some relationship to the returns on other assets, it follows that share prices must rise over time if the yield is to remain stable.

---

[2] We shall later refer to the *payout ratio*. The payout ratio is 1 *minus* the retention ratio.

Preferred shares pay a fixed dividend (and in that sense are like a bond). Preferred shareholders rank behind bondholders, however. Thus, in periods of low earnings bondholders may be paid when preferred shareholders (and ordinary shareholders also of course) get nothing. Furthermore, unlike bondholders, preferred shareholders have no power to declare the firm insolvent. Predictably, there are many variations on the preference theme. With *cumulative preferred shares*, unpaid dividends are cumulated and become payable when earnings permit. *Convertible preferred shares* carry rights to convert to ordinary shares on specified terms and at specified times. And there are other variations.

The fact that the income stream from ordinary shares is uncertain naturally makes share valuation more difficult (than, say, bond valuation). The difficulties are further increased because it is difficult to establish precisely the degree of risk for any individual share and thus it is difficult to calculate an appropriate rate of discount.

The dominant approach to valuing company shares is known as **fundamental analysis**. This is the approach that we took in Section 11.4. An alternative, which attracts occasional attention, is known as **technical analysis**. In the next section, 17.3, we shall look in some detail at the pricing or valuation of ordinary company shares, concentrating mainly on the former methods, though saying a little also about the latter. Because the behaviour of share prices is subject to so many, and often unpredictable, influences, we devote Section 17.4 to what causes changes in share prices, rather than summarizing the relevant variables in two boxes as we did for bonds.

17.3 Equity pricing

17.3.1 Dividend models

In Chapter 11 we had an introduction to equity pricing which consisted of discounting a share's dividend payments. This approach gives rise to a series of what are called **dividend models** of share valuation and it grows out of the conventional approach to asset valuation with which we are now familiar. This approach says that the present value of an asset consists of the sum of its future earnings, each discounted at an appropriate rate which recognizes the time we have to wait and the risk or uncertainty attaching to the earnings.

Recall from above that company shares have no redemption date or redemption value. In that sense, equities are like perpetual or irredeemable bonds. If we assume that dividend payments go on forever at a constant level, then:

$$PV = \frac{D_1}{(1+K)} + \frac{D_2}{(1+K)^2} + \frac{D_3}{(1+K)^3} + \dots \quad (17.1)$$

or, more compactly:

$$PV = \sum_{t=1}^{t=\infty} \frac{D_t}{(1+K)^t} \quad (17.2)$$

where D stands for the dividend payment and K for the discount rate. If D is given and the payments go on for ever, Equation 17.2 simplifies to:

$$PV = \frac{D}{K} \quad (17.3)$$

which is the same formula as we used for valuing a perpetual bond in Section 11.3.2, except that D, the dividend, replaces C, the coupon, and K replaces i, the rate of interest.

In the last chapter we discounted the coupons of perpetual bonds by the current long-term interest rate and by simple rearrangement of terms we could show that the long-term interest rate by which we were discounting was also the rate of return that perpetual bondholders would receive if they bought bonds at a price which was equal to the present value arrived at as a result of that discounting. Doing the same here gives us:

$$K = \frac{D}{P} \quad (17.4)$$

The discount rate thus *is* the rate of return. Furthermore, *in equilibrium*, it must be the case that the rate of return that investors receive must be the *required* rate of return. (If you are doubtful, ask yourself 'why should investors accept anything else?' If the actual return is not equal to the required rate, investors are free to sell (or buy), causing prices and yields to change until they get the return they require.) So now we may say that, in equilibrium, the rate at which future earnings are discounted is the investors' required rate of return.

There is one further equivalence which we need to note. In Equation 17.4, K is also the cost of capital for a firm which is financed solely by the issue of shares with a constant dividend payment. K is the return that investors require and this is the return that they actually receive because the firm pays the current level of dividend. If it wishes to raise new capital by issuing new shares at this price, then the firm must accept the future commitment to pay this level of dividends. Imagine for a moment that the firm cut its dividend, trying to reduce the cost of its new capital. If $\overline{K}$ is the *required* rate of return, investors will accept the new issue of shares only when the price falls to a level that preserves the value of $\overline{K}$. Let us repeat: if $\overline{K}$ is the rate of return required by investors, then this is the cost that the firm has to pay for new capital.

As we have seen, the required rate of return for equities is represented by $\overline{K}$ and this is the same $\overline{K}$ which we saw derived, in Chapter 8, with the help of the capital pricing model. For an asset, A, recall:

$$\overline{K}_A = K_{rf} + \beta_A(K_m - K_{rf})$$

where K_{rf} is the risk-free rate of interest, $K_m - K_{rf}$ is the whole market risk premium and β_A is an index of the riskiness of asset A when compared with the market as a whole. Thus, in Equation 17.3, we discount the perpetual, and constant, dividend stream by a rate, $\overline{K}$, which takes into account the current level of risk-free rates, the market's pricing of average or benchmark risk as represented by the whole market portfolio, and the riskiness of the asset itself.

However, while equities may be like perpetual bonds in having no redemption date or value, the assumption of constant dividend payments is clearly quite unrealistic. We noted above that equities are riskier than bonds precisely because their dividend payments can fluctuate for a variety of reasons. Furthermore, with the passage of time one would expect dividends on average to grow. This is because new investment enlarges the firm's productive capital, leading to larger output, and also because dividends are paid out of money profits and inflation will cause money values to increase, even when there is no change in volume. We could make the model rather more realistic, therefore, by allowing dividends to grow.

The simplest assumption that we can make about growth is that growth occurs at a constant rate, g. Thus:

$$PV = \frac{D_1}{(1 + \overline{K})} + \frac{(1 + g)D_1}{(1 + \overline{K})^2} + \frac{(1 + g)^2 D_1}{(1 + \overline{K})^3}$$
$$+ \frac{(1 + g)^3 D_1}{(1 + \overline{K})^4} + \dots \qquad (17.5)$$

Simplifying Equation 17.5 by using the formula for the sum of a geometric progression, and assuming that the market prices the share at its present value, then:

$$P_0 = PV = \frac{D_1}{(\overline{K} - g)} \qquad (17.6)$$

where P_0 is the current price. Equation 17.6 is known as the **constant growth model**, or **Gordon growth model** after Gordon (1962).

Notice that we can rearrange Equation 17.6 in order to show that the required rate of return, $\overline{K}$, is the sum of the dividend yield and the rate of growth of dividends.

$$\overline{K} = \frac{D_1}{(P_0)} + g \qquad (17.7)$$

Notice also that g is the rate of capital appreciation, so that Equation 17.7 is equivalent to writing the total return on a share as its current yield plus its capital growth. The equivalence between the growth of dividends and the rate of capital appreciation can be seen when we consider that if:

$$P_0 = \frac{D_1}{(\overline{K} - g)} \qquad (17.8)$$

Exercise 17.1 Share valuation – dividend models

Wyndham Wines plc is a company whose dividends have been growing at a steady 15 per cent for the past few years. Last year it paid a dividend of 30p. Its shares are calculated to have a β-coefficient of 1.4, while the risk-free rate of interest is 6 per cent and the market risk premium is 10 per cent.

Using Equation 17.6, calculate a 'fair price' for Wyndham Wines' shares.

Suppose now that the central bank raises the official interest rates by 1 per cent, the market risk premium and the share's β-coefficient being unchanged. What effect will this have on the price of Wyndham Wines' shares?

Suppose now that in the course of the year Wyndham Wines announces the disposal of a soft-drinks subsidiary in Spain. This part of the business has always had highly variable earnings and analysts calculate that selling it off should reduce Wyndham Wines' β-coefficient to 1.3. Calculate a new fair price.

(Answers are in Box 17.1.)

BOX 17.1 Some solutions

The fair price is given by Equation 17.6:

$$P_0 = D_1/(K - g)$$

If we take the data given in Exercise 17.1 for purposes of illustration, we can calculate an initial fair price of Wyndham Wines' shares as follows:

$$D_1 = D_0(1 + g) = 30(1 + 0.15) = 34.5\text{p}$$

$$\overline{K} = K_{rf} + \beta(K_m - K_{rf}) = 6\% + 1.4(10\%) = 20$$

$$g = 15\%$$

Thus:

$$P_0 = 34.5/(0.2 - 0.15) = 690\text{p or } £6.90$$

If the central bank raises official interest rates from 6 per cent to 7 per cent and all else is unchanged, then we have to recalculate $\overline{K}$.

$$\overline{K} = 7\% + 1.4(10\%) = 21\%$$

Substituting 21 per cent in the denominator,

$$P_0 = 34.5/(0.21 - 0.15) = 575\text{p or } £5.75$$

If Wyndham Wines reduces its β-coefficient by disposing of a problem subsidiary, then, with all else unchanged, $\overline{K} = 7\% + 1.3(10\%) = 20\%$. Thus:

$$P_0 = 34.5 \div (0.2 - 0.15) = 690\text{p or } £6.90$$

The price returns to its original level.

---

then the price in the next period must be:

$$P_1 = \frac{D_2}{(\overline{K} - g)} \quad \text{where } D_2 = D_1(1 + g) \qquad (17.9)$$

Thus:

$$P_1 = \frac{D_1}{(\overline{K} - g)}(1 + g) \qquad (17.10)$$

Substituting Equation 17.8 into Equation 17.10:

$$P_1 = P_0(1 + g) \qquad (17.11)$$

The change in price between one period and the next takes place at the rate $(1 + g)$. That g is the percentage capital gain is then easily shown by rearranging Equation 17.11:

$$P_1 = P_0 + gP_0 \qquad (17.12)$$

and thus:

$$g = \frac{P_1 - P_0}{P_0} \qquad (17.13)$$

In Equation 17.6, $\overline{K}$ must be greater than g in order to yield a finite result. In practice, this condition is likely to hold if we remember that $\overline{K}$ is the cost of capital to firms. Imagine for a moment that the situation were reversed, that is, $g > \overline{K}$ The growth rate would exceed the cost of capital. This would be extraordinarily fortunate for any firm and the firm would expand as rapidly as it could. Its demand for capital would push up $\overline{K}$ and this would be further reinforced as other firms were attracted into the market. As a result of this expansion, demand would eventually be satisfied and g would fall. The rise in $\overline{K}$ and the fall in g would eventually reverse the inequality. $\overline{K} < g$ is not a sustainable condition.

Consider now the origins of g. Assume, for a moment, constant prices. The growth of the firm's earnings depends upon how much it adds to its capital stock, that is, its net investment, and the productivity of that additional investment. Let E_t stand for the firm's earnings, v_t for net investment and ϕ for the **payout ratio** – the fraction of earnings paid out as dividends. (All variables are in per-share form.) Then:

$$v_t = (1 - \phi)E_t \qquad (17.14)$$

Assume that the investment generates a return of ω per year, then earnings will increase by ωv_t per year. Thus:

$$E_{t+1} = E_t + \omega v_t = E_t[1 + \omega(1 - \phi)] \qquad (17.15)$$

And since:

$$E_t[1 + \omega(1 - \phi)] = E_t(1 + g) \qquad (17.16)$$

by definition, then

$$g = \omega(1 - \phi) \qquad (17.17)$$

Exercise 17.2 Share prices and yields

In Exercise 17.1 we saw that the required rate of return on Wyndham Wines plc's shares was 20 per cent p.a.

1 Using the information given in Exercise 17.1, identify separately the dividend yield component and the capital gain component.

2 Suppose that there is a reduction in the market price of risk so that the market risk premium falls to 9 per cent, risk-free rates remaining at 6 per cent and the β-coefficient remaining at 1.4. What happens to (a) the total return on Wyndham Wines' shares and (b) the dividend yield?

If we now substitute Equation 17.17 into Equation 17.6 we are on the verge of some interesting discoveries.

$$P_0 = \frac{(D_1)}{\overline{K} - \omega(1 - \phi)} \tag{17.18}$$

Remember that ϕ is the payout ratio (or 1 *minus* the retention ratio), the fraction of earnings paid out as a dividend. We can now rewrite the numerator of (17.6):

$$P_0 = \frac{\phi E_1}{\overline{K} - \omega(1 - \phi)} \tag{17.19}$$

Notice that changing the payout ratio changes both the numerator and the denominator, and *in the same direction*. A reduction in the payout ratio reduces the dividend payment, but it also increases the growth rate. This is what, intuitively, one would expect. If the firm pays out less as dividends, retaining more of its earnings in order to invest more, one might expect that shareholders will lose dividend income but one might also expect some compensation in the form of faster capital gain. Indeed, we can show that if a firm is in the long-run equilibrium position where the return on new capital investment is just equal to its cost of capital that is, $\overline{K} = g$, and we also assume:

- taxation which does not discriminate between capital gains and income
- zero transactions costs in buying and selling equities

then the compensation when the payout ratio changes is complete. The reduction (for example) in dividend yield will be just matched by the increase in capital gain, leaving the cost of capital and the return to shareholders unchanged. This is known as the Miller–Modigliani (1961) **dividend irrelevance hypothesis**. Box 17.2 provides a numerical illustration.

BOX 17.2 Dividend payouts and the value of shares

If we assume that a firm uses all retained earnings to finance new investment and that there is no other source of investment funds, then Equations 17.6 and 17.19 are equivalent. Imagine now a firm whose earnings or profits are the equivalent of 50p per share and it has a policy of paying out half of its earnings as dividends, retaining the rest for investment projects which produce a real return of 20 per cent p.a. In equilibrium, the return on capital projects will equal the required rate of return and so this too is 20 per cent p.a. Assume, finally, that its earnings growth rate has been steady at 10 per cent p.a. for the last few years. Then, from Equation 17.19 we can see that:

$$P_0 = 0.5(50p)/[0.2 - 0.2(1 - 0.5)]$$
$$= 25p / [0.2 - 0.1]$$
$$= 25p/0.1 = 250p = £2.50$$

Suppose now that the firm takes the decision to invest more of its earnings and raises the retention ratio to 60 per cent. If all else is unchanged, then:

$$P_0 = 0.4(50p)/[0.2 - 0.2(1 - 0.4)]$$
$$= 20p /[0.2 - 0.12]$$
$$= 20p/0.08 = 250p = £2.50$$

In these circumstances, the dividend policy pursued by the firm has no effect upon the value of its shares (and no effect upon the cost of capital, which remains at 20 per cent). But remember the assumptions that we made:

- The cost of capital must be just equal to the return on capital.
- Income and capital gains must be treated equally by the tax system.
- There must be no transaction costs in the buying and selling of shares.

The last two conditions are important to shareholders. If, for example, capital gains are taxed at a lower rate than income, then shareholders will prefer a lower payout ratio in order to earn more of their return through capital gain. Furthermore, because they keep more of their 20 per cent return after tax, they will be willing to accept a pre-tax rate of return of less than 20 per cent and the cost of capital to the firm will consequently be lower.

As another example, retired shareholders may prefer income to capital gain and thus would demand a higher return (impose a higher cost of capital) if a firm operated a low payout ratio. But if there are no transactions costs, they should have no objection to low payouts and large capital gains because they will be able to create an income by selling some shares every so often, without diminishing the value of their shareholding. This is one of several practices available to shareholders which have become known as the 'home-made alternative'.

Thus the assumptions are important. Dividend policy will *not* be irrelevant if they do not hold.

Because the Gordon model assumes a constant rate of growth of dividends throughout the whole period of the company's life, it is often referred to as a **one-period model**. Clearly, the assumption that firms grow at a constant rate throughout their life is unrealistic. More typically, we might expect that a firm would grow at a rapid rate in the early years (this could be the period when g is temporarily greater than $\overline{K}$). During this first period, earnings growth may still be constant, but at a high rate. After this initial period, earnings grow more slowly. In this second period, earnings growth may well be constant again, but at a lower rate. In practice, many analysts would take this long-run steady-state growth rate to be equal to the growth rate of nominal *GDP*, since the growth rate of the economy as a whole consists of nothing more than the sum of the growth rates of its productive units. A simple **two-period model** can therefore be constructed in which the current price is calculated by discounting a series of earnings expected to grow at a constant rate, g_1, for a period of N years, and then at a new constant rate of g_2 indefinitely after N.[3]

In the simplest two-period model, the transition from an unusual to a permanent growth rate is assumed to occur instantly, in one sudden step. This too is rather unrealistic. It is more probable that the end of a high growth period (for example) is indicated by a decline in the growth rate *over a period*, until it settles at the permanent level. This gives rise to a **three-period model**, in which there is a high growth phase, a transition phase and a permanent growth phase. Figure 17.1 shows the behaviour of earnings growth in a simple two-period model (the solid line) and compares it with the behaviour of earnings growth in a three-period model (the dashed line).[4]

17.3.2 Price earnings ratios

In the last section we defined ϕ, the payout ratio, as 1 *minus* the retention ratio. If we let λ be the retention ratio, then we can rewrite Equation 17.17 as:

$$g = \omega\lambda \qquad (17.20)$$

Substituting into Equation 17.7 gives:

$$\overline{K} = \frac{D_1}{P_0} + \omega\lambda \qquad (17.21)$$

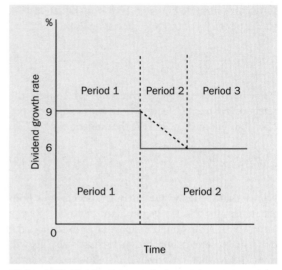

Figure 17.1 Dividend growth in 2- and 3-period models

Recall, from the last section, that ω, the return on the firm's investment projects, could be less than, equal to, or greater than its cost of capital. Thus $\omega = a\,\overline{K}$, where $a = {<}1,\ 1$ or ${>}1$. As we also said in the last section, we might normally expect firms to invest in all those projects up to the point where the productivity of capital just matches the cost of capital (that is, $a = 1$). Recall furthermore that dividends are equal to the fraction of earnings paid out ($D_0 = \phi E_0$) or $(1 - \lambda)E_0$. This being so, then:

$$\overline{K} = \frac{(1 - \lambda)(1 + \omega\lambda)E_0}{P} + \overline{K}\lambda \qquad (17.22)$$

Assume for the moment that a firm is investing in all projects in which the project returns just match the cost of capital as dictated by the return required by shareholders, i.e.:

$$\omega = \overline{K} \qquad (17.23)$$

Then substituting Equation 17.23 into 17.22 and rearranging yields:

$$\overline{K}(1 - \lambda) = \frac{(1 - \lambda)(1 + \omega\lambda)E_0}{P} \qquad (17.24)$$

---

3   See Elton and Gruber (1995) Ch. 18 for details.

4   The mathematics are explained in Elton and Gruber (1995) Ch. 18.

and

$$\overline{K} = \frac{(1 + \omega\lambda)E_0}{P} = \frac{E_1}{P} \qquad (17.25)$$

What we can now see is that in these (rather special) circumstances:

$$\overline{K} = \frac{D_1}{P} + g = \frac{E_1}{P} \qquad (17.26)$$

That is to say, the required rate of return will be equal to the dividend yield plus capital appreciation and this in turn will be equal to total earnings divided by the share price. What is special about the circumstances? The answer is that in Equation 17.23 we made ω, the firm's return on its real capital projects just equal to the cost of capital, i.e. to the required rate of return, $\overline{K}$. Look at what happens in Equation 17.25 if we allow ω to vary. Increasing the value of ω increases the value of E_1/P (and vice versa) so that it is no longer equal to $\overline{K}$. Any firm which has a return on its real capital equipment which exceeds its cost of capital ($\omega > \overline{K}$) will have a ratio of E_1/P which exceeds the rate of return required by shareholders. This is not a long-run equilibrium position. Any firm in this situation is receiving a signal that it can increase profits by raising additional funds from shareholders at the rate $\overline{K}$ and investing them in projects which yield the rate ω. Any firm in these circumstances is a growth firm.

Now look at the situation from the shareholders' point of view. We have just seen that any firm which has a return on its real capital equipment which exceeds its cost of capital ($\omega > \overline{K}$) will have a ratio of E_1/P which exceeds the rate of return required by shareholders. Provided that E_1/P exceeds $\overline{K}$, the shares offer the prospect of excess returns. Every shareholder will want to buy them. The effect will be to push up the price, and to reduce the ratio E_1/P. Thus, we would expect a firm with good growth prospects to have a lower E_1/P ratio than a firm with a slow growth outlook.

In the UK, it is more usual to talk about the inverse of the ratio E_1/P, and to refer to it as the **price/earnings** or **P/E ratio**. Everything said about the E/P ratio still applies of course – but in reverse. A firm whose real projects offer an actual return which exceeds the required return will find that its P/E ratio is bid *up* until a new equilibrium between the *actual* and *required* rates is re-established. Box 17.3 provides an illustration of the process.

BOX 17.3 High growth means high P/E

Sarum Sausages plc has earnings per share this year of 46.51p. Until now, it has enjoyed earnings growth of 7.5 per cent p.a. and on this basis expects to have earnings per share of 50p next year. It regularly retains one-half of its earnings for investment in new plant and equipment, which earns a return which just meets the cost of capital. It is financed entirely by the issue of ordinary shares and its cost of capital is 15 per cent p.a. Using Equation 17.6, we can calculate the share price based on this information.

$$P_0 = \frac{25p}{(0.15 - 0.075)} = \frac{25p}{0.075} = 333p$$

However, this year it plans to introduce a new product – wild boar sausages – and calculates that this will raise the overall return on its capital equipment to 20 per cent p.a.

The first question we might ask is what will happen to the actual return on Sarum's shares, if everything else, including their price, remains as it is.

$$P_0 = \frac{25.58p}{(0.15 - 0.10)} = \frac{25.58p}{0.05} = 511.6p$$

Using Equation 17.7, we can show that at their current price (£3.33) Sarum's shares would yield a return well in excess of that currently required by shareholders once it invests in the new line since earnings (and dividends) would be growing at 10 per cent p.a.

$$K = \frac{25.58p}{333} + 0.1 = 0.177 \quad \text{or} \quad 17.7 \text{ per cent}$$

At the current price and the rate of growth promised by the new investment the *actual* return to shareholders would be 17.7 per cent against the *required* rate of 15 per cent. We know that this means the shares will be highly desirable and that additional demand for the shares will push up the price until it reaches £5.12, at which level the *actual* return on the shares will match the *required* return of 15 per cent.

Now look at the P/E ratio in the normal growth phase and the fast growth phase. In the earlier situation the P/E ratio was 333/50 = 6.66. When it became apparent that Sarum Sausages faced a particularly rapid period of earnings, however, the ratio jumped to 511.6/51.16 = 10.

It is a short and simple step now to see how the information contained with a firm's P/E ratio can be combined with knowledge of the required rate of return to evaluate the price of a share for a company with *any* type of growth prospects, with a view to buy/sell recommendations. We have merely to find the value for P which makes the ratio E_1/P (the inverse of the P/E ratio) equal to the required return (in Equation 17.26). This is illustrated in Box 17.4.

As a means of evaluating the price of a share, however, one might raise two questions about the use of P/E ratios in this way. Firstly, one might ask, how is it *fundamentally* different from the dividend discount model? We are still, as in the dividend discount model, checking the market price to see whether or not it provides the required rate of return where the required rate of return is still being established by reference to the capital asset pricing model. Furthermore, one might ask, if it is not fundamentally different, does it perhaps have some advantage in convenience? The

answer to that is 'not obviously'. In the dividend discount model, we discounted the dividends actually declared by the firm, after allowing for their rate of growth. In Box 17.5, we substituted earnings for dividends but then we needed to know the retention ratio and the rate of return on the firm's investment projects relative to its cost of capital. There is no obvious economy of information or ease of calculation in doing that.[5]

When it comes to the use of P/E ratios in practice, therefore, we should not be surprised if their application is rather different from our illustration above. When we first met the practice of asset valuation (in Section 11.3) we noted that analysts are often interested in *relative* valuation. That is to say they are more concerned with the question of whether an asset yields a return which is greater than other assets with similar characteristics (or, equivalently, of whether its price is lower). It is for purposes of relative valuation that the P/E ratio is more commonly used. We look now at how that is done.

The price/earnings ratio tells us the price that an investor has to pay in order to buy a claim on a flow of earnings (which might be paid out as dividends or retained for reinvestment and capital growth). Other things being equal, an investor would prefer to pay the lowest price per pound of earnings. Thus, a firm with a P/E ratio below the norm for the sector in which it operates might be considered 'cheap'. Notice, however, that this is only an indication that the share is *relatively* cheap. There is nothing in *this* use of P/E ratios to justify the *absolute* level of prices of shares in this sector. Notice also that the share will be relatively cheap if we have indeed compared it with other shares where 'other things are *genuinely* equal'. A low P/E ratio may not indicate underpricing; it may simply indicate that something about the firm gives its earnings a higher degree of risk and makes it less attractive relative to its earnings. Conversely, a firm with a high P/E ratio may not be overpriced. It may be that there are characteristics of the firm that suggest that it has very good growth prospects. Its currently high price, relative to earnings, means that shareholders receive a low dividend yield (D_1/P_0) but this is compensated by a high

---

BOX 17.4 Share pricing by P/E ratio

Consider again the situation facing Sarum Sausages in Box 17.3. From Equation 17.20 we know that its new investment should cause earnings growth over the year of $\omega\lambda$, the return on its investment multiplied by the retention ratio. The growth rate in this case, therefore, is $0.2 \times 0.5 = 0.1$ or 10 per cent. In the next period, therefore, Sarum's earnings should be 51.16p per share.

Using Equation 17.6 again we can calculate the equilibrium price in the next time period assuming that shareholders still impose a cost of capital of 15 per cent.

$$P = \frac{(1 - 0.5)51.16}{0.15 - 0.1} = \frac{25.58}{0.05} = 511.6\text{p}$$

At a price below £5.12, shares in Sarum Sausages plc are cheap and would be an obvious 'buy' recommendation. At any price above £5.12 the shares would be expensive and investors would be recommended to sell before the market re-prices them correctly.

---

[5] Furthermore, there are considerable drawbacks to working with earnings since a firm's published earnings can vary considerably according to the accounting methods being used. This is not an issue we can pursue here but it is widely discussed in textbooks of corporate finance. There is a very good illustration of the problem in Blake (2000).

BOX 17.5 *Financial Times* share price data

The table in this box shows the information published by the *Financial Times* on 6 October 2007, about shares in the 'Media' sector. The name of the company is followed by one or more symbols whose meaning has to be checked in the notes to the whole table. They mainly indicate further information which is available.

The table next shows the price at the close of trading on 5 October and then the change in the price between the beginning and end of trading. Most prices are quoted in pence; those which are quoted in pounds would be shown '£'. The next two columns show the highest and lowest price reached in the course of the last 52 weeks. This provides some context in which to view the current price. 'Yield' is short for 'dividend yield' and shows the pre-tax dividend per share divided by the share price. The next column gives the price/earnings ratio. The final 'volume' column shows the number of shares traded on 5 October.

MEDIA

	Notes	Price	+ or −	52 week High	52 week Low	Yield	P/E	Volume 000s
Aegis	†	125	−	155	114	1.6	18.8	6,049
Blmsbury . .	†	145	+1	255.50	142	2.6	32.7	39
BSkyB	✠	696	+3	721	521	2.2	24.5	7,463
Centaur . . .		115.25	+0.25	155	108	3.0	16.1	90
Chime Cm .	†	49	−1	59.50	42.50	1.3	14.8	38
Chrysalis . .	♣	103.25	+0.50	165.50	94	1.3	52.1	1,303
CityofLn . . .		94	−	149	71.50	2.1	−	46
Creston . . .	♣	115.75	−0.25	203.50	99	2.3	12.3	12
DlyMailA . .	†	656	+7	875.50	606.50	2.1	24.5	3,855
Ekay.	♣	14	−	38.50	14	2.1	14.1	0
EMAP		922	+2	937.50	685	3.4	28.2	2,086
EntRghts . .		21.75	−0.25	37.25	**21.75**	−	34.1	573
Eurmony. . .	†	521.50	+1.50	713.50	486.25	3.4	13.1	56
Future		44.25	−1.75	48	38.25	2.3	28.7	153

Source: *Financial Times*, 6 October 2007. Reprinted with permission.

capital growth rate, g. We must be careful to compare like with like.

Because analysts commonly use P/E ratios in their assessment of share value, the P/E ratio is one of the essential pieces of information that the *Financial Times* publishes daily. Box 17.5 shows an extract from the information published by the *FT* on 6 October 2007.

As Box 17.5 shows, P/E ratios can vary quite substantially, even within one sector, but it is important to remember only to compare P/E ratios for companies which are strictly comparable. (There is further discussion of the data in Box 17.5 in Section 17.5 below.)

Used in this way, to try to identify anomalies in relative pricing, we can now see that there are major differences between the dividend discounting approach to share valuation and the P/E approach. Firstly, as we said above, comparing P/E ratios is an exercise in *relative* evaluation. We cannot ever say that a share is 'fairly priced'. Judged by absolute standards, having regard to risk and the market price of risk, for example, a whole sector of shares may be grossly overvalued, but we still have to say about a company whose P/E ratio lies below the sector norm for no apparent reason that it is *undervalued*. The reason for this lies in the second contrast between the two methods. Used in the way we have just described, P/E ratios tell us nothing explicit about the quantity of risk or about the price of risk. All the influences on a share's price, except earnings themselves, are bundled up in a collective way in the ratio. Finally, it is worth noting that, in order to be useful, the P/E ratio approach has to assume that equity markets are to some degree inefficient, at least for short periods. That is to say that the approach relies upon being able to find shares which are mispriced relative to others. There is simply no point in examining P/E ratios if we begin from the assumption that the market is so efficient that share prices are always 'correct' share prices.

17.3.3 Asset values

It is not uncommon, when reading commentaries on share prices, to meet the statement that 'the current share price is at a premium (or discount) to the firm's **asset value**'. What the former means is that the present price of the share gives the firm a value which is greater than one would arrive at by valuing its component assets individually and then summing the component values. The implication of the statement, of course, is that the share price is 'too high', should be lower, will probably fall shortly when the market recognizes the anomaly, and should be sold (or at least not bought). Notice immediately that this is again a statement about *relative* value, though this time the comparison is with the underlying assets of the same firm rather than with another firm. As it stands, it says nothing about the underlying assets being correctly valued in any absolute sense. One could defend asset valuation as a source of absolute values, *if* one could argue that the underlying asset values were absolutely correct. If that were so, then a statement that the share price (for example) is at a premium to asset value tells us *both* that it is too high relative to asset values but also that it is absolutely too high, since the underlying assets are correctly valued in an absolute sense. The question this poses, however, is how do we arrive at an absolute valuation for the underlying assets? The answer to that is that we can only get it by the standard practice of discounting the future earnings of those assets by some appropriate, risk-adjusted, discount rate. And if we do that, then we are essentially back to a discounted dividend model of valuation. Thus, if asset valuation is to mean anything strictly different from the approach we outlined in Section 17.2.1, then we have to treat it as another approach to relative valuation which might be useful in certain circumstances.

Why might one want to use it? One clue is given to us when we examine why the value of the firm, represented by its share price, might differ from the value of its component assets. This often happens because the component assets are valued on the basis of the going market price for similar assets. Thus, one might consider what price could be got for the firm's premises, sold simply as commercial premises. To this one would add the market price of any equipment, sold separately from the site. In addition, there would be market prices for its vehicles, office furniture, stocks of raw materials, finished goods and so on. It is not difficult now to see why share value and asset value (defined in this way) might differ. It is usually the case that the assets, when sold off separately, have to compete with a large number of very similar second-hand assets. However, when combined together in the hands of a skilled management which is able to produce a unique good or service for which there is high demand, the value of the assets when *constituting the firm* could be considerably higher. This is another way of saying that the valuation of the component assets is incomplete. There is something else which adds value when they are combined as this particular firm. The obvious omission is the management or 'human capital' and the reason that it is left out of the valuation is that there is no recognized market for human capital (since the abolition of slavery). The problem is recognized as particularly acute in certain industries. Firms specializing in marketing and other media-related activity provide frequent examples. Their tangible, marketable assets often consist of little more than premises, office furniture and the usual computing and communications equipment. None of this is highly specialized and once placed on the market it competes with a large volume of similar equipment. The bulk of the 'value' of such firms lies in the management and employees. It is their creative skill that enables the firm to generate large earnings relative to its asset value.

On the face of it, therefore, asset valuation does not look generally very useful as a means of determining a share's (and firm's) value. However, we can say that evaluating a share's price by looking at the value of the underlying assets is particularly useful whenever the question of selling the underlying assets arises. Such a situation is almost invariably associated with mergers and takeovers for two reasons.

Firstly, the share price relative to asset value may enable us to identify 'bargains'. If, for example, a firm's share price values it at a discount to its assets, this is saying that the firm can be bought at a price which is less than that which could be realized by selling its assets on the secondhand market. This makes the firm an obvious target for takeover, since the bidding (or predator) firm knows that once it has possession it faces a choice of profitable strategies. It might decide to keep the target firm in operation, using its own management to improve its performance. If this looks unattractive, it can simply close the firm and sell the assets for a higher price than the price it paid.

Secondly, the takeover of a thriving firm may be encouraged if the predator firm thinks that it can sell part of the target business for a profit. In this case, selling some of the target firm's assets is being used to finance the takeover. Doing this successfully depends upon being able to identify some assets in the target firm which are contributing less than their market value to the price of the share. This seems to be possible where the target firm is large and consists of several quite distinct operations. In this situation, the firm's accounts will often make it possible to identify the contribution to total earnings (or dividends) that each division makes. This enables analysts (and predators!) to say whether the earnings of the assets in their present use gives them a value which is greater or less than their value on the open market. In the late 1980s there were a number of takeovers which resulted in the subsequent sale of some or all of the assets taken over. The practice was common enough to acquire its own name, 'asset stripping'.

Where the price of a share values the firm at a discount to its asset value, this is a signal to buy since the undervaluation is not likely to persist for the reasons we have just seen.[6]

17.3.4 Technical analysis

An entirely different approach to the valuation of equities is known as **technical analysis**, or *chartism* to give its popular name. The core of technical analysis uses visual representations of past price movements to identify patterns which, it is believed, repeat themselves. Typically, the past price movement of a security will be plotted using a line or point and figure chart. The analyst then focuses upon the most recent price movement in order to identify a pattern. These patterns go under a variety of colourful names, such as 'head and shoulders', 'wedges', 'flags' and so on.

Once such a pattern has been identified, the behaviour of the share in the more distant past can be searched for signs of a similar pattern and, most importantly, the behaviour of the price at the end of that pattern. Sometimes, there will be no comparable pattern in the share's history. Then the analyst will look for the same pattern in similar shares in order to see what happened next in their case. (See also Box 18.4.)

Clearly, we have come a long way from explaining a share's price by reference to its fundamentals. Nothing explains the price in technical analysis except the past movement in the share's price. This is interesting, and makes technical analysis highly controversial in the eyes of many. This is because technical analysis conflicts with the efficient markets hypothesis (which we discuss in Chapter 26). The weakest form of the EMH suggests that all the information that can be obtained from *past* movements in a share's price is already incorporated in the share's *current* price. Thus, if a 'head and shoulders' pattern means that the price is pausing before a major fall, and it is known that this is what a head and shoulders pattern means, then shareholders will sell instantly and the price will fall so quickly that no one can take advantage of the information. According to the weak form EMH, the only thing that can change a share's price is 'news' and news, by definition, is unpredictable. If this is the case,

---

MORE FROM THE WEB
Technical analysis

There are thousands of Internet sites offering information about 'finance' and 'financial markets'. Most of these are aimed at the private investor and are frankly designed to persuade people to get involved in the stock market, often using, and paying for, some service offered by the website.

Among the more educational, however, are three which provide a serious discussion of technical analysis. These are:

www.investorsintelligence.com/x/default.html

In October 2007 this site was providing free online access to a number of 'educational' papers on the subject of technical analysis.

www.technicalanalysis.org.uk/
www.investopedia.com/university/technical

---

[6] Identifying and recommending shares that value the firm at less than its asset value has often been one strategy followed by newspaper share tipsters.

then the ability of technical analysts to predict price movements successfully must be the result of luck. It will not be sustained; their predictions will eventually go through a correspondingly bad patch and *in the long run* technical analysis will not enable analysts to earn above average returns.

Nonetheless, technical analysis remains very popular. It also contributes to the **liquidity of the market** since it increases the diversity of views about a share's price. If technical analysis leads some investors to have views about a share's next movement that differ from those of other investors, this simply helps to ensure that there will always be some people willing to buy when others are willing to sell.

17.4   Share price movements

We begin by distinguishing between the behaviour of share prices in the aggregate (what might be called 'equity market movements') and the behaviour of individual share prices. We then distinguish between the short run and the long run.

17.4.1 Whole market – short run

As with bonds, in the short run the supply of equities is fixed. In a market diagram, the supply curve is vertical.[7] The demand curve slopes downward, indicating that when prices are lower (and yields higher) *relative to other assets*, there will be a greater willingness to hold equities. With a given stock, changes in prices (and yields) are the result of demand shifts. Prices will change when investors' perception of the value or fair price of shares in general changes. If something happens to cause investors to put a lower value on shares, for example, the demand curve shifts downward until shares in general seem attractive again at the new price and yield. To explain changes in the *general* level of prices we have to look at general or 'whole market' events.

Look again at Equation 17.6. We know that share prices will change if there are changes to D_1, g or $\overline{K}$. Investor perceptions of future dividends in general will obviously be responsive to changes in the outlook

for the economy as a whole. The movement from boom to recession, for example, or the prospect of a tighter fiscal policy will lead to a 'downgrading' of dividend forecasts. A reduction in the numerator, of course, reduces the value of shares. Similar events might also lead to a downward revision of g, the rate at which future earnings and dividends are expected to grow. Remember also that firms' payout ratios are irrelevant to shareholders only if the tax system is neutral between income and capital gains and transaction costs are zero. Imagine that a newly elected left-wing government reveals plans for higher tax rates on 'unearned' income, perhaps arguing that this will encourage firms to retain earnings (reduce their payout ratios) and increase their investment. As we saw in Box 17.2, shareholders might be quite indifferent to this, if their lower dividends are replaced by larger capital gains, *provided that they can make a costless sale* of a few shares every time they require income. If they cannot, then this tax change will push share prices down, since shareholders will insist on higher pre-tax yields to compensate for the higher tax on dividends.

For many firms, a fall in the exchange rate will lead to an upward revision of g, since imports from competitors will be dearer and the firm's own exports will become cheaper in foreign markets. As a general rule, therefore, a depreciation in the exchange rate helps equity markets, notwithstanding the fact that governments may try to prevent the depreciation, or at least to slow it down, by raising interest rates. An interesting exception to this rule in Europe is the Italian equities market, which almost invariably moves positively with the euro/dollar exchange rate. A depreciation causes share prices to fall because there are relatively few large exporting firms quoted on the Italian exchanges and so the market has only to take account of the implications for inflation and interest rates. Both are likely to increase and this will depress prices, as we see in the next paragraph.

The largest source of market-wide influences, however, is always likely to be found in interest rates or expectations of interest rate movements. Recall that $\overline{K}$ in Equation 17.6 is the sum of a risk-free rate and a risk premium derived from the market's current pricing of risk in general ($K_m - K_{rf}$) and the firm's relative risk characteristics, β. A change in β, of course,

---

[7]   Readers who want to refresh their memory of this should go back to the discussion surrounding Figure 11.2.

reflects a change in the characteristics of the firm itself and is therefore not relevant in this context. However, a change in official interest rates causes a change in K_{rf} and, other things being equal, must cause a change in $\overline{K}$. (Precisely this case is discussed in Case study 1, see page 590.) Notice that a general change in $\overline{K}$ would follow also if there were a change in the market's risk aversion. If, for example, investors generally took the view that equities as a class of assets were becoming more risky, then the market risk premium $(K_m - K_{rf})$ would widen, increasing $\overline{K}$ for all equities and leading to lower prices.

17.4.2 Individual shares – short run

Individual shares will, of course, be affected by all those events that affect the prices of shares in general. However, there will in addition be firm-specific events which have their impact on D_1, g and $\overline{K}$. The first two may obviously be boosted by news of new product developments or by the granting of new patents giving a firm protection to exploit a particular product for a specified period. Conversely, a firm's share price is likely to react badly when a profitable patent comes to an end or a rival develops a competing or superior product. Through most of 1996, the shares in 'privatized utilities' in the UK were depressed because of plans by the Labour Party to impose a windfall tax if they formed the next government (unrealized in the event). The argument behind the windfall tax was that these ex-nationalized firms had been sold to the private sector at too low a price (at a cost to the general taxpayer in other words) and that since then shareholders had made unreasonable gains. Throughout Europe and the United States, firms are subject to legislation to deter restrictive practices and the development of monopolies which might work against the public interest. News that a firm is to be investigated by the anti-monopoly authorities is often sufficient to cause a fall in its share price – not just because it may have to end some monopoly practice which has been profitable in the past (driving down D_1 and g), but simply because the inquiry itself is expected to divert a large amount of management time and effort which would have gone into running the firm into preparing answers to the regulator's questions. Another development that often gives rise to the most spectacular short-term price rises is news of a takeover bid, especially if that takeover bid is resisted. The market regards the bid as evidence either that the bidding firm can operate the assets of the target firm more efficiently (raising future levels of D and perhaps g as well) or simply that the target company is underpriced. (This raises serious questions about the efficiency with which the market values firms, an issue we discuss in Chapter 26.) Even if shareholders doubt that the firm will be more profitable in the long run, a contested bid almost invariably results in the bidding firm having to make one or more higher offers. Naturally, if it raises the price at which it is prepared to buy the shares, their price goes up.

It is possible also for firm-specific events to have their impact on $\overline{K}$. Recall that the firm-specific component of $\overline{K}$ is β, an index of the firm's riskiness relative to a whole market portfolio. Many large corporations consist of a widely diversified range of subsidiaries, often the result of past takeovers and mergers. It is not unusual for some subsidiaries to perform better than others, nor is it unusual for subsidiaries to have different risk characteristics. (These differences were often the reason for combining them in the first place!) Where this is the case, then the β-coefficient of the whole corporation, β_c is just the value-weighted average of the β's of the individual subsidiaries. Formally:

$$\beta_c = \sum w_s \cdot \beta_s$$

where w_s is the value of each subsidiary expressed as a fraction of total firm value, and β_s is the β-coefficient of each subsidiary. We can now see that the acquisition (or disposal) of any subsidiary whose individual β differs from the corporation average, β_c, must cause a change in β_c. Thus, even if interest rates remain unchanged and there is no change in the market's pricing of risk, the riskiness of the firm itself can change, causing a rise (or fall) in the required rate of return, $\overline{K}$.

Before leaving this discussion of short-term changes in share prices, remember that price movements only need events to be *expected*. If people *expect* an announcement of lower profits, they will sell as quickly as possible. They will certainly sell before the announcement itself; in fact the selling will drive prices down. And the selling will drive prices down even if the expectation turns out to be wrong. If the expectation is wrong, share prices may recover again after the announcement but that does not alter the fact that expectation caused the first movement. On the other hand, if the expectation turns out to be correct, there will be no further movement in prices at the time of the announcement. That is why, in Case study 1, the *Financial Times* report of the fall in US interest rates places so much stress upon the unexpected nature of the event. Asset prices fell because the rise in interest rates was 'news'. If it had been expected, it would already have been incorporated in the price and would have had little, if any, effect. In Section 11.5 we included a quotation from John Maynard Keynes which suggested an even more extreme role for expectations. According to Keynes, one did not even have to expect a piece of genuine economic news in order to make buying or selling the rational thing to do. One only had to think that other people expected some news and were going to buy or sell. Indeed, one might forget about news altogether and simply concentrate on what one thinks other people are going to do. If this is true then prices are not moved by events ('level 1') or even *expectations of events* ('level 2') but by *expectations of other people's expectations* ('level 3'). In Keynes' words:

> We have reached the third degree where we devote our intelligences to anticipating what average opinion expects the average opinion to be. And there are some, I believe, who practise the fourth, fifth and higher degrees.
>
> Keynes, *General Theory*, 1936, p. 156.

17.4.3　Whole market – long run

In the long run, the aggregate stock of company shares will expand. The supply curve will shift to the right. This happens because new firms are established and existing firms convert to joint-stock or 'corporate' status. Naturally, some firms will fail, while some firms will find it advantageous to buy in some of their existing shares. Nonetheless, one would expect a net increase in the aggregate stock of shares over time.

The speed at which this happens will depend to some extent on the state of the economy. When the economy is booming, firms have more need for new capital for expansion. Furthermore, it is likely that share prices themselves will be high in a boom because investors expect good profits and a high rate of

growth of dividends. In Section 11.3.1 we went to some trouble to establish that the required rate of return on shares, $\overline{K}$, was the equivalent of the firm's cost of capital. High share prices, therefore, are equivalent to a low cost of capital.[8] When the cost of capital is low, firms will be encouraged to expand.

The net flow of new issues is likely to be particularly marked if the cost of equity capital is low relative to other sources of funds. This too can happen in a boom where a rise in the rate of inflation looks likely. Higher inflation rates may lead to higher interest rates and thus a reduction in the present value of all assets, but for equities higher inflation will mean a more rapid growth in nominal profits and, *ceteris paribus*, a higher rate of growth of dividends. There is no such compensation for bondholders whose returns are fixed in nominal terms. Thus, in the later stages of a boom, when investors become concerned about inflation, it is not unusual for bond yields to rise relative to equity yields and thus for shares to become, relatively, a cheaper source of capital than bonds.

In the long run, then, we would expect a net increase in the stock of company shares, though the rate of expansion may fluctuate. In a market diagram, the continued rightward shift of the supply curve, other things unchanged, suggests a downward movement in prices, and a continuous shift to the right suggests a continuous downward price trend. This, clearly, is wrong. Share prices do sometimes fall dramatically and they do sometimes experience periods of long gentle decline but they do not suffer from a continuous decline. Equally, seen from the yield side, yields do not rise continuously with time. In the long run, real yields (that is, allowing for inflation) are commonly assumed to be 'stationary'.[9] From this, we are driven to the conclusion that, in the long run, the demand curve also shifts to the right, that is, the demand for shares also increases. And it is easy to see why this should be the case, especially if we recall the discussion in Sections 1.2.3 and 1.2.4. There is a *net* demand for financial assets every time a unit or sector saves in excess of its real investment. If we take households, for example, a sector which normally runs a financial surplus, households make a *net* acquisition

---

[8] An informal way to understand this is to remember that in return for a given dividend payment the issue of one extra share raises more capital if its price is high than it does when its price is low.

[9] 'Stationary' in a formal, statistical, sense means that a time series has a constant mean, variance and covariance. In other words, it does not matter from where we draw a sample of observations in the series, we get the same values. Clearly, this condition cannot hold if the data is subject to a time-related trend.

of financial assets every year. A *net* acquisition means an acquisition in excess of disposals. Thus, each year there is a demand by households to add to their stock of wealth, and company shares, directly or indirectly via a managed mutual fund, will be part of the additional wealth that they wish to acquire.

As with shifts in supply, there will be fluctuations in the rate of shift. In a boom, with low unemployment and high incomes, the scope for aggregate saving will be greater and out of this greater saving there will be a more rapid acquisition of financial assets. The behaviour of demand for shares over time will also depend upon the attractiveness of shares as an investment relative to other assets. In the UK, for example, it was a frequent complaint from industry that there were too many incentives for households to accumulate housing wealth. These incentives included tax relief on mortgage interest payments and capital gains tax exemption on the sale of homes. Successive governments in the 1980s and 1990s began reducing the real value of the interest tax relief on house purchase and created tax incentives for investment in company shares using what were initially known as 'Personal Equity Plans' (PEPs) and later 'Individual Savings Accounts' (ISAs). Differences in the rate of growth of demand for and supply of company shares over time will lead to occasional trends in prices and yields, but these are trends which are quite quickly reversed.

17.4.4 Individual shares – long run

Individual shares will, of course, be subject to the same long-run influences that apply to the equity market as a whole. Individual shares suffer from discriminatory tax regimes and benefit from market-side inducements to buy shares. Beyond these influences it is difficult to isolate long-run effects on *individual* shares because any long-run tendency is usually a signal for something to change. If, for example, a firm's share price establishes a long-term downward trend because of declining earnings, and this performance is unique to that particular firm within a profitable sector, then the declining price is a sign of management failure and the firm will quickly become a takeover target. By contrast, an *individual* firm which is a runaway success will quickly find other firms diversifying into its area of activity and the growth in profits will eventually slow.

It is easier to identify trends for whole sectors or categories of firms. The fortunes of whole sectors tend to be associated with structural changes in the economy, or with long-term technological change. Thus, after 1921, dividends on the shares in coal mining and railway companies steadily declined, and with them went the value of the shares. In both cases, the problem was one of the long-run development of rival products and technologies. By contrast, in the 1990s a new and fashionable sector emerged, under the general heading of 'biotechnology'. These were firms set up to exploit recent technological breakthroughs in the manipulation of the genetic code in DNA. The ultimate prize was seen as the development of effective drugs for cancer, AIDS, arthritis and other afflictions which had so far resisted all conventional treatments. Many companies enjoyed the sight of their newly issued shares increasing rapidly in price even before they had produced any products for sale. This may be a sector set for long-run growth.

17.5 Equity market characteristics

Equities are issued in all countries by firms wishing to raise long-term capital but who have decided for some reason against the issue of long-term bonds. Table 17.1 gives some indication of the scale of this activity for a range of European bourses.

There are many ways in which the scale of stock market activity can be compared. As with bonds, raising new capital involves making new issues of shares (or additional issues of existing shares). This is the primary function of a stock market and one might therefore use that as the basis for comparison. The final column of Table 17.1 shows how much was raised in the first quarter of 2007 and, on this basis, the London Stock Exchange comes second in the list though by only a very small margin. On any other basis, London's paramount position is obvious. Turnover figures record all the sales/purchases in a given period and for virtually all the exchanges it is clear that turnover greatly exceeds the funds raised by new issues – confirming that by far the greater part of stock market activity is secondary activity. Capitalization refers to the total value of all shares listed on the exchange. Looking at the London turnover figures (for the first quarter 2007) it seems clear that total trading on the London Stock Exchange is

Table 17.1 European equity markets in July 2007

	Capitalization[1]	Listed shares (no.)		Turnover[2]	New issues[2]	
	(€m)	Domestic	Foreign	(€m)	Shares (no.)	Funds raised (€m)
Deutsche Börse	1,393,265	657	98	263,311	10	n/a
Euronext[3]	2,991,708	951	n/a	9,435	9	n/a
Italian exchange	784,664	298	6	130,844	12	1,564
London Stock Exchange	2,885,449	2,615	686	397,514	55	7,660
Oslo Børs	245,543	205	37	23,244	0	222
Spanish Exchanges	1,123,540	3,419	37	206,637	14	1,919
Warsaw	150,440	300	16	5,768	9	416

[1] Domestic equity only, end-July 2007. [2] Domestic equity only, July 2007. [3] Amsterdam, Brussels and Paris.

Source: Compiled from data in the Federation of European Stock Exchanges Database. *Last Month Report*, http://www.fese.be/en/?inc=page&id=10.

approximately equal to just over half its total capitalization and getting on for 53 times the value of new funds raised.

17.5.1 Primary markets

As with bonds, the bulk of trading in equities involves the buying and selling of existing stock. However, a major consequence of this secondary market activity is that it supports a primary market in which investors are more willing to buy new issues, and provide new funds, knowing that they can subsequently sell the stocks quickly and cheaply if they so wish.

In most financial centres, the methods for making *new* issues of new ordinary company shares involve either a sale to the general public – a **public offer for sale** – or a **placing**. In each case a financial institution, usually a merchant bank or a securities trader, **underwrites** the issue. Underwriting involves the purchase of the stock on agreed terms from the issuer with the promise to distribute it subsequently to shareholders using one of the methods just described. The advantage to the issuing firm is that it knows both the quantity of funds that the issue will raise and the cost of those funds. Indeed, these will be agreed with the underwriter sufficiently far in advance that they will form part of the basis on which the firm decides whether or not to go ahead with the issue. Clearly, the underwriter is accepting a degree of risk in providing this service. Firstly, there is the risk that the issue may be overpriced with the result that the

underwriter cannot subsequently dispose of the whole issue at that price or better. Secondly, there is the risk that although the price initially agreed was correct, the market falls between the time that the underwriter takes up the new issue and distributes it to shareholders. Again, the underwriter is left with unsold stock. Because of the risk involved, it is common for large issues to be underwritten by a **syndicate**, a group of merchant banks or securities dealers.

New issues will take place when either a firm decides to raise funds by adding to the number of shares already in issue, or when a firm decides to raise funds by 'going public' for the first time. The former case is often described as a **rights issue** since existing shareholders are given a guaranteed opportunity to buy shares in the new issue, provided that they exercise the right within a specified period. The purpose of this is to protect existing shareholders from the enforced dilution of their holding in the firm. 'Rights' give the shareholder the opportunity to maintain his or her percentage of the ownership of the firm.

With rights issues, it is possible also to compare the price of new shares at the time of issue with those already being traded. It is usual to observe a discount. This is difficult to explain by reference to economic theory. Since the new shares, after issue, have exactly the same characteristics, benefits and risks as existing shares (indeed are indistinguishable from pre-existing shares) it is hard to see why they should have a different value. The explanation that is often advanced is that the discount represents a price that underwriters are prepared to pay to preserve their reputation. A new issue which is undersubscribed is often the source of comment in the financial press and might be thought to suggest poor judgement on the part of the underwriter(s). This might make it harder for them to attract underwriting business in future. If this is true, it is worth considering carefully who is really paying the price of protecting this reputation. If we assume that the need to sell at a discount to existing prices is built into the negotiations between the firm and the underwriter, then part at least of the discount at least is being met by the firm. In accepting that the shares will ultimately be issued at a discount, it is accepting a smaller volume of funds and thus a higher cost of capital than may be necessary.

17.5.2 Secondary markets

As we saw in Chapter 16, various trading structures are possible in securities markets. At the moment, the London Stock Exchange is mainly a 'quote-driven, continuous' market, although 'order driven' trading in the shares included in the FTSE-100 index began in October 1997. Prior to 1986, quotes were made by jobbers who held inventories of stock and acted on their own behalf as principals. Under the pre-1986 rules, they could deal only with brokers, who acted as investors' agents. The same rules limited broking and jobbing firms to partnerships with unlimited liability and also permitted firms to work to a scale of fixed minimum commissions. During the 1960s and 1970s a number of pressures built up for change (Cobham, 1992). The event that finally forced a reappraisal of these arrangements was the removal of exchange controls in the autumn of 1979. Even before this, a certain amount of trading in UK securities was being carried out in other centres, mainly in New York where deregulation, economies of scale and new technology meant much lower commissions. The ending of exchange controls opened the flood gates. UK fund managers diversified rapidly into overseas securities, dealing with overseas market makers. It was clear not just that minimum commissions made London uncompetitive but that the Stock Exchange member firms were simply too small to take on the large increased holdings of international stocks that investors now required and to exploit the economies of scale that the new trading and information technology offered. In the course of 1985 Stock Exchange members came to accept: (a) opening up membership of the

> **MORE FROM THE WEB**
> **Stock exchange trading**
>
> While most major stock exchanges provide vast amounts of information, this is aimed largely at potential investors and at firms considering applying for a listing. Neither of these is assumed to be very interested in trading methods. The best place to look for any relevant information is under the heading 'members' since members are mainly the exchanges dealers or market-makers.
>
> Just a reminder – the main European exchanges are:
>
> > www.londonstockexchange.com
> > www.euronext.com
> > www.deutsche-boerse.com
>
> The one partial exception to this is Euronext whose website includes a pdf document titled 'Euronext: organisation and procedures'. This can be accessed from the home page by clicking on 'Private Investor' and then on 'Documents Centre'. (The 'Education Centre' also has some useful items.)
>
> Probably more use, and certainly informative and entertaining, is the 'howstuffworks' website. Go to: www.howstuffworks.com/stocks.htm.
>
> This will display a page entitled 'How stocks and the stock markets work'. This provides an introduction but also has a drop-down contents list which gives access to more specialized discussions of 'A stock exchange' and 'Exchanges and brokers'. Other topics include the use of stocks and the stock market from firms' point of view.

Exchange to corporations with limited liability; (b) the ending of minimum commissions; and (c) the replacement of the broker–jobber roles by single capacity market makers. This opened the way for large financial institutions to become members and to invest heavily in the new screen-based technology.

Since 1986, it is these single capacity market makers who provide the quotes for the London market. The Stock Exchange regulations require market makers to quote continuous two-way prices at which they are prepared to deal in return for which they can display their quotes on the SEAQ (Stock Exchange Automated Quotations system) screens and have access to stock borrowing facilities and the TALISMAN electronic settlement system.

One obvious consequence of Big Bang was the arrival of many new firms and an injection of large amounts of capital into the London Stock Exchange. For some years, the obvious question was whether or not this increase in capital and participants improved the functioning of the market. For some years, therefore, the Stock Exchange published a quarterly, *Quality of Markets Review*. The criteria for assessment were (and remain):

1 **Liquidity**: measured by 'turnover' (the value of transactions per period) and 'velocity' (the value of transactions as a proportion of the total value of securities listed).

2 **Depth**: measured by the degree of competition and the ability of the market to trade large quantities of stock without affecting price. Trends in the former can be established by monitoring the number of market-makers for each type of stock and in the latter by examining the difference between the bid–offer price for different bargain sizes.

3 **Visibility**: refers to the amount of information that is available to market participants.

4 **Transaction costs**: measured by commission levels and bid–offer spreads.

The benefits of Big Bang quickly became apparent, although figures for turnover and velocity were adversely affected by the 1987 stock market crash and did not recover until 1998. But visibility has certainly increased dramatically, aided by technological developments which allow large amounts of information to be available on-screen at the touch of a button. Bid–offer spreads and commissions have generally declined for all bargain sizes. For some years, in the early 1990s, it looked as though 'retail' investors were being left out of the benefits by commissions which remained stubbornly high for the smallest deals. But even this problem declined from the mid-1990s with the development of internet and online brokerage services. Even the data provided to the general public by the Stock Exchange itself has increased. Instead of a quarterly review of market efficiency, the London Stock Exchange now publishes monthly and annual reports which contain data for primary and secondary, main and AIM markets, and which show much greater detail than that required to judge 'quality'. The reports are available online at the Stock Exchange's website (www.londonstockexchange.com).

Many of the major upheavals of the London market have since been reproduced in other European markets, partly because of the competition that the reformed London market posed.[10] If we summarize the core of the London reforms as having four elements – continuous electronic trading, dual capacity, liberalization of commissions and freedom of entry – then by 1990 the *Paris Bourse* had adopted them all, Frankfurt moved to a similar system in 1995 and Madrid and Milan were committed to reform on lines identical to the Paris model. In detail, the Paris arrangements differ from those of London in so far as the market makers (*Sociétés de Bourse*) operate a computerized auctioneer system of trading. They do not normally quote continuous two-way prices but execute deals when buy and sell orders cross. In the typology of Figure 16.7, Paris (and the other European markets following the same pathway) are 'continuous auction' rather than 'continuous dealer' markets. More information about the auction markets of Amsterdam, Brussels and Paris can be found by following the links from www.euronext.com detailed on p. 373.

In a continuous auction market, buyers and sellers submit orders to the market maker specifying respectively an upper and lower limit at which they are prepared to trade. Buy orders are then matched to sell orders, so far as possible, by computer and a price is struck and declared. Any offers which cannot be executed at that price are kept until the price moves within their limit or the instruction to buy or sell is withdrawn. Compared with the quote-driven or dealer system it is immediately apparent that the order-driven system apportions the risk rather differently. In a dealer system, the dealer holds inventories of stocks on his or her own behalf, to which s/he adds the sell stocks that s/he receives and from which s/he executes buy orders. Clearly the price of this inventory will fluctuate with changes in the market price of stocks. Meanwhile, the buyer/seller has the advantage of knowing with certainty the price at which his or her order will be executed. In an auction system, the market maker holds no significant inventories and accepts no stocks except in so far as s/he matches them instantly with a buyer. The counterparties to the transaction, however, cannot know in advance the exact price at which their order will be carried out. The risk to the latter is moderated by the setting of price limits

---

[10] For a detailed discussion of the reforms in French and German securities markets after 1986 see Story (1995), especially pp. 24–53.

and by the fact that auction markets, just like dealer markets, display continuous and detailed trading information on screen which enables potential buyers and sellers to see the price at which the last trade was carried out and any trend that might be developing.

It is difficult with such a short period for comparison to draw general conclusions about the quality of market provided by the London and European models since only Paris and London have any established record. The papers by Pagano and Roell (1990, 1992) attempt some preliminary suggestions. An interesting finding is that for average size deals in the 16 stocks traded on both SEAQ (in London) and CAC (in Paris), the *fourchette*, effectively the bid–ask spread, in Paris, is smaller than the *touch*, in London. Even more interesting was their observation that the touch on these stocks in London doubled when the CAC was closed. However, the average size of deal in Paris was smaller than in London and there were very few large trades. Thus, in terms of our indicators above, there is some evidence that transaction costs are lower on deals in Paris but also that the market lacks depth and visibility when compared with London. The lower transaction costs observed in continental auction systems explain the decision to adopt trading of FTSE-100 shares in London from October 1997.

With motives similar to those which drove the Paris reforms, the German government announced far-reaching plans for the equities market in 1992. The proposals to create *Finanzplatz Deutschland* (the 'German financial marketplace') include: bringing the country's eight stock exchanges together into one major market in Frankfurt;[11] abolishing the stock exchange turnover tax; creating a centralized regulatory body; encouraging the creation of a futures and options exchange; the introduction of money market mutual funds; and the computerization of stock trading. We noted at the beginning of this chapter that personal ownership of shares is limited in Germany. This is just one aspect of the lack of an 'equity culture'. The stock market plays a very small role in the financing of firms. There are fewer than 900 listed companies and liquidity is very limited in all but the few largest firms. Bank finance plays a much more important role and even where firms are listed, the shares are very often held by a few institutions, mainly banks themselves. Even insurance companies, large holders of equities in the UK and USA, hold over 80 per cent of their portfolios in government bonds.

The last few years have seen the merging and consolidation of a number of major stock exchanges. The London Stock Exchange, one of the largest, was frequently the object of takeover speculation in the early 2000s with New York's NASDAQ the favoured bidder. In October 2007, the London Stock Exchange announced that it was merging with the Italian exchanges – the *Borsa Italiano*. More significant was the merger between Euronext (already a consortium of Paris, Amsterdam and Portuguese exchanges) and the New York Stock Exchange in March 2007.

For firms, the listing of their shares on an organized stock exchange carries many advantages. Principal among these is that very large amounts of capital can be raised at a reasonable cost because the ownership and risk is widely dispersed among investors who can relinquish their commitment quickly and easily. However, 'listing' invariably carries considerable costs and obligations. Costs come in the form of payments to the exchange itself and also in the form of 'disclosure requirements'. Firms with a stock exchange listing are required to make certain categories of financial information continuously available to the general public and to publicize any major changes that occur to their circumstances. These obligations are intended to reduce the information advantage which firms have over their shareholders and thus provide some degree of protection for the latter. Because of these costs, small and medium-sized firms are often deterred from applying for a listing on a major stock exchange and this has led most countries to develop second- (or even third-) tier markets, with lower charges and less demanding obligations. For example, in the UK until the mid-1990s small firms were able to join the Unlisted Securities Market (USM) which opened in 1980. The desire by the European Union to standardize stock exchange listing requirements (see *Bank of England Quarterly Bulletin*, May 1990) led to the conditions for USM membership becoming so similar to those of the main markets that the two were merged in 1996. The requirement for a

---

[11] Germany is a federal state and the tendency for each of the *Länder* to have its own financial institutions and regulators is a legacy of the decentralization of the financial system forced upon Germany by the Allies in the period of post-war reconstruction (Marsh, 1992). In practice, there are three major securities markets: Frankfurt, Düsseldorf and Munich. The figures from all eight exchanges are aggregated in the Deutsche Börse figures in Table 17.1.

market with low entry and compliance costs remained, however, and this has been provided since 1996 by AIM, the alternative investment market.

17.5.3 Reading the *Financial Times*

Up-to-date information on activity in equity markets is carried in all serious newspapers that report business news. It is also available increasingly these days on television screen text services such as Ceefax or Teletext. For professional investors, very detailed and sophisticated 'real-time' data is available by telecommunication from commercial suppliers. One of the most comprehensive services of information readily available to the general public, however, is provided by the *Financial Times*, in its UK and European and US editions.

Data on share prices, changes, yields and P/E ratios is listed on two pages headed 'London Share Service'. Shares are grouped according to the principal activity of their firms. Look again at Box 17.5 which contains data for the media sector. The purpose of the groupings is, obviously, to make it easy for investors to find the company in which they are interested (companies are listed alphabetically within each sector) but it also has the important effect of making it easier for investors to compare data across similar types of firm. When we discussed P/E ratios (and the data in Box 17.5), recall, we stressed how important it is to compare like with like. As we would expect, the data for individual shares includes the price at the previous day's close, the change during the day, the highest and lowest price within the last 52 weeks, the dividend yield (before tax) and the P/E ratio.

Commentary on equity price behaviour is spread over three pages. The first of these, 'Markets', is the last page of the 'Companies and Markets' section and summarizes events in the major stock markets around the world. The last two inside pages, 'Markets & Investing' focus more on the recent behaviour of selected shares/companies. The two pages headed 'London Share Service' carry the data for companies listed on the London Stock Exchange and AIM as well as a number of tables relating to stock price indices.

Because there are so many different shares listed, the only manageable way to describe and to measure the behaviour of the market as a whole, and especially over a long period of time, is to use an index number.

One obvious and important use for such an index is to tell us the rate of return on a broad portfolio of stocks which could be used to approximate K_m, the whole market return, in the capital asset pricing model. The *Financial Times* publishes nine broad-based share price indices, which it has developed with the help of the Faculty and Institute of Actuaries. (We saw in the last chapter that the latter decide on the design and the components of the index, while the *FT* collects the data and calculates the index value.) The most commonly quoted index is probably the *Financial Times Stock Exchange 100* (FTSE-100 or 'Footsie' for short). This is a 'real-time' index, meaning that it reflects changes in the price of its constituents as they actually happen. It was introduced in February 1984 (the others began in 1962) when a new futures contract based on UK equity prices was launched and needed a continuous record of market price movements. The components of the index are the 100 largest UK firms judged by their market capitalization. It is thus a weighted average, unlike the US 'Dow Industrial Average' which is, as its name implies, simply the average of (the largest) 30 industrial firms. Membership changes, obviously, as firms merge, or get taken over, and as relative market values change. There is a certain amount of status involved in membership of the FTSE-100 but more important from a practical point of view is that there appears to be a 'membership effect'. When a firm joins the index, its share price tends to rise (and to fall, when it leaves). This is because the performance of many investment funds is judged against the index and therefore fund managers feel it appropriate to hold a significant stake in each of the index's constituents in their fund. The other FTSE indices are larger. The *FTSE All-Share* contains over 800 stocks. Other indices contain 250 or 350 shares or include only small companies (the *FTSE SmallCap*). Being much larger, movements in these indices are calculated less frequently, usually on a daily basis. The statistical calculation of these indices is explained by the *Financial Times* itself (Greenhorn, 1985) and the details of the constituent firms (in each index) and their weighting within the index are published quarterly in the *FT*. The 'London Stock Exchange' page also has a table containing index data for 37 industrial groups. For every index, the data provided includes the current value of the index, the previous day's change, and the index value for each of the three previous days and a year ago. In addition, the figures include the average gross dividend yield for the stocks in the index as well as 'net cover' (the number of times by which earnings exceed dividend payments)[12] and the P/E ratio. We are reminded again of the importance and frequency of relative valuation since these are intended to be useful benchmarks against which to judge the characteristics of individual shares. Many of these indices are also listed on the 'London Share Service' pages.

As with London, other markets also express general movements in asset prices by the use of indices. The French CAC (*Cotation Assistée en Continu*) index began in 1987 when the Paris Bourse reforms began. Like the FTSE-100 it is recalculated continuously while the market is open. It is also a weighted average index, the weights being derived from the comparative capitalization of the 40 shares included in it. As with most share price indices, the *n* shares which comprise the index are the *n* largest shares (by capitalization) in the market, but the CAC-40 takes the largest firms from each sector, rather than the 40 largest in the market as a whole.

The German *DAX* (*Deutscher Aktienindex*) is another index which calculates a total return by adding dividend payments to the change in capital value of a weighted average of the top 30 shares. Germany has a number of regional markets which, though smaller than Frankfurt, are more significant than regional exchanges in France or the UK. The DAX incorporates price changes from all the country's exchanges. It is a real-time index, unlike the *Commerzbank* index which is calculated only once a day and is based upon a weighted average of the top 60 shares quoted on the Düsseldorf exchange.

17.6 Summary

'Equities' are ordinary company shares. Their holders are the legal owners of the firm and their shares bring them benefits in the form of dividend payments, which are a claim on the firm's profits, and capital appreciation, as the firm's earnings increase. The 'fundamental' analysis of shares involves the discounting of future dividend earnings though analysts sometimes use P/E ratios and asset values. 'Technical' analysis, by contrast, studies the past behaviour of share prices. Like all prices, the prices of shares change when there is a shift in demand, or supply, or both. With shares, such shifts occur when investors change their view of the appropriate value for the share, whether this view comes from dividend discounting, asset values or past price movements. There are many events that cause investors' valuations to change. More importantly, we need to remember that the price of any financial asset will change merely because investors expect an event to happen, whether it actually does so or not.

Once issued, shares are traded in secondary markets where a variety of trading arrangements are possible. Since 'Big Bang' the London Stock Exchange has been organized as a continuous dealer market although major shares are now traded on a continuous auction basis. Continental equity markets have been caught up in the reform trend in order to compete with London and have acquired similar characteristics. However, European markets have generally opted for continuous auction rather than continuous dealer trading structures.

Key concepts in this chapter

Articles of association	Equities
Asset values	Fundamental analysis
Authorized shares	Gordon growth model
Common stock	Liquidity of the market
Constant growth model	Memorandum
Depth of the market	One-period model
Dividend	Ordinary shares
Dividend irrelevance hypothesis	Payout ratio
Dividend models	Placing

---

[12] For example, 'net cover' of 2 means that earnings were twice the level of dividends. Thus, taking the reciprocal of net cover is one way of estimating the payout ratio (see Section 17.3.1).

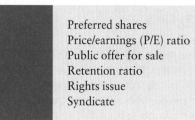

Preferred shares   Technical analysis
Price/earnings (P/E) ratio   Three-period model
Public offer for sale   Transaction costs
Retention ratio   Two-period model
Rights issue   Underwrite
Syndicate   Visibility

Questions and problems

1 Wilton Wayfarers plc is a chain of travel agents whose earnings have grown steadily at 12 per cent p.a. for several years and are expected to do so for the foreseeable future. Calculate the equilibrium price for their shares if the three-month treasury bill rate is 6 per cent, the shares have a β-coefficient of 1.2 and the return on the FTSE-100 portfolio is currently 18 per cent.

2 What new price would you predict for these shares if the Bank of England raised the treasury bill rate to 7 per cent, *ceteris paribus*?

3 What is rate of return to shareholders in (2) above?

4 Why is this rate of return also the firm's cost of capital?

5 Explain what is meant by the *retention ratio*.

6 Explain why an increase in the retention ratio may have no effect on the value of a firm's shares. Specify carefully the assumptions that you need to make for this to be true and work a numerical example to illustrate it.

7 Explain what is meant by a P/E ratio and discuss how it may be used to value the shares of a firm.

8 In Box 17.5, *Euromoney* (a financial magazine) has a P/E ratio of 13.7, while *Daily Mail* (a daily newspaper) has a P/E ratio of 24.5. Does this mean that *Daily Mail* is overpriced? Explain your answer.

9 After careful consideration, Wilton Wayfarers plc decides to drop African adventure holidays from its range of package tours since political uncertainties have made earnings from these tours extremely variable. It decides to put more effort into marketing European weekend breaks, for which there has always been a steady demand. Use the capital asset pricing model to analyse the likely effect upon the required rate of return on Wilton's shares and use a supply and demand diagram to show how this change will affect the share's price.

10 Explain what is meant by a 'quote-driven continuous market' for securities. What advantages does it have over other types of trading arrangement?

Further reading

D Blake, *Financial Market Analysis* (London: McGraw-Hill, 2000) Ch. 6
K Boakes, *Reading and Understanding the Financial Times* (London: Financial Times Prentice Hall, 2008), Topic 6

Z Bodie, A Kane and A Marcus, *Essentials of Investment* (New York: McGraw-Hill, 4e, 2001) Ch. 13
M Brett, *How to Read the Financial Pages* (London: Random House, 5e, 2000) Chs 6–9

M Buckle and J Thompson, *The UK Financial System* (Manchester: Manchester University Press, 1995) Ch. 8

D Cobham, 'The equity market', in D Cobham (ed.) *Markets and Dealers: The Economics of the London Financial Markets* (London: Longman, 1992)

D Cobham and S Bonetti, 'Financial markets and the City of London', in D Cobham (ed.) *Markets and Dealers* (London: Longman, 1992)

E J Elton and M J Gruber, *Modern Portfolio Theory and Investment Analysis* (Chichester: John Wiley, 5e, 1995) Chs 18, 19

Euromoney (monthly) and *Euromoney Country Surveys* (annual) (London: Euromoney Publications)

Federation of European Stock Exchanges 'Statistics and Market Research' (www.fese.be)

J K Galbraith, *The Great Crash, 1929* (London: Penguin, 1961)

P M Garber, 'Famous first bubbles', *Journal of Economic Perspectives*, 4(2), 1990, 35–54

M J Gordon, *The Investment, Financing and Valuation of the Corporation* (Irwin: Homewood Ill, 1962)

A Greenhorn, *A Guide to Financial Times Statistics* (London: FT Business Information, 1985)

JM Keynes, *General Theory of Employment, Interest and Money* (London: Macmillan, 1936)

M Livingston, *Money and Financial Markets* (Oxford: Blackwell, 3e, 1996) Ch. 19

London Stock Exchange, (www.londonstockexchange.com) 'About the Exchange'/

D Marsh, *The Bundesbank* (London: Heinemann, 1992) Ch. 6

M H Miller and F Modigliani, 'Dividend policy, growth and the valuation of shares', *Journal of Business*, 1961, 163–96

OECD, *Financial Market Trends* (triannual) (OECD: Paris)

OECD, *Financial Statistics*, part 1, § 1 and 2 (monthly) (OECD: Paris)

M Pagano and A Roell, 'Trading systems in European stock exchanges: Current performance and policy options', *Economic Policy*, 10, 1990, 65–115

M Pagano and A Roell, 'Auction and dealership markets: What is the difference?', *European Economic Review*, 1992

J Rutterford and M Davsion, *An Introduction to Stock Exchange Investment* (London: Palgrave, 3e, 2007)

T Schoen, *The French Stock Exchange* (Chichester: Wiley, 1995)

B M Smith, *A History of the Global Stock Market: From Ancient Rome to Silicon Valley* (Chicago: Chicago University Press, 2004)

J Story, 'The politics and markets of German financial services', *Institute for German Studies Discussion Paper*, No. IGS95/3 (Birmingham: University of Birmingham, 1995)

R Vaitilingam, *The Financial Times Guide to Using the Financial Pages* (London: Pearson Education, 4e, 2001)

Websites

www.deutsche-boerse.com
www.euronext.com
www.fese.be
www.howstsuffworks.com
www.investopedia.com
www.londonstockexchange.com
www.moneyextra.com

Chapter 18 Foreign exchange markets

What you will learn in this chapter:

■ Reasons for the growth of the foreign exchange market

■ How to read the *Financial Times* currency tables

■ The meaning of effective interest rates and real interest rates

■ The relationship between spot and forward rates of exchange

■ The roles played by arbitrageurs and speculators

■ The problems associated with forecasting rates of exchange

■ The difficulties in interpreting news in foreign exchange markets

18.1 Introduction

The foreign exchange (forex) market allows payments to be made across national boundaries by establishing the prices of national currencies in terms of other currencies. The product (foreign exchange) consists of national currencies, each of which has an exchange rate with every other currency. Exchange rates should, in theory, be determined in markets by the forces of demand and supply, although in practice the exchange of the currencies of most developing countries is so heavily controlled by governments that the official rates of exchange have little to do with market forces.

Market participants can be split into five groups:

- *End users* of foreign exchange: firms, individuals and governments that need foreign currency in order to acquire goods and services from abroad or to move capital as part of their regular economic activities.

- *Market-makers*: large international banks which hold stocks of currencies to allow the market to operate continuously and which make their profits through the spread between buying and selling rates of exchange.

- *Speculators*: banks, firms and individuals that attempt to profit from outguessing the market.

- *Arbitrageurs*: banks that make profits from buying in one market at the same time as selling in another, taking advantage of small inconsistencies which develop between markets.

- *Central banks* which, on behalf of their governments, enter the market to attempt to influence the international value of their currency – perhaps to protect a fixed rate of exchange, or to manage to varying degrees an allegedly market-determined rate.

It is clear from this list that it is possible to play multiple roles in the market. For instance, international banks may act in up to four capacities, while firms and governments may be end users on occasions, speculators on others.

In Section 11.4 we met the notion that the price of an asset can be explained by the rational behaviour of end users of the asset trying consistently to maximize the benefit from some real economic activity. In such a case, the price may be said to be determined by its underlying **fundamentals** which we take to be the basic influences on the supply of and demand for

currencies by end users. We need then to identify the fundamentals of exchange rates and to consider how changes in them should be expected to influence exchange rates. Economics also generally teaches that market exchange rate changes must reflect a movement away from a previously existing equilibrium position towards a new equilibrium. We shall see, however, that exchange rates fluctuate much more than economic theories suggest is likely. Thus, we need both to look at important ideas in attempted explanation of long-term movements in exchange rates such as interest rate parity and purchasing power parity and to consider possible reasons for the very rapid day-to-day fluctuations that we see in the market.

18.1.1 The growth in the size and complexity of the market

The increasing interdependence of countries in recent years has led to a dramatic growth in the proportion of financial transactions with an international aspect. As exports and imports have grown as a percentage of the GDP of all developed countries, so too has the proportion of firms earning foreign exchange and/or requiring foreign currencies to purchase raw materials or intermediate goods. Because exchange rates may change rapidly, such firms are exposed to **foreign exchange risk** – the risk that losses may arise from rises or falls in the value of a currency in terms of the domestic currency. Firms have sought to protect themselves against this risk and to seek profits through speculation. The desire to protect against risk has led to the development of markets designed to provide insurance (forward, futures and options markets) and the exploitation of techniques such as interest rate and currency *swaps* which involve the simultaneous exchange of spot and forward contracts. As Table 18.1 overleaf shows, the market grew rapidly up until 1998, went into reverse between 1998 and 2001 but then resumed its rapid rise.

The table shows that the estimated average daily turnover at April 2007 exchange rates grew by 30.7 per cent between 1992 and 1995 and 43.5 per cent between 1995 and 1998 but then fell back by 13.9 per cent between 1998 and 2001. However, daily turnover then grew by 37.3 per cent between 2001 and 2004 and by 65 per cent in the most recent three years. Thus, at April 2007 exchange rates, turnover has grown by approximately 9 per cent per annum over the past fifteen years. A significant factor in the

Table 18.1 Global foreign exchange market turnover[1]
Daily averages in April (US$bn)

	1989	1992	1995	1998	2001	2004	2007
Spot transactions	317	394	494	568	386	621	1,005
Outright forwards	27	58	97	128	130	208	362
Foreign exchange swaps	190	324	546	734	656	944	1,714
Estimated gaps in reporting	56	43	53	61	28	107	129
Total 'traditional' turnover	590	820	1,190	1,490	1,200	1,880	3,210
Turnover at April 2007 exchange rates[2]	*n/a*	*880*	*1,150*	*1,650*	*1,420*	*1,950*	*3,210*

[1] Adjusted for local and cross-border double-counting.   [2] Non-US dollar legs of foreign currency transactions were converted from current US dollar amounts into original currency amounts at average exchange rates for April of each survey year and then reconverted into US dollar amounts at average April 2007 exchange rates.

Source: BIS (2007) *Triennial Central Bank Survey. Foreign Exchange and Derivatives Market Activity in 2007*, table 1, p. 5, http://www.bis.org/publ/rpfx07.pdf.

decline in turnover was the introduction of the euro at the beginning of 1999, eliminating trading among the previously separate euro area currencies. The reduction in foreign exchange transactions within the euro area following the advent of the euro is shown in Table 18.3. In April 1998, euro area currencies were involved in 52.5 per cent of all foreign exchange transactions. By April 2001, this had fallen to 37.6 per cent.

Table 18.1 also shows the steady increase in the value of outright forwards and foreign exchange swaps transactions relative to spot transactions. In 1989, spot transactions made up 53.7 per cent of the average daily turnover in the market but by 2007 they accounted for only 31.3 per cent. As is shown in Table 18.2, the London market remains clearly the biggest market and over half of all turnover occurs on

Table 18.2 Geographical distribution of foreign exchange market turnover[1]
Daily averages in April in percentages

Country	1989	1995	2001	2004	2007	Country	1989	1995	2001	2004	2007
UK	25.6	29.5	31.2	31.3	34.1	Sweden	1.8	1.3	1.5	1.3	1.1
USA	16.0	15.5	15.7	19.2	16.6	Luxembourg	n/a	1.2	0.8	0.6	1.1
Switzerland	7.8	5.5	4.4	3.3	6.1	Italy	1.4	1.5	1.0	0.8	0.9
Japan	15.5	10.3	9.1	8.3	6.0	India	n/a	n/a	0.2	0.3	0.9
Singapore	7.7	6.7	6.2	5.2	5.8	Korea	n/a	n/a	0.6	0.8	0.8
Hong Kong	6.8	5.7	4.1	4.2	4.4	Norway	0.6	0.5	0.8	0.6	0.8
Australia	4.0	2.5	3.2	3.4	4.2	Netherlands	1.8	1.7	1.9	2.0	0.6
France	3.2	3.7	3.0	2.7	3.0	Spain	0.6	1.1	0.5	0.6	0.4
Germany	n/a	4.8	5.5	4.9	2.5	Taiwan	n/a	n/a	0.3	0.3	0.4
Denmark	1.8	2.0	1.4	1.7	2.2	Austria	n/a	0.8	0.5	0.6	0.4
Canada	2.1	1.9	2.6	2.2	1.5	Mexico	n/a	n/a	0.5	0.6	0.4
Russia	n/a	n/a	0.6	1.2	1.3	South Africa	n/a	0.3	0.6	0.4	0.4
Belgium	1.4	1.8	0.6	0.8	1.2	Other	1.2	1.3	1.5	2.0	2.9

[1] Adjusted for local double-counting ('net-gross'). Estimated coverage of the foreign exchange market ranged between 90 and 100 per cent in most countries.

Source: Adapted from BIS (2001) *Triennial Central Bank Survey. Foreign Exchange and Derivatives Market Activity in 2001*, table B.7; BIS (2007) *Triennial Central Bank Survey. Foreign Exchange and Derivatives Market Activity in 2007*, table 5, p. 9, http://www.bis.org/publ/rpfx07.pdf.

the London and New York markets. Among the smaller markets, there are some interesting trends, for example the growth of foreign exchange markets (admittedly from a low level) in Russia and India, reflecting the increased strength of their economies.

Although people associate the demand for foreign exchange with the needs of international trade, these have accounted for only a small proportion of the large increase in foreign exchange transactions over the past twenty years. A much higher proportion derived from the great increase in international capital mobility. Both large multinational firms and governments have sought to tap international capital

markets to widen their access to funds and/or to lower the costs of borrowing. To meet these demands, international banks have grown hugely in size, new markets have opened up and expanded and new instruments have been developed. As well as the growth shown here in spot and forward exchange rate transactions, there have been major developments in derivatives contracts on foreign exchange and interest rates. The complexity of the market is shown by the fact that some 90 per cent of all transactions were in the interbank market, rather than involving end users. As Table 18.3 shows, the importance of specific currencies also changes over time: trades involving

Table 18.3 Currency distribution of foreign exchange market turnover[1]
Percentage shares of average daily turnover in April

Currency	1992	1995	1998[2]	2001	2004	2007
US dollar	82.0	83.3	87.3	90.3	88.7	86.3
Euro	–	–	–	37.6	37.2	37.0
Deutsche mark	39.6	36.1	30.1	–	–	–
French franc	3.8	7.9	5.1	–	–	–
ECU and other EMS	11.8	15.7	17.3	–	–	–
Japanese Yen	23.4	24.1	20.2	22.7	20.3	16.5
Pound sterling	13.6	9.4	11.0	13.2	16.9	15.0
Swiss franc	8.4	7.3	7.1	6.1	6.1	6.8
Australian dollar	2.5	2.7	3.1	4.2	5.5	6.7
Canadian dollar	3.3	3.4	3.6	4.5	4.2	4.2
Swedish krona[2]	1.3	0.6	0.4	2.6	2.3	2.8
Hong Kong dollar[3]	1.1	0.9	1.3	2.3	1.9	2.8
Norwegian krone[3]	0.3	0.2	0.4	1.5	1.5	2.2
New Zealand dollar[3]	0.2	0.2	0.3	0.6	1.0	1.9
Mexican peso[3]	–	–	0.6	0.9	1.1	1.3
Singapore dollar[3]	0.3	0.3	1.2	1.1	1.0	1.2
Korean won[3]	–	–	0.2	0.8	1.2	1.1
South African rand[3]	0.3	0.2	0.5	1.0	0.8	0.9
Danish krone[3]	0.5	0.6	0.4	1.2	0.9	0.9
Russian rouble[3]	–	–	0.3	0.4	0.7	0.8
Polish zloty[3]	–	–	0.1	0.5	0.4	0.8
Indian rupee[3]	–	–	0.1	0.2	0.3	0.7
Chinese renminbi	–	–	0.0	0.0	0.1	0.5
Other currencies	7.6	7.1	9.5	8.1	7.9	9.9
All currencies	**200.0**	**200.0**	**200.0**	**200.0**	**200.0**	**200.0**

[1] Because two currencies are involved in each transaction, the sum of the percentage shares of individual currencies totals 200 per cent instead of 100 per cent. The figures relate to reported 'net-net' turnover, i.e. they are adjusted for both local and cross-border double-counting.   [2] From 1992 to 1998, the data cover local home currency trading only. Included as main currency from 2007.
[3] From 1992 to 1998, the data cover local home currency trading only.

Source: BIS (2007) *Triennial Central Bank Survey. Foreign Exchange and Derivatives Market Activity in 2007*, table 3, p. 7, http://www.bis.org/publ/rpfx07.pdf.

sterling fell from 15 per cent to 11 per cent between 1989 and 1998, only to rise again to 16.9 per cent in 2004 following the advent of the euro and then fall back to 15 per cent in 2007. The US dollar remains by far the most used currency, still being involved in over 85 per cent of daily turnover.

The combination of increasing international interdependence and uncertainty has given governments a greater interest than ever in movements in the international value of their currencies. The increased volatility of exchange rates, as the world has lurched between systems of fixed and floating exchange rates, with varying degrees of government intervention, has led to much attention being paid to attempts to forecast changes in them. To understand why exchange rates fluctuate as much as they do, we need to look closely at the nature of exchange rates and the functioning of foreign exchange markets.

18.2 Foreign exchange rates in the *Financial Times*

On its website and every Monday in the newspaper, the *Financial Times* publishes a table of world currencies which covers approximately 200 countries and some 150 different currencies,[1] ranging from the Afghanistan Afghani to the Zimbabwe dollar, including such well-known currencies as the tugrik, the colón and the dong. As well as each currency being used by residents within their own country, there is certain to be some international demand for it to allow the purchase by foreigners of domestic goods and services (every country has some foreign tourists, journalists and diplomats). The international demand for most currencies, however, is small. Foreign citizens and firms are unwilling to accept many currencies in settlement of debt and governments do not hold them in their foreign exchange reserves or use them to intervene in currency markets. This may be because of foreign exchange risk or *sovereign* or *political* risk – the fear that government regulations may prevent or restrict the conversion of a currency into other currencies.

Currencies that are not fully convertible are not part of international liquidity (the world money supply). Only the currencies of a few industrial countries are willingly held by other governments and are part of the international trading system. A small number of these currencies (key currencies) are freely used in transactions not involving the issuing countries and are used by central banks to intervene in foreign exchange markets (intervention currencies). Nonetheless, there remains the potential for a set of market-determined exchange rates for each currency. Even where such a market does not exist officially, there are black markets, expressing demand and supply conditions.

Such demand and supply conditions can be shown in a standard diagram. However, care needs to be taken in the definition of the rate and in the labelling of the axes of exchange rate diagrams. Because an exchange rate is a relative price, it can be expressed in either direction – if the pound goes up against the dollar, the dollar goes down against the pound. If we are interested in the exchange rate of the euro (€) it is logical to think of it as our medium of exchange, or numéraire, and to express the price of all other currencies in terms of the euro. This should lead us to ask:

> How much in euro does it cost to buy $1, ¥100 (Japanese yen), £1 (British pound or sterling) or SFr1 (Swiss francs) . . . ?[2]

The answer to this question takes the form:

> €0.707 = $1;   €0.610 = ¥100;
>
> €1.442 = £1;   €0.601 = SFr1.[3]

We are quoting the price of the foreign currency in each case (the domestic currency is being quoted against the foreign currency). This is known as the **direct quotation** (denoted by E_S) of the exchange rate and is the form used in most countries. Figure 18.1 shows the expression of market conditions in this form.

Note that on the vertical axis we have the price of the foreign currency ($) in terms of the home currency (€) – the price of US$1 in euro. On the horizontal axis, we have the quantity of the foreign currency ($) supplied and demanded. Note further that if there is an

---

[1] Although most countries have their own currencies for internal purposes, not all countries do so, because there are some monetary unions in which a single currency is used in a number of independent countries.

[2] For ease of expression, currencies whose basic unit has only a low value are quoted in terms of tens or hundreds. Thus, exchange rates are expressed in tens for the Swedish krona while the Japanese yen is expressed in terms of hundreds, for example, US$0.863 = ¥100 (Japanese yen).

[3] These are the exchange rates quoted in the *Financial Times* on 3 October 2007.

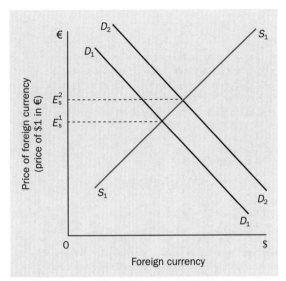

Figure 18.1 Supply and demand using direct quotations

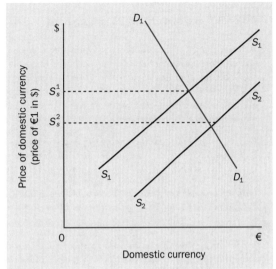

Figure 18.2 Supply and demand using indirect quotations

increase in demand for dollars (the demand curve shifts up from D_1D_1 to D_2D_2), the exchange rate rises (from E_S^1 to E_S^2). That is, it now costs more euro to buy $1 than before – the value of the euro has fallen. Thus, an increase in the exchange rate of a currency expressed in direct quotation indicates that the value of the currency has fallen.

For British students in particular, there is a complication because the UK uses the **indirect quotation** (denoted by S_S) of the exchange rate in which the price of the domestic currency is expressed. This asks how much foreign currency exchanges for one unit of the domestic currency (foreign currencies are quoted against the domestic currency):

What is the price of €1 in US dollars, sterling, yen, Swiss francs . . . ?

The answers are in the form:

€1 = $1.4154;   €1 = £0.6934

€1 = ¥164.018;   €1 = SFr1.6635

This method conflicts with the normal idea of a price but it does have one advantage. The relevant diagram has the price of the domestic currency (euro) in foreign currency (US dollars) on the vertical axis and the quantity of the domestic currency demanded and supplied on the horizontal axis. Now, an increase in demand for dollars will be shown as an increase in the supply of euro in order to acquire the extra dollars.

The supply curve for euro moves down (from S_1S_1 to S_2S_2) and the exchange rate falls (from S_S^1 to S_S^2) – meaning here that the value of the euro also falls (see Figure 18.2). Thus, if we were to keep to indirect quotation, a 'fall in the value of the domestic currency' would have the same meaning as a 'fall in the exchange rate of the domestic currency'.

Box 18.1 provides additional information on the expression of exchange rates and Exercise 18.1 gives you some practice in the manipulation of rates.

The *Financial Times* publishes a table of exchange rates each day. We reproduce as Table 18.4 on page 387 the currency rates table published on 3 October 2007. The table shows spot rates of exchange for a wide range of currencies against the dollar, the euro and the pound. For four currencies (the yen, sterling, the US dollar and the euro) forward rates of exchange are given for one month, three months and one year ahead. In these cases, the first row provides the spot rate of exchange.

You will note an oddity about the way in which two rates are quoted in Table 18.4. If you look at the dollar column you see that most rates are quoted 'against the dollar' – the amount of the foreign currency exchanged for $1: $1 = Won 913.850 = SKr6.5089 = SFr1.1753 = T$32.5770 = Bt34.2500 and so on. However, when you arrive at the exchange rate for the UK, you find £1 = $2.0411, the dollar quoted against the pound (the direct quotation of the

---

BOX 18.1 Bid and offer rates of exchange

Whether using direct or indirect quotation above, we have provided only one exchange rate in each case. This is, however, the mid-point between two exchange rates: the *bid rate* – the rate at which market makers are prepared to buy – and the *offer rate* – the rate at which they are prepared to sell. If we are using direct quotation, we are talking in terms of the buying and selling of the foreign currency and bid rates will be below offer rates in order to provide market makers with a profit. With indirect quotation, market makers are quoting the price of the home currency and bid rates will be above offer rates. For example:

Direct quotation of sterling (sterling against the euro and the dollar)
Bid rate: £0.6969 = €1   Offer rate: £0.6945 = €1   Mid-point: £0.6957 = €1
Bid rate: £0.4896 = $1   Offer rate: £0.4906 = $1   Mid-point: £0.4901 = $1

Indirect quotation of sterling (the euro and the dollar against sterling)
Bid rate: £1 = €1.4443   Offer rate: £1 = €1.4495   Mid-point: £1 = €1.4469
Bid rate: £1 = $2.0395   Offer rate: £1 = $2.0484   Mid-point: £1 = $2.0440

As well as providing a profit for market-makers, the difference between the two rates (the *bid–offer* or *bid–ask* spread) covers their costs and reflects the degree of risk involved in holding the foreign currency in question. For example, there are many transactions every day between the euro and the US dollar (the market is very deep) and so there is little chance of sudden, large movements in the exchange rate. Consequently, the bid–offer spread is likely to be only a very small percentage. For less commonly traded currencies such as the New Zealand dollar, bid–offer spreads are likely to be larger. Spreads are often quoted in terms of *points* or *pips*, where a point is .0001 and a pip is .00001. Hence, the bid–offer spread where the rates are £0.6969 − £0.6945 = €1 is 24 points or 240 pips.

---

dollar). The indirect quotation, $1 = £0.4899, is provided in brackets). We then return to the indirect quotation of the dollar: $1 = Peso 22.9250 = Bolivar 2147.30 = Dong 16085.00. However, for the euro, we are back to the direct quotation of the dollar, €1 = $1.4154 with again the indirect quotation

($1 = €0.7065) provided in brackets. The *Financial Times* tells you this in the explanatory notes at the bottom of the table: 'The closing mid-point rates for the euro and £ against the $ are shown in brackets. The other figures in the dollar column of both the euro and sterling rows are in the reciprocal form in line with market convention.' That is, the conventions of the London foreign exchange market.

For each exchange rate, we are given the *closing mid*, the mid-point between bid and offer rates of exchange at the close of the London exchange on the previous trading day. Thus we see that the mid-point between bid and offer rates for the South Korean won at the close of the London market on 2 October 2007 were:

$1 = Won 913.850   €1 = Won 1293.42
£1 = Won 1865.21

We are also given the *day's change*, the amount that the mid-point changed during the previous day's trading. If we stay with the exchange rate of the South Korean currency, we see that the rate of the won against the US dollar changed by +0.1000 during trading on 2 October. Thus, the rate at the close on 1 October must have been (913.850 − 0.10) = 913.750. Because exchange rates are, for the most part, being quoted indirectly, a plus sign here will indicate that a

---

Exercise 18.1

You are given the following bid and offer rates for indirect quotations of the dollar against the euro, sterling and the yen. See Box 18.1 for information on bid and offer rates.

   $1 = €0.7060–0.7070
   $1 = £0.4894–0.4904
   $1 = ¥115.4–116.4

1 Calculate the mid-points and the direct quotation of each of these rates.

2 Calculate the exchange cross rates between:
   (a) the euro and the pound sterling;
   (b) the pound sterling and the yen;
   (c) the euro and the yen.

Table 18.4 Currency rates in the *Financial Times*

Oct 2	Currency	DOLLAR		EURO		POUND	
		Closing mid	Day's change	Closing mid	Day's change	Closing mid	Day's change
Argentina	(Peso)	3.1463	−0.0025	4.4531	−0.0316	6.4217	−0.0116
Australia	(A$)	1.1323	+0.0090	1.6026	+0.0028	2.3111	+0.0162
Bahrain	(Dinar)	0.3769	−	0.5334	−0.0034	0.7693	−0.0008
Bolivia	(Boliviano)	7.6750	−	10.8628	−0.0684	15.6651	−0.0157
Brazil	(R$)	1.8291	+0.0039	2.5888	−0.0107	3.7333	+0.0042
Canada	(C$)	1.0003	+0.0071	1.4157	+0.0012	2.0416	+0.0124
Chile	(Peso)	507.925	−1.6250	718.892	−6.8349	1036.70	−4.3613
China	(Yuan)	7.5061	−	10.6238	−0.0668	15.3203	−0.0154
Colombia	(Peso)	2016.00	−4.1500	2853.35	−23.853	4114.76	−12.612
Costa Rica	(Colon)	518.560	+0.0450	733.944	−4.5511	1058.41	−0.9710
Czech Rep.	(Koruna)	19.4599	+0.1781	27.5425	+0.0805	39.7186	+0.3241
Denmark	(DKr)	5.2668	+0.0322	7.4543	−0.0010	10.7497	+0.0551
Egypt	(Egypt £)	5.5765	−0.0110	7.8927	−0.0653	11.3819	−0.0340
Estonia	(Kroon)	11.0549	+0.0691	15.6465	−	22.5635	+0.1185
Hong Kong	(HK$)	7.7640	−0.0057	10.9887	−0.0773	15.8467	−0.0276
Hungary	(Forint)	177.839	+1.6555	251.705	+0.7750	362.979	+3.0177
India	(Rs)	39.8500	−	56.4017	−0.3547	81.3359	−0.0817
Indonesia	(Rupiah)	9090.50	+5.5000	12866.20	−73.072	18554.20	−7.3989
Iran	(Rial)	9310.00	−	13176.90	−82.859	19002.20	−19.085
Israel	(Shk)	4.0090	+0.0218	5.6742	−0.0047	8.1826	+0.0362
Japan	(¥)	115.885	+0.2300	164.018	−0.7037	236.527	+0.2323
One Month		115.436	+0.0145	163.513	+0.0156	235.445	+0.0285
Three Month		114.640	+0.0130	162.516	+0.0155	233.521	+0.0143
One Year		111.608	−0.0340	158.481	+0.0058	225.546	−0.0233
Kenya	(Shilling)	66.8500	−0.1500	94.6162	−0.8086	136.444	−0.4435
Kuwait	(Dinar)	0.2795	−0.0001	0.3955	−0.0026	0.5704	−0.0008
Malaysia	(M$)	3.4055	+0.0105	4.8200	−0.0154	6.9508	+0.0145
Mexico	(New Peso)	10.9193	−0.0041	15.4547	−0.1030	22.2869	−0.0307
New Zealand	(NZ$)	1.3168	+0.0091	1.8638	+0.0013	2.6878	+0.0160
Nigeria	(Naira)	125.150	−0.0500	177.131	−1.1850	255.437	−0.3587
Norway	(NKr)	5.4393	+0.0728	7.6985	+0.0553	11.1019	+0.1377
Pakistan	(Rupee)	60.7450	+0.0750	85.9754	−0.4339	123.984	+0.0288
Peru	(New Sol)	3.0475	−0.0205	4.3133	−0.0563	6.2201	−0.0481
Philippines	(Peso)	44.9150	+0.0650	63.5705	−0.3072	91.6738	+0.0407
Poland	(Zloty)	2.6659	+0.0216	3.7732	+0.0070	5.4412	+0.0387
Romania	(New Leu)	2.3742	+0.0233	3.3603	+0.0120	4.8458	+0.0427
Russia	(Rouble)	24.9522	+0.0853	35.3161	−0.1005	50.9287	+0.1230
Saudi Arabia	(SR)	3.7395	−	5.2927	−0.0333	7.6325	−0.0076
Singapore	(S$)	1.4848	+0.0077	2.1015	−0.0022	3.0305	+0.0128
Slovakia	(Koruna)	24.0884	+0.2829	34.0935	+0.1885	49.1656	+0.5285
South Africa	(R)	6.9230	+0.0419	9.7985	−0.0020	14.1302	+0.0713
South Korea	(Won)	913.850	+0.1000	1293.42	−7.9908	1865.21	−1.6690
Sweden	(SKr)	6.5089	+0.0633	9.2124	+0.0323	13.2850	+0.1160
Switzerland	(SFr)	1.1753	+0.0087	1.6635	+0.0019	2.3988	+0.0153
Taiwan	(T$)	32.5770	+0.0030	46.1079	−0.2857	66.4913	−0.0606

▶

Table 18.4 *continued*

Oct 2	Currency	DOLLAR		EURO		POUND	
		Closing mid	Day's change	Closing mid	Day's change	Closing mid	Day's change
Thailand	(Bt)	34.2500	−0.0050	48.4757	−0.3120	69.9060	−0.0804
Tunisia	(Dinar)	1.2541	+0.0057	1.7750	−0.0030	2.5597	+0.0092
Turkey	(Lira)	1.2131	+0.0115	1.7170	+0.0055	2.4760	+0.0210
U A E	(Dirham)	3.6723	+0.0005	5.1976	−0.0320	7.4953	−0.0065
UK (0.4899)*	(£)	2.0411	−0.0021	0.6935	−0.0037	–	–
One Month		2.0396	–	0.6945	–	–	–
Three Month		2.0370	−0.0001	0.6960	–	–	–
One Year		2.0209	+0.0004	0.7027	–	–	–
Uruguay	(Peso)	22.9250	−0.2000	32.4469	−0.4889	46.7911	−0.4556
USA	($)	–	–	1.4154	−0.0089	2.0411	−0.0021
One Month		–	–	1.4165	−0.0001	2.0396	–
Three Month		–	–	1.4176	−0.0002	2.0370	−0.0001
One Year		–	–	1.4200	+0.0002	2.0209	+0.0004
Venezuela†	(Bolivar)	2147.30	–	3039.18	−19.111	4382.75	−4.4018
Vietnam	(Dong)	16085.00	–	22765.90	−143.16	32830.30	−32.974
Euro (0.7065)*	(Euro)	1.4154	−0.0089	–	–	1.4421	+0.0076
One Month		1.4165	−0.0001	–	–	1.4399	–
Three Month		1.4176	−0.0002	–	–	1.4369	–
One Year		1.4200	+0.0002	–	–	1.4232	–
SDR	–	0.6430	+0.0017	0.9100	−0.0033	1.3123	+0.0021

Rates are derived from WM/Reuters at 4 pm (London time).   *The closing mid-point rates for the Euro and £ against the $ are shown in brackets. The other figures in the dollar column of both the Euro and Sterling rows are in the reciprocal form in line with market convention. †Official rates set by Venezuelan government is 2150 mid per USD; the WM/Reuters rate is for the valuation of capital assets. Some values are rounded by the F.T. The exchange rates printed in this table are also available on the internet at http://www.FT.com/marketsdata.
Euro Locking Rates: Austrian Schilling 13.7603, Belgium/Luxembourg Franc 40.3399, Finnish Markka 5.94573, French Franc 6.55957, German Mark 1.95583, Greek Drachma 340.75, Irish Punt 0.787564, Italian Lira 1936.27, Netherlands Guilder 2.20371, Portuguese Escudo 200.482, Slovenia Tolar 239.64, Spanish Peseta 166.386.
Source: *Financial Times*, 3 October 2007. Reprinted with permission.

currency has weakened against the currency in the relevant column (the dollar, the euro or the pound). You will see in Table 18.4 that the won weakened against the dollar on 2 October 2007, but strengthened against both the euro and the pound, implying that the dollar had strengthened against both the euro and the pound. This can be confirmed by looking down the table to the rates for the dollar, where you will find a negative sign in the columns showing the change in the value of the dollar against the euro and the pound −0.0089 and −0.0021, respectively).

When we look at the figures for the day's change we need to remember that, although the London foreign exchange market closes officially at 4 p.m., foreign exchange trading does not stop at that time. The market does not have a physical location. Trading takes place via computer link, telephone and telex among the major participants and thus can continue after 4 p.m. In addition, trading takes place on foreign exchange markets in other countries. The value of currencies goes on changing across the world in a number of major markets whose trading hours overlap. The three principal forex markets are London, New York and Tokyo but these markets do not cover the whole 24 hours and significant markets have developed elsewhere, notably in Los Angeles, Hong Kong, Singapore, Bahrain, Zurich, Frankfurt and Paris. When the London market opens the next day,

---

BOX 18.2 **Official versus tourist rates of exchange**

There are two obvious differences between official and tourist exchange rates. Firstly, tourist rates are worse for both buyers from and sellers to the foreign exchange office – there is a much bigger spread between bid and offer rates. Secondly, foreign exchange offices often make commission charges as well as benefiting from the wider bid/offer spread. How can one explain this?

Remember that the spread (+ commission charges) covers costs and provides profits for dealers. Tourist transactions are on average small and administrative costs are likely to be high relative to turnover. This is particularly likely since exchange offices are usually centrally located in high property rental areas and, for the convenience of customers, keep generous hours and hold a wide range of currencies, some of which may have quite large risk associated with them. Part of the large spreads and charges can, then, be explained by the costs of providing the service.

In addition, however, there is certainly an element of what the market will bear. The principal forex markets are characterized by large numbers of operators and a high degree of knowledge of available rates. The considerable degree of competition forces profit margins down to very low levels, although market-makers still do very well in absolute terms because of the size of the transactions.

There is a much lower level of consumer knowledge in tourist forex markets and a much smaller degree of competition among suppliers. By and large, tourists take the rate that they are offered, grumble about it though they may.

---

rates will have changed, perhaps considerably, from those quoted as the closing London rates in the *Financial Times*. It is also worth noting that the exchange rates quoted in the Currency Rates table of the *Financial Times* are rather different from the exchange rates available to tourists and other small users of foreign currencies. This issue is dealt with in Box 18.2.

18.2.1 Exchange cross rates

From the information provided in Table 18.4, it is possible to calculate through the dollar, the exchange rate between any pair of the non-dollar currencies listed. That is, it is possible to calculate the **exchange cross rate**, defined as an exchange rate calculated from two other rates, for instance the exchange rate of the euro against the Swedish krona (SKr) derived from the $/SKr and the $/€ rates. It is possible also to calculate cross rates using the euro or the pound but, in practice, all cross rates are calculated through the US dollar. Indeed, the cross exchange rate is sometimes defined as the exchange rate between two non-dollar currencies calculated through the US dollar. Let us calculate the cross rate of Swedish krona against the dollar. To do this, we need to multiply the exchange rate of the Swedish krona against the dollar (the indirect quotation of the dollar) by the exchange rate of the dollar against the euro (the direct quotation of the dollar):

SKr/$ × $/€

From Table 18.4 we have:

$1 = SKr6.5089   and   €1 = $1.4154

These, remember, are the mid-points between the bid and offer rates of exchange.

Multiplying the two rates gives us €1 = SKr9.2126. We can see that this is very slightly different from the exchange rate given for the Swedish krona against the euro in the table (9.2124). This is almost certainly simply because we are using mid-points and this often involves doing some rounding up of numbers.

MORE FROM THE WEB
Exchange rates on the *Financial Times* website

On the website of the *Financial Times* (www.ft.com), click on 'Markets data' and then 'Currencies' and under 'Currencies in print' you will find headings for the pound, dollar and euro spot and forward, the dollar against minor currencies and exchange cross rates. Above these is a currency converter allowing you to convert any one of 25 currencies against each of the others in either direct or indirect quotation. Finally, there is the World Currencies table giving you exchanges rates of the currencies used by over 200 countries against the dollar, the pound, the euro and the yen. You will find this under 'FT Guide to World Currencies'.

Exercise 18.2

Using the exchange rates provided in Table 18.4, calculate the following cross rates of exchange through the US dollar:

1   the Swedish krona (SKr) against the Swiss franc (SFr);

2   South Korean won against the Taiwanese dollar (T$);

3   the Venezuelan bolivar against the Bolivian boliviano.

However, from time to time exchange rates across currencies or in different markets do move out of line, providing opportunities for arbitrage.

As a second example, consider the cross rate between the Swedish krona and the Swiss franc. Assume this time that we want the rate for the Swiss franc against the Swedish krona. We can do this by: SFr/$ × $/SKr. Table 18.4 gives us SFr/$ = 1.1753. However, to obtain $/SKr, we need to take the reciprocal of the rate provided for the dollar in the table, i.e. 1/6.5089. This gives us: SKr1 = $0.1536 and our cross rate will be: SFr/SKr = 0.1805. That is, SKr1 = SFr0.1805. Exercise 18.2 gives some practice in calculating cross rates.

To make life easier, the *Financial Times* publishes on its website a table of exchange cross rates involving nine currencies. The exchange cross rates table for exchange rates at the close on 2 October 2007 is reproduced here as Table 18.5.

By taking a currency in the left-hand column and reading across the table, we find the exchange rates of eight other currencies against that currency (the indirect quotation). We have, for example:

€1 = C$1.416 = DKr7.454 = ¥164.0
   = NKr7.699 = SKr9.212 = SFr1.663
   = £0.693 = $1.415

To find the exchange rate of the currency against other currencies (the direct quotation), find the currency across the top of the table and read down. In this way, we find from the Swiss franc (SFr) column that:

SFr1.175 = C$1;   SFr2.232 = DKr10;
SFr1.663 = €1;   SFr1.014 = ¥100;
SFr2.161 = NKr10;   SFr1.806 = SKr10;
SFr2.399 = £1   and   SFr1.175 = $1.

The table also allows us to find quickly the amount of a currency quoted in direct quotations – by glancing at the diagonal running from left to right.

18.2.2 Exchange rate indices, real exchange rates and currency baskets

It may be useful to know what is happening to the value of a currency in general as well as to specific exchange rates. Since the pound might, for example, rise against the dollar but fall against the euro and the yen, exchange rate indices are prepared showing the average performance of a currency against a basket of other currencies. Because the pound's relationship

Table 18.5 Exchange cross rates

Oct 2		C$	DKr	Euro	¥	NKr	SKr	SFr	£	$
Canada	C$	1	5.265	0.706	115.9	5.438	6.507	1.175	0.490	1
Denmark	DKr	1.899	10	1.342	220.0	10.33	12.36	2.232	0.930	1.899
Euro	Euro	1.416	7.454	1	164.0	7.699	9.212	1.663	0.693	1.415
Japan	¥	0.863	4.545	0.610	100	4.694	5.617	1.014	0.423	0.863
Norway	NKr	1.839	9.683	1.299	213.1	10	11.97	2.161	0.901	1.838
Sweden	SKr	1.537	8.092	1.085	178.0	8.357	10	1.806	0.753	1.536
Switzerland	SFr	0.851	4.481	0.601	98.60	4.628	5.538	1	0.417	0.851
UK	£	2.042	10.75	1.442	236.5	11.10	13.28	2.399	1	2.041
USA	$	1	5.267	0.707	115.9	5.439	6.509	1.175	0.490	1

Danish kroner, Norwegian kroner and Swedish kronor per 10; yen per 100.

Source: *Financial Times*, 3 October 2007. Reprinted with permission.

with some currencies is much more important than with others from the point of view of the UK's over-all trading position, an exchange rate index (the **effective exchange rate**) shows changes in the value of a currency against a *weighted average* of the values of a number of other currencies. Weights are based on the importance in trade of different currencies, taking into account competition in third markets. Thus, an exchange rate index for the pound would give a much higher weight to the euro than, for instance, to the Canadian dollar.

The Bank of England prepares two effective exchange rates for sterling – the Bank of England index and the broad effective exchange rate index. Since 1999, it has published an effective exchange rate index for the euro area. It also prepares indices for currencies of other countries of some importance for UK exports and imports. These indices (with the exception of the broad sterling index) are reported in the Effective Index Rates table on the Market Data page of the *Financial Times*. We reproduce this table again from the *FT* of 3 October 2007 as Table 18.6. We see from the explanatory notes at the foot of this table that the base for the sterling rate was January 2005 whereas for all other currencies the base was the average of 1990 exchange rates.

MORE FROM THE WEB
Effective exchange rates

The Bank of England (www.bankofengland.co.uk) publishes on its website all of the effective exchange rate indices mentioned above but also sets out definitions and the current and past weights used in the calculation of the two sterling indices. On the home page, choose 'Statistics', then 'Interest and exchange rates' and from the list of tables provided choose 'Effective exchange rates' and proceed from there. The tables of past and current weights allow you to see the changes that have taken place in the UK's trade pattern in the last quarter of a century.

Table 18.6 Effective exchange index rates

	Oct 2	Oct 1	Mth ago	FT
Australia	99.9	100.4	95.1	
Canada	113.8	114.6	108.7	
Denmark	108.4	108.5	108.1	
Japan	118.4	118.3	120.3	
New Zealand	113.4	113.8	106.8	
Norway	107.6	108.4	104.0	
Sweden	82.7	83.2	80.5	
Switzerland	107.3	107.6	107.4	
UK	102.8	102.4	104.4	
USA	86.2	85.8	88.8	
Euro	98.36	98.68	96.14	

New Sterling ERI base Jan 2005 = 100. Other indices base average 1990 = 100. Index rebased 1/2/95. For further information about ERIs see www.bankofengland.co.uk.

Source: *Financial Times*, 3 October 2007. Reprinted with permission.

In Table 18.6, we see that the effective exchange rate of sterling on 2 October 2007 was 102.8. Since the base of the index was January 2005, the index was telling us that the pound had strengthened slightly against the weighted average of currencies of some importance to the UK in trade over the previous two and three-quarter years. The weights for the calculation of this index are changed each year, taking into account changes in the UK's pattern of trade. The weights in use in October 2007 included 26 countries, 11 of which were euro area countries.[4] Countries are included if their share of either UK imports or UK exports was 1 per cent or higher in the most recent three-year period. The weights attached to each currency reflect then direct exports to and imports from the countries in the index as well as competition with UK exports in third markets. In October 2007, the euro area countries had a combined weight in the index of 54 per cent, the principal contributors to which were Germany (13 per cent), France (8.9 per cent), Netherlands (6.6 per cent), Spain (5.8 per cent) and Ireland (5.7 per cent). Other countries in the index included the USA (16.5 per cent), China (5.6 per cent) and Japan (4.7 per cent).

The broad effective exchange rate index for sterling includes all currencies of countries whose share of UK imports or exports is 0.5 per cent of the total or higher. In 2007, this added another 11 currencies to the index.

The spot exchange rate we have dealt with so far is also known as the *nominal exchange rate*. A firm may become uncompetitive in foreign markets either

---

[4] Twelve countries, in fact, but Belgium and Luxembourg are treated as one country in trade statistics.

because the value of its domestic currency has risen (causing the prices of its products expressed in foreign currencies to rise) or because the prices in domestic currency of its products have risen. Consequently, to judge the competitive position of a country's firms against those of another country, we must adjust the nominal exchange rate to reflect the differences between the inflation rates in the two countries. This gives us the **real exchange rate** between two currencies. The formula for calculating the real exchange rate depends on whether the nominal rate is quoted in indirect or direct terms. Assume an exchange rate of £1 = $2.0393 (the indirect quotation of the pound sterling). Assume further that the UK's expected inflation rate over the next year is 2 per cent per annum as against 4 per cent for the USA. We might then calculate the real exchange rate of sterling as:

$$S_R = S_S + (\pi_D^e - \pi_F^e)S_S \qquad (18.1)$$

where S_R and S_S are respectively the real and nominal exchange rates, both in indirect quotation, and π_D^e and π_F^e are the domestic (UK) and foreign (US) expected inflation rates respectively. Thus, the real exchange rate of sterling is:

£1 = $2.0393 + (1.02 − 1.04)2.0393 = $1.9985

The real exchange rate being below the nominal exchange rate indicates that British goods will in the future be more competitive (because of the lower expected inflation rate) than is suggested by the nominal rate. Expressing the exchange rate in direct form, we have £0.4904 = $1 and the real exchange rate formula becomes:

$$E_R = E_S + (\pi_F^e - \pi_D^e)E_S \qquad (18.2)$$

where E_R and E_S are respectively the real and nominal exchange rates, both in direct quotation. This gives:

$1 = £0.4904 + (1.04 − 1.02)0.4904 = £0.5002

Now, the higher future competitiveness of UK goods is indicated by the real exchange rate being *above* the nominal rate.

We saw above that an effective exchange rate index of a currency is calculated against a weighted basket of other currencies. Currency baskets have other uses. Before the introduction of the euro in January 1999, the official currency of the European Union for the preparation of accounts and the calculation of payments was the *ecu* (*European currency unit*), a weighted average of the currencies of the members of the EU.

Another important currency basket still in use in the world economy is the Special Drawing Right (SDR). The SDR is a weighted average of four currencies (the US dollar, the yen, the euro and the pound sterling). Its value on 2 October 2007 is given at the bottom of Table 18.4 as $1 = SDR0.6430; €1 = SDR0.9100; £1 = SDR1.3123. All IMF accounting is in SDRs. They were initially intended to play a major role in the development of the international monetary system and were issued to countries in the 1970s and early 1980s to form part of the international reserves of IMF members. However, there have been no further issues and they now make up only a very small proportion of international reserves.

18.2.3 Spot and forward rates of exchange

As Table 18.1 showed, a little under one-third of foreign exchange transactions are **spot** transactions – purchases/sales of foreign currency for immediate delivery, which means that the transaction must be completed within two working days of the contract being made (the date of the actual payment of funds is called the value date). **Forward** rates of exchange relate to contracts entered into now for promised delivery in the future. The most common periods for forward contracts are one month and three months, although much longer periods are possible especially for heavily traded currencies. We noted above that for four currencies, Table 18.4 gives forward foreign exchange rates for one month, three months and one year's time. We shall mainly be using Table 18.4 here. However, if you want forward rates for other currencies, you can go to the *Financial Times* website, www.ft.com, where separate tables are provided for the pound, dollar and euro. The pound spot forward table for

2 October 2007 is reproduced here as Table 18.7. This provides spot rates for around fifteen countries fewer than can be found in the currency rates table in the newspaper but provides one-month, three-months and one-year forward rates for all but one of the 35 currencies currently quoted in the table against the principal currency. It has another advantage in that as well as giving the forward exchange rates, it tells you the percentage *per annum* premium or discount (%PA) at which a currency is trading in the forward market. You will notice that Table 18.7 also gives you the Bank of England index for sterling and the other effective indices listed in Table 18.6.

Let us return for the moment to Table 18.4 and consider the *one month* details for the four currencies for which we have forward rate information there. The one-month rate for the euro against the pound is given as €1.4399, below the spot rate of €1.4421 – the exchange rate for pounds one month in advance was lower than the spot rate by €0.0022. In other words, against the pound the euro was trading at a **forward premium** of €0.0022. This can be expressed as an annual rate obtained by multiplying the one-month premium (€0.0022) by 12 to convert it into an annual figure, dividing by the spot exchange rate (€1.4421), and multiplying by 100 to produce a percentage rate:

$$\frac{(0.0022)12}{1.4421} \times 100 = 1.83\,\% \qquad (18.3)$$

MORE FROM THE WEB
Exchange rates

There are several websites that give both current exchange rates for many currencies and long historical runs of data. Two of the most useful are: http://www.oanda.com/ and http://fx.sauder.ubc.ca/ (University of British Columbia). Both are North American sites but both allow you to express dates in the European manner. You will find on the former site historical data under the heading 'Currency Tools'. It even includes the tugrik back to 1998. You can also prepare your own cross exchange rate table for up to 20 currencies. The site has many other facilities. The latter site has fewer facilities and deals with fewer currencies. It lacks, we're sorry to say, the tugrik but does include the leu, the tolar and the lempira.

We could also calculate the annual percentage rates for the euro three-months forward against the pound, remembering to multiply the premium by 4, rather than by 12. Using the figures in Table 18.4 produces a figure of 1.44 per cent whereas 12 months forward, the premium was 1.31 per cent.

The Japanese yen and the US dollar were also trading at a premium against the pound. The forward rates in Table 18.7 give a more mixed picture for the forward rates of the pound, with 23 currencies at a forward premium against the pound and 11 currencies at a *forward discount* against the pound. The countries whose currencies were at a forward discount were Hungary, Russia, Turkey, Argentina, Brazil, Mexico, Australia, Indonesia, New Zealand, the Philippines and South Africa. These all have negative signs in the % columns in Table 18.7. What might these countries have in common? To answer this question we need to look at the important idea of interest rate parity, which we do in Section 18.3. Before looking at this, however, you should try Exercise 18.3. It provides some practice in the calculation of forward premiums and discounts.

Exercise 18.3

You are given the following indirect quotations of the euro, sterling and the yen against the US dollar (that is, the value in each of the other currencies of $1):

	EURO	POUND	YEN
Spot	0.7065	0.4899	115.885
One month	0.7060	0.4903	115.436
Three month	0.7054	0.4909	114.640
One year	0.7042	0.4948	111.608

1 Which two of the three currencies quoted here were trading at a forward premium against the US dollar?

2 Calculate the annual percentage rate of each of the following:

  (a) the percentage per annum forward discount or premium of the yen against the dollar one month forward;

  (b) the percentage per annum forward discount or premium of the euro against the dollar three months forward;

  (c) the percentage per annum forward discount or premium of the pound against the dollar one year forward.

Table 18.7 Pound spot forward against the pound

Oct 2		Closing mid-point	Change on day	Bid/offer spread	Day's mid high	Day's mid low	One month Rate	One month %PA	Three months Rate	Three months %PA	One year Rate	One year %PA	Bank of Eng. Index
Europe													
Czech Rep.	(Koruna)	39.7186	0.3241	871–500	39.7670	39.3830	39.6224	2.9	39.4573	2.6	38.8703	2.1	–
Denmark	(DKr)	10.7497	0.0551	470–523	10.7537	10.6957	10.7340	1.7	10.7089	1.5	10.6133	1.3	108.4
Hungary	(Forint)	362.979	3.0177	716–242	363.242	359.430	363.470	–1.6	364.152	–1.3	367.355	–1.2	–
Norway	(NKr)	11.1019	0.1377	964–073	11.1148	10.9793	11.0964	0.6	11.0872	0.5	11.0719	0.3	107.6
Poland	(Zloty)	5.4412	0.0387	363–461	5.4461	5.3974	5.4355	1.3	5.4251	1.2	5.4034	0.7	–
Russia	(Rouble)	50.9287	0.1230	173–400	50.9710	50.7245	51.0387	–2.6	51.1829	–2.0	51.2974	–0.7	–
Slovakia	(Koruna)	49.1656	0.5285	291–021	49.2021	48.6340	49.0897	1.9	48.9202	2.0	48.3271	1.7	–
Sweden	(SKr)	13.2850	0.1160	797–902	13.3153	13.1759	13.2620	2.1	13.2254	1.8	13.0986	1.4	82.7
Switzerland	(SFr)	2.3988	0.0153	979–997	2.4024	2.3856	2.3913	3.7	2.3788	3.3	2.3279	3.0	107.3
Turkey	(Lira)	2.4760	0.0210	728–792	2.4792	2.4497	2.5018	–12.5	2.5449	–11.1	2.7288	–10.2	–
UK	(£)												102.8
Euro	(Euro)	1.4421	0.0076	418–424	1.4426	1.4345	1.4399	1.8	1.4369	1.4	1.4232	1.3	98.36
SDR	–	1.3123	0.0021										
Americas													
Argentina	(Peso)	6.4217	–0.0116	183–250	6.4337	6.4181	6.4437	–4.1	6.5122	–5.6	6.8264	–6.3	–
Brazil	(R$)	3.7333	0.0042	308–358	3.7360	3.6912	3.7442	–3.5	3.7621	–3.1	3.8702	–3.7	–
Canada	(C$)	2.0416	0.0124	408–423	2.0424	2.0259	2.0396	1.2	2.0354	1.2	2.0176	1.2	113.8
Mexico	(New Peso)	22.2869	–0.0307	790–947	22.3355	22.1950	22.3176	–1.7	22.3784	–1.6	22.7184	–1.9	–
Peru	(New Sol)	6.2201	–0.0481	163–239	6.2239	6.2163	6.2138	1.2	6.2060	0.9	6.1838	0.6	–
USA	($)	2.0411	–0.0021	408–413	2.0446	2.0371	2.0396	0.8	2.0370	0.8	2.0209	1.0	86.2

FT

Pacific/Middle East/Africa

Australia	(A$)	2.3111	0.0162	102–120	2.3148	2.2827	2.3126	–0.8	2.3154	–0.7	2.3389	–1.2	99.9
Hong Kong	(HK$)	15.8467	–0.0276	440–493	15.8812	15.8143	15.8402	0.5	15.8111	0.9	15.6658	1.1	–
India	(Rs)	81.3359	–0.0817	157–560	81.3560	80.7510	81.2943	0.6	81.2736	0.3	81.1586	0.2	–
Indonesia	(Rupiah)	18554.2	–7.3989	468–615	18596.8	18500.3	18607.5	–3.4	18674.2	–2.6	18886.1	–1.8	–
Iran	(Rial)	19002.2	–19.0853	896–147	–	–	–	–	–	–	–	–	–
Israel	(Shk)	8.1826	0.0362	754–897	8.1903	8.1264	8.1708	1.7	8.1508	1.6	8.0916	1.1	118.4
Japan	(¥)	236.527	0.2323	468–587	236.780	235.020	235.445	5.5	233.521	5.1	225.546	4.6	–
Kuwait	(Dinar)	0.5704	–0.0008	702–705	0.5713	0.5692	0.5687	3.4	0.5674	2.1	0.5616	1.5	–
Malaysia	(M$)	6.9508	0.0145	448–568	6.9574	6.9271	6.9367	2.4	6.9098	2.4	6.7942	2.3	–
New Zealand	(NZ$)	2.6878	0.0160	867–888	2.6979	2.6639	2.6937	–2.7	2.7054	–2.6	2.7631	–2.8	113.4
Philippines	(Peso)	91.6738	0.0407	319–156	91.7576	91.4316	91.7158	–0.6	91.7615	–0.4	91.6449	0.0	–
Saudi Arabia	(SR)	7.6325	–0.0076	265–385	7.6403	7.6111	7.6236	1.4	7.6099	1.2	7.5421	1.2	–
Singapore	(S$)	3.0305	0.0128	294–315	3.0332	3.0159	3.0211	3.7	3.0040	3.5	2.9358	3.1	–
South Africa	(R)	14.1302	0.0713	183–421	14.1772	13.9444	14.1847	–4.6	14.2944	–4.6	14.8242	–4.9	–
South Korea	(Won)	1865.21	–1.6690	447–595	1868.01	1862.11	1861.57	2.3	1854.38	2.3	1833.24	1.7	–
Taiwan	(T$)	66.4913	–0.0606	709–117	66.7938	66.3683	66.2409	4.5	65.7990	4.2	64.0963	3.6	–
Thailand	(Bt)	69.9060	–0.0804	770–349	70.0040	69.8050	69.7908	2.0	69.5583	2.0	68.5482	1.9	–
U A E	(Dirham)	7.4953	–0.0065	940–965	7.5081	7.4800	7.4827	2.0	7.4600	1.9	7.3719	1.6	–

Euro Locking Rates: Austrian Schilling 13.7603, Belgium/Luxembourg Franc 40.339, Finnish Markka 5.94573, French Franc 6.55957, German Mark 1.95583, Greek Drachma 340.75, Irish Punt 0.787564, Italian Lira 1936.27, Netherlands Guilder 2.20371, Portuguese Escudo 200.482, Spanish Peseta 166.386. Bid/offer speads in the Euro Spot table show only the last three decimal places Bid, offer, mid spot rates and forward rates are derived from THE WM/REUTERS CLOSING SPOT and FORWARD RATE services. Some values are rounded by the F.T.

Source: *Financial Times*, 3 October 2007. Reprinted with permission.

18.3 Interest rate parity

To begin to examine why some currencies are at a forward discount and others at a forward premium, consider the position of three investors A, B and C, each of whom has €1m to invest in a secure form for three months. A buys Italian government securities at existing euro interest rates. B sells the euro for sterling and uses it to buy British government securities that bear a higher interest rate than Italian securities. Suppose, however, that over the three months, the value of sterling falls relative to that of the euro. Then, when B comes to reconvert the pounds into euro, he may have incurred a loss – the higher interest rate on British securities may have been more than offset by the decline in the value of the UK currency. An operation of this kind is known as **uncovered interest rate arbitrage** – it is *interest rate arbitrage* because it seeks to take advantage of interest rate differentials; it is *uncovered* because the investor is not protected against exchange rate risk.

C takes advantage of the existence of the forward exchange market to obtain cover against this risk. Thus, at the same time that she buys British government securities, C sells three months forward the amount of sterling that she will receive in three months' time. In this way, she locks in the existing forward exchange rate. Then, when the British securities mature, C simply fulfils the forward contract and finishes up back in euro. She has engaged in **covered interest arbitrage**, having taken no risk in the process. Clearly, the actions of A and C are directly comparable and, in a well-informed market, the rates of return available to A and C quickly move to equality. A's rate of return is the interest rate on three-month Italian government securities. C's rate of return consists of two elements:

■ the interest rate on three-month British government securities;

■ the forward exchange premium or discount involved in selling sterling forward.

Assume next that, at the beginning of the three-month period, the euro and sterling were trading with no forward premium or discount (spot and forward rates were exactly the same) but that British interest rates were higher than euro interest rates for comparable securities. Clearly, then, C's investment strategy would be better than A's and

large numbers of investors would follow C. In other words, they would:

(a) sell Italian securities (forcing their price down and pushing the yield on them up);

(b) buy sterling spot (forcing up the spot exchange rate of the pound – increasing the number of euro needed to buy £1);

(c) buy British securities (forcing their price up and yields on them down); and

(d) cover their exchange rate risk by selling sterling three months forward (forcing down the three-month forward exchange rate of sterling).

This process would continue until the rates of return available on the strategies of A and C came into equality (with some small allowance for the transactions costs involved), establishing **covered interest parity**. What is the final outcome? Euro interest rates start below sterling rates, but euro interest rates rise while sterling rates fall. Thus, the interest rate differential between the two currencies is reduced. The spot exchange rate of the pound rises while the forward rate falls, opening up a difference between the two (forward, the pound trades at a discount). The arbitrage opportunity remains until the interest rate differential between the two currencies equals the forward discount on the pound (again, allowing for transactions costs). This establishes a general rule:

> The currency of the country in which interest rates are higher trades at a forward discount; the currency of the country with the lower interest rates trades at a forward premium.

We can go further. If there are no opportunities for profitable arbitrage (there is covered interest parity) and there are no transaction costs, then the differential between the two interest rates (known as the **interest agio**) should equal the forward discount on the currency of the high interest rate country (the **exchange agio**). We can express the exchange agio for euro/sterling in terms of the direct quotation of the euro (the domestic currency) against the pound (the foreign currency).

$$\frac{i_D - i_F}{1 + i_F} = \frac{E_F - E_S}{E_S} = \frac{E_F}{E_S} - 1 \qquad (18.4)$$

where i_D and i_F are the interest rates in the domestic (euro) and foreign (UK) currencies respectively; E_S and E_F are the spot and forward rates of exchange (expressed in direct quotation). It follows then that:

$$E_F = \left[1 + \left(\frac{i_D - i_F}{1 + i_F}\right)\right] E_S \qquad (18.5)$$

Consider an example. In the *Financial Times* of 3 October 2007, the one-year interest rate on the pound was quoted as 6.11 per cent (0.0611); that on the euro as 4.69 per cent (0.0469). Thus, the difference between the two rates was 1.42 per cent (0.0142) or 142 basis points. The spot rate of exchange of the euro in direct quotation was €1.44421 = £1. We should then have had:

$$E_F = \left[1 + \left(\frac{0.0469 - 0.0611}{1.0611}\right)\right] \times 1.4421 \quad (18.6)$$

That is, the one-year forward rate of sterling should have been £1 = €1.4228, with the euro at a one-year forward premium of €0.0193 per £.

To express exchange rates in indirect quotation and still have our signs correct, we must change the formula to:

$$\frac{i_D - i_F}{1 + i_F} = \frac{S_S - S_F}{S_F} \qquad (18.7)$$

and:

$$S_F = \left[\frac{1}{\left[1 + \left(\frac{i_D - i_F}{1 + i_F}\right)\right]}\right] S_S \qquad (18.8)$$

The indirect quotation of the euro against sterling on the day in question was €1 = £0.6934. The forward discount should have been £0.0094 and the forward exchange rate €1 = £0.7028. For ease of expression, we have been dealing here with a 12-month period. To calculate the expected three-month or one-month forward rate we must divide the annual interest rate differential by four or 12. Thus, the one-month interest rates on the euro and sterling at the close of the markets on 2 October 2007 were 4.35 and 6.0 respectively. The interest rate differential was 1.65 per cent (or 165 basis points) but these were per annum rates. Using the same spot exchange rate of £1 = €1.4421, our formula in Equation 18.5 gives us an annual forward discount for sterling of €0.0224. To obtain the forward discount for one month we divide this by 12, giving a one-month forward discount of €0.0019 and a one-month forward exchange rate of £1 = €1.4402.

Because of transaction costs, we would not have expected our estimate to be perfectly correct, but a glance at the real figures shows that we come very close to the actual figures. On the day in question we have:

one month:
Actual £1 = €1.4399 or €1 = £0.6945 (sterling forward discount 1.83 per cent p.a.)
Estimate £1 = €1.4402 or €1 = £0.6943 (sterling forward discount 1.58 per cent p.a.)

one year:
Actual £1 = €1.4232 or €1 = £0.7027 (sterling forward discount 1.31 per cent p.a.)
Estimate £1 = €1.4228 or €1 = £0.7028 (sterling forward discount 1.34 per cent p.a.)

We would not always expect a calculation using the above formulae to produce results so close to the actual market figures. This is because in our calculations, we have been making a number of assumptions quite apart from the absence of transactions costs. The interest rates we used were taken from the 'Market Rates' table in the *Financial Times*. These were not the precise interest rates payable on Italian and UK government securities respectively. In the Italian/UK case the interest rate differential may have been quite close to the interest rate differential on government securities but this would not be true where the markets judged there to be a greater risk of default associated with one country's government securities. This indeed was the position before the formation of the euro with Italian government securities issued in lira. The risk premium on Italian government securities in that period included two elements – exchange rate risk to cover the possibility of a fall in the value of the lira and default risk based on the view of the international credit rating agencies that Italian government debt was too high. With Italy now in the euro area, the risk of the lira falling in value relative to other euro area currencies has disappeared but Italian government securities still carry slightly higher interest rates than, say, German government securities to cover the extra possibility of default. Indeed, in October 2006, two of the largest international credit rating agencies downgraded Italian government securities. The closeness of our estimates to the actual figures is, however, a good indication that covered interest rate parity does generally hold in foreign exchange markets.

We are now easily able to see what the eleven countries whose currencies were at a forward discount to the pound in October 2007 had in common. We do this in Box 18.3.

18.4 Exchange rate arbitrage

The interest rate parity theorem provides an example of interest rate arbitrage. **Exchange rate arbitrage** involves taking advantage of differentials in the price of a currency in different markets – buying in one market and selling in another to make a profit. Such arbitrage transactions may be classified in terms of the number of markets involved. Thus we may have transactions in two markets (two-point arbitrage), three markets (three-point arbitrage) or more. Two-point arbitrage operations are very simple, taking advantage of small variations in the one exchange rate in two markets. For example, if the spot exchange rate of the euro were €1.43 = £1 in London and €1.45 = £1 in Frankfurt, arbitrageurs could profit from the differential by buying euros in Frankfurt and selling them immediately in London, forcing up the demand for euros

in Frankfurt, and causing the rate there to fall below €1.45 = £1; and increasing the demand for sterling in London, pushing the London rate above €1.43 = £1. The arbitrage operation would close the gap between the two rates. As always, the rates would not come exactly into line because of the existence of transactions costs, but the rates should move to being transactions-costs close – sufficiently close to remove any further possible arbitrage profits.

Three-point arbitrage occurs where exchange rates among different currencies are mutually inconsistent. Arbitrageurs then attempt to profit from these inconsistencies and in the process eliminate discrepancies and establish mutually consistent exchange cross rates. Assume that the following three market rates applied in the Frankfurt market:

$$\$1 = SKr6.5089$$
$$€1 = \$1.4154$$
$$€1 = SKr9.5541$$

We wish to consider the possibility that these rates are mutually inconsistent. Our first step is to take any pair of these market rates and use them to calculate the exchange cross rates consistent with them. We have already carried out this exercise for the first two rates in Section 18.2.1. There we discovered that the exchange cross rate for SKr against the euro was:

$$€1 = SKr9.2126$$

Thus, it is clear that the market price (€1 = SKr9.5541), *relative to the other pair of exchange rates*, is over-valuing the euro in terms of the SKr (the SKr is under-valued against the €). In other words, the three market rates are mutually inconsistent and a profitable arbitrage opportunity exists. We could have arrived at the same conclusion by using the $/€ and SKr/€ rates to calculate the cross rate for Swedish krone against the dollar or by using the SKr/$ and the SKr/€ rates to calculate the cross rate for the dollar against the euro.

To realize an arbitrage profit, it is necessary to follow two rules:

1 buy cheap and sell dear;

2 finish in the currency in which you started.

Assume we hold dollars. Our aim must be to organize our transaction to make sure that at some point we sell euros for SKr, in order to take advantage of the inconsistency we discovered by calculating the cross rate (if we buy € with SKr, we shall make a loss). In order to be able to do this, we must take the following steps:

Step A: Sell $ for €;

Step B: sell € for SKr;

Step C: sell SKr for $.

Make sure you understand each of these steps. In step A, since the direct form of the exchange rate for the dollar is given (dollar against the euro), you will need to take the inverse of the rate we have given you to find the number of euro you will obtain for your dollars. However, for step B, you are given the indirect rate for the euro (SKr against the euro) and you need simply multiply. What form of the exchange rate are you given for step C?

You should calculate the arbitrage profit on the assumption that you start with $1m. If you do not finish up with a profit of slightly over 3.7 per cent, try it again. Exercise 18.4 provides another example for you to try. In practice, the calculation would be a little more difficult than is suggested here because you would be faced with bid and offer rates for each exchange rate and you would need to choose the correct rate of the pair, depending on whether you were buying or selling.

Three things should be noted here. Firstly, the profit rate in our exercises is much higher than would occur in practice. Arbitrageurs would notice profit opportunities and act to take arbitrage profits before they reached the size we have assumed. Profit rates on each arbitrage transaction are usually, therefore, very small but this profit may be made in moments and the arbitrageur bears no risk of loss. He undertakes the above steps simultaneously and starts and finishes in the same currency.

Secondly, step A causes the price of the dollar in terms of the euro to rise above €1.4154; step B causes the price of the euro to fall below SKr9.5541; and step C, the price of dollars to rise above SKr6.5089. These changes continue until any possibility of profit from arbitrage is removed.

Thirdly, the same steps apply if we start and finish in a different currency from pounds, but the order of the steps is different. A Swedish arbitrageur starting and finishing in SKr would:

Step A: Sell SKr for $;

Step B: Sell $ for €;

Step C: Sell € for SKr.

18.5 Foreign exchange risk and speculation

We have talked about the existence of foreign exchange risk. A market agent bearing risk is said to have an *open position in the market*. There are two types of open position – an agent may go *long* (take a **long position**) by having assets in a currency greater than his or her liabilities in the same currency. The risk then is that the currency will weaken, reducing the value of the position. An agent who goes *short* (takes a **short position**) has liabilities in a currency greater than assets. The risk is that the currency will strengthen, increasing the debt in that currency. The act of moving from an open position to a closed position in the market (that is, covering exchange rate risk) is known as **hedging**. Consider hedging more formally.

Consider the case of a German firm which, on 2 October 2007, expected to receive Danish krone (DKr)100,000 in three months' time. The anticipated sum was worth €13,415 at the then current spot exchange rate of €1 = DKr7.4543, but had the Danish krone depreciated over those three months to, say, €1 = DKr8, the German firm would have received only €12,500, incurring a foreign exchange loss. If, however, it had on 2 October contracted to sell Danish kroner forward at the then 3-months' forward

---

> **Exercise 18.4**
>
> 1 Imagine you are a German arbitrageur in the following example:
>
> **Actual exchange rates**
> €1 = $1.4154
> $1 = ¥115.885
> €1 = ¥168.023
>
> Start with €1,000,000.
>
>   (a) List the steps you need to take to make a profit.
>
>   (b) Calculate the percentage rate of profit you would make (assuming no transactions costs).
>
> 2 Check your answer by using the same figures but starting and finishing in yen.

rate of €1 = DKr7.4528, it would have received €13,418 and would have avoided the loss. The existence of a long position (net foreign currency asset) and the failure to cover (hedge) this position exposed the German firm to an unfavourable and avoidable movement in the Danish krone spot exchange rate. Of course, by making the forward market trade, the firm would also have denied itself a possible profit had the Danish krone appreciated over the three months in question.

Take next the case of an Irish firm which must pay ¥1 million in three months' time for goods from Japan. At a current spot exchange rate of €1 = ¥164.018, this would cost €6,097. If, however, the yen were to strengthen against the euro to, say, €1 = ¥150 over the period, the firm would find itself paying €6,667 and would suffer a foreign exchange loss of €570. This might be avoided by hedging through the forward exchange market: buying yen forward at a rate of, say, €1 = €162.516. This would have cost €6,153 and the loss would have been limited to €56, the cost of the forward transaction.

How else might these firms cover themselves against foreign exchange risk? In our second example, it would have been possible to pay three months ahead, that is, to *lead* the payment. The loss in this case would have been the loss of interest on €6,097 for three months. Someone with a bill due now in a foreign currency which they feel will fall in value in the future may endeavour to pay late (to *lag* the payment). Again, foreign exchange risk can be covered using only the spot market. Thus, the Irish firm could buy yen in the spot market, invest them in Japanese securities for three months at Japanese interest rates and then use the yen at the end of the period to pay for the goods supplied. The German firm could borrow DKr at the beginning of the period, convert them into euro at the spot exchange rate and use the DKr received in three months' time to pay off the loan. The cost of this operation would have been the interest paid on the DKr loan.

The forward market, however, provides a more convenient way of hedging. In the German example, it would have been necessary to find someone in Denmark willing to lend at reasonable interest rates. In the Irish case, either of the alternatives requires the firm to have funds now and to tie those funds up for three months. Other instruments useful for the hedging of risk, notably futures, options and swaps, are dealt with in Chapters 19 and 20.

Although the forward market was developed as a means of providing insurance against risk, it has come to be used principally as a means of **speculation**, which involves the taking on of risk (moving to an open position). Firms sometimes engage in speculation in an attempt to make additional profits to those produced by their normal activities. For example, the German firm may choose not to hedge against the exchange rate risk in the expectation that the currency in which it is long (the Danish krone) will strengthen, increasing the return on the transaction. Equally, the Irish firm may choose not to insure itself against forex risk in the hope that the yen will weaken against the euro, allowing the firm to settle its bill at a lower cost in euros.

As well, a market agent may engage in speculation in a currency in which she has no other interest and may do this on either the spot or forward market. Most obviously, if a French speculator thinks that a currency, say the dollar, is likely to strengthen against the euro, she may borrow funds in euro and use them to buy dollars spot, hold the dollars in the form of a liquid security and, if the dollar strengthens, cash in the security, reconvert the dollars to euro, and pay off the loan, leaving a profit. Alternatively, she may use the forward market, selling euro for dollars forward. Then, when the dollar strengthens, she buys euro for dollars at the new spot rate and sells euro to meet the requirement of the forward contract. This would again leave the agent with a profit. Of course, if the value of the dollar fell rather than rose, both strategies would produce losses. The use of the forward market does not require the speculator to have available or borrow the full amount of the transaction at the beginning of the period, although she will need to have sufficient funds available to persuade the market-maker that she will be able to meet the forward contract when it falls due. Thus it is likely that acting through the forward market requires some of the funds needed for the transaction to be tied up for a shorter period than does acting through the spot market. This, in turn, means that the per annum rate of profit from a forward transaction is likely to be higher than for the equivalent spot market transaction.

You should next consider how a speculator might make use of the forward market to profit from a belief that his or her home currency, say the euro, is likely to fall in value in the next month.

18.5.1 Attitudes to speculation

Speculators provide liquidity to a market. Thus, it is argued, their presence provides a benefit for agents who wish to use the market for normal business or hedging purposes. For example, in the absence of the activities of speculators, the number of people wishing to buy or sell a relatively minor currency forward may be so small that no market-maker is prepared to offer forward contracts involving that currency. Again, if only a small number of a particular forward contract (involving, say, US dollars and Australian dollars) were sold, the risks to the market maker would be high and the bid/offer spread on the contract would be large. Thus, firms wishing to hedge against risks associated with holding Australian dollars would find it expensive to do so. The presence of speculators deepens the market, reduces the volatility of the exchange rates and leads to a lowering of the cost of using the market.

In addition, as we have already seen, it is claimed that speculators act to ensure the efficient operation of markets, linking present and future prices of assets. This favourable view holds speculation to be stabilizing, always moving the market towards its equilibrium. Destabilizing speculators – those trying to bet against the natural direction of the market – would, it is argued, lose since market forces are so strong that it is not possible to act against them. For example, suppose market forces determine that the value of a currency must fall. Speculators make their profit by seeing this in advance of other people and selling the currency with the aim of buying it back later at a lower price. Thus their action forces the value down towards its new equilibrium value. Again, speculators who realize that a rise/fall from an equilibrium is likely to be only temporary act on the correct assumption that the exchange rate returns to its previous level after the effects of the temporary shock wear off. They sell/buy the currency when it has deviated sufficiently from its equilibrium value for the return to equilibrium to compensate them for the trouble and risk of engaging in the transaction. In doing this, they help to push the currency back to the original equilibrium position. Successful speculators thus are said to ensure that movements to new equilibrium positions occur more smoothly than otherwise would be the case and that equilibrium positions are stable. Since the aim of speculation is to make a

profit, it follows that unsuccessful speculators quickly leave the market. Only successful speculators remain in the market. This support for speculation is an important part of the argument that markets left to themselves produce stable equilibrium exchange rates and thus is a major element in the case for floating rates of exchange.

Arguments against speculation claim that some speculators do lose – they are not the core of professionals in the market but a part of the large fringe of traders, tourists and central banks that take open positions in foreign exchange but to whom the activity is peripheral. If this is so, it does not follow that the outcome of speculation is always to move the market in the direction in which it would otherwise have gone.

Of greater weight is the proposition that markets do not always work well and that this allows the possibility of profitable destabilizing speculation. Markets might, for example, fail because of time lags, different speeds of adjustment of different prices, lack of information or asymmetric information. In such circumstances, speculators might attempt to amplify price movements. This is more likely where trading volumes are low (thin markets) and market agents form expectations extrapolatively. For instance, speculators might be able to sell a currency sufficiently heavily to force its value down; others within the market observe the fall and assume it will continue. Thus, they also sell, pushing the price down further still. Speculators are then able to buy back in at the lower price, taking their profit.

We have also seen, the suggestion that even speculators may be risk averse, limiting the amount they bet on any economic outcome that is less than a sure thing. In such a case, their actions would not succeed, for example, in bringing into line forward and future spot rates of exchange.

18.6 Reasons for exchange rate changes – theory and practice

We now know a good deal about the way in which exchange rates are expressed but we have yet to say anything about why exchange rates are what they are or why they change. Yet exchange rates clearly do change a great deal over quite short periods of time. We can see this clearly by looking at some figures for the value of the euro against the US dollar on the first trading day of each year since the launch of the euro in January 1999:

1999	$1 = €0.84219	2000	$1 = €0.96981
2001	$1 = €1.05656	2002	$1 = €1.10689
2003	$1 = €0.96495	2004	$1 = €0.79419
2005	$1 = €0.75230	2006	$1 = €0.83479
2007	$1 = €0.75262		

And, of course, we have seen earlier in this chapter that on the 2 October 2007, the rate was $1 = €0.70605.

How might we explain such large changes as these? Naturally, economists begin with the presumption that prices (exchange rates) must derive from the demand for and supply of currencies originating from end users and that their behaviour is underpinned by rational economic motives. This leads to the view that exchange rates should be determined by the market *fundamentals* but leaves us to explain what these fundamentals are.

Economic theory also suggests that exchange rate changes must reflect a movement away from a previously existing equilibrium towards a new equilibrium position. Unfortunately, it is hard to discern in the everyday behaviour of the markets any tendency towards anything we might think of as equilibrium. It is difficult even to define an equilibrium position. One common idea is that the equilibrium exchange rate is the rate that produces balance in the balance of payments. Since countries trade with many partners, and balance of payments equilibrium does not require balance with each trading partner, this does not give us a clear idea of the desirable exchange rate between the domestic currency and any one foreign currency. Nonetheless, the balance of payments is often taken as a starting point in attempts to understand exchange rate changes and the fundamentals of exchange rates are identified as economic factors that are important influences on the current and capital accounts of the balance of payments.

Early exchange rate theories concentrated on the current account of the balance of payments and were concerned with factors influencing a country's competitiveness in international trade. We thus had real factors such as relative labour productivity across countries and rates of economic growth. However, as we saw in considering real exchange rates above, competitiveness is also influenced by relative rates of inflation. This led to the powerful idea of explaining exchange rates in terms of **purchasing power parity** (PPP) – the idea that goods of the same quality should sell at the same price, when expressed in a common currency, in all countries.

18.6.1 The determinants of spot exchange rates – purchasing power parity

PPP starts with the proposition that if, at the existing exchange rate, goods were cheaper in the USA than in the UK, UK citizens would switch to US-produced *goods*. To do this they would sell sterling and acquire dollars, forcing down the value of the pound relative to the dollar. This process would continue until US-produced goods no longer had a competitive advantage and the movement of goods from the US to the UK would stop. This would occur when prices in the two countries expressed in a common currency were equal. This gives the absolute form of PPP – spot exchange rates in equilibrium are a reflection of differences in price levels in different countries. Since we are generally interested not in absolute exchange rates but rather in changes from existing rates, PPP is usually expressed in relative terms: that changes in spot exchange rates reflect differences in inflation rates among countries. Using the direct quotation (E) of the exchange rate, this can be written:

$$\frac{\pi_D^e - \pi_F^e}{1 + \pi_F^e} = \frac{E_{t+1}^e - E_S}{E_S} \qquad (18.9)$$

where π_D^e is the expected inflation rate in the domestic country (UK), π_F^e the expected inflation rate in the foreign country (USA), E_{t+1}^e the expected future spot rate of exchange at time $t + 1$ and E_S the spot rate of exchange at time t. Assuming expected inflation rates in the UK of 2 per cent per annum and in the USA of 1 per cent per annum and a spot exchange rate £0.4899 = $1 would give an expected exchange rate in one year's time on the basis of relative purchasing power parity of £0.4947 = $1. In other words, the dollar would need to be stronger in one year's time if UK goods were to maintain PPP, given the higher inflation rate in the UK. The formula for the same calculation in indirect quotation is:

$$\frac{\pi_D^e - \pi_F^e}{1 + \pi_F^e} = \frac{S_S - S_{t+1}^e}{S_{t+1}^e} \qquad (18.10)$$

Using a spot rate of exchange of £1 = \$2.0411, we obtain a future spot rate of exchange of £1 = \$2.0211.

But how useful is PPP in the explanation of exchange rates? The theory as we have expressed it here clearly leaves out the various costs of moving goods from one country to another and the many barriers to international trade such as tariffs, quotas and differential tax rates. It also assumes that consumers have full information about both the quality of goods produced in other countries and their prices and that they have no loyalty to home-produced goods. We would not, therefore, expect PPP to provide anything like an exact explanation of exchange rate changes and certainly not to contribute much to an understanding of the changes in the exchange rate of the euro against the dollar listed at the beginning of this section. We might think that PPP would perform better in accounting for exchange rate changes between the currencies of countries geographically close and we should expect it to do better in looking at exchange rates over long periods of time. Even in the long run, however, the supporting evidence for PPP is thin.

Yet it remains a powerful idea and is included in most economists' models of exchange rate determination. It is also the basis of the popular and much-reproduced Big Mac index of prices. Everyone would include relative rates of inflation as one of the market fundamentals of exchange rates. One could, of course, go further and consider the causes of differences in inflation rates among countries and, depending upon one's views of the causes of inflation, include in the fundamentals the pressure of demand, unemployment rates or rates of growth of the money supply among the relevant market fundamentals.

18.6.2 The capital account of the balance of payments and relative interest rates

Perhaps the major weakness of PPP is that in a modern economy there are many other reasons for demanding a foreign currency than a desire to purchase the goods and services of that country. Indeed, we noted at the beginning of this chapter that the needs of international trade have accounted for only a small proportion of the increase in the turnover in foreign exchange markets in recent years. Thus, as international capital flows increased from the 1960s onward, theories

began to pay more attention to the capital account of the balance of payments. This had two major impacts.

Firstly, theories stressed the role of relative interest rates. This led to the question of what determined interest rates. One approach was to make use of the Fisher effect which we explained in Section 9.3.1. We saw there that the Fisher effect is the assumption that in equilibrium real interest rates will be the same in all countries and hence that differences in nominal interest rates on different currencies will reflect only the differences in expected inflation rates between the respective countries. We could use this to help us explain the differences in interest rates on, say, euro and sterling. We could say that, with real interest rates equal across countries and the foreign exchange market in equilibrium, the difference in nominal interest rates on euro and sterling depends on the difference between the expected inflation rates in the euro area and the UK. Treating the euro area as the domestic country (D) and the UK as the foreign country (F), we could write

$$\frac{i_D - i_F}{1 + i_F} = \frac{\pi_D^e - \pi_F^e}{1 + \pi_F^e} \qquad (18.11)$$

This is sometimes known as the Fisher closed hypothesis. Notice that the term on the right-hand side in Equation 18.11 is the same as the terms on the left-hand side in Equations 18.9 and 18.10 for PPP. Thus, expected inflation rates are equal to *both* the expected change in spot exchange rates and the difference in interest rates. It follows that in equilibrium, differences in interest rates must equal the expected changes in the spot rates of exchange. This is sometimes known as the international Fisher effect or the Fisher open hypothesis:

$$\frac{E_{t+1}^e - E_S}{E_S} = \frac{i_D - i_F}{1 + i_F} = \frac{S_S - S_{t+1}^e}{S_{t+1}^e} \qquad (18.12)$$

This establishes a relationship between the forward rate of exchange (which is known in the present) and the future spot rate of exchange which is unknown. Covered interest parity establishes, remember, a link between interest rate differentials and forward premiums/discounts. But the combination of purchasing power parity and the Fisher effect establishes a link between interest rate differentials and expected changes in the exchange rate.

The principal problem with this is that real rates of interest are not equal across countries. The theory that they should be equal, like the theory underlying PPP, assumes perfect markets with full information and perfect capital mobility. If these did exist, we should expect capital to move from capital-rich countries in which the real rate of return on capital were low to capital-scarce countries with high real rates of return on capital until real rates of interest were equal across countries. This would be ensured by uncovered interest arbitrage. In practice, neither information nor international capital mobility is perfect and we need to add the existence of default risk, exchange rate risk and political or sovereign risk which require interest rates of many countries to include risk premiums if they are to attract capital. Indeed, private capital barely flows at all to the poorest countries despite the existence of very high rates of interest. As we noted in Section 9.3.1, Irving Fisher himself advanced many reasons why the nominal interest rates should not, in practice, be expected to follow the rate of inflation very closely. It is hardly surprising then that the open Fisher hypothesis has not tested at all well as a theory of exchange rates. Despite this, we can, as we did with PPP, accept that interest rate differentials are important and add them to a list of fundamentals of the exchange rate.

The second impact of the concentration on capital flows as influences on exchange rates was to the importance of expectations about future interest rates, future inflation rates and future exchange rates themselves. Market participants will often be concerned more with what might happen to interest rates and inflation rates than with their current values. This implies a greater concern with what other people in the market are likely to do and introduces a strong psychological element into decisions as to which currency to buy or sell and when to buy or sell it. Under these circumstances, each piece of information ('news') that comes to the market needs to be carefully interpreted to try to discover its meaning for the future and the impact it is likely to have on other market agents. Further, the attempt to outguess the market requires judgements about the future behaviour of policymakers and the likely impact on economies of political and other news that might influence the composition and/or behaviour of governments.

Because a great deal of the activity in forex markets is based on expectations concerning future exchange rates, much effort has gone into the development of models aimed at forecasting these rates. We have so far come across two approaches in this chapter – (a) applying specific rules such as PPP and (b) the more general use of a range of market fundamentals likely to have an impact on the current and capital accounts of the balance of payments and hence on the demand for and supply of currencies. However, (b) leaves mat-

ters very open and so a wide range of **fundamentalist models** have been developed incorporating theories of the current and capital accounts of the balance of payments, the role of inflation, and theories of expectations formation. Fundamentalist models may be classified in a variety of ways.

One common classification is into *flow models*, those based on current account performance, and stock or *asset models* which stress the role of the capital account. Flow models incorporate relative prices (PPP), differences in the rate of productivity increase, and/or the relative rates of growth of domestic and world income. *Stock models* include relative interest rates and rates of growth of money supplies as well as exchange rate expectations and PPP among the market fundamentals. Most early fundamentalist models implied that real exchange rates should change relatively slowly over time. This left the major problem of explaining the volatility of exchange rates following the collapse of the Bretton Woods fixed exchange rate system of the International Monetary Fund in 1972.

One approach has been to attribute the volatility to the actions of governments and the intervention of central banks in the market. Governments, it has been argued, have often followed interventionist monetary policies which have kept exchange rates away from their equilibrium levels. Central banks have often bought and sold currencies (in effect acting as speculators) for political motives, attempting to influence the value of their own currencies or as part of a coordinated attempt to influence the values of important world currencies such as the dollar and the yen.

Another approach has been to incorporate time lags into models to explain why an exchange rate may not, once an equilibrium position has been disturbed, move directly and rapidly to a new equilibrium. One significant class of models of this kind has been the overshooting exchange rate models (deriving from Dornbusch, 1976). These continue to assume the existence of long-run equilibrium rates of exchange and incorporate both uncovered interest rate and purchasing power parity. They also typically assume rational expectations and so market participants are assumed to make the best available use of all relevant information and to employ the best available model for forecasting future exchange rates. The result is that market agents are assumed to know what the long-run equilibrium exchange rate is. Nonetheless, despite this knowledge, exchange rates are held to overshoot their long-run equilibrium positions. That is, in the process of moving to a new equilibrium, an exchange rate first shoots well beyond it in the opposite direction. This result is achieved by assuming that different elements in the model adjust at different speeds. For instance, one might assume that the money market in an economy adjusts instantaneously but that the goods market is slow to adjust to new influences. An alternative is to assume that the prices of tradable goods adjust quickly to international pressures but that the prices of non-tradables change only slowly.

Unfortunately, all of the fundamentalist models have problems. Flow models assume either that capital is completely immobile or that prices are fixed or both. Simple stock models assume that domestic and foreign assets are perfect substitutes for each other and that a maintained interest rate differential produces a continual flow of capital. This does not happen in practice. PPP plays an important part in all stock models and we have noted that empirical evidence provides little support for PPP. Expectations are important in many stock models but there is uncertainty as to how to model them. None of the models do well in testing, many performing worse than a simple random walk model. One study (by Meese and Rogoff, 1983) tested the predictions over the late 1970s of three fundamentalist models (a monetary model; Dornbusch's overshooting model; and a stock model which added current account factors to the Dornbusch model) together with those of a model stating simply that the exchange rate in the following period would be the same as in the current period. They found that the last model performed best! Models based on fundamentals faced particular difficulties in the first half of the 1980s as the dollar continued a prolonged increase in value (reaching its peak in February 1985) against all economic logic. This led to a number of developments in exchange rate theories.

Models were developed which attempted to explain sudden and apparently inexplicable jumps in the value of a currency through the phenomenon of **rational bubbles** (bubbles in which all participants know the correct model for the determination of the exchange rate but nonetheless the actual rate moves sharply away from equilibrium until eventually the bubble bursts). Models that explain these jumps but which continue to assume that the market is characterized by rational behaviour, start in a disequilibrium position and show how rational decisions may cause the market to move further away from equilibrium rather than returning to it.

For example, in trying to explain the inexorable rise in value of the US dollar between 1981 and 1985, Dornbusch started with an overvalued exchange rate.

Investors were assumed to be risk neutral, and so a strategy that has a risk of high losses if things go wrong but a potential for high profits if they go right is equivalent to one in which potential losses and profits are both low. Investors had to compare two probabilities: that the exchange rate would return to equilibrium and that it would go on rising. The further the exchange rate was currently above the equilibrium rate, the greater was the potential loss for investors if it fell back to equilibrium and the greater the required profits had to be if the rate kept on rising. To put it another way, the greater the risk of a crash, the faster the rate of appreciation had to be to compensate for potential losses. Investors were thus obliged to go on buying the currency, pushing the rate up further and further, although there was no economic justification for doing so.

Some models allowed for the existence of two kinds of forecasters in the market. In Goodhart's (1988) model, for example, dealers make their decisions on the basis of a weighted average of the forecasts of market efficiency theorists and modellers of fundamentals, with the weights determined by the relative past success of the two forecasts. Again the model starts with an overvalued exchange rate. In the absence of news, the market efficient forecast is for no change while fundamentalists predict that the exchange rate will fall to equilibrium. Assume next that a random shock forces it further away from equilibrium. Both forecasts will be wrong but the market efficiency forecast will be less wrong and in the next period the weights are changed to reflect this, causing the predicted fall in the exchange rate to be smaller. Dealers thus buy more of the overvalued currency, forcing the rate up yet further.

An alternative approach has been to reject rationality in its narrow economic sense. It is argued that much trading in forex markets is based on 'noise' – information that is irrelevant to market price and only confuses market participants – rather than 'news' and that this results in excessive volatility. Frankel and Froot (1990) developed a model similar to Goodhart's, except that the bubble is not rational but speculative, being the outcome of self-confirming market speculations. Again there are two types of forecasters but this time they are fundamentalists and chartists. Fundamentalists (using an overshooting model) forecast a depreciation of the dollar which would be rational if there were no chartists. Chartists extrapolate recent trends based on an information set that includes no fundamentals. Box 18.4 indicates some of the features of exchange rate behaviour of interest to

---

BOX 18.4 Forecasting foreign exchange rates with the use of charts (technical analysis)

Forecasters who make use of charts of past foreign exchange rates are attempting only to forecast the very short term. They assume that current demand and supply conditions can best be understood by examining the way exchange rates have been moving. Forecasting is based principally upon three elements in the charts.

1 Trends
Whether an exchange rate has been rising or falling and the gradient of the trend – relatively flat trends are regarded as being more sustainable; steep trends as more volatile and subject to change. Trends can be established by constructing a channel of two parallel lines which encompass all the exchange rate movements. If an exchange rate then breaks out of its current channel there is a suggestion that the present trend is about to be reversed. Analysis of trends can be supplemented by calculation of moving averages.

2 Support and resistance levels
A support level is a rate at which the currency appears to be strongly demanded. Thus, it is difficult for the exchange rate to fall below this level. A resistance level is the reverse – a rate which it is difficult for the currency to rise above. Support and resistance levels thus establish the width of the current channel in which the currency is trading. It is usually felt that if support or resistance levels are breached, the currency will fall sharply below the previous support level or rise sharply above the prior resistance level.

3 Pattern recognition
This is the recognition of visual patterns in the chart – either continuation patterns (including 'flags' and 'triangles') which suggest that the rate will continue to follow its current overall tendencies; or reversal patterns (such as 'head and shoulders'). In addition, chartists make use of information on momentum (the speed at which exchange rates change) and velocity (the rate of change of moving averages of exchange rates).

---

chartists and the extent to which market practitioners often combine fundamentalism and **chartism** (also known as **technical analysis**).

In Frankel and Froot's model, portfolio managers base their decisions on a weighted average of the forecasts of fundamentalists and chartists. Starting from an overvalued dollar (explained by overshooting), fundamentalists forecast depreciation but are incorrect. Consequently, portfolio managers increase the weight they assign to the forecasts of the chartists. In doing this, they reduce their weighted-average expectations of depreciation, raise their demands for the dollar and thus bring about the dollar's continued appreciation. According to this view, in 1985 the dollar entered a new stage, with an ever-worsening current account deficit leading to the reversal of the overvaluation caused by the bubble. Frankel and Froot thus show how (non-rational but) sensible behaviour can generate not simply short-run volatility in exchange rates but also, and more importantly, large and cumulative exchange rate misalignments. More recent work has attempted to set such models within the framework of chaos theory in which very small changes in a system can produce dramatic results.

Speculators are also sometimes divided into those who think short term (which in this context refers to one week or less) and those with long-run horizons (up to three months), with short termers holding **extrapolative expectations** and long termers **regressive expectations**. Much then depends on which group dominates the market at any particular time.

A number of special counter-examples have been developed to Friedman's (1953) argument, outlined above, that destabilizing speculators on average lose and are driven out of the market. Most of these involve heterogeneous actors, for instance 'suckers' who lose and 'sharpies' who win. In the simplest counter-example, based on the theory of rational speculative bubbles, each market participant loses if he does not go along with the herd.

The process of developing and testing models of foreign exchange determination continues but the performance of these models continues to leave much to be desired. The best that can be hoped for is reasonable forecasts over very long periods. Exchange rates change too much for there to be much hope of success of accounting for the variations in the euro/dollar relationship between 1999 and 2007 let alone of forecasting accurately how the rates might change in the near future. If this were possible, of course, there would be no one in the market practising technical analysis, no possibility of profit from speculation and no need for hedging. We can see some of the difficulty by looking at reports on the daily activity in foreign exchange markets.

Any reading of these reports quickly makes it clear how difficult it is, in practice, to interpret news and to decide what information is relevant to the determination of the exchange rate. It is common, for instance, for a market to adjust to news but then to go through a process of reinterpretation, sometimes drawing different inferences from it, other times discarding it altogether as irrelevant. Again, different sets of economic indicators often provide apparently conflicting

information about the state of different aspects of the economy and hence of exchange rate fundamentals. There is always a degree of uncertainty as to what is genuine news and what is not.

It is hardly surprising that there are difficulties in interpreting news since, as we have seen, perfect models of the determinants of exchange rates do not exist. Particular problems with the impact of news arise when market participants are using different models or are switching between one model and another. Box 18.5 provides an example of the difficulties of interpreting news in the foreign exchange market.

BOX 18.5 The market interpretation of news

The following extract is from the article 'Dollar index sinks to lowest ebb' by Peter Garnham on page 31 of the *Financial Times*, 29/30 September 2007.

> The dollar finished a tumultuous third quarter on the currency markets firmly on the back foot, hitting a record low against a raft of currencies. The dollar index, which tracks its value against a basket of six leading currencies, dropped to a low of 77.66 yesterday, its weakest level since the Federal Reserve launched the data series in 1973. Analysts said weak US data, including a plunge in house sales to their lowest in nearly a decade and a drop in consumer confidence to a two-year trough, had heightened expectations that the Federal Reserve would cut interest rates further. David Woo at Barclay's Capital said he remained bearish on the dollar . . .
>
> 'The US economy faces the most downside risks and, given the dependence of the US on foreign willingness to fund its current account deficit, the prospects for the dollar are bleak,' he said . . .
>
> Analysts said the euro was supported by data for consumer price inflation in the eurozone, which rose by an annual 2.1 per cent in September. That was the highest in more than a year and above the European Central Bank's 2 per cent target . . .
>
> Marc Chandler at Brown Brothers Harriman said the figures kept alive market expectations of another eurozone interest rate rise in late 2007. 'The data leave the ECB between a rock and a hard place and officials are likely to remain hawkish, though we think the recent tightening of credit and the softening trend in the economy suggest the Bank will be on hold for an extended period,' he said.

Source: *Financial Times*, 29/30 September 2007. Reprinted with permission.

Comment

Here we do have some stress on fundamentals – inflation rates, interest rates, the level of demand in the US and euro area economies – but it is all directed at trying to guess what the monetary authorities at the Fed and the ECB are likely to do next. The dollar, we are told, is likely to stay weak because the Fed might cut its official interest rate while the ECB might increase its interest rate. The former seemed more likely because the dollar is already weak (effective exchange rate at its lowest since 1973), demand in the economy low (low sales of houses) and likely to stay low (low consumer confidence), meaning that unemployment is likely to be more of a problem for the US economy than inflation. A cut in interest rates would weaken the dollar. This is particularly true because the US has a long-term deficit on the current account on its balance of payments producing an excess supply of dollars. There must therefore always be a large inflow of capital into the US to support the value of the dollar. This is much less likely if US interest rates are falling. In Europe, the signals are more mixed and it seems less clear what the ECB will do. Inflation is a little on the high side (very slightly above the ECB target) suggesting a likely increase in interest rates which would cause the dollar to weaken even further in relation to the euro. But the euro area economy is 'softening' – starting to weaken with falling rates of economic growth and increasing unemployment. This would suggest a cut in interest rates and so Mr Chandler thinks they are likely to leave interest rates unchanged for some time (they will be 'on hold for an extended period') even though he thinks the officials remain hawkish (more worried about inflation than anything else and more likely, other things being equal, to increase interest rates than to cut them).

18.7 Summary

The forex market is the market in which one national currency is traded for another. The market has grown hugely in recent years because of the rapid growth in international capital mobility and the volatility of exchange rates following the breakdown of the Bretton Woods fixed exchange rate system in the early 1970s. This volatility has greatly increased the need of firms to protect themselves against foreign exchange risk and has provided the opportunity to exploit exchange rate variations for profit.

Because exchange rates are prices of one currency in terms of another, they can be expressed in two ways – direct and indirect quotation. Currencies may be traded spot (for immediate delivery) or forward (delivery normally one month, three months or one year ahead). Exchange rate indices may be prepared expressing the average value of a currency against a basket of currencies or the real value of one currency against another, allowing for differences in expected rates of inflation.

To understand the relationship between spot and forward rates of exchange we need to look at the role of interest rate arbitrage – capital moves to take advantage of differences in interest rates on different currencies but there are risks because exchange rates change and buying a foreign currency to benefit from a higher interest rate on that currency might produce a loss if the foreign currency weakens. This risk can be eliminated (covered) by using forward foreign exchange markets. It follows that there is a close relationship between differences in interest rates on currencies and differences between spot and forward rates of exchange. In any pair of currencies, the one with the higher interest rate will trade at a forward discount.

Exchange rate arbitrageurs and speculators both play important roles in the foreign exchange market. As well as helping to bring about covered interest rate parity, arbitrageurs act to ensure that exchange rates are mutually consistent through exchange rate arbitrage. The contribution of speculators is much more controversial. They make use of instruments (such as forward exchange rates) initially developed to provide protection against foreign exchange risk to seek profits. The fact that this is possible indicates that foreign exchange markets are, in fact, far from perfect. This is indicated also by the failure to develop reliable models for the forecasting of future rates of exchange.

It is extremely difficult to predict what is likely to happen to exchange rates in the future. Important ideas have been formulated, notably purchasing power parity and interest rate parity and a variety of types of models have been constructed and tested but nothing has proved particularly helpful in the short to medium term. Because of the importance of expectations and psychological factors in the market, it is particularly difficult for market participants to interpret the significance for future exchange rates of new information (news) coming to the market.

Key concepts in this chapter

Chartism (technical analysis)	Hedging
Covered interest arbitrage	Indirect quotation
Covered interest parity	Interest agio
Direct quotation	Interest rate parity
Effective exchange rate	Purchasing power parity (PPP)
Exchange agio	Rational versus speculative bubbles
Exchange cross rates	Real exchange rate
Exchange rate arbitrage	Regressive expectations
Extrapolative expectations	Short versus long positions
Foreign exchange risk	Speculation
Forward premiums and discounts	Spot and forward exchange rates
Fundamentalist models	Uncovered interest rate arbitrage

Questions and problems

1 List as many items as you can of 'news' which would be likely to cause the value of your domestic currency to fall. Explain why in each case.

2 Explain the following terms in the context of the foreign exchange market:

(a) Covered interest arbitrage
(b) Long positions in a foreign currency
(c) Hedging
(d) Three-point foreign exchange arbitrage

3 Examine the 'Effective Index Rates' table from the *Financial Times* and answer the following questions:

(a) What information do the numbers in the table provide?
(b) What is meant by the words 'index rebased'?
(c) List the currencies that have, on average, strengthened since 1990.

4 In the 'Market Rates' column of the *Financial Times* of 3 October 2007, the three-month interest rate on sterling was quoted as 6.22 per cent; the three-month rate on US dollars was given as 5.22 per cent. On the same day, the spot rate of exchange for the pound against the dollar was: \$1 = £0.4899. On the assumption of perfect interest parity what would one have expected the forward premium/discount on sterling to have been? Why might the actual figure have been different from this?

5 (a) Describe the arbitrage operation that would produce a profit if the following set of spot exchange rates prevailed in a foreign exchange market, explaining how you arrived at your answer:

    US\$1 = NKr5.4393
    US\$1 = €0.7065
    €1 = NKr7.4985

(b) What impacts would such an arbitrage operation have on the above set of exchange rates?

6 Examine the 'Currency Rates' table from any copy of the *Financial Times* and answer the following questions:

(a) What information is being given by the columns headed: 'Closing mid' and 'Day's change'?
(b) To what do the rows labelled 'Three month' refer?
(c) Why are the euro and sterling rows in the dollar column given in reciprocal form?

7 Find a copy of the Big Mac Price Index (the Hamburger Standard) – try, for example, http://www.oanda.com/products/bigmac/bigmac.shtml. Consider the figures in the light of PPP. Why might PPP be particularly unlikely to apply to the trade in hamburgers?

8 You are given the following information:

Spot exchange rate €1 = ¥164.018

Expected euro area inflation rate for next year = 2.2%

Expected Japanese inflation rate for next year = 0.2%

Three-month money market interest rate for the euro = 4.77%

Three-month money market interest rate for Japan = 1.04%

On the basis of these figures calculate:

(a) the real exchange rate of the yen against the euro; and
(b) the approximate three-month forward exchange rate of the yen against the euro.

9 Explain and defend the argument that speculation in markets is desirable.

10 How might one use the spot markets to obtain protection against foreign exchange risk? What advantages do the forward markets have for this purpose?

11 Explain the following:

(a) the relationship between spot and forward rates of exchange;
(b) purchasing power parity;
(c) the difference between a rational and a speculative bubble in the foreign exchange market.

Further reading

Bank for International Settlements, *Triennial Central Bank Survey of Foreign exchange and derivatives market activity in April 2007 – preliminary global results* (Basle, September 2007) [table 1 (t18.1), table 3 (t18.2), table 5 (t18.3)]

A Buckley, *Multinational Finance* (Harlow: FT Prentice Hall, 5e, 2003) Chs 4, 5, 7, 8

L S Copeland, *Exchange Rates and International Finance* (Harlow: FT Prentice Hall, 4e, 2004) Chs 1–3, 5, 7, 8

R Dornbusch, 'Expectations and exchange rate dynamics', *Journal of Political Economy*, 96, 1976, 1161–76

J A Frankel and K A Froot, 'Chartists, fundamentalists and trading in the forex market', *American Economic Review*, May 1990, 181–5

M Friedman, 'The case for flexible exchange rates', in *Essays in Positive Economics* (Chicago: Chicago University Press, 1953) 157–203

P Garnham, 'Dollar index sinks to lowest ebb', *Financial Times*, 29/30 September 2007, p. 31

H D Gibson, *International Finance. Exchange Rates and Financial Flows in the International System* (London: Longman, 1996) Chs 2 and 3

C A E Goodhart, 'The foreign exchange market: The random walk with a dragging anchor', *Economica*, 55, 1988, 437–60

R A Meese and K Rogoff, 'Empirical exchange rate models of the seventies: Do they fit out of sample?', *Journal of International Economics*, 14, 1983, 3–24

F Taylor, *Mastering Foreign Exchange and Currency Options* (London: FT Prentice Hall, 2e, 2003)

Websites

www.bankofengland.co.uk
www.bis.org
www.ft.com
http://fx.sauder.ubc.ca/
www.fxstreet.com
www.imf.org
www.oanda.com

Chapter 19 | Derivatives – the
financial futures
markets

What you will learn in this chapter:

■ What derivatives are and why derivatives markets have grown
so quickly

■ What financial futures are and how futures exchanges
are organized

■ How to read financial futures information in the
Financial Times

■ What determines the pricing of financial futures in general

■ How pricing rules may be applied to different types of
financial futures

19.1 Introduction

One of the most striking developments in financial markets over the past quarter of a century has been the establishment and growth of financial derivatives markets. A derivative is a financial instrument based upon the performance of separately traded commodities or financial instruments. Many agricultural and mining products are traded on commodities markets by firms who are end users of those products. Equally, bond markets and foreign exchange markets allow end users to borrow or lend funds or to obtain foreign exchange. It is possible then to construct contracts which promise to deliver those products at some time in the future or give the right to buy or sell them in the future. These contracts may then be traded in markets different from the original commodities and financial markets (usually referred to as cash markets). Such contracts are known as **derivatives**. They are linked to the cash market through the possibility that a delivery of the primary commodity or instrument might occur. For example, if a trader is to carry out a promise to deliver an instrument in three months' time he will at some time during that three months need to buy the instrument in the cash market. It follows that the value of a derivative and hence its price varies as the price in the cash markets fluctuates. In practice, derivatives seldom lead to the exchange of the underlying instrument. Instead, contracts are *closed out* or allowed to lapse before the delivery.

Derivatives, then, are forward contracts that allow market agents to gamble on movements in the prices of other instruments without being required actually to trade in them. Their initial purpose was to allow traders to hedge risks that they faced in the cash markets as a part of their normal business activity by offsetting one type of risk (resulting, for example, from being long in the cash market) with the opposite risk in a derivatives market. Clearly, however, these markets provide additional possibilities for speculators to take on risk in the expectation that they will be able to outguess the market. In the case of *financial derivatives*, the underlying instrument is financial: bonds, currencies, or stock exchange indices. Derivatives may be divided into three groups:

(a) outright contracts

(b) options, and

(c) complex derivatives that combine elements of outright contracts and options.

Outright contracts establish a commitment to buy, sell or exchange the underlying asset. Consequently, the payoffs on outright contracts are related symmetrically to the upwards and downwards movements of the prices of the underlying assets. *Forward contracts* are outright contracts to buy or sell a given asset at a specified later date when the contract is signed. A different type of outright contract is the *swap*. A swap is a contract for the exchange of payments calculated on different bases, for example the exchange of fixed-rate and floating-rate interest payments on a loan. *Options*, on the other hand, give only the right to buy or sell the underlying asset. Since the right to buy or sell need not be exercised, no definite commitment to buy or sell the underlying asset is established. Consequently, payoffs respond asymmetrically to price movements in cash markets. A major recent development in financial derivatives markets has been the creation and marketing of *credit derivatives*. This term covers a number of types of swap associated with the transfer of credit risk. Because they are relatively new we deal with them in Section 24.3.3 in the chapter on financial innovation.

Derivatives may be traded on organized exchanges with the exchange acting as an intermediary or directly between counterparties in over-the-counter (OTC) markets. Exchange trading establishes a tradable instrument that may be sold on to a third party. OTC contracts cannot be sold on in this way. A forward contract traded on an organized exchange is known as a **future**.

Although derivatives trading based upon commodities (agricultural products or minerals) has existed for several centuries, the need for financial derivatives markets was not seen until the early 1970s when the globalization of business, which had been proceeding apace for the previous 20 years, confronted the increased volatility of foreign exchange rates and increasing and fluctuating rates of inflation. As firms were exposed to increasing amounts of risk, risk management (or financial engineering) became a major concern of business. The most obvious form of *exchange rate risk* relates to current individual transactions (transactions exposure) – the possibility that apparently profitable activities will turn into losses because of unfavourable movements in exchange rates. More generally, the whole future trading performance of a foreign branch or subsidiary may suffer as a result of exchange rate changes, depending on the impact they have on factors such as relative inflation rates, interest rates, profit margins and market share (economic exposure). A different form of risk exists, however, for transnational firms with subsidiaries in other countries – the loss of value of foreign assets in the consolidated balance sheet of the parent company (translation exposure). In addition, the participation of firms in distant and foreign markets led not only to increased exchange rate risk but also to greater default, market and sovereign risk.

Responses were many. To help counter foreign exchange risk, firms developed internal techniques relating to accounting systems and payment and invoicing procedures. Governments of developed countries became involved, providing exchange rate guarantees and other forms of insurance, in effect subsidizing the foreign activities of their exporting firms. Developments in international capital markets allowed firms to borrow more easily in foreign currencies against anticipated future payments in those currencies. The growth of Eurocurrency markets, in particular, allowed firms to obtain foreign currency overdrafts to offset long positions in major currencies. Forward foreign exchange markets developed and banks began to use them more imaginatively, offering, for example, optional date forward contracts in which a firm is given an option regarding the maturity date within a specified period and is charged the premium or discount that applies to the most costly of the settlement dates within the period.

These, and other activities, aimed to remove or reduce the risk faced by firms in particular transactions. An alternative approach in a generally risky environment is to oppose one form of risk to another and hence scope existed for the creation of new instruments which themselves carried risk but which firms could use to balance risks in other elements of their portfolios. More importantly, increases in the range of available instruments allowed firms to diversify their portfolios of assets further. By so doing, they were able to reduce overall risk.

At the same time as firms were becoming increasingly international, they were merging or taking over other firms in different industries – the number of conglomerates was increasing. It was only a matter of time before large firms began to see trading in financial instruments as equivalent to any other part of their business. Risky situations came to be seen as opportunities for making profits that were equivalent to profits made from selling cars, chemicals or airline tickets. This great growth in financial activity was necessarily accompanied by a vast growth in international banking, with banks acting as guarantors, providing

> **MORE FROM THE WEB**
>
> For a timeline of some of the important dates in the history of CBOT (Chicago Board of Trade) and CME (Chicago Mercantile Exchange) see http://www.cmegroup.com/timeline.html.

information and expertise and speculating on their own behalf in the new markets. Banks, seeking to manage the risk they were taking on in order to meet the needs of end users, increasingly engaged in transactions with other banks to the point where interbank transactions have come to make up a very high proportion of total financial activity.

The great growth in derivatives is indicated by the very rapid increase in the number and size of the exchanges on which they are traded. In the 1980s and 1990s many new derivatives exchanges were opened. Recently, there has been a good deal of consolidation through mergers and takeovers. In 2007, the two big Chicago exchanges that started life as commodities markets, the Chicago Board of Trade (CBOT) and the Chicago Mercantile Exchange (CME) merged to form the CME Group. The European Exchange (Eurex) was the result of a 1998 merger between German and Swiss derivatives exchanges (*Deutsche Terminbörse* and the Swiss Options and Financial Future Exchange). Euronext was formed by a merger of the Paris, Amsterdam, Brussels and Lisbon Stock Exchanges and later took over the London International Financial Futures Exchange (LIFFE). In 2007, Euronext merged with the New York Stock Exchange (NYSE) to form NYSE Euronext.

It is these relatively new instruments and markets that we need to explore in this chapter and the next. We deal with futures in this chapter and in Chapter 20 consider options, swaps and more complex derivatives.

19.2 The nature of financial futures

A futures contract is a forward contract traded on a derivatives exchange. It is an agreement to exchange a given asset at a specified later date at a price established when the contract is signed. The buyer goes long in the cash market, that is, he contracts to take delivery of the underlying instrument in the future. The seller goes short, contracting to deliver the instrument in the future. An exchange-traded contract is standardized in terms of both time period and amount. It specifies the quantity and quality of the underlying asset as well as the date of delivery and the agreed price at which delivery of the underlying asset will take place, should delivery actually occur. Thus, the three-month Euroswiss futures contract offered by Euronext.liffe specifies an amount of SFr1 million, while the US dollar currency futures offered by the CME group specifies an amount of €125,000. Bond futures specify the amount of the bond and its interest rate coupon, for instance, a $100,000 nominal 20-year treasury bond with a 7 per cent coupon. As long as single contracts are for relatively small amounts, this does not reduce the flexibility of the market by much since it is always possible for a market agent to increase his or her exposure by buying or selling a number of contracts on the same underlying asset for the same period.

In contrast, OTC forward contracts are direct contracts between a bank and another market agent. The amount of the contract and its terms are determined by the two counterparties. Flexibility is possible in the time period as well as in the amount. Crucially, an OTC forward transaction does not produce a tradable instrument that can be sold on to a third party in the way that futures can.

Until recently, all trading at futures exchanges took place in trading *pits*, areas of the trading floor devoted to the trade of a particular contract. This method of trading between members, which allowed all traders to hear every negotiated price, is known as **open outcry**. However, financial futures exchanges have developed automated systems which allow screen-based trading and all electronic exchanges have been opened. Open outcry hangs on in a small number of commodity exchanges but in most places will soon be a memory from a more colourful past.

Most financial futures contracts have four delivery dates per year. There are a number of very precise delivery details including lists of eligible assets which will satisfy the delivery requirements of a contract and methods of determining the final **settlement price**. However, delivery does not usually occur as buyers and sellers of futures contracts are not normally end users of the underlying asset. Traders using futures to hedge against risk to which they are exposed in the cash market are seeking to lock into existing exchange or interest rates on future transactions. In such cases, the period for which the hedge is needed is unlikely to coincide with the time period of the futures contract. Once a firm has traded out of its open position in the cash market, it will no longer need the hedge in the futures market.

Financial futures may also be traded by speculators who wish to profit from the rises or falls they expect to occur in interest rates, exchange rates or stock exchange indices. Through futures, they can take a view about trends in cash markets without having to purchase the underlying currency or financial instrument. A speculator who felt that interest rates were likely to rise or a currency's value decline could go short in the relevant asset by selling a futures contract. Traders who are using the futures market to create an open position in this way usually close the position once they have achieved their profit objectives. If it does not seem likely that they will make the hoped-for profit, they will probably cut their losses before delivery is due. Investors wishing to cancel out the obligation to deliver or to accept delivery of the instrument can do so by entering into an offsetting (or reversing) contract. That is, if a market agent has entered into a contract to deliver a particular instrument, he can offset this by taking out another contract which requires him to take delivery of the same amount of the same instrument on the same date. His obligations under the two contracts then cancel out. In some cases, such as futures based upon equity market indices or interest rates on short-term deposits, no delivery is possible and traders meet their obligations by making cash payments based upon the changes in the value of the index or interest rate in question.

To reduce default risk and hence to make futures more easily tradable, futures exchanges make use of a **clearing house** which covers any default arising from a contract. Therefore, although all futures contracts involve a buyer and a seller, the obligation of each is to the clearing house, not to each other. That is, after the transaction has been recorded, the clearing house substitutes itself for the counterparty and becomes the seller to every buyer and vice versa. Therefore, the only default risk faced by someone entering into a futures contract stems from any doubts about the creditworthiness of the clearing house itself. This is, in turn, reduced in a number of ways. Firstly, all transactions must take place through members of the exchange who act as brokers for anyone wishing to invest in the market. The number of members (or seats on the exchange) is limited. Seats on an exchange may be purchased from existing members but new members must demonstrate their creditworthiness to the exchange. In addition, the members of the exchange must keep with the clearing house special accounts (margin accounts) that are adjusted from day to day to ensure that members are always able to settle their debts to the clearing house. Investors must, in turn, maintain similar accounts with the members of the exchange. This is known as trading on **margin,** and futures positions are said to be margined on a **marked-to-market** basis. These rules should mean that the clearing house is able to guarantee the performance of every contract entered into on the exchange.

The first step in the system is that an investor must, at the start of the contract period, pay into a margin account a small percentage (the **initial margin**) of the value of the contract. The size of the initial margin is intended to reflect the maximum daily loss likely to arise on the contract and so will be related to the volatility of the price movements of that instrument. Initial margins are generally between 1 and 5 per cent of the value of the contract. Margin accounts must then be adjusted daily to reflect gains or losses on a contract over the day. Assume a contract has a commencing value of $10,000 with each counterparty paying an initial margin of $500 into their margin accounts. Assume next that during the first day's trading, the contract's value rises to $10,100, representing a loss for the seller and a gain for the buyer of the contract. The clearing house would then transfer $100 from the seller's margin account to that of the buyer. Should the price rise again the next day, a similar transfer would occur. If the balance in the seller's account fell below a specified level (the **maintenance margin**), she would be required to make additional payments into the account (the **variation margin**) in order to keep the account at or above an acceptable minimum balance. On the other hand, the buyer could, in this case, withdraw the daily profits from her margin account. Some exchanges (for example, Euronext.liffe) set the maintenance margin at the same level as the initial margin.

Of course, should the value of the above contract fall below £10,000, the buyer's margin account would fall and she might be required to make additional payments. Failure to make such payments immediately would lead to the closure of the contract against the defaulting party. The system of marking accounts to market daily prevents losses from accumulating, and the holding of margins by the clearing house removes most default risk.

Daily gains and losses on contracts are determined by the settlement price, which is set by the settlement committee of the exchange. It is normally the closing price for the day (the last price at which the contract has traded). However, if a contract has not traded for some time prior to the market's close, the committee may set a different settlement price in an attempt to reflect accurately the trading conditions at the close of the market. The freedom that the settlement committee has to fix the settlement price also allows it to protect the clearing house from the remaining default risk that might arise from very large daily swings in the price of a contract. They may do this by setting price limits – maximum movements up and down from the previous day's settlement price. If these limits would otherwise be broken, the market closes **limit-up** or **limit-down**. The aim is to prevent losses going above the amounts held in margin accounts, forcing or tempting losers to default. The hope is that the temporary closure of the market might lead traders to reassess their positions. However, the system of price limits has its disadvantages. As long as the market remains closed positions cannot be closed out and contracts become illiquid, destroying one of the major advantages of futures contracts, their tradability. For this reason, many exchanges do not operate price limits during the delivery month of a contract.

The relative smallness of the margin requirements is responsible for another important aspect of futures markets – their high *gearing* (or leverage). If all goes well, the effective rate of profit on a futures contract can be very high. To see this, consider the following simple example. Assume that in March an investor buys a €125,000 contract on US dollars for delivery in June at a price of €1 = $1.40. The contract value is $175,000. Assume an initial margin of 2 per cent ($3,500). Assume next that the value of the euro rises steadily over the contract period to €1 = $1.50 and the contract price rises in line with it. The value of the contract would have been rising steadily and no further margin payments would have been required. At the end of June, the investor takes delivery of the euro at €1 = $1.40 and sells it spot at €1 = $1.50. The buyer of the contract makes a profit (and the seller a loss) of $12,500 (125,000 × $0.10) but has only had to lay out $3,500, giving a per annum rate of return of over 1,400 per cent! Alternatively, he could take his profit by reversing the contract – taking out another contract to *sell* €125,000 in June at the now higher contract price.

Sadly, however, life is not quite as easy as this. In addition to making margin payments, investors must pay brokers a negotiated commission for executing orders. Commission (sometimes referred to as the direct cost of the contract) is charged on both the opening and the closing of a position and is normally payable either when the position is closed or when delivery takes place. More seriously, the value of the euro may have fallen, requiring the investor to advance more margin. Suppose that the day after the contract was taken out, the value of the euro fell to €1 = $1.35. The value of the contract would have fallen to $168,750 and (on the assumption that the maintenance margin was the same as the initial margin) a variation margin payment of $6,250 would need to be made. If, the euro later rose in value, some of this variation margin could be withdrawn, but an investor would need to be fortunate not to have to make some variation margin payments over the life of a contract and thus the average amount held in the margin account over the contract period is likely to be above the initial margin. The possibility that additional margin payments may have to be made on a daily basis also requires an investor to keep a certain amount of his or her assets in a very liquid form. Of course, if the value of the euro did not rise again during the life of the contract, the investor would be required on the delivery date to buy euro at $1.40 and would only be able to sell them spot for $1.35, producing a loss of $6,250. Again, the investor could avoid having to receive and then re-sell sterling by reversing the contract before the delivery date but this would not reduce the loss. Futures contracts, therefore, provide the prospect of high rates of return but involve considerable risks.

MORE FROM THE WEB

There is a great deal of educational material about financial derivatives on the web and many glossaries of terms. You could try, for example, the website of the International Swaps and Derivatives Association (ISDA) on http://www.isda.org. Click on 'Education' and then on 'Product Descriptions'. There is also a useful annotated bibliography and a helpful set of links. There you will find links to a variety of helpful sites including http://www.margrabe.com/, http://www.numa.com and, probably best, http://www.finpipe.com.

19.3 Reading the *Financial Times*

On the 'Market Data' page of the *Financial Times*, a table of a range of short-term interest rate futures is provided. It can also be found on the *Financial Times* website under Markets Data: Bonds & Rates. In Table 19.1, we reproduce the table for 2 October 2007.

All the contracts in Table 19.1 are contracts on three-month time deposits. The buyer of such a contract would, on delivery, receive a time deposit at an eligible bank of the amount specified in the contract. For example, the Euroswiss 3m contract is for a deposit of SFr1 million; the Eurodollar 3m contract is for $1 million; and the sterling 3m contract for a deposit of £500,000. The gamble in such contracts relates to changes in short-term interest rates relative to those rates at the time the contract is negotiated. Contract prices are quoted in terms of *points of 100%* or *100-rate*. That is, the price of the contract is quoted in the form of subtractions from 100 per cent – a price of 95.38 represents an annual interest rate of 4.62 per cent (100 − 95.38). The minimum price movement (or *tick size*) on most of these contracts is one basis point (0.01 per cent). In the case of a $1 million three-month time deposit, a change in the price of one basis point translates into a change in the value of the contract of $25 (0.01 per cent per annum interest on $1 million for three months). This is known as the *tick value* of the contract. The tick value provides a simple way of quoting the profit or loss on a contract – a profit of 10 ticks on the Three Month Eurodollar Futures contract is a profit of $250; a 10 tick profit on the Three Month Euroswiss contract is SFr250.

Quoting the price as an index maintains the usual inverse relationship between the price of a financial instrument and the yield on it. As explained in Section 19.4 below, although the settlement price at the time of delivery is based on the spot interest rate on the last trading day of the contract, the interest rate implied by the futures price during the life of the future can differ from the interest rate on the underlying asset in the cash market. Some examples of the relationship between futures prices shown in Table 19.1 and spot market interest rates are shown in Box 19.1.

For each contract listed in Table 19.1, prices are quoted for a series of delivery dates. Delivery days are in December, March, June and September. The delivery day on each contract is the first business day after the last trading day, and the last trading day is the

Table 19.1 Interest rate futures

Oct 2		Open	Sett	Change	High	Low	Est. vol	Open int.
Euribor 3m*	Dec	95.39	95.38	−0.02	95.39	95.37	74,592	871,140
Euribor 3m*	Mar	95.63	95.62	−0.02	95.63	–	109,402	620,089
Euribor 3m*	Jun	95.73	95.73	−0.01	95.73	95.71	92,367	443,242
Euribor 3m*	Sep	95.76	95.79	+0.00	95.79	95.75	74,174	415,094
Euroswiss 3m*	Dec	97.19	97.18	−0.02	97.20	97.17	4,904	80,954
Euroswiss 3m*	Mar	97.20	97.18	−0.01	97.20	97.16	3,118	54,943
Sterling 3m*	Dec	93.96	93.99	+0.01	93.99	93.96	42,324	513,539
Sterling 3m*	Mar	94.28	94.31	+0.00	94.32	94.27	34,200	532,002
Sterling 3m*	Jun	94.44	94.48	+0.02	94.50	94.42	44,912	498,767
Sterling 3m*	Sep	94.52	94.56	+0.02	94.58	94.48	45,457	351,294
Eurodollar 3m†	Dec	95.11	95.08	−0.03	95.11	95.06	223,920	1551,776
Eurodollar 3m†	Mar	95.43	95.42	+0.00	95.46	95.39	277,258	1508,827
Eurodollar 3m†	Jun	95.59	95.60	+0.02	95.64	95.54	277,781	1358,828
Eurodollar 3m†	Sep	95.66	95.69	+0.04	95.72	95.60	243,836	1220,497
Fed Fnds 30d‡	Oct	95.260	95.270	−0.010	95.275	95.260	7,175	82,348
Fed Fnds 30d‡	Nov	95.435	95.435	–	95.445	95.410	14,581	98,311
Fed Fnds 30d‡	Dec	95.560	95.560	+0.000	95.570	95.535	8,635	56,642
Euroyen 3m††	Dec	99.140	99.135	−0.010	99.145	99.130	47,456	956,998
Euroyen 3m††	Mar	99.105	99.105	−0.010	99.110	99.095	25,571	728,039
Euroyen 3m††	Jun	99.065	99.065	−0.015	99.075	99.060	15,242	378,737

Contracts are based on volumes traded in 2004.

Sources: * LIFFE, † CME, ‡ CBOT, †† TIFFE.

Source: *Financial Times*, 3 October 2007. Reprinted with permission.

BOX 19.1 Short-term interest rate futures prices and short-term interest rates

Table 19.1 is taken from the *Financial Times* of 3 October 2007 and the settlement prices given are for the previous day. Delivery dates (the third Wednesday of the month) for the December, March, June and September contracts were thus approximately three months, six months, nine months and twelve months ahead. By comparing the interest rates implied by the futures prices with the interest rates for similar periods in the 'Market Rates' table on the same day, we can make an interesting point. Consider the Three Month LIFFE sterling contract shown in Table 19.1. From the settlement prices (Sett) for this contract, we can derive the following interest rates:

December 6.01%; March 5.69%; June 5.52%; September 5.44%

£ LIBOR market interest rates on the same day were:

one month	6.14625%
three months	6.25875%
six months	6.25500%
one year	6.14750%

The official repo rate at the time was 5.75%. Although there are differences between the two sets of rates, it is clear that the derivatives price is related to the underlying money markets. Both sets of figures suggest the possibility of an early increase in the official rate but the interest rates implied by the prices of the futures suggest likely reductions in interest rates in the early months of 2008. This is not reflected in the market rates. It is also clear that the interest rate derived from the futures price is consistently below the market rates. Can you think of a reason why this might be so? (We discuss this case in Box 19.2 later in the chapter.)

Exercise 19.1

US$ LIBOR money market interest rates on the 2 October 2007 were:

one month	5.12625%
three months	5.24000%
six months	5.16250%
twelve months	4.97563%

Would you expect the price of three-month Eurodollar futures shown for December to be higher or lower than that for the following September? Check your answer with Table 19.1.

third Wednesday of the delivery month. Table 19.1 has seven columns. These are as follows:

- Open: the price of the contract at the beginning of business.
- Sett: the settlement price – the price at which contracts are settled at the end of the day.
- Change: the change in the settlement price from the previous day – in many cases this is not equal to the difference between the first two columns. For example, September Three Month Sterling Futures have an opening price of 94.52 and a settlement price of 94.56 but the change is given as only +0.02, suggesting that few contracts had changed hands the previous day and that the opening price the following morning had been different from the previous settlement price.

- High: the highest price reached for the contract on the day.
- Low: the lowest price reached for the contract on the day.
- Est. vol: the estimated number of contracts entered into during the day.
- Open int: **open interest** – the number of outstanding contracts on the previous trading day.

A table of currency futures, also for 2 October 2007, is shown as Table 19.2. It is available on the *Financial Times* website but is no longer regularly in the newspaper. It provides similar information to the interest rate futures table except that prices here are quoted in exchange rates. For example, for €-Sterling futures offered by the New York Board of Trade NYBOT[1] we are told that a contract is for €100,000 while for the

Table 19.2 Currency futures

Oct 2		Open	Latest	Change	High	Low	Est. vol	Open int.
€-Sterling*	Dec	0.6987	0.6962	−0.0028	0.6985	0.6954	435	10,482
€-Yen*	Dec	162.87	162.71	−0.87	162.84	162.65	1,467	10,562
$-Can $†	Dec	1.0094	1.0030	−0.0070	1.0094	0.9996	39,130	139,774
$-Euro €†	Dec	1.4252	1.4175	−0.0085	1,4260	1.4160	157,454	209,987
$-Euro €†	Mar	1.4254	1.4187	−0.0084	1,4255	1.4176	284	1,380
$-Sw Franc†	Dec	0.8604	0.8550	−0.0054	0.8610	0.8535	37,673	74,661
$-Yen†	Dec	0.8720	0.8711	−0.0008	0.8752	0.8698	69,381	176,656
$-Yen†	Mar	0.8820	0.8796	−0.0008	0.8835	0.8787	89	8,625
$-Sterling†	Dec	2.0396	2.0377	−0.0031	2.0423	2.0337	52,041	93,905
$-Aust S†	Dec	0.8912	0.8832	−0.0088	0.8921	0.8779	35,549	92,873
$-Mex Peso†	Dec	91325	91300	−125	91475	91025	12,139	25,471

Sources: * NYBOT; Sterling €100,000 and Yen: €100,000.   †CME: Australian $: A$100,000, Canadian $: C$100,000, Euro: €125,000; Mexican Peso: 500,000, Swiss Franc: SFr125,000; Yen: Y12.5m ($ per Y100); Sterling: £62,500. CME volume, high & low for pit & electronic trading at settlement. Contracts shown are based on the volumes traded in 2004.

Source: *Financial Times*, 3 October 2007. Reprinted with permission.

---

[1]   In 2006, NYBOT became a wholly owned subsidiary of the Intercontinental Exchange (ICE).

$-Euro contract offered by the Chicago Mercantile Exchange (CME)[2] each contract is for €125,000 and so on. The price in both of these cases is quoted *per euro*. That is, the price reflects the indirect quotation of the euro – how much €1 exchanges for in sterling and US dollars respectively. The price shown in Table 19.2 for the $-Euro future for December delivery is €1 = $1.4252. The settlement price for December delivery for the €-Sterling future is €1 = £0.6987.

Table 19.3 reproduces a *Financial Times* table showing a sample of bond futures for 2 October 2007. This table is also now available regularly only on the *FT*'s website. Bond futures are typically based on notional government bonds. The table indicates down the left-hand side the bonds on which the futures are based together with the names of the exchanges offering the contracts. For example, Euro-Bobl-Eurex is a contract offered by Eurex on a notional medium-term debt instrument issued by the German Federal

Government with a term of 4.5 to 5.5 years and a coupon of 6 per cent. The contract size is €100,000. Kofex relates to a future offered by the Korean Futures Exchange on a notional three-year bond. We can see that there are two ways of expressing the quotation here. Interest rates in the USA are quoted in 32nds of 1 per cent. Hence, prices on notional US treasury bond futures are quoted in that way with 106–215 being read as 106 21.5/32 (that is, 106 43/64). In Europe, on the other hand, interest rates are quoted in decimals, hence the closing prices of 112.73 and 113.13 for Euro-Eurex.

Another important point stems from the fact that long-term bond futures are based on notional bonds since, in the unlikely event that the contract leads to the delivery of bonds, the seller of the contract is extremely unlikely to be able to deliver a bond with the exact characteristics of the notional bond. Thus, the exchange establishes a list of eligible bonds, any one

Table 19.3 Bond futures

Oct 2		Open	Close	Change	High	Low	Est. vol	Open int.
Euro-Eurex	Dec	112.58	112.73	−0.01	112.93	112.36	1023,243	1395,148
	Mar	113.00	113.13	−0.01	113.34	112.83	340	1,555
Japan 10yr-TSE	Dec	134.87	134.89	−0.20	134.88	134.78	51,295	123,012
US Tr long-CBOT	Dec	111–28	112–00	+0–09	112–10	111–14	319,539	918,556
	Mar	111–27	111–29	+0–10	112–07	111–27	110	1,651
US Tr 10yr-CBOT	Dec	109–135	109–195	+0–085	109–255	109–055	1113,817	2250,978
	Mar	108–265	109–050	+0–090	109–100	108–245	5,095	76,980
Euro-Bobl-Eurex	Dec	107.68	107.75	−0.04	107.89	107.55	508,719	1110,202
	Mar	107.87	107.89	−0.04	107.87	107.87	302	10,211
Euro-Schatz-Eurex	Dec	103.370	103.380	−0.025	103.440	103.305	504,863	1446,267
	Mar	–	103.380	−0.025	–	–	750	344
US Tr 5 yr-CBOT	Dec	107–010	107-045	+0–055	107–095	106–260	477,326	1603,080
	Mar	106–215	107-000	+0–070	106–215	106–215	724	5
Long gilt-Liffe	Dec	106.81	107.25	+0.19	107.32	106.71	108,496	307,786
	Mar	–	107.33	+0.19	–	–	–	–
SFE 3 yr	Dec	93.54	93.55	−0.01	93.55	93.53	18,675	576,231
Kofex 3 yr	Dec	106.66	106.72	+0.04	106.73	106.65	33,264	159,181

Contracts shown are among the most heavily traded in 2004. Open interest figures and are for the previous day. CBOT volume, high & low for pit & electronic trading at settlement. For more contract details see: www.eurexchange.com, cbot.com, tse.or.jp, liffe.com. Changes based on prev sett price. US data in 32nds.

Source: *Financial Times*, 3 October 2007. Reprinted with permission.

---

[2]　Now part of the CME Group together with CBOT.

of which may be used to effect delivery. For example, the notional bond may have a period to maturity of 20 years and a coupon rate of 9 per cent while the eligible list established by the exchange might include bonds with periods of maturity between 15 and 25 years and coupon rates ranging from 6 to 12 per cent. This causes a complication at the point of delivery because the buyer of the contract must pay for the bond actually delivered whereas the final settlement price of the futures contract will be based on the notional price. To overcome this problem, the exchange publishes a **price factor** or **conversion factor** for each eligible bond that reflects the difference in value between the notional bond and the actual bond delivered. The final settlement price for the notional bond is multiplied by the price factor (which may be either greater than or less than one). This accounts for some of the high closing prices quoted such as 134.89 for a notional 10-year bond with the Tokyo Stock Exchange (TSE). The bonds available for delivery in these cases must have characteristics quite different from the notional bonds or very profitable arbitrage opportunities would exist between the bond market and the futures market.

Another complication arises because, although both futures contracts and bonds trade at clean prices, bonds have accrued interest added on whereas futures contracts do not. Consequently, allowance has to be made for interest accrued between the date of the coupon prior to the delivery of the bond and the delivery date. These two modifications mean that the buyer of the contract must pay for the bond delivered to him, the final settlement price for the notional bond plus any unpaid interest accrued on the bond.

Of the bonds eligible for delivery, the seller always chooses the bond which is cheapest for him to deliver – the cheapest to deliver (CTD) bond. Delivery may take place on any day of the delivery month, although in practice it is always on either the first or the last day of the month. If the current yield on the bond that is to be delivered is greater than the money market interest rate, the seller will retain the bond until the last day of the month before delivering it. On the other hand, if money market interest rates are higher, he will deliver the bond on the first day of the month.

Stock exchange index futures and futures on a selection of individual stocks are found in the stock exchange pages of the *Financial Times*. The Equity Index Futures table currently provides information on a FTSE-100 (Financial Times Stock Exchange Index) futures

---

MORE FROM THE WEB

Contract details for the various futures referred to in *Financial Times* tables can be obtained from the websites of the exchanges involved.

For example, for **Eurex**, consult www. eurexchange.com On the home page, click on 'Products' under the heading 'Direct Links' and then select 'Interest rate derivatives' and then 'Eurex Bonds' will give you contract sizes, the form of price quotation and delivery days for the contracts available. Addresses of other derivatives exchanges mentioned in Tables 19.1, 19.2 and 19.3 are:

Chicago Board of Trade (CBOT) www.CBOT.com, now part of the **CME Group** with **Chicago Mercantile Exchange (CME)** www.cme.com

LIFFE now **Euronext.liffe** and part of **NYSE Euronext** www.euronext.com

Korean Futures Exchange (Kofex), since 2005 part of the **Korea Exchange (KRX)** http://eng.krx.co.kr/a

New York Board of Trade (NYBOT), since 2006 a subsidiary of **Intercontinental Exchange (ICE)** and since September 2007 known as **ICE Futures US** www.theice.com

Sydney Futures Exchange (SFE), since 2006 part of the **Australian Securities Exchange (ASX)**, www.asx.com.au

Tokyo Financial Futures Exchange (TIFFE), since 2005 known as **Tokyo Financial Exchange (TFX)** www.tfx.co.jp/en/

Tokyo Stock Exchange (TSE), http://www.tse.or.jp/english/

---

contract as well as on a selection of contracts on the indices of other exchanges including the Tokyo Stock Exchange's Nikkei 225 index, the Standard and Poor's (S&P) 500 index, the Dow Jones Industrial Average (DJIA) and a range of indices of European stock markets. Prices are quoted directly in terms of the index.

19.4 The pricing of futures

We have said above that very few, if any, end users of the underlying instrument use the futures market as a means of buying or selling that instrument. Thus, we have three principal types of agent – hedgers, speculators and arbitrageurs. For ease, hedgers can be assumed to be participants with open positions in the cash market who are using the futures market to offset their cash risk.[3] They may either be long in the cash market and wish to go short in the futures market or vice versa. Speculators, in effect, provide the insurance for hedgers by being prepared to take an open position. If hedgers in general wish to go short in the futures market, they can only sell contracts if speculators are prepared to go long and vice versa.

A major role in determining the pricing of futures is, however, played by arbitrageurs. The nature of their role can be seen by looking at forex futures. The existence of a forward market in foreign exchange as well as forex futures contracts means that there are two markets in what is essentially the same product. Consequently, arbitrage is possible between the two markets and this should ensure that variations in the forward exchange rate of the euro should be reflected in changes in the price of a euro futures contract. If this did not occur, there would be a profit opportunity for arbitrageurs. Almost all forex futures contracts are priced in terms of dollars per unit of the other currency. Suppose the three-month forward value of the dollar per euro fell from €1 = \$1.40 to €1 = \$1.45 but the price of the equivalent futures contract did not change. Arbitrageurs would be able to buy euro futures contracts allowing delivery of euro in three months' time at an exchange rate of \$1.40 to the euro and, at the same time, sell euro three months forward at the higher exchange rate. At the end of the three months, they would take delivery of the euro under the futures contract and sell them under the terms of the forward contract, making a risk-free profit. The increased demand for the futures contract would force up the futures price while the sale of euro in the forward market would push down its forward exchange rate, changing its relationship with the spot rate and opening up possibilities for interest rate arbitrage. We would not return to equilibrium until the spot and forward exchange rates and the price of the futures contract had come into line and all arbitrage profit opportunities had been removed. This is not to say that prices in the futures, forward and spot markets move exactly together. We shall see that there is a financing cost associated with arbitraging between spot and futures markets; there are always transactions

> **MORE FROM THE WEB**
>
> A great deal of information on the state of international derivatives markets is provided by the Bank for International Settlements (www.bis.org). Every six months, a report is published on OTC derivatives market activity. The *BIS Quarterly Review* (downloadable in pdf format) also publishes regular reports on international banking and financial market developments. Go to the BIS home page and click on 'Publications and Statistics'.

costs; and futures and forwards contracts while dealing in essentially the same product are not exactly the same. Among other things, futures contracts involve daily cashflow settlements while forward contracts do not.

Nonetheless, the prices of futures must be linked through arbitrage to the prices of the underlying instrument in the cash market. This link provides the basic theory for the determination of futures prices (the cost-of-carry model). It stems from the fact that buying the underlying asset and holding it for three months is always an alternative to buying a futures contract requiring one to take delivery of the asset in three months' time. Equally, going short in the cash market is an alternative to selling a futures contract which may require its delivery in the future. Further, on the delivery date itself, the value of a futures contract is determined by the cash price of the underlying asset.

19.4.1 The cost-of-carry model of futures pricing

According to the cost-of-carry model, futures prices depend on the price of the underlying instrument and the cost of holding it from the date of purchase to the delivery date. For financial instruments, the principal **cost of carry** is the financing cost. If a trader buys a financial instrument and holds it for three months, the financing cost (or cost of carry) is the interest paid or forgone on the funds needed to purchase the instrument

---

[3] In practice, hedgers could be using futures markets to diversify their portfolio and so reduce specific risk as part of a general risk management strategy.

less any yield obtained on it while it is being held. That is:

$$Cc = P_s(i - c) \qquad (19.1)$$

where Cc is the cost of carry; P_s is the cash price of the underlying asset; i is the interest rate payable on the funds borrowed to purchase the instrument and c is any yield on the asset during the period in which it is held. The costs of borrowing in futures markets are usually low both because those borrowing are normally large financial institutions and because the purchased instrument may act as collateral for the loan. In our examples below, we shall assume that traders in the futures market are able to borrow at money market rates and in any examples we shall use figures from the Market Rates columns of the *Financial Times*.

The basic cost-of-carry rule for all futures is that the futures price, *in a perfect market*, must be equal to the cash price of the instrument plus the carrying charges necessary to carry the commodity forward to delivery.

$$P_f = P_s + Cc \qquad (19.2)$$

and

$$P_f = P_s(1 + i - c) \qquad (19.3)$$

where P_f is the futures price.

This is known as the **fair price** of futures and is the price that produces for the purchaser of a futures contract a risk-free rate of profit just equal to the costs of carry. This derives from the arbitrage opportunity which would exist in a perfect market if the futures price were different from the cash price of the instrument. If the futures price were greater than the cash price (including carrying costs), an arbitrageur could borrow and use the funds obtained to buy the instrument in the cash market while, at the same time, selling a futures contract promising delivery of the same amount of the instrument at the end of the period of the loan. On the delivery date, he would meet the requirements of the futures contract by delivering the instrument he had been holding and would use the funds received to repay the loan, leaving an arbitrage profit. No risk would have been involved in this 'cash-and-carry' operation. On the other hand, if the cash price were too high relative to the futures price, there would be a reverse cash-and-carry arbitrage opportunity. An arbitrageur could sell the instrument short, lend the proceeds of the short sale and buy a futures contract promising delivery at time t. At t, he would

collect the proceeds from the loan (including interest) and pay for the instrument delivered under the terms of the futures contract. This would, in turn, be used to remove the short position in the asset, again leaving an arbitrage profit.

This example ignores the transactions costs that exist on both sides of the market, including fees to have orders executed (brokerage, commissions, exchange fees), any taxes payable, and the bid–offer spread found in all markets. Inclusion of these costs provides an area of indeterminacy for the futures price. If we were to assume that transactions costs were a fixed percentage, T, of the transaction amount and that these costs applied to the cash market but not the futures market, the above equation would become:

$$P_s(1 - T)(1 + i - c) \leq P_f \leq P_s(1 + T)(1 + i - c) \qquad (19.4)$$

This equation defines the no-arbitrage band, outside of which there would be scope for arbitrage. If the futures price were to rise above the band, traders would buy the instrument in the cash market and sell the futures, forcing the futures price down and the cash price up, removing the arbitrage opportunity. With the futures price below the band, the reverse strategy would be profitable. In practice, transactions costs and hence the width of the no-arbitrage band vary among traders – a non-exchange member, for instance, faces much higher costs than a member. But for the market as a whole, the futures price should stay within or be rapidly forced back into the band set by the trader with the lowest transactions costs. With some financial futures, particularly stock exchange indices futures, attempting to arbitrage between cash and futures markets is not risk free. This opens up a further possibility for differences emerging between cash and futures prices.

The next question we must ask is where, within the no-arbitrage band, the futures price will settle. In essence, this becomes a question of the price at which speculators will provide the insurance required by hedgers. From the point of view of the speculator, the important question is the relationship between the futures price and the future cash price of the underlying asset at the point of delivery specified in the futures contract. Thus, in order to decide what price she is willing to pay, a speculator needs to form an expectation of the future cash price. In a certain world, that expectation would always be correct and the futures would be priced to give the risk-free rate of return equal to the cost of carry. Under rational expectations and with risk-neutral speculators, the market average expectation of the future cash price would be correct and this expectation would determine the current futures price. Again only the risk-free profit in the cost-of-carry model would be received. The difference between the futures price and the current cash price of the underlying asset (known as the **basis**) would be equal to the cost of carry.

If the cost of carry is positive (that is, $i > c$) and thus the futures price is above the cash price, the situation is known as a **contango**. In this case, the futures price is falling towards the cash price as the delivery day approaches since the amount of interest which must be paid to finance the holding of the underlying instrument is falling as the time to delivery shortens. If the futures price is below the cash price ($i < c$) we have what is known as **backwardation**. Then the futures price is rising towards the cash price as the delivery date approaches. These same ideas can be applied to a series of forward contracts for different time periods since again arbitrage is possible. Consider two three-month Eurodollar contracts, with December and March delivery dates respectively. Just as it is possible to go long by buying the instrument and holding it rather than buying a futures contract, it is possible to buy a December forward contract, take delivery, and then hold the instrument until March as an alternative to buying a future with a March delivery date. Thus, the relationship between the fair prices for a December futures contract (P_1^f) and a March contract (P_2^f) is given by the cost of carry:

$$P_2^f = P_1^f + P_1^f(i - c) \qquad (19.5)$$

If the cost of carry is positive ($i > c$), contracts with more distant delivery dates will be trading at a premium to those with nearer dates. This is a **normal contango**. Where futures with more distant delivery dates are trading at a discount we have **normal backwardation**.

So far, we have been assuming risk-neutral speculators. But what if speculators are risk averse? Then they demand a risk premium and the current futures price varies from the cash price by more or less than the cost of carry, although it must always remain within the no-arbitrage band. The direction in which it varies will depend on the nature of the risk speculators are taking. If hedgers are long in the cash market and wish to go short in the futures market, speculators will need to go long in the futures market (buy the contract) if they are to provide the insurance hedgers

are seeking. The risk for speculators would then be that the future cash price would be less than the futures price (they would have to sell the instrument when it was delivered to them at a lower price than they had paid for the future). To reduce this risk, they would wish to pay a lower price for the future than the expected cash price. In other words, the risk premium built into the price of the future would be negative and – as long as the risk premium were greater than any excess of i over c – we should have backwardation. If this were the normal state of affairs in the market, futures with more distant delivery dates would be trading at a discount and we would have normal backwardation.

For many years, dating back to Keynes (1930) and Hicks (1946), it was largely assumed that hedgers were firms that produced or utilized the underlying instrument and much of the research literature on futures markets (notably commodity futures) was based on the normal-backwardation theory (Phillips and Weiner, 1994). It follows from this theory that if expectations are on average correct, speculators as a group receive a rate of return greater than the risk-free rate which would have been justified. That is, on average, speculators should gain and hedgers should lose. More recently, it has been demonstrated by Grossman and Stiglitz (1980) and by Kyle (1985) that differential information can affect prices and profits in financial markets. Shleifer and Summers (1990) have also developed a model based on asymmetrically informed market participants, with the less informed referred to as 'noise traders'. A literature has also developed based on portfolio theory (for example, the capital asset pricing model). Working on the assumption that forward and futures markets are perfectly integrated with markets for other assets, it has reached the conclusion that risk premiums are not related to hedging, because speculators can costlessly enter forward and futures markets, and diversify the non-systematic risk assumed in these markets by combining them in portfolios with other assets. Hirshleifer (1988) has integrated the traditional theories of risk premiums based on hedging with the portfolio approach and has shown that non-marketability of claims on profits, together with fixed costs of entering asset markets, yield predictions similar to those of the simple normal backwardation model. In contrast, the asymmetric-information view of trader performance predicts that traders with better information gain at the expense of 'noise' traders. If traders who operate in the cash market have superior information about future supply and demand conditions, the prediction of the normal-backwardation model can be reversed.

Let us next apply the general approach outlined here to some specific types of financial futures.

19.4.2 Pricing interest rate futures

We begin by considering short-term interest rate futures. We assume initially a perfect market and ignore any special features of a futures contract. Assume that the contract is based on three-month Eurodollar interest rates as in the contract offered by CME shown in Table 19.1. Thus, if the futures contract has 90 days to run to the delivery date and is for an eligible bill with a maturity on delivery of 90–92 days, a trader wishing to apply an arbitrage strategy would buy a 180-day bill so that it would have the correct properties on the delivery date 90 days hence. Because of this, the price of interest rate futures depends on **forward-forward interest rates** – interest rates for periods commencing at points of time in the future. Forward-forward rates are implied by the current rates for different maturities. Consider the following example.

In October 2007, the per annum rates of interest on three months' and six months' money in the euro area were 4.77 per cent and 4.73 per cent respectively. The forward-forward rate three months ahead is then the rate we would need to receive on funds deposited for three months at, say, the end of December in order to ensure that funds invested at the beginning of October for three months and then reinvested for another three months at the end of December would produce the same return after six months as funds invested at the beginning of October at the spot six months' rate. That is, the forward-forward rate compounded with the spot three months' rate must equal the spot six months' rate. Expressing interest rates in decimals, we can write:

$$(1 + i_f)(1 + i_s) = (1 + i_l) \tag{19.6}$$

where i_s and i_l are the spot interest rates on the shorter-term (in our case three months) and the longer-term deposits (in our case six months) respectively and i_f is the implied forward-forward interest rate s time periods ahead. From Equation 19.6, we can write:

$$i_f = \frac{(1 + i_l)}{(1 + i_s)} - 1 \tag{19.7}$$

and using the euro rates above, remembering to divide the per annum rates by four and two to find the yield for three months and six months respectively, we get:

$$i_f = (1.0237/1.0119) - 1 = 0.0117$$

Multiplying this by four to obtain a per annum rate gives us 0.0468 and, in percentage terms, the forward-forward interest rate three months ahead is 4.68 per cent. It is entirely logical that in a case like this where the yield curve is sloping downwards the forward-forward interest rate should be lower than both the three months' and six months' spot rates. Exercise 19.2 provides some practice in calculating forward-forward interest rates.

Next, we need to see exactly why forward-forward interest rates (often referred to as the implied repo rate) are important for interest rate futures prices. Consider the following set of actions of an arbitrageur:

1 She sells a futures contract requiring the delivery in three months' time of a bill maturing three months from the delivery date.

2 To allow her to deliver the required bill in three month's time, she buys a 180-day treasury bill (yielding i_l).

Exercise 19.2 Forward-forward interest rates

US$ LIBOR interest rates on 2 October 2007 were:

one month	5.12625%
three months	5.24000%
six months	5.16250%
one year	4.97563%

1 Calculate the forward-forward interest rates:

  (a) for two months, one month ahead;

  (b) for three months, three months ahead;

  (c) for six months, six months ahead;

  (d) for nine months, three months ahead.

2 What general conclusions can you come to about the relationship between spot interest rates and forward-forward rates, by comparing your answers with the spot rates for the different time periods in the USA and with the euro area example in the text?

3 To pay for the treasury bill, she borrows in the money market for three months (at i_s).

No risk is involved here. At the end of three months, she settles the futures contract by delivering the treasury bill she has been holding and uses the funds received to pay back the loan. All that is really going on is the purchase of a 180-day treasury bill which is resold three months ahead. In a perfect market and with no transactions costs, all that our arbitrageur should be able to ask for this bill in three months' time is the interest rate on three-month money three months ahead, that is, the three-month forward-forward interest rate three months from now. Since, in this example, the means used for carrying out the purchase

and re-sale of the treasury bill is the futures contract, that contract should be priced to yield the forward-forward interest rate. We have already seen that this is determined by the relationship between the spot rate of interest on money for six months and the spot rate of interest on three-month money. If the price of the futures contract were too high, yielding greater than the forward-forward rate, the arbitrage strategy above would produce a profit for the arbitrageur. On the other hand, if the yield on the futures contract were below the forward-forward interest rate, the reverse strategy would produce an arbitrage profit. Box 19.2 uses these rules to return to the question of the pricing of LIFFE sterling futures raised in Box 19.1.

BOX 19.2 **Pricing sterling interest rate futures**

In Box 19.1 we reported that the implied interest rates on three-month LIFFE sterling interest rate futures on 2 October 2007 were December 6.01%; March 5.69%; June 5.52%; September 5.44%. We asked you to consider why these rates were consistently below the equivalent money market interest rates.

Using the formula in Equation 19.7, we can calculate the following forward-forward interest rates on sterling using the LIBOR interest rates given in Box 19.1:

Forward-forward rate

(a) for two months one month ahead   6.28%
(b) for three months three months ahead   6.155%
(c) for six months six months ahead   5.857%

Using the rule that the *fair price* of a short-term interest rate future should be given by the relevant forward-forward interest rate, (a) should correspond approximately to the implied interest rate from the December forward contract price (6.01%); (b) to that implied by the March forward contract price (5.69%) and (c) to that implied by the September contract (5.44%). In fact, the forward-forward rates lie comfortably above the rates implied from the futures contracts, just as the market interest rates did, although (b) and (c) are closer to the rates given by the futures prices than are the money market rates.

Why might this have been so? Remember that the existence of transactions costs establishes a no-arbitrage band within which the prices of futures settle. Remember also that the price within this band at which prices do settle depends on expectations regarding the future price of the underlying asset – in this case interest rates on short-term deposits. The UK had had a period of steadily rising interest rates that had started in November 2003 when the Monetary Policy Committee of the Bank of England increased its repo rate from 3.5 to 3.75%. The latest rise from 5.5% to 5.75% had been in July 2007. However, the subprime mortgage problem in the USA and a 50 basis point cut in the official rate there in September 2007 led to increasing speculation that interest rates had peaked and might soon begin to come down. Nonetheless, the MPC had voted unanimously to keep interest rates unchanged in September. Thus, the general market view was that interest rates were likely to fall in the early months of 2008. This anticipated interest rate began to be reflected in interest rate future prices, accounting for the implied rates from futures contracts lying below the fair price established by forward-forward interest rates. We can see this by looking at changes in the settlement price of the June contract between July and October 2007 (implied interest rate is in brackets):

2 July   93.71 (6.29%)   1 August   93.84 (6.16%)   3 September   93.96 (6.04%)
2 October   94.48 (5.52%)

We can formalize the above argument as follows. From Equation 19.3, we have the price of a futures contract as:

$$P_f = P_s(1 + i - c) \tag{19.3}$$

Since we are dealing here with a bill, there is no return on the bill while it is being held and $c = 0$. Thus we have:

$$P_f = P_s(1 + i_s \cdot n_{sm}) = P_s + (i_s \cdot n_{sm})P_s \tag{19.8}$$

where P_s is the spot price of the bill, i_s is the financing cost of holding the bill until the futures delivery date (three months in our example) and n_{sm} is the period to redemption expressed as a fraction of a year. We then need the expression for the spot price of the asset underlying the future. This is the six-month bill, held for three months and then delivered to meet the futures contract with three months to delivery. The price of this bill, expressed in terms of the interest rate rather than the discount rate can be written as:

$$P_s = \frac{M}{(1 + i_l \cdot n_{sm})} \tag{19.9}$$

where M is the par value and i_l is the interest rate on the bill. Making use of Equation 19.6 above, we can write this as:

$$P_s = \frac{M}{(1 + i_s \cdot n_{sm})(1 + i_f \cdot n_{sm})} \tag{19.10}$$

where i_f is the forward-forward interest rate from s to l.

Substituting Equation 19.10 into Equation 19.8 gives us:

$$P_f = \frac{M}{(1 + i_f \cdot n_{sm})} \tag{19.11}$$

and from Equation 19.7 above, we can write the fair price of our futures contract as:

$$P_f = \frac{M}{\dfrac{(1 + i_l \cdot n_{sm})}{(1 + i_s \cdot n_{sm})} - 1} \tag{19.12}$$

You will notice that this is different from what we do in Box 19.2 above where we have obtained a per annum interest rate implied by a futures price simply by subtracting the price from 100. This is, in fact, what futures exchanges do. Thus the expression for the fair price of futures becomes:

$$P_f = 100 - i_f$$

This may only be an approximation to Equation 19.12, but it does have the advantage of simplicity.

For a particular contract, say for three-month eurodollar futures where the contract is for $1 million, the fair price of the contract would be:

$$P_f = (100 - i_f) \cdot M/100 = (100 - i_f) \cdot \$1m/100$$

Of course, as in our general discussion above, the addition of transactions costs would introduce an element of freedom for futures prices. We would now have to say that the futures yield would have to be above or below the relevant forward-forward interest rate by more than necessary to meet transactions costs before arbitrage would be profitable. Also as in the general case, if we were to include a risk premium we could produce either backwardation or a contango.

To adapt this approach to long-term bond futures, we must allow for the coupon payments (thus c in Equation 19.3 is positive rather than being zero as it is with short-term interest rate futures). This has the effect of lowering the net financing cost associated with an arbitrage operation although the amount paid for the asset will be higher than in the short-term interest rate futures case since the bond must be purchased at face value, rather than at a discount. We must also take into account the complications on delivery noted in Section 19.3. Suppose the futures contract has a delivery date three months ahead and is for a notional 20-year bond. The **cash-and-carry** arbitrage operation does not require the arbitrageur to buy now a bond which will, in three months' time, have 20 years to run to maturity. Rather, he will buy now the cheapest-to-deliver bond that will satisfy the contract. He must therefore borrow funds at money market rates to buy this bond and will pay the dirty price for it. The cost of carry will be given by the dirty price of the bond

---

MORE FROM THE WEB

We mentioned earlier the existence on the web of many glossaries of financial terms. Some are more detailed than others but if you are having a problem with a term such as 'contango', you could try one or more of: http://www.pathtoinvesting.org/index.htm; http://www.riskglossary.com/; or http://biz.yahoo.com/f/g/cc.html. For material on pricing as well as definitions, try http://www.quantnotes.com/fundamentals/.

times the money market interest rate less the amount of accrued interest on the bond over the three months to the delivery which will depend on the coupon of the CTD bond. To establish the fair price of the notional bond, we must then divide by the price factor (PF) on the CTD bond. We can modify Equation 19.3 to:

$$P_f = \frac{P_s}{PF}(1 + i \cdot n_{sm} - c \cdot n_{sm})\frac{P_s}{PF} \qquad (19.13)$$

Again, an actual futures price may vary from the fair price because of transactions costs and the incorporation of a risk premium.

19.4.3 Pricing currency futures

Establishing the fair price of a currency future is simply an exercise in covered interest rate parity. Assume a British firm needs euro in three months' time (it is short in euro) and it wishes to lock in the existing £/€

exchange rate (hedging against the risk that the pound would weaken over the following three months). It could do this by purchasing a futures contract on euro with a delivery date three months ahead (or it could buy euro forward). Alternatively, it could borrow for three months in sterling at UK interest rates, convert the funds borrowed into euro at the existing spot exchange rate and invest the euro at euro area interest rates for three months. At the end of the period, it would collect the euro from its investment, meet its obligations in the euro area, and repay its sterling loan.

These two strategies produce the same results and thus the fair price of the futures contract should depend on the spot exchange rate and the difference between interest rates in the UK and the euro area. As we demonstrate in Box 19.3, we can write the fair price of the currency future by rewriting Equation 18.4 as:

$$\frac{P_f - E_s}{E_s} = \frac{i_d - i_f}{1 + i_f} \qquad (19.14)$$

BOX 19.3 The fair price for currency futures and covered interest parity

Assume a UK firm needs €1 million in three months' time to pay for goods already ordered from a German firm. It sets out to lock in the current exchange rate, using spot markets only. Thus, it will need to invest in the euro area: €1m/(1 + i€) where i€ is the spot interest rate in the euro area. Assuming this to be 4 per cent, it will require €990,099.

To obtain this, it will need to convert into euro £[1,000,000/(1 + i€)] · E_s where E_s is the spot exchange rate of sterling in direct quotation. Assume this to be: €1 = £0.6935. That is, it will need to convert £686,634 into euro. It borrows this amount at UK interest rates and at the end of the three months must repay this amount plus interest:

{[€1,000,000/(1 + i€)] · E_S} · (1 + $i_£$)

With UK interest rates at 6 per cent, this will amount to £696,934. Thus, the actual exchange rate obtained for the transfer of funds will be £696,934/1,000,000 = €1 or £0.6969 = €1.

We have omitted transactions costs here and so can assume that this should be the fair price of a currency future for the delivery of euro three months ahead. That is,

P_f = {[€1,000,000/(1 + i€)] · E_S} · (1 + $i_£$)

We may generalize the equation by letting:

$i_£ = i_d$; i€ = i_f (domestic and foreign interest rates respectively)

and €1,000,000 = 1 (contract). Then:

P_f/E_S = (1 + i_d)/(1 + i_f)

which we may rearrange and write as:

($P_f - E_S$)/E_S = ($i_d - i_f$)/(1 + i_f) = $i_d - i_f$

which is the covered interest parity condition.

where P_f is the price of the futures contract. In our example above i_d, the domestic interest rate, is the interest rate on the pound, i_f the euro rate and E_s the exchange rate of sterling expressed in direct quotation. This may be approximated as:

$$\frac{P_f - E_s}{E_s} = i_d - i_f \qquad (19.15)$$

Therefore, the fair price of a currency futures contract is the same as the price of the equivalent forward contract under conditions of interest rate parity. There will be differences between forward and futures prices when allowance is made for the margins payments under futures contracts and the interest forgone on margin payments. It must also be remembered, however, that traders wishing to buy foreign currency forwards from banks will be required to maintain deposits with the bank to insure the bank against default risk, and so the differences between forward and futures prices are likely in practice to be very small.

19.4.4 Equity index futures prices

The general rules apply also to the pricing of equity index futures and we could reproduce Equation 19.3, with c now being the dividend yield on shares held. However, a number of complications can be seen when the nature of the cash-and-carry arbitrage strategy is considered. Let us take the steps involved in the similar strategy for short-term interest rate futures listed in Section 19.4.1 and observe the differences.

(a) The arbitrageur sells a futures contract requiring the delivery in three months' time of the stock exchange index. But an index cannot be delivered. Rather, stock exchange index futures are settled on the delivery date by cash payments reflecting the change in the value of the index over the period of the contract. Thus, the risk to the seller of the index is that the share price index will have risen during that time.

(b) To remove this risk of having to make a cash payment, the arbitrageur would need to construct, at the beginning of the period, a portfolio of all the shares in the stock exchange index in question, in the exact proportions used in the calculation of the index. The portfolio would be held until the delivery date of the futures contract and then sold in its entirety. The portfolio of shares would rise in value in the exact proportion as the index and the cash profit on the shares could be used to meet the required cash payments under the futures contract. The purchase of the shares would have the extra bonus that dividends would be received while the shares were being held and the fair price of the futures contract would be lower to this extent.

(c) To pay for the portfolio of shares, the arbitrageur borrows in the money market for the period of the contract.

Now consider the problems in step (b). Firstly, it would be impossible to construct the required portfolio instantaneously at the beginning of the period and thus prices might move against the arbitrageur while the portfolio was being constructed. That is, share prices might begin to rise, making it more expensive to acquire the required portfolio. Secondly, it is likely to be very difficult, if not impossible, to build up a portfolio exactly the same as that used in the calculation of the index. Given stock exchange rules regarding the minimum size of parcels of shares, a portfolio that exactly represented the index might need to be very large. To the extent that the portfolio held was different from the notional portfolio used to calculate the index, the level of systematic or market risk associated with the portfolio might be different from that of the index. Hence it is not possible to have a genuinely risk-free arbitrage strategy in the case of stock exchange indices. In addition, the transaction costs associated with acquiring the necessary shares would be likely to be much higher than they would be if purchasing a single bill or bond in the cash market. Therefore, the no-arbitrage band is bound to be much wider in the case of stock exchange index futures.

Finally, the dividend payments cause complications because, unlike bond coupon payments, they will not occur regularly throughout the period during which the shares are held and their size will be uncertain. This makes futures prices more volatile than the index itself. Suppose a number of dividend payments on the shares are bunched together. As soon as they are paid, the benefits of acquiring the representative portfolio of assets will fall (in terms of Equation 19.3, c will fall sharply) and the fair price of the futures will rise sharply. Meanwhile the index, which does not take dividend payments into account, will remain unaffected.

19.5 Summary

Risks facing firms have increased in a number of ways as they have become bigger and more international in nature and as exchange rates have become more volatile and future inflation rates more uncertain. To help counter these risks, new markets have grown up in financial derivatives – contracts to exchange based upon the performance of separately traded financial instruments. As part of this growth, financial futures markets have developed in which standardized contracts on short- and long-term interest rates, foreign exchange rates and stock exchange indices are traded on specialized exchanges. To reduce default risk and increase the tradability of futures, clearing houses have been established which take over counterparty obligations on all contracts. Exchange members must keep accounts with the clearing house, which are adjusted daily to reflect profits and losses on all contracts. This system of margin payments means that futures are highly geared. Although very few exchanges of the underlying instruments actually occur under futures contracts, the possibility that delivery might be required ensures that the prices of futures will be closely linked (although not identical) to the prices on the cash markets through potential arbitrage strategies. These arbitrage strategies allow the fair price of futures – the price that provides the risk-free rate of profit – to be calculated. This rate of profit will always equal the net cost of carry, the net cost of holding the underlying instrument for the duration of the futures contract. In practice, transaction costs create a no-arbitrage band within which the price of the futures must lie and the actual futures price may vary from the fair price to include a risk premium. The basic fair pricing rule can be modified to suit the particular characteristics of the different types of financial futures.

Key concepts in this chapter

Backwardation	Initial margin
Basis	Limit-up/Limit-down
Cash and carry strategy	Margins
Clearing house	Marked to market
Contango	Normal backwardation
Conversion factor	Normal contango
Cost of carry	Open interest
Derivatives	Open outcry
Fair price	Price factor
Forward-forward interest rates	Settlement price
Futures	Variation margin

Questions and problems

1 Explain each of the following:
   (a) the role of a clearing house in a futures market;
   (b) the potential advantages and risks of trading on margin in futures markets;
   (c) contango;
   (d) normal backwardation.

2 Outline the relative advantages and disadvantages of each of the following as instruments for providing protection against foreign exchange risk:
   (a) forward foreign exchange markets;
   (b) futures contracts in foreign exchange.

▶

3 What are the characteristics of futures and futures exchanges which serve to increase the tradability of futures?

4 Money market interest rates on the Danish krone on 2 October 2007 were:

one month	4.16 per cent
three months	4.41 per cent
six months	4.69 per cent
one year	4.72 per cent

Calculate the forward-forward interest rates:

(i) for two months, one month ahead;

(ii) for three months, three months ahead;

(iii) for six months, six months ahead;

(iv) for nine months, three months ahead

5 You are given the following information:

Spot euro interest rates on three-month money: 4.77 per cent

Spot US interest rates on three-month money: 5.22 per cent

$/€ exchange rate: $1.4154 = €1

(a) Calculate the fair price for a euro futures contract with a delivery date three months ahead.

(b) Why might the actual futures price differ from the fair price?

(c) Describe the arbitrage strategy which would produce a profit if the actual futures price was (i) above the fair price, (ii) below the fair price.

(d) Allow for transactions costs of 2 per cent of the value of the contract and calculate the no-arbitrage band for the futures price.

6 In Section 19.4.2 above, we write:

If the price of the futures contract were too high, yielding greater than the forward-forward rate, the arbitrage strategy above would produce a profit for the arbitrageur. On the other hand, if the yield on the futures contract were below the forward-forward interest rate, the reverse strategy would produce an arbitrage profit.

Outline the reverse strategy referred to here.

7 Assume that at the beginning of March 2008, three-month Euribor futures offered by Euronext.liffe stood at:

Jun 96.02   Sep 95.98   Dec 95.90

What term would you use to describe this relationship between futures contracts of different periods? What is the opposite situation? What might the above set of figures imply that hedgers were using short-term interest rate futures to achieve?

8 You are given the following figures for the end of September:

Spot dirty price of cheapest to deliver long gilt = £97.25

Price factor of cheapest to deliver long gilt = 0.9815625

Sterling money market interest rate for three months = 6.29 per cent

Coupon rate on the cheapest to deliver long gilt = 8 per cent

Calculate the fair futures price for the December long gilt contract.

9 Why is so much attention given to the form of delivery of the underlying product on futures contracts when delivery hardly ever occurs?

Further reading

S J Grossman and J Stiglitz, 'On the impossibility of informationally efficient markets', *American Economic Review*, 70, June 1980, 393–408

J R Hicks, *Value and Capital* (London: Oxford University Press, 2e, 1946)

D Hirshleifer, 'Residual risk, trading costs, and commodity futures risk premia', *Review of Financial Studies*, 1, Summer 1988, 173–93

H S Houthakker and P J Williamson, *The Economics of Financial Markets* (Oxford: Oxford University Press, 1996) Chs 9, 10

J C Hull, *Options, Futures and Other Derivatives* (Harlow: Pearson Education, 6e, 2005)

J M Keynes, *A Treatise on Money*, Vol. II (London: Macmillan, 1930)

A S Kyle, 'Continuous auctions and insider trading', *Econometrica*, 53, November 1985, 1315–35

G M Phillips and R J Weiner, 'Information and normal backwardation as determinants of trading performance: evidence from the North Sea Oil forward market', *Economic Journal*, 104 (436), 1994, 76–95

A Shleifer and L H Summers, 'The noise trader approach to finance', *Journal of Economic Perspectives*, 4, Spring 1990, 19–33

J L Stein, *The Economics of Futures Markets* (Oxford: Blackwell, 1986)

F Taylor, *Mastering Derivatives Markets* (Harlow: Pearson Education, 3e, 2006)

Websites

www.asx.com.au
www.bankofengland.co.uk
www.bis.org
www.CBOT.com
www.cme.com
http://eng.krx.co.kr/a
www.eurexchange.com
www.euronext.com
www.tfx.co.jp/en/
www.theice.com
www.tse.or.jp/english/

Chapter 20 Options, swaps and other derivatives

What you will learn in this chapter:

■ The nature and uses of options

■ How to read options tables in the *Financial Times*

■ The factors determining options prices

■ The nature and uses of swaps

■ The advantages of different kinds of financial derivatives

■ The advantages and disadvantages of financial derivatives in general

20.1 Introduction

Two other instruments whose use has grown rapidly in financial markets in recent years have been options and swaps. Both instruments help firms hedge risk but both have also become associated with speculation and spectacular financial disasters. In this chapter we look at the nature of these instruments and also at the advantages and disadvantages of derivatives generally. From Sections 20.2 to 20.5 we look at the use of and the pricing of options. Section 20.6 deals with swaps while Section 20.7 compares the different types of derivatives and Section 20.8 considers issues associated with derivatives generally.

20.2 Options

Options are available on all types of financial instruments – short-term interest rates, foreign exchange rates, bonds, stock indices and derivatives contracts – there are even options on options.

An option gives the right to buy or sell a given amount of a financial instrument or commodity at an agreed price (known as the **exercise** or **strike price**) within a specified time, but does not oblige investors to do so. Just as with futures, options contracts are drawn up between two counterparties, the purchaser and the writer (seller) of the option. They may be registered with and traded through a futures and options exchange or may be arranged over-the-counter (OTC) between the two counterparties. Options contracts are offered both on cash securities (short- and long-term interest rates, exchange rates, equities of individual companies, and stock exchange indices) and on other derivatives contracts. For options on cash securities (premium paid options), the buyer pays the full price or **premium** of the option at the time of purchase. For options on derivatives contracts (premium margined options), buyers and sellers are margined and marked to market in the same way as with futures.

OTC options (non-tradable, custom-made options constructed by banks for their customers) make up a high proportion of the total value of options sold. Traditional options which are also not tradable continue to exist in stock markets. The major developments in recent years have been the large increase in the number of specialized futures and options exchanges, the development of increasing numbers of traded options contracts and the growth of **exotic options** tailored to the specific needs of investors.

The buyer of a **call option** acquires the right to buy the specified instrument. For example, an investor who thinks that the euro will rise against the US dollar could buy a \$/€ option, giving the right to buy euro at a specified price, say \$1.40 = €1. The holder of the option then has the right to acquire euro at that price at any time during the life of the option and is thus in a position to benefit from a rise in the spot price of the euro. If the spot exchange rate were to rise to \$1.45 = €1, the option holder could acquire euro at \$1.40 under the terms of the option and sell them in the spot market at \$1.45. The buyer of a call option thus assumes a long position in the underlying instrument (in this case euro). As the price of the underlying instrument rises, so too will the profit that can be made from exercising the option. Consequently, the premium that must be paid to acquire the option rises and this allows the holder of a call option to realize his or her profit by selling the option on, rather than by exercising it. If the option did not rise as the price of the underlying asset rose, there would be a profitable arbitrage opportunity. Box 20.1 overleaf provides a more detailed example relating to interest rate options.

The buyer of a **put option** acquires the right to sell and thus assumes a short position in the specified instrument. That is, the buyer of a put option stands to gain from a *fall* in the price of the underlying asset. Therefore, someone who buys a put option at \$1.40 = €1 will be hoping that the value of the euro will fall below that level. They will then be able to buy euro in the spot market at, say \$1.35 = €1 and then exercise the option in order to sell the euro at \$1.40. In this case, as the euro falls, the profitability of a put option in euro will rise and the premium that other investors are prepared to pay in order to acquire such an option will increase. As above, the holder of the put option may realize his or her profit by selling the option on, rather than by exercising it.

Just as in the futures market, the holder of an option sells it (closes out his or her market position) by entering into a reversing contract. That is, in the first case above in which we assumed that the euro was rising, a holder of a call option in euro 'sells' the option by writing (that is, selling) a call option on the same instrument for the same expiry (or expiration) date, in effect cancelling his or her right to buy euro.

BOX 20.1 Arbitraging between the cash and options markets

Assume that the strike price of a three-month American option on a short-term interest rate (a three-month bank deposit) is 95; the premium is 0.25 per cent of the specified amount of the deposit which is £100,000. Thus, if the option is exercised, the writer of the option will pay the buyer interest on £100,000 for three months at a rate of 5 per cent p.a. (£1,250); the premium paid for buying the right to this payment is £250. The market rate of interest on the type of deposit specified is 5 per cent. The option is then said to be *at-the-money* – the value of the right granted by the option is equal to the market value of the underlying instrument. The current value of the option (the option's **intrinsic value**), the profit available from exercising it, would be zero. The buyer of the option could obtain from a prime bank exactly the same interest as is available from exercising the option.

Underlying deposit:	£100,000
Strike price:	95 (implying 5% p.a. interest rate)
Market rate of interest:	5% p.a.
Intrinsic value of option:	£0
Premium:	0.25% of underlying deposit = £250
Period to expiry:	Three months

Traders might still buy this option because the option grants the buyer more than the intrinsic value since interest rates might fall and the intrinsic value of the option rise before the expiry date. This right to benefit from a future rise in the price of an instrument is known as the option's **time value**.

Assume next that one month later (the option still has two months to expiry date), the current market rate of interest falls to 2 per cent but the premium on the option does not change. The option holder could then exercise the option and receive £1,250 from the writer when a deposit of £100,000 with a bank (the alternative) would yield only £500. The option would be *in-the-money* – the value of the right granted by the option is greater than the market value of the underlying instrument and it would be profitable to exercise the option. We would have:

Underlying deposit:	£100,000
Strike price:	95
Market rate of interest:	2% p.a.
Intrinsic value of option:	£750
Premium:	0.25% = £250
Period to expiry:	2 months

Clearly, large numbers of traders would wish to buy this option but no one would be willing to write it since a writer would have to pay a much higher rate of interest than was available to them on an equivalent deposit. The premium would have to rise *at least* to 0.75 per cent of the underlying deposit. Of course, it might rise higher because of the time value remaining to the option holder – the possibility that the market interest rate might fall further in the following two months.

Had the interest rate risen above 5 per cent in this case, an option with a strike price of 95 would have been *out-of-the-money*.

However, the increase in the price of the euro will have meant that the premium received for the sale of the call option will be greater than the premium paid on the initial call option.

The example of a call option given above states that the option can be exercised at any time during its life up until (and including) the expiry date. Such an option is known as an **American option**. There exist also **European options** and **Bermudan options**. European options only allow the exercise of the option on the expiry date whereas Bermudan options permit the option to be exercised on any one of a number of specified dates. Most traded options are American options.

Like futures contracts, few options produce a delivery of the underlying asset because profitable market positions are generally closed out before expiry while unprofitable options are left to lapse, with the buyer losing only the premium. Therefore, the profit for most buyers of options is given by the change in the option premium between its purchase and sale. Options, then, like futures, give traders the opportunity to speculate on the likely direction of a market without actually trading in that market.

For hedgers who are short in the underlying asset, a call option establishes a maximum price for it:

- if the price in the cash market rises, the hedger may exercise the option at the lower strike price; or

- pay the higher price for the instrument in the cash market but set against this the profit obtained from selling the option.

However, if the spot market price falls, the hedger obtains the benefit of the fall and has only to set against this the premium paid for the option. Thus, the option provides protection from the spot price moving in one direction, without removing the profits that might arise if the price moves in the opposite direction. This is not the case in trading in other derivatives contracts. The reverse arguments hold for hedgers who are long in the underlying asset. For them, a put option establishes a minimum price for the underlying asset. If the spot price falls, the premium of the put option rises and the holder may either exercise the option at the strike price (preventing a loss) or sell the underlying asset at the lower spot price and sell the option in order to offset the loss incurred in the spot market. If the spot price rises, the holder of the option can benefit from the higher price in the cash market and allow the option to lapse. Thus, holding a long position in the cash market and buying a put option produces the same result as does buying a call option when the trader has no position in the cash market – in both cases, the holder of the option benefits from a rise in the price of the instrument in the cash market. For this reason the combination of being long in an instrument and holding a put option is sometimes known as a **synthetic call option**.

Whether a trader chooses an outright derivatives contract (such as a future) or an option will depend on what he thinks is likely to happen to the price of the underlying asset and on his attitude towards risk. A trader who has a long position in the cash market and who is convinced that the price of the instrument in

question will not fall may well choose not to hedge at all. If he is certain that the price will fall, he may either sell the instrument or take an offsetting short position by selling forwards. This eliminates entirely his exposure to the price fall. The trader is only likely to choose options if he is uncertain in which direction the price will move. Even then, if he thinks that the price is more likely to fall than to rise, outright forward contracts are preferable to options. Options are preferable if the trader has no view or thinks that the price is more likely to rise than fall. Many mixed strategies are possible. Box 20.2 overleaf sets out some examples.

Options are highly geared (leveraged) because the options price is only a small percentage of the price of the underlying asset. In the example in Box 20.1, the buyer of the call option may have made a profit of £750 for an outlay of only £250 in one month – a net per annum profit rate of 2,400 per cent.

Although it carries a considerable risk, a trader may prefer to hedge or speculate by writing options rather than buying them. Writing a call option offers protection against a price fall since in this case the option will not be exercised and the writer will collect the premium on the option. In the same way, writing a put option offers protection against a price rise. Writing options is only effective, however, if the price changes are relatively small and it carries the risk that if prices go against the writer, the loss may become very large. For example, a trader who writes a call option on the $/€ exchange rate at a strike price of $1.40 agrees to sell euro at that price. If the euro increases in value and the writer is short in euro, he will need to acquire them in the spot market at the higher price and the amount he loses will depend on the size of the contract (€100,000) and the amount the price rises. If the euro rose to $1.41, the loss would be $1,000 (100,000 × $0.01); if it rose to $1.46, the loss to the writer would be $6,000 (100,000 × $0.06) and so on. The writer cannot abandon a losing option in the way that the buyer can.

The trading of options contracts on organized exchanges guards against the risk that the writer of an option might default by not being able to deliver the underlying asset to the holder of a call option or by being unable to accept it from the holder of a put option. To buy an option, a trader must have an account with a brokerage firm holding a membership on the options exchange. The buyer pays for the option at the time of the trade and no other payments

---

BOX 20.2 Mixed strategies in options trading

It is possible to combine call and put options and the buying and writing of options to try to profit from expected conditions in the market. Some such options are:

A. Cases where a trader either buys or writes options but does not do both

straddle – a call + a put at the same strike price and expiry date

strangle – a call + a put for the same expiry date but at different strike prices

strap – two calls + one put with the same expiry dates; the strike prices might be the same or different

strip – two puts + one call with the same expiry date; again strike prices might be the same or different

In general, the buyer of these options is hoping for market prices to move sharply but is uncertain whether they will rise or fall. The buyer of a strap will gain more from a price rise than from a price fall; the buyer of a strip will gain more from a price fall. The writer in all four cases is hoping that the market will remain stable with little change in price during the life of the option.

B. Spreads: combinations of buying and writing options

butterfly – *buying* two call options, one with a low exercise price, the other with a high exercise price + *writing* two call options with the same intermediate strike price **or** the reverse

condor – similar to a butterfly except that the call options which are written have different intermediate prices

Both a butterfly and a condor are *vertical* spreads – all options bought or sold have the same expiry date but different strike prices. *Horizontal* spreads have the same strike prices but different expiry dates. With *diagonal* spreads both the strike prices and the expiry dates are different.

Other mixed strategies have equally improbable names. They include: vertical bull call; vertical bull spread; vertical bear spread; rotated vertical bull spread; and rotated vertical bear spread.

---

are required apart from a commission to the broker. However, because the writer of an option enters into an open-ended commitment, he may need large financial reserves to meet his obligations and the broker may require financial guarantees from option writers. A writer may write a **covered call** (the writer already owns the underlying asset and deposits it with the broker) or a **naked call**. In the latter case, the broker may require from the writer substantial deposits of cash or securities to ensure that he is able to meet his commitment. As in a futures market, the buyer and writer of an exchange-traded option have obligations not to a specific individual but to the clearing house of the exchange that manages the exercise process and the standardization of contract terms. This is not the case with over-the-counter (OTC) options where the relationship between buyer and writer is direct.

 ### Principal types of options on financial assets

20.3.1 Short-term interest rate options (STIRs)

The *Financial Times* provides information on the trading of three short-term interest rate options contracts – a Eurodollar option offered by the Chicago Mercantile Exchange[1] and Euribor and Short Sterling contracts offered by Euronext.liffe. In all of these cases, the underlying asset is a futures contract on a time deposit. Thus, for CME's three month Eurodollar option it is a Eurodollar time deposit futures contract. The tables are now available on the *FT* website rather than in the newspaper. Table 20.1 shows details of the three contracts for 2 October 2007.

---

[1] Now part of the CME Group, together with the Chicago Board of Trade (CBOT). The two exchanges merged in 2007.

Table 20.1 Interest rate options

■ THREE MONTH EURODOLLAR OPTIONS $1m (CME)   FT

Strike price	CALLS			PUTS		
	Dec	Mar	Jun	Dec	Mar	Jun
94.75	0.37	0.70	0.87	0.05	0.04	0.06
94.875	0.29	0.60	0.77	0.08	0.07	0.08
95	0.21	0.50	0.68	0.13	0.08	0.11
95.125	0.15	0.42	0.59	0.19	0.14	0.15

Prev day's data: volume, 597,359; calls, 374,709; puts, 222,650; open interest, 23,153,108.   Source: Reuters/CME.

■ EURIBOR OPTIONS (Euronext.liffe) €1m 100-rate

Strike price	CALLS				PUTS			
	Oct	Dec	Mar	Jun	Oct	Dec	Mar	Jun
95125	0.250	0.258	0.510	0.630	–	0.008	0.015	0.030
95250	0.130	0.155	0.395	0.518	0.005	0.030	0.025	0.043
95375	0.033	0.088	0.295	0.420	0.033	0.088	0.050	0.070
95500	0.010	0.040	0.213	0.335	0.135	0.165	0.093	0.110

Prev day's data: volume, 63,431; calls, 34,288; puts, 29,143; open interest, 1,140,9.   Source: Reuters/EUREX.

■ SHORT STERLING OPTIONS (Euronext.liffe) £500,000 100-rate

Strike price	CALLS				PUTS			
	Oct	Dec	Mar	Jun	Oct	Dec	Mar	Jun
93625	0.373	0.430	0.730	0.905	0.008	0.060	0.045	0.050
93750	0.255	0.330	0.620	0.790	0.015	0.090	0.060	0.060
93875	0.155	0.245	0.520	0.693	0.040	0.135	0.085	0.088
94000	0.080	0.178	0.425	0.595	0.090	0.188	0.115	0.115
94125	0.035	0.120	0.350	0.510	0.170	0.255	0.165	0.155
94250	0.015	0.075	0.275	0.425	0.275	0.335	0.215	0.195

Prev day's data: volume, n/a; calls, n/a; puts, n/a; open interest, n/a.   Source: Reuters.

Source: *Financial Times*, 3 October 2007. Reprinted with permission.

The size of the time deposit underlying each contract is given at the top of each table ($1 million, €1 million, £500,000). The various strike prices are shown down the left-hand side of each table. Since the asset on which the option is being offered is a short-term interest rate future, the strike price is obtained by subtracting from 100 the time deposit interest rates available. Thus, the Euribor options shown here were options on three-month Euribor futures at four different interest rates: 4.875 per cent, 4.750 per cent, 4.625 per cent and 4.5 per cent.

The table provides details of premiums on only a limited number of expiry dates – for Euribor and Short Sterling options October and December 2007 and March and June 2008; for the Eurodollar option December, March and June only. In fact, in all three cases contracts are available terminating in both quarterly months (March, June, September and

December) and some serial (non-quarterly) months with the effect that there are terminating dates available in all months.

The statement that a contract terminates in a particular month does not mean the end of the month. The usual arrangement for the type of option we have here (true in all three cases above) is that trading terminates on the second bank business day before the third Wednesday of the contract month. Thus, for CME's Eurodollar December 2007 option quoted in Table 20.1, the last trading date and settlement date was 17 December 2007.

In Table 20.1, premiums of call and put options are quoted for each strike price and time period. Premiums here are quoted as a percentage of the contract value but may also be quoted in points, with each point representing a given unit of currency.

In the case of **short-term interest rate options**, the option's price rises when the market interest rate falls since the exercise of the option would deliver to its holder a rate of interest higher than the market interest rate. Below each table the number of contracts traded the previous day and the total number of contracts outstanding (open interest) are provided. Exercise 20.1 asks you to consider the significance of some of the premiums quoted in Table 20.1.

Exercise 20.1

Consider Table 20.1, which relates to 2 October 2007. One-month, three-months and one-year Euro LIBOR interest rates on that day were 4.3825, 4.79188, and 4.71750 per cent respectively.

1 Why were the premiums for October calls on Euribor options lower than for puts for only the highest strike price?

2 Why were the premiums for June calls so much higher than for October calls?

3 What do the premiums on short sterling options tell you about sterling interest rates on 2 October 2007?

The three contracts considered here are only a very small sample of the range of short-term interest rate options available. Box 20.3 provides some other examples.

BOX 20.3 Some short-term interest rate options contracts

As well as the 3-month Eurodollar option dealt with in the text, CME offers an option on a 13 Week US Treasury Bill, and options on a Euroyen futures contract, and an international money market one-month LIBOR futures contract. It also offers a Eurodollar Mid-Curve option. A Mid-Curve option is an option on a futures contract that expires twelve calendar months from the next quarterly month nearest to the expiry of the option. That is, for options with January, February and March expiry months, the future delivery month will be March the following year, for April, May and June options, June the following year and so on.

■ **Euronext.liffe**, in addition to the Euribor and Short Sterling futures above, offers options on Eurodollar and Euroswiss futures contracts and Mid-Curve options on Eurodollar, Euribor and Short Sterling.

■ **Eurex** offers options on 3-month Euribor futures.

All of the other futures and options exchanges offer similar products.

20.3.2 Currency options

Currency options are options on futures contracts in currencies. The majority of currency options are for the US dollar against a non-dollar currency and a call option gives the right to buy the non-dollar currency. Exercise prices are stated in US cents. They are offered for many currencies. For example, CME offers American options on futures contracts for the US dollar against the Australian dollar, the Brazilian real; the British pound, the Canadian dollar, the Chinese renminbi, the Czech koruna, the euro, the Hungarian forint, the Israeli shekel, the yen, the Korean won, the Mexican peso, the New Zealand dollar, the Polish zloty, the Russian rouble, the South African rand and the Swiss franc. They also offer European-style options on the pound, the Canadian dollar, the euro and the Swiss franc and a number of options on futures contracts involving two non-dollar currencies: euro/pound, euro/yen, euro/Swiss franc, euro/koruna, euro/forint and euro/zloty as well as a contract on a dollar index.

Currency options tables are no longer provided by the *Financial Times* but we are still able to explain the principal features of currency options contracts with the help of past *FT* tables. We reproduce here as Table 20.2 information from 2004 on three currency options offered by CME – $/€, $/yen and $/£. There is an interesting by-product of using old figures – compare the exchange rates quoted here from 2004 with the 2007 exchange rates used elsewhere in this book.

Since these contracts are for a future on a dollar against a non-dollar currency, the exercise prices are stated in US cents. Thus, the strike price of 1.2100 on the $/€ contract in Table 20.2 is an exchange rate of $1.21 = €1, the direct quotation of the dollar. The

holder of a call option gains if the non-dollar currency rises in value. On 15 March 2004 (the day to which the tables refer) the spot exchange rate of the dollar against sterling was $1.795 = £1. Thus, options with strike prices of $1.80 and above were out-of-the-money, accounting for their low call premiums. Put options for the same strike prices were, of course, in-the-money since holders of put options would have been able to buy sterling on the cash foreign exchange market at $1.795 and then claim the future the price of which would have risen as sterling had risen. This accounts for the fall in call premiums and the rise in

Table 20.2 Currency options

■ US$/€ OPTIONS (CME)   FT

Strike price Mar 15	CALLS			PUTS		
	Apr	May	Jun	Apr	May	Jun
12100	2.08	–	3.14	0.89	1.72	2.12
12200	1.63	2.17	2.88	1.34	2.08	2.53
12300	1.04	1.72	2.26	2.19	2.80	3.26
12400	0.92	1.34	1.87	2.86	3.41	3.86

Previous day's data: volume, 2,476; calls, 1,433; puts, 3,909; open interest, 51,772.   Source: Reuters/CME.

■ US$/YEN OPTIONS (CME)

Strike price Mar 15	CALLS			PUTS		
	Apr	May	Jun	Apr	May	Jun
8900	–	–	2.61	0.23	0.51	0.71
9000	1.38	1.74	1.97	0.47	0.83	1.06
9100	0.80	1.18	1.43	0.89	1.27	1.52
9200	0.44	0.78	1.04	1.53	1.87	2.13

Previous day's data: volume, 270; calls, 565; puts, 853; open interest, 35,834.   Source: Reuters/CME.

■ US$/UK£ OPTIONS (CME)

Strike price Mar 15	CALLS			PUTS		
	Apr	May	Jun	Apr	May	Jun
1790	–	–	3.34	2.36	–	3.70
1800	1.45	2.53	3.09	2.91	3.70	4.26
1810	1.36	–	–	3.53	–	–
1820	0.91	1.80	2.31	4.27	4.96	5.47

Previous day's data: volume, 1,115; calls, 431; puts, 1,546; open interest, 12,509.   Source: Reuters/CME.

Source: *Financial Times*, 16 March 2004. Reprinted with permission.

put premiums as the strike price rises. That is, the *intrinsic value* of the call option is lower and that of the put option higher as the strike price rises. The intrinsic value is negative for out-of-the-money options but the premiums remain positive because of the *time value* possessed by an option (see Box 20.1).

The increase in the premium of both calls and puts for any one strike price as the length of time to expiry increases, reflects the greater time value possessed by options that have more time to expiry. Thus, the highest premium shown for the $/£ option in Table 20.2 (5.47 for a June put) arises both because the option was already in-the-money and because it had three months to run until expiry during which time the

value of sterling might have fallen in the cash market. The $/€ exchange rate in the foreign exchange market on 15 March 2004 was $1.225 = €1, meaning that call options with strike prices of $1.21 and $1.22 were in-the-money while put options with a strike price of $1.23 and $1.24 were in-the-money.

20.3.3 Bond options

Options are also offered by different derivative exchanges on a variety of bonds. Table 20.3 shows details of three options on notional US, Japanese and German government bonds offered by the Chicago

Table 20.3 Bond options

■ **US TREASURY 10 YEAR OPTIONS $100,000** (CBOT) **FT**

Strike price	.... CALLS			.... PUTS		
	Nov	Dec	Jan	Nov	Dec	Jan
109	0–63	1–15	1–16	0–24	0–40	1–06
110	0–30	0–46	–	0–56	1–07	–
111	0–12	0–25	0–34	1–38	1–50	–
112	0–05	0–13	0–22	–	2–37	–

Prev day's data: volume, 230,974; calls, 108,054; puts, 122,920; open interest, 2,515,162.   Source: Reuters/TSE.

■ **10 YEAR JAPANESE GOVT BOND OPTIONS** (TSE)

Strike price	.... CALLS			.... PUTS		
	Oct	Nov	Dec	Oct	Nov	Dec
1345	0.32	0.80	–	0.01	0.37	0.65
1350	0.01	0.27	–	0.49	0.96	–
1355	0.01	0.27	–	0.49	0.96	–
1360	0.01	0.14	0.27	1.57	–	1.08

Prev day's data: volume, n/a; calls, n/a; puts, n/a; open interest, n/a.   Source: Reuters/TSE.

■ **EURO BUND OPTIONS £100,000** (Eurex)

Strike price	.... CALLS			.... PUTS		
	Nov	Dec	Mar	Nov	Dec	Mar
112.5	0.69	1.03	–	0.42	0.92	1.10
113	0.55	0.80	–	–	–	–
113.5	0.34	0.55	–	–	–	–
114	0.20	0.40	–	–	–	–

Prev day's data: volume, n/a; calls, n/a; puts, n/a; open interest, n/a.   Source: Reuters/Eurex.

Source: *Financial Times*, 3 October 2007. Reprinted with permission.

Board of Trade (CBOT, now part of the CME Group), the Tokyo Stock Exchange (TSE) and Eurex respectively.

The US example is an option on a 10-year US Treasury Note futures; the Japanese example an option on a 10-year Japanese government bond futures; and the German example an option on the Euro Bund futures contract offered by Eurex. That is, the underlying instrument is a futures contract offered on a notional long-term debt instrument issued by the German Federal Government. In each case, the exercise of the option creates a corresponding futures position for both purchaser and seller.

You should note that in all three cases the option premiums for calls falls as the strike prices increase, indicating that the market expected interest rates to rise and, hence, bond prices to fall in the near future.

20.3.4 Equity index options

Exchanges also offer a variety of options on stock exchange indices. For example, Euronext liffe offer options on a variety of indices of the Amsterdam, Belgian, London and Paris stock exchanges. Table 20.4 overleaf shows options on three stock exchange indices:

- on the Financial Times Stock Exchange Index of the share prices of the 100 largest companies quoted on the London Stock Exchange (FTSE-100), offered by Euronext.liffe;
- on the German DAX (offered by Eurex);
- on the Japanese Nikkei 225, offered by the Osaka Securities Exchange (OSE).

These tables no longer appear in the *Financial Times* but, even with rather old figures, they remain useful. All three options set out here are European-style options and thus can only be exercised on the expiry date, not at any time during the life of the option as with American options.

The FTSE index option is organized with strike prices along the top and expiry dates down the left-hand side. The reverse is done for the other contracts shown. The premiums for options on stock exchange indices are calculated in terms of index points not as a percentage of the contract value. With all three options one can again see that the premium on both calls and puts rises as the period to expiry lengthens. Equally, the premium on calls falls and that on puts rises as the strike price increases.

20.4 The pricing of options

We have seen that the premium of an option on a given day consists of two elements: the *intrinsic value* – the profit that would be made by exercising the option on that day; and the *time value* – a measure of the chances that the option will become profitable before the expiry date. We have seen above, in looking at contract premiums that one element of the time value of an option is just the length of time that an option has to run to expiry since the longer that period is, the greater must be the chance that the price of the underlying asset will change, affecting the profitability of the option. Options pricing is, however, rather more complicated than this suggests since the chances of a change occurring in an underlying price depend not only on the length of time but also on the volatility of the price in question. Where the underlying price has a high variance (that is, it changes frequently and by relatively large amounts), the time value of an option will be greater for each period to expiry than where the underlying price is generally relatively stable. It is true that a volatile price may fall sharply as well as rise sharply but falls in price are relevant only to the point at which the option is at-the-money at the time of expiry – greater falls in price, making the value of the option negative at the time of expiry, will simply cause the option to be abandoned. It follows that sharp price movements upwards have a much stronger impact on the possible profitability of an option and also that volatility will always be positively related to the premium.

Further, the intrinsic value and time value are related. If an option is presently deeply out-of-the-money (it has no intrinsic value), the chances that (for any given time period and volatility of the cash price) a change

---

Exercise 20.2

At the close of the London Stock Exchange on 26 April 2004, the FTSE-100 index stood at 4571.8.

(a) Which of the options contracts on the FTSE-100 index shown in Table 20.4 were then in-the-money? Why?

(b) Explain the difference between the cost of a call option and a put option at a strike price of 4825.

Table 20.4 Equity index options

■ FTSE 100 INDEX OPTION (Euronext.liffe) £10 per full index point															26 April	FT
	4225		4325		4425		4525		4625		4725		4825		4925	
	C	P	C	P	C	P	C	P	C	P	C	P	C	P	C	P
May	349½	4½	252	7	160	14½	79½	33½	26	79½	5½	159	1	254	¾	353
Jun	365½	15½	273	22½	185½	34½	109½	58	52½	100	21	168	6½	253	1½	347½
Jul	391	29½	301½	40	216½	55	143½	82	81½	120	40	178½	17½	256	7	345½
Aug	401½	48	316	62½	236½	83	166	112½	107	153½	63½	210	33½	280	16	362½
Sep	422½	65	339½	80½	262	101½	192	130	131½	168	83	218	48	281	25	356½

Calls, 9,615; puts, 11,934. *Underlying index value. Premiums shown are based on settlement prices.

■ DAX INDEX OPTIONS (Eurex)						
Strike price	.... CALLS			.... PUTS		
26 Apr	Jun	Sep	Dec	Jun	Sep	Dec
4100	143.2	254.8	327.8	100	184.5	232
4150	113	–	–	110.5	192.3	–
4200	88	193	268	144	214	–

Calls, 67,285; puts, 75,869; volume, 143,154. Previous day's open interest, 4,119,747.   Source: Reuters/Eurex.

■ NIKKEI 225 OPTIONS (Osaka)						
Strike price	.... CALLS			.... PUTS		
26 Apr	May	Jun	Jul	May	Jun	Jul
11500	725	780	880	25	115	200
12000	305	440	545	125	280	380
12500	80	215	315	410	540	625
13000	10	90	165	–	–	–

Calls, na; puts, na; volume, na. Previous day's open interest, na.   Source: Reuters.

Source: *Financial Times*, 27 April 2004. Reprinted with permission.

in price will make the instrument profitable must be less than if the option is only just out-of-the-money or at-the-money. Equally, if an option is deeply in-the-money, the chances that the cash price will go on rising, continuing to increase the profitability of the option, are less than if the intrinsic value of the option is lower. We can put this more formally as: the further the strike price is from the prevailing spot rate (the deeper in- or out-of-the-money the option is) the lower will be its time value as the risk-adjusted probability of

gain on the contract to the buyer declines. Box 20.4 discusses the relationship between time value and intrinsic value in the context of the European- and American-style options.

The value of a call option and hence the premium on it will also be higher, the higher is the risk-free rate of interest. This arises because of the choice which is always available to buy the underlying asset in the cash market as an alternative to buying an option. One advantage of the option is that only the premium

---

BOX 20.4 Premiums on European and American stock exchange indices

European options can only be exercised on the expiry date whereas *American options* can be exercised on any day up to and including the date of expiry. Thus, prior to the expiry date an American option has both intrinsic value and time value whereas a European option effectively only has time value. However, on the expiry date itself, European and American options have the same value – they both only have intrinsic value given by the difference between the strike price and the underlying price. There is no time left for the underlying price to change.

Remember also that short of the expiry date American options that are out-of-the-money have no intrinsic value and so, like European options, they only have time value. However, as we note in the text, the time value of the two types of option will differ because an out-of-the-money American option might acquire intrinsic value and be exercised prior to the expiry date. This cannot happen with a European option since it only has intrinsic value on the expiry date and so for options that are currently out-of-the-money, the premiums for American options should be higher than for European options. But how much higher?

Remember, too, from the text that for deeply out-of-the-money options, *ceteris paribus*, the chances that a change in price would make the option profitable are less than if the option were only just out-of-the-money or at-the-money. Thus, the difference between the time value and hence the premiums of European and American options should be smaller the more deeply out-of-the-money they currently are.

---

needs to be paid and thus the difference between the cost of buying the asset directly in the cash market and the premium paid on the option is available to be invested. If we wish to make the two strategies comparable, the amount made available for investment by buying the option should be invested in a risk-free form, hence the use of the risk-free rate of interest. It follows that increases in interest rates will cause options to become more attractive relative to a direct purchase in the cash market. The value of the option and the premium paid for it increase with increases in the rate of interest.

We can sum up this discussion by saying that the premium of an option will, *ceteris paribus*, be:

1 positively related to the cash price (P_s) of the underlying asset since increases in P_s increase the intrinsic value of the option;

2 negatively related to the strike price (P_x) since decreases in the strike price increase the intrinsic value of the option;

3 positively related to the amount of time that the option has to run before expiry (n_m) since the longer this period is the greater the time value of the option is;

4 positively related to the volatility of the cash price of the underlying asset since the greater the volatility of the cash price the greater is the chance that the cash price will rise to high levels before expiry (the higher the volatility, the higher the time value of the option); and

5 positively related to the risk-free rate of interest (i_{rf}) since the higher is the rate of interest the more attractive the option is relative to a purchase of the underlying asset in the cash market.

The next step is to establish the band within which an options price must fall if there are not to be profitable arbitrage opportunities. Consider the premium of an American call option. Even if it is deeply out-of-the-money, a call option must always have a positive value before expiry because there must always be some chance that the cash price will change sufficiently to give the option intrinsic value by the expiry date. At the point of expiry, however, the option could have zero value, in which case it would lapse. Thus:

$$Pm^c \geq 0 \qquad (20.1)$$

where Pm^c is the premium of a call option.

However, it is also true that the premium of an American call option must be at least equal to its intrinsic value at any time or the immediate exercise of the option would be profitable:

$$Pm^c \geq P_s - P_x \qquad (20.2)$$

But by developing the argument in point 5 above, we can develop another pricing rule. Compare two strategies: (i) buying the underlying asset in the cash market now and holding it for three months; (ii) buying a three-month European call option and exercising it at the strike price at expiry. The gain in following strategy (ii) is the difference between the present cash price and the premium. At the point of expiry, however, strategy (ii) will deliver only the difference between the cash price at that time and the strike price:

$$(P_s^2 - Px) \geq 0$$

where P_s^2 is the cash price at expiry. Thus, the maximum loss associated with strategy (ii) will be the value of P_x in three months' time. To compare this with the present gain, we need to discount it back to the present and, since we might have invested the amount saved in the present from strategy (ii) at the risk-free rate of interest, we should use that rate of interest to discount back the strike price. Thus we have:

$$P_s - Pm^c \geq P_x e^{-i_{rf} n_m} \qquad (20.3)$$

where $P_x e^{-i_{rf} n_m}$ is the discounted value of the cash price and hence:

$$Pm^c \geq P_s - P_x e^{-i_{rf} n_m} \qquad (20.4)$$

That is, the premium of the call option must at least equal the present cash price minus the discounted strike price. This rule must also hold for an American option since an American option must be more valuable than a European option because it adds the time value of the option between the present and the expiry date to the intrinsic value of the option at expiry.

Equation 20.4 formalizes the argument above that an increase in the risk-free rate of interest (i_{rf}) increases the premium of a call option since it reduces the present value of the strike price at the point of expiry ($P_x e^{-i_{rf} n_m}$). From Equation 20.4, we can also see that the premium must be greater than the difference between the cash price and the strike price ($P_s - P_x$) since the strike price is discounted back from the expiry date. The expression on the right-hand side of Equation 20.4 ($P_s - P_x e^{-i_{rf} n_m}$) can be negative although, as we saw in Equation 20.1, an option premium will never fall below zero. Thus, it is usual to combine Equations 20.1 and 20.4 into:

$$Pm^c \geq max(0, P_s - P_x e^{-i_{rf} n_m}) \qquad (20.5)$$

We can now use Equations 20.1, 20.2 and 20.4 to establish boundary conditions for the pricing of options as shown in Figure 20.1.

Writing, $P_x e^{-i_{rf} n_m}$ as P_x^f for ease, we can interpret the diagram in the following way. Given the cash price of the underlying asset, the greatest value an option can assume will be where the strike price is zero. With a zero strike price (P_x), Equation 20.4 tells us that the call option premium will just equal the cash price.

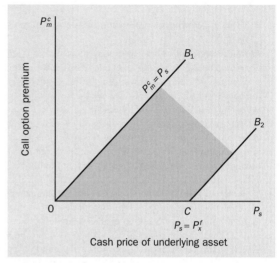

Figure 20.1 Option pricing limits

That is, the maximum premium for an option is shown along the ray from the origin $0B_1$ which is at 45 degrees to the horizontal axis. The minimum price of any option will be zero and this will occur where the cash price is less than or equal to the discounted strike price P_x^f. For any given value of P_x^f, as P_s rises above P_x^f, the option premium will rise in line with the cash price (along the line CB_2). However, since P_x^f will change with changes in the strike price, the risk-free rate of interest, and the time to the expiry date of the option, it is clear that the premium may fall anywhere in the shaded area between $0B_1$ and CB_2. Exercise 20.3 gives practice in the calculation of the minimum price of a call option.

A number of options pricing models have been developed to allow the calculation of options premiums within the band illustrated in Figure 20.1. Expectations regarding the likely future cash price of the underlying asset are crucial in such calculations since it is the future cash price that will determine the profitability or otherwise of the option. We have seen, in particular, that the expected volatility of the cash price above the level at which it is greater than the discounted strike price ($P_s > P_x^f$) is very important here since that indicates the chances of the cash price reaching high levels and thus producing high profits. Assets with stable prices are less likely to produce large profits and hence will have lower time value.

The usual assumption for the pricing of options is that future volatility can be estimated from the past

---

Exercise 20.3 Boundaries on options

Assume that for April \$/£ call options on the Chicago Mercantile Exchange in Table 20.2 contracts had one month to run to expiry and that the risk-free interest rate in the USA was the rate then available for one-month money in the US money market (1.1 per cent). Thus, to discover the maximum call option premium for a strike price of 1.21 we discount back the strike price at a rate of 0.011 for one month and subtract the figure we obtain from the spot price on the day (\$1.2225).

Read example A below and then supply the missing figures for examples B and C.

A. Strike price \$1.21

1   Discounting back \$1.2100 at 0.011 for one month gives \$1.209.

2   Subtracting \$1.209 from the spot price of \$1.2225 gives \$0.0135.

The premiums are, however, expressed in cents per €. Therefore, the minimum premium should be 1.35 US cents per €. We also know from Equation 20.2 in the text that the premium must be at least equal to the intrinsic value of the option. This was \$1.2225 − \$1.21 = \$0.0125 = 1.25 cents. A price of 1.35 cents thus lies above the intrinsic value and we return to the position that the minimum price should have been 1.35 cents per euro.

   We see from Table 20.2 that the actual premium for April contracts with a strike price of \$1.21 was, in fact, 2.08 cents.

B. Strike price \$1.23

1   Discounting back \$1.23 at 0.011 for one month gives (B1).

2   Subtracting (B2) from the spot price of (B3) gives (B4).

3   The premium for a call option at \$1.23 should have been above (B5).

4   The actual premium on this option in Table 20.2 is (B6).

C. Strike price \$1.24

1   Discounting back \$1.24 at 0.011 for one month gives (C1).

2   Subtracting (C2) from the spot price of (C3) gives (C4).

3   The premium for a call option at \$1.24 should have been above (C5).

4   The actual premium on this option in Table 20.2 is (C6).

D. Comment on the difference between your answers for B5 and B6 and C5 and C6.

---

volatility of the cash price in question. Thus, the premium for a call option to buy euro (with dollars) will be influenced by the past distribution of the \$/€ rate about its mean. The greater the variance of the rate in the past, the higher will be the option premium. This is the basis of the best known of the various theoretical models for pricing options, the Black–Scholes options pricing model which is based upon shares on which no dividends are paid. Detailed treatment of options pricing models is beyond the scope of this book but we can get a feel of the nature of the Black–Scholes model by modifying Equation 20.4 as follows:

$$Pm^c = P_s N(d_1) - P_x e^{-i_{rf} n_m} N(d_2) \qquad (20.6)$$

Here the cash price (P_s) and the discounted strike price ($P_x e^{-i_{rf} n_m}$) are multiplied by $N(d_1)$ and $N(d_2)$ respectively. This provides a measure of possible future profit levels given the past variance (σ) of the cash price of the underlying asset. Formally, $N(d_1)$ and $N(d_2)$ are cumulative weighted normal probability values of d_1 and d_2, which are calculated in their turn as follows:

$$d_1 = \frac{\ln (P_s/P_x) + [i_{rf} + (1/2)\sigma^2] n_m}{\sigma \sqrt{n_m}} \qquad (20.7)$$

and

$$d_2 = d_1 - \sigma \sqrt{n_m} \qquad (20.8)$$

where n_m is the length of time the option has to run to expiry and i_{rf} is the risk-free rate of interest. That is, the probabilities are derived from a log normal distribution of possible cash prices. The weighting takes into account the fact that low values of the cash price are of no significance since the option premium cannot fall below zero. In general, the greater is the expected volatility of the cash price and the longer the time to expiry, the more dispersed the distribution will be. The more dispersed the distribution, the higher will be the probability of extreme values occurring. Thus, the more dispersed the distribution, the greater will be the weighted sum of potential profits to the buyer and the higher the premium will be.

Similar principles may be used to calculate theoretical premiums for put options and for exotic options. Of course, the market is likely to use calculations from models such as the Black–Scholes options pricing model as a guide. If buyers and writers held rational expectations, they would take into account all the information that might affect future volatility, not just calculations based on the dispersion of past cash prices. In a market where expectations differ from one investor to another, speculators will be attempting to make profits by guessing better what will happen than the average investor. We have seen in Box 20.2 that investors use strategies which enable them to profit if they guess correctly that the market will be more or less volatile than the average investor believes. In Box 20.7, where we look at the collapse of the British bank Barings, we see that the trader, Nick Leeson, was betting on Japanese share prices remaining stable, which had been the recent experience. In fact, they became very volatile.

<table>
<tr><td>20.5</td><td>Exotic options</td></tr>
</table>

There are many variations on the simple call and put options dealt with above. They are known as *exotic options*. We explain some of them here.

An **interest rate cap** is an option in which the buyer receives money at the end of each period in which an interest rate exceeds the agreed rate. In an **interest rate floor**, the buyer receives a payment if the interest rate is below the agreed rate. They are both, thus, equivalent to a series of European call options (or caplets) with an option expiring at the end of each period.

MORE FROM THE WEB

Do you need some more examples? Many glossaries and explanations of financial products are available on the web. For exotic options and other derivatives try, for example, www.finpipe.com/exoptions.htm.

This site also provides a good set of internet links. A useful introduction to derivatives is available on the Bank of England website, downloadable in pdf format: www.bankofengland.co.uk/ccbs. Choose the 'Handbooks in Central Banking' link and then you will find a list of handbooks available. Financial Derivatives is No. 17.

Consider an example of an interest rate cap. A firm raising capital at floating rates in the market may have a target interest rate it feels it can afford on its loan but fears that interest rates might rise during the life of the loan pushing its cost of capital up. It seeks to hedge against this risk by taking out an interest rate cap for the amount of the loan on a floating interest rate (say LIBOR). Assume it does this for six months with an expiry date at the end of each of month and that Libor is currently 4.5 per cent. Then, on any expiry date that LIBOR is above 4.5 per cent (the strike price below 95.5), the option holder receives a payment based on the interest rate difference and the agreed capital sum. If interest rates rise, the firm will have to pay more for its capital but this is offset by the payment it receives under the terms of the option. If interest rates do not rise, the caplets expire unexercised in the usual way and the firm has protected itself at the cost of the option premium. An interest rate floor might be attractive to a firm that has lent money at a floating interest rate and is seeking to hedge against falling interest rates. Interest rate caps or floors can be modified to limit the total payment possible over the life of the option. Then they become **bounded interest rate caps** or **bounded interest rate floors**. Another possible modification relates not to the size of the payout but to the size of the premium. The terms of the option might state that an additional premium must be paid if Libor reaches a particular level. Then the option becomes a **contingent premium cap** or **floor**.

Barrier options are over-the-counter options designed to meet the particular needs of customers. They are also known as *knock-in* or *knock-out* options which means that they come into being (knock-in) or lapse (knock-out) when specified prices of the underlying asset are reached. There are four types of barrier options: calls and puts, each with a knock-out or knock-in feature.

Barrier cap or **barrier floor** options (knock-in options) pay nothing at expiry unless they are first brought to life as a result of the price of the underlying asset reaching a specified level (the barrier cap or barrier floor). Thus, the interest rate cap example above could be modified by inserting a barrier of, say, 4.75 per cent for LIBOR. Then, LIBOR might rise above 4.5 per cent but no payment would be due until it reached 4.75 per cent. If LIBOR rose above 4.75 per cent, payment would occur and would be based on actual LIBOR at the exercise date – 4.5 per cent. In a barrier floor, the barrier might be set at, say, 4.25 per cent. These options may be modified further by accepting a ceiling to the amount of the payout, making them bounded barrier caps or bounded barrier floors. Alternatively, the amount to be paid might be magnified according to an agreed formula when the barrier is reached and the option comes into life. This is known as a **balloon option**. A knock-out option begins life as a standard option but is killed off if the cash price or interest rate touches the barrier. Yet another possibility is for limits to be placed on the number of payouts that can be made. For example, an interest rate cap with six possible payout dates may be limited to three payouts. This is known as a 'flexible cap' option. Where the option holder is allowed to select which three payouts to accept (assuming that more than three would be triggered during the life of the option), we have a 'chooser flexible cap' option. Naturally, there are also 'flexible floors' and 'chooser flexible floors'.

There are many other variations. For example, it is possible to take out options which will only pay out if the underlying variable (e.g. an interest rate or an exchange rate) finishes up within a range. Assume in our example of the firm concerned about the cost to it of the capital it needs to raise. It might only become unhappy if interest rates rise by, say, 1 per cent. Therefore, it wants an option which knocks in when LIBOR reaches 5.5 per cent. However, it believes that it is quite impossible for LIBOR to go beyond 7 per cent during the life of the option. It thinks it would be a waste of money to insure itself against something that it thinks will never happen and so wants an option which knocks out at a LIBOR of 7 per cent. This is a **double barrier option**. It pays out on each specified date if LIBOR is between 5.5 and 7 per cent but not otherwise.

Because they might never come into existence or might be killed off, barrier options are much cheaper than conventional options. They are often used in the foreign exchange market by chartists who feel strongly that exchange rates will not fall below support levels or rise above resistance levels. Box 20.5 overleaf discusses the use of barrier options.

Credit risk derivatives or credit derivatives were devised by banks to help manage their own credit risks but were then marketed to clients. The most popular has been the credit default option which protects the buyer against the default of a specific company or country. For example, an option might be taken out by a company which expects to be paid €20m in three years' time when it completes a project in a foreign country. But since the country in question has defaulted on similar payments in the past, the company wants insurance against default risk. Hence it may take out an option with a bank which requires it to pay the premium in annual or semi-annual portions to the bank. In the event of a default, or a breach of other criteria agreed at the start of the option, the company will receive a payment.

The bank arranging the option will use outstanding bonds issued by the country concerned as a benchmark for setting the premium but since the bank will be hedging its own position by issuing bonds of a similar amount to investors, the company will have to pay above the yield on the outstanding bonds to attract buyers for the bonds backing the transaction. In the event of a default, there are various ways in which the size of the bank's payment may be calculated and the formula chosen by the company will influence the premium of the option. Credit risk derivatives are also sometimes bought by a fund manager holding, say, double-A rated bonds to compensate him if the securities were downgraded to single-A. For further details on credit derivatives see Section 24.3.3.

Other exotic options include:

- **Lookback options:** options that give the right to buy (lookback call) or sell (lookback put) at the lowest price reached by the underlying asset during the life of the option.
- **Asian options:** options whose intrinsic value is calculated by comparing the strike price with the average spot price over the period of the option.

BOX 20.5 The use of a barrier option

A German company which imports oil, paying in US dollars, expects a bill for $1 million in three months' time. The current exchange rate is $1.42 = €1. If the company is happy with that rate, it might buy a three-month euro call at that exercise price. This would protect the firm against the euro weakening and, if the euro strengthened, in the following three months the option could be allowed to lapse and the $1 million bought spot at a more favourable rate.

A *knock-out* euro call would give the same protection against the weakening of the euro (downside protection) but only until the exchange rate falls to a level below which the firm thinks it is unlikely to go. For example, a knock-out option with the same strike price and a barrier set at $1.38 = €1 might cost much less than the standard option because the more extreme possibilities of loss to the writer would be cut off by the option being knocked out. If, at any time within the three months, the spot rate touched $1.38, and the option ceased to exist, the firm could buy the necessary euro in the spot market at that rate and put it on deposit until needed.

Barrier options are also used in investment products to enhance yield or to allow investors to express a view on two or more assets with a single instrument. For example, it would be possible to have a call option on a basket of French equities which knocked out if the euro appreciated by more than a given percentage against the dollar. This would be an example of an *outside barrier* – the barrier asset (the exchange rate) is different from the asset on which the basic option is written.

Another popular application during periods of low interest rates has been to use two knock-out options to create structured notes which pay high returns provided an underlying asset remains within a certain range. A typical example is a one-year dollar-denominated bond which yields 200 basis points more than conventional one-year paper provided the dollar/euro exchange rate remains within the range $1.38–1.42 = €1. The narrower the range, and hence the more likely that the option would be knocked out, the greater the yield would be.

- **Average strike rate options**: options where the strike rate is the average of the underlying index over the life of the option and so can only be calculated at the expiry date.

- **Options on options (compound options)**: an option that gives the right but not the obligation to buy or sell an option at a later date. Again, there are many variations among which is the **chooser option** where the buyer can decide at the point at which he must choose whether or not to accept the second option whether that option is a call or a put.

- **Basket options**: currency-protected options in which the payout is based on the average performance of a pre-determined basket of underlying assets (e.g. interest rates, currencies, equities, commodities).

- **Cliquet options**: options in which the strike price is re-set periodically at the cash price of the underlying asset. A variation on this is the **coupe option** where the strike price is either re-set at the current cash price or left at the original strike price, whichever is worse from the point of view of the option holder.

- **Flex options**: options offered by the Chicago Board Options Exchange (CBOE) which allow an institutional OTC customer to choose any strike price and expiry date up to five years. Initially they applied to the CBOE's Standard and Poor's 100 and 500 Stock Index baskets and had an underlying value of $10m, much larger than the standard index options contracts.

- **Warrants**: options to purchase or sell an underlying asset at a given price and time or series of prices and times. A warrant differs from a call or put option by ordinarily being issued for longer than a year. With covered warrants the shares that

---

MORE FROM THE WEB

The list of exotic options we have provided here is only a beginning. You can find many more types on the web. Begin with http://www.business.com/ and put 'exotic options' into the search box and you should arrive ar a page which gives you addresses of a number of firms but also a long, long list of types of options. Clicking on each of these will lead you to a page of description with examples and some discussion on pricing. For more detail on CBOE's flex options above, try www.cboe.com.

holders receive, if they exercise their warrants, already exist. Thus, the issuer of covered warrants is usually a bank that has bought up underlying shares. On the other hand, when companies issue warrants, usually in conjunction with bonds, it is generally a means of raising funds by creating new shares if the warrants are exercised.

20.6 Swaps

Swaps are exchanges of cashflows. They are attempts by firms to manage their asset/liability structure or to reduce their cost of borrowing. Cashflows generated by many different types of financial instruments may be swapped. Simple swaps such as interest rate and currency swaps are sometimes known as plain vanilla swaps. There are many variations on these.

An **interest rate swap** is an exchange of a cashflow representing a fixed rate of interest on a notional capital sum with that representing a floating rate on the same sum in the same currency. There is no exchange of the principal amount. They are potentially useful because the fixed and floating capital markets are distinct markets and firms wishing to borrow may not have equal access to both. For example, a firm may be quite large in a regional market and be able to borrow from regional banks at fine floating interest rates (that is, the rate at which banks themselves obtain their money – the basis rate or interbank rate – plus a small fixed rate spread). Nonetheless, it may be insufficiently well known to be able to launch a fixed interest rate bond without offering a high coupon because of the high risk premium that will be demanded in the bond market for holding bonds issued by a little known firm (because the firm is only regional it may be given a low credit rating by the international agencies).

Taking the floating rate loan, however, exposes the firm to the risk that interest rates may rise. The firm may be able to obtain better fixed interest rate terms in the national capital market on relatively short-term loans but will still face the interest rate risk if it wishes a long-term loan because the interest rate may change when it seeks to rollover the loan. The firm may be able to hedge the risk in a variety of ways. It could, for example, sell a long-term interest rate futures contract. Then, if the interest rate rises, the firm loses on its loan but this loss is offset by the profit made on the

futures contract. Again, the firm could hedge by buying a put (or writing a call) option on long-term interest rates or interest rate futures. Yet another possibility is for it to swap the interest rate payments it must make to its bank with a fixed interest rate flow of another firm that has been able to obtain a suitably priced fixed interest rate loan but would prefer a floating rate loan.

The default risk in a swap of future cash streams between firms is overcome in the swaps market by arranging the swap through a bank (the swap bank or hedge bank) which acts as a guarantor to both parties and charges a fee that takes into account the risk that one of the firms will default on their payments to the bank. This type of business has advantages to the bank because it earns a fee for its services without advancing any of its capital or using up any of its credit lines – it is off-balance-sheet business. Box 20.6 overleaf provides an example of how an interest rate swap might work to benefit all parties.

This is an example where payments are swapped but receipts may also be swapped. Yet again, since the capital sums are only notional, it is possible to speculate on the possibility of an interest rate rise or fall through interest rate swaps. For example, a speculator might feel that interest rates are likely to fall and so offer a floating rate stream (which will fall as market interest rates decline) in exchange for a fixed rate stream which will not. If the speculator is right about the direction of interest rate change she will profit from the swap. The price of a swap (the charge made by the swap bank for its services) depends on the bank's estimate of the extent of default risk, the ease with which it can obtain a counterparty and the term structure of interest rates in the bond market.

A **currency swap** has three stages:

- an initial exchange of principal: the two counterparties exchange principal amounts at an agreed exchange rate. This can be a notional exchange since its purpose is to establish the principal amounts as a reference point for the calculation of interest payments and the re-exchange of the principal amounts;

- exchange of interest payments on agreed dates based on outstanding principal amounts and agreed fixed interest rates;

- re-exchange of the principal amounts at a predetermined exchange rate so the parties end up with their original currencies.

BOX 20.6 An interest rate swap

A major British defence industry supplier, Death Mines plc, wishes to borrow £1m for 12 years at a fixed interest rate to finance a new investment project. It could do so by issuing a straight Eurobond but, as the international market has some doubts about the future of medium-sized arms suppliers, it would have to pay a coupon of 9 per cent which it regards as too high. The firm's own bank is willing to lend Death Mines the required amount via a one-year floating rate note at a rate of 1.5 per cent over the London Inter-Bank Offered Rate (LIBOR), currently at 5 per cent, and rollover the loan annually.

The floating rate loan is much cheaper at the moment, but LIBOR could easily rise over the period of the loan to such a level that Death Mines will finish up losing on the project. Thus, it enters into a contract with a swap bank, Border International, to pay to it 6 per cent on the principal, receiving in exchange LIBOR.

The position of Death Mines now is:

Pays to its own bank	LIBOR + 1.5%
Pays to Border	6%
Receives from Border	LIBOR
Net position – fixed rate loan at	7.5%

But what of Border International? It has taken on a risk that LIBOR will increase. To cover this, it must either find a counterparty that wishes to take the reverse action to Death Mines or hedge the risk through, perhaps, options or futures (this is known as warehousing). Let us assume that Border International finds a counterparty – a large US multinational, Global Heat. Global Heat is a prime borrower and so can borrow on the Eurobond market on the finest terms, but prefers a floating rate loan as it is willing to gamble on interest rates falling in the future. Thus, it issues a straight £1m Eurobond with a coupon of 5.375 per cent. Then it enters into a contract with Border International to pay Border LIBOR in exchange for a fixed return of 5.75 per cent.

The position of Global Heat now is:

Pays on its straight Eurobond	5.375%
Receives from Border	5.75%
Pays to Border	LIBOR
Net position: floating rate loan at	LIBOR – 0.375%

Border International's Position now is:

Receives from Death Mines	6%
Pays to Death Mines	LIBOR
Receives from Global Heat	LIBOR
Pays to Global Heat	5.75%
Net position – profit of	0.25% (25 basis points)

Again this may be done to hedge risk, to speculate on changes in exchange rates or to attempt to lower the cost of borrowing by borrowing in the currency in which the most favourable interest rates are available and then swapping into the currency that the firm needs to carry out its business. Whether this will be cheaper will depend among other things on the bid–offer spread.

There are many variations on simple currency swaps. In a **cross-currency basis swap** two floating rate cash streams are swapped. This may be possible because the banks that have made the two loans are using a different basis rate for the calculation of their floating interest rates. The most commonly used basis rate in the London market is LIBOR (the London Inter-Bank Offered Rate). The US dollar prime rate is also widely used. Thus, a basis rate swap may involve, for example, an exchange of a sterling cash stream representing a floating interest rate based upon Libor with a dollar cash stream representing a floating rate based upon the US$ prime rate.

A **cross-currency coupon swap** is a currency swap involving a fixed interest stream and a floating interest stream. In other words, it is a combination of an interest rate swap and a fixed rate currency swap – both the interest rate structure and the currency are exchanged.

Other types of swap include **equity swaps** which are agreements to exchange the rate of return on an equity or an equity index for a floating or fixed rate of interest. Equity swaps can be used as an alternative to futures and options for hedging but are most attractive to fund managers trying to outperform an index. The fund manager receives a stream of payments replicating the return of a direct investment in an equity index and makes in return a stream of payments usually based on LIBOR. An equity swap may increase a fund manager's ability to increase returns but because swaps, unlike futures, can run for up to 10 years, the default risk is greater, although exposure to it is limited by payments normally being made every three months and because there is no exchange of principal.

In a **commodity swap** the counterparties exchange cash flows, at least one of which is based on a commodity price or commodity price index. A high proportion of the market is made up of oil-related transactions. A **diff swap** (or *quanto swap*) is the exchange of the cashflows on an asset or liability in one currency for those in another. A firm making a diff swap separates foreign exchange and interest rate exposure, by paying interest rates based on one currency while taking the foreign exchange risk of another. For example, a company with US dollar liabilities, paying say 7 per cent interest, would prefer to be paying euro interest rates of 4.5 per cent but may not want to be exposed to the risk of changes in the value of the euro. Under a diff swap, the company agrees to receive dollar LIBOR and to pay a margin over euro LIBOR in dollars. The structure takes advantage of different-shaped yield curves to create immediate cost savings for the borrower and allows an investor to receive higher interest rates without changing currency exposure. Such an agreement typically runs from three to five years and so the risk for either borrower or investor is that the shape of one or both yield curves will change more quickly than expected, turning expected benefits into losses. Diff swaps became common when US and European interest rates diverged sharply. They involve *correlation risk* – an assumption that there will be a correlation between an interest rate movement and that of the currency. With a *LIBOR-in-arrears swap*, the borrower essentially takes a bet that implied forward rates are wrong by having LIBOR set, say, six months in arrears.

It is also possible to combine a zero coupon bond with an interest rate swap (known as a zero coupon swap). Then there are *swaptions* – options that give the right to enter into a swap within a specified period. Because swaps are off-balance-sheet business but carry risks for the swap bank there was a concern in the past that banks might take on more risk through swaps than was justified by the size of their capital backing. As a consequence, the rules adopted by a number of countries (known as the Basel rules, see Chapter 25), which try to ensure that the capital backing of banks is adequate for the type of business in which they are engaged, make allowances for off-balance-sheet business. Because currency swaps involve both default risk and exchange rate risk, they require higher capital backing under the Basel rules and this has slowed down their expansion relative to interest rate swaps.

20.7 Other investment products and derivative contracts

There are yet other products and strategies that do not fit neatly under the futures, options and swaps headings. Some of these are clearly derivatives, others relate to forward markets or offer other forms of protection to investors.

Among those related to forward markets are **safes** (synthetic agreements for forward foreign exchange). These are forward contracts that do not require an exchange of principal. This means that banks need to devote less capital to them and are less exposed to default risk. There are two types of Safe: the Exchange Rate Agreement (ERA) which protects the purchaser against a change in the forward foreign exchange spread; and the Forward Exchange Agreement (FXA) which gives protection against a change in the spot rate as well as the forward spread. **Dynamic hedging** is a strategy involving the buying and selling of forward contracts in the market in order to replicate options. It became popular in foreign exchange markets after the problems in the European Monetary System in 1992 which caused options prices to rise sharply.

Other products which clearly are derivatives include:

- **Insurance risk contracts:** futures and options on catastrophe insurance, health, and homeowner's and reinsurance risk.

■ **Contracts for difference (CFDs):** cash-settled agreements traded on margin to exchange the difference in value of a particular share, future, option or index between the time at which a contract is opened and the time at which it is closed. The contract is effectively renewed at the close of each trading day and rolled forward if desired. Positions can be kept open indefinitely, provided the investor has enough margin in his account to support the position. CFDs are settled, in the case of futures, on the difference between the purchase and sale prices; with options on the difference between the exercise price and the settlement price. Thus, there is no underlying asset. Rather, CFDs involve a swap of cashflows and have been compared to borrowing money and then using this to buy shares. While the contract remains open, the investor's account with the provider will be debited or credited to reflect interest and dividend adjustments. CFDs can be used to maintain either short or long positions. Investors with long positions receive dividends and pay interest and so it can become expensive to maintain long positions for any length of time. Investors with short positions receive interest and pay dividends. Commission is paid on each side of the contract. Contracts can be closed at any time. In practice there is no minimum contract value though, normally, the smallest contract value will be £10,000. Because they are traded on margin they, as do other derivatives, offer considerable leverage opportunities but also involve considerable risk. CFDs have become increasingly popular in recent years.

■ **Principal-protected notes** (PPNs) (also known as equity-protected notes) are synthetic or structured products created by financial engineers who combine derivatives either with other derivatives or with a traditional investment such as a stock or a bond. They guarantee to return at least 100 per cent of the original investment provided that the

PPN is held to maturity. Typically, a bank acts as the guarantor of the invested principal. PPNs are sold as equivalent to bonds and have several things in common with them – they have a face value, a term to maturity (usually six to ten years) and a return of principal at maturity. However, unlike bonds, there is no guaranteed periodic coupon. The return on a PPN depends on the terminal value of an embedded option and so is really a derivative with several features in common with traditional fixed-income products.

In addition, investors may engage in **spread betting** – betting as to whether an asset or a market will rise or fall and by how much. The bet can be on a wide range of futures including share price indices, commodities and currencies. Spread betting on financial assets is classified as gambling rather than as investment but is administered by the Financial Services Authority.

20.8 Comparing different types of derivatives

20.8.1 Exchange-traded versus OTC options

Exchange-traded options have five principal advantages over over-the-counter options:

1 the existence of the clearing house guarantees all trades and virtually eliminates the default risk present in OTC trades;

2 price discovery is easier from exchange-based trading than in OTC markets because exchange-traded options contracts are reported immediately and prices are widely distributed;

3 markets for exchange-based options are more liquid than bilateral OTC trades since there are many traders;

4 exchange-traded options are highly tradable because they are standardized whereas OTC options, being non-standard and redeemable only at the bank where they were bought, have a low re-sale value;

5 exchange-based options are lower in price than options with OTC derivatives since there will almost always be some irreducible residual risk that a bank is forced to take onto its own book, despite the fact

---

MORE FROM THE WEB

For more information on contracts for difference (CFDs), try http://www.contracts-for-difference.com/. For additional information on principal-protected notes, try http://www.investopedia.com/articles/bonds/07/principal_protected.asp.

that it will attempt to minimize its risks by arranging offsetting contracts with other customers/banks and/or by taking a position in exchange-traded options.

Against these, we must set the fact that OTC options are designed to meet the specific requirements of each customer in terms of size, strike price and expiry.

20.8.2 OTC outright contracts versus futures

There may be important cashflow differences between OTC outright and futures contracts because, whereas net profits on a futures hedge are accrued on a daily basis, the net profits on an OTC forward hedge are only realized on the actual date of currency delivery (assuming the forward contract is not closed out prematurely). A different type of problem connected with the use of futures contracts to hedge an exposed currency position arises in cases where the lifetime of the futures contract continues beyond the intended date of currency delivery. This problem stems from the fact that the difference between the futures and spot rates may not tend uniformly towards zero as the delivery date for the futures contract approaches, which is the assumption that underlies calculations of the forward rate. Eventual convergence is certain, but in the meantime as the basis moves to compensate for changes in interest rate differentials between countries, so the futures hedge will tend to be in either profit or loss. Clearly, the further the anticipated date of actual currency conversion is from the futures delivery date, the less the natural tendency towards zero of the basis will dominate other factors and hence the less efficient the hedge.

20.8.3 Outright contracts versus options

Outright contracts lock in an investor to a given exchange rate. Thus, the contract provides a hedge if the exchange rate moves in the direction that would have produced a loss, but there is an opportunity loss if the currency moves in the opposite direction. Currency options, on the other hand, do not lock in an investor to a particular exchange rate since the option does not have to be exercised.

20.9 The use and abuse of derivatives

We have seen that financial derivatives allow firms to hedge against erratic price and interest rate movements while also attracting speculators because of their high gearing. These two aspects of the market have led to conflicting attitudes regarding their overall contribution to financial markets. Supporters of derivatives markets argue that they perform a number of important roles. They are said to:

- facilitate the hedging of risk through sophisticated risk management, and by so doing improve the productivity of investments;

- respond more quickly to new information than the cash markets and allow people who do not participate in derivatives trading to forecast accurately what will happen to future cash market prices and use this information to make better consumption, pricing and investment decisions – this is known as the 'price discovery' role of derivatives;

- assist in the standardization of commodity or financial instrument contracts in the cash markets because derivatives contracts are highly standardized themselves;

- contribute to the integration of global capital markets, hence improving the global allocation of savings and fostering higher investment levels;

- help to combat the adverse effects of volatile commodity prices on the economies of developing countries because forward prices tend to be less volatile than spot prices, giving commodity producers an opportunity to reduce the volatility of the price of their output through hedging;[2]

- facilitate speculation which provides liquid markets enabling hedgers to protect themselves from risk in the most efficient way possible.

Doubts have been expressed about the price discovery role since it is dependent on the efficient markets hypothesis (see Chapter 26). However, the main

---

[2] This role was emphasized in a 1994 World Bank report which referred to a study of the oil futures market in the late 1980s where it was suggested that a producer routinely hedging 15 months in advance could cut price volatility by a half.

doubts expressed about the benefits of derivatives have centred on the role of speculation and the difficulties that the increasing complexity of derivatives products have caused for regulators. Support for the attack on derivatives trading has come from problems in markets as a whole and from examples of spectacular losses by individual companies and banks.

For example, derivatives trading was widely held to be partly to blame for the 1987 stock market crash. The argument was that stock market traders were pessimistic and expected a fall in the price of stocks when the exchanges opened after a weekend. Large orders to sell arrived at brokerage houses prior to opening and, as the market started falling, many traders automatically sold futures in the shares of the major corporations. This destabilized stock markets and contributed to the panic selling of stocks and shares. This view of the crash led to a general concern that high turnover in derivatives, particularly that involving large-scale arbitrage techniques, may contribute to the volatility of the cash market. This is strenuously denied by the derivatives markets themselves, but worries have been expressed at a high level. Towards the end of April 1994 finance ministers from the Group of 10 leading industrial countries agreed on the need to strengthen cooperation in gathering statistics and assessing the implications for the world financial system of the innovative segments of financial markets. There was also a call for improved disclosure requirements and sufficient capital adequacy standards among financial institutions to underpin their risky activities.

Certainly there is some evidence that Wall Street equity prices have been affected by heavy activity in stock index contracts, especially around expiry dates, and there is a possible theoretical argument to support the view that derivatives trading makes the cash markets more volatile and nervy. This is that, in the past, people who thought prices in a market were becoming too high would speculate and express their bearish feelings by leaving the market. This would exert downward pressure on prices and help to stabilize them. Now, however, such firms stay in the market but protect themselves against risk using derivatives markets. No sale is made and bearish opinion loses its restraining influence on prices. Thus, although spreading risks through derivatives reduces risks for the individual, it increases risk for the system as a whole. This in turn provides big profit opportunities

for the uninsured speculators but increases risks of bankruptcies.

Concern about the systemic risks associated with derivatives trading have become prominent again in recent years. This derives partly from the vast size and continued rapid growth of the derivatives sector. According to the Bank for International Settlements, in 2007 the total face value of all derivatives contracts on and off exchanges reached $450,000bn – a fourfold increase since the start of the decade, and several times larger than the entire gross domestic product of the global economy. A second contributing factor to the renewed worry comes from fears about the speed with which the exposure of companies to risk can change, the continued lack of understanding by management of derivatives and the risks associated with them and the inadequate evaluation by firms of the risks they face. A third element in the argument is that markets continue to become more international. Thus, most people continue to accept the view that the use of derivatives can not only help to protect individual companies from risk but also increase the resilience of the financial system as a whole, certainly to the extent that relatively small (from a global perspective) shocks, can be contained. However, there are severe doubts among policymakers and regulators about the outcome of a large shock and the possibility of contagion. Markets are now so international they cannot be controlled by any single authority and no one has clear responsibility for the international system in crisis.

Individual company losses through derivatives have in recent years become almost routine. We shall look at a small selection here.

MORE FROM THE WEB

Until recently, there was an excellent website with contemporary newspaper and other reports of major financial scandals on the website of Roy Davies, a librarian at Exeter University – www.ex.ac.uk/~RDavies/.

At the time of writing, Exeter University appeared to be reorganizing its website and the financial scandals site had disappeared. With luck it will return with a different address. In the meantime, for links to a number of sites with material on financial scandals, try http://www.eagletraders.com/advice/financial_scandals.htm.

Perhaps the most spectacular was the collapse of the British merchant bank Barings in 1995. It is explained in Box 20.7.

Another interesting case arose from the attempt made in the late 1980s by Hammersmith and Fulham local authority in London to profit from speculation in interest rate swaps, but they ran up huge losses instead. They entered the sterling interest rate swaps market on 1 December 1983. Council officers had visited LIFFE where the idea of using swaps to reduce the sensitivity of the council's borrowings to interest rate fluctuations was explained to them. An independent inquiry in 1991, however, showed that such was the level of the user's understanding that the leader of the council and the finance department were not clear whether they were interested in futures or options transactions. The council's activities in the money markets intensified in May 1987 when it began to become involved in swap options and other complex transactions, eventually totalling 550 transactions.

At the time, interest rates were falling and the local authorities gambled on their continued fall. Thus, in 1988 when the base rate of interest in the UK was 7.5 per cent, local authorities swapped fixed interest rate for floating interest rate loans of the same value with hedging banks. The only payments made were for the net liabilities on whichever was the higher – the fixed or the floating rate. Thus if interest rates had continued to fall the local authorities would have profited. Their aim was to pick correctly the trough in interest rates and at that stage to reverse the swap,

---

BOX 20.7 The case of Barings

The British merchant bank, Barings Brothers, was bankrupted in 1995 after losses of more than £860 million accrued on the Singapore and Osaka derivatives exchanges. The bank was the victim of its own star trader, Nick Leeson, and the absence of management controls to monitor his activities. Leeson was responsible for both trading and back office records of his deals at Simex (the Singapore International Monetary Exchange). He had started by running a hedged position in futures on the Japanese Nikkei stock exchange index and to make money by arbitrage – taking advantage of different prices on the Singapore and Osaka exchanges. However, he stopped hedging the purchases made in Singapore and between 1992 and 1995 built up positions in futures and options contracts on the Nikkei 225 index. Initially this proved highly profitable for Barings and the management asked few questions about his activities.

Leeson bought futures positions on the Nikkei index such that he was betting against the volatility of the market. That is, he would make losses if the index either rose or fell by large amounts but would profit from the index remaining stable. Everything seemed secure enough until early 1995 since during 1994 the Nikkei index had stayed within a narrow range. However, in early 1995, the combination of a large earthquake in Kobe in Japan and a turn in investor sentiment against Japanese markets drove the Nikkei index sharply down. This meant that Leeson needed to make daily margin payments with the clearing house. He assumed that the Nikkei index would soon recover and financed the required margin payments by writing put options on the contract. The hope was that when the Nikkei index again rose, these put options would be abandoned, leaving Leeson with the premiums as profit. He began writing the put options in early February. Further contracts were agreed in mid-February to provide cash to cover losses as the Nikkei index continued to fall. At least 20,000 contracts were bought expiring in mid-March. Each point of the Nikkei 225 futures contract carries a value of ¥1,000, and so with the Nikkei 225 trading at levels between 18,000 and 20,000 in the first few weeks of the year, each future would have had a value of some ¥18–20 million. With 20,000 contracts, the fall in the index from 19,600 to 17,600 produced losses of ¥40 billion on the put options in addition to the losses on the initial futures and options contracts. The writing of the put options transformed an already highly geared trading strategy into a perilous double-or-quits game.

Leeson concealed the growing losses from the Bank for some time in the hope that the market would suddenly turn around and he would be saved at the last moment. This did not happen and when the desperate position finally became known he had built up total losses that far exceeded the capital of the bank. The bank collapsed. Most of Barings' employees were saved by Internationale Nederlanden Group which bought Barings and took on its losses. ING paid £1 for the bank. Leeson was later jailed in Singapore for the falsification of records in the attempt to conceal his activities.

moving back to a fixed interest rate, probably at a lower rate than their original interest payments.

However, the local authorities were taken unawares by the sharp jump in interest rates which saw the base rate of interest rise to 15 per cent in 1989. They were then, under the terms of the contract, required to pay large amounts to the banks – the difference between the now very high floating rates and the fixed rate on their original loans. Despite the volume of contracts and the size of the risk, there was never any monitoring system established to track the performance and possible dangers of their derivative business. But the ratepayers of the most indebted local authorities were rescued by the courts, which ruled that it had been illegal for the local authorities to use their funds in this way and therefore that the contracts were unenforceable. The banks thus found themselves exposed to **legal risk**.

Yet another famous case was that of Metallgesellschaft (MG), the fourteenth largest industrial concern in Germany. The strategy of its US affiliate, MG Refinery and Marketing Inc., was to sell petrol, diesel and heating oil products to customers on fixed price contracts up to 10 years ahead. It then protected itself against price movements by hedging the full amount with futures and OTC swap contracts. Over the previous 10 years, spot prices had mostly exceeded near future prices (backwardation). This meant that hedging in short-dated futures would produce profits as each expiring contract yielded more than it cost. However, in 1993, a contango occurred, upsetting MG's calculations and shocking its banks. Every $1 fall in the spot oil price meant an extra $160 million of margin payments. Also complicating the question was the fact that MG was losing money every time it rolled over its oil futures contracts. On each rollover date, as it sold expiring futures contracts and bought new ones to carry the hedge forward, MG had to pay more for the new contracts than it received for the old ones because of the contango. This rollover cost amounted to $20–30 million in each of October and November and would have been $50 million in December. MG had to pay out over $900 million in the form of additional margin on its futures positions, and extra collateral to counterparties on over-the-counter swaps.

This resulted in a severe liquidity crisis, leading to an emergency line of credit from banks and a forced unwinding of most of the company's derivative positions. Longer-term hedging contracts would have been available – but at a higher price. It was the funding cost of the short-term hedging strategy that led to the heavy losses. Had winter come earlier (causing the spot oil price to rise), the crisis would have been averted, but there was no guarantee that it would not have arisen later. In January 1994, 150 German and international banks, headed by Deutsche and Dresdner Bank, mounted a DM3.4 billion rescue operation to save Metallgesellschaft from bankruptcy.[3]

The large American firm, Procter and Gamble, was in 1994 required to make $102 million after-tax charges on its profits arising from swap transactions losses. It later sued Bankers Trust, claiming that Bankers Trust did not 'accurately and fully' disclose information about the derivatives contract. Procter and Gamble had been using derivatives instruments to cut the cost of its borrowing and manage its exposure to interest rate and foreign exchange for years. However, the company took out two highly geared swaps contracts, designed by Bankers Trust to allow Procter and Gamble to swap fixed interest rate loans for floating interest rate loans, on the assumption that US and German interest rates would stay low. When interest rates rose sharply, Procter and Gamble lost money on the contracts, which they later said were inconsistent with the company's internal policy on the use of derivatives. Bankers Trust were also sued at the same time on similar grounds by another American company, Gibson Greetings.[4]

Tokyo Securities lost ¥32 billion, one-third of the firm's net assets, in 1994. Kashima Oil, a Japanese company, lost $1.5 billion in foreign exchange derivative trading. The head of bond trading at the US securities firm, Kidder Peabody, was fired in 1994 for allegedly creating $350 million of fictitious profits. The firm was broken up largely as a result. In 1991, another US securities firm, Salomon Brothers, had to pay several hundred million dollars in fines and compensation after its head of bond trading was found to have faked customer bids in treasury auctions. The new management had to write off several hundred

---

[3]   For details of these cases see F Guerrera, A Parker and C Pretzlik, 'As criticism of derivatives grows, regulators push for tougher accounting rules', *Financial Times*, 10 March 2003; and 'Lex Column: Oil Futures', *Financial Times*, 10 February 2006.
[4]   For details of these cases see R Waters, 'US bank settles derivatives law suit', *Financial Times*, 28 October 1994; and R Waters, 'P & G sues bank over big loss on derivatives', *Financial Times*, 28 October 1994.

million dollars more early in 1995 for past bookkeeping errors. The Japanese car manufacturer, Mazda, lost ¥65 billion on its foreign exchange transactions in 1993/94.

On the other hand, the Italian clothing firm, Benetton, achieved a one-off gain of 50 billion Italian lira from some well-timed currency hedges when the lira strengthened against the DM by almost 10 per cent in three months in 1993.

The Australian bank, Westpac, suffered from **tax risk** in 1992 when it was forced to pay an unexpected tax liability and penalties of nearly $80 million in the USA because of conflicting tax treatment of swaps and forward contracts in the USA and Australia. In 1991, Allied-Lyons lost £150 million in foreign exchange dealings, through writing currency options. This can lead to unlimited losses. This case is treated in Exercise 20.4.

A trader at Daiwa, one of Japan's largest and once one of its most respected financial institutions, incurred losses of millions of dollars a week on the trading of government bonds. The total losses amounted to $1.1 billion. He hid those losses over 11 years by selling securities which the bank held but which belonged to its customers. To avoid suspicion, he continued to pay interest on those securities by forging bank statements. He confessed in July 1995 but the management then took steps designed to conceal the losses from the US authorities. The losses were not revealed to the world at large until September. Thus, in November, Daiwa was ordered by the US authorities to close its US operations and the company was accused of conspiring to defraud the United States by having lied to, misled and deceived US authorities. Specifically, Daiwa was accused of using its international treasury division in Tokyo to repurchase US treasuries, making up for the missing ones sold by the trader and covering up what it was doing by preparing false documents, including bank statements, internal records and a report issued to the Federal Reserve Board on 31 July, stating the bank's balance sheet.

Between 1997 and 2002 John Rusnak, working in Baltimore for Allfirst Bank (at the time a subsidiary of Allied Irish Bank), made losses of $691 million on forward purchases of yen, allegedly hedged by combinations of options and covered up through the development of fictitious options.

Many of these cases have had international implications. However, the most dangerous case from the point of view of world markets in general has been the

---

Exercise 20.4

Read the following extract from the *Financial Times* and answer the questions that follow:

> Allied-Lyons' losses of approximately £150m, attributed to 'abnormal foreign exchange exposures', arose because the company took a strong view on the direction of the dollar, and got it wrong. It is standard practice for companies with a large portion of dollar-based income from both operations and exports, as Allied-Lyons has, to hedge against adverse currency movements.
>
> But Allied-Lyons appears to have gone further, taking heavy positions on the expectation of dollar weakness. The company took positions in both derivative and cash markets, writing call options on the dollar, and selling the dollar short in the foreign exchange market, according to analysts . . .
>
> Although it is quite common for large companies to write call options, it is a practice approached with caution. In buying a call option, the option holder can only lose the nominal cost of the option . . . Writing – that is, selling – a call option, on the other hand, leaves the writer with unlimited exposure . . .

Source: 'Price of being bucked by the trend', by Tracy Corrigan and Stephen Fidler, *Financial Times*, 20 March 1991. Reprinted with permission.

Questions

1 What is meant by 'hedging against adverse currency movements'? How might Allied-Lyons have hedged?

2 What must they have done in order to go short in dollars?

3 What is a call option in dollars?

4 Under what circumstances will the writer of a call option in dollars lose?

5 Explain why such losses may be unlimited.

---

near collapse in September 1998 of the US hedge fund Long-Term Capital Management (LTCM). Hedge funds were originally US equity funds that hedged against market declines by holding short, as well as long, positions. However, LTCM was using derivatives to take large bets on the direction of markets. Using a very complex system, LTCM risked 40 times its capital, a total exposure of $200 million.

Although LTCM's board included Myron Scholes and Robert Merton who had won the Nobel Prize for Economics for their work on the pricing of options, their system could not cope with the financial crisis that had developed in South-East Asia and Russia. As Tracey Corrigan wrote in the *Financial Times* of 26/27 September 1998, 'all the complex formulae and computer models that the best brains had produced simply did not work when financial crisis spilt over from the emerging markets'.

LTCM was, in the event, rescued by the New York Federal Reserve, which recruited 14 financial groups to help. Prior to the rescue there were genuine fears that LTCM's collapse would have led to the collapse of a large number of major world banks. Even with the rescue, UBS, Europe's largest bank, had to accept a loss of £406 million.

In 2007 an Italian bank, Banca Italease, lost €687m in over-the-counter derivatives trading linked to interest rates. The Bank of Italy dismissed all but three members of the board of directors for failing to limit the bank's rapidly growing exposure to the derivatives. Banca Italease was also instructed by the Bank of Italy to seek an increase in capital to return its risk–asset ratio (see Section 25.4) to an acceptable level and to cease selling derivatives contracts.[5]

20.10 Summary

Options are financial instruments that give the right to buy or sell an underlying financial instrument. Options are traded both on exchanges and over-the-counter and have many features in common with outright contracts – they are highly geared and are used by both hedgers and speculators. Options have advantages over outright derivatives contracts in certain circumstances. In particular, they may be used to provide protection against the market moving in one direction without removing the prospect of gain if the market moves in the opposite direction. The price or premium of an option can be divided into the option's intrinsic value (the profit that would be made if the option were exercised immediately) and its time value (a measure of the possibility that the option's value might increase before the expiry date). Arbitrage possibilities between the cash market and the options market establish boundaries within which the option premium must lie but the actual premium depends on the market's estimate of the future volatility of the price of the underlying instrument.

Swaps are also widely used for hedging and speculation and for changing the structure of a company's balance sheet or reducing the interest it must pay on a loan. The most common form of swaps are exchanges of interest rate streams or cashflows in different currencies. There are very many variations on both swaps and options. Derivatives of all kinds perform a number of roles in financial markets and are strongly supported by many people. However, concern has been expressed about the effects of derivatives trading on the volatility of the underlying markets and the rapid growth of ever more complex derivatives trading has made life difficult for regulators and company managers alike. One consequence of this has been the very large losses regularly experienced by companies through the use of the derivatives markets.

Key concepts in this chapter

American option	Bounded interest rate caps/floors
Asian options	Call option
Average strike rate options	Chooser option
Balloon option	Cliquet options
Barrier cap/floor	Commodity swap
Barrier options	Contingent premium cap/floor
Basket options	Contracts for difference
Bermudan option	Coupe option

---

5   E Backus, 'Italease appoints new board', *Financial Times*, 10 September 2007.

Covered call	Legal risk
Credit risk derivatives	Lookback options
Cross-currency basis swap	Naked call
Cross-currency coupon swap	Premium
Currency swaps	Options
Diff swap	Options on options
Double barrier option	Principal-protected notes
Dynamic hedging	Put option
Equity swap	Safes
European option	Short-term interest rate options (STIRs)
Exotic options	Spread betting
Flex options	Strike/exercise price
Insurance risk contracts	Synthetic call option
Interest rate caps/floors	Tax risk
Interest rate swaps	Time value
Intrinsic value	Warrants

Questions and problems

1 Explain each of the following:

 (a) fixed rate currency swaps;

 (b) an 'in-the-money' option.

2 Explain the statement made by the Chairman of the Chicago Board of Trade (CBoT) in the following extract:

 The Chicago Board of Trade will launch an oats futures options contract on May 1. Options on oats will provide a variety of hedging possibilities. The American Oats Association in Minneapolis said that producers were more likely to use options than futures. According to the CBoT chairman, by purchasing options a hedger can establish price ceilings and floors, and still benefit if cash prices change in his favor.

3 Find out as much as you can about the activities and procedures of the international credit-rating agencies.

4 Answer the following questions concerning interest rate swaps:

 (a) Why might a borrower wish to enter into such a swap?

 (b) Why might such a swap be possible?

 (c) What risk does the guaranteeing bank run?

5 Consider Table 20.1 and answer the following questions:

 (a) Why do short sterling call options for March with strike prices at 95875 or above have premiums of 0?

 (b) Why do the premiums on put options increase as the strike price increases?

 (c) What do the premiums on Euribor options tell you about euro interest rates on 15 March 2004?

6 Find examples of companies having hedged through the use of derivatives products other than those mentioned in the text.

7 Find more information about some of the examples of company problems mentioned in the text.

8 Find as many examples as you can of exotic options and variations upon plain vanilla swaps.

9 What factors are likely to influence the price that a swap bank will charge for participating in a currency swap?

10 Why do you think so many types of derivatives have been developed over such a short period?

Further reading

A Buckley, *Multinational Finance* (Harlow: Financial Times Prentice Hall, 5e, 2003)

H S Houthakker and P J Williamson, *The Economics of Financial Markets* (Oxford: Oxford University Press, 1996) Ch. 8

J C Hull, *Options, Futures and Other Derivatives* (Harlow: Pearson Education, 5e, 2003)

F Taylor, *Mastering Derivatives Markets* (London: Financial Times Pitman Publishing, 3e, 2006)

F Taylor, *Mastering Foreign Exchange and Currency Options* (London: Financial Times Prentice Hall, 2e, 2003)

R Waters, 'US bank settles derivatives law suit', *Financial Times*, 28 October 1994

R Waters, 'P & G sues bank over big loss on derivatives', *Financial Times*, 28 October 1994

Websites

www.bankofengland.co.uk
www.cboe.com/
www.contracts-for-difference.com/
www.euronext.com
www.finpipe.com
www.ft.com
www.investopedia.com

Part 6 Current Issues

Chapter 21 The internal European
market

What you will learn in this chapter:

■ The objectives of the Single European Act of 1986

■ The approach to estimating gains from the creation of the
internal market and criticisms of it

■ The reasons for the slowness of progress towards a single
European financial market

■ The advantages of home-country regulation of financial
services

■ The extent of progress towards a single European market in
banking, the securities market, and insurance

■ The impact on the internal market of the increase in
membership of the EU to 27 countries

21.1 Introduction

Although the early history of the European Union was concerned largely with the removal of tariffs among member states and the establishment of a common commercial policy towards the rest of the world, the Treaty of Rome had required nothing short of a **single European market** (**SEM**) in all goods and services. To this end, the 1957 Treaty had specified the dismantling of all non-tariff barriers to the free movement of goods among members. The progressive abolition of all restrictions on the freedom to supply services, such as banking, insurance and communications services, across frontiers was also sought and this was to be accompanied by the free movement of labour and capital. All discrimination based on nationality was to disappear.

Progress in the removal of tariffs was quite rapid but, although the European Commission battled constantly towards the goal of a **single market** in all areas of production, the gains throughout the 1970s and early 1980s were small. The first stage of integration was complete by the mid-1980s but many of the other objectives of the Rome Treaty had not been achieved. Indeed, non-tariff barriers within the EU had almost certainly increased between 1975 and 1985, partly as a response to the removal of tariffs among members. Advances had been even slower in services, notably transport and financial services, than in other sectors of the economy. At the same time, there was increasing concern over slow rates of growth in much of the EU in comparison with apparently more dynamic economies elsewhere. Consequently, it was felt that a new drive was needed to deepen integration among member countries. Thus, the 1986 **Single European Act** (**SEA**) was intended to achieve both the removal of non-tariff barriers to trade and the free movement of labour and capital by the beginning of 1993.

A further step towards the deepening of economic integration was taken with the movement towards a single currency culminating in the establishment of the euro area at the beginning of 1999. At the same time as integration among members has been growing, the membership has widened from the original six countries of 1957 to 27 from 1 January 2007.

In Section 21.2 we look at the objectives and achievements of the SEA and progress made towards the full achievement of the SEM. Section 21.3 looks at the attempt to achieve a single European financial market while Section 21.4 considers specific sections of the financial services industry from this point of view. Section 21.5 outlines the European Commission's Financial Services Action Plan and we look briefly at some of the implications of enlargement in 21.6. The movement to a single currency is treated in Chapters 22 and 23.

21.2 The objectives and achievements of the Single European Act

Objectives were set by the SEA in relation to three main types of non-tariff barriers to trade and factor mobility.

With regard to **physical barriers** created by customs formalities and controls, objectives included the simplification of administrative checks and their movement away from borders, the elimination of all internal frontiers and controls on people and capital as well as on goods and services, and the development of a common transport policy.

In relation to **technical barriers** such as different technical specifications of products, it was intended to harmonize regulations or, failing this, to have mutual recognition of each other's standards, to remove exchange controls, and to establish the equivalence of qualifications.

Under the heading of **fiscal barriers** came the much more difficult to achieve goal of the harmonization of taxation rates and systems, especially in the fields of indirect and corporation taxes.

The SEA also stressed the desirability of opening up each country's public purchasing to competition from other member states; ensuring a firmer application of competition policy; and incorporating the social charter. However, there were no credible plans for dealing with differences in external trade policy and the Commission's attitude towards subsidies was unclear. There was also uncertainty over the degree to which **harmonization** could give way to **mutual recognition** in the completion of the **internal market**.

The European Commission argued that the movement to a single European market would produce gains of a number of types for the EU:

1 It would extend the static gains attributed to the removal of tariffs between countries – net trade creation. This is a measure of trade creation minus trade diversion. *Trade creation* is the replacement of high-cost domestic output of one member state by the lower-cost output of another member state.

Trade diversion is the diversion of output from low-cost outside sources of supply to a higher-cost source within the integrated area. It was held that the gains from the dismantling of non-tariff barriers might be even greater than from the removal of tariffs because it would not involve any loss of government revenue. Further, trade diversion was likely to be less since removing some non-tariff barriers (such as different product standards and definitions) would help outside producers as well as those in EU member states.

2 It would produce many dynamic gains in the form of economies of scale, increased competition resulting in reductions in X-inefficiency and international price discrimination, and an increase in the variety of products available across the market.

3 Any gains made under items 1 and 2 would lead to increased investment both from within and without the EU, further adding to the increase in welfare attributable to the internal market.

Just how large the gains would be, however, was extremely difficult to say. A major attempt was made to estimate the possible gains from the internal market in a report, running to 16 volumes, prepared for the European Commission on the 'Costs of non-Europe' (Cecchini *et al.*, 1988; Emerson *et al.*, 1992). Unsurprisingly, the estimates in this report have been subject to much discussion and criticism.

The study approached the problem from both microeconomic and macroeconomic angles. The microeconomic analysis focused, sector by sector, on three types of benefits:

1 *direct* gains of the removal of trade barriers;

2 *indirect* gains of increased market integration from the removal of barriers to competition such as those connected with public purchasing and technical standards;

3 *efficiency* gains from the greater exploitation of economies of scale and the reduction of X-inefficiency.

The welfare effects on each sector of industry were estimated within a partial equilibrium framework in which, importantly, it was assumed that employment would remain constant. Thus, it was assumed that workers displaced from inefficient firms would be able to move quickly and easily into other jobs. The welfare gains were estimated at between 4.3 per cent

and 6.4 per cent of GDP for the EU as a whole. These were said to be cautious estimates, implying that the true effects could be yet higher.

From a macroeconomic angle, the estimated gain was 4.5 per cent of EU GDP. However, it was argued that these gains would help to ease pressures on the macroeconomic management of the economy and hence allow further gains. Taking this into account, one estimate put the likely once-and-for-all medium-term gain at 7.5 per cent of EU GDP, together with the creation of five million jobs.

Several writers complained that these estimates were far too optimistic. They argued, in particular, that the Cecchini gains assumed that all members would implement all directives and accept the unpleasant consequences of intensified competition without resorting to subsidies and hidden discrimination; that firms would compete and not collude or merge to avoid the extra competitive pressures; that the Commission would be able to enforce the competition rules; and that Court of Justice rulings would be obeyed by all. Many thought that all of this was unlikely.

There was criticism, too, that the report failed to take full account of the costs of the restructuring that would be needed in many economies for the SEA to achieve its objectives. It was assumed that any resources made unemployed by the 1992 process would be fully re-absorbed by the end of 1992. Some writers argued that parts of the EU could experience a downward spiral in employment as a result of the SEA programme as companies lost market share to more efficient producers in the 'core' of the EU. The possibility of regional problems arising from the internal market programme was certainly taken seriously and both the SEA and the 1992 Treaty on European Union talked of the need for economic and social cohesion to overcome problems of regional imbalance within the Union but the Cecchini estimates ignored such costs. Despite the scepticism about the estimates of the likely gains and the worries about regional imbalance, there was widespread support for the move to a single European market even from people who were later much less welcoming towards the movement to a single currency.

21.2.1 Progress towards the SEM

Frontier controls were abolished and most of the proposed legislative changes had been adopted by the Council of Ministers by the target date of 1 January

1993. However, in some areas, notably financial services, major pieces of legislation had been adopted rather late. For example, the directive to allow for cross-frontier trade in life insurance only came into force in July 1994. The Sutherland Report (1992) also pointed out that some directives were being transposed only slowly into the national laws of the member states. This was still a problem in 2007 in relation to financial integration. Twice a year the European Commission publishes a scoreboard[1] (in which the speed of transposing EU directives into national legislation is recorded.

In July 2007 the scoreboard showed that the Commission's average transposition deficit, having reached a low of 1.2 per cent in December 2006, had risen again in 2007 – from 1.2 per cent to 1.6 per cent. This calculation excluded the two new members, Romania and Bulgaria. Had they been included the deficit would have been 1.8 per cent. Sixteen of the other 25 member states were meeting the European Council's target of a 1.5 per cent deficit, nine of whom had reached the new target of 1 per cent (to be reached by January 2009). The poorest performers were Portugal, Luxembourg, Italy and Greece.

The report was also concerned about the increase in the number of infringement cases. An infringement arises when a member state incorrectly transposes EU directives into its national law or when internal market legislation is not correctly applied in a member state. In the first part of 2007, the average number of infringement cases open against the 25 members rose from 50 in December 2006 to reach 53 by 1 May 2007, with Malta, Poland and Ireland having a particularly bad six months in terms of the number of new infringement cases opened against them. Overall, Italy remained much the worst performer in operating fully and correctly the internal market directives with 153 infringement cases still open against it. Next in order of poor performance were Spain, France and Greece. The greatest failure both to correctly transpose and then to correctly apply internal market directives occurs in environmental matters followed by taxation and customs union issues. There has also always been concern that penalties for breaking internal market laws were much harsher in some countries than in others. It is one thing to implement the laws, another to enforce them.

When the Commission discovers an infringement by a member country of EU internal market legislation, it first issues a warning letter. If this fails to produce an adequate response, the Commission sends a reasoned opinion stating in detail what the member is doing wrongly and what needs to be done to rectify the position. If this has no effect, the Commission takes the member country to the European Court of Justice.

The Commission also remains concerned about the interferences with competition in the internal market brought about by the continued existence of differences in taxation systems and rates among member states. A completely different worry has been that small and medium-sized firms and consumers often appear to have little knowledge of new internal market laws, reducing the likelihood of the mutual recognition of technical regulations.

Failure to implement correctly internal market rules by member states, of course, undermines the arguments for the internal market based upon expected increases in internal trade flows. It limits the process of restructuring that the SEA was intended to bring about and, in the words of the member of the European Commission responsible for the internal market, means that 'citizens and businesses are being denied the very benefits to which their governments have themselves agreed.'[2]

MORE FROM THE WEB

For up-to-date news on the single market, go to the European Commission site: www.europa.eu. Choose one of the 23 languages in which you are welcomed. Then, if you have chosen English, from the subject headings in the centre of the page select 'Internal Market' and then 'Internal Market' again, 'General Policy Framework', 'Monitoring and Reporting' and, finally 'Internal Market Scoreboard' which will lead you to all the editions of the scoreboard since its first publication in November 1997. There is much other relevant material on the internal market pages including a great deal on the Financial Services Action Plan.

---

[1]   http://ec.europa.eu/internal_market/score/index_en.htm#score.
[2]   Internal Market Scoreboard, 16 July 2007, p. 5.

21.3 The single financial market (European Financial Common Market – the EFCM)

A single market in financial services required:

- the free mobility of capital, implying the removal of exchange controls, the disappearance of exchange rate uncertainties and the full acceptance of the right to raise capital and to invest in all EU markets;

- the right of establishment by firms in other member states;

- the right to supply cross-border services;

- the acceptance of common supervisory regulations; and

- the harmonization of taxes.

It was always going to be difficult to meet all or even the majority of these requirements, especially because the financial services industry has always been politically sensitive and had been highly regulated everywhere. There were two principal reasons for this heavy regulation – the risk that the failure of one firm might endanger a country's whole financial system (*systemic risk*) and the common assumption that purchasers of financial services need high levels of consumer protection.

Not only were many governments reluctant to reduce the level of financial regulation but also they were unwilling to allow regulation to pass from their control. Because financial services have such a central role in the economy, governments and regulatory authorities have been reluctant to allow national markets to be dominated by foreign institutions, leading to action to prevent foreign firms from competing with local companies. This could be done in a variety of ways. For example, it could be made expensive or even illegal for foreign firms to establish local branches or to take over of domestic companies. In that case, foreign firms could still compete from outside (cross-border trade) but this was much less important in financial services than in trade in goods. Alternatively, foreign firms could be prevented from introducing new products by limiting them to providing the same range of services as domestic firms were allowed to offer under national law. In general, regulation of all firms operating in a country by the domestic government (**host-country regulation**) acted to remove much of any competitive

advantage the foreign firms might have had and thus tended to reinforce other tendencies towards a fragmented and inefficient financial services industry across Europe. There had been movement towards an integrated market in some areas of finance such as wholesale banking, but other areas such as retail banking and insurance had remained fragmented. Even for corporate business, EU national financial systems were, by the 1980s, far from integrated, with differences remaining between them in regulation, taxation, the competitive environment and the role of the state.

The demand for a competitive and efficient financial system across Europe therefore led to a demand for **home-country regulation** (the single passport) with each firm being authorized and regulated by the authorities in the country in which its head office was located. For example, the branches of a German firm in other EU countries would be supervised by the German regulating authority and would need to comply with German laws. Reluctant governments, however, quickly pointed out that home-country regulation also involved competitive distortions and inequality of treatment among firms because different firms operating in the one country would be subject to different laws enforced, very likely with varying levels of severity.

21.3.1 The Treaty of Rome and the single financial market

The reluctance on the part of governments to give up control of financial firms operating in their national markets explained the greater resistance to a single market in financial services than in other areas of production. This reluctance was evident even in the Treaty of Rome itself. It is true that the Treaty's many objectives included:

- the right of establishment – the freedom of firms to locate anywhere in the market;

- the freedom of firms to supply services across national borders; and

- the free movement of capital.

However, Article 67 of the Treaty which expressed the objective of the free movement of capital implied that this was of secondary interest, being required only to the extent needed to ensure the proper functioning of the common market. In any case, much of the force of the objectives was lost by the inclusion in the Treaty of general exceptions which ensured that the freedom to supply financial services across borders remained, in practice, limited. For instance, Article 73 of the Treaty included an escape clause allowing governments to place restrictions on capital mobility during balance of payments crises. In any case, the Treaty only specified the liberalization of payments in connection with current transactions and did nothing towards the achievement of the other requirements for a common financial market.

A ruling of the European Court of Justice reduced still further the likelihood of a movement to a **single financial market** by allowing governments to impose specific regulatory requirements on cross-border suppliers of services provided that:

- the specific requirements were objectively justified by the general interest; and

- the host country could not achieve the same end by applying other, less restrictive, measures (the principle of proportionality).

The first Council of Ministers directives on finance appeared in 1960 and 1962. These made some progress towards the goal of capital mobility by introducing a limited degree of liberalization of payments in connection with capital transactions. Capital movements were divided into four groups, for two of which unconditional liberalization was required. These covered transactions related to foreign trade or to foreign direct investment and operations in listed securities. A third category, including the buying and selling of unit trusts, and unlisted securities, long-term commercial credits and medium-term financial credits were granted conditional liberalization. On the other hand, governments were free to impose any restrictions they chose on the fourth category, which included dealings in money market instruments, short-term financial credits and transactions in bank deposits. Even in areas specifying freedom from restrictions, the directives had very little impact. Although they were binding on member governments, the choice of method of achieving the end result was left to individual governments and this allowed scope for many differences in interpretation and practice.

Despite this, in the 1960s there was extensive liberalization of financial markets in direct investments, commercial credits and the acquisition of securities on foreign stock exchanges; but the 1970s saw this trend reversed in several member states, notably France and Italy. This occurred largely because of the turmoil in international currency markets in that decade. Consequently, the advance towards capital mobility was, until 1980, moderate, especially in comparison with the increases occurring in intra-Union trade in goods. In 1979, the UK removed all capital controls and in the following few years Germany, the Netherlands and Luxembourg followed suit. Then, as the foreign exchange markets calmed down and, in the middle 1980s, the stability of the European Monetary System (EMS) increased, exchange controls were eased in most other member states.

However, exchange controls were only one of the barriers to free capital mobility, which in turn was only one of the barriers to a single market in financial services. Despite the relative stability among exchange rates in the second half of the 1980s, significant interest rate differentials remained among member states and exchange rate uncertainties were to return in the 1990s. The free flow of capital was also hindered by differences in tax regimes among countries, particularly relating to the taxation of profits, and by differences among national capital markets. For example, the takeover of firms was more difficult in Germany than in the Netherlands or the UK. This was held to be partly because of the role of the major banks as shareholders and as the holders of proxies for other shareholders in Germany. Differences in investor and consumer attitudes may also have been important in maintaining the fragmentation of the market.

Finally, in the 1970s and 1980s governments continued to favour local companies by enforcing limitations on cross-border trade in financial services and barriers to the free location of financial institutions and other suppliers of financial services. For example, all countries required foreign firms to obtain formal authorization before they could set up branches although only Spain imposed limits on their establishment. In all countries except the UK, dedicated capital had to be provided, increasing the cost to firms of establishing branches abroad. Many countries retained restrictions on the acquisition by foreigners of domestic financial firms, especially of major domestic banks, with most countries requiring the notification of anything more than minor shareholdings in banks. A little progress was made in specific segments of the financial services industry in the 1970s, especially in relation to the right of establishment, but much remained to be achieved.

21.3.2 The Cockfield Report, the SEA and the change of strategy

The approach to be taken in the SEA towards the financial services industry was developed in the Cockfield Report, prepared for the European Commission in 1985. The aim was to move towards complete mobility of capital and to the integration of banking, insurance and securities trading.

The report saw the removal of restrictions on international capital mobility as an integral part of the full development of a common market in financial services but also as essential for the completion of the internal market in all its dimensions. This was argued on three grounds:

1 that freedom of capital was necessary for the achievement of totally integrated markets for all goods and services and also for promoting the free movement of labour across borders;

2 that freedom of capital would provide a powerful incentive for governments to adopt macroeconomic policies which would lead to price and exchange rate stability; and

3 that opening up the capital market would widen the freedom of choice for European investors and contribute to a more efficient allocation of savings.

The report also tackled the question of home-country versus host-country regulation. Prior to the Cockfield Report, the Commission had operated on the basis of Article 100 of the Treaty of Rome which implied that a common market in financial services could not come about until regulatory arrangements had been harmonized between members. Harmonization requires that all countries agree precisely on a common set of laws and can only take place with a spirit of compromise and much good will. However, the Treaty of Rome had also indicated that regulation would be based on host country and national principles and this gave each national authority an incentive to attempt to impose its regulatory system on other member states. Under these circumstances few were prepared to make any concessions regarding their own arrangements. The Cockfield Report argued that if a single market in financial services was to be achieved by 1992 a change of strategy was needed.

The report thus proposed the drawing of a clear distinction between what had to be harmonized and what could be left to mutual recognition of national regulations and standards. Mutual recognition had become important within the European Union as a result of a ruling by the European Court of Justice in 1979 which denied Germany the right to ban the import of *Cassis de Dijon* from France on the grounds that its alcoholic content was lower than that required by German law. The force of this ruling was that failure to meet a national law was not, in itself, sufficient reason for refusing to import a good or service from another member state. This, in turn, meant that full harmonization of national laws was not needed for the movement to a single market – all that was required was acceptance (or recognition) of each other's laws. A refusal to recognize the laws of other member states required a demonstration that to do so would cause a threat to public health or the rights of the consumer, or would damage fiscal supervision or the fairness of commercial transactions. Mutual recognition of national laws was clearly much easier to achieve than the harmonization of them.

The Cockfield Report further proposed that in cases of mutual recognition, regulation would be based on home-country requirements. In other words, if two members had different regulations in an area in which the Commission decided that harmonization was not needed, the regulations of the country in which the financial institution was registered or licensed would apply to it no matter where it was doing business. This accepted the principle of freedom of establishment and the cross-border provision of services within the Union since an institution authorized in one country would be deemed to be similarly authorized in all other member states.

The requirement to indicate areas where harmonization was necessary meant that, for each harmonization initiative, the Commission would decide whether or not national regulations were excessive and constituted a barrier to trade. In the banking sector, for instance, it was agreed that harmonization of regulation was needed in the following areas: authorization criteria; minimum capital requirements; the definition of own funds (equity capital); large exposure limits; deposit-protection arrangements; control of the major shareholdings in banks; limits on banks' involvement in non-bank sectors; and the quality of accountancy and internal control mechanisms. Anything else could be left to mutual recognition.

21.3.3 The Cecchini Report and the financial services industry

The Cecchini Report foresaw a number of benefits from the movement to a single market in financial services including:

- lower prices of financial services resulting from the measures needed to complete the single market;
- an increase in general efficiency in the economy arising because financial services are a major input into industry;
- increased access to a wider range of markets, instruments and services, allowing increased portfolio diversification and raising welfare by improving the risk/return combination;
- more efficient allocation of capital, conveying generalized benefits to the economy as a whole.

The potential gains to consumers seemed to be substantial given the wide disparities in prices between member states for apparently standardized financial products. According to Cecchini, prices were likely to fall furthest in Belgium, France, Italy and Spain. The report discovered particularly wide price differences in motor vehicle insurance, home loans, consumer credit, foreign exchange drafts and most securities operations. The study considered eight countries (the original six members of the EU plus Britain and Spain) and estimated that across these countries the single market would produce an average price reduction in financial services of 10 per cent (ranging from 4 per cent in the Netherlands to 21 per cent in Spain). The potential price falls in the Cecchini Report are shown in Table 21.1. The increased competition, producing the reduced price dispersion, would, the report claimed, increase the value added in financial services by the equivalent of 0.7 per cent of GDP.

Table 21.1 Cecchini Report estimates of potential price falls

	Belgium	Germany	Spain	France	Italy	Netherlands	UK
Banking							
Consumer credit	−41	136	39	105	n/a	31	121
Credit cards	79	60	26	−30	89	43	16
Mortgages	31	57	118	78	−4	−6	−20
Letters of credit	22	−10	59	−7	9	17	8
Foreign exchange	6	31	196	56	23	−46	16
Travellers' cheques	35	−7	30	39	22	33	−7
Commercial loans	−5	6	19	−7	9	43	46
Insurance							
Life	78	5	37	33	83	−9	−30
Home	−16	3	−4	39	81	−17	90
Motor	30	15	100	9	148	−7	−17
Commercial, fire, theft	−9	43	24	153	245	−1	−27
Securities							
Private equity	36	7	65	−13	−3	114	123
Private gilts	14	90	217	21	−63	161	36
Institutional equity	26	69	153	−5	47	26	−47
Institutional gilts	284	−4	60	57	92	21	N/a
Theoretical, potential price falls							
Banking	15	33	34	25	18	10	18
Insurance	31	10	32	24	51	1	4
Securities	52	11	44	23	33	18	12
Total	23	25	34	24	29	9	13

Source: The economics of 1992: a study for the European Commission, *European Economy*, Vol. 35, OPOCE (1988), reproduced with permission of Pricewaterhouse Coopers.

MORE FROM THE WEB

Oddly enough, a short summary of the Cecchini Report can be found on the website of the library of Pittsburgh University (Archive of European Integration), see http://aei.pitt.edu/3813/01/000209_1.pdf. For an outline of an even more optimistic view of the benefits of 1992 than Cecchini, see the views of Richard Baldwin on the website of CEPR (Centre for Economic Policy Research), http://www.cepr.org/Pubs/bulletin/meets/245.htm.

There are three types of objection to the Cecchini estimates. Firstly, there were doubts about the way existing price differences were measured. The calculations were based on identifying standardized financial products. Each country's prices for these products were then compared with the average of the four lowest prices for the product and the discrepancies were converted into potential price falls. These were then scaled down to produce figures for expected price falls in each country, making some allowance for the fact that price differences might arise from factors other than a lack of competition. But it was arguable that this scaling down was insufficient. In practice, products cannot easily be standardized. For instance, price differences in insurance markets may reflect differences in risk. Again, for many products the prices charged by banks reflect a customer's total business with the bank (relationship pricing). Thus, there are many cross-subsidies, making it difficult to isolate the price of one financial product from others. It may also be argued that the benchmark prices used for computing the potential price falls were artificial prices that existed in no one country of the union.

Secondly, the estimates implicitly assumed that observed price differences were accounted for principally by lack of competition. But wide price differences may arise also because of differences among countries in the efficiency of financial systems, regulatory taxes, the competitive environment and the extent to which economies of scale are exploited. In principle, these differences should all be attacked by increased competition but this may be limited by location, information and transaction costs. These latter are, in turn, influenced by exchange rate uncertainties. In addition, there may be different structures of cross-subsidies within banks and other financial institutions. Although some cross-subsidies may reflect

differences in competitive conditions between markets, not all do so. Significant price differences are bound to remain for specific financial products within countries despite an increase in competition resulting from the removal of regulatory and other barriers.

Thirdly, the report assumed that the 1992 arrangements would raise competitive pressures in financial systems. But entry costs, scale constraints and imperfect information may cause markets to remain partially segmented.

We have already noted the possible impact of national differences in the structure of capital markets. It may be the case that national or regional differences in consumer tastes are less pronounced in the field of financial services than in other products. On the other hand, the importance to people of many single financial decisions and the consequent fear of loss may increase consumer loyalty to local firms.

Thus, although there was no doubt that the changes introduced in the SEA and the subsequent directives would compete away some existing restrictive practices and collusive agreements and overcome some protective regulatory arrangements, the Cecchini figures for gains to consumers were optimistic.

21.3.4 The EFCM and the periphery

Just as there has been a general concern about the impact of the move to a single market on the peripheral (poorer) members of the EU, particular worries have surfaced with regard to the movement to a European Financial Common Market. With regard to the peripheral countries, it has been argued that the movement to a single financial market across Europe may produce either of two outcomes. The relatively low profits of peripheral country banks may discourage the restructuring of the European banking system (Grilli, 1989), leaving peripheral banking systems relatively underdeveloped with many banks remaining essentially regional. This would accentuate the differences between core and peripheral countries and could increase the financial fragility of the peripheral countries since banks with a narrow base are more at risk from external shocks because of their inability to diversify.

Alternatively, restructuring may occur with core country banks taking over banks within the periphery (Gibson and Tsakalotos, 1993). This may have a variety of consequences for the periphery, including the reduction of specialist regional advice and service

MORE FROM THE WEB

For a paper by two Italian economists, Pietro
Alessandrini and Alberto Zazzaro, on the impact of
financial integration on the banks and development
of the periphery see: http://www.ersa.org/ersaconfs/
ersa98/papers/132.pdf.

within the periphery as the 'over-branched' peripheral
banks are slimmed down in search of efficiency gains
and better profit performance. The accompanying centralization of bank administration and decision making may also lead to a large reduction in available
knowledge of the level of risk associated with potential
borrowers. This too may increase the risks of financial
fragility or may produce credit rationing, making it
more difficult for small entrepreneurs to obtain funds
for investment. In either case, banking developments
could contribute to a widening of real income differences between rich and poor member states.

However, none of these worries have led the
poorer countries to oppose the movement to the
EFCM. They have obtained derogations with regard
to a number of directives to allow them to delay implementation for some years but have generally put
their faith in enhanced regional policies and the concern for economic and political cohesion in the EU.

21.4 Progress towards the EFCM

21.4.1 Freedom of capital movements

The Single European Act, 1986 set the end of 1992 as
the date for removal of all controls and in 1985 and
1986 liberalization rules were agreed which removed
all restrictions from the third category of capital
movements under the 1960s directives, such as the
buying and selling of unit trusts and unlisted securities. The *Capital Liberalization Directive*, adopted in
June 1988, then completely liberalized all capital
movements. Eight of the then 12 member states were
given until July 1990 to achieve this. Spain, Portugal,
Ireland and Greece were allowed until the end of 1992
to meet the terms of the directive, with Greece and
Portugal permitted to apply for a further extension to
1995. Despite some reinstatement of controls following the EMS crisis in 1992, all of these four countries

eventually liberalized all capital movements and the
addition of Sweden, Finland and Austria to the union
caused no further problems in this regard. Under the
Treaty on European Union (Maastricht Treaty), the
old capital mobility articles of the Rome Treaty were
replaced by new provisions prohibiting all restrictions
on the movement of capital and on payments between
member states. The safeguard clauses which had been
retained in the *Capital Liberalization Directive* were
removed and even restrictions on capital movements
and payments between member states and non-
member states were prohibited. Only one escape
clause remains and this only relates to movements of
capital to and from non-member states.

The complete freedom of capital movements is by no
means an unmixed blessing and arguments have been
made in recent years for taxing the international movement of capital in an attempt to restore to governments
some control over their macroeconomic policies. However, if one views capital mobility strictly in terms of the
movement to a single European market in financial services, it had to be regarded as essential. Clearly, a major
element in it has now been achieved. A further step towards full capital mobility was taken with the adoption
of a single currency by 11 EU members from January
1999, with Greece becoming a twelfth member in
January 2001, Slovenia joining in January 2007 and
Cyprus and Malta from January 2008. The consequent
removal of exchange rate risk brought interest rates
rapidly into line across the euro area. In March 1997,
Eurocurrency interest rates were between 3 and 4 per
cent higher in Spain, Portugal and Italy than in Belgium,
Denmark, Germany, the Netherlands and France, and
were higher still in Greece. However, by 2007 interest
rate differences across the euro area had been greatly
reduced, as can be seen in Table 21.2. This shows a
selection of interest rates for household deposits and
loans across member countries in July 2007.

Some interest rates, such as on consumer loans to
households and, in particular, bank overdraft rates,
continue to vary from country to country but this is
often because the conditions attached to these types of
loans vary among countries.

21.4.2 The banking industry

The banking industry was one of the most highly regulated industries in the EU and operated with widely
varied regulatory practices. In general, barriers to the

Table 21.2 Selected interest rates for households in euro area countries, July 2007

	€ area average	BE	DE	IE	GR	ES	FR	IT	LU	NL	AT	PT	SI	FI
Deposits maturity up to 1 year	3.86	4.05	3.84	×	4.00	3.88	3.83	2.68	3.56	3.92	3.94	3.73	3.36	4.11
Deposits maturity up to 2 years	3.49	4.00	3.66	3.84	3.91	3.44	3.63	2.28	3.53	3.88	3.22	2.78	3.29	3.74
Bank overdrafts	10.38	10.66	11.79	13.53	14.12	–	10.77	8.72	×	7.06	7.57	11.68	10.74	11.33
Loans for consumption 1 to 5 years	6.77	7.73	5.98	×	9.25	8.37	6.59	7.98	5.84	–	6.47	10.90	7.40	5.60
Loans for house purchase over 5 years	4.89	4.53	5.12	5.06	5.12	4.81	4.38	5.42	4.75	4.81	5.23	5.14	6.81	4.80

Note: × data not available; – the related transactions do not exist or the data is subject to statistical confidentiality.

Source: European Central Bank (2007) Euro area and national MFI interest rates (MIR): July, http://www.ecb.int/stats/money/interest/interest/html/interest_rates_2007–07.en.html. This information may be obtained free of charge through the ECB website www.ecb.int. Reprinted with permission.

supply of cross-border services were more of a problem than those related to location. In some countries laws and regulations restricted the right of non-resident banks and financial institutions to conduct business with residents.

Prior to the SEA, there had been two major directives relating to the banking industry: the *First Banking Directive on Coordination of Regulations Governing Credit Institutions* of 1977; and the 1983 *Directive on the Supervision of Credit Institutions on a Consolidated Basis.*

The *First Banking Directive* required member states to establish systems for authorizing and supervising banks and other credit institutions that take deposits and lend money. It required such institutions to be licensed. Once licensed, they would be allowed to conduct business in other member countries provided they were authorized to do so by the host government and complied with the conditions and supervision applied to local banks. To be authorized, a credit institution was required to have separate capital from its owners, to meet an initial capital requirement, and to

have at least two directors and a reputable and experienced management. However, authorization could not legally be withheld on the sole ground that the head office was in another member state. As we have seen, the host-country principle on which the directive was based meant that a German bank in Spain, for example, could only do what Spanish laws allowed its own banks to do in Spain.

The *Directive on the Supervision of Credit Institutions on a Consolidated Basis (1983)* established the common principle that bank activities were to be supervised on the basis of their worldwide activities. Thus, capital requirements were to relate to their global balance sheet position, preventing banks from seeking to avoid capital requirements by arranging business through less strictly regulated financial centres. This derived from the growing international concern with the solvency of banks, particularly at the commencement of the international debt crisis of the developing countries.

Since the SEA, there have been a series of directives on the banking industry, most notably the *Second*

Banking Coordination Directive, which came into force on 1 January 1993. This was based on the Cockfield Report strategy of home-country regulation and mutual recognition. It gave the right to banks to establish branches and to trade in financial services throughout the EU on the basis of a single licence obtained from the home-country authorities. The directive included some exceptions to home-country control. Host countries retained the right to control bank liquidity for monetary policy purposes and had to comply with host-nation consumer protection and similar laws in the public interest. There was some ambiguity in relation to the scope of the consumer protection qualification. However, the directive eliminated the requirement for branches of foreign banks to maintain dedicated capital for their local operations.

The directive covered much else. It set out a detailed list of bank activities to which the directive applied. This, as is shown in Box 21.1, was very broad and included much of what is generally included under the heading of securities or investment business in addition to activities more widely considered as banking. This accepted the principle of universal banking on which the German banking industry was organized.

The directive established the right of banks with head offices in other EU countries to pursue all the listed activities in a host country, including those that host-country laws might forbid to local banks. Essentially, banks were allowed to participate fully in securities business either directly or through subsidiaries. Nonetheless, despite the apparently comprehensive nature of the list, difficulties of interpretation remained. For example, Davis and Smales (1990) raised the question of variable-rate mortgage lending which was legal in the UK but not in Belgium. If this were regarded as a technique, Belgium would be required to allow UK banks to market the product in Belgium. On the other hand, if it were regarded as a basic activity, Belgium could prevent UK banks from marketing it under the consumer protection exception since it was not listed separately from mortgage lending. This is a difficulty associated with any listing that attempts to be comprehensive, especially in a period of rapid change and innovation. Difficulties associated with the regulation of banks engaged in both banking and securities business are discussed in Chapter 25.

The directive included rules regarding the exchange of information between home- and host-country

---

BOX 21.1 **What a universal bank might do**

According to the EU's *Second Banking Directive*, EU banks may engage in all of the following activities:

1 Acceptance of deposits and other repayable funds from the public.

2 Lending to include consumer credit, mortgage credit, factoring, financing of commercial transactions (including forfaiting).

3 Financial leasing.

4 Money transmission services.

5 Issuing and administering means of payment (for example credit cards, travellers' cheques and bankers' drafts).

6 Guarantees and commitments.

7 Trading for own account or for account of customers in:

   (a) money market instruments (cheques, bills, CDs, and so on);

   (b) foreign exchange;

   (c) financial futures and options;

   (d) exchange and interest rate instruments;

   (e) transferable securities.

8 Participation in share issues and the provision of services related to such issues.

9 Advice to undertakings on capital structure, industrial strategy and related questions, and advice and services relating to mergers and the purchase of undertakings.

10 Money broking.

11 Portfolio management and advice.

12 Safekeeping and administration of securities.

13 Credit references services.

14 Safe custody services.

Source: The Second Banking Directive 89/646/EEC in *Official Journal of the EC*, L386, Vol. 12, 30 December 1989, Annex, © European Communities. In short, banks may participate in all activities considered in this book (with the exception of central banking) and a good deal besides.

regulators and harmonized minimum standards of authorization and prudential supervision. This included setting minimum requirements for the size of own funds (equity capital). The authorities in all countries were given the right to supervise ownership and control to prevent cross-financing and conflicts of interest. Hence, disclosure of the identity of a bank's most important shareholders was required and limits on banks' shareholdings in other financial and non-financial companies were harmonized.

A number of other directives, ancillary to the *Second Banking Directive*, were approved in 1989 and later years in order to meet the harmonization requirements for banking. Box 21.2 lists these directives.

21.4.3 Securities markets

A genuine single financial market across the EU needed to apply much more broadly than to banking. It was accepted that if competition were to be fair for all firms across the EU, free access was required to all sources of capital. It was also accepted that if savings were to be utilized as effectively as possible, investors should have free access to all investment products irrespective of their country of origin. With the very rapid development of financial markets and the great increase in new financial products from the early 1970s onwards, the securities (or investment) industry (which covers securities trading, unit trusts,

---

BOX 21.2 EU banking directives

The principal ancillary banking directives to the *Second Banking Coordination Directive* have been:

Own Funds Directive
Bank Solvency Ratio Directive
Second Consolidated Supervision Directive
Money Laundering Directive
Annual and Consolidated Accounts Directives
Large Exposures Directive
Deposit Guarantee Directive
Market Risks Directive

They aimed at providing a common regulatory framework for banking. The first five all came into force from 1 January 1993 together with the *Second Banking Directive*. The *Own Funds Directive* and the *Bank Solvency Ratio Directive* were concerned with the adequate capitalization of banks. The *Own Funds Directive* harmonized the definition of the minimum capital base of credit institutions. The *Bank Solvency Ratio Directive* harmonized the minimum prudent solvency ratio for banks. Both directives followed the principles and figures set out in the Basel capital adequacy rules of the Bank for International Settlements, discussed in Chapter 25. The *Money Laundering Directive* set out requirements for the transparency of banking conditions relating to cross-border financial transactions. There were two directives on bank accounts. One described the layout, nomenclature and terminology for bank balance sheets, profit-and-loss statements and consolidated accounts of banks and greatly improved the comparability of bank accounts across member states. The second laid down the accounting obligations of bank branches of foreign banks in member states.

The *Large Exposures Directive* (in operation since the start of 1994) strengthened the capital adequacy provisions in the other directives by requiring credit institutions to report annually on all large exposures to individual borrowers amounting to more than 15 per cent of their own funds (equity capital) or of the largest exposures, even if less than 15 per cent. The *Deposit Guarantee Directive* has since January 1995 required members to establish deposit guarantee schemes, financed by banks, to protect depositors in the event of a credit institution's financial collapse. Finally, rules on the monitoring of market risks incurred by credit institutions were incorporated into a directive operative from January 1996.

These various directives were consolidated into a single text in 2000. Several have been updated since and additional directives on a variety of topics added. Full details are available at www.europa.eu.int. Point at 'Documents' and choose 'Summaries of Legislation', then 'Internal Market', and finally 'Financial Services'.

broking and market-making, portfolio management, underwriting and investment advice as well as issues related to the access of companies to foreign stock exchanges and the quotation of securities on foreign stock exchanges) was becoming increasingly significant. However, it was also an area in which markets developed much more rapidly in some member states than others. This caused anxiety in some countries that increased competition across the EU would damage, if not destroy, their underdeveloped markets and institutions. Under these circumstances, progress towards a single market was bound to be slow.

Nonetheless, strong efforts were made in some segments of the industry from the late 1970s on, notably in regard to the harmonization of the different regulations of the member states on the admission of securities to stock exchange listing and the information provided to investors. In 1979, the *Directive Coordinating the Conditions for the Admission of Securities to Official Stock Exchange Listing* set out the minimum conditions to be met by issuers of securities, including minimum issue price, a company's period of existence, free negotiability, sufficient distribution, and the provision of appropriate information to investors. Member states were free to impose stricter requirements. This was the first of four directives (the others followed in 1980 and 1982) which were designed to make it easier for companies to list their shares or raise capital on other EU stock exchanges. Directives concerned with information to investors covered the disclosure of large shareholdings in companies, the provision of information in prospectuses and insider dealing.

The new SEA principles of minimum harmonization, mutual recognition, a single passport and home-country regulation were applied in two directives on the marketing of unit trusts in 1985 and 1988. These allowed a unit trust which had been approved in one member country to be sold anywhere in the EU without further authorization provided it met investor protection requirements in force in the host country.

The first major securities industry directive based on SEA principles was the *Investment Services Directive* (ISD) which came into force in June 1992. It extended the single passport principle to non-bank investment firms generally. This extension was essential because the *Second Banking Directive* had given this right to banks carrying out securities business but did not grant it to non-banks in this area. There was a particular problem because, as we have noted, the banking industry in some member states had traditionally been organized on universal banking principles whereas in other member states (notably the UK), the two forms of business had been separated. Thus, if the *Investment Services Directive* had not been agreed, banks engaged in securities business would have been given a competitive advantage over non-bank firms. The *Investment Services Directive* thus provided for the removal of barriers to both the provision of cross-border securities services and the establishment of branches throughout the EU for all firms. It also liberalized the rules governing access to stock exchanges and financial futures and options exchanges.

The difference in the organization of banking and securities industries among member countries led to problems in relation to capital adequacy. If capital adequacy rules had not been extended to cover non-bank securities firms, then they, in their turn, would have been given a competitive advantage over banks engaged in securities business who were required to meet capital adequacy rules. However, as we explain in Chapter 25, it was widely argued that the same rules should not apply to both forms of business. This ultimately led to the *Capital Adequacy Directive* of 1993 which applied to both investment firms and to the securities activities of banks.

21.4.4 Insurance services

As with other financial services, the insurance industry has typically been highly regulated. There are particular reasons for this in the nature of some kinds of insurance. Firstly, specifically in the area of life insurance, contracts are very long term with the consequence that a policyholder faces a significant default risk, especially since the insurance companies themselves face major problems in the assessment of risk and maturity transformation. But information on the ability of a company to meet its financial obligations many years ahead is difficult to come by and expensive.

Secondly, the risks being insured may be very large relative to other aspects of a policyholder's annual or even lifetime income. Few people are sufficiently wealthy to be able to afford not to have their house or even their motor vehicle insured. Third-party payments on motor vehicle accidents are potentially so large that insurance against it is a legal requirement for drivers.

Thirdly, the nature of the product is far from transparent. The complexity of the risks being insured and of the terms of settlement of contracts means that the problem of 'the small print' in contracts is of more importance in insurance than in most mass consumer industries and that open and honest professional advice is a crucial element of the industry. Consumer protection is thus a very important issue in insurance.

It is not surprising, then, that there has always been a tendency to regulate the insurance industry quite tightly. The special features of insurance have also, until quite recently, favoured local insurance companies. Consumers have, on balance, felt more confident in assessing the reliability of local companies. Equally, until insurance companies became very large and began to act entirely on the basis of probability, there were advantages for domestic over international companies. The result of all of this has been that legal barriers have strongly reinforced other factors in the fragmentation of insurance into a number of relatively isolated national markets. With the exception of reinsurance, which deals with very large and often international risks, the insurance industry has, in all EU countries other than the UK, been well protected from foreign competition.

From the beginning, the European Commission acknowledged the additional problems associated with the long average length of contracts in life insurance by the issuing of separate directives for life and non-life insurance. Hence, 1973 saw the promulgation of the *First Non-Life Insurance Directive*. The *First Life Insurance Directive* followed in 1979. Both of these directives followed the principle of host-country regulation. They established the right of companies to operate in other member states, but harmonization of regulations across the EU was very slow. Several members strongly resisted attempts to open up their insurance markets to greater competition. In Germany, for example, non-German firms were required to have a local establishment and were taxed at rates that the European Commission considered discriminatory. In 1986 the European Court of Justice made a ruling that the restrictions imposed on insurance companies from other member states by Germany, France, Ireland and Denmark were partly illegal. In particular, the Court attacked the practice of requiring establishment and local authorization before a company could participate in the co-insurance of large risks situated outside of its home country.

The court ruling, together with the increased role for qualified majority voting introduced in the Single European Act, encouraged the European Commission to attempt to incorporate the home-country regulation principle into insurance directives. They were, however, inhibited from replacing the requirement of full harmonization of the rules regarding the authorization of companies by mutual recognition because of the sensitivity of the consumer protection issue in a significant part of the insurance industry. Consumer protection was, remember, one of the areas which, under the 1979 *Cassis de Dijon* court ruling, could be used to justify the rejection of the standards applied by other member states.

The Commission tackled the problem by following the 1986 Court of Justice ruling that had made a distinction between the insurance of large risks (including all marine, transport and aviation risk) and small commercial risks and personal insurance. Whereas host-country regulation was preserved for the latter category, the Commission felt able to apply the home-country regulation principle to the former category on the grounds that large companies or people responsible for insuring large risks are much better able to collect and assess information about insurance companies than is the average consumer.

Thus, in the *Freedom of Services Directive for Non-Life Insurance*, for small-risk business the regulations of the country in which the policyholder resides apply while for large-risk business the regulations of the country in which the company is licensed apply. Large-risk business was defined to cover policies for companies with more than 500 employees or more than £15 million turnover. Motor insurance was brought within the scope of the Non-Life directive by the *Motor Insurance Services Directive* of 1990.

The distinction between large and small risks could not be made in the *Second Life Assurance Directive* and so a different distinction was made to bring in an element of home-country regulation. Host-country regulation applied except where the initiative for a cross-border policy came from the policyholder rather than the company – then the home-country regulation principle applied. Should the initiative for a cross-border policy come from the insurance company, on the other hand, host-country rules would apply and the provisions applicable would be those of the country in which the risk was situated. Host countries also retained responsibility for the regulation of branches of foreign companies, although 'well-established' companies covering large risks were, under the terms of the directive, simply required to notify the host authorities of their intention to provide services in the host country.

Despite continued resistance from some members and problems over the distortion of competition by different tax relief treatment on premiums, the Commission pushed ahead and in July 1994 the *Third Non-Life Insurance Directive*, the *Third Motor Insurance Directive* and the *Third Life Assurance Directive* came into force, introducing the full single passport, home-regulation regime to the insurance industry, although derogations gave extra time for implementation, ranging from the end of 1995 to the end of 1998, to Spain, Portugal and Greece. Although home-country regulation applies, a role remains for host institutions. In practice, most insurance companies establish a local presence because of the need to provide follow-up customer sales and service. Local rules on sales techniques and advertising apply but cannot be used to discriminate against foreign companies. In certain circumstances, host states can exercise control over particular products, for instance mandatory third-party motor insurance. Finally, policyholders are protected by the application of domestic contract law.

21.5 The Financial Services Action Plan

In the late 1990s the European Commission remained concerned over progress towards a common financial market. Legislation was still required to overcome interferences with competition across the market. Member states were being slow in implementing the existing directives and there were inconsistencies in the way different members were implementing them. The hoped-for benefits of an integrated financial market were being slow to appear. In retail financial markets, for instance, the expected gains in terms of the reduction in disparities in prices for financial services among members had not been forthcoming. As an example, the Commission reported that fixed commissions for private equity transactions were still 17 times more expensive in the dearest member state than in the cheapest.

Consequently, the **Financial Services Action Plan (FSAP)** was developed. The aim of the plan was to put in place a series of measures to ensure deep and liquid capital markets and to remove the remaining

MORE FROM THE WEB

The EU itself publishes a mountain of material on the internal market. However, there are also many other useful sites. For example, for the application of the Financial Services Action Plan to the UK see the website of the Financial Services Authority www.fsa.gov.uk/. Click on 'FSA Library', then 'Other publications', then 'EU information' and, finally, 'General EU documents' to find documents about the FSAP. Also, try the UK Treasury website, http://www.hm-treasury.gov.uk/. Clicking on 'Financial Services' leads you to the heading for European Union Financial Services.

barriers to the cross-border provision of retail financial services. There were three elements in the strategy adopted by the Commission:

- to develop a flexible approach to prudential and other rules to ensure that legislation could be adapted to the rapidly changing needs of financial institutions and markets;

- to introduce some additional legislation notably in relation to pension funds and consumer compensation;

- to achieve more satisfactory enforcement of the existing rules through higher rates of implementation of directives and more uniform interpretation of EU legislation.

Separate plans were developed for wholesale and retail financial markets and in relation to the issues of supervisory cooperation and taxation. Areas of concern to the Commission included:

- *Wholesale markets* – prospectuses for the public offering of equities; the financing of small business start-ups; investment restrictions on supplementary pension funds; financial reporting; problems arising from the *Investment Services Directive*; and takeover bid procedures.

- *Retail financial markets* – the restriction of host-country requirements to private individuals; the transparency of host-country rules relating to consumer protection; the level of consumer compensation and the handling of consumer complaints; the need to increase consumer confidence in financial services; safeguards relating to the behaviour of insurance intermediaries; and the adoption of proposals on electronic money and the distance selling of financial services.

- *Supervisory cooperation* – increased coordination between the different supervisory bodies across the EU; ensuring conformity of banking supervision rules with those of the Basel Committee; prudential problems posed by financial conglomerates; and the adoption of proposals relating to the winding-up and liquidation of banks and insurance companies.

- *Taxation* – tax distortions to the allocation of savings and harmful taxation competition between financial centres; and the taxation of financial products preventing cross-border marketing, particularly obstacles to cross-border membership of pension funds.

Other issues mentioned included systemic risk, fraud, money laundering and the need to enforce rules on competition and state aid. The Financial Services Action Plan identified 42 possible measures to be taken – a mixture of new directives, amendments to directives, political agreements, Commission communications and recommendations, and the application of existing regulations.

In 2000 the Council of Finance Ministers asked the Commission to develop indicators to assess the state of financial integration. In response, the Commission publishes special tables on the transposition of financial services directives into national legislation. The tables published on 15 August 2007 dealt with 25 directives dated between 2000 and 2004 all of which had been due to be transposed into national legislation by the end of January 2007. The slowness of response of many member countries to Commission directives is well illustrated by transposition performance in relation to the 2004 *Directive on Markets in Financial Instruments* (MiFID) – an important extension of the *Investment Services Directive* of 1993, which we consider in Box 21.3. MiFID was intended to come into operation in November 2007. The Commission deadline for transposition of this directive into national laws was 31 January 2007 but by August 2007 only 11 of the 27 members had notified the Commission that they had incorporated the directive into their own laws. A further three had indicated that they had partially transposed the directive. That left 13 members who had not incorporated the directive at all into their own laws. Only seven members had notified the Commission that they had transposed all 25 of the directives. The worst performers in terms of the transposition of directives were Spain (the worst), Hungary, Malta, the Czech Republic and Belgium.

In addition to this transposition record, from May 2004 the Commission has published the annual reports of the *Financial Integration Monitor* which aims to assess the degree of financial integration that

---

BOX 21.3 Directive on Markets in Financial Instruments (MiFID)

MiFID is an extension of the *Investment Services Directive* of 1993 and was agreed by the EU in two steps in 2004 and 2006 to come into force from November 2007. Both ISD and MiFID have set down rules for the organization and conduct of business of financial sector firms across the EU and have sought to harmonize a number of features of the operation of regulated financial markets. However, there are signficant changes to the regulatory framework in MiFID to reflect developments in financial services and markets between 1993 and 2007. MiFID seeks to:

(a) **widen the scope** of ISD by adding to the range of investment services that can be granted a European passport (that is, approved for home regulation across the EU) the provision of investment advice and trading in commodity derivatives, credit derivatives and financial contracts for differences. It also seeks to take account of the number of firms now operating across a number of regulated financial markets by applying all of the rules that apply to regulated financial markets to multilateral trading facilities (MTFs);

(b) **increase the degree of harmonization** by incorporating more detailed requirements governing the organization and conduct of the business of investment firms and of the operation of regulated markets and MTFs as well as including new transparency requirements for equity markets and more extensive transaction reporting requirements;

(c) **facilitate cross-border business** by making more clear how responsibility is allocated between home and host state for investment firms authorized to operate across the internal market (that is, improving the passport that firms are granted); and

(d) **increasing the number of firms** subject to the new *Capital Requirements Directive* (CRD) of 2006 relating to the regulatory capital a firm must hold.

has taken place in the EU and its impact on competition, efficiency and stability. The 2004 report dealt only with the EU15. It showed increased but uneven financial integration across the internal market. Full or close to full integration had been achieved in the euro-denominated and government bond markets and most of the other wholesale markets were becoming more integrated. However, financial markets remained very diverse among member countries, especially those catering for retail markets such as the market for consumer loans to households. Market-based financing had gained in importance, financial markets had become more liquid and there had been an increase in the range of financing techniques and products but bank lending remained the predominant source of external finance in the EU15. Again, all member states had shared in the broadening and deepening of European financial markets but important differences remained among the national markets. Two of these were noted in particular:

■ the three principal sources of finance (bank loans, securities and bonds) play a different role as a source of finance in the different member state economies;

■ there are marked differences between countries in the products used (pension, insurance and mutual funds) to manage the long-term savings and pensions of households and employees.

The 2005 report looked at retail markets in more detail and concluded that the integration of these markets had been largely limited to cross-border establishment for accessing local markets. The report, however, suggested that the greater use of online facilities by consumers might eventually assist in the integration of retail financial markets. The report also commented on the high level of foreign, mainly EU15, ownership of financial institutions in the new member states at that stage – 70 per cent of total banking assets were foreign-owned compared with 24 per cent in the EU15. The 2006 report concentrates on institutional investors, the external dimension of the EU financial sector and on the state of integration in the EU insurance, pension fund and investment fund sector, all of which have expanded rapidly in recent years.

Despite worries about the slowness of member states in transposing financial services directives into their own legislation and the doubts about the effectiveness of some of the directives introduced as a result of the Financial Services Action Plan, the Commission felt that sufficient had been done to warrant further planning for the future. Thus, in 2005, the European Commission published a White Paper setting out its financial services strategy for the period 2005–2010.

This continues to make the assumptions that underlie all of the drive towards the integration of financial markets across Europe, in particular that the more integrated financial markets are, the more efficient the allocation of resources and long-run economic performance will be and that financial market integration represents one of the best chances for gains from further European integration. The White Paper sets out five objectives for the period 2005–2010:

1 to consolidate progress towards financial integration and to ensure the enforcement of the existing rules;

2 to incorporate better regulation into all policymaking;

3 to enhance supervisory convergence;

4 to create more competition between service providers;

5 to expand the EU's influence in helping to bring about global capital markets.

It places greater stress than did the FSAP on integration in retail markets and in the removal of barriers to cross-border banking.

21.6 Enlargement to 27

On 1 May 2004, the EU grew from 15 to 25 members with the inclusion of the Czech Republic, Poland, Hungary, Slovakia, Slovenia, Latvia, Lithuania, Estonia, Malta and Cyprus.[3] Then, on the 1 January 2007, the addition of Bulgaria and Romania brought the number of member states to 27. Entry negotiations had begun in 1998 with the applicant countries

---

3 This excludes, for the present at least, the Turkish-ruled northern part of the island of Cyprus.

being required to meet the conditions established by the EU in 1993 (the Copenhagen criteria). These were:

■ the existence of stable institutions guaranteeing democracy;

■ the rule of law, respect for and protection of human rights and minorities;

■ the existence of a functioning market economy;

■ the capacity to cope with market forces and competitive pressures within the Union; and

■ the ability to take on the obligations of membership, including economic and monetary union.

Entry treaties for the first ten new members were signed in April 2003 and these were ratified in the new member countries following the holding of national referendums. Bulgaria and Romania were thought not to have met all conditions at that time but in 2002 a road map had been drawn up to help to ease their path to accession.

Preparing for membership required the new countries to accept the 80,000 pages of EU law (the *acquis communautaire*), to improve their administrative, bureaucratic and judicial systems and to tighten security at the new external borders of the EU. The EU15 provided financial and administrative help in this process. Many of the EU programmes and policies apply to the new member states immediately but others were phased in through transitional arrangements. Full integration for the EU10 was achieved in 2007.

The new members were a mixture of large and small countries but the overall effect was to add considerably to the size of the internal market. Several of the new members have per capita incomes well below the average of existing EU members, which gave rise to a number of fears in both the new and old member countries. These related particularly to the movement of labour, the ability of agriculture in the new member countries to compete, the buying up of property in the new member countries, and the problems associated with developing a new European constitution to allow the effective working of the various EU institutions.

Fears among the EU15 regarding the movement of labour from the new members led 12 of the 15 (the exceptions being the UK, Ireland and Sweden) to impose restrictions on the movement of labour from the new members for a period of seven years. However, in 2006, it having appeared that the impact of migration from the new members to the UK, Ireland and Sweden had, on balance, been positive for those economies, six other members of the EU15 removed the restrictions and four more eased them. Nonetheless, political pressure within the UK caused the imposition there of temporary restrictions on the movement of labour from Bulgaria and Romania.

It will be difficult for some time to assess the full impact on all countries of the expansion although, perhaps not surprisingly, the Commission has taken a positive view of developments since 2004. In a communication from the Commission to the European Council in May 2006, it argued that the first two years of the expansion from 15 to 25 had seen the new member states continue to grow more rapidly than the EU15, helping to reduce the difference in average income between the two groups of countries and that the increased integration had contributed to economic policy discipline and the credibility of economic policy. Interest rates in the new members had moved closer to those of the EU15 and budget deficits had been corrected to the extent that public debt was higher in the EU15 than in the new member states. The Commission judged that fears among the EU15 regarding the relocation of industries and the loss of employment to the new member states had not been warranted. Problems remained, in particular regarding unemployment levels in the new member states, but the Commission's view was certainly optimistic.

Transitional arrangements applied to many elements of financial integration but the new members accepted the same implementation deadlines for all FSAP measures as did the older members. The European Commission accepted that the enlargement would accentuate the diversity of financial structures and levels of financial development as well as increasing the number of infringements of EU directives. However, the Commission also looked favourably upon the early impact of the new enlargement on financial markets and institutions. There was a surge in the growth of credit in the new member states and cross-border investment and the penetration rate of foreign banks was higher than among the members of the EU15. The cost of borrowing had fallen although interest rates were still significantly higher in some economies, notably those of Poland and Slovenia. Banks in the EU15 had benefited from expansion into the new member economies.

Table 21.3 Regional GDP per inhabitant in the EU27 in 2004 (in PPS,* EU27 = 100)

	The fifteen highest:			The fifteen lowest:	
1	Inner London (UK)	303	1	North East (Romania)	24
2	Luxembourg (Luxembourg)	251	2	Severozapaden (Bulgaria)	26
3	Brussels (Belgium)	248	3	Yuzhen central (Bulgaria)	26
4	Hamburg (Germany)	195	4	Severen central (Bulgaria)	26
5	Vienna (Austria)	180	5	South – Muntenia (Romania)	28
6	Île de France (France)	175	6	South-West Oltenia (Romania)	29
7	Berkshire, Buckinghamshire and Oxfordshire (UK)	174	7	Severoiztochen (Bulgaria)	29
8	Oberbayern (Germany)	169	8	Yugoiztochen (Bulgaria)	30
9	Stockholm (Sweden)	166	9	South-East (Romania)	31
10	Utrecht (Netherlands)	158	10	North-West (Romania)	33
11	Darmstadt (Germany)	157	11	Lubelskie (Poland)	35
12	Prague (Czech Republic)	157	12	Podkarpackie (Poland)	35
13	Southern and Eastern (Ireland)	157	13	Central (Romania)	35
14	Bremen (Germany)	156	14	Podlaskie (Poland)	38
15	North Eastern Scotland (UK)	154	15	West (Romania)	39

*PPS = purchasing power standard.
Source: Eurostat, News Release, 23/2007, 19 February 2007 © European Communities, 1995–2007. Reprinted with permission.

This optimism of the European Commission regarding the universal benefits of EU enlargement needs to be tempered by a realization of the extent of the regional problem that remains and the extent to which this has increased with the most recent enlargement. Figures released by Eurostat in February 2007 for GDP per capita in the 268 NUTS-2[4] regions of the EU27 show the enormous difference in living standards across the Union. Expressed as an index with the average GDP per capita for the EU27 equal to 100, the range was from 303 in the richest region (Inner London) to 24 (north-east Romania). Table 21.3 shows the fifteen highest and the fifteen lowest regions in this classification. It is true that 12 of the 15 lowest regions are in Bulgaria and Romania; the other 3 are in Poland. Thus, the table says nothing at all about any impact that membership of the EU might have on regional differences.

Even at a national level the variation is striking as can be seen in Table 21.4. And, if one concentrates only on the EU12, all members since 1981, excluding the African and West Indian *départements* of France d'Outre-Mer, one still finds three regions (two in Greece, one in Portugal) below 60 in the regional lists.

Expansion beyond 27 seems certain with the most likely current candidate being Croatia. Formal negotiations began with Turkey and Croatia in October 2005 and may be completed with Croatia within a few years. Turkey's future membership remains open to doubt in part because the prospect of Turkish membership has produced a quite large degree of political hostility in several of the existing member countries. An application for membership by the former Yugoslav Republic of Macedonia was formally accepted by EU leaders in December 2005 but with no date for entry negotiations to begin. The EU is also looking at further enlargements in the Western Balkans with the fairly distant possibility of eventual membership for Bosnia and Herzegovina, Serbia, Montenegro and Albania.

---

[4]   NUTS = Nomenclature of Territorial Units for Statistics.

Table 21.4 National GDP per inhabitant in the EU27 in 2004 (in PPS,* EU27 = 100)

1	Luxembourg	251	15	Greece	84.8
2	Ireland	141.4	16	Slovenia	83.3
3	Netherlands	130	17	Czech Republic	75.2
4	Austria	128.7	18	Portugal	74.8
5	Denmark	124.5	19	Malta	74.4
6	Belgium	124.4	20	Hungary	64
7	UK	123	21	Slovakia	56.7
8	Sweden	120.3	22	Estonia	55.7
9	Germany	115.8	23	Lithuania	51.1
10	Finland	115.5	24	Poland	50.7
11	France	112.3	25	Latvia	45.5
12	Italy	107.4	26	Romania	34.0
13	Spain	100.7	27	Bulgaria	33.2
14	Cyprus	91.4			

*PPS = purchasing power standard.
Source: Eurostat, News Release, 23/2007, 19 February 2007 © European Communities, 1995–2007. Reprinted with permission.

21.7 Summary

Progress towards a fully integrated European economy had begun to slow down by the early 1980s. Although tariffs among member states had been removed, there were still many barriers to intra-EU trade. The removal of these barriers would increase competition and allow the fuller exploitation of economies of scale, leading to increased efficiency, lower costs, and higher levels of investment and rates of economic growth. The Single European Act 1986 thus sought to deepen integration through the removal of all non-tariff barriers to trade in both goods and services and to the mobility of capital and labour.

Estimates were made of considerable welfare gains which would accrue to Europe through the movement to the single market and these were published in the Cecchini Report. Criticisms followed that the estimates were overly optimistic and that regional and structural problems might result. Nonetheless, there was widespread acceptance of the single market programme.

The removal of barriers to trade within financial services and to the mobility of capital had been even slower than in other areas of the European economy. One major reason for this lay in the unwillingness of national regulatory authorities to cede control of activities in their own national markets. This had led to progress in the harmonization of regulations across

the EU being very slow. To speed up the movement to a single financial market, a change of strategy was incorporated in the Single European Act. The objective of complete harmonization of regulations was replaced with the much more easily attainable mutual recognition of national standards and regulations. A second major change was the move from host-country regulation of the firms of other member states within a country to home-country regulation. This allowed a company to operate anywhere within the EU on the basis of a single licence obtained from the regulatory authorities in its home market.

These new principles were incorporated in directives aimed at the creation of a single market in the three categories of financial services – banking, the rapidly growing securities market and insurance. The Financial Services Action Plan led to a set of 42 directives aimed at further integration of financial markets and by 2007 the great majority of these directives had been transposed into national legislation. Nonetheless, the Commission felt that a good deal remained to be done to realize all of the possible benefits available from financial integration and a strategy was developed for the period 2005–2010 to continue the process.

The enlargement of the EU to 27 clearly complicated the movement to a single market in financial services but the initial judgement of the 2004 expansion to 25 members has been favourable.

Key concepts in this chapter

Financial Integration Monitor
Financial Services Action Plan (FSAP)
Fiscal barriers to trade
Harmonization
Home-country regulation
Host-country regulation
Internal market

Mutual recognition
Physical barriers to trade
Single European Act (SEA)
Single European market (SEM)
Single financial market
Single market
Technical barriers to trade

Questions and problems

1 What disadvantages do you see in the movement to the SEM?

2 List as many technical barriers to trade as you can think of.

3 Why is the measurement of gains from the movement to a single market so difficult?

4 What was special about the financial services industry which led progress towards the harmonization of national laws to be so slow?

5 List the arguments in favour of host-country regulation and discuss them. Why did the European Commission favour home-country regulation?

6 Have you seen examples in your town or region of the development of a single European financial market? What have they been?

7 Why is consumer protection such an important issue in insurance?

8 What is the ultimate limit to the membership of the EU? How would you define 'Europe' in this connection? What has been the basis of the political hostility to Turkish membership?

Further reading

R E Baldwin, 'On the growth effects of 1992', *Economic Policy*, 9, 1989, 248–81

P Cecchini *et al.*, *The European Challenge 1992: The benefits of a single market*, Report of the Cost of Non-Europe Steering Committee (Aldershot: Wildwood House, 1988)

E Davis and C Smales, 'The integration of European financial services', in J Kay (ed.), *1992: Myths and Realities* (London: London Business School, 1990), 205–41

M Emerson *et al.*, *The Economics of 1992* (Brussels: Commission of the EC, 1988)

European Commission, *Completing the Internal Market*. White Paper from the Commission to the European Council (Brussels: European Commission, 1985) ('The Cockfield Report')

European Commission, The Second Banking Directive 89/646/EEC, *Official Journal*, L386, 12, 30 December 1989, Annex [box 21.1]

H D Gibson and E Tsakalotos, 'European integration and the banking sector in southern Europe: competition, efficiency and structure', *Banca Nazionale del Lavoro Quarterly Review*, September 1993, 299–326

V Grilli, 'Europe 1992: Issues and prospects for the financial markets', *Economic Policy*, 9, 1989

P Sutherland *et al.*, *The Internal Market after 1992: Meeting the Challenge*, Report to the European Commission by the High Level Group on the Operation of the Internal Market (1992)

Price Waterhouse, 'The Economics of 1992', Study for the European Commission, in *European Economy* (1988)

Websites

http://epp.eurostat.cec.eu.int/pls/portal/docs
www.europa.eu.int
www.fsa.gov.uk
www.hm-treasury.gov.uk

Chapter 22 The European
Monetary System
and monetary union

What you will learn in this chapter:

■ The background to and the early history of the EMS

■ The plans for monetary union in the Maastricht Treaty

■ The principal reasons for the ERM problems in the early 1990s

■ The nature of the movement to the European single currency

■ Views on the success of the introduction of the single currency

■ An understanding of the issues concerning future membership
  of the monetary union

22.1 Introduction

The European Monetary System (EMS) was established in 1979 for a mixture of economic and political reasons. The central element in the system was the **Exchange Rate Mechanism (ERM)**, a fixed exchange rate arrangement that sought to restrict the extent to which volatile exchange rates interfered with fair competition among EU producers. From an economic viewpoint, fixed exchange rates became essential once the International Monetary Fund's fixed exchange rate system had started to come under pressure in the late 1960s. Under the IMF system, the exchange rates of EU countries could vary against each other by a maximum of ±2 per cent.[1] However, in August 1969, the French franc was devalued by 11.11 per cent and later the Deutschmark was revalued by over 9 per cent. In December 1971, the band that each currency had to maintain against the dollar was increased to 2.25 per cent, widening the allowable variation in the value of one European currency against another to ±4.5 per cent. The combination of the wide band and possible changes in the exchange rate parity was thought to interfere too much with the fairness of competition among producers in different EU states and to raise the possibility of countries acting to push down the relative values of their currencies in order to improve the competitiveness of their industries.

Volatile exchange rates also caused a specific problem for the Common Agricultural Policy (CAP) of the EU. The policy had been designed in the 1960s on the assumption that the exchange rates among the EU currencies would remain unchanged. Prices in the CAP were fixed in terms of the EUA – the European Unit of Account, the forerunner of the Ecu. A fall in the value of the franc, say, against the dollar and the EUA meant that farm prices in France would rise in terms of French francs but remain the same elsewhere. This would give French farmers an advantage over other farmers within the Union and encourage them to increase production, adding to the already strong incentives for European farmers to overproduce. In 1971 a formal system of levies and subsidies (known as MCAs – Monetary Compensatory Amounts)

was introduced. This established a dual system of exchange rates – the actual market rate and the Green rate of exchange which was used to convert farm prices set in EUAs into national currencies. Countries whose market exchange rates fell below their Green rates would pay MCAs, those whose market rates rose above their Green rates would receive MCAs. Although MCAs adjusted to some extent for the exchange rate changes in terms of fairness, these modifications to the CAP meant that there was no longer a system of common prices throughout the Union.

Although the Treaty of Rome had contained nothing about **monetary integration**, there had always been considerable support on political grounds for the idea that it should eventually occur. Proposals for steps to be taken towards a single currency and a single monetary policy were made as early as 1961. Serious discussion of monetary integration began at The Hague summit in December 1969 and this was followed in 1971 by the Werner Committee report which recommended the achievement of **monetary union** by 1980. Any possibility that this might happen was removed by the volatility of exchange rates following the complete breakdown of the Bretton Woods International Monetary Fund system of fixed exchange rates in 1972.

This also destroyed any chance of success for the system of fixed exchange rates, known as the **Snake in the Tunnel**, which was established in Europe in April 1972 and struggled on until March 1979, when the EMS replaced it. The Snake attempted to limit the freedom of European currencies to move against each other to ±2.25 per cent around the established **central rates** – half the freedom that had been possible under the modified IMF arrangements. However, only Benelux, West Germany and Denmark remained members of the Snake for the seven years of its existence. At various times, France, the UK, Sweden, Norway and Italy all entered and left. The 'fixed' parities were altered 31 times.

Details of the exchange rate mechanism of the EMS are provided in Box 22.1.

An attempt was made to allow for the problems of particular countries by requiring those that had not survived within the Snake to maintain the value of

---

[1] All currencies were required to remain within a band *against the US dollar* of ±1 per cent, which meant that all non-dollar currencies could vary against other non-dollar currencies by ±2 per cent, with currency A being at times 1 per cent above its parity with the dollar and currency B being 1 per cent below its dollar parity; at other times the reverse might apply.

BOX 22.1 The Exchange Rate Mechanism of the EMS

The ERM was based on a **parity grid** which tied each currency to every other currency in a system of mutually agreed and consistent rates. Under a parity grid, whenever a currency diverges from parity, all other exchange rates also diverge from the agreed rate. Hence, all countries must respond to bring about the re-establishment of parity. It was thus intended that the burden of maintaining the fixed exchange rate system would be shared equally among all members; those with strong and weak currencies alike. Central rates (parities) in the EMS were established against the European Currency Unit (Ecu), a weighted average of the value of the currencies of all EU members.

As the system operated from its inception in 1979 until the collapse early in August 1993, each of the currencies in the ERM had to stay within a band either of ±2.25 per cent (narrow band) or ±6 per cent (broad band) around its central rate against the Ecu (at the time of the collapse, the peseta and the escudo were the only two of the nine currencies within the broad band). In August 1993, the band for all members was widened to ±15 per cent, although Germany and the Netherlands agreed separately to retain the old narrow band for the relationship between their currencies.

The parity grid, showing the required relationship of each country against every other currency in the mechanism, was derived from the central rates of each currency against the Ecu. In addition to being required to stay within its band against the Ecu, each currency had to stay within the same band against every other currency. In practice, currencies under pressure within the mechanism fell out of their bands against individual currencies before they fell out of their bands against the Ecu.

Intervention points were calculated at 75 per cent of the permitted divergence of a currency from its central parity against the Ecu. When a currency reached an intervention point, the central bank in question was required to intervene in the market, buying or selling its own currency in order to keep the currency within its band. Adjustments to central parities were allowed from time to time, although these were meant to stop under Stage II of the EMU process.

---

their currency within a very wide band of ±6 per cent around the central rates that were established against the Ecu.[2] Despite this attempt at increased flexibility, the mechanism faced many early problems and seven adjustments were made to central rates in the first four years. After much talk in 1982 and early 1983 of French withdrawal and of the system's virtual collapse, things began to settle down and there were only three further realignments prior to the general realignment of January 1987. Towards the end of this period of relative exchange rate stability, talk began to be heard again about the possibility of a movement to monetary union. Box 22.2 overleaf summarizes this last section by showing the changes in central parities in the ERM between 1979 and 1996.

The period up until September 1992 was one of capital liberalization and a determined attempt to achieve exchange rate stability as a step towards monetary union. The only change in central rates in over 5½ years was a small reduction in the central rate of the lira to allow it to move from the ±6 per cent band to the ±2.25 per cent band. There was growing evidence of inflation rates among members converging on the lower rate of inflation experienced by Germany. For several countries, this convergence of inflation rates was accompanied by large increases in unemployment but most governments seemed prepared to accept this as a necessary cost of lower inflation. In 1990, the EMS was generally held to have been a success because it had reduced the variability of members' bilateral exchange rates.

The second half of the 1980s also saw a renewed political push towards monetary integration. In 1985, when member countries adopted the Single European Act, they increased the need for the progressive development of economic and monetary union (EMU). In June 1988 the Council of Europe set up a committee under Jacques Delors, the President of the European Commission, to study and make proposals regarding the necessary stages for the achievement of EMU. The result, submitted in April 1989, was *The Report of the Committee on Economic and Monetary Union*, also

---

[2]   Only Italy accepted this offer at the beginning, although later Spain (1989), the UK (1990) and Portugal (1992) all accepted the 6 per cent band on joining the ERM.

BOX 22.2 Central parity changes in the ERM

(All figures are percentage changes in central rates against the Ecu)

Period One – 1979 to 1983: the early problems

13 Mar 1979	ERM comes into operation
24 Sep 1979	DM +2; krone −2.9
30 Nov 1979	Krone −4.8
23 Mar 1981	Lira −6
5 Oct 1981	Lira, Fr franc −3; DM, guilder +5.5
22 Feb 1982	Bel/Lux franc −8.5; krone −3
14 June 1982	Fr franc −5.75; lira −2.75; DM, guilder +4.25
21 Mar 1983	Fr franc, lira −2.5; DM +5.5; punt −3.5; Bel/Lux franc +1.5; krone +2.5; guilder +3.5

Period Two – 1983 to 1987: settling down

22 Jul 1985	Lira −6; all others +2
7 Apr 1986	Fr franc −3; DM, guilder +3; krone, Bel/Lux franc + 1
4 Aug 1986	Punt −8
12 Jan 1987	Bel/Lux franc +2; DM, guilder +3

Period Three – 1987 to 1992: stability

1 Jun 1989	Peseta joins ERM
5 Jan 1990	Lira's band narrowed from ±6 to ±2.25, implicitly changing central rate by −3.7
8 Oct 1990	Sterling joins ERM
6 Apr 1992	Escudo joins ERM

Period Four – 1992 to 1996: renewed disturbance

14 Sep 1992	Lira −3.5; all others +3.5
16 Sep 1992	Sterling suspended from ERM
17 Sep 1992	Lira suspended from ERM; peseta −5
23 Nov 1992	Peseta, escudo −6
30 Jan 1993	Punt −10
13 May 1993	Peseta −8; escudo −6.5
2 Aug 1993	Bands widened to ±15
1 Jan 1995	Schilling joins ERM
6 Mar 1995	Peseta −7; escudo −3.5
14 Oct 1996	Markka joins ERM
25 Nov 1996	Lira rejoins ERM

---

known as the Delors Report. It set out the goal to be reached, the reasons for it and its possible implications, as well as specifying the desired stages leading up to EMU. The Delors Report was accepted as the basis for the debate at the European summit held in Madrid on 26 June 1989. Its principal recommendations were then incorporated into the Treaty on European Union, agreed upon at Maastricht in December 1991.[3]

22.2 The Treaty on European Union and the plans for monetary union

The Treaty on European Union set out the nature, functions and constitution of the new central banking system which would manage the single currency, monetary policy and foreign exchange in monetary union. It also explained how fiscal and budgetary

policy would be managed and set out the stages through which EMU would be reached. The first stage was seen retrospectively as having commenced in July 1990 with the liberalization of capital flows and the integration of financial markets under the single market programme. During this first stage, all EU countries were to become full members of the ERM in the narrow band and there was to be an increase in the coordination of national monetary policies.

Stage 2 was to begin in January 1994 with the establishment of the European Monetary Institute (EMI) which would have the task of preparing the way for monetary union. Responsibility for the execution of monetary, exchange rate and fiscal policy would still rest with the member states. However, the EMI would plan monetary policy, monitor the policies of member states, and advise member governments. Changes would only be allowed to central exchange rates in the ERM under exceptional circumstances.

---

[3] Although it was agreed upon at Maastricht, the Treaty on European Union was not signed until 7 February 1992 and did not come into force until 1 November 1993, following slowness in ratification of the Treaty by many countries.

The EMI would be replaced at the beginning of Stage 3 by the European Central Bank (ECB) which, together with the central banks of the member states, would form the European System of Central Banks (ESCB). In Stage 3 exchange rates would be irrevocably fixed and national currencies would eventually be replaced by a single currency. The ECB would take over from the EMI, and would assume responsibility for exchange rate and monetary policies. A decision was required before the end of December 1996 as to when Stage 3 would commence. If, however, no date had been set by the end of 1997, the third stage would start on 1 January 1999.

With regard to membership of the monetary union, the Treaty set out a number of **convergence** conditions, which EU member states would need to meet to be allowed to join. Membership would require:

1 demonstration that the country's inflation rate had converged on the lowest rates of inflation within the union – to be judged specifically by whether the average rate of inflation, observed over a period of one year before the decision regarding membership, was within 1.5 percentage points of the average of the three lowest national rates;

2 evidence that the inflation convergence was durable – to be shown by a long-term interest rate within 2 percentage points of the average of the long-term interest rate of the three countries with lowest inflation;

3 a sustainable **government financial position** defined as (i) a general government budget deficit no greater than 3 per cent of GDP at market prices and (ii) a ratio of gross public debt to GDP at market prices no greater than 60 per cent – unless this debt ratio is falling 'at a satisfactory pace';

4 observance of the normal fluctuation margins provided for by the ERM of the EMS for at least two years with no devaluations against any other member currency.

A majority of the EU member states were required to be economically fit for monetary union if the currency union were to go ahead from December 1996 but it would be established on 1 January 1999 (with membership being determined by July 1998) no matter how few member states were eligible.

The specific numbers included in the convergence conditions had nothing in particular to recommend them. At the time of the signing of the Treaty on European Union, they looked to be achievable targets for many EU member states while appearing sufficiently tough to hope to persuade financial markets that the monetary policies pursued after 1999 would be strong, **anti-inflationary** policies.

22.3 The problems of the 1990s

At the beginning of 1992, everything seemed to be going well for the EMS and hopes were high of meeting the deadlines of the Treaty on European Union for the formation of EMU by 1997 or by 1999 at the latest. Yet by September of that same year, two major currencies (sterling and the lira) had been forced out of the ERM while three others (the peseta, the escudo and the punt) had devalued. Three more currencies (the French franc, the Danish krone and the Belgian franc) remained under severe pressure at various stages in the following months and in August 1993 the allowable band around central rates within which countries were required to keep their exchange rates was widened to ±15 per cent in order to preserve the central rate of the French franc and to make life more difficult for speculators.

What had gone wrong? Both economic and political factors contributed to the crisis. Part of the problem was that by 1992 exchange rates were well out of line following the prolonged period without adjustment of central rates. Although inflation rates had converged to a considerable extent, the differences that remained had meant that a number of countries had become seriously uncompetitive at the existing exchange rates.

Popular concerns regarding the increased speed of integration of the EU had added to the economic problem of misaligned exchange rates. In Britain's case this was nothing new. The British government's doubts had been expressed at the Maastricht conference by its insistence that Britain be given the right to opt out of membership of the single currency. In other member states, uncertainty about the future had clearly increased and this was shown by the narrowness with which the referendum held in France to approve the Treaty on European Union was passed and the loss of the first referendum held in Denmark on the same question. The increase in doubt about the future of the EU expressed itself in foreign exchange markets through a weakening of currencies already weakened by worries about competitiveness.

The liberalization of capital flows among member states under the Single European Act provided the final element. This allowed speculators to exploit the difficulties of weak currencies. They knew that if they sold weak currencies in large quantities for sufficient periods of time, governments would be forced either to devalue their currencies or to leave the ERM. If they left the ERM, their currencies, now floating freely outside the ERM, would be very likely to fall sharply. In either event, speculators who had sold the weak currencies would be able to buy them back at much lower rates and make large per annum rates of profit. Because central banks could no longer impose capital controls and because the capital movements were so very large, central banks were in no position to resist the downward pressure on weak currencies. Where they tried and failed, as with the Bank of England, they experienced very large losses.

There were two apparent solutions.

1   to lower interest rates generally across the EU to help countries in recession;

2   to realign the exchange rates within the EMS with the weak currency countries accepting devaluation.

The first would have required the *Bundesbank* to lower its interest rate. This it was unwilling to do for two reasons – one local and one related to the aims of the EMS as a whole. The local, if very large, problem that Germany faced was the absorption by West Germany of the very weak East German economy following German reunification in 1989. The German government had, for internal economic and political reasons, exchanged the Deutschmark for the East German currency, the Ostmark, at equal value. This had increased the total German money supply much more than total German production had increased as a result of reunification and raised fears of increasing inflation. These fears were augmented by the promise of the government not to increase taxation rates during the reunification process. Public expenditure and budget deficits inevitably increased.

The *Bundesbank*'s natural response was to raise interest rates, rather than to lower them as the UK wanted. This made sense in terms of the system as a whole, if one accepted that a major advantage of the EMS was that it allowed inflation-prone countries to lower their rates of inflation by linking their currencies to that of low-inflation Germany. This possibility would have disappeared had inflation rates in Germany climbed sharply.

The second possible solution, the devaluation of the weak currencies, also faced problems. It would have increased inflationary pressures in those countries and caused doubts about their future determination to fight inflation. The UK, in particular, was unwilling to accept an organized, ordered devaluation. The increase in tensions between the *Bundesbank* and the British government caused further doubts in the foreign exchange market and led to more downward pressure being exerted on sterling. Italy was also thought to be uncompetitive at the existing central rates and speculators spread their attack to the lira. Spain and Portugal were able to contain the pressure to some extent both because they were still in the 6 per cent band of the EMS and because they were able to reintroduce controls over the flow of capital.[4]

This period of exchange rate turmoil marked the beginning of a long period of doubt about both the prospects of monetary union occurring in 1999 and the countries likely to qualify to join at its beginning. Doubts were intensified as it became clear that most EU members would have grave difficulty in meeting the convergence conditions laid down at Maastricht. The principal difficulty related to the requirement of a sustainable government financial position. European economies experienced deep recessions in the early 1990s and this inevitably led to budget deficits in most countries well beyond the limit of 3 per cent of GDP.

In addition to the problems over government finances, the exchange rate disturbances of 1992 and 1993 had made the achievement of the fourth convergence condition very difficult. To begin with, by March 1997, the UK had not rejoined the ERM and Greece and Sweden were still to become members. The narrow band had all but been destroyed and, with bands of ±15 per cent, the phrase 'observance of the normal fluctuation margins provided for by the ERM' in the Maastricht Treaty had very little meaning. The exchange rate changes had also interfered with the convergence of inflation rates.

---

[4]   Spain and Portugal had both been given until the end of 1992 to remove all capital controls under the SEA.

22.4 The movement to monetary union

By 1997 doubts about monetary union had risen to the extent that postponement of the 1999 starting date seemed increasingly likely. At that stage few countries seemed likely to meet all the convergence criteria by July 1998.

The governments of France and Germany remained strongly committed to the single currency on political grounds but faced increasing doubts from their own populations. France had unemployment of over 12 per cent and had experienced both social and industrial unrest. There was a strong feeling that the high unemployment was at least partly the result of the policy of maintaining the value of the franc in terms of the German mark in order to keep alive hopes of the single currency. This had required constant downward pressure on government expenditure but yet more cuts in expenditure would be needed to push government borrowing below 3 per cent of GDP. Meanwhile, Germany had high unemployment also, although this could still be seen to a significant extent as one of the costs of reunification. Of more concern to the German supporters of monetary union were the widespread fears that the replacement of the Deutschmark by the single currency would mean higher inflation.

In the event, the political problems were overcome and the strong drive to meet the conditions together with some generous accounting interpretations of the facts allowed the European Council to argue that almost all of the countries that had wished to be part of the first wave of membership of the union had either met the conditions or were moving towards them with sufficient speed. This was most dubious in relation to Italy whose public debt remained stubbornly well above the desired 60 per cent of GDP. However, Italy had been a founding member of the EU in 1957 and had always been a strong supporter of integration. Further, it was a large country and, from a trading point of view, it was much better to have it as a member of the single currency than not.

Consequently, of the 12 countries that wished to join from January 1999, only Greece was failed on the convergence criteria and the single currency commenced with 11 participating members. Three members of the EU – the UK, Denmark and Sweden – chose to remain outside of the monetary union at least for the time being. Greece was judged to have done sufficiently well in relation to the convergence criteria within the following two years and became a member of the single currency from 1 January 2001. Table 22.1 shows the exchange rates used for the conversion of the founding 11 currencies to the euro at the beginning of 1999 and those for the drachma (2001), the tolar (2007) and the Cyprus pound and Maltese lira (2008).

Table 22.1 Conversion rates of single currency countries to the euro[1]

Country	Old currency	Conversion rate
Austria	Schilling (Sch)	€1 = Sch13.7603
Belgium	Franc (BFr)	€1 = BFr40.3399
Germany	Deutschmark (DM)	€1 = DM1.95583
Spain	Peseta (Pta)	€1 = Pta166.386
Finland	Markka (FM)	€1 = FM5.94573
France	Franc (FFr)	€1 = FFR6.55957
Ireland	Punt (I£)	€1 = £0.787564
Italy	Lira (L)	€1 = L1936.27
Luxembourg	Franc (LFr)	€1 = LFr40.3399
Netherlands	Guilder (Fl)	€1 = Fl2.20371
Portugal	Escudo (Es)	€1 = Es200.482
Greece	Drachma (Dr)	€1 = Dr340.75
Slovenia	Tolar (SIT)	€1 = SIT239.640
Cyprus	Pound (CYP)	€1 = CYP0.585274
Malta	Lira (MTL)	€1 = MTL0.429300

[1] From 1 January 1999 with the exception of the drachma (joined 1 January 2001), the tolar (1 January 2007) and the Cyprus pound and Maltese lira (joined 1 January 2008).

22.5 Monetary union developments

After agreement was reached regarding the number of members of monetary union, progress towards the full establishment of the monetary union commenced. The European Central Bank (ECB) and the European System of Central Banks (ESCB) were established on 1 June 1998 and in September agreement was reached with Denmark and Greece, two of the countries not in the first wave of single currency membership, over the formation of a replacement for the old ERM (ERM II). Under this agreement, Denmark agreed to keep its currency within a band of 2¼ per cent around its central rate with the euro. Greece, on the other hand, stuck with the existing 15 per cent band. Sweden and the UK chose not to be a part of ERM II, which meant that their currencies would float against the euro when it was established. During the second half of 1998 important decisions were made by the Governing Council of the ECB regarding post-monetary union monetary policy. These are included in the list of important monetary union dates in Box 22.3 and are discussed in Chapter 23.

The euro was formally established on 1 January 1999 and trading in the currency commenced on 4 January. Although the euro was a fully established currency from that date, euro notes and coins were not issued until 1 January 2002. Before that date, national currencies remained in use throughout the **euro area**.

In many ways the euro was a success. In the first five years, however, the attention of economic and political commentators was directed almost entirely to the weakness of the euro against other currencies, particularly the US dollar. A confident opening for the euro saw it rise above an exchange rate of €1 = $1.18 by the time markets closed in the USA. However, the euro's value began to fall immediately after this and, despite occasional small recoveries, it fell steadily to a low of $0.8252 during trading on 26 October 2000, a loss of value of over 30 per cent. Although it then began to rise again and went above $0.95 in early January 2001, it could not sustain the recovery and fell back below $0.90 in mid-March 2001. It hovered around $0.90 until late 2002, when it was able for the first time in three years to maintain a rate above parity in relation to the dollar. In 2003 the value of the euro increased steadily, going above $1.25 by the year's end. It continued to perform strongly in 2004 rising above $1.36 by the year end. Some weakness late in 2005 saw it drift back below the rate on the first day of trading but lasted only a few days. The generally poor performance of the dollar against all of the major currencies led to the value of the euro rising strongly against the dollar in 2007. The weakness of the euro was no longer an issue. The exchange rate performance of the euro is discussed in Chapter 23, along with the monetary policy followed by the ECB. Table 22.2 shows annual average exchange rates for the euro against the dollar, yen and pound from 1999 to 2006.

Leaving aside the value of the euro, what else do we need to look at to decide if the introduction of the euro can be considered a success? Three types of economic argument are usually put forward in support of the European single currency. Two of these are microeconomic.

Firstly, increased **price transparency** across national borders in the euro area together with lower production costs should lead to increased competition and increases in efficiency. These, in turn, should produce increases in trade and higher rates of economic growth. Price transparency increases because the single currency makes it much more difficult for producers to charge different prices in different markets, allowing efficient firms to compete more effectively. Production costs are lowered by the removal of the uncertainty associated with exchange rate changes. This saves exporters, importers and investors active throughout the area the costs involved in covering

Table 22.2 Annual average exchange rates of the euro, 1999 to 2006

Year	US$ per euro	Japanese yen per euro	£ sterling per euro
1999	1.0658	121.32	0.65874
2000	0.9236	99.47	0.60948
2001	0.8956	108.68	0.62187
2002	0.9456	118.06	0.62883
2003	1.1312	130.97	0.69199
2004	1.2439	134.44	0.67866
2005	1.2441	136.85	0.6838
2006	1.2556	146.02	0.68173

Source: European Central Bank Statistical Data Warehouse http://sdw.ecb.europa.eu/browse.do. This information may be obtained free of charge through the ECB website www.ecb.int. Reprinted with permission.

BOX 22.3 Monetary union developments 1998–2007

1 Jun 1998	Establishment of ECB and ESCB
26 Sep 1998	Denmark and Greece agree to participate in ERM II
13 Oct 1998	ECB announces a target inflation rate for the euro area of less than 2%
1 Dec 1998	ECB announces a reference value for monetary growth (M3) of 4.5%
22 Dec 1998	ECB sets its main refinancing interest rate (refi) at 3%
31 Dec 1998	Conversion rates of the 11 participating currencies in the euro established from 1/1/99
4 Jan 1999	Trading begins in euros; rate against US$ at close €1 = $1.1789
9 Apr 1999	ECB cuts refi from 3% to 2.5%
5 Nov 1999	ECB raises refi from 2.5% to 3%
27 Jan 2000	Euro falls below parity with the US dollar for the first time: €1 = $0.9976
4 Feb 2000	ECB raises refi from 3% to 3.25%
17 Mar 2000	ECB raises refi from 3.25 to 3.5%
28 Apr 2000	ECB raises refi from 3.5% to 3.75%
9 Jun 2000	ECB raises refi from 3.75% to 4.25%
19 Jun 2000	Greece granted membership of the single currency from 1 Jan 2001
28 Jun 2000	ECB changes refinancing operations from fixed to variable interest rate system
1 Sep 2000	ECB raises minimum refi from 4.5% to 4.75%
22 Sep 2000	ECB, US, UK and Japanese central banks intervene in currency markets to support euro
28 Sep 2000	Danish referendum decides against membership of the euro area: 53.1% to 46.9%
6 Oct 2000	ECB raises minimum refi from 4.5% to 4.75%
26 Oct 2000	Euro falls to US$0.8252, lowest level between start of 1999 and October 2007
10 May 2001	ECB cuts minimum refi from 4.75% to 4.5%
31 Aug 2001	ECB cuts minimum refi from 4.5% to 4.25%
18 Sep 2001	ECB cuts minimum refi f from 4.25% to 3.75%
9 Nov 2001	ECB cuts minimum refi from 3.75% to 3.25%
1 Jan 2002	Introduction of euro notes and coin
15 Jul 2002	euro rises above parity with the US dollar: €1 = $1.0024
6 Dec 2002	ECB cuts minimum refi from 3.25% to 2.75%
17 Mar 2003	ECB cuts minimum refi from 2.75% to 2.5%
23 May 2003	euro rises temporarily above rate on 4/1/99: €1 = $1.179
6 Jun 2003	ECB cuts minimum refi from 2.5% to 2.0%
14 Sep 2003	Sweden votes solidly against membership of euro area: 56.1% against 41.8%
27 Nov 2003	euro again rises above rate on 4/1/99 and stays there for 2 years €1 = $1.1902
28 Dec 2004	euro reaches a new high of €1 = $1.3633
8 Nov 2005	euro slips temporarily below rate on 4/1/99, reaching a low of €1 = $1.1667 on 15 Nov
6 Dec 2005	ECB raises minimum refi from 2% to 2.25%
8 Mar 2006	ECB raises minimum refi from 2.25% to 2.5%
15 Jun 2006	ECB raises minimum refi from 2.5% to 2.75%
9 Aug 2006	ECB raises minimum refi from 2.75% to 3%
11 Oct 2006	ECB raises minimum refi from 3% to 3.25%
13 Dec 2006	ECB raises minimum refi from 3.25% to 3.5%
1 Jan 2007	Slovenia joins euro area becoming 13th member
14 Mar 2007	ECB raises minimum refi from 3.5% to 3.75%
13 Jun 2007	ECB raises minimum refi from 3.75% to 4.0%
1 Oct 2007	Euro reaches new high against US dollar: €1 = $1.4232
1 Jan 2008	Malta and Cyprus join euro area increasing membership to 15

All exchange rates in this table are official ECB rates based on the regular daily concertation procedure between central banks within and outside the European System of Central Banks, which normally takes place at 2.15 p.m. (14:15) ECB time.

MORE FROM THE WEB

The once extremely useful site, http://www.eui.eu/RSCAS/Research/Eurohomepage/, once a magnificent site for anything about the single currency and monetary policy in Europe, hasn't been updated for a long time and many of the links no longer work. However, if you are willing to put up with the frustration, there is still a great deal of useful material to be found. For arguments stressing the success of the euro see speeches of ECB officials on http://www.ecb.int/press/key/date/2005/html/sp050318.en.html.

Searching the net under 'success of the euro' turns up a great deal of material, for and against, at various levels.

exchange rate risk relating to exposures within the euro area. It also removes the exchange rate risk premium previously built into the interest rates of many countries. The lower costs brought about by the single currency reduce the barriers to cross-border trade and investment and should encourage small and medium-sized companies that have, in the past, been active only in the domestic market to enter the markets of the neighbouring countries, further increasing the degree of competition within the euro area.

Secondly, the use of the single currency should have an important impact on the development of financial markets. We have seen in Chapter 21 that the level of competition across financial markets in the EU was low and many European financial markets were relatively underdeveloped. There was hope that financial integration would have a large impact on the efficiency of financial firms and that this would be a considerable benefit to both producers and consumers in the EU. The progress towards financial integration after the signing of the Single European Act in 1986 had been slow and it was hoped that the adoption of a single currency would help in this process. It was expected, in particular, that a deep and liquid bond market in euro would develop, making it easier for companies to raise finance in the domestic capital market, without incurring exchange rate risks. This would, it was hoped, provide support for merger and acquisition activity by euro area firms as well as improved efficiency and competitiveness and would make it easier for new firms and firms undertaking risky investment projects to raise capital. Equally, the

introduction of the single currency was expected to boost integration efforts in equities and derivatives markets and payment and settlement systems.

The final argument in support of the single currency related to the encouragement of policies that would produce macroeconomic stability. In part, this was held to derive from the application of the Maastricht convergence conditions for monetary union membership together with the use of the Stability and Growth Pact to govern national fiscal policies within monetary union. In addition, the adoption by all member countries of a politically independent central bank in the lead up to membership of the single currency and the independence of the ECB itself would remove monetary policy from the political arena and increase stability. This would be beneficial to firms and would also encourage member countries to carry out important restructuring of economies, notably of labour markets and tax systems.

Criticisms have concerned the once-and-for-all inflation effects of the adoption of the new currency, and the existence of a single interest rate across all member countries irrespective of differences in levels of demand pressure and unemployment, potential deleterious impacts on particular countries and regions within countries.

It is difficult to make judgements about the performance of the euro under these headings partly because several of the possible advantages relate to long-term potential gains and cannot yet be fully assessed. In addition, it is often difficult to separate out the impact of one change (in this case, the movement to the single currency) from other changes occurring at the same time. The integration of financial markets across the EU, for example, is the goal of the European Financial Common Market Programme and the Financial Services Action Plan which apply to all 27 EU members and are quite independent of monetary integration. Again, financial integration across Europe is being hastened by globalization and this is also independent of monetary integration.

Nonetheless, a number of claims have been made. For example, between 1998 and 2006, exports and imports of goods within the euro area rose from about 26 per cent to 32 per cent of GDP while imports and exports of services rose from 5 to 7 per cent of GDP. Further, there was an even greater increase in extra-euro area trade with exports and imports of goods rising from around 24 per cent to almost 33 per cent of GDP in this period while extra-euro-area services trade rose from 8 per cent to almost 10 per cent of GDP.[5] How much of this is attributable to the single currency is difficult to say but it is reasonable to suggest that it has contributed. There has also been a considerable increase in intra-euro-area foreign direct investment since 1994 and, since the introduction of the euro, a sharp increase in cross-border mergers and acquisitions within the manufacturing sector of euro area countries.

The ECB has produced a set of indicators suggesting a considerable increase in the level of integration within the euro area financial and banking markets since the introduction of the euro. These include:

■ the cross-country standard deviation of interest rates in the interbank money market has fallen greatly;

■ the euro corporate bond market has grown significantly, with bonds issued by euro area non-financial corporations growing from 3.9 per cent of GDP in 1999 to 12.5 per cent in 2006;

■ euro area residents doubled their holdings of equities issued in another euro area country between 1997 and 2005;

■ the share of long-term debt securities issued in the euro area and held by residents of other euro area countries has risen markedly.

As well as making these points, Jean-Claude Trichet, the President of the ECB, has argued[6] that the degree of synchronization of business cycles across the euro areas has grown since the 1990s and that the euro area is now more resilient to external developments than individual members were before the introduction of the euro.

Since the problem of the 'weak' euro has disappeared, economic arguments against the single currency have largely centred on the relatively good economic performance of two of the three countries which might have entered the single currency but have chosen so far not to do so – the UK and Sweden. Although Denmark also chose not to enter the single currency, its currency has been closely linked to the euro through ERM II throughout the period. Table 22.3

Table 22.3 Rate of growth of GDP in EU15 countries, 1999–2006

Country	1999	2000	2001	2002	2003	2004	2005	2006	Average 1999–2006
Austria	3.3	3.4	0.8	0.9	1.1	2.4	2.0	3.2	2.14
Belgium	3.3	3.9	0.7	1.4	1.0	2.7	1.5	3.0	2.19
Finland	3.9	5.0	2.6	1.6	1.8	3.7	2.9	5.5	3.38
France	3.0	4.0	1.8	1.1	1.1	2.0	1.2	2.0	2.03
Germany	1.9	3.1	1.2	0.0	−0.2	1.2	0.9	2.7	1.35
Greece	3.4	4.5	4.5	3.9	4.9	4.7	3.7	4.2	4.2[1]
Ireland	10.7	9.4	5.8	6.0	4.3	4.3	5.5	6.0	6.5[1]
Italy	1.9	3.6	1.8	0.3	0.0	1.2	0.1	1.9	1.35
Luxembourg	8.4	8.4	2.5	3.8	1.3	3.6	4.0	5.8	4.73[1]
Netherlands	4.7	3.9	1.9	0.1	0.3	2.0	1.5	2.9	2.16
Portugal	3.9	3.9	2.0	0.8	−0.7	1.3	0.5	1.3	1.63
Spain	4.7	5.0	3.6	2.7	3.0	3.2	3.5	3.9	3.7
Denmark	2.6	3.5	0.7	0.5	0.4	2.1	3.1	3.3	2.03
Sweden	4.5	4.3	1.1	2.0	1.7	4.1	2.9	4.4	3.13
United Kingdom	3.0	3.8	2.4	2.1	2.7	3.3	1.9	2.7	2.74

[1] IMF Staff estimates.

Source: WORLD ECONOMIC OUTLOOK: SPILLOVERS AND CYCLES IN THE GLOBAL ECONOMY by IMF. Copyright 2007 by International Monetary Fund. Reproduced with permission of International Monetary Fund in the format Textbook via Copyright Clearance Center.

---

[5]   All figures in this section from Jean-Claude Trichet, President of the ECB, 'The process of European economic and financial integration', speech at conference held in Malta, 1 October 2007, http://www.ecb.int/press/key/date/2007/html.
[6]   Jean-Claude Trichet, ibid.

Table 22.4 Unemployment in EU15 countries, 1999–2006

Country	1999	2000	2001	2002	2003	2004	2005	2006
Austria	3.9	3.6	3.6	4.2	4.3	4.8	5.2	4.8
Belgium	8.5	6.9	6.6	7.5	8.2	8.4	8.4	8.3
Finland	10.2	9.8	9.1	9.1	9.0	8.8	8.4	7.7
France	10.5	9.1	8.4	8.7	9.4	9.6	9.7	9.0
Germany	7.5	6.9	6.9	7.7	8.8	9.2	9.1	8.1
Greece	12.1	11.4	10.8	10.3	9.7	10.5	9.9	8.9
Ireland	5.6	4.3	3.9	4.4	4.6	4.4	4.4	4.4[1]
Italy	10.9	10.1	9.1	8.6	8.4	8.0	7.7	6.8
Luxembourg	2.9	2.5	2.3	2.6	3.5	3.9	4.2	4.4
Netherlands	3.2	2.9	2.2	2.8	3.7	4.6	4.7	3.9
Portugal	4.4	3.9	4.0	5.0	6.3	6.7	7.6	7.7
Spain	15.6	13.9	10.6	11.5	11.0	9.2	8.5	7.8
Denmark	5.7	5.4	5.2	5.2	6.2	6.4	5.7	4.5
Sweden	5.6	4.7	4.0	4.0	4.9	5.5	5.8	4.8
United Kingdom	6.0	5.5	5.1	5.2	5.0	4.8	4.8	5.4

[1] IMF Staff estimates.

Source: WORLD ECONOMIC OUTLOOK: SPILLOVERS AND CYCLES IN THE GLOBAL ECONOMY by IMF. Copyright 2007 by International Monetary Fund. Reproduced with permission of International Monetary Fund in the format Textbook via Copyright Clearance Center.

and Table 22.4 show economic growth and unemployment figures respectively for the EU15 from 1999 to 2006.

Certainly the performance of the big countries – Germany, Italy and France – can be seen to be poor over the period but, in truth, these figures don't tell us a great deal. Since we cannot credit or blame the single currency for the events of the early years, we are dealing here with very few years and, again, it is difficult to separate membership of the single currency from everything else that might have affected unemployment and growth rates in these economies. If we treat Ireland, Luxembourg and Greece as special cases, Sweden's performance was relatively good and the UK's performance was better over the period both in terms of growth and unemployment, than that of the member countries of equivalent size. But we cannot know how Sweden and the UK would have performed had they been within the single currency. We also need to repeat that most of the gains meant to accrue from monetary union are long-term in nature.

22.6 The euro area – future membership prospects

The addition of Slovenia (from January 2007), Malta and Cyprus (from January 2008) into the euro area took the membership to 15. The combined population of the euro area (2007 EU figures) is now 316 million of the EU total population of 491 million. This left 12 EU member states outside the single currency – Denmark, the UK, Sweden, 7 of the 10 countries that became members of the enlarged monetary union on 1 May 2004 and the two most recent EU members, Bulgaria and Romania.

In the Maastricht Treaty negotiations, Denmark and the UK were granted derogations from participating in the monetary union until such time as the countries themselves requested membership. Denmark has since confirmed the decision to remain outside the single currency in two referendums, the second being on 28 September 2000. Because the margin in favour of remaining outside the euro area was quite high in this referendum (53.1 to 46.9 per cent), it was unlikely that the question would again be put to the vote for some years. This continued to be the position in 2007. Denmark remains a member of ERM II and its currency is thus closely linked to the euro. This has meant that the annual average exchange rate of the Danish krone against the euro has stayed within a very narrow range over the past eight years:

1999 €1 = DKr7.4432;   2000 €1 = DKr7.4631;

2001 €1 = DKr7.4357;   2002 €1 = DKr7.4243;

2003 €1 = DKr7.4446;   2004 €1 = DKr7.7.4381;

2005 €1 = DKr7.4605;   2006 €1 = DKr7.4560

Thus, Denmark would have obtained and will continue to obtain any benefits arising from increased macroeconomic stability and is under no great pressure to join the euro area in the near future.

The Swedish Parliament decided in 1997 that Sweden would not participate in the monetary union from its inception in 1999 and was given the status of a country with a derogation from the need to join the euro by the European Council in 1998. It has for some time met all of the economic criteria for membership with the exception of maintaining a stable relationship between its currency and the euro. It has never joined ERM II and so its currency has fluctuated much more against the euro than has Denmark's. Annual averages have ranged from €1 = SKr8.4465 (for the year 2000) to €1 = SKr9.2849 (for 2005), although the relationship has been more stable recently than in earlier years. Sweden has also once rejected membership in a referendum, more recently and by a larger margin than in the case of Denmark. Its economy has performed well in recent years outside of the single currency and so there is no immediate prospect that Sweden will join.

The UK government indicated in 1998 its willingness in principle to join the single currency but added that it would only do so when the economic case for membership was 'clear and unambiguous'. In June 2003, the UK Treasury confirmed its view that the economic conditions it had set for membership had not yet been attained. If, and when, the decision is taken in the future that UK membership can be fully justified in economic terms, the question will be put to a referendum. The details of the UK Treasury's enquiry into UK membership of the euro area is considered in detail below.

Of the new member countries, we have seen that Slovenia, Malta and Cyprus have already joined. The remaining nine are committed to adopting the euro but vary considerably in terms of how soon that is likely to happen. Estonia, Latvia, Lithuania and Slovakia have all joined ERM II. With their currencies thus closely linked to the euro, they are the most likely candidates for relatively early membership. The most hopeful is Slovakia which has a target date for joining of 1 January 2009 and was judged by an OECD report of 5 April 2007[7] to be on track to meet this. The main difficulties the OECD foresaw were problems of adjustment after membership, especially in maintaining macroeconomic stability, rather than with meeting the entry criteria.

Estonia, Latvia and Lithuania are similar small economies with the same problem – inflation. Estonia originally aimed to adopt the euro at the beginning of 2007 but this was postponed to 2008 and then to 2010. This date has also been abandoned and there is currently no target date but it is not likely to be possible until 2011 or later. Almost all shops show prices in euro as well as in the Estonian currency (kroon) and many shops accept euro. The latest ECB/EU convergence report on Estonia suggested that many of the Maastricht requirements were being met.[8] The budget was in surplus for 2005 and forecast to remain so in 2006 and the debt/GDP ratio was extremely low (it was forecast to be only 4.0 per cent in 2006). Because Estonia does not have a developed bond market in kroon, no harmonized long-term interest rate was available for judging the interest rate requirement for entry but there was no indication of a problem in this regard. However, according to IMF figures, inflation,

---

[7] OECD, 'Economic survey of the Slovak Republic 2007: Catching up with advanced European countries and entering the euro area', OECD, 2007, http://www.oecd.org/document/30/0,3343,en_2649_201185_38292446_1_1_1_1,00.html.
[8] European Central Bank, *Convergence Report*, December 2006, http://www.ecb.int/pub/pdf/conrep/cr200612en.pdf.

having fallen to only 1.3 per cent in 2003, has recently been rising steadily, reaching 4.4 per cent in 2006. Further, inflation was forecast to be 4.8 per cent in 2007 and 5.3 per cent for 2008, well above the euro area average and thus well above the reference point (approximately 2.8 per cent in early 2007) under the Maastricht criteria. The increase in inflation had occurred during a period of extremely rapid economic growth which had caused capacity constraints and a tight labour market pushing wages and other costs up. Estonia also faced rising gas prices, and other factors likely to increase inflation in the coming years were identified in the convergence report. There was no immediate prospect of inflation being brought under control.

Latvia has similar inflation problems for much the same reasons and this has also caused the postponement of its likely date for entry into the euro area. It had originally anticipated adopting the euro in January 2008 but the earliest date now being suggested is 2012. Latvia, too, had a budget surplus and a low government debt/GDP ratio. It also met the long-term interest rate criterion but its inflation performance was worse than that of Estonia. The problem had originally been caused by high import prices following a devaluation of the currency before Latvia's entry into the EU. It had then been greatly exacerbated by a tight labour market, especially in the services sector, by increasing gas prices and by the effects of harmonizing taxes within the EU. Again the ECB was able to identify a number of factors likely to keep inflation well above the single currency entry reference rate for a number of years into the future. IMF estimates of the inflation rate were 7.3 per cent for 2007 and 6.5 per cent for 2008.

Lithuania also had intended to join the euro as early as possible after accession to the EU, had set a target of January 2007 and had applied for membership. However, it was rejected by the European Commission because of its high inflation rate. In fact, the May 2006 ECB convergence report on Lithuania showed an inflation rate over the period being considered of only 2.7 per cent, just above the then reference value for inflation (but, as we have seen, below the 2.8 per cent rate needed the following year). Lithuania had been rejected not so much on its current performance as on the inflationary pressures that the ECB saw ahead. As with Estonia and Latvia, these mainly related to increasing labour costs and gas prices and

the increases in excise taxes on fuel, alcohol and tobacco needed to bring the taxes to EU levels. Nonetheless IMF estimates of inflation for 2006, 2007 and 2008 of 3.8, 3.5 and 3.4 per cent respectively indicate a rather smaller problem than for Estonia and Latvia. The government now suggests 2010 or later for its accession to the euro. The question may be complicated by political factors since there is evidence of considerable opposition to membership among the Lithuanian people.

This leaves us to consider briefly the five EU members currently not members of ERM II and so not meeting the exchange rate requirement for entry to the euro – the Czech Republic, Hungary, Poland, Bulgaria and Romania. Although the koruna had not been a member of ERM II, the strength of the Czech economy (growth rates of around 6 per cent for 2005 and 2006) had been associated with an appreciation of the currency against the euro until early 2006 followed by a period of stability. Thus, there did not appear to be a problem associated with locking the koruna into the euro at a fixed rate. In 2006, the Czech Republic's difficulties from the point of view of euro membership seemed to start and end with its budget deficits of around 3.5 per cent of GDP, above the level of 3 per cent specified in the Maastricht Treaty. There was no problem with the overall government debt/GDP ratio which, at around 31 per cent, is well below Maastricht's target of 60 per cent. At the time of the ECB convergence report of December 2006, there was also no problem with the level of long-term interest rates and inflation was below the reference rate. It will not be easy, however, for the government to meet the budget deficit target and there are indications of increasing inflation. IMF forecasts are for an inflation rate of 2.9 per cent in 2007 and 3.0 per cent in 2008. The Czech government's 2010 target date for entry has now been dropped and 2012 is probably the earliest date at which membership of the euro area is possible.

Hungary has much more severe budget problems and a higher inflation rate than the Czech Republic and is, therefore, rather further away from euro membership than the Czech Republic. As can be seen in Table 22.5, long-term interest rates were also above Maastricht reference levels. IMF estimates also suggest a worsening of inflation – rising to 6.4 per cent in 2007 although dropping back to 3.8 per cent in 2008. Following the very high budget deficit, Hungary's deputy

Table 22.5 Economic indicators of convergence: EU non-euro area members without derogation, 2006

Country	Inflation (annual % increase in HICP)	Long-term interest rate	General government surplus or deficit (−)	General government gross debt (% of GDP)
Bulgaria[3]	7.4	–	3.3	22.8
Czech Republic	2.2	3.8	−3.5	30.9
Estonia	4.3	–	2.5	4.0
Hungary	3.5	7.1	−10.1	67.6
Latvia	6.7	3.9	−1.0	11.1
Lithuania	3.8[1]	3.8[2]	−0.6	18.9
Poland	1.2	5.2	−2.2	42.4
Romania[3]	6.6	–	−1.9	12.4
Slovakia	4.3	4.3	−3.4	33
reference value	2.8	6.2	−3.0	60

[1] IMF estimate. [2] Figure for 2005. [3] Figures from Eurostat, http://epp.eurostat.ec.europa.eu/portal.

Source: European Central Bank (2006) *Convergence Reports*, December 2006 for all countries except Lithuania (May 2006), Bulgaria and Romania. This information may be obtained free of charge through the ECB website www.ecb.int. Reprinted with permission.

finance minister announced in March 2007[9] that no target date for euro entry would be set until the social welfare system had been overhauled. The government would work with the central bank to prepare a 'road map' for euro entry by the middle of 2008 but even that was unlikely to contain a target date for entry.

Poland's principal problem also relates to its government accounts. Table 22.5 shows Poland as having achieved all Maastricht convergence requirements in 2006 including those relating to the government accounts. However, these figures were based on statistical procedures changed by Eurostat in 2004. Applying the new rules would have, according to estimates in the ECB's convergence report, raised the budget deficit to 4.2 per cent and increased the government debt/GDP ratio to 49.3 per cent. The Polish government also foresees problems ahead and has set a target for introduction of the euro of the beginning of 2012. The president has also spoken of holding a referendum on the subject although this is not required. Poland does not have an opt-out from membership of the single currency. In any case, it seems likely that a referendum on euro membership would be carried comfortably.

Bulgaria and Romania have not been the subject of recent ECB convergence reports. Bulgaria has spoken

of a target date of the second half of 2009 or the beginning of 2010 but is not yet a member of ERM II, although the value of its currency (the lev) is fixed to the euro. Remaining outside the euro leaves open the possibility of future devaluations or revaluations. There is as yet no timetable for entry agreed with the ECB. The country clearly has no problem concerning its government accounts since 2006 figures show a 3.3 per cent budget surplus and a government debt/GDP ratio of 22.8 per cent. However, inflation in 2006 was 7.4 per cent although the IMF estimate was for it to fall to 3.6 per cent by 2008. Romania, as one of the two newest members of the EU and as the poorest of the 27 members, also faces severe difficulties in meeting entry criteria and has adopted a more realistic timetable than have some other countries. It plans to join ERM II by 2012 and to join the single currency in 2014. Again, there are no problems with public debt (2006 budget deficit 1.9 per cent; government debt/GDP 12.4 per cent) but it had in 2006 an inflation rate of 6.6 per cent.

Quite apart from the problem of meeting the convergence criterion, countries such as Romania must think carefully about the impact of single currency membership on their underdeveloped economies.

---

[9] *Budapest Business Journal* (BBJ), 'Hungary's euro adoption hinges on economy overhaul', 23 March 2007, http://www.bbj.hu/news/news.

22.6.1 The UK and membership of the euro area

Technically, the UK was not eligible to join the euro area at the beginning of January 1999 because sterling had not been a member of the exchange rate mechanism (ERM) of the EMS for at least two years immediately prior to the establishment of the monetary union (sterling had been in the ERM only from 1990 to 1992). In practice, sterling would almost certainly have been granted membership from January 1999, but the government chose to exercise its opt-out and remain outside. The government had expressed a general willingness to join but only when the necessary conditions for membership to be favourable to the British economy were met.

These conditions were formalized in July 1997 by the then Chancellor of the Exchequer, Gordon Brown, in the form of **five economic tests**. The UK's readiness for membership was then examined by the UK Treasury in terms of these five tests. The exercise was repeated by the Treasury in 2003.

The five economic tests were:

1 Are business cycles and economic structures compatible so that we and others could live comfortably with euro interest rates on a permanent basis?

2 If problems emerge is there sufficient flexibility to deal with them?

3 Would joining EMU create better conditions for firms making long-term decisions to invest in Britain?

4 What impact would entry into EMU have on the competitive position of the UK's financial services industry, particularly the City's wholesale markets?

5 In summary, will joining EMU promote higher growth, stability and a lasting increase in jobs?

Let us consider in turn what each of these involves.

1 *Are business cycles and economic structures compatible so that we and others could live comfortably with euro interest rates on a permanent basis?*

There are three separate issues here:

■ whether external shocks are likely to affect the UK economy in the same way as they do the other EU countries;

■ whether the timing of business cycles in the UK is similar to that in the rest of Europe – if not, the UK economy might require interest rate cuts when other euro area countries require interest rate increases or vice versa;

■ whether the UK economy is sufficiently different from the rest of the EU in other ways – in production, tax, financial and wage-setting systems and in institutional structures – that a change in a common European monetary policy might have a significantly different impact on the UK economy from that experienced by other members.

The October 1997 Treasury assessment of the five tests stressed the crucial nature of business cycle convergence and argued that the timing of the UK business cycle remained significantly different from that of the rest of the EU and that forward-looking measures indicated that significant differences would remain into 1999 and beyond. In the Treasury's second evaluation of the tests, in June 2003, it concluded that significant progress had been made on convergence since 1997 and that UK business cycles were now more convergent with the euro area generally than was the case for some other euro area members. However, concern over structural differences, notably in the housing market, led to the view that, on balance, the test was still not being met. Since convergence is a continuing process, there is likely to be some date in the future when the Treasury will judge that the UK economy is sufficiently integrated with the rest of the euro area to be able to live comfortably with euro interest rates. However, there is a strong element of judgement here and different people view the matter in different ways. It is also possible that membership of the single currency would speed up the process of integration. Further, it is possible that the problem with a single monetary policy for Europe is as much a regional as a national one – that is, if the UK were a member of the single currency area, a particular interest rate decision might suit, say, the regions centred on Paris, Hamburg, Madrid and London but cause unhappiness in the south of Germany, north-east France, the Basque country of Spain, and Scotland. In the debate about UK compatibility with the rest of the euro area, there is probably a tendency to overstate the extent to which all parts of the UK economy are similar. Nonetheless, it is true that interest rate changes can have significantly different impacts on national economies.

2 *If problems emerge is there sufficient flexibility to deal with them?*

This principally concerns the flexibility of the labour market and the ability of the UK economy to withstand economic shocks, including those induced by inappropriate monetary policy decisions, given that the shock could no longer be mitigated by the adjustment of the exchange rate between sterling and the euro. The role of labour market flexibility is not free from controversy. There are two concerns. The first is with the ability of the euro area as a whole to recover from negative economic shocks because of labour market inflexibility arising from government regulations regarding wages, working hours, employer rights to fire workers and, in general, the 'freedom of management to manage'. The EU's concern with social policy and workers' rights is often pointed to as a basic reason for slow EU growth in comparison with growth rates in the USA. The second issue is the lack of labour market mobility across the euro area. It is normally argued that the much greater degree of labour mobility in national economies such as the USA provides a safety valve for regional pressures as labour moves from high to low unemployment areas, helping to balance the unequal impact of asymmetric shocks or policies. Labour mobility might be hampered again by labour market practices as well as by other aspects of social policy and regulations governing the housing market and pensions. It is not clear that the weakening of employment and social policy would have much effect on euro area labour mobility, given the continuing language and cultural differences and lack of information regarding employment opportunities and living conditions across national boundaries. It is also not clear whether greater labour market mobility always has a positive impact.

MORE FROM THE WEB

The full 2003 Treasury assessment of the five economic tests is still available on the Treasury website: http://www.hm-treasury.gov.uk/. Choose 'International issues' on the home page, then 'The Euro' and then 'UK Membership of the Single Currency'. There are also many summaries of the main points at various levels. For a simple summary see, for example, http://www.historylearningsite.co.uk/euro.htm.

The Treasury 2003 evaluation concentrates on UK labour market flexibility, arguing that the slower is the progress on flexibility within the EU, the more important it is to have a high level of labour market flexibility in the UK. It concludes that, although labour market flexibility has increased considerably in the UK since 1997, it is not certain that it has improved sufficiently. Again, this is a matter of judgement.

3 *Would joining EMU create better conditions for firms making long-term decisions to invest in Britain?*

It is difficult to say much about this in advance. Euro interest rates are lower than those in the UK, in part because of the continued presence of an exchange rate risk premium on sterling. It is likely, therefore, that entry into the euro would reduce the cost of capital for UK firms. Small and medium-sized enterprises might also benefit from greater financial integration consequent on membership of the euro area. It is further possible that as foreign direct investment (FDI) in the euro area increases with the single currency, the UK's share of this would fall were it to remain outside for a prolonged period. Indeed, the UK's share of FDI flows into the EU did fall between 1999 and 2003. However, investment decisions of firms are influenced by many factors and we cannot definitely know what would have happened to incoming investment had sterling joined the euro area in 1999. As we have seen in Section 22.5, the UK economy has, in the period of the life of the euro, performed well in terms of GDP growth and unemployment in comparison with the large economies in the euro area, those of Germany, France and Italy and this must have helped to persuade firms to stay in or come to the UK. A period of weakness in the UK economy or a period of sharp growth in, say, France and Germany could easily produce a greater fall in the UK's share of FDI flows irrespective of whether the UK joins the euro area.

Were the UK to join, the question would remain counterfactual since we should not know what would have happened had the UK not joined. We have a certain amount of anecdotal evidence. Several large firms have made it clear that they would prefer the UK to be in the euro area and might possibly relocate from the UK into the euro area if the UK remains outside the single currency for much longer. There have also been some investment decisions in favour of the euro area against the UK that have been said to relate largely to the UK's being outside the area. However, it is hard to judge these statements and actions. Some of the unhappiness on the part of foreign firms with the UK's failure to join the single currency in 1999 has stemmed from the strength of sterling against the euro. Nonetheless, the Treasury evaluation concluded that the quantity and quality of investment in the UK would very likely increase with euro area membership. The Treasury, however, hedges its bets by making this judgement dependent on the assumption that sustainable and durable convergence had been achieved before membership. Thus, the third test becomes subject to the first one, which then assumes greater importance.

4   *What impact would entry into EMU have on the competitive position of the UK's financial services industry, particularly the City's wholesale markets?*

There is no obvious reason why the City of London should benefit from the UK remaining outside the single currency. Thus, the question appears to be whether continued failure to join might cause the City to lose business to Paris or Frankfurt. There is no evidence that this has occurred since January 1999 and it seems likely that the City of London would remain strong in wholesale financial markets whether the UK joined the euro or not. Nonetheless there are probable additional benefits for the financial services industry from membership of the euro area as European financial markets become increasingly integrated through the EU's Financial Services Action Plan. The Treasury, therefore, concluded that this test had been met. Yet it remains difficult to quantify the potential gains here in order to weigh them against other possible losses.

5   *In summary, will joining EMU promote higher growth, stability and a lasting increase in jobs?*

The Treasury 2003 evaluation notes the increase in intra-euro-area trade in recent years and attributes this to the single currency. It concludes, on this basis, that membership of the single currency could lead to a significant increase in UK trade within the euro area and that this, in turn, could lead to a small but sustained increase in potential output. This suggests that membership could help promote higher growth and a lasting increase in jobs. However, this potential growth is outweighed in the Treasury view by the concerns over macroeconomic stability, in particular that it would be harder to maintain stability within the

euro area than outside it. Two particular worries are expressed.

The first of these relates to the monetary policy of the European Central Bank (ECB). It has not been clear from the early years of operation of the ECB precisely what its aim is in relation to inflation. The ECB is charged with maintaining price stability but this is not defined in the Treaty on European Union. The ECB has quantified price stability as an inflation rate below but near to 2 per cent. However, experience suggests that it has been happy with rates between 1 and 3 per cent. Uncertainty over objectives and more general concerns about lack of transparency in ECB monetary policy has translated into worries that monetary policy may be inconsistent and difficult to anticipate. We deal with this issue in detail in Section 23.6.

The second problem arises from the EU's attempt to constrain the fiscal policy freedom of euro area member countries by the application of the **Stability and Growth Pact**. Article 103 of the Treaty on European Union specifies that where the European Council finds economic policies of a member state that endanger the proper functioning of economic and monetary union, it may make policy recommendations to that member's government and may publish them. In all areas other than that of fiscal deficits, members need not accept these recommendations. Article 104c forbids member states to have excessive budget deficits and charges the European Commission with the task of monitoring the budgetary situation and the stock of government debt of member states. The Commission may report to the Council that an excessive deficit exists. The Council may then make policy recommendations that the member state in question *is obliged to follow*. Failure to do so may ultimately lead to the imposition of financial sanctions in the form of a non-interest-bearing deposit or a fine.

Detail was added to this clause by the agreement of the Stability and Growth Pact of 1997, which set out rules for government borrowing of euro area members after January 1999. These rules converted the 3 per cent of GDP limit on budget deficits in the Maastricht convergence conditions into a permanent ceiling that might only be breached under exceptional circumstances. These were defined as a natural disaster or a fall in GDP of at least 2 per cent over a year. This would only occur in a severe recession. In cases where GDP has fallen between 0.75 per cent and

2 per cent in a single year, EU finance ministers have discretion over whether to impose penalties. Members who break the 3 per cent barrier in other circumstances are required to make heavy non-interest-bearing deposits with the European Central Bank. These deposits would be converted into fines should the member's budget deficit remain above the 3 per cent limit. Since there is discretion in the application of fines, it is still unclear to what extent the Stability and Growth Pact will ultimately be enforced. Member countries have been warned and threatened with action but nothing more has yet occurred. Nonetheless, the threat remains.

From a macroeconomic stabilization point of view, the firm application of the pact would make little sense since the fines would make it more difficult for governments to get their borrowing back below 3 per cent of GDP and would very likely require a higher level of unemployment to achieve it. The restriction of fiscal policy in this way would thus remove another element of flexibility in the management of national economies and would increase the costs associated with the loss of freedom to change exchange rates. The UK would like two changes to the interpretation of the pact.

Firstly, it does not see a problem with public sector deficits produced by increases in government investment since successful investment should contribute to future economic growth and permit the repayment of government debt without forcing interest rates up. It would also allow the UK government to continue its current heavy investment programmes in health and education to overcome underinvestment in these areas over many years. Allowing this freedom to break the 3 per cent deficit limit would be in accord with Gordon Brown's 'golden rule' of public finance – that over the economic cycle, the government should borrow only to invest and not to fund current spending. Secondly, the UK argues that governments that do not have a high public debt/GDP ratio should be allowed greater freedom in fiscal policy than those countries that do. That is, the rules should be applied strictly only to member countries with a debt problem. The Treasury concluded in 2003 that if the macroeconomic framework were to change in the direction favoured by the UK, the fifth test would also be passed.

There has been little indication that these views will be accepted. However, after the operation of the Stability and Growth Pact had been effectively suspended in late 2003, when it became clear that France and Germany were unwilling to take the actions needed to return their budget deficits to below the required 3 per cent of GDP, the rules were relaxed in March 2005 and an attempt was made to make the pact more enforceable. In 2007, excessive deficit procedures were still continuing against 7 of the 27 EU members but sanctions had yet to be taken against a member country.

We thus have some tests passed and some not. As one would expect, joining a single currency area at any time would carry with it some economic advantages and some disadvantages. However, the Treasury plainly does not see the exercise as one of weighing these up. One of the five tests – the first, relating to economic convergence – turns out to be more important than the others. We have seen that the Treasury's view that the UK currently fails this test was one of judgement, rather than of clear-cut fact. It follows that there is little possibility that at any time in the future membership will be 'clearly and unambiguously' to the UK's economic advantage. This is hardly surprising since little economic analysis of future events produces 'clear and unambiguous' support for anything.

The problem, then, with the five economic tests is that they are sufficiently open to interpretation that the decision when to hold a referendum on membership remains much more likely to be decided by political factors. There is nothing, of course, inherently wrong with this since there can be little doubt that the single currency is to a significant extent a political project and political advantages of greater European integration should not be left out of the equation.

Quite apart from the five economic tests, there is a severe political problem associated with UK membership of the euro. The UK has always been the member country most sceptical of the benefits of deeper integration across the EU and the most fearful of the ideas of federation and political union in Europe. This has been strongly translated into opposition against UK membership of the euro area and it seems very unlikely that any referendum put to the British people in the foreseeable future on the subject of membership of the euro area would be passed. Indeed, it is sufficiently improbable to discourage UK governments from holding a referendum on the question. In addition, the current Prime Minister, Gordon Brown, the inventor and long-time custodian of the five economic tests, has always seemed personally very dubious about the benefits of euro membership for the UK. The Conservative Party, the principal Opposition party, has, despite strong internal differences of opinion in the past, remained opposed to UK membership and so UK membership seems an increasingly distant prospect. This view is reinforced by the fact that there has been no suggestion that a new assessment of the five economic tests be undertaken by the UK Treasury in the near future and no Treasury statement on the issue since the publication of the 2003 report. European issues and UK membership of the euro have now disappeared from the home page of the Treasury's website and been incorporated under the broad heading of 'International Issues'.

22.7   Summary

There have always been strong political and economic motives behind the desire to move to monetary union. The need for closer monetary integration only became urgent, however, with the breakdown of the fixed exchange rate Bretton Woods system from the late 1960s on. Plans to move to a single currency by 1980 came to nothing and the fixed exchange rate system established in 1972, the Snake, failed. The European Monetary System (EMS) was established in 1979 to attempt to limit exchange rate uncertainty within the EU. After some difficult years, the system appeared to be settling down. This, together with the passing of the Single European Act in 1986, encouraged hopes for a renewed attempt to move to monetary union. The Delors Report recommended a three-stage process for achieving economic and monetary union and this was confirmed at the Maastricht conference in December 1991, with 1 January 1999 being set as the latest date by which monetary union must occur.

Optimism about monetary union was badly dented by the major currency disturbances of 1992 and 1993 which led to sterling and the lira being suspended from membership of the exchange rate mechanism of the EMS and to the bands within which currencies were allowed to move within the mechanism being dramatically widened. Despite this, a strong determination to achieve monetary union remained on the part of the European Commission and of several governments. As the starting date became closer, however, doubts arose about the ability of many governments, most importantly those of Germany and France, to meet the conditions for the single currency membership laid down at Maastricht. In the event, 11 countries were allowed to join the single currency, the euro, which was established on schedule at the beginning of January 1999. Greece became the twelfth member at the beginning of 2001, Slovenia joined from the beginning of 2007 and Cyprus and Malta from the beginning of 2008.

Most discussion of the performance of the euro during its early years was concentrated on the falling value of the euro, especially against the US dollar but concerns about this disappeared as the euro commenced a long period of appreciation against the US dollar. In other ways, the establishment of the euro has been argued to have been a success, especially to the extent that its existence has helped the EU to reap more fully the benefits of the Single European Market. Nonetheless, doubts about the benefits of membership have remained strong in the three members of the EU15 which have chosen to remain outside the euro area – Denmark, Sweden and the UK – and there seems no prospect that any of the three will join in the near future.

On the other hand, all 12 countries that have joined the EU since 2004 are committed to joining the euro area under the terms of their accession to the EU and all have expressed a desire to do so as soon as possible. However, many have problems in meeting the convergence conditions for membership established by the Maastricht Treaty. By early 2008, three of the twelve had become part of the single currency but entry for the others seems likely to be spread out over many years with no further expansion in membership occurring before 2010.

The UK government was in favour of membership in principle but had committed itself to a referendum to be held only after five economic tests laid down by the Treasury could be judged to have been met. The UK Treasury judged in 2003 that the tests had not at that time been met and there is no indication that a further assessment is being planned in the near future. Political and popular opposition to UK membership of the single currency makes it unlikely that anything will happen for some years.

Key concepts in this chapter

Central rates
Convergence
Euro area
Exchange Rate Mechanism (ERM)
Five economic tests
Government financial position

Monetary integration
Monetary union
Parity grid
Price transparency
Snake in the Tunnel
Stability and Growth Pact

Questions and problems

1 Explain the reasoning behind each of the Maastricht convergence conditions.

2 What were the *economic reasons* for wanting monetary integration in Europe?

3 Consider the argument that monetary union was a necessary extension of the European single market.

4 Why was it important that Germany should be a member of the European single currency?

5 Why did Denmark, Sweden and the UK choose to stay outside the single currency when it was established? Were the reasons the same in each case?

6 Consider the difficulties in coming to a conclusion on each of the UK Treasury's five economic tests for membership of the single currency.

7 What are the advantages and disadvantages of having a weakening currency?

8 What problems might economies such as those of Romania and Bulgaria face if they join the single currency too soon?

Further reading

L S Copeland, *Exchange Rates and International Finance* (Harlow: FT Prentice Hall, 4e, 2004) Ch. 11
P De Grauwe, *The Economics of Monetary Integration* (Oxford: Oxford University Press, 6e, 2005)
HM Treasury, *UK Membership of the Single Currrency: An Assessment of the Five Economic Tests* (London: HM Treasury, October 1997)
HM Treasury, *UK Membership of the Single Currrency: An Assessment of the Five Economic Tests*, Cm 5776 (London: HM Treasury, June 2003)

Websites

www.ecb.int/home
http://epp.eurostat.ec.europa.eu/portal
www.eui.eu/RSCAS/Research/Eurohomepage/
http://europa.eu/index_en.htm
http://fx.sauder.ubc.ca/euro/
www.historylearningsite.co.uk/euro.htm
www.hm-treasury.gov.uk
www.imf.org/
www.oberlin.edu/faculty/dcleeton/s
http://specials.ft.com/euro/index.html

Chapter 23 The European Central Bank and euro area monetary policy

What you will learn in this chapter:

- The possible forms of determining monetary policy in a monetary union

- The reasons for making the ECB politically independent

- The reasons for concern about the size of the budget deficits of EMU members

- The rules governing the European Central Bank and its operations

- The way in which euro area monetary policy has been practised since 1999

- The nature of the questions to be resolved concerning post-EMU monetary policy

23.1 Introduction

In a **currency area** with completely fixed exchange rates *and* full freedom of capital flows, there must be a **common monetary policy**. Imagine that each member of such an area tried to operate its own monetary policy. Suppose that one member decided to have a tighter monetary policy than the rest. As soon as it raised interest rates, capital would flow into the country from other member states. This must happen since, with completely fixed exchange rates, there would be no foreign exchange risk and so no distinction between covered and uncovered interest parity. Capital would move until interest rates were again the same in all member states. Exactly where the common interest rate finished up would depend on the monetary policies and relative strengths of the member states, but there would be only one interest rate for the area as a whole.

But how should the common monetary policy be determined? There are two possible models:

1 the *asymmetric leadership model*: one country's monetary policy dominates those of other members and effectively becomes the monetary policy for the entire area;

2 the *joint-decision model*: governments or central banks of member countries meet together and decide upon the common monetary policy through discussion and compromise.

This leaves us to ask who becomes the leader in the asymmetric leadership model. Again there are two possibilities:

1 that the system is organized around one currency which thus necessarily becomes the leader – this was the case with the US dollar in the Bretton Woods fixed exchange rate system;

2 that a currency becomes the leader because the market and other governments feel that it is most likely to retain its value – this is likely to be the currency which is thought likely to have, over a run of years, the lowest average rate of inflation since, within a fixed exchange rate system, higher rates of inflation will quickly make a country's goods uncompetitive in international markets.

If exchange rates are not fully fixed and/or if there are effective controls on the flow of capital, member countries may be able to determine their own monetary policies to a considerable extent. We have seen that, apart from the five years between 1987 and 1992, the EMS was not a fully fixed exchange rate system. Even between 1987 and 1992, the possibility of changes in central rates was sufficiently powerful that there was very little change over the period in foreign exchange risk premiums. Equally, up until 1990, many members still had capital controls in place. Thus members had some freedom over their own monetary policies. Nonetheless, it is generally accepted that the Deutschmark was the leading currency within the system and that German monetary policy had a quite strong influence on the policies of other countries. Why was this so?

Firstly, Germany had, over a long period, built up a reputation as a low-inflation country. It was also the biggest and most powerful economy in the system. Secondly, it was believed that its institutional arrangements were such that it would go on delivering low inflation into the future. That is, its monetary policy was run by its central bank, the *Bundesbank*, which was constitutionally independent of the democratic political process. Further, the control of inflation was the major, although not the only, objective set down in the *Bundesbank*'s constitution (the significance of these points is explained in Section 14.6. and the general arguments for and against the independence of central banks is summarized in Box 23.1).

The importance given to this institutional arrangement was seen in the period immediately after German unification. The way in which the West and East German monetary systems were unified, combined with the unwillingness of the German government to raise tax rates to pay for the inevitable increase in government expenditure following reunification, led to a temporary increase in inflation above the levels normally associated with Germany. Given the severe difficulties faced by the inefficient industry of the old East Germany, there would have been a strong temptation for any government in control of monetary policy to run an easy, low interest rate policy to encourage investment and expansion. The financial markets were confident, however, that the *Bundesbank* would not follow such a policy. Thus, although French inflation was lower than German inflation for some time, there was no great switch of funds from DMs to French francs. The markets held to the view that the DM was still the more trustworthy currency in the medium to

---

BOX 23.1 The independence of central banks and the rate of inflation

In Section 14.6, we have examined the arguments for the view that central banks should be independent of the democratic political process. These depend on the existence of a close association between the degree of independence of central banks and low rates of inflation. The argument depends on a number of contentious theoretical and empirical points which we summarize here:

FOR

1 Democratic political systems are inflationary and do not take the long-run costs of expansionary policies fully into account because:

  (a) politicians aim to maximize votes;
  (b) voters believe that expansionary policy reduces unemployment;
  (c) there is no long-run trade-off between inflation and unemployment.

2 Independent central bankers can precommit themselves credibly to a low-inflation policy rule in the way that governments cannot because:

  (a) central bankers do not face re-election;
  (b) it is known that governments benefit from inflation through seigniorage – the gains which accrue to the issuer of a currency because it obtains real resources in return for non-interest-bearing, non-repayable debt.

3 Empirical evidence appears to show a relationship between the degree of central bank independence and low rates of inflation.

AGAINST

1 The apparent empirical relationship is suspect because it depends on a subjective assessment of the degree of independence of central banks.

2 Even if there is a statistical relationship, this does not prove causality. Other factors may be responsible for low inflation. Thus, low German inflation may have been due to:

  (a) the system of universal banking which is lending-based rather than securities-based;
  (b) the separation of prudential supervision of the banking system from monetary policy;
  (c) the federal system of government;
  (d) Germany's historical experience of high inflation;
  (e) the form of organization of labour markets in Germany.

3 Removal of the control of monetary policy from the democratic system has income redistribution effects: favouring those who benefit from low inflation, notably the financial sector, at the expense of the rest of the population.

---

long term. This is an example of the importance of a central bank's reputation (see Section 14.6).

A full monetary union with a single currency must, *a fortiori*, have a common monetary policy since the possibility, which must continue to exist in any fixed exchange rate system, that exchange rate parities might be changed, is completely removed. The question still remains as to how that monetary policy will be determined. Placing the operation of policy in the hands of a single, supranational central bank such as the **European Central Bank (ECB)**, does not determine what that bank's monetary policy should be. The policy could be decided either by member governments or by central bankers or by a combination of both. For a country such as Germany, used to both low inflation and a politically independent central bank, there was a serious concern here – that the inclusion in

the monetary union of countries with a record of high inflation and/or current economic problems would provide incentives to operate a loose monetary policy. Thus, a monetary policy decided by discussion and compromise would have been weaker and more inflationary than the existing German policy.

One solution was to apply strict entry conditions designed to keep such countries out of the union *and* to introduce rules that would carry those strict conditions through into policy after the formation of the monetary union (the Stability and Growth Pact). However, the case for monetary union was at least as strongly political as economic and it did not make political sense to restrict membership to a small number of countries with a history of low inflation. In any case, in a period of impending national elections, any government, whatever the country's past inflation performance, might be tempted to ease monetary policy. As we have noted in Section 14.6, the obvious answer to this was to model the European Central Bank on the *Bundesbank*, making it independent of all member governments and establishing for it a constitution that stressed the objective of low inflation. This was what was proposed in the Maastricht Treaty.

Before looking at the nature of the European Central Bank, however, we need to consider rather more closely the problems that this structure was meant to counter.

23.2 Inflation, exchange rate and default risk in monetary union

The concern with inflation had a number of sources. One stemmed from conventional economic theory. The majority of economists had, by the early 1980s, come to accept a model of the economy in which government attempts to expand the economy through monetary and fiscal policy would lead both to higher inflation and, in the long run, to increased unemployment. Low inflation was thus seen as a prerequisite for future economic growth. The evidence for this proposition was weak but the most successful European economy, that of Germany, had had low inflation over a long period. Thus, it was felt that, although there might be high short-run costs in terms of higher unemployment in getting inflation down, these would be outweighed by the long-run benefits of low inflation.

The current economic theory also taught that the most important element in becoming a low-inflation economy was to establish anti-inflation credibility – that is, to convince the markets that the government was serious in its determination to reduce inflation and to keep it low. If a government could do this, it was held, the short-run costs of producing low inflation would be much reduced. One way of trying to achieve this anti-inflation credibility was to link the economy to low-inflation Germany in a fixed exchange rate system dominated by German monetary policy. This explained the significance of the determination expressed in the Maastricht conditions for convergence on a *low* rate of inflation.

At least two other elements entered the picture as seen by Germany. The first was historical. Even in the 1990s, the folk memory of the economic, social and political devastation wrought by the very high German inflation of the early 1920s appeared to be strong. Probably of greater importance, however, was the understandable fear of savers in a low-inflation economy that the real value of their savings would be rapidly eroded by high future inflation. This fear was given apparent credence by the behaviour of the financial markets which assumed that post-union monetary policy would be weaker than the existing German policy. From the early 1990s, this assumption was built into long-term German interest rates, with the yield curve rising sharply for maturities beyond 1999. Thus, for Germany, the crucial economic issue became the external value of the single currency after 1999.

The Maastricht convergence condition regarding the government financial position was, in part, related to the desire to produce and maintain low inflation since there was concern that heavily indebted governments would have an additional incentive to push for an expansionary common monetary policy, since a low interest rate would reduce the interest burden upon them and a higher inflation rate would reduce the real value of their debt. However, there was an extra question – the possibility of individual governments attempting to act as free riders. The potential difficulty arose because a monetary union does not require a common fiscal policy. Indeed, to have a fully common fiscal policy requires a high degree of political as well as economic integration.

Members of the monetary union would thus be free to set their own budgets and determine their own budget deficits. With monetary policy in the hands of the European Central Bank they would not be able to finance those deficits by borrowing from their own central banks as in the past; but they would still be able to issue and sell their own government securities. In the monetary union, these securities would be denominated in euros. With no foreign exchange risk, heavily indebted countries would be able to sell their debt at a lower interest rate than previously.

Further, the market for euro-denominated bonds would be so large that individual countries in a large monetary union might hope to increase the budget deficit and finance this by selling additional government securities without causing interest rates to rise. A previously existing constraint on fiscal policy would have been removed. But if several countries behaved in this way, the outcome would be a significant increase in the total amount of the government debt of euro area countries on the market, with the consequence that interest rates across the union would be forced up. Governments with tight fiscal policies would have to accept part of the burden of their more freely spending partners in the form of higher interest rates or support an easier monetary policy from the European Central Bank, with the associated risk of higher inflation.

There was yet another issue. Prior to monetary union, the interest rate on a country's government securities reflected default risk as well as foreign exchange risk. Indeed, where governments attempted to remove the element of foreign exchange risk by denominating their debt in a foreign currency, the credit-rating agencies often attached a lower credit rating to the debt, signalling to the market that the interest rate paid on that debt should reflect a higher default risk. Thus, there was a second constraint on government fiscal policy. If they allowed their indebtedness to grow too large, the credit agencies would lower the credit rating of the government and force the government to pay higher interest rates on their debt, making it more likely that total indebtedness would continue to grow. It was possible to construct a model in which a country's total government debt might grow explosively. Governments could, thus, not afford to allow the market's assessment of their default risk to become too high.

But what would happen to default risk after monetary union? It was arguable that prior to union an Italian default on part of its public debt would have very little impact on any other country. On the other hand, the default of a member of a monetary union on debt payments in the single currency might easily have a spillover effect on market confidence in other euro-denominated debt. Hence it was widely assumed that the European Central Bank would not be prepared to allow any of the monetary union members to become, in effect, bankrupt – that it would be bound to step in and **bail out** the country in trouble with a consequent increase in the money supply and the risk of greater inflation. The impact of a country believing that it was bound to be bailed out would be to remove also the constraint on its spending imposed by default risk. If the markets believed that any member would be bailed out by the European Central Bank, the relevant credit rating for any euro-denominated debt would be the credit rating of the European Central Bank itself.

This would give free-spending governments total freedom to go on spending and it might also lower the

credit rating of the European Central Bank, again causing interest rates on all euro-denominated debt to rise. Monetary union would give governments a clear incentive to operate expansionary fiscal policies. Any country that chose not to do so would not obtain the benefits of increased public expenditure but would incur costs as a result of the expansionary policies of other member governments. This possibility explains the importance attached to the government financial position in the Maastricht convergence conditions and to the Stability and Growth Pact.

23.3 Monetary institutions and policy in the single currency area

Monetary policy in the single currency area is conducted by the **European System of Central Banks (ESCB)**, consisting of the European Central Bank (ECB) and the national central banks of the member states. The ESCB is governed by the Governing Council and the Executive Board of the ECB. To ensure the independence of the ESCB from both the European Commission and the governments of the member states, the national central banks, although continuing to be owned by their governments, were also required to become independent of the political process in their own countries.

Article 105(2) of the Treaty on European Union set the ESCB four basic tasks:

1 to define and implement monetary policy of the Community;

2 to conduct foreign exchange operations;

3 to hold and manage the official foreign exchange reserves of the member states; and

4 to promote the smooth operation of payments systems.

Remember from Section 14.6 that the link between central bank independence and low inflation requires a 'conservative' independent central bank and that one way of creating and maintaining a conservative policy outlook is to oblige the independent central bank to place more weight on inflation than on output by ranking policy objectives and ensuring that all other objectives are subsidiary to low inflation.

Article 105(1) of the Treaty thus established the primary objective of the ESCB as the maintenance of **price stability**. The ESCB was also enjoined, *without* *prejudice to the goal of price stability*, to support the EU's general economic policies and to act in accordance with the principle of an open market economy with free competition, favouring an efficient allocation of resources. The general economic policies of the EC are stated in Article 2 of the Treaty as being 'to promote throughout the Community a harmonious and balanced development of economic activities, sustainable and non-inflationary growth respecting the environment, a high degree of convergence of economic performance, a high level of employment and social protection, the raising of the standard of living and quality of life, and economic and social cohesion and solidarity among Member States'. Article 3a further requires that in attempting to achieve all of this, member states and the Community should comply with the guiding principles of stable prices, sound public finances and monetary conditions, and a sustainable balance of payments. This gave the ESCB a set of objectives similar to those of the *Bundesbank*, which was obliged by law to safeguard the currency while supporting the general economic policy of the German Federal Government.

Although pursuit of general economic policy objectives is not meant to prejudice the achievement of price stability, there is clearly scope for interpretation under circumstances in which an apparent conflict exists between tightening monetary policy and one or more of the general objectives. 'Price stability', after all, does not necessarily mean the lowest possible level of inflation. Indeed, with a central bank composed of people from a number of countries with different economic conditions and problems, one might expect a range of interpretations of price stability. Nonetheless, control of inflation is clearly intended to be central. Further, the objective of low inflation is statutorily protected since the ESCB's objectives can only be changed by the unanimous decision of the Council of Ministers. The European Parliament has no influence on the objectives of monetary policy.

The possibility of the system's objectives being interpreted in different ways makes the issue of the composition of the ECB extremely important and raises the question of how to ensure the political independence of the decision makers within the system. Box 23.2 sets out a number of factors widely accepted as relevant to the degree of political independence of a central bank. The ECB does generally very well on these criteria.

The Executive Board of the ECB, which runs the bank, comprises a president, vice-president and four other members appointed by the heads of state on a recommendation from the European Council after

---

MORE FROM THE WEB

It is always worth knowing something about the people in charge of economic policy as well as the dry rules governing the composition of boards and committees. The ECB provides a picture of the Governing Council of the ECB so that in 2007 you were able to see that it was composed of 18 men in suits and one woman. There is a zoom facility so that you can have a close up view of their smiling faces. Try http://www.ecb.int/ecb/orga/decisions/govc/html/membersgcbig.en.html. Further down the page you will find individual photos and the curriculum vitae of the six Executive Board members on the Governing Council. To find more about the national central bank governors you will need to consult each central bank's website (see 'Links' on the ECB's home page for addresses). For example, for the Governor of the Bank of Finland (in 2007 Erkki Liikanen) see http://www.bof.fi/en, click on 'Bank of Finland' and 'Bank of Finland's Board'.

BOX 23.2 Features important in determining the independence of a central bank

1 Statutory guarantees of independence or non-interference

2 The existence of statutory objectives for the central bank and the nature of those objectives

3 The methods of appointment and removal of the governor, senior officers and the board of directors

4 The length of the governor's term of office

5 The presence or absence of government officials on the bank's board

6 The extent to which the bank is bound by instructions from the government and the range of instruments at the bank's disposal

7 The limits on central financing of the government

8 The ease with which any of the above features can be altered by government

consultation with the European Parliament and the Governing Council of the ESCB. All six members are required to be 'persons of recognized standing and professional experience in monetary or banking matters'. In other words, they should be representatives from the world of finance, making it very likely that their interpretation of 'price stability' will be conservative.

The term of office for Executive Board members is eight years and is non-renewable. Members of the Executive Board may be compulsorily retired but only for 'misconduct', which is defined to include the taking of instructions from a member government. Compulsory retirement can only be achieved through the European Court of Justice on the application of the ECB Council or the Executive Board. Governors of national central banks must be appointed for at least five years and may end their terms prematurely only for serious cause, notified either by themselves or the ECB council. That is, they cannot be removed by their own national governments. The long and non-renewable term is meant to avoid the possibility of Board members following the wishes of governments in the hope of being reappointed to their positions.

The Governing Council consists of the Executive Board plus the governors of the national central banks. Thus, the membership rose to 21 with the entry of Cyprus and Malta to the monetary union at the beginning of 2008. Voting, on all issues except those related to the bank's capital, is on a one-person one-vote basis, with decision by simple majority. This makes it possible for the representatives of the national central banks to outvote the Executive Board members on the Governing Council and for the smaller members to outvote large members such as Germany on all issues other than those related to the ECB's capital. This provided an extra reason for the insistence that the national central banks be politically independent.

The number of members of the Governing Council with voting rights will be capped at the present number of 21: six permanent voting rights for the members of the Executive Board and 15 voting rights for the Governors of national central banks. When there are more than 15 member states and thus more than 21 members of the Governing Council, voting rights for the Governors will be allocated on the basis of a rotation system (see Box 23.3). All members will have the right to attend and to speak.

Where the bank's capital is involved, voting power is proportional to the member states' subscribed capital and the Executive Board has no votes. The subscribed capital, in turn, is determined by equal weighting of (1) the member states' shares of the population and (2) GDP at market prices, averaged over the previous five years. Subscriptions are to be revised every five years.

The ECB is responsible for the note issue, open market operations, the setting of minimum reserve requirements and other aspects of monetary control but can make use of the national central banks to carry out open market operations. The ECB supplies liquidity to the banking system subject to the availability of 'adequate collateral' (Statute, Article 18). However, in an attempt to overcome the potential problems discussed in Section 23.2, the ESCB is not permitted to lend to governments except through the acquisition of their paper in the secondary market. Overdraft or other credit facilities by the ECB or national central banks to any EU or member state public body are explicitly prohibited by Article 104 of the Treaty.

To strengthen the control of high-spending member governments, the Maastricht Treaty forbad **excessive government deficits** and the '**bailing out**' of indebted member governments by EU governments or institutions. This should mean that member governments continue to face default risk with the consequence that bond issues of different governments should continue to carry different rates of interest to reflect the market's assessment of the default risk associated with each government's debt issue.

In practice, this has not occurred.[1] There are three possible reasons for this. Firstly, the financial markets might not believe that the 'no bail out' rule would apply if a member did default on its loans. Secondly, the worry about countries running large budget deficits in a monetary union might have been unjustified because of their inability to finance these deficits through monetary expansion. Thirdly, the exercise of the Stability and Growth Pact together with the power granted by the Maastricht Treaty to the European Council to monitor economic developments in each of the member states might have been effective in persuading high spending countries to keep a tight control of their budgets.

---

[1] See Table 21.2.

BOX 23.3 The voting rotation system for the ECB Governing Council

When the number of national central bank governors rises above 15, the votes of the governors will be limited to 15. The six Executive Board members will always retain their independent votes. The allocation of votes to the central bank governors will require them to be divided into groups. When the number of governors is between 16 and 22, there will be two groups, the central bank governors of the five largest member states will form the first group with country size being determined by the member state's share of the euro area's aggregate GDP at market prices (given 5/6 weighting in the calculation) and the member state's share of the euro area's total aggregated balance sheets of the monetary financial institutions (given 1/6 weighting). The remaining governors will form group 2. Thus, if there are 20 member states, 5 will be in group 1 and 15 in group 2. Group 1 governors will have 4 votes and thus each group 1 governor will be able to vote at 4 of every 5 meetings. Group 2 governors will have 11 votes. Thus, with 20 governors on the Governing Council, 4 will miss out at each meeting. Each governor will vote at 73.3 per cent of all meetings. There is, however, a problem when there are 16–18 governors as following the rules above would mean that the five biggest countries would vote less often than the smaller ones – and this the five biggest countries would not like at all. Indeed, it is specified in the amendment to Article 10.2 of the Statute of the European System of Central Banks and of the ECB approved in March 2003 that the 'frequency of voting rights of the governors allocated to the first group shall not be lower than the frequency of voting rights of those of the second group'. Thus, if Slovakia succeeds in joining the euro area in 2009, bringing the number of governors to 16, there will need to be an adjustment to the rules.

When the number of governors goes above 22, things become more complex. Then there will be three groups: Group 1 with the 5 largest countries as members as before; Group 2 with a membership of half the total number of governors (rounded up); Group 3 consisting of the remaining governors (of the smallest countries).

With 23 member states and therefore 23 governors on the Governing Council, there will be 5 members in Group 1, 12 in Group 2 and 6 in Group 3. With 24 governors, the numbers will be 5, 12 and 7. Group 1 will have four votes, group 2 eight votes and group 3 three votes.

For a discussion of this method of rationing votes and of various alternatives see: Katrin Ullrich, 'Decision-making of the ECB: reform and voting power', Discussion Paper no. 04-70, ZEW, Centre for European Economic Research, September, 2004, http://opus. zbw-kiel.de/volltexte/2004/2358/pdf/dp0470.pdf.

The Maastricht Treaty separated the operation of monetary policy from the **prudential supervision** of credit institutions and the stability of the financial system. The latter remains the responsibility of the member states, although the ESCB is expected to ensure the smooth conduct of policies relating to prudential supervision and the ECB may, with the unanimous approval of the European Council and the approval of the European Parliament, be given specific tasks in this area (Article 105.6). In general, this conforms to the German model in which prudential supervision was not carried out by the *Bundesbank* but by the separate *Aufsichtsamt* (the Federal Banking Supervisory Office). The UK also changed to this arrangement with the independence of the Bank of England in 1997 when the supervisory role was taken away from the Bank of England and given to the Financial Services Authority (FSA).

Any attempt to place significant power in the hands of an unelected body such as the ECB raises the question of the **accountability** of that body to governments and, ultimately, to the citizens of the member states. Accountability under the Maastricht Treaty is weak, as seemed bound to be the case where the aim was to prevent as far as is possible the contamination of the central bank by the attitudes and policies of the democratic political system. What accountability there is takes a number of forms. Firstly, the ECB is subject to audit and is under the jurisdiction of the Court of Justice. Secondly, the President of the European Council and a member of the European Commission are allowed to attend meetings of the Governing Council of the ECB but are not allowed to vote. Thirdly, the ECB is required to report annually on its activities to the Council and the European Parliament and the President and other members of the Executive Board are heard by the relevant committees of the Parliament at either side's request.

The aim of these regulations was to create a strongly independent central bank. Indeed, it is, in a sense, more politically independent than the *Bundesbank* itself. One argument given for this view is that when the *Bundesbank* and the German government held different views regarding economic policy, the *Bundesbank* had a single and united opponent which was able to point to its electoral support. Within the monetary union, the counterpart of the German government is a group of governments which may have different political persuasions and whose countries may be experiencing different economic problems. Consequently, there is unlikely to be a single united political view to contrast with that of the Executive Board of the ECB.

In addition, the *Bundesbank* central council included the 11 presidents of the German *Länder* (regions) and this regional representation probably kept the *Bundesbank* more in touch with the real problems of the economy than is the case with the General Council of the ECB.

And yet, despite all of the attempts to preserve the political independence of the ECB, to enforce strict convergence conditions for membership and forbid loose budgetary policies, the view of both the financial markets and leading economists prior to the establishment of the single currency was that the euro, in the long term, would be a weak currency. One basis for this view was that the high proportion of intra-EU trade of monetary union members would mean that the EU would, like the USA, be a substantially closed economic area with its external trade possibly making up considerably less than 20 per cent of GDP. This, it was held, would cause the ECB to be less concerned about the external value of the euro than the *Bundesbank* was about the DM and more likely to behave like the US Federal Reserve – pursuing internal price stability but being largely indifferent to the impact of the exchange rate on foreign trade. This would make it more open to pressures for weaker monetary policy in order to stimulate economic growth, particularly given the slow growth and high rates of unemployment in much of the EU in the late 1990s. A supporting argument was that the euro, as a broader-based reserve currency than the DM, would be less likely to be driven artificially high on occasions.

23.4 The form of monetary policy in the euro area

Several issues relating to the operation of policy needed to be settled in advance of 1999. There were three principal issues:

- the interpretation of the phrase 'price stability';
- whether to target the inflation rate directly or to target an intermediate variable such as the rate of growth of the money supply;
- the choice of the policy instrument.

The definition of price stability

The ECB made its own interpretation of price stability, referring to it as a 'quantitative definition of price stability' rather than as a target because the Bank denies that it is engaged in inflation targeting (ECB, 2001). However, we are also told that the quantitative definition 'provides a yardstick against which the public can hold the ECB accountable' (ECB, 2001, p. 38) and that:

> The ECB is required to provide an explanation for sustained deviations from this definition and to clarify how price stability will be re-established within an acceptable period of time.
>
> ECB, 2001, p. 38.

This makes it sound close enough to a target for us to use the word. The Governing Council of the ECB announced a definition of price stability as a 'year-on-year increase in the **Harmonised Index of Consumer Prices (HICP)** for the euro area of below 2%'.[2] This was qualified to make clear that 'prolonged declines in the level of the HICP index, would not be deemed consistent with price stability'.[3] This implied a medium-term range of 0 to 2 per cent but left open the possibility of the rate of inflation falling below zero in the short run and of being very close to zero even in the medium term. This caused concern that the policy might be too strict, particularly given the problems surrounding the use of price indices in general and the HICP in particular. According to Eurostat, the

---

[2] European Central Bank, 'The stability-oriented monetary policy strategy of the Eurosystem', *Monthly Bulletin*, January 1999, 39–50, p. 46.
[3] ibid.

statistics bureau of the EU, the HICP takes account of the latest economic research. However, national price indices are probably more likely to overestimate inflation than the reverse; the same is likely to be true of the HICP. Early practice with, from June 2000, the inflation rate spending much time at or above 2 per cent calmed these worries and then in May 2003 the ECB's Governing Council eased the Bank's statement of the meaning of price stability to:

> The primary objective of the ECB's monetary policy is to maintain price stability. The ECB aims at inflation rates of below, but close to, 2% over the medium term.

This is the statement one now finds on the monetary policy page of the Bank's website. It differs from the 2 per cent target faced by the Bank of England in two ways. Firstly, inflation rates slightly below 2 per cent are clearly regarded as preferable to those slightly above 2 per cent. Secondly, the use of the phrase 'over the medium term' introduces an element of doubt regarding the judgement of current performance. The arrangement in the UK is straightforward – an inflation rate more than 1 per cent above or below the target is regarded as a failure requiring the Monetary Policy Committee to explain what has gone wrong and what it intends to do about it. The ECB is under no such pressure to explain deviations from the 'near 2 per cent inflation' definition of inflation it faces.

This greater vagueness in the ECB's case is understandable for two obvious reasons, the first deriving from the problems of operating a monetary policy for a large number of countries. Plainly, a low inflation rate calculated across a number of economies might well involve falling prices in some national economies and this needs to be taken into account in making an assessment of the meaning of the measured inflation rate for all economies. An inflation rate for the euro area of, say, 1.8 per cent is not likely to be acceptable if it is associated with deflation in some member states. This problem is complicated by any doubts attached to the accuracy of the HICP.

A rather different problem derives from the fact that the HICP is a measure of headline inflation. That is, the measure is influenced by all factors including external shocks, even if these have only short-term effects, and policy changes, although they might be intended to reduce longer-term inflationary pressure. This contrasts with the idea of framing the inflation target in terms of core or underlying inflation which seeks to measure sustained domestic inflationary

pressure. The use of a headline rate leaves an element of uncertainty as to how the central bank is likely to react to an external shock.

The ECB has argued that it retains a degree of flexibility because its concern is with medium-term inflationary trends, but this leaves open the question of the length of the medium term. It has defended the choice of a quantitative definition of price stability as a means of providing both accountability and transparency in monetary policy. However, the greater the degree of flexibility in interpretation of its objective that the ECB allows itself, however understandable this is, the less transparent is its monetary policy and the more uncertain financial markets are likely to be about the basis of ECB decisions.

23.4.1 Intermediate or final target?

The ECB had to decide whether simply to target the ultimate objective – the achievement of a low inflation rate – or to choose an intermediate target through which it would hope to control the rate of inflation. The likely intermediate target was some measure of the money supply.

We have seen in Chapters 12 and 13 that there is no possibility of, or justification for, using the money supply as an instrument of policy, but the use of a money supply intermediate target was defended by a number of economists at the time of the establishment of the ECB and its approach to monetary policy.

The argument related to the length of time lags. The full effects of a change in short-term interest rates on the rate of inflation might not be felt for two years or longer. If we add in the numerous exogenous influences on the rate of inflation, it is easy to see the difficulties facing central banks. As we have seen in Chapter 14, the central bank will seek additional information about the performance of the economy and the inflationary pressure present in the economy to help it make its judgements regarding adjustments in the interest rate. One idea still popular in 1998 was that of establishing an intermediate target which responded more quickly to interest rate changes than the rate of inflation itself and which had fewer external influences upon it. An intermediate target is only useful, however, if it is stably related to the instrument and to the final target.

A variety of intermediate targets have been proposed including the rate of growth of the money supply.

Clearly, the time lag between changes in short-term interest rates and changes in the rate of growth of the money supply are relatively short and there are fewer exogenous influences upon the money supply than on the inflation rate itself or on other intermediate targets proposed such as changes in the level of aggregate demand. However, the use of an intermediate money supply target would only make sense if there were a stable short-run demand function for money. In the UK, the short-run money demand function had been manifestly unstable over the 20 years before 1998 and the use of a money supply target in the UK had been abandoned very quickly. Germany, on the other hand, had continued to specify a target for broad money. Although, in practice, the *Bundesbank* had appeared to pay at least as much attention to the rate of inflation itself as to the broad money target, it had continued to recommend the use of a broad money target for the ECB. This was despite the existence of evidence that in the second half of the 1990s, the German demand for money function was starting to become unstable because of financial liberalization and increased financial innovation in Germany. As well as causing short-term instability in the demand for money function, financial liberalization had made it harder for central banks to control the money supply because it had become harder to influence relative interest rates between money and other financial assets.

This meant that there were sufficient uncertainties to make it inadvisable to depend on a single measure of the money supply as an intermediate target. A money supply target could have been based on past relationships between the money supply and inflation or on the basis of a model of the economy of the monetary union but there was a serious possibility that it would be of little use in making monetary policy decisions. In addition, a failure to achieve the single money supply target would have added to the uncertainty regarding the strength of the ECB's monetary policy.

Thus, instead of a money supply target, the ECB set a monetary growth reference point for a broad measure of the money supply, M3. M3 consists of currency in circulation plus certain liabilities of monetary financial institutions (MFIs) resident in the euro area and, in the case of deposits, the liabilities of some institutions that are part of central government (such

as Post Offices and Treasuries). These liabilities included in M3 are:

- overnight deposits;
- deposits with an agreed maturity of up to two years;
- deposits redeemable at notice up to three months;
- repos;
- debt securities with maturity of up to two years;
- money market funds and money market paper (net).

The monetary growth reference value was established as the first pillar of the ECB's monetary stability strategy. The second pillar of the strategy is a broadly based assessment of the outlook for price developments and the risks to price stability, using other available indicators. These other indicators include the output gap, forecasts of economic growth and a forecast of the rate of inflation itself. Factors taken into account are considered in more detail below.

The monetary growth reference value was set at 4.5 per cent per annum and has been left unchanged. This figure was based on what the ECB referred to as the plausible assumptions of a medium-term rate of growth of 2 to 2.5 per cent per annum and an annual decline in the velocity of money of 0.5 to 1 per cent, together with the target rate of inflation of less than 2 per cent.[4] The ECB made it quite clear from the beginning that the figure of 4.5 per cent for monetary growth was not a target and that figures above 4.5 per cent would certainly not automatically trigger interest rate rises. The reference value is also described as a medium-term concept. In the view of the ECB, temporary deviations from it are not unusual and do not necessarily have implications for future price developments.

23.4.2 Choice of policy instrument

The choice of instrument

The ECB had first to decide upon its system for providing liquidity to the banking system. This is done principally through the main refinancing operations, weekly open market operations that provide liquidity to the banking system through repurchase agreements

---

[4] This appears to give a range for inflation of 1–2 per cent, hence the suggestion in Svensson (2000) of 1.5 per cent as the point inflation target of the ECB.

(repos) with a maturity of two weeks. Initially, this operated through a system of fixed-rate tenders, with the fixed rate known as the **main refinancing rate –** 'refi' for short. This rate became the focus of attention at the regular announcement of the interest rate decision of the ESCB's Governing Council.[5]

In a fixed-rate tender, when the total amount for which banks bid is greater than the amount the central bank is prepared to lend, each bank receives the same proportion of the amount for which they bid. This encourages banks to bid for more than they really want since they know they are unlikely to receive all that they bid for and they know the interest rate they will have to pay on the funds they receive. This gives an advantage to large banks, which have the collateral to be able to support large bids for funds. It also makes it difficult for the central bank to judge the true demand for money in the system.

Thus, it quickly became clear that the ECB would prefer a variable-rate tender in which banks indicate how much they are willing to borrow from the central bank at various rates. A cut-off rate of interest is then declared. Bids above this cut-off rate are fully filled while bids at the cut-off rate are filled proportionately. This gives the central bank a better idea of the state of demand in the market and of market expectations about future interest rates. The official refinancing rate is then simply a minimum rate of interest – no funds are provided by the central bank below this rate but it is quite possible for funds to be lent to the banks above this rate. For this reason, the ECB was wary about changing to the variable-rate system. This was particularly the case because the large single currency economies were in recession during the first year of the ECB's operation. This had led the bank to cut the refinancing rate from 3 per cent to 2.5 per cent on 9 April 1999 and it had a clear desire at this point to keep interest rates low. During this period only about 5 per cent of total bank bids for funds were being met by the ECB and there was little doubt that the interest rate at which funds were actually provided under a variable-rate system would be higher than the minimum rate.

The change to a variable-rate tender was made on 28 June 2000. By then, the main refinancing rate was on its way up as the ECB became more concerned about inflation. Nonetheless, the ECB wished to keep interest rates as steady as possible under the new system and so moved to variable-rate tenders just after it had increased the refinancing rate by a half percentage point – a larger increase than many in the market had expected. Changing the system at that time made it less likely that the rates at which funds would actually be provided to the banks would be much above the official refinancing rate.

The main refinancing operations of the ECB are supported by two other types of open market operations: longer-term refinancing operations and fine-tuning operations. Longer-term financing operations are conducted monthly through repurchase agreements with a three-month maturity. The purpose of these is to prevent all liquidity in the money market from having to be rolled over every two weeks and to provide access to longer-term refinancing. As their name suggests, fine-tuning operations are conducted irregularly with the aim of smoothing the impact on interest rates of unexpected liquidity fluctuations in the money market. Structural operations are also possible – these are intended to adjust the structural liquidity of the Eurosystem in relation to the banking system.

When the refinancing rate is announced by the ESCB's Governing Council, two other rates are also declared. These are the ECB's rates on its marginal lending facility and on its deposit facility. The marginal lending facility provides the possibility of emergency overnight borrowing to meet liquidity needs. The rate of interest for such borrowings is always set above the refinancing rate. On 22 January 1999, after a brief adjustment period, the marginal lending interest rate was set 150 basis points (1.5 per cent) above the main refinancing rate. From 9 April 1999, this difference was reduced to 100 basis points (1 per cent) and the gap between the two rates has remained unchanged from that date. The deposit rate applies to overnight deposits and is always set below the refinancing rate. The gap between these two rates has also stayed steady at 100 basis points (1 per cent) since 9 April 1999. The main refinancing rate (refi) is by far the most important of the ECB's rates.

Another question was whether to support the control of short-term interest rates with the requirement that banks hold mandatory **minimum reserve ratios**. Before monetary union, this was practised in the majority of EU member countries in the belief that it allowed

---

[5] Interest rate decisions are announced fortnightly, except in August when there is normally only one meeting of the Council.

the central bank more easily to manage short-term interest rates by creating a predictable demand for reserves at the central bank under circumstances in which bank balance sheets were growing rapidly in response to increased demand for credit. However, because reserves held at the central bank usually do not receive interest, the ratios act as a tax upon banks and as the required reserves grow banks push up interest rates on loans to make up for the lost interest and to restore their overall rates of profit. This in turn puts downward pressure on the demand for credit. The Bank of England argued that minimum reserve ratios were not required in deep and liquid financial markets since the central bank could achieve its objectives in such markets solely through open market operations. In addition, it was suggested that the use of minimum reserve ratios conflicted with the Maastricht Treaty requirement that policy should be conducted in accordance with the principle of an open market economy with free competition, favouring an efficient allocation of resources.

Despite these objections, the ECB settled for a minimum reserves system with banks required to hold with the national central bank members of the ESCB a reserve ratio of 2 per cent of the liability base. This was defined to include: overnight deposits; deposits with agreed maturity up to two years; deposits redeemable at notice up to two years; debt securities issued with agreed maturity up to two years; and money market paper. A lump-sum allowance of €100,000 may be deducted from an institution's reserve requirement. The Governing Council argued that without the use of a minimum reserve system, the ESCB would be faced with a relatively high volatility of money market interest rates and would need to engage frequently in open market operations. This could undermine the operational efficiency of monetary policy as markets have difficulty in distinguishing policy signals made by the ECB from technical adjustments necessary to reduce the volatility of interest rates. Further, it argued that a reserve ratio system would safeguard the role of

national central banks as providers of liquidity to the banking system. However, the Council acknowledged the burden that such a system places on banks if reserves are required at the central bank without the receipt of interest. It thus decided to pay interest on the required minimum reserves holdings at the ECB's main refinancing interest rate.

23.5 ECB monetary policy and the euro

It is difficult to judge the effectiveness of ECB monetary policy. Firstly, we must allow for the time lags in monetary policy and accept that the performance of the euro area economy in 1999 and perhaps a good proportion of 2000 had more to do with the monetary policies of the central banks of the member countries before 1999 and with the attempt by various governments to meet the Maastricht convergence criteria. Secondly, despite the setting of an inflation target and a monetary growth reference value, it has not been easy to know precisely what the ECB has been attempting to do.

In practice, the interest rate decisions appear to suggest that a medium-term average rate of inflation of 2 per cent would be perfectly acceptable and that monthly figures between 2 and 3 per cent do not, in themselves, suggest a failure of policy. Thus, the Governing Council appears to become concerned when the monthly rate moves above 2 per cent only if there is evidence of growing inflationary pressure that would continue in the medium term, pushing the rate higher. However, it is difficult to know how long the medium term is in the minds of the members of the Governing Council. It has also been difficult to determine the attitude of ECB members towards the desired value of the euro.

We have mentioned the doubts that surrounded the likely policy of the ECB and hence the likely strength of the euro following its launch in January 1999. The constitution had been designed partly to convince the markets that the euro area would be a low inflation area with a strong currency. However, the ECB was a new institution and new institutions ultimately only establish a reputation through their behaviour over a number of years. In January 1999, no one knew precisely how the ECB would behave.

Despite these doubts, no one forecast the dramatic fall that took place in the value of the euro, particularly against the US dollar and the Japanese yen, in its first two years of life. The extent of this fall is shown in Table 23.1 which provides exchange rates of the US$, yen and pound sterling principally on those days on which the ECB announced a change in its main refinancing rate.

The euro, having begun trading on 4 January 1999 at a rate of €1 = $1.1743 rose slightly on the first two days but from then until the 26 October 2000 (when it seemed to have finally reached its low), fell 30 per cent against the dollar, 33.2 per cent against the yen and 18.4 per cent against the pound sterling.

It then recovered briefly but soon fell back to below a rate of €1 = $0.90. In the first half of 2002, however, it began a steady climb, rose above parity towards the end of 2002 and reached new highs in late 2003. In February 2004, the euro reached a peak of $1.2858 before again falling back. The rate then remained remarkably stable for much of 2004 before another upward swing took the euro up to another new high of $1.3621 on New Year's eve of that year. We then saw a fairly steady but slow weakening of the euro taking it back down to €1 = 1.1797 on the last day of trading

Table 23.1 Exchange rates of the euro against the dollar, the yen and sterling, 1999–2004

Date	$/€	¥/€	£/€	refi (% rate)	US Fed funds – refi (%)
4 Jan 99	1.1789	133.73	0.7111	3.0	+1.75
9 Apr 99	1.0778	130.75	0.6724	2.5	+2.25
5 Nov 99	1.0408	109.79	0.6397	3.0	+2.25
4 Feb 00	0.9835	105.99	0.6195	3.25	+2.5
17 Mar 00	0.9672	102.31	0.6146	3.5	+2.25
28 Apr 00	0.9085	97.48	0.5794	3.75	+2.25
9 Jun 00	0.949	101.42	0.631	4.25	+2.25
1 Sep 00	0.8902	94.77	0.6135	4.5	+2.0
6 Oct 00	0.8703	94.82	0.6014	4.75	+1.75
26 Oct 00	**0.8252**	**89.3**	**0.5807**	**4.75**	**+ 1.75**
11 May 01	0.8773	107.35	0.6181	4.5	0
31 Aug 01	0.9158	108.65	0.6285	4.25	−1.0
18 Sep 01	0.9256	108.5	0.6304	3.75	−0.75
9 Nov 01	0.893	107.47	0.6144	3.25	−1.25
6 Dec 02	1.0006	125.02	0.6377	2.75	−1.5
7 Mar 03	1.1039	128.68	0.6867	2.5	−1.5
6 Jun 03	1.1813	139.28	0.7093	2.0	−1.0
31 Dec 03	1.263	135.05	0.7048	2.0	−1.0
31 Dec 04	1.3621	139.65	0.70505	2.0	+0.25
5 Jul 05	1.1883	133.03	0.67735	2.0	+1.25
6 Dec 05	1.1783	142.64	0.67905	2.25	+1.75
8 Mar 06	1.1914	140.35	0.68605	2.5	+2.0
15 Jun 06	1.261	144.84	0.68225	2.75	+2.25
9 Aug 06	1.2879	148.17	0.6753	3.0	+2.25
11 Oct 06	1.2543	149.96	0.67575	3.25	+2.0
13 Dec 06	1.3265	155.34	0.6728	3.5	+1.75
14 Mar 07	1.3183	153.66	0.68535	3.75	+1.5
13 Jun 07	1.3287	162.52	0.6745	4.0	+1.25
1 Oct 07	**1.4232**	**164.76**	**0.69735**	**4.0**	**+ 0.75**

Source: European Central Bank (2007) Statistical Data Warehouse, http://sdw.ecb.europa.eu/ (extracted 11 October). This information may be obtained free of charge through the ECB website www.ecb.int. Reprinted with permission.

of 2005 virtually unchanged from its rate on the opening day of euro trading seven years earlier. The euro was generally stronger in 2006 and the year ended at a rate of €1 = $1.316. The rate remained steady for the first part of 2007 but then, as the dollar weakened further against all major currencies, the euro rose again to reach its latest high of $1.4232 on 1 October 2007.

Thus, in a little under eight years the value of the dollar against the euro had swung between $0.8252 and $1.4232. A little later in October 2007, a new high had also been recorded in the ¥/€ exchange rate of €1 = ¥166.96, giving it a range since the establishment of the euro. The lowest figure recorded at that time was that of €1 = ¥89.3 in October 2000. At 1 October 2007, the $/€ rate was 20.7 per cent higher, the ¥/€ rate 24.8 per cent higher and the £/€ rate 1.4 per cent lower than they had been at the beginning of January 1999. We then need to ask what exactly had happened. Why did the euro fall so sharply and quickly in the first two years of its life?

The fall in the value of the euro was clearly partly a reflection of the strength of the US dollar as the US economy continued to grow rapidly and European firms invested heavily in the USA. This is reflected in the final column in Table 23.1 which shows the difference on the date in question between the Federal Reserve's target Fed funds rate and the ECB's main refinancing rate. This stood at 1.75 per cent when the euro was established but rose above that as the Fed engaged in a series of interest rate rises in 1999 and the first half of 2000. Simply on interest rate parity grounds it seems unsurprising that the dollar was strengthening against the euro.

In addition, because the markets had no clear notion of how low the ECB was prepared to see the euro fall before it took action, market agents frequently 'tested the market' – they sold euro to see if falls would produce some indication of likely future action by the ECB. This doubt about the policy likely to be followed by the ECB was increased by the tendency of members of the Executive Board to make conflicting statements about the euro. The markets did not like this apparent lack of leadership. Nor were they convinced that the ECB would, despite its constitution, be truly immune to political pressure. This concern was strengthened by the confusion over the length of the term of office of the first President of the ECB, Wim Duisenberg of the Netherlands.

Duisenberg was appointed in 1998 to serve an eight-year term. However, there had been conflict over his appointment because of the fear of some member states, notably France, that Duisenberg's approach to policy would be too conservative and that monetary policy might be deflationary. It was generally understood that there had been a behind-the-scenes agreement that Duisenberg would not serve his full term of office and would be replaced by a French nominee, although the exact terms of the agreement were unclear. There was a widespread view that Duisenberg would serve only four years, although he consistently denied this. In the event, in February 2002, he announced that he would be retiring from the job on his 68th birthday, on 9 July 2003. By then, he had served just over five years of his term of office.

In addition to the worry about leadership, because the euro was a new currency, there was no firm view as to the long-run exchange rate indicated by economic fundamentals. The starting exchange rate of the euro was simply a weighted average of the values of the 11 participating currencies at the end of December 1998. There was no reason to believe that the new currency would behave in the same way as this weighted average had done before 1999. Indeed, it was probably the case that recessions in the major economies would have a more depressing impact on expectations about the future of the European economy than was suggested by the weights applied in the old ERM.

Under these circumstances, other factors that might normally not have had much impact on the currency provided additional excuses for selling the euro. These included the resignation of the President and members of the European Commission and the NATO bombing of Serbia and Kosovo. The feeling was that only genuine news about improved fundamentals of the currency would push the value of the euro up, whereas it would fall merely because of rumour and political uncertainty. Thus, the fall resulted from a mixture of genuine economic news, the existence of uncertainty about the attitudes of the authorities and a variety of short-term political factors. The doubts about when the euro would 'bottom out' encouraged speculators to continue to sell the euro.

For most of 1999, the ECB was able to take a relaxed view of the value of the euro. At this time, the major European economies were in recession with high levels of unemployment and low rates of growth. There was little inflationary pressure in these economies and the HICP showed inflation rates comfortably below the ECB's objective of 'less than but close to 2 per cent'. This is shown clearly in Table 23.2,

Table 23.2 Inflation and unemployment rates, money growth rate and official interest rate for the euro area, January 1999–August 2007

Date		Inflation rate[1]	Money growth rate[2]	Unemployment rate[3]	Interest rate[4]
1999	Jan	0.8	6.2	9.5	3.0
	Apr	1.1	5.3	9.3	2.5 (9 April)
	Nov	1.5	5.8	8.6	3.0 (5 Nov)
2000	Feb	1.9	5.9	8.4	3.25 (4 Feb)
	Mar	1.9	6.0	8.3	3.5 (17 Mar)
	Apr	1.7	5.9	8.2	3.75 (28 Apr)
	Jun	2.1	4.7	8.1	4.25 (9 Jun)
	Sep	2.5	4.2	8.0	4.5 (1 Sep)
	Oct	2.4	4.2	7.9	4.75 (6 Oct)
2001	Jan		Greece joins euro area		
	May	3.1	4.4	7.8	4.5 (11 May)
	Aug	2.3	5.9	7.8	4.25 (31 Aug)
	Sep	2.2	6.8	7.8	3.75 (18 Sep)
	Nov	2.0	7.8	7.9	3.25 (9 Nov)
2002	Jun	1.9	7.2	8.2	3.25
	Sep	2.1	7.1	8.3	3.25
	Dec	2.3	7.0	8.5	2.75 (6 Dec)
2003	Mar	2.5	8.2	8.6	2.5 (7 Mar)
	Jun	1.9	8.5	8.7	2.0 (6 Jun)
	Dec	2.0	7.1	8.8	2.0
2004	Mar	1.7	6.2	8.8	2.0
	Jul	2.3	5.4	8.8	2.0
	Dec	2.4	6.6	8.7	2.0
2005	Mar	2.1	6.5	8.8	2.0
	Sep	2.6	8.3	8.4	2.0
	Dec	2.2	7.3	8.4	2.25 (6 Dec)
2006	Mar	2.2	8.5	8.2	2.5 (8 Mar)
	Jun	2.5	8.4	7.9	2.75 (15 Jun)
	Aug	2.3	8.2	7.8	3.0 (9 Aug)
	Oct	1.6	8.5	7.7	3.25 (11 Oct)
	Dec	1.9	9.9	7.5	3.5 (13 Dec)
2007	Jan		Slovenia joins euro area		
	Mar	1.9	11.0	7.1	3.75 (14 Mar)
	Jun	1.9	10.9	6.9	4.0 (13 Jun)
	Aug	1.7	11.6	6.9	4.0

[1] Annual rate of growth of Harmonised Index of Consumer Prices.

[2] Annual rate of growth of M3.

[3] Unemployment as a percentage of the labour force.

[4] ECB's main refinancing (refi) rate at the end of month (date of interest rate change in brackets).

Source: European Central Bank (2007) Statistical Data Warehouse, http://sdw.ecb.europa.eu/ (extracted 11 October). This information may be obtained free of charge through the ECB website www.ecb.int. Reprinted with permission.

which sets out changes in the ECB's main refinancing rate since January 1999, together with inflation, unemployment, and money growth rate figures over the period for the euro area. We need to note that at the beginning of 2001, Greece became a member of the euro area, requiring some small adjustment of the statistics. We should also note that the base of 100 for the HICP represents average 1996 prices. At the beginning of the operations of the ECB in January 1999, the HICP stood at 102.8.

In the first half of 1999, there was little desire to invest within Europe and the ECB was able to keep interest rates low to help the recovery of the European economy. The HICP remained almost stationary for much of the year. The ECB's initial interest rate of 3 per cent was lowered in early April to 2.5 per cent and was then left unchanged for seven months. By November, however, although the inflation rate was still well within the target range, it had begun to rise. The monetary growth rate had climbed to 6.2 per cent, the euro was plunging towards parity with the dollar and unemployment, while still high, was beginning to fall. The ECB responded to what they saw as developing inflationary pressure by pushing the main refinancing rate back to 3 per cent.

The euro continued to fall, breaching parity with the dollar for the first time on 27 January 2000. Despite a temporary fall in January 2000, the monetary growth rate remained well above the reference value and unemployment continued slowly to decline. The ECB responded with a series of quarter-point interest rises in February, March and April and a half-point rise in June, although as we see in Table 23.1, this was only keeping pace with the interest rate rises occurring in the USA. Under pressure from the rising interest rates, monetary growth fell back towards the reference value and the euro picked up to some extent. This was misleading since it began to fall again sharply in August and September. Meanwhile the inflation rate continued to rise, reaching 2.5 per cent in September. The ECB appeared now to be genuinely concerned about the possible inflationary effects of the weakening currency. Interest rates were again increased in September, and on 22 September 2000 the ECB joined with the central banks of the USA, Japan and the UK to purchase euro in the attempt to prop up the currency. This, together with a further interest rate rise in October, had no immediate effect and the euro reached a low of $0.8252 on 26 October.

Nonetheless, the euro area economy appeared soon after to be responding to the ECB's rate rises. By January 2001, the inflation rate had fallen towards the target range; the monetary growth rate had fallen below the reference value; and the fall in unemployment had virtually come to a halt. The ECB felt able to relax. Following the October 2000 increase, the main refinancing rate was left unchanged for seven months. During this period, however, the US economy had started to head towards recession and fears of a global recession had begun to emerge. The Federal Reserve had begun to slash US interest rates and the financial markets were expecting the ECB to follow suit. The problem for the ECB was that monetary growth was again starting to move up and the inflation rate was under pressure from rising world oil prices as well as the weak euro. The impact on the HICP of the temporarily high world oil price provides a good example of the problem of using a headline rate of inflation as the target of monetary policy. It is at least possible that the ECB was unduly slow to cut interest rates because of the high rate of inflation as shown by the HICP, which reached a peak of 3.1 per cent in May 2001.

Following the May cut, the ECB resisted pressure for further cuts until the end of August. In the period between May and August, the inflation rate began to decline but remained well outside the target range. Monetary growth continued to rise. The 11 September attack on the World Trade Centre in New York and the Pentagon in Washington DC led to increased worries about world recession and the ECB responded with a half-point cut in rates on 18 September and a further quarter-point cut in November. By this time inflation had fallen to 2.1 per cent, just outside the target range.

The monetary growth rate continued to climb but this was dismissed by the ECB. It argued that the relatively high growth of M3 was the result of people shifting into the liquid and relatively safe short-term assets that make up M3 because of the uncertainty following the September 11 attacks. Support for this view was drawn from the fact that the growth of private sector credit had been continuously falling over recent months. The ECB felt that the main refinancing rate, which stood after the November cut at 3.25 per cent, had been reduced sufficiently. There was some criticism that the ECB was not responding sufficiently to the threat of world recession. In 2001, the US Federal Open Market Committee had reduced the

Federal funds rate by 4.25 percentage points (from 6 per cent to 1.75 per cent) while the ECB had cut its main refinancing rate from only 4.75 per cent to 3.25 per cent. Even the UK's MPC had cut its repo rate by more (from 6 per cent to 4 per cent) despite the fact that the UK economy appeared to be better placed to withstand a world recession than the large economies in the euro area.

However, the ECB continued to feel that it had done enough and did not make another change until December 2002. Then, with the inflation rate still just outside the target range and with money supply growth still well above the reference range, the ECB felt able to cut the refi rate by 50 basis points. The key to this decision was the continued sluggishness of euro area economies, the stubborn refusal of unemployment to fall below 8 per cent and the upward movement of the euro above parity with the US dollar. This reduction appeared to have little effect. The euro continued to increase in value but this was hardly surprising since the Fed funds rate was by then 1.5 percentage points below the main refinancing rate, a large turnaround from the beginning of 1999.

Further cuts in the refi rate followed in March and June 2003. By then, the refi rate had fallen 275 basis points from the peak reached in late 2000, more than the 250 basis points fall in the UK's repo rate. Of course, by this time the Fed funds rate had fallen to 1 per cent and the euro continued to rise, threatening the exports of the large euro area countries. By 2004, talk was again of rising interest rates. Interest rates in the UK were already on the way up and were expected to rise in the USA if not before, then soon after the presidential election in November. The ECB, however, felt the need to resist the upwards movement. Inflation rose to 2.5 per cent in May and stayed above 2 per cent for the rest of the year. Monetary growth was above the reference level but unemployment remained high. Despite the Fed's rush of interest rate increases, the dollar was weakening against the euro. By December 2004, the Fed funds rate had risen above the refi for the first time for three-and-a-half years. Increases in the ECB's rate would only have put further upward pressure on the euro.

The ECB faced the same problem throughout 2005. Inflation remained a fraction above 2 per cent for much of the year and the monetary growth rate was well above its reference value but unemployment remained high. The $/€ exchange rate finally began to respond to the increases in the Fed funds rate, drifting down, especially from May onwards and spending much of the second half of the year not much above (or on occasions even slightly below) the rate at the beginning of January 1999. By September the pressure on the ECB to move interest rates up was growing. Inflation reached 2.6 per cent over that month and the monetary growth rate had risen to 8.3 per cent, indicating the possibility of more inflation problems ahead. Unemployment had (if ever so slowly) started to come down and there was by then no immediate worry about an overvalued euro.

In the event, the ECB did not act until December and then it embarked on a steady series of interest rate rises, continuing through 2006 and lasting into 2007. Inflation and monetary growth remained above the ECB's desired levels until September but unemployment was continuing to come down. Although the Fed had continued its series of rate rises until late June 2006, the dollar had weakened a little against the euro but not sufficiently to cause any worry. Despite the fall in inflation rate to well below 2 per cent in September and October, the ECB continued with its rate rises, pushing the refi up in both October and December. After all, it could be argued that evidence from both the money supply figures and the labour market suggested the need for further tightening of monetary policy.

This remained the position during the first two-thirds of 2007. The ECB's policy of continuing interest rate rises appeared to be justified by the inflation rates which perfectly met the requirement of an inflation rate just below 2 per cent. The money supply and labour market figures could be held to justify the further interest rate rises of March and June 2007. However, beyond June, the $/€ exchange rate was again beginning to become worryingly high especially following the Fed's half-point interest rate cut in September. The ECB was again facing a potential conflict brought about by concern over the value of the €.

In the light of the performance of the euro and the targets established for itself by the ECB, what can we say about European monetary policy since 1999? Much depends on the interpretation of the 'medium term' element in the ECB's statement of its inflation objective. Up until the end of August 2004, the ECB had been responsible for monetary policy for 104 months but, given what we have said about time lags in monetary policy, it seems reasonable to judge its performance in terms of its price objective from, say, the beginning of 2001, a total of 80 months. In that period, using the ECB's figures, the annual rate of inflation has been below 2 per cent in 21 months and above it in 50 months. However, the difficulty of the task is such that any central bank must be allowed some leeway, especially if the aim is a medium-term one. Let us allow the ECB the same degree of freedom that the UK government allows the Bank of England's MPC (1 per cent above or below target), and interpret the 'below, but close to, 2 per cent' as a target of 1.9 per cent and consider the ECB's inflation performance in terms of the range 0.9 to 2.9 per cent. This seems reasonable particularly in the light of the problems associated with the HICP and the use of a headline rate of inflation. This leaves us with only one failure, a rate of inflation of 3.1 per cent in May 2001 but we have seen that the ECB suggested that this was largely due to the special factor of sharply rising oil prices.

One might, of course, argue that a rate of inflation below 1.5 per cent would be much too low given that low rates of inflation across the area may well involve recession in some economies. In this case, one might suggest that the central bank should be less concerned with a rate of inflation above 2 per cent than with a rate significantly below 2. Since the lowest the HICP rate of inflation has been since the beginning of 2001 is 1.6 per cent (and then only in two months), this appears to be the attitude the ECB is taking.

We have said that the market was, at the beginning of the life of the euro, uncertain as to the ECB attitude to the desirable value of the euro. This seems to have become clearer over time. As a relatively closed economy wishing specifically to encourage intra-area trade, the euro area is able to take a relatively relaxed view of the value of the euro in terms of its impact on both the balance of trade of the area and the rate of inflation. Nonetheless, external trade remains important for many member states and a very weak euro will ultimately become a problem from the point of view of inflation. The \$/€ rate clearly became too low for the ECB in September–October 2000 and has recently become uncomfortably high. The ECB's behaviour appears to suggest that within a range of, say, \$1 = €0.90 to \$1 = €1.30, the value of the euro does not provide a reason for a change in the refi, although it may on occasion provide supporting evidence for a change indicated on other grounds. Of course, it is undesirable for a number of reasons to have large swings in the external value of the currency over relatively short periods but there is clearly a problem that the

ECB can do little about associated with asynchronous US and euro area business cycles.

This leaves us with the difficulty of the monetary growth monetary growth reference value of 4.5 per cent. Monetary growth has not been at or below this figure in any month since May 2001. The ECB has argued on several occasions that the rate of growth of M3 has been above the reference level for temporary and irrelevant factors. But if this happens frequently it is not easy to see the value of attempting to use the rate of growth of M3 as an intermediate target of monetary policy. It seems odd that monetary growth continues to be acknowledged as the 'first pillar' of policy when all that occurs is that 'developments of M3 are continuously and thoroughly analysed by the ECB in the broader context of other monetary indicators and information from the second pillar to assess their implications for the risks to price stability over the medium term'.[6]

23.6 Possible reforms at the ECB

The ECB has faced criticism because of both its perceived lack of transparency and accountability and its monetary policy strategy. Svensson (2000) suggested that claims by the ECB that it is open and credible carried little weight when it was clear that it was less accountable than the central banks of New Zealand, Sweden and the UK. Most criticism was based on the failure of the ECB to publish details of voting and the minutes of the meetings at which interest rate decisions are taken or forecasts made of the future rate of inflation, and on the Bank's refusal to state a precise inflation target. It was argued that this lack of a precise target made it difficult to judge how the Bank was interpreting its mandate. It was also argued that the lack of transparency of ECB monetary policy made it more likely to take the financial markets by surprise – see, for example, Case study 6. However, this problem appears to have eased as markets have become more familiar with the behaviour of the ECB. Some adjustments have been made. For example, economic forecasts made by ECB staff are now published. The ECB is certainly well aware of the transparency issue and discusses it on its website. Recent academic discussion has been much more favourable towards the Bank and its practices than in the early years.

---

[6] ECB, *Monthly Report*, December 2001, p. 5.

MORE FROM THE WEB

For comments on ECB performance at various stages of its short life, you could consult a 2002 report with ideas of possible reform by Patrick Artus and Charles Wyplosz in *Analyses, Economiques* on http://www. cae.gouv.fr/lettres/CAE-I-05-GB.pdf. See also http:// www.ecb.int/press/key/date/2004/html/sp041009. en.html and http://www.ecb.int/press/key/date/2004/ html/sp040709.en.html for a 2004 interview with and speech by Jean-Claude Trichet, the president of the ECB, with some responses to Artus and Wyplosz. For useful commentary and judgement on ECB transparency see www.qub.ac.uk/polproj/reneg/contested_ meanings/Begg_transparency_draft%20aug05.doc for a draft version of a paper by the British economist Neville Begg and www.zei.de/download/zei_wp/ B00-16.pdf mentioned in Section 14.6. You will find much more simply by entering 'ECB transparency' or 'ECB reform' in Google.

Reform proposals other than those associated with transparency have concentrated on the inflation targets set, the role of the monetary growth reference value in the policy deliberations and the use of the Stability and Growth Pact although this derives from the EU as a whole rather than the ECB. Proposals regarding these have included the move to the use of a core rate of inflation in place of the headline rate provided by the HICP and a raising of the target rate to a range of 1–3 per cent. There have also been suggestions that the euro area should move to the UK system of having the inflation target set by the political system, for example by the European Parliament. These suggestions have sometimes taken place in a political context such as the demand for ECB reforms by Nicolas Sarkozy, the French President, during the election campaign of 2007. Sarkozy, like others before him, was unhappy at the priority the ECB gives to inflation in its policy decisions over economic growth and unemployment. However, Sarkozy later drew back from his criticisms and there seems little prospect of any important change occurring in the ECB's procedure or policy.

23.7 Summary

In a currency area with completely fixed exchange rates *and* full freedom of capital flows, there must be a common monetary policy. Such a policy could be determined by a single leader or on the basis of a joint decision by governments or central banks. The EMS did not have both fully fixed exchange rates and fully mobile capital but the Deutschmark had been the strongest currency in the system partly because of Germany's reputation for low inflation and partly because the political independence of the *Bundesbank* was seen as a guarantee that low inflation would continue. With monetary union, a supranational central bank, the European Central Bank, was established to conduct the common monetary policy. Its constitution was designed to make the ECB politically independent.

Many of the decisions made about the European Central Bank in the Treaty on European Union can be explained by a consideration of the fears which prospective members had about the operation of the system. Above all, there was the fear that the common monetary policy might be inflationary. This was thought possible to the extent that the policy became a compromise among countries with different attitudes towards inflation. Thus it was deemed necessary to design a set of institutions that would overcome the potential problems.

The Maastricht Treaty thus modelled the European Central Bank on the *Bundesbank* and included rules aimed to prevent member countries from running excessive government deficits. Despite this, financial markets still had doubts about the likely strength of the euro. The ECB sought to overcome this by designing a monetary policy that stressed price stability. It chose a target rate of inflation of below but close to 2 per cent and set a monetary growth reference point although this was to be only one of the two pillars of its policy. Its judgements on interest rates also take into account a set of other indicators, including the rate of inflation itself. The ECB followed the *Bundesbank* in choosing a system of reserve ratios for commercial banks.

Despite everything that was done to convince the markets before January 1999, the ECB was a new institution and had no reputation. The markets were thus uncertain as to how it would act. In practice, there appeared to be no clear leadership and the markets responded to the climate of uncertainty and the weakness of the European economy by pushing the value of the euro sharply down against the dollar. Later, however, it rose above its 1999 starting value and has since gone much higher. The ECB's monetary policy has been criticized for its lack of transparency.

Key concepts in this chapter

Accountability
Bailing out a bankrupt country
Common monetary policy
Currency area
European Central Bank (ECB)
European System of Central
    Banks (ESCB)

Excessive government deficits
Harmonised Index of Consumer Prices
    (HICP)
Main refinancing rate (refi)
Minimum reserve ratios
Price stability
Prudential supervision

Questions and problems

1 Explain the conflict between a low-inflation policy and a weak euro.

2 Why was it thought that a monetary union with many members would be more inflationary than one with only a few members?

3 Why might credit-rating agencies rate a country's debt denominated in its own currency more highly than its debt denominated in a foreign currency?

4 Why might it be considered undesirable by all the members of a monetary union for one member to default on its government debt?

5 Does it matter if a country's central bank is only weakly accountable to the country's political institutions?

6 Compare and contrast the monetary policy system and practice of the Bank of England with those of the European Central Bank.

7 Why might interest rates differ in different countries, even within a monetary union?

8 In Table 23.1 compare 4 January 1999 with 6 December 2005 and then look at other dates on which the difference between the Fed funds rate and the refi was +1.75 per cent. Can one say anything about the impact of interest rates on exchange rates and/or about the likely long-run value of the $/€ rate of exchange?

9 What reasons are there for a country or monetary union wanting to have a strong currency?

Further reading

P Artus and C Wyplosz, 'The European Central Bank', *Analyses, Economiques*, Vol. I-05, Dec 2002
I Begg, 'Contested meanings of transparency in central banking', *Comparative European Politics*, 2007, 5, 36–52
P De Grauwe, *The Economics of Monetary Union* (Oxford: Oxford University Press, 6e, 2005)
European Central Bank, *The Monetary Policy of the ECB* (Frankfurt: ECB, 2001) downloadable from http://www.ecb.int/pub/pdf/other/monetarypolicy2001en.pdf
European Central Bank, 'The stability-oriented monetary policy strategy of the Eurosystem', *Monthly Bulletin*, Jan 1999, 39–51
European Central Bank, *The implementation of monetary policy in the euro area: General documentation on Eurosystem monetary policy instruments and procedures* (Frankfurt: ECB, 2006) downloadable from http://www.ecb.int/pub/pdf/other/gendoc2006en.pdf
European Central Bank, 'Interpreting monetary developments since mid-2004', *Monthly Bulletin*, July 2007, 51–74
L E O Svensson, 'The first year of the eurosystem: inflation targeting or not?', *American Economic Review, Papers and Proceedings*, 90 (2), 2000, 95–9

Websites

www.bankofengland.co.uk
www.ecb.int/home
http://epp.eurostat.ec.europa.eu/portal
http://europa.eu/index_en.htm
www.oberlin.edu/faculty/dcleeton/s
http://specials.ft.com/euro/index.html

Chapter 24 Financial innovation

What you will learn in this chapter:

- Why financial innovation takes place

- How regulation, technology and the changing economic environment combined in the stimulation of off-balance-sheet activity and liability management

- How financial innovation can pose problems for financial regulators and for the conduct of monetary policy

24.1   Introduction

One function of a financial system is to channel funds between the end users of the system, that is to say from surplus to deficit units. In so doing, the components of the system – markets and institutions – provide a range of services for which ultimate lenders and borrowers are prepared to pay. Some measure of the value end users place upon the facilities can be gained from the commissions, fees and spreads charged by providers of the services. As with any other profit-driven economic activity, suppliers are looking continually for products which can be differentiated (or at least presented as differentiated) from those of their competitors and for ways of finding competitive cost advantages. The result is a continually evolving menu of financial products and processes.

However, not all new products and processes survive. This leads some commentators (for example, Finnerty, 1992) to distinguish between 'trivial' and 'non-trivial' innovations. The latter are those that continue to supply a need even after the original stimulus to their development has disappeared. The fact that there seems still to be a place for lasting innovations is often taken as evidence that financial markets are still 'incomplete'.

The difficulty of distinguishing between 'trivial' and 'non-trivial' innovations, however, is that it can only be done with hindsight. This is fine for financial commentators and the writers of textbooks but it is very difficult for practitioners – people working in the financial services industry – to know which of the changes taking place all around them are changes that really matter for the industry and its clients and which are transient and of little consequence. The Centre for the Study of Financial Innovation, whose work we refer to on the next page, is an independent 'think-tank' with a predominantly professional membership. It is clear from the range of its work and interests that it is obliged to treat almost every current development as a potentially significant financial innovation.

Financial innovation, therefore, is no more a novelty of the 1990s than is innovation in consumer durables. Indeed, financial innovation is not even confined to recent times. In Chapter 12 we noted that money today consists largely of bank deposits – the liabilities of private firms working for profit – and that this poses considerable difficulties for the authorities which often wish to control the growth of money. From a monetary point of view, therefore, the developments which replaced precious metals and then notes and coin with bank deposits were among the most important and these took place in the sixteenth and nineteenth centuries. Partnerships and lotteries are two more examples of what were once upon a time 'innovations', designed to help raise finance for firms and for the state respectively.

Continuous as the process of financial innovation may be, however, the innovations of the 1980s and 1990s can be seen as the latest stage or phase of a longer wave of rapid change which dates from the mid-1960s. Sametz (1992), for example, identifies the first stage, running from 1965 to 1972, when a combination of regulatory inflexibility and rising inflation and interest rates produced the first certificates of deposit and money market mutual funds. The second phase ran from 1973 to 1982, when the increased volatility of interest, inflation and exchange rates combined to produce hedging instruments such as options and futures contracts. The third phase, running from 1982, has been driven by increased volatility in security prices, of which the 1987 crash is the most conspicuous example, and by increased merger and acquisition activity.

In this chapter we shall look firstly at some of the theories which try to explain why financial innovation takes place. There is no completely satisfactory theory of financial innovation. As we have just seen, different 'causes' are likely to appear at different times. Then, in Section 24.3, we shall look at two cases, off-balance-sheet activity and retail liability management, which illustrate the interaction of regulation, technology and the economic environment as 'causes' and show how they in turn produce new dilemmas for the regulatory authorities. These are only two of many innovations. Many of the others, particularly where they involve the development of new products in new markets, are treated in detail elsewhere in this book and we shall make cross-references to them as appropriate. In Section 24.4 we look at the impact of retail liability management on the demand for money and the conduct of monetary policy. This section, therefore, returns us to some of the important issues raised earlier in Chapters 12, 13 and 14. Section 24.5 summarizes.

24.2   Theories of innovation

The immediate cause of innovation is the prospect of profit. It is driven by the desire, on the one hand, of financial firms to increase profit and by the desire, on the other, of lenders and borrowers to be able to carry out their lending and borrowing on terms which offer them the prospect of a greater increase in their wealth for a given level of risk than was available previously. But this rather basic statement of economic motivation does not take us very far. It merely raises the subsequent question of why the possibilities of profitable innovation occur when they do and in particular why they seem to occur more at certain times than at others. The answer to this must be that profitable opportunities arise with changes in the economic environment. It is when we try to identify the relevant changes that the picture becomes complicated. What sort of changes in the economic environment are important in stimulating financial innovation?

When it comes to explaining the burst of innovative activity since the 1960s, the three most frequently cited influences are: *regulation* (and *deregulation*), *technology* and *volatility*. The economic environment has been changed by all three of these over the past 40 years or so, and all three are undoubtedly relevant but they interact in a continuous and complex way and so the challenge becomes one of imposing some sort of order. This can be done either by chronology in which one influence dominates at a particular time (as with Sametz above); or by treating some as acting upon demand (for example, volatility) and others (for example, technology) upon supply; or by treating some as originating outside the financial system itself, volatility and technology being the most promising candidates, in that order, while others are seen as originating within the financial system initially as a response to the other disturbances but then helping to carry the developments forward. Following this approach, one can distinguish between 'exogenous' and 'endogenous' factors. The brief survey here is organized chronologically. We look firstly at regulation as something that has always been present in financial systems and has always been an inducement to innovation; then we look at volatility and technological change, which are among the circumstances peculiar to the 1970s and 1980s, Sametz's second and third waves. But, before we begin, we take a look at Table 24.1 overleaf, which tries to impose some order on what is a very complex picture. (See Lewis and Mizen (2000) tables 12.1 and 12.2 for a slightly different approach.) Notice that it is divided into three columns. The first of these is headed 'causes' and contains the three most relevant environmental changes that we have just listed. In the second column, we have listed the innovations (products and services) for which each of these causes was largely responsible. This is a simplification, since most innovations were influenced by more than one cause, but it is reasonable to argue that in most cases there was a principal cause, more important than the other two. The third column we have headed 'consequences'. This is because we want to emphasize the broader significance of these innovations. Each innovation has its own justification in providing a product or service that consumers regard as an improvement on what went before. But some innovations have a wider significance for

Table 24.1 Financial Innovation

Causes	Results	Implications
Regulation and deregulation	Eurodollar markets	Money substitutes
	Money market mutual funds	New monetary instruments
	CDs	Evade quantity controls
	'Bill leak'	Securitization
	Off-balance-sheet activity	Rise in money's own rate
	Increased competition	Money's own rate market related
		Liability management
Volatility	Swaps	Risk reduction
	Options	Loan demand less interest elastic
	Futures	
	Variable rate lending	
Technology	Globalization	Economies in cash holding
	24hr markets	Larger debit and credit positions
	Programme trading	(fall in velocity)
	Derivatives	Liability management
	ATMs	Credit derivatives
	EFTPOS	
	Credit checking	
	Cheaper intermediation	
	Cheaper entry	
	(contestable markets)	

monetary and financial economics. This is often because they change agents' behaviour in a major way which in turn forces us to change our view of how a modern monetary economy works. Quite often, this change in behaviour causes problems for the authorities, which find that their monetary and financial policies, based on old patterns of behaviour, are less effective than they were. As the table shows, not all new products and services have this wider significance.

We turn now to the argument that regulation has long been central to the process of financial innovation. This is most strongly associated with Kane (1981, 1984, 1988), who coined the term **regulatory dialectic** to describe the continuous interaction between financial firms which seek to minimize the burden of regulation and the authorities which modify the rules of regulation in response to the latest products and practices of financial firms. Kane's thesis was based largely upon US experience and the circumstances surrounding the growth of Eurodollar deposits, the growth of repurchase agreements and

money market mutual funds. The first developed after 1966 while the others took off in the 1970s. All were a response to **Regulation Q**, which limited banks' ability to pay interest on deposits. The regulation was circumvented in the first case by overseas US banks whose deposits were outside US jurisdiction; in the second case by repurchasing at a loss securities lent for a specified period (the loss amounting to interest); and in the third case by pooling retail deposits and investing them in short-term money market instruments (which became technically the source of the interest) while allowing withdrawals on demand. In the UK, an obvious parallel was the 'bill leak' which occurred at intervals in the 1970s when the 'corset' or supplementary special deposits scheme was in operation. Under the corset, banks were limited to target rates of growth in their interest-bearing liabilities (roughly, interest-bearing deposits) and were subject to financial penalties on a scale which increased steeply with the degree of overshoot. Like all direct controls, the corset frustrated both sides of the market with the predictable effect that eventually both sides would collude in circumvention. Circumvention began with large corporations borrowing in the money markets by issuing their own commercial bills but developed rapidly when firms discovered that the discount on the bills (the cost of funds) would be much smaller if the bills carried the guarantee of a major bank. The advantage to banks was that the fee income from these 'acceptances' partly replaced the interest income forgone on the loans they were prevented from making. This incident introduced UK banks to the advantages of 'off-balance-sheet' activity which developed rapidly in many directions thereafter. Chapter 13 discusses banks' involvement with 'swaps', another example of off-balance-sheet activity, and Chapter 25 discusses some of the regulatory issues that are raised by banks engaging in business which is not represented in the structure of assets and liabilities in their balance sheets.

Both Hester (1981) and Silber (1983) similarly emphasize the role of regulation. Hester also focused on innovations in the USA after 1960. Many of these, he concluded, were the result of monetary policy decisions and the outcome of most was beneficial since regulation led to inefficiency. A feature of Hester's argument, however, was the simultaneous emphasis upon the underlying conditions which made innovation worthwhile. These included high and variable interest rates (which determined the 'cost' of Regulation Q) and the progress in information technology which lowered the cost of circumventory action. In Silber, regulation appears as a special case in a more general theory of innovation. Financial firms are assumed to maximize utility (essentially profit) subject to a balance sheet constraint. Innovation is thus a profit-oriented response to some externally imposed constraint. Innovation is usually a response to *changes* which may either force a reduction in the utility of the firm or increase the cost of adhering to the constraint. Within this framework, a new regulation reduces utility while changing conditions (such as higher interest rates) may make compliance more costly.

Financial innovation also occurs at times and in places where regulation is not an obvious burden to intermediaries. Indeed, some of the most far-reaching (in their effects) innovations in the UK in the 1970s and 1980s came about during periods of overt slackening of regulation. **Competition and Credit Control (CCC)** facilitated the first stage of liability management while legislation in 1983 and 1986 to put banks and building societies onto a more equal footing took

it a stage further (as we shall see in Section 24.3). For this reason alone, some attention to the underlying economic conditions is required. As we have seen, both the level and volatility of interest rates have been cited as instrumental in the inducement to innovate, either in conjunction with regulation (by determining the cost of compliance) or alone (by increasing the level of financial risk).

We saw earlier that Sametz regards **financial volatility** as central to the innovation process since the 1970s. Balance of payments surpluses and deficits have been both absolutely larger and larger also in relation to their respective GDPs than at any earlier period. Commodity prices have shown larger swings and nominal interest and exchange rates have also been extremely volatile. Recall (from Chapter 16) that a doubling in nominal interest rates will almost halve the value of a long-dated fixed interest bond and interest rates often doubled and halved in the 1970s and 1980s. Relevant information about future price movements thus became increasingly expensive, if not impossible, to obtain, and accordingly (on this view) it has been markets and intermediaries that have been able to develop practices and products that help to manage the risk associated with price and rate fluctuations that have prospered. It is no coincidence that the most rapid growth in the 1970s and 1980s has taken place in financial futures (Chapter 19), interest rate and currency swaps, and traded options markets (Chapter 20). The growth of variable rate lending in US banking is another obvious response to volatility. This increase in the instability of financial and economic conditions, as we have seen, is generally recognized even in quarters where other stimuli are also thought to have been critical. Both Goodhart (1986) and Lewis (1988) have given it particular emphasis.

Whether it comes as a response to the frustrations of regulation or in response to increasing risk, financial innovation takes place only when it seems likely to be profitable. The role of technology in financial as in other activity is to lower the costs of production and possibly also the costs of entry. We take firstly the costs of production.

Conventional banking operations were once very labour intensive. Furthermore, those activities that required the storage and transmission of information were limited by the speed with which paper and people could be moved from one place to another. The development of ever more powerful and compact computers and more importantly the simultaneous development of communications networks allowing remote operators virtually instant access to centrally stored information has widened the range of services financial firms can offer. It has also increased the speed with which those services can be supplied, lowered their cost, changed dramatically the conditions (and locations) of work for those employed in the industry and changed the relationship between the supplier and consumer of financial services.

At one extreme, one thinks of the high speed and low cost with which firms based in London can transact business in Tokyo or New York, through their local subsidiaries. Indeed, the existence of local subsidiaries is itself dependent upon the cheap and instant interchange of information between the subsidiary and head office. The globalization of money and capital markets would simply not have been possible without these developments.

Equally, the development of new instruments and their markets would not have been possible without the facility of 'real-time' computer access. The pricing of options, currency futures and derivative instruments generally is a non-trivial arithmetic exercise which requires appropriate computer software and, again, instant access.

Seemingly less glamorous, but with effects which we shall see later are just as far-reaching, technology has had its effect upon retail consumers. Cash dispensing automated teller machines (ATMs) first appeared in the mid-1970s and have spread rapidly ever since. In the 1980s rival institutions combined their ATMs into networks to give customers even easier access to their accounts. In the 1990s, the same technology was extended to electronic funds transfer (EFT) with the result that stores can provide cash withdrawal facilities. Two processes are at work here. Firstly, the electronic handling of transactions is much cheaper than paper-based transfer, not just in labour but also in its requirement for premises. For years banks defended bank charges and later the non-payment of interest on checkable deposits on the grounds that they needed the endowment effect to subsidize the high cost of the money transmission system. One of the reasons that UK banks have been able to pay interest on sight deposits since 1983 is that the unit cost of payments has fallen.

Another sense in which technology has contributed to cost reduction is through the lowering of the costs of entry into the provision of financial services, making financial markets more **contestable**. Building societies

have been able to enter the money transmission business because electronic transfer of funds merely requires an extension to their existing computing capacity where previously it would have required prohibitive expenditure on labour and premises. The case of retail stores provides an even clearer illustration. Once computer terminals had been installed at checkouts, originally to improve the management of stocks, it required only software modifications, and a secure link to cooperating banking institutions, to enable the same equipment to debit a customer's account for the purchase of goods. Debiting the account for cash was an obvious next step. The cost of entering the cash management part of banking business is now so low for any nationwide organization which has a large number of retail outlets linked to a central computer that it is difficult to see where this development will end. In the opening months of 1997, the hot news in the UK was the competition between major food retailers to provide further banking services, including current accounts with overdraft facilities. In 2004, it was the rapid growth of hedge fund activity in London and the risk that investment banks were taking on in providing services to these funds.

The cost-reducing potential of technology has a number of implications for monetary economics. Firstly, a reduction in transactions costs lowers the costs of intermediation generally. Other things being equal, people will be willing to hold larger simultaneous debit and credit positions leading to a larger money stock and lower velocity than hitherto. Pushing in the opposite direction, as we see in Section 24.3, however, the reduction of **transactions costs** and the ability to access current balance information more quickly and cheaply may encourage people to hold fewer precautionary balances and to economize on cash holdings in particular, with whatever consequences that may have for the ratio of bank deposits to monetary base.

24.3 Three case studies

As we saw in the last section there are many points of contact between policy and innovation. There are times, for example, when monetary policy imposes constraints upon agents within the financial system and upon the end users. Innovations are a rational response to these constraints when the costs of compliance, often affected by the prevailing economic conditions, exceed the cost of innovation, often affected by technological change. Some innovations produce consequences that affect the outcomes of policymakers' plans and raise the question of re-regulation.

Two significant innovations which illustrate this process at work, and also have potentially interesting monetary consequences, are the switch towards '**off-balance-sheet activities**', including **securitization**, by banks; and a variety of new products and practices developed by UK banks and building societies as *deregulation* threw them into direct competition in the 1980s – a package of developments we shall call '**retail liability management**'. A third is the rapid growth of **credit risk derivatives**. Other examples of innovations, not discussed here but treated elsewhere in this book, are Eurocurrencies (in Chapter 15), Eurobonds and strips (in Chapter 16), futures (Chapter 19) and options and other derivatives (Chapter 20). Readers making a comprehensive study of financial innovation should consult the relevant sections as well as reading what follows here.

24.3.1 Off-balance-sheet operations

'Off-balance-sheet' operations are activities that generate income for banks without creating assets or liabilities which normal accounting procedures would place in their balance sheets. Once again, it is worth noting that there is nothing very remarkable in this. Firms search continually for new services and products to offer to customers. Their success or failure shows in the profit and loss account. We would not expect to see new activities directly reflected in balance sheet changes: the effect on assets and liabilities could be very large or very small. So what is so remarkable about banks engaging increasingly in activities which are only indirectly reflected in balance sheets? The interest that attaches to off-balance-sheet operations by banks stems from a traditional, and rather limited, model of bank behaviour which sees bank income and profit generated more or less exclusively by the maturity and risk transformation that banks carry out specifically by mismatching their assets and liabilities. On this view, an expansion of traditional bank business necessarily requires a corresponding increase in (on-balance-sheet) assets and liabilities.

This still risks an overstatement of the novelty of off-balance-sheet activity, however. One of the earliest functions of UK banks was the guaranteeing or 'acceptance' of commercial bills; trustee work, executorships and financial advice generally, also have a long tradition. As with most other innovations, the interest in off-balance-sheet operations lies not in their novelty but in their recent rapid expansion and increasing variety. A survey by Lewis (1988) listed some 60 off-balance-sheet activities. These were divided roughly equally between 'financial services' and those giving rise to 'contingent claims'. The former included activities such as tax and financial planning, investment advice, portfolio management, insurance broking, credit/debit card services and (most recently) estate agency. The latter included the issuing of guarantees of many kinds, securities underwriting, market making in securities and arranging swap and hedging transactions. One of the themes running through the growth of off-balance-sheet operations, and much discussed in the financial innovation literature, is securitization. This refers both to the increasing use by ultimate lenders and borrowers of capital markets, in preference to bank intermediation, and to the practice by banks themselves of selling off loans from their asset portfolio, by turning them into marketable securities – shifting them off the balance sheet.

The securitization of bank loans has developed furthest in the USA where there is a highly developed market for *mortgage-backed securities*. The tradition of mortgage lenders transferring the original loan to a second investor has its origin in the 1930s when the Federal Government began offering insurance for mortgages made to certain disadvantaged social groups. Because the mortgages were guaranteed, investors were prepared to take them over from the originator. However, the development of an active secondary market in securities dates from the 1970s when the Federal Government reorganized the Federal National Mortgage Association (FNMA or 'Fannie Mae') and established two new agencies – the Government National Mortgage Association (GNMA or 'Ginnie Mae') and the Federal Home Loan Mortgage Corporation (FHMLC or 'Freddie Mac'). Their purpose was to issue securities backed by both insured and uninsured mortgages. The basic security is the **passthrough**. The agency puts together a pool of mortgages and sells *shares* in the pool to investors who earn a corresponding share of the payments (of interest and principal) made by the borrowers. The principle of the passthrough, although it originated in the securitization of mortgages, is now a commonly

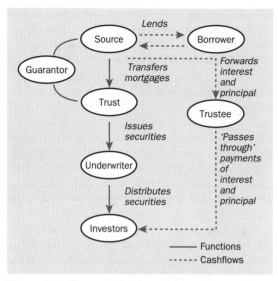

Figure 24.1 The securitization process

adopted securitization technique and is therefore worth considering in a little detail. Figure 24.1 illustrates the steps.

The source of the loan is any financial intermediary, say a bank or savings and loan, which makes secured loans. In the short run, until sufficient new loans have been created to justify pooling, the loans stay on the intermediary's balance sheet. At intervals, however, a collection of loans is pooled and placed with a trust, administered by a trustee. The trust issues securities which are then passed to an underwriter who distributes them to the general public in the normal way. The proceeds of the sale return to the source of the loan. If, as we have assumed, the source is a private commercial organization it may purchase a guarantee for the loans which naturally enhances the attractiveness of the ultimate securities. (When the source is one of the government agencies this step will be omitted.) Throughout the life of the loan the borrower makes payment to the originator of the loan in the usual way and the intermediary passes the income to the trustee. The trustee deducts its own expenses and those of the original lender (in continuing to collect and monitor the payments) and distributes ('passes through') the income to the investors.

We have described the passthrough as a share. This is because it has many of the characteristics of an ordinary company share. In particular, the income associated with it may fluctuate as a result of

pre-payment. This arises when borrowers choose to repay the loan before its scheduled terminal date. This has the effect of boosting investors' income now but lowering it for the remaining life of the security. For the lender, the attractiveness of securitization has always been greatest for fixed rate loans (as US mortgages usually are) since such loans are subject to interest rate risk – the lender suffering when interest rates rise. Securitization has the advantage for the lender that the interest rate risk is moved to the holders of the securities. Recall that borrowers are paying a fixed rate of interest. When interest rates fall, it becomes attractive to prepay the loan and to replace it with another loan at the new, lower, fixed rate. If this happens on a sufficiently large scale, the holders of the security find that they receive all their income early and then face reinvestment risk – the risk that they will not be able to reinvest their funds for the period that they originally intended at the original rate of return.

Reinvestment risk is a particular problem for life assurance and pension funds for whom security of long-term interest is essential (see Section 21.3). For these institutions, passthroughs are less attractive than bonds which offer a fixed return for a fixed period. Where the loan-backed security takes the form of a bond, however, the prepayment risk remains with the trustee (and thus with the originator of the loan). For this reason, the yield on passthroughs is usually greater than the yield on bonds.

Clearly, at an institutional level, one can view this growth of off-balance-sheet activities as representing a significant change in banking operations. On a more theoretical level, however, one should take seriously the argument that off-balance-sheet activities are essentially the same as the 'traditional on-balance sheet lending and borrowing operations of banks [which] can be seen to be packages of information and risk-sharing (or insurance) services' (Lewis, 1988, p. 396). By taking a customer's deposit a bank (traditionally) creates a very secure, very liquid asset, repayable at par, and turns it into a long-term liability for a borrower. The bank protects both from risk by its superior information and by its size. The interest rate 'spread' is the price that lenders and borrowers pay for this service. Nothing is fundamentally different when a bank accepts a bill or issues a standby letter of credit. The holder of the bill (or letter) enjoys a transfer of risk to the bank for which s/he pays by accepting a lower interest rate on the loan than would have been the case without the bank's guarantee; the borrower pays a fee to the bank for the benefit of the lower interest charge required by the market. Furthermore, the bank is willing to accept the risk in the guarantee because it has information which enables it to make a reasonable assessment of the individual default risk and to price it bearing in mind the average default rate on the total pool of guarantees.

When it comes to identifying the consequences, actual and potential, of the expansion of off-balance-sheet activity, one can say, as with the growth of Euromarkets, that by supplying services that customers want, banks are helping to mobilize funds which might otherwise have lain idle and are generally adding to the liquidity of the financial system. Similar implications can be traced in the case of off-balance-sheet activity. In the last section, for example, we observed that one consequence of the 'corset', which penalized the growth of interest-bearing deposits in the UK in the 1970s (and thus reduced the attractiveness of lending), was the 'bill leak'. Banks found it more profitable to accept commercial bills issued by their clients. Corporate borrowers were thus still able to borrow, on terms very close to those that would have prevailed on a bank loan. Spending, presumably, grew at much the same rate that it would have done without the corset, thwarting the authorities' intentions and at the same time removing whatever useful information may until then have been contained in the growth rates of the monetary aggregates. The growth of off-balance-sheet operations, just like the growth of Eurocurrency business, widens the scope for disintermediation to follow as a response to any form of monetary control that targets banks' balance sheets.

Other possible consequences of concern to the authorities involve questions of efficiency and stability. Firstly, there is a question of *moral hazard*. This arises from the regulatory authorities in most countries being also the lender of last resort. It may be, for example, that banks' willingness to offer guarantees of various kinds relies itself upon the banks' knowledge that they have access to liquidity support services offered by central banks and, furthermore, that guaranteed access to this support might encourage more reckless excursions into new activities than would otherwise be the case. For reasons of efficiency, regulators wish to see that banks are not operating with unfair advantage. They wish to see equal opportunities available to all market participants and

not just to banks enjoying access to lender of last resort facilities.

Moral hazard arises also from the widespread availability of deposit and other forms of customer insurance in developed financial systems. Indeed, one of the arguments sometimes advanced for the specific off-balance-sheet innovations is the **moral hazard hypothesis** – banks know that their customers are protected and are thus encouraged to take greater risks. This is often combined with the **regulatory tax hypothesis** that argues that off-balance-sheet activity develops specifically to avoid capital, reserve and other regulatory requirements designed to make the system stable. Viewed from this perspective, the regulators' main concern is to control banks' exposure to risks which banks have been encouraged to take on as a result of earlier actions by the regulators themselves.

Clearly, off-balance-sheet activity exposes banks to many types of risk (as does on-balance-sheet business). Most of the regulators' attention has focused upon credit or default risk which banks incur mainly through guarantees and acceptances. The approach has been to try to incorporate off-balance-sheet commitments as part of total assets in calculating a ratio of capital to (risk-adjusted) assets. The details are discussed in Chapter 25.

The growth of Euromarkets and off-balance-sheet activity both owe something to the constraints imposed on traditional banking business by regulation. We turn now to a group of developments where interest lies rather more in their effect on the operation of monetary policy.

24.3.2 Retail liability management

To the consumer of financial services in the UK, one of the most visually obvious features of the 1980s has been the diversification of financial institutions and the breakdown of traditional demarcations. Retail banks have become mortgage lenders, market-makers in securities, unit trust companies, insurance agents and, with a sense of timing paralleled only by their judgement of the merits of Third World lending, estate agents. Building societies have become banks (virtually in most cases, literally in some). They too have taken on insurance and estate agency and the provision of legal services. *Within* banking, traditional divisions have become blurred as retail banks join others in raising funds in wholesale markets and moving away from their traditional function of 'direct' lending, to advising commercial clients on a wide range of financial matters, offering acceptances and guarantees and other off-balance-sheet facilities as we noted above.

A further breach of traditional demarcations has developed with major stores establishing their own financial subsidiaries, firstly to market credit accounts to the store's customers and later to offer interest on positive balances on credit accounts which involved regular customer payments. In 1988 Marks and Spencer launched its own unit trust, and selected branches of Tesco began to provide cash withdrawal facilities at checkouts in the 1990s.

Looking at developments from the point of view of the retail consumer, the first and potentially the most far-reaching development of the 1980s was the entry of banks into the mortgage market in 1981. From this stemmed the break-up of the building societies' interest rate cartel in 1983, the rise in building society deposit and advances rates to market clearing levels and the consequent demise of mortgage rationing. As building societies moved onto the offensive, they dabbled in money transmission services by issuing chequebooks (of limited attraction without the benefit of cheque guarantee cards) and set about lobbying the government for a change in the Building Societies Act 1962 which limited their sources of funds to retail deposits on which interest had to be paid net of tax and restricted their lending to first mortgages secured on property.

Pushing on an open door where deregulation was concerned, the societies were quickly rewarded with the **Building Societies Act 1986**, which broadened both the sources and destinations of societies' funds. In particular, large societies were permitted a limited amount of unsecured personal lending. This apparently minor change had momentous results. Since societies could now legally permit customers to be overdrawn, they could, for the first time, issue cheque guarantee cards. This made building society cheque accounts indistinguishable from those of banks except for the considerable advantages that societies paid interest on all positive balances, stayed open longer and were generally seen as more user-friendly by the public. The change in building society regulation, therefore, ensured that banks which had, since 1983, grudgingly paid interest on selected cheque accounts with restricted use, would have to follow. The first announcement came from Lloyds Bank in December 1988. The

increasing tendency to pay interest on sight deposits has a number of possible consequences. If it narrows the spread between lending and deposit rates, it is one way by which the cost of bank intermediation may fall. Borrowing to finance spending becomes cheaper relative to using existing liquid assets; at the same time, money's own rate increases relative to other assets. In short, money and bank debt both become more attractive. We look briefly at the implications for the demand for money in the next section.

The willingness to hold higher levels of bank (and building society) debt relative both to income and to other liquid assets and liabilities was quite likely further encouraged by a reduction in the **non-pecuniary costs of borrowing** for many people. The unsecured personal bank loan (as opposed to overdraft) is a product strictly of the 1970s when it became available to established bank customers in exchange for the prior completion of an application form requesting extensive personal information. In the 1980s the forms got shorter and the development of credit-rating agencies using computer data files removed the delay. What once involved an interview with a bank manager became available on demand from high street stores. Furthermore, a combination of advertising, unsolicited postal offers of credit and unrequested increases in established credit limits not only made borrowing easier, but transformed its image. The stigma of 'debt' was eventually replaced by the status of 'credit'.

Furthermore, the increasing tendency to pay interest at rates that move with the general level of market rates made it increasingly difficult to engineer changes in **relative rates** for monetary control purposes. The cheapening of bank and building society debt and the loss of control over interest relativities are both related to the general issue of monetary control, an issue to which we turn in a moment.

24.3.3 Credit risk derivatives

A major area of growth in recent years has been the market for credit risk derivatives. A credit risk derivative can be defined as:

> a contract which allows one party (the protection buyer or risk seller) to transfer the credit risk of a reference asset to one or more other parties (the protection seller or risk buyer) without transferring the reference asset.

The protection that is being bought is similar to the protection that one could get from an insurance contract or a guarantee. Earlier in this chapter we referred to the 'bill leak' whereby a third party with exceptionally high credit standing (a bank) sold a guarantee of creditworthiness in order to make a market in commercial bills between firms wanting credit and lenders unwilling to take on the whole of the risk. From the protection buyer's point of view, a credit derivative achieves much the same result. But these derivatives do so with much more flexibility. This is because the derivative can in principle be based on *any* underlying asset (the 'reference' asset) while traditional forms of guarantee were linked to a very narrow range and also because they can be designed to compensate for the risk inherent in a wide range of activities, rather than the classic case of default. Furthermore, credit risk derivatives differ from the 'standard' insurance contract in that they offer a known level of compensation, provided only that the 'defined credit event' occurs. This compensation is assured, regardless of the actual loss the protection buyer may suffer. Unlike an insurance contract, therefore, where the insured is compensated only for the loss actually experienced (which is unknown at the time of the contract) the derivative has a known value and this is essential if is to be traded. In short, they open up a market in protection against 'credit events' which offers a flexible hedge against adverse events to protection buyers and new investment opportunities to protection sellers.

There is some dispute about when the market for credit risk derivatives began, but the US financial press in 1993 was making reference to deals done by Merrill Lynch and J P Morgan. By 1996 the market was expanding rapidly. In 2002 the British Bankers' Association was estimating the size of the market at US$2 trillion with the prospect of doubling again by 2004.

Credit risk derivatives come in many shapes and sizes. Box 24.1 summarizes the main types. In the illustration that follows we look at the details of one of the commonest types – the single name credit default swap (CDS).

To begin with, we imagine two banks, A and B. Over the years, each has developed specialist knowledge about certain types of lender and has a portfolio of loans which is concentrated in this area of expertise. Let us suppose that Bank A has many clients from the leisure and entertainment industries while Bank B has a majority of its loans with the retailing and distribution

---

BOX 24.1 A sample of credit risk derivatives

Credit default swap
A credit default swap offers protection to a lender in the event of default by a specific borrower.

Total return swap
A total return swap exchanges the cashflow from a named asset (interest + capital gain/loss) for a pre-determined rate of interest (usually a spread over LIBOR). In this case the pre-determined rate of interest gives the protection buyer a guaranteed income while the seller receives an uncertain income which will be affected by any credit event.

Credit spread swap
The holder of an asset paying a variable interest rate is anxious to protect his or her cashflow relative to the return on some other asset. This may be a risk-free asset or some other benchmark asset (e.g. LIBOR). The protection seller offers to pay a rate of interest which will vary so as to deliver this spread, in exchange for the actual spread earned by the reference asset. The seller gains if the spread widens and loses if it narrows.

Basket swaps
A basket swap is like a credit default swap except that 'the basket' contains a number of reference assets. The derivative is normally triggered by the first asset in the basket to default.

---

sector. Both banks are exploiting their superior knowledge of screening and monitoring, and perhaps also some economies of scale, but we know from Chapter 2 that they are forgoing at least some of the benefits of diversification by holding these specialized portfolios. One solution would obviously be for each bank to develop its lending to other sectors but this might be inefficient if it means going into markets with which it is unfamiliar. (Instead of reducing risk, it might even increase it.) An alternative is for each bank to enter into an agreement to 'buy' part of the risk of the other bank's portfolio, without transferring any part of the portfolio or reducing portfolio concentration. In exchange for a fee from Bank A, Bank B agrees to pay (a fixed amount of) compensation if a defined event occurs, and vice versa. Figure 24.2 shows the process we have just described. What we have described is a bilateral deal, but in principle there

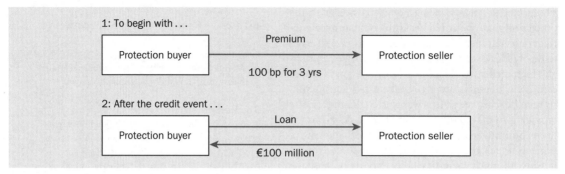

Figure 24.2 A single name credit default swap

is no reason why shares in the risks of these portfolios should not be bought and sold between third parties.

In Figure 24.2, a bank buys protection for a €100m loan for three years by issuing a single name CDS to an investor. For this benefit, the bank agrees to pay 1 per cent interest (100 bp) per annum. In the event of default by the borrower, the seller of protection agrees to pay €100m. In this particular deal, the buyer agrees to transfer the loan (and whatever residual value it may have) to the seller. This is a very simple deal and the possibilities of variation are considerable. The term and the principal can take any value. The premium can be fixed, as here, or it can be fixed relative to

some benchmark such as LIBOR. The contract can specify that the underlying asset must be transferred (as here), in which case the seller of the protection will be entitled to whatever value can be recovered, or the asset may remain with the buyer of protection. Box 24.2 lists the key terms which each contract must specify.

The pricing of credit risk derivatives is beyond the scope of this book. A text like Jarrow and Turnbull (1999, Ch. 18) will supply the deficiency and some guidance can be obtained from the sources referred to in 'More from the web: Credit risk derivatives'. But a glance at the example in Figure 24.2 will help explain

---

BOX 24.2 Elements of a credit risk derivatives contract

The key terms which must be agreed in any credit risk derivative contract include:

The underlying or reference asset(s)
The asset can be any credit asset. Bonds and loans are the most common. In a basket swap, all the component assets must be specified.

The credit event
This could be the default on a payment; insolvency; deterioration in credit rating; change in a credit spread; restructuring of a business. The terms must be precisely specified, e.g. as to whether there is any grace period in respect of payments in default, or the threshold below which the credit rating must not fall.

'Materialization'
This is related to the credit event in that 'materiality' clauses endeavour to specify incontrovertible criteria for judging that the credit event has actually occurred.

Payment terms
These are the payments made by the buyer of protection and are usually periodic over the life of the contract. They may be specified as a percentage of the value of the underlying asset or they may be specified as a margin over some benchmark, variable, interest rate. Frequency and date of payment must also be agreed.

Payment in case of a credit event
Clearly there needs to be agreement as to the compensation paid in the case where a credit event triggers the contract. This will involve the fixed sum being paid by the protection seller but it will need to state whether the seller receives the underlying asset. Some credit spread swaps are triggered only if the spread narrows beyond a certain point. This could happen at any time in the contract and so the contract must include a means of arriving at a value for the compensation to be paid having regard to the remaining length of the contract.

the variables that will be relevant to the pricing. First of all, we note that the seller of protection is earning a premium of 1 per cent. Given the size of the loan being protected, this will produce a cashflow of €1m for each of three years. If we wish to put a *price* on this contract then a present value can be found for this in the normal way. The more interesting question concerns the variables which generate the premium of 100bp. Recall that the buyer is insuring a loan on which it is charging a given rate of interest consisting of the risk-free rate plus a risk premium, both of which are market-determined. The buyer is then, in effect, using a slice of that premium to buy protection. Why is the seller prepared to settle for a price which may be less than (and certainly will not be more than) the market risk premium on loans of this kind? Firstly, we need to remember the basic point that the seller is receiving a fee only for the *protection*. Unlike the seller, it is not funding the loan. The whole point of credit risk derivatives, we saw at the beginning of this section, was to separate the risk in an asset from the principal of the loan. That said, it may still be that the seller is charging a premium which is less than the risk premium charged by the lender. But this merely reflects the portfolio preferences of the protection seller and in particular the preferences towards this particular risk. It may be, for example, that the protection seller is looking for exposure to the type of risk on offer because s/he has little exposure to this sector and thinks that the sector has a low covariance with other sectors to which it has considerable exposure. This is the case that we saw with the two banks at the beginning of this section. While Bank A would require a substantial risk premium to induce it to lend any more to clients in the entertainment field, Bank B is happy to accept some risk exposure in this field at a lower cost because it helps diversify its portfolio.

When it comes to deciding exactly what to charge for this protection one obvious variable will be the risk of default. Another will be the prospects of recovering any value in the case of a credit event triggering the compensation and there will also be the seller's own costs of operation to consider. This last point is often put in terms of the seller's cost of capital, partly on the grounds that the cost of capital is a major cost for any firm. But given the Basle capital adequacy directives, it is quite likely that a bank buying risk will have to set aside a certain amount of capital in order to stay within the rules.

MORE FROM THE WEB
Credit risk derivatives

Because of their recent development, but more especially because of the very rapid growth in the market for credit risk derivatives, websites are at least as useful as published textbooks. Two websites which provide an explanation of credit risk derivatives and how they work are:

www.credit-deriv.com/creprime.htm
www.finpipe.com/crederiv.htm

Both sites have useful links to other sources.

Because of the centrality of risk, central banks are inevitably interested in the growth of this market and useful articles can usually be found among their publications. For the Bank of England, the best place to look is the *Financial Stability Report* at www.bankofengland.co.uk/publications/fsr.

One thing is for sure, typing 'credit risk derivatives' in any web browser will produce an overwhelming response.

24.4 The demand for money and monetary policy

In the early chapters of this book we repeatedly stressed that the successful conduct of monetary policy, especially where that policy includes targeting monetary growth rates, relies heavily upon a stable demand for money function. An obvious comment to make about financial innovation, therefore, is that it must surely make it more difficult to operate monetary policy and in particular to operate any monetary policy, such as following a money growth rule, which relies upon a stable demand for money function (see Chapter 13). In this section we explore numerous ways in which changes in the financial system can lead to changes in the demand for money. We begin by suggesting a number of ways in which one could imagine this happening in principle. The purpose of this is to emphasize the large number of channels through which institutional changes might work and the difficulty of judging *a priori* which of several contradictory results a given innovation is likely to have. Even so, our list is not exhaustive. Towards the end of the section, we make brief reference to recent empirical work on the demand for money which has tried to identify and incorporate the impact of one or more aspects of financial innovation.

Interest rates

As we saw in Chapter 13, which rate of interest should be chosen to represent the opportunity cost of holding money has been a perennial problem. What is and what is not a close substitute for money changes over time. Furthermore, the 'closeness' of substitutes varies with the definition of money, something which itself varies as innovations in very liquid assets take place. In a study of UK households' demand for money, for example, one might have taken some measure of building society share and deposit rates up until 1989 when M3 (which excluded building society deposits) was replaced by M4 (which included them). Even with a constant definition of money, however, the closest substitutes will change through time. Taking the 1980s again, it would be interesting to know whether the aggressive marketing of National Savings instruments, including new products paying more closely market-related interest rates, made NS rates more relevant than, say, bond rates. For firms, the development of the CD and the interbank market from the end of the 1960s explains the appearance of those rates of interest in money demand studies. The Eurocurrency markets offer a new, possibly relevant, set of rates. Furthermore, while theoretical considerations may dictate the relevance of, say, long rather than short rates the appropriate choice in practice requires knowledge of institutional detail. In this case the obvious choice might seem to be the rate on long-dated gilts, and this would be correct in a financial system where secondary trading was thin and costly and where securities were generally held to maturity. The growth and development of the secondary gilts market, however, and the changes especially since 'Big Bang' have made all gilts extremely liquid. As we noted in Chapter 17, long gilts, like shorts, can be sold cheaply and easily for cash in 24 hours.

Whether or not absolute changes in the rate(s) on non-money assets represent changes in the opportunity cost of money depends, of course, on what is happening to money's 'own rate'. In a world where bank deposits do not pay interest, money's explicit own rate is zero and absolute changes in rates on non-money assets necessarily indicate changes in opportunity cost. An intermediate situation applies where deposits pay interest but at rates which are probably low but above all are very sticky. This was a situation which

prevailed in the UK until the changes in *Competition and Credit Control* in 1971. Once deposits begin to pay market-related rates then changes in money's own rate mean that it is changes in the 'spread' or differential between the rate on money and the rate on other assets that indicate a change in opportunity cost. Furthermore, where some deposits (and notes and coin) still pay no interest and where banks offer premium rates for differing terms and conditions, theory suggests that money's own rate should be indicated by a weighted average of deposit rates.

In theory at least, the spread between money's own rate and the rate charged on bank lending should also influence the demand for money since spending in excess of income can be financed either by running down liquid assets or by borrowing. It has been pointed out by Goodhart (1984) that when the rate on overdrafts and the rate on deposits are equal, the demand for overdrafts will become infinite. The significance of this observation is widely recognized in studies of the demand for bank lending. It is less frequently recognized that there is also an implication for the demand for money since the attraction of overdrafts when this spread approaches zero arises from a reluctance to run down liquid assets. Clearly, the growth of interest-bearing deposits and the resulting changes in money's own rate are involved here as well. Furthermore, financial innovation may be implicated in changes in the other part of the spread, the cost of bank lending. As we shall see in the next section, competition between banks and building societies to lend for house purchase in the 1980s led households in the UK to build up their holdings of floating rate debt. This altered dramatically the composition of their bank debt as the share made up of personal loans and overdrafts diminished while the share of mortgage debt rose. Until the fall in property prices began in 1990, mortgage lending was charged at rates very close to base rates with the result that at any given level of interest rates the average cost of bank debt, weighted by its components, was falling. The attractiveness of borrowing from banks while building up liquid assets was possibly further reinforced by the increasing ease with which bank credit became obtainable – a decline in the non-pecuniary costs of borrowing. Again, the next section details the rise in personal sector indebtedness and its consequences; it should be remembered that this was the counterpart to a steady rise in the demand for money relative to income and to the dramatic decline in income velocity.

Velocity and the scale variable

As we noted in Chapter 13, when economists today refer to velocity, they are almost always referring to **income velocity**, that is to say GDP/M, or PY/M – in contrast to Irving Fisher's use of **transactions velocity**, PT/M. The most commonly expressed reason for this seems to be that since we are ultimately concerned with money's influence on *output* (or the price of output), PY is more relevant than PT. As we shall see shortly, this runs the risk of ignoring links that may run in the other direction – from spending to money.

Limiting our discussion to income velocity for the moment, it is clear that velocity can change in any direction, depending on the precise form that innovations take. The more traditional view, which associates innovation with the development of near-money substitutes, would lead us to expect a fall in the demand for money relative to GDP. As the need for asset balances declines, the existing money stock is able to finance more (income) transactions. On this view, innovation is associated with rising velocity. On the other hand, and this is a compelling argument given developments in the UK in the 1980s, if innovation leads to the development of increasingly close money substitutes that bear interest, then this may be followed by a rise in money's own rate relative to other rates which *increases* its attraction as a liquid asset. This is simply restating the earlier interest rate argument in velocity rather than demand terms.

There may, however, be much more subtle connections between innovation and velocity which we can explore only if we go back to the idea of transactions velocity, PT/M. Total transactions are larger than 'income' transactions by an amount which reflects, *inter alia*, the volume of intermediate transactions involved in the production process (itself a reflection of the degree of integration in production), the volume of financial transactions and the volume of transactions in existing assets or 'secondhand goods'. The latter of course includes a very large proportion of total house sales/purchases. In adopting PY rather than PT the point is often made that total transactions are likely to be stably related to income transactions and that the distinction between the two is, therefore, unlikely to matter. This is certainly convenient, but not very compelling. Clearly Fisher (1926) did not think it probable and Keynes (1930) explicitly denied its likelihood in

the first volume of the *Treatise*. Various attempts have been made in recent years to develop a PT series and to compare its movements with PY or GDP. Following Keynes and using cheque and electronic payments data, Bain and Howells (1991) constructed a PT series which showed a dramatic upward divergence from GDP, from a multiple of approximately two to three between 1979 and 1989. Interestingly, this study deliberately omitted all transactions through the CHAPS and 'Town Clearing' systems. These are 'same day' payments mechanisms used predominantly by financial firms but also in the settlement of housing transactions. Including CHAPS and Town Clearing data not only makes the PT/PY multiple much larger but also increases dramatically the divergence over time. It seems at least worth considering the possibility, therefore, that financial innovation could have a fairly direct effect upon *transactions* velocity by causing a rise in financial and 'secondhand' transactions relative to those involving newly produced goods and services. Howells and Hussein (1997) found that the demand for UK broad money is much better explained by PT, represented by the Bain/Howells series, than by PY, where PY includes only GDP transactions.

This distinction between income and transactions velocities, and the possibility that financial innovation may somehow be implicated, raises another interesting possibility although it is more strictly related to supply and only indirectly to the demand for money. The endogeneity argument, as we saw in Chapter 13, is based upon (deposit-creating) advances being demand-determined. The demand for bank lending originates ultimately from the expenditure needs of deficit units. The desire to spend in excess of one's income can reflect a desire for newly produced goods or services or for financial assets or for secondhand goods. There seems no good reason, therefore, why GDP rather than PT should appear in bank lending equations. Indeed, theory suggests the reverse. Suppose now that the demand for bank lending were shown to be sensitive to PT rather than to GDP. Bank lending follows total transactions and grows more rapidly than if it were closely linked to GDP. Bank lending and the money supply grow more rapidly than income and income velocity must fall. Financial activity thus not only affects transactions velocity but is causally implicated in the fall in income velocity. Of course, in equilibrium, the resulting deposits must be held. It would be interesting to see the effect of using a *PT* series as the scale variable in demand for money studies.

Transactions costs

Since Baumol (1952) and Tobin (1956) brought inventory-theoretic considerations to bear upon transactions demand it has been recognized that brokerage charges (for changing bonds into money), or the 'shoe leather cost' of going to the bank to change deposits into cash or non-money assets into deposits, should play some part in determining the quantity of money people wish to hold and the form in which they wish to hold it.

Such charges, explicit and implicit, are amongst the costs most likely to be reduced by technological innovation in the banking and payments systems. Firstly, we should note that electronic communication and ATMs lower the cost of entry into some areas of banking activity. Where competition increases we should expect a narrowing of spreads and a desire to hold both larger deposits and larger debts than hitherto. More specifically, where extensive (and expensive) specialist labour and premises would previously have been required, cash deposit and withdrawal facilities can now be offered by retail stores whose computer networks already allow for payment by credit and debit cards. Three obvious consequences could follow from this. Firstly, there is an opportunity to economize on non-interest-bearing cash and an increased desire to hold deposits, giving banks command over a greater proportion of monetary base. Secondly, the virtual automatic access to credit lines provided by plastic cards raises the theoretical question of whether this unused credit should be included in a 'truer' measure of money and at the same time reinforces the point we made above that easier credit makes it more attractive to hold both debit and credit positions simultaneously. On the other hand, ATMs, which typically offer current balance statements and more especially on-screen home banking services, could reduce considerably the need for significant holdings of precautionary balances by making it easier for people to manage their money balances with precision.

Predictably, attempts to incorporate the effects of financial innovation in empirical work have been most marked with respect to interest rates and a recognition that variations in money's own rate, where the demand for broad money is at issue, could be significant. The own rate can be entered implicitly

as an element in the differential between money's own rate and the rate on other assets or explicitly with the rate on other assets appearing independently. Adam (1991), for example, estimated long- and short-run equations from quarterly data for UK real M3 1975–86 using a weighted average own rate on money, with the weights and interest rates reflecting each of the components of M3. Other, opportunity cost, interest rates were the yield on bonds (including capital gains) and on Eurodollar deposits (adjusted for expected depreciation of sterling), recognizing thus the 'innovations' of Euromarkets and the abolition of exchange controls. Both money's own rate and the rate on foreign assets were significant in the long-run equation.

In Chapter 13 we noted that empirical work on the demand for money had employed a variety of scale variables in an attempt to capture the effect of, variously, income, wealth or transactions. This variety is driven more from the controversies which still surround the motives for holding money, however, than by a recognition that financial innovation has changed the appropriate variable. If, as we have said several times, the boom in financial activity in recent years has caused non-income transactions to rise as a proportion of total transactions then it would be interesting to see the effect of using a *PT* rather than *PY* series as the scale variable. A recent comparison of the demand for broad money in the UK and Germany (Biefang-Frisancho Mariscal *et al.*, 1995) found the coefficient on real GNP for Germany was close to unity, while for the UK it was nearly 1.7. The latter is what one would expect if the demand for money were following a *PT* series which was growing more rapidly than GNP. It may not be coincidence that *PT* has diverged from *PY* in the UK since the mid-1970s while it has not done so in Germany.

Most explicit attempts to include the effects of institutional change on the demand for money have focused upon long-run changes, rather in the spirit of the quantity theory that while velocity may change it does so only in the long run and as the result of institutional factors. Institutionally related variables used in studies have included bank offices per head of population, the proportion of the labour force employed outside of agriculture, and the ratio of currency to total money stock and of non-bank to bank financial assets. Other efforts have involved the inclusion of past peak levels of interest rates on the grounds that the incentive to innovation, as we saw in Section 24.2, comes from changes in costs of which interest rates are an important part. The argument is then that an innovation, once adopted, is not usually reversed even when interest rates fall. Clearly, however difficult it may be to measure the effects empirically, the scope for financial innovations to modify the demand for money, in various contradictory ways, are considerable. Consider the following:

■ liability management affects money's own rate and thus the opportunity cost of holding money;

■ a change in financial transactions relative to GNP transactions may make GNP an inappropriate scale variable;

■ a reduction in transactions costs may reduce the demand for precautionary balances but may also lead to more borrowing and larger debit and credit positions;

■ by creating ever closer money substitutes, innovation may lead to an increase in velocity;

■ cheaper access to cash may reduce the demand for cash and thus reduce α, the public's cash ratio, with implications also for money supply;

■ better access to balance sheet information may reduce the demand for precautionary balances;

■ better access to financial innovation generally may make agents more sensitive to interest rate differentials leading to more frequent switching between components of broad money.

From this, one can theorize *a priori* virtually any effect one chooses upon the demand for money. Figure 24.3 shows five money demand curves. The rate of interest is an absolute rate on alternative assets and money is assumed (for the moment) not to pay interest. Let M_d^0 be the 'original' curve. Consider firstly the possible effects of liability management where this results most notably in money starting to pay market-related interest rates. If the demand curve in Figure 24.3 shows the demand for broad money, then the increasing practice of liability management, leading to an increase in the proportion of money that pays interest, shifts the curve outward from M_d^0 to M_d^1. More money is demanded at any rate of interest. If, however, the figure depicts the demand for narrow money, while liability management results in interest being paid only on the components of the broader aggregates,

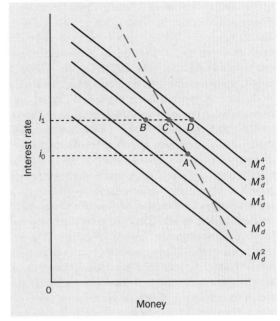

Figure 24.3 Financial innovation and the money demand curve

then M_d^0 will shift to the left, to M_d^2. Similar effects follow from any of the innovations which lead to an economizing on money holdings.

Now consider the effect of a rise in interest rates. We start on curve M_d^1. When money does not pay interest, a rise in the general level of interest rates from i_0 to i_1 moves us up M_d^1 in the normal way. When money's own rate is market-related, however, the rise in interest rates on non-money assets is accompanied by a rise in money's own rate and the demand curve *shifts out*, reflecting the increase or improvement in money's 'services'. In Figure 24.3, the demand curve shifts to M_d^3 and the quantity of money demanded is reduced from A to C rather than to B. If we plot the change in quantity against the change in price, we trace out the false demand curve shown by the long-dashed line. It is this that presumably leads to the oft-made but strictly incorrect assertion that liability management makes the demand for money less interest elastic. If we were to redraw Figure 24.3 with the genuine opportunity cost under liability management, that is, the bond rate minus own rate *spread*, on the vertical axis then the confusion is clearly exposed. Liability management delivers a smaller change in the spread and so we move a smaller distance along a *given* demand curve. In the case where money's own rate moved perfectly with the bond rate, there would be no change at all in the spread and we would stay at one point on the curve. In Figure 24.3 as drawn with a simple, absolute, rate on the vertical axis, this would be shown by a rightward shift of the curve to M_d^4, sufficient to offset completely the movement up it A to D.

Remember that in Chapter 13, where we discussed the history of monetary targeting and techniques of monetary control, we saw that the rationale for monetary targets is a stable relationship between money growth rates and the rate of growth of spending – a stable velocity. Furthermore, we noted that the main instrument that central banks have at their disposal for influencing monetary growth is changes in short-term interest rates. Ideally a change in official dealing rates would cause a change in **relative interest rates**. When official rates are increased (for example) the return on non-money assets rises in relation to the return on money. Money becomes less attractive and people hold fewer deposits. The rise in rates also increases the cost of borrowing. The flow of new loans diminishes and the money supply expands more slowly. The reduction in the demand for loans will be further reinforced if the switch from deposits to non-money assets makes it cheaper for firms to borrow by issuing liabilities which are taken up in preference to deposits. But all this begins with, and depends upon, the central bank's ability to change relative rates when it changes its official dealing rates. This becomes increasingly difficult as money pays interest and as the rate that it pays moves in line with changes in other rates. At the same time, sharp changes in the interest-bearing proportion of money, such as that witnessed in the UK in the 1980s, mean that the average 'own rate' on money changes. When this happens, people hold more (or less) money relative to spending. Velocity is no longer stable.

24.5 Summary

Innovation is a natural and continuous process in a competitive economic environment. However, it is stimulated by changes in the economic environment and these changes are more pronounced at some periods than others. Typically relevant changes are those involving regulation, technology and volatility of financial flows. Each of these has played a major role in stimulating groups of financial innovations during the past 30 years.

Examples of financial innovation are scattered throughout this book, but in this chapter we looked at three particular forms of innovation, which are both widespread and significant either for the regulatory authorities or for the conduct of monetary policy. The first of these is the development of off-balance-sheet activity. This originated as a response to regulation but has blossomed – particularly in the form of securitization of loans – as a response to reducing the risk exposure of institutions which make fixed rate loans in periods of volatile interest rates. The second is retail liability management. This began in response to deregulation and has had major impacts on the demand for money and on the ability of the authorities to control monetary growth. The third is the rapid expansion in the use of credit risk derivatives which provide a particular form of insurance against risk.

Key concepts in this chapter

Building Societies Act 1986	Passthrough
Competition and Credit Control (CCC)	Pre-payment
Contestable markets	Regulation Q
Credit risk derivatives	Regulatory dialectic
Financial volatility	Regulatory tax hypothesis
Income velocity	Relative interest rates
Money's own rate	Retail liability management
Moral hazard hypothesis	Securitization
Non-pecuniary costs of borrowing	Transactions costs
Off-balance-sheet operations	Transactions velocity

Questions and problems

1   Why does financial innovation occur?

2   Explain, using examples, how regulation, technological change and volatility can encourage financial innovation.

3   Why has financial innovation been such a feature of the past 25 years?

4   Explain what is meant by 'off-balance-sheet operations' and give three examples.

5   Explain the basic principles underlying the creation of loan-backed securities.

6   What are the characteristics of a 'passthrough' security? Why might these characteristics limit the attractiveness of this type of security for some types of investor?

7   What is meant by 'retail liability management'? Explain how it has been encouraged by deregulation.

8   Discuss the impacts, potential and actual, of liability management on the demand for money.

9   Why has retail liability management made control of the money supply more difficult?

Further reading

C S Adam, 'Financial innovation and the demand for M3 in the UK 1975–86', *Oxford Bulletin of Economics and Statistics*, 53, 1991, 401–24

K Bain and P G A Howells, 'The income and transactions velocities of money', *Review of Social Economy*, XLIX, 1991, 383–95

W Baumol, 'The transactions demand for cash: an inventory theoretic approach', *Quarterly Journal of Economics*, 66, 1952, 545–56

B Bernanke, 'Regulation and financial innovation', Speech to the Federal Reserve Bank of Atlanta's 2007 Financial Markets Conference, Sea Island, Georgia, 15 May 2007 (www.federalreserve.gov/newsevents/speech/bernanke20070515a.htm)

V Bessis, *Risk Management in Banking* (Chichester: Wiley, 2e, 2002) Ch. 60

I Biefang-Frisancho Mariscal, H M Trautwein, P G A Howells, P Arestis and H Hagemann, 'Financial innovation and the demand for money in the UK and in West Germany', *Weltwirtschaftliches Archiv*, June 1995, 302–25

J D Finnerty, 'Financial engineering', in P Newman, M Milgate and J Eatwell (eds), *The New Palgrave Dictionary of Money and Finance* (London: Macmillan, 1992)

I Fisher, *The Purchasing Power of Money* (New York: Macmillan, 2e, 1926)

C A E Goodhart, *Monetary Theory and Practice: The UK Experience* (London: Macmillan, 1984)

C A E Goodhart, 'Financial innovation and monetary control', *Oxford Review of Economic Policy*, 2 (4), 1986, 79–102

D D Hester, 'Innovations and monetary control', *Brookings Papers on Economic Activity*, 1, 1981, 141–89

P G A Howells and K A Hussein, 'The demand for money in the UK: transactions as the scale variable', *Economics Letters*, 1997, 371–7

R Jarrow and S Turnbull, *Derivative Securities* (New York: Thomson, 2e, 1999) Ch. 18

E J Kane, 'Accelerating inflation, technological innovations and the decreasing effectiveness of banking regulation', *Journal of Finance*, 36 (2), 1981, 33–67

E J Kane, 'Technological and regulatory forces in the developing fusion of financial services competition', *Journal of Finance*, 39 (3), 1984, 24–41

E J Kane, 'How market forces influence the structure of financial regulation', in W S Haraf and R M Kushmeider (eds), *Restructuring Banking and Financial Services in America* (Washington DC: American Enterprise Institute, 1988)

J M Keynes, *Treatise on Money*, Vol. 1 (London: Macmillan, 1930)

M K Lewis, 'Off-balance sheet activities and financial innovation in banking', *Banca Nazionale del Lavoro Quarterly Review*, 167, December 1988

▶

M K Lewis and P D Mizen, *Monetary Economics* (Oxford: Oxford University Press, 2000)

A W Sametz, 'Financial innovation and regulation in the United States', in P Newman, M Milgate and J Eatwell (eds), *The New Palgrave Dictionary of Money and Finance* (London: Macmillan, 1992)

W L Silber, 'The process of financial innovation', *American Economic Review*, 73 (2), 1983, 89–95

J Tobin, 'The interest elasticity of transactions demand for cash', *Review of Economics and Statistics*, 38, 1956, 241–7

P Tufano, 'Financial Innovation' (www.people.hbs .edu/ptufano/fininnov_tufano_june2002.pdf)

Websites

www.bankofengland.co.uk
www.credit-deriv.com
www.csfi.org.uk
www.fenews.com
www.finpipe.com
www.frbatlanta.org

Chapter 25 The regulation of
financial markets

What you will learn in this chapter:

■ Why financial systems are heavily regulated

■ The nature of market failure in financial markets

■ The arguments against regulation based on agency capture,
moral hazard and compliance costs

■ The arguments for and against self-regulation

■ The nature of the problem of competitive laxity

■ The problems caused for regulators by globalization and
financial innovation

■ The difficulties in regulating a financial system composed of
separate national systems with different banking traditions

25.1 Introduction

The financial services industry has always been politically sensitive and, consequently, heavily regulated. The political sensitivity of the industry stemmed from its origin in money-lending which many religions have equated with usury.[1] The rejection by Christianity of usury up until the early years of the Renaissance led to money-lending being dominated by non-Christian outsiders which, in turn, intensified the distaste for it, even while the services of money-lenders were becoming increasingly demanded. Shakespeare's *The Merchant of Venice* shows a society which accorded moral superiority to the shipping of goods from one country to another over the lending of money even though the former depended on the latter.

There have also been more specific reasons for concern about the practice of the industry. Up until the past quarter of a century or so, the term 'financial services' referred principally to the banking and insurance industries. The specific reasons for the demand for regulation of these two industries have been rather different. For the banking industry, the basic problem has been its reliance on public confidence. The fractional reserve banking system – the holding of only relatively small reserves against deposits – vastly increases the potential profitability of banks but, at the same time, leaves them at risk from loss of public confidence which may cause a run on their deposits. The risk of collapse is made greater by the contrast between the liquid nature of bank liabilities (deposits) and the illiquid nature of their assets (loans). This creates the possibility of a solvent bank with sound but illiquid assets being faced with a liquidity problem as in the Northern Rock case in the UK in 2007 (discussed in Case study 4). Further, the assets of a bank are likely to have a significantly lower value when the bank is in liquidation than when it is a going concern. Consequently, a collapse will generally result in a heavy loss to creditors.

There are two principal areas of concern in relation to bank collapse. The first is the prospect of *contagion* – the collapse of one bank leading to the collapse of others with the possibility of damage occurring to the whole financial industry. This, in turn, might have very serious consequences for the real economy. Contagion might arise to the extent that a failure of one bank causes a loss of confidence in banking in general. Thus, a run on a bank may occur because it becomes known that it is in a difficult financial position – perhaps it has made a number of dubious loans that are not likely to be repaid. This could either lead the public to become more discriminating in their choice of bank, in which case there would be no danger for soundly managed banks, or it could lead to many depositors wishing to withdraw their funds from the banking system in general, causing problems for all banks. A second possible source of contagion is the very high level of interbank dealings which is a common feature of modern finance – the collapse of a large bank might create a significant quantity of bad debts for other banks. It is possible as well that the default of a major borrower might encourage other borrowers to default. This was one of the fears in the early years of the international debt crisis of the developing countries which started in 1982 with the decision by Mexico to default on debt repayments.

The second concern with regard to possible bank collapse relates to consumer protection. The efficiency of a modern economy is greatly enhanced by the development of the financial system and thus it is desirable that as many people as possible participate in that system. It follows that collapses of financial institutions within a sophisticated financial system are bound to affect many people, small savers as well as large. Further, most people who take part in financial transactions have very little knowledge of either the products or the processes of the system. In addition, prices in financial markets depend heavily on expectations and can thus move very sharply as a result of market optimism or pessimism. This means that large profits (and losses) can, on occasions, be made with great rapidity. It is hardly surprising, then, that greed, chicanery and gullibility are present to a greater extent in financial markets than in many others. A recent example with grave political and social consequences was the collapse of the pyramid savings schemes in Albania in early 1997.

In markets where the potential losers may be thought to be people with ready access to financial resources and information, it may seem reasonable to

---

[1]   It is the strict Islamic rejection of usury that has led to the quite rapid development in recent years of Islamic banking which eschews the taking of interest.

follow the principle of *caveat emptor*.[2] It would, however, take a bold politician to ignore the plight of small savers threatened with the loss of their life savings. The safest response is to attempt to regulate the market in the hope of preventing such situations from occurring and/or to provide insurance where they do arise. Box 25.1 considers some contrasting British cases from this point of view.

Deposit-taking institutions have been subject to heavy regulation because their liabilities form the means of payment. Thus, bank regulation aims to guarantee the integrity of the transactions medium and to prevent the process of financial intermediation from failing.

Special features that explain the high level of regulation of the insurance market include the very long term of some contracts, the size of many of the risks being insured relative to policyholders' incomes, and the lack of transparency of many of the products. Until quite recently, in other financial markets – for equities, bonds, bills, derivatives – only the funds of professional investors were at risk. Now, however, many people have at least an indirect interest in the performance of such markets through unit trusts, investment trusts and pension funds managed for them by professional fund managers. More of us than ever before have a reason for wishing financial markets to be sound and transparent.

BOX 25.1 Attitudes towards losers in financial markets

1 Lloyd's of London names
Lloyd's of London is an insurance market organized into 400 syndicates supplying a range of insurance services. Syndicates are backed by 'names' who guarantee to meet any syndicate losses from their personal wealth on a basis of unlimited liability. In profitable years, 'names' do not have to provide funds and thus earn a rate of return on money that can also be invested elsewhere. However, in the late 1980s and early 1990s, several syndicates experienced years of large losses and 'names' backing these syndicates were called upon to pay large sums. It was claimed that some losses were the result of manipulation by professionals in the market and the market felt obliged to provide some compensation to losers in order to try to salvage its own reputation. Many court actions were undertaken by 'names'. Nonetheless, there was very little public sympathy for 'names'. It was widely believed that they were happy to accept the high returns without being prepared fully to accept the accompanying risk.

2 UK private pensions
In the late 1980s, new legislation opened up the possibility of people taking out private pension plans. Large insurance companies saw this as a major new market and set about persuading large numbers of people to switch from their existing pension schemes operated by their employers to private pension plans or to take out personal pensions rather than joining employers' schemes. Between April 1988 and June 1994, many people were misled by insurance companies into believing they would be better off with a personal pension plan when the reverse was the case. When this became clear, there was widespread public and political anger. The industry regulators imposed fines on the companies involved and required that compensation be paid. However, the form of compensation was not agreed until some years after the problem become known. The mis-selling review was not completed until early 2003. Compensation offered by the insurance companies was over £11.5bn and fines of more than £10m were levied on the companies. The administration costs of the review were £2bn.

Losers and the search for remedy
We have seen in the personal pensions case and shall see again with regard to split investment trusts in Box 25.4 that there is sometimes a case for losers in financial markets to be rescued. On other occasions, as with bank deposit insurance, losers are, up to set limits, insured against loss. In the personal pension example, industry regulators sought recompense for the wronged parties. However, although losers may in some circumstances obtain help from an ombudsman, they mostly must seek legal remedy, as with Lloyd's names above and the Mirror Group pensioners considered in Box 25.2. We mentioned another interesting legal case in Section 20.9, with the ratepayers of Hammersmith and Fulham being rescued by the courts from the folly of their council officials. Other cases abound. All these cases raise, in different ways, the question of the extent to which people should be held responsible for their actions in complex financial markets.

---

[2] Let the buyer beware.

25.2 The difficulties of regulation

The case for regulation can be put in more technical terms than we have done above. Regulation is necessary, we could say, because of *market failure*. Market failure might arise for any number of reasons – because of the presence of elements of monopoly or oligopoly; because confidence in the financial system is a social benefit which will not be adequately valued by individuals in the market; because of the lack of perfect knowledge and so on. A particular form of the lack of perfect information is **asymmetric information** – the ignorance of consumers relative to producers in highly technical markets. Although not all the arguments are convincing, there is a firm basis of support for some level and form of regulation of financial markets. We do, however, face a number of difficulties.

Firstly, regulation can cause problems as well as solve them. This has been at the base of the strong demand over the past quarter of a century for **deregulation** – for greater freedom from government control – in all areas of the economy, not least in financial markets. These demands have been supported by the development of the 'economic theory of regulation' which stresses a number of undesirable features of regulation. The theory[3] derives from the idea of **agency capture** – that the regulatory process will inevitably be captured by producers and used in their interests rather than in the interests of consumers. The theory of regulation points to four major failings of regulation:

- Regulation creates *moral hazard*. That is, it causes people to behave in a counterproductive way. For example, a belief that the government will ensure the safety of deposits with all financial institutions leads savers to deposit their money without giving thought to the behaviour of the company with whom they bank. This, in turn, allows dubious organizations to survive. Equally, the belief that they will always be rescued from collapse causes financial institutions to take greater risks in their lending policies in search of higher returns. Moral hazard is discussed in Section 24.3.1 in relation to off-balance-sheet activity and makes a strong appearance on the discussion of the Northern Rock case study (Case study 4, see page 603). Another much-quoted example of moral hazard in operation was the risky behaviour of Savings and Loans Associations in the USA in the 1980s (see Box 4.1).

- The regulatory process is likely to be captured by producers since the activities of regulators are much more important to each of the relatively small number of producers than to each of the much larger number of consumers. Further, the next career move of regulators is often into the industry they have been regulating and so they may not wish to offend producers, and/or regulators may be ex-practitioners who share the judgements and values of the producers.

- Regulation creates **compliance costs** (the costs of adhering to the regulations) for producers. The effects of such costs depend on the degree of competition in the industry and the nature of the costs. If producers are able to pass the costs on to consumers, the result is higher prices and lower output. On the other hand, fixed compliance costs will have no impact on marginal costs and, in a genuinely competitive industry, will not affect output. Complying with regulations may also have benefits for firms. They might, for example, be required to keep better records than they would have chosen to do voluntarily and might later discover advantages in having done so.

- The need to comply with regulations increases the costs of entry into and exit from markets. This helps to preserve monopoly positions and make cartels more stable.

Combining the last two arguments produces the proposition that regulation inhibits competition and thus reduces the efficiency with which financial markets help to allocate the economy's scarce resources. However, even if we accept that regulation restricts competition, it is by no means the only factor in financial markets that does so and there is no guarantee that a reduction in regulation will lead to increased competition. The deregulation argument may work in two ways.

- Regulation keeps out new entrants who, if they could enter, would force existing firms in the market to be more efficient and would compete prices down, removing monopoly rents.

- Regulation prevents mergers and acquisitions and allows small inefficient firms to remain in business. Thus, deregulation would lead to mergers which would result in economies of scale, economies of scope and the replacement of poor management by superior management.

---

[3] The theory was developed in Stigler (1971).

With regard to the first of these, the benefits of lower prices which might arise from deregulation have to be weighed against costs such as possible reductions in the stability of the system and increased risk of loss for consumers. Unfortunately for the second proposition, studies of the very considerable merger activity that took place in US banking in the 1980s and 1990s have produced no convincing evidence of increased efficiency or profitability.[4] On the other hand, if there were significant economies of scale, and mergers occurred to take advantage of them, it would become difficult for new entrants to come into the market, even in the absence of regulation.

It therefore seems that none of the criticisms of regulation provide sufficient reason to reject all regulation, though they do point to matters that must be taken into account in decisions as to how much regulation there should be and what form it should take.

With regard to the form of regulation, we must first ask who should carry out the regulation – the government or a government agency, or the industry itself (**self-regulation**). The argument for self-regulation has two elements. Firstly, the industry has a commercial incentive to protect its own reputation and so members will be prepared to pay to achieve this, thus overcoming one of the principal market failure arguments for government regulation. Secondly, practitioners understand the needs of the industry and are likely to interfere less with its efficient functioning. This counters a common complaint against public regulatory bodies that, because they will be heavily criticized over the collapse of firms but not praised for actions that lead to lower prices, they will always impose excessive safety standards, raising the cost of regulation to both producers and consumers.

The assumption then is that self-regulation is almost certain to be lighter than regulation by an external body. There is a danger, however, that self-regulation may turn out to be an awkward halfway house. To begin with, it must be supported by some government regulation at least to the extent that firms are legally required to join the industry regulatory scheme. Otherwise, an incentive would be created for some firms to act as free riders, hoping to benefit from any increase in reputation of the industry resulting from the behaviour of firms within the regulatory organization without paying the costs of membership.

More importantly, self-regulation will only create less moral hazard than public regulation to the extent that it leaves an element of risk for both consumers and producers. The problem is that once an element of risk exists, the degree of risk has to be assessed to allow a judgement to be made of the risk/return profile of an investment. This should cause no worries to professionals, but the general public faces two types of difficulty. Firstly, it may be time-consuming and costly to acquire the necessary knowledge to assess risk accurately. Secondly, the ability of non-experts in a field to assess risk is notoriously poor. There is a strong tendency for people to respond to risk by adopting one or other extreme position. They may, as responses to food scares show, eschew a product or activity completely as soon as an element of risk is made clear. Alternatively, they may, as people's behaviour as car drivers and smokers attests, believe that risk only exists for other people. Thus, the possibility of consumers assessing risk at all accurately is remote, especially in markets that are characterized by asymmetric information and where producers have both the incentive and the capacity to mislead consumers.

Further, the existence of consumers who are, in the field of finance, risk takers or who underestimate the true level of risk ensures that dubious firms will continue to survive despite the apparent reduction of moral hazard. On the other hand, those who are risk averters or who overestimate the true risk may be driven away from products from which they might have benefited.

Nor does self-regulation perform particularly well in terms of the other complaints about regulation. By definition, self-regulation places regulation in the hands of the producers. Indeed, it places it in the hands of *existing* producers and provides an incentive for them to use regulation to increase barriers to entry to the industry. Thus, it may lead to a lowering of some kinds of compliance costs, but not necessarily all.

Many of the problems of self-regulation can be illustrated by a consideration of the operation of the UK's *Financial Services Act* of 1986. The Act set up a regulatory system for the City of London with the aim of creating a flexible system of self-regulation which inspired confidence in both market practitioners and investors. It established a new principal regulatory authority, the Securities and Investment Board (SIB), which recognized three types of organization: a number of self-regulatory organizations (SROs) which were composed of investment practitioners and which were given the responsibility of regulating their own segment of the industry; a group of recognized

---

4 See Rhoades (1992).

professional bodies (RPBs) whose task it was to maintain the standards of the lawyers, accountants, insurance brokers and actuaries who participate in the market; and a number of regulated exchanges.

The Act covered all financial services. An initial problem was with the classification of the industry for the purpose of defining membership of the SROs. This is far from easy because of the overlapping of activities. For example, life assurance firms not only provide insurance but also run pension funds, have an interest in housing finance, engage in fund management and provide investment advice. Banks also participate in a variety of fields and overlap with insurance companies in some ways. This problem increased with the *functional integration* of financial services firms. A single firm may now[5] be engaged in banking, insurance and securities business.

The argument that self-regulation is desirable because practitioners understand best the needs and working of an industry requires that regulation should be undertaken by experts. The complexity of the various elements of the industry, in turn, means that the regulatory needs of the various activities will be different and that there should be a number of SROs each dealing with a precise segment of the industry. Yet this is bound to produce some overlap among the SROs. It follows that if the legal requirement is for firms to join only one regulatory organization, some will be able to choose which organization to join and the separate SROs may find themselves competing for members.

This introduces the possibility of **competitive laxity** with those regulating authorities that try to maintain high standards losing out to those that choose to reduce standards in the interests of their members. In this way, the regulating authorities might act as trade associations, looking after the interests of their members, and underplaying the role of consumer protection. Some regulators may attempt to maximize membership by keeping subscriptions low, reducing their ability to supervise the behaviour of members. A case in point in Britain in the early 1990s was FIMBRA (the Financial Intermediaries, Managers and Brokers Regulatory Association), one of the original SROs set up by the Financial Services Act. FIMBRA kept its subscriptions low and as a result soon ran into financial problems. It then had to be rescued by loans

---

MORE FROM THE WEB

A good way to stay in touch with what is happening regarding the regulation of financial markets in the UK is to read the press releases on the Financial Services Authority (FSA) website. Go to www.fsa.gov.uk. On the home page, click on 'Communication Documents' and then on 'Press Releases'. This gives access to all FSA's press releases since 1999. A press release usually provides a short summary of the issue under consideration, gives 'Notes for Editors' which provide a little background information and provides links to allow you to obtain more detail if you need it.

---

from its larger members, causing it to be heavily dependent on a small number of members who could transfer to other associations if the actions of FIMBRA did not suit them. One of the consequences of the weakening of the regulatory system in this way was the Maxwell pension fund scandal which is set out in Box 25.2.

In addition, as the Chairman of Britain's Securities and Investment Board (SIB), Andrew Large, admitted in 1993, self-regulation is often seen to equate with self-interest. This was particularly true of the City of London self-regulatory system as a result of the uncovering of a large number of illegal activities and institutional collapses in the late 1980s and 1990s.

The system was given the benefit of the doubt for some years on the grounds that a complex system needed time to settle down. However, in 1997, 11 years after the Financial Services Act, the industry was still struggling to cope with issues such as the failure of agents to seek the best prices for clients and the giving of unsuitable investment advice. It was clear that a more trusted system was needed and in May 1997 the government announced the return to full statutory regulation under a single regulator, the **Financial Services Authority (FSA)**. We look at the FSA in Section 25.3.

The difficulties faced by financial regulators everywhere have been increased by the *globalization* of financial markets. In the period since 1980 there has been a very rapid growth in the stock of cross-border bank assets and cross-border securities transactions. Both the sheer size and the interdependence of markets now pose problems. The Bank for International Settlements (BIS) has warned that essentially local

---

[5] A significant amount of functional integration has always existed in countries such as Germany and Austria in which banks have been universal – able to provide a wide range of banking and securities services. On the other hand, self-regulation has not been practised in those countries.

BOX 25.2 Maxwell and the pension funds

On 31 October 1991 the body of the newspaper tycoon, Robert Maxwell, was discovered floating in the sea off the Canary Islands. During the subsequent unravelling of the affairs of the Maxwell group of companies, including Maxwell Communications Corporation (MCC) and Mirror Group Newspapers (MGN), massive fraud was discovered relating to the pension funds of the Maxwell companies.

Two types of problems were uncovered. The first was the management of the pension funds in the interests of the Maxwell family rather than the investors in the fund. When Maxwell had taken control of the MGN fund in 1985, investments were largely in UK blue chip equities. By April 1990, more than half of the 20 largest investments in the fund's portfolio were in companies with which Maxwell had a connection or in his own private interests. This was clearly contrary to general trust law which lays down three obligations for trustees:

- to diversify investments;
- to avoid exposing beneficiaries to undue risk;
- to act reasonably.

However, much worse was to follow. During 1991, Maxwell siphoned off up to £1 billion from the pension funds of his companies in the form of unsecured loans for his own use in defending his seriously troubled empire. When the Maxwell companies collapsed, this money was lost, leaving several of the funds unable to meet their obligations to pay pensions to employees and former employees.

How could this have happened?

Pension funds accounts are required by law to be kept separate from company accounts. A board of 'independent' trustees is appointed to oversee the running of the fund. However, Maxwell was able to appoint his own trustees and did so to good effect. There was a gradual erosion of representation of employees on the board and most trustees appeared to know little of what was being done in their name. Maxwell managed the funds through his own private management firm, Bishopgate Investment Management (BIM). It was subject to inspection by auditors and to regulation by one of the SROs, IMRO (the Investment Management Regulatory Organization).

A report compiled by the House of Commons social security select committee later described the events as a 'spectacle to make even Pontius Pilate blush' as everyone in the City seemed mainly concerned to deny blame. The report concluded that if the regulators had 'acted with the proper degree of suspicion . . . and if professional advisers' care had been commensurate with their fees . . . then the Maxwell pension funds would have been secure' (*Financial Times*, 10 March 1992, p. 8).

The report particularly criticized the accountancy firm, Coopers & Lybrand Deloitte, which had detailed serious shortcomings in the way BIM managed the pension funds as early as February 1991 but had reported this only to the pension fund manager and only rarely attended meetings of the trustees of the funds. IMRO was also heavily criticized. It had investigated BIM only five weeks before Maxwell's death but had claimed to find nothing wrong. It had failed, said the select committee, to spot stealing on a massive scale. It added that self-regulation was little short of tragic comedy.

events might have disruptive implications for the whole international financial system. Globalization has also caused fears of competitive laxity among national regulatory authorities. A national authority may feel that too strict regulation could leave its own country's firms at a competitive disadvantage in comparison with firms based in countries with less stringent rules. Since much of the financial services industry is footloose, strict regulation in one country may cause firms to move their operations to other countries, possibly resulting in a considerable loss of income and employment to the country attempting to operate a responsible regulatory regime. To the extent that regulations are loosened everywhere and/or that firms do move to more poorly regulated areas, the level of systemic risk through contagious financial disorders may be increased.

Financial innovation and rapid technological change in the financial services industry have posed yet more major problems for regulators. The development of screen-based trading systems, securitization and the rapid growth in the availability of new, sophisticated derivatives have all complicated the job of the authorities. Especial concern has been expressed over the growth of off-balance-sheet risk and the risk posed by fast-changing on-balance-sheet positions. The traditional regulatory, accounting and legal framework for financial organizations which depended on the regular scrutiny of balance sheets has been left behind by such developments. We look at these questions in Section 25.4 below.

We can sum up by saying that regulation of financial services faces many serious problems and may, under certain circumstances, make matters worse. We have seen, however, that self-regulation does not provide a simple remedy for such problems. We shall see in Section 25.4 that government regulators have no choice but to work with the industry itself in the operation of regulatory regimes, but there remains a strong case for regulatory bodies which are external to the industry. Certainly, the difficulties of regulation do not justify complete deregulation of the industry. It has been frequently argued by those in favour of deregulation that financial markets are not different in kind from other markets but only in degree and so should not be treated any differently. However, large differences in degree are equivalent to differences in kind. Financial markets are of great importance to the economy as a whole and to a large number of individual consumers. Views about their regulation cannot satisfactorily be derived from the treatment of non-financial markets.

25.3 The Financial Services Authority (FSA)

The Financial Services Authority (FSA) was set up as the single regulator for all financial firms and markets in the UK with its powers being confirmed by the *Financial Services and Markets Act* (FSMA), which received royal assent in June 2000. It is an independent non-governmental body with a Board appointed by the Treasury. The Board, currently of 14 members including nine non-executive members, establishes the overall policy of the organization while day-to-day decisions are the responsibility of the Chief Executive. A formal link with the Bank of England is established by the presence on the Board of the Deputy Governor (Financial Stability) of the Bank. The FSA is financed by fees from authorized firms and exchanges.

The FSA is directly accountable to HM Treasury and through it to the UK Parliament. It has, in addition, established a number of independent panels which monitor the extent to which the FSA is meeting its statutory objectives from the point of view of different interest groups – the Consumer Panel, the Practitioner Panel, and the Smaller Businesses Practitioner Panel. There is also a Complaints Commissioner and the Financial Services and Markets Tribunal which passes judgement in cases where disagreements arise between the FSA and firms or individuals about the FSA's regulatory decisions.

The FSA had been launched in 1997, taking over from a number of regulatory and self-regulatory organizations including the Securities and Investment Board, the Building Societies Commission, the Friendly Societies Commission, the Insurance Directorate of HM Treasury and the Registry of Friendly Societies. In the early years, these organizations continued to act on behalf of the FSA while it built up its organization, determined its regulatory philosophy and prepared its handbook of rules and guidance.

In June 1998 the FSA took over direct regulation of the banking sector from the Bank of England. The FSA is now responsible for enforcing the Banking Act, 1987 and the relevant European Union banking directives. The content of the Banking Act is covered in Section 3.2. In July 1998, the FSA produced its own guide to bank supervisory policy, although this remained heavily dependent on previous publications of the Bank of England. Although it had become the banking regulator, the FSA needed to coordinate with the Bank of England because the Bank retained the responsibility for maintaining the stability of the financial system including overseeing the payment systems and considering risks across the system as a whole. The allocation of responsibilities for regulation and financial stability in the UK were set out in the Memorandum of Understanding (1997, updated 2006, available at http://www.fsa.gov.uk/pubs/mov/fsa_hmt_boe.pdf) between the Bank, HM Treasury and the FSA.

The FMSA set the FSA four objectives: market confidence; consumer awareness; consumer protection; and fighting financial crime. The FSA has added to these a set of principles of good regulation and summarizes its statutory objectives and principles in terms of:

■ promoting efficient, orderly and fair markets;

■ helping retail consumers achieve a fair deal; and

■ improving its business capability and effectiveness.

In its approach to these objectives, the FSA accepts risk as inherent in financial markets and does not seek to discourage appropriate risk taking by regulated

---

BOX 25.3 Financial Ombudsman Service

As well as setting up the FSA, the Financial Services and Markets Act 2000 established a single financial services ombudsman to help settle disputes between consumers and financial firms. This combined the work of four separate complaints procedures under the previous regulatory system. The introduction of an ombudsman into a regulatory system has two purposes – to increase public confidence in financial markets and thus to encourage consumers to participate in these markets despite the manifest risks of doing so; and to attempt to redress a perceived imbalance in financial markets resulting from consumer ignorance and asymmetric information.

The ombudsman can consider complaints about a wide range of financial matters and the service is free to consumers. The decisions of the ombudsman are binding on firms but not on consumers. Consumers, having first complained to the firm with which they have a grievance, can take their cases to the ombudsman. If the decision there is not to their liking, they retain the ability to go to court. The ombudsman does not, as the FSA can do, either punish or fine firms for breaking rules.

The ombudsman service applies compulsorily to all firms regulated by the FSA for certain types of complaints. In addition, firms not regulated by the FSA can volunteer to participate in the service. Further, firms that are regulated by the FSA can volunteer to have the ombudsman consider types of complaints that are not part of the ombudsman's compulsory jurisdiction. Through consultation, the Financial Ombudsman Service has sought to widen the range of complaints with which it deals.

In the year ended 31 March 2006, 112,923 new cases were referred to the case handling teams – the number of cases has increased greatly since 2001 when 31,347 new cases were dealt with. Unsurprisingly, the biggest area for complaints was mortgage endowments (69,149 new cases – 61 per cent of the total). Next came other investment-related cases (15,795 cases, 14 per cent), followed by insurance-related cases (14,270, 13 per cent) and then banking-related cases (13,709, 12 per cent). For more details see http://www.financial-ombudsman.org.uk/.

---

firms or investors. It believes that it is not practicable to try to develop a regime in which there are no failures of financial firms; nor is it desirable to try to do so since this would produce heavy-handed and expensive regulation that would restrict innovation and interfere with competition.

Under the single regulator system, each firm obtains from the FSA a single authorization to carry out financial business in the UK with an associated list of permissions setting out what the FSA allows it to do – under the old regulatory system, many firms had held a number of authorizations from different regulatory bodies. Single compensation and ombudsman schemes were also developed and from the second half of 2001 all financial firms were, for the first time, subject to a single regime for tackling 'market abuse', a non-criminal offence that was added to the already existing criminal offences of insider trading and market manipulation. Three categories of market abuse have been defined: misuse of information; giving false or misleading impressions; and market distortion.

The FSMA also requires the FSA to be efficient and economic in its use of resources and thus it focuses its efforts on what it sees as the most significant risks to the achievement of its statutory objectives. This approach to regulation has been described as both 'principles based' and 'light touch' and has been highly praised in other parts of the world, notably the USA. Sir Callum McCarthy, Chairman of the FSA, denies that either of these phrases correctly describes its regulatory practice, preferring 'risk-based regulation' as a description.[6] This indicates that, in allocating its resources, the FSA takes into account the risk of failure faced by particular firms and the impact that such a failure would have on the FSA's statutory objectives. Thus, where the FSA judges both the risk of failure and the potential impact of failure to be high, the firm is subject to 'close and continuous' attention, but this applies to less than one per cent of the 29,000 firms regulated. However, firms that are judged to present a very small threat to the FSA's objectives may never be inspected or inspected only relatively infrequently. This places great weight on the judgement of degree of risk.

The FSA has a fine line to walk. A single regulator, even one that prefers to operate on the basis of broad principles rather than detailed regulations, is bound to

---

[6]   See Callum McCarthy, 'Financial regulation: myth and reality', speech at the FSA British American Business London Insight Series and Financial Services Forum, 13 February 2007, http://www.fsa.gov.uk/pages/Library/Communication/Speeches/2007/0213_cm.shtml.

maintain a large rule book and will always be subject to the criticism that it is too large and bureaucratic and imposes heavy compliance costs on firms. On the other hand, it has been criticized for moving too far in the opposite direction and failing adequately to observe and prevent developing risks facing consumers.

Particular problems over which the FSA has been criticized include split capital investment trusts (see Box 25.4), Equitable Life and endowment mortgages and, more recently, the Northern Rock affair. In relation to Equitable Life (see Section 3.5), the FSA was criticized for its failure to spot problems and to follow up issues that had been uncovered although it was partly excused because the problem had developed during the period in which the FSA was being set up (between January 1999 and December 2000) during most of which, regulation was being carried out on the FSA's behalf by its predecessor, the Personal Investment Authority (PIA).

The mis-selling of endowment mortgages also began well before the FSA came into existence and the criticism of the FSA related not to the occurrence of the problem itself but to the way it was handled once it had been uncovered. Millions of people had in the 1980s and 1990s chosen to take out interest-only mortgage loans accompanied by endowment insurance policies. This meant that the amount owing was not reduced at all during the life of the loan but the endowment policy was expected to grow sufficiently to pay off the original amount borrowed at the end of the period and could, indeed, if bonuses were high, return to the policyholder at the end of the period a sum greater than that needed to repay the mortgage. However, endowment mortgage loans run the risk that the bonus rate paid on the policies will be insufficient to repay the loan. Bonus rates depend on the performance of the investments made by the insurance company which, in turn, are affected by the performance of the stock and bond markets.

Thus, when the performance of endowment policies deteriorated sharply because of low inflation and low interest rates in the 1990s, it became clear that many of them would not meet the mortgage in full at the end of the loan period. Things were made worse by falling share prices late in 2000. Policyholders were faced with either having to meet the difference at the end of the period or to make top-up payments to the insurance company to ensure that the mortgage would be paid off. Was this just an unfortunate result of the change in economic conditions and a case of 'let the buyer beware'? After all, people had opted for the endowment mortgages in the hope that they would produce a higher return than the less risky straight repayment mortgage. However, it soon became clear that many policyholders had not been told by the insurance companies that their policies carried any risks. These policies had then been 'mis-sold' (sold under false pretences), an offence under the 1986 Financial Services Act. In October 2000, the FSA accepted that this might have happened in hundreds of thousands of cases. Companies who had sold endowment mortgages were required to calculate the position of all policies sold after 29 April 1988, the date that the Financial Services Act came into force, and to write to all policyholders setting out their positions.

People who believed they had been mis-sold endowment mortgages were able to apply for redress to the Financial Ombudsman Service or, where the company that sold the policy had gone out of business, to the Financial Services Compensation Scheme. Some insurance companies pledged to make up shortfalls whether or not the policies had been mis-sold. People sold endowment mortgages before 29 April 1988 had little chance of receiving compensation, although some companies agreed to allow the Financial Ombudsman Service to consider on a voluntary basis complaints of mis-selling before that date.

The FSA also imposed large fines on a number of insurance companies for mis-selling under the market abuse powers granted by the FSMA but it did not undertake a case-by-case review of the problem, arguing that this was not needed because the vast majority of policyholders were better off, despite the disappointing performance of their endowment policies, than they would have been had they taken up a straight repayment mortgage in the first place. Therefore, they would not be entitled to compensation even if the risks of the endowment mortgage had not been explained to them. The main issues for the FSA were to make sure that all policyholders knew their position and what they had to do to overcome the problem and to deter companies from mis-selling policies in the future.

Consumer organizations and the FSA's Consumer Panel were unhappy with this. They argued that people who had realized that they had been mis-sold an endowment policy and had then converted to a simple repayment mortgage would have lost. This problem was partially overcome when the Financial Ombudsman Service said that these people would be entitled to compensation for the loss provided they could

BOX 25.4 Consumer protection – split capital investment trusts

By M Richards and R Budden

Split capital investment trusts are investment trusts – companies listed on the London Stock Exchange that raise funds to invest in other companies. Investors benefit from both dividend income and capital growth. Split capital trusts typically have two types of shareholders with different investment needs – those interested principally in income who collect dividends and expect their capital returned at the end of the trust's life; and those interested in growth who opt for zero dividend preference shares (zeros), receiving in return for forgoing dividends a share in all the capital growth of the fund at the end of its life.

In the late 1990s, when share prices were booming, split capital trusts were heavily marketed and extravagant promises were made. High annual rates of return were mentioned and the trusts were said to be 'low risk'. Shares in the trusts were bought, in particular, by parents saving for school fees and pensioners wanting income or lump sums. But when share prices began to fall sharply in 2000, many trusts did not have enough cash to pay the scale of dividend they had promised. Some trusts borrowed heavily to buy more shares (they became heavily geared) and also invested in each other (cross-holdings). One trust lost over 68 per cent of its value in one year. By October 2002, eight split capital trusts had called in the receivers and up to 40 of the 120 trusts were thought to be in serious trouble. Perhaps 50,000 people lost money in the trusts, some losing heavily. There were stories of pensioners losing their homes.

Initially it was thought that losers had little chance of compensation. The investment industry sought to blame the buyers of zeros. Further, since investment trusts are technically companies rather than regulated funds, the Financial Services Authority claimed no responsibility for them and the Financial Ombudsman Service could only deal with them on a voluntary basis.

However, in February 2003, the House of Commons Treasury Select Committee issued a report on the trusts, which accused one of the biggest firms in the sector, Aberdeen Asset Management, of recklessly misleading promotion. More generally, it suggested widespread conflicts of interest and collusive behaviour in the sector, possibly amounting to corruption. This considerably increased the prospects of investors suing companies for mis-selling. The Treasury Committee chair called for compensation with extra cash where collusion or corruption could be shown.

Following an investigation into the selling of splits, the FSA proposed to the firms involved that they take part in collective settlement negotiations leading, where appropriate, to firms compensating investors and taking disciplinary action against staff. This led to the establishment of Fund Distribution Limited (FDL) to administer the payment of compensation to aggrieved investors. FDL made an initial offer of 40 pence for every pound lost, in return for which investors were required to give up the chance of securing potentially higher payouts through the courts or by use of the ombudsman service, an offer accepted by almost all of the 25,000 eligible investors. FDL made two distributions amounting to 50.663 pence in the pound to eligible investors between May and December 2006. A total of £143.5m was paid to 24,661 eligible investors. The FSA also proposed the introduction of a number of safeguards on the operation of splits in the future. These included a limit to be placed on the extent to which firms can cross-invest in each other, changes to the nature and content of warnings about the risks to capital, and the strengthening of the independence of the company from its investment manager.

The split capital investment trusts affair illustrates several points:

(a) The notion of *moral hazard* – the existence of a powerful regulator and an ombudsman leads small investors to feel their investments are secure. They do not, as a result, always read the 'small print' attached to financial products, even though it could be argued that the high rates of return offered should have alerted investors to the degree of risk they faced.

(b) The difficulty in determining the extent of consumer responsibility for their loss. Was this really a case of mis-selling with innocent consumers being misled by dissembling or dishonest professionals? Or were consumers led into the investment partly by greed – the promised high rates of return causing them to act in a foolish way? This raises the question of how much consumer protection should be provided.

(c) The damage to the industry caused by cases such as these – the Association of Investment Trust Companies felt the need to set up a hardship fund to help out even before any decision had been made as to whether mis-selling had occurred, seeking contributions from fund managers who wanted to restore the battered reputation of the investment trust sector.

Sources: M Richards, 'Split cap victims pick up the pieces on offer', *Financial Times*, 11 November 2006 and R Budden, 'Second payment to splits victims', *Financial Times*, 23 August 2006. Reprinted with permission.

show that they had been mis-advised. Nonetheless, there was concern that the FSA had not acted speedily enough and had not done enough to ensure that all people mis-sold policies would be adequately compensated. From the FSA's point of view, the matter had been effectively resolved when, on 15 July 2005, it announced an independent research finding that most of the 2.2 million households whose endowment policy was still linked to their mortgage, and who were facing a shortfall, had taken some positive action to deal with it. This returns us to the general question of the extent to which financial regulators could or should attempt to protect consumers in financial markets from loss or whether their remit should be the much more general one of ensuring both the fairness and the efficiency of the financial system.[7]

The difficulty of judging which firms and/or activities are likely to put the statutory objectives of the FSA at risk is well illustrated by the Northern Rock problems of 2007 (see Case study 4, page 603), which led to severe criticism of the FSA. In discussing the risk-based approach to regulation and its implications for the way in which resources are used, Sir Callum McCarthy, in a speech made in February 2007,[8] said:

> We have, for example, over a number of years made a substantial shift in the relative resources devoted to bank supervision and supervision of insurance companies, switching resources from the former to the latter in response to our view of the risks in those sectors.

Much of the criticism levelled at the FSA in October 2007 related to its failure to foresee the potential dangers at Northern Rock raising the possibility that the movement of resources away from bank supervision had been overdone. A rather different criticism of the regulatory response to the Northern Rock problem related to the question of coordination between the FSA and the Bank of England. We deal with this in Section 25.4. For a view of the overall performance of the FSA as a financial regulator see Case study 6, page 608.

25.3.1 The FSA and financial capability

We have seen that the second statutory objective of the FSA relates to consumer awareness. The FSA sees

this as not only worthwhile in itself but also of importance in terms of both consumer protection and market confidence. Firms are more easily able to mis-sell products to consumers because of the high degree of consumer ignorance regarding financial services. Clearly, if the FSA could help to increase financial capability among consumers it would help to overcome market abuse. Further, high-profile failures in markets such as illustrated by the long queues of Northern Rock depositors seeking to withdraw their deposits, are very likely to damage confidence in financial markets. Consequently, the FSA quite early decided to move resources away from current regulatory issues towards its educational role, with expenditure on financial education increasing from £3.6 million in 2003/04 to £17.1 million planned for 2007/08.

There are two different but related questions associated with the nature of consumer participation in financial markets. The first concerns the extent to which people participate in financial markets. One important element of this is 'financial exclusion' which we deal with in Box 25.5. It relates to people who do not participate in financial markets at all and can be seen as one aspect of the social deprivation felt by groups of poor people. Certainly, lack of financial capability is not the sole reason for this and it must be tackled by policies that involve a good deal more than improved financial education. A second level of non-participation involves people who are not strictly 'financially excluded' but who are not regular savers. Research into the extent of financial exclusion in Wales in 2005[9] indicated that one in seven people did not have a bank account. These could clearly be identified as financially excluded. The research also suggested that only 42 per cent (below the UK average of 55 per cent) of people in Wales could be classed as regular savers. Again, this low level of regular saving is not caused solely by lack of financial capability although lack of knowledge of available products and lack of confidence in financial institutions and markets no doubt contributes. In a study of the financial education needs of people in their 40s in 2004, about half said that the complexity of financial products and services has put them off addressing their own financial needs.[10]

---

[7]   Financial Services Authority, 'Endowments – consumers act but FSA keeps close eye on complaints', Press Release, 15 July 2005, http://www.fsa.gov.uk/pages/Library/Communication/PR/2005/081.shtml.

[8]   Sir Callum McCarthy, op. cit.

[9]   See http://www.fsa.gov.uk/financial_capability/tools/library-inclusion.html.

[10]   See http://www.fsa.gov.uk/financial_capability/tools/library-work.html.

BOX 25.5 The FSA and financial exclusion

'Financial exclusion' is the exclusion of significant numbers of people from financial services: from particular sources of credit, insurance, bill payment services and accessible and appropriate deposit accounts. People may be excluded as a result of the policies and behaviour of the financial services industry or they may be 'self-excluded' because of the type of financial products available or their assumptions about the likely behaviour of financial institutions. That is, they might not apply for financial services because they assume they will be rejected.

Poor members of the community, in particular, lone parents, people with disabilities, the unemployed, and those on low wages, are the most likely to be financially excluded. For them, financial exclusion is one aspect of general deprivation – a major element within 'social exclusion', which implies a lack of economic, political or social citizenship. However, financial exclusion is not limited to the poor. There may be problems also for ethnic minorities as well as for those who do not conform to the standard picture of creditworthy people used by financial institutions in risk assessment.

According to research estimates published by the FSA, around 7 per cent of households in Britain (1.5 million) have no basic bank or building society account. Around 20 per cent of adults lack a current account, while 27 per cent of employees do not have an occupational or private pension. Up to a quarter of households have no home contents insurance and 45 per cent have no life insurance cover.

Exclusion from financial services carries a number of costs for those excluded. It denies them the ability to borrow and thus to arrange their financial affairs optimally or it forces them to borrow from 'unofficial' sources, possibly at very high interest rates; it denies them discounts on many bills available to people able to pay by direct debit; it greatly reduces their ability to deal with household and personal emergencies because of their lack of insurance and it greatly reduces their ability to plan for the future and to cope with old age and sickness. Because financial exclusion is concentrated both among particular groups and geographically, whole communities are disadvantaged in these ways.

Although dealing with financial exclusion is not a direct responsibility of the FSA, it has acknowledged the need to consider the impact of its regulations on the more vulnerable sectors in society. In July 2000, in conjunction with the University of Bristol, the FSA published a report entitled *In or Out – Financial Exclusion*. This identifies the following ways of tackling financial exclusion:

- improving financial literacy and lowering psychological barriers to using financial services;

- increasing access through outlets such as supermarkets, post offices and credit unions;

- providing simple and low cost financial products;

- providing appropriate regulation of benchmarked products to reduce costs;

- ensuring appropriate regulation for not-for-profit organizations such as credit unions and proposed community banks to provide vulnerable consumers with adequate levels of protection.

The second question deals with people who can and do purchase financial products but who are inadequately informed about them. In the Welsh research, for example, one in five people admitted to having bought a financial product without fully understanding its terms and conditions. These are people relatively easily able to be mis-sold financial products. The figure of one in five in this category considerably understates the problem of inadequate consumer awareness of financial products, given the numbers and types of people mis-sold products in the split capital investment trust and endowment mortgage affairs and the length of the Northern Rock queues.

All of these questions are of interest to the FSA and they have become involved in research and education in a number of ways. For example, it leads the National Strategy for Financial Capability and in June 2005 launched the Financial Capability Innovation Fund which provides grants to encourage and support projects by voluntary and community groups aiming to help people become more financially capable. The FSA also provides support to a number of organizations

> **MORE FROM THE WEB**
>
> Another good source for regulation stories is the website of the Financial Ombudsman Services: www.financial-ombudsman.org.uk. Click on 'News'. On the News page, you will find headings of recent news items with links to full reports. Again, if you need old news, you will be able to consult stories for each year back to 1998.

concerned with financial education in schools. The FSA is also strongly interested in the training and practice of financial advisers.

25.4   Banking regulation

We have mentioned two regulatory issues in banking:

- the possibility of contagion as the result of a run on one bank turning into a *panic* which might lead to a serious reduction in liquidity for the system as a whole;

- the need for consumer protection, given the nature of the banking industry and the cost and difficulty of acquiring knowledge.

We have added to these the need to cause as little moral hazard as possible, to keep compliance costs low and to interfere as little as possible with competition either by creating barriers to entry or exit or by favouring some institutions over others within the market.

A common approach to ensuring the stability of the banking industry has been to prevent banks from participating in the more risky aspects of finance by limiting them to deposit creation and lending functions. Thus, we have seen in earlier chapters that in both the United States and Italy, legislation passed during the 1930s rigidly separated commercial banking from investment banking and other financial activities. Since banks could provide a wider range of financial services not just in their own name but through the acquisition of other companies, this had to be supported by legislation that restricted the ability of banks to acquire non-banking firms and vice versa. In the United States, for example, the *Bank Holding Act, 1956* sought to prevent companies owning banks from being allied with insurance companies, securities firms and commercial enterprises. Such a separation fitted well with the British and American model of banking in which the various kinds of banking business were typically provided by different types of banking organization. In particular, deposit-taking banks concentrated on short-term lending. This contrasted with the universal banking model common in northern Europe.

Other approaches to ensuring the stability of banks have included guaranteeing the liquidity of the overall banking system by giving the central bank the role of lender of last resort to the system, seeking to prevent runs on individual banks by introducing some form of deposit insurance scheme, placing limitations on interest payments on deposits to prevent competition for deposits (liability management), and establishing barriers to entry also with the intention of limiting competition among banks.

We have seen that all of these restrictions have come under challenge in recent years. High and variable inflation and interest rates put pressure on traditional specialized savings institutions. In the United States this was magnified by legal restrictions on rates of interest payable on retail deposits. As financial services became an increasingly international industry, governments became concerned about the competitiveness of their domestic financial industries hobbled by tight regulation. In a world of increasingly mobile capital, firms found their way around existing restrictions and sooner or later forced legislative changes which gave them greater freedom. Diversification of asset bases provided benefits in an increasingly risky environment and firms sought to benefit from economies of both scale and scope. The financial conglomerate was born. All of this was fostered by an anti-government mood in the worlds of both business and finance.

In such a world, fears of instability have increased and the issue of bank supervision at both national and international levels has grown in importance. In supervising banks, regulatory authorities are concerned particularly with questions of capital adequacy, liquidity, asset quality and the concentration of risks.

Capital adequacy is central because a bank's capital must be sufficient to absorb losses and to finance the operation of its business. The modern approach to the assessment of a bank's capital adequacy is based on a calculation of its **risk–asset ratio**. This involves a number of steps:

- a definition of the elements of capital for supervisory purposes;

- the allocation of weights to different broad categories of asset (e.g. cash, government securities, loans to banks, loans to firms and households);
- the expression of capital as a percentage of total risk-weighted assets.

The weights applied in the second step reflect the degrees of risk associated with the different categories of assets. More risky assets have higher weights. Thus, an increase in the proportion of a bank's assets regarded as risky increases the size of its risk-weighted assets and lowers the ratio of capital to risk-weighted assets.

Liquidity relates to the ability of a bank to meet its obligations on time, especially in relation to repayment of interbank borrowings and customer deposits. This is essential if a bank is to maintain its reputation. Given that the survival of a bank depends on the retention of the confidence of its depositors, the maintenance of reputation is critical. Thus, banks must actively manage liquidity. Banks seek to do this in three ways. Firstly, they hold a stock of readily marketable liquid assets that can be turned into cash quickly in response to unforeseen needs. Secondly, in doing this, they identify mismatches between potential receipts and payments in future periods. Thirdly, banks respond to potential mismatches of this kind by borrowing in the market to smooth out cashflows in particular time periods. Regulators may attempt to ensure the continued liquidity of banks by, for example, imposing a required minimum liquidity ratio (a ratio of assets of short maturity to total deposits) and/or by setting limits on mismatches or net positions in particular time bands. In doing the latter, they would allow liquid assets to be included in the calculation at a maturity earlier than their final repayment date to reflect their marketability.

The main issue in relation to the quality of a bank's assets is the ability of its borrowers to service and repay loans. The poor quality of the loans of many banks has been a central element in the problems faced by the Japanese banking system in recent years. It was also an issue in the international debt crisis of developing countries of the 1980s and in the 2007 subprime mortgages problems in the USA. The early identification of problem loans is important if remedial action is to succeed. One way of doing this is to employ a grading system that classifies loans in the range from trouble-free to problematic or, worse,

non-performing. Some countries, including the USA, assign ratings to individual loans in the attempt to evaluate the quality of banks' assets on a consistent basis.

The concern about risk concentration comes from the dangers that arise when banks make very large loans to a small number of borrowers. If loans to a few borrowers make up a high proportion of a bank's assets, then default on these loans can create serious problems. Thus, the greater the concentration of loans, the larger is the potential for loss on the part of the bank. The usual regulatory response is to limit exposures to single counterparties, or groups of counterparties, to the equivalent of some proportion of the bank's capital base. Overexposure to a few borrowers was particularly in evidence in the international debt crisis of the 1980s. Dangers can also arise for banks if deposits come from a narrow range of sources, if individual deposits are large and volatile, if income derives from a small number of transactions or activities, if there is overspecialization in the bank's product range, or if a high proportion of loans are made against one particular kind of collateral.

Quite apart from the difficulties concerning the regulation of individual banks, coordination problems might arise between the bank regulating authority and the central bank. By 1998, when the responsibility for the regulation of banks in the UK was transferred to the FSA, it had become widely accepted that, from the point of view of monetary policy, the regulation of a country's banks should not be left to the country's central bank. However, the central bank necessarily retains responsibility for maintaining the stability of the financial system as a whole since only it is in a position to change its lending policy to the banking sector and so influence the liquidity of the financial system as a whole. The Northern Rock affair in the UK in 2007 (see Case study 4, page 603) illustrated a potential problem here. Was the run on Northern Rock's deposits principally the result of an easily foreseen problem at Northern Rock? Was it principally due to a lack of liquidity in the financial system as a whole? Or was it the result of a mixture of these two? In the first case, one could lay the regulatory failure at the door of the FSA. In the second case, one could argue that the Bank might have acted sooner than it did to ease the lack of liquidity in the system. In the third case, there is a suggestion of a failure of coordination. It is for this reason that in its leading article, the *Financial Times* of 9 October 2007 included among its ten questions for the FSA:

> We would like to know: five, when you first felt concerned about the liquidity of Northern Rock, what caused that concern, and what you did about it? Six, we want to know what you told the Bank of England, whether you asked the Bank to intervene, and when?

A great deal of work has gone on in recent years to standardize and coordinate bank supervision and regulation across all countries. This has centred on the work of the Basel Committee of the Bank for International Settlements (BIS). The Basel Committee decisions are considered in Section 25.5. The European Union has included the various Basel proposals in its banking directives, and these in turn have been incorporated into the domestic legislation of EU member countries.

25.5   The impact of globalization and financial innovation – the Basel Committee

The globalization of the banking industry led to a great increase in international interbank lending and increased dramatically the possibility that the collapse of a bank in one country could cause serious losses for banks in other countries. Regulators became strongly aware of this danger with the collapse in 1974 of both the Franklin National Bank in New York and the Herstatt Bank in Germany. At the same time, there was increasing worry over the gravitation of banks to the least regulated national jurisdictions with resulting competition in regulatory laxity between financial centres. One outcome of these concerns was the setting up of a standing committee of bank supervisors under the auspices of the Bank for International Settlements (BIS). The committee comprised representatives of the bank supervisors of the 11 Group of Ten countries[11] and of Luxembourg. Its formal title was the Committee on Banking Regulation and Supervisory Practices but it has become known as the Basel Committee. It sought to link together the different regulatory regimes in different countries in order to ensure that all banks were supervised according to certain broad principles.

The initial concern of the committee was to establish guidelines for the division of responsibilities among the national supervisory authorities and this led to the signing of the Basel Concordat in December 1975 by the central bank governors of the Group of Ten. This distinguished between 'host' and 'parent' authorities and between branches and subsidiaries of foreign banks. Under the Concordat, the supervision of foreign banking establishments was to be the joint responsibility of parent and host authorities. Host authorities were to be responsible for the supervision of the liquidity of foreign banks. Solvency was to be the responsibility of the parent authority in the case of foreign branches and of the host authority in the case of foreign subsidiaries. Great stress was laid upon the exchange of information between host and parent authorities.

The Concordat was voluntary but all countries represented on the committee adopted its rules. However, it soon became clear that there was a good deal of confusion over the interpretation of the rules. The confusion increased following the adoption in 1978 of a rule that the international business of banks should be conducted on a consolidated basis to limit the opportunities for regulatory evasion since this appeared to conflict with the earlier granting of responsibility for the solvency of foreign subsidiaries to host authorities. A second problem was that the different supervisory standards among countries led some countries, notably the USA, to be more reluctant than others to share or delegate supervisory responsibilities. The collapse of Banco Ambrosiano's Luxembourg subsidiary in the summer of 1982 caused particular concern as neither the Luxembourg nor the Italian authorities would accept responsibility for either supervision or emergency support of the bank, in part because the Luxembourg subsidiary was technically a holding company rather than a bank. In an attempt to overcome the various problems, the Concordat was revised in 1983 with the revision being based upon the principle of consolidated supervision and provisions designed to ensure adequate supervisory standards. The aim was to encourage national authorities to lock out foreign banks originating from permissive jurisdictions and to prevent their own banks from conducting their international operations from poorly regulated centres. The adoption of the principle of consolidated

---

[11]   USA, UK, Japan, Germany, France, Italy, Canada, Netherlands, Belgium, Sweden and Switzerland.

supervision was intended to make the solvency of foreign subsidiaries a joint responsibility of parent and host authorities. Foreign bank subsidiaries were required to be financially sound in their own right, while also being supervised as integral parts of the group to which they belonged. Responsibility for the supervision of liquidity of both foreign branches and subsidiaries was to remain with host authorities. The new agreement also introduced more precise guidelines for the supervision of holding companies.

Despite the changes in the revised Concordat, problems remained and these were highlighted by the pressure placed on the international banking system by the debt crisis of the developing countries during the early 1980s. When, early in 1982, the Mexican government declared a moratorium on debt repayments, there was a potential crisis for international banks which had lent Mexico vast amounts over the previous eight years and possibly for the whole international financial system. Several banks had lent to Latin American countries (especially Mexico, Argentina and Brazil) considerably more than their total capital. In 1982, claims of selected US banks on five major Latin American debtors ranged from between 140 and 260 per cent of the paid-in capital of the banks. In many cases, loans to a single country were more than half the bank's capital. Thus, if Mexico had continued to default on its repayments and if other countries had followed suit, a number of banks would have been wiped out. This possibility raised the spectre of the contagious bankruptcy of many other banks. The IMF, the World Bank and the USA combined to help banks out of these particular problems, but the view took hold that a degree of harmonization of supervisory standards was needed among national regulatory authorities.

The principal outcome of this was the Basel minimum capital adequacy guidelines for international banks approved in July 1988 which established common prudential risk-adjusted ratios for banks to apply from the beginning of 1993. In discussing the risk–asset approach above, we mentioned the need to define the elements of capital for supervisory purposes. The Basel agreement initially distinguished between two types of capital:

Tier I capital (core capital) consists principally of shareholders' equity, disclosed reserves and the current year's retained profits, which were readily available to cushion losses – these must be verified by the bank's auditors.

Tier II capital (supplementary capital) comprises funds available but not fully owned or controlled by the institution, such as 'general' provisions that the bank has set aside against unidentified future losses and medium or long-term subordinated debt issued by the bank.

Tier II capital cannot be more than 100 per cent of Tier I capital for the purpose of calculating the risk–asset ratio. A third type of capital (Tier III) was later defined.

Tier III capital consists of:

(a) subordinated debt of at least two years' maturity which is subject to a 'lock-in' clause (that is, it can only be repaid with permission from the regulatory authorities if repayment would cause the bank to breach its capital ratio); and

(b) accumulated profit arising from the trading book (that is, securities and investment activities not traditionally regarded in the UK as banking business).

The weights to be attached to bank assets included: cash 0; loans to the discount market 0.1; interbank lending 0.2; home mortgage loans 0.5; other commercial loans 1. The Basel Committee proposed a lower limit of 8 per cent for the ratio of total capital to risk-adjusted assets, though national bank supervisors had some discretion in applying this to different types of bank and countries were free to impose a higher minimum requirement on their own banks. In the UK, the FSA sets each UK incorporated bank a separate target minimum capital adequacy requirement for both its banking and investment business, with the 8 per cent risk–asset ratio of the Basel Accord being an absolute minimum requirement for all banks. The agreement sought both to strengthen the soundness and stability of the international banking system and to ensure competitive equality among international banks.

Although the acceptance of the risk–asset approach was regarded as an important step towards increased financial stability in the world economy, as with all such measures, the application of the ratio influenced bank behaviour in ways that made regulation more difficult and may have increased overall risk in the system. In particular, an initial response of banks was to increase further the already growing proportion of their income derived from securitized off-balance-sheet activities. Box 25.6 provides a simplified example of the impact of asset securitization on risk–asset calculations.

BOX 25.6 Risk–asset ratios and off-balance-sheet activities – a simplified example

A bank had the following set of assets:

Asset	Face value	Risk weighting	Risk-weighted value
Cash	50	0	0
Loans to discount market	150	0.1	15
Interbank loans	300	0.2	60
Home mortgage loans	1,550	0.5	775
Loans to small and medium-sized firms	2,150	1	2,150
Total			3,000

Under the rules of the Basel Accord of 1988, the bank was required to hold a minimum of 8 per cent of its risk-weighted assets as capital for regulatory purposes, 50 per cent of which had to be in the form of Tier I capital. Thus, it was required to hold 8 per cent of 3,000 = 240. Tier II capital gives greater flexibility than Tier I capital and the bank chooses to do no more than meet the minimum requirement. Thus, it holds 120 in Tier I capital and 120 in Tier II capital. The bank then decides to increase its competitiveness by holding less capital and to seek to make up for any lost income through securitization and acting in the swaps market. It takes two steps:

1 it securitizes its home mortgage loans, removing them from its balance sheet and increases its loans to firms, which earn a higher rate of interest;

2 it also acts as a guarantor for swap deals to the value of 500, which also does not appear on the balance sheet.

The bank's risk-weighted balance sheet position now is:

Asset	Face value	Risk weighting	Risk-weighted value
Cash	50	0	0
Loans to discount market	150	0.1	15
Interbank loans	300	0.2	60
Loans to small and medium-sized firms	2,425	1	2,425
Total			2,500

The bank now has to hold only 200 capital and is able to reduce its Tier I capital to 100. Funds that previously had to be kept readily available to cushion possible losses could be used more productively.

When one takes into account the risk associated with the securitized home mortgages and the interest rate swaps together with the increase in loans to firms, it seems clear that the bank now faces more risk than previously. Yet it was required under the Basel Capital Accord of 1988 to hold less capital against the possibility of default.

It is easy to see why this type of activity worried the Basel Committee and led to the proposals in the Basel II Capital Accord regarding securitized assets.

Modifications were proposed to the Basel Accord to take this into account by making allowance for off-balance-sheet credit exposures. The idea was to convert these exposures into balance sheet equivalent amounts using a formula that takes account of the likely extent of the default risk involved. This proposal was taken into account in the preparation of the Basel II Capital Accord (see below). The question at issue then becomes the extent to which the formula used is such that an incentive still remains for banks to continue to move towards off-balance-sheet business.

Further changes to the accord were proposed to incorporate capital requirements for over-the-counter derivatives with the capital adequacy requirement being determined by estimates of current and potential credit exposure, taking into account the nature of the counterparty.

Other developments followed. In April 1990 an addendum to the Basel Concordat aimed to encourage more regular and structured collaboration between supervisors, with provision being made for supervisory consultations at the authorization stage. In the same

MORE FROM THE WEB

For stories on the regulation of international financial markets go first to www.bis.org, the website of the Bank for International Settlements. On the left-hand side of the home page you will find a heading for the Basel Committee. Point at it and subheadings appear including the latest news on Basel II. It is also worth looking up the Financial Stability Institute, the heading for which is immediately below that for the Basel Committee. For information on financial stability, try also the Bank of England www.bankofengland.co.uk and click on 'Financial Stability', one of the headings at the top of the home page.

year, the Committee tried to deal with the single most important cause of bank failures, excessive concentration of default risk. It did this by recommending common definitions and procedures related to large exposures, recommending maximum limits on single exposures of 25 per cent of the capital base.

That serious problems remained, however, became clear with the forced closure of the Bank of Credit and Commerce International (BCCI) in July 1991. BCCI's corporate structure was based on a non-bank holding company in Luxembourg which owned two separate banking networks incorporated in Luxembourg and the Cayman Islands. The holding company was unregulated and so consolidated supervision of the group was not possible, allowing BCCI to hide its problems by shifting assets between national jurisdictions. The Basel Committee responded to the BCCI affair by issuing a set of minimum standards for supervision of international banks.

However, other problems were coming to the fore, particularly with the very rapid growth in derivatives trading worldwide. The speed at which the risks of derivatives can be transformed and the complexity of the transformation process result in a loss of transparency. This makes risk assessment much more difficult and, it was argued, weakened both market discipline and regulatory oversight, leading to greatly increased systemic risks. Risk was increased also, it was thought, because end users frequently did not understand how derivatives worked and the management of banks and securities houses often did not

understand what their dealers were doing. This last problem is magnified to the extent that pay systems reward traders hugely for success in achieving profits and provide them with little incentive to follow cautious strategies. We have also considered in Section 20.8 the argument that derivatives trading increases the volatility of financial asset prices. Finally, there were concerns over the concentration of derivatives trading among a few major financial institutions, with the possibility that the failure of a large derivatives dealer could both inflict large losses on counterparties and also damage the liquidity of the derivatives market.

One approach to the potential increase in default risk has been to encourage the use of **netting agreements** which create a single legal obligation covering multiple transactions between two counterparties, allowing them to reduce both the amount and the number of payments in comparison to settlements on a gross basis. In the USA, the International Swap Dealers Association (ISDA) drew up a master agreement which allows an intermediary to reconcile all of its transactions with a defaulted counterparty and come up with a final net payment, permitting the amount of capital set aside to support the business to be reduced by 50 per cent since the capital adequacy rules only have to be applied to the net value of transactions payments. In line with this, the Basel Committee amended the 1988 accord by reducing the capital that must be held against derivatives credit exposures which are subject to bilateral netting, subject to banks being able to demonstrate to their supervisors the legal enforceability of netting arrangements in all relevant jurisdictions. Regulators have also acted to include derivatives transactions in large exposure limits, along with conventional on-balance-sheet exposures.

The initial Basel proposals were concerned with *credit risk* – the risk that the bank's counterparty might not pay on the due date. Later Basel proposals were concerned with *market risk* – the risk that movements in the prices of financial instruments lead to loss. This had not been treated at all in the 1988 Accord. In April 1993[12] the Basel Committee published proposals for minimum capital requirements to cover banks' exposure to market fluctuations. Derivatives were to be converted into positions in the relevant underlying asset and become subject to capital

---

[12] Basel Committee on Banking Supervision (1993).

requirements designed to capture specific and general market risk. However, this was criticized on the grounds that static capital adequacy rules cannot capture the risk profiles of individual institutions. It was argued that a much more sophisticated approach was needed which made use of the complex risk management models used by the major derivatives dealers with regulators acting to validate the models and set the risk parameters used in the estimate of the overall value-at-risk against which capital must be held.

In July 1994,[13] the Basel Committee and the International Organization of Securities Commissions (IOSCO) produced a joint policy statement on the oversight of the risk management process by senior management; the measurement, control and reporting of risk exposures; and the internal controls and audits regarding risk management. In April 1995, following the collapse of Barings, the Basel Committee agreed to allow banks to use their own computer models to assess the risks arising from market volatility, rather than complying with standardized measures of volatility and risk for particular financial instruments. Also, for the first time, capital charges were required to cover commodities risks. The Committee later supported a number of steps to improve the quality of risk management. These included *stress tests* which examine the overall impact of a worst case scenario (such as a repeat of the 1987 stock market crash) on a bank's capital base. In addition, it supported the separation of the trading and settlement arms of banks' trading divisions.

There are still worries about the reliability of the computer models with regard to the more complex derivatives products and about the ability of regulators to evaluate the models. It is also feared that the use of the models will greatly reduce the transparency of financial markets because only banks and regulators will know the basis on which risks have been measured. Nonetheless, there seems little choice but to move further in the direction of the use of these models and this is, indeed, what the Basel Committee has decided to do.

In June 1999, the Basel Committee issued a proposal for a new capital adequacy framework that will replace the 1988 accord and be known as the Basel II Capital Accord. An extensive consultation process followed the publication of the new proposals and a second consultative paper was published in January 2001. Further consultations were needed with the industry, however, and a third version was published. This incorporated many of the modifications to the original accord discussed above, notably the use of internal risk models to assess credit risk, the allowance for market risk and operational risk in the standardized calculation of the risk–asset ratio and the attempt to deal with the greater use of off-balance-sheet **asset securitization** by banks. Basel II applies to large complex organizations. To ensure that risks within entire banking groups are considered, the Basel II Capital Accord has been extended on a consolidated basis to holding companies of banking groups.

Other banks will remain Basel I institutions but amendments are also being made to Basel I to enhance the risk sensitivity of the Basel I rules and to mitigate potential competitive distortions from the introduction of Basel II. Basel II came into operation at the end of 2006.

The new capital framework consists of three pillars:

1 minimum capital requirements, developing and expanding on the standardized rules set forth in the 1988 accord;

2 a supervisory review of an institution's capital adequacy and internal assessment process; and

3 the effective use of market discipline to strengthen disclosure and encourage safe and sound banking practices.

The three pillars are seen as part of a single package and are to be implemented together.

The new Capital Accord has been designed to improve the extent to which regulatory capital requirements reflect underlying risks and to address specifically the financial innovation that has occurred in recent years. It also aims to reward the improvements in risk measurement and control that have occurred and to provide incentives for these to continue.

Despite earlier rumours that the new accord would abandon the standardized formula for the risk-weighting of assets, this is being maintained. The definition of capital is not being modified and the minimum ratio of capital to risk-weighted assets including operational and market risks will remain at 8 per cent for total capital. Tier II capital will also continue to be limited to 100 per cent of Tier I capital.

---

[13]   Basel Committee on Banking Supervision (1994).

Under the new accord, the denominator of the minimum total capital ratio will consist of two parts:

1 the sum of all risk-weighted assets for credit risk; plus

2 12.5 times the sum of the capital charges for market risk and operational risk.

Assuming that a bank has $875 of risk-weighted assets, a market risk capital charge of $10 and an operational risk capital charge of $20, the denominator of the total capital ratio would equal $875 + [(10 + 20) \times 12.5)]$ or $1,250.[14]

The major difference from the 1988 accord lies in the greater emphasis on banks' own assessment of the risks to which they are exposed in order to make the overall approach more sensitive to different kinds and degrees of risk, allowing the incorporation of a much wider range of grades of assets. The use of a bank's internal risk model is known as an **internal ratings-based (IRB) approach**. This is to be introduced at two levels: foundation and advanced. A foundation IRB approach combines a significant external assessment of risk factors with elements of a bank's own risk assessment. Thus, banks that meet robust supervisory standards will make their own assessment of the probability of default associated with assets but estimates of additional risk factors, such as the loss incurred by the bank given a default and the expected exposure at default, will be made externally through the application of standardized supervisory estimates. The advanced IRB approach will be available to banks that meet even more rigorous supervisory standards and will allow more of the risk components to be estimated internally by the bank. However, the Committee has stopped short of permitting banks to calculate fully their capital requirements on the basis of their own portfolio credit risk models.

The Basel Committee, while acknowledging that asset securitization can be an efficient way for a bank to redistribute its credit risks to other banks and non-bank investors, has become increasingly worried by the way in which some banks have been using it to avoid maintaining a sufficient level of capital for their risk exposures. Thus, the Basel II accord develops standardized and IRB approaches for treating the explicit risks that traditional securitizations pose for banks.[15] The accord sets out operational, disclosure, and minimum capital requirements for securitizations.

The new accord does not aim to raise the total amount of regulatory capital required by banks but big banks with sophisticated risk management systems should be able to hold less capital and therefore strengthen their competitive position. Other banks might have to hold more capital to reflect the wider range of risks than under the old rules and a more finely tuned assessment of the credit risk associated with different assets. The calculation of credit risk will also depend on how exposed a bank is to a single borrower or sector. Further, for the first time, there will be a requirement to hold capital to cover operating risk. Securitized loans will need more capital set aside than in the past unless the risk is completely transferred out of the bank. However, there will be greater allowance for factors that reduce risk, such as collateral or guarantees.

In order to counter concerns expressed in the banking industry over the implementation of the IRB approaches and the methods regulators will use to ensure that they are evenly applied between different banks and regulatory authorities, the new accord includes an extensive auditing system and enhanced requirements for disclosure. Another concern expressed by some bankers and regulators is that capital requirements have a pro-cyclical impact on bank lending – encouraging banks to lend when economies are doing well but discouraging loans in recessions, thus making economic cycles more pronounced. Under the old accord this happened because more loans become problematic during recessions and the valuation of banks' capital falls, requiring banks to set aside more regulatory capital to maintain the minimum capital asset ratio. Under the new proposals, this will continue to happen but, in addition, the more sensitive assessment of risk applied to assets will increase the calculation of risk-weighted assets. That is, in a recession the numerator will fall and the denominator rise, making it more difficult for banks to make new loans. There is some evidence that this had a serious impact on the US economy in the early

---

[14]   This example is taken from Basel Committee on Banking Supervision (2001).

[15]   A traditional securitization is defined in the new accord as involving the legal or economic transfer of assets or obligations by an originating institution to a third party, referred to as a 'special purpose vehicle' (SPV). An SPV issues asset-backed securities, which are claims against specific asset pools.

1990s, especially in making it difficult for small and medium-sized companies without access to the capital markets to raise funds.

The reverse happens in booms. Credit-risk models can attempt to take this into account but there is doubt that they can do it adequately. These worries need to be balanced against the view that the new accord will remove distortions from the regulatory framework and, by so doing, should encourage lending to sound borrowers and discourage lending to bad ones.

The Basel Committee continues to act in a number of other ways to improve the quality of international bank regulation. In 1997, it published, again in response to the financial crises of the 1980s and 1990s, the Basel Core Principles for Effective Banking Supervision and its Methodology, which set out (in 25 principles) globally agreed minimum standards for banking regulation and supervision covering such areas as bank licensing, bank ownership, capital adequacy, risk management, consolidated supervision, ways to deal with problematic situations in banks and the division of tasks and responsibilities between home and host authorities. The principles were updated in 2006, improving the criteria for assessing interest rate, liquidity and operational risks as well as strengthening those against money laundering, terrorist financing and fraud prevention. Periodical assessments of compliance with the core principles are carried out. Sometimes these are self-assessment by individual countries. However, assessments are also carried out by the IMF and the World Bank as part of what is known as the Financial Sector Assessment Program. These assessments have led to many countries taking measures to improve their supervisory systems and methods.

25.6 The regulation of universal banking in the EU

We have discussed EU financial regulation in Chapter 21. We noted there that the European Commission has followed developments in the Basel Accord. For example, in May 1996 it proposed the amendment of the *First Banking Directive*, the *Bank Solvency Ratio Directive* and the *Capital Adequacy Directive* to change supervisory rules for banks to introduce more sophisticated capital requirements for default risks

involved in OTC derivatives in line with the Basel Committee changes. The *Bank Solvency Ratio Directive* was also amended in 1996 to encourage bilateral netting agreements, allowing the offsetting of mutual claims and liabilities from OTC derivatives contracts.

Here, however, we are concerned with a particular problem related to the regulation of banking that arose in the EU because of the different banking traditions of its members. We have seen that a significant proportion of German banks engaged in a wide range of securities operations as well as in the narrow banking activities of deposit taking and making commercial loans. Thus, when the European Commission put forward its proposals for the regulation of EU-wide banking in the *Second Banking Coordination Directive* of 1989, regulatory authorities in a member state were allowed to grant their home banks a licence to offer a wide variety of services throughout all member states (see Box 21.1 for the list of these activities).

In its attempt to ensure the stability of the EU banking system, the *Second Banking Directive* and the *Bank Solvency Ratio Directive* of 1989 adopted the Basel capital adequacy ratios discussed above. This, however, left non-bank securities houses, notably those in the UK, unregulated at EU level – neither guaranteed a single passport to trade freely across the EU nor subject to capital adequacy and solvency rules. The former left the British financial industry at a serious competitive disadvantage relative to that of Germany and made the *Investment Services Directive* which came into force in June 1992 essential, extending the single passport principle to non-bank investment firms generally. The latter then placed German banks and their subsidiaries engaged in securities trading at a competitive disadvantage relative to the British non-bank securities firms. To overcome this, the *Capital Adequacy Directive* (CAD) of 1993 had to apply to both investment firms and to the securities activities of banks.

One problem with this solution is that the argument for official protection of investment firms is less clear than for banks. A major difference is that the assets of securities houses consist largely of marketable securities, making them much less vulnerable than banks to contagious liquidity and solvency crises. Thus, there is much less chance than in the case of banks that they will cause systemic problems with their associated social costs.

Systemic problems may, of course, arise for banks within a financial market regime characterized by increasing integration of banking and securities business to the extent that banks engage in securities business directly or through a subsidiary, or lend to investment firms. This, however, does not provide a justification for the regulation of separate investment firms. It has been argued that, if both banks and securities houses are to be regulated, different techniques should be applied with the emphasis being on solvency for banks but on liquidity for securities houses.

The CAD solution made the securities activities of banks subject to a capital adequacy regime separate from that of the banking business. This approach is known as the **trading book model** since the bank is being required, for the purposes of capital adequacy, to keep its trading business separate from its banking business. The *trading book* covers trading for short-term gain, while the *banking book* relates to longer-term investment or hedging. Only certain types of instrument can be held in the trading book but some types of instrument can be held in either the trading book or the banking book depending on the purpose for which they are being held. A single instrument cannot be held simultaneously in both books. Items held in the banking book are subject to the risk-weighting scheme described above. Items in the trading book are subject to capital charges. The size of these capital charges varies with the nature of the risk. The capital charges for all trading book items are added together and a measure known as Notional Risk Weighted Assets is produced. This allows the capital adequacy requirement for both the banking and trading books to be expressed as a single unit.

This approach ensures competitive equality between the securities arms of universal banks and separate investment firms, but in so doing it assumes that banks engaged in securities business can genuinely prevent problems in one part of its activities from spreading to the other. In Dale's (1996) view, the approach puts competitive equality before that of the soundness and stability of the system.

25.7 Summary

The financial services industry has always been heavily regulated. This has been particularly true of banking because of the vulnerability of banks to a loss of public confidence. The collapse of a single bank arouses fears that it might be contagious, causing problems for the banking industry as a whole and hence for the provision of the economy's medium of exchange. Important consumer protection issues also arise in the failure of banks.

The case for regulation is based upon the existence of various types of market failure, notably the existence of asymmetric information, while strong arguments against regulation are centred on the ideas of moral hazard, agency capture and compliance costs. Regulation increases the costs of entry and exit for new firms and thus may inhibit competition. In some circumstances, regulation may even increase the instability of an industry. A compromise position is to support regulation but to argue in favour of self-regulation on the grounds that practitioners have an interest in maintaining the reputation of their industry and are in the best position to understand the impact of regulation on the industry. Nonetheless, several problems have emerged in self-regulatory schemes.

Financial markets have been greatly influenced by globalization and financial innovation, both of which have caused particular problems for regulators. Globalization has led to the need for coordination of activities among bank supervisors and for the development of common regulatory standards to avoid competitive laxity among the supervising authorities. As the EU financial services directives have shown, however, it is not easy to devise common regulatory standards among countries with differently organized financial systems.

Key concepts in this chapter

Agency capture	Financial Services Authority (FSA)
Asset securitization	Internal ratings-based approach (IRB)
Asymmetric information	Netting agreements
Competitive laxity	Risk–asset ratios
Compliance costs	Self-regulation
Deregulation	Trading book model

Questions and problems

1 Why might the existence of asymmetric information lead bankers to be conservative in their lending policies?

2 How does asymmetric information produce a role for credit-rating agencies? What dangers might there be in the financial services industry becoming too dependent on credit-rating agencies?

3 How important is moral hazard as a determinant of people's behaviour? Provide examples of moral hazard related both to everyday life and to the financial services industry.

4 Under what circumstances might regulation decrease rather than increase the stability of an industry?

5 Discuss the view that self-regulation cannot cope with the problem that what is good for the industry as a whole may not be good for individual practitioners.

6 Why has globalization of the financial services industry made the problems faced by regulators more difficult?

7 Explain the basis of the distinction between the types of capital in the Basel Concordat.

8 Why is it thought that simple capital adequacy ratios are insufficient as a basis for supervising the activities of firms engaged in securities trading?

9 What aspects of the regulatory problem were highlighted by:

(a) the collapse of Baring's Bank in 1995?
(b) the collapse of BCCI in 1991?
(c) the Northern Rock difficulties of 2007?

Further reading

Basel Committee on Banking Supervision, *Supervisory Recognition for Netting for Capital Adequacy Purposes*, Consultation Proposal (Geneva: BIS, April 1993)

Basel Committee on Banking Supervision, *Risk Management Guidelines for Derivatives* (Geneva: BIS, July 1994)

Basel Committee on Banking Supervision, *Overview of the New Basel Capital Accord* (Geneva: BIS, January 2001)

R Dale, *Risk and Regulation in Global Securities Markets* (Chichester: John Wiley & Sons, 1996)

D Gowland, *The Regulation of Financial Markets in the 1990s* (Aldershot: Edward Elgar, 1990)

H S Houthakker and P J Williamson, *The Economics of Financial Markets* (Oxford: Oxford University Press, 1996), Ch. 11

S A Rhoades, 'Banking acquisitions', in P Newman, M Milgate and J Eatwell (eds), *The New Palgrave Dictionary of Money, Banking and Finance* (London: Macmillan, 1992)

G J Stigler, 'The theory of economic regulation', *Bell Journal of Economics and Management, Science*, 2 (1), 1971, 3–31

D Ware, *Basic Principles of Bank Supervision* (Handbook No. 7, Bank of England Centre for Central Bank Studies) – available on www. bankofengland.co.uk

Websites

www.bankofengland.co.uk
www.bis.org
www.financial-ombudsman.org.uk
www.fsa.gov.uk
www.ft.com

Chapter 26 Financial market efficiency

What you will learn in this chapter:

- The meanings of the term 'efficiency' when applied to financial markets

- The forces tending to make financial markets efficient

- The distinctions between various forms of the efficient market hypothesis

- The implications which follow from financial market efficiency

- Some ways in which efficiency can be tested

26.1   Introduction

It is perhaps appropriate that the final chapter of this book should take us back to where we began. In Chapter 1 we explained that a fundamental purpose of a financial system is to help funds to move from those with a financial surplus to those with a financial deficit. In Section 1.5 we discussed the many benefits that would flow from this, among which should be a higher level of saving and investing and a higher rate of economic growth.

These are large potential benefits and so it seems reasonable to ask questions about the efficiency with which financial systems work. One such question we met in Chapter 2 when we saw that some critics feel that the UK and US so-called market-based financial systems encourage 'short-termism'. Understandably, therefore, a substantial amount of effort has gone into investigating financial market efficiency.

In these investigations 'efficiency' has been defined quite narrowly. In saying that any market is efficient, one could mean any one of several things. Firstly, one might mean that the market is **operationally efficient**. This would mean that trading is carried out quickly, reliably, and at minimum cost. If one were interested in this kind of efficiency, one might look back at the chapters in Part 2 of this book where we saw that most financial systems have very high levels of activity and turnover in relation to the net flows of funds actually channelled between lenders and borrowers. On the other hand, one might ask whether a market was **allocationally efficient**. This would mean that the resources being allocated, 'funds' in the present case, were going to their most productive use. If one were interested in this kind of efficiency one would certainly want to know whether firms with long-term projects found funds unreasonably expensive to raise compared with firms with short-term projects (the short-termism hypothesis) or whether firms with a long-established record of profit growth found funds very expensive while firms with no track record could raise funds easily. Finally, one might ask whether a market was **informationally efficient** in the sense that prices were based on the best information available. If one were interested in this kind of efficiency, one would want to see whether it was possible to seek out information that enabled one to make better predictions of future prices than those that the market made

for itself. Notice that in order for a market to be allocationally efficient it must also be informationally efficient since allocation decisions are made in response to prices. Thus prices must be 'correct' in the sense that they incorporate all information. Indeed, allocational efficiency imposes an even stricter condition which is that the information in question must relate wholly and exclusively to 'fundamentals'. We shall see the significance of this in a moment.

In practice, the financial market literature is concerned with **pricing efficiency**. 'Efficient', when applied to financial markets, means quite simply that:

security prices fully reflect all relevant information.

Since we know that, all other things given, the price fixes the return on assets and vice versa, it is immaterial whether we write the definition in terms of prices or rates of return.

Notice that, as we have written it, the definition requires that prices reflect all **relevant information**. But this then raises a further question. 'Relevant to what?' Well, relevant to the pricing of securities, obviously. But we already know that security prices could be driven by a range of quite different factors. The best place to look is in Sections 11.4 and 11.5. In Section 11.4 we introduced models of asset valuation involving a risk-adjusted discount rate, the current income payment and an earnings forecast. These, we stressed at some length, are often described as an asset's fundamentals. On the other hand, we said in Section 11.5 that asset prices *might* be driven by other things, including the belief, in a boom for example, that there is always someone prepared to pay a higher price whatever the fundamentals may be (the 'bigger fool' hypothesis). The definition that we have given of an efficient financial market, even if we add the word 'relevant', is strictly agnostic as to what information it is that should be incorporated. As we noted above, if we want markets to be allocatively efficient, we want them to be informationally efficient but we also need to know that the relevant information that is playing its part is information about the asset's fundamentals, since it is these fundamentals that are linked to productivity and social rates of return.[1] The situation where markets are informationally efficient *and* the information involved relates to fundamentals is described by Elton and Gruber (1995) as **market rationality**. We shall follow this practice but it is fraught with danger because the lesser question of whether markets are informationally efficient (regardless

---

1   If this has been forgotten or remains obscure, a glance at Section 11.4 might be useful.

of the information source) hinges upon whether traders form their expectations *rationally*. Clearly, these are references to two quite different 'rationalities': that of agents in using information to form expectations, and that of markets in choosing a pricing model which relies only on fundamentals. We must be very careful not to confuse the two. With this in mind, we shall take the issue of informational efficiency first and turn to market rationality at the end.

Thus, in the next section we set out the **efficient market hypothesis (EMH)** and we distinguish between different 'levels' at which it may operate. In Section 26.3 we look at the implications of the hypothesis and in Section 26.4 at ways of testing the hypothesis and at some of the evidence. In Section 26.5 we turn to the question of market rationality, looking at the implications and the evidence in the one section. In Section 26.6 we provide a brief introduction to a body of work which has developed in recent years under the heading of '**behavioural finance**' and which is very critical of the EMH. As usual, the final section provides a summary.

26.2 The efficient market hypothesis

As we noted above, the hypothesis states that the current price of securities incorporates all relevant information or, equivalently, that securities yield rates of return which incorporate all available information.

Looking at rates of return first, we know from Equation 11.3 that the total return on a security is the sum of its dividend yield (dividend divided by price) plus any capital appreciation (or loss). Thus, where K is the rate of return, P_0 is the purchase price, D_1 is the dividend paid during the holding period and g is the rate of capital appreciation:

$$K = D_1/P_0 + g \qquad (26.1)$$

Recall then that the rate of capital appreciation is merely the change in price divided by the price paid, then:

$$K = \frac{D_1}{P_0} + \frac{P_1 - P_0}{P_0} \qquad (26.2)$$

where P_1 is the price in the next period.

Imagine a security, a company share say, where the next dividend, D_1, is known.[2] Then the rate of return, $\hat{K}$, *expected* at the beginning of the period, is uncertain by virtue of the fact that we do not know, but can only form *expectations of*, P_1. Thus:

$$\hat{K} = \frac{P_1 - P_0 + D_1}{P_0} \qquad (26.3)$$

Since efficient market theory argues that people use all available information in forming expectations of future events, then $\hat{K}$ is an **optimal forecast** of K, and since making an optimal forecast of K requires that we make an optimal forecast of P_1, then $\hat{P}_1$ must be an optimal forecast of P_1. Thus:

$$\hat{K} = K^{of} \quad \text{and} \quad \hat{P}_1 = P_1^{of}$$

where the superscript *of* stands for optimal forecast.

The efficient market hypothesis is persuasive at first sight since it is merely an application of the basic economic proposition that people act as rational maximizers.[3] We have made the assumption throughout this book that agents are risk-averse wealth maximizers. If they do not form expectations of the future in the optimal way, then they will be forgoing wealth maximizing opportunities: 'irrational' expectations are costly. Suppose, for example, that when directors sell shares in their own companies this is generally followed by announcements of lower than expected earnings. We know (from Chapter 17) that lower than expected earnings will cause a share's price to fall and the holders of that share will suffer a reduction in wealth. However, if there is a regular observable pattern of directors' sales followed by poor earnings announcements, agents who are genuinely wealth maximizers and genuinely rational will seek out this information[4] and incorporate it into what they think shares are worth. Thus a director's disposal will itself act as a signal to sell as well-informed ('rational') investors try to avoid a capital loss, and the subsequent reduced earnings announcement will have no effect on the price, which will already have incorporated this information.

Another way of looking at the forces pushing agents to make optimum forecasts based on all information is to think of 'equilibrium' prices or returns. By 'equilibrium' we mean those prices which produce

---

[2]   In many cases of course it will not be known but this makes little difference to the analysis. We should simply have to assume that the forecasts of D_1 also use all available information.

[3]   The efficient market hypothesis is just one application of the 'theory of **rational expectations**' first set out in 1961 by John Muth.

[4]   The Saturday issue of the *Financial Times* lists the major sales (and purchases) by directors of shares in their own company.

rates of return that are just equal to what people require (again, for the moment we say nothing about the origin of this valuation). Let us call the equilibrium return[5] K^* and the corresponding equilibrium price P^*. Then it follows that if an optimal forecast of K exceeds $\overline{K}$, informed investors will wish to buy the corresponding asset in order to benefit from the abnormally high return. Buying the share will of course cause the price to rise and the forecast return to fall until the optimal forecast just equals the required or equilibrium return. Conversely, if the optimal forecast of returns is that they are below what investors require, then well-informed investors again will try to benefit, this time trying to avoid a capital loss, by selling the corresponding asset. Its price will fall until, again, the optimal forecast return rises to that required by the market. Using our symbols, we can summarize:

$$\text{If } K^{of} > \overline{K}, P \uparrow \rightarrow K^{of} \downarrow$$
$$\text{If } K^{of} < \overline{K}, P \downarrow \rightarrow K^{of} \uparrow$$

We turn now to what the EMH does *not* imply. This is important since finding that the implications of the EMH are not confirmed in practice is one way of casting doubt upon it. But if the implications themselves are incorrect, this rejection will be unjustified.

Firstly, *the EMH does not say that prices will always be correct*. It merely says that the expectations that people form are the best possible forecasts in the prevailing situation. Thus, it will frequently be the case that our forecast of price in the next period, $\hat{P}_1$, will be:

$$\hat{P}_1 = P_1 + \varepsilon \tag{26.4}$$

where ε is an error term. What the EMH *does* say is that there is nothing in the behaviour of the error term which enables us to improve our forecast. If, for example, ε were always positive this would mean that our forecast of the price was always too high. In these circumstances, we could improve the forecast by adjusting it downwards. In this example, the error term is *systematically* positive. In fact, we can always improve the forecast if the error term behaves in any way that suggests a systematic connection with the forecast. We simply have to find out how the error term behaves and make the appropriate adjustment. This leads to an important conclusion which is best stated

formally. If our forecasts are to be *optimal* forecasts (and the EMH holds) then it must be the case that the forecast errors have a mean value of zero and that they have zero covariance with the forecast. Thus, a market can make forecast errors of future prices (and yields) and still be efficient, provided that there was no way of doing anything better. Box 26.2 provides an interesting example of the UK money markets failing to make correct forecasts of movements in short-term interest rates; notice, however, that the errors were soon corrected!

Secondly, *the EMH does not require people to use all information in forming their expectations*. This would be realistic only if information were costless. We noted above that one of the forces that drives markets towards efficiency is the motivation of traders in those markets. Their incentive to trade efficiently is the desire not to forgo profitable opportunities. But an opportunity in which it costs more to acquire the information than could possibly be lost by making a second-best forecast is not a profitable one. Since information costs are generally positive, we should better say that the EMH implies that prices reflect all that information whose marginal cost is less than the marginal benefit from incorporating it in the decision.

Lastly, *the EMH does not require everyone to behave as well-informed, rational, risk-averse wealth maximizers*. The fact that we can always find some trader somewhere who makes a 'silly' or at least highly questionable decision does not disprove the EMH. Market prices are determined by the actions of the majority. Provided that there are numerous well-informed traders looking for unexploited profit opportunities, market prices will be driven, by a process known as arbitrage, to the point where they reflect all profitable information.

Since Fama (1970) it has been standard practice to identify three *levels* at which the EMH can be said to hold,[6] where each level is distinguished by the stringency of the demands which it places on the information to be incorporated in the price. The first is the **weak form**, in which all information contained in the past behaviour of the asset's price is included. This amounts to saying that studying past trends tells us nothing about the next price movement because any useful information in those past trends has already been exploited. The price has already moved. In the

---

[5] Defined as the required rate of return, K^* is simply equivalent to $\overline{K}$ which was the symbol we used in Chapters 11 and 17.
[6] The definition of each was modified slightly in a more recent paper (Fama, 1991).

semi-strong form, all publicly available information is incorporated in the current price. This amounts to saying that studying current publicly available information – about the growth of retail sales or a firm's latest earnings, for example – is no guide to future movements and for the same reason. Any information that could be extracted is already in the price. In the **strong form**, all information – public and private – is incorporated. This makes the most stringent demands on information since it says that even the information available only to those closely concerned with the firms has already been taken up and incorporated in the price.

This distinction between 'levels' of the EMH is important. Firstly, in the next section, we shall see that each level of the EMH has different implications for financial markets and investors' strategies, and in Section 26.4 we shall see that different empirical tests are required for each level.

26.3 Implications of the EMH

The main or the fundamental implication of the EMH is that if markets are efficient then it is impossible for investors to exploit information in order to earn excess returns over a sustained period of time. 'Excess' here means in excess of the equilibrium or required rate of return, howsoever that is determined. In these circumstances it is sometimes said that the process determining security prices makes for a **fair game model**. Based on the information available at time, t, an investor makes an estimate of what an asset's return will be between t and $t + 1$ (or between 0 and 1 in our examples above). As we saw in the last section, an investor will compare this expectation with the equilibrium or required return for an asset of that type. The estimate may be higher or lower than equilibrium and the investor will accordingly buy or sell. Sometimes the eventual outturn will show that the return was correctly estimated; sometimes it will show the estimate was too high and sometimes too low. If prices are determined by a fair game process, there should be no relationship between the investor's estimates of deviations from the required return and the actual deviation from the required return as it turns out to be at $t + 1$. As we have said all along, systematic errors can be corrected and the EMH says that, in general, they will be.

It is sometimes said that if the EMH holds then returns follow a *random walk*. As we shall see in a moment, the **random walk model** is a restricted version of the fair game model, but the origin is the same. If past information is already incorporated in the price, the only information that can cause a price change is *news*, and news by its nature is unpredictable. Sometimes the news will be good and sometimes it will be bad. Prices (or returns) which respond to this news will thus follow a random pattern. Strictly speaking, a random pattern of returns means that each return is independent of the one before. Furthermore, the returns are identically distributed over time: they are drawn, in other words, from a constant distribution of returns. This condition need not apply in the fair game model and indeed for many shares one would not expect it. A firm with a large investment programme aimed at changing its core business, for example, may be entering markets with a higher risk/return combination. In this situation, successive returns will not be independent but will be increasing. Even so, the information about the firm's change of direction cannot be used to earn excess returns since its risk is also increasing and the returns will follow a fair game process even though they do not follow a random walk.

We shall see shortly that there are all sorts of practical, subsidiary implications that follow from the fundamental point that information cannot be used to extract excess returns, but first we need to note that each of the three forms of the EMH carry this implication for different types of information. We consider the implications of each form in turn.

Firstly, if the market is weak-form efficient then it will be impossible to earn consistent excess returns by using any information extracted from the past behaviour of asset returns (or prices). Imagine the case of a share whose price and dividends have increased steadily over the past few years, giving a consistent rate of return. *If* there is any information in this trend that suggests that it will continue, then this is already built into the price that people are prepared to pay for it. Equally, any useful information that might be conveyed by the price of a share which recently declined sharply and is now recovering is already incorporated in today's price. Investors could, if they wished, construct portfolios based on shares of either type. Thus a naive, risk-averse investor, believing that the past is a good guide to the future, might be tempted to invest in shares of the first type, turning his or her back on shares whose returns may fall again shortly. However, the message of the weak-form EMH is that neither strategy, investing in 'steady growth' or in 'recovery' shares simply on the evidence of past price movements, will yield a return which is consistently above that required by the market for shares of each risk class.

Secondly, if the market is semi-strong-form efficient, then it is impossible to earn excess returns from the exploitation of current, publicly available information. According to this view, the investor who studies firms' announcements about earnings, sales, new products, changes in capital structure and so on, will be no more able to buy shares at a price which yields excess returns than s/he would if s/he bought those shares that gave him or her the desired combination of risk and return at any time that suited him or her. The effect of any announcements that have been made is already incorporated in the price. If it were possible to devise 'rules' or 'clues' that allowed announcements to be anticipated, then these rules and clues would also be exploited in order to anticipate the announcement and again the effect on the price would already have occurred by the time our investor could act. The same goes for market-wide information. We know, for example, that a change in interest rates causes bond prices to change in the opposite direction. But bond prices do not wait for the change in interest rates to occur. This is because changes in rates are to some degree predictable on the basis of what we know the government's objectives to be, we know the model of the economy that it is using in order to achieve those objectives and we can see the present direction of the economy. Thus, if we know that the government is following a strict money supply rule (as it did in the UK from 1980 to 1985) then the rapid growth of bank lending becomes a leading indicator of interest changes and so bond prices responded to information about bank credit. In this situation, the semi-strong version of the EMH says that no excess returns can be made from studying bank lending trends since any information which is known to be interest relevant will already be incorporated in bond prices.

In its strong form, the EMH says that even information available only to privileged groups of investors is incorporated in the price. Consequently, this information is also unhelpful as a source of excess returns. This is clearly the most demanding of the three forms of the EMH and looks implausible at first glance. It seems obvious to most people that someone working in a large corporation, for example, could become aware of profitable information even before the directors. Imagine a drug or biotechnology company whose profits are extremely sensitive to scientific breakthroughs. Common sense suggests that it must be possible for researchers to become aware of a major breakthrough before this is known to managers who cannot understand the research data until it is interpreted. Someone in such a position must surely be able to earn excess returns. In most countries s/he will also earn a spell in gaol since **insider trading**, trading on information available only to those inside the firm, is illegal. Undoubtedly it is possible to earn excess returns by breaking the law, in financial markets just as much as in other walks of life. The question addressed by the strong form of the EMH is whether this can be done by legally exploiting information available only to the few. In practice, as we shall see shortly, this usually means 'is it possible for professional analysts to earn excess returns by studying the characteristics and behaviour of individual firms?'

Notice that what is at issue in all these forms of the EMH is the speed with which the particular category of information is incorporated into the price. If markets are informationally efficient, it is the speed with which information (of whatever category) is used that prevents investors from earning excess returns. The possibility that markets might be so efficient that investors cannot profit from exploiting information of any kind itself has further implications. We have space to discuss only limited examples.

If the EMH says that it is impossible for investors to exploit information so as to earn excess returns for any sustained period of time, then this suggests that there is little point in expending effort in searching for **bargains**. There are no bargains. There will be 'cheap' securities and 'expensive' ones (that is, securities with high yields and low yields respectively) but this will be because of the degree of risk that attaches to them or to some other characteristic(s) on which the market bases its valuation. 'Bargains' are anomalies. But if the market is informationally efficient, all relevant information is incorporated in the price by the time the investor comes to buy it. In these circumstances, the best investment strategy is to buy a portfolio of shares and to hold them for a long period in order to minimize transaction costs. A portfolio (rather than a single asset) is necessary in order to diversify risk and it is tempting to say that the investor should assemble a portfolio of shares that matches his or her risk/return preferences. But if we remember the discussion in

Section 8.5, we recall that there is at least a theoretical case that the 'best' combination of risk and return comes from holding part of one's wealth in a portfolio that replicates the whole market of risky assets and allocating the rest to a risk-free asset. In practice, this reasoning gives rise to the **index tracker funds** marketed by most unit trust or mutual investment funds. Investors' funds are used to buy units in a portfolio of shares which matches, if not the whole market portfolio, at least the portfolio of shares that make up some representative index. Having assembled that portfolio, the fund managers have little to do but adjust the portfolio on the comparatively rare occasions that the composition of the index changes. In other words, they pursue a 'buy and hold' strategy on behalf of investors. Since this absorbs little management time and effort, compared with all the research and analysis that goes into trying to pick 'winners', charges on tracker funds are much lower than on actively managed funds. In the UK at least, investors' returns from index tracker funds have been in the top quartile of unit trusts ranked by return over the last ten years. This performance, combined with low charges, has made them a popular recommendation from consumer organizations, though they remain a small proportion of the whole range of funds available. One might say that their success is some evidence in favour of the EMH, but the investing public appears to remain sceptical and is prepared to pay for specialist advice which it thinks can beat the market. Box 26.1 shows why. It tells the story of a fund manager who was brought back to manage a fund which had performed badly since he had left. In the year after June 2006 he managed to improve the performance to such an extent that it moved from 13th to second out of 22 funds investing in emerging markets. And if a manager can improve performance on that scale, this suggests that he should be able to 'beat the market'. But two cautions are necessary. Firstly, we must always remember that 'beating the market' involves earning an *excess return for a given level of risk*. There is no argument that one can earn more by taking on more risk – indeed that is standard wisdom in finance. If we read the article carefully it looks as though the manager's performance passes this test. It says that the fund is 'benchmarked against the MSCI Global

---

BOX 26.1 Fund management and efficient markets FT

Gartmore Turnround
By Hugo Greenhalgh

For Christopher Palmer, manager of Gartmore's £310m Emerging Markets Opportunities fund, August's volatility demonstrated just how much the emerging markets have matured since the heady days of the late 1990s . . .

. . . This is Mr Palmer's second stint as manager of the fund. Following Gartmore's management buy-out in 2006, he was parachuted back in to turn round performance. Since his return in June that year the fund has moved from 13th out of 22 funds in the Global Emerging Markets sector to second. According to Morningstar, the fund has returned 62.3 per cent since June 2006, compared with an average peer group growth of 49.9 per cent.

Looking for growth opportunities across the sectors, the manager works with his team of five analysts to identify stocks on a purely bottom-up basis. Countries act as catalysts rather than benchmarks and he remains flat on a sector basis. 'Just because our model might favour Korea, for example, doesn't mean we will necessarily go overweight. We look at what the performance of these stocks tells us.'

Focusing on 'growth-orientated managers with a twist', Mr Palmer says he looks for stocks with growth potential likely to exceed the consensus.

Overall the fund is benchmarked against the MSCI Global Emerging Markets index, but it operates with one eye firmly attuned to micro

rather than macro-movements. 'We look for companies with high levels of cash flow and relatively low levels of corporate debt.'

With just 87 holdings, the fund, which usually ranges between 75 and 90 positions, is fairly concentrated given the scope of its investment universe. 'Any position we hold is a high conviction overweight,' Mr Palmer says.

. . .

The themes are the rise of the middle-class consumer and rapid industrialisation. 'There has been massive investment into countries, such as China and India, to lift them from agricultural societies to have higher levels of GDP,' Mr Palmer says.

Source: *Financial Times*, 8 October 2007. Reprinted with permission.

Emerging Markets Index'. In other words, the test is to beat the other funds (which make up the index) which are investing in similar markets and taking on similar levels of risk. We are not told what the return on the index was but it must have been broadly similar to the average performance of the group itself which is given as 49.9 per cent. So here is someone who can, apparently, beat the market.

But the second test is not so easily passed. This is the requirement that the market can be beaten *consistently*, so as to rule out the possibility of pure chance. It is impossible to draw a firm conclusion about this from the report although it suggests that this is a manager with a 'reputation' for good performance.

If the EMH calls into question the wisdom of investors trying to select assets that beat the market, it also calls into question the wisdom of paying for specialist advice in order to make the selection. If the market is strong-form efficient and prices incorporate *all* relevant information, regardless of its source, then *no one* has an informational advantage and so paying for advice is a waste of money. However, if the market is only semi-strong efficient, then it might be possible that professional research, conducted by analysts who concentrate on just one sector of the market or just one narrowly defined set of assets, *might* succeed in uncovering bargains. The question then for investors is 'does the superior information generate excess returns, greater than the cost of acquiring it?' As we shall see in the next section, one of the tests of the strong-form EMH involves looking at the returns to investors generated by actively managed mutual funds *after* their charges have been deducted. On the face of it, financial markets throughout the world appear to accept some degree of informational inefficiency. If the market were strong-form efficient there could be no superior alternative to 'buy and hold'. However, we saw in Chapter 3 that turnover figures for securities of all kinds were many times greater than the net acquisitions made by investment institutions on behalf of investors. Securities markets are very active and this must, to some degree, represent a view that superior returns can be made by moving, and moving frequently, between assets. Furthermore, investors clearly are prepared to pay for professional advice and those that offer it can earn substantial salaries. In January 1997, the UK media were briefly fascinated by a story of a female fund manager who had been sacked from a post in which she had reportedly been

> **MORE FROM THE WEB**
> **The efficient market hypothesis**
>
> For an issue which is so controversial and has dominated finance for a generation, it is not surprising that there are hundreds of websites devoted to it, or featuring it as one issue among many. Fortunately, many of these sites are interlinked so that if we only highlight two, that will give access to 20 or more. If that is not sufficient, just type 'efficient markets' into a search engine – and prepare to be swamped.
>
> Two sites that we have referred to elsewhere in this book are: www.investopedia.com/university/ concepts; (among the concepts listed is the EMH, which is clearly explained with additional reading and links to other sites) and www.investorhome.com/ emh.htm (this takes you directly to a rather more informal discussion of the EMH; again there are links to other sites and the major contributors to the debate).

earning over £1m per annum. More interestingly, from our point of view, however, is the background to the story in which it was alleged by her employers that she had been preparing to move to a rival firm and had been encouraging selected colleagues to move with her. The extensive commentary which accompanied these events made it clear that investment institutions supported an active transfer market for successful and very highly paid fund managers.

The fact that some professionals are particularly sought after for their apparent ability to beat the market seems to suggest that the market is to some degree at least inefficient. Indeed, one might ask whether the mere existence of so much financial analysis and financial advice is evidence of inefficiency. If an efficient market is one in which investors cannot beat the returns from a 'buy and hold' strategy, then devoting considerable resources to looking for bargains seems pointless. But we need to be careful with this evidence. Firstly, the fact that a lot of skilled work goes into researching firm-specific and whole market conditions is one of the reasons why financial markets possess whatever informational efficiency they do possess. There is a paradox here. If the market is efficient, the research is unnecessary but without the research the market will not be efficient. Secondly, remember that market efficiency does not require that *all* investors make the best use of available information. Many will; these are the 'information traders' whose role we discussed in Section 16.6. But we also identified 'noise traders', those who buy and sell in response to their own view of how a security's price is going to move. Noise traders, whether they realize it or not, behave *as if* the market is inefficient and provide a ready market for advice, tips and so forth.

The EMH has implications for corporate finance as well as private investment. Recall (from Chapter 17) that the market value of a firm is the market value of the securities in issue. Furthermore, the dividends paid on equities and the interest paid on any bonds are components of the firm's cost of capital. If, as we said above, there are no bargains for shareholders – prices accurately reflect the market's valuation of the securities' characteristics – then there is nothing that firms can do to influence the price of their own bonds and shares. This could be important in a variety of contexts. In a contested takeover, for example, it is advantageous to both sides to maximize the value of their shares since, for the target, this makes it more expensive for the predator to buy, while, for the predator, a high share price means that fewer of its own shares have to be offered in any deal with the shareholders of the target company. A firm wishing to raise capital via a new issue of shares will also find a high share price advantageous since, for the current level of dividend payments, each new share brings in more funds than would be the case if the price were low: a high share price means a low cost of capital. In both these (and other) cases, firms might be tempted to manipulate information in order to raise their share price – bringing forward 'good' information and suppressing 'bad', for example. But if the market is strong-form efficient this should not work. There is no inside information which only the firm can exploit. Any 'news' that it tries to create is already in the price. The market must be only semi-strong-form efficient if this type of operation is to succeed. So far as one can judge from their behaviour, firms are divided in their views. Many bitterly contested takeovers are fought out with expensive public relations techniques designed to influence investors' perceptions of firms' value by suggesting that the share price does not incorporate all relevant information. On the other hand, the infamous Guinness takeover battle for the Distillers company in 1986 resulted in the Guinness chairman and associates being sentenced to prison for organizing an illegal share support operation.

Essentially, this involved paying inducements to selected investors to encourage them to buy Guinness shares in the hope that this would push up the price and so strengthen Guinness's position. This suggests a belief on the part of the Guinness side that the market was so efficient that there was nothing they could do to strengthen their position by manipulating information. The only way to move their shares' price was to pay others to buy them.

26.4 Testing the EMH

In its weakest form, the EMH says that returns (or price changes) cannot be predicted from information about the past behaviour of returns (or prices). As we saw in the last section, this amounts to saying that events in the next time period are unrelated to those in the last. Tests of the weak form of the EMH therefore consist of tests for the absence of correlation between returns (or prices) in successive time periods. Two commonly used tests which do this directly are (regression) tests for **serial correlation** and **'runs' tests**. A less direct approach is to see whether traders can make abnormal profits by adopting a trading rule based on past data patterns. We look at each in turn.

26.4.1 Regression tests for serial correlation

'Serial correlation' simply means that successive values of a variable are related. Thus the value of the variable today is to some extent determined by yesterday's value. As we have seen, the EMH denies this since any information available in yesterday's price would already have been exploited in determining today's price. It is quite easy to test for serial correlation using the standard regression techniques employed to test many hypotheses in economics. If we make today's return, K_t, the dependent variable, our question is 'is K_t dependent, in any significant, way upon K_{t-1} or K_{t-2} . . . etc?' If we simply test for dependence upon the previous period's price then we estimate the equation:

$$K_t = a + bK_{t-1} + \varepsilon_t \qquad (26.5)$$

If the EMH holds, then b should be zero, or at least it should not be significantly different from zero when subject to standard tests of significance. However, since the explanatory variable, K_{t-1}, is simply the lagged dependent variable, estimating the value of b is equivalent to estimating the correlation coefficient between K_t and K_{t-1} and many of the studies which use this approach prefer to report their results in terms of correlation coefficients. The reported correlation coefficients in most studies are extremely small (though not actually zero), typically less than 0.1 per cent. (Less than one-tenth of 1 per cent of the variation of today's return is explained by yesterday's return. See Elton and Gruber, 1995, Ch. 17.)

26.4.2 Runs tests

'Runs' tests are another way of examining successive price (or return) *changes*. If the EMH holds then successive changes should be unrelated. This lack of a relationship sets a limit to the number of days on which a 'run' of consecutive price rises (for example) can occur. Too many in succession is more than coincidence. Thus, a large number of short runs tends to favour the EMH; a small number of long runs does not.

The tests are done by examining the behaviour of a price series over time and identifying each day's price as a '+' (a rise), a '−' (a fall) or a '0' (no change). A succession of days with the same sign is a run and so our price series will be divided into a series of runs. Notice that the shorter the runs, the more runs there must be in a given series. (If each sign were always followed by a different sign, the runs would all have the value 1, and the number of runs would equal the number of observations in the series!) Fortunately, we can be reasonably precise about the number (and length) of runs that we would expect if successive changes turn out to be the same only by chance. Firstly, we calculate the total number of '+'s, '−'s, and '0's and we note the number of runs, which we might denote v. Appropriate statistical tables will give us the critical value of v, given the number of '+'s, '−'s and '0's. Such critical values are usually given for a 5 per cent level of significance. Remember that more runs indicates less association. Then if, for example, our table tells us that $v_{crit} = 11$, while our data gives us a total of seven runs, we know that there is only a 5 per cent chance of such a small number (long length) of runs occurring by chance. By contrast, there is a 95 per

cent probability that the runs indicate some degree of association between successive changes.

The evidence of large-scale runs tests is that actual runs are often slightly fewer than one would expect from probability tables and this suggests some very slight evidence for positive correlation. But it is very slight: in many cases the actual runs are almost identical with the expected value and the closeness becomes very striking when the change is measured over longer periods, weeks say, rather than days.

26.4.3 Filter tests

The tests that we have so far described are tests for a linear relationship between current returns and past returns. As we have seen, there is little evidence of serial correlation. However, finding that price changes and returns are not related in a linear manner does not mean that there is no relationship. It might be that they follow a more complex pattern. If this were true, then it might still be possible to earn excess returns by exploiting this more complex pattern and this possibility can be explored by formulating a trading rule based on the assumption of some pattern and comparing the resulting investment returns with a policy of simple 'buy and hold'. This argument forms the basis of 'filter rules' (and of some aspects of 'chartist' or 'technical' analysis).

Let us suppose, as seems reasonable, that the price of a security, instead of being rigidly fixed at a point, oscillates from day to day within fairly narrow bands around its equilibrium. The price breaks out of these bands only when genuinely relevant news arrives and the price moves towards a new equilibrium. Investors who buy when the price breaks through the upper band (or sell when the price falls through the lower band) will benefit. The trick, of course, is to identify the bands and this is done by formulating a 'filter rule' which says, for example, 'buy when the price rises by 5 per cent from its previous low and sell when it declines by 3 per cent from its previous high'. Here the filters, 5 per cent and 3 per cent, are being used to identify an unusually large price change which marks progress to a new equilibrium level (rather than a day-to-day fluctuation). In theory, the numerical value of the filter could be anything. It is simply a question of what (if any) filter works and that involves repeated testing.

Perhaps unsurprisingly, given the outcomes from regression and runs tests, **filter tests** do not suggest that there are past patterns of behaviour which can be profitably exploited. Certainly this is true when we allow for taxes and transactions costs.

A market that fails the tests for weak-form efficiency cannot be semi-strong or strong-form efficient. The converse, though, is not true and thus, since many tests suggest that markets are at least weak-form efficient, economists are naturally curious to know whether that efficiency extends in any cases to the semi-strong or even, possibly, the strong form. We look at one common way of testing each form.

The semi-strong form of the EMH says that publicly available news is so quickly incorporated in security prices that no advantage can be gained from studying this information. One way of testing whether or not this is true is to study the behaviour of prices with respect to public announcements of news. The methodology of **event studies**, as these are known, is fairly straightforward and can be described in a series of steps:

1 Identify a sample of firms which experienced a major public announcement.

2 Identify the announcement day and number it 'zero'.

3 Define a period (say 30 days) either side of day zero.

4 For each firm, compute the actual return on each day.

5 Compute a 'normal' return for each day. Practice varies here but one common approach is to average the actual return on each day of other (unselected) firms in the same sector.

6 Compute the 'abnormal' return on each day by comparing the actual return with the normal return calculated in (5).

7 Some studies cumulate the abnormal return, but the crucial step is:

8 Examine the abnormal return (or the cumulated abnormal return) with respect to time.

If the market is semi-strong-form efficient then most of the abnormal return will be earned before or on the day of the announcement and it will not be possible, after the announcement, to use the news in order to earn abnormal returns. These tests, which were very popular in the 1970s and 1980s, generally found that the UK and US equity markets were semi-strong-form efficient and that information was incorporated in prices too rapidly for investors to be able to make subsequent excess returns.

If markets are strong-form efficient, then even private information is incorporated sufficiently quickly that it cannot be exploited to make consistent excess returns. Remember (from the last section) that what we are interested in here is the question of whether it is possible *legally* to benefit from the use of private information. In practice, this comes down to the question of whether 'private' information can be purchased legitimately at a price which allows above average returns to be earned and that in turn means that the tests of the strong-form EMH are usually tests of the performance of fund managers who have access to professional analysis and research. We might think it reasonable that analysts who follow closely the behaviour of a small number of firms or a particular sector, and who enjoy occasional briefings by firms' financial managers, might well acquire useful information before it is available to the general public. If there is an advantage (and the market is thus strong-form *in*efficient) then managed funds should outperform a simple buy and hold strategy which could be proxied by a broad-based stock market index.

There have been many tests of managed fund performance over the years. However, many suffer from what is known as 'survivorship bias'. That is to say, the very unsuccessful ones tend to last only for short periods with the result that studies that look at the performance of a sample of funds over a long period of time are looking at a sample of funds which, *by definition*, have a better average performance than the whole population of managed funds. Even so, the evidence from most of these studies does not suggest that there is much advantage to be gained from buying specialist information. The costs of that information are passed on to investors through bid–ask spreads and management charges and it is not generally the case that, once these are allowed for, investors would have done better than by buying and holding a portfolio selected (by themselves) based upon an index. Indeed, Elton and Gruber (1995, p. 437) cite studies where, with survivorship bias removed, managed funds perform worse than an index and, furthermore, where the underperformance is *positively* related to the scale of the management charges. In these circumstances, the apparent lack of interest in index tracker funds (noted above) is all the more surprising.

26.5 Market rationality

So far, we have been concerned with whether or not financial markets incorporate information into the pricing of assets sufficiently quickly that no one can have an informational advantage. We can pose this question about three different types of information and this gives rise to the three forms of the EMH. But we have not yet said anything about what information is relevant or anything about *how* it is incorporated. All our tests so far tell us is that whatever information drives security prices and howsoever it is seen to be relevant to those prices, it does not seem possible to obtain this information in order to earn excess returns.

And yet much more is often claimed for the EMH. For example, it is often implied (and sometimes stated) that if the EMH holds then assets will be priced according to their fundamentals and funds will (with a few additional assumptions) be subject to optimum allocation. This does not strictly follow from the EMH alone. Markets could be informationally efficient in the sense of making optimal forecasts on the basis of current information but 'optimal' only means that those forecasts are on average correct and cannot be improved upon. What it is that is driving prices is unspecified. It may be that markets are responding (super-efficiently) to information which drives prices but which economists cannot see to have any rational connection with prices whatsoever. The question of what information is relevant, and the model which links it to prices, is a separate question from the one of informational efficiency. Nonetheless, it is undoubtedly the case that many who would like to feel that the EMH holds would like also to feel that financial markets are efficient at directing limited funds to those uses that are in some sense better than others and so it is worth considering the additional conditions that are necessary.

To do this, we need only look back, quite briefly, to Section 11.4 where we discussed the 'fundamentals' of asset valuation. In Section 11.4 we were arguing that the capital asset pricing model gave us a *rational* explanation of how security prices were determined. The CAPM says that prices will adjust until the asset yields just that rate of return required by investors and then goes on to explain how that required rate is determined. The required rate of return is explained throughout as the result of attempts to maximize returns, subject to constraints, by rational investors. Furthermore, by establishing the required return as a rational process, the model then in effect imposes that return as the *cost* of capital to firms. Only those firms which have real investment projects that match this cost will have access to the funds. The ability of those investment projects to match the cost of capital depends upon the physical productivity of capital and the revenue for which its output can be sold. This in turn depends upon consumers' willingness to pay and this, as all first-year economics students know, is carried to the point where the satisfaction from the marginal unit consumed is just equal to its price. *If* prices (and returns) are driven by the process described by the CAPM, then the pricing of financial assets is just one small part of a grand rational process in which everyone is doing the best they can to maximize their own wellbeing subject to constraints. If financial markets are informationally efficient, and prices are determined by the CAPM, then the informational efficiency is indeed important to an efficient and benevolent allocation of funds. But none of our tests so far shed any light on this question. We need something different.

The major challenges to the view that the market prices securities rationally, as well as efficiently, consist of volatility tests and the examination of major market movements such as the 1987 crash.

Volatility tests compare the actual variance in share prices with the variance in theoretical prices. Theoretical prices are those that one would have expected had securities been priced according to fundamentals in a model such as the CAPM. These can be calculated, *ex post*, using actual changes in dividend discount rates (resulting from changes in interest rates and/or in the market risk of an asset) and actual changes in dividends. The most famous of these tests was carried out by Shiller (1981) and it shows that long runs of US stock prices show much greater volatility than could be accounted for by the changes in fundamentals that actually occurred.

The other obvious challenge to the proposition that markets always produce rational valuations of securities comes from the spectacular booms and slumps that have occasionally hit asset markets. These range, chronologically, from the Dutch Tulip Mania of the sixteenth century to the 'dotcom' boom of 2000 and include the 1929 Wall Street crash and the eighteenth century South Sea and Mississippi bubbles as well as the crash of October 1997. The argument of critics here again is that prices changed too far and too fast to be justified by any change in fundamentals. In the 1987 crash, for example, both the London and New York markets saw prices fall by 25 per cent in one day. *Ex post*, it is difficult to see any news that could have caused investors to reappraise either the discount rate, the current level of expected dividends or the earnings growth rate by an amount sufficient to cause a price change of this magnitude (but see Case study 3 for a discussion of the required change in earnings growth). However, it is worth looking at the symposium of papers collected by Stiglitz (1990) to see just how careful one needs to be in looking at historic information through the eyes of those who had to interpret it at the time. What might look to us in retrospect to be evidently foolish interpretations of information may not have been without foundation for those trying to understand it at the time.

BOX 26.2 Irrational behaviour is correlated

In Section 26.6 we refer to evidence that the irrational behaviour of investors is not random. Errors do not cancel out. On the contrary, errors are correlated and so we observe firms with a string of good news becoming overvalued and vice versa. From an investment strategy point of view, this kind of behaviour suggests that a 'contrarian' approach is the way to 'beat the market' and make consistent excess returns. The following article, taken from the *Financial Times* of 29 May 2004, points to further evidence of 'noise traders' tending to adopt a herd-like behaviour with the result that their collective actions cause overvaluations. In this case the behaviour is based upon the view that a firm engaged in 'new' technology where there is a good prospect of earnings growth, deserves a valuation that assumes that rapid growth will go on for ever. Once again, the evidence suggests that a strategy of doing the opposite from the herd would have produced better returns in the long run. Notice the reference towards the end to the position of the fund manager who is obliged to follow short-term fashions. This is another factor which limits ability of arbitrage to eliminate irrational prices. Many arbitrageurs are fund managers. They, in particular, face the risk that prices move against them before they can close an arbitrage deal. They cannot run the deal with an infinite time horizon (closing only when price anomalies are eliminated) because their performance is evaluated at short-term intervals.

Don't be a mug when buying growth stocks

PHILIP COGGAN
THE LONG VIEW

Every so often in capitalist economies a great business opportunity presents itself. The media are full of it. Investors clamour to support it. And usually it turns out to be a trap.

When the opportunity is obvious, many businesses attempt to exploit it. New capacity is created that often overwhelms the rosy forecasts of higher demand. Competition then drives down returns and many of the new entrants are forced out of business.

This theory, dubbed the capital cycle approach, has been used as a guiding principle for almost two decades by Marathon Asset Management. The fund management group has collected some of its investment commentaries in a book* covering, in particular, the excesses of the late 1990s.

The tendency for competition to drive excess returns back down to the cost of capital has been highlighted before – by Andrew Smithers and Stephen Wright in their book *Valuing Wall Street*, for example. And the frequent failure of technological innovations to reward investors was well made by Sandy

Nairn in his book *Engines That Move Markets*. Nevertheless, given how often investors have been fooled in the past, the rule is always worth repeating.

Indeed, Marathon points out that the cycle works profitably the other way round. Many investors shun well-established industries where there is little sign of growth. But those industries are often marked by an absence of new investment in capital. Eventually, a reduction in competition leads to higher returns for those that remain.

Sometimes this process can be frustrated when governments, or generous bankruptcy laws, intervene

▶

BOX 26.2 *continued*

to prevent excess capacity being destroyed (the airline industry is a good example). Nevertheless the general rule, according to Marathon, is that 'it is better to invest in a mature industry where competition is declining than in a growing industry where competition is expanding'.

Stock markets form a vital part of the process. New issues are far more likely to occur in expanding sectors that in declining ones. Investment bank analysts have a tendency to project rosy earnings forecasts well into the future. Such forecasts usually fall prey to the 'fallacy of composition' in which a range of companies are all given a high value on the basis of their ability to exploit an expanding market.

When sectors are hot, shares rarely look cheap in terms of conventional measures such as dividend yield, historic price–earnings ratios or asset values. So the temptation is to find new measures such as Ebitda (earnings before interest, tax depreciation and amortisation) or new concepts such as 'first-mover advantage' or 'network effects' to justify the high valuations. Few are willing to say that the emperor has no clothes.

Those high valuations duly have an effect on the actions of managements. If companies are valued at a premium to the replacement cost of their capital, there is an incentive for them to invest more capital. Or as journalist Edward Chancellor writes in his introduction: 'When a hole in the ground costs $1 to dig but is priced in the stock market at $10, the temptation to reach for a shovel becomes irresistible.'

The telecommunications sector in the 1990s provided a golden example of the capital cycle in operation. The old national telecoms monopolies were facing competition from new entrants. Mobile telephone technology was reaching the 'tipping point' where it was transformed from a minority,

---

While telecoms companies were soaring in value and index weight, few investors had the courage to sell

business use into adoption by the vast majority of the population. The development of the internet offered the potential for vast amounts of data to be transmitted down phone lines including, for example, entertainment to be piped directly into people's homes.

Investors drooled in anticipation at the profits these new business opportunities would bring. Marathon reports that, in April 1999, Colt Telecom was valued at about five times the capital it *planned* to invest during the next five years. Level 3 Communications had virtually no revenues but planned to invest $10bn in a fibreoptic network; its enterprise value (equity plus debt) was more than $30bn.

Sure enough, more capital was invested in telecoms capacity, to the tune of $500bn in the US and Canada, equivalent to $5,000 per household. It was hard to imagine how such companies could hope to earn an economic return from such investment, especially as long-term

phone charges were declining. But the companies kept on investing; how could they not? To admit to investors there was a problem with excess capacity would risk collapsing the house of cards; but every extra investment only made the collapse more certain.

Investment banks, eager to earn fees from the raising of capital by telecoms companies, had no incentive to point out the potential for disaster. And while telecoms companies were soaring in value and index weight, few investors had the courage to sell.

The problem investors face in standing back from the herd in that the cycle can take a very long time to unfold. Investors can be proved right in the long run but appear wrong in the short term as share prices in the sector soar and rivals rake in the profits. More than six years elapsed between Marathon's initial forebodings about the telecoms sector, for example, and the eventual share price collapse. That was plenty long enough for fund managers to get fired and lose their jobs.

Growth stocks usually disappoint in the end. A study by Sanford Bernstein of the 1965–1998 period found that only 19 per cent of growth stocks still qualified for that category after 10 years; after 20 years, the proportion fell to 5 per cent.

Of course, there will always be exceptions. But for every Microsoft, there are many more failures. Paying stratospheric valuations for growth stocks is a mug's game.
Capital Account: A Money Manager's Reports on a Turbulent Decade, published by Texere, 283 pp., £24.99 in UK, $39.95 in US
philip.coggan@ft.com

Source: *Financial Times*, 29 May 2004. Reprinted with permission.

26.6 Behavioural finance

Although the events referred to in the last paragraph have undoubtedly made people feel uneasy about the EMH, it nonetheless retains a strong appeal. To deny it is either to suggest that people *do not* make the best use of available information or that they are careless about their own self-interest. These are profoundly disturbing possibilities to anyone brought up in the orthodox traditions of economics where the presence of rational, utility-maximizing individuals is axiomatic. Throw out the EMH and what, if anything, might be left?

But these puzzling cases (and other anomalies) persist and recent years have seen a radically different approach begin to emerge under the name of 'behavioural finance'.

> At the most general level, behavioural finance is the study of human fallibility in competitive markets.
>
> Shleifer, 2000, p. 23.

Behavioural finance theory rests on two foundations, whose significance we will explore below. The first is best called '**investor sentiment**' which is a theory of how real-world investors form their beliefs and valuations. The second is that there are serious practical limits to the possibilities of arbitrage. The first can be seen as a theory of why investors might cause an 'irrational' price to emerge while the second is an explanation of why that price might not be corrected. Behavioural finance has made more progress with the limited arbitrage hypothesis than the theory of investor sentiment. Let us see now why they matter, beginning with **arbitrage**.

To understand the importance of arbitrage, we need first to recall that the EMH rests upon three theoretical foundations. The first is that investors are rational (and make the best use of information about fundamentals etc.). The second is that while *some* investors may not be rational (these are the 'noise traders' we referred to earlier) their irrational trades cancel and leave prices and returns to be determined by investors who are rational. Note that this amounts to saying that the decisions of noise traders are uncorrelated. Both of these foundations are weak. Investors do all sorts of strange things. They follow the advice of financial pundits (whose superior information is impossible under the EMH); they hang on too long to securities whose prices are falling. The latter is the

result of a psychological trait which Odean (1998) calls 'loss aversion'. They are reluctant to sell because this turns a notional loss into a real one. But they sell securities showing a gain 'too soon'. The loss function seems steeper than the gain function. They trade too much. They buy expensively managed mutual funds (again on the basis that their managers have some superior information). If we assume that investors understand that there is a systematic relationship between risk and return then it is very difficult to explain how rational investors can behave as described by Benartzi and Thaler (1995), who found that investors were more inclined to buy equities when confronted with evidence of long-term returns than they were when shown only the evidence of volatility of returns. And so it goes on.

The third foundation is that even if irrational traders behave in the same way (their decisions *are* correlated) then profitable opportunities for arbitrage will force noise traders out of business, leaving pricing to rational investors. Given that we do have evidence of irrational behaviour and even of correlated irrational behaviour, the role of arbitrage might be considered the 'argument of last resort' for the emergence and maintenance of efficient prices. If this fails, then the EMH is in serious trouble. This is why the argument in behavioural finance that the possibilities of profitable arbitrage are distinctly limited is absolutely fundamental to the debate. We look at this in more detail.

A common definition of arbitrage is that it involves the simultaneous purchase and sale of the same asset in two different markets at advantageous prices. This is just a rather formal way of saying that if the same asset has a different price in two different markets, there is a (riskless) profit to be made by buying the cheap asset and selling the expensive one. Clearly such trades will tend to bring prices in the two markets into equality, so arbitrage is an important underpinning of the law of one price. Just as important, however, is the fact that an arbitrage deal delivers a riskless profit and therefore traders who are well informed and can carry out these trades will make a profit. At the same time, the ill-informed, or noise traders, will be the ones who are buying the overpriced securities sold by the arbitrageurs (and selling the underpriced securities to them). This cannot go on for ever. Eventually, the noise traders must lose all their wealth, drop out of the market and leave pricing to the well-informed arbitrageurs.

586 CHAPTER 26 FINANCIAL MARKET EFFICIENCY

But behavioural finance asks us to think more carefully about what arbitrage involves in practice. For the trade to be riskless, the arbitrageur has to be able to sell (or sell short) an asset which is overpriced and buy (ideally) the same asset cheaply. The practical problem to which this gives rise is that there is often no (underpriced) close substitute available for the asset which is overpriced. Suppose a trader thinks that stocks in the FTSE-250 index are generally overpriced. S/he can borrow (and sell short) those stocks in the anticipation that the price will later fall. To make the deal riskless, however, s/he has to be able to buy the same portfolio at a lower price. This is because s/he has to return the FTSE-250 stocks to the lender at the end of the deal at *their then market value*. Suppose s/he holds no alternative at all. In other words s/he has simply sold shares which s/he has borrowed. If (unexpectedly) the portfolio is hit by good news between the day of the sale and the date for their return to the lender, then the trader will have to enter the market and buy the shares at a higher price than that for which they were sold. The only way that the arbitrageur can be sure to make a riskless profit is if s/he was able to buy at the beginning, at a lower price, the same set of shares that s/he has sold (or sold short). In these circumstances, any unexpected news that affects the price of the borrowed shares will automatically affect the value of the shares which are held. This is the problem of being able to find a suitable 'hedge'. Obviously, this tends to be easier when the arbitrage involves a single security and increases in difficulty as we try to hedge portfolios.

MORE FROM THE WEB
Behavioural finance

Behavioural finance is also well represented by sites on the internet, though there maybe fewer than those devoted to the EMH.

Two excellent sites are: www.behaviouralfinance.net, which provides a very extensive glossary of terms (and reading) of importance to behavioural finance. To get the best from the site, of course, it helps to have some idea of how the terms fit into the story.

A better pace to start for absolute beginners is probably: www.finpipe.com, which begins with an introductory essay and then many links to take the issue further.

Another practical problem is one of time. If an arbitrage deal is done with imperfect substitutes (or no substitute at all) then there is the risk that prices which are expected to converge eventually might diverge before the deal has to be closed. For example, the arbitrageur borrows and sells short an asset which is overpriced at the same time buying another (but not identical one) which seems underpriced. The loan will be for a specified period. During that time the overpriced asset might rise further in price. And if the hedge is imperfect, it will not move in the same way and will not offer full protection to the holder. Alternatively, it might be that the hedge itself, while underpriced, falls further.

The point of these (and other possible examples) is that the riskless arbitrage deal is more plausible in theory than in practice. In practice, arbitrageurs are forced to take risk and this will limit their ability to guarantee the elimination of mis-pricing. (See Shleifer, 2000, pp. 13–16.)

But why should mispricing occur in the first place? This is where a theory of how investors process information and form judgements is required. At the moment, behavioural finance draws much of its inspiration from work in psychology but it is not impossible that work in experimental economics will shed light on this in future. Two important behavioural hypotheses in the current literature are 'conservatism' (Edwards, 1968) and 'representativeness' (Tversky and Kahneman, 1974). Together they show (as the result of experimentation) that people are slower to modify or update their understanding than is warranted by the evidence but that once they cross this threshold, they regard what may be random occurrences as confirming a pattern. The classic experiment involves the tossing of a coin which is *known* to the experimental subjects to be unfair in the sense that it has (say) a 70:30 bias. But the subjects do not know in which way it is biased – 70 per cent heads or 70 per cent tails. So far as the subjects are concerned, therefore, the probability of each bias is 0.5. The experimenter then begins tossing the coin (which we will assume is heads biased). At each successive toss the outcome is the same and subjects are asked after each toss to give their estimate of the probability that the bias is indeed heads. Predictably, their estimate of the probability, beginning at 0.5, rises quite quickly in the face of repeated outcomes of heads. But the striking thing is that in the early stages it does not rise as quickly as it 'should' if the subjects were following truly Bayesian principles. Equally interesting is the discovery that after a few tosses the underestimate of the Bayesian probability switches to an overestimate. The early tosses in a series seem not to have the impact that they warrant, while the later ones are seized on as evidence that the world is more certain than it really is. The first is evidence of 'conservatism': news has to be repeated until its real significance is appreciated. The second is evidence of the 'representativeness': if news recurs often enough, it is treated as belonging to a pattern and the possibility of randomness is discounted.

It is not difficult to see how these tendencies could be translated to a financial context. For example, we assume that investors have a particular view about a company and the value of its stock. They then receive news about the firm to which their response is less than would be the case if they acted according to true Bayesian principles. But the news keeps coming and eventually is interpreted, falsely, as part of a trend which is going to continue for ever. In the first phase, investors underreact to the news and in the second phase they overreact.

Evidence that this is in fact what happens comes from numerous studies but the easiest to understand are those where a stock which experiences a sustained period of poor news subsequently outperforms stocks which have been the subject of good news. This evidence suggests that the firm with consistent good news and earnings has become overvalued while the stocks with a run of bad news are undervalued. Investors can therefore earn abnormal returns by betting against this overreaction to news by buying the bad news stocks and selling the good news stocks. The best known of these studies was carried out by De Bondt and Thaler (1985) who, for each year since 1933, constructed a ('losers') portfolio of the worst performing stocks and a ('winners') portfolio of the best performing stocks judged by their performance in the three previous years. They then computed the performance of each portfolio in the five years following its formation. Averaging the results across the approximately 50 'winner' portfolios and 50 'loser' portfolios showed a clearly superior return for the 'loser' portfolios. It is impossible to avoid the conclusion that the good news portfolios had been overvalued while the bad news portfolios were undervalued.

Why people should behave in such a way that they are led to make persistent under- and overvaluations is a mystery but it is one on which experimental psychology may eventually shed some light. Certainly, looking at research into human behaviour in other branches of the social sciences seems more likely to produce satisfying answers than simply *assuming* that people with superior information are bound to impose the correct valuation on everyone else.

26.7 Summary

Markets can be efficient in a number of ways, but the term 'efficient markets' is usually understood to refer to informational efficiency and this in turn refers to the speed with which markets react to information. If markets are informationally efficient then prices adjust so quickly to new information that it is impossible for any agent to exploit information in order to make consistent excess profits. The degree of informational efficiency is distinguished by reference to the type of information to which markets respond quickly. If current security prices incorporate all the information contained in past price behaviour, they are said to be 'weak-form' efficient. Markets which are 'semi-strong-form' efficient incorporate all publicly available information too quickly for any trader to exploit it profitably while markets which are 'strong-form' efficient react quickly even to information which is not universally available.

Tests of the EMH tend to support the hypothesis in its weaker forms. The evidence is not quite so convincing for the strong form of the hypothesis though it still seems unlikely that investors can derive sufficient advantage from private information to make consistent excess profits after allowing for the cost of acquiring the information.

The EMH only says that investors use information to make the best possible forecast of future prices and/or yields. In this respect, it assumes that investors behave 'rationally' by learning from any past mistakes or being driven from the market. Thus the EMH assumes that investors apply their information to the 'best' model of security pricing, where 'best' means the one that the market appears to use. What this model may be is a separate issue. It could be that the market values assets according to their 'fundamentals', in the manner described by the CAPM. If that is the case, then fluctuations in security prices and returns should reflect fluctuations in these fundamentals and we could then describe markets as behaving 'rationally'. However, the evidence for market rationality is not as convincing as the evidence for the EMH. The alternative, suggested by behavioural finance, is that many investors simply do not attempt to find the best information but instead, for reasons we do not yet fully understand, adopt 'rules of thumb' which lead to persistent errors, which arbitrage is unable to eliminate.

Key concepts in this chapter

Allocative efficiency	Market rationality
Arbitrage	Operational efficiency
Bargains	Optimal forecast
Behavioural finance	Pricing efficiency
Efficient market hypothesis (EMH)	Random walk model
Event studies	Rational expectations
Fair game model	Relevant information
Filter tests	Runs tests
Index tracker funds	Semi-strong-form EMH
Informational efficiency	Serial correlation
Insider trading	Strong-form EMH
Investor sentiment	Weak-form EMH

Questions and problems

1 Distinguish between the meanings which can be attached to 'efficiency' when applied to financial markets.

2 What forces tend to make financial markets informationally efficient?

3 Distinguish between the different forms of the efficient market hypothesis.

4 How might an investment strategy appropriate for a market which is informationally efficient differ from one appropriate for a market which is inefficient?

5 How might you test for 'weak' and 'semi-strong' efficiency?

6 You suspect that directors' purchases/sales of shares in their own firms are an indicator of future share price movements. How would you test whether such information could be profitably exploited?

7 Explain what is meant by 'investor sentiment'.

8 Why might arbitrage fail to eliminate mispricing?

Further reading

S Benartzi and R Thaler, 'Myopic loss aversion and the equity premium puzzle', *Quarterly Journal of Economics*, 110, 1995, 73–92
K Boakes, *Reading and Understanding the Financial Times* (London: Financial Times Prentice Hall, 2008), Topic 7
Z Bodie, A Kane and A J Marcus, *Essentials of Investments* (New York: McGraw-Hill, 4e, 2001) Ch. 9

D M Cutler, J M Poterba and L H Summers, 'What moves stock prices?', *Journal of Financial Economics*, 1989, 4–12
P Coggan, 'Don't be a mug when buying growth stocks', *Financial Times*, 29 May 2004
W F M De Bondt and R Thaler, 'Does the stock market overreact?', *Journal of Finance*, 40, 1985, 793–805

W Edwards 'Conservation in human information processing', in B Kleinmitz (ed.) *Formal Representation of Human Judgment* (New York: Wiley, 1968)

E J Elton and M J Gruber, *Modern Porfolio Theory and Investment Analysis* (New York: Wiley, 5e, 1995)

E Fama, 'Efficient capital markets: A review of theory and empirical work', *Journal of Finance*, 25 (2), 1970, 383–417

E Fama, 'Efficient capital markets II', *Journal of Finance*, 26 (5), 1991, 1575–1617

P Garber, 'Famous first bubbles', *Journal of Economic Perspectives*, 4 (2), 1990, 35–54

B Malkiel, A *Random Walk Down Wall Street* (New York: Norton, 1973)

J Muth, 'Rational expectations and the theory of price movements', *Econometrica*, 29, 1961, 315–35

T Odean, 'Are investors reluctant to realize their losses?', *Journal of Finance*, 53, 1998, 1775–98

R J Shiller, *Irrational Exuberance* (Woodstock: Princeton University Press, 2000)

R J Shiller, 'Do stock prices move too much to be justified by subsequent changes in dividends?', *American Economic Review*, 1981, 421–36

A Shleifer, *Inefficient Markets: An Introduction to Behavioural Finance* (Oxford: Oxford University Press, 2000)

G Stiglitz (ed.), 'Symposium on "bubbles"', *Journal of Economic Perspectives*, 4 (2), 1990, 1–34

A Tversky and D Kahneman, 'Judgment under uncertainty: Heuristics and biases', *Science*, 185, 1974, 1124–31

Websites

www.behaviouralfinance.net
www.finpipe.com
www.investopedia.com
www.investorhome.com

Case study 1 The structure of banking and conflicts of interest

In the spring of 2002, the international banking world was shocked by the discovery that several US investment banks had behaved towards their clients in a way which revealed glaring conflicts of interest. The episode brings together a number of aspects which we have touched on at various points in the book. For example, it reveals the sharp difference in focus between retail and investment banks (Section 2.3); it also illustrates the fears that some people expressed at the time of the 'Big Bang' reforms of the London Stock Exchange in 1986 (Section 17.5.2); it provides another reason why the price of shares may not always reflect the underlying fundamentals of the firm (Section 11.5) and thus it contributes to the debate about financial market efficiency and the question of whether some people have an information advantage (Section 26.3).

In Section 2.3 we distinguished between different types of banking activity. Retail banks, we said, were banks which offered loan and deposit, money transmission and a range of other services to the personal sector. Such banks are likely to be parts of a large banking conglomerate, other parts of which would be engaged in wholesale banking. Barclays and HSBC in the UK, Citigroup in the USA and Deutsche Bank in Germany are obvious examples. Very likely this would include corporate banking – offering similar services to retail banks but designed for the corporate sector – and investment banking. The latter would involve advising firms in mergers and acquisitions, making new issues of shares and bonds for firms, mutual fund management, equity and bond analysis and even acting as a market-maker in a range of shares. While retail banks were likely to be part of a conglomerate which included wholesale banks, we noted that the

opposite was not the case. Many wholesale banks are 'free-standing' specialists in corporate or investment banking. Among the largest and best known of the latter are firms like Goldman Sachs, Merrill Lynch, Lehman Brothers, Morgan Stanley and Credit Suisse First Boston (CSFB).

In May 2002 the *Financial Times* reported that some share analysts at Merrill Lynch in New York had been publishing judgements about the shares in some companies which they knew to be false. As the story grew, the New York district attorney, Elliot Spitzer, ordered an investigation and evidence began to appear in the form of colourful emails which were being sent to colleagues within the bank. One of the analysts, central to the scandal, was named Henry Blodget and the investigation found emails which he had sent to investment management colleagues within the bank warning them that some companies (particularly in the dotcom and telecoms sectors) were virtually worthless and that their shares were overvalued. These private judgements were quite different from the public reports which he was writing and sending out to fund managers and to private clients of the bank.

The accompanying extract from the *Financial Times* was written towards the end of the affair, in April 2003, and it shows the reason for this deception in paragraphs two and three where Blodget is reported as celebrating the amount of 'banking' business the analysts are bringing in and rating it as much more important than the research they are supposed to be doing. Much of the work done by an investment bank is to assist firms in negotiations over mergers and acquisitions (negotiations which may become very aggressive if an unwelcome takeover bid is launched) and to make new share and bond issues for the firm. This is the really profitable part of the business and so investment banks compete keenly for the role of adviser to the largest firms. Consequently, M&A activity (as it is often called) is also where the really big salaries and bonuses are earned. Clearly no investment bank will want to upset a client firm by publishing adverse reports about it to the investing community. The *Financial Times* refers to the case of GoTo where a junior analyst is worried that some retail investors (taking the published analysis in good faith) might lose the whole of their retirement savings by following the advice on GoTo, just because Merrill Lynch did not want to upset GoTo's chief financial officer by telling the truth. Hence share analysts at some investment banks were, it seems, under great pressure to find positive things to say publicly, even about firms which they thought privately were poorly run and managed or had poor profit outlooks. As the *Financial Times* report says, in the case of Internet Capital Group, the private view was that it was 'a disaster' with 'no "operations" here to fall back on' and yet they gave it a favourable rating in public.

Global settlement: Blodget pays out $4m and gets life ban

By Charles Pretzlik

Henry Blodget, Merrill Lynch's former star technology analyst, has agreed to pay $4m to settle charges of misconduct from US securities regulators. He will also be barred from the securities industry for life.

According to court documents filed by the Securities and Exchange Commission, 'from at least July 1999 through June 2001, research analysts at Merrill Lynch were subject to inappropriate influence by investment banking at the firm'. The complaint, filed in the US District Court for the Southern District of New York, alleges the bank published 'false or misleading research', published 'exaggerated or unwarranted research or research that lacked a reasonable basis'. It also said the bank failed properly to supervise research and investment banking. In a March 1999 e-mail, Mr Blodget said: 'We are now up to 11–12 internet banking transactions in the pipeline . . . The current schedule for this week . . . is 85 per cent banking, 15 per cent research.'

Merrill bankers used research as bait for investment banking business. In an April 2000 e-mail, one banker asked: 'Do you think we should aggre-ssively link coverage with banking – that is what we did with Go2Net (Henry [Blodget] was involved).' The documents also indicate that Merrill's draft research and proposed rating changes were sometimes shown to the companies being covered ahead of time, as well as to investment banking colleagues, despite internal rules banning this.

In February 2001 a Merrill analyst sent an unpublished report to Tyco's chief financial officer with the following note: 'PLEASE REVIEW ASAP. I WILL NOT SEND ID OUT UNTIL I HEAR FROM YOU FIRST! LOYAL TYCO EMPLOYEE!'

It is also clear that analysts came under pressure from colleagues in investment banking seeking to influence coverage of stocks. Merrill research management acknowledged this in an October 2000 e-mail to Mr Blodget. 'I think we are off base on how we rate stocks and how much we bend backwards to accommodate banking etc,' it said. The regulators said that on two companies, GoTo.com and InfoSpace, Merrill published research that failed to reflect its analysts' privately expressed negative views, 'making the reports materially false and misleading'. On the day that Merrill initiated coverage of GoTo, 11 January 2001, Mr Blodget received an e-mail from an institutional client which asked: 'What's so interesting about Goto [sic] except banking fees????' Mr Blodget replied: 'Nothin.'

While working on the initial research report on GoTo, a junior analyst said in an e-mail that retail investors might lose their retirement 'because we don't want [GoTo's CFO] to be mad at us'. On InfoSpace, Mr Blodget wrote e-mails reporting 'enormous skepticism'.

A September 2000 report into Internet Capital Group provided a favourable rating. Yet in a private e-mail about it two weeks later, Mr Blodget wrote: 'This has been a disaster . . . There really are no "operations" here to fall back on, so there really is no "floor" to the stock.'

Merrill will pay $100m in penalties, plus $75m over five years to fund independent research and $25m to fund investor education.

Source: *Financial Times*, 29 April 2003. Reprinted with permission.

In Section 17.5.2, we explained that, prior to 1986, the London Stock Exchange was closed to public corporations. The only firms allowed to trade on the LSE were partnerships. This restricted their size, prevented economies of scale and allowed them to survive only by operating a set of fixed commissions which were much higher than large US banks were charging for dealing in shares on the NYSE. When the decision was finally made to sweep all this away and to allow large firms to set up stockbroking and/or market-making facilities in the London Stock Exchange, it was clear to everyone that the firms wishing to join would be international investment banks. A conflict of interest was immediately foreseen. If investment banks were specialists in researching the value of companies and their shares and in floating new issues, it was clearly possible that they might use some of this specialist and inside information to give themselves an advantage when it came to making markets in various stocks. This was not quite the same conflict as emerged in the Blodget case – the problem at Merrill Lynch was that one part of the bank had specialist knowedge about the value of firms and shares while another part of the firm was managing investments for bank clients and another part was advising firms on M&As and new issues. If the clients in the M&A/new issue part of the bank were to be kept happy they needed to see flattering reports. But then someone needed to tip off the investment managers that they should not believe what their colleagues were publishing. But the principles were the same. In the case of 'Big Bang' the London Stock Exchange insisted that if investment banks wished to become market-makers then they must put up what were famously called 'Chinese Walls' between the various departments of the bank. These 'walls' were a set of rules which were intended to prevent the flow of information from one part of the bank to another. Provided the wall was intact, the theory went, the analysts would have no incentive to tell two different stories. With the wall in place, they would not be able to tip off their own fund managers that their public reports were false and so publishing a misleading report would run the risk that the bank's own managers would believe and act on it. Eventually, as part of the settlement, the US banks involved (in addition to Merrill Lynch – Bear Stearns, CSFB, Goldman Sachs, Lehman Brothers and Citigroup) agreed to pay large amounts in compensation and fines ($400m in the case of Citigroup) and to introduce structural reforms to insulate research analysts from the influence of investment bankers.

Questions for discussion

1 Why might the CFO at GoTo have been 'mad' if Merrill Lynch had published an adverse report about his firm?

2 What does this incident suggest about the strong form of the efficient markets hypothesis?

3 How effective do you think that the reported settlement is likely to be in preventing more cases of this kind?

Further reading

A M Santomero and David F Babbel, *Financial Markets, Instruments and Institutions* (New York: McGraw-Hill, 2e, 2001) Ch. 21

Case study 2 The dotcom phenomenon

One of the most startling features of recent stock market history was the dramatic rise and fall in popularity and value of technology stocks in the course of roughly two years between early 1999 and March 2001. The background to this was a steady rise in share prices which had begun with the recovery after the 1987 crash and had begun to increase in speed from about 1995. The upward trend was most dramatic in the USA, more moderate in the UK and the EU, decidedly bumpy in SE Asia where markets suffered a temporary fall in 1997–98 and largely absent in Japan. During 1997 it became apparent that the rise in prices was more marked in some sectors than in others and that these sectors shared one common feature, namely, their ability to exploit the latest developments in communications technology. Collectively, the stocks became known as 'TMT' or 'Technology, Media and Telecom' stocks. Within this grouping, the so-called 'dotcoms' were companies which were going to exploit the advantages of the internet, usually by establishing an internet site which enabled people to browse, select and pay for goods, services or information 'online'. And it was this subset of TMT stocks which saw the most dramatic action.

The two articles reprinted here appeared in the *Financial Times* almost exactly a year apart. The first was published in March 2000, when technology stocks were at their peak. It refers specifically to the extraordinary behaviour of investors towards dotcom stocks and shows that the *FT* was already worried that they were taking excessive risks with shares whose prices could not be justified. The second describes what happened in the following year. In retrospect, the episode is quite entertaining. But there are serious aspects to it as we shall try to show by drawing on some of the theory we have discussed in earlier chapters.

The first article begins by pointing out that even cautious investors are likely to be exposed to high-risk investment in dotcom companies. The reason for this is that the share price of some of these firms was so high that their market capitalization (number of shares × price) put them amongst the 100 largest UK firms. As such, they became eligible for membership of the FTSE-100 share price index. Clearly, since market capitalization varies with share price, even in normal times eligibility for membership can come and go, especially for firms with a value around the 100th

threshold. In order to prevent high-frequency oscillations, the FTSE membership rules employ a filter which requires that firms outside the index have actually to achieve a capitalization which puts them at least as high as 90th before entry, while a firm which is in the index has to drop in value to 110th before being excluded. But these were not normal times and the quarterly revisions to the index saw new dotcoms being added in March 2000 and excluded again in June. The important point being made in the article, however, is that once a firm is a member of the FTSE-100 (and many other indices for that matter) its shares are immediately bought by fund managers. This may be because the fund has been set up in order to replicate (or 'track') an index or because it has rules which require managers to put at least a given percentage of the fund into the shares of large companies, in the traditional view that 'large' means 'safe'. Consequently anyone with a pension fund or index tracker fund could, in the spring of 2000, have found themselves exposed to these very high-risk companies.

The other side of this picture, as the article notes in the third paragraph, is that long-established firms, with good profit records and a long history of supplying the general public with goods and services which it certainly needs (Thames Water was an example) found themselves dropped from the index in favour of a firm for whose output there was no definite demand.

One of the firms involved in this dramatic rise in value was Lastminute.com, whose shares were floated on Tuesday, 14 March 2000. As the second article reports, after the initial announcement of Lastminute's forthcoming flotation, the demand for dotcom shares pushed prices to the point where the issuing bank decided to raise the indicative price of the shares from a range of 190–230p to 320–380p, an increase of 67 per cent. We return to this later.

The rest of the first article draws attention to the risks associated with investing in these companies, suggesting that it is something that ought to be done by specialist venture capital fund managers. It also gives three reasons for the extraordinary boom in dotcoms. The first of these is the slackening of listing rules by many stock exchanges. The London Stock Exchange, like many others, used to insist that firms coming to the market have a well-established trading record. The second is that the technology behind 'e-commerce' firms meant that they had to move quickly in order to get any advantage from being the first to think of an idea. If they had to trade for several years before getting a listing, their competitors would have ample time to catch up. And, thirdly, the technology also required large amounts of capital at the time of initial start-up. It was not possible to start in a small way and expand subsequently.

Looking back from a year later, the second article begins by recalling that the dotcom boom required people to behave in ways that broke most rules of sound business. It also gives evidence of the frenzy by referring to the 88 per cent rise in the NASDAQ index over a five-month period. NASDAQ stands for National Association of Securities Dealers Automated Quotations. It is based in New York and the majority of the shares listed are technology firms which means that movements in the overall price of NASDAQ shares provides quite a good indication of what is happening to technology stocks, at least in the USA. On 10 March 2000, the index stood at its all-time high of 5049. Exactly one year later it had lost 59 per cent of its value. The article then goes on to show what this dramatic decline meant for individual firms like Clickmango.com, QXL and Oxygen Holdings.

What neither article explains directly, but is obviously a major question looking back, is why investors were so willing to pay very high prices for shares in companies with no profits, whose technological characteristics made them extremely risky. Each article offers a clue, however, which we can interpret with the help of earlier discussion. The first article comments that 'the market is applying a lower discount rate to the future earnings of high-tech companies than the venture capital industry would'. The Gordon growth model which we have used throughout this book, $P = D_1/(K - g)$, is not entirely appropriate in this context because the firms in question had no current earnings (let alone paid dividends) but it suggests the article can be interpreted as saying that the reason prices were so high was that a lot of investors were employing a much lower value for K than would normally be the case. Why should this be so? It is unlikely to be because of a false estimate of the risk-free rate. It seems more likely that they were employing too low (even a zero?) risk premium.

It may be, however, that in these circumstances we need to abandon conventional approaches to valuation. Look at the closing sentence of the second article.

Here is a fund manager saying that when prices are going up (even if you have doubts about the wisdom) your clients expect you to buy in order to earn them a slice of the profit: '. . . you are not paid to sit on your hands while others are making money'. This is the dilemma that faces all fund managers. Their responsibility is to their investing clients and if their investing clients want maximum short-term profit then the manager must follow market sentiment whether or not he or she thinks it soundly based. And the pressures for short-term performance are considerable. Many newspapers run annual league tables of fund performance in which managers are implicitly judged against an index or against other fund managers. If you are a manager, it is no use saying to your clients when you come bottom of the league, that your decision not to buy dotcom stocks was correct 'in theory' or 'will be proved right in the long run'. In the long run, your clients will have left and you will have been sacked. This is the insight (inverted) behind Keynes' remark quoted in Section 11.5. It is no use offering a price for an asset which you may think theoretically correct, if you think the market will value it at twice that amount three months hence.

Although it is not mentioned in either of the articles, we should also remember the background that we outlined at the beginning, namely that in the UK and USA shares had been rising almost continuously for more than ten years. As time goes by, memories fade (and the most experienced personnel retire). There comes a time when few can remember that prices can also fall. Furthermore, it may be that markets, rightly or wrongly, are coming to see an additional role for central banks. In Sections 2.3 and 9.4, we refer to 'lender of last resort' as a key function of central banks. As we explain, this is usually understood to mean lender to *banks* in the event of a system-wide liquidity shortage. But there have been occasions in recent years where central banks, led by the Federal Reserve, have reduced interest rates seemingly in response to potential problems in financial *markets*. It happened in the October 1987 crash (from which recovery was quite rapid). It happened again in the SE Asia crises in 1997, again in 1998 when it looked as though a major US hedge fund (Long-Term Capital Management) was going to collapse and one might argue that this is also a possible interpretation of the Fed's rate cuts in March and April of 2001. In these circumstances, if central banks are underwriting the risk of equity investment, we are

WE ARE ALL VENTURE CAPITALISTS NOW

By Martin Dickson

We are all capitalists now, according to the aphorism that echoed through the post-communist 1990s. But a more accurate slogan for the new millennium might be: 'We are all venture capitalists now'.

For these days anyone with a pension fund, an index tracker fund or a direct holding in many of the newly quoted dotcom companies has some exposure to the kind of high-risk, high-return investments more normally associated with the venture capital industry.

The trend has been highlighted by two events this week: the remarkable changes in the FTSE 100 index, where profitable 'old economy' stocks have been replaced by a clutch of loss-making high-technology ones; and the flotation of Lastminute.com, the small online retailer. Such a stampede seems to be developing for its shares that it could be valued at close to £1bn when dealings start on Tuesday, even though it is not expected to turn a profit until 2004.

The venture capital industry specialises in funding very young companies that have a good idea but an unproven business model and makes its money when its companies are sold, either in a flotation or to another group. Once upon a time the industry aimed to get a decent return on its initial investment in five to seven years. But nowadays high-technology companies are being brought to market much more quickly and often at a much earlier stage in development, well before their business model is proven. Take, for example, Freeserve, the internet portal. Ironically, it has joined the FTSE 100 in the very week that the model on which it was founded – funding free internet access by creaming off part of the telecoms bills run up by customers – was dealt a probably mortal blow by rivals.

Three factors explain this rush to market. First, the rules have changed. Stock exchanges across the western world, anxious to be seen as innovative and scared to be left behind by rivals, have relaxed listing rules. The London Stock Exchange has largely dropped its requirement that a company have a three-year trading record before admission to its main market: Lastminute.com's web site was set up only 18 months ago.

Second, companies with good e-commerce ideas need to move quickly to establish 'first mover' advantage and if their growth requires very large amounts of capital they may need to tap the equity markets.

Third, there are companies that could well meet their financial requirements from within the venture capital industry but are coming to market quickly – 'a short flip' in the jargon – to capitalise on the insatiable demand and extraordinary high prices they can get for these stocks.

'Today the market is applying a lower discount rate to the future earnings streams of high-tech companies than the venture capital industry would,' according to one leading figure in the sector. Translated into plain English that means stock market investors are often prepared to make wildly optimistic assumptions about prospects for these companies, although venture capitalists who understand them are not . . .

Lastminute.com provides an example of the kinds of risk to which investors are being exposed. Its revenues are minuscule, its losses are growing, and its business model is, to put it politely, far from proven. Its big idea sounds initially plausible – selling online last minute goods, such as cheap flights – but it is questionable whether there is a market here that cannot be tapped more efficiently by industry heavyweights.

Investors who buy high-tech stocks at such an early stage of development may be rewarded with high returns, but they are taking on huge risks without any means of controlling them, apart from the hope of selling quickly if the market turns sour. And over the long term, the odds are stacked against them. Venture capitalists reckon that for every 10 investments they make, only two will be unqualified successes, two will be total write-offs and six will cause them problems. That is a hell of a gamble if you are buying into a company at a sky-high dotcom price . . .

Source: *Financial Times*, 11 March 2000. Reprinted with permission.

What a difference a year can make to a dream

By Thorold Baker

Twelve months ago, dotcom mania was at its peak. And nowhere was it more obvious than in the panelled rooms of one City investment house. Sitting across the table from two dotcom entrepreneurs, an experienced investment banker was struck by the hideous realisation that the men facing him were trying to float nothing more than an idea for more than £100m. And they had no relevant experience.

'You don't understand,' the ebullient chief executive said. 'This is not about performance, it is about a concept. If we started executing the plan it would lose its purity and investors wouldn't be interested.' The discussion was short and the company never reached the stock market. But, for a few months at the beginning of last year, investors' seemingly insatiable appetite for dotcom companies put normal business rules on hold.

Nasdaq, the US technology market that helped drive dotcom mania on both sides of the Atlantic, rose an astonishing 88 per cent in less than five months. It ended its seemingly unstoppable rise on Friday, March 10 – a year ago today – but the week leading up to the peak typified the frenzy surrounding anything 'dotcom'. That week started with Alta Vista, the internet search engine, grabbing the headlines by becoming the first in the UK to offer unlimited access to the web for a flat fee – a promise it admitted five months later it could not afford and never actually launched. The same day saw the start of bidding in the UK for third-generation mobile phone licences. The five 3G licences were originally

expected to raise £1.5bn. But the competitors – beguiled by the prospect of huge revenues from mobile internet services – entered a bidding frenzy that ended in a £22.5bn windfall for the Treasury and saddled the companies with a pile of debt that has scared investors off the sector ever since.

The action of dotcom investors, like 3G bidders, seems incomprehensible in the cold light of day. But at the time people would pay almost any price for a piece of the action. Their excitement about the dotcom revolution was outweighed only by a sense of panic that they might miss the opportunity of a generation.

Michael Ross, chief executive of Figleaves.com, which sells lingerie online, says: 'You had to be pretty stubborn to sit on the sidelines and predict doom instead of getting involved. People were making real money and many of those who did take the risk still have the fortunes to prove it.' Everybody had a dotcom idea to discuss in the pub. Most never came near fruition. Instead, people ranging from the Queen – who invested in Getmapping.com, an internet mapping company – to housewives, professionals, manual workers and students got involved by investing in dotcoms listed on the seemingly unstoppable stock markets, where demand far outstripped the supply of shares.

'We all invested in a few (dotcoms). You look at it now and think you must have been a bit crackers.'

A favourite was Lastminute.com. Thursday March 9 saw Lastminute – probably the most hyped dotcom flotation of all – raise the price range

for its imminent flotation by an unprecedented 67 per cent following huge retail demand. The following day Nasdaq hit an all-time high of 5,049. A year on the picture could scarcely be more different. Nasdaq has lost 59 per cent of its value, completely choking off the flood of internet flotations. Many would-be entrepreneurs who rushed into risky start-ups have returned even faster to the security of a monthly salary in a profitable company.

The red-hot venture capital market – which famously gave Clickmango.com's youthful founders £3m in only eight days to set up a natural health products e-tailer – has turned off the taps, replacing the flow of dotcom millionaires with a steady drip of internet collapses – including Clickmango itself. Private investors have also been burned. Oxygen Holdings – which soared 29-fold on its debut in February 2000 after raising £2.2m to invest in students' dotcom ideas – has tumbled more than 96 per cent from its peak value of £214m and now sits below its float price. Other favourites such as QXL.com, the online auctioneer, and Durlacher, the internet investment company, have fallen by a similar amount.

Trading volumes, which rose 50 per cent from normal levels in the first quarter of 2000, have returned to earth as the appetite for risk has disappeared. The latest figures from Autif, the fund management industry body, show sales of technology funds falling from £878m in March 2000 to £74m in January this year.

The dotcoms themselves, says one venture capitalist, are having a 'breath-holding contest'. The focus

▶

has changed in a year from trying to build a business as fast as possible, with scant regard to losses, to conserving cash at any cost to remain the last man standing. Lastminute cannot have imagined how important the extra cash it earned by raising its float price would be.

Some dotcoms will make it. But as their number dwindles, it would be hard to believe the frenzy of last year had ever happened were it not for everyday reminders: the range of specialist internet magazines on newsagents' shelves; the huge cash piles that some companies raised at the top of the market and still control; and the underlying uptake of the internet, which has made it a part of everyday life for many.

Michael Jackson, chairman of Elderstreet, the venture capitalist, remains philosophical about the whole experience: 'We all invested in a few (dotcoms). You look at it now and think you must have been a bit crackers,' he says. 'But at the end of the day you are not paid to sit on your hands while others are making money.'

Source: *Financial Times*, 10 March 2001. Reprinted with permission.

entering a new era in which conventional beliefs about the required premium for equity holding are all wrong. It also raises issues of 'moral hazard' (see Section 2.4). If investors believe that the central bank will prop up financial markets as well as banks, they may become much less cautious about investing in risky projects.

So much for possible *causes*; what about the implications of the 'boom and bust'? Clearly some people will have made substantial profits by buying and selling at the right time. Others will have made substantial losses by doing the opposite. There must, therefore, have been some redistribution of wealth.

More importantly, the rapid rise in TMT (the broader category) stocks after 1997, and its effect in increasing people's wealth, seems likely to have had some considerable impact on consumption spending in the USA, where household saving dropped effectively to zero. (There is no need to save, if your wealth is going to increase without it.) The subsequent decline in prices has had the opposite effect and is closely woven into the delicate balance between a slowdown in growth and a genuine recession that faced the US and other economies in early 2001.

What we should also consider are the implications for capital allocation. In Section 1.5.3, we noted that one of the ways in which the performance of a financial system can affect the rest of the economy is through its 'allocative efficiency', its ability to allocate funds to their most productive use. Ideally, for such allocative efficiency to exist, one would wish that the best-managed firms were the most profitable firms. If markets valued their shares according to Equation 11.6, the good management and the good earnings would be reflected in a 'high' share price. A high share price would mean a low cost of capital (Section 17.4.3) and this would be some encouragement to such firms

to borrow, to invest and expand. The result would be an increase in output from a firm which had a proven record of providing what society valued, in the most efficient way (see Sections 11.5 and 26.5).

But contrast this with what happened in case of dotcom firms. These were firms, we said earlier, which had earned no profits. There was, strictly speaking, no evidence that they were providing things which people wanted at a price which would justify their production. Nonetheless, these firms attracted large capital flows in the hope that they would eventually meet a genuine demand. Furthermore, as the price of the shares increased, their cost of capital fell. Consider again Lastminute.com. Its advisers originally expected that each share sold would raise about £2 for the firm. But such was the frenzy of buying of dotcom shares that, in the few weeks between the issue of the prospectus and the opening of the subscription the advisers realized that each share could probably be sold for over £3. This was a firm whose issue price was raised by 67 per cent between announcement of flotation and the sale of the shares. The effect of this was immediately to increase by one-half the amount of capital raised for any commitment to pay future dividends. An imaginary dividend of 20p per share would have represented a cost of capital of 10 per cent at the original flotation price. At the revised price, the cost would have been 6.67 per cent (20p/£3), a reduction in the unit cost of capital of one-third. Meanwhile, 'old economy' firms with a proven track record of satisfying consumer demand found their cost of capital rising. This must have been especially galling for old economy firms who found themselves squeezed out of the FTSE-100 index. Outside the index, their shares became less attractive to fund managers, and fell in price accordingly. Being squeezed out of the index increased their capital costs.

Questions for discussion

1 Imagine that you are a fund manager and you observe share prices in one particular sector rising very rapidly, accompanied by much comment in the press that these companies are going to have a very profitable future. Using the valuation principles outlined in Chapter 11, you personally believe that the shares are severely overvalued already. What policy would you adopt on behalf of your fund and why?

2 How would you interpret the 'dotcom' phenomenon in the light of the 'efficient market hypothesis' discussed in Chapter 26?

Case study 3 Efficient markets: contrasting evidence

In Chapter 26 we discussed the widely held belief that financial markets are informationally efficient – participants make the best use of all relevant information in making judgements about the appropriate price at which assets should trade. We also pointed out that this hypothesis is often combined with an unwritten assumption that the information in question is information about 'fundamentals', with the result that markets price assets efficiently and rationally. This is an age-old controversy, not least because the implications (a) appear to conflict with casual observation of the way markets actually behave – with a great deal of volatility – and (b) suggest that many of the specialists working in financial markets are wasting their time in trying to earn superior returns from investment analysis. These two themes are represented in the two articles reprinted here from the *Financial Times*. The first was written in April 2001, after a sharp fall in stock prices generally and a very dramatic fall in technology stocks in particular (in fact, the article has several connections with issues discussed in Case study 2). The second was written about a year earlier, when prices were still around their peak. The first casts some doubt upon the EMH; the second tends to support it. But both raise interesting issues which we touch on in Chapter 26, and elsewhere in this book.

The first article states the core of the EMH in the second paragraph and points out that it is usually combined with a supplementary assumption that the information which is being efficiently used is information which is required for a 'rational' valuation of assets. It is not, for example, information about the consumption of Prozac, but information about 'expected earnings per share growth, interest rates and the equity risk premium'. This is information which relates to what is often called a share's 'fundamentals' and it is the sort of information which is necessary in order for capital markets to allocate funds in a socially beneficial way. We discussed the role of 'fundamentals' in the optimum allocation of funds in Sections 11.4, 26.5 and in Case study 2.

The problem with the EMH for many observers is described in the opening paragraph. Prices seem sometimes to fluctuate by more than could be accounted for by revisions to 'fundamentals'. The 1987 crash is quoted as an example. Later on the article quotes the fate of Cisco Systems and Deutsche Telekom in the recent technology share crash. To explain events like this by reference to the EMH we have either to suppose that radically new information about fundamentals was suddenly discovered, which in turn means either (a) that there was an actual shift in fundamentals on a dramatic scale, or (b) that fundamentals had been changing less dramatically for some period of time and this fact had lain undiscovered. The latter seems unlikely because 'These are not speculative minnows but widely-owned giants subjected to high levels of reporting and analysis.' (It is always possible that vital information about small, obscure firms fails to get publicized but these big firms were subject to high levels of continuous, professional analysis.) The alternative, then, is that the fundamentals really did change in quite a big way. But the obvious problem with this idea is that it is impossible to understand why 'they ever went so high in the first place'. What changes in fundamentals could possibly account for this?

The article goes on to consider recent changes in market behaviour which suggest alternative possible explanations. In Chapter 26, we went to some lengths to stress the dual hypotheses which are commonly rolled together under the EMH heading. The efficient use of information itself is not enough to produce the optimum allocation of capital; that requires that the information relates to fundamentals. In the light of this, it is worth noting that in the 'problems at three levels' which the article gives us as contributing to this volatility, there is little suggestion that markets became any less efficient at processing and using information. Indeed, the first 'problem' actually refers to *improved access to information* as the result of financial websites which were springing up across the internet. The EMH, strictly defined, remains intact. But the other two 'problems' clearly suggest that the information that market participants focused on was increasingly divorced from fundamentals. The first of these is that analysts and fund managers became increasingly concerned with *relative* performance and valuation. Thus, provided a share's price looked reasonable relative to others in the same sector, the price was justified. No one was checking whether the whole sector was overvalued in an absolute sense. (We discuss this concern with relative valuation in Section 17.3.2 and the second article also draws attention to it.) Furthermore, the article says towards the end, the performance of analysts and fund managers themselves is increasingly judged in relative terms. A fund manager who can show that he has matched the returns on some index is viewed as successful. The fact that the index may be rising (or falling) for reasons which may not be well founded is irrelevant. Indeed, any manager that tried to be independent would quickly be fired. (We came across this problem from a different direction in Case study 2.) This second explanation would appeal to anyone familiar with the basic ideas of behavioural finance that we discussed in Section 26.6. Irrational behaviour is frequently correlated. This pushes prices to unrealistic levels. But arbitrage, which is supposed to remove price anomalies, is risky, *especially when there is no satisfactory hedge* (typically the case with whole sectors) and when *the potential arbitrageur faces a short time horizon* (as is the case with the fund managers referred to in the article).

Markets behaving badly

By Barry Riley

Are the financial markets, and their participants, of sound mind? Over the years, perhaps naively, I have generally given them at least the benefit of the doubt, in aggregate . . . One of the fundamental concepts is market efficiency. This implies that prices accurately reflect information generally known and understood (although the quality of that knowledge may vary). There is also a more general economic hypothesis of rational expectations, that individuals anticipate the future in a coherent way. In the stock market this implies that values can be modelled statistically in terms of factors like expected earnings per share growth, interest rates and the equity-risk premium.

Set against these hypotheses, however, are the behavioural theories. These explore much less rational possibilities, such as that people will follow fashions and be influenced by peer group pressures. The explanation for financial manias may be psychological, or even chemical: indeed, recently an American doctor sent me a paper that seriously discussed the possibility that Wall Street's bubble reflected the ever-rising consumption of Prozac which, he said, fuelled over-optimism.

Setting the pill bottle aside, how can we interpret the markets' recent gyrations? After all, the Nasdaq – at its peak the world's biggest exchange – has crashed in value by two-thirds within 13 months. This week it was down 6 per cent on Tuesday, up 9 per cent on Thursday; yesterday it was tumbling again.

Cisco Systems, which for just a day or two during mad March last year was the world's most valuable company, worth $550bn, has since (at the recent low point) suffered a shareprice collapse of 84 per cent. The drop at Deutsche Telekom has been 70 per cent. These are not speculative minnows but widely-owned giants subjected to high levels of reporting and analysis.

Clearly, confidence in rationality has been shaken although, as is usual in the aftermath of a big fall, the puzzling aspect is not why values have tumbled but why they ever got so high in the first place. From a selfish point of view the distortions have made it easier to predict the future: it is possible to forecast price trends in an inefficient market but in a completely efficient one you never have a better than 50 per cent chance of getting the up-or-down decision right. However, looking at the markets from an economic point of view, they have become distorted and maybe dangerous: capital has been allocated wrongly, with vast sums now being dissipated before our very eyes in ill-conceived internet projects and telecoms over-expansion.

There have been problems at three levels. The one that received the most publicity during the bubble was the enormous increase in stock market speculation during the late 1990s by private individuals; millions were lured into the more fashionable sectors of the equity markets, notably technology. Improved access to information and dealing facilities through the internet fuelled this expanded participation, often by so-called 'day traders'. Rational valuation took an extended holiday.

Setting the pill bottle aside, how can we interpret the markets' recent gyrations?

Second, professional investors have failed to provide a proper balance. Portfolio managers have been drawn towards relative performance, with the help of increasingly varied and complicated stock market indices, and risk-control models. Thus Vodafone, which accounted

for 13 per cent of London's All-Share Index at one stage, was generally regarded as a low-risk holding relative to the index, whereas in absolute terms it actually carried a high risk, though with a share price down 'only' 51 per cent it has not turned out to be as risky as some (not yet, anyway). Fund managers who held out against the irrational fashions of 1999 and early 2000 faced a big risk of being washed away by the tide, although if they survived they will have performed very well recently.

Third, the market's institutional structures have become unstable. Investment banks, and their executives, became irresponsibly greedy, a trend that culminated in the wave of flotations of immature companies, often scarcely past the start-up stage. Stock exchanges, sometimes themselves new, competed aggressively for the quotations of these unproven and risky enterprises, degrading their own listing standards in the process. Quality was abandoned. Now we read that the Neuer Markt is having trouble persuading some of its listed companies to report their results within its three-month time limit. Accounting standards have become seriously distorted, in the US technology sector at any rate, by the huge handouts of stock options. Many of those options are presumably now worthless, but that poses the problem that workforces no longer locked in will crumble away.

Amid all the hysteria the community of investment analysts, with some honourable exceptions, was focused on keeping the bubble inflated. In the technology sector, earnings forecasts were hoisted higher and higher . . . Again, as with portfolio managers, an important problem is that analysts are chasing relative accuracy: in this case, how far their forecasts diverge from the consensus, rather than whether they turn out to be right or not in absolute terms. Only the ones who stray away from the herd feel vulnerable.

A nasty bear market has been needed to resolve these many distortions and, of course, it has all happened before. Perhaps it is disappointing that better information and technology have not really helped the capital markets to operate more reliably. Perversely, facts and analysis, however vast the quantity, can more easily be brought to bear to justify wrong prices than to generate correct ones.

A full post mortem on rationality will have to wait until the dust has settled. My interim report is that human nature, often dominated by shortsightedness and greed, will always be the most important factor. The efficient market hypothesis must co-exist with behavioural theory.

Source: *Financial Times*, 7 April 2001. Reprinted with permission.

The other problem mentioned is that regulations and market structures became weaker during the boom, so that firms with weak fundamentals were able to get a stock exchange listing.

And the costs of all this? As we said in Section 26.5, the optimum allocation of funds requires the most effective use of information and that it be related to fundamentals. If either of these conditions fails, then funds could go anywhere. Unsurprisingly in the circumstances described here, 'capital has been allocated

wrongly, with vast sums now being dissipated before our very eyes in ill-conceived internet projects and telecoms over-expansion'.

The second article applies a rather more formal test to the EMH. Recall that the 'strong-form' of the hypothesis asserts that *all* relevant information (past, current public and even current private information) is incorporated into market prices so quickly that no one can benefit from privately obtained information. The sort of private information envisaged is the information

FINANCE WEEK:

It takes a cracker . . . : Tracker funds look the better bet but even they have problems

THE LONG VIEW

By Barry Riley

It's a simple point, but evidently one well worth repeating. For the second year running Virgin Direct has hired the Edinburgh-based performance measurement experts WM to do a demolition job on active managers of UK unit trusts. Virgin, if you need reminding, only runs a 'passive' fund that tracks the FTSE Actuaries All-Share Index using a fixed formula and computerized technology rather than the ace stockpickers employed by most unit trust companies.

Well, they are supposed to be aces. Right now huge sums are cascading, for instance, into fashionable technology funds. Top-performing funds are heavily promoted, especially with the tax-favoured Isa sales season nearing its peak. But most of this churning of portfolios is a waste of effort. WM has examined data on the UK All Companies unit trust and open-ended investment companies (OEICS) sector going back 20 years. Out of 58 funds that survived for the whole period only seven outperformed the All-Share Index. As for the performance of those that fell by the wayside, usually through mergers – don't even ask.

Not that tracker funds provide a perfect alternative. Only two have even been around for more than 10 years. They all underperform the index, too, if only slightly, because they have costs, which the index does not. However, WM has worked out that over any recent five-year period investors in an active fund had no better than a one-in-four chance of beating the return of a tracker fund. Over longer periods the active funds tend to fall away even more.

But won't you be all right if you pick the right fund? That is how fund promoters and financial advisers justify their activities (and commissions). But the statisticians at WM have searched for persistent performance and have struggled to find any. The best they can say is that good performance by top quartile active funds tends to be clustered in three-year sequences. The central year features an average of 6 per cent outperformance, with another 1.5 per cent the previous year and the same again the year after.

This is interesting as an indication of how long particular investment styles tend to work. The trouble is, investors cannot spot the opportunity until year two. And since it usually costs 5 or 6 per cent to switch between unit trusts it will hardly be worth their while to chase these temporarily successful funds.

But surely a fund that has performed well over a decent period of, say, five years has demonstrated its quality and durability? Unfortunately, WM's analysis shows that such funds have only performed with random results in subsequent five-year periods. Brilliant investment teams tend to break up (or their luck runs out). There can also be important momentum effects in unit trusts. The successful ones draw in heavy inflows of new money, which tend to push up the prices of the managers' favourite stocks. But the funds become too big to be managed easily, money starts to leave and the whole process can go into reverse.

There is now a phenomenal momentum effect in the technology

sector which has developed into an astonishing bubble. It may still have some distance to run, but when it tops out the downside risks will be enormous, and the fund managers, however brilliant, will not be able to do much about it. The unit trust industry has always found it much easier to sell yesterday's fashions than tomorrow's winners.

Virgin Direct's not entirely independent advice is that you should stick to tracker funds as the core of your portfolio, and if you dabble in active funds at the margin it will not matter so much if they disappoint. But there are potential problems with tracker funds. They depend on a continuing bull market in equities: they will track an index downwards just as remorselessly as upwards.

There are also fashions in tracking. Several years ago several unit trust managers launched funds that tracked the better-known and smaller (and therefore cheaper to track) FTSE 100 Index rather than the more cumbersome All-Share. For a while the Footsie surged ahead of the All-Share, partly because of the new tracker money chasing the market leaders – but last year the Footsie underperformed by 4 per cent and it has continued to lag. Moreover, marketing men will develop the tracking concept through funds matching global multinational indices, SmallCap indices and the Techmark Index, among others. Picking the right index could become as tricky as picking the best active manager.

Anyway, indices can contain their own booby-traps. This is

especially so when a growing volume of tracking money is reinforced by 'closet index' funds, the supposedly 'active' portfolios that hug the indices so that managers can control their risks against their benchmarks.

We are seeing a powerful Vodafone effect, with the weighting of the mobile company pushed up to 15 per cent of the Footsie (and even 12 per cent of the All-Share). There is an eruption of new issues with low free floats (that is, most of the stock remains unavailable, as nearly 80 per cent does at lastminute.com, for example) and a growing fashion for Freeserve-style partial spin-offs of subsidiaries, creating what used to be called pyramids.

Just four sectors now account for more than 60 per cent of the Footsie Index, and 10 individual stocks account for 50 per cent. The degree of concentration is making index tracking riskier, and the Vodafone effect means even the All-Share tracker unit trusts are in breach of the standard statutory risk control, a 10 per cent ceiling on each individual investment.

Wednesday's quarterly index updating resulted in an unprecedented nine changes to the 100 constituents of the Footsie, and 38 to the mid-cap 250 Index. One interpretation of this turmoil is that investors are adapting to the New Economy; another is that enormous index-related distortions are largely responsible. Modern indices were invented to measure investors, not drive them.

The risks of tracker funds are still not nearly as great as for active funds, however. Last year broke all recent records for variability, and investment returns on the 232 funds measured by WM varied between 102 per cent and 6 per cent. There is evidence that some active managers are taking big risks in order to beat the index-matching competition.

You need a cracker to beat a tracker. But you will be very lucky to find one.

Source: *Financial Times*, 11 March 2000. Reprinted with permission.

---

that can be obtained only by very close, professional scrutiny of individual firms and their markets. This is the sort of work which is carried out by analysts on behalf of fund managers. An obvious test of this version of the EMH (as we point out in Section 26.4) is therefore whether fund managers can obtain returns which are consistently better than would be obtained by simply buying and holding a diversified portfolio of shares such as those which make up an index.

Virgin Direct is a mutual fund which operates only one type of fund. This is described as a 'passive' fund because it requires very little management and very little buying and selling of shares. This is because the fund is 'formula driven', where the formula is some chosen index. In Virgin's case it is the FTSE All-Share (which we know from Section 17.5.3 means that the fund consists of about 800 shares). The quantities of each are held in the same proportions as they appear in the index, so that the Virgin Direct fund can be regarded as an accurate, but miniature, replication of the All-Share Index. Passive funds are often known as 'tracker funds', because their performance is bound to track or follow exactly the performance of the index. They are popular because, being formula driven, they are cheap to run. No stock selection is necessary and no expensive analysis is required to justify the selection. (In Section 3.6 we explain that one way in which clients pay the managers of unit trusts is via a 'spread' between buying and selling prices, often of around 5 per cent. In tracker funds, this spread is commonly zero.)

Such tracker funds, therefore, provide one essential part of a test of the benefits of active management. They provide a benchmark.

The article reports that Virgin Direct commissioned the WM company to examine the returns to investors from investing in broad-based actively managed unit trusts and OEICS (see Chapter 3) and compare them with those from tracker funds. The comparison was to be made on a 20-year sample, in order to rule out short-term 'chance'. There were only 58 such funds in existence for the whole 20-year period and only seven of these produced better returns than would have been achieved by 'holding the index'. The evidence suggests that the EMH (or at least one of its implications) is correct.

On the face of these results, one might imagine that the appropriate investment strategy is to buy a tracker fund and forget about it. Furthermore, it might be thought that it does not matter which, since each fund tracks a broad-based index and there is no room for management skill (or lack of it) to make any difference to returns. But most of the article goes on to explain that things are not so simple.

Firstly, the returns from all tracker funds fail to match those from the index on which they are based. This is because some management costs remain.

(An annual management charge of around 0.5 per cent is deducted from the income to the fund.)

Secondly, while it maybe a virtue of tracker funds that there is no room for management discretion, this does mean that when an index is falling, the managers have no option but to stay invested in the shares that are declining. They cannot, for example, sell shares and hold money until the decline stops. (The article was drawing attention to this in March 2000 when investors had no experience of tracker funds in falling markets.)

Thirdly, there is the question of which tracker fund to choose (in effect a question of which index to follow). The common assumption is that all tracker funds are widely diversified and therefore have relatively low risk (for the reasons we discuss in Section 8.3).

But, the article points out, some indices are larger than others. The FTSE Actuaries All-Share gives, by definition, the greatest degree of diversification available from investing in UK stocks. By contrast, the FTSE-100 contains only 100 shares and these, in March 2000, were heavily skewed towards technology stocks because the recent fashion for TMT shares had turned some of these firms into the largest UK companies. Investing in a FTSE-100 tracker fund meant putting 15 per cent of your portfolio into the single firm, Vodafone, and half of one's portfolio would be in just 10 stocks.

Even so, as the article concludes, this is a lot less risky than investing in an actively managed fund, especially if the fund concentrates upon a particular sector, or particular region. And one pays less for it.

Questions for discussion

1 What does the article mean when it says that 'rational valuation took a holiday'?

2 Why does concentrating upon *relative* valuation encourage 'irrational' valuation?

3 Explain what is meant by a 'tracker fund'. What are its supposed advantages from an investor's point of view?

4 What was the problem (in 2000), according to the *Financial Times*, in investing in a tracker fund based upon the FTSE-100 index.

Case study 4 The Northern Rock affair

The Northern Rock bank converted from a building society in October 1997 (see Table 3.3). Like other ex-building societies, its origins showed on the asset side of its balance sheet in the concentration of its loans in the form of mortgages secured on domestic dwellings. Most of these loans had been granted according to conventional criteria (regarding credit history, income etc.) and although 'subprime' lending played a part in the crisis that unfolded in September 2007, there was no suggestion that Northern Rock itself had engaged in reckless lending or that its assets were of anything but the highest quality. In one respect, however, the Northern Rock had broken with its building society roots. This was on the liabilities side where, instead of the customary retail deposits dominating, the bank relied heavily upon loans from the interbank market.

This formed the link with the so-called 'subprime' market.

The problem of subprime lending almost certainly had its origin in a long-run of financial stability, rising markets, and low inflation which produced low nominal interest rates. One of the major constraints that borrowers face in taking out a loan is the ability of their income to 'service' it, that is, to meet the interest payments. These payments are the product of the capital sum borrowed and the nominal rate of interest. With inflation apparently well under control for a number of years, some commentators began to argue that it had been defeated 'for good' and that we were entering a new regime of low inflation/interest rates. In these changed circumstances, conventional measures used in the screening of applications for credit were held to be inappropriate. Thus, instead of limiting loans to, say, three times a person's income, multiples of five and six began to appear. Furthermore, borrowers with poor credit records (in some cases a history of default) were granted loans, again on the grounds that circumstances had changed, long term, for the better and that past record was not necessarily a guide to the future. In some cases, the loan:income multiple was in practice higher even than lenders intended. This came about, more in the USA than elsewhere, as a result of 'self-certification'. This was a situation where borrowers were trusted to provide accurate information in their application, the lender taking no steps to check that the figures, for income, for example, were correct. In some cases, it was subsequently argued, financial advisers had *encouraged* clients to apply for mortgages they could ill-afford, making false statements if necessary, in order to earn a commission when the loan was completed.

This was clearly a risky form of behaviour on the part of lenders and, during the summer of 2007, some commentators who were worried about the implications began to refer to the 'mis-pricing of risk' – meaning that lenders were failing to appreciate the scale of risk to which they were exposing themselves.

The risk started to become apparent when three events came together. Firstly, interest rates had begun to rise in 2006 and in the early summer of 2007 the consensus was that further rises would probably be necessary. Secondly, many of the subprime deals had been offered with the incentive of a rate of interest that was fixed for the first one or two years. This period was coming to an end for many borrowers who were finding that market interest rates were some 150 bp above the rates that they were used to paying (albeit with difficulty). Thirdly, the US housing market in particular had started to show signs of weakness towards the end of 2006 and there were reports of falling prices in the summer of 2007. Although this did not increase the risk of default in itself, it certainly made the consequences worse for the lenders – who would find that the collateral was worth substantially less than the loan.

All of this would have been bad enough. It would have created a number of financial institutions whose solvency was threatened by that fact that they had assets on their books which were worth a lot less than had been supposed and were possibly worth a lot less than their liabilities. (Recall from Section 2.3 that a bank whose assets are worth less than its

liabilities is insolvent.) But it was made worse as a result of the practice of 'securitization' that we discussed in Section 24.3. This, it will be recalled, involved the originator of the loan (the bank or building society) bundling a number of loans together and selling them on to another institution which would finance their purchase by issuing a bond or similar tradable security. Since there had been a rapid growth in these 'mortgage-backed securities' and they were widely distributed throughout the financial system, it was very difficult to tell which institutions were facing the greatest risk of default. So the situation created was one where everyone knew that banks as a whole faced higher levels of risk but no one could tell where most of the risk lay. It is hard to imagine a situation better calculated to increase the *perception* of risk than one where it is known to exist but is hidden.

The result was that banks wanted suddenly to increase their own liquidity and at the same time cut their lending to other banks that might just possibly be at risk. This led to a rise in interbank rates relative to the official rate of interest set by the central bank. Interest rates rise, even though the policymaker did not want this. And during August 2007 it was quite common for interbank rates to be 150 bp above the official rate. Bear in mind that when central banks change the official rate they do so by 25 bp, this jump in interbank rates was the equivalent of several policy increases rolled into one and the authorities became seriously worried that this 'credit crunch' might cause a recession.

From the Northern Rock's perspective, this was serious because it was relying on interbank funds to support its mortgage lending. We know, from Section 15.2 that interbank loans are very short term and so Northern Rock was having constantly to re-borrow in the interbank market at rapidly rising cost if it could borrow at all. The difficulty (and cost) of obtaining such funds in the interbank market led it to increase its borrowing from the Bank of England, using the new standing facility (discussed in Section 15.4). Once this became public knowledge, it was immediately interpreted by Northern Rock savers as a sign that their deposits might be at risk and many branches were besieged by customers wishing to make withdrawals. There can scarcely have been a better demonstration of the difference between liquidity and solvency. As we stressed at the outset, there was no question about the Northern Rock's asset quality or

'Inflexible' King finally forced to bend

By Peter Thal Larsen, Chris Giles, Jean Eaglesham and Lina Saigol

The Bank of England's decision to ease its hardline stance on intervention in the money markets followed a 24-hour period in which it came under increasing pressure from bankers and politicians to prevent the financial crisis from spreading.

At a meeting at the Bank on Tuesday evening, its governor, Mervyn King, was told yet again by executives of Britain's banks that his position – set out in a letter to the Treasury select committee the previous week – risked damaging confidence in a banking system already undermined by the run on Northern Rock.

According to those present, Mr King dropped hints that the Bank might consider action in the money markets. But, to the exasperation of his audience, he also repeated his long-held view that it should not bail out the shareholders of institutions that had engaged in irresponsible lending. 'The feeling was that you're in the headmaster's study and you've been really naughty. There has to be pain and someone has to suffer,' one bank chief said. Mr King's hardline stance was also at odds with that adopted earlier in the day by the Financial Services Authority regulator.

At an FSA meeting with bank chiefs, Hector Sants, the authority's chief executive, is reported to have implored them to pull together to ease the liquidity problems. He urged

them to continue providing liquidity to the interbank market in order to prevent the problems that caused Northern Rock to tumble from spreading to other smaller lenders, such as Alliance & Leicester and Bradford & Bingley.

But Mr Sants also stressed that the FSA was not able to intervene in the money markets on its own. This prompted some to question the tripartite approach to financial regulation, whereby responsibilities are split between the Bank, the FSA and the Treasury.

In the past month bankers have made increasingly desperate pleas for the Bank to broaden the range of collateral against which it is willing to lend in an effort to ease the liquidity crisis in the money markets . . .

By Monday lunchtime the Bank knew that Northern Rock depositors were to get a full guarantee of their cash from the government. This was strongly supported by senior officials, who hoped that the chancellor's action would draw a line under the bank run and restore calm to the financial markets.

At the time, insiders scorned the suggestion that the Bank should take the kind of action it announced yesterday. The agreed position of senior officials was that widening the collateral accepted by the Bank would send a message to commercial lenders that the central bank would always provide them with liquidity.

By yesterday morning that stance had crumbled. The Bank insisted the decision was its alone – although others, including the FSA and the Treasury, were interested parties. The Bank believes that it can argue its corner at today's select committee hearings, where it is bound to face a grilling. Nevertheless, it remains unclear what circumstances had changed so dramatically since Monday. Yesterday the Treasury refused to be drawn on the pressure applied to the Bank by ministers. Disclosure of details of talks between the chancellor and the Bank could create a false sense of divisions within the tripartite system 'when it's not divided', said a government insider. But officials made no secret of ministers' support for the U-turn.

Northern Rock's executives reacted angrily to the Bank's volte-face. After watching panicked customers rushing to withdraw their savings, they wondered why Mr King had not acted a few weeks earlier. Other bankers felt the same. 'Northern Rock was avoidable,' one executive said yesterday. 'Had it been a French or German bank it would have been able to borrow from the ECB. Intellectually and theoretically Mervyn King was correct. But he showed no flexibility when it was needed most.'

Source: *Financial Times*,
20 September 2007. Reprinted
with permission.

its solvency. But a piece of information which was misinterpreted by depositors was sufficient to create a liquidity crisis from nowhere. And, as we know from Section 2.3, once depositors start a mass withdrawal, this will *create* a crisis even for a well-run bank. It is precisely this situation that the lender of last resort (LoLR) is intended to prevent. One of the many interesting

features of this crisis was the struggle that the LoLR (the Bank of England in this case) had in trying to reassure depositors that all was well. To begin with the Bank made reassuring statements about Northern Rock's assets and about its willingness to provide liquidity. But depositors still queued to withdraw. What this illustrates is that once confidence is shaken, withdrawal becomes a one-way bet. The LoLR may make reassuring promises and these may be true, but if you have the slightest doubt and all you have to do is stand in a queue, you might as well stand in the queue. The confidence created by the LoLR has to be enough to stop the queue forming in the first place. In the event, the UK government had to announce that it would guarantee *all* deposits, and not just all the deposits of the Northern Rock but the entire deposits of the UK banking system.

The article suggests that Northern Rock episode raised two further issues that we have touched on. The first of these is of 'moral hazard'. We have stressed in several places (e.g. in Sections 2.3 and 2.4.3) that providing insurance to agents runs the risk of encouraging them to behave more recklessly in future. This is almost certainly the main reason for the Bank of England's rather cautious approach to helping Northern Rock as reported in the *Financial Times* article. The Bank was willing to provide assistance through the normal LoLR channels but the article makes it clear that the banking industry as a whole felt that more drastic action was required. In particular, there was the argument that the Bank should widen the range of assets against which it was prepared to lend. In Section 15.4 we saw that central banks normally conduct repurchase agreements involving gilts or government bonds. The industry's argument here was twofold. Firstly, if the Bank of England were prepared to accept a wider range of assets this would give banks more assets against which they could borrow on normal terms; secondly, widening the range to include mortgage-backed securities would have the effect of restoring some confidence in the securities themselves. Eventually, as the article shows, the Bank agreed but the delay made it look indecisive.

Finally, there is the issue of having regulation of the banking system in effect divided between the Bank, the Treasury and the Financial Services Authority. Recall that in Section 3.2 we said that the decision to transfer banking supervision from the Bank of England to the FSA in 1998 was deliberate and was intended to avoid conflicts of interest arising from the Bank's instrument independence. There is no reason to doubt that conflict of interest is reduced, but it may be at the cost of coherence and determination when a crisis strikes.

Questions for discussion

1 A month after the crisis at Northern Rock began, the bank's shares had fallen in value by about 80 per cent. How would you explain that change in value using the ideas that we developed in Chapter 17?

2 Can you explain in more detail the problems hinted at in the article that result from having responsibility for the banking system divided between a central bank and a government regulatory body?

Further reading

K Boakes, *Reading and Understanding the Financial Times* (London: Financial Times Prentice Hall, 2008), Topic 12

Case study 5 Exchange rate explanations – interpreting the news

The accompanying article is the Currencies report on the Market News & Comment page of the *Financial Times* of 17 October 2007 and on www.ft.com. These daily reports seek to explain events in the foreign exchange market in London on the previous day. This article emphasizes the importance of interest rate expectations in markets and other fundamentals but also short-term influences, indicating the difficulties

Pound slips after Bank minutes

By Peter Garnham and Neil Dennis

Sterling lost ground on Wednesday after the minutes from the Bank of England's October meeting revealed one of the central bank's Monetary Policy Committee voted for an interest rate cut.

The minutes showed eight members of the nine-strong committee voted to hold UK interest rates steady at 5.75 per cent earlier this month, with David Blanchflower calling for rates to be lowered by 25 basis points.

Paul Robson at RBS said the minutes would reinforce negative sentiment on the pound after Tuesday's soft UK consumer price inflation report.

'Blanchflower, is the committee's primary dove, so if anyone was going to vote for a cut it was always going to be him', he said. 'While other members will need more convincing, the minutes do raise the chances of an early rate cut. This leaves the pound set to underperform.'

However, after initial losses, the pound regained some poise as investors focused on expectation-beating UK employment data.

Jonathan Loynes at Capital Economics said data showing UK unemployment fell by 13,000 in September while average earnings growth rose to 3.7 per cent showed that the UK economy was yet to show signs of weakening significantly following the recent market turmoil.

'We continue to expect the first cut in [UK] rates to be delayed until the first quarter of next year,' he said.

After falling as low as $2.0288 against the dollar, the pound bounced back to stand up 0.1 per cent at $2.0345, while the pound advanced 0.1 per cent to £0.6966 against the euro.

Meanwhile, Japan's yen benefited for a second-successive session, while the Australian and New Zealand dollars were dumped as investors continued to abandon carry trades.

With the risk outlook clouding due to uncertainties over global growth and mounting inflationary pressures, traders have increasingly turned away from carry trade bets – where profits made on interest rate differentials can be instantly wiped out by volatile price moves.

Meanwhile, warnings ahead of this weekend's G7 meeting regarding one-way currency bets were reiterated by a Japanese finance ministry official on Tuesday.

Falling equity markets in Asia added to the loss of risk appetite after India introduced curbs on foreign capital inflows into its equity market. Japan's Nikkei 225 Average fell more than 1 per cent.

'The yen has continued to strengthen against the majors driven mainly by the decline in global stock indices, which has prompted investors to liquidate high yielding currency positions,' said Lee Hardman at the Bank of Tokyo-Mitsubishi UFJ.

The Australian dollar fell 0.7 per cent to Y103.48, while the New Zealand dollar shed 0.9 per cent to ¥86.93. Sterling fell 0.2 per cent to ¥237.31, while the dollar was off 0.2 per cent to ¥116.60.

Elsewhere, the dollar was little changed at $1.4170 against the euro.

Source: *Financial Times*, 17 October 2007. Reprinted with permission.

---

involved in forecasting day-to-day changes in exchange rates.

Consider first of all the pound and the news the market received about exchange rate fundamentals:

(a) **Interest rates.** We have no interest rate rises here. However, we have one piece of news that persuaded some people in the market that a fall in UK interest rates might be imminent. This seems a fairly weak piece of news. One member of the MPC had voted for an interest rate cut and he was the 'leading dove' – the member of the committee always likely to be the most in favour of interest rate cuts. Still, this was enough, given the previous 'negative sentiment' to persuade some people to sell sterling causing it to weaken. This negative sentiment came from news about:

(b) **Inflation.** There had been a 'soft UK consumer price inflation report' – an inflation rate lower than expected which would also have favoured a possible future cut in interest rates. But, having fallen a little, the pound began to rise again (it 'recovered some poise') because of news about:

(c) **Unemployment.** There had been some 'expectation-beating UK employment data'. Unemployment had fallen and the growth in earnings was bigger than expected, despite the 'recent market turmoil' – which was referring to the problems in financial markets stemming from the sub-prime mortgage problem in the USA and the subsequent problems at Northern Rock. This militated against an interest rate cut in the near future.

We had, therefore, one expert thinking that perhaps UK interest rates would fall soon (because of the vote in the MPC and the lower than expected inflation rate) and that the pound would 'underperform', but another expert thinking that interest rates wouldn't fall (because of the fall in unemployment). You can see that the principal thing going on here is trying to guess what the authorities will do next and when they will do it.

Next, consider what we are told about the performance of the yen. We are told that it strengthened for the second successive day and that the New Zealand and Australian dollars had weakened. We are given one explanation: the abandonment of 'carry trades'. If you don't know what these are, you can probably almost work it out from the text. If not . . . read on.

The net return from holding an asset is referred to as the 'carry' of the asset. It might be positive or negative. A carry trade is thus one in which a trader hopes to increase the carry from holding currencies. The aim is to borrow a currency with a low interest rate and use it to buy currencies with a high rate of interest. In this case the currency borrowed was yen (the international market rate on yen for short-term money was 0.58 per cent). The currencies that had been being bought were the Australian and New Zealand dollars. The official Australian interest rate at the time was 6.5 per cent; that in New Zealand 8 per cent). However, the traders doing this were engaged in uncovered interest arbitrage – that is, it carried a risk. The risk was that the value of the currencies being bought would weaken and that when the loans in yen had to be repaid and the Australian and New Zealand dollars sold to allow this, the trader would lose. Thus, it was a 'one-way currency bet'. Remember from Chapter 18 that if the traders had wanted to protect themselves they could have done so by selling the Australian and NZ currencies forward – but the cost of doing this would not have made the whole transaction worthwhile. Traders engaged in carry trade take risks in order to make good profits.

This means that if, for some reason, the markets suddenly seem more risky than previously, the carry trade appears much less attractive and traders sell off the high interest rate currencies (that is, they 'liquidate high yielding currency positions') pushing their value down. Next we need to ask what had happened to cause the greater feeling of risk. The article gives several reasons.

Questions for discussion

1 What are the reasons the article gives for the increased feeling of risk in currency markets?

2 Why might traders have expected the 'recent market turmoil' to have caused the UK economy to weaken?

3 In what way is the title of the article a little misleading?

4 Why might the Australian and New Zealand dollars be more attractive as destinations for carry trade money than, say, the pound sterling?

5 Does the carry trade have any longer-term impact on exchange rates?

Case study 6 Judging the regulator – the FSA, praise and blame

In 1997, the Financial Services Authority (FSA) was announced as the single regulator of all financial services in the UK, with its powers being confirmed by the Financial Services and Markets Act (FSMA) of 2000. There was immediate criticism from those who thought that a single regulator was bound to be bureaucratic and heavy-handed and would impose large compliance costs on financial firms. The FSA, however, has sought to adopt an approach to regulation described variously as 'principles based', 'light touch' and 'risk-based' and to greatly reduce the size and complexity of its rule book. Nonetheless, Tony Blair, the then Prime Minister, claimed in a speech in May 2005 that the FSA was seen by some respectable businesses as 'hugely inhibiting of efficient businesses'. Despite this, the FSA's approach won praise especially from abroad, and in June 2006 the *Financial Times* produced the following favourable interim judgement:

The regulator judged

Most employers reward productivity. But it is the curse of regulators that, though they are paid to regulate, the more rules they manufacture or enforce, the more likely they are to be criticised. On the other hand, *if a watchdog fails to intervene, it risks being damned for its inaction* [our emphasis]. In the six years since it was formally created from a merger of other watchdogs, Britain's Financial Services Authority has largely neutralised this double-edged curse. It has earned a reputation, both at home and abroad, as a successful 'light-touch' authority . . .

But it is already clear that the FSA has dealt with many of the concerns expressed when it came into being. At the time, the risks of setting up a 'super-regulator' seemed evident. Sceptics warned that the new authority would be too heavy-handed; it

would be unable to deal with the differing priorities of wholesale and retail financial services providers and customers; it would hamstring the growth of the City. There are those who believe the FSA has too frequently succumbed to those risks. Bigger customers of the authority – notably banks and insurers – have a tendency to complain about heavy-handedness. The FSA's consumer panel pointed out earlier this week that the regulator had not championed retail customers' interests sufficiently in five areas of concern. But critics tend to forget that six years is not a long time for a new regulator to establish a strong and consistent reputation. The FSA . . . has already demonstrated a maturity that has made it a model for other regulators. Far from diminishing the attractiveness of the UK as a financial centre,

the FSA has become an asset, often cited (at least privately) by foreign bankers as a reason for doing business in and with the City. Credit for the level-headed approach must go to the FSA's leadership, which has avoided the temptation to use the wide powers of the original legislation to create an overbearing regulator. True, the FSA has not yet been tested by a big financial catastrophe or scandal . . .

Vigilance, robust self-criticism and external review will always be necessary. But Sir Callum, Sir Howard Davies, his predecessor, and their management teams have set the FSA on a positive course that even the most incompetent future leaders of the authority will have difficulty reversing.

Source: *Financial Times*, 22 June 2006. Reprinted with permission.

Now we move forward to June 2007 for the following:

LOMBARD:

When a financial failure would be a success

By John Authers

When everyone from Hank Paulson, US Treasury secretary and ex-head of Goldman Sachs, to Eliot Spitzer, New York governor and former scourge of Wall Street, looks to London for lessons in how to regulate the financial services sector, it is tempting to break out the bowlers and furled umbrellas and take a self-congratulatory stroll through the City.

Not so fast, says a report from the Centre for the Study of Financial Innovation. The "light touch" UK approach may be extolled by outsiders, but those in the line of fire are complaining about increasing regulation.

The target of the CSFI's study – if a report as painfully even-handed as this one can be said to have a target – is the Financial Services Authority, which started sucking up various regulatory authorities, commissions and organisations almost 10 years ago. The concentration of supervisory power in one place was generally held to be a step forward. But the CSFI working group questions it. The one-stop-shop is all very well, it suggests, but customers are left out in the cold with their noses pressed to the window . . .

The problem is that the politicians that rejoice in the FSA's international reputation as a proportionate,

principles-based regulator are *the same politicians that would crucify the agency if it allowed a firm to collapse on their watch* [our emphasis]. In this way, nervousness permeates the whole system and rules, rather than principles, proliferate. A similar chain of events led to the perpetration of the Sarbanes–Oxley act in the US. The FSA is taking the right steps but, as the CSFI report implies, its biggest challenge may be to persuade staff that an occasional financial failure can actually be a good thing.

Source: *Financial Times*, 6 June 2007. Reprinted with permission.

Now we move further forward to September/October 2007 after the Northern Rock episode. On 1 October a *Financial Times* leading article offered:

The right response to Northern Rock

There comes a moment, when something has gone badly wrong for a large group of people, that the cry goes up, 'Never again!'. In the coming weeks there will be strident demands for reform to prevent another illiquidity episode and bank run like that suffered by Britain's Northern Rock. But the lessons from this crisis are not simple and nor are the obvious changes necessarily the best.

At least four issues flow from the crisis. First is banking supervision and whether Northern Rock's troubles were preventable. Second is the system for managing the crisis. Third is whether the limited insurance of bank deposits in the UK contributed to the run. Fourth is the Bank of England's highly public support operation for Northern Rock, which had the same effect as a lion ambling up to a herd of zebras: a mass depositor stampede.

British banks are supervised by the Financial Services Authority *and it would be easy, though unfair, to blame it for Northern Rock's woes* [our emphasis]. Evidence of supervisory culpability may yet emerge, but liquidity is hard to measure or guarantee, and the trouble appears to be limited to one small bank. The FSA clearly erred by not forcing Rock to stress-test itself for turmoil of this severity, but a system where no bank ever got into trouble would be a system that was too strict by far.'

Source: *Financial Times*, 1 October 2007. Reprinted with permission.

Then came headlines such as:

MPs grill FSA chiefs over Northern Rock

By Jennifer Hughes and Kate Burgess

Source: *Financial Times*, 9 October 2007. Reprinted with permission.

and

FSA owns up to Rock failings

By Jennifer Hughes, Peter Thal Larsen and Jane Croft

Source: *Financial Times*, 10 October 2007. Reprinted with permission.

We also had another *FT* leading article:

FSA in the dock

The FSA is responsible for the supervision of liquidity-starved bank Northern Rock and, alongside the Treasury and Bank of England, for handling financial crises. It has questions to answer, questions about why the Rock was so vulnerable to a liquidity crisis, about its role in the Bank of England rescue, and about the debacle by which that rescue turned into a bank run . . .'

Source: *Financial Times*, 9 October 2007. Reprinted with permission.

The *FT* thought that the FSA had ten questions to answer. We also had differing views as to what should follow regarding banking supervision in the UK.

Return regulation to the Bank of England

By Peter Oppenheimer

The key lesson of Northern Rock is that the monetary policy reform package of 1997 was misconceived and unviable. Giving formal independence to the Bank of England in setting interest rates was harmless enough – a matter of degree rather than of principle, and in fact designed to enhance the Treasury's independence of Downing Street more than the Bank's independence of the Treasury. The blunder was to remove the Bank's authority to regulate the banking sector and to imagine that the Financial Services Authority could do the job instead.

Source: *Financial Times*, 2 October 2007. Reprinted with permission, © Peter Oppenheimer.

Questions for discussion

We have several questions, for us and for you.

1 How many types of complaints against the FSA are mentioned in the extracts here? Have there been other types of criticism?

2 How would one now judge the overall performance of the FSA as a financial regulator?

3 Is the idea of a single regulator for the whole financial system a good one?

4 Should banking supervision in the UK be returned to the Bank of England?

5 In February 2007, seven months before the Northern Rock troubles, Sir Callum McCarthy said:

> First, there is the problem that, while a non-zero failure policy is accepted, and even applauded, ex ante, after the event of a failure there is a general tendency to act as if failure of a financial institution should be equated with failure of the regulatory regime.

In the light of Northern Rock:

(a) Do you think that politicians and members of the public do accept a 'non-zero failure policy' for financial institutions?

(b) Should the Northern Rock regulatory failure be judged just as the failure of a financial instiution? Or was it a failure of the regulatory regime?

Further reading

J Authers, 'When a financial failure would be a success', Lombard column, *Financial Times*, 6 June 2007

Financial Times, 'The regulator judged', leading article, 22 June 2006

Financial Times, 'The right response to Northern Rock', leading article, 1 October 2007

Financial Times, 'FSA in the dock', leading article, 9 October 2007

J Hughes and K Burgess, 'MPs grill FSA chiefs over Northern Rock', *Financial Times*, 9 October 2007

J Hughes, P Thal Larsen and J Croft, 'FSA owns up to Rock failings', *Financial Times*, 9 October 2007

▶

C McCarthy, 'Financial regulation: myth and reality', speech at the FSA British American Business London Insight Series and Financial Services Forum, 13 February 2007

P Oppenheimer, 'Return regulation to the BoE', *Financial Times*, 2 October 2007

Websites

www.fsa.gov.uk
www.ft.com/indepth/northernrock
www.ft.com/indepth/subprime
http://news.bbc.co.uk

Case study 7 The 'who' and 'why' of financial exclusion

Consider the following cases:

1 Disabled, unemployed ex-soldier, a seller of *The Big Issue*, who had a government cheque for £17,366 in backdated disability pension and a regular pension. Nonetheless, he was unable to open an account at HSBC, Lloyds, Barclays or NatWest.

2 Recently divorced woman with a cheque for £21,000 after the sale of her home, who was turned away by every bank and building society she approached.

3 Head of a media agency who had just recently moved jobs in order to increase his earnings but was refused a mortgage.

4 Receptionist who did shift work and needed her own transport to get her to and from the office but had trouble borrowing money from mainstream banks and building societies in order to have her car repaired.

5 Unemployed artist, 33, who was unable to borrow £180 to attend a two-day course at the London College of Fashion.

6 Fifty-three-year-old bankrupt who had suffered two heart attacks and was struggling to pay off several debts including a doorstep loan of £800 with an APR of 80 per cent. He had a bank account but no facility to borrow.

7 Lone parent on a run-down northern housing estate who had borrowed £300 for 12 months to buy a washing machine from a finance company that specialized in loans to low income families and who collected repayments weekly from door-to-door. The APR on the loan was 150 per cent and so the £300 washing machine cost £450.

What do these people have in common?

They suffer from financial exclusion, defined in Box 25.5 as exclusion from financial services of one sort or another: from particular sources of credit, insurance, bill payment services and accessible and appropriate deposit accounts. The reasons for their exclusion are not the same.

In the first three cases, the problem is not a lack of immediate resources. The ex-soldier lived in a housing collective and had neither a driving licence nor a utility bill bearing his name, the usual forms of identification required by banks before they will open an account. He presented his army certificate and letters bearing his name and address from his landlord and local council but none of the banks found these acceptable. A lack of correct identification was also the problem of the recently divorced woman. The media agency head could not get a mortgage because he had had his current job for less than six months. Important questions on all credit assessment forms include the length of time you have been in your current job and at your current address.

The receptionist was unable to borrow because she had had a court judgement against her for debt when she had been much younger. The artist was, of course, unemployed but also, although he had been at his current address for more than a year, he had previously had a period in which he had 'no fixed abode'. The heart-attack victim had been bankrupted and also had a poor health record. The purchaser of the washing machine was rejected by mainstream banks and building societies because of her low income and the fact that she was a lone parent.

In each of these cases, one can understand the position of mainstream financial intermediaries which need to make credit assessments and wish to avoid loan defaults. However, in the modern world in which financial services play such a large part in most people's lives, the costs of financial exclusion can be extremely high, can have a major impact on an individual's quality of life and can make it impossible for those excluded to struggle out of their present difficulties.

Questions for discussion

1 What are 'doorstep lenders' and 'loan sharks'? How can one justify an APR of 80 per cent or 150 per cent?

2 Which features of recent developments in the financial services industry might have increased the amount of financial exclusion?

3 To what extent is financial exclusion a social problem as well as a personal one?

4 What has been done in recent years to try to reduce the amount of financial exclusion?

Case study 8 Financial scandals and the impact on markets: Parmalat

A. The story

Parmalat was probably Italy's best known food company. It was established by Calisto Tanzi who, in 1961, having inherited his father's delicatessen, set up a dairy plant near Parma in northern Italy to challenge a then existing Italian milk monopoly. Parmalat became Italy's first producer of branded milk and greatly expanded its market through the production of UHT milk. It expanded strongly, and by 2002 was the fourth largest food products group in Europe with consolidated sales in that year of €7.6bn. It had grown by gradually moving into new product lines (including yoghurt and fruit juice) and by making a large series of acquisitions, particularly abroad.

Only about a quarter of Parmalat's sales were in Italy; almost two-thirds of total sales were in non-European markets. The group had 37,000 employees, of whom about 4,000 were in Italy. At the end of 2002, the group was composed of 213 companies in 50 countries. The shares of Parmalat Finanziaria, which controlled the industrial firm, were listed on the stock exchange in the 1990s. The company's financial reports were formally audited. The company was well known for sport sponsorships and had bought the Italian Serie A football club, Parma.

Parmalat accompanied its strategy of expansion abroad with a large-scale internationalization of its financial operations. Acquisitions and investments were financed by entering into debt. Through various group companies Parmalat obtained very substantial financing on the international capital market. Starting in 1997, the group made 32 bond issues for a total of around €7bn. Several leading international banks granted substantial loans and underwrote more than 80 per cent of the group's bond issues. Even in the second half of 2003, top foreign banks continued to purchase Parmalat bonds, for a total in excess of €1bn.

Despite the heavy indebtedness of the company, financial institutions and markets seemed happy with the acquisition strategy. At the beginning of 2003 Parmalat's shares were brought into the index of the 30 largest companies listed on the Italian stock exchange. According to Antonio Fazio, then the Governor of the *Banca d'Italia*, in August 2003, nine out of 14 international financial analysts advised investors to buy the company's securities, and another three recommended holding existing investments. In November, seven out of 14 analysts still recommended purchase and two continued to favour holding existing investments. Studies by two international banks were released giving positive judgements on the group's prospects and the relative value of its shares. In the early days of December 2003, the rating still reflected a positive opinion of the company's ability to redeem its bonds.

However, by the beginning of the second week in December it had become clear that Parmalat would have difficulty meeting a debt repayment to a group of investors who had bought 18 per cent of Parmalat's large Brazilian subsidiary but who had then exercised an option to sell it back to Parmalat following the failure of the subsidiary to be quoted on the Brazilian stock exchange. Parmalat claimed that it would be able to meet the payment by recovering a €500m ($590m) investment in a mysterious hedge fund in the Cayman Islands tax haven. As the accompanying article suggests, the funds turned out to be non-existent. The company had been engaged in false accounting, the concealment of liabilities, the inflation of assets and the forging of bank statements. It was thought that the fraud (practised for over a decade) could be for as much as $16.8bn. Parmalat had been using Enron-style accounting to hide liabilities and move money around among subsidiaries but the claimed funds, as in the case of the deposit supposedly held by its subsidiary Bonlat, sometimes did not exist.

The company filed for bankruptcy. Calisto Tanzi was arrested. Questions were asked also about the company's accounting firm, the US-based Grant Thornton, which had audited Parmalat's books until 1999 and had continued to audit the books of Bonlat, the subsidiary with the missing $4.9bn. Grant Thornton claimed that it had been the victim of a fraud but the head of the Italian branch of the company resigned and his partner was suspended

---

LEX:

Parmalat

Assume the worst, then prepare to be disappointed. First Parmalat's 'liquid' $590m investment in the Epicurum hedge fund disappeared. Now €3.95bn of securities and cash supposedly held on account by Bonlat, its subsidiary, have vanished into the Cayman Trough. Bank of America has informed Bonlat's auditors that it has no account in that name and denies the authenticity of a document certifying the existence of this rather spectacular amount. Creditors had already called on Enrico Bondi in search of a corporate doctor. They are now dialling 112 for the Carabinieri.

The Cayman Trough is four miles deep. Yet even in this depth of water one might have expected to see the odd ripple from such a spectacular implosion. Parmalat's collapse, however, has sent only the faintest of cat's-paws across the surface of the international capital markets. Parmalat's own shares were remarkably buoyant in the grey market yesterday, as traders were forced to buy in order to cover their short positions. But the share prices of some Italian

banks, which are estimated to be exposed to at least €1bn of Parmalat's €2bn bank debt, have suffered; Capitalia, which has admitted €393m of exposure, dipped 4.6 per cent yesterday, and Banca Intesa, with €360m of exposure, lost 4.1 per cent. The knock-on effect on credit spreads for other issuers has, by contrast, been negligible.

It might be argued that the collapse of a small Italian dairy should have little impact beyond the Gulf of Genoa. Parmalat's debt, however, has found its way into many corners of the financial system. Credit rating agency Moody's found 61 European collateralised debt obligation structures, which repackage debt into securities with varying ratings and returns, with an aggregate €602m of exposure to Parmalat. Even UK unit trusts have not come out unscathed. Many funds bought the company's sterling perpetuals; for example, it was the second-largest holding in New Star's high-yield bond fund as recently as October.

The whole saga ought, moreover, to reawaken suspicions about the

quality of information contained in audited accounts. The same applies to credit ratings – S&P yesterday downgraded Parmalat to D, for default, yet only 11 days ago it gave the company an investment-grade rating.

Some investment bank-dealing desks have taken the opportunity to widen spreads on corporate bonds. However, corporate investment-grade credit spreads are uncomfortably tight, offering only the skimpiest of risk premiums over government bonds. Credit quality may be stabilising, but downgrades still out-number upgrades, and negative credit reviews by the rating agencies have started to tick up again. While investors continue to pour money into the asset class, corporate bonds may still gain ground. But current prices do not give adequate compensation for the risk involved – a risk of which Parmalat provides an all-too graphic illustration.

Source: www.FT.com, 19 December 2003. Reprinted with permission.

after warrants had been issued for their arrest. As well as the charges in Italy, the SEC in the USA charged Parmalat with fraudulently offering $100m of unsecured notes to US investors and of inflating its assets by at least $5bn. In late May 2004, Italian prosecutors sought to have 32 Parmalat executives on trial. Several former executives later pleaded guilty to misleading investors, received gaol sentences and testified in the trial of Mr Tanzi. Three Bank of America bank officers were also charged, accused of deliberately misleading the market to believe Parmalat's balance sheet was stronger than it actually was.

In the usual Italian manner, trials and charges are still continuing. In July 2007, two prominent bankers, Cesare Geronzi and Matteo Arpi, were indicted by a judge in Parma: Geronzi for contributing to the fraudulent bankruptcy of Parmalat, Arpi for failing to prevent fraud committed by others.

Parmalat was subsequently rebuilt as a company and again listed on the Italian stock exchange. In 2006, the new management of the company sought to take legal action against banks whom it believed assisted in the fraud.

B. The impact on the markets

At the time of writing, the Parmalat fraud was still being investigated. However, there had been a number of effects on financial markets in the immediate aftermath.

- After the collapse of another large group, Cirio, in November 2002, Italian companies felt that it would be more difficult for them to gain access to the Eurobond market. Consequently, in 2003, during which bond issues in the euro area were increasing, Eurobond issues by Italian private sector non-financial companies fell to €13.8bn, compared with €19.5bn on average in the previous four years. It was thought likely that this decline would intensify following the Parmalat scandal. This indeed happened. By the end of 2006, the stock of bonds issued by non-financial firms had fallen back to the 1998 figure of 3 per cent of GDP compared with 7 per cent for the euro area.

- Following Parmalat, financing conditions worsened in the Euromarket for riskier Italian borrowers, although this seemed not to be true for Italian investment-grade bond issuers.

- The movement of bond prices in the secondary market in early 2004 suggested that investors had become more selective with regard to Italian firms issuing unrated or high-yield securities (those rated below BBB- or Baa3). Average yields on a sample of euro-denominated fixed rate securities of this type rose by about three percentage points between the beginning of December 2003 and the end of February 2004, but this did not happen to comparable foreign bonds. Movements in credit default swap spreads gave much the same message.

- The Parmalat crisis had a significant impact on some segments of the Italian stock market, notably in the food processing sector where share prices (excluding Parmalat) fell by 2.9 per cent between the beginning of December 2003 and the end of January 2004 – share prices in this sector rose in this period in both Germany and France.

- The quality of banks' loan portfolios deteriorated. The downgrading of bank loans to the companies caught up in the Parmalat group's collapse caused the ratio of new bad debts to outstanding loans to rise from 1 per cent to 1.2 per cent and the stock of bad debts to rise from 4.5 to 4.7 per cent of total lending.

- According to the *Banca d'Italia*, the Parmalat collapse would not have a serious direct impact on the Italian banking system. In November 2003 Italian banks' exposure to companies controlled by the Tanzi family came to around €3bn. However, the loans were highly fragmented, involving at least 120 intermediaries, and were commensurate with the capital base of the banks. The loans of the ten Italian banking groups most exposed to Parmalat amounted to 2.3 per cent of their supervisory capital. The EU limits on risk concentration (the *Large Exposures Directive* – see Box 21.2) had been respected.

- However, the Parmalat collapse had serious consequences for its bondholders. In the aftermath of the collapse, Parmalat bond prices fell sharply from around par to about 20 per cent of their nominal value. The impact on savers was greater because of the lack of development in the Italian financial system of the securities sector. This means that it is not easy for Italian investors to spread their holdings of shares and bonds among various issuers. This, in turn, makes savers highly vulnerable to the collapses of individual firms.

Questions for discussion

1 According to the then Governor of the *Banca d'Italia*, 'The Parmalat affair is the outcome of the repeated perpetration of criminal acts in the management of the company. The circumstances surrounding the case once again show that failure to observe the law and the lack of a firm ethical base for the conduct of economic agents can be a serious impediment to the functioning of the economic and financial system' (Fazio, 2004). Discuss the problem facing regulators, in the light of:

   (a) the importance of consumer confidence to financial markets, but

   (b) the concern of financial markets regarding overzealous and costly regulation.

2 How has financial regulation been changed in the USA and Italy in response to the Enron, WorldCom and Parmalat scandals?

3 In a leading article on 23 December 2003, the *Financial Times* said that rating agencies in the Parmalat affair 'carry responsibility for their sheer gullibility'. Do you think this is a fair criticism? (See the letter in reply on 24 December 2003 from the Executive Managing Director of Standard and Poor's in Paris.)

4 What has happened in the trials of Parmalat executives and others since October 2007?

Further reading

Banca d'Italia, 'The single monetary policy, financial intermediaries and markets in the euro area and Italy', *Economic Bulletin*, 38, March 2004, 56–77 (Rome: Banca d'Italia)

Banca d'Italia, 'The impact of the Cirio and Parmalat crises on the market for Eurobonds issued by Italian non-financial companies', *Economic Bulletin*, 38, March 2004, 72 (Rome: Banca d'Italia)

A Fazio, 'Fact-finding with regard to the relationship between firms, financial markets

and the protection of savings', *Economic Bulletin*, 38, March 2004, 87–100 (Rome: Banca d'Italia)

Websites

www.bancaditalia.it
www.ft.com
www.guardian.co.uk/parmalat/
http://search.bloomberg.com/s

Accrued interest
The interest that accrues to the seller of a bond between the last coupon payment date and the date of sale. It is paid to the seller by the buyer and makes the difference between the clean price and the dirty price.

Adaptive expectations
Expectations formed on the basis of the average values of past events.

Adverse selection
The situation where the demand for insurance comes mainly from those most likely to produce the outcomes insured against.

Agency capture
The situation where a regulatory process is 'captured' by those it is supposed to regulate and turned to their advantage.

Allocative efficiency
The best economic use of scarce resources – that use of resources which maximizes consumer utility. In the case of financial markets, this requires that funds go to their most productive use.

American option
The option to buy or sell an asset at a pre-determined price at any time within the period of the option contract.

Asymmetric information
The situation where one party in a bargain has information which is superior to that of the other.

Backwardation
The state of a futures contract in which the price of the future is below the cash price of the underlying asset. The price of the future will be rising towards the cash price as the delivery date approaches.

Basis point
One one-hundredth of a percentage point (i.e. $1\% = 100$ bp).

β-coefficient
An index which relates the amount of market risk in an asset to the risk in a whole market portfolio.

Call option
An option which gives the buyer an opportunity to purchase an asset within the time specified in the contract.

Capital risk
The risk that the capital value of an asset at the time of disposal may differ from the value expected.

Cash and carry strategy
The process of arbitrage between the futures market and the cash market that establishes the boundaries within which the futures price must lie.

Clean price
The price (usually of a bond) excluding any accrued interest.

Competitive laxity
Competition for customers by financial centres in the form of relaxing the rules by which financial institutions

must abide, resulting in the weakening of the regulation of the financial system.

Compliance costs
The costs of complying with regulation for those being regulated.

Contango
The state of a futures contract in which the price of the future is above the cash price of the underlying asset. The price of the future will be falling towards the cash price as the delivery date approaches.

Correlation coefficient of return
The extent to which the returns on two assets are correlated. The more closely the returns move together, the closer the correlation coefficient is to unity.

Coupon
The fixed, periodic, payment on a bond.

Coupon rate
The coupon payment on a bond, expressed as a percentage of its par value.

Covariance
A measure of the extent to which two (or more) asset prices vary together from their average values.

Covered call
A call option (q.v.) where the underlying asset is owned by the writer (seller) of the option.

Covered interest arbitrage
The act of moving funds from one country to another to gain from higher interest rates while protecting oneself in the forward foreign exchange market against spot exchange rate changes.

Credibility
The likelihood, as judged by market agents, of an announced economic policy or existing fixed exchange rate being maintained by the government.

Currency substitution
The use of or holding of a foreign currency by domestic residents, usually as a protection against expected depreciation of the domestic currency.

Currency swap
The exchange between two borrowers of the interest payments of different types of loans e.g. fixed and floating interest rate loans, loans in different currencies or loans using different basis rates.

Default risk
The probability that a borrower may fail to make payments of interest or repayment of principal at the scheduled time.

Direct quotation
The practice of quoting the exchange value of a currency by saying how many units of that currency is required to buy a single unit of another currency.

Dirty price
The price of a bond including any portion of the next coupon payment that may have accrued to the seller between the last coupon payment and the date of sale.

Discount basis
The rate of return on an asset quoted as a rate of discount on the principal *plus the interest payment*.

Disintermediation
The switching of lending/borrowing away from banks and other financial institutions to direct lending/borrowing or lending/borrowing via financial markets.

Dividend yield
The dividend payment on a share expressed as a percentage of the share's price.

Divisia
A measurement of the total stock of money which weights each component of the money stock according to its liquidity characteristics.

Duration
The average length of time taken to receive a series of income payments (usually from a bond).

Efficient market hypothesis
The proposition that prices of financial assets adjust instantaneously to all relevant news.

European option
The option to buy or sell an asset at a pre-determined price on a date specified in the contract.

Exchange agio
The sum payable for the convenience of exchanging one type of money for another, e.g. spot dollars for forward dollars – hence, in this case, the forward premium or discount on a currency.

Extrapolative expectations
The belief that the value of a variable, which has just changed, will go on changing in the same direction, e.g. that rising equity prices will go on rising.

Fair game model
A model of an efficient market in which all errors are random and hence there is no relationship between an investor's estimate of the deviation from the required or equilibrium rate of return and the actual deviation from that rate of return.

Financial deficit
The situation where planned consumption plus real investment spending exceed income.

Financial surplus
The situation where income exceeds planned consumption plus real investment.

Fisher effect
The assumption that in equilibrium real interest rates will be the same everywhere and hence that differences in nominal interest rates on different currencies will reflect only the differences in inflation rates in the respective countries.

Forward premium/discount
The difference between the spot and forward exchange rates.

Functional integration
The development of financial conglomerates, with mergers and takeovers leading to single firms being engaged in many financial functions, e.g. banking, insurance and securities business.

Hedge fund
A mutual investment fund open to a limited range of professional investors. The fund can engage in a wider (and riskier) range of strategies than a conventional fund open to the general public.

Hoarding
Saving. Usually associated with the idea of people holding money despite the loss of interest involved because of the fear of the prices of financial instruments falling.

Income risk
The probability that the rate of return from an asset will differ from what was expected.

Indirect quotation
The practice of quoting the exchange value of a currency by saying how many units of another currency can be bought with one unit.

Inflation premium
That part of the nominal interest rate which compensates for (strictly speaking expected) inflation.

Informational efficiency
The speed with which relevant information is incorporated into prices.

Initial margin
The percentage of the value of a futures contract that an investor must lodge with the clearing house at the beginning of a futures contract, against the possibility that the futures contract will experience losses.

Interest rate parity
Equality of interest rates in different countries, making allowances for expected changes in exchange rates (uncovered interest rate parity) or for the forward premium/discount of a currency (covered interest rate parity).

Interest rate swap
The exchange of interest rates on two loans – one a fixed interest rate loan, the other a floating interest rate loan.

Interest yield
The coupon payment on a bond divided by the market price of the bond.

Intermediation
Lending/borrowing carried out via a bank or other financial institution.

Law of Large Numbers
The Law of Large Numbers says that in repeated, independent, trials with the same probability p of success in each trial, the chance that the percentage of successes differs from the probability p by more than a fixed positive amount converges to zero as the number of trials becomes very large.

Lender of last resort
The sole supplier of bank reserves in the event of a system-wide shortage.

Liability management
Attempts by a financial institution to control the volume and type of its liabilities by varying the terms offered to holders of those liabilities.

Liquidity
The extent to which an asset can be converted to money, quickly, cheaply and for a known capital sum.

Liquidity preference theory
The theory that the rate of interest is determined by the demand for money (liquidity preference) and the supply of money.

Liquidity premium
The price people are prepared to pay (usually in the form of a lower return) for a liquid asset compared with an illiquid one.

Loanable funds theory
The theory that the rate of interest is determined by people's willingness to save and the demand for funds to invest in real capital assets.

Marked to market
The process by which margins are adjusted on the basis of daily price changes in the markets for assets underlying futures contracts. Investors must either pay additional margin to the clearing house or may draw funds from their margin accounts depending on the direction in which prices have moved in the cash markets.

Market efficiency
Usually refers to 'informational efficiency' (q.v.) but could refer to allocative (q.v.) or operational (q.v.) efficiency, or all three.

Market risk
The extent to which returns on assets vary because of events which affect the whole market portfolio of risky assets.

Market segmentation
The formal or informal division of markets into smaller segments influenced by different supply and demand conditions.

Maturity transformation
The difference between the average maturity of a financial institution's liabilities and its assets.

Monetary base
Notes and coin outside the central bank plus banks' deposits with the central bank.

Money illusion
Mistaking changes in nominal values for changes in real values; failing to allow for inflation.

Money's own rate
The rate of return on money. Usually calculated as the average rate of return on all deposits in the money stock, weighted by their respective proportion of the total money stock.

Monitoring
The process by which financial intermediaries attempt to ensure that loans are being used for the intended purpose and in an effective way and hence are likely to be repaid on time.

Moral hazard
The tendency of agents who are insured to behave more recklessly because of their insurance cover.

NAIRU

The 'non-accelerating inflation rate of unemployment'. That rate of unemployment at which aggregate demand pressure is consistent with a constant rate of inflation.

Naked call

A call option (q.v.) where the underlying asset is not owned by the writer (seller) of the option.

Natural rate of unemployment

The percentage of the labour force that is recorded as unemployed when the labour market is in equilibrium.

Netting agreements

The accounting practice of offsetting profits and losses on different contracts or in different currencies in the attempt to lower the overall level of risk.

Operational efficiency

The speed and cost at which a market enables transactions to be carried out.

Payout ratio

The fraction of a firm's earnings which it pays as a dividend to shareholders (= 1 − retention ratio).

Portfolio choice

The decision to hold one's wealth in a variety of different assets.

Portfolio equilibrium

The situation where the distribution of wealth across a range of assets shows no tendency to change.

Portfolio theory

The principles involved in making the decision on how to hold one's wealth in a variety of different assets.

Price/earnings (P/E) ratio

The price of a company share divided by the earnings per share. A measure of the price that has to be paid for a share of a firm's profits.

Private equity

Equity investment in firms which are not listed on a public stock exchange.

Purchasing power parity

The situation where the exchange rate between two currencies represents the difference between the price levels in the two countries.

Put option

The option to sell an asset at a pre-determined price at some time in future.

Random walk

A time series in which the change from one period to the next in the value of the variable in question (e.g. an asset price) is purely random.

Rate of discount

The rate of return implied by the difference between the price paid for the asset and the amount the holder will receive when the asset matures.

Rational expectations

Expectations that would be formed by agents making the best use of available information.

Real interest rate

The nominal rate of interest *minus* the expected rate of inflation (strictly) but in practice often the nominal rate *minus* the actual rate of inflation.

Redemption yield

The rate of return on an asset (usually a bond) held to redemption, taking account of the reinvestment of coupon income and any difference in current price and redemption price.

Reinvestment risk

The risk that when a bond matures and the holder wishes to reinvest the proceeds interest rates will have fallen.

Reputation

The view taken by the market of the long-term policy performance of governments or central banks based on past performance and the constitutional constraints imposed on the authority in question.

Retention ratio

The fraction of its earnings retained by a firm for reinvestment in the business (= 1 − the payout ratio).

Return
The cashflow generated by an asset (usually expressed as a *rate*).

Risk
The probability that an outcome differs from what was expected.

Risk premium
The additional rate of return, over and above the return on a risk-free asset, required to persuade investors to hold a risky asset.

Search costs
The costs, in money and time, of finding an opportunity to trade.

Securitization
The transformation of a non-tradable asset/liability into one which can be bought and sold between third parties.

Serial correlation
A time series in which the change from one period to the next in the value of the variable in question (e.g. an asset price) is correlated with past values of the variable.

Specific risk
The variability in an asset's return caused by events specific to that particular asset.

Strike price
In an auction, the situation where all bidders pay the (same) minimum price necessary to clear the market. In an option, the price of the underlying asset at which it becomes profitable to exercise the option.

Synthetic call option
The combination of being long in the underlying cash market and, at the same time, holding a put option.

Term premium
The additional rate of return, over and above the rate on a short-dated asset, required to persuade investors to hold assets with a long period to maturity.

Term structure
The pattern of returns available on assets differentiated solely by their term to maturity.

Time inconsistency
The failure to maintain an announced policy because the original policy brings about changes in circumstances that then require policy authorities to alter the policy in order to maximize its welfare.

Total risk
The combination of specific risk, which relates to a particular type of asset, and market risk, which derives from events that effect all types of asset. Total risk is measured by the standard deviation of returns from the mean.

Transaction costs
Administrative costs of buying and selling in a market, including commissions and taxes.

Variation margin
The proportion of the value of a futures contract that must be held with the clearing house against the possibility of losses arising on the contract. Often the variation margin is the same proportion of the value as the initial margin.

Velocity
Total output at current market prices, divided by the stock of money in circulation.

Venture capital
Equity capital subscribed by private, professional, investors to young, growing (and therefore risky) businesses.

Venture capital fund
A pooled investment vehicle in which private individuals (often forming a partnership) borrow from others in order to invest in businesses which find it hard to get finance from other sources.

Yield basis
The rate of return on an asset calculated, like a conventional rate of interest, on the basis of the sum laid out in order to earn the return.

2.3

(a) mis-estimation; (b) random fluctuation; (c) parameter change.

2.4

Flooding claims will be highly positively correlated. An overflowing river has the potential to inundate many properties simultaneously. Furthermore, this positive correlation may well not be simply a local matter. The path of a river can extend across a number of counties and bad weather after a long wet period can affect many parts of the country simultaneously, with the result that flood alerts can be outstanding in many localities at the same time. With total insurance pay-outs on flood-related claims as high as £5bn in the last five years, as indicated in the article, insurers truly face a catastrophe risk. Hence their threat to refuse cover unless the government continues to accept the cost of reducing substantially the risk that insurers face.

As is the case with flooding, losses are likely to be highly correlated at time of war and, on a smaller scale, when there are riots or civil commotion. All may be regarded as catastrophe risks, explaining the response of exclusion clauses.

2.5 (a)

The answer lies between these two extremes. It is clearly not a simple matter of transferring the individual's longevity risk onto the annuity provider since the latter will aim to use the LLN to reduce the longevity risk it faces itself. However, we know from our examination of insurers' residual risks (see Section 2.4.2), that the LLN cannot entirely eliminate the risks inherent in providing insurance cover. Similar considerations apply here, notably that the annuity-providing intermediary is exposed to risks of mis-estimation and parameter change. Basing its calculations on mortality statistics (sample data), it will aim to ensure that the lump sum payments received from clients when they retire (taking into account the returns it can earn on them) will be sufficient to cover the pension payments made to clients of average longevity. However, since even sample averages of life spans will vary around their mean, the intermediary's calculations may turn out to have underestimated the true average longevity of its client group and, in any case, advances in medicine may cause average longevity to increase at a faster rate than it anticipates. Hence longevity risk does not simply disappear.

2.6

Changes (a) to (d) will all tend to make the scheme underfunded either now or in the future. An increase in the rate of benefit and an increase in the life expectancy will immediately increase the accrued liabilities of the scheme. A decrease in investment profitability will make it more difficult to cover liabilities already accrued, while a decrease in contribution rates will make it more difficult to cover liabilities that will accrue in the future so that, over time, the scheme will cease to be fully funded.

On the other hand, an increase in labour turnover (e) as well as a round of redundancies (f) will, *ceteris paribus*, tend to make the scheme overfunded. For, leaving the firm before retirement for whatever reason may in some schemes reduce the size of the pension that a worker may ultimately be paid on the basis of the contributions he or she has already made and hence reduce the liabilities of the scheme.

Finally, the impact of a rise in the inflation rate (g) could be either positive or negative. For it may increase the rate of return on the fund's investments. On the other hand, if pensions are index-linked it will increase the scheme's liabilities.

2.7

$$\text{Annual pension} = \frac{23}{80} \times £26,400 = £7,590$$

$$\text{Lump sum} = \frac{3}{80} \times 23 \times £26,400 = £22,770$$

2.9

1 (a) Both risks are borne by the employee; (b) Yes, the pension is or can be perfectly portable since the worker can transfer the value of the fund he or she has accrued at any point in time to a defined contribution scheme operated by another employer; (c) No, in addition to the risks referred to in (a), the value of the individual worker's fund is entirely dependent on what he or she has paid in.
2 This is a policy issue for the readers to weigh up for themselves. They should consider the advantages and disadvantages of defined benefit schemes discussed earlier, the advantages of defined contribution schemes and their disadvantages as indicated in Question 1.

9.1

1 3.8 per cent and 4 per cent.
2 4.3 and 5 per cent.
3 The difference in methods at low rates is 0.2 per cent, while at the higher rates the difference is 0.7 per cent.

12.1

1 3,500
2 $150 \div 3,000 = 0.05$
3 10
4 10
5 0.040/0.0547/0.0547/0.0495
6 3,530
7 0.0495/0.0495/0.0495
8 0.0495
9 1,010/1,010/1,010
10 No change
11 $D_p = 3,015$ $C_p = 515$
12 $135 \div 3,015 = 0.0448$

12.2

1 $350 \div 3,000 = 0.05$
2 $300 \div 3,000 = 0.10$
3 $(0.10 + 1.0) \div (0.05 + 0.10) = 1.1 \div 0.15$
$$= 7.33$$
4 $1.1 \div 0.17 = 6.47$
5 $1.08 \div 0.17 = 6.35$

14.1

1 $2\% + 2\% = 4\%$
2 $2\% + 4\% = 6\%$
3 $2\% + 6\% = 8\%$

14.2

1 2%
2 4%
3 I would expect a *real* wage increase of 2%
4 I would expect no change in *real* wages.

14.3

1 7.5%
2 6%

15.1

1 12%
2 12.12%
3 £99,540

15.2

1 £205,000
2 £200,195
3 12.82%

15.3

1 8.83%
2 £6,013,150

17.2

1 Dividend yield $= D_1/P = 34.5/690p = 5\%$
Capital gain $= g = 15\%$
2 (a) $K = 6\% + 1.49(9\%) = 18.6\%$
(b) Dividend yield $= K - g = 18.6\% - 15\%$
$$= 3.6\%$$

18.1

1 $\$1 = €0.7065$; $€1 = \$1.2706 - 1.4144$;
$€1 = \$1.4154$

$1 = £0.4899; £1 = $2.0391 − 2.0433;
£1 = $2.0412
$1 = ¥115.9; ¥100 = $0.8591 − 0.8666;
¥100 = $0.8628

2 (a) £1 = €1.4421; €1 = £0.6934
  (b) £1 = ¥236.575; ¥100 = £0.4227
  (c) €1 = ¥164.04; ¥100 = €0.6096

18.2

1 We need SKr/$ × $/SFr = 6.5089/1 × 1/1.1753
  = 6.5089 × 0.8508 and SFr1 = SKr5.5378

2 We need Won/$ × $/T$ = 913.850/1 ×
  1/32.5770 =913.850 × 0.0307 and T$1 =
  Won 28.055

3 We need Bolivar/$ × $/Boliviano = 2147.3/1 ×
  1/7.6750 = 2147.3 × 0.1303 and Boliviano 1 =
  279.79

18.3

1 euro and yen
2 (a) 4.65% p.a. premium
  (b) 0.62% p.a. premium
  (c) 1.0% p.a. discount

18.4

1 (a) Calculate the cross rate for yen against the
      euro through the dollar (€1 = ¥164.02); ob-
      serve that the market is undervaluing the yen
      against the euro (€1 = ¥168.023); realize that
      to make a profit you will need to sell euro for
      yen (always sell the overvalued currency).
      Therefore, the steps required are: (i) sell €
      for ¥; (ii) sell ¥ for $; (iii) sell $ for €.
  (b) 2.44 per cent.

19.1

Higher; in Table 19.1, we see the prices: December
95.08; September 95.69.

19.2

1 (a) 5.274% p.a.   (b) 5.019% p.a.
  (c) 4.668% p.a.   (d) 4.824% p.a.
2 All forward/forward rates in this exercise are
  below the spot rates because interest rates were
  expected to fall over the following 12 months.

20.1

1 The money market interest rates for one month
  (4.3825 per cent), three months (4.79188) and one
  year (4.71750) tell us that the market expected
  euro short-term interest rates to rise in the near future but then reach a peak in 2008. The market
  was balanced at 95375 (implying an interest rate of
  4.625 per cent). No one wished to buy at implied
  interest rates below that and hence call options
  were unpopular. On the other hand, no one
  thought interest rates would rise in the immediate
  future as high as 4.875 and so no one wished to sell
  at 95125. There was no market for put options at
  that price.
2 October calls had only a couple of weeks to run
  and so had a much lower time value than June
  calls.
3 Interest rates available to participants in the market must have been around 6 per cent but were expected to fall in the first part of 2008 – premiums
  for calls and puts were more or less balanced at
  9400 for October and December but for June even
  at a strike price of 94250 (implied interest rate of
  5.75 per cent) calls were significantly more expensive than puts.

20.2

Those with strike prices of 4225, 4325, 4425 and
4525 since the strike price was below the FTSE index.
This is clear from the options premiums on call options. As the strike price approaches the current value
of the index, the index is less in-the-money and the
premium falls. Notice that even call options that are
out-of-the-money (FTSE index below the strike price)
have a positive premium because of the time value of
the option, although this is very small for May options because of the short time to expiry.

20.3

B. 1. $1.4241; 2. $1.4241; 3. $1.4284; 4. $0.0043;
   5. 0.43 cents; 6. 1.08 cents.
C. 1. $1.4341; 2. $1.4341; 3. $1.4284;
   4. −$0.0057; 5. zero; 6. 0.72 cents.
D. The rule we have used for establishing the minimum price of a call option is for a European
   option. The Philadelphia Stock Exchange contract
   in Table 20.2 is an American option and thus
   the premiums will allow for the extra element in

the time value, deriving from the possibility of American options being exercised before the expiry date. Thus, it is not surprising that B6 and C6 lie comfortably above the minimum price calculated as B5 and C5.

20.4

1 Acting in financial markets to protect oneself against the risk the value of a currency in which one is long falling in value *or* against the value of a currency in which one is short rising in value.

Allied-Lyons were initially long in dollars and thought the dollar would fall in value. They might have hedged by:
  (i) selling dollars forward;
  (ii) selling futures contracts in dollars;
  (iii) buying put options or writing call options in dollars.

2 Acting as in (a) to a sufficient extent to reverse the existing long position, e.g. selling *more* dollars forward than they expected to receive.

3 A contract giving the right to buy dollars before or at expiry date of the option at the strike price specified in the contract.

4 If the value of the dollar rises.

5 Because the writer must pay the excess of the spot price of the dollar over the strike price, no matter how high the dollar rises. The writer of the option has to meet his or her obligation to provide dollars to the buyer.

Index